The Penguin Factfinder

The Penguin
Factfinder

Edited by David Crystal

PENGUIN BOOKS

PENGUIN BOOKS

Published by the Penguin Group
Penguin Books Ltd, 80 Strand, London WC2R 0RL, England
Penguin Group (USA) Inc., 375 Hudson Street, New York, New York 10014, USA
Penguin Group (Canada), 90 Eglinton Avenue East, Suite 700, Toronto, Ontario, Canada M4P 2Y3
(a division of Pearson Penguin Canda Inc.)
Penguin Ireland, 25 St Stephen's Green, Dublin 2, Ireland (a division of Penguin Books Ltd)
Penguin Group (Australia), 250 Camberwell Road, Camberwell, Victoria 3124, Australia
(a division of Pearson Australia Group Pty Ltd)
Penguin Books India Pvt Ltd, 11 Community Centre, Panchsheel Park, New Delhi – 110 017, India
Penguin Group (NZ), 67 Apollo Drive, Mairangi Bay, Auckland 1310, New Zealand
(a division of Pearson New Zealand Ltd)
Penguin Books (South Africa) (Pty) Ltd, 24 Sturdee Avenue, Rosebank 2196, South Africa

Penguin Books Ltd, Registered Offices: 80 Strand, London WC2R 0RL, England

www.penguin.com

The New Penguin Factfinder first published 2003
The second edition published as The Penguin Factfinder 2005
This revised third edition published 2007
1

Copyright © Crystal Reference Systems Ltd, 2003, 2005, 2007

Set in 8/8.5pt Swift in QuarkXPress™
Typeset by Crystal Reference Systems Ltd, Holyhead
Printed in England by Clays Ltd, St Ives plc

ISBN: 978-0-141-02622-0

ABOUT THIS BOOK

The Penguin Factfinder contains more facts than any other book of its kind. We also believe it is much easier to use than other such books. What might seem at first the most simple of books – a collection of bits of information for use in the home, at school or in the office – is actually the product of much hard thinking about how best to organize the information, and, indeed, what the nature of this information is.

What is a fact?

> Something that has really occurred or is actually the case; something certainly known to be of this character; hence a particular truth known by actual observation or authentic testimony, as opposed to what is merely inferred, or to a conjecture or fiction; a datum of experience, as opposed to the conclusions which may be based upon it.

This definition, one of the longest in the *Oxford English Dictionary*, gives a hint of the difficulty involved in saying what exactly counts as a 'fact' and thus of the difficulties facing any editor who has to decide what should be included in a book of them. At first glance, the answer is obvious: there are facts about objects and animals (what are the characteristics of X?), people (who is X?), places (where is X?), and times (when did X happen?), and these facts can be numerical (how many X? how often did X happen?), verbal (how to describe X?), and tabular (how to classify X?).

At second glance, the situation becomes more complicated (and more interesting). There are facts about fictions (X in mythology or literature) and fictions about facts (disputes over the longest or largest X). There are situations where we cannot decide whether something is fiction or fact (the changing politics of country X). There are near-facts (estimates of X), transient facts (world records about X), qualified facts (the majority of X), arguable facts (the most important X), politically biased facts (the growth or decline of X), and contrived facts (neat classifications of X). A factbook must not ignore these awkward and marginal cases, but having included them it must always remember to warn readers if 'there's something they should know' before swallowing a 'fact' whole. Examples of this advice are given on p. 42 (about longest rivers) and p. 420 (about saints' days). Many bitter arguments (such as those that arise out of a disputed answer in a quiz game) could be avoided if more attention were paid to this issue.

What isn't a fact?

On the other hand, certain notions are not part of a factbook. Definitions of words, for example, really have no place. It is a fact that Memphis and its necropolis is a World Heritage Site (p. 46). However, if you don't know what a necropolis is you had best look the word up in a dictionary. Nor do explanations of concepts have any place in a factbook. If, to continue the example, you are unclear about who would be buried in a necropolis, you had better look this up in an encyclopedia. A factbook is not intended to do the job of a glossary, a manual, or a textbook.

Nor is a fact a single, isolated piece of information. An enquirer may have a single question in mind, and want a single fact for an answer, but any factbook worth its salt should show how this enquiry fits into a broader frame of reference. No fact exists in isolation. Everything is part of a pattern. It is therefore important to show the pattern. A factbook should say to a reader: 'You asked about X, and here's the answer – but don't forget there's also Y and Z, which can help you understand X further. And, while you're here, have a look at Y and Z anyway, as they're interesting too.' A good factbook, once entered, should put questions in perspective, and also be difficult to leave. There should be a strong temptation to stay awhile, and browse. In *The Penguin Factfinder*, the organization of information into fields of meaning, sequenced logically, and grouped hierarchically, provides both motivation and means. If the job is done well, answering factual questions proves to be the least trivial of pursuits.

Selecting the facts

A factbook could, in theory, be any size, from a few dozen to thousands of pages. Whatever the size, two considerations are paramount. There should be a balance between the various areas of knowledge covered; and there should be a pragmatic principle at work by which the editor tries to answer those questions that readers are most likely to ask.

Balance is relatively easy to achieve, by devising a scheme that works systematically through the various well-recognized domains of enquiry. In *The Penguin Factfinder*, this is handled by starting with the most general perspective (the Universe) and finding a coherent path (one of many possible) through physical, biological, historical, geographical, and social domains.

Justifying the selection within each domain is less simple, and any editor has to fall back on the well-tried principle that 'one can please all of the people some of the time ...' In the present case, the task was much aided by the experience of running an encyclopedia Datasearch project in the early 1990s. This project enabled readers of the encyclopedia to interrogate its database to obtain further information about topics that interested them. By keeping a record of the types of enquiry, it proved possible to develop a sharpened sense of the kinds of things people wanted to know about. Examining the question-lists of innumerable pub quiz competitions, and other such games, has provided a further dimension.

Finding your way about

A factbook should be as accurate and as up-to-date as the state of knowledge permits, and *The Penguin Factfinder* team has made every effort to ensure that these criteria are met. Full use has been made of the database compiled for *The Penguin Encyclopedia*, which is continually being updated, and which has been used since 1986 to generate a wide range of reference books, notably the Cambridge and Chambers factfinders of the 1990s. The comprehensive coverage of the *Encyclopedia* has helped to guarantee the breadth of the present project; and many specialized reference books have proved to be of great value in developing the project's depth of detail. Directly or indirectly, over 250 experts have been involved in generating the information that the *Factfinder* contains.

But it is no use having marvellously up-to-date and accurate facts if readers cannot find them. Critical to the success of any factbook, therefore, is an appropriate means of information retrieval. This is where most factbooks fall down. They may advertise that there are 'hundreds of thousands of facts' within their covers, but if it proves impossible to find the answer to a simple question without having to spend several minutes combing through the pages, the factbook has to be judged a failure. The solution is simple: proper indexing, with a preparedness to set aside sufficient space so that the project gets the index it deserves.

There are, broadly speaking, two ways into a factbook, and both are represented in *The Penguin Factfinder*:

- One way suits the person who is interested in a general area of knowledge, and who wishes to explore it systematically. This person may not have a specific question in mind, only a vague uncertainty or need for clarification. Often a precise question does not become apparent until a range of possible answers has been presented. Such enquirers need a thematic guide to the factbook, where the various types of information are presented conceptually, with as much logical order relating the concepts as it is possible to impose. The logic underlying *The Penguin Factfinder* is shown on p. ix. Using this information, it should be possible to 'home in' quickly on a broad area, and then to focus on a chosen topic.

- The other way suits the person who does have a precise question in mind – a who, a what, a when, a where. For this person, a thematic approach is of relatively little value. If you wish to find out a fact about the *gull*, for example, you want to be able to go immediately to wherever in the book this item is located, and not waste time searching for it unfruitfully under such a heading as *sea birds* (it is in fact a shore bird). Similarly, under which heading would you look for information about a particular thing or person? (Does the *Forth Bridge* appear under Communications, Scotland, or UK? Is *Leonardo da Vinci* under sculptors, architects, or painters?) All of this uncertainty is avoided through the expedient of an in-depth letter-by-letter index, with appropriate cross-references to handle alternative points of entry. Thus, in the index to this book, *Forth Bridge* is under *F* and *Leonardo da Vinci* is under *L*. The headings are there, too (*bridges* under *B* etc.), as an alternative route to themes and sub-themes. The index of *The Penguin Factfinder* is far and away the most comprehensive ever prepared for a book of this kind, and it is space well used.

In short, the opening pages present in a thematic way the various fields or systems of information dealt with in this book. The closing pages present in an alphabetical way the items those systems contain. This dual perspective has been called, in lexicography, an 'index-to-system' approach, and it is the first time that it has been used to its full potential in a factbook. Such an approach adds coherence, increases speed of item look-up, makes the information more accessible, and promotes flexibility by providing alternative routes to answering a question. I hope that, after using the book, this is an opinion that readers will share.

David Crystal

Crystal Reference Systems Ltd

Editor
David Crystal

Associate Editor
Ann Rowlands

Assistant Editor
Hilary Crystal

Taxonomy Editor
Jan Thomas

Database Management
Tony McNicholl
Dan Wade

Database Assistance
Peter Preston
Todd Warden-Owen

Administration
Ian Saunders
Rob Phillips

Typesetting
Crystal Reference Systems Ltd, Holyhead

Penguin Books

Editor
Kristen Harrison

Cartography
David Graham

Production
Katja Kiebs

David Crystal was born in 1941 and spent the early years of his life in Holyhead, North Wales. He went to St Mary's College, Liverpool, and University College London, where he read English and obtained his Ph.D. in 1966. He was a lecturer in linguistics at the universities of Bangor and Reading, becoming Professor of Linguistic Science at Reading in 1975, and is now Honorary Professor of Linguistics at the University of Wales, Bangor. He is editor of *The Penguin Encyclopedia* and related publications, the former editor of the Cambridge family of general encyclopedias, compiler of several dictionaries, and author of publications on the theory and practice of reference works. He currently directs research in a company which manages a large reference database and which is developing systems for improving document classification and internet search. A past president of the Society of Indexers, in 2001 his book *Words on Words* (co-authored with Hilary Crystal) was awarded the Wheatley Medal for an outstanding index. In 1995 he was awarded the OBE for services to the English language.

AREAS OF KNOWLEDGE

This page shows how *The Penguin Book of Facts* is divided into broad areas of knowledge. Also indicated (in roman numerals) are the pages where you will find a much more detailed breakdown of each section in the Table of Contents which follows. For really specific queries, you should use the Index at the back of the book.

TABLE OF CONTENTS

PART ONE

The Universe

THE COSMOS

Star distances

Star	Distance (l y)[a]
Proxima Centauri	4.24
Alpha Centauri A	4.34
Alpha Centauri B	4.34
Barnard's Star	5.97
Wolf 359 (CN Leonis)	7.80
Lalande 21185	8.19
UV Ceti A	8.55
UV Ceti B	8.55
Sirius A	8.67
Sirius B	8.67
Ross 154	9.52
Ross 248 (HH Andromedae)	10.37
Epsilon Eridani	10.63
Ross 128 (Fl Virginis)	10.79
L 789-6	11.12
GX Andromedae	11.22
GQ Andromedae	11.22
61 Cygnus A	11.22
61 Cygnus B	11.22
HD 173739	11.25
Epsilon Indi	11.25
Tau Ceti	11.41

[a]l y = light years.

Star magnitudes

Star	Common name	Magnitude	Distance (l y)[a]
Alpha Canis Majoris	Sirius	−1.47	8.7
Alpha Carinae	Canopus	−0.72	98
Alpha Centauri	Rigil Kentaurus	−0.29	4.3
Alpha Boötis	Arcturus	−0.04	36
Alpha Lyrae	Vega	0.03	26
Alpha Aurigae	Capella	0.08	45
Beta Orionis	Rigel	0.12	815
Alpha Canis Minoris	Procyon	0.34	11
Alpha Orionis	Betelgeuse	0.50 (v)	520
Alpha Eridani	Achernar	0.50	118
Beta Centauri	Hadar	0.60 (v)	490
Alpha Crucis	Acrux	0.76	370
Alpha Aquilae	Altair	0.77	16
Alpha Tauri	Aldebaran	0.85 (v)	68
Alpha Scorpii	Antares	0.96	520
Alpha Virginis	Spica	0.98	220
Beta Geminorum	Pollux	1.15	35
Alpha Piscis Austrini	Fomalhaut	1.16	23
Beta Crucis	Mimosa	1.20 (v)	490
Alpha Cygni	Deneb	1.25	1600
Alpha Leonis	Regulus	1.35	85

[a]l y = light years.
(v) = variable.

The constellations

Latin name	Astronomical name	Latin name	Astronomical name	Latin name	Astronomical name
Andromeda	Andromeda	Cygnus	Swan	Pavo	Peacock
Antlia	Air Pump	Delphinus	Dolphin	Pegasus	Winged Horse
Apus	Bird of Paradise	Dorado	Goldfish/Swordfish	Perseus	Perseus
Aquarius (Z)	Water Bearer	Draco	Dragon	Phoenix	Phoenix
Aquila	Eagle	Equuleus	Little Horse	Pictor	Easel
Ara	Altar	Eridanus	River Eridanus	Pisces (Z)	Fishes
Aries (Z)	Ram	Fornax	Furnace	Piscis Austrinus	Southern Fish
Auriga	Charioteer	Gemini (Z)	Twins	Puppis	Ship's Stern
Boötes	Herdsman	Grus	Crane	Pyxis	Mariner's Compass
Caelum	Chisel	Hercules	Hercules		
Camelopardalis	Giraffe	Horologium	Clock	Reticulum	Net
Cancer (Z)	Crab	Hydra	Sea Serpent	Sagitta	Arrow
Canes Venatici	Hunting Dogs	Hydrus	Water Snake	Sagittarius (Z)	Archer
Canis Major	Great Dog	Indus	Indian	Scorpius (Z)	Scorpion
Canis Minor	Little Dog	Lacerta	Lizard	Sculptor	Sculptor
Capricornus (Z)	Sea Goat	Leo (Z)	Lion	Scutum	Shield
Carina	Keel	Leo Minor	Little Lion	Serpens	Serpent
Cassiopeia	Cassiopeia	Lepus	Hare	Sextans	Sextant
Centaurus	Centaur	Libra (Z)	Scales	Taurus (Z)	Bull
Cepheus	Cepheus	Lupus	Wolf	Telescopium	Telescope
Cetus	Whale	Lynx	Lynx	Triangulum	Triangle
Chamaeleon	Chameleon	Lyra	Harp	Triangulum Australe	Southern Triangle
Circinus	Compasses	Mensa	Table	Tucana	Toucan
Columba	Dove	Microscopium	Microscope	Ursa Major	Great Bear
Coma Berenices	Berenice's Hair	Monoceros	Unicorn	Ursa Minor	Little Bear
Corona Australis	Southern Crown	Musca	Fly	Vela	Sails
Corona Borealis	Northern Crown	Norma	Level	Virgo (Z)	Virgin
Corvus	Crow	Octans	Octant	Volans	Flying Fish
Crater	Cup	Ophiuchus	Serpent Bearer	Vulpecula	Little Fox
Crux	Southern Cross	Orion	Orion		

Z = zodiac constellation.

The northern sky

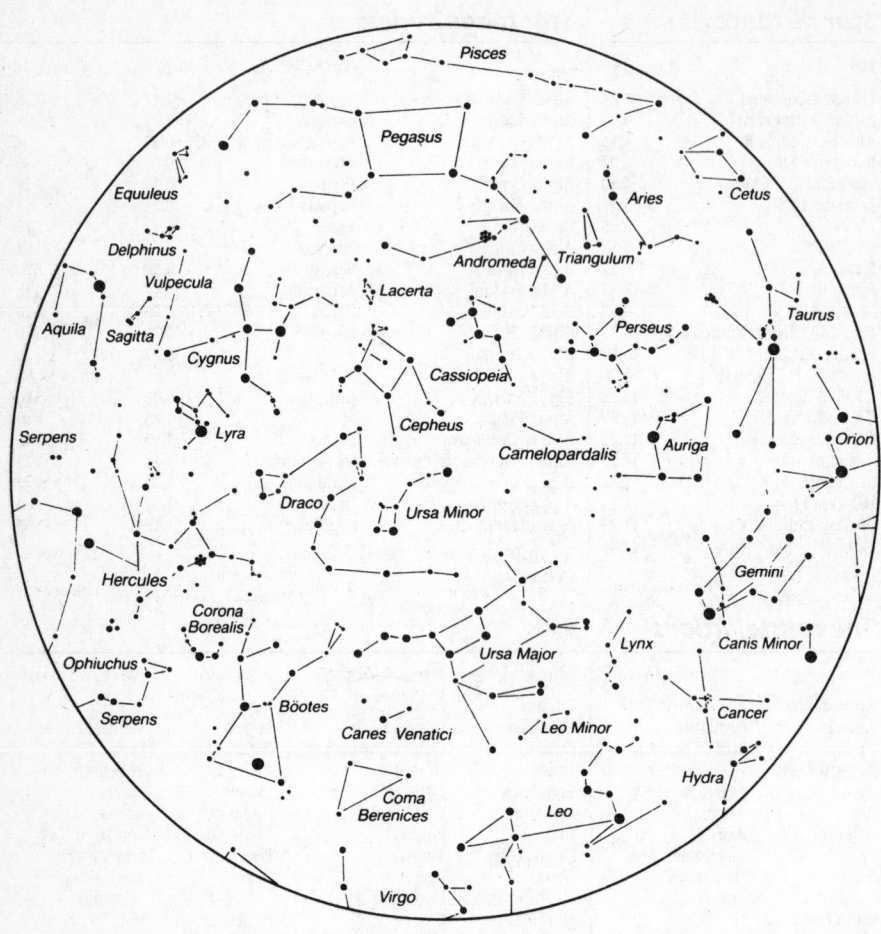

'Alpha' stars within constellations[a]

Name	Constellation	Name	Constellation	Name	Constellation
Achernar	Eridanus	Alnair	Grus	Atria	Triangulum Australe
Acrux	Crux	Alphard	Hydra	Betelgeuse	Orion
Acubens	Cancer	Alphekka	Corona Borealis	Canopus	Carina
Al Giedi	Capricornus	Alpheratz	Andromeda	Capella	Auriga
Al Rijil	Centaurus	Altair	Aquila	Castor	Gemini
Aldebaran	Taurus	Ankaa	Phoenix	Choo	Ara
Alderamin	Cepheus	Antares	Scorpius	Cor Caroli	Canes Venatici
Alkes	Crater	Arcturus	Boötes	Deneb	Cygnus
Alkhiba	Corvus	Arneb	Lepus	Diadem	Coma Berenices

[a]'Alpha' denotes the brightest star in a constellation.

The southern sky

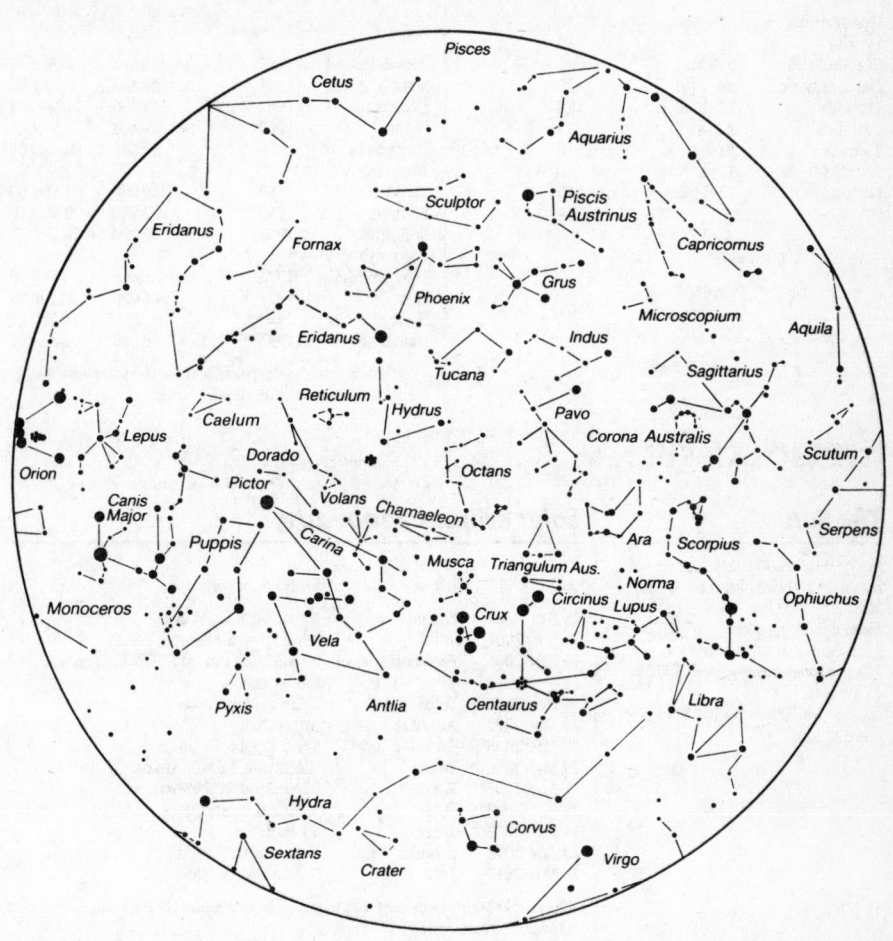

Name	Constellation	Name	Constellation	Name	Constellation
Dubhe	Ursa Major	Phakt	Columba	Sadalmelik	Aquarius
Fomalhaut	Piscis Austrinus	Polaris	Ursa Minor	Shedir	Cassiopeia
Hamal	Aries	Praecipua	Leo Minor	Sirius	Canis Major
Kaïtain	Pisces	Procyon	Canis Minor	Spica	Virgo
Kitalpha	Equuleus	Rasalgethi	Hercules	Svalocin	Delphinus
Markab	Pegasus	Rasalhague	Ophiuchus	Thuban	Draco
Men	Lupus	Rasalmothallah	Triangulum	Unukalhai	Serpens
Menkar	Cetus	Regulus	Leo	Vega	Lyra
Mirphak	Perseus	Rukbat	Sagittarius	Zubenelgenubi	Libra

Meteor showers

Name	Dates of maximum	Hourly rate
Quadrantids	3–4 Jan	100
Lyrids	21–2 Apr	10
Eta Aquarids	5–6 May	35
Delta Aquarids	28–9 Jul	20
Perseids	12–13 Aug	75
Orionids	22 Oct	25
Taurids	4 Nov	10
Leonids	17–18 Nov	10
Geminids	13–14 Dec	75

Historic comets

Name	First seen	Period of orbit (years)	Date of last perihelion[a] passage
Arend-Roland	1957	not known	8 Apr 57
Mrkos	1957	not known	1 Aug 57
Humason	1962	3 000	14 May 62
Ikeya	1963	not known	21 Mar 63
Ikeya–Seki	1965	879.88	21 Oct 65
Tago-Sato-Kosaka	1969	420 000	21 Dec 69
Bennett	1970	1 680	20 Mar 70
Kohoutek	1973	75 000	28 Dec 73
Kobayashi–Berger–Milon	1975	not known	5 Sep 75
West	1976	500 000	25 Feb 76
Halley	240 BC	76.1	9 Feb 86
Hale-Bopp	1995	6 580	1 Apr 97

[a]'Perihelion' refers to the position of the closest approach to the Sun of an object in an elliptical orbit.

THE SOLAR SYSTEM

The Sun

Age 4 500 000 000 years
Diameter 1 392 000 km/864 950 mi
Mass 2×10^{30} kg
Mean density 1.4 g/cm^3
Luminosity 3.9×10^{27} kW
Effective surface temperature 5 770 K/ 5 496.8 °C
Average orbital velocity 107 210 kph/ 66 620 mph

Solar eclipses 2000–2015

Date	Extent of eclipse	Visible from parts of[a]
25 Dec 2000	Partial	N America, Caribbean
21 Jun 2001	Total	S America, S Atlantic, Africa
14 Dec 2001	Annular[b]	Hawaii, SW Canada, W & C America, Caribbean
4 Dec 2002	Total	S Africa, Australia
23 Nov 2003	Annular	Antarctica
8 Apr 2005	Annular/Total	S & C Pacific, C America
29 Mar 2006	Total	C Atlantic, W & N Africa, C Asia
1 Aug 2008	Total	Greenland, N & C Asia
22 Jul 2009	Total	S Asia, C Pacific
11 Jul 2010	Total	S Pacific
13 Nov 2013	Annular/Total	N Australia, S Pacific
20 Mar 2015	Total	N Atlantic, Arctic

[a] The eclipse begins in the first area named. [b] In an annular eclipse a ring-shaped part of the Sun remains visible.

Planetary data (1)

Major planet	Distance from Sun				Sidereal period[a]	Axial rotation (equatorial)	Diameter (equatorial)	
	maximum		minimum					
	(million km)	(million mi)	(million km)	(million mi)			(km)	(mi)
Mercury	69.4	43.0	46.8	29.0	88 d	58 d 16 h	4 878	3 032
Venus	109.0	67.6	107.6	66.7	224.7 d	243 d	12 104	7 520
Earth	152.6	94.6	147.4	91.4	365.26 d[b]	23 h 56 m 4 s	12 756	7 926
Mars	249.2	154.5	207.3	128.5	687 d	24 h 37 m 22 s	6 794	4 222
Jupiter	817.4	506.8	741.6	459.8	11.86 y	9 h 55 m 41 s	142 984	88 846
Saturn	1512	937.6	1346	834.6	29.46 y	10 h 14 m	120 536	74 898
Uranus	3011	1867	2740	1699	84.01 y	17.2 h[c]	51 118	31 764
Neptune	4543	2817	4466	2769	164.79 y	16.11 h[c]	49 532	30 778

[a]'Sidereal period' refers here to the period of revolution around the Sun with respect to the stars.
[b] Precisely 365 d 5 h 48 m 46 s.

[c] Different latitudes rotate at different speeds.
y: years d: days h: hours m: minutes s: seconds
km: kilometres mi: miles.

Planetary data (2)

Major planets

Mercury
Atmosphere hydrogen, helium, neon; *satellites* 0; *features* lunar-like crust, crustal faulting, small magnetic field.

Venus
Atmosphere carbon dioxide; *satellites* 0; *features* shrouded in clouds, 70% rolling plains, 10% highlands, 20% lowlands, craters.

Earth
Atmosphere nitrogen, oxygen; *satellites* 1; *features* liquid water oceans filling lowland regions between continents, permanent ice caps at each pole, unique in supporting life, magnetic field.

Mars
Atmosphere carbon dioxide; *satellites* 2; *features* cratered uplands, lowland plains, massive volcanic regions.

Jupiter
Atmosphere hydrogen, methane; *satellites* 63; *features* covered by clouds, craters, volcanic features, dark ring of dust, magnetic field.

Saturn
Atmosphere hydrogen, helium; *satellites* 46 (the exact number is not yet determined); *features* several cloud layers, magnetic field, thousands of rings.

Uranus *Atmosphere* methane, helium, hydrogen; *satellites* 27; *features* clouds, layers of mist, magnetic field, c. 11 rings.

Neptune
Atmosphere methane, hydrogen; *satellites* 13; *features* unable to detect these telescopically from Earth.

The 'asteroid belt' is found mainly in a large series of orbits lying between Mars and Jupiter.

Dwarf planets
(take more than 200 years to orbit the Sun)

Eris
Pluto
Charon
Ceres

Main planetary satellites

	Year discovered	Distance from planet (km)	Distance from planet (mi)	Diameter (km)	Diameter (mi)
Earth					
Moon	–	384 000	238 000	3 476	2 155
Mars					
Phobos	1877	937 800	582 700	27	17
Deimos	1877	2 346 000	1 458 000	15	9
Jupiter					
Metis	1979	128 000	79 000	40	25
Adrastea	1979	129 000	80 000	24	15
Amalthea	1892	181 000	112 000	270	168
Thebe	1979	222 000	138 000	100	60
Io	1610	422 000	262 000	3 650	2 260
Europa	1610	671 000	417 000	3 140	1 950
Ganymede	1610	1 070 000	665 000	5 260	3 270
Callisto	1610	1 883 000	1 170 000	4 800	3 000
Leda	1974	11 100 000	6 900 000	20	12
Himalia	1904	11 480 000	7 134 000	186	116
Lysithea	1938	11 720 000	7 283 000	36	22
Elara	1905	11 740 000	7 295 000	80	50
Ananke	1951	21 200 000	13 174 000	30	19
Carme	1938	22 600 000	14 044 000	40	25
Pasiphae	1908	23 500 000	14 603 000	50	30
Sinope	1914	23 700 000	14 727 000	36	22
Saturn					
Pan	1990	134 000	83 000	10	6
Atlas	1980	138 000	86 000	40	25
Prometheus	1980	139 000	86 000	100	60
Pandora	1980	142 000	88 000	100	60
Epimetheus	1980	151 000	94 000	140	90
Janus	1966	151 000	94 000	200	120
Mimas	1789	186 000	116 000	390	240
Enceladus	1789	238 000	148 000	500	310
Calypso	1980	295 000	183 000	30	19
Telesto	1980	295 000	183 000	30	19
Tethys	1684	295 000	183 000	1 060	660
Dione	1684	377 000	234 000	1 120	700
Helene	1980	377 000	234 000	15	9
Rhea	1672	527 000	327 000	1 530	950
Titan	1655	1 222 000	759 000	5 150	3 200
Hyperion	1848	1 481 000	920 000	480	300
Iapetus	1671	3 560 000	2 212 000	1 460	910
Phoebe	1898	12 950 000	8 047 000	220	137
Uranus					
Miranda	1948	130 000	81 000	480	300
Ariel	1851	191 000	119 000	1 160	720
Umbriel	1851	266 000	165 000	1 170	730
Titania	1787	436 000	271 000	1 580	980
Oberon	1787	583 000	362 000	1 524	947
Neptune					
Triton	1846	355 000	221 000	2 705	1 681
Nereid	1949	5 510 000	3 424 000	340	210

The near side of the Moon

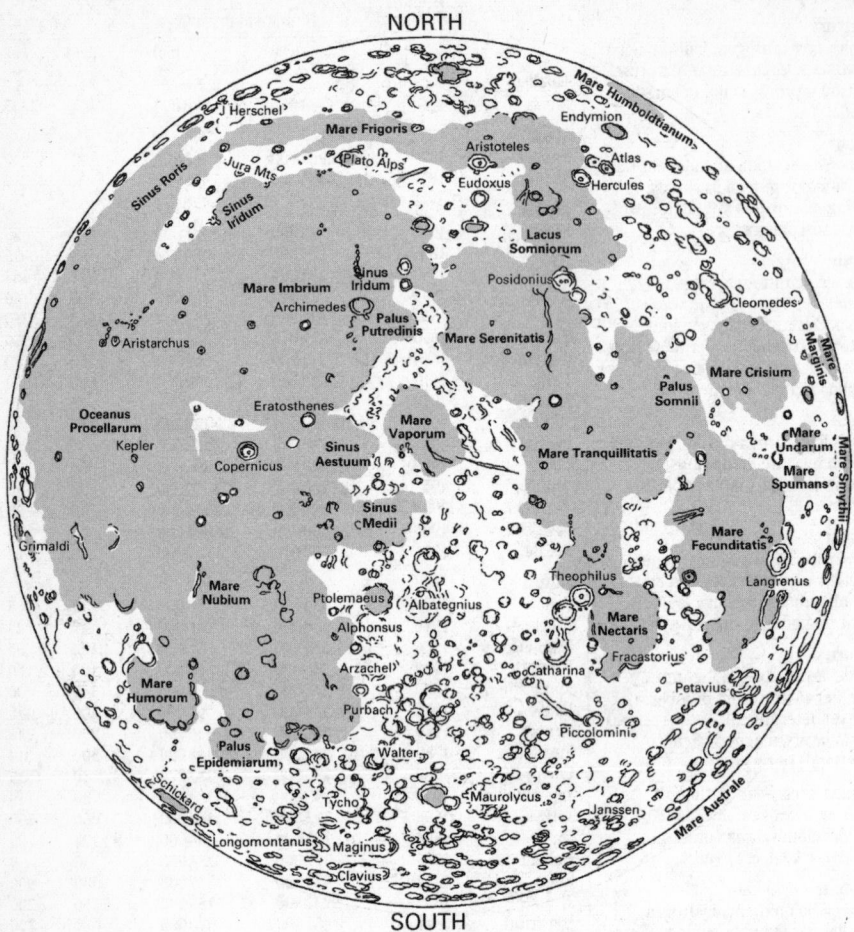

NORTH

J Herschel
Mare Frigoris
Jura Mts
Plato Alps
Aristoteles
Atlas
Endymion
Mare Humboldtianum
Sinus Roris
Sinus Iridum
Eudoxus
Hercules
Mare Imbrium
Sinus Iridum
Lacus Somniorum
Posidonius
Cleomedes
Aristarchus
Archimedes
Palus Putredinis
Mare Serenitatis
Mare Crisium
Palus Somnii
Mare Marginis
Eratosthenes
Mare Vaporum
Oceanus Procellarum
Sinus Aestuum
Mare Undarum
Mare Smythii
Kepler
Copernicus
Mare Tranquillitatis
Mare Spumans
Sinus Medii
Mare Fecunditatis
Grimaldi
Mare Nubium
Ptolemaeus
Albategnius
Theophilus
Langrenus
Alphonsus
Mare Nectaris
Arzachel
Catharina
Fracastorius
Petavius
Mare Humorum
Purbach
Piccolomini
Palus Epidemiarum
Walter
Maurolycus
Janssen
Mare Australe
Schickard
Tycho
Longomontanus
Maginus
Clavius

SOUTH

The lunar 'maria'[a]

Latin name	English name	Latin name	English name
Lacus Somniorum	Lake of Dreams	Mare Serenitatis	Sea of Serenity
Mare Australe	Southern Sea	Mare Smythii	Smyth's Sea
Mare Crisium	Sea of Crises	Mare Spumans	Foaming Sea
Mare Fecunditatis	Sea of Fertility	Mare Tranquillitatis	Sea of Tranquillity
Mare Frigoris	Sea of Cold	Mare Undarum	Sea of Waves
Mare Humboldtianum	Humboldt's Sea	Mare Vaporum	Sea of Vapours
Mare Humorum	Sea of Humours	Oceanus Procellarum	Ocean of Storms
Mare Imbrium	Sea of Showers	Palus Epidemiarum	Marsh of Epidemics
Mare Ingenii	Sea of Geniuses	Palus Putredinis	Marsh of Decay
Mare Marginis	Marginal Sea	Palus Somnii	Marsh of Sleep
Mare Moscoviense	Moscow Sea	Sinus Aestuum	Bay of Heats
Mare Nectaris	Sea of Nectar	Sinus Iridum	Bay of Rainbows
Mare Nubium	Sea of Clouds	Sinus Medii	Central Bay
Mare Orientale	Eastern Sea	Sinus Roris	Bay of Dew

[a]'Maria' refers to the lowland areas of the moon flooded by lava 3.5 thousand million years ago.

The far side of the Moon

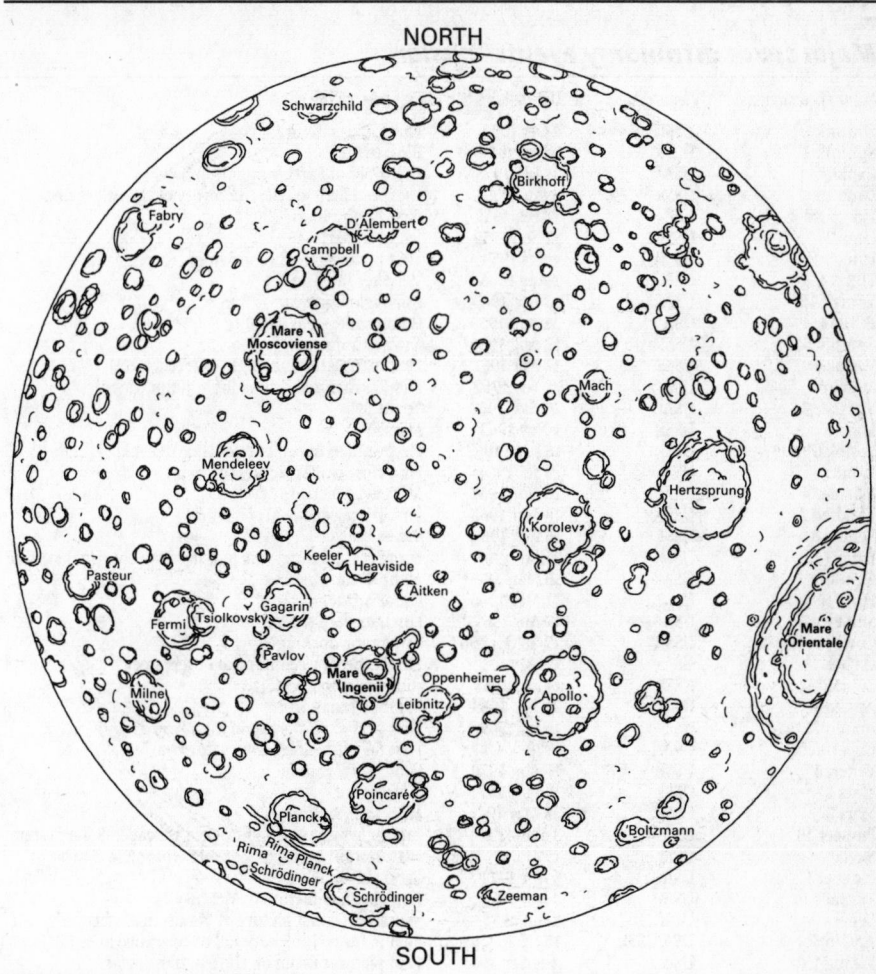

NORTH

SOUTH

Lunar eclipses 2000–2010

Date	Extent of eclipse	Time of mid-eclipse (universal)	Date	Extent of eclipse	Time of mid-eclipse (universal)
21 Jan 2000	Total	04.45	17 Oct 2005	Partial[u]	12.03
16 Jul 2000	Total	13.57	14 Mar 2006	Partial	23.47
9 Jan 2001	Total	20.22	7 Sep 2006	Partial[u]	18.51
5 Jul 2001	Partial[u]	14.55	3 Mar 2007	Total	23.21
30 Dec 2001	Partial	10.29	28 Aug 2007	Total	10.37
26 May 2002	Partial	12.03	21 Feb 2008	Total	03.26
24 Jun 2002	Partial	21.27	16 Aug 2008	Partial[u]	21.10
20 Nov 2002	Partial	01.46	9 Feb 2009	Partial	14.38
16 May 2003	Total	03.40	7 Jul 2009	Partial	09.38
9 Nov 2003	Total	01.18	6 Aug 2009	Partial	00.39
4 May 2004	Total	20.30	31 Dec 2009	Partial[u]	19.23
28 Oct 2004	Total	03.04	26 June 2010	Partial[u]	11.38
24 Apr 2005	Partial	09.55	21 Dec 2010	Total	08.17

[u]Umbral; all others are penumbral

SPACE EXPLORATION

Major space astronomy events/missions

Name of event/mission	Country/agency	Date of launch	Event description
Sputnik 1	USSR	4 Oct 1957	First Earth satellite
Sputnik 2	USSR	3 Nov 1957	Biosatellite
Explorer 1	USA	31 Jan 1958	Discovery of Earth's radiation belts
Luna 1	USSR	2 Jan 1959	Escaped Earth gravity; discovery of the solar wind
Vanguard 2	USA	17 Feb 1959	First Earth photo
Luna 2	USSR	12 Sep 1959	Lunar impact
Luna 3	USSR	4 Oct 1959	First lunar photo (hidden side)
TIROS 1	USA	1 Apr 1960	Weather satellite
Transit 1B	USA	13 Apr 1960	Navigation satellite
ECHO 1	USA	12 Aug 1960	Communications satellite
Sputnik 5	USSR	19 Aug 1960	Orbited animals
Vostok 1	USSR	12 Apr 1961	First manned orbital flight (Yuri Gagarin)
Mercury	USA	20 Feb 1962	First US manned orbital flight (John Glenn)
Mariner 2	USA	26 Aug 1962	Venus flyby
Mars 1	USSR	1 Nov 1962	Mars flyby
Vostok 6	USSR	16 June 1963	First woman in orbit (Valentina Tereshkova)
Ranger 7	USA	28 Jul 1964	First close-up TV pictures of lunar surface
Mariner 4	USA	28 Nov 1964	Mars flyby pictures
Voskhod 2	USSR	18 Mar 1965	First spacewalk (AA Leonov)
Venera 3	USSR	16 Nov 1965	Venus impact
Luna 9	USSR	31 Jan 1966	Lunar soft landing; first picture from the lunar surface
Gemini 8	USA	16 Mar 1966	Manned docking
Luna 10	USSR	31 Mar 1966	Lunar orbiter
Surveyor 3	USA	17 Apr 1967	Lunar surface sampler
Cosmos 186/188	USSR	22/28 Oct 1967	Automatic docking
OAO 2	USA	1968	First orbiting astronomical observatory
Zond 5	USSR	14 Sep 1968	Animals moon orbit
Apollo 8	USA	21 Dec 1968	Manned lunar orbit
Apollo 11	USA	16 Jul 1969	First person on the moon (Neil Armstrong)
Copernicus	USA	1970	First far ultra-violet observatory
Venera 7	USSR	17 Aug 1970	Venus soft landing
Mars 2	USSR	19 May 1971	Mars orbit
Mars 3	USSR	28 May 1971	Mars soft landing
Pioneer 10	USA	3 Mar 1972	Jupiter flyby; crossed Pluto orbit; escaped Solar System
Skylab	USA	1973	High-resolution images of solar corona in X-rays
Pioneer 11	USA	6 Apr 1973	Saturn flyby
Mariner 10	USA	3 Nov 1973	First detailed picture of Mercury
Venera 9	USSR	8 Jun 1975	Venus orbit; first picture of Venusian surface
Apollo/Soyuz	USA/USSR	15 Jul 1975	First manned international co-operative mission
Viking 1, 2	USA	Aug/Sep 1975	First pictures taken on the Martian surface
Voyager 1, 2	USA	Aug/Sep 1977	First images of Jupiter, Saturn, Uranus, and Neptune
IUE	USA/UK/ESA	1978	First international space observatory
ISEE C	USA	12 Aug 1978	Comet intercept
STS 1	USA	12 Apr 1981	First launch of *Columbia* space shuttle
STS 6	USA	4 Apr 1983	First launch of *Challenger*
Soyuz T 9	USSR	27 Jun 1983	Construction in space
STS 9	USA	28 Nov 1983	First flight of the ESA spacelab
STS 41 D	USA	30 Aug 1984	First launch of *Discovery*
STS 51 A	USA	8 Nov 1984	Recovery of satellites 'Westar 6' and 'Palapa B2'
Vega 1	USSR	15 Dec 1984	Halley flyby
STS 51 J	USA	3 Oct 1985	First launch of *Atlantis*
Giotto	ESA	1986	First high-resolution image of Halley's nucleus
STS 26	USA	29 Sep 1988	First launch after *Challenger* disaster
Magellan	USA	5 May 1989	Global radar map of Venus
STS 34	USA	18 Oct 1989	*Galileo* launch
Muses A	Japan	24 Jan 1990	Two satellites placed in orbit round the moon
STS 31	USA/ESA	24 Apr 1990	Launch of Hubble Space Telescope
STS 41	USA/ESA	6 Oct 1990	Launch of *Ulysses*; first flight above the solar poles
STS 37	USA	5 Apr 1991	Launch of Compton Gamma Ray Observatory
STS 47	USA	7 May 1992	First launch of *Endeavour*

Major space astronomy events/missions (continued)

STS 49	USA/ESA	31 Jul 1992	Launch of *Eureca* (European recoverable carrier)
STS 59	USA	2 Dec 1993	Hubble Space Telescope repaired in space
STS 69	USA/Russia	29 Jun 1995	*Atlantis* docked with *Mir* space station
Mars Pathfinder	USA	4 Dec 1996	Microrover's first exploration of Mars surface, Jul 1997
Cassini	NASA/ESA/ASI	15 Oct 1997	Cassini Orbiter to Saturn, with Huygens probe to Titan
DSI	USA	24 Oct 1998	Deep Space 1, first technology demonstration probe
Mars Surveyor	USA/NASA	Apr 2001	*Odyssey* spacecraft launched to orbit Mars
STS 111	USA/NASA	Jun 2002	*Endeavour* is 14th shuttle mission to the ISS
Mars Express	ESA	Jun 2003	Mission to Mars: remote sensing orbiter and small lander named *Beagle 2* (lost during landing)
Mars Exploration Rover	NASA	Jun 2003	Rover probe (*Spirit*) landed on Mars, Jan 2004; sent back coloured images of surface
Smart 1	ESA	28 Aug 2003	Europe's first mission to the Moon: Lunar probe to map surface composition; mission completed Sep 2006
Rosetta probe	ESA	Mar 2004	Probe to rendezvous with comet 67P/Churyumov-Gerasimento in 2014
Cassini–Huygens	NASA/ESA/ASI	Jul 2004	First space vehicle to go into orbit around Saturn; Huygens probe landed on Titan, Jan 2005
Mercury Messenger	NASA	Aug 2004	Probe launched to reach Mercury in 2011
STS 114	USA/NASA	26 Jul 2005	*Discovery* shuttle damaged on take off; pioneering spacewalk to effect repairs
Venus Express	ESA	9 Nov 2005	Europe's first mission to Venus
New Horizons	NASA	19 Jan 2006	First mission to Pluto; to arrive 2015
STS 115	NASA	9 Sep 2006	Completion of 12-day *Atlantis* mission to re-start construction of International Space Station

(ESA = European Space Agency; ASI = Italian Space Agency)

Satellite launch centres

Country	Launch base	Organization responsible	First launch
USA	Cape Canaveral	US Air Force/NASA	31 Jan 1958 (Explorer 1)
	Kennedy Space Center	NASA	9 Nov 1967 (Apollo 4)
	Vandenberg AFB	US Air Force/SAMTO/NASA	28 Feb 1959 (Discoverer 1)
	Wallops Island	NASA Goddard Space Flight Center	16 Feb 1961 (Explorer 9)
USSR (now CIS)	Kapustin Yar, or Volgograd cosmodrome	Ministry of Defence/Academy of Sciences/Intercosmos	16 Mar 1962 (Cosmos 1)
	Plesetsk, or Northern cosmodrome	Ministry of Defence/Academy of Sciences	17 Mar 1966 (Cosmos 112)
	Tyuratam Leninsk, or Baikonur cosmodrome	Ministry of Defence/Academy of Sciences	4 Oct 1957 (Sputnik 1)
Australia	Woomera Range	WRE/British DTI/ELDO	29 Nov 1967 (Wresat)
Brazil	Alcantara Launch Centre	Ministry of Aeronautics/COBAE/CTA	2 Nov 1977 (VLS, unsuccessful)
China	Jiuquan SLC	Ministry of Defence/MOA	24 Apr 1970 (SKW1/Tungfanghung)
	Xichang SLC	MOA	29 Jan 1984 (STW1)
France	Guianan Space Centre at Kouru	CNES/ESA/Arianespace	10 Mar 1970 (Dial)
	Hammaguir/Colombia Bechar	CIEES/CNES	26 Nov 1965 (A1 'Asterix')
India	SHAR/Sriharikota Range	ISRO	18 Jul 1980 (Rohini RS1)
Italy	San Marco platform	CRA/University of Rome	26 Apr 1967 (San Marco 2)
Japan	Kagoshima Space Centre	ISAS/University of Tokyo	11 Feb 1970 (Ohsumi)
	Tanegashima Space Centre	Nasda	9 Sep 1975 (ETS1/Kiku)
Sweden	Esrange, Kiruna	Swedish Space Corporation	20 Nov 1966 (Centaure)

THE UNIVERSE

International space launchers

The major launch vehicles in use and some of their important predecessors. The data refer to lift capacity (given in kg/lb, in most cases to the nearest hundred) and year of launch.

LEO: low Earth orbit (c.200 km/125 mi)
GEO: geosynchronous Earth orbit (36 000 km/22 500 mi)
ETO: elliptical transfer orbit (intermediate between LEO and GEO)

USSR/CIS/Russia

Cosmos
500 kg/1 800 lb
to LEO
(1964)

Cyclone
4 500 kg/10 000 lb
to LEO
(1966)

Soyuz/Molniya
7 300 kg/16 000 lb
to LEO
1 600 kg/3 500 lb
to ETO
(1960)

Proton
18 900 kg/41 600 lb
to LEO
1 600 kg/3 500 lb
to GEO
(1965)

Cosmos
16 000 kg/35 000 lb
to LEO
(1985)

Energia
100 000 kg/
220 000 lb
to LEO
(1987)

China   India   Japan

   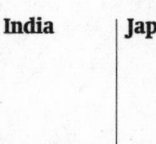  

Long March 1
225 kg/500 lb
to LEO
(1970)

Long March 2
1 900 kg/
4 200 lb
to LEO
(1975)

Long March 3
900 kg/
2 000 lb
to GEO
(1984)

SLV-3
45 kg/100 lb
to LEO
(1980)

MU-3
180 kg/400 lb
to LEO
(1971)

N-2
700 kg/
1 500 lb
to GEO
(1981)

H-1
300 kg/700 lb
to LEO
(1986)

European Space Agency

Ariane 1
1 700 kg/3 700 lb
to ETO
(1979)

Ariane 3
2 400 kg/5 200 lb
to ETO
(1984)

Ariane 4
4 200 kg/9 200 lb
to GEO
(1987)

Ariane 5
6 500 kg/14 300 lb
to GEO
(1995)

International space launchers (continued)

United States of America

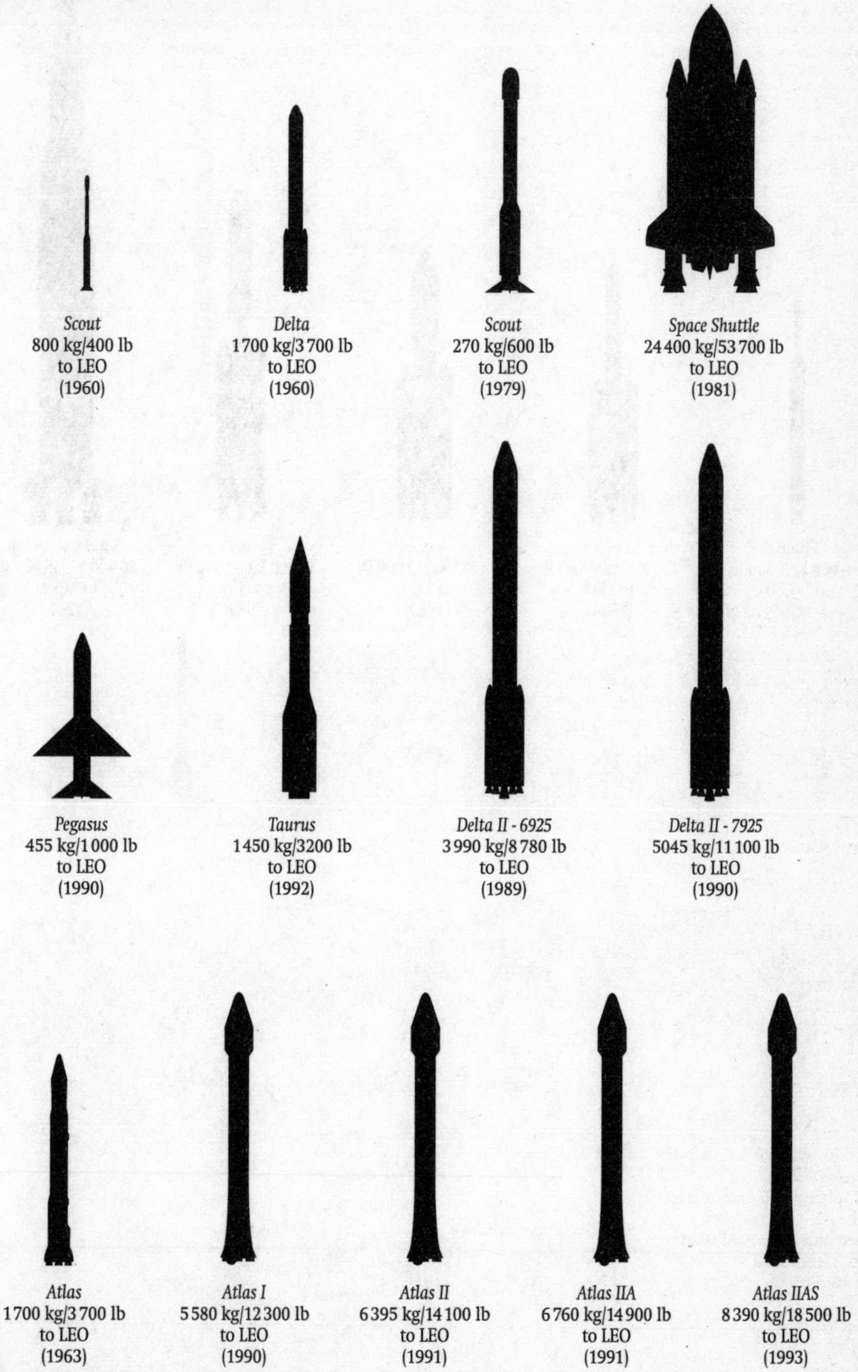

Scout
800 kg/400 lb
to LEO
(1960)

Delta
1700 kg/3700 lb
to LEO
(1960)

Scout
270 kg/600 lb
to LEO
(1979)

Space Shuttle
24400 kg/53700 lb
to LEO
(1981)

Pegasus
455 kg/1000 lb
to LEO
(1990)

Taurus
1450 kg/3200 lb
to LEO
(1992)

Delta II - 6925
3990 kg/8780 lb
to LEO
(1989)

Delta II - 7925
5045 kg/11100 lb
to LEO
(1990)

Atlas
1700 kg/3700 lb
to LEO
(1963)

Atlas I
5580 kg/12300 lb
to LEO
(1990)

Atlas II
6395 kg/14100 lb
to LEO
(1991)

Atlas IIA
6760 kg/14900 lb
to LEO
(1991)

Atlas IIAS
8390 kg/18500 lb
to LEO
(1993)

THE UNIVERSE

International space launchers (continued)

Titan 3B
3 900 kg/8 600 lb
to LEO
(1966)

Titan 34D
13 600 kg/30 000 lb
to LEO
(1984)

Titan III
14 515 kg/32 000 lb
to LEO
(1989)

Titan IV
17 700 kg/39 000 lb
to LEO
(1989)

Saturn V Apollo
20 400 kg/45 000 lb
to Moon
(1967)

PART TWO

The Earth

HISTORY

The developing world

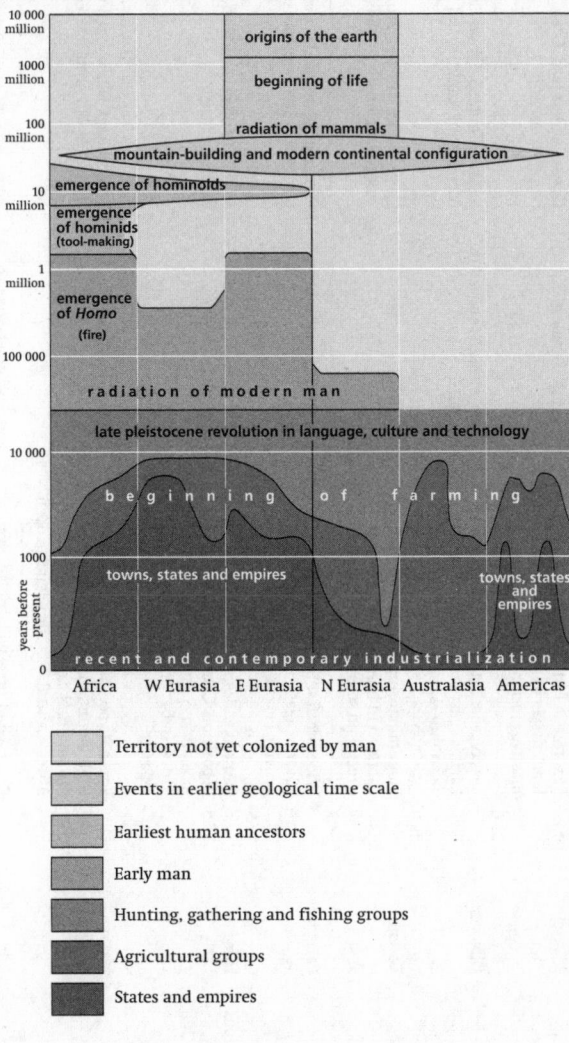

origins of the earth

beginning of life

radiation of mammals

mountain-building and modern continental configuration

emergence of hominoids

emergence of hominids (tool-making)

emergence of *Homo* (fire)

radiation of modern man

late pleistocene revolution in language, culture and technology

beginning of farming

towns, states and empires

towns, states and empires

recent and contemporary industrialization

Africa   W Eurasia   E Eurasia   N Eurasia   Australasia   Americas

years before present

10 000 million
1000 million
100 million
10 million
1 million
100 000
10 000
1000
0

- Territory not yet colonized by man
- Events in earlier geological time scale
- Earliest human ancestors
- Early man
- Hunting, gathering and fishing groups
- Agricultural groups
- States and empires

Major ice-age periods

A schematic presentation of the major glacial periods (dark grey) in the Earth's history. It is likely that a number of glaciations occurred within each epoch. Note the change in scale on the time axis at 1 000 million years ago.

THE EARTH

Age (million years)		
	Pleistocene/Quaternary	
	Cenozoic	Tertiary
100	Mesozoic	Cretaceous
		Jurassic
200		Triassic
		Permian
300	Permo-Carboniferous (Gondwanan)	
	Palaeozoic	Carboniferous
		Devonian
400		Silurian
	Ordovician	Ordovician
500		Cambrian
600	Precambrian Varangian	
700		
800	Sturtian	
900		
	Gnejsö	
1000		
2000	Huronian	
3000		
4000		

THE EARTH

Geological time scale

Eon	Era	Period	Epoch	Million years before present	Geological events	Sea life	Land life
Phanerozoic	Cenozoic	Quaternary	Holocene		Glaciers recede. Sea level rises. Climate becomes more equable.	As now.	Forests flourish again. Humans acquire agriculture and technology.
				0.01			
			Pleistocene		Widespread glaciers melt periodically, causing seas to rise and fall.	As now.	Many plant forms perish. Small mammals abundant. Primitive humans established.
				2.0			
		Tertiary	Pliocene		Continents and oceans adopting their present form. Present climatic distribution established. Ice caps develop.	Giant sharks extinct. Many fish varieties.	Some plants and mammals die out. Primates flourish.
				5.1			
			Miocene		Seas recede further. European and Asian land masses join. Heavy rain causes massive erosion. Red Sea opens.	Bony fish common. Giant sharks.	Grasses widespread. Grazing mammals become common.
				24.6			
			Oligocene		Seas recede. Extensive movements of Earth's crust produce new mountains (eg Alpine–Himalayan chain).	Crabs, mussels, and snails evolve.	Forests diminish. Grasses appear. Pachyderms, canines, and felines develop.
				38.0			
			Eocene		Mountain formation continues. Glaciers common in high mountain ranges. Greenland separates. Australia separates.	Whales adapt to sea.	Large tropical jungles. Primitive forms of modern mammals established.
				54.9			
			Palaeocene		Widespread subsidence of land. Seas advance again. Considerable volcanic activity. Europe emerges.	Many reptiles become extinct.	Flowering plants widespread. First primates. Giant reptiles extinct.
				65			
	Mesozoic	Cretaceous	Late Early		Swamps widespread. Massive alluvial deposition. Continuing limestone formation. S America separates from Africa. India, Africa and Antarctica separate.	Turtles, rays, and now-common fish appear.	Flowering plants established. Dinosaurs become extinct.
				97.5			
		Jurassic	Malm Dogger Lias		Seas advance. Much river formation. High mountains eroded. Limestone formation. N America separates from Africa. Central Atlantic begins to open.	Reptiles dominant.	Early flowers. Dinosaurs dominant. Mammals still primitive. First birds.
				144 163 188			
		Triassic	Late Middle		Desert conditions widespread. Hot climate slowly becomes warm and wet.	Ichthyosaurs, flying fish, and crustaceans appear.	Ferns and conifers thrive. First mammals, dinosaurs, and flies.
				213 231			

THE EARTH

Era	Period	Epoch	Million years	Geology	Life	Flora / Development
Palaeozoic		Early	243	Break up of Pangea into supercontinents Gondwana (S) and Laurasia (N).	Some shelled fish become extinct.	Deciduous plants. Reptiles dominant. Many insect varieties.
	Permian	Late	248	Some sea areas cut off to form lakes. Earth movements form mountains. Glaciation in southern hemisphere.		
		Early	258			
	Carboniferous	Pennsylvanian	286	Sea-beds rise to form new land areas. Enormous swamps. Partly-rotted vegetation forms coal.	Amphibians and sharks abundant.	Extensive evergreen forests. Reptiles breed on land. Some insects develop wings.
		Mississippian	320			
	Devonian	Late	360	Collision of continents causing mountain formation (Appalachians, Caledonides, and Urals). Sea deeper but narrower. Climatic zones forming. Iapetus ocean closed.	Fish abundant. Primitive sharks. First amphibians.	Leafy plants. Some invertebrates adapt to land. First insects.
		Middle	374			
		Early	387			
	Silurian	Pridoli	408	New mountain ranges form. Sea level varies periodically. Extensive shallow sea over the Sahara.	Large vertebrates.	First leafless land plants.
		Ludlow	414			
		Wenlock	421			
		Llandovery	428			
			438			
	Ordovician	Ashgill	448	Shore lines still quite variable. Increasing sedimentation. Europe and N America moving together.	First vertebrates. Coral reefs develop.	None.
		Caradoc	458			
		Llandeilo	468			
		Llanvirn	478			
		Arenig	488			
		Tremadoc	505			
	Cambrian	Merioneth	525	Much volcanic activity, and long periods of marine sedimentation.	Shelled invertebrates. Trilobites.	None.
		St David's	540			
		Caerfai	590			
Proterozoic / Precambrian	Vendian		650	Shallow seas advance and retreat over land areas. Atmosphere uniformly warm.	Seaweed. Algae and invertebrates.	None.
	Riphean	Late	900	Intense deformation and metamorphism.	Earliest marine life and fossils.	None.
		Middle	1300			
		Early	1600			
	Early Proterozoic		2500	Shallow shelf seas. Formation of carbonate sediments and 'red beds'.	First appearance of stromatolites.	None.
Archaean	Archaean (Azoic)		4600	Banded iron formations. Formation of the Earth's crust and oceans.	None.	None.

STRUCTURE

The Earth

Age 4 500 000 000 years
Area 509 600 000 km²/197 000 000 sq mi
Mass 6.0 × 10²⁴ kg
Land surface 148 000 000 km²/57 000 000 sq mi
(c.29% of total area)
Water surface 361 000 000 km²/140 000 000 sq mi
(c.71% of total area)
Circumference (equator) 40 076 km/24 902 mi
Circumference (meridian) 40 000 km/24 860 mi
Diameter (equator) 12 757 km/7 927 mi

Diameter (meridian) 12 714 km/7 900 mi
Period of axial rotation 23 h 56 m 4.0996 s
Lithosphere 80 km/50 mi thick
Thickness of upper mantle 700 km/430 mi
Thickness of lower mantle 2 200 km/1 370 mi
Thickness of outer core 2 250 km/1 400 mi
Radius of inner core 3 480 km/2 160 mi
Density of core 13.09 g/cm³
Temperature at core 4 500°C

The structure of the Earth

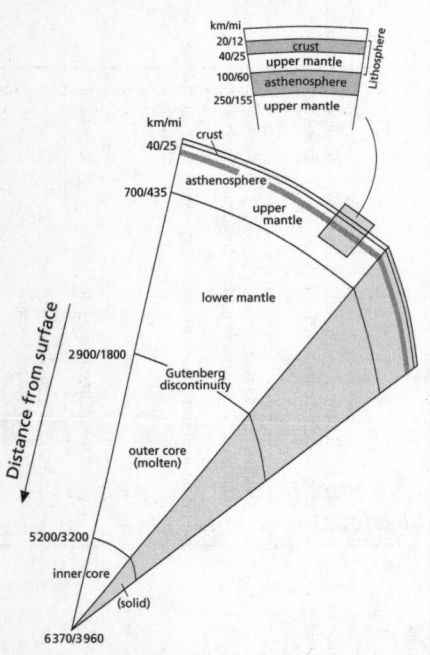

Earth's crust composition

This pie chart shows percentages of the most abundant elements in the Earth's crust.

a Oxygen 46.6%

b Silicon 27.72%

c Aluminium 8.13%

d Iron 5.0%

e Calcium 3.63%

f Sodium 2.83%

g Potassium 2.59%

h Magnesium 2.09%

i Other elements 1.41%

Chemical composition of rocks

Oxide component (%)	Type of rock						
	Granite	Basalt	Amphibolite	Schist	Shale	Sandstone	Limestone
SiO_2	70.8	49.0	49.3	63.3	62.4	94.4	5.2
TiO_2	0.4	1.0	1.2	1.4	1.1	0.1	0.1
Al_2O_3	14.5	18.2	16.9	17.9	16.6	1.1	0.8
Fe_2O_3	1.6	3.2	3.6	3.6	3.2	0.4	0.3
FeO	1.8	6.0	6.8	2.6	2.1	0.2	0.2
MgO	0.9	7.6	7.0	1.6	2.5	0.1	7.9
CaO	1.8	11.0	9.5	1.9	1.7	1.6	42.6
Na_2O	3.3	2.5	2.9	1.3	0.9	0.1	0.1
K_2O	4.0	0.9	1.1	3.1	3.0	0.2	0.3
H_2O	0.8	0.4	1.5	2.6	5.2	0.3	0.7
CO_2					1.0	1.1	41.6

Mineral composition of rocks

Mineral component (%)	Type of rock						
	Granite	Basalt	Amphibolite	Schist	Shale	Sandstone	Limestone
Quartz	30			32	17	97	3
Alkali feldspar	60	5				1	1
Plagioclase	5	45	42	18			
Pyroxene		40					
Amphibole			50				
Olivine		5					
Biotite	4			5	7		
Muscovite				38	1	1	
Magnetite	1	5	3	3	1	1	1
Staurolite				2			
Clay minerals					80		1
Calcite					1		94

Mohs scale of hardness

Friedrich Mohs (1773–1839) introduced a simple definition of hardness, according to which one mineral is said to be harder than another if the former scratches the latter. The Mohs scale is based on a series of common minerals, arranged in order of increasing hardness.

Mineral	Composition	Simple hardness test	Hardness
Talc	$Mg_3Si_4O_{10}(OH)_2$	Crushed by finger nail	1
Gypsum	$CaSO_4 \cdot 2H_2O$	Scratched by finger nail	2
Calcite	$CaCO_3$	Scratched by copper coin	3
Fluorite	CaF_2	Scratched by glass	4
Apatite	$Ca_5(PO_4)_3F$	Scratched by penknife	5
Orthoclase (feldspar)	$KAlSi_3O_8$	Scratched by quartz	6
Quartz	SiO_2	Scratched by steel file	7
Topaz	$Al_2SiO_4F_2$	Scratched by corundum	8
Corundum	Al_2O_3	Scratched by diamond	9
Diamond	C		10

Layers of the atmosphere

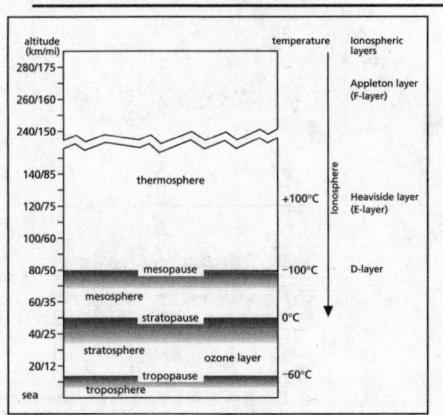

The composition of dry air at sea level

Gas	Volume (%)
Nitrogen (N_2)	78.08
Oxygen (O_2)	20.95
Argon (Ar)	0.93
Carbon dioxide (CO_2)	0.031
Neon (Ne)	0.0018
Helium (He)	0.00052
Krypton (Kr)	0.00011
Xenon (Xe)	0.0000087
Hydrogen (H_2)	0.00005
Methane (CH_4)	0.0002
Nitric oxide (NO)	0.00005
Ozone (O_3)	0.000002 (winter) 0.000007 (summer)

THE EARTH

World minerals map

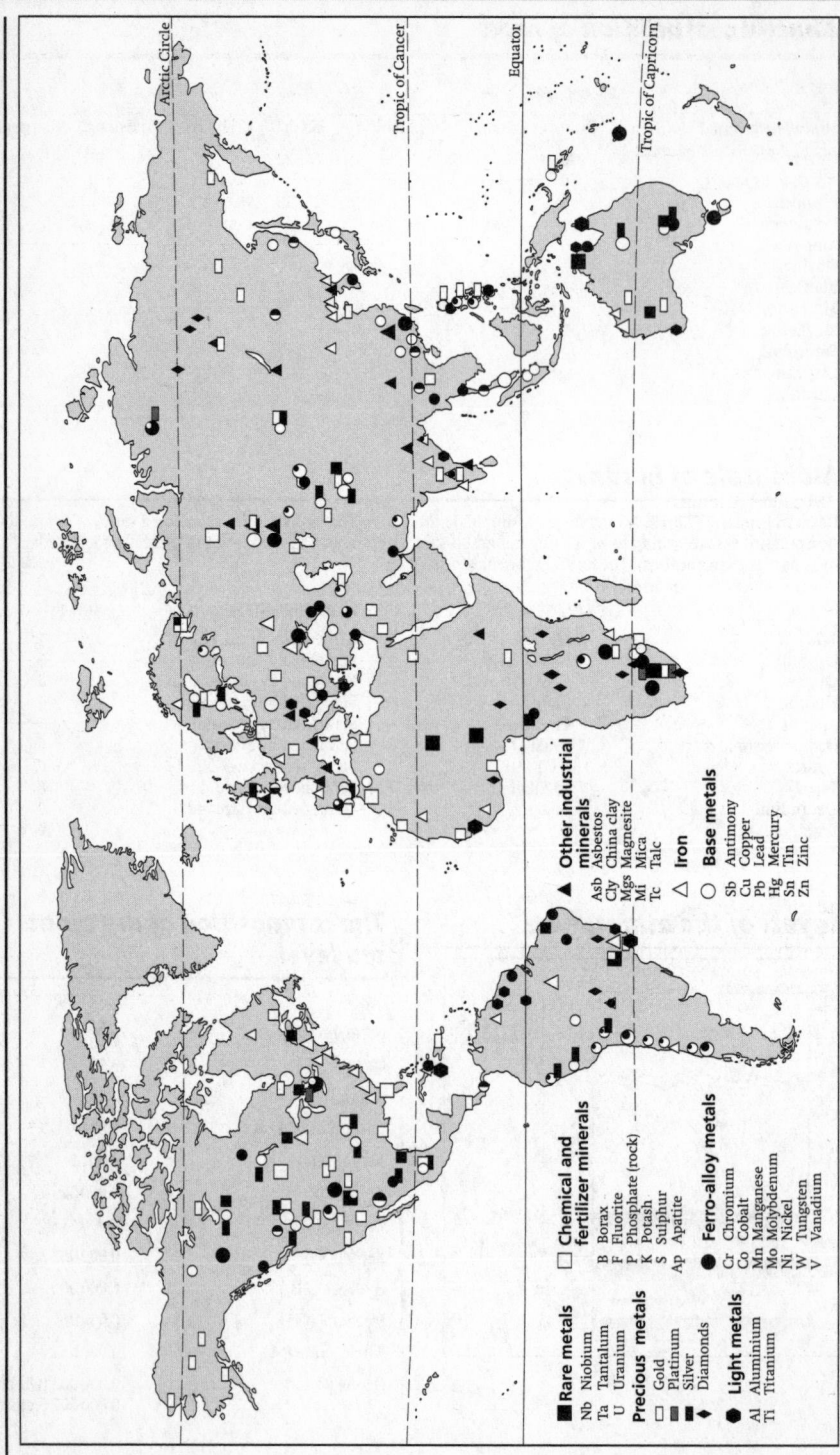

Rare metals
Nb Niobium
Ta Tantalum
U Uranium

Precious metals
Gold
Platinum
Silver
Diamonds

Light metals
Al Aluminium
Ti Titanium

Chemical and fertilizer minerals
B Borax
F Fluorite
P Phosphate (rock)
K Potash
S Sulphur
Ap Apatite

Ferro-alloy metals
Cr Chromium
Co Cobalt
Mo Molybdenum
Mn Manganese
Ni Nickel
W Tungsten
V Vanadium

Other industrial minerals
Asb Asbestos
Cly China clay
Mgs Magnesite
Mi Mica
Tc Talc

Iron

Base metals
Sb Antimony
Cu Copper
Pb Lead
Hg Mercury
Sn Tin
Zn Zinc

Arctic Circle
Tropic of Cancer
Equator
Tropic of Capricorn

Continental drift

240 million years ago
The single supercontinent *Pangea* is formed, with a single superocean, *Panthalassa*.

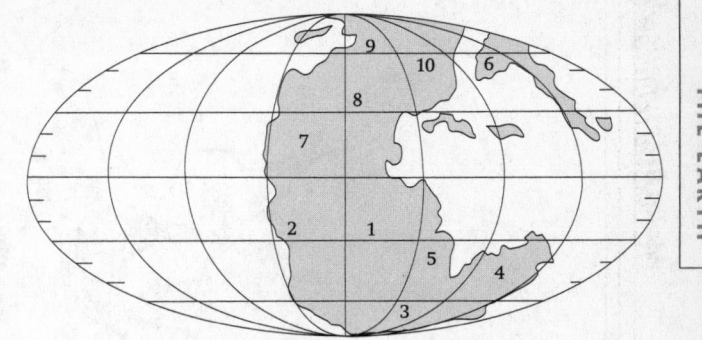

120 million years ago
Tethys, a broad gulf, divides Pangea into two huge landmasses: *Laurasia* in the north; *Gondwana* in the south.

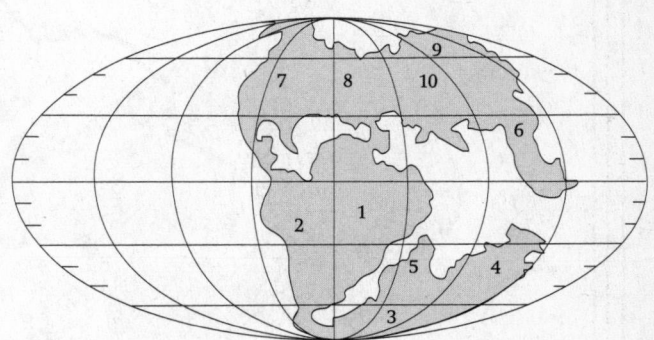

60 million years ago
Laurasia and Gondwana have split to begin to form the continents as we know them today.

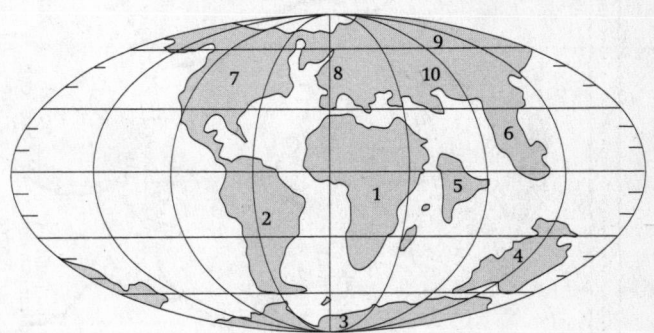

Major lithospheric plates

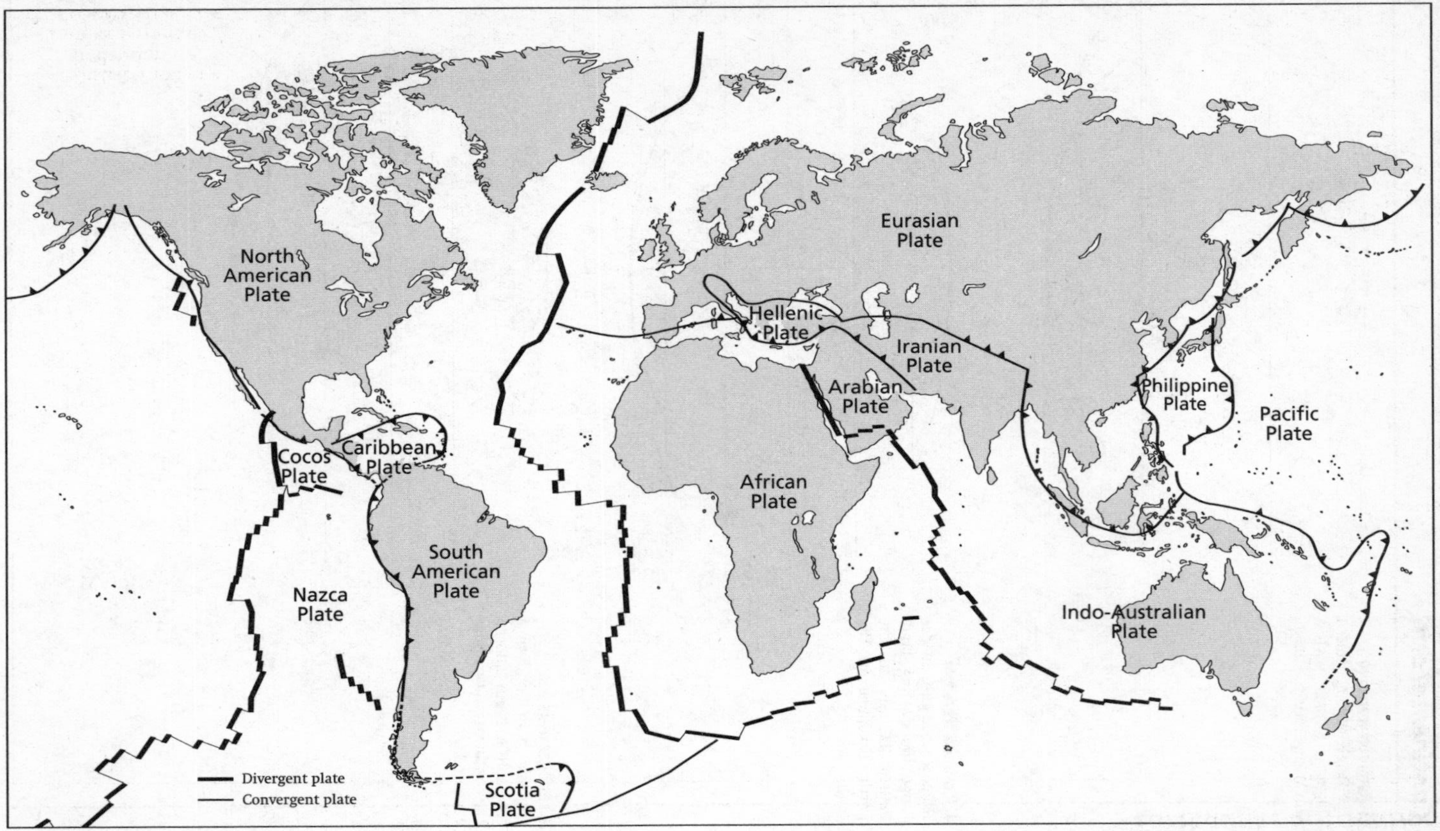

Eurasian Plate

Pacific Plate

Philippine Plate

Indo-Australian Plate

Iranian Plate

Arabian Plate

Hellenic Plate

African Plate

North American Plate

Caribbean Plate

Cocos Plate

South American Plate

Nazca Plate

Scotia Plate

—— Divergent plate
— Convergent plate

Earthquake distribution

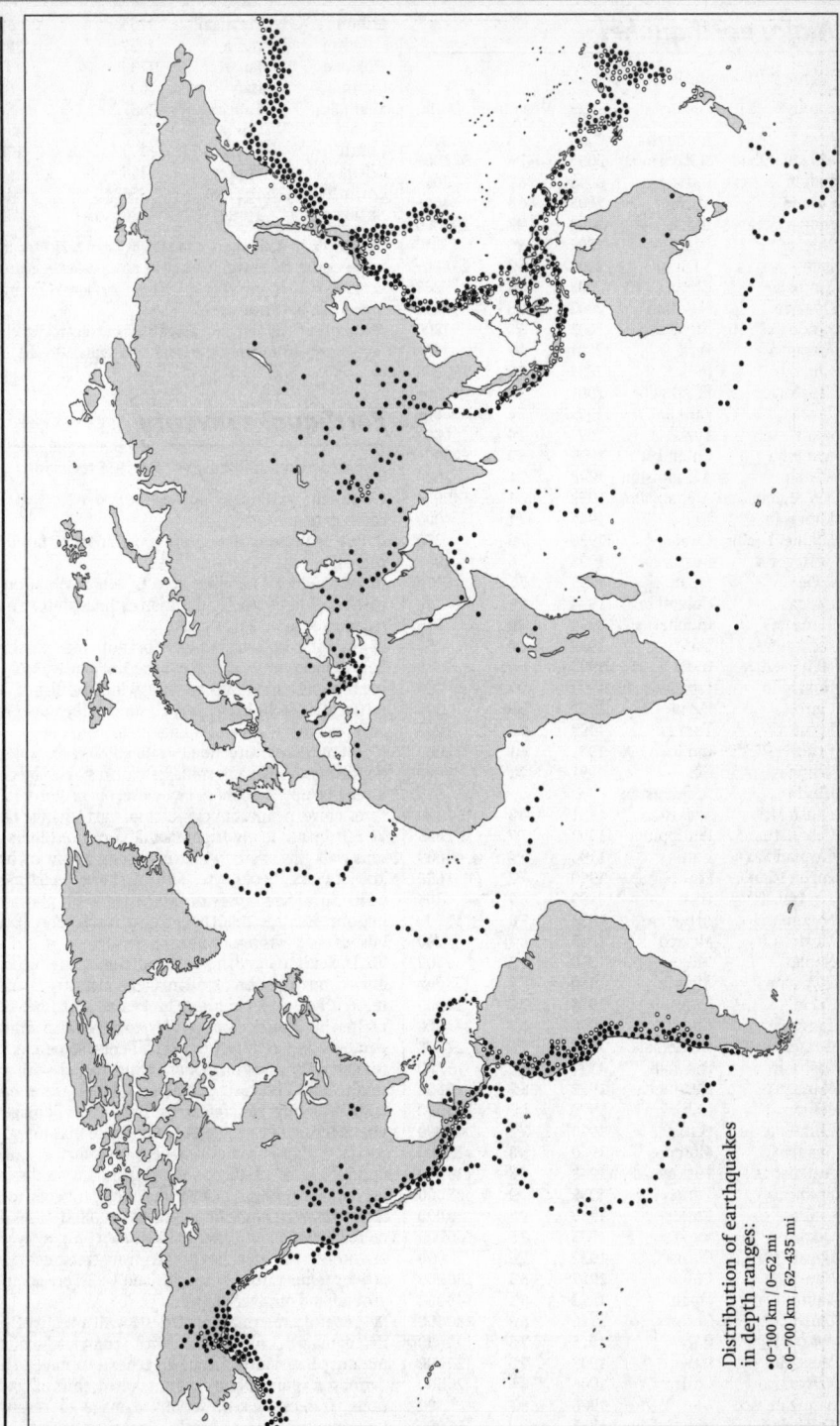

Distribution of earthquakes
in depth ranges:
● 0–100 km / 0–62 mi
○ 0–700 km / 62–435 mi

Major earthquakes

All magnitudes on the Richter scale[a]

Location	Country	Year	Magnitude	Deaths
Java	Indonesia	2006	6·3	6000+
Muzaffarabad	N Pakistan	2005	7·6	87000+
Indian Ocean	Indonesia	2005	8·7	1000+
Zarand	SE Iran	2005	6·4	400+
Indian Ocean	Indonesia[b]	2004	9·3	300000
Niigata	Japan	2004	6·8	40
Bam	S E Iran	2003	6·3	26000+
Xinjiang	China	2003	6·8	268
Quazvin	N W Iran	2002	6·3	230
Hindu Kush Mts	Afghanistan	2002	6·1	1800
Arequipa	Peru	2001	7·9	100+
Gujarat	India	2001	7·9	100000
El Salvador	El Salvador	2001	7·7	680+
Taiwan	Taiwan	1999	7·6	2000+
Izmit	Turkey	1999	7·4	15000+
Armenia	Colombia	1999	6·0	2000+
Rostaq	Afghanistan	1998	7·1	2000
NW Afghanistan	Afghanistan	1998	6·1	4000+
Khorasan	Iran	1997	7·1	4000
Lijiang, Yunan	China	1996	7·0	250
Neftegorsk	Russia	1995	7·6	1989
Kobe	Japan	1995	7·2	5477
Cauca	Colombia	1994	6·8	269
Sumatra	Indonesia	1994	7·0	215
Los Angeles	USA	1994	6·8	57
Maharashtra	India	1993	6·4	9748
Hokkaido	Japan	1993	7·7	200
Cairo	Egypt	1992	5·9	500
Erzincan	Turkey	1992	6·2	2000
Uttar Pradesh	India	1991	6·1	1000
Georgia	CIS	1991	7·2	100
Hindu Kush Mts	Afghanistan/ Pakistan	1991	6·8	1300
Cabanatuan	Philippines	1990	7·7	1653
Caspian Sea	Iran	1990	7·7	40000
Luzon Island	Philippines	1990	7·7	1600
San Francisco	USA	1989	6·9	100
N Armenia	Armenia	1988	7·0	25000
Mexico City	Mexico	1985	8·1	7200
Naples	Italy	1980	7·2	4500
El Asnam	Algeria	1980	7·3	5000
Tabas	Iran	1978	7·7	25000
Tangshan	China	1976	8·2	242000
Guatemala City	Guatemala	1976	7·5	22778
Kashmir	Pakistan	1974	6·3	5200
Managua	Nicaragua	1972	6·2	5000
Tehran	Iran	1972	6·9	5000
Chimbote	Peru	1970	7·7	66000
Agadir	Morocco	1960	5·8	12000
Ashkhabad	Turkmenistan	1948	7·3	19800
Erzincan	Turkey	1939	7·9	23000
Chillan	Chile	1939	7·8	30000
Quetta	India	1935	7·5	60000
Gansu	China	1932	7·6	70000
Nan-Shan	China	1927	8·3	200000
Kanto	Japan	1923	8·3	143000
Gansu	China	1920	8·6	180000
Avezzano	Italy	1915	7·5	30000
Messina	Italy	1908	7·5	120000
Valparaiso	Chile	1906	8·6	20000
San Francisco	USA	1906	8·3	500
Calabria	Italy	1783		50000
Lisbon	Portugal	1755		70000
Calcutta	India	1737		300000
Hokkaido	Japan	1730		137000
Catania	Italy	1693		60000
Shemaka	Caucasia	1667		80000
Shensi	China	1556		830000
Chihli	China	1290		100000
Cilicia	Turkey	1268		60000
Corinth	Greece	856		45000
Antioch	Turkey	526		250000

[a]A logarithmic scale, devised in 1935 by Charles Richter, for representing the energy released by earthquakes. A figure of 2 or less is barely perceptible, while an earthquake measuring over 5 may be destructive.
[b]Epicentre off NW Sumatra caused a major tsunami which devastated territories in and around the Indian Ocean.

Earthquake severity

Modified Mercalli intensity scale (1956 revision)

I Not felt; marginal and long-period effects of large earthquakes.
II Felt by persons at rest, on upper floors or favourably placed.
III Felt indoors; hanging objects swing; vibration like passing of light trucks; duration estimated; may not be recognized as an earthquake.
IV Hanging objects swing; vibration like passing of heavy trucks, or sensation of a jolt like a heavy ball striking the walls; standing cars rock; windows, dishes, doors rattle; glasses clink; crockery clashes; in the upper range of IV, wooden walls and frames creak.
V Felt outdoors; direction estimated; sleepers wakened; liquids disturbed, some spilled; small unstable objects displaced or upset; doors swing, close, open; shutters, pictures move; pendulum clocks stop, start, change rate.
VI Felt by all; many frightened and run outdoors; persons walk unsteadily; windows, dishes, glassware break; knickknacks, books, etc, fall off shelves; pictures off walls; furniture moves or overturns; weak plaster and masonry D crack; small bells ring (church, school); trees, bushes shake visibly, or heard to rustle.
VII Difficult to stand; noticed by drivers; hanging objects quiver; furniture breaks; damage to masonry D, including cracks; weak chimneys broken at roof line; fall of plaster, loose bricks, stones, tiles, cornices, also unbraced parapets and architectural ornaments; some cracks in masonry C; waves on ponds, water turbid with mud; small slides and caving in along sand or gravel banks; large bells ring; concrete irrigation ditches damaged.
VIII Steering of cars affected; damage to masonry C and partial collapse; some damage to masonry B; none to masonry A; fall of stucco and some masonry walls; twisting, fall of chimneys, factory stacks, monuments, towers, elevated tanks; frame houses move on foundations if not bolted down; loose panel walls thrown out; decayed piling broken off; branches broken from trees; changes in flow or temperature of springs and wells; cracks in wet ground and on steep slopes.
IX General panic; masonry D destroyed; masonry C heavily damaged, sometimes with complete collapse; masonry B seriously damaged; general damage to foundations; frame structures, if not bolted, shift off foundations; frames racked; serious damage to reservoirs; underground pipes break; conspicuous cracks in

ground; in alluviated areas sand and mud ejected, earthquake fountains, sand craters.

X Most masonry and frame structures destroyed with their foundations; some well-built wooden structures and bridges destroyed; serious damage to dams, dykes, embankments; large landslides; water thrown on banks of canals, rivers, lakes, etc; sand and mud shifted horizontally on beaches and flat land; rails bent slightly.

XI Rails bent greatly; underground pipelines completely out of service.

XII Damage nearly total; large rock masses displaced; lines of sight and level distorted; objects thrown into the air.

Note

Masonry A Good workmanship, mortar and design; reinforced, especially laterally, and bound together using steel, concrete etc; designed to resist lateral forces.

Masonry B Good workmanship and mortar; reinforced, but not designed in detail to resist lateral forces.

Masonry C Ordinary workmanship and mortar; no extreme weakness like failing to tie in at corners, but neither reinforced nor designed against horizontal forces.

Masonry D Weak materials, such as adobe; poor mortar; low standards of workmanship; weak horizontally.

THE EARTH

Major volcanoes and eruptions

Name	Location	Height (m)	(ft)	Major eruptions (year/s)	Last eruption (year)
Aconcagua	Argentina	6960	22831	extinct	
Ararat	Turkey	5198	18350	extinct	Holocene
Awu	Sangir Is	1327	4355	1711, 1856, 1892, 1968	1992
Bezymianny	Russia	2800	9186	1955–6, 1984	1997
Coseguina	Nicaragua	847	1598	1835	1859
El Chichón	Mexico	1349	4430	1982	1982
Erebus	Antarctica	4023	13200	1947, 1972, 1986	1991
Etna, Mt	Italy	3236	10625	122, 1169, 1329, 1536, 1669, 1928 1964, 1971, 1986, 1992, 1994, 2001	2002
Fuji	Japan	3776	12388	1707	1707
Galunggung	Java	2180	7155	1822, 1918, 1982	1984
Hekla	Iceland	1491	4920	1693, 1845, 1947–8, 1970, 1981, 1991	2000
Helgafell	Iceland	215	706	1973	1973
Hudson	Chile	1740	5742	1971, 1973	1991
Jurullo	Mexico	1330	4255	1759–74	1774
Katmai	Alaska	2298	7540	1912, 1920, 1921, 1931	1974
Kilauea	Hawaii	1247	4100	1823–1924, 1952, 1955, 1960, 1967–8, 1968–74, 1983–7, 1988, 1991, 1992	1994
Kilimanjaro	Tanzania	5895	19340	extinct	Pleistocene
Klyuchevskoy	Russia	4850	15910	1700–1966, 1984, 1985	1994
Krakatoa	Sumatra	818	2685	1680, 1883, 1927, 1952–3, 1969	1980
La Soufrière	St Vincent	1232	4048	1718, 1812, 1902, 1971–2	1979
Laki	Iceland	500	1642	1783, 1784, 1938	1996
Lamington	Papua New Guinea	1780	5844	1951	1956
Lassen Peak	USA	3186	10453	1914–15	1921
Mauna Loa	Hawaii	4172	13685	1859, 1880, 1887, 1919, 1950, 1984	1987
Mayon	Philippines	2462	8084	1616, 1766, 1814, 1897, 1968, 1978, 1993	2001
Nyamuragira	Democratic Republic of Congo	3056	10026	1921–38, 1971, 1980, 1984, 1988, 1991	2002
Paricutín	Mexico	3188	10460	1943–52	1952
Pelée, Mont	Martinique	1397	4584	1902, 1929–32	1932
Pinatubo	Philippines	1758	5770	1391, 1991, 1992	2001
Popocatépetl	Mexico	5483	17990	1920, 1943	1999
Rainier, Mt	USA	4392	14416	1st-c BC, 1820	1882
Ruapehu	New Zealand	2796	9175	1945, 1953, 1969, 1975, 1986, 1995	1996
St Helens, Mt	USA	2549	8364	1800, 1831, 1835, 1842–3, 1857, 1980, 1986, 1991	2005

Structure

Major volcanos and eruptions (continued)

Santorini/ Thera	Greece	556	1824	1470 BC, 197 BC, AD 46, 1570–3, 1707–11, 1866–70	1950
Stromboli	Italy	931	3055	1768, 1882, 1889, 1907, 1930, 1936, 1941, 1950, 1952, 1986, 1990	1994
Surtsey	Iceland	174	570	1963–7	1967
Taal	Philippines	1448	4752	1911, 1965, 1969, 1977	1988
Tambora	Sumbawa	2868	9410	1815	1880
Tarawera	New Zealand	1149	3770	1886	1973
Unzen, Mt	Japan	1360	4462	1360, 1791, 1991, 1994	1996
Vesuvius	Italy	1289	4230	79, 472, 1036, 1631, 1779, 1906	1944
Vulcano	Italy	502	1650	antiquity, 1444, 1730–40, 1786, 1873, 1888–90	1890

Major tsunamis

Tsunamis are long-period ocean waves produced by movements of the sea floor associated with earthquakes, volcanic explosions, or landslides. They are also referred to as *seismic sea waves*, and in popular (but not technical) oceanographic use as *tidal waves*.

Location of source	Year	Height (m)	Height (ft)	Location of deaths/damage	Deaths
Indian Ocean	2004	10	32	NW Indonesia, Sri Lanka, SE India, Thailand, Myanmar, Indian Ocean territories, E Africa	150000+
Bismarck Sea	1998	10	32	NW Papua New Guinea	3000
Mindoro	1994	15	49	Philippine Is	60
Banyuwangi	1994	5	16	Indonesia	200
Sea of Japan	1983	15	49	Japan, Korea	107
Indonesia	1979	10	32	Indonesia	187
Celebes Sea	1976	30	98	Philippine Is	5000
Alaska	1964	32	105	Alaska, Aleutian Is, California	122
Chile	1960	25	82	Chile, Hawaii, Japan	1260
Aleutian Is	1957	16	52	Hawaii, Japan	0
Kamchatka	1952	18.4	60	Kamchatka, Kuril Is, Hawaii	many
Aleutian Is	1946	32	105	Aleutian Is, Hawaii, California	165
Nankaido (Japan)	1946	6.1	20	Japan	1997
Kii (Japan)	1944	7.5	25	Japan	998
Sanriku (Japan)	1933	28.2	93	Japan, Hawaii	3000
E Kamchatka	1923	20	66	Kamchatka, Hawaii	3
S Kuril Is	1918	12	39	Kuril Is, Russia, Japan, Hawaii	23
Sanriku (Japan)	1896	30	98	Japan	27122
Sunda Strait	1883	35	115	Java, Sumatra	36000
Chile	1877	23	75	Chile, Hawaii	many
Chile	1868	21	69	Chile, Hawaii	25000
Hawaii	1868	20	66	Hawaii	81
Japan	1854	6	20	Japan	3000
Flores Sea	1800	24	79	Indonesia	400–500
Ariake Sea	1792	9	30	Japan	9745
Italy	1783	?	?	Italy	30000
Ryukyu Is	1771	12	39	Ryukyu Is	11941
Portugal	1775	16	52	W Europe, Morocco, W Indies	60000
Peru	1746	24	79	Peru	5000
Japan	1741	9	30	Japan	1000
SE Kamchatka	1737	30	98	Kamchatka, Kuril Is	?
Peru	1724	24	79	Peru	?
Japan	1707	11.5	38	Japan	30000
W Indies	1692	?	?	Jamaica	2000
Banda Is	1629	15	49	Indonesia	?
Sanriku (Japan)	1611	25	82	Japan	5000
Japan	1605	?	?	Japan	4000
Kii (Japan)	1498	?	?	Japan	5000

Recent hurricanes

A hurricane (H) is an intense, often devastating, tropical storm which occurs as a vortex spiralling around a low-pressure system. Wind speeds are high – above 120 kmh/75 mph. Hurricanes originate over tropical oceans and move in a W or NW direction in the northern hemisphere, and SW in the southern hemisphere, losing energy as they reach land. They are also known as *typhoons* in the western N Pacific and *cyclones* in the Bay of Bengal. Hurricane naming began in 1950, using the phonetic alphabet of the time (Able, Baker, etc.), changing to female first-names in 1953, and alternating male and female names for Atlantic Basin hurricanes in 1979, and introducing male names a year later.

Name	Location	Year	Deaths	Damage (US $bn)
Typhoon Saomai	SE China	2006	255+	1.4
H Wilma	Mexico, Cuba, Florida	2005	17	n.a.
Typhoon Longwang	SE China	2005	65+	1.5
H Rita	US Gulf Coast	2005	10	6
H Katrina	US Gulf Coast	2005	13 000+	50
Typhoon Nanmadol	Philippines	2004	1000+	n.a.
Typhoon Tokage	Japan	2004	82	n.a.
H Jeanne	Dominican Republic, Haiti, Florida	2004	2000+	n.a.
H Ivan	Florida, S USA, Grenada, SE Caribbean Is	2004	103	n.a.
H Frances	Florida	2004	2	4.4
H Charley	West Florida	2004	26	7.4
Typhoon Rananim	East China	2004	164	1.85
Typhoon Megi	S & N Japan, S Korea	2004	13	n.a.
Cyclone Heta	South Pacific, Niue	2004	1	n.a.
Typhoon Maemi	South Korea, Kyongsang	2003	117	4.1
Typhoon Dujuan	China	2003	23	n.a.
Cyclone Zoë	Pacific, Solomon Is	2002	none	n.a.
H Michelle	Cuba, Florida, C America	2001	20	n.a.
H Iris	Belize	2001	18	n.a.
Cyclone	Orissa, India	1999	9000+	n.a.
H Floyd	Caribbean, E Coast America	1999	17	n.a.
H Mitch	C America	1998	8347	5.0
H Georges	Caribbean, US Gulf Coast	1998	581	2.0

Name	Location	Year	Deaths	Damage (US $bn)
Typhoon Linda	Vietnam, South Coast	1997	358	n.a.
H Pauline	Mexico	1997	240+	n.a.
H Opal	Florida, Gulf Coast	1995	19	n.a.
H Marilyn	Virgin Is, Puerto Rico	1995	9	n.a.
H Luis	Caribbean	1995	12	n.a.
Typhoon Angela	Philippine Is	1995	500+	n.a.
H Andrew	S Florida, Bahamas	1992	88	26.5
H Iniki	Kauai, Hawaii	1992	3	1.0
H Bob	NE USA	1991	17	1.5
Cyclone	Bangladesh	1991	200 000	
H Hugo	South Carolina	1989	49	7.0
H Gilbert	Caribbean, Mexico	1988	318	5.0
H Joan	Caribbean	1988	216	
H Elena	Mississippi, Alabama, NW Florida	1985	2	1.25
H Gloria	E USA	1985	15	0.9
H Juan	Louisiana	1985	12	1.5
H Kate	Florida	1985	16	0.3
Cyclone	Bangladesh	1985	11 000	
H Alicia	N Texas	1983	18	2.0
H Allen	S Texas	1980	235	0.3
H David	Florida	1979	2400	0.3
H Frederic	Alabama, Mississippi	1979	31	2.3
H Eloise	NW Florida	1975	100	0.49
H Carmen	Louisiana	1974	1	0.15
H Fifi	Honduras, C America	1974	10 000	1.0
Cyclone Tracey	Darwin, Australia	1974	65	1.0

CLIMATE

World temperatures

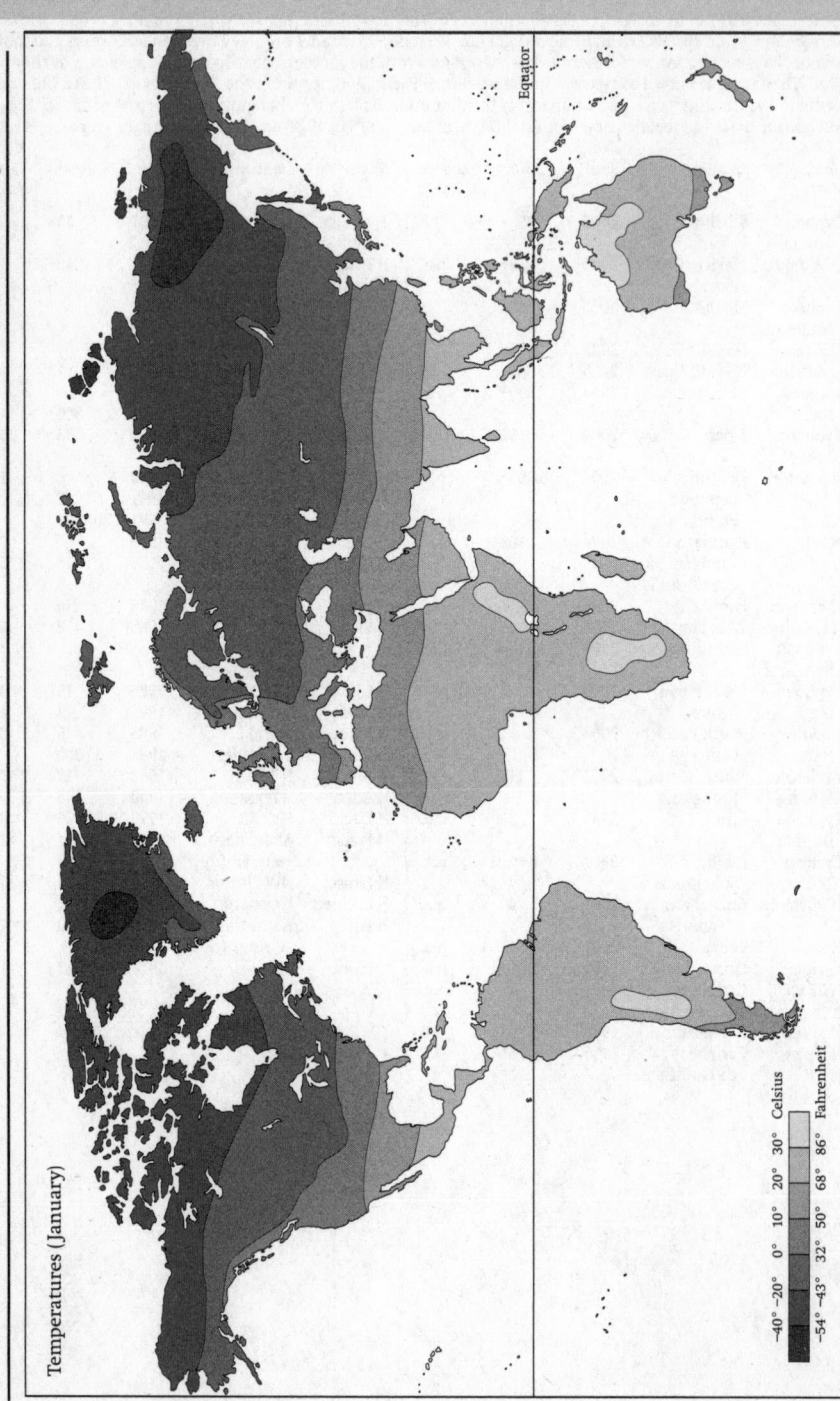

Temperatures (January)

Equator

Celsius
-40° -20° 0° 10° 20° 30°
-54° -43° 32° 50° 68° 86° Fahrenheit

Temperatures (July)

Equator

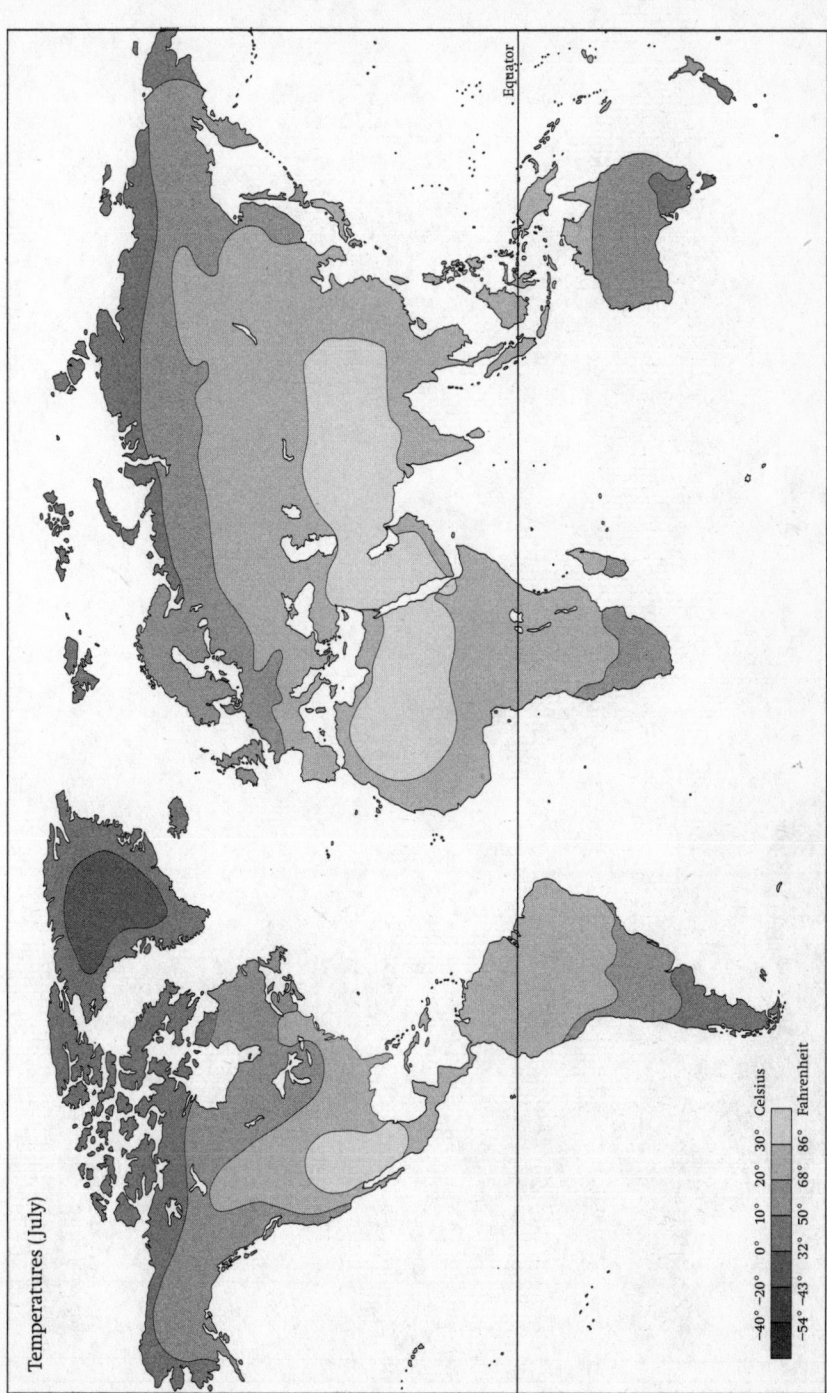

−40°	−20°	0°	10°	20°	30°	Celsius
−54°	−43°	32°	50°	68°	86°	Fahrenheit

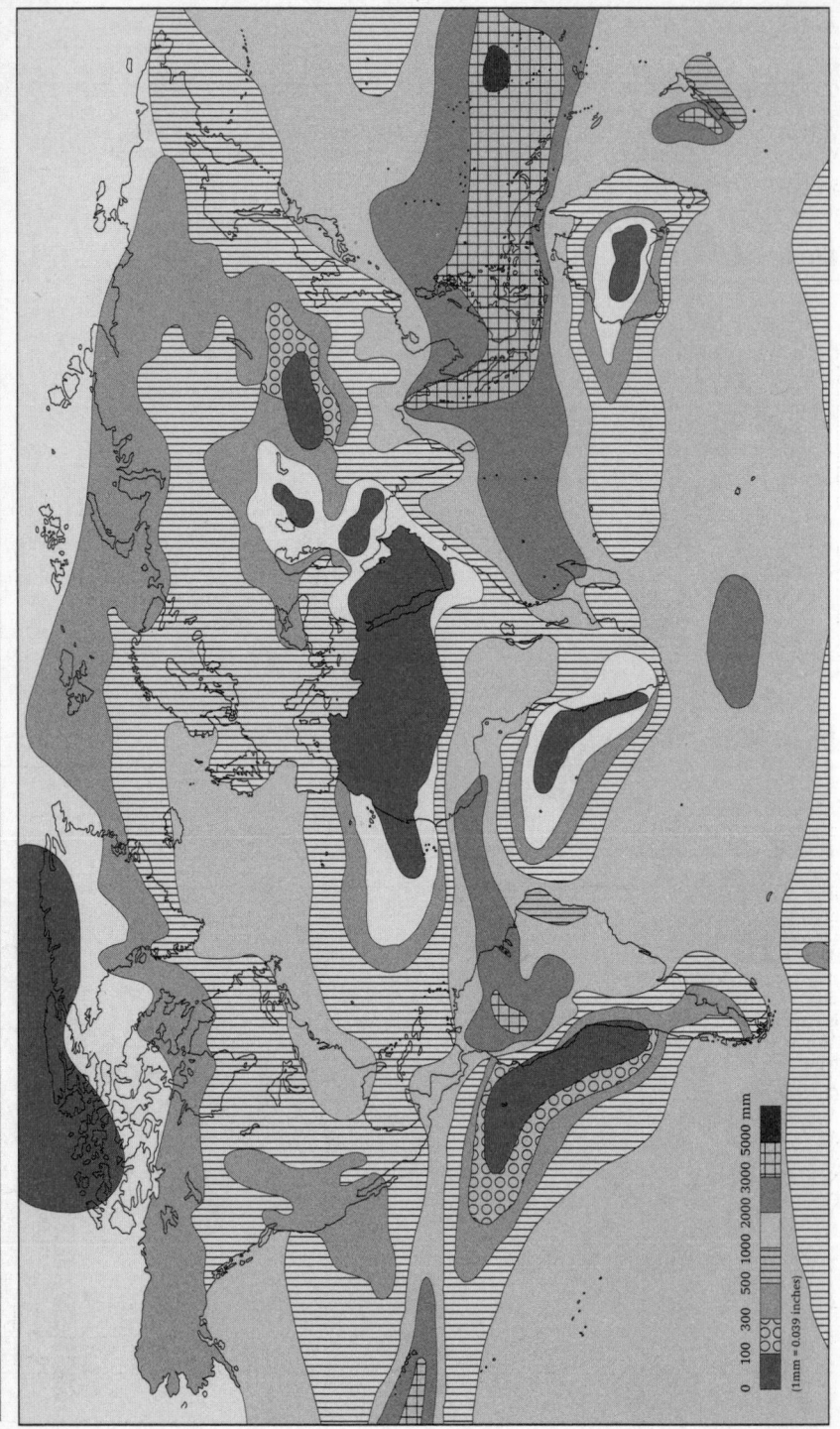

0   100   300   500   1000   2000   3000   5000 mm

(1mm = 0.039 inches)

Meteorological records

Hottest place	El Azizia, Libya	58˚C / 136.4˚F (hottest recorded temperature)
Coldest place	Vostok, Antarctica	−89˚C / −128.20˚F (coldest recorded temperature)
Driest place	Arica-Antofagasta, Pacific coast, Chile	0.1 mm / 0.004 in (annual mean rainfall)
Wettest place	Mawsynram, Meghalaya State, India	861 mm / 467 in (annual mean rainfall)
Windiest place	Honolulu, Hawaii	380 kmh/236 mph (highest recorded gust)

Source: UK Met Office (Hadley Centre)

Cloud types

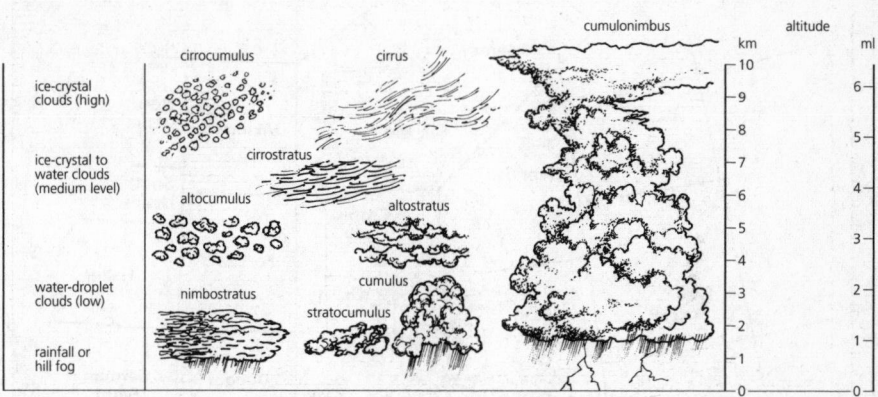

Depressions

Plan view of the six idealized stages in the development and final occlusion of a depression along the polar front in the northern hemisphere. Stage 4 shows a well-developed depression system and stage 5 shows the occlusion. The cross-section is taken along the line AB in stage 4. The cloud types are:

Cb – cumulonimbus;
As – altostratus;
Ac – altocumulus;
Cs – cirrostratus;
Ns – nimbostratus;
Ci – cirrus.

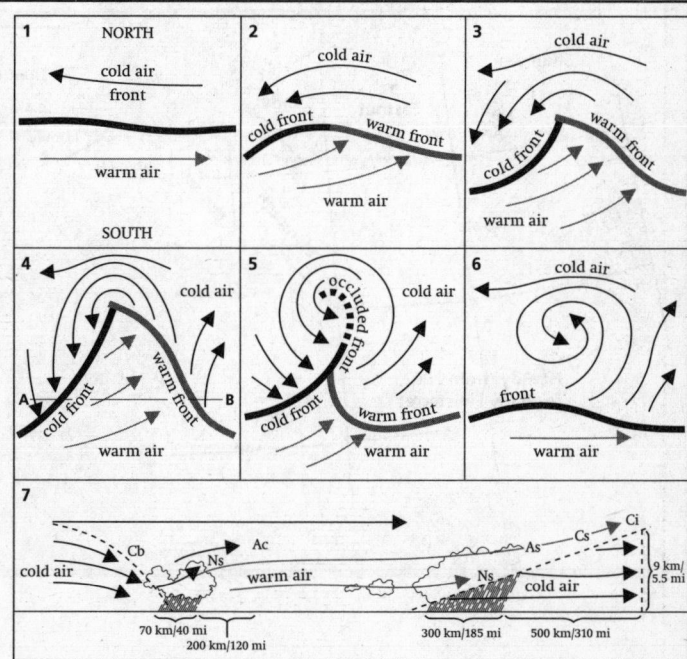

THE EARTH

Meteorological sea areas around the British Isles

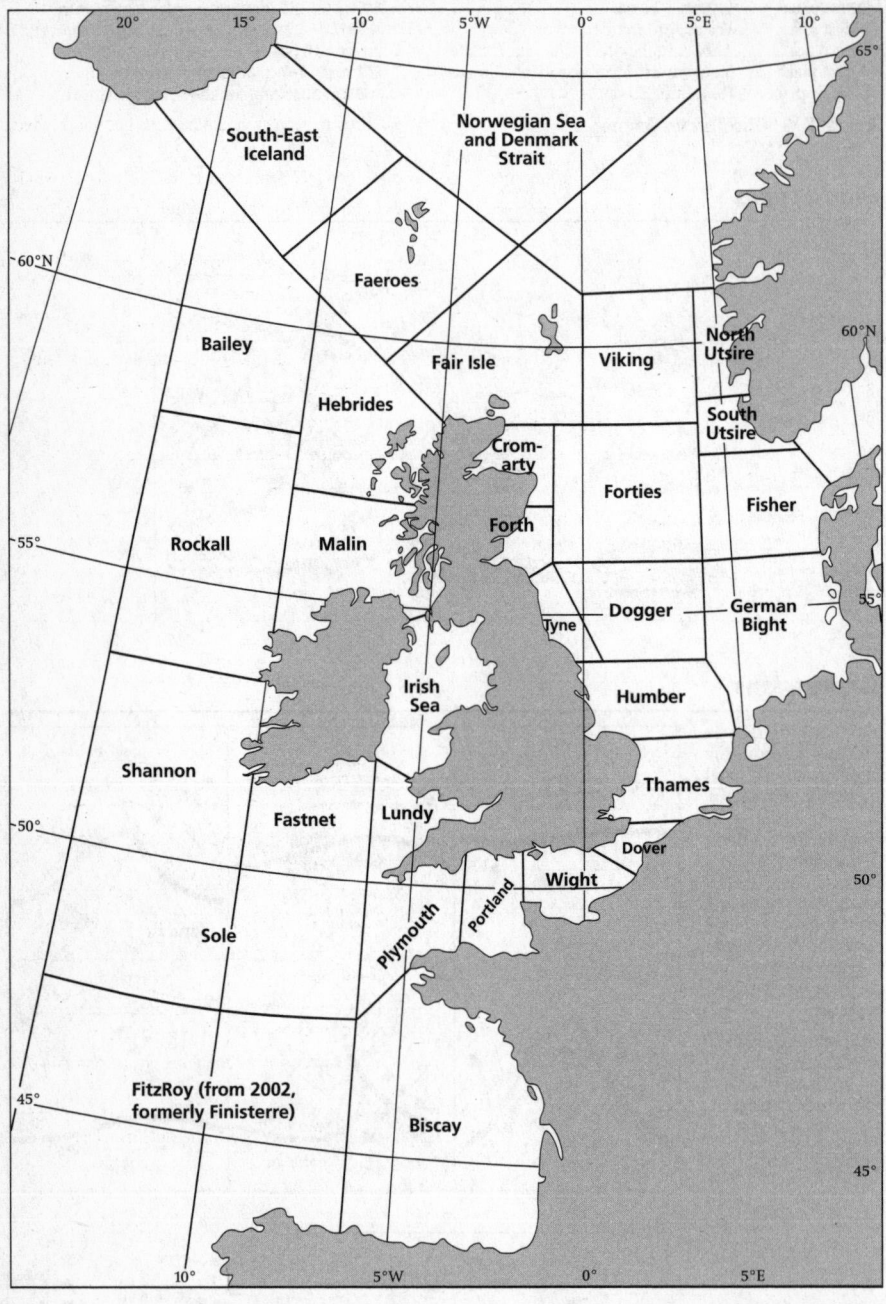

Wind force and sea disturbance

Beaufort number	Wind speed		Wind name	Observable wind characteristics
	(kmh)	*(mph)*		
0	<1	<1	Calm	Smoke rises vertically
1	1–5	1–3	Light air	Wind direction shown by smoke drift but not by wind vanes
2	6–11	4–7	Light breeze	Wind felt on face; leaves rustle; vanes moved by wind
3	12–19	8–12	Gentle breeze	Leaves and small twigs in constant motion; wind extends light flag
4	20–8	13–18	Moderate	Raises dust, loose paper; small branches moved
5	29–38	19–24	Fresh	Small trees begin to sway
6	39–49	25–31	Strong	Large branches in motion; difficult to use umbrellas
7	50–61	32–8	Near gale	Whole trees in motion; difficult to walk against wind
8	62–74	39–46	Gale	Breaks twigs off trees; impedes progress
9	75–88	47–54	Strong gale	Slight structural damage caused
10	89–102	55–63	Storm	Trees uprooted; considerable damage occurs
11	103–17	64–72	Violent storm	Widespread damage
12–17	>118	>73	Hurricane	

Sea disturbance number (Beaufort)	Average wave height		Observable sea characteristics
	(m)	*(ft)*	
0 (0)	0	0	Sea like a mirror
0 (1)	0	0	Ripples like scales
1 (2)	0.3	0–1	More definite wavelets
2 (3)	0.3–0.6	1–2	Large wavelets; crests beginning
3 (4)	0.6–1.2	2–4	Small waves becoming longer; fairly frequent white horses
4 (5)	1.2–2.4	4–8	Moderate waves with longer form; many white horses; some foam spray
5 (6)	2.4–4	8–13	Large waves forming; more white foam crests; spray
6 (7)	4–6	13–20	Sea heaps up; streaks of white foam blown along
6 (8)	4–6	13–20	Moderately high waves of greater length; well-marked streaks of foam
6 (9)	4–6	13–20	High waves; dense streaks of foam; sea begins to roll; spray affects visibility
7 (10)	6–9	20–30	Very high waves with overhanging crests; generally white appearance of surface; heavy rolling
8 (11)	9–14	30–45	Exceptionally high waves; long white patches of foam; poor visibility; ships lost to view behind waves
9 (12–17)	14	>45	Air filled with foam and spray; sea completely white; very poor visibility

THE EARTH

World physical map

SURFACE

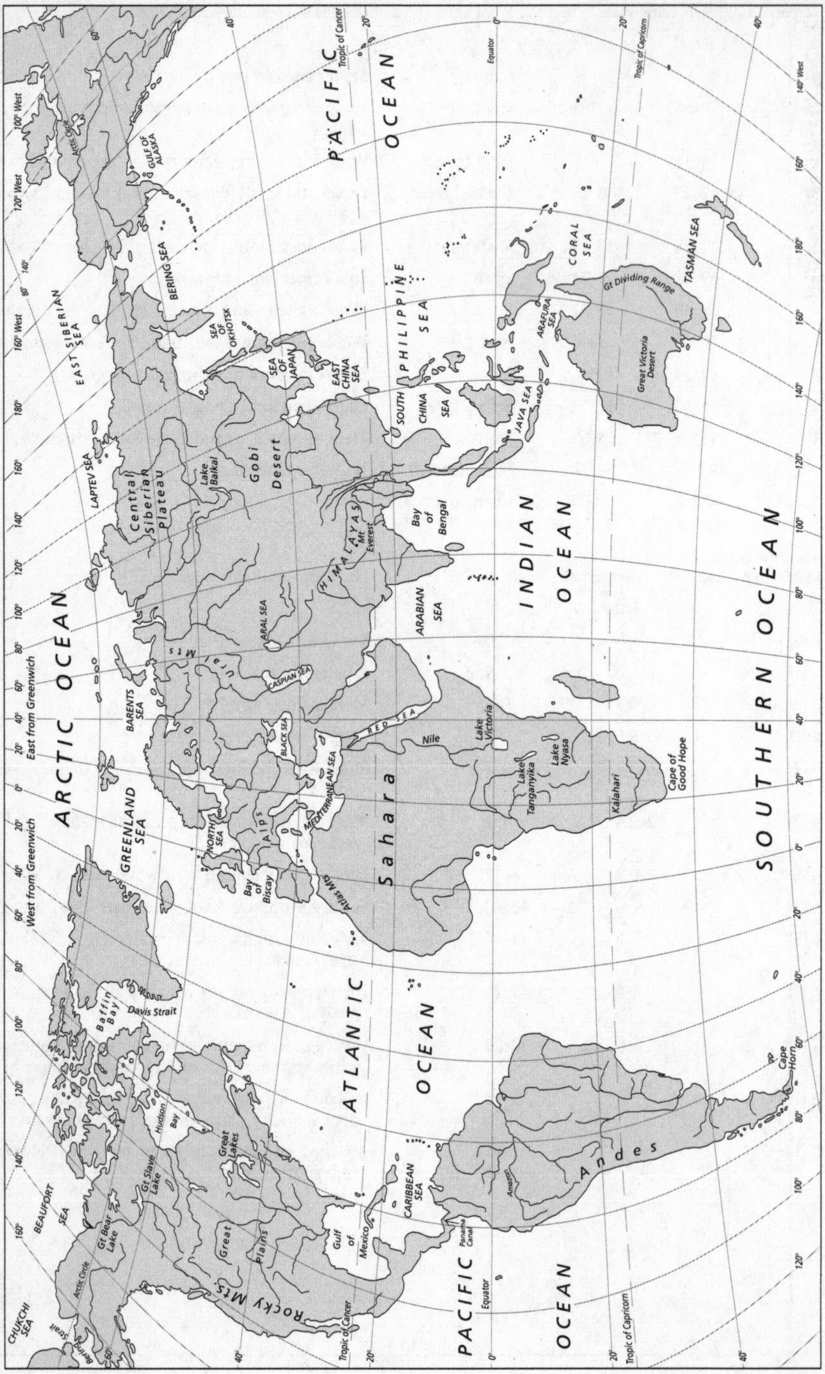

Major ocean-surface currents

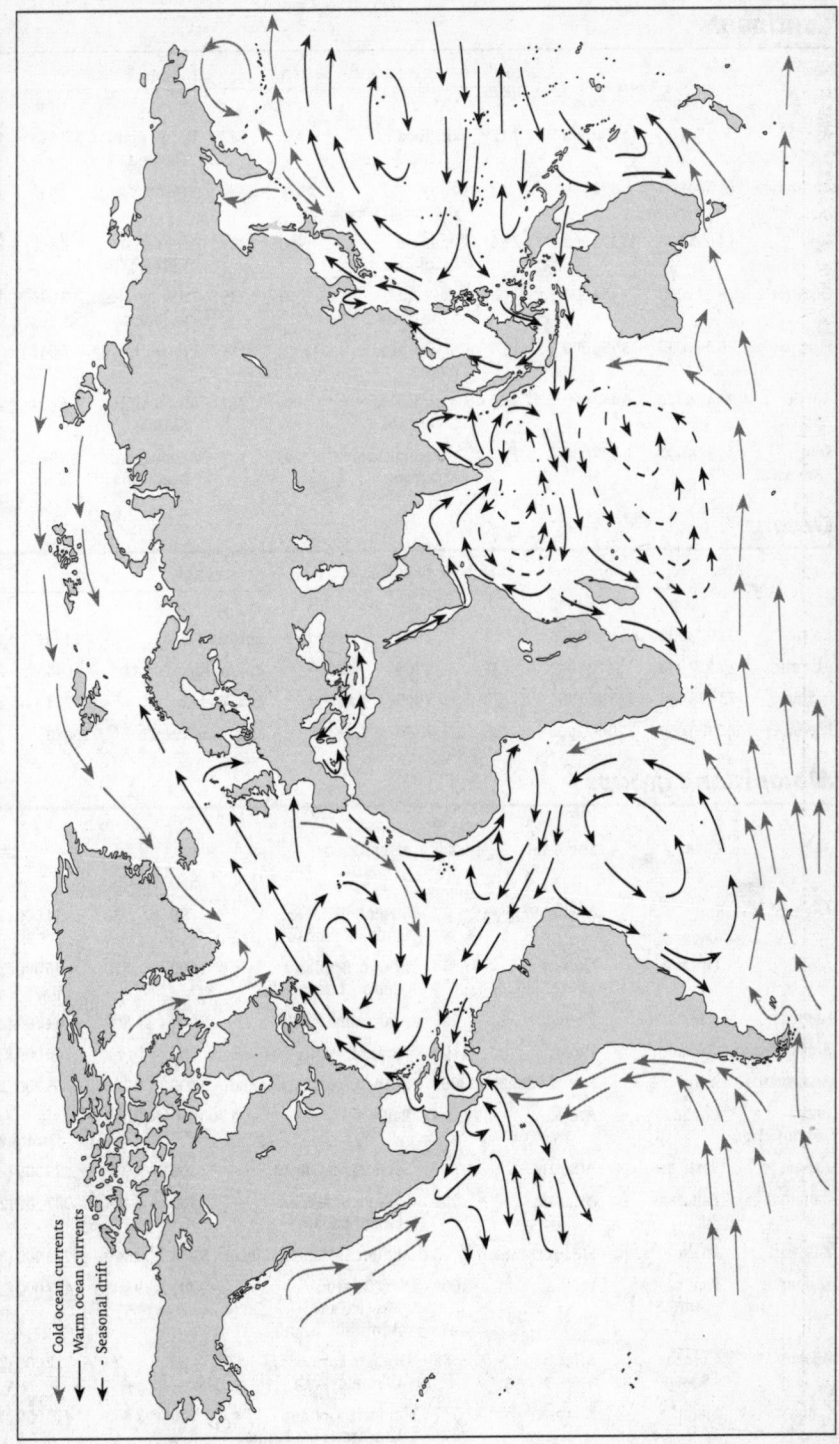

Cold ocean currents
Warm ocean currents
- Seasonal drift

Continents

Name	Area (km²)	(sq mi)	% of total	Lowest point below sea level	(m)	(ft)	Highest elevation	(m)	(ft)
Africa	30 970 000	11 690 000	20.2	Lake Assal, Djibouti	156	512	Kilimanjaro, Tanzania	5 895	19 340
Antarctica	15 500 000	6 000 000	9.3	Bently subglacial trench	2 538	8 327	Vinson Massif	5 140	16 864
Asia	44 493 000	17 179 000	29.6	Dead Sea, Israel/Jordan	400	1 312	Mt Everest, China/Nepal	8 848	29 028
Oceania	8 945 000	3 454 000	6	Lake Eyre, S Australia	15	49	Puncak Jaya, Indonesia	5 030	16 500
Europe	10 245 000	3 956 000	6.8	Caspian Sea, Russia	29	94	Elbrus, Russia	5 642	18 510
North America	24 454 000	9 442 000	16.3	Death Valley, California	86	282	Mt McKinley, Alaska	6 194	20 320
South America	17 838 000	6 887 000	11.9	Peninsular Valdez, Argentina	40	131	Aconcagua, Argentina	6 960	22 831

Oceans

Name	Area (km²)	(sq mi)	% of total	Average depth (m)	(ft)	Greatest depth	(m)	(ft)
Arctic	13 986 000	5 400 000	3	1 330	4 300	Eurasia Basin	5 122	16 804
Atlantic	82 217 000	31 700 000	24	3 700	12 100	Puerto Rico Trench	8 648	28 372
Indian	73 426 000	28 350 000	20	3 900	12 800	Java Trench	7 725	25 344
Pacific	181 300 000	70 000 000	46	4 300	14 100	Marianas Trench	11 040	36 220

Major island groups

Name	Country	Sea/Ocean	No. of islands	Main islands	Area (km²)	(sq mi)	Inhabitants
Aeolian	Italy	Mediterranean	7	Stromboli, Lipari, Vulcanö, Salina	90	30	11 000 (2000e)
Åland	Finland	Gulf of Bothnia	6554	Eckerö, Lemland, Vardö, Lumparland	1 500	570	25 000 (2000e)
Aleutian	USA	Pacific	150	Andreanof, Adak	18 000	6 800	14 500 (2000e)
Alexander	Canada	Pacific	1100	Baranof, Prince of Wales	na	na	40 000 (2000e)
Andaman	India	Bay of Bengal	300+	N Andaman, S Andaman	8 300	3 200	288 000 (2000e)
Arctic Archipelago	Canada	Arctic	na	Baffin	1 300 000	500 000	largely uninhabited
Azores	Portugal	Atlantic	9	São Miguel, Flores	2 300	900	239 000 (2000e)
Bahamas	Bahamas	Atlantic	700	New Providence, Grand Bahama	13 900	5 400	287 500 (2000e)
Balearic	Spain	Mediterranean	5	Mallorca, Menorca, Ibiza	5 000	1 900	712 000 (2000e)
Bismarck	Papua New Guinea	Pacific	2 000	New Britain, New Ireland, Admiralty Island	49 700	19 200	473 000 (2000e)
Bijagos	Guinea-Bissau	Atlantic	88	Orango, Formoza, Caravela, Roxa	50	30	27 000 (2000e)
Canary	Spain	Atlantic	7	Tenerife, Gomera, Lanzarote, Las Palmas	7 300	2 800	1 475 000 (2000e)

Name	Country	Sea/Ocean	No. of islands	Main islands	Area (km²)	(sq mi)	Inhabitants
Cape Verde	Cape Verde	Atlantic	10	Barlavento group, Sotavento group	4 000	1 500	411 500 (2000e)
Caroline	USA	Pacific	680	Yop, Pohnpei, Truk	1 300	500	153 000 (2000e)
Channel	UK	English Channel	4	Guernsey, Jersey, Sark, Alderney	200	80	151 600 (2000e)
Commander	Russia	Bering Sea	4	Bering, Medny	1 800	700	750 (2000e)
Comoros	Republic of Comoros	Mozambique Channel	4	Grand Mohore, Anjouan, Moheli, Mayotte	1 900	700	580 500 (2000e)
Cook	New Zealand	Pacific	15	Palmerston, Rarotonga, Mangaia	240	90	20 400 (2000e)
Cyclades	Greece	Aegean	c.220	Andros, Mikonos, Paros	2 600	990	99 300 (2000e)
Dodecanese	Greece	Aegean	12	Rhodes, Kos, Patmos	2 700	1 000	175 000 (2000e)
Falkland	UK	Atlantic	200	W Falkland, E Falkland, S Georgia	12 200	4 700	2 000 (2000e)
Faroe	Denmark	Atlantic	22	Strømø, Østerø	1 400	540	40 200 (2000e)
Fiji	Fiji	Pacific	844	Viti Levu, Vanua Levu	18 330	7 080	823 000 (2000e)
Galapagos	Ecuador	Pacific	16	Santa Cruz, Santiago	7 800	3 010	12 100 (2000e)
Gotland	Sweden	Baltic	2	Gotland, Fårö	3 140	1 210	60 000 (2000e)
Greenland	Denmark	N Atlantic, Arctic	2	Greenland, Disko	2 175 600	840 000	60 000 (2000e)
Hawaiian	USA	Pacific	8	Hawaii, Oahu	16 760	6 470	1 052 000 (2000e)
Hebrides	UK	Atlantic	10+	Lewis, Skye, Mull		na	40 000 (2000e)
Ionian	Greece	Aegean	7	Kerkira, Levkas	2 300	890	200 000 (2000e)
Japan	Japan	Pacific	1000+	Honshu, Hokkaido, Kyushu, Shikoku	370 000	145 000	126 434 000 (2000e)
Juan Fernandez	Chile	Pacific	3	Robinson Crusoe, Alejandro Selkirk, Santa Clara	180	70	500 (2000e)
Kuril	Russia/Japan	Pacific	56	Shumsu, Iturup	15 600	6 000	20 000 (2000e)
Laccadive	India	Arabian Sea	27	Laccadive, Amaindivi	30	10	61 000 (2000e)
Lofoten	Norway	Norwegian Sea	5	Hinnoy, Austvagoy	1 420	550	24 500 (2000e)
Madeira	Portugal	Atlantic	4	Madeira	790	310	259 000 (2000e)
Malay Archipelego	Indonesia, Malaysia, Philippines	Pacific/ Indian	20 000	Borneo, New Guinea, Sumatra, Jarva, Philippine Is (>> p.40)	329 750	127 280	322 000 000 (2000e)
Maldives	Republic of Maldives	Indian	1 190	Male	300	120	310 500 (2000e)
Malta	Republic of Malta	Mediterranean	5	Malta, Gozo	320	120	383 000 (2000e)
Mariana	Mariana Is	Pacific	14	Saipan, Tinian, Rota	470	180	72 000 (2000e)
Marquesas	France	Pacific	10	Nukultiva	1 190	460	9 300 (2000e)
Marshall	Marshall Islands	Pacific	1 200+	Bikini	180	70	68 000 (2000e)
Mascarene	France	Indian	3	Réunion, Mauritius, Rodrigues	na	na	1 969 000 (2000e)
Melanesia		Pacific	na	Solomon, Bismarck, Fiji, New Guinea	540 000	210 000	6 578 000 (2000e)
Micronesia		Pacific	na	Caroline, Gilbert, Marshall, Kiribati	3 270	1 260	390 000 (2000e)

THE EARTH

Major island groups (continued)

Name	Country	Sea/Ocean	No. of islands	Main islands	Area (km²)	(sq mi)	Inhabitants
New Hebrides	Republic of Vanuatu	Pacific	72	Espiritu Santo	14 760	5 700	193 000 (2000e)
New-foundland	Canada	Atlantic	na	Newfoundland	405 720	156 650	636 000 (2000e)
New Zealand	New Zealand	Pacific	4+	North, South	268 810	103 760	3 698 000 (2000e)
Nicobar	India	Bay of Bengal	19+	Great Nicobar	1 625	625	40 000 (2000e)
Novaya Zemlya	Russia	Arctic	5	North, South	81 300	31 400	no permanent population
Orkney	UK	North Sea	20	Mainland, Ronaldsay	980	380	20 400 (2000e)
Philippines	Republic of the Philippines	Pacific	7 100	Luzon, Mindanao, Samar	300 680	110 680	80 961 000 (2000e)
Polynesia		Pacific	na	Hawaii, Tonga, Kiribati, Easter, Samoa	17 200	10 700	1 900 000 (2000e)
Queen Charlotte	Canada	Pacific	150	Graham	6 361	2 455	5 900 (2000e)
São Tomé and Príncipe	Republic of São Tomé & Príncipe	Atlantic	2	São Tomé, Príncipe	970	370	160 000 (2000e)
Scilly	UK	English Channel	140	St Mary's, St Martin's	20	10	1 970 (2000e)
Seychelles	Republic of Seychelles	Indian	115	Mahé, La Digue	450	170	80 000 (2000e)
Shetland	UK	North Sea	500+	Mainland, Unst	1 400	550	23 100 (2000e)
Society	France	Pacific	2	Tahiti	1 500	590	193 000 (2000e)
Solomon	Solomon Islands	Pacific	6+	New Georgia, San Cristobal	27 560	10 640	470 000 (2000e)
South Orkney	UK	Atlantic	2	Coronation, Laurie	620	240	uninhabited
Sri Lanka	Republic of Sri Lanka	Indian	2	Sri Lanka, Mannar	65 610	25 200	19 355 000 (2000e)
Taiwan	Republic of China	China Sea/Pacific	na	Taiwan	36 000	13 900	22 319 000 (2000e)
Tasmania	Australia	Tasman Sea	5+	Tasmania, King Flinders, Bruny	67 800	26 200	501 000 (2000e)
Tierra del Fuego	Argentina/ Chile	Pacific			73 700	28 500	78 200 (2000e)
Tristan da Cunha	UK	Atlantic	5	Gough, Inaccessible, Nightingale	100	40	370 (2000e)
Tuamotu	France	Pacific	80	Rangiroa, Hao, Fakarava	800	320	13 500 (2000e)
Tuvalu	Tuvalu	Pacific		Funafuti Atoll, Nanumea	30	10	10 700 (2000e)
Virgin	USA	Caribbean	50+	St Croix, St Thomas	340	130	121 000 (2000e)
Virgin	UK	Caribbean	36	Tortola, Virgin Gorda	150	60	19 600 (2000e)
Zanzibar	Tanzania	Indian	3	Zanzibar, Tumbatu	1 600	640	494 000 (2000e)

na – data not available.

Considerable variation will be found among sources giving area estimates for island groups, because of the difficulty in deciding where the group boundary line should lie.

All estimates above 100 km²/sq mi have been rounded to the nearest 10, and all above 1 000 km²/sq mi to the nearest 100.

Largest seas

Name	Area[a]	
	(km²)	(sq mi)
Coral Sea	4791000	1850200
Arabian Sea	3863000	1492000
S China (Nan) Sea	3685000	1423000
Mediterranean Sea	2516000	971000
Caribbean Sea	2516000	971000
Bering Sea	2304000	890000
Bay of Bengal	2172000	839000
Sea of Okhotsk	1590000	614000
Gulf of Mexico	1543000	596000
Gulf of Guinea	1533000	592000
Barents Sea	1405000	542000
Norwegian Sea	1383000	534000
Gulf of Alaska	1327000	512000
Hudson Bay	1232000	476000
Greenland Sea	1205000	465000
Arafura Sea	1037000	400000
Philippine Sea	1036000	400000
Sea of Japan	978000	378000
E Siberian Sea	901000	348000
Kara Sea	883000	341000
E China Sea	664000	256000
Andaman Sea	565000	218000
North Sea	520000	201000
Black Sea	508900	196000
Red Sea	453000	175000
Baltic Sea	414000	160000
Celebes Sea	280000	110000

Oceans are excluded.
[a]Areas are rounded to nearest 1000 km²/sq mi.

Largest islands

Name	Area[a]	
	(km²)	(sq mi)
Greenland	2175600	830780
New Guinea	790000	305000
Borneo	737000	285000
Madagascar	587000	227600
Baffin	507000	196000
Sumatra	425000	164900
Honshu (Hondo)	228000	88000
Great Britain	219000	84400
Victoria, Canada	217300	83900
Ellesmere, Canada	196000	75800
Sulawesi (Celebes)	174000	67400
South I, New Zealand	151000	58200
Java	129000	50000
North I, New Zealand	114000	44200
Newfoundland	109000	42000
Cuba	110860	42790
Luzon	105000	40400
Iceland	103000	40000
Mindanao	94600	36500
Novaya Zemlya (two islands)	90600	35000
Ireland	70280	27100
Hokkaido	78500	30300
Hispaniola	77200	29800
Sakhalin	75100	29000
Tierra del Fuego	71200	27500

[a]Areas are rounded to the nearest three significant digits.

Largest lakes

Name/location	Area[a]	
	(km²)	(sq mi)
Caspian Sea, Iran	371000	143240[b]
Superior, USA/Canada	82260	31760[c]
Victoria, E Africa	62940	24300
Huron, USA/Canada	59580	23000[c]
Michigan, USA	58020	22400
Tanganyika, E Africa	32000	12350
Baikal, Russia	31500	12160
Great Bear, Canada	31330	12100
Aral Sea, Kazakhstan	30000	11580[b]
Great Slave, Canada	28570	11030
Erie, USA/Canada	25710	9920[c]
Winnipeg, Canada	24390	9420
Malawi/Nyasa, E Africa	22490	8680
Balkhash, Kazakhstan	18300	7000[b]
Ontario, Canada/USA	19270	7440[c]
Ladoga, Russia	18130	7000
Chad, W Africa	10000–26000	4000–10000
Maracaibo, Venezuela	13010	5020[d]
Patos, Brazil	10140	3920[d]
Onega, Russia	9800	3800

[a]Areas given to the nearest 10 km²/sq mi. Caspian & Aral Seas, entirely surrounded by land, are classified as lakes. [b]Salt lakes. [c]Average of areas given by Canada & USA. [d]Salt lagoons.

Pollution is reducing the size of many lakes, notably the Aral Sea, which is now less than half its original size. Lake Chad has shrunk by 95% since 1960s; Lake Balkash shrank by 770 sq mi/1995 sq km in 2003.

Largest deserts

Name/location	Area[a]	
	(km²)	(sq mi)
Sahara, N Africa	8600000	3320000
Arabian, SW Asia	2330000	900000
Gobi, Mongolia and NE China	1166000	450000
Patagonian, Argentina	673000	260000
Great Basin, SW USA	492000	190000
Chihuahuan, Mexico	450000	175000
Great Sandy, NW Australia	450000	175000
Great Victoria, SW Australia	235000	125000
Sonoran, SW USA	310000	120000
Kyzyl-Kum, Kazakhstan/Uzbekistan	300000	115000
Takla Makan, N China	270000	105000
Kalahari, SW Africa	260000	100000
Kara-Kum, Turkmenistan	260000	100000
Kavir, Iran	260000	100000
Syrian, Saudi Arabia/Jordan/ Syria/Iraq	260000	100000
Nubian, Sudan	260000	100000
Thar, India/Pakistan	200000	77000
Ust'-Urt, Kazakhstan/Uzbekistan	160000	62000
Bet-Pak-Dala, Kazakhstan	155000	60000
Simpson, C Australia	145000	56000
Dzungaria, China	142000	55000
Atacama, Chile	140000	54000
Namib, SE Africa	134000	52000
Sturt, SE Australia	130000	50000
Bolson de Mapimi, Mexico	130000	50000
Ordos, China	130000	50000
Alashan, China	116000	45000

[a]Desert areas are very approximate, because clear physical boundaries may not occur.

THE EARTH

Highest mountains

Name	Height[a]		Location
	(m)	(ft)	
Everest	8850	29030	China–Nepal
K2	8610	28250	Kashmir–Jammu
Kangchenjunga	8590	28170	India–Nepal
Lhotse	8500	27890	China–Nepal
Kangchenjunga S Peak	8470	27800	India–Nepal
Makalu I	8470	27800	China–Nepal
Kangchenjunga W Peak	8420	27620	India–Nepal
Llotse E Peak	8380	27500	China–Nepal
Dhaulagiri	8170	26810	Nepal
Cho Oyu	8150	26750	China–Nepal
Manaslu	8130	26660	Nepal
Nanga Parbat	8130	26660	Kashmir–Jammu
Annapurna I	8080	26500	Nepal
Gasherbrum I	8070	26470	Kashmir–Jammu
Broad-highest	8050	26400	Kashmir–Jammu
Gasherbrum II	8030	26360	Kashmir–Jammu
Gosainthan	8010	26290	China
Broad-middle	8000	26250	Kashmir–Jammu
Gasherbrum III	7950	26090	Kashmir–Jammu
Annapurna II	7940	26040	Nepal
Nanda Devi	7820	25660	India
Rakaposhi	7790	25560	Kashmir
Kamet	7760	25450	India
Tirich Mir	7690	25230	Pakistan
Muz Tag Ata	7550	24760	China
Communism Peak	7490	24590	Tajikistan
Pobedy Peak	7440	24410	China–Kyrgyzstan
Ulugh Muztagh	6973	22876	Tibet
Aconcagua	6960	22830	Argentina
Ojos del Salado	6910	22660	Argentina–Chile

[a]Heights are given to the nearest 10 m/ft.

Highest waterfalls

Name	Height[a]		Location
	(m)	(ft)	
Angel (upper fall)	807	2648	Venezuela
Itatinga	628	2060	Brazil
Cuquenan	610	2000	Guyana–Venezuela
Ormeli	563	1847	Norway
Tysse	533	1749	Norway
Pilao	524	1719	Brazil
Ribbon	491	1612	USA
Vestre Mardola	468	1535	Norway
Roraima	457?	1500?	Guyana
Cleve-Garth	450?	1476?	New Zealand

[a]Distances are given for individual leaps.

Deepest caves

Name/location	Depth	
	(m)	(ft)
Jean Bernard, France	1494	4900
Snezhnaya, Russia	1340	4397
Puertas de Illamina, Spain	1338	4390
Pierre-Saint-Martin, France	1321	4334
Sistema Huautla, Mexico	1240	4067
Berger, France	1198	3930
Vqerdi, Spain	1195	3921
Dachstein-Mammuthöhle, Austria	1174	3852
Zitu, Spain	1139	3737
Badalona, Spain	1130	3707
Batmanhöhle, Austria	1105	3626
Schneeloch, Austria	1101	3612
GES Malaga, Spain	1070	3510
Lamprechtsofen, Austria	1024	3360

Longest rivers

Name	Outflow	Length[a]	
		(km)	(mi)
Nile–Kagera–Ruvuvu–Ruvusu–Luvironza	Mediterranean Sea (Egypt)	6690	4160
Amazon–Ucayali–Tambo–Ene–Apurimac	Atlantic Ocean (Brazil)	6570	4080
Mississippi–Missouri–Jefferson–Beaverhead–Red Rock	Gulf of Mexico (USA)	6020	3740
Chang Jiang (Yangtze)	E China Sea (China)	5980	3720
Yenisey–Angara–Selenga–Ider	Kara Sea (Russia)	5870	3650
Amur–Argun–Kerulen	Tartar Strait (Russia)	5780	3590
Ob–Irtysh	Gulf of Ob, Kara Sea (Russia)	5410	3360
Plata–Parana–Grande	Atlantic Ocean (Argentina–Uruguay)	4880	3030
Huang He (Yellow)	Yellow Sea (China)	4840	3010
Congo (Zaire)–Lualaba	Atlantic Ocean (Angola–Democratic Republic of Congo)	4630	2880
Lena	Laptev Sea (Russia)	4400	2730
Mackenzie–Slave–Peace–Finlay	Beaufort Sea (Canada)	4240	2630
Mekong	S China Sea (Vietnam)	4180	2600
Niger	Gulf of Guinea (Nigeria)	4100	2550

[a]Lengths are given to the nearest 10 km/mi, and include the river plus tributaries comprising the longest watercourse.

The Earth's largest drainage basins

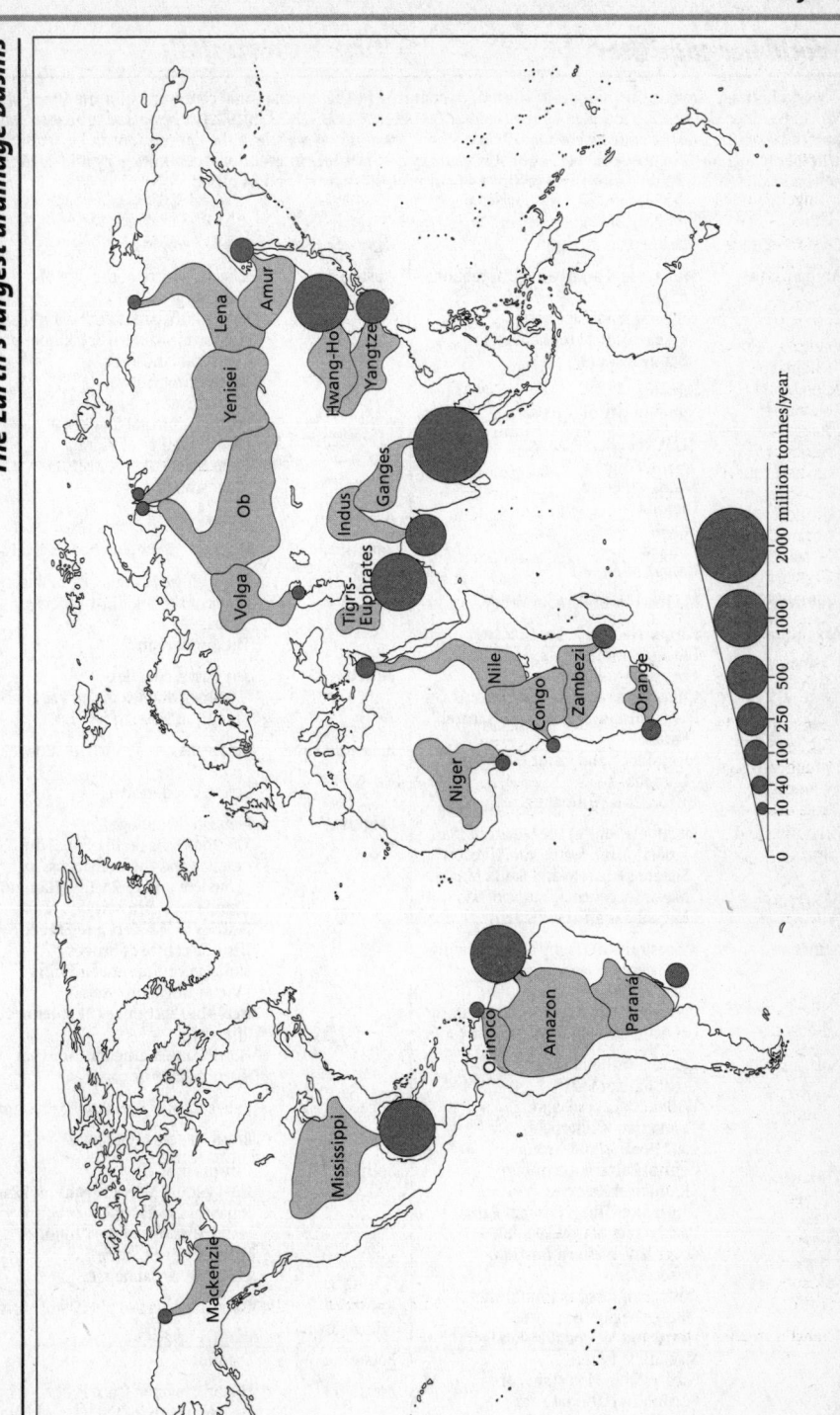

2000 million tonnes/year

2000 1000 500 250 100 40 10 0

Lena
Amur
Yenisei
Hwang-Ho
Yangtze
Ob
Ganges
Indus
Volga
Tigris-Euphrates
Nile
Congo
Zambezi
Orange
Niger
Amazon
Orinoco
Paraná
Mississippi
Mackenzie

THE EARTH

World heritage sites

A world heritage site is a site (natural or cultural) recognized by the international community (in the shape of the World Heritage Convention founded by the General Conference of UNESCO in 1972) as possessing universal value, and thus coming under a collective responsibility. A country nominates a site to the Convention, and a decision on whether to include it in the world heritage list is made by a 21-member international committee. By mid-2006 there were 830 sites in 138 states (below), comprising 644 cultural, 162 natural and 24 mixed.

*Transboundary property

Contracting state	Name of property
Afghanistan	Minaret and archaeological remains of Jam
	Cultural landscape and archaeological remains of the Bamiyan Valley
Albania	Butrinti
	Museum-city of Gjirokastra
Algeria	Al Qal'a of Beni Hammad
	Tassili n'Ajjer
	M'Zab Valley
	Djémila
	Tipasa
	Timgad
	Kasbah of Algiers
Andorra	Madriu-Claror-Perafita Valley
Argentina	Parque Nacionale Los Glaciares
	Iguazu National Park
	Peninsula Valdes
	Cueva de las Manos, Rio Pinturas
	Ischigualasto – Talampaya Natural Parks
	Jesuit Block and Jesuit Estancias of Cordoba
	Quebrada de Humahuaca
Argentina and Brazil	Jesuit Missions of the Guaranis: San Ignacio Mini, Santa Ana, Nuestra* Señora de Loreto and Santa Maria Mayor (Argentina), ruins of São Miguel das Missões (Brazil)
Armenia	Monasteries of Haghpat and Sanahin
	Monastery of Geghard and Upper Azat Valley
	Cathedral and churches of Echmiatsin and archaeological site of Zvartnots
Australia	Kakadu National Park
	Great Barrier Reef
	Willandra Lakes Region
	Tasmanian Wilderness
	Lord Howe Island Group
	Central Eastern Australian Rainforest Reserves
	Uluru-Kata Tjuta National Park
	Wet Tropics of Queensland
	Shark Bay, Western Australia
	Fraser Island
	Australian fossil mammal sites (Riversleigh/Naracoorte)
	Heard and McDonald Islands
	Macquarie Island
	Greater Blue Mountains Area
	Purnululu National Park
	Royal Exhibition Building and Carlton Gardens

Contracting state	Name of property
Austria	Historic centre of the city of Salzburg
	Palace and gardens of Schönbrunn
	Hallstatt-Dachstein Salzkammergut cultural landscape
	Semmering Railway
	City of Graz
	Wachau cultural landscape
	Historic centre of Vienna
	Ferto-Neusiedlersee cultural landscape*
Azerbaijan	Walled City of Baku
Bahrain	Qal'at al-Bahrain archaeological site
Bangladesh	The Historic Mosque City of Bagerhat
	Ruins of the Buddhist Vihara at Paharpur
	The Sundarbans
Belarus	Mir Castle complex
	Cultural complex of the Radziwill family at Nesvizh
Belarus/Poland	Belovezhskaya Pushcha/Bialowieza Forest*
	Struve Geodetic Arc*
Belgium	Flemish Béguinages
	The Four Lifts on the Canal du Centre and their environs, La Louvière and Le Roeulx (Hainault)
	Grand-Place, Brussels
	Belfries of Flanders and France*
	Historic centre of Bruges
	Major town houses of architect Victor Horta, Brussels
	Neolithic flint mines at Spiennes (Mons)
	Notre Dame Cathedral, Tournai
	Plantin-Moretus complex
Belize	Belize Barrier Reef Reserve System
Benin	Royal Palaces of Abomey
Bolivia	City of Potosi
	Noel Kempff Mercado National Park
	Imperial capital of Tiwanaku
	Jesuit Missions of the Chiquitos
	Historic city of Sucre
	El Fuerte de Samaipata
Bosnia– Herzegovina	Old bridge area of old city of Mostar
Botswana	Tsodilo
Brazil	Historic town of Ouro Preto
	Historic centre of the town of Olinda
	Historic centre of Salvador de Bahia

Contracting state	Name of property
	Sanctuary of Bom Jesus do Congonhas
	Iguaçu National Park
	Brasilia
	Serra da Capivara National Park
	Historic Centre of São Luis
	Discovery Coast Atlantic Forest Reserves
	Southeast Atlantic Forest Reserves
	Diamantina town historic centre
	Pantanal Conservation Complex
	Jau National Park
	Fernando de Noronha and Atol das Rocas Reserves
	Chapada dos Veadeiros and Emas National Parks
	Goias town historic centre
Bulgaria	Boyana Church
	Madara Rider
	Thracian tomb of Kazanlak
	Rock-hewn churches of Ivanovo
	Ancient city of Nessebar
	Rila Monastery
	Srebarna Nature Reserve
	Pirin National Park
	Thracian tomb of Sveshtari
Cambodia	Angkor
Cameroon	Dja Faunal Reserve
Canada	L'Anse aux Meadows National Historic Park
	Nahanni National Park
	Dinosaur Provincial Park
	Anthony Island
	Head-Smashed-In Buffalo Jump Complex
	Wood Buffalo National Park
	Canadian Rocky Mountains Parks (including Burgess Shale)
	Quebec (historic area)
	Gros Morne National Park
	Lunenburg old town
	Miguasha Park
Canada and United States of America	Tatshenshini-Alsek/Kluane National Park, Wrangell – St. Elias National Park and Reserve, and Glacier Bay National Park*
	Waterton Glacier International Peace Park*
Central African Republic	Manovo-Gounda Floris National Park
Chile	Rapa Nui National Park
	Churches of Chiloe
	Historic quarter of Valparaiso
	Humberstone and Santa Laura Saltpeter works
	Sewell mining town
China (People's Rep. of)	Mount Taishan
	The Great Wall
	Imperial Palace of the Ming and Qing Dynasties in Beijing and Shenyang
	Mogao Caves

Contracting state	Name of property
	The Mausoleum of the First Qin Emperor
	Peking Man Site at Zhoukoudian
	Mount Huangshan
	Wulingyuan scenic and historic interest area
	Jiuzhaigou Valley scenic and historic interest area
	Huanglong scenic and historic interest area
	Mountain resort and outlying temples, Chengde
	Temple and cemetery of Confucius, and the Kong Family mansion in Qufu
	Ancient building complex in the Wudang Mountains
	Potala Palace, Lhasa
	Lushan National Park
	Mount Emei and Leshan Giant Buddha
	Old town of Lijiang
	Ancient city of Ping Yao
	Classical gardens of Suzhou
	Summer Palace in Beijing
	Temple of Heaven in Beijing
	Mount Wuyi
	Dazu rock carvings
	Mount Qincheng and Dujiangyan irrigation system
	Xidi and Hongcun ancient villages, S Anhui
	Longmen Grottos
	Imperial tombs of Ming and Qing dynasties
	Yungang Grottos
	Three parallel rivers of Yunnan protected areas
	Capital cities and tombs of Ancient Koguryo Kingdom
	Historic centre of Macao
	Sichuan giant panda sanctuaries
	Yin Xu
Colombia	Port, fortresses and group of monuments, Cartagena
	Los Katios National Park
	Historic centre of Santa Cruz de Mompox
	Archaeological national park of Tierradentro
	Archaeological park of San Agustin
	Malpelo fauna and flora sanctuary
Congo, Democratic Republic of	Virunga National Park
	Kahuzi-Biega National Park
	Garamba National Park
	Salonga National Park
	Okapi Wildlife Reserve
Costa Rica	Cocos Island National Park
Costa Rica/ Panama	Talamanca Range – La Amistad Reserves/La Amistad National Park*
	Guanacaste conservation area
Côte d'Ivoire	Tai National Park
	Comoé National Park

THE EARTH

World heritage sites (continued)

Contracting state	Name of property
Croatia	Old city of Dubrovnik
	Historical complex of Split with the Palace of Diocletian
	Plitvice Lakes National Park
	Episcopal Complex of the Euphrasian Basilica in the historic centre of Porec
	Historic city of Trogir
	Cathedral of St James, Sibenik
Cuba	Old Havana and its fortifications
	Trinidad/Valley de los Ingenios
	San Pedro de la Roca Castle, Santiago de Cuba
	Desembarco del Granma National Park
	Vinales Valley
	First coffee plantations in the SE of Cuba
	Alejandro de Humboldt National Park
	Urban historic centre of Cienfuegos
Cyprus	Paphos, Tombs of the Kings
	Painted churches at Troodos region
	Choirokoitia
Czech Republic	Historic centre of Prague
	Historic centre of Český Krumlov
	Historic centre of Telč
	Pilgrimage church of St John of Nepomuk at Zelena Hora
	Historic centre of Kutna Hora, with St Barbara church and the cathedral of Our Lady at Sedlec
	Lednice-Valtice cultural landscape
	Holašovice historical village reservation
	Gardens and castle at Kromeríz
	Litomysl Castle
	Holy Trinity Column, Olomouc
	Tugendhat Villa, Brno
	Jewish quarter and St Procopius' Basilica in Trebic
Denmark	Roskilde Cathedral
	Jellings mounds, runic stones, and church
	Kronborg Castle
	Ilulissat Icefjord
Dominica	Morne Trois Pitons National Park
Dominican Republic	Colonial city of Santo Domingo
Ecuador	Galapagos Islands
	City of Quito
	Sangay National Park
	Santa Ana de los Rios de Cuenca historic centre
Egypt	Memphis and its necropolis – the Pyramid fields, Giza to Dahshur
	Ancient Thebes with its necropolis
	Nubian monuments from Abu Simbel to Philae

Contracting state	Name of property
	Islamic Cairo
	Abu Mena
	St Catherine area
	Wadi Al-Hitan (Whale Valley)
El Salvador	Joya de Caren archeological site
Estonia	Historic centre (old town) of Tallinn
	Struve Geodetic Arc*
Ethiopia	Simen National Park
	Rock-hewn churches, Lalibela
	Fasil Ghebbi, Gondar Region
	Lower valley of the Awash
	Tiya
	Aksum
	Lower valley of the Omo
Finland	Old Rauma
	Fortress of Suomenlinna
	Petäjävesi old church
	Verla Groundwood and Board Mill
	Bronze Age Burial Site of Sammallahdenmaki
	Struve Geodetic Arc*
France	Mont-Saint-Michel and its bay
	Chartres Cathedral
	Palace and park of Versailles
	Vézelay, church and hill
	Decorated grottoes, Vézère Valley
	Palace and park of Fontainebleau
	Château and estate of Chambord
	Amiens Cathedral
	The Roman theatre and its surroundings and the 'Triumphal Arch' of Orange
	Roman and romanesque monuments of Arles
	Cistercian abbey of Fontenay
	Royal Saltworks of Arc-et-Senans
	Place Stanislas, Place de la Carrière and Place d'Alliance in Nancy
	Church of Saint-Savin sur Gartempe
	Cape Girolata, Cape Porto and Scandola Natural Reserve and Piana Calanches in Corsica
	Pont du Gard (Roman aqueduct)
	Strasbourg – Grande Ile
	Paris, banks of the Seine
	Cathedral of Notre-Dame, former Abbey of Saint-Remi and Tau Palace, Reims
	Bourges Cathedral
	Historic centre of Avignon
	Canal du Midi
	Historic fortified city of Carcassonne
	Routes of Santiago de Compostela in France
	Historic city of Lyon
	Jurisdiction of Saint-Emilion
	Loire Valley, including château and estate of Chambord
	Provins, town of mediaeval fairs
	Le Havre, the city rebuilt by Auguste Perret
France/Spain	Pyrénées – Mount Perdu

THE EARTH

Contracting state	Name of property
Gambia	James Is and related sites
	Stone circles of Senegambia
Georgia	City-museum reserve of Mtskheta
	Bagrati Cathedral and Gelati Monastery
	Upper Svaneti
Germany	Aachen Cathedral
	Speyer Cathedral
	Würzburg Residence with the court gardens and Residence Square
	Pilgrimage church of Wies
	The Castles of Augustusburg and Falkenlust at Brühl
	St Mary's Cathedral and St Michael's Church at Hildesheim
	Roman monuments, cathedral and Liebfrauen-Church in Trier
	Hanseatic city of Lübeck
	Palaces and parks of Potsdam and Berlin
	Abbey and Altenmünster of Lorsch
	Mines of Rammelsberg and the historic town of Goslar
	Town of Bamberg
	Maulbronn Monastery complex
	Collegiate church, castle, and old town of Quedlinburg
	Völklingen Ironworks
	Fossil site of Messel Pit
	Cologne Cathedral
	Bauhaus and its sites in Weimar and Dessau
	Luther memorials in Eisleben and Wittenberg
	Classical Weimar
	Museumsinsel (Museum Island), Berlin
	Wartburg Castle
	Garden Kingdom of Dessau-Worlitz
	Monastic Island of Reichenau
	Zollverein Coal Mine Industrial Complex, Essen
	Upper Middle Rhine Valley
	Stralsund and Wismar historic centres
	Dresden Elbe Valley
	Town Hall and Roland in Bremen marketplace
	Frontiers of the Roman Empire*
	Old town of Regensburg with Stadtamhof
Germany / Poland	Muskauer Park*
Ghana	Forts and castles, Volta, Greater Accra, Central and Western Regions
	Ashanti traditional buildings
Greece	Temple of Apollo Epicurius at Bassae
	Archaeological site of Delphi
	The Acropolis, Athens
	Mount Athos
	Meteora
	Paleochristian and Byzantine monuments of Thessalonika
	Archaeological site of Epidaurus

Contracting state	Name of property
	Mediaeval city of Rhodes
	Archaeological site of Olympia
	Mystras
	Delos
	Monasteries of Daphni, Hossios Luckas, and Nea Moni of Chios
	Pythagoreion and Heraion of Samos
	Archaeological site of Vergina
	Mycenae and Tiryns archaeological sites
	Historical sites on Island of Patmos
Guatemala	Tikal National Park
	Antigua Guatemala
	Archaeological park and ruins of Quirigua
Guinea and Côte d'Ivoire	Mount Nimba Strict Nature Reserve*
Haiti	National History Park – Citadel, Sans Souci, Ramiers
Honduras	Maya site of Copan
	Rio Platano biosphere reserve
Hungary	Budapest, the banks of the Danube with the Buda Castle Quarter
	Hollokö
	Millenary Benedictine Monastery of Pannonhalma and its natural environment
	Hortobagy National Park
	Pecs (Sopianae) early Christian cemetery
	Tokaji wine region cultural landscape
Hungary / Slovak Republic	Caves of the Aggtelek and Slovak Karst*
Iceland	Thingvellir National Park
India	Ajanta Caves
	Ellora Caves
	Agra Fort
	Taj Mahal
	The Sun Temple, Konarak
	Group of monuments at Mahabalipuram
	Kaziranga National Park
	Manas Wildlife Sanctuary
	Keoladeo National Park
	Churches and convents of Goa
	Khajuraho group of monuments
	Group of monuments at Hampi
	Fatehpur Sikri
	Group of monuments at Pattadakal
	Elephanta Caves
	Brihadisvara Temple, Thanjavur
	Sundarbans National Park
	Nanda Devi National Park
	Buddhist monuments at Sanchi
	Humayun's Tomb, Delhi
	Qutb Minar and its monuments, Delhi
	Darjeeling Himalayan Railway
	Mahabodhi Temple Complex at Bodh Gaya
	Rock shelters of Bhimbetka

THE EARTH

World heritage sites (continued)

Contracting state	Name of property
	Champaner-Pavagadh Archaeological Park
	Chhatrapati Shivaji Station
Indonesia	Komodo National Park
	Ujung Kulon National Park
	Borobudur Temple compound
	Prambanan Temple compound
	Sangiran early man site
	Lorentz National Park
	Tropical Rainforest Heritage of Sumatra
Iran	Tchogha Zanbil
	Persepolis
	Meidan Emam, Esfahan
	Takht-e Soleyman
	Pasargadae
	Bam and its cultural landscape
	Soltaniyeh
	Bisotun
Iraq	Hatra
	Ashur (Qal'at Sherqat)
Ireland	Archeological ensemble of the Bend of the Boyne
	Skellig Michael
Israel	Masada National Park
	Old City of Acre
	The white city of Tel-Aviv
	Biblical Tels – Megiddo, Hazor, Beer Sheeba
Italy	Rock Drawings in Valcamonica
	The Church and Dominican convent of Santa Maria delle Grazie with 'The Last Supper' by Leonardo da Vinci
	Historic centre of Florence
	Venice and its lagoon
	Piazza del Duomo, Pisa
	Historic centre of San Gimignano
	I Sassi di Matera
	Vicenza city and Palladian villas of the Veneto
	Historic centre of Siena
	Historic centre of Naples
	Crespi d'Adda
	Renaissance city of Ferrara
	Castel del Monte
	The *trulli* of Alberobello
	Early Christian monuments of Ravenna
	Historic centre of Pienza city
	18th-c Royal Palace at Caserta with park, Aqueduct of Vanvitelli and San Leucio Complex
	Residences of the Royal House of Savoy
	Botanical garden (Orto Botanico), Padua
	Portovenere, Cinque Terre, and the Islands (Palmaria, Tino and Tinetto)
	Cathedral, Torre Civica and Piazza Grande, Modena

	Archaeological areas of Pompeii, Herculaneum and Torre Annunziata
	Costiera Amalfitana
	Archaeological area of Agrigento
	Villa Romana del Casale
	Su Nuraxi di Barumini
	Cilento and Vallo di Diano National Park with archaeological sites of Paestum and Velia, and the Certosa di Padula
	Historic centre of Urbino
	Archaeological area and Patriarchal Basilica of Aquileia
	Villa Adriana
	Aeolian Islands
	Assisi
	City of Verona
	Villa d'Este, Tivoli
	Late Baroque towns of the Val di Noto
	Sacri Monti of Piedmont and Lombardy
	Etruscan Necropolises of Cerveteri and Tarquinia
	Val d'Orcia
	Syracuse and rocky necropolis of Pantalica
	Le Strade Nuove and system of Palazzi dei Rolli at Genoa
Italy/Holy See (each according to its jurisdiction)	Historic Centre of Rome, the properties of the Holy See (Vatican City) in that city enjoying extraterritorial rights, and San Paolo Fuori le Mura*
Japan	Buddhist monuments in the Horyu-ji area
	Himeji-jo
	Yakushima
	Shirakami-Sanchi
	Historic monuments of ancient Kyoto, Uji, and Otsu cities
	Historic villages of Shirakawa-go and Gokoyama
	Hiroshima Peace Memorial (Genbaku Dome)
	Itsukushima Shinto Shrine
	Historic monuments of ancient Nara
	Shrines and temples of Nikko
	Gusuku sites and properties of the Kingdom of Ryukyu
	Sacred sites and pilgrimage routes in the Kii mountain range
	Shiretoko
Jerusalem	Old city of Jerusalem and its walls (*site proposed by Jordan*)
Jordan	Petra
	Quseir Amra
	Um er-Rasas
Kazakhstan	Mausoleum of Khoja Ahmed Yasawi
	Petroglyphs within archaeological landscape of Tamgaly

Contracting state	Name of property
Kenya	Mount Kenya National Park/Natural Forest
	Lake Turkana National Parks
	Lamu old town
Korea, North	Complex of Koguryo tombs
Korea, South	Sokkuram Buddhist Grotto
	Temple of Haiensa Changgyong P'ango (location of the wood blocks of Tripitaka Koreana)
	Chongmyo Shrine
	Ch'angdokkung Palace Complex
	Hwasong Fortress
	Koch'ang, Hwasun and Kanghwa Dolmen sites
	Kyongju historic sites
Laos	Town of Luang Prabang
	Vat Phou and ancient settlements within Champasak cultural landscape
Latvia	Historic centre of Riga
Lebanon	Anjar
	Baalbek
	Byblos
	Tyre
	Wadi Qadisha (the Holy Valley) and the Forest of the Cedars of God (Horsh Arz el-Rab)
Libya	Archaeological site of Leptis Magna
	Archaeological site of Sabratha
	Archaeological site of Cyrene
	Rock-art sites of Tadrart Acacus
	Old town of Ghadamès
Lithuania	Vilnius historic centre
	Curonian Spit*
	Kernave archaeological site
	Struve Geodetic Arc*
Luxembourg	Old quarters and fortifications of Luxembourg city
Macedonia, (Former Yugoslav) Republic of	Ohrid Region with its cultural and historical aspects and its natural environment
Madagascar	Tsingy de Bemaraha Strict Nature Reserve
	Royal Hill of Ambohimanga
Malawi	Lake Malawi National Park
	Chongoni rock art area
Malaysia	Gunung Mulu National Park
	Kinabalu Park
Mali	Old towns of Djenné
	Timbuktu
	Cliff of Bandiagara (Land of the Dogons)
	Tomb of Askia
Malta	Hal Saflieni Hypogeum
	City of Valletta
	Megalithic temples of Malta
Mauritania	Banc d'Arguin National Park

Contracting state	Name of property
	Ancient *ksour* of Ouadane, Chinguetti, Tichitt and Oualata
Mauritius	Aapravasi Ghat
Mexico	Sian Ka'an
	Pre-Hispanic city and national park of Palenque
	Historic centre of Mexico City and Xochimilco
	Pre-Hispanic city of Teotihuacan
	Historic centre of Oaxaca and archaeological site of Monte Alban
	Historic centre of Puebla
	Historic town of Guanajuato and adjacent mines
	Pre-Hispanic city of Chichen-Itza
	Historic centre of Morelia
	El Tajin, Pre-Hispanic City
	Whale Sanctuary of El Vizcaino
	Historic centre of Zacatecas
	Rock paintings of the Sierra de San Francisco
	Earliest 16th-c monasteries on the slopes of Popocatepetl
	Prehispanic town of Uxmal
	Historic monuments zone of Querétaro
	Hospicio Cabañas, Quadalajara
	Historic monuments zone of Tlacotalpan
	Archaeological zone of Paquimé, Casas Grandes
	Archaeological monuments zone of Xochicalco
	Historic fortified town of Campeche
	Ancient Maya city of Calakmul, Campeche
	Franciscan missions in the Sierra Gorda of Querétaro
	Luis Barragán house and studio
	Islands and protected areas of the Gulf of California
	Agave landscape and ancient industrial facilities of Tequila
Moldova	Struve Geodetic Arc*
Mongolia	UVS Nuur Basin*
	Orkhon Valley cultural landscape
Montenegro	Durmitor National Park
	Tara River Gorge
	Region of Kotor
Morocco	Medina of Fez
	Medina of Marrakesh
	Ksar of Aït-Ben-Haddou
	Historic city of Meknes
	Archaeological site of Volubilis
	The Medina of Tétouan (formerly known as Titawin)
	Medina of Essaouira (formerly Mogador)
	Portuguese city of Mazagan
Mozambique	Island of Mozambique
Nepal	Sagarmatha National Park

THE EARTH

World heritage sites (continued)

Contracting state	Name of property
	Vale of Kathmandu
	Royal Chitwan National Park
	Lumbini, birthplace of the Lord Buddha
Netherlands	Schokland and its neighbourhood
	Defence Line of Amsterdam
	Mill network at Kinderdijk-Elshout
	Historic area of Willemstad, inner city and harbour, the Netherlands Antilles
	Ir. D F Woudagemaal
	Droogmakerij de Beemster (Beemster Polder)
	Rietveld Schroder House
New Zealand	Te Wahipounamu – South West New Zealand (Westland/Mount Cook National Park and Fiordland National Park, previously inscribed on the World Heritage List, are part of this site)
	Tongariro National Park
	New Zealand Sub-Antarctic Islands
Nicaragua	Ruins of Leon Viejo
Niger	Aïr and Ténéré Natural Reserves
	W National Park of Niger
Nigeria	Sukur cultural landscape
	Osun-Osogbo Sacred Grove
Norway	Urnes Stave Church
	Bryggen
	Røros
	Rock drawings of Alta
	Vegaøyan – the Vega archipelago
	Struve Geodetic Arc*
	Geirangerfjord and Naerøyfjord west Norwegian fjords
Oman	Bahla Fort
	Archaeological sites of Bat, Al-Khutm, and Al-Ayn
	Arabian oryx sanctuary
	Frankincense Trail
	Aflaj irrigation systems of Oman
Pakistan	Archaeological ruins of Moenjodaro
	Taxila
	Buddhist ruins of Takht-i-Bahi and neighbouring city remains at Sahr-i-Bahlol
	Historical monuments of Thatta
	Fort and Shalamar Gardens in Lahore
	Rohtas Fort
Panama	The fortifications on the Caribbean side of Panama: Portobelo-San Lorenzo
	Darien National Park
	Historic district of Panama, with Salón Bolivar
	La Amistad National Park*
	Coiba National Park and special zone of marine protection

Contracting state	Name of property
Paraguay	Jesuit Missions of La Santisima Trinidad de Parana and Jesus de Tavarangue
Peru	City of Cuzco
	Historic sanctuary of Machu Picchu
	Chavin (archaeological site)
	Huascarán National Park
	Chan Chan Archaeological Zone
	Manu National Park
	Rio Abiseo National Park
	Historic centre of Lima
	The lines and geoglyphs of Nasca and Pampas de Jumana
	City of Arequipa historic centre
Philippines	Tubbataha Reef Marine Park
	Baroque churches of the Philippines
	Terraced rice-fields of the Philippine cordilleras
	Puerto-Princesa Subterranean River National Park
	Historic town of Vigan
Poland	Kraków's historic centre
	Wieliczka Salt Mine
	Auschwitz Concentration Camp
	Historic centre of Warsaw
	Old city of Zamość
	Medieval town of Torun
	Castle of the Teutonic Order in Malbork
	Kalwaria Zebrzydowska
	Churches of Peace in Jawor and Swidnica
	Wooden churches of Southern Little Poland
	Park Muzakowski*
	Centennial Hall in Wroclaw
Portugal	Central zone of the town of Angra do Heroismo in the Azores
	Monastery of the Hieronymites and Tower of Belem in Lisbon
	Monastery of Batalha
	Convent of Christ in Tomar
	Historic centre of Evora
	Monastery of Alcobaça
	Cultural landscape of Sintra
	Historic centre of Oporto
	Prehistoric rock-art sites in Côa Valley
	Laurisilva of Madeira
	Alto Douro wine region
	Guimaraes historic centre
	Landscape of the Pico Island vineyard culture
Romania	Danube Delta
	Biertan and its fortified church
	Monastery of Horezu
	Churches of Moldavia
	Sighisoara historic centre
	Dacian fortresses of the Orastie Mts
	Wooden churches of Maramures
Russian Federation	Historic centre of St Petersburg and related groups of monuments

Contracting state	Name of property
	Khizi Pogost
	Kremlin and Red Square in Moscow
	Historic monuments of Novgorod and surroundings
	Cultural and historic ensemble of Solovetsky Islands
	The White Monuments of Vladimir and Suzdal
	Architectural ensemble of the Trinity Sergius Lavra in Sergiev Pasad
	Church of the Ascension, Kolomenskoye
	Komi virgin forests
	Lake Baikal
	Volcanoes of Kamchatka
	Golden Mountains of Altai
	Western Caucasus
	Ensemble of Ferapontov Monastery
	Historic and architectural complex of Kazan Kremlin
	Curonian Spit*
	Central Sikhote-Alin
	Citadel, ancient city and fortress buildings of Derbent
	Natural System of Wrangel Island Reserve
	Ensemble of the Novodevichy Convent
	Uvs Nuur Basin*
	Historic centre of city of Yaroslavl
	Struve Geodetic Arc*
Saint Kitts and Nevis	Brimstone Hill Fortress National Park
Saint Lucia	Pitons Management Area
Senegal	Island of Gorée
	Niokolo-Koba National Park
	Djoudj National Bird Sanctuary
	Island of Saint-Louis
	Stone circles of Senegambia
Serbia	Stari Ras and Sopocani
	Studenica Monastery
	Medieval monuments in Kosovo
Serbia and Montenegro (former)	Region of Kotor
	Durmitor National Park
Seychelles	Aldabra Atoll
	Vallée de Mai Nature Reserve
Slovakia	Vlkolinec
	Banská Stiavnica historic town
	Spissky Hrad and its associated cultural monuments
	Aggtelek caves and Slovak Karst*
	Bardejov town conservation reserve
Slovenia	Škocjan Caves
Solomon Islands	East Rennell
South Africa	Greater St Lucia Wetland Park
	Robben Island
	Fossil hominid sites of Sterkfontein, Swartkrans, Kromdraai and environs
	Ukhahlamba/Drakensberg Park

Contracting state	Name of property
	Mapungubwe cultural landscape
	Cape Floral Region Protected Areas
	Vredefort Dome
Spain	Historic centre of Córdoba
	The Alhambra Generalife, and Albayzcin, Granada
	Burgos Cathedral
	Monastery and site of the Escorial, Madrid
	Parque Güell, Palacio Güell and Casa Mila, in Barcelona
	Altamira Cave
	Old town of Segovia and its aqueduct
	Monuments of Oviedo and the Kingdom of the Asturias
	Santiago de Compostela (Old Town)
	Old town of Avila with its extra-muros churches
	Mudejar architecture of Teruel
	Historic city of Toledo
	Garajonay National Park
	Old town of Cáceres
	The Cathedral, the Alcazar and the Archivo de Indias, in Seville
	Old city of Salamanca
	Poblet Monastery
	Archeological ensemble of Mérida
	Royal Monastery of Santa Maria de Guadalupe
	The Route of Santiago de Compostela
	Doñana National Park
	Historic walled town of Cuenca
	La Lonja de la Seda de Valencia
	Las Médulas
	The Palau de la Música Catalana and Hospital De Sant Pau, Barcelona
	San Millán Yuso and Suso monasteries
	University and historic precinct of Alcalá de Henares
	Rock-art of the Mediterranean Basin on the Iberian Peninsula
	Ibiza, biodiversity and culture
	San Cristobal de La Laguna
	Archaeological ensemble of Tarraco
	Palmeral of Elche
	Roman Walls of Lugo
	Catalan Romanesque churches of the Vall de Boi
	Archaeological site of Atapuerca
	Aranjuez cultural landscape
	Renaissance monumental ensembles of Ubeda and Baeza
	Pyrénées-Mont Perdu*
	Vizcaya Bridge
Sri Lanka	Sacred city of Anuradhapura
	Ancient city of Polonnaruva
	Ancient city of Sigiriya
	Sinharaja Forest Reserve
	Sacred city of Kandy
	Old town of Galle and its fortifications
	Golden Temple of Dambulla

World heritage sites (continued)

Contracting state	Name of property
Sudan	Gebel Barkal and sites of the Napatan region
Suriname	Central Suriname Nature Reserve
	Historic inner city of Paramaribo
Sweden	Royal Domain of Drottningholm
	Birka and Hovgården
	Engelsberg Ironworks
	Rock carvings in Tanum Skog-skyrkogården
	Hanseatic town of Visby
	Church village of Gammelstad, Luleå
	The Laponian area
	Naval port of Karlskrona
	High Coast
	Agricultural landscape of Southern Öland
	Mining area of the Great Copper Mountain in Falun
	Varberg Radio Station
	Struve Geodetic Arc*
Switzerland	Convent of St Gall
	Benedictine convent of St John at Müstair
	Old city of Berne
	Three castles, defensive wall and ramparts of Bellinzone market town
	Jungfrau-Aletsch-Bietschhorn
	Monte San Giorgio
Syria	Ancient city of Damascus
	Ancient city of Bosra
	Site of Palmyra
	Ancient city of Aleppo
	Crac des Chevaliers and Qal'at Salah El-Din
Tanzania	Ngorongoro conservation area
	Ruins of Kilwa Kisiwani and Songo Mnara
	Serengeti National Park
	Selous Game Reserve
	Kilimanjaro National Park
	Stone town of Zanzibar
	Kondoa rock art sites
Thailand	Thungyai-Huai Kha Khaeng wildlife sanctuaries
	Historic town of Sukhothai and associated historic towns
	Historic city of Ayutthaya and associated historic towns
	Ban Chiang archaeological site
	Dong Phayayen-Khao Yai forest complex
Togo	Koutammakou, the land of the Batammariba
Tunisia	Medina of Tunis
	Site of Carthage
	Amphitheatre of El Djem
	Ichkeul National Park
	Punic town of Kerkuane and its necropolis

Contracting state	Name of property
	Medina of Sousse
	Kairouan
	Dougga/Thugga
Turkey	Historic areas of Istanbul
	Göreme National Park and the rock sites of Cappadocia
	Great Mosque and hospital of Divrigi
	Hattusha
	Nemrut Dag
	Xanthos-Letoon
	Hierapolis-Pamukkale
	City of Safranbolu
	Archaeological site of Troy
Turkmenistan	State historical and cultural park 'Ancient Merv'
	Kunya-Urgench
Uganda	Bwindi Impenetrable National Park
	Rwenzori Mountains National Park
	Tombs of Buganda Kings at Kasubi
Ukraine	Kiev: Saint Sophia Cathedral and related monastic buildings, and Lavra of Kiev-Pechersk
	L'viv – the ensemble of the historic centre
	Struve Geodetic Arc*
United Kingdom	The Giant's Causeway and Causeway coast
	Durham Castle and Cathedral
	Ironbridge Gorge
	Studley Royal Park including the ruins of Fountains Abbey
	Stonehenge, Avebury and associated sites
	The castles and town walls of King Edward in Gwynedd
	St Kilda
	Blenheim Palace
	City of Bath
	Hadrian's Wall
	Palace of Westminster, Abbey of Westminster, and Saint Margaret's Church
	Henderson Island
	The Tower of London
	Canterbury Cathedral, St Augustine's Abbey, and St Martin's Church
	Edinburgh old and new towns
	Gough Island Wildlife Reserve
	Maritime Greenwich
	Heart of Neolithic Orkney
	Historic town of St George and related fortifications, Bermuda
	Blaenavon industrial landscape
	Derwent Valley mills
	Dorset and East Devon coast
	New Lanark
	Saltaire
	Royal Botanic Gardens, Kew
	Liverpool – maritime mercantile city

Contracting state	Name of property
	Cornwall and West Devon mining landscape
United States of America	Mesa Verde
	Yellowstone
	Grand Canyon National Park
	Everglades National Park
	Independence Hall
	Redwood National Park
	Mammoth Cave National Park
	Olympic National Park
	Cahokia Mounds state historic site
	Great Smoky Mountains National Park
	La Fortaleza and San Juan historic site in Puerto Rico
	The Statue of Liberty
	Yosemite National Park
	Chaco Culture National Historical Park
	Monticello and University of Virginia in Charlottesville
	Hawaii Volcanoes National Park
	Pueblo de Taos
	Carlsbad Caverns National Park
	The Statue of Liberty
	Yosemite National Park
	Chaco Culture National Historical Park
	Monticello and University of Virginia in Charlottesville
	Hawaii Volcanoes National Park
	Pueblo de Taos
	Carlsbad Caverns National Park
	Kluane/Wrangell-St Elias/Glacier Bay/Tatshenshini-Alsek*
	Waterton Glacier International Peace Park*
Uruguay	Historic quarter of Colonia del Sacramento

Contracting state	Name of property
Uzbekistan	Itchan Kala
	Historic centre of Bukhara
	Historic centre of Shakhrisyabz
	Samarkand
Venezuela	Coro and its port
	Canaima National Park
	Ciudad Universitaria de Caracas
Vietnam	The complex of Hué monuments
	Ha Long Bay
	Hoi An ancient town
	My Son sanctuary
	Phong Nha-Ke Bang National Park
Yemen	Old walled city of Shibam
	Old city of Sana'a
	Historic town of Zabid
Zambia/Zimbabwe	Victoria Falls/Mosi-oa-Tunya*
Zimbabwe	Mana Pools National Park, Sapi, and Chewore Safari Areas
	Great Zimbabwe National Monument
	Khami Ruins National Monument
	Matobo Hills

National Parks in England and Wales

Name (Date of designation)	Location	Area (km²)	(sq mi)
Brecon Beacons (1957)	Powys, Dyfed, Gwent, Mid Glamorgan	1351	522
Dartmoor (1951)	Devon	954	368
Exmoor (1954)	Somerset, Devon	693	268
Lake District (1951)	Cumbria	2292	885
New Forest (2005)	S Hampshire	571	220
Northumberland (1956)	Northumberland	1049	405
North York Moors (1952)	North Yorkshire, Cleveland	1436	554
Peak District (1951)	Derbyshire, Staffordshire, South Yorkshire, Cheshire, West Yorkshire, Greater Manchester	1438	555
Pembrokeshire Coast (1952)	Dyfed	584	225
Snowdonia (1951)	Gwynedd	2142	817
The Broads[a] (1988)	Norfolk and Suffolk	303	117
Yorkshire Dales (1954)	N Yorkshire, Cumbria	1769	683

[a]Does not bear the title National Park but is part of the Association of National Park Authorities.

National Parks in Scotland

Name (Date of designation)	Location	Area	
		(km²)	(sq mi)
Loch Lomond and the Trossachs (2002)	W Central Scotland	1600	618
Cairngorms (2003)	NE Central Scotland	4000	1544

National Parks in the USA

Park (Date authorized)	Location	Area	
		(ha)	(ac)
Acadia (1916)	SE Maine	15 770	38 971
American Samoa (1988)	American Samoa	3 642	9 000
Arches (1929)	E Utah	29 695	73 379
Badlands (1929)	SW South Dakota	98 461	243 302
Big Bend (1935)	W Texas	286 565	708 118
Biscayne (1968)	SE Florida	72 900	180 128
Bryce Canyon (1923)	SW Utah	14 502	35 835
Canyonlands (1964)	SE Utah	136 610	337 570
Capitol Reef (1937)	S Utah	97 895	214 904
Carlsbad Caverns (1923)	SE New Mexico	18 921	46 755
Channel Islands (1938)	S California	100 910	249 354
Crater Lake (1902)	SW Oregon	64 869	160 290
Death Valley (1994)	California, Nevada	1 362 879	3 367 627
Denali (1917)	S Alaska	1 645 248	4 065 493
Dry Tortugas (1992)	Florida	26 184	64 700
Everglades (1934)	S Florida	566 075	1 398 800
Gates of the Arctic (1978)	N Alaska	2 854 000	7 052 000
Glacier (1910)	NW Montana	410 188	1 013 595
Glacier Bay (1925)	SE Alaska	1 569 481	3 878 269
Grand Canyon (1908)	NW Arizona	493 059	1 218 375
Grand Teton (1929)	NW Wyoming	125 661	310 516
Great Basin (1986)	E Nevada	31 206	77 109
Great Smoky Mountains (1926)	SW North Carolina, SE Tennessee	210 550	520 269
Guadalupe Mountains (1966)	W Texas	30 875	76 293
Haleakala (1916)	Maui Is, Hawaii	11 956	28 655
Hawaii Volcanoes (1916)	Hawaii Is, Hawaii	92 745	229 177
Hot Springs (1832)	C Arkansas	2 358	5 826
Isle Royale (1931)	NW Michigan	231 398	571 796
Joshua Tree (1994)	California	320 825	792 749
Katmai (1918)	SW Alaska	1 792 810	4 430 125
Kenai Fjords (1978)	S Alaska	229 457	567 000
Kobuk Valley (1978)	N Alaska	692 000	1 710 000
Lake Clark (1978)	S Alaska	987 000	2 439 000
Lassen Volcanic (1907)	N California	43 047	106 372
Mammoth Cave (1926)	C Kentucky	21 230	52 452
Mesa Verde (1906)	SW Colorado	21 078	52 085
Mount Rainier (1899)	SW Washington	95 265	235 404
North Cascades (1968)	N Washington	204 277	504 781
Olympic (1909)	NW Washington	370 250	914 890
Petrified Forest (1906)	E Arizona	37 835	93 493
Redwood (1968)	NW California	44 280	109 415
Rocky Mountain (1915)	C Colorado	106 762	263 809
Saguaro (1994)	Arizona	36 875	91 116
Sequoia and Kings Canyon (1890, 1940)	E California	349 539	863 700
Shenandoah (1926)	N Virginia	78 845	194 826
Theodore Roosevelt (1947)	W North Dakota	28 497	70 416
Virgin Islands (1956)	St John, Virgin Islands	5 947	14 695
Voyageurs (1971)	N Minnesota	88 678	219 128
Wind Cave (1903)	SW South Dakota	11 449	28 292
Wrangell-St Elias (1978)	SE Alaska	3 297 000	8 147 000
Yellowstone (1872)	Idaho, Montana, Wyoming	898 350	2 219 823
Yosemite (1890)	E California	307 932	760 917
Zion (1909)	SW Utah	59 308	146 551

PART THREE

The Environment

CLIMATE

The climate system

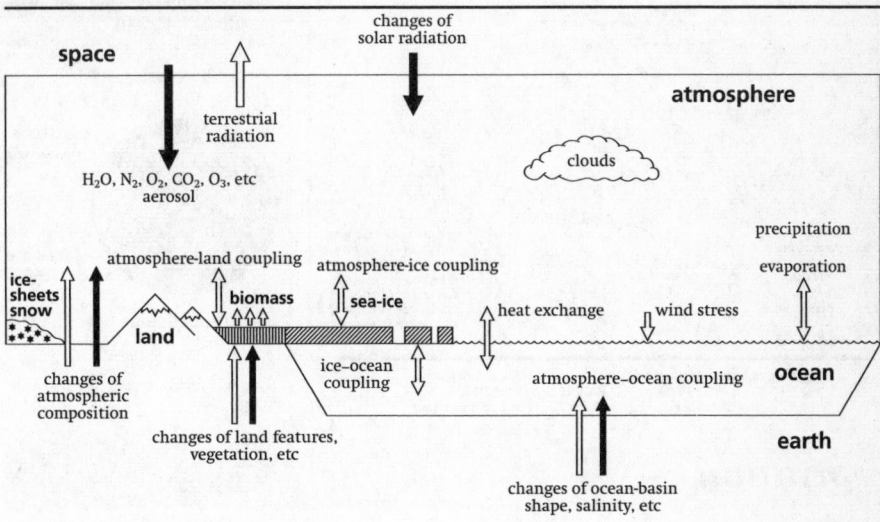

Schematic illustration of the climate system components and interactions (from Houghton, J.T. (ed), 1984, *The Global Climate*; Cambridge University Press).

Climate alterations produced by cities

Element	Compared to rural environs	Element	Compared to rural environs
Contaminants		Snowfall: inner city	5–10% less
Condensation nuclei	10 times more	Snowfall: lee of city	10% more
Particulates	10 times more	Thunderstorms	10–15% more
Gaseous admixtures	5–25 times more		
		Temperature	
Radiation		Annual mean	0.5–30°C/0.9–54°F more
Total on horizontal surface	0–20% less	Winter minimums (average)	1–2°C/1.8–3.6°F more
Ultraviolet: winter	30% less	Summer maximums	1–3°C/1.8–5.4°F more
Ultraviolet: summer	5% less	Heating degree days	10% less
Sunshine duration	5–15% less		
		Relative humidity	
Cloudiness		Annual mean	6% less
Clouds	5–10% more	Winter	2% less
Fog: winter	100% more	Summer	8% less
Fog: summer	30% more		
		Wind speed	
Precipitation		Annual mean	20–30% less
Amounts	5–15% more	Extreme gusts	10–20% less
Days with less than 5 mm/0.2 in	10% more	Calm	5–20% more

THE ENVIRONMENT

The greenhouse effect

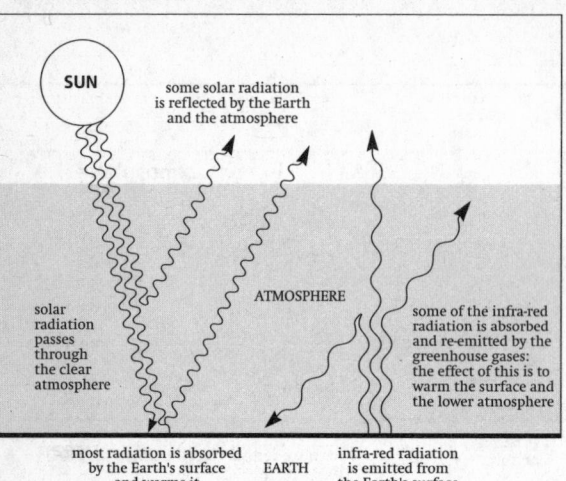

SUN

some solar radiation
is reflected by the Earth
and the atmosphere

ATMOSPHERE

solar
radiation
passes
through
the clear
atmosphere

some of the infra-red
radiation is absorbed
and re-emitted by the
greenhouse gases:
the effect of this is to
warm the surface and
the lower atmosphere

most radiation is absorbed
by the Earth's surface
and warms it

EARTH

infra-red radiation
is emitted from
the Earth's surface

Greenhouse gases

The share of greenhouse warming due to different greenhouse gases. The contribution from ozone may also be significant, but cannot be quantified at present.

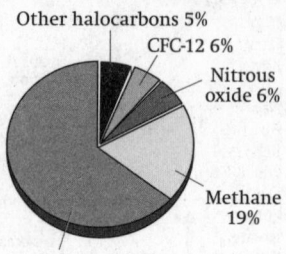

Other halocarbons 5%

CFC-12 6%

Nitrous
oxide 6%

Methane
19%

Carbon dioxide 64%

Source: World Resources Institute, 1998.

POLLUTION

Pollutants and the ecosystem

Pathways of pollutants and other substances in ecosystems.

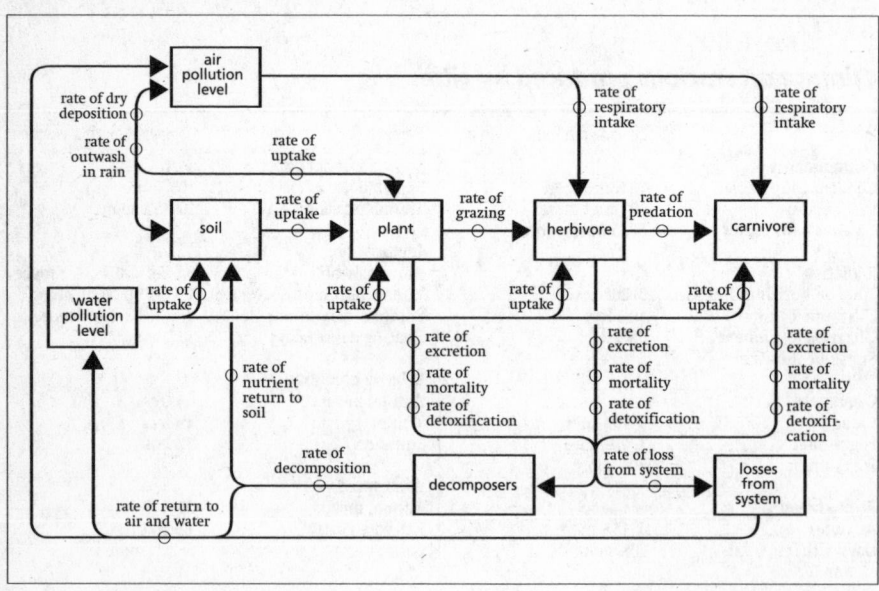

Carbon dioxide

Carbon-dioxide (CO_2) emissions from energy use[a] 1980–99 (1 tonne = 0.984 tons).

	Carbon (million tonnes)							Marine bunkers[b]	Aviation[c]
	1980	1990	1995	1996	1997	1998	1999	1999	1999
Canada	429	421	452	464	480	488	489	3.5	3.1
Mexico	244	297	314	325	339	357	358	2.6	8.2
USA	4765	4846	5116	5255	5460	5506	5585	82.6	56.8
Japan	913	1049	1134	1162	1161	1135	1158	16.7	18.9
Korea	124	234	364	402	430	376	410	20.7	1.4
Australia	212	260	278	297	311	309	322	2.5	7.2
New Zealand	17	23	27	29	31	30	31	0.9	2.0
Austria	57	57	57	60	61	61	61	0.0	1.5
Belgium	126	106	114	122	119	122	119	14.0	4.5
Czech Republic	165	150	125	127	129	122	111	0.0	0.4
Denmark	61	50	58	70	61	58	53	4.1	2.3
Finland	59	53	55	65	63	60	58	1.8	1.1
France	472	364	344	367	345	372	361	9.2	15.8
Germany	1074	967	866	891	865	858	822	6.6	20.5
Greece	45	69	72	73	77	81	82	9.8	2.9
Hungary	81	68	59	60	58	57	58	0.0	0.6
Iceland	2	2	2	2	2	2	2	0.2	0.4
Ireland	26	32	34	35	36	38	40	0.5	1.5
Italy	370	397	412	406	411	420	421	7.6	10.1
Luxembourg	12	10	8	8	8	7	7	0.0	1.0
Netherlands	154	156	170	178	175	171	167	40.2	10.1
Norway	29	28	30	30	33	34	37	2.7	1.7
Poland	437	348	336	364	348	323	310	1.7	0.8
Portugal	25	40	49	48	50	55	61	1.9	1.6
Russian Federation	–	2351	1575	1551	1483	1440	1486	0.0	26.2
Slovak Republic	63	55	41	41	39	38	39	0.0	0.0
Spain	192	212	239	229	247	254	272	18.7	7.8
Sweden	69	49	51	52	49	50	48	4.8	1.5
Switzerland	40	41	38	39	41	41	40	0.0	4.5
Turkey	73	138	157	173	184	185	183	0.9	1.5
UK	584	572	552	563	537	540	535	7.3	18.8
N. America	5438	5564	5882	6044	6278	6351	6432	88.6	68.1
OECD Europe	4217	3965	3871	4004	3936	3949	3886	132.0	110.9
EU-15	3327	3134	3083	3168	3103	3146	3106	126.5	101.0
OECD	10923	11095	11555	11938	12147	12148	12239	261.3	208.4
Non-OECD Europe	375	398	278	284	272	263	232	3.4	2.9
Africa	410	600	678	691	707	720	730	23.9	13.8
Asia	744	1381	1904	2023	2119	2082	2131	73.3	40.7
China	1487	2429	3072	3228	3162	3087	3051	22.7	10.0
Former USSR	3234	3544	2473	2399	2278	2230	2281	0.8	29.8
Latin America	577	622	746	792	822	865	864	26.6	11.0
Middle East	353	584	805	857	839	862	886	11.6	18.1
Total non-OECD	7179	9557	9957	10274	10199	10110	10175	162.1	126.3
World	18102	20652	21512	22213	22346	22258	22414	423.5	334.7

Notes:
[a] Anthropogenic CO_2, emissions from energy use only. Oil held in international marine bunkers is presented separately. Oil and gas for non-energy purposes and the use of biomass fuels are excluded. Peat is included.
[b] International marine bunkers represent quantities delivered to seagoing ships of all flags, including warships and fishing vessels. Quantities are assigned to the country in which these bunkers are situated.
[c] Emissions from fuels used in international air transport.
RUS: 1990, 1991: Secretariat estimates
China: including Hong Kong

Source: IEA-OECD Environmental Data, 2002.

* Much of the data in the following sections comes from the Organization for Economic Cooperation and Development (OECD).
OECD Europe refers to all EU member countries of OECD, plus Austria, Finland, Iceland, Norway, Sweden, Switzerland, and Turkey.
OECD refers to all members of OECD Europe, plus Canada, US, Japan, Australia, and New Zealand.

THE ENVIRONMENT

Emissions of major greenhouse gases, end 1990s

1000 tonnes CO$_2$ equivalent

	Year	CH$_4$	N$_2$O	HFCs	PFCs	SF$_6$	CO$_2$ emissions from: energy use	ind. processes[a]	Total CO$_2$[b]	Total GHG[c]
Canada	1999	90 000	54 000	900	6 000	1 700	506 000	39 000	546 000	69 900
Mexico	1998	169 274	14 710	–	–	–	350 380	44 346	394 726	578 710
USA	2000	614 500	425 300	121 300	–	–	5 623 300	161 900	5 840 000	7 001 200
Japan	1999	27 023	16 536	19 497	11 043	8 351	1 147 945	53 233	1 224 980	1 307 430
Australia	1999	117 663	29 649	–	1 001	4	332 860	7 898	340 776	489 092
N. Zealand	1999	33 594	12 397	210	74	33	27 656	2 867	30 523	76 831
Austria	2000	9 402	2 515	1 033	25	677	53 414	12 187	66 102	79 754
Belgium	2000	10 995	13 422	804	–	–	114 126	11 209	127 040	151 930
Czech Rep.	1999	10 900	8 100	412	3	111	118 600	2 400	121 600	141 126
Denmark	2000	5 753	9 083	730	28	59	51 287	1 453	52 852	68 505
Finland	2000	3 930	7 183	502	22	17	58 457	1 072	62 305	73 958
France	2000	60 296	76 891	6 973	1 672	2 279	380 370	17 478	401 923	542 299
Germany	2000	60 583	60 080	7 700	1 709	3 442	831 759	26 149	857 908	991 421
Greece	2000	10 890	11 010	4 281	148	–	95 682	7 877	103 727	129 652
Hungary	1999	14 343	11 259	154	574	101	56 490	2 709	60 117	86 547
Iceland	1999	286	220	59	133	5	1 930	656	2 738	3 441
Ireland	2000	12 800	9 661	–	–	–	41 239	2 576	43 815	66 277
Italy	2000	37 676	41 643	1 786	209	328	433 717	25 802	461 822	543 464
Luxembourg	2000	478	94	–	–	–	4 707	682	5 399	5 949
Netherlands	2000	20 638	16 980	3 913	1 531	327	171 714	1 360	173 527	216 916
Norway	2000	6 814	5 154	232	899	891	33 705	7 251	41 273	55 263
Poland	1999	47 250	23 250	–	–	–	319 088	10 609	329 739	400 239
Portugal	2000	13 134	8 258	–	157	1	57 395	5 070	63 150	84 700
Russian Fed.	1996	389 424	40 920	5 915	30 262	–	1 477 000	18 920	1 495 920	1 962 441
Slovak Rep.	1999	4 658	2 745	66	14	13	41 326	3 549	44 875	52 370
Spain	2000	38 363	30 497	9 878	409	209	285 260	19 903	306 632	385 987
Sweden	2000	5 874	6 916	369	266	77	51 144	4 600	55 855	69 356
Switzerland	1999	4 567	3 615	366	28	125	41 181	2 238	44 826	53 527
Turkey	2000	18 986	5 441	–	–	–	210 462	16 893	227 355	251 782
UK	2000	50 960	43 878	9 316	668	1 540	529 424	13 111	542 743	649 106
North America		873 800	494 000	–	–	–	6 479 700	245 200	6 780 700	8 278 900
OECD Europe		449 600	397 900	–	–	–	3 982 500	196 800	4 197 300	5 103 600
EU15		341 800	338 100	47 300	6 800	9 000	3 159 700	150 500	3 324 800	4 059 300
OECD		1 501 600	950 500	–	–	–	11 970 600	506 100	12 574 300	15 255 800

Notes:
[a] All emissions from industrial processes, except those from fuel combustion.
[b] Without emissions from land use change and forestry.
[c] CO$_2$ without emissions from land use change and forestry, CH$_4$, N$_2$O, HFCs, PFCs, SF$_6$.
USA Data reported for HFCs refer to HFCs, PFCs and SF.
CZE HFCs, PFCs, SF: potential emissions.
TUR CH$_4$: excludes emissions from landfills and coal mining.
TOT Rounded figures, exclude Korea.

Source: UNFCCC, EEA
OECD Environmental Data, 2002.

THE ENVIRONMENT

Carbon-dioxide (CO₂) emissions by source^a, 1980–99

million tonnes

	Transport^b 1980	Transport^b 1999	Bunkers^c 1980	Bunkers^c 1999	Energy transformation^d 1980	Energy transformation^d 1999	Industry^e 1980	Industry^e 1999	Other^f 1980	Other^f 1999
Canada	128.3	151.4	6.1	6.5	107.0	172.3	102.8	89.8	89.9	90.1
Mexico	67.3	97.8	5.2	10.8	62.3	155.1	59.8	62.7	23.3	32.7
USA	1237.6	1692.9	109.1	139.4	1936.2	2668.4	795.9	555.8	697.9	605.4
Japan	156.7	252.8	40.8	35.5	333.3	448.4	251.9	260.6	127.0	165.6
Korea	14.4	81.4	1.1	22.1	27.2	164.9	35.5	75.7	46.7	78.9
Australia	49.3	72.2	5.9	9.7	99.7	189.6	47.6	50.5	11.1	14.4
N. Zealand	6.7	12.2	1.7	2.9	2.2	7.6	4.7	7.9	2.8	2.1
Austria	12.8	17.4	0.4	1.5	12.8	16.6	15.8	13.9	15.7	13.8
Belgium	16.1	24.7	8.9	18.5	40.6	29.1	34.3	32.0	33.0	30.7
Czech Rep.	6.8	11.5	0.9	0.4	57.4	61.4	69.9	25.0	37.9	12.1
Denmark	9.1	12.5	3.0	6.4	26.5	28.0	8.3	5.1	18.7	8.1
Finland	8.4	12.3	2.3	2.9	20.8	22.7	14.8	14.0	11.5	6.8
France	89.7	136.3	18.4	25.0	136.2	61.5	120.3	79.4	119.6	103.5
Germany	130.2	178.4	19.6	27.1	440.3	341.3	234.5	128.7	252.9	176.6
Greece	9.6	19.8	5.0	12.7	19.6	44.4	10.6	9.6	5.9	10.4
Hungary	8.5	9.0	0.4	0.6	34.0	29.0	22.8	7.4	20.4	15.1
Iceland	0.5	0.6	0.1	0.5	0.0	0.0	0.5	0.6	0.7	0.8
Ireland	4.6	9.7	0.9	2.1	8.2	15.8	6.0	4.9	7.2	9.5
Italy	71.8	113.4	17.5	17.7	119.3	148.1	93.5	79.0	78.8	82.0
Luxembourg	1.3	4.2	0.2	1.0	1.7	0.1	7.4	1.6	1.5	1.6
Netherlands	22.4	31.3	32.4	50.3	49.4	66.1	35.7	34.8	46.3	38.5
Norway	8.6	13.1	1.6	4.4	3.4	14.4	10.9	6.9	5.5	3.9
Poland	28.1	30.0	2.9	2.5	234.0	172.1	67.3	48.1	82.9	54.3
Portugal	6.9	16.8	2.3	3.5	6.5	26.2	7.9	12.4	2.8	5.0
Russian Fed.	–	182.5	–	26.2	–	889.3	–	192.4	–	197.6
Slovak Rep.	3.7	4.2	0.0	0.0	12.3	12.2	25.6	14.4	10.7	9.4
Spain	45.5	89.6	7.8	26.4	70.4	101.9	53.7	47.7	19.9	27.5
Sweden	17.0	22.1	3.2	6.3	10.2	10.1	20.1	10.4	26.6	9.2
Switzerland	10.5	15.1	2.1	4.5	1.3	1.3	8.7	6.1	19.3	18.6
Turkey	16.8	33.8	0.1	2.4	16.6	73.8	21.0	43.3	17.4	30.4
UK	90.5	132.1	16.6	26.1	257.8	200.7	104.7	74.4	119.9	112.0
N. America	1433.2	1942.1	120.4	156.7	2105.5	2995.8	958.6	708.3	811.1	728.2
Australia	56.0	84.4	7.6	12.5	101.9	197.2	52.3	58.3	13.9	16.5
OECD Europe	619.3	937.9	146.3	242.8	1578.3	1476.6	994.0	699.5	955.2	779.5
EU-15	536.0	820.7	138.2	227.4	1219.4	1112.4	767.3	547.7	760.4	635.0
OECD	2279.7	3298.6	316.3	469.7	4146.1	5282.9	2292.3	1802.3	1953.9	1768.6
Non-OECD Europe	26.8	32.6	3.0	6.2	120.0	124.5	136.0	44.5	77.3	22.9
Africa	83.3	123.8	25.9	37.7	158.3	323.6	123.9	133.9	45.4	78.8
Asia	128.8	382.4	36.5	114.0	247.6	929.8	268.3	586.5	76.3	171.2
P. Rep. China	82.7	220.6	7.0	32.8	344.4	1420.2	660.3	979.4	323.0	354.3
Former USSR	278.6	236.3	87.4	30.7	1283.1	1205.9	904.2	373.4	597.4	385.3
Latin America	181.8	288.0	28.1	37.5	144.4	227.0	155.4	212.4	64.8	108.8
Middle East	77.8	164.8	39.1	29.7	106.9	383.1	101.3	204.3	38.0	189.4
Total non-OECD	859.7	1448.4	227.0	288.5	2404.5	4614.2	2349.3	2534.3	1222.1	1310.7
World	3139.4	4747.0	543.3	758.2	6550.6	9897.1	4641.6	4336.6	3176.1	3079.4

Notes:

^{a} Anthropogenic CO₂, emissions from energy use only. Oil held in international marine and aviation bunkers is presented separately. Oil and gas for non-energy purposes and the use of biomass fuels are excluded. Peat is included.

^{b} Includes transport in the industry sector and covers road, railway, air, internal navigation, transport of materials by pipeline and non-specified transport.

^{c} International marine (quantities are assigned to the countries in which bunker deliveries were made) and aviation bunkers.

^{d} Electricity and heat plants, refineries.

^{e} Refineries excluded.

^{f} Agriculture, commerce, residential sectors.

Source: OECD-IEA.
OECD Environmental Data, 2002.

THE ENVIRONMENT

Total emissions of traditional air pollutants[a], late 1990s

	Total emissions (1000 tonnes)					Per capita emissions (kg/cap.)					Emissions per unit of GDP (kg/1000 USD)[d]				
	SOx	NOx	CO	Part[b]	VOC[c]	SOx	NOx	CO	Part[b]	VOC[c]	SOx	NOx	CO	Part[b]	VOC[c]
Canada	2691	2056	10145	1736	2670	89.7	67.4	338.3	58.5	89.0	3.7	2.6	14.0	2.5	3.7
Mexico	1168	1152	5928	–	999	12.2	12.0	62.0	–	10.4	1.6	1.6	8.1	–	1.4
USA	17116	23037	85648	2762	15763	62.7	84.4	313.8	10.1	57.8	2.0	2.6	9.8	0.3	1.8
Japan	870	1654	3636	169	1842	6.9	13.1	28.7	1.3	14.5	0.3	0.5	1.2	0.1	0.6
Korea	1146	1083	977	420	–	24.7	23.3	21.0	9.0	–	1.8	1.7	1.5	0.7	–
Australia	1818	2565	18166	–	1917	95.8	135.2	957.8	–	101.1	4.0	5.7	40.1	–	4.2
N. Zealand	44	202	843	44	174	11.6	53.4	222.3	11.7	45.8	0.7	3.1	12.8	0.7	2.6
Austria	41	184	906	77	239	5.0	22.7	112.1	9.5	29.5	0.2	0.9	4.6	0.4	1.2
Belgium	205	364	1026	65	295	20.1	35.7	100.6	6.4	28.9	0.9	1.5	4.3	0.3	1.2
Czech Rep.	265	397	649	57	247	25.8	38.6	63.2	5.6	24.0	2.0	3.0	4.9	0.4	1.9
Denmark	28	208	656	28	131	5.2	38.9	123.1	5.3	24.5	0.2	1.5	4.8	0.2	1.0
Finland	76	236	535	48	162	14.6	45.6	103.4	9.3	31.3	0.6	1.9	4.3	0.4	1.3
France	837	1654	8013	–	2341	14.2	28.1	136.2	–	39.8	0.7	1.3	6.3	–	1.8
Germany	831	1637	4952	259	1651	10.1	19.9	60.3	3.2	20.1	0.4	0.9	2.7	0.1	0.9
Greece	540	382	1500	–	397	51.4	36.4	142.8	–	37.8	3.7	2.6	10.2	–	2.7
Hungary	592	221	737	127	149	58.5	22.0	72.9	12.6	14.8	5.7	2.1	7.2	1.2	1.4
Iceland	9	26	26	–	8	33.4	91.8	93.3	–	29.1	1.3	3.5	3.5	–	1.1
Ireland	158	119	285	–	95	42.2	31.8	76.1	–	25.4	1.7	1.3	3.1	–	1.0
Italy	923	1485	6051	–	1671	16.0	25.8	105.0	–	29.0	0.8	1.2	4.9	–	1.4
Luxembourg	3	17	49	–	13	7.0	38.8	111.6	–	30.1	0.2	0.9	2.6	–	0.7
Netherlands	100	408	680	44	–	6.3	25.8	43.0	2.8	–	0.3	1.1	1.8	0.1	–
Norway	28	240	606	53	349	6.4	53.7	135.8	11.8	78.1	0.2	2.1	5.3	0.5	3.0
Poland	1511	838	3463	464	599	39.1	21.7	89.6	12.0	15.5	4.3	2.4	9.9	1.3	1.7
Portugal	375	369	1095	–	484	37.6	37.0	109.7	–	48.5	2.5	2.4	7.2	–	3.2
Russian Fed.	5877	3029	16225	3182	3019	39.9	20.5	110.0	21.6	20.5	6.0	3.1	16.7	3.3	3.1
Slovak Rep.	179	130	310	58	101	33.2	24.1	57.5	10.7	18.7	3.3	2.4	5.6	1.1	1.9
Spain	1592	1299	3706	–	1820	40.4	33.0	94.1	–	46.2	2.4	2.0	5.6	–	2.7
Sweden	71	267	911	–	431	8.0	30.2	102.8	–	48.6	0.4	1.4	4.6	–	2.2
Switzerland	28	105	400	30	175	3.9	14.8	56.0	4.2	24.6	0.1	0.6	2.1	0.2	0.9
Turkey	2226	951	3779	–	726	33.3	14.2	56.6	–	10.9	5.3	2.3	9.0	–	1.7
UK	1187	1603	4760	186	1566	19.9	26.9	80.0	3.1	26.3	1.0	1.3	3.9	0.2	1.3
N. America	21000	26200	101700	–	19400	52.4	65.3	253.6	–	48.4	2.0	2.6	9.9	–	1.9
OECD Europe	11800	13100	45100	–	13600	22.8	25.3	87.1	–	27.1	1.3	1.4	4.8	–	1.5
EU-15	7000	10200	35100	–	11300	18.6	27.1	93.4	–	31.4	0.9	1.3	4.4	–	1.5
OECD	36700	44900	170400	–	37000	32.9	40.3	152.8	–	35.1	1.5	1.9	7.1	–	1.6

Notes:
[a] Man-made emissions. Data refer to 2000 or to the latest available year from 1996 on.
[b] The size of the particulates being measured varies from country to country.
[c] Emissions of non-methane VOCs.
[d] GDP at 1995 prices and purchasing power parities.

Source: OECD Environmental Data, 2002

Pesticide pollution

Consumption of pesticides[a], latest year available.

	Year	*Active ingredients (tonnes)* Pesticides total	Insecticides	Fungicides	Herbicides	Other pesticides
Canada	1994	29 206	3 426	3 780	21 910	90
Mexico	1993	36 000	–	–	–	–
USA	1997	353 802	41 730	24 040	213 188	74 843
Japan	1993	64 500	–	–	–	–
Korea	1997	24 814	9 161	7 332	6 043	2 278
Australia	1999	34 200	8 700	3 000	22 000	500
N. Zealand	1998	3 368	718	702	1 847	102
Austria	2000	3 563	334	1 598	1 609	22
Belgium	2000	9 973	918	3 057	5 217	373
Czech Rep.	2000	4 303	158	1 007	2 599	539
Denmark	2000	2 841	41	614	1 982	204
Finland	2000	1 150	55	178	862	55
France	2000	94 693	3 103	52 834	30 845	7 911
Germany	2000	31 850	2 357	9 641	16 610	3 242
Greece	1998	11 479	2 505	4 731	2 303	1 940
Hungary	2000	5 472	771	1 590	2 682	429
Iceland	2000	4	1	0	3	0
Ireland	1997	2 325	73	679	1 261	312
Italy	1996	48 050	8 992	25 074	9 888	4 096
Luxembourg	1999	421	19	186	198	18
Netherlands	2000	9 644	1 008	4 460	2 605	1 571
Norway	2000	380	11	53	283	33
Poland	2001	8 855	549	2 815	4 748	743
Portugal	1998	14 382	1 079	10 475	1 914	914
Russian Fed.	1997	25 961	1 686	12 110	12 152	13
Slovak Rep.	2001	3 444	178	537	2 144	585
Spain	1998	35 070	10 173	11 984	9 413	3 500
Sweden	1998	1 629	27	300	1 269	33
Switzerland	1999	1 528	188	708	613	19
Turkey	1995	33 243	14 850	4 937	7 583	5 873
UK	2000	32 989	667	5 282	22 702	4 339

Notes:

[a] Unless otherwise specified, data refer to active ingredients. Insecticides: acaricides, molluscicides, nematocides and mineral oils. Fungicides: bactericides and seed treatments. Herbicides: defoliants and dessicants. Other pesticides: plant growth regulators and rodenticides.

Source: FAO, national statistical yearbooks, UNECE, UNEP, ECPA. OECD Environmental Data, 2002.

THE ENVIRONMENT

Amounts of waste generated[a]

Amounts of waste generated, by source, selected countries.

Amount (thousand tonnes)

	Agriculture, forestry, ...	Mining & quarrying	Manufact. ind.	Energy prod.	Water purific. & distrib.	Construct.	Other	Municipal	Total
USA	–	–	–	–	–	–	–	208 520	–
Japan	91 450	17 660	120 050	7 500	7 910	76 240	78 590	51 450	451 250
Korea	–	–	39 810	–	–	28 750	–	16 950	85 510
Australia	560	–	37 040	11 000	–	10	–	–	–
N. Zealand	–	–	1 750	–	–	–	–	1 450	3 200
Austria	–	–	–	–	2 330	27 500	14 300	4 500	48 630
Belgium	–	620	13 780	1 290	130	–	–	5 470	34 850
Czech Rep.	10 440	2 480	9 110	6 950	1 440	4 840	2 840	3 370	41 450
Denmark	–	–	2 950	1 180	1 480	3 220	1 120	3 080	13 030
Finland	24 000	28 000	15 910	1 270	140	35 000	–	2 200	106 520
France	–	–	101 000	–	–	–	–	30 740	–
Germany	–	56 160	47 960	–	3 930	231 000	–	44 090	398 310
Greece	7 780	3 900	6 680	9 320	–	1 800	–	3 900	33 130
Hungary	58 000	180	2 030	7 880	–	80	10	4 980	73 160
Iceland	–	–	10	–	–	–	50	200	250
Ireland	64 580	3 510	5 110	450	40	2 700	–	2 060	78 450
Italy	240	350	22 990	–	9 510	20 590	7 190	26 610	87 480
Luxembourg	–	–	–	–	–	–	–	280	–
Netherlands	17 000	330	9 780	1 550	100	16 100	3 050	9 220	57 130
Norway	–	–	3 550	–	–	1 540	760	1 400	7 250
Poland	–	45 800	58 980	18 100	1 910	140	550	12 230	137 710
Portugal	–	4 690	12 800	490	–	60	–	4 300	22 350
Slovak Rep.	4 380	940	4 340	2 920	480	70	4 970	1 700	19 800
Spain	114 000	22 760	29 240	–	540	–	–	24 470	–
Sweden	–	63 820	19 780	–	–	–	–	4 000	–
Switzerland	–	–	1 470	–	200	6 390	–	4 680	12 740
Turkey	–	3 620	12 840	12 200	–	–	–	24 940	–
UK	87 000	118 000	50 000	13 000	42 000	72 000	25 000	33 200	440 200

[a] Latest year available. Data prior to 1993 not taken into account. Data are rounded.

Source: OECD Environmental Data, 2002.

Sewage sludge production and disposal[a]

	Year	Total (dry weight) (1000 tonnes)	Disposal methods (%) Agricultural use	Landfill	Incineration	Other[b]
Canada	1992	500	–	–	–	–
USA	1995	7 000	54	18	19	9
Japan	1995	1 689	–	20	66	14
Korea	1999	1 593	–	40	2	58
Australia	1998	120	93	–	–	–
Austria	1998	212	20	17	32	31
Belgium	1998	78	36	33	23	9
Czech Rep.	1999	198	77	19	–	4
Denmark	1998	154	59	13	21	3
Finland	1997	136	39	10	–	51
France	1997	814	–	–	–	–
Germany	1998	2 482	32	8	16	44
Greece	1997	38	–	–	–	–
Hungary	1998	87	36	47	1	17
Iceland	1999	0.20	–	–	–	–
Ireland	1999	38	24	45	–	31
Italy	1993	2 177	10	57	1	32
Luxembourg	1999	17	70	19	–	11
Netherlands	1998	350	–	29	46	25
Norway	1999	104	59	12	0	29
Poland	1999	354	–	58	1	41
Portugal	1992	25	11	29	–	58
Slovak Rep.	1998	117	72	28	–	–
Spain	1997	689	–	48	–	–
Sweden	1998	221	25	46	–	29
Switzerland	1998	200	39	7	51	3
Turkey	1997	2 838	5	21	0	74
UK	1999	1 000	56	11	21	12

[a] Sludge produced in public sewage treatment plants, unless noted otherwise.
[b] Composting, dumping at sea, and other methods.

Source: OECD Environmental Data, 2002.

THE ENVIRONMENT

Production, movement, and disposal of hazardous waste[a]

1000 tonnes

	Year [b]	Production A	Imports[c] B	Exports[c] C	Amounts to be managed A+B+C	Recovery	Physico-chem & biolog. tr	Thermal tr	Landfill	Release into water	Other
Canada	1999	-	-	663	268	-	-	-	-	-	-	-
	2000	-	-	560	324	-	-	-	-	-	-	-
Mexico	1999	-	3 183	265	33	3 415	-	-	-	-	-	-
	2000	-	3 706	276	97	3 885	-	-	-	-	-	-
USA	1997	N	36 901	-	-	36 901	4 769	1 598	1 491	26 092	-	-
	1999	N	36 312	-	-	36 312	3 484	1 223	1 361	17 722	-	-
Japan	1999	-	-	2	3	-	-	-	-	-	-	-
	2000	-	-	4	2	-	-	-	-	-	-	-
Korea	1999	N	2 733	-	-	2 733	1 372	-	466	262	145	488
	2000	N	2 779	-	-	-	1 400	-	603	336	181	259
Australia	1998	-	-	2	31	-	-	-	-	-	-	-
	1999	-	-	1	34	-	-	-	-	-	-	-
N. Zealand	1998	-	-	13	1	-	-	-	-	221	-	-
	1999	-	-	16	0.4	-	-	-	-	222	-	-
Austria	1998	N	918	15	68	865	-	-	-	-	-	-
	1999	N	972	16	109	879	-	-	-	-	-	-
Belgium	1998	N	-	-	-	-	542	-	113	636	-	-
	1999	N	-	437	748	-	634	-	129	631	-	-
Czech Rep.	1998	-	3 417	-	3	3 414	1 002	1 183	16	276	-	267
	1999	-	2 393	-	2	2 391	381	1 203	5	147	-	170
Denmark	1998	N	374	44	137	281	224	-	-	57	-	-
	1999	N	386	86	153	319	256	-	-	63	-	-
Finland	1992	N	559	5	22	542	202	450	44	23	-	86
	1997	N	485	11	42	454	61	62	59	234	10	-
France	1998	-	-	-	-	-	222	302	1 361	803	-	-
	1999	-	9 000	1 450	158	10 292	-	-	-	-	-	-
Germany	1997	-	-	268	601	10 836	3 300	1 827	1 109	3 789	-	812
	1998	-	-	396	568	11 372	3 757	1 975	1 113	3 740	-	787
Greece	1992	-	450	-	0.1	450	88	-	-	-	-	-
	1997	-	280	-	1.4	-	96	7	-	176	-	-
Hungary	1998	N	3 915	-	-	-	-	-	-	-	-	-
	1999	N	3 646	-	-	-	-	-	-	-	-	-
Iceland	1998	-	7	-	1	6	-	-	6	-	-	-
	1999	-	8	-	2	6	-	-	6	-	-	-
Ireland	1996	N	328	-	52	276	139	7	46	-	-	-
	1998	N	370	-	100	271	153	13	66	41	0.2	0.1
Italy	1997	-	3 401	-	80	3 705	880	1 132	282	791	-	620
	1998	-	4 058	-	91	4 948	1 903	1 199	560	605	-	680
Luxembourg	1997	N	143	40	140	43	-	-	-	20	-	-
	1998	N	201	23	184	40	-	-	-	-	-	-
Netherlands	1998	N	1 600	246	267	-	278	601	246	372	-	-
	1999	N	1 500	200	314	-	283	532	290	353	-	-
Norway	1997	N	619	36	46	609	-	-	-	-	-	-
	1998	N	608	47	32	623	119	335	-	-	-	-
Poland	1999	N	1 134	-	-	-	400	-	-	113	-	-
	2000	N	1 601	-	-	-	477	-	-	96	-	-
Portugal	1997	N	595	3	32	566	-	-	-	-	-	-
	1998	-	-	5	45	-	-	-	-	-	-	-
Russian Fed.	1998	-	107 060	-	-	-	-	-	-	-	-	-
	1999	-	108 070	-	-	-	-	-	-	-	-	-
Slovak Rep.	1998	-	1 400	-	1	1 399	226	695	68	292	-	25
	1999	-	1 400	0.3	1	1 400	288	607	107	203	-	103
Spain	1998	-	-	112	73	-	-	73	-	-	-	-
	1999	-	-	113	53	-	-	53	-	-	-	-
Sweden	1994	N	139	88	26	201	-	-	-	-	-	-
	1995	N	-	109	25	-	-	-	-	-	-	-
Switzerland	1998	N	1 043	20	123	940	73	277	371	219	-	-
	1999	N	1 016	-	113	903	70	234	366	234	-	-
United Kingdom	97/98	N	4 878	129	18	4 989	-	-	-	-	-	-
	98/99	N	4 846	86	14	4 918	-	-	-	-	-	-

Notes:

[a] Hazardous waste refers to waste streams controlled according to the Basel Convention on Transboundary Movements of Hazardous Wastes and their disposal. National definitions often differ, and caution should be exercised when using these figures. "N" indicates national or other definition.

[b] In this column, "-" indicates Basel definition.

[c] Imports, exports: should refer to actual amounts moved, but may in some cases refer to total authorisations (notifications) granted.

[d] Landfill also includes land treatment, deep injection, surface impoundment and specially engineered landfill. Release into water includes inland and marine waters as well as sea-bed insertion. Other includes other treatment or disposal methods such as permanent storage.

Source: OECD Environmental Data, 2002.

THE ENVIRONMENT

Nuclear waste: spent fuel arisings[a] 1987–2015

tonnes of heavy metal

	1987	1988	1989	1990	1991	1992	1993	1994	1995	1996	1997	1998	1999	2000	2001	2005	2010	2015
Canada	1500	1500	1300	1213	1383	1690	1690	1690	1690	1690	1340	1515	1200	1180	1300	1500	1900	1900
Mexico	-	-	-	-	-	-	-	19	20	39	42	22	22	45	22	42	21	21
USA	1621	1700	2000	2200	2100	2300	2100	1867	2100	2300	2100	1900	1960	2360	1630	2170	1930	1860
Japan	1060	830	790	688	995	869	876	713	914	852	964	897	996	998	996	980	1160	1520
Korea	-	-	-	-	-	261	342	211	216	247	364	370	481	675	634	730	730	730
Australia	-	-	-	-	-	-	-	-	-	-	-	-	-	-	-	-	-	-
N. Zealand	-	-	-	-	-	-	-	-	-	-	-	-	-	-	-	-	-	-
Austria	-	-	-	-	-	-	-	-	-	-	-	-	-	-	-	-	-	-
Belgium	140	135	122	120	120	102	95	99	121	123	80	165	78	110	144	114	141	-
Czech Rep.	-	-	-	-	-	-	-	-	46	45	45	43	43	41	42	82	82	82
Denmark	-	-	-	-	-	-	-	-	-	-	-	-	-	-	-	-	-	-
Finland	76	73	73	74	63	60	67	67	68	68	71	72	74	74	72	213	243	243
France	750	900	1000	1120	1200	1050	1150	1190	1200	1264	1130	1165	1141	1141	1146	1100	964	871
Germany	380	320	360	490	510	500	490	490	470	450	450	450	430	420	420	420	380	380
Greece	-	-	-	-	-	-	-	-	-	-	-	-	-	-	-	-	-	-
Hungary	-	-	-	-	-	-	-	-	52	55	55	80	48	47	46	43	43	22
Iceland	-	-	-	-	-	-	-	-	-	-	-	-	-	-	-	-	-	-
Ireland	-	-	-	-	-	-	-	-	-	-	-	-	-	-	-	-	-	-
Italy	13	-	-	-	-	-	-	-	-	-	-	-	-	-	-	-	-	-
Luxembourg	-	-	-	-	-	-	-	-	-	-	-	-	-	-	-	-	-	-
Netherlands	14	14	15	17	15	15	15	14	14	14	12	12	12	12	10			
Norway	-	-	-	-	-	-	-	-	-	-	-	-	-	-	-	-	-	-
Poland	-	-	-	-	-	-	-	-	-	-	-	-	-	-	-	-	-	-
Portugal	-	-	-	-	-	-	-	-	-	-	-	-	-	-	-	-	-	-
Slovak Rep.	-	-	-	-	-	-	-	-	-	-	-	-	43	43	59	243	289	184
Spain	206	235	191	187	160	168	151	177	168	158	192	97	139	180	136	157	155	157
Sweden	236	250	190	230	250	250	200	212	213	235	238	238	240	250	310	200	200	200
Switzerland	80	85	85	85	85	85	85	71	77	64	64	64	64	64	64	64	64	64
Turkey	-	-	-	-	-	-	-	-	-	-	-	-	-	-	-	-	25	50
UK	919	884	910	1022	1022	997	1080	1286	1713	781	820	865	789	650	650	738	450	158
N. America	3121	3200	3300	3413	3483	3990	3790	3576	3810	4029	3482	3437	3182	3585	2952	3712	3851	3781
OECD Europe-19	2814	2896	2946	3345	3425	3227	3333	3606	4044	3157	3057	3128	2967	2901	2952	3006	2622	-
EU-15	2734	2811	2861	3260	3340	3142	3248	3535	3967	3093	2993	3064	2903	2837	2888	2942	2533	-
OECD-25	6995	6926	7036	7446	7903	8086	7999	7895	8768	8038	7503	7462	7145	7484	6900	7698	7633	-

Notes:

[a] Spent fuel arisings expressed in tonnes of heavy metal; from 2001 onwards: national projections.

USA 2000: provisional data.
JPN For fiscal year, 2001–2015: LWR fuel and HWR fuel only.
KOR LWR fuel and HWR fuel only.
FIN 2015: Secretariat estimates.
GER 2010, 2015: Secretariat estimates.
NLD 2001: Secretariat estimates.
SLO 2000: provisional data.
SPA 2000: provisional data.
SWE 2000: provisional data; 2010, 2015: Secretariat estimates.
UK 2000: provisional data; 2001: Secretariat estimates.

Source: OECO-NEA Environmental Data, 2002.

Water pollution

Water quality of lakes, annual mean concentration of phosphorus and nitrogen, selected lakes, 1980–1999.

Country	Lake	Total phosphorus (mgP/l)					Total nitrogen (mgN/l)				
		1980	1990	1995	1997	1999	1980	1990	1995	1997	1999
Canada	Ontario	0.015	0.010	0.008	–	–	0.31	0.53	–	–	–
	Huron	0.005	0.005	–	–	–	0.48	0.46	–	–	–
Mexico	Chapala	0.280	0.240	–	0.380	–	0.21	0.15	–	0.12	–
	Catemaco	–	–	0.008	–	–	–	0.08	0.04	0.01	–
	Chairel	–	0.040	0.020	0.020	–	–	–	0.11	0.13	–
USA	Twin-Portage (Ohio)	0.700	–	–	–	–	4.95	–	–	–	–
Japan	Biwa (N)	0.010	0.009	0.010	0.009	0.008	0.29	0.28	0.33	0.32	0.32
	Biwa (S)	0.027	0.025	0.023	0.021	0.020	0.41	0.40	0.47	0.42	0.40
	Kasumigaura	0.080	0.066	0.100	0.100	0.091	1.00	1.10	0.96	0.89	0.93
Korea	Chunchonho	–	0.014	0.064	0.025	0.014	–	0.60	1.20	1.52	1.60
	Chungiuho	–	0.044	0.023	0.027	0.019	–	0.62	1.75	3.06	2.59
	Paldang	–	0.048	0.041	0.041	0.036	–	1.36	1.87	2.39	2.24
Austria	Mondsee	0.025	0.009	0.008	0.008	–	0.48	0.62	0.57	–	–
	Ossiachersee	0.012	0.014	0.009	–	–	–	0.33	0.47	–	–
Denmark	Dons Norreso	–	0.222	0.105	–	–	–	4.93	4.05	–	–
Finland	Pääjärvi	0.011	0.013	0.012	0.013	–	1.35	1.29	1.05	1.01	–
	Päijänne	0.010	0.008	0.006	0.006	–	0.45	0.51	0.48	0.48	–
	Yli-Kitka	0.006	0.008	0.006	0.005	–	0.17	0.22	0.22	0.23	–
France	Parentis-Biscarrosse	–	0.084	0.091	0.050	0.076	–	0.86	1.00	0.89	0.88
	Cazaux-Sanguinet	–	0.026	–	0.013	–	–	0.28	–	0.44	–
	Lac d'Annecy	–	0.010	0.008	–	–	–	0.07	0.27	–	–
Germany	Bodensee	0.079	0.036	0.022	0.017	–	0.87	0.96	1.01	0.98	–
Hungary	Fertö	–	–	0.089	0.087	0.049	–	–	–	–	–
	Balaton	0.010	0.030	0.069	0.110	0.056	0.93	0.82	0.69	1.06	0.94
Ireland	Ennell	0.027	0.017	0.020	0.017	–	0.47	0.47	0.25	0.48	0.29
	Derg	0.020	–	0.055	0.048	0.032	1.20	–	0.52	1.23	–
Italy	Maggiore	0.036	0.015	0.009	0.010	–	0.91	0.99	0.82	0.84	–
	Como	0.078	0.047	0.038	0.046	–	–	0.96	0.88	0.89	–
	Garda	0.020	0.015	0.017	0.015	–	–	0.41	0.32	0.35	–
	Orta	0.004	0.004	0.001	0.002	–	9.90	4.71	2.70	2.30	–
Luxembourg	Esch/Sûre	–	0.050	0.045	–	–	–	3.55	3.25	5.15	3.42
	Weiswampach	–	0.600	0.200	0.500	0.019	–	0.90	3.16	2.48	2.48
Norway	Mjoesa	0.009	0.007	0.005	0.007	0.052	0.41	0.38	0.49	0.44	0.44
	Randsfjorden	0.004	0.004	0.005	0.007	0.003	0.51	0.54	0.54	0.53	0.51
Poland	Sniardwy	–	0.140	–	0.043	–	–	1.08	–	0.90	–
	Hancza	–	–	–	0.025	–	–	–	–	0.68	–
Sweden	Mälaren	0.034	0.025	0.023	0.018	0.031	0.71	0.61	0.69	0.67	0.87
	Vättern	0.009	0.007	0.006	0.004	0.005	0.63	0.73	0.71	0.83	0.78
Switzerland	Léman	0.083	0.055	0.041	0.038	0.039	0.66	0.69	0.67	0.67	0.66
	Constance	0.079	0.036	0.023	0.018	0.014	0.93	1.19	1.21	1.21	1.19
Turkey	Kurtbogazi	0.110	0.050	–	–	–	0.43	–	–	–	–
	Sapanca	0.030	0.030	0.040	–	–	0.94	–	0.17	–	–
	Altinapa	–	0.110	0.110	–	–	1.55	–	1.76	1.84	1.64
UK	Neagh	0.108	0.096	0.120	–	–	0.48	0.77	0.42	–	–
	Lomond	0.009	0.019	0.009	–	0.000	0.30	0.13	0.39	–	0.37

Source: OECD Environmental Data, 2002.

THE ENVIRONMENT

DEFORESTATION

Forests of the world: areas and carbon stocks

Forest type	Area		Carbon stocks in plants (thousand million tonnes of carbon)	Carbon stocks in detritus and soil (thousand million tonnes of carbon)
	(millions km²)	(millions sq mi)		
Tropical forests (both evergreen, and in primary form)	8.6	3.3	202	288
Temperate-zone forests	8.2	3.2	65	161
Boreal forests	11.7	4.5	127	247
Woodland and shrublands	12.8	4.9	57	59
Rest of Earth's land surface	103.3	39.9	109	720
Totals	144.6	55.8	560	1475

World distribution of various types of forest

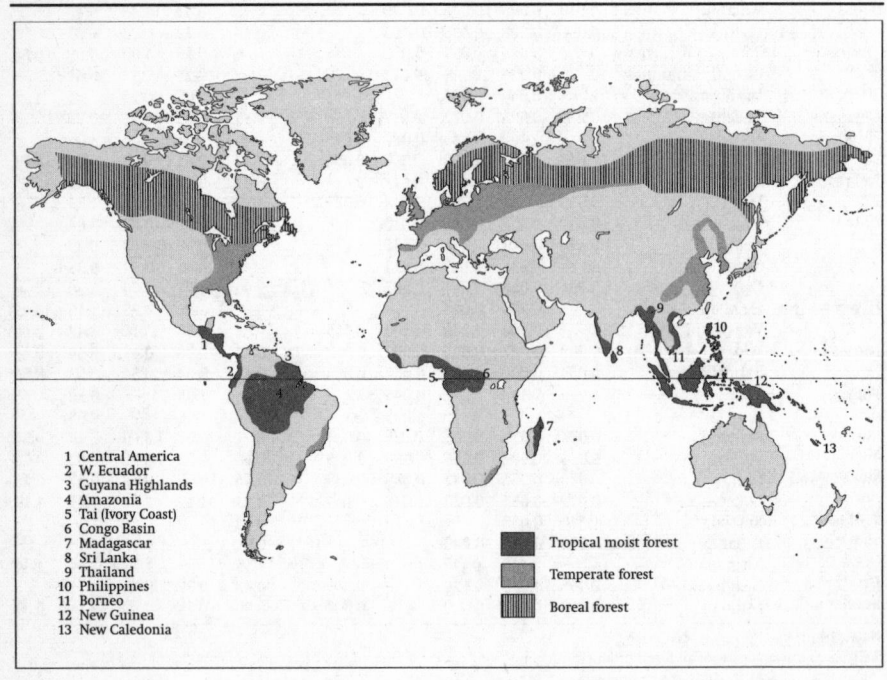

1 Central America
2 W. Ecuador
3 Guyana Highlands
4 Amazonia
5 Tai (Ivory Coast)
6 Congo Basin
7 Madagascar
8 Sri Lanka
9 Thailand
10 Philippines
11 Borneo
12 New Guinea
13 New Caledonia

■ Tropical moist forest
▨ Temperate forest
▥ Boreal forest

Forests, Grasslands, and Drylands

	Forest Area						Drylands[a]		Grassland Area		
	Total Forest		Natural Forest		Plantations						
	Area (1000 ha) 2000	Annual % change 1990–2000	Area (1000 ha) 2000	Annual % change 1990–2000	Area (1000 ha) 2000	Annual % change 1990–2000	Av. area (1000 ha) 1950–81	% of total land area	Shrub-lands 1992–3	Savan-nas (1000 km²) 1992–3	Herbaceous Grasslands 1992–3
World	3 869 455	(0.2)	3 682 722	–	186 733	–	5 060	–	23 343	16 013	10 542
Asia (excl. Middle East)	504 180	(0.1)	375 824	(0.1)	110 953	5.3	1 078	–	4 003	1 061	4 054
Europe[b]	1 035 344	0.0	1 007 236	0.1	32 015	0.0	488	–	3 650	686	715
Middle East & N. Africa	29 104	0.2	20 448	–	6 533	–	553	–	2 476	76	596
Sub-Saharan Africa	486 571	(0.9)	478 576	–	6 210	–	1 121	–	2 513	7 749	1 830
North America	470 564	0.1	209 755	0.1	16 238	0.8	547	–	4 531	415	1 334
C. America & Caribbean	78 737	(1.1)	76 556	(1.2)	1 295	(0.5)	138	–	437	348	333
South America	885 618	(0.4)	875 163	(0.5)	10 455	6.7	444	–	1 674	3 168	1 101
Oceania	201 271	(0.2)	194 718	(0.2)	2 848	0.6	661	–	4 023	2 505	567
Developed	1 725 231	0.1	1 377 765	–	63 695	–	2 168	–	13 483	3 745	4 190
Developing	1 962 481	(0.5)	1 817 491	(0.2)	122 764	4.4	2 862	–	9 825	12 263	6 341

Notes:
[a] Drylands area is determined using aridity zones; arid, semi-arid and dry sub-humid zones are included. Hyper-arid (bare sand deserts) are excluded.
[b] Regional totals are from the original source and are not calculated by WRI.

Sources: Food and Agriculture Organization of the United Nations (FAO), United Nations Environment Program-Global Resource Information Database, Global Land Cover Characteristics Database (GLCCD).

Production and Trade of Selected Forest Products

	Forest Harvest (annual average)				Forest Product Trade[a] (annual average)			
			Total Roundwood		Imports		Exports	
	Industrial roundwood	Wood fuel	Cubic metres (000)	Percent change	Value US$	Percent change	Value US$	Percent change
	Cubic metres (000) 1999–01		(000) 1999–01	since 1989–91	(000) 1999–01	since 1989–91	(000) 1999–01	since 1989–91
World	1 562 331	1 783 827	3 346 157	(0)	145 067 983	34	137 242 617	40
Asia (excl. Middle East)	212 283	788 651	1 000 934	(0)	35 788 387	39	16 687 740	43
Europe	453 753	104 841	558 595	–	61 128 623	–	64 285 067	–
Middle East & N. Africa	–	–	–	–	5 572 653	18	357 380	132
Sub-Saharan Africa	66 437	501 242	567 679	22	1 128 877	65	2 626 913	62
North America	601 350	74 262	675 612	1	28 776 190	75	41 756 000	35
C. America & Caribbean	13 122	80 139	93 260	9	3 598 353	127	376 127	74
South America	150 213	186 781	336 994	23	2 943 727	145	5 089 167	93
Oceania	46 406	12 207	58 613	40	1 882 227	17	2 429 283	69
Developed	1 133 524	197 709	1 331 233	–	105 268 280	–	110 863 573	–
Developing	424 616	1 585 550	2 010 165	8	35 550 783	77	22 744 127	56

Notes:
[a] Refers to the aggregate of all forest products, including industrial roundwood, fuelwood and charcoal, sawnwood, wood-based panels, wood pulp (including recovered paper), and paper and paperboard.

Source: Food and Agriculture Organization of the United Nations (FAO).

THE ENVIRONMENT

RECENT NOTABLE ENVIRONMENTAL DISASTERS

Date	Event	Location	Consequence
1970	Collision of the tanker *Othello*	Tralhavet Bay, Sweden	17 640 000–29 400 000 gallons of oil spilled.
1971	Overflow of water storage space at Northern States Power Company's reactor	Monticello, Minnesota, USA	50 000 gallons of radioactive waste dumped into Mississippi River. Contamination of St Paul water system.
1972	Collision of the tanker *Sea Star*	Gulf of Oman	33 810 000 gallons of oil spilled.
1974	Explosion of container of cyclohexane	Flixborough, UK	28 deaths.
1975	Fire at Brown's Ferry reactor	Decatur, Alabama, USA	$100 million damage. Cooling water level lowered significantly.
1976	Leak of toxic gas TCDD	Seveso, Italy	Topsoil had to be removed in worst contaminated areas.
1976	Grounding of the supertanker *Urquiola*	La Coruña, Spain	Spillage of 29 400 000 gallons of oil.
1977	Well blow-out at Ecofisk oil field	North Sea	Spillage of 8 200 000 gallons of oil.
1977	Fire on the *Hawaiian Patriot*	Northern Pacific	Spillage of 29 106 000 gallons of oil.
1978	Grounding of the Cyprus tanker *Amoco Cadiz*	Portsall, France	Spillage of 65 562 000 gallons of oil. Pollution of 160 km/99 mi of French coast.
1979	Uranium released from secret nuclear fuel plant	Erwin, Tennessee, USA	Approximately 1000 people contaminated.
1979	Collision of *Burmah Agate*	Galveston Bay, Texas	Spillage of 10 700 000 gallons of oil.
1979	Release of radioactive steam after water pump breaks down	Three Mile Island, Pennsylvania, USA	Pollution by radioactive gases. Partial core meltdown in reactor.
1979	Blowout in Ixtoc oil well	Gulf of Mexico	176 400 000 gallons of oil spilled.
1979	Collision of the *Atlantic Empress* and *Aegean Captain*	Trinidad and Tobago	88 200 000 gallons of oil spilled.
1980	Chemical spill due to Sandoz factory fire	Basel, Switzerland	Rhine polluted for 200 km/124 mi.
1983	Blow-out in Nowruz oil field	Persian Gulf	Spillage of 176 400 000 gallons of oil.
1984	Union Carbide pesticide plant leaks toxic gas	Bhopal, India	Death of 2 352 people officially. Unofficially, an estimated 10 000 died.
1986	Explosion of nuclear reactor	Chernobyl, Ukraine	Official death toll 50. Radioactive cloud spread across Europe contaminating farmland. Long-term effects on inhabitants of surrounding areas.
1987	Abandoned radiotherapy unit containing radioactive material leaks	Goiana, Brazil	Radioactive contamination affected 249 people.
1988	Accident at water-treatment works resulting in aluminium sulphate being flushed into local rivers	Camelford, Cornwall, UK	Local people suffer from stomach and skin disorders. Thousands of fish killed.
1989	Grounding of the tanker *Exxon Valdez* on Bligh Reef	Prince William Sound, Alaska, USA	Spillage of 10 080 000 gallons of oil; 1 170 km/1 162 mi of Alaskan coastline polluted. More than 3 600 km²/1 390 sq mi contaminated. Thousands of birds and animals killed.
1991	Break-up of the Greek tanker *Kiriki*	Cervantes, W Australia	Spillage of 5 880 000 gallons of crude oil and pollution of conservation and fishing areas.
1991	Oil fields set alight by Iraqi forces during the Gulf War	Kuwait	Spillage estimated between 25 000 000–130 000 000 gallons. Air pollution and potential increase in acid rain.
1992	Grounding of the Greek oil tanker *Aegean Sea*, with subsequent fire	La Coruña, Spain	Spillage of an estimated 16 000 000 gallons of crude oil, creating a slick 19 km/12 mi long and 2 km/1 mi wide and causing contamination of 80 km/50 mi of Spanish coastline. Serious pollution of sealife and clam and oyster fisheries.
1993	Break-up of the tanker *Braer* on the rocks of Fitful Head	Shetland, Scotland, UK	Spillage of 26 000 000 gallons of oil. Slick contained to 180–270 m/200–300 yd, but serious pollution of fishing grounds and fish farms, as well as sea animals and birds.

Date	Event	Location	Consequence
1994	Rupture of oil pipeline	Usinsk, Russia	Spillage of 4 300 000 gallons of oil, causing extensive pollution of surrounding Arctic habitat.
1996	Cargo Freighter *North Cape* ran aground	Block Island Sound, off Rhode Island	Spillage of 820 000 gallons of home heating oil.
1996	Oil tanker *Sea Empress* grounded on rocks	Milford Haven, Wales, UK	Spillage of 73 450 tonnes of oil causing long-term environmental and socio-economic effects.
1997	Super-tanker *Diamond Grace* runs against reef	Tokyo Bay	Spillage of 13 400 tons of crude oil. Many people taken ill from fumes.
1998	Waste spill at Aznalcóllar mineral plant	Southern Spain	Toxic waste poisons thousands of hectares of farmland and threatens Doñana National Park.
2000	Waste spill at Baia-Mare mine	Romania	Spillage of 100 tonnes of cyanide into rivers in Romania and Hungary.
2002	Blazing bushfires	Arizona, USA	Wildlife devastated; 30 000 people forced from their homes.
2002	Sinking of tanker *Prestige*	NW Spain	Spillage of at least 3 million gallons of fuel oil, before the vessel split and sank, taking rest of its 20-million-gallon cargo to the seabed; over 400 km/250 mi of coastline polluted.
2002	Collision of freighter *Tricolor* with container ship	English Channel	Sank with cargo of 3000 cars; became hazard to shipping; oil spillage.
2003	Blazing forest fires	S and C Portugal	Crops and livestock lost, massive soil erosion; many homes lost.
2004	Blazing forest fires	S Portugal and S Spain	Thousands of hectares destroyed.
2004	Fire at Iraq chemical plant	Nr Mosul, Iraq	Largest recorded man-made release of sulphur dioxide (600 000 tonnes). US$40 million of damage to local crops; respiratory problems in local people.
2005	Blazing bush fires	Eyre Peninsula, S Australia	145 000 hectares of forest and farmland destroyed; 9 deaths.
2005	Forest fires	C and N Portugal	180 000 hectares of forest and farmland destroyed; many homes and farms lost; 15 deaths.
2006	Forest fires	Galicia, NW Spain	100+ fires started deliberately; 70 000 hectares devastated; 4 deaths, hundreds evacuated.

THE ENVIRONMENT

FLORA AND FAUNA

State of mammals, birds, and fish[a]

Species:	Mammals known	Mammals threatened[b] No.	Mammals threatened[b] %	Mammals decreasing No.	Mammals decreasing %	Birds known	Birds threatened[b] No.	Birds threatened[b] %	Birds decreasing No.	Birds decreasing %	Fish known	Fish threatened[b] No.	Fish threatened[b] %	Fish decreasing No.	Fish decreasing %
Canada	193	33	17.1	–	–	426	41	9.6	–	–	1021	72	7.1	–	–
Mexico	491	118	24.0	–	–	1054	122	11.6	–	–	2122	61	2.9	–	–
USA	466	49	10.5	–	–	1090	79	7.2	–	–	2640	64	2.4	–	–
Japan	200	48	24.0	B	B	700	90	12.9	B	B	183	44	24.0	–	–
Korea	100	17	17.0	–	–	417	59	14.1	–	–	905	12	1.3	–	–
Australia	315	73	23.2	–	–	777	94	12.1	–	–	4195	28	0.7	–	–
New Zealand	46	7	15.2	2	4.3	170	43	25.3	15	8.8	1048	8	0.8	2	0.2
Austria	82	29	35.4	13	15.9	219	81	37.0	42	19.2	58	38	65.5	13	22.4
Belgium	57	18	31.6	10	17.5	167	46	27.5	53	31.7	46	25	54.3	6	13.0
Czech Republic	90	30	33.3	2	2.2	220	123	55.9	36	16.4	65	19	29.2	–	–
Denmark	50	11	22.0	2	4.0	219	29	13.2	10	4.6	38	6	15.8	4	10.5
Finland	59	7	11.9	–	–	240	32	13.3	–	–	68	8	11.8	–	–
France	122	24	19.7	20	16.4	357	51	14.3	51	14.3	415	31	7.0	28	6.7
Germany	79	29	36.7	8	10.1	240	70	29.2	18	7.5	66	45	68.2	–	–
Greece	116	44	37.9	12	10.3	422	55	13.0	37	8.8	107	26	24.3	–	–
Hungary	83	59	71.1	–	–	373	70	18.8	–	–	81	26	32.1	14	17.3
Iceland	4	–	–	–	–	75	26	34.7	3	4.0	5	–	–	–	–
Ireland	31	2	6.5	–	–	193	42	21.8	17	8.8	27	9	33.3	–	–
Italy	118	48	40.7	46	39.0	473	87	18.4	37	7.8	85	27	31.8	39	45.9
Luxembourg	64	33	51.6	–	–	130	65	50.0	–	–	43	12	27.9	–	–
Netherlands	64	10	15.6	20	31.3	170	46	27.1	41	24.1	28	23	82.1	–	–
Norway	88	3	3.4	–	–	222	17	7.7	17	7.7	195	–	–	–	–
Poland	83	15	18.1	9	10.8	235	63	26.8	24	10.2	55	20	36.4	15	27.3
Portugal	98	17	17.3	17	17.3	313	43	13.7	39	12.5	43	8	18.6	12	27.9
Slovak Republic	90	20	22.2	15	16.7	341	49	14.4	46	13.5	84	20	23.8	–	–
Spain	118	25	21.2	–	–	368	52	14.1	–	–	68	20	29.4	–	–
Sweden	65	15	23.1	16	24.6	245	47	19.2	74	30.2	164	13	7.9	35	21.3
Switzerland	79	27	34.2	A	A	197	84	42.6	–	–	47	21	44.7	A	A
Turkey	135	30	22.2	–	–	450	30	6.7	–	–	192	19	9.9	–	–
United Kingdom	64	14	21.9	23	35.9	544	35	6.4	50	9.2	54	6	11.1	–	–
Russian Federation	320	40	12.5	–	–	732	56	7.7	–	–	277	34	12.3	–	–

Notes: Capital letters in the table refer to estimates of the number of species in each category: A = some species; B = several species.
[a] Latest year available.
[b] 'Threatened' refers to the sum of species 'critically endangered', 'endangered', and 'vulnerable' (new IUCN categories), or to the sum of species 'endangered' and 'vulnerable' (old IUCN categories).

Source: OECD Environmental Data, 2002.

State of reptiles, amphibians, and invertebrates[a]

Species:	Reptiles known	threatened[b] No.	%	decreasing No.	%	Amphibians known	threatened[b] No.	%	decreasing No.	%	Invertebrates known	threatened[b] No.	%	decreasing No.	%
Canada	42	18	42.9	–	–	42	12	28.6	–	–	34552	12	–	–	–
Mexico	704	111	15.8	–	–	290	42	14.5	–	–	29501	–	–	–	–
USA	368	26	7.1	–	–	222	8	3.6	–	–	–	–	–	–	–
Japan	97	18	18.6	B	B	64	14	21.9	B	B	35200	423	1.2	B	B
Korea	29	3	10.3	–	–	14	2	14.3	–	–	11853	19	0.2	–	–
Australia	770	49	6.4	–	–	203	27	13.3	–	–	92000	–	–	–	–
New Zealand	61	11	18.0	4	6.6	4	1	25.0	2	50.0	22973	14	0.1	243	1.1
Austria	16	14	87.5	1	6.3	21	21	100.0	–	–	-45000	2291	–	516	–
Belgium	4	2	50.0	2	50.0	13	4	30.8	5	38.5	939	373	39.7	431	45.9
Czech Republic	11	11	100.0	3	27.3	20	18	90.0	9	45.0	43734	165	0.4	40	0.1
Denmark	7	–	–	1	14.3	14	5	35.7	9	64.3	3674	561	15.3	220	6.0
Finland	5	2	40.0	–	–	5	1	20.0	–	–	26600	759	2.9	–	–
France	38	6	15.8	16	42.1	39	11	28.2	13	33.3	38500	110	0.3	–	–
Germany	14	11	78.6	–	–	21	12	57.1	2	9.5	30570	4869	15.9	–	–
Greece	59	4	6.8	2	3.4	20	–	–	–	–	32800	–	–	–	–
Hungary	16	16	100.0	16	100.0	16	16	100.0	16	100.0	>43000	>400	>0.9	9	–
Iceland	–	–	–	–	–	–	–	–	–	–	1300	–	–	–	–
Ireland	3	1	33.3	–	–	3	1	33.3	–	–	–	–	–	–	–
Italy	58	21	36.2	25	43.1	38	16	42.1	27	71.1	56500	2435	4.3	–	–
Luxembourg	6	6	100.0	6	100.0	14	13	92.9	13	92.9	30000	–	–	–	–
Netherlands	7	6	85.7	5	71.4	16	9	56.3	7	43.8	27700	–	–	–	–
Norway	5	1	20.0	1	20.0	6	3	50.0	2	33.3	17870	367	2.1	–	–
Poland	9	3	33.3	2	22.2	18	0	0.00	2	11.1	30000	3500	11.7	800	2.7
Portugal	34	3	8.8	–	–	17	–	–	–	–	–	–	–	–	–
Slovak Republic	12	5	41.7	–	–	18	8	44.4	–	–	24875	1301	5.2	–	–
Spain	56	11	19.6	–	–	25	4	16.0	–	–	25000	391	1.6	–	–
Sweden	6	3	50.0	3	50.0	13	6	46.2	5	38.5	28500	1010	3.5	1810	6.4
Switzerland	14	11	78.6	C	C	17	16	94.1	A	A	2251	839	37.3	C	C
Turkey	106	17	16.0	A	A	22	3	13.6	B	B	–	–	–	–	–
United Kingdom	9	–	–	4	44.4	14	–	–	2.0	14.3	22778	976	4.3	–	–
Russian Federation	75	9	12.0	–	–	27	5	18.5	–	–	104000	118	0.1	–	–

Notes: Capital letters in the table refer to estimates of the number of species in each category: A = some species; B = several species; C = a large part of species.

[a] Latest year available.
[b] 'Threatened' refers to the sum of species 'critically endangered', 'endangered', and 'vulnerable' (new IUCN categories), or to the sum of species 'endangered' and 'vulnerable' (old IUCN categories).

Source: OECD Environmental Data, 2002.

State of vascular plants, mosses, lichens, fungi, and algae[a]

	Species: known	Vascular plants threatened[b] No.	%	decreasing No.	%	Mosses Species known	Lichens Species known	Fungi Species known	Algae Species known
Canada	4 120	116	2.8	–	–	965	2 000	9 310	5 303
Mexico	10 819	323	3.0	–	–	960	–	6 000	2 702
USA	22 200	118	0.5	–	–	–	–	–	–
Japan	7 000	1 665	23.8	–	–	1 800	1 000	16 500	5 500
Korea	3 971	58	1.5	–	–	691	497	1 128	3 609
Australia	25 000	1 085	4.3	–	–	3 500	2 000	10–20 000	28 000
New Zealand	2 400	119	5.0	249	10.4	513	1 200	3 500	1 100
Austria	2 950	1 157	39.2	166	5.6	>800	2 100	>5 000	>4 000
Belgium	1 202	383	31.9	275	22.9	502	168	–	–
Czech Republic	2 700	1 170	43.3	185	6.9	848	1 534	30 000	15 000
Denmark	1 050	102	9.7	53	5.0	900	950	6 000	450
Finland	3 200	180	5.6	–	–	883	1 452	4 798	5 000
France	6 020	387	6.4	261	4.3	2 000	3 000	5–10 000	4 500
Germany	3 001	772	25.7	168	5.6	1 121	1 691	5 441	2 653
Greece	5 700	177	3.1	79	1.4	–	–	1 200	–
Hungary	2 500	495	19.8	386	15.4	600	700	2 000	3 800
Iceland	485	37	7.6	10	2.1	600	620	300	238
Ireland	1 309	9	0.7	–	–	533	1 050	3 500	–
Italy	5 599	270	4.8	185	3.3	3 000	2 145	10 000	6 200
Luxembourg	1 258	153	12.2	220	17.5	468	1 000	1 000	600
Netherlands	1 392	486	34.9	–	–	539	619	3 293	–
Norway	1 195	100	8.4	–	–	1 064	430	6 000	5 500
Poland	2 300	279	12.1	138	6.0	671	1 500	4 000	>10 000
Portugal	3 095	255	8.2	–	–	628	800	2 500	–
Slovak Republic	3 352	903	26.9	–	–	909	1 508	2 469	3 008
Spain	8 000	509	6.4	600	7.5	1 012	2 500	10 000	31
Sweden	2 272	326	14.3	–	–	1 058	2 038	4 000	34
Switzerland	2 617	579	22.1	–	–	1 025	1 800	5 000	–
Turkey	3 072	237	7.7	–	–	750	–	–	–
United Kingdom	2 230	201	9.0	–	–	>1 000	>1 700	>20 000	15–20 000
Russian Federation	11 400	201	1.8	–	–	1 370	3 000	–	–

Notes:
[a] Latest year available.
[b] 'Threatened' refers to the sum of species 'critically endangered', 'endangered', and 'vulnerable' (new IUCN categories), or to the sum of species 'endangered' and 'vulnerable' (old IUCN categories).

Source: OECD Environmental Data, 2002.

THE ENVIRONMENT

Biosphere reserves and wetlands, 2002

	Biosphere reserves[a]	Wetlands[b]	
	No. of sites	No. of sites	Total area
Canada	11	36	130 515
Mexico	12	7	11 571
USA	47	18	11 899
Japan	4	11	837
Korea	1	2	10
Australia	12	56	53 102
New Zealand	–	5	389
Austria	5	11	1 180
Belgium	–	6	79
Czech Republic	6	10	419
Denmark	–	27	7 365
Finland	2	11	1 387
France	8	15	5 791
Germany	14	31	6 729
Greece	2	10	1 635
Hungary	5	21	1 541
Iceland	–	3	590
Ireland	2	45	670
Italy	5	46	571
Luxembourg	–	1	3
Netherlands	1	18	3 249
Norway	–	23	702
Poland	9	8	905
Portugal	1	12	661
Slovak Republic	4	12	378
Spain	20	38	1 582
Sweden	1	51	5 145
Switzerland	2	8	79
Turkey	–	9	1 593
United Kingdom	9	156	7 588
Russian Federation	25	35	103 238
OECD	179	707	258 165
World	408	1 179	1 021 268

Notes: [a] As of 16 May 2002   [b] As of 5 July 2002
Source: UNESCO-MAB, Ramsar Convention Bureau. OECD Environmental Data, 2002.

CONSERVATION

Environmental programmes

CLIMAP	Climatic Applications Project (WMO)	ISCCP	International Satellite Cloud Climatology Project
COADS	Comprehensive Ocean Air Data Set		
GAW	Global Atmospheric Watch	IUCN	International Union for Conservation of Nature and Natural Resources
ERBE	Earth Radiation Budget Experiment		
ERS	Earth Resources Satellite	JGOFS	Joint Global Ocean Flux Study
GEWEX	Global Energy and Water Cycle Experiment	SAGE	Stratospheric Aerosol and Gas Experiment
GMCC	Geophysical Monitoring of Climatic Change	TOGA	Tropical Ocean and Global Atmosphere
ICRCCM	Intercomparison of Radiation Codes in Climate Models	UNEP	United Nations Environment Programme
		WCRP	World Climate Research Programme
IGAC	International Global Atmospheric Chemistry Programme	WOCE	World Ocean Circulation Experiment
IGBP	International Geosphere-Biosphere Programme		

THE ENVIRONMENT

Major protected areas,[a] late 1990s

	Protected areas			of which IUCN categories (%)					
	Total size (km²)	Percentage of national territory	per 1000 inhabitants (ha.1000 cap.)	1a/1b[b]	II[c]	III[d]	IV[e]	V[f]	VI[g]
Canada	953 103	9.6	3 178.4	3	42	0	42	10	3
Mexico	159 759	8.2	170.1	8	5	0	13	19	56
USA	1 988 444	21.2	741.8	20	13	3	20	6	38
Japan	25 590	6.8	20.3	1	51	0	19	29	0
Korea	6 838	6.9	14.9	0	0	0	5	95	0
Australia	597 528	7.7	3 225.7	39	39	1	0	0	20
N. Zealand	63 338	23.5	1 684.1	25	45	5	4	22	0
Austria	24 512	29.2	303.7	0	1	0	21	78	0
Belgium	859	2.8	8.4	0	0	0	14	86	0
Czech Rep.	12 776	16.2	124.0	1	6	0	6	88	0
Denmark	13 796	32.0	261.1	2	0	0	85	13	0
Finland	28 407	8.4	552.7	23	15	0	27	0	34
France	55 723	10.1	95.1	3	5	0	6	86	0
Germany	96 193	26.9	117.2	0	0	0	5	94	0
Greece	3 408	2.6	32.5	0	49	5	31	9	6
Hungary	8 449	9.1	83.9	0	25	0	5	71	0
Iceland	9 805	9.5	3 619.4	0	18	3	8	71	0
Ireland	653	0.9	17.8	0	72	0	28	0	0
Italy	27 530	9.1	47.9	0	17	0	12	71	0
Luxembourg	168	6.5	39.9	0	0	0	3	97	0
Netherlands	4 820	11.6	30.9	5	6	5	28	4	52
Norway	24 555	7.6	546.8	10	66	0	1	23	0
Poland	29 291	9.4	75.8	0	6	0	3	91	0
Portugal	6 036	6.6	60.6	2	12	1	18	67	0
Russian Fed.	938 900	5.5	635.9	56	16	0	28	0	0
Slovak Rep.	10 605	21.6	197.0	1	19	0	5	76	0
Spain	42 418	8.4	107.9	0	5	0	41	54	0
Sweden	36 547	8.1	413.1	42	14	0	34	10	0
Switzerland	7 447	18.0	105.1	2	0	0	32	66	0
Turkey	29 985	3.8	46.3	2	31	0	43	8	16
UK	50 001	20.4	84.7	0	0	0	6	94	0
OECD Europe	523 984	10.4	101.9	5	10	0	17	65	3
OECD	4 318 584	12.4	392.4	17	23	2	21	14	24
World	13 232 275	9.9	227.2	15	30	1	19	8	27

Notes:

[a] IUCN management categories I–VI. National classifications may differ.

[b] Strict nature reserves/Wilderness areas: protected areas managed mainly for science/wilderness protection.

[c] National parks: protected areas managed mainly for ecosystem protection and recreation.

[d] National monuments: protected areas managed mainly for conservation of specific natural features.

[e] Habitat/species management areas: protected areas managed mainly for habitat and species conservation through management intervention.

[f] Protected landscapes/seascapes: protected areas managed mainly for landscape/seascape conservation and recreation.

[g] Managed resource protected areas: protected areas managed mainly for the sustainable use of natural ecosystems.

Source: WCMC, IUCN, OECD Environmental Data, 2002.

Multilateral conventions on the environment

			Number of parties				Entry into Force
			OECD		Total		
Type[a]	Subject	Place and date	Signed	Ratified[b]	Signed	Ratified[b]	
General							
A	Prior consultation concerning setting up near border of permanent storage of explosive substances	Brussels, 1950	3	3	3	3	–
T	Antarctic	Washington, 1959	24	24	45	45	23.06.1961
	Protocol to Antarctic treaty (environmental protection)	Madrid, 1991	23	17	29	29	14.01.1998
C	Nordic environmental protection	Stockholm, 1974	4	4	4	4	05.10.1976
C	Transfrontier co-operation bet. territorial communities or authorities	Madrid, 1980	20	19	33	27	22.12.1981
	Additional protocol	Strasbourg, 1995	11	6	18	10	01.12.1998
	Second protocol	Strasbourg, 1998	8	4	15	7	–
C	Benelux convention on nature conserv. & landscape protect.	Brussels, 1982	3	3	3	3	01.10.1983
C	Control of transboundary movements of hazardous wastes & their disposal	Basel, 1989	29 +EU	28 +EU	149	149	05.05.1992
	Amendment	Geneva, 1995	11 +EU	11 +EU	27	27	–
	Protocol (liability & compensation for damage)	Basel, 1999	8	–	13		–
A	Transboundary co-op. with a view to preventing or limiting harmful effects for human beings, property or the environment in the event of accidents	Stockholm, 1989	4	4	4	4	09.08.1989
C	Safety in the use of chemicals at work (ILO 170)	Geneva, 1990	3	3	9	9	04.11.1993
C	Environmental impact assessment in transboundary context	Espoo, 1991	23 +EU	19 +EU	43	38	10.09.1997
C	Protection of Alps	Salzburg, 1991	5 +EU	5 +EU	9	9	06.03.1995
	Protocol (nature protection and landscape conservation)	Chambery, 1994	5 +EU	–	9		–
	Protocol (town and country planning and sustainable development)	Chambery, 1994	5 +EU	–	9		–
	Protocol (mountain agriculture)	Chambery, 1994	5 +EU	–	9		–
	Protocol (mountain forests)	Brdo, 1996	5	–	8		–
	Protocol (tourism)	Brdo, 1996	5	–	8		–
	Protocol (energy)	Bled, 1998	5	–	7	1	–
	Protocol (land conservation)	Bled, 1998	5	–	8	1	–
	Protocol (transport)	Lucerne, 2000	5	–	7	1	–
C	Transboundary effects of industrial accidents	Helsinki, 1992	21 +EU	13 +EU	31	23	–
C	Civil liability for damage resulting from activities dangerous to the environment	Lugano, 1993	7	–	9	–	–
C	North American agreement on environmental co-operation	1993	3	3	3	3	01.01.1994
C	Prevention of major industrial accidents (ILO 174)	Geneva, 1993	3	2	7	7	03.01.1997
C	Prohibition of development, production, stockpiling & use of chemical weapons and their destruction	Paris, 1993	29	23	174	145	29.04.1997
T	Energy Charter	Lisbon, 1994	24 +EU	20 +EU	51	45	16.04.1998
	Protocol (energy efficiency & related environmental aspects)	Lisbon, 1994	24 +EU	20 +EU	51	44	16.04.1998
C	Regional convention on hazardous and radioactive wastes (Waigani Convention)[c]	Port Moresby, 1995	2	2	15	10	21.10.2001
A	Transfrontier co-op. with Saarlorlux-Rhineland-Palatinate regions	1996	4	–	4	–	–
A	Transfrontier co-op.	Karlsruhe, 1996	4	–	4	–	01.09.1997
C	Access to environmental information & public participation in environmental decision-making	Aarhus, 1998	21 +EU	2	44	18	30.10.2001
C	Protection of the environment through criminal law	Strasbourg, 1998	11	–	13	–	–
C	Prior informed consent procedure for hazardous chemicals & pesticides (PIC)	Rotterdam, 1998	25 +EU	6	74	18	–
C	European landscape convention	Florence, 2000	14	1	23	1	–
Atmospheric pollution							
A	Adoption of unif. cond. of approv. & recipr. recogn. of approv. for motor veh. equip. & parts	Geneva, 1958	18	18	23	23	20.06.1959
C	Protection against hazards of poisoning arising from benzene (ILO 136)	Geneva, 1971	9	9	36	36	27.07.1973
C	Prev. & control of occup. hazards caused by carcinog. subst. & agents (ILO 139)	Geneva, 1974	15	15	35	35	10.06.1976
C	Protec. of workers against occup. hazards in the working env. due to air poll. noise and vibrat. (ILO 148)	Geneva, 1977	13	13	41	41	11.07.1979
C	Long-range transboundary air pollution	Geneva, 1979	24 +EU	24 +EU	50	48	16.03.1983
	Protocol (financing of EMEP)	Geneva, 1984	23 +EU	23 +EU	38	38	28.01.1988
	Protocol (reduction of sulphur emissions or their transboundary fluxes by at least 30%)	Helsinki, 1985	15	15	22	22	02.09.1987
	Protocol (control of emissions of nitrogen oxides or their transboundary fluxes)	Sofia, 1988	21 +EU	20 +EU	29	28	14.02.1991
	Protocol (control of emissions of volatile organic compounds or their transboundary fluxes)	Geneva, 1991	20 +EU	16	27	21	29.09.1997
	Protocol (further reduction of sulphur emissions)	Oslo, 1994	20 +EU	18 +EU	27	23	05.08.1998
	Protocol (heavy metals)	Aarhus, 1998	23 +EU	9 +EU	36	10	–
	Protocol (persistent organic pollutants)	Aarhus, 1998	23 +EU	7	36	8	–
	Protocol (abate acidification, eutrophication and ground-level ozone)	Gothenburg, 1999	22	–	31	1	–
C	Protection of the ozone layer	Vienna, 1985	29 +EU	29 +EU	184	184	22.09.1988
	Protocol (substances that deplete the ozone layer)	Montreal, 1987	29 +EU	29 +EU	183	183	01.01.1989
	Amendment to protocol	London, 1990	29 +EU	29 +EU	163	163	10.08.1992
	Amendment to protocol	Copenhagen, 1992	29 +EU	29 +EU	140	140	14.06.1994

THE ENVIRONMENT

Type[a]	Subject	Place and date	OECD Signed	OECD Ratified[b]	Total Signed	Total Ratified[b]	Entry into Force
	Amendment to protocol	Montreal, 1997	20 +EU	19 +EU	78	78	10.11.1999
	Amendment to protocol	Beijing, 1999	7	7	27	27	25.02.2002
C	Framework convention on climate change	New York, 1992	28 +EU	28 +EU	186	186	21.03.1994
	Protocol	Kyoto, 1997	27 +EU	20 +EU	111	74	–
A	Exchange of emissions data in the Black Triangle	1996	3	–	3	–	–
C	Persistent organic pollutants	Stockholm, 2001	28 +EU	2	115	5	–

Inland waters pollution

Type[a]	Subject	Place and date	OECD Signed	OECD Ratified[b]	Total Signed	Total Ratified[b]	Entry into Force
P	Establish tripartite standing committee on polluted waters	Brussels, 1950	3	3	3	3	08.05.1950
A	Protection of Lake Constance against pollution	Steckborn, 1960	3	3	3	3	10.11.1960
	Regulation (water withdrawal)	Bern, 1966	3	3	3	3	25.11.1967
P	Constitution of int'l commission for protection of Mosel against pollution	Paris, 1961	3	3	3	3	01.07.1962
	Complementary protocol (int'l commi. for protection of Mosel & Sarre)	Brussels, 1990	3	3	3	3	01.01.1993
	2d compl. prot. (to int'l commi. protec. of Mosel and Sarre, and to first compl. prot.)	Maria Laach, 1992	3	3	3	3	
A	Int'l commission for protection of Rhine against pollution	Bern, 1963	5 +EU	5 +EU	6	6	01.05.1965
	Supplementary agreement	Bonn, 1976	5 +EU	5 +EU	6	6	01.02.1979
C	Protection of Rhine against chemical pollution	Bonn, 1976	5 +EU	5 +EU	6	6	01.02.1979
C	Protection of Rhine from pollution by chlorides (modf. by exchanges of letters)	Bonn, 1976	5	5	5	5	05.07.1985
	Protocol	Brussels, 1991	5	5	5	5	–
C	Protection of Rhine	Bern, 1999	5 +EU	3 +EU	6		–
A	Restriction of use of certain detergents in washing & cleaning products	Strasbourg, 1968	10	10	10	10	16.02.1971
	Protocol	Strasbourg, 1983	7	5	7	5	01.11.1984
A	International commission for protection of R Elbe	Magdeburg, 1990	2 +EU	2 +EU	2	2	–
C	Protection & use of transboundary water courses & international lakes	Helsinki, 1992	19 +EU	18 +EU	35	33	06.10.1996
	Protocol (water and health)	London, 1999	19	3	36	6	–
C	Co-operation for protection & sust. use of R Danube	Sofia, 1994	3	1	9		–
A	Protection of the Meuse	Charleville-Mézières, 1994	3	3	3	3	–
A	Protection of the Scheldt	Charleville-Mézières, 1994	3	3	3	3	–
A	Int'l commission for protection of R Oder against pollution	Wroclaw, 1996	3 +EU	–	3	–	–
C	Disposal of waste & waste water from navigation on Rhine	Strasbourg, 1996	6	–	6	–	–
C	Law of non-navigational uses of international watercourses	New York, 1997	8	5	19	11	–

Marine pollution

Type[a]	Subject	Place and date	OECD Signed	OECD Ratified[b]	Total Signed	Total Ratified[b]	Entry into Force
C	Prevention of pollution of sea by oil	London, 1954	25	25	72	72	20.01.1978
	Amendments to convention (protection of Great Barrier Reef)	London, 1971	13	13	27	27	–
C	Limitation of liability of owners of sea-going ships	Brussels, 1957	8	6	51	45	31.05.1968
	Protocol	Brussels, 1979	9	7	13	8	06.10.1984
C	International council for exploration of the sea	Copenhagen, 1964	16	16	19	19	22.07.1968
	Protocol	Copenhagen, 1970	16	16	19	19	12.11.1975
C	Intervention on high seas in cases of oil pollution casualties (INTERVENTION)	Brussels, 1969	23	21	78	77	06.05.1975
	Protocol (pollution by substances other than oil)	London, 1973	19	18	44	44	30.03.1983
C	Civil liability for oil pollution damage (CLC)	Brussels, 1969	4	3	80	77	19.06.1975
	Protocol	London, 1976	21	21	55	55	08.04.1981
	Protocol	London, 1992	23	23	80	80	30.05.96
C	Int'l fund for compensation for oil pollution damage (FUND)	Brussels, 1971	2	1	26	26	16.10.1978
	Protocol	London, 1976	18	18	33	33	22.11.1994
	Protocol	London, 1992	22	22	75	75	30.05.96
C	Prevention of marine pollution by dumping of wastes & other matter (LC)	Lond'n, Mexico, Moscow Washington, 1972	26	26	78	78	30.08.1975
	Amendments to Annexes (incineration at sea)	1978	24	24	75	75	11.03.1979
	Amendments to convention (settlement of disputes)	1978	17	17	20	20	–
	Amendments to Annexes (list of substances)	1980	26	26	78	78	11.03.1981
	Protocol (prevention of marine pollution by dumping of wastes & other matter	London, 1996	16	10	20	16	–
C	Prevention of marine pollution by dumping from ships & aircraft	Oslo, 1972	13	13	13	13	07.04.1974
	Protocol	1983	13	13	13	13	01.09.1989
C	Prevention of marine pollution from land-based sources	Paris, 1974	13 +EU	12 +EU	14	13	06.05.1978
	Protocol	Paris, 1986	12 +EU	12 +EU	13	13	01.09.1989
C	Protection of North-East Atlantic marine env. (Oslo-1972 and Paris-1974)	Paris, 1992	15 +EU	15 +EU	16	16	25.03.1998
	Protocol (prevention of pollution from ships) (MARPOL PROT)	London, 1978	29	29	119	119	02.10.1983
	Annex III	London, 1978	26	26	100	100	01.07.1992
	Annex IV	London, 1978	18	18	84	84	–
	Annex V	London, 1978	28	28	104	104	31.12.1988
	Annex VI	London, 1997	2	–	4		–
C	Protection of marine environment of Baltic Sea area	Helsinki, 1974	5 +EU	5 +EU	10	10	03.05.1980
C	Protection of marine environment of Baltic Sea area (amendment)	Helsinki, 1992	5 +EU	5 +EU	10	10	17.01.2000
C	Protection of Mediterranean Sea against pollution	Barcelona, 1976	5 +EU	5 +EU	21	21	12.02.1978
	Protocol (dumping from ships and aircraft)	Barcelona, 1976	5 +EU	5 +EU	21	21	12.02.1978

Type[a]	Subject	Place and date	OECD Signed	OECD Ratified[b]	Total Signed	Total Ratified[b]	Entry into Force
	Protocol (dumping from ships & aircraft or incineration at sea)	Barcelona, 1995	3 +EU	3 +EU	–	10	–
	Protocol (pollution by oil & other harmful substances in cases of emergency)	Barcelona, 1976	5 +EU	5 +EU	21	21	12.02.1978
	Protocol (pollution from land-based sources)	Athens, 1980	5 +EU	5 +EU	21	21	17.06.1983
	Protocol (pollution from land-based sources & activities)	Syracuse, 1996	4 +EU	4 +EU	–	8	–
	Protocol (specially protected areas)	Geneva, 1982	5 +EU	5 +EU	21	21	23.03.1986
	Protocol (specially protected areas & biological diversity)	Monaco, 1996	5 +EU	3 +EU	17	8	12.12.1999
	Protocol (pollution from exploitation of continental shelf, seabed & subsoil)	Madrid, 1994	3	–	11	2	–
	Protocol (pollution by transboundary movements of hazardous wastes & their disposal)	Izmir, 1996	4	1	11	3	–
A	Protection of waters of Mediterranean coastline (RAMOGE)	Monaco, 1976	2	2	3	3	1981
C	Limitation of liability for maritime claims (LLMC)	London, 1976	19	19	37	37	01.12.1986
	Amendment to convention	London, 1996	8	3	9	6	–
C	Law of the sea	Montego Bay, 1982	27 +EU	23 +EU	200	137	16.11.1994
A	Relating to implementation of part XI of convention	New York, 1994	26 +EU	22 +EU	115	103	28.07.1996
A	Implementation of provisions of convention relating to conservation & management of straddling fish stocks & highly migratory fish stocks	New York, 1995	23 +EU	6	70	30	–
M	Memorandum of understanding on port state control	Paris, 1982	17	17	19	19	01.07.1982
C	Protection & development of marine environment of wider Caribbean region	Cartagena, 1983	5 +EU	5	24	21	11.10.1986
	Protocol (oil spills)	Cartagena, 1983	5	5	23	21	11.10.1986
	Protocol (specially protected areas & wildlife)	Kingston, 1990	5	1	16	9	18.06.2000
A	Co-operation in dealing with pollution of North Sea by oil & other harmful subst.	Bonn, 1983	8 +EU	8 +EU	9	9	01.09.1989
	Amendment	Bonn, 1989	8 +EU	8 +EU	9	9	01.04.1994
C	Protection, management & development of marine & coastal environment of Eastern African region	Nairobi, 1985	1 +EU	1	8	6	30.05.1996
	Protocol (protected areas & wild fauna & flora in Eastern African region)	Nairobi, 1985	1 +EU	1	8	6	30.05.1996
	Protocol (co-operation in combating marine pollution in cases of emergency in Eastern African region)	Nairobi, 1985	1 +EU	1	8	6	30.05.1996
C	Protection of natural resources & environment of South Pacific region	Noumea, 1986	5	4	15	12	22.08.1990
	Protocol (prevention of pollution by dumping)	Noumea, 1986	5	5	15	11	22.08.1990
	Protocol (co-operation in combating pollution emergencies)	Noumea, 1986	5	4	15	12	22.08.1990
A	South Pacific Regional Environment Programme (SPREP)	Apia, 1993	4	3	22	14	31.8.1995
C	Salvage	London, 1989	18	15	41	38	14.07.96
C	Establishing marine scientific organization for North Pacific Region (PICES)	1990	3	3	6	6	24.03.1992
C	Oil pollution preparedness, response & co-operation (OPRC)	London, 1990	21	20	72	64	13.05.1995
A	Co-op. for protection of coasts and waters of NE Atlantic	Lisbon, 1990	3 +EU	2 +EU	5	3	–
C	Protection of Black Sea against pollution	Bucharest, 1992	1	1	6	6	15.01.1994
	Protocol (combating pollution by oil & other harmful subst. in emergency situation)	Bucharest, 1992	1	1	–	–	–
	Protocol (protection of Black Sea marine environment against pollution from dumping)	Bucharest, 1992	1	1	–	–	–
	Protocol (protection of Black Sea marine env. against poll. from land based sources)	Bucharest, 1992	1	1	–	–	–
A	Co-op. in prevention of marine poll. from oil & other dangerous chemicals	Copenhagen, 1993	5	5	5	5	1998
M	Memorandum of understanding on port state control in Asia-Pacific region	Tokyo, 1993	5	5	20	17	01.04.1994
C	Liability & compensation for damage in connection with carriage of hazardous & noxious substances by sea	London, 1996	8	–	8	2	–

Flora and fauna

Type[a]	Subject	Place and date	OECD Signed	OECD Ratified[b]	Total Signed	Total Ratified[b]	Entry into Force
C	Preservation of fauna & flora in their natural state	London, 1933	6	4	11	9	14.01.1936
C	Nature protection & wild life preservation in the Western Hemisphere	Washington, 1940	2	2	22	19	01.05.1942
C	Regulation of whaling	Washington, 1946	19	19	48	48	10.11.1948
	Protocol	Washington, 1956	19	19	43	43	04.05.1959
C	Protection of birds	Paris, 1950	13	9	15	10	17.01.1963
A	Plant protection for the Asia & Pacific region	Rome, 1956	7	7	25	25	02.07.1956
C	Conservation of North Pacific fur seals	Washington, 1957	3	3	4	4	14.10.1957
	Extension	Washington, 1969	3	3	–	–	in force
A	Measures for conservation of Antarctic fauna & flora	Brussels, 1964	10	10	17	17	in force
C	Benelux convention on hunting & protection of birds	Brussels, 1970	3	3	3	3	01.07.1972
C	Wetlands of int'l importance especially as waterfowl habitat	Ramsar, 1971	29	29	127	127	21.12.1975
	Protocol	Paris, 1982	29	29	122	122	01.10.1986
C	Conservation of Antarctic seals	London, 1972	12	11	17	16	11.03.1978
C	Protection of new varieties of plants (revised)	Geneva, 1972	25	25	50	50	1972
	Amendments	Geneva, 1978	23	23	48	48	08.11.1981
	Amendments	Geneva, 1981	10	10	19	19	24.04.1998
C	Int'l trade in endangered species of wild fauna & flora (CITES)	Washington, 1973	29	28	159	156	01.07.1975
A	Conservation of polar bears	Oslo, 1973	4	4	5	5	26.05.1976
C	Conservation of nature in the South Pacific	Apia, 1976	3	3	7	7	28.06.1990
C	Conservation of migratory species of wild animals	Bonn, 1979	20 +EU	20 +EU	79	79	01.11.1983

THE ENVIRONMENT

Type[a]	Subject	Place and date	OECD Signed	OECD Ratified[b]	Total Signed	Total Ratified[b]	Entry into Force
A	Conservation of bats in Europe	London, 1991	15	14	26	25	16.01.1994
A	Conservation of small cetaceans of the Baltic & the North Seas	New York, 1992	8 +EU	8	9	8	20.03.1994
A	Conservation of cetaceans of Black Sea, Mediterranean Sea & contiguous Atlantic area	Monaco, 1996	6 +EU	1	15	8	01.06.2001
A	Conservation of African-Eurasian migratory waterbirds	The Hague, 1996	13 +EU	8	38	31	01.11.1999
C	Conservation of European wildlife & natural habitats	Bern, 1979	22 +EU	22 +EU	45	45	01.06.1982
C	Conservation of Antarctic marine living resources	Canberra, 1980	18 +EU	18 +EU	28	28	07.04.1982
A	Tropical timber	Geneva, 1983	23 +EU	23 +EU	52	52	01.04.1985
	Revised agreem.	New York, 1994	23 +EU	23 +EU	57	57	01.01.1997
A	Conservation of wetlands & their migratory birds	1998	3	3	3	3	–
A	Co-op. on research, conservation & managt. of marine mammals in the N. Atlantic	Nuuk, 1992	2	–	4	–	–
C	Biological diversity	Rio de Janeiro, 1992	29 +EU	28 +EU	190	184	29.12.1993
P	Biosafety	Montreal, 2000	26 +EU	1	106	7	–
M	Memorandum of understanding to establish trilateral committee for wildlife, plants & ecosystem management	1996	3	3	3	3	–

Fisheries

Type[a]	Subject	Place and date	OECD Signed	OECD Ratified[b]	Total Signed	Total Ratified[b]	Entry into Force
T	Spitsberg	1920	1	1	1	1	1994
C	Establishment of inter-American tropical tuna commission	Washington, 1949	4	4	12	12	03.03.1950
C	High seas fisheries of North Pacific Ocean	Tokyo, 1952	3	3	3	3	12.06.1953
	Protocol	Tokyo, 1978	3	3	3	3	15.02.1979
C	Conservation of anadromous stocks (North Pacific Ocean)	Moscow, 1992	3	3	4	4	16.02.1993
C	Fishing & conservation of living resources of the high seas	Geneva, 1958	16	12	58	37	20.03.1966
A	Protection of salmon in Baltic Sea	Stockholm, 1962	4	4	4	4	01.03.1966
	Protocol	Stockholm, 1972	4	4	4	4	24.11.1976
C	Fisheries	London, 1964	13	12	13	12	15.03.1966
C	Int'l convention for conservation of Atlantic tunas (ICCAT)	Rio de Janeiro, 1966	9	9 +EU	40	37	21.03.1969
C	Conduct of fishing operations in North Atlantic	London, 1967	16	12	17	13	26.09.1976
C	Conservation of living resources of Southeast Atlantic	Rome, 1969	7	7	17	17	24.10.1971
C	Future multilateral co-operation in Northwest Atlantic fisheries (NAFO)	Ottawa, 1978	9 +EU	9 +EU	17	17	01.01.1979
C	South Pacific Forum Fisheries Agency	Honiara, 1979	2	2	16	16	10.07.1979
C	Multilateral co-operation in North-East Atlantic fisheries	London, 1980	7 +EU	7 +EU	11	10	17.03.1982
C	Conservation of salmon in North Atlantic Ocean	Reykjavik, 1982	7 +EU	7 +EU	9	9	01.10.1983
T	South Pacific fisheries	Port Moresby, 1987	3	3	13	13	15.06.1998
C	Prohibition of fishing with long driftnets in South Pacific	Wellington, 1989	4	3	15	7	17.05.1991
	Protocol	Noumea, 1990	1	1	1	1	28.02.1992
	Protocol	Noumea, 1990	1	–	2	1	05.10.1993
T	Cooperation in fisheries surveillance & law enforcement in the South Pacific region	Honiara, 1992	2	1	17	14	20.05.1993
C	Conservation of Southern Pacific bluefin tuna	Canberra, 1993	3	3	3	3	20.05.1994
A	Establishment of Indian Ocean Tuna Commission	Rome, 1993	5 +EU	5 +EU	20	20	27.03.1996
A	Promote compliance with int'l conservation & managt. measures by fishing vessels on the high seas	1993	6 +EU	6 +EU	22	22	–
C	Conservation & managt. of pollock resources in C. Bering Sea	Washington, 1994	4	–	6	–	–

Nuclear

Type[a]	Subject	Place and date	OECD Signed	OECD Ratified[b]	Total Signed	Total Ratified[b]	Entry into Force
C	Third party liability in field of nuclear energy	Paris, 1960	17	14	18	15	01.04.1968
	Supplementary convention	Brussels, 1963	14	11	14	11	04.12.1974
	Additional protocol to convention	Paris, 1964	17	14	17	14	01.04.1968
	Additional protocol to supplementary convention	Paris, 1964	14	11	14	11	04.12.1974
	Protocol amending convention	Brussels, 1982	17	14	17	14	07.10.1988
	Protocol amending supplementary convention	Brussels, 1982	14	11	14	11	01.08.1991
	Jnt protocol relating to applic. of Vienna & Paris Conv'ns	Vienna, 1988	18	9	32	21	27.04.1992
C	Liability of operations of nuclear ships	Brussels, 1962	5	2	17	7	–
C	Civil liability for nuclear damage	Vienna, 1963	6	4	39	33	12.11.1977
	Protocol to amend Vienna convention	Vienna, 1997	4	–	15	4	–
T	Banning nuclear weapon tests in atmosphere, outer space & under water	Moscow, 1963	28	27	130	118	10.10.1963
T	Prohibition of nuclear weapons in Latin America	Mexico, 1967	1	1	–	–	–
C	Civil liability in maritime carriage of nuclear material	Brussels, 1971	12	10	18	16	15.07.1975
C	Prohib. emplacement of nuclear & mass destruct. weapons on sea-bed, ocean floor and subsoil	London, Moscow, Washington, 1971	28	28	108	86	18.05.1972
C	South Pacific nuclear free zone treaty	Rarotonga, 1985	5	2	11	11	11.12.1986
C	Early notification of nuclear accident	Vienna, 1986	29	29	102	87	27.10.1986
C	Assistance in case of nuclear accid't or radiological emergency	Vienna, 1986	29	24	103	83	26.02.1987
C	Nuclear safety	Vienna, 1994	28	27	72	53	24.10.1996
C	Supplementary compensation for nuclear damage	Vienna, 1997	4	–	13	3	–
C	Joint convention on safety of spent fuel manag't. & on safety of radioactive waste	Vienna, 1997	23	18	42	27	18.06.2001

Notes:
[a] A – Agreement; C – Convention; M – Memorandum; P – Protocol; T – Treaty.
[b] Includes accessions, acceptances, approvals and successions.
[c] In full: Convention to ban the importation into Forum island countries of hazardous wastes and radioactive wastes and to control the transboundary movement and management of hazardous wastes within the South Pacific.

Source: OECD Environmental Data, 2002.

PART FOUR

Natural History

CLASSIFICATION OF LIVING ORGANISMS

It has been estimated that between 3 million and 20 million different kinds of organism are alive in the world today. Large numbers of other organisms have become extinct, and some of these are preserved as fossils. Most modern schemes of classification of living organisms are based upon the pioneering work of the Swedish biologist Carl von Linné (in Latin, Carolus Linnaeus; 1707–78), who established the practice of *binomial nomenclature*, by which all organisms are given two names, traditionally printed in italics. The first name is that of the *genus*, and is common to a group of closely related organisms. The second is that of the *species* and is unique to a particular type of organism. Higher levels of classification show a hierarchy of relationships. These are illustrated here using the human species as an example.

Classification of the human species

Taxonomic level

Kingdom	Animalia	(animals)
Phylum (division)[a]	Chordata	(chordates)
Subphylum	Vertebrata	(vertebrates)
Class	Mammalia	(mammals)
Order	Primates	
Family	Hominida	(hominids)
Genus	*Homo*	
Species	*sapiens*	

[a] In classifiying plants, fungi and bacteria, the term *division* is used rather than *phylum*.

The five kingdoms

While almost all modern systems of classification use the same basic taxonomic system, there are several different ways of grouping living organisms together. This book uses the popular Whittaker system, which divides the living world into five kingdoms.

Kingdom	Members of kingdom
Prokaryotae*	Monera, or bacteria
Protoctista	Algae, protozoans, slime moulds
Fungi	Mushrooms, moulds, lichens
Animalia	Animals
Plantae	Plants

* The kingdom Prokaryotae is sometimes given to include the viruses. Other systems describe viruses as being outside normal systems of classification.

ANIMALS

The animal kingdom is usually divided into about 30 phyla, which differ enormously in size and are listed here in order of primitive to advanced.

Classification of animals

Phylum	Common name/examples	No. of species	Comments
Placozoa	*Trichoplax adhaerens*	1	The only species in the phylum, this is the simplest animal known. No tissues, organs, or symmetry.
Porifera	Sponges	10 000	All aquatic: vast majority in sea-water, 150 in fresh water. No tissues, organs, or symmetry.
Cnidaria	Coelenterates; *Hydra*; true jellyfish; corals; sea anemones	9 500	Nearly all marine. Radially symmetrical with tissues and organs; have stinging cells (nematocysts) on tentacles.
Ctenophora	Comb jellies; sea gooseberries	90	Aquatic; transparent.
Mesozoa	Mesozoans	50	Small, worm-like organisms.
Platyhelminthes	Flatworms; flukes; tapeworms	15 000	Ribbon-shaped and soft-bodied; the least complex of the animals that have heads.
Nemertina	Ribbon worms or proboscis worms	900	Characteristic feature is long, sensitive anterior proboscis, used to explore the environment and capture prey.
Gnasthostomulida	Jaw worms or gnasthostomulids	80	Microscopic marine worms.
Gastrotricha	Gastrotrichs	400	Aquatic microscopic animals with cilia on their bodies.

NATURAL HISTORY

Classification of animals (continued)

Phylum	Common name/examples	No. of species	Comments
Rotifera	Rotifers or wheel animals	2 000	Aquatic microscopic animals with their anterior end modified into a ciliary organ called a *corona*, the beating of which resembles a rotating wheel.
Kinorhyncha	Kinorhynchs	150	Small worm-like marine animals.
Loricifera	Loriciferans	10	Tiny marine animals whose abdomen is covered by a girdle of spiny plates called a *lorica*.
Acanthocephala	Spiny-headed worms	600	Gut parasites of vertebrates, usually of carnivores.
Entoprocta	Entoprocts	150	Small marine animals, mostly sedentary, living in colonies attached to rocks, shells, algae, or other animals.
Nematoda	Nematodes or roundworms	>80 000	Unsegmented, more or less cylindrical worms which occur free-living in all types of environment, and also as parasites of plants and animals. It has been estimated that there may be as many as 1 million species of nematode in the world (ie vast numbers of undiscovered species). In terms of numbers of individuals, nematodes are the most abundant group of multicellular animals.
Nematomorpha	Horsehair worms; hair-worms; Gordian worms	240	Very long, thin worms which are parasitic in insects and crustaceans as juveniles, and free-living in water as adults.
Ectoprocta	Ectoprocts	5 000	Small aquatic animals, mostly colonial.
Phoronida	Horseshoe worms; phoronids	10	Marine worms with as many as 1 500 hollow tentacles. Live in tubes which they secrete and strengthen with sand or shell fragments.
Brachiopoda	Lamp shells	335	Bottom-living marine animals with shells with two valves. They thrived during the Palaeozoic era – more than 30 000 extinct species have been described.
Mollusca	Molluscs, including snails, slugs (gastropods), clams, mussels, oysters (bivalves), octopus, squid (cephalopoda)	110 000	The second largest phylum of animals, molluscs live in aquatic or moist environments, are soft-bodied, and are usually protected by a calcareous shell which is secreted by a fold of the body wall called the *mantle*.
Priapulida	Priapulids	10	Small carnivorous marine worms.
Sipuncula	Peanut worms	>300	Unsegmented marine worms, which live in crevices or are burrowing.
Echiura	Spoon worms	140	Unsegmented marine worms, which burrow in marine deposits.
Annelida	Annelids, including earthworms, leeches, ragworms	8 900	Worms with a well-developed coelom, and with the body divided up into a number of more or less similar segments. Terrestrial, freshwater, or marine.
Tardigrada	Water bears; tardigrades	380	Minute animals which live in films of water around mosses and other low terrestrial features. Four pairs of stubby legs armed with terminal claws.

Phylum	Common name/examples	No. of species	Comments
Pentastoma	Tongue worms	70	Parasitic worms in the respiratory passages of air-breathing vertebrates. They have a chitinous cuticle which is periodically moulted to allow growth.
Onychophora	Velvet worms; onychophorans	80	Soft-bodied, segmented animals with many paired but unjointed legs. Confined to humid tropics.
Arthropoda	Arthropods, including crustaceans (shrimps, barnacles, woodlice, crabs), scorpions, mites, ticks, spiders, insects, centipedes, millipedes	>2 000 000	By far the largest animal phylum, with more species than all the other phyla combined (more than 800 000 species of insects alone have been described; some zoologists think there may be as many as 10 million). Arthropods are segmented animals with paired, jointed appendages on some or all of their body segments.
Pogonophora	Beard worms	100	Extremely slender, gutless, tube-living marine worms.
Echinodermata	Echinoderms, including starfish, sea urchins, sea cucumbers	6 000	Marine, mostly bottom-dwelling animals, usually displaying five-fold symmetry. The fluid-filled tube feet are used for locomotion and feeding.
Chaetognatha	Arrow worms	>100	Small, slender, torpedo-shaped marine planktonic animals which are voracious carnivores.
Hemichordata	Hemichordates	90	Small soft-bodied animals which inhabit shallow U-shaped burrows in sandy or muddy sea bottoms.
Chordata	Mammals; birds; amphibians; reptiles; fish; plus a small number of invertebrates	45 000	The best known phylum of Animalia, containing all the species which, in the minds of many, are considered 'animals'. Chordates are distinguished by having (i) the walls of their pharynx, at some stage in their life cycle, perforated by gill clefts; (ii) a hollow dorsal nerve cord; (iii) an axial cartilaginous rod – the *notochord* – lying immediatedly beneath the nerve cord. Most chordates have backbones and are called *vertebrates*, but two of the three subphyla are small *invertebrate* groups.

Animal records

Size

This table shows the largest species in the animal kingdom, plus some others of particular interest. Unless otherwise stated: (i) *largest* means bulkiest and heaviest; (ii) the size given is the largest size regularly attained by the species, not that of individual 'record-holders'.

	Species	Dimension	Size (m)	(ft)	Comments
Mammals					
Cetacea	Blue whale *(Balaenoptera musculis)*	Length	35.0	115	The largest and longest-living mammal, and the largest animal ever known.
	Sperm whale *(Physeter catadon)*	Length	25.0	82	The largest-toothed mammal and the largest marine carnivore[a].
Marine carnivores	Sperm whale (see above)				
	Southern elephant seal *(Mirounga leonina)*	Length	6.0	20	The largest seal.

NATURAL HISTORY

Animal records (continued)

	Species	Dimension	Size (m)	(ft)	Comments
Ungulates	African elephant (Loxodonta africana)	Height	3.2	10.5	The largest land mammal.
	Giraffe (Giraffa camelopardalis)	Height	5.5	18.0	The tallest land mammal.
Terrestrial carnivores	Kodiak bear (Ursus arctos middendorffi)	Length	2.4	7.8	The largest land carnivore.
	Indian tiger (Panthera tigris tigris)	Length	3.15	10.3	The largest member of the cat family.
Primates	Eastern lowland mountain gorilla (Gorilla gorilla graueri)	Height (standing)	1.88	6.2	The largest and tallest primate[b].
Rodents	Capybara (Hydrochoerus hydrochoerus)	Length	1.4	4.6	The largest rodent.
	Coypu (Myocastor coypus)	Length	0.9	2.9	
Marsupials	Red kangaroo (Megaleia rufa)	Height	2.15	7.1	The largest marsupial.
Birds	Ostrich (Struthio camelus)	Height	2.75	9.0	The largest and tallest bird.
Reptiles	Estuarine or saltwater crocodile (Crocodylus porosus)	Length	4.8	15.7	The largest reptile.
Snakes	Anaconda (Eunectes murinus)	Length	8.5	27.8	The largest snake.
	Reticulated python (Python reticulatus)	Length	10.0	32.8	The longest snake.
Lizards	Komodo monitor (Varanus komodoensis)	Length	2.25	7.4	The largest lizard.
	Salvadori monitor (Varanus salvadori)	Length	4.75	15.6	The longest lizard.
Amphibians	Giant salamander (Andrias davidianus)	Length	1.2	3.9	The largest amphibian.
Fishes					
Marine	Whale shark (Rhincodon typus)	Length	13.0	43.0	The largest marine fish.
Freshwater	Sturgeon (Acipenseridae spp.)	Length	5.0	16.4	The largest freshwater fish.
	European catfish (Siluridae spp.)	Length	4.0	13.1	
Molluscs	Atlantic giant squid (Architeuthis dux)	length	17.0	56.0	The largest mollusc and the largest invertebrate.
	Pacific giant octopus (Octopus dofleini)	length	10.0	32.8	
Crustaceans					
Marine	Giant spider crab (Macrocheira kaempferi)	Claw span	2.7	8.8	The largest crustacean.
	North Atlantic lobster (Homarus americanus)	Length	1.06	3.5	The heaviest crustacean.
Freshwater	Crayfish (Astacopsis gouldi)	Length	0.6	1.9	The largest freshwater crustacean.
Worms	Bootlace worm (Lineus longissimus)	Length	40.0	131.0	The longest worm.
Jellyfish	Arctic giant (Cyanae capillata arctica)	Diameter	2.2	7.2	The largest jellyfish.
		Length of tentacles	35.0	115.0	
Insects	Goliath beetle (Scarabaeidae spp.)	Length	0.11	0.4	The largest insect.
	Queen Alexandra's birdwing (Ornithoptera alexandrae)	Wing-span	0.28	0.9	The largest butterfly.
Spiders	Goliath bird-eating spider (Theraphosa leblondi)	Leg-span	0.25	0.8	The largest spider.

[a] Discounting the filter-feeding baleen whales (eg the blue whale) which feed on small crustaceans such as krill.

[b] Humans (Homo sapiens) regularly exceed this height. In fact, the tallest recorded human, Robert Pershing Wadlow (1918-40), who measured 2.72 m/8.9 ft at his death, is probably the tallest ever primate.

spp. = species

Weight

	tonnes
Blue whale	120
Sperm whale	50
Right whale	50
Whale shark	43
Basking shark	40
African elephant	6
White shark	5
Elephant seal	4
Hippopotamus	3
Manta ray	3
White rhinoceros	2
Moonfish	2
Saltwater crocodile	1.5
American bison	1.5
Leatherback turtle	0.8
Kodiak bear	0.74
Gorilla	0.35
Anaconda	0.23

	km/h	mph
Horizontal flight		
Birds		
Peregrine falcon	200	124
Teal	120	75
Oystercatcher	100	60
Swan	90	55
Duck	85	53
Partridge	84	52
Pheasant	60	35
Crane	50	30
Gull	40	25
Crow	40	25
Fish		
Flying fish	90	55
Insects		
Dragonfly	75	45
Hawkmoth	50	30
Hoverfly	14	9
Bumblebee	11	7

	km/h	mph
Fish		
Sailfish	110	68
Swordfish	90	55
Blue shark	70	44
Tuna	70	44
Salmon	40	25
Trout	37	23
Pike	33	20

Speed on the ground

	km/h	mph
Mammals		
Cheetah	110	68
Roe deer	98	61
Antelope	95	59
Lion	80	50
Red deer	78	48
Hare	70	44
Horse	69	43
Zebra	65	40
Greyhound	60	35
Giraffe	50	30
Wolf	45	28
Elephant	40	25
Birds		
Ostrich	50	30
Reptiles		
Crocodile	13	8
Mamba	11	7

Speed in the air

	km/h	mph
Mammals		
Bat	20–50	12–30
Birds		
Diving		
Peregrine falcon	350	217
Golden eagle	300	185

Speed in water

	km/h	mph
Mammals		
Dolphin	64	40
Killer whale	55	34
Sea lion	40	25
Birds		
Penguin	40	25
Reptiles		
Leatherback turtle	35	22

NATURAL HISTORY

Mammals

Order	Family	Common name/examples	No. of species	Distribution of order	General characteristics of order
Monotremes	Ornithorhynchidae	Platypus	1	Australia	Lay eggs from which young are hatched.
	Tachyglossidae	Echidna (spiny anteater)	2		
Marsupialia	Didelphidae	Opossums	65	Australia, S and C America	Premature birth of young and continued development outside the womb.
	Thylacinidae	Tasmanian wolf	1		
	Dasyuridae	Native cats; marsupial mice	48		
	Myrmecobiidae	Numbat	1		
	Notoryctidae	Marsupial moles	2		
	Peramelidae	Bandicoots	22		
	Thylacomyidae	Burrowing bandicoots	20		
	Caenolestidae	Rat opossums	7		
	Phalangeridae	Phalangers; cuscuses	15		
	Burramyidae	Pigmy possums; feathertail gliders	6		
	Petauridae	Gliding phalangers	25		
	Macropodidae	Kangaroos; wallabies	47		
	Phascolarctidae	Koala	1		
	Vombatidae	Wombats	4		
	Tarsipedidae	Honey possum	1		
Insectivora	Erinaceidae	Hedgehogs; gymnures	14	Europe, N and S America, Asia, Australia	Active mainly at night; do not need to rely on vision for orientation.
	Talpidae	Moles	22		
	Tenrecidae	Tenrecs	20		
	Potamogalidae	Otter shrews	3		
	Chrysochloridae	Golden moles	11		

Mammals (continued)

Order	Family	Common name/examples	No. of species	Distribution of order	General characteristics of order
	Solenodontidae	Solenodon, almiqui	2		
	Soricidae	Shrews	291		
	Macroscelididae	Elephant shrews	28		
	Tupaiidae	Tree shrews	15		
Chiroptera	Pteropodidae	Old World fruit bats; flying foxes	154	Europe, N and S America, Asia, Africa, Australia	Insectivorous; nocturnal; migrate annually to and from summer roosts and winter migration sites; use echolocation for orientation; order defined by true flight.
	Rhinopomatidae	Mouse-tailed bats	3		
	Emballonuridae	Sheath-tailed or sac-winged bats	50		
	Nycteridae	Slit-faced or hollow-faced bats	13		
	Megadermatidae	False vampires	5		
	Hipposideridae	Old World leaf-nosed bats	60		
	Rhinolophidae	Horseshoe bats	70		
	Noctilionidae	Bulldog bats	2		
	Mormoopidae	Insectivorous bats	9		
	Phyllostomatidae	American leaf-nosed bats	120		
	Desmodontidae	Vampire bats	3		
	Natalidae	Funnel-eared bats	4		
	Furipteridae	Smoky bats	2		
	Thyropteridae	Disk-wing bats	2		
	Myzopodidae	Old World sucker-footed bats	1		
	Vespertilionidae	Common bats	290		
	Mystacinidae	New Zealand short-tailed bats	1		
	Molossidae	Free-tailed bats	90		
Rodentia	Aplodontidae	Mountain beaver or sewellel	1	Europe, Asia, N and S America, Africa, Australia	One pair of upper and lower incisors which grow throughout life; broadly herbivorous; gnawing mechanism; clawed digits.
	Sciuridae	Squirrels; chipmunks; marmots	250		
	Cricetidae	Field mice; deer mice; voles; lemmings; muskrats	560		
	Muridae	Old World rats and mice	450		
	Heteromyidae	Mice; pocket mice; kangaroo rats	75		
	Geomyidae	Pocket gophers	40		
	Zapodidae	Jumping and birch mice	10		
	Dipodidae	Jerboas	25		
	Spalacidae	Mole rats	3		
	Rhizomyidae	Bamboo rats; African mole rats	18		
	Octodontidae	Octodonts; degus	7		
	Echimyidae	Spiny rats; rock rats	40		
	Ctenomyidae	Tuco-tucos	26		
	Abrocomidae	Abrocomes or chinchilla rats	2		
	Chinchillidae	Chinchillas; viscachas	6		
	Capromyidae	Hutias; coypus	10		
	Dasyproctidae	Pacas; agoutis	13		
	Dinomyidae	Pacarana or Branick's paca	1		
	Caviidae	Cavies; guinea pigs; maras	12		
	Hydrochoeridae	Capybaras	2		
	Erethizontidae	New World porcupines	8		
	Petromuridae	Rock or dassie rat	1		
	Thryonomyidae	Cane rats	2		
	Bathyergidae	Blesmols or African mole rats	9		
	Hystricidae	Old World porcupines	15		
	Castoridae	Beavers	2		
	Anomaluridae	Scaly-tailed squirrels	7		
	Ctenodactylidae	Gundis	8		
	Pedetidae	Cape jumping hare or springhaas	1		
	Gliridae	Dormice	20		
	Seleveniidae	Jumping dormouse	1		

Order	Family	Common name/examples	No. of species	Distribution of order	General characteristics of order
Edentata	Myrmecophagidae	Anteaters	3	S and N America	Reduced dentition; long sticky tongue; powerful clawed forefeet.
	Bradypodidae	Tree sloths	5		
	Dasypodidae	Armadillos	20		
Lagomorpha	Ochotonidae	Pikas	14	Asia, N America, Europe, S Africa, S America, Australia	Herbivorous; well-developed incisors which grow continuously from roots; elongation of the limbs distally.
	Leporidae	Hares; rabbits	46		
Carnivora	Canidae	Dogs; foxes; wolves; jackals	35	Europe, Asia, N America, S America, Africa, Australia	High level of intelligence; highly developed sense of smell; varied dentition; well-developed carnassials.
	Ursidae	Bears; giant panda	7		
	Otariidae	Eared seals; walrus	15		
	Procyonidae	Raccoons; coatis; lesser panda	15		
	Mustelidae	Weasels; otters; skunks; badgers; mink	65		
	Phocidae	Earless seals	20		
	Felidae	Cats	35		
	Viverridae	Civets; mongooses; genet	70		
	Hyaenidae	Hyenas	4		
Cetacea	Balaenidae	Right whales	3	S America, Africa, N America, Europe, Asia, Antarctica, Australia	Breathe through blowholes; tapered body; develop young internally and give birth at sea; long breeding period; hearing is major sense; migrate seasonally.
	Eschrichtiidae	Grey whales	1		
	Balaenopteridae	Rorquals; humpbacks	8		
	Platanistidae	River dolphins	4		
	Delphinidae	Dolphins; killer whales	30		
	Phocoenidae	Porpoises	6		
	Monodontidae	Beluga; narwhal	2		
	Physeteridae	Sperm whales	3		
	Hyperoodontidae (formerly Ziphiidae)	Beaked whales	15		
	Stenidae	Long-snouted dolphins	4		
Proboscidea	Elephantidae	African elephant, Asian elephant	2	Africa, Asia	Bulky bodies and elongated snout; each toe has heavy hoof nail; no canine teeth; herbivorous.
Sirenia	Dugongidae	Dugong	1	Australia, S America, Africa	Herbivorous; totally aquatic; torpedo-shaped bodies; tough, almost hairless skin; body contains much fat.
	Trichechidae	Manatees	3		
Perissodactyla	Equidae	Horses; asses; zebras; donkeys	7	Africa, Europe, Asia	Herbivorous; high-crowned grinding teeth.
	Tapiridae	Tapirs	4		
	Rhinocerotidae	Rhinoceroses	5		
Artiodactyla	Tragulidae	Chevrotains	4	Asia, Africa, C and S America	Ruminants; herbivorous; cloven-hoofed; moderately large brain; migrate seasonally.
	Antilocapridae	Pronghorn	1		
	Giraffidae	Giraffe; okapi	2		
	Cervidae	Deer	35		
	Bovidae	Cattle; goats; sheep; antelopes; gazelles	110		
	Camelidae	Camels; llamas	4		
	Suidae	Pigs	8		
	Tayassuidae	Peccaries	3		
	Hippopotamidae	Hippopotamuses	2		
Tubulidentata	Orycteropodidae	Aardvark	1	S Africa	Long, tapering tail used for burrowing; tubular snout; sticky tongue; rootless teeth.

Mammals (continued)

Order	Family	Common name/examples	No. of species	Distribution of order	General characteristics of order
Primates	Lemuridae	Lemurs	14	Africa, Asia, S America (man is distributed worldwide)	Omnivorous; multi-purpose dentition; large brain; body position upright; five-digit hands and feet; stereoscopic vision.
	Cheirogaleidae	Dwarf lemurs; mouse lemurs	4		
	Indriidae	Indris; sifaka; avahi	4		
	Daubentoniidae	Aye aye (lemur)	1		
	Lepilmuridae	Sportive lemurs	2		
	Galagidae	Galagos	7		
	Lorisidae	Lorises; pottos; bushbabies	12		
	Tupaiidae	Tree shrews	17		
	Tarsiidae	Tarsiers	3		
	Callitrichidae	Tamarins; marmosets	15		
	Cebidae	New World monkeys	30		
	Cercopithecidae	Old World monkeys	72		
	Hylobatidae	Gibbons; siamang	7		
	Pongidae	Great apes: gorilla, chimpanzee, orangutan	4		
	Hominidae	Man	1		

Length of pregnancy in some mammals

Animal	Gestation period[a]	Animal	Gestation period[a]	Animal	Gestation period[a]
Camel	406	Hamster	16	Pig	113
Cat	62	Hedgehog	35–40	Rabbit	32
Cow	280	Horse	337	Rat	21
Chimpanzee	237	Human	266	Reindeer	215–45
Dog	62	Hyena	110	Seal, northern fur	350
Dolphin	276	Kangaroo	40	Sheep	148
Elephant, African	640	Lion	108	Skunk	62
Ferret	42	Mink	50	Squirrel, grey	44
Fox	52	Monkey, rhesus	164	Tiger	105–9
Giraffe	395–425	Mouse	21	Whale	365
Goat	151	Opossum	13		
Guinea pig	68	Orangutan	245–75		

[a]Average number of days.

Classification of birds

This table uses the Voous taxonomic sequence running from what are supposed to be the most primitive families to the newest ones.

Order	Family	Common name/ examples	No. of species	Distribution of family	General characteristics of order
Struthioniformes	Struthionidae	Ostrich	1	Africa	The ostrich is the world's largest living bird. Swift-running, flightless and gregarious; ground-nesting; feeds on vegetable matter.
Rheiformes	Rheidae	Rheas	2	S America	Swift-running, flightless ground-nesting birds which feed on vegetation and insects. Ostrich-like with short wings and no tailfeathers.
Casuariiformes	Casuariidae	Cassowaries	3	Australia and adjacent islands	Large, flightless, running birds with three toes and rough, hair-like plumage.
	Dromaiidae	Emu	1		

Order	Family	Common name/ examples	No. of species	Distribution of family	General characteristics of order
Apterygiformes	Apterygidae	Kiwis	3	New Zealand	Small-eyed, flightless, tailless birds with vestigial wings. They nest in burrows; are mainly nocturnal, insectivorous, and forest-dwelling.
Tinamiformes	Tinamidae	Tinamous	45	S and C America	Terrestrial, ground-nesting birds which can fly but do so rarely. They have patterned plumage; feed on vegetation; and live in grassland, brush, and forest.
Sphenisciformes	Spheniscidae	Penguins	16	Antarctica, Australia, Africa, S America	Black-and-white, flightless, aquatic birds. They nest in burrows or on the ground and are good swimmers, living off fish, squid, and crustacea. Walk upright or glide on their stomachs. Specially adapted feet feature a highly efficient heat-exchange mechanism to ensure survival in cold climates.
Gaviiformes	Gaviidae	Divers or loons	4	N America, Eurasia	Black and brown diving birds which breed on inland lakes and nest on the ground. They eat mostly fish, and winter on sea coasts. Clumsy on land, their legs are adapted for swimming and diving.
Podicipediformes	Podicipedidae	Grebes	20	Africa, Europe, Asia, Australia, N and S America	Large grey and brown short-winged diving birds with partly webbed feet. They eat fish, and nest on the water. They inhabit freshwater lakes in the summer and sea coasts in winter. Some are migratory.
Procellariiformes	Diomedeidae	Albatrosses	14	Seas worldwide	Generally long-winged, partly webbed-toed seabirds which feed on fish and nest on isolated islands and cliffs. Some species discharge oil in self-defence.
	Procellariidae	Petrels; fulmars; shearwaters	55		
	Hydrobatidae	Storm petrels	20		
	Pelecanoididae	Diving petrels	4		
Pelecaniformes	Pelecanidae	Pelicans	7	All continents	Diverse order of diving birds, found in marine and freshwater coastal habitats worldwide. They nest on cliffs or in trees; have a diet of mostly fish; and are generally web-toed.
	Sulidae	Gannets; boobies	9	N Atlantic, S Africa, Australasia, tropical oceans	
	Phaethontidae	Tropicbirds	3	Tropical oceans	
	Phalacrocoracidae	Cormorants	29	Worldwide	
	Fregatidae	Frigatebirds	5	Tropical oceans	
	Anhingidae	Darters	4	N and S America, Africa, Asia, Australasia	

NATURAL HISTORY

Classification of birds (continued)

Order	Family	Common name/ examples	No. of species	Distribution of family	General characteristics of order
Ciconiiformes	Ardeidae	Herons; bitterns	60	Worldwide except northernmost America and Eurasia	Upright, wading birds with specialized bills. Their toes are sometimes webbed and the middle claw is often serrated, or pectinate, for preening.
	Scopidae	Hammerhead	1	SW Arabia, Sub-Saharan Africa	
	Balaenicipitidae	Whale-headed stork	1	Africa	
	Ciconiidae	Storks	17	N America, Eurasia	
	Threskiornithidae	Spoonbills; ibises	31	Worldwide	
	Phoenicopteridae	Flamingos	5	Tropical zones	
Anseriformes	Anatidae	Ducks; geese; swans	147	Worldwide except Antarctica	Marsh-dwelling waterbirds which eat mostly vegetation and nest on the ground.
	Anhimidae	Screamers	3	S America	
Falconiformes	Cathartidae	Vultures (New World)	7	Americas	Birds of prey, or *raptors*. Expert fliers, they have hooked beaks and talons; and are generally large, heavily feathered birds with excellent eyesight and good hearing.
	Sagittariidae	Secretary-bird	1	Sub-Saharan Africa	
	Pandionidae	Osprey	1	Worldwide	
	Falconidae	Falcons; caracaras	60	Worldwide except Antarctica	
	Accipitridae	Kites; Old World vultures; harriers; hawks; eagles; buzzards	217	Worldwide except Antarctica	
Galliformes	Megapodidae	Megapodes	9	E Indies, Malaysia, New Guinea, Australia	The Galliformes, or gamebirds, have short, rounded wings, ill-adapted for sustained flight. They have large feet and claws, and are usually omnivorous in diet. The male plumage is often brilliant. Many are endangered owing to habitat destruction and over-hunting.
	Cracidae	Guans; curassows; chachalacas	42	Americas	
	Tetraonidae	Grouse	16	Eurasia, Americas	
	Phasianidae	Pheasants; quail; partridge	180	Worldwide, except N Eurasia and S America	
	Numididae	Guineafowl	7	Sub-Saharan Africa	
	Meleagrididae	Turkeys	2	N and S America	
Gruiformes	Mesitornithidae	Mesites	3	Madagascar	Diverse order of ground-feeding birds, generally with brown or grey plumage and long, rounded wings.
	Turnicidae	Buttonquails; hemipodes	16	Sub-Saharan Africa, China, Australia, Philippines, Mediterranean	
	Pedionomidae	Plains wanderer or collared hemipode	1	Australia	
	Gruidae	Cranes	15	All continents except S America and Antarctica	
	Aramidae	Limpkin	1	Americas	
	Psophiidae	Trumpeters	3	S America	
	Rallidae	Rails	130	Worldwide	
	Heliornithidae	Finfoots	3	Tropical America, tropical Africa and SE Asia	
	Rhynochetidae	Kagu	1	New Caledonia	
	Eurypygidae	Sunbittern	1	S America	
	Cariamidae	Seriemas	2	S America	
	Otididae	Bustards	22	Africa, Eurasia, Australia	

Order	Family	Common name/ examples	No. of species	Distribution of family	General characteristics of order
Charadriiformes (Sub-order Charadrii)	Jacanidae	Jacanas or lily-trotters	7	Americas, Africa, SE Asia, N Australia	Diverse order of mostly small to medium-sized shorebirds and seabirds.
	Rostratulidae	Painted snipe	2	S America, SE Asia, Australia	They generally have long, narrow wings, except for
	Haematopodidae	Oystercatchers	6	All continents	auks whose shorter wings
	Charadriidae	Plovers; lapwings	62	Worldwide	can act as paddles
	Scolopacidae	Sandpipers	81	All continents	underwater.
	Recurvirostridae	Avocets; stilts	7	All continents	
	Phalaropodidae	Phalaropes	3	N Eurasia, N America	
	Dromadidae	Crab plover	1	Indian ocean coastlines	
	Burhinidae	Stonecurlews or thick-knees	9	All continents except N America	
	Glareolidae	Pratincoles; coursers	17	Eurasia, Africa, Australia	
	Thinocoridae	Seed snipe	4	S America	
	Chionididae	Sheathbills	2	Antarctica and sub-Antartic islands	
(Sub-order Lari)	Stercorariidae	Skuas; jaegers	6	Worldwide	
	Laridae	Gulls	45	Worldwide	
	Sternidae	Terns; noddies	42	Worldwide	
	Rynchopidae	Skimmers	3	Tropical Africa, SE Asia, eastern N America, C and S America	
(Sub-order Alcae)	Alcidae	Auks	22	Northern hemisphere seas	
Columbiformes	Pteroclididae	Sandgrouse	16	Africa, S Europe, Asia	Small to medium-sized arboreal and terrestrial
	Columbidae	Pigeons; doves	300	Worldwide except Antarctica	birds with thick, heavy plumage.
Psittaciformes	Psittacidae	Parrots; lories; cockatoos; lovebirds; macaws; budgerigars	330	All continents except Antarctica	The parrots have zygodactyl toes: two pointing forward, and two backward, enabling them to climb and hold objects. They have strong, hooked bills – (with mobile upper mandible) used for cracking nuts, holding things and climbing – as a 'third foot'. Often colourful, they nest in trees and on ledges and have a largely vegetarian diet.
Cuculiformes	Musophagidae	Turacos	22	Sub-Saharan Africa	Diverse order of arboreal and terrestrial birds. Many
	Cuculidae	Cuckoos; anis; roadrunner; coucals	128	Worldwide	cuckoos are brood parasites, relying on other species to raise
	Opisthocomidae	Hoatzin	1	S America	their young.
Strigiformes	Strigidae	Owls (typical)	124	Worldwide except Antarctica	The owls are nocturnal raptors found in grassland and woodland habitats,

NATURAL HISTORY

Classification of birds (continued)

Order	Family	Common name/ examples	No. of species	Distribution of family	General characteristics of order
	Tytonidae	Barn owls	10	Worldwide except C Asia, New Zealand and Antarctica	usually nesting in cavities. Their large, forward-facing eyes peer out of a facial disc and give them binocular vision. Owls can turn their heads in either direction more than 180°, and also have acute hearing.
Caprimulgiformes	Caprimulgidae	Nightjars or goatsuckers	70	Open habitats in temperate and tropical regions	These are generally insectivorous. Some hibernate and many are
	Podargidae	Frogmouths	12	SE Asia, Australia	migratory. They have
	Aegothelidae	Owlet-nightjars	8	Australia, SE Asia	wide, gaping mouths
	Nyctibiidae	Potoos	5	S America	with hooked beaks, large
	Steatornithidae	Oilbird	1	S America	eyes and short legs with weak feet. Many species are two-coloured, featuring grey and red phases.
Apodiformes	Apodidae	Swifts	80	Worldwide	Aerial birds that depend
	Hemiprocnidae	Crested swifts	3	SE Asia	on their flying skills for
	Trochilidae	Hummingbirds	320	Americas	food. Swifts are insectivorous and migratory. While on the wing they feed, mate, collect nest material, drink, and even, in some species, pass the night at high altitudes. Hummingbirds feed on nectar, supplemented with insects.
Coliiformes	Coliidae	Mousebirds or colies	6	Sub-Saharan Africa	These acrobatic, highly social birds live in scrub and bushes, feeding on fruit and vegetation – often becoming agricultural pests.
Trogoniformes	Trogonidae	Trogons	35	America, Asia, Sub-Saharan Africa	Colourful, sedentary, arboreal birds that feed on fruit and insects. They nest in tree cavities and termite mounds.
Coraciiformes	Alcedinidae	Kingfishers	87	Worldwide	The three anterior toes on
	Todidae	Todies	5	W Indies	these birds are united, an
	Momotidae	Motmots	8	S America	adaptation for perching
	Meropidae	Bee-eaters	24	Africa, Eurasia, Australia	and tree-climbing. Many are brightly coloured,
	Leptosomatidae	Cuckoo-roller	1	Madagascar, Comoros Islands	some are social. All nest in cavities, digging holes
	Coraciidae	Rollers	16	Africa, Eurasia, Australia	in, for example, earth banks or rotten trees.
	Upupidae	Hoopoe	1	Africa, Eurasia	
	Phoeniculidae	Woodhoopoes	6	Sub-Saharan Africa	
	Bucerotidae	Hornbills	45	Sub-Saharan Africa, SE Asia	

Order	Family	Common name/ examples	No. of species	Distribution of family	General characteristics of order
Piciformes	Galbulidae	Jacamars	15	S America	These birds are zygodactylous (see Psittaciformes). Colourful and arboreal, they feed on vegetation and insects, and nest in holes.
	Bucconidae	Puffbirds	30	S America	
	Capitonidae	Barbets	76	Americas, Sub-Saharan Africa, SE Asia	
	Indicatoridae	Honeyguides	15	Sub-Saharan Africa, Himalayas, SE Asia	
	Ramphastidae	Toucans	40	S America	
	Picidae	Woodpeckers; piculets; wrynecks	200	Worldwide	
Passeriformes (Sub-order Eurylaimi)	Eurylaimidae	Broadbills	14	Africa, Asia	Around 5 200 species, well over half of all birds, belong to the order Passeriformes, the perching birds or passerines. The order includes the most familiar garden birds – tits, chickadees, robins and sparrows – as well as other species found in virtually all land habitats. No passerine is a true water bird, though the dippers come close. Most are small or medium-sized birds (the largest species are the raven and the Australian lyrebird). The perching feet have four well-developed, separate toes. These are very vocal, singing birds. The male is often more brightly coloured than the female. Most are opportunistic feeders, being dependent on high-energy foods such as seeds and insects. Monogamy is the norm.
(Sub-order Menurae)	Menuridae	Lyrebirds	2	SE Australia	
	Atrichornithidae	Scrub-birds	2	W and E Australia	
(Sub-order Tyranni)	Furnariidae	Ovenbirds	220	C and S America	
	Dendrocolaptidae	Woodcreepers	48	S America	
	Formicariidae	Antbirds	230	S America	
	Tyrannidae	Tyrant flycatchers	375	Americas	
	Pittidae	Pittas	29	Africa, SE Asia, Australia	
	Pipridae	Manakins	53	S America	
	Cotingidae	Cotingas	65	S America	
	Conopophagidae	Gnateaters	9	S America	
	Rhinocryptidae	Tapaculos	29	S America	
	Oxyruncidae	Sharpbill	1	S America	
	Phytotomidae	Plantcutters	3	S America	
	Xenicidae	New Zealand wrens	4	New Zealand	
	Philepittidae	Sunbird asities	4	Madagascar	
(Sub-order Oscines)	Hirundinidae	Swallows; martins	74	Worldwide	
	Alaudidae	Larks	75	All continents	
	Motacillidae	Wagtails; pipits	54	Worldwide	
	Pycnonotidae	Bulbuls	120	S Asia, Africa	
	Laniidae	Shrikes	69	N America, Africa, Eurasia	
	Campephagidae	Cuckoo-shrikes	72	Africa, Australia, S and E Asia	
	Irenidae	Leafbirds	14	S and E Asia	
	Prionopidae	Helmet shrikes	9	Sub-Saharan Africa	
	Vangidae	Vanga shrikes	13	Madagascar, Comoros	
	Bombycillidae	Waxwings; silky flycatchers	8	N Eurasia, S America	
	Dulidae	Palmchat	1	S America	
	Cinclidae	Dippers	5	N Africa, Eurasia, W America	
	Troglodytidae	Wrens	60	NW Africa, Eurasia, N and S America	
	Mimidae	Mockingbirds	30	Americas	
	Prunellidae	Accentors	13	N Africa, Eurasia, S Asia	

Classification of birds (continued)

Order	Family	Common name/ examples	No. of species	Distribution of family	General characteristics of order
	Subfamilies of the family Muscicapidae				
	Turdidae	Thrushes	305	Worldwide	
	Timaliidae	Babblers	252	Africa, S Asia, Australasia, N America	
	Sylviidae	Warblers (Old World)	350	Worldwide	
	Muscicapinae	Flycatchers (Old World)	155	Australasia, Old World	
	Malurinae	Fairy-wrens	26	Australia, New Guinea	
	Paradox- ornithinae	Parrotbills	19	Asia, Europe	
	Monarchinae	Monarch flycatchers	133	Sub-Saharan Africa, S Asia, Australasia	
	Orthonychinae	Logrunners	20	SE Asia, Australia	
	Acanthizinae	Australian warblers	65	SE Asia, Australasia	
	Rhipidurinae	Fantail flycatchers	39	SE Asia, Australasia	
	Pachycephalinae	Thickheads	46	SE Asia, Australasia	
	Paridae	Tits	46	Africa, Eurasia, N America	
	Aegithalidae	Long-tailed tits	7	Eurasia, N America	
	Remizidae	Penduline tits	10	Africa, Eurasia, N America	
	Sittidae	Nuthatches	21	N America, Eurasia, N Africa, Australia	
	Climacteridae	Australasian treecreepers	8	Australia, New Guinea	
	Certhiidae	Holarctic treecreepers	5	Eurasia, Africa, N America	
	Rhabdornith- idae	Philippine treecreepers	2	Philippines	
	Zosteropidae	White-eyes	85	Sub-Saharan Africa, S and E Asia, Australasia	
	Dicaeidae	Flowerpeckers	50	SE Asia, Australasia	
	Pardalotidae	Pardalotes or diamond eyes	5	Australia	
	Nectariniidae	Sunbirds; spiderhunters	116	Old World tropics, Africa to Australia	
	Meliphagidae	Honeyeaters	169	Australasia, S Africa	
	Ephthianuridae	Australian chats	5	Australia	
	Subfamilies of the family Emberizidae				
	Emberizinae	Old World buntings; New World sparrows	281	Worldwide except SE Asia and Australasia	
	Catambly- rhynchinae	Plush-capped finch	1	S America	
	Thraupinae	Tanagers; honeycreepers	233	Americas	
	Cardinalinae	Cardinals and grosbeaks	37	S America	
	Tersininae	Swallow tanager	1	S America	
	Parulidae	Wood warblers	119	Americas	
	Vireonidae	Vireos; pepper shrikes	43	Americas	
	Icteridae	American blackbirds	94	Americas	
	Subfamilies of the family Fringillidae				
	Fringillinae	Fringilline finches	3	Eurasia, Canary Islands	
	Carduelinae	Cardueline finches	122	Worldwide except Australia	

Order	Family	Common name/ examples	No. of species	Distribution of family	General characteristics of order
	Drepanidinae	Hawaiian honeycreepers	23	Hawaiian Islands	
	Estrildidae	Waxbills	124	Africa, S Asia, Australia	

Subfamilies of the family Ploceidae

	Ploceinae	True weavers	95	Africa, S Asia	
	Viduinae	Widow birds	10	Sub-Saharan Africa	
	Bubalornithinae	Buffalo weavers	3	Sub-Saharan Africa	
	Passerinae	Sparrow weavers; sparrows	37	Africa, Eurasia	
	Sturnidae	Starlings	106	Africa, Eurasia, Australia, New Zealand	
	Oriolidae	Orioles; figbirds	28	Africa, Eurasia, Australia	
	Dicruridae	Drongos	20	Sub-Saharan Africa, S Asia, N and E Australia	
	Callaeidae	New Zealand wattlebirds	3	New Zealand	
	Grallinidae	Magpie larks	2	Australia	
	Corcoracidae	Australian mudnesters	2	E Australia	
	Artamidae	Wood swallows	10	SE Asia, Australia	
	Cracticidae	Bell magpies	9	New Guinea, Australia	
	Ptilonorhynch-idae	Bowerbirds	18	New Guinea, Australia	
	Paradisaeidae	Birds of paradise	43	New Guinea, Australia	
	Corvidae	Crows; magpies; jays	113	Worldwide	

Incubation and fledgling periods

Bird family	Incubation period (days)	Fledgling period (days)
Hole nesters		
Bee-eaters	20	23
Hornbills	35	46
Kingfishers	22	29
Owls	30	30
Rollers	18	28
Swifts	20	44
Open nesters		
Anis	13	11
Cuckoos	12	22
Passerines	13	13
Pigeons	15	17
Turacos	17	28
Seabirds		
Wandering albatross	78	280
Fulmar	49	49
Gannet	44	90
King penguin	53	360
Adelie penguin	33	51
Giant petrel	59	108
Storm petrel	41	63
Shag	30	53
Common tern	23	30
Sandwich tern	23	35

Wingspans

Common name (Latin name)	Length	
	(m)	(ft)
Wandering albatross (*Diomedea exulans*)	3.5	11.5
Marabou stork (*Leptoptilos dubius*)	3.3	11.0
Andean condor (*Vultur gryphus*)	3.2	10.5
White pelican (*Pelicanus onocrotalus*)	3.1	10.0
Lammergeier (*Gypaetus barbatus*)	2.7	9.0
Mute swan (*Cygnus olor*)	2.3	7.5
Crane (*Grus grus*)	2.3	7.5
Golden eagle (*Aquila chrysaetos*)	2.2	7.2
White stork (*Ciconia ciconia*)	2.1	7.0
Grey heron (*Ardea cinerea*)	1.9	6.0
Northern gannet (*Sulla bassana*)	1.8	5.9
Canada goose (*Branta canadensis*)	1.8	5.9
Greater flamingo (*Phoenicopterus ruber*)	1.65	5.4
Herring gull (*Larus argentatus*)	1.6	5.2
Osprey (*Pandion haliaetus*)	1.6	5.2
Barn owl (*Tyto alba*)	0.9	3.0

NATURAL HISTORY

Life-history features

Species	Maximum recorded age (years)	Annual adult mortality (%)	Age of first breeding (years)	No. of eggs	Body weight (g)	Body weight (oz)
Blue tit	10	70	1	12–14	11	0.4
European robin	13	52	1	4–6	18	0.6
Song sparrow	8	44	1	4–6	30	1.0
House sparrow	12	50	1	3–6	30	1.0
European starling	20	50	1–2	4–6	80	3.0
American robin	10	48	1	4–6	100	3.5
European blackbird	20	42	1	3–5	80–110	3.0–4.0
Barn swallow	16	63	1	4–6	20	0.7
Common swift	21	15	2	2–3	36–50	1.0–2.0
Tawny owl	18	26	2	2–4	680–750	24.0–26.5
Mourning dove	17	55	1	2	140	5.0
Woodpigeon	16	36	1	2	450–550	16.0–19.0
Atlantic puffin	22	5	4	1	350–550	12.0–19.0
Black-legged kittiwake	21	14	4–5	2–3	300–500	10.5–17.5
Herring gull	36	6	3–5	3	750–1 250	26.5–44.0
Curlew	32	26	2	4	575–800	20.0–28.0
Redshank	17	31	1–2	4	110–155	4.0–5.5
Lapwing	23	32	1–2	4	200–300	7.0–10.5
Avocet	25	22	2–3	4	250–400	9.0–14.0
Pheasant	8	58	1–2	8–15	900–1 400	32.0–49.0
Kestrel	17	34	1–2	4–6	190–240	6.5–8.5
Buzzard	26	19	2–3	2–4	550–1 200	19.0–42.0
Osprey	32	18	2–3	2–3	1 200–2 000	42.0–71.0
Mallard	29	48	1–2	9–13	850–1 400	30.0–49.0
Tufted duck	15	46	1–2	8–11	550–900	19.0–32.0
Eider	18	20	2–3	4–6	1 200–2 800	42.0–99.0
Barnacle goose	23	9	3	3–5	1 400–1 600	49.0–56.5
Mute swan	22	10	3–4	5–8	10 000–12 000	353.0–424.0
Grey heron	25	30	2	4–5	1 600–2 000	56.5–71
White stork	26	21	3–5	3–5	3 000–3 500	106.0–123.5
Shag	21	16	3–4	3–4	1 750–2 250	62.0–79.0
Short-tailed shearwater	31	5	5–8	1	530	19.0
Royal albatross	36	3	8–10	1	8 300	293.0
Yellow-eyed penguin	18	10	2–4	2	5 200	183.5

Reptiles

Order	Family	Common name/ examples	No. of species	Distribution	General characteristics of order
Chelonia	Dermatemydidae	Central American river turtle	1	C America, Mexico	Aquatic and terrestrial reptiles – turtles, terrapins and tortoises. These have a rigid body shell comprising a dorsal carapace and a ventral plastron, into which most species draw their head and legs for protection. The jaws are beaked, without teeth.
	Chelydridae	Common and alligator snapping turtles	2	N and S America	
	Kinosternidae	Mud and musk turtles	21	Tropical regions	
	Testudinidae	Tortoises	40	All continents except Australia	
	Platysternidae	Big-headed turtle	1	SE Asia	
	Emydidae	Common turtle	76	Abundant in northern hemisphere	
	Cheloniidae	Sea turtles	5	Worldwide	
	Dermochelyidae	Leatherback turtle	1	Worldwide	
	Carettochelyidae	New Guinea plateless turtle	1	New Guinea	
	Trionychidae	Soft-shell turtles	20	All continents except S America and Australia	
	Pelomedusidae	Side-necked turtles	14	Africa, S America	

Order	Family	Common name/ examples	No. of species	Distribution	General characteristics of order
	Chelyidae	Snake-necked turtles	31	Australia, S America	
Rhynchocephalia	Sphenodontidae	Tuatara	1	New Zealand	Primitive nocturnal reptile, feeds on snails, worms, occasionally small lizards and birds.
Squamata (Sub-order Sauria)	Gekkonidae	Geckos	650	Worldwide	The Squamata are a large and very diverse order comprising three suborders, Sauria (lizards), Serpentes or Ophidia (snakes), and Amphis-baenia (worm lizards). This order contains the great majority of living reptiles. Lizards vary in size from a few centi-metres (some geckos) to about 3 m/10 ft in length (the Komodo dragon). They feed as herbivores, insect-ivores or as predators of small vertebrates. The skull is made up of several separate mobile elements (a form of modification known as cranial kinesis). Limbs may be reduced in burrowing forms.
	Pygopodidae	Flap-footed lizards	15	Australia, New Guinea	
	Dibamidae	Burrowers	3	Philippines, Vietnam, New Guinea	
	Iguanidae	Iguanas	600	N and S America, W Indies, Galapagos, Fiji, Madagascar	
	Agamidae	Agamid lizard	300	Tropical regions worldwide	
	Chameleontidae	Old World chameleons	85	Africa, W Asia, India	
	Scincidae	Skinks	800	Worldwide except polar regions	
	Cordylidae	Girdle-tailed lizards	50	S Africa, Madagascar	
	Lacertidae	Old World terrestrial lizards	150	Europe, Asia, Africa	
	Teiidae	Whiptail lizards	200	Tropical regions	
	Anguidae	Glass lizards; alligator lizards; galliwasps	67	Americas	
	Anniellidae	California legless lizards	2	California	
	Xenosauridae		4	Mexico, China	
	Helodermatidae	Gila monster lizard; bearded lizard	2	N America, Mexico	
	Varanidae	Monitor lizards	30	Tropical regions	
	Lanthanotidae	Earless monitor lizard	1	Borneo	
	Xantusiidae	Night lizards	12	C America, Cuba	
(Sub-order Serpentes)	Typhlopidae	Blind snakes; worm snakes	200	Tropical regions	Snakes have no limbs, have long, cylindrical scaly bodies, lidless eyes and highly mobile jaws (cranial kinesis). They eat animals (or eggs), killing by suffocation, by biting, or by venom, and cannot chew. They moult their skin several times each year.
	Letotyphlopidae	Slender blind snakes	40	N and S America, SW Asia, Africa	
	Xenopeltidae	Sunbeam snake	1	India	
	Uropeltidae	Shieldtail snakes	50	S Asia	
	Boidae	Pythons; boas; woodsnakes	60	Tropical regions	
	Acrochordidae	Wart snakes	2	Australia, E Indies, SE Asia	
	Colubridae	Terrestrial, arboreal and aquatic snakes	>1500	Worldwide	
	Viperidae	Vipers; rattlesnakes; moccasins	180	Europe, Asia, Africa, not Australia	
	Elapidae	Cobras; mambas; coral snakes	170	Asia, Africa, N and S America	
	Hydrophiidae	Sea snakes	50	Indian and Pacific oceans	

NATURAL HISTORY

Reptiles (continued)

Order	Family	Common name/examples	No. of species	Distribution	General characteristics of order
(Sub-order Amphisbaenia)	Amphisbaenidae	Worm lizards	100	Africa, C and S America, SE Asia and Seychelle Islands	Small, limbless burrowing lizards with concealed eyes and wedge-shaped skulls to aid with digging. They eat small animals.
Crocodilia	Alligatoridae	Alligators; caiman	7	S America, Africa, Asia, Australia	Small to very large (7 m/23 ft) carnivorous, amphibious reptiles. Heavy cylindrical body armoured with bony plates; elongated snout; webbed toes; powerful tail; mainly nocturnal.
	Crocodilidae	True crocodile	13		
	Gavialidae	Gavial or gharial	1	India	

Amphibians

Order	Family	Common name/examples	No. of species	Distribution	General characteristics of order
Trachystomata		Sirens	3	N America	Aquatic, eel-like amphibians; no hindlimbs; forelimbs tiny; without external eyes or ears.
Gymnophiona		Caecilians	160	C and S America, Africa, SE Asia, Seychelle Islands	Caecilians are limbless, worm-like subterranean amphibians with annuli (rings) along length of body.
Urodela or Caudata	Hynobiidae	Asiatic salamanders	30	N Asia (from Ural Mountains to Japan and Taiwan)	The tailed amphibians salamanders and newts. Adults aquatic or terrestrial, occasionally arboreal; eggs and larvae primitively aquatic. Feed on slow-moving invertebrates (worms, slugs and snails).
	Cryptobranchidae	Giant salamanders; hellbenders	3	N America, China and Japan	
	Sirenidae	Sirens; dwarf sirens	3	SE United States, Mexico	
	Proteidae	Olm	1	Balkan peninsula	
	Necturidae	Mud puppies	5	N America	
	Amphiumidae	Congo eels	3	SE United States	
	Salamandridae	Salamanders and newts	42	Europe, N Africa, Middle East, S Asia, N America	
	Ambystomatidae	Mole salamanders; axolotl	33	N America	
	Plethodontidae	Lungless salamanders	210	Americas, S Europe	
Anura	Leiopelmatidae	Primitive frogs	4	New Zealand, N America	The frogs and toads. Tail absent; hindlimbs enlarged for jumping. Adults aquatic or terrestrial, occasionally arboreal or burrowing. Eggs
	Discoglossidae	Fire-bellied toads; midwife toads	8	Europe, Asia, N America, Philippines	
	Rhinophrynidae	Burrowing toad	1	C America	
	Pipidae	Tongueless frogs	14	Africa, S America	

Order	Family	Common name/ examples	No. of species	Distribution	General characteristics of order
	Pelobatidea	Spadefoots	59	Europe, Asia, N America, Australia	and larvae (tadpoles) typically aquatic, but reproductive
	Myobatrachidae	Terrestrial, arboreal and aquatic frogs	95	New Guinea, Australia, South Africa	strategies vary. Largely insectivorous. (Smooth wet-skinned
	Rhinodermatidae	Mouth-breeding frog	1	S America	species of Anura are
	Leptodactylidae	Terrestrial neotropical frogs	650	Americas, Caribbean	usually known as frogs, rough dry-
	Bufonidae	True toads	235	Worldwide	skinned species as
	Brachycephalidae	Terrestrial toads	2	Brazil	toads, but there is no
	Dendrobatidae	Arrow-poison frogs	70	C and S America	technical difference
	Pseudidae	Fully aquatic frogs	5	S America	between the two.)
	Centrolenidae	Leaf frogs	60	C and S America	
	Hylidae	Tree frogs	400	Worldwide	
	Ranidae	True frogs	850	Worldwide	
	Sooglossidae	Terrestrial frogs	3	Seychelle Islands	
	Microhylidae	Narrow-mouthed frogs	230	Africa, Asia, N and S America, Australia	

Fishes

There have been many different systems of fish classification, and today there is still much debate about taxonomy. Most systems divide the world of fishes into three: the jawless fishes, the cartilaginous fishes and the bony fishes. This table lists some of the best-known types of fish.

Order	Common name/ examples	No. of species	Distribution	General characteristics of order
Class Agnatha (jawless fishes)				
Cyclostomata	Lampreys	30	Cool, fresh, and coastal waters of all continents, except Africa	Eel-shaped body; well-developed dorsal and caudal fins; horny teeth; feed on the blood of other fishes; only breed in fresh water.
	Hagfishes	30	Cold, marine bottom waters; equatorial oceans	soft-skinned; nearly cylindrical; eyes vestigial, covered by skin; feed on dead or moribund fishes or invertebrates; locate food by scent; only breed in marine water.
Class Chondrichthyes (fishes with a cartilage skeleton)				
Selachii	Sharks	>200	Tropical and temperate zones; particularly New Zealand, S Africa	Large group of predatory fishes belonging to nineteen separate families; streamlined bodies; highly sensitive sense of smell; attacks on humans very rare, usually occur in water warmer than 21°C (70°F); an exception, however, is the white shark, which is also the most dangerous; others include hammerheads (very mobile using rudder effect of head), tiger and sand sharks; largest are the whale and basking sharks.

NATURAL HISTORY

Fishes (continued)

Order	Common name/ examples	No. of species	Distribution	General characteristics of order
Batoidei	Rays; skates; stingrays	>300	All oceans from tropical to temperate latitudes	Bottom dwellers, preying on other animals on sea floor; differ externally from sharks having gill openings confined to lower surface; eyes on dorsal surface; many armed with thorns, tubercles or prickles; stingrays live in shallow, coastal waters; if provoked, will lash back their tails; electric rays are sluggish, stun invertebrates and fishes by shocks produced from electric organs. Skates lie on bottom, often partially buried; rise in pursuit of prey, particularly herring; trap victims by swimming over them and settling upon them; their egg cases ('mermaid's purses') are often washed ashore.

Class Osteichthyes (fishes with a bony skeleton)

Order	Common name/ examples	No. of species	Distribution	General characteristics of order
Dipnoi	Lungfishes	6	Freshwater; Australia, Africa, N America	Voracious, eating aquatic animals, including own species; most grow to substantial size; sac-shaped, pneumatic organs that lie along alimentary tract, whose structure and function are like primitive lungs of amphibians.
Acipenseriformes	Sturgeons	25	Marine and freshwater; Europe, Asia, N America	Braincase mostly cartilaginous; ground feeding by dragging tactile, whisker-like barbels over bottom; toothless mouth with protractile lips surrounded by taste buds; food fish for humans, source of caviar.
	Paddlefishes	2	Marine and freshwater; China and N America	Braincase mostly cartilaginous; feed by straining plankton through gill system; elongated, paddle-shaped snout composed entirely of cartilage, measuring one-third of the total body length.
Polypteriformes	Bichirs or reedfishes	11	Tropical swamps and rivers in C Africa	Inhabit edges of streams and flood plains, concealed by day, forage for worms, insect larvae, small fishes by night.
Elopiformes	Bonefishes	4	Coastal and deep waters of warm oceans	Specialized bottom feeders; grubs with snout for worms and shellfish which they crush with rounded palatal teeth.
	Tarpons	2	Warm coastal waters Atlantic	Fast-swimming predator; swim bladder lung-like, partially compartmented, highly vascularized; obligate air breathers, can die from asphyxiation if prevented from reaching surface.
	Ladyfish	6	Warm coastal waters circumtropical	Fast-swimming predators; appear to 'roll' at sea surface apparently for intake of air; open duct to swim bladder when air is taken through mouth.

Order	Common name/ examples	No. of species	Distribution	General characteristics of order
Anguilliformes	Eels	>500	Marine and freshwater; of Europe and N America; some in shallow water or deep sea	Elongate, cylindrical body form; carnivorous until maturity; morays and congers inhabit rock crevices, others form vast colonies of individuals in tropical reef areas; return to sea to spawn.
Clupeiformes	Herrings	190	Virtually worldwide in marine waters, and in many bodies of freshwater	Teeth usually absent or weakly developed; single schools of herring estimated to include many millions.
	Anchovies	200	Widespread in surface coastal waters of tropical and temperate seas; a few anadromous (returning to fresh water to spawn)	Snout projects beyond very wide mouth; upper and lower jaws usually armed with rows of minute teeth; found in large schools, some spreading over 100 m/330 ft, contracting to writhing sphere of thousands of fishes only a few metres across at approach of a predator.
Osteoglossiformes	Bony tongues	6	Freshwater; rivers and lakes, turbid waters or regions with dense aquatic vegetation	Strongly-toothed jaws; large mouth; well-developed swim bladder; some species, upper portion of ear (for balance) completely separated from lower part (for hearing).
	Freshwater butterfly fish	1	Freshwater; Africa	Greatly expanded wing-like pectoral fins (behind gills) which are used for short flights to the air, either to escape predators or to catch insects.
Salmoniformes	Salmons; trouts; chars; smelts; graylings; whitefishes	150	Widespread, marine or freshwater. Salmon common in N Atlantic; return to freshwater to breed	Trim, fusiform body; powerful caudal (tail) muscles; commonly migrate upstream to spawn; very important food fishes.
	Pikes; mudminnows	10	Freshwater; northern hemisphere	Long bodies; dorsal and anal fins positioned posteriorly, adipose fin absent.
Ostariophysi	Carps; minnows; barbs; suckers; loaches	3 500	Fresh to brackish waters: Africa, S and C America, Eurasia	Small to medium-sized fishes; upper jaw protractile, jaw teeth usually absent. Body covered in scales.
	Catfishes	2 500	Low saline, brackish freshwater or marine	Order of small to very large freshwater fishes; oral incubation of eggs by some species; most active at night or under conditions of reduced light.
Characiformes	Tetras; darters; piranhas	>1 300	Freshwater: S and C America, Africa	Mostly small, colourful fishes; upper jaw projectile, jaws bearing teeth; of prime importance in aquarium trade.
Paracanthopterygii	Toadfishes	45	Primarily marine, mainly tropical and temperate shallow waters along continental coasts; occasionally freshwater	Generally have two dorsal fins; nine venomous species restricted to coast and rivers of C and S America.
	Trout-perches	8	All freshwater; N America	Live under conditions of dim light; can be found in clear water of the Great Lakes at depths of about 64 m/210 ft.
	Codfishes	800	Primarily marine, shallow-water, some deep-sea types, worldwide distribution; particularly N Atlantic	Largest of order, growing to about 2 m/6.5 ft in length and attain weights that may exceed 90 kg/200 lb; migrate over long distances, gathering in late winter and early spring to spawn, each species goes to particular area.

NATURAL HISTORY

Fishes (continued)

Order	Common name/ examples	No. of species	Distribution	General characteristics of order
Atheriniformes	Flying fishes	50	Surface marine waters, worldwide	Surface fishes of the open ocean where they breed; capable of leaping or skipping on surface to escape predators; tail (caudal) fin usually asymmetrical, lower lobes longer than body so while out of water lower lobe vibrates as a scull driving fish along.
	Needlefishes; garfishes	25	Mostly temperate and tropical marine; a few freshwater	Pelagic (inhabiting the open ocean); predatory habit highly developed; long, formidable toothed jaws elongated into strong-toothed beak; breed near shore.
	Cyprinodonts	500	Tropical and subtropical distribution, including hot springs of Africa and America	Diminutive; many important as experimental animals in biological research; among hardiest of fishes, some surviving in rigorous environments, including water temperatures in hot springs approaching coagulation point of protoplasm.
Gasterosteiformes	Sticklebacks	11	Fresh, brackish, and marine waters of northern hemisphere	Small, scaleless fishes; short jaws armed with sharp teeth; body more nearly fusiform (tapered at both ends).
	Tube snout	1	NE Pacific Ocean	Elongated, slender, cylindrical body, tipped by prolonged snout; small toothed mouth has hinged upper jaw; scale-less body armoured with series of embedded bony plates.
	Sea horses	24	Widely distributed; marine	Bony rings instead of scales; use coiled tail to grip seaweed and other plants/objects; propulsion by means of dorsal fin (midline of back); tiny pectoral fin used for steering; rise or settle to another depth by changing air volume within the bladder.
Scorpaeniformes	Scorpion fishes; rockfishes; redfishes; turkeyfishes; gunards	330	Tropical, temperate, and northern seas	Live on coral or rocky bottom; many possess remarkable degree of concealing coloration and shape; dorsal fin spines long and numerous; head spiny; body scaly; some with venom glands on fin spines.
Perciformes				The largest group of fishes, comprising about 7000 species in 150 families.
	Perches	125	Freshwater temperate species	Possess numerous short, fine, pointed teeth; prefer quiet waters; pike-perches semi-migratory, prefer quiet, running waters.

Order	Common name/ examples	No. of species	Distribution	General characteristics of order
	Tunas	40	Open waters of tropics and warm seas of world	May travel across entire Pacific Ocean from California coast to Japan, or reverse, to spawn; one of the larger predatory perciforms; carnivorous; well-developed vascular system under skin, associated with sustained high-speed swimming and a body temperature a few degrees higher than surrounding water.
	Marlins	7	Worldwide in warm seas	Greatest game fishes of the ocean; black marlin is the largest at 900 kg/2 000 lb.
Pleuronectiformes	Flatfishes	2	Indo-Pacific and Africa	Asymmetrical; found in depths up to 1 000 m/3 300 feet, most occur on continental shelf in less than 200 m/650 ft of water; swim by undulating movement of body and fins; lie on bottom, generally covered by sand or mud, with only eyes protruding; eyes can be raised, lowered and moved independently.
	Flounders	300+	Marine and freshwater, tropic and temperate seas	Either right-eyed (dextral) or left-eyed (sinistral); asymmetrical; feed primarily on crustaceans, other bottom invertebrates and small fish; when feeding lie motionless and then pounce on close prey.
	Soles	100+	Tropic and temperate seas, some freshwater	Asymmetrical; strongly compressed; eyes, usually small, on one side (dextral); mouth curved downward; caudal fin with numerous rays.
Tetraodontiformes	Box fishes	25	Prominent around coral reefs, open sand and grassy flats; worldwide	Carapace closed behind anal and usually behind dorsal fin; no ventral keel; blow jet of water out of mouth onto sand bottom to expose burrowing invertebrates.
	Puffer fishes	7	Prominent around coral reefs, open sand and grassy flats; worldwide	Poisonous flesh, at least during certain seasons of year; most of highly poisonous substance contained in viscera; flesh can be eaten if professionally cleaned.
	Ocean sunfishes	3	Prominent around coral reefs, open sand and grassy flats; tropical and subtropical oceans worldwide	Massive, crushing jaws and teeth; feed extensively on soft-bodied invertebrates, such as jellyfishes.

Insects

Order	Common name/ examples	No. of species	Distribution	General characteristics of order
Collembola	Springtails	2 000	Worldwide	Blind, primitively wingless insects with entognathous mouthparts (ie contained within an invagination of the head). They leap by means of a forked springing organ on the underside of the abdomen.
Diplura	Diplurans	660	Worldwide	Small, slender, blind, whitish insects, with entognathous mouthparts; found in damp soil, under logs and stones.

NATURAL HISTORY

Insects (continued)

Order	Common name/ examples	No. of species	Distribution	General characteristics of order
Protura	Proturans	120	Worldwide	Primitively wingless; white; blind; no antennae; reduced mouthparts; found under bark, stones or rotting vegetation.
Thysanura	Bristletails; silverfish	600	Worldwide	Primitive wingless insects found amongst decaying wood etc, in human habitations, and in association with ants and termites; feed on fungi, lichens, algae, pollen, or decaying vegetable matter.
Ephemeroptera	Mayflies	2000	Worldwide, except Antarctica	Some species carnivorous, but majority are herbivorous. Life cycle consists of four stages. Nymph can live for 2 weeks to 2 years; the adults are winged and non-feeding, living from 2 to 72 hours, during which time they mate.
Odonata	Dragonflies; damselflies	5000	Worldwide	Carnivorous, often brightly coloured; aquatic larvae; adults have powerful predatory mouthparts and two pairs of richly veined wings. Larvae feed on aquatic larvae, tadpoles, worms, and small fishes; adults on flying insects.
Orthoptera	Grasshoppers; locusts; crickets	24000	Worldwide	Wings, when present, number four; chewing mouthparts; mostly plant feeders. Hindlimbs usually specialized for jumping; many species produce sounds by rubbing together forewings. Of immense economic importance.
Phasmida (Phasmoptera)	Stick insects; leaf insects	2500	Tropical areas	Arboreal; nocturnal; feed on plant juices; camouflage and mimicry highly developed.
Blattaria	Cockroaches	3700	Worldwide	Depressed body; long legs; forewings hard or leathery; hindwings membranous, but may be reduced or absent. Typically live on the ground, under stones, or in litter and wood debris. Some are household pests.
Embioptera	Webspinners	200	Tropical regions	Inhabit extensive galleries or labyrinths of silk on bark, litter, moss, lichens, or within the soil. Body slender; legs short; females and some males wingless.
Zoraptera	Zorapterans	20	Tropical regions	Tiny insects resembling slender termites.
Dermaptera	Earwigs	1500	Worldwide	Feed as scavengers or predators with large pincers variously used for predation, defence, courtship, and grooming. Wings frequently reduced or absent.
Mantodea	Mantids; mantises	1800	Tropical and subtropical areas	Predatory insects in which body shape is highly adapted for camouflage; head very mobile, eyes large; in some species female eats male headfirst during copulation.
Isoptera	Termites or white ants	2000	Europe, Australia, Asia, N America	Cellulose-eating, social insects that construct nests which vary in size from a few centimetres to several metres. Caste system includes morphologically distinct soldiers and workers.
Phthiraptera	Sucking lice (Anoplura); biting lice (Mallophaga); booklice and barklice (Psocoptera)	3400	Worldwide	Parasites of birds or mammals; eyes reduced or absent; reduced antennae; mouthparts mandibulate or piercing.

Order	Common name	No. of species	Distribution	General characteristics of order
Thysanoptera	Thrips	5 000	Tropical regions	Fringed wings, bristles on body wall; mouthparts specialized for piercing and sucking. Feed on plant juices, fungi, spores, pollen, or body fluids of other arthropods. Some species hibernate in winter in cold climates.
Homoptera	Cicadas; hoppers; whiteflies; aphids; scale insects	45 000	Worldwide	Plant feeders with mouth parts adapted for sucking plant sap; wings number two or four when present. Many are crop pests.
Hemiptera	True bugs	35 000	Worldwide	Sucking mouthparts adapted to pierce plant or animal tissue; most species terrestrial, a few aquatic; well-developed compound eyes; scent glands usually present. Many are crop pests.
Neuroptera	Alderflies; dobsonflies (Megaloptera); lacewings (Plannipennia); snakeflies (Raphidiodea)	4 500	Worldwide	Biting mouthparts; two pairs of similar wings. Alderflies and dobsonflies have aquatic larvae. Snakeflies arboreal, characterized by elongate and highly mobile thorax.
Trichoptera	Caddisflies	7 000	Worldwide	Moth-like; wings covered with hairs; long antennae; large compound eyes; larvae almost exclusively aquatic.
Lepidoptera	Butterflies; moths; skippers	138 000	Worldwide	Two pairs of wings, covered by dustlike scales; four stages of life; day-flying; herbivorous; complete metamorphosis occurs (larvae are caterpillars). Adults typically with slender, coiled, sucking proboscis.
Coleoptera	Beetles; weevils	250 000	Worldwide	Two pairs of wings, front pair modified into horny covers; antennae variable; large compound eyes; mouthparts adapted for chewing; hard outer skeleton; complete metamorphosis.
Hymenoptera	Ants; bees; sawflies; wasps	130 000	Worldwide except polar regions	Pollinators of wild and cultivated flowering plants; some species have complex social organization; complete metamorphosis; four membranous wings; mouthparts adapted for chewing and sucking; larvae usually maggot-like.
Strepsiptera	Stylopids	400	Worldwide	Parasites of other insects; male winged, female wingless and larvae-like.
Mecoptera	Scorpion flies	450	Mostly tropical, subtropical areas	Inhabit moist forests feeding on nectar or preying on other insects.
Diptera	True flies	150 000	Worldwide	Forewings membranous, hindwings modified as minute club-like balancing organs (halteres). Feed on plant and animal juices or other insects; two wings; sucking mouthparts; some pupae aquatic. Many are disease vectors, though many are also beneficial as pollinators.
Siphonaptera	Fleas	1 750	Worldwide	Wingless; parasitic; mouthparts adapted to piercing and sucking; larvae elongated and often enclosed in cocoons. Feed mainly on mammals, but also some birds. Disease vectors.

PLANTS

Classification of plants

Phylum	Common name/examples	No. of species	Comments
Bryophyta	Liverworts (*Hepaticae*); hornworts (*Anthocerotae*); mosses (*Musci*)	24 000	Small plants living in moist habitats (their sperm must swim through water to reach their eggs). Reproduce by spores.
Psilophyta	Whiskferns	12	Simple vascular plants lacking true roots and, in some species, leaves. Reproduce by spores.
Lycopodophyta	Club mosses	1 000	Small, terrestrial or epiphytic (ie grow on other plants); needle or scale-like leaves arranged spirally on stem. Reproduce by spores.
Sphenophyta or Equisetophyta	Horsetails; scouring rushes	20	Primarily found in moist, muddy habitats; stems creeping underground and producing erect annual or perennial stems with tiny leaves whorled into sheaves around stem. Jointed hollow stems and rough, ribbed texture caused by the mineral silica. Reproduce by spores.
Filicinophyta or Pteridophyta	Ferns	12 000	Vascular plants which reproduce by spores; stems mostly creeping, large leaves (megaphylls) with branching veins. The most complex, diverse and abundant of the plant phyla that do not form seeds.
Cycadophyta	Cycads	100	Evergreen perennial shrubs or trees with stems that are usually unbranched but thickened by some secondary growth. Palm-like or fern-like compound leaves; they contain symbiotic cyanobacteria in special roots.
Ginkgophyta	Ginkgo; maidenhair tree	1	Native to China but cultivated worldwide, the ginkgo is a tall tree with deciduous fan-shaped leaves; the only living descendant of a once-large group.
Coniferophyta or Pinatae	Conifers	550	By far the most familiar of the gymnosperms (plants having naked seeds); usually evergreen shrubs or trees with simple needle-like leaves, spirally arranged. Commercially important for timber, pulp, turpentine, and resin products.
Gnetophyta	Gnetophytes (cone-bearing desert plants)	70	Cone-bearing desert plants. Resemble flowering plants in many ways; were once thought to be a link between conifers and angiosperms.
Angiospermophyta or Magnoliophyta	Angiosperms; flowering plants	>230 000	The dominant land vegetation of the Earth, including nearly every familiar tree, shrub, or garden plant that produces flowers and seeds. Characterized by the aggregation of sexual reproductive structures with specialized shoots (flowers), which typically comprise four kinds of modified leaves: sepals, petals, stamens (male organs), and carpels (female organs).

World vegetation map

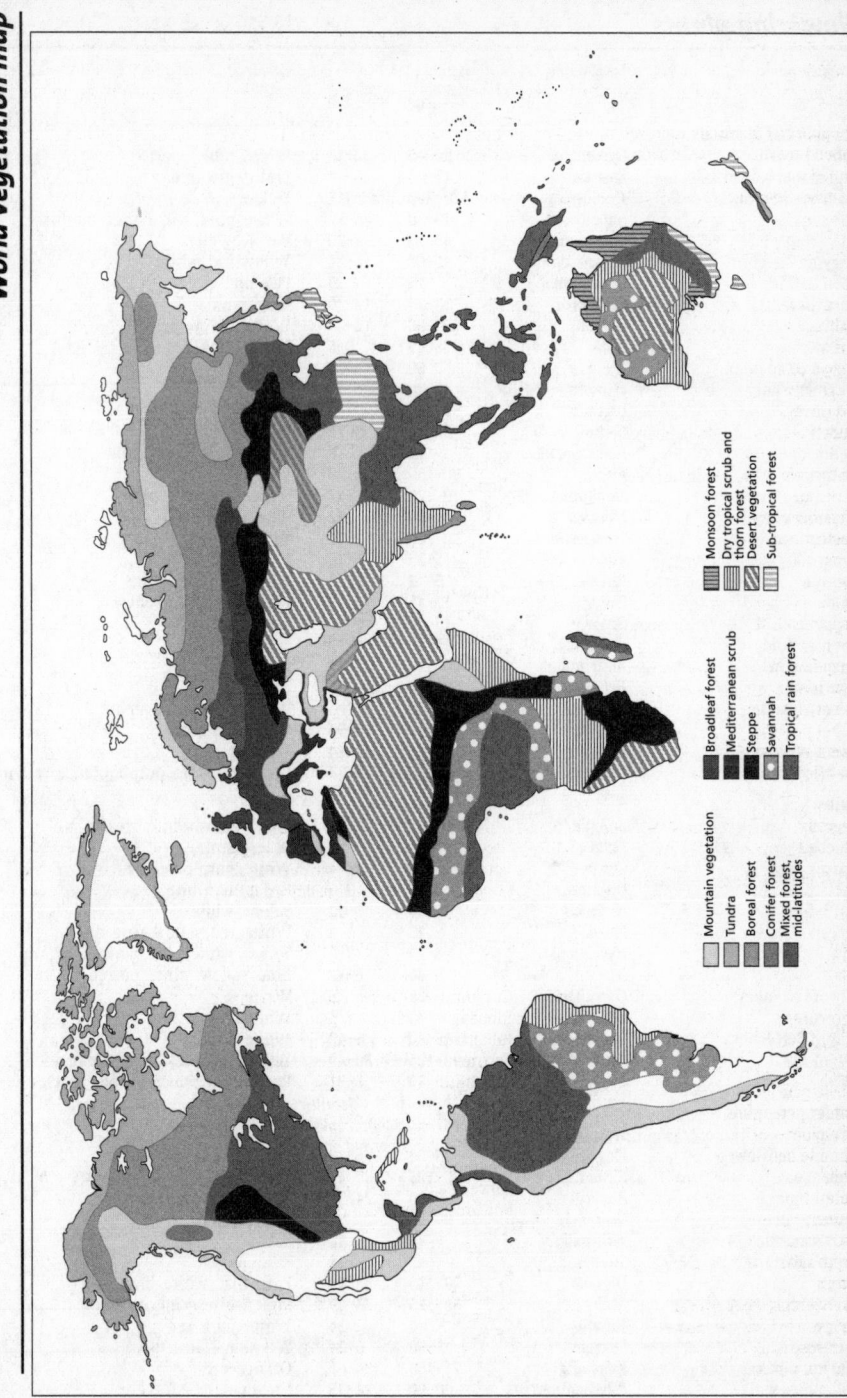

Mountain vegetation
Tundra
Boreal forest
Conifer forest
Mixed forest, mid-latitudes

Broadleaf forest
Mediterranean scrub
Steppe
Savannah
Tropical rain forest

Monsoon forest
Dry tropical scrub and thorn forest
Desert vegetation
Sub-tropical forest

NATURAL HISTORY

Flowering plants

Common name	Latin name	Height (cm)	Height (in)	Colour
Annuals and biennials				
Baby's breath	Gypsophila	30–45	12–18	White, pink
Begonia	Begonia	15–45	6–18	Pink, white, red
Black-eyed Susan	Thunbergia	120–300	47–118	Yellow
Busy Lizzie	Impatiens	15–30	6–12	White, pink, red, orange, mauve
Canterbury bell	Campanula	45–75	18–30	Purple, white
Chrysanthemum	Chrysanthemum	45–60	18–24	Yellow, red, white
Corn cockle	Agrostemma	75	30	Pale lilac
Cornflower	Centaurea	30–75	12–30	Blue, pink
Dahlia	Dahlia	30–60	12–24	White, red, yellow
Daisy	Bellis	8–15	3–6	White, pink, red
Flower of an hour	Hibiscus	60	24	Cream
Forget-me-not	Myosotis	15–30	6–12	Blue
Foxglove	Digitalis	90–150	35–59	Purple
Godetia	Godetia	20–60	8–24	Pink, orange
Heliotrope	Heliotropium	45	18	White, dark blue, purple
Hollyhock	Althea	90–150	35–59	Pink
Larkspur	Delphinium	30–120	12–47	White, pink, red, blue
Morning glory	Ipomoea	180–360	71–142	Blue, purple, red
Nasturtium	Tropaeolum	30–180	12–71	Yellow, orange
Pansy	Viola	15–25	6–10	Violet, yellow
Petunia	Petunia	15–45	6–18	Pink, red ,blue, white
Phlox	Phlox	15–45	6–18	Pink, red, white, yellow
Poppy	Papaver	15–90	6–35	Red, pink, white
Pot marigold	Calendula	15–30	6–12	Yellow, orange
Snapdragon	Antirrhinum	90–120	35–47	Crimson, scarlet
Sunflower	Helianthus	60–300	24–118	Yellow
Sweet alyssum	Alyssum	8–15	3–6	White, purple, lilac, pink
Sweet pea	Lathyrus	30–240	12–94	Orange, crimson
Sweet William	Dianthus	30–60	12–24	White, red
Wallflower	Cheiranthus	20–60	8–24	Crimson, white, purple, orange, cream
Bulbs				
Begonia	Begonia	30–45	12–18	Pink, yellow, white, cream
Bluebell	Scilla	8	3	Blue, purple
Crocus	Crocus	8–10	3–4	White, purple, yellow
Cyclamen	Cyclamen	8–15	3–6	Red, pink, white
Daffodil	Narcissus	15–30	6–12	Yellow, white
Freesia	Freesia	15	6	White, red, yellow, pale blue
Hyacinth	Hyacinthus	8–15	3–6	Yellow, white, blue, pink, violet, red
Iris	Iris	15–30	6–12	Blue, yellow, white, purple
Lily of the valley	Convallaria	20	8	White
Snowdrop	Galanthus	13	5	White
Star of Bethlehem	Ornithogalum	15–30	6–12	White
Sword lily	Gladiolus	90–125	35–49	Yellow, red, pink, peach, orange
Tulip	Tulipa	20–80	8–31	Red, yellow, white, purple, peach
Border perennials				
Campion	Lychnis	90	35	Red, pink
Chinese bellflower	Platycodon	15–30	6–12	White, pink, pale blue
Clematis	Clematis	90–125	35–49	Blue, white
Columbine	Aquilegia	60–90	24–35	Yellow, red, blue
Crane's-bill	Geranium	45	18	Violet, pink
Lady's mantle	Alchemilla	45	18	Yellow
Lamb's ear	Stachys	45	18	Lilac, pink
Lupin	Lupinus	90–125	35–49	Pink, lilac, white, blue
Michaelmas daisy	Aster	60–125	24–49	Pink, white, crimson, blue
Peony	Paeonia	60	24	White, pink, red
Primrose	Primula	15–60	6–24	Yellow, red, lilac
Red hot poker	Kniphofia	75–155	30–61	Orange-red
Solomon's seal	Polygonatum	60–90	24–35	Cream
Speedwell	Veronica	45–155	18–61	Blue, pink, white
Violet	Viola	10–15	4–6	Violet, white, lilac, pink

Shrubs

Common name	Latin name	Height (cm)	(in)	Colour
Azalea	*Rhododendron*	180	71	Pink, red, white, yellow
Bay laurel	*Laurus*	610	240	Yellow
Broom	*Genista*	210	83	Yellow
Butterfly bush	*Buddleia*	250	98	Purple, white, mauve
Camellia	*Camellia*	180–250	71–98	Red, pale pink, white, bright pink
Fatsia	*Fatsia*	300	118	White
Firethorn	*Pyracantha*	370	145	Red, yellow
Fuchsia	*Fuchsia*	180	71	Red
Gorse	*Ulex*	180	71	Yellow
Heather	*Erica*	20–60	8–24	White, purple, yellow
Holly	*Ilex*	1500	590	Red
Honeysuckle	*Lonicera*	210–300	83–118	Pink, cream
Hydrangea	*Hydrangea*	90–150	35–59	Pale blue, white, pink, purple
Japonica	*Chaenomeles*	120–90	47–75	Red, white
Jasmine	*Jasminum*	300	118	Yellow
Lavender	*Lavandula*	90	35	Blue
Lilac	*Syringa*	370	145	Purple, white, lavender, lilac
Magnolia	*Magnolia*	150–610	59–240	White, red
Myrtle	*Myrtus*	300	118	White
Oleaster	*Elaeagnus*	230–300	90–118	White
Periwinkle	*Vinca*	20–5	8–10	White, blue
Rhododendron	*Rhododendron*	180	71	Red, purple, pink, white
Silk tassel bush	*Garrya*	275	108	White
Veronica	*Hebe*	30–300	12–118	Blue, white
Viburnum	*Viburnum*	180–300	71–118	White, pink, red, blue
Winter sweet	*Chimonanthus*	275	108	Yellow

Trees

Common name	Latin name	Varieties	Height (m)	(ft)
Alder	*Alnus*	Common; Italian; golden leaf	20	65
Antarctic beech	*Nothofagus*	False beech	12	39
Ash	*Fraxinus*	Common; raywood; manna	18	59
Avocado	*Persia*	*americana*; *drymifolia*	18	59
Bamboo	*Bambusoidae*	*Dendrocalamus strictus*; *Bambusa arundinacea*	36	118
Baobab	*Andansonia*	*digitata*; *gregorii*	9–12	29–39
Beech	*Fagus*	Dawyck; fern-leaved; weeping; copper; golden	30	98
Birch	*Betula*	Silver; Swedish	10	33
Coconut palm	*Cocus nucifera*	Coconut palm	30	98
Cypress	*Chamaecyparis*	Lawson cypress	30–6	98–118
Elm	*Ulmus*	Wych; Dutch; English; weeping; Chinese	27–36	88–118
False acacia	*Robinia*	*frisia*; *pseudoacacia*	18	59
Flame tree	*Delonix regia*	Flame tree	15	49
Flowering cherries	*Prunus*	Ornamental almond; ornamental plum; ornamental peach; ornamental cherry	6–12	20–39
Flowering crab	*Malus*	John Downie; golden hornet; Japanese; Montreal beauty; profusion; Van Eseltine; *lemoinei*	6–15	20–49
Golden rain	*Laburnum*	Common; scotch; *vosii*	4	13
Gum	*Eucalyptus*	Gum; snow gum	15	49
Handkerchief	*Davidia*	*involucrata*	15	49
Hawthorn	*Crataegus*	*monogyna*; Paul's scarlet; *crusgalli*; *orientalis*; *prunifolia*	4	13
Hazel	*Corylus*	Common; *aurea*, corkscrew; filbert; giant; *purpurea*	3–9	10–29
Honey locust	*Gleditsia*	Sunburst; *elegantissima*	7	23
Hornbeam	*Carpinus*	Common	12	39
Horse chestnut	*Aesculus*	Red; common	18	59
Indian bean	*Catalpa*	Indian bean; *aurea*	6	20
Judas	*Cercis*	Judas; white Judas	4	13

Trees (continued)

Common name	Latin name	Varieties	Height (m)	(ft)
Juniper	Juniperus	communis; virginiana; sabina; chinensis; phoenicea; horizontales; thuinfera	3-6	10-20
Larch	Larix	European; golden	24-30	79-98
Lime	Tilia	Common; large-leaved; American	24-7	79-88
Mango	Mangifera indica	Mango	18	59
Maple	Acer	Field; Norway; purple Norway; sycamore	6-9	20-9
Mountain ash	Sorbus	Rowan; Joseph rock; Swedish whitebeam	15	49
Mulberry	Morus	Black mulberry	6	20
Oak	Quercus	English; sessile; Turkey; red; holm; willow	24	78
Ornamental pear	Pyrus	pendula	6	20
Palm	Palmae	Sugar; cohune; palmyra; silver; coconut; carnaulsa; doum; coco de mer; date; royal; cabbage	20	65
Paulownia	Paulownia	tomentosa	7	23
Pea	Caragana	pendula; dwarf	4	13
Pine	Pinus	Scots; Corsican; Austrian; Monterey	18-36	59-118
Plane	Platanus	London plane	24	79
Poplar	Populus	White; grey; aurora; Italica; aspen	24	79
Pride of India	Koelreuteria	paniculata	6	20
Sweet chestnut	Castanea		30	98
Sweet gum	Liquidambar	styraciflua	45	148
Tree of heaven	Ailanthus	altissima	20	65
Tulip	Liriodendron	tulipifera	35	115
Tupelo	Nyssa	sylvatica	9	29
Walnut	Juglans		30	98
Willow	Salix	Golden; weeping; American; Kilmarnock; purple; corkscrew	3-9	10-29
Yew	Taxus baccata	Common; Irish	4-15	13-49

Plants as foodstuffs

Temperate fruits

Common name	Latin name	Family
Apple	Malus pumila	Rosaceae
Pear	Pyrus communis	Rosaceae
Quince	Cydonia vulgaris	Rosaceae
Peach; nectarine	Prunus persica	Rosaceae
Sweet cherry	P. avium	Rosaceae
Sour cherry; cooking cherry; morello	P. cerasus	Rosaceae
Plum	P. domestica	Rosaceae
Bullace; damson	P. insititia	Rosaceae
Gage; greengage; mirabelle	P. insititia var italica, var syriaca	Rosaceae
Cherry plum	P. cerasifera	Rosaceae
Japanese plum	P. salicina	Rosaceae
American plum	P. americana	Rosaceae
Apricot	P. armeniaca	Rosaceae
Medlar	Mespilus germanica	Rosaceae
Raspberry	Rubus idaeus	Rosaceae
American red raspberry	R. ideaus var strigosus	Rosaceae
Black raspberry	R. occidentalis	Rosaceae
Blackberry; bramble	R. fruticosus	Rosaceae
Evergreen blackberry	R. laciniatus	Rosaceae
Cloudberry	R. chamaemorus	Rosaceae
Pacific dewberry	R. ursinus	Rosaceae

Common name	Latin name	Family
Loganberry; boysenberry; veitchberry	R. × loganbaccus	Rosaceae
Wineberry	R. phoenicolasius	Rosaceae
Strawberry	Fragaria × ananassa (= F. virginiana × F. chiloensis)	Rosaceae
Gooseberry	Ribes uva-crispa (= R. grossularia)	Rosaceae
Blackcurrant	R. nigrum	Rosaceae
Redcurrant	R. rubrum	Rosaceae
Fig	Ficus carica	Moraceae
Olive	Olea europaea	Oleaceae
Mulberry; black mulberry	Morus nigra	Moraceae
Red mulberry	M. rubra	Moraceae
Grape	Vitis vinifera	Vitaceae
Frost grape	V. riparia; V. vulpina	Vitaceae
Bush or sand grape	V. rupestris	Vitaceae
Fox or skunk grape	V. labrusca	Vitaceae
Muscadine; bullace grape	V. rotundifolia	Vitaceae
Bilberry	Vaccinium myrtillus	Ericaceae
Cranberry	V. oxycoccus; V. macrocarpon	Ericaceae
Cowberry	V. vitis-idaea	Ericaceae
Lowbush blueberry	V. angustifolium	Ericaceae
Highbush blueberry	V. corymbosum	Ericaceae
Strawberry tree	Arbutus unedo	Ericaceae
Chinese gooseberry; kiwiberry	Actinidia chinensis	Actinidiaceae

Tropical and subtropical fruits

Common Name	Latin name	Family
Sweet orange	Citrus sinensis	Rutaceae
Sour, Seville or bitter orange	C. aurantium	Rutaceae
Lime	C. aurantiifolia	Rutaceae
Lemon	C. limon	Rutaceae
Rangpur lime; mandarin lime	C. × limonia	Rutaceae
Shaddock; pummelo	C. maxima	Rutaceae
Citron	C. medica	Rutaceae
King orange	C. × nobilis	Rutaceae
Grapefruit	C. × paradisi	Rutaceae
Mandarin; satsuma; tangerine; clementine	C. reticulata	Rutaceae
Kumquat	Fortunella japonica	Rutaceae
Loquat; Japanese medlar	Eriobotrya japonica	Rosaceae
Breadfruit	Artocarpus altilis	Moraceae
Jackfruit	A. heterophyllus	Moraceae
Cherimoya	Annona cherimolia	Annonaceae
Custard apple; bullock's heart	A. reticulata	Annonaceae
Soursop; guanabana	A. muricata	Annonaceae
Sugarapple; sweetsop	A. squamosa	Annonaceae
Banana; edible plantain	Musa acuminata; M. × paradisiaca	Musaceae
Fehi banana	M. fehi	Musaceae
Avocado; aguacate; alligator pear	Persaea americana (= P. gratissima)	Lauraceae
Coconut	Cocos nucifera	Palmae
Date	Phoenix dactylifera	Palmae
Pineapple	Ananas comosus	Bromeliaceae
Mango	Mangifera indica	Anacardiaceae
Cashew apple	Anacardium occidentale	Anacardiaceae
Granadilla; passion fruit	Passiflora edulis	Passifloraceae
Sweet granadilla	P. ligularis	Passifloraceae
Yellow granadilla	P. laurifolia	Passifloraceae
Sweet calabash	P. maliformis	Passifloraceae
Curuba	P. mollissima	Passifloraceae
Giant granadilla	P. quadrangularis	Passifloraceae
Papaw; pawpaw	Carica papaya	Caricaceae
Durian	Durio zibethinus	Bombacaceae
Mangosteen	Garcinia mangostana	Guttiferae
Rambutan	Nephelium lappaceum	Sapindaceae
Longan	Euphoria longan	Sapindaceae
Akee	Blighia sapida	Sapindaceae
Guava	Psidium guajava	Myrtaceae
Cape gooseberry	Physalis peruviana	Solanaceae
Tomatillo; jamberry	P. ixocarpa	Solanaceae
Mammey apple; mammee	Mammea americana	Guttiferae
Sapodilla	Manilkara sapota	Sapotaceae
Sapote	Pouteria sapota (= Calocarpoum sapota)	Sapotaceae
Tamarind	Tamarindus indica	Leguminosae

Common name	Latin name	Family
Carambola; caramba; blimbing; bilimbi	Averrhoa carambola	Oxalidaceae
Persimmon	Diospyros kaki	Ebenaceae
Pomegranate	Punica granatum	Punicaceae
Litchi; lychee	Litchi chinensis	Sapindaceae

Vegetables

Common name	Latin name	Family
BRASSICAS		
Cabbage, spring		Cruciferae
Cabbage, savoy		Cruciferae
Cauliflower		Cruciferae
Broccoli; calabrese	Brassica oleracea	Cruciferae
Kale		Cruciferae
Brussel sprouts		Cruciferae
Turnip; swede	B. campestris	Cruciferae
Pak-choi	B. campestris, subspecies chinensis	Cruciferae
Pe-tsai	B. campestris, subspecies pekinensis	Cruciferae
LEAF AND STEM VEGETABLES		
Asparagus	Asparagus officinalis	Liliaceae
Wild asparagus	A. acutifolius	Liliaceae
Chives	Allium schoenoprasum	Liliaceae
Celery	Apium graveolens	Umbelliferae
Fennel	Foeniculum vulgare var vulgare	Umbelliferae
Florence fennel; finocchio	F. vulgare var azoricum	Umbelliferae
Chicory; asparagus chicory; witloof; belgian endive	Cichorium intybus	Compositae
Radicchio; red verona chicory; treviso chicory; castelfranco chicory	C. intybus	Compositae
Grumolo; broad-leaved chicory	C. intybus	Compositae
Endive; escarolle; batavian endive	C. endivia	Compositae
Lettuce; cabbage lettuce; cos lettuce	Lactuca sativa	Compositae
Wild lettuce	L. taraxaciflora	Compositae
Spinach; summer or round-seeded, winter or prickly-seeded	Spinacia oleracea	Chenopodiaceae
Spinach beet	Beta vulgaris var cicla	Chenopodiaceae
Seakale beet; Swiss chard	B. vulgaris var cicla	Chenopodiaceae
Orache	Atriplex hortensis	Chenopodiaceae
New Zealand spinach	Tetragonia expansa	Aizoaceae

NATURAL HISTORY

Plants as foodstuffs (continued)

Common name	Latin name	Family
Amaranth spinach	Amaranthus caudatus; A. hybridus; A. tricolor	Amaranthaceae
Sea kale	Crambe maritima	Cruciferae
Bamboo shoots	Bambusa arundinacea B. beecheyana; B. vulgaris; Phyllostachys dulcis; P. pubescens etc	Gramineae
Globe artichoke	Cynara scolymus	Compositae
Cardoon	C. cardunculus	Compositae
Okra; gumbo; lady's fingers	Hibiscus esculentus (= Abelmoschus esculentus)	Malvaceae
Jew's mallow	Corchorus olitorius	Tiliaceae
Jute	C. capsularis	Tiliaceae
Water spinach	Ipomoea aquatica	Convolvulaceae
Rhubarb, garden	Rheum rhabarbarum	Polygonaceae

ROOT VEGETABLES

Common name	Latin name	Family
Radish	Raphanus sativus	Cruciferae
Winter radish	R. sativus cv 'Longipinnatus'	Cruciferae
Black salsify	Scorzonera hispanica	Compositae
Salsify; oyster plant	Tragopogon porrifolius	Compositae
Carrot	Daucus carota subspecies sativus	Umbelliferae
Parsnip	Pastinaca sativa	Umbelliferae
Celeriac; turnip-rooted celery	Apium graveolens var rapaceum	Umbelliferae
Arracacha	Arracacia xanthorrhiza	Umbelliferae
Turnip-rooted parsley; hamburg parsley	Petroselinum crispum var tuberosum	Umbelliferae
Chervil, turnip-rooted	Chaerophyllum bulbosum	Umbelliferae
Jerusalem artichoke	Helianthus tuberosus	Compositae
Chinese artichoke	Stachys tuberifera	Labiatae
Oca	Oxalis tuberosa	Oxalidaceae
Ulluco; ullucu	Ullucus tuberosus	Basellaceae
Anu; anyu	Tropaeolum tuberosum	Tropaeolaceae
Yam bean	Pachyrhizus erosus	Leguminosae
Yam bean; potato bean	P. tuberosus	Leguminosae
Sacred or East Indian lotus	Nelumbo nucifera	Nymphaeaceae
Kaffir potato; Hausa potato	Plectranthus (Coleus) esculentus	Labiatae
Onion	Allium cepa	Liliaceae
Shallot	A. cepa var aggregatum (= A. ascalonicum)	Liliaceae
Welsh onion; Japanese onion	A. fistulosum	Liliaceae
Garlic	A. sativum	Liliaceae
Leek	A. porrum	Liliaceae

Fruit vegetables

Common name	Latin name	Family
Tomato	Lycopersicum esculentum	Solanaceae
Aubergine	Solanum melongena	Solanaceae
Cucumber	Cucumis sativa	Cucurbitaceae
Gherkin	C. anguria	Cucurbitaceae
Bitter gourd; bitter cucumber	Momordica charantia	Cucurbitaceae
Bottle gourd; calabash gourd; white gourd	Lagenaria siceraria	Cucurbitaceae
Snake gourd	Trichosanthes cucumerina	Cucurbitaceae
Wax, ash gourd	Benincasa hispida	Cucurbitaceae
Chayote; christophine pumpkins; marrows; squashes	Sechium edule	Cucurbitaceae
Breadfruit	Artocarpus altilis	Moraceae
Jackfruit	A. heterophyllus	Moraceae
Pepper; sweet pepper	Capsicum annuum	Solanaceae
Avocado; alligator pear	Persea americana	Lauraceae

Root crops

Common name	Latin name	Family
TEMPERATE		
Turnip	Brassica campestris ssp rapifera	Cruciferae
Swede; rutabaga	B. napus var napobrassica	Cruciferae
Mangel; mangel-wurzel; mangold	Beta vulgaris ssp vulgaris	Chenopodiaceae
Beet; sugarbeet; beetroot	B. vulgaris ssp vulgaris	Chenopodiaceae
Potato	Solanum tuberosum	Solanaceae
TROPICAL		
Sweet potato	Ipomoea batatas	Convolvulaceae
Topee-tambu	Calathea alloula	Marantaceae
Cassava; manihot	Manihot esculenta	Euphorbiaceae
Taro; tanier cocoyams; arrowroots		
Yam, white Guinea	Dioscorea rotundata	Dioscoreaceae
Yam, yellow Guinea	D. cayenensis	Dioscoreaceae
Yam, greater	D. alata	Dioscoreaceae
Yam, bitter	D. dumetorum	Dioscoreaceae
Yam, Asiatic	D. esculenta	Dioscoreaceae
Yam, American	D. trifida	Dioscoreaceae

Legumes and pulses

Common name	Latin name	Part consumed
COOL TEMPERATE AND WARM TEMPERATE		
Garden pea	Pisum sativum	Seeds; young pods
Field pea	P. arvense	Seeds
Asparagus pea; winged pea	Tetragonolobus purpureus	
French, kidney, haricot, green, runner, string, salad, wax bean	Phaseolus vulgaris	Young pods; seeds
Runner; scarlet runner	P. coccineus	Young pods
Butter, sieva, civet, Madagascar, Carolina sewee bean	P. lunatus	Seeds
Lima bean	P. limensis	Seeds
Soybean	Glycine max (G. soja)	Seeds; sprouts; oil
Lentil	Lens culinaris	Seeds
Broad bean	Vicia faba	Seeds
Lupin	Lupinus albus; L. pilosus; L. luteus; L. mutabilis	Seeds
Carob bean; locust bean; St John's bread	Ceratonia siliqua	Pods
TROPICAL		
Tepary bean	Phaseolus acutifolius var latifolius	Seeds
Cluster bean; guar	Cyamopsis tetragonolobus	Young pods; seeds
Goa bean; asparagus pea; winged pea	Psophocarpus tetragonolobus P. palmettorum	Young pods
Yam bean; chopsui potato	Pachyrhizus erosus; P. tuberosus	Young pods; roots
Lablab; hyacinth	Dolichos lablab	Pods; seeds
Madras gram; horse gram	D. biflorus	Seeds
Chick pea	Cicer arietinum	Seeds
Bambara; groundnut; kaffir pea	Voandzeia subterranea	Seeds
Kersting's groundnut	Kerstingiella geocarpa	Seeds
Tamarind	Tamarindus indica	Pulp from pods; seeds
Moth bean	Vigna aconitifolia	Seeds
Adzuki bean	V. angularis	Seeds
Cowpea	V. unguiculata	Seeds
Black-eyed pea	V. unguiculata subspecies unguiculata	Seeds
Yard long bean	V. unguiculata subspecies sesquipedalis	Pods
Black gram	Vigna mungo (Phaseolus mungo)	Seeds; young pods
Green gram; mung bean	V. radiata (Phaseolus aureus)	Seeds; pods; sprouts

Common name	Latin name	Part consumed
Rice bean	V. umbellata	Seeds
Jack bean	Canavalia ensiformis	Young pods; seeds
Sword bean	C. gladiata	Young pods; seeds
Groundnut	Arachis hypogaea	Seeds; oil
Pigeon pea; Cajan congo pea; red gram	Cajanus cajan	Seeds
African locust bean	Parkia filicoidea; P. biglobosa	Seeds; pulp of pod
Yam bean	Sphenostylis stenocarpa	seeds

Main cereal crops

Common name	Latin name
Wheat	Triticum
wild emmer	T. diococcoides
cultivated emmer	T. diococcum
einkorns	T. monococcum var monococcum; var boeoticum
hard (durum)	T. durum
turgidum	T. turgidum
bread	T. aestivum var aestivum
spelt	T. spelta
club	T. compactum
Barley	Hordeum vulgare
two-rowed	H. distichum
six-rowed	H. hexastichum
Rye	Secale cereale
Maize (US corn)	Zea mays
Rice	Oryza sativa
African rice	O. glaberrima
Oats	Avena
hexaploid	A. sativa; A. byzantina; A. nuda
tetraploid	A. abyssinica
diploid	A. strigosa; A. brevis
Sorghum	Sorghum bicolor
Millets	
finger or African bulrush; pearl bajra; common; proso	Eleusine coracana; Pennisetum americanum; Panicum miliaceum
Japanese barnyard; sanwa	Echinachloa frumentacea
Foxtail, German and Italian	Setaria italica
Teff	Eragrostis tef
Fonio; fundi	Digitaria spp
Koda; kodo	Paspalum scrobiculatum

Sugar and starch crops

Common name	Latin name	Family
SUGAR PLANTS		
Sugar cane	Saccharum officinarum	Gramineae
Sugar beet	Beta vulgaris	Chenopodiaceae
Sugar maple	Acer saccharum	Aceraceae

Plants as foodstuffs (continued)

Common name	Latin name	Family
Black maple	A. nigrum	Aceraceae
Barley (germinating)	Hordeum vulgare	Gramineae
Sweet sorghum; sorgo	Sorghum bicolor	Gramineae
Wild date palm	Phoenix sylvestris	Palmae
Palmyra palm	Borassus flabellifer	Palmae
Toddy palm; sago palm; jaggery palm	Caryota urens	Palmae
Coconut palm	Cocos nucifera	Palmae
Gomuti palm; sugar palm	Arenga pinnata	Palmae
Honey palm; syrup palm	Jubaea chilensis	Oleaceae
Nypa palm	Nypa fruticans	Oleaceae
Manna ash	Fraxinus ornus	Oleaceae

STARCH PLANTS

Common name	Latin name	Family
Potato	Salanum tuberosum	Solanaceae
Cassava; manioc	Manihot esculenta	Euphorbiaceae
Arrowroot	Maranta arundinacea	Marantaceae
Queensland arrowroot	Canna edulis	Cannaceae
Taro	Colocasia esculenta	Araceae
Giant taro	Alocasia macrorrhiza	Araceae
Dasheen	Colocasia esculenta var globifera	Araceae
Giant swamp taro	Cyrtosperma chamissonis (C. edule)	Araceae
Tanier; cocoyam	Xanthosma atrovirens; X. sagittifolium; X. violaceum	Araceae
East Indian arrowroot	Curcuma angustifolia	Zingiberaceae
Fijian arrowroot; Tahitian arrowroot	Tacca leontopetaloides (T. pinnatifida)	Taccaceae
Greater Asiatic yam	Dioscorea alata	Dioscoreaceae
White Guinea yam	D. rotundata	Dioscoreaceae
Yellow Guinea yam	D. cayenensis	Dioscoreaceae
Air potato	D. bulbifera	Dioscoreaceae
Cush-cush; yampee	D. trifida	Dioscoreaceae
Sago palm	Metroxylon rumphii; M. sagu	Palmae
Sago palm; gomuti palm	Arenga pinnata	Palmae
American cabbage palm; caribe palm	Oreodoxa oleracea; Roystonea oleracea	Palmae

Common name	Latin name	Family
Kaffir bread	Encephalartos caffer	Zamiaceae
Bread tree	E. altensteinii	Zamiaceae
Sago palm; queen sago	Cycas circinalis	Cycadaceae
Japanese sago palm	C. revoluta	Cycadaceae
Maize	Zea mays	Gramineae
Wheat	Triticum spp	Gramineae
Rice	Oryza sativa	Gramineae

Edible nuts

Common name	Latin name	Main areas of cultivation
Hazelnut; cob; European filbert	Corylus avellana	Turkey; Italy; Spain; France; England; Oregon
Giant filbert	C. maxima (C. americana)	(As above)
Turkish cobnut	C. colurna	Turkey
Sweet chestnut	Castanea sativa	S Europe; N America
American chestnut	C. dentata	N America
Japanese chestnut	C. crenata	Japan; N America
Chinese chestnut	C. mollissima	China; Korea; N America
Almond	Prunus amygdalus (= P. dulcis)	Mediterranean; SW Asia; N America
Sweet almond	P. amygdalus var amygdalus	Americas
Bitter almond	P. amygdalus var amara	
Walnut	Juglans regia	Europe; Asia; N America
Black walnut; eastern walnut	J. nigra	N America
Butternut	J. cinerea	N America
Japanese walnut	J. ailanthifolia	Japan; N America
Chinese walnut	J. cathayensis	China; N America
Pecan	Carya illinoinensis	N America
Shagbark hickory	C. ovata	N America
Shellbark hickory	C. laciniosa	N America
Brazil nut; paranut	Bertholletia excelsa	Amazon region (wild)
Sapucaia; sapucaia	Lecythis sabucayo	S America (wild)
Monkey nut	L. usitata	S America (wild)
Cashew nut	Anacardium occidentale	Tropical S America; India; E Africa
Coconut	Cocos nucifera	India; Sri Lanka; Malaysia; Indonesia; Philippines

Common name	Latin name	Main areas of cultivation	Common name	Latin name	Main areas of cultivation
Macadamia; Australia, or Queensland nut (smooth shell)	Macadamia integrifolia	Australia; California	Betel nut	Areca catechu	Old World tropics
Macadamia nut (rough shell)	M. tetraphylla	Australia; California	Kola	Cola nitida	W Africa; Caribbean
Moreton bay chestnut	Castanospermum australe	Australia (wild)		C. acuminata	W Africa; Brazil
Oysternut	Telfairia pedata	E Africa	Water chestnut	Trapa natans; T. bicornis;	E Asia; Malaysia;
Peanut; ground nut	Arachis hypogaea	India; tropical Africa; China		T. maximowiczii	India
			Pine nut; pine kernel	Pinus pinea; P. pinaster	Mediterranean Mediterranean
Pilt nut	Canarium luzonicum; C. ovatum	Philippines	Swiss stone pine	P. cembra	Europe
			Mexican stone pine	P. cembroides	Mexico
Java almond	C. commune	Java			
Pistachio	Pistacia vera	E Mediterranean; India; S USA			

Herbs and spices

Common name	Latin name	Forms	Area of origin
Anise	Pimpinella anisum	Seeds; leaves	Middle East, now Southern Russia; Turkey; India; parts of Europe
Basil	Ocimum basilicum	Leaves	Europe
Bay	Laurus nobilis	Leaves	Mediterranean
Bergamot	Monarda didyma	Flowers; leaves	N America
Caraway	Carum carvi	Seeds (ground); leaves; tap roots	Temperate Asia; Europe; N America
Cardamom	Elettaria cardomomum	Pods; seeds (dried)	India; Middle East
Chervil	Anthriscus cerfolium	Leaves	S Russia, now Europe
Chilli	Capsicum annuum	Whole (fresh or dried)	N America; Europe
Chives	Allium schoenoprasum	Stems; flowers	Europe
Cinnamon	Cinnamomum zeylanicum	Bark (dried or ground)	Sri Lanka
Cloves	Eugenia aromatica	Buds (whole and ground)	SE Asia; Indonesia; Madagascar; Tanzania; Sri Lanka; Malaysia; Grenada
Coriander	Coriandrum sativum	Leaves; seeds (ground)	S Europe; Middle East
Cumin	Cuminum cyminum	Seeds (whole and ground)	The East; India; Egypt; Arabia
Dill	Anethum graveolens	Leaves; seeds	Scandinavia; Germany; C and E Europe
Fennel	Foeniculum vulgare	Leaves; stalks; seeds	S Europe
Ginger	Zingiber officinale	Root	Tropical Asia; Middle East; S Europe
Juniper	Juniperus communis	Berries	S Europe
Lovage	Levisticum officinale	Leaves; seeds; stems	Europe
Marjoram	Origanum majorana	Leaves	Mediterranean regions
Mint	Mentha	Leaves	Europe; Middle East
Mustard	Brassica nigra; B. juncea; B. alba	Seeds	Europe (white mustard – Mediterranean region)
Nutmeg	Myristica fragrans	Whole; ground	SE Asia
Oregano	Oregano vulgare	Leaves	Mediterranean regions
Paprika	Capsicum tetragonum	Fresh (whole); dried (ground)	Mexico; Spain; Morocco; Hungary
Parsley	Petroselinum crispum	Leaves	S Europe, now all the world's temperate regions
Poppy seeds	Papaver somniferum	Seeds	Middle East; India, N America; Europe
Rosemary	Rosmarinus officinalis	Leaves; flowers	Mediterranean region
Saffron	Crocus sativus	Flowers (dried and ground)	Mediterranean countries, particularly Spain

NATURAL HISTORY

Herbs and spices (continued)

Common name	Latin name	Forms	Area of origin
Sage	*Salvia officinalis*	Leaves	N Mediterranean coast
Sassafras	*Sassafrass albidum, S. officinalis*	Leaves; bark (dried)	N America
Sesame seeds	*Sesamum indicum*	Seeds	Africa; India; China
Sorrel	*Rumex acetosa, R. scutatus*	Leaves	Europe; particularly France
Tamarind	*Tamarindus indica*	Pulp	E Africa; S Asia
Tansy	*Chrysanthemum vulgare*	Leaves	Europe
Tarragon	*Artemisia dracunculus*	Leaves	Siberia; now Europe
Thyme	*Thymus vulgaris*	Leaves	Mediterranean regions
Turmeric	*Curcuma longa*	Root (whole or ground)	India; China; Middle East
Vanilla	*Vanilla plainfolia*	Pods	S Mexico; Madagascar; C America; Puerto Rico; Réunion

FUNGI

Phylum	No. of species	Class	Examples	Characteristics of class
Zygomycota	600	Mucorales	Black bread mould (*Rhizopus stolonifer*); *Mucor*	Many saprozoic on dung or organic debris. Others parasites of invertebrates, other fungi, and plants.
		Entomophthorales	*Basidiobolus*	Most parasites of animals, mainly insects.
		Zoopagales	*Cochlonema; Endocochlus*	Parasites of amoebas, nematodes, and other small animals.
Ascomycota	15 000	Hemiascomycetae	Yeasts, eg baker's yeast (*Saccharomyces cerevisiae*)	Morphologically simple. Short mycelia or none at all.
		Euascomycetae	Morels; truffles (*Tuber*); most fungal partners in lichens; *Neurospora*	Largest and best known class of Ascomycota.
		Loculoascomycetae	*Mycosphaerella; Elsinoe*	Many are parasites of economically important food plants.
		Laboulbeniomycetae	*Rhizomyces; Amorphomyces*	Parasites of insects.
Basidiomycota	25 000	Heterobasidiomycetae	Jelly fungi; rusts; smuts	
		Homobasidiomycetae	Common mushrooms; shelf fungi; coral fungi; puffballs; earthstars; stinkhorns; bird's nest fungi	Contains most of the fungi known as mushrooms and toadstools.
Deuteromycota (Fungi Imperfecti)	25 000	Sphaeropsida	*Clypeoseptoria aparothospermi*	
		Melanconia	*Cryptosporium lunasporum*	
		Monilia	*Penicillium; Candida albicans*	Pathogenic yeasts; other yeasts that do not form asci or basidia.
		Mycelia Sterilia	*Rhizoctonia*	

PART FIVE

Human Beings

EARLY HUMANS

Evolution of early humans

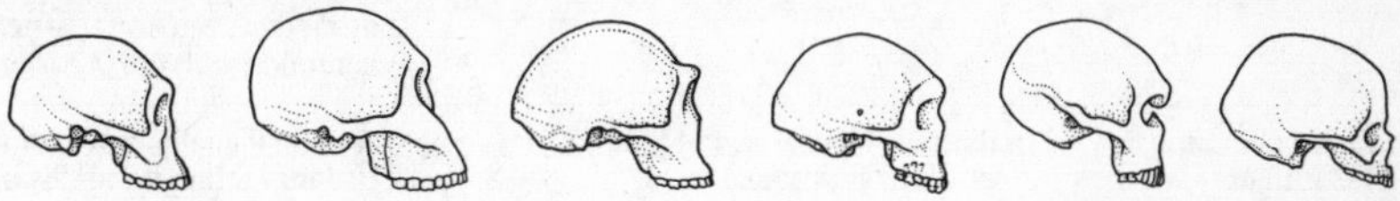

	Homo habilis (small)	*Homo habilis* (large)	*Homo erectus*	'Archaic *Homo sapiens*'	Neanderthals	Early modern *Homo sapiens*
Height (m/ft)	c.1/3	c.1.5/5	1.3–1.5/4–5	?	1.5–1.7/5–5.5	1.6–1.85/5.3–6
Physique	Relatively long arms	Robust but 'human' skeleton	Robust but 'human' skeleton	Robust but 'human' skeleton	As 'archaic *H. sapiens*', but adapted for cold	Modern skeleton; ?adapted for warmth
Brain size (ml)	500–650	600–800	750–1250	1100–1400	1200–1750	1200–1700
Skull form	Relatively small face; nose developed	Larger, flatter face	Flat, thick skull with large occipital and brow ridge	Higher skull; face less protruding	Reduced brow ridge; thinner skull; large nose; midface projection	Small or no brow ridge; shorter, high skull
Jaws/teeth	Thinner jaw; smaller, narrow molars	Robust jaw; large narrow molars	Robust jaw in larger individuals; smaller teeth than *H. habilis*	Similar to *H. erectus* but teeth may be smaller	Similar to 'archaic *H. sapiens*'; teeth smaller except for incisors; chin development in some	Shorter jaws than Neanderthals; chin developed; teeth may be smaller
Distribution	Eastern (+ southern?) Africa	Eastern Africa	Africa, Asia, Indonesia (+ Europe?)	Africa, Asia, Europe	Europe and W Asia	Africa and W Asia
Known date (years ago)	2–1.6 million	2–1.6 million	1.8–0.3 million	400000–100000	150000–30000	130000–60000

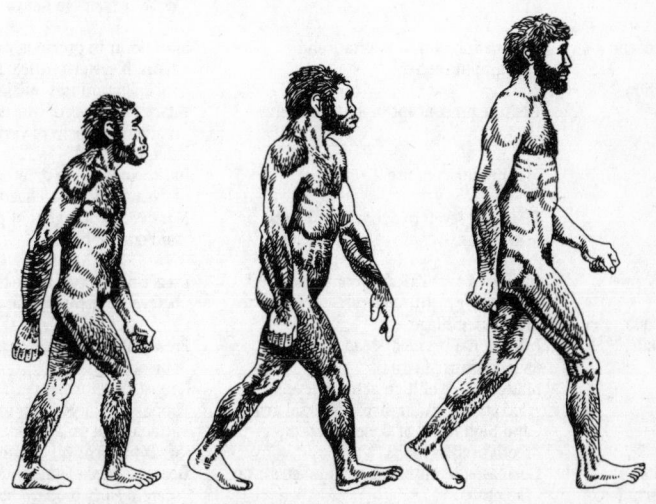

Homo habilis   *Homo erectus*   *Homo sapiens*

HUMAN BEINGS

Early human behaviour and ecology

Hominids and time periods (years ago)	Inference	Nature of the evidence
A Hominid ancestors ?8–5 million	Equatorial African origin.	Humans are genetically closest to African apes, which today are distributed across equatorial Africa; earliest hominid fossils are in eastern Africa.
B Earliest hominids 5–3 million	Habitually bipedal on the ground; occasionally arboreal.	Postcranial anatomy of fossils from Hadar in Ethiopia (but disagreements about similarity to modern human bipedalism and degree of arboreality).
	Inhabited a mosaic of grassland, woodland and thick shrub.	Faunas from Laetoli in Tanzania, Hadar and Makapansgat in South Africa.
3–2 million	Occupation of open savannas.	Fossil pollen and fauna.
	Emphasis on a fibrous plant diet in robust australopithecines.	Microwear on teeth; large teeth and jaws.
	First known manufacture of stone tools.	Tools from Ethiopia, Kenya, Malawi, and Democratic Republic of Congo dated between 2.5 and 2.0 million years.
C Plio-Pleistocene hominids 2.0–1.5 million (Stone technology and changes in diet, brain size, etc. are usually associated with *Homo*)	Increased commitment to bipedalism on the ground.	Postcranial anatomy associated with archaic *Homo* established.
	Increased dexterity related to tool use and toolmaking, and possibly foraging.	Anatomy of hand bones and characteristics of stone tools and cores.
	Stones and animal bones carried repeatedly to specific sites.	Earliest known complex sites with many stone artifacts and fossils.
	Use of tools to procure and process food.	Bone and stone tools with distinctive traces of use.
	Dietary increase in protein and fat from large animals.	Cut marks made by stone tools on animal bones.
	Scavenging and possible hunting of large animals; processing of animals at specific spots.	Limb bones of animals concentrated at undisturbed archaeological sites.
	Increased cognitive capacities associated with making tools, foraging, social arrangements, and/or developing linguistic skills.	Increase in brain size from about a third to a half that of modern humans.
	Changes in maturation rate.	Implied by brain size increase and possible changes in tooth development.
	Increased mobility and predator defence.	Large stature evident in skeletal remains of early *Homo erectus* from West Turkana in Kenya.
D Early Pleistocene hominids 1.5–0.1 million	Occupation of new habitats and geographic zones.	Sites occur in previously unoccupied areas of eastern Africa; first appearance of hominids outside Africa.
	Definite preconception of tool form.	Biface handaxes of consistent shape made from rocks of varying original shape.
	Manipulation of fire.	Indications of fire differentially associated with archaeological sites.
	Increased levels of activity and stress on skeletons.	Massive development of postcranial and cranial bones.
E Late Pleistocene hominids 100 000–35 000 (Neanderthals)	Increased sophistication of toolkit and technology; still slow rate of change to tool assemblage.	Larger number of stone-tool types than before; complex preparation of cores.
	Intentional burial of dead and suggestions of ritual.	Preservation of skeletons, some with objects.
	Maintenance of high activity levels (locomotor endurance; powerful arms) and high levels of skeletal stress (eg teeth used as tools).	Robust skeletons, especially thick leg bones and large areas for muscle attachment on arm bones; prominent wear patterns on incisor teeth.
35 000–10 000 (fully modern *Homo sapiens*)	Decreased levels of activity and stress on skeleton.	Decrease in skeletal robusticity (also seen in early modern humans before 35 000 years ago).

Hominids and time periods (years ago)	Inference	Nature of the evidence
	Enhanced technological efficiency.	Innovations in stone- and bone-tool production (eg blades and bone points).
	Innovations in hunting and other foraging activities, including systematic exploitation of particular animal species.	Evidence of spearthrower and harpoon, and trapping and netting of animals; animal remains in archaeological middens.
	Colonization of previously uninhabited zones.	For example, sites in tundra in Europe and Asia; colonization of the Americas (Australasia was probably first inhabited around 50000 years ago).
	Elaboration of artistic symbolic expression and notation.	Engraving, sculpting and painting of walls and figurines; repetitive marks on bones; jewellery.
	Surge of technological and cultural differentiation and change.	Variation in toolkits over space and time.
	Harvesting and first cultivation of grains; first domestication of animals.	Evidence of seeds and fauna from sites dating to the end of the Pleistocene.

THE BODY

DNA

DNA or *deoxyribonucleic acid* contains the genetic information for most living organisms. Each human cell contains about 2 m/6.6 ft of DNA supercoiled on itself such that it fits within the cell nucleus (less than 10 μm (micrometres) in diameter).

DNA consists of four *bases* (adenine [A], guanine [G], thymine [T], and cytosine [C]), a sugar (2-deoxy-D-ribose), and phosphoric acid, arranged in the famous *double helical* structure discovered by geneticists James Watson and Francis Crick in 1953. In the helical structure, A pairs only with T, and G only with C.

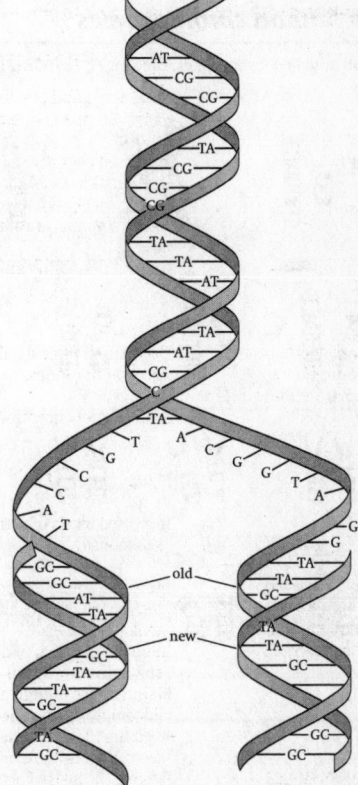

DNA structure and replication, following Watson and Crick. The two strands of the double helix separate, and a new strand is assembled alongside each, the base sequence being determined by complementary pairing with the base sequence of the existing strand.

The genetic code

The four DNA bases A, G, T, and C, like the letters of the alphabet, can be used to store information. This genetic information is passed on via RNA or *ribonucleic acid* (consisting of the four bases adenine, guanine, cytosine, and uracil [U]), which provides a template for the assembly of amino acids in a particular sequence, thereby building a protein.

A group of three DNA or RNA bases is known as a *triplet* or *codon*, and codes for a particular amino acid. Information is passed from DNA to RNA by *complementary pairing*: A pairs only with U, and G only with C.

Genetic code in RNA triplets

1st base	2nd base				3rd base
	U	C	A	G	
U	Phenylalanine	Serine	Tyrosine	Cysteine	U
	Phenylalanine	Serine	Tyrosine	Cysteine	C
	Leucine	Serine	—[a]	—[a]	A
	Leucine	Serine	—[a]	Tryptophan	G
C	Leucine	Proline	Histidine	Arginine	U
	Leucine	Proline	Histidine	Arginine	C
	Leucine	Proline	Glutamine	Arginine	A
	Leucine	Proline	Glutamine	Arginine	G
A	Isoleucine	Threonine	Asparagine	Serine	U
	Isoleucine	Threonine	Asparagine	Serine	C
	Isoleucine	Threonine	Lysine	Arginine	A
	Methionine	Threonine	Lysine	Arginine	G
G	Valine	Alanine	Aspartic acid	Glycine	U
	Valine	Alanine	Aspartic acid	Glycine	C
	Valine	Alanine	Glutamic acid	Glycine	A
	Valine	Alanine	Glutamic acid	Glycine	G

[a] Chain termination.

The human chromosomes

The 46 human chromosomes, showing the banding patterns characteristic of each, grouped according to convention.

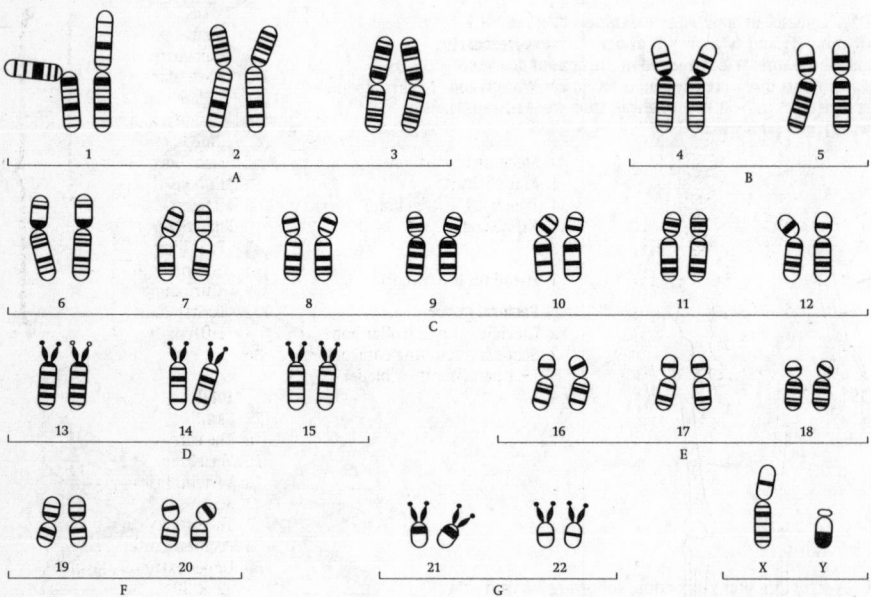

The human skeleton

The bones of the skeleton are often divided into two groups: the *axial skeleton* comprises the bones of the vertebral column, skull, ribs, and sternum; and the *appendicular skeleton* comprises the remainder.

1 Skull, displaying the frontal bone, and the front parts of the parietal and temporal bones. **2** Maxilla. **3** Mandible. **4** Clavicle. **5** Humerus. **6** Radius. **7** Ulna. **8** Sternum. **9** Scapula (obscured in this view by the upper ribs). **10** Ribs. **11** Vertebral column, displaying (from above to below) cervical, thoracic, lumbar, sacral, and coccygeal vertebrae. **12** Ilium. **13** Sacrum. **14** Coccyx. **15** Femur. **16** Kneebone. **17** Fibula. **18** Tibia. **19** Bones of the hand, comprising the eight carpals, the five metacarpals, the three phalanges in each finger, and the two phalanges in the thumb. **20** Bones of the foot, comprising the seven tarsals, the five metatarsals, the two phalanges in the big toe, and the three phalanges in the other toes.

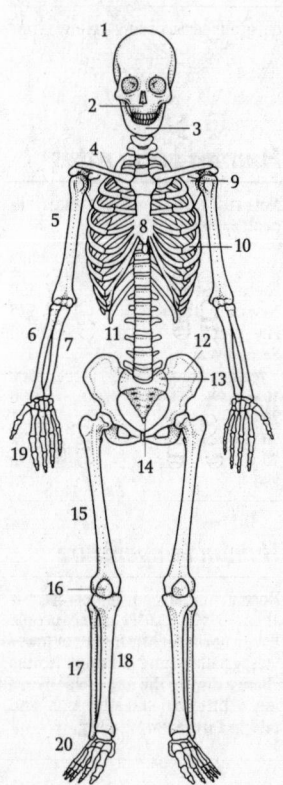

Bones of the human body

Skull
1 Occipital
2 Parietal – 1 pair
1 Sphenoid
1 Ethmoid
2 Inferior nasal conchae
1 Frontal – 1 pair, fused
2 Nasal – 1 pair
2 Lacrimal – 1 pair
2 Temporal – 1 pair
2 Maxilla – 1 pair
2 Zygomatic – 1 pair
1 Vomer
2 Palatine – 1 pair
1 Mandible – 1 pair, fused
   (jawbone)
__
22

The ears
2 Malleus (hammer) ⎫
2 Incus (anvil) ⎬ ossicles
2 Stapes (stirrups) ⎭
__
6

Vertebrae
7 Cervical
12 Thoracic
5 Lumbar
1 Sacral – 5, fused to form the
   sacrum
1 Coccyx – between 3 and 5,
   fused
__
26

Vertebral ribs
14 Ribs, 'true' – 7 pairs
10 Ribs, 'false' – 5 pairs of which 2
   pairs are floating
__
24

Sternum (breastbone)
1 Manubrium
1 'The body' (sternebrae)
1 Xiphisternum
__
3

1 Hyoid (in the throat)

Pectoral girdle
2 Clavicle – 1 pair (collar bone)
2 Scapula (including coracoid)
   – 1 pair (shoulder blade)
__
4

Upper extremity (each arm)
1 Humerus
1 Radius ⎫
1 Ulna ⎬ forearm
   Carpus:
1 Scaphoid
1 Lunate
1 Triquetral
1 Pisiform
1 Trapezium ⎫ wrist
1 Trapezoid
1 Capitate
1 Hamate ⎬ hand
5 Metacarpals
   Phalanges:
2 First digit
3 Second digit
3 Third digit ⎫ fingers
3 Fourth digit
3 Fifth digit
__
30

Pelvic girdle
   Ilium, ischium and pubis
   (combined) – 1 pair of hip
2 bones, innominate

Lower extremity (each leg)
1 Femur (thighbone)
1 Tibia
1 Fibula
1 Patella (kneebone)
   Tarsus:
1 Talus
1 Calcaneus
1 Navicular
1 Cuneiform medial
1 Cuneiform, inter-
    mediate
1 Cuneiform, lateral
1 Cuboid ⎬ ankle / foot
5 Metatarsals
   Phalanges:
2 First digit
3 Second digit
3 Third digit ⎫ toes
3 Fourth digit
3 Fifth digit
__
30

Total
22 Skull
6 The ears
26 Vertebrae
24 Vertebral ribs
3 Sternum
1 Throat
4 Pectoral girdle
60 Upper extremity (arms) –
   2 × 30
2 Hip bones
60 Lower extremity (legs) –
   2 × 30
___
208

Muscles and internal organs

In human beings the musculature normally accounts for some 40% of the total body weight. There are 639 named muscles in the human anatomy.

1 Trapezius muscle
2 Deltoid muscles
3 Triceps muscles (the biceps, at the front of the arm, cannot be seen from this view)
4 Latissimus dorsi muscle
5 Gluteus maximus muscle (largest muscle in the body)
6 Kidney
7 Trachea
8 Lungs
9 Heart
10 Liver (only a small part of the liver can be seen in this illustration)
11 Stomach
12 Spleen
13 Colon
14 Small intestine
15 Appendix
16 Bladder

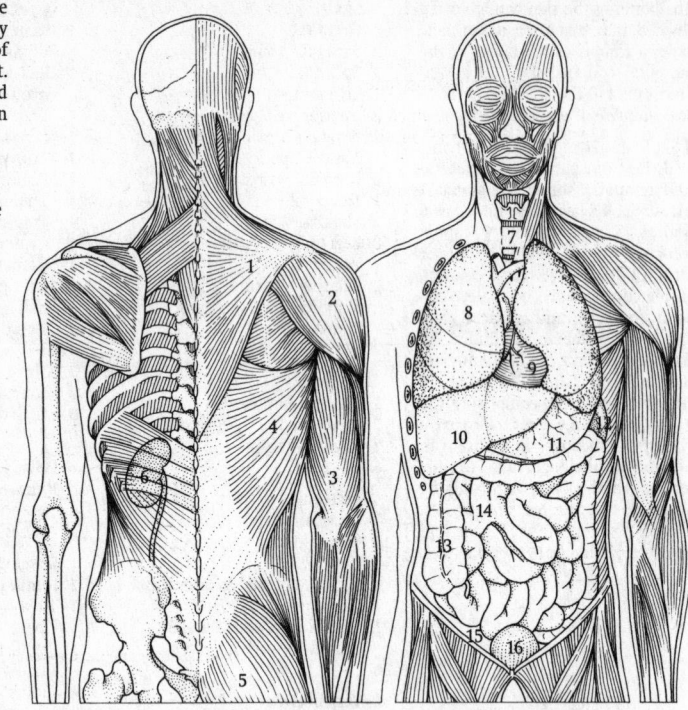

The heart

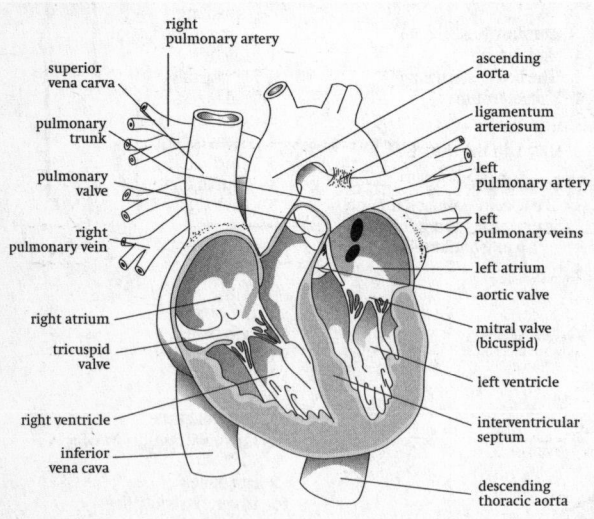

right pulmonary artery
superior vena carva
pulmonary trunk
pulmonary valve
right pulmonary vein
right atrium
tricuspid valve
right ventricle
inferior vena cava

ascending aorta
ligamentum arteriosum
left pulmonary artery
left pulmonary veins
left atrium
aortic valve
mitral valve (bicuspid)
left ventricle
interventricular septum
descending thoracic aorta

Human pulse rates

Normal resting pulse rates in healthy persons.

	Beats per minute
Foetus *in utero*	150
New born (full term)	140
First year	120
Second year	110
5 years	100
10 years	90
20 years	71
50 years	72
70 years	75
>80	78

Human temperature

Normal human body temperature is about 37°C (98.6°F); some people have a norm slightly higher or lower – especially young children. Norms change during the day – usually rising a little by mid-afternoon and falling a little during sleep.

The composition of blood

In an average human being blood accounts for 7–8% of body weight. Blood consists of:

Plasma: Water (90%), proteins (7%), nutrients, salts, nitrogen waste, carbon dioxide, hormones

Red blood cells (erythrocytes), 54% of which is haemoglobin. Normal count = 4–6 million per mm³

White blood cells (leukocytes). Normal count = 4 500–11 000 per mm³

Platelets (thrombocytes). Normal count = 150 000–300 000 per mm³

The brain in section

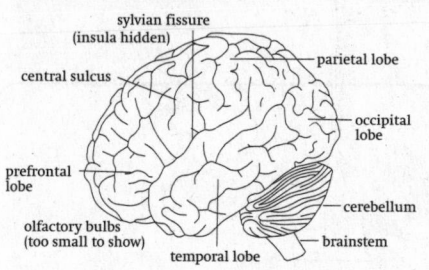

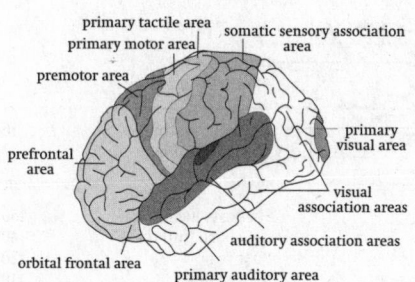

The ear

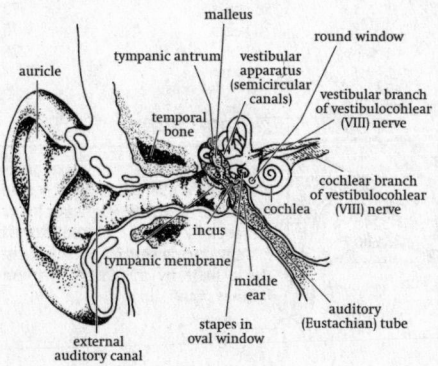

The eye

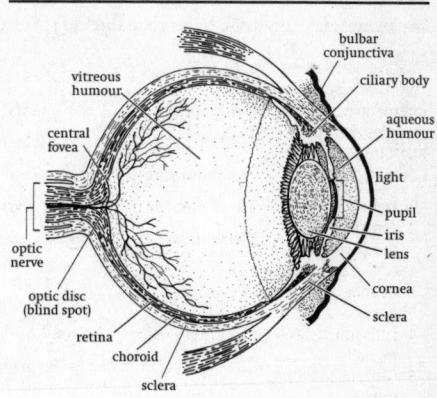

Normal eye

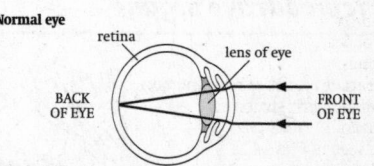

The image is in focus on the retina without a correcting lens in front.

Short-sighted or near-sighted eye (myopia)

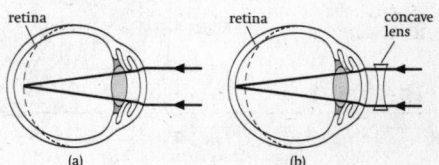

(a) The eye is too long and the image is not in focus on the retina.
(b) The use of a concave lens brings the image into focus.

Long-sighted or far-sighted eye (hypermetropia)

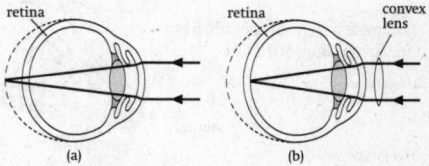

(a) The eye is too short and the image is not in focus on the retina.
(b) The use of a convex lens brings the image into focus.

The teeth

The approximate times of eruption and shedding of teeth.

Milk			Permanent	
	Eruption	*Shed*		*Eruption*
Incisor 1	6–10 months	6–7 years	Incisor 1	7–8 years
Incisor 2	8–12 months	7–8 years	Incisor 2	8–9 years
Canine	16–22 months	10–12 years	Canine	10–12 years
Molar 1	13–19 months	9–11 years	Premolar 1	10–11 years
Molar 2	25–33 months	10–12 years	Premolar 2	11–12 years
			Molar 1	6–7 years
			Molar 2	12 years
			Molar 3	17–21 years

Note: The lower teeth usually appear before the equivalent upper teeth.

The reproductive organs

Females
Main female organs of reproduction
and surrounding structures

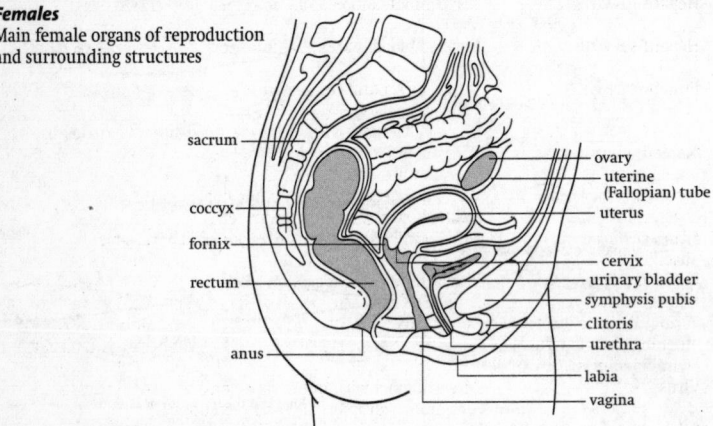

Males
Main male organs of reproduction
and surrounding structures

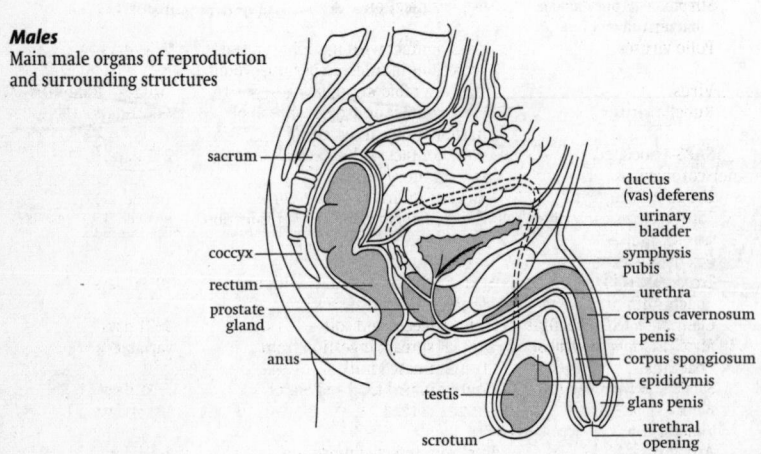

MEDICAL MATTERS

Communicable diseases

Name	Cause	Transmission	Incubation period
AIDS (Acquired Immune Deficiency Syndrome)	Human Immuno-deficiency Virus (HIV)	Sexual relations; sharing of syringes; blood transfusion	several years
Brucellosis	*Brucellus abortus* or *B meliteusis* bacteria	Cattle or goats	3–6 years
Chickenpox (varicella)	Varicella zoster virus (US) Herpes zoster virus (UK)	Infected persons; articles contaminated by discharge from mucous membranes	10–21 days
Cholera	*Vibrio cholerae* bacterium	Contaminated water and seafood	a few hours – 5 days
Common cold	Numerous viruses	Respiratory droplets of infected person	1–4 days
Diphtheria	*Corynebacterium diphtheriae* bacterium	Respiratory secretions and saliva of infected persons or carriers	2–6 days
Encephalitis	Viruses	Bite from infected mosquito	4–21 days
Gas gangrene	*Clostridium welchii* bacterium	Soil or soil-contaminated articles	1–4 days
Gonorrhoea	*Neisseria gonorrhoeae* bacterium	Urethral or vaginal secretions of infected persons	3–8 days
Hepatitis A (infectious)	Hepatitis A virus	Contaminated food and water	15–50 days
Hepatitis B (serum type B)	Hepatitis B virus	Infected blood; parenteral injection	6 weeks – 6 months
Infectious mononucleosis (US) Glandular fever (UK)	Epstein-Barr virus	Saliva; direct oral contact with infected person	2–6 weeks
Influenza	Numerous viruses (types A, B, C)	Direct contact; respiratory droplets, possibly airborne	1–4 days
Legionnaires' disease	*Legionella pneumophila* bacterium	Water droplets in contaminated hot-water systems, cooling towers, etc.	1–3 days
Leprosy	*Mycobacterium leprae* bacillus	Droplet infection (minimally contagious)	variable
Malaria	*Plasmodium* protozoa	Bite from infected mosquito	6–37 days
Measles (rubeola)	Rubeola virus	Droplet infection	10–15 days
Meningitis	Various bacteria (bacterial meningitis) and viruses (viral meningitis)	Respiratory droplets	varies with causative agent
Mumps	Virus	Direct contact with infected persons; respiratory droplets and oral secretions	14–21 days
Paratyphoid fevers	*Salmonella* bacteria	Ingestion of contaminated food and water	1–14 days
Pneumonia	*Streptococcus pneumoniae* bacterium	Droplet infection	1–3 weeks
Poliomyelitis	Polio viruses	Direct contact with nasopharyngeal secretions of infected persons; vomit	7–21 days
Rabies	Virus	Bite from rabid animal	10 days – 6 months
Rubella (German measles)	Rubella virus	Direct contact or droplet spread of nasopharyngeal secretion	14–21 days
SARS (severe acute respiratory syndrome)	SARS-associated coronavirus	Direct contact with infected persons, or respiratory droplets	2–7 days
Scarlet fever	Group A haemolytic *Streptococcus* bacteria	Direct or indirect contact with infected persons, or droplet infection	1–5 days
Shingles	*see* chickenpox	*see* chickenpox	
Smallpox (variola)	Poxvirus variola	Direct contact; droplet	7–14 days
Syphilis	*Treponema pallidum* bacterium	Sexual relations; contact with open lesions; blood transfusion	10–90 days
Tetanus (lockjaw)	*Clostridium tetani* bacillus	Animal faeces and soil	3–21 days
Tuberculosis	*Mycobacterium tuberculosis* bacillus	Droplet spread; ingestion from contaminated milk	variable
Typhoid fever	*Salmonella typhi* bacillus	Contaminated food and water	7–21 days
Whooping cough (pertussis)	*Bordetella pertussis* bacterium	Droplet spread	10–21 days
Yellow fever	Arbovirus	Bite from infected mosquito	3–6 days

HUMAN BEINGS

The geography of HIV infection

At the end of 2001 it was estimated that some 35 million people were infected with HIV (23.5 million in sub-Saharan Africa). By 2005, the estimated figure had risen to 40 million.

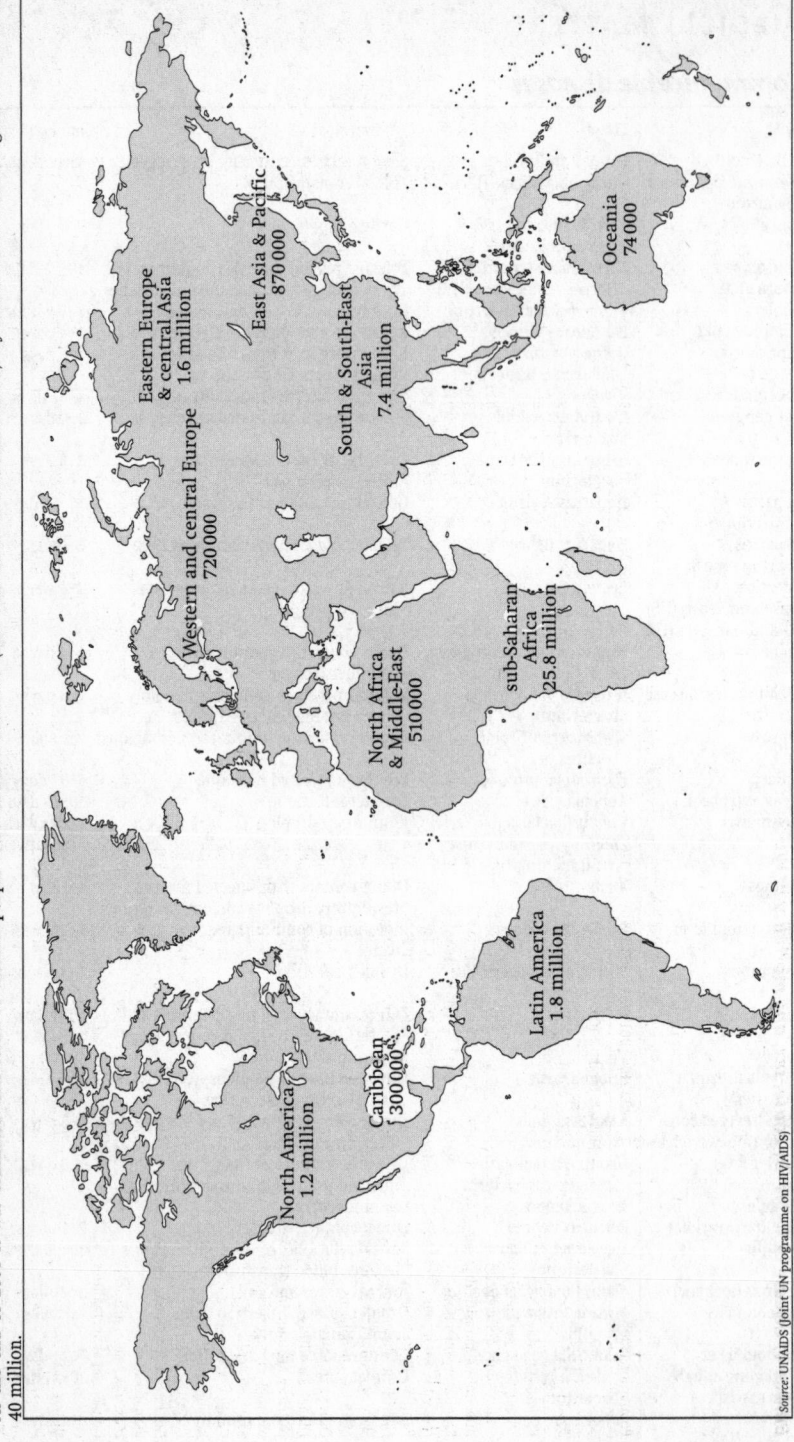

North America
1.2 million

Caribbean
300000

Latin America
1.8 million

Eastern Europe
& central Asia
1.6 million

Western and central Europe
720000

North Africa
& Middle-East
510000

sub-Saharan
Africa
25.8 million

East Asia & Pacific
870000

South & South-East
Asia
7.4 million

Oceania
74000

Source: UNAIDS (Joint UN programme on HIV/AIDS)

Burden of disease in DALYs[a] by cause, sex, and mortality in WHO Regions,[b] estimates for 2001

Cause[c]	Both sexes (000)	% total	Africa — High child, high adult	Africa — High child, v. high adult	The Americas — V. low child, low adult	The Americas — Low child, low adult	The Americas — High child, high adult	Eastern Mediterranean — Low child, low adult	Eastern Mediterranean — High child, high adult	Europe — V. low child, low adult	Europe — Low child, low adult	Europe — Low child, high adult	South-East Asia — Low child, high adult	South-East Asia — High child, high adult	Western Pacific — V. low child, low adult	Western Pacific — Low child, low adult
	(000)	% total	(000)	(000)	(000)	(000)	(000)	(000)	(000)	(000)	(000)	(000)	(000)	(000)	(000)	(000)
Population (000)	6 122 210		301 878	353 598	328 176	437 142	72 649	141 835	351 256	412 512	219 983	214 683	297 525	1 262 285	154 919	1 546 770
Total DALYs	1 467 257	100	147 899	209 985	46 520	81 270	17 427	23 007	113 214	53 075	38 936	59 212	61 290	357 554	16 430	241 438
I Communicable diseases, maternal & perinatal conditions & nutritional deficiencies	615 737	42.0	105 097	156 359	3 250	17 105	6 761	5 691	61 446	2 579	7 029	4 999	20 403	167 749	1 064	56 205
Infectious & parasitic diseases	359 377	24.5	71 903	117 144	1 422	7 424	3 709	2 227	32 514	958	2 388	2 530	11 018	82 977	358	22 805
Respiratory infections	94 037	6.4	13 111	16 761	425	2 139	965	1 115	10 615	677	2 056	893	2 497	30 407	394	11 983
Maternal conditions	30 943	2.1	4 783	6 546	189	1 158	496	446	3 684	156	329	266	1 404	8 623	59	2 805
Perinatal conditions	98 422	6.7	11 091	10 829	739	5 257	1 100	1 289	11 174	489	1 666	712	3 828	35 667	127	14 453
Nutritional deficiencies	32 958	2.2	4 209	5 079	476	1 127	490	615	3 460	299	591	599	1 656	10 075	125	4 158
II Noncommunicable conditions	672 865	45.9	30 030	36 075	38 642	50 328	8 432	13 282	39 329	46 259	27 473	42 170	31 866	144 703	13 720	150 556
Malignant neoplasms	76 716	5.2	2 956	3 881	5 555	4 513	883	1 084	2 824	8 554	3 330	5 486	3 027	10 630	2 743	21 248
Other neoplasms	1 773	0.1	31	44	104	136	22	35	191	176	38	65	333	271	68	259
Diabetes mellitus	15 446	1.1	358	460	1 388	1 798	226	418	833	1 083	526	682	1 098	3 417	377	2 783
Nutritional/endocrine disorders	8 232	0.6	754	897	802	1 181	252	242	629	637	177	184	402	537	229	1 310
Neuropsychiatric disorders	191 260	13.0	7 868	9 412	13 845	18 598	2 927	4 234	10 555	14 727	7 015	8 858	8 538	39 553	3 757	41 373
Sense organ disorders	38 742	2.6	2 086	2 234	1 681	1 793	307	879	2 457	2 234	1 024	1 819	2 995	10 585	806	7 841
Cardiovascular diseases	144 471	9.8	5 388	5 976	6 950	7 194	1 001	2 935	8 855	9 201	8 495	16 440	6 104	35 427	2 391	28 115
Respiratory diseases	62 842	4.3	3 126	4 144	2 986	4 848	761	674	3 125	3 195	1 699	2 149	2 366	14 042	1 053	18 674
Digestive diseases	50 173	3.4	2 864	3 506	1 705	3 759	782	545	3 622	2 447	2 027	2 682	2 523	12 791	706	10 214
Genitourinary system diseases	15 010	1.0	1 271	1 509	595	1 055	265	349	1 114	549	565	725	823	2 729	225	3 236
Skin diseases	2 171	0.1	335	425	73	171	42	21	145	88	37	133	241	309	19	133
Musculoskeletal diseases	29 798	2.0	1 037	1 144	1 923	2 178	304	485	1 203	2 448	1 468	1 902	1 564	5 085	982	8 077
Congenital abnormalities	28 083	1.9	1 715	2 161	685	2 284	514	962	3 121	566	679	697	1 191	7 616	221	5 670
Oral diseases	8 148	0.6	242	282	352	820	147	419	655	353	393	347	661	1 712	141	1 623
III Injuries	178 656	12.2	12 771	17 551	4 628	13 837	2 235	3 960	12 439	4 237	4 434	12 042	9 021	45 102	1 646	34 677
Unintentional	129 853	8.9	9 403	10 886	3 053	7 288	1 679	3 296	9 033	3 121	3 371	7 614	7 032	36 900	994	26 184
Intentional	48 802	3.3	3 369	6 666	1 575	6 549	555	738	3 406	1 116	1 063	4 428	1 989	8 203	653	8 493

Notes:
[a] Disability-Adjusted Life Years. [b] These figures were produced by WHO using the best available evidence. They are not necessarily the official statistics of Member States.
[c] Estimates for specific causes may not sum to broader cause groupings due to omission of residual categories.

Source: World Health Organization, World Health Report, 2002.

HUMAN BEINGS

HUMAN BEINGS

Phobias

An A to Z of phobias arranged by technical term

Technical term	Everyday name	Technical term	Everyday name	Technical term	Everyday name
Acero-	Sourness	Enete-	Pins	Nepho- (nephelo-)	Clouds
Achulo-	Darkness	Entomo-	Insects	Noso- (patho-)	Disease
Acro-	Heights	Eoso-	Dawn	Ocho-	Vehicles
Aero-	Air	Eremo-	Solitude	Odonto-	Teeth
Agora-	Open spaces	Ergo-	Work	Oiko-	Home
Aichuro-	Points	Erythro-	Blushing	Olfacto-	Smell
Ailouro-	Cats	Geno-	Sex	Ommato-	Eyes
Akoustico-	Sound	Geuma- (geumato-)	Taste	Oneiro-	Dreams
Algo-	Pain	Grapho-	Writing	Ophidio-	Snakes
Amaka-	Carriages	Gymnoto-	Nudity	Ornitho-	Birds
Amatho-	Dust	Gyno-	Women	Ourano-	Heaven
Andro-	Men	Hamartio-	Sin	Pan- (panto-)	Everything
Anemo-	Wind	Hapto-	Touch	Partheno-	Girls
Angino-	Narrowness	Harpaxo-	Robbers	Patroio-	Heredity
Anthropo-	Man	Hedono-	Pleasure	Penia-	Poverty
Antlo-	Flood	Helmintho-	Worms	Phasmo-	Ghosts
Apeiro-	Infinity	Hemato-	Blood	Phobo-	Fears
Arachno-	Spiders	Hodo-	Travel	Photo-	Light
Astheno-	Weakness	Homichlo-	Fog	Pnigero-	Smothering
Astra-	Astral	Horme-	Shock	Poine-	Punishment
Ate-	Ruin	Hydro-	Water	Poly-	Many things
Aulo-	Flute	Hypegia-	Responsibility	Poto-	Drink
Aurora-	Northern Lights	Hypno-	Sleep	Pterono-	Feathers
Bacillo-	Microbes	Ideo-	Ideas	Pyro-	Fire
Baro-	Gravity	Kakorraphia-	Failure	Rypo-	Soiling
Baso-	Walking	Katagelo-	Ridicule	Satano-	Satan
Batracho-	Reptiles	Keno-	Void	Sela-	Flashes
Belone-	Needles	Kineso-	Motion	Sidero-	Stars
Bronto- (tonitro-)	Thunder	Klepto-	Stealing	Sito-	Food
Cheima- (cheimato-)	Cold	Kopo-	Fatigue	Sperma- (spermato-)	Germs
Chiono-	Snow	Kristallo-	Ice	Stasi-	Standing
Chrometo-	Money	Lalo-	Stuttering	Stygio- (hade-)	Hell
Chromo-	Colour	Linono-	String	Syphilo-	Syphilis
Chrono-	Duration	Logo-	Words	Thalasso-	Sea
Chrystallo-	Crystals	Lysso- (mania-)	Insanity	Thanato-	Death
Claustro-	Closed spaces	Mastigo-	Flogging	Thasso-	Sitting
Cnido-	Stings	Mechano-	Machinery	Theo-	God
Cometo-	Comets	Metallo-	Metals	Thermo-	Heat
Cyno-	Dogs	Meteoro-	Meteors	Toxi-	Poison
Demo-	Crowds	Miso- (myso-)	Contamination	Tremo-	Trembling
Demono-	Demons	Mono-	One thing	Triskaideka-	Thirteen
Dermato-	Skin	Musico-	Music	Xeno-	Strangers
Dike-	Justice	Muso-	Mice	Zelo-	Jealousy
Dora-	Fur	Necro-	Corpses	Zoo-	Animals
Eisoptro-	Mirror	Nelo-	Glass		
Elektro-	Electricity	Neo-	Newness		

Phobias (continued)

An A to Z of phobias arranged by everyday name

Everyday name	Technical term	Everyday name	Technical term	Everyday name	Technical term
Air	Aero-	Glass	Nelo-	Ridicule	Katagelo-
Animals	Zoo-	God	Theo-	Robberies	Harpaxo-
Astral	Astra-	Gravity	Baro-	Ruin	Ate-
Birds	Orthino-	Heat	Thermo-	Satan	Satano-
Blood	Hemato-	Heaven	Ourano-	Sea	Thalasso-
Blushing	Erythro-	Heights	Acro-	Sex	Geno-
Carriages	Amaka-	Hell	Stygio- (hade-)	Shock	Horme-
Cats	Ailouro-	Heredity	Patroio-	Sin	Hamartio-
Closed spaces	Claustro-	Home	Oiko-	Sitting	Thasso-
Clouds	Nepho- (nephelo-)	Ice	Kristallo-	Skin	Dermato-
Cold	Cheima-	Ideas	Ideo-	Sleep	Hypno-
Colour	Chromo-	Infinity	Apeiro-	Smell	Olfacto-
Comets	Cometo-	Insanity	Lysso- (mania-)	Smothering	Pnigero-
Contamination	Miso- (myso-)	Insects	Entomo-	Snakes	Ophidio-
Corpses	Necro-	Jealousy	Zelo-	Snow	Chiono-
Crowds	Demo-	Justice	Dike-	Soiling	Rypo-
Crystals	Chrystallo-	Light	Photo-	Solitude	Eremo-
Darkness	Achluo-	Machinery	Mechano-	Sound	Akoustico-
Dawn	Eoso-	Man	Anthropo-	Sourness	Acero-
Death	Thanato-	Many things	Poly-	Spiders	Arachno-
Demons	Demono-	Men	Andro-	Standing	Stasi-
Disease	Noso- (patho-)	Metals	Metallo-	Stars	Sidero-
Dogs	Cyno-	Meteors	Meteoro-	Stealing	Klepto-
Dreams	Oneiro-	Mice	Muso-	Stings	Cnido-
Drinks	Poto-	Microbes	Bacillo-	Strangers	Xeno-
Duration	Chrono-	Mirrors	Eisoptro-	String	Linono-
Dust	Amatho-	Money	Chrometo-	Stuttering	Lalo-
Electricity	Elektro-	Motion	Kineso-	Syphilis	Syphilo-
Everything	Pan- (panto-)	Music	Musico-	Taste	Geuma- (geumato-)
Eyes	Ommato-	Narrowness	Angino-	Teeth	Odonto-
Failure	Kakorraphia-	Needles	Belone-	Thirteen	Triskaideka-
Fatigue	Kopo-	Newness	Neo-	Thunder	Bronto- (tonitro-)
Fears	Phobo-	Northern Lights	Aurora-	Touch	Hapto-
Feathers	Pterono-	Nudity	Gymno-	Travel	Hodo-
Fire	Pyro-		(gymnoto-)	Trembling	Tremo-
Flashes	Sela-	One thing	Mono-	Vehicles	Ocho-
Flogging	Mastigo-	Open spaces	Agora-	Void	Keno-
Flood	Antlo-	Pain	Algo-	Walking	Baso-
Flute	Aulo-	Pins	Enete-	Water	Hydro-
Fog	Homichlo-	Pleasure	Hedono-	Weakness	Astheno-
Food	Sito-	Points	Aichuro-	Wind	Anemo-
Fur	Dora-	Poison	Toxi-	Women	Gyno-
Germs	Sperma-	Poverty	Penia-	Words	Logo-
	(spermato-)	Punishment	Poine-	Work	Ergo-
Ghosts	Phasmo-	Reptiles	Batracho-	Worms	Helmintho-
Girls	Partheno-	Responsibility	Hypegia-	Writing	Grapho-

HUMAN BEINGS

Commonly used drugs

Common name	Drug type	Use	Comments
Adrenaline	Bronchodilator	Counteracts cardiac arrest; relieves severe allergic reactions; and controls symptoms of asthma.	Constricts blood vessels and is used to control bleeding in surgery.
Anabolic steroids	Male sex hormones	Increase muscle bulk and body growth. Help increase production of blood cells in some forms of anaemia.	Risk of serious side-effects. Abused by some athletes to improve performance.
Aspirin	Analgesic; anti-inflammatory; anti-platelet	Relieves pain; reduces fever; helps prevent blood clots from forming.	Introduced by Hermann Dresser, 1893. Can cause irritation to the stomach and even bleeding.
AZT (azidothymidine)	Anti-viral drug	Suppresses activity of the virus that causes Aids, and can alleviate symptoms.	Effective only in certain cases, and not a cure.
Beta blockers	Beta blockers	Treat angina, hypertension, and irregular heart rhythms. Can also prevent migraines.	Minor side-effects of reduced circulation and reduced capacity for strenuous exercise.
Chloral hydrate	Sleeping drug	Short-term treatment of insomnia.	Suitable for use by children.
Cimetidine	Anti-ulcer drug	Reduces level of acid and pepsin, and promotes healing of stomach and duodenal ulcers.	Also affects actions of certain enzymes in the liver. Prescribed only when possibility of stomach cancer has been ruled out.
Codeine	Narcotic analgesic	Relieves mild pain. Also effective as a cough suppressant.	Introduced at turn of century. Can be habit-forming, but addiction seldom occurs if drug used for limited period.
Cortisone	Corticosteroid	Treats rheumatoid arthritis. Anti-inflammatory drug.	Discovered by Edward Calvin Kendall, 1934, as adrenal cortisone extracts.
Co-trimoxazole	Antibacterial	Treats respiratory, constipating, and urinary tract infections.	Can have side-effects of nausea and vomiting.
Diazepam	Benzodiazepine anti-anxiety drug	Treats anxiety, insomnia. Also prescribed as muscle relaxant.	Can be habit-forming if taken over a long period.
Digoxin	Digitalis drug	Slows down rate of heart. Controls tiredness, breathlessness, and fluid retention.	Treatment must be monitored carefully.
Ethambutol	Antituberculosis	Used with other antituberculosis drugs it helps boost their effects.	Side-effect can be eye damage.
Frusemide	Loop diuretic	Treats fluid retention caused by heart failure and some liver and kidney disorders.	Discovered 1960.
Ibuprofen	Analgesic; anti-inflammatory	Treats symptoms of rheumatoid arthritis as well as headaches and menstrual pain.	Few-side effects and does not cause bleeding in the stomach.
Insulin	For diabetes	Supplements or replaces natural insulin in diabetes mellitus.	Isolated by Frederick Banting, C H Best, 1921. Only effective treatment for juvenile diabetes.
Magnesium hydroxide	Antacid	Neutralizes stomach acid. Also acts as laxative.	
Morphine	Narcotic analgesic	Relieves severe pain.	Discovered by Friedrich Serturner, 1805. Derives from opium and can be addictive.
Paracetamol/ acetaminophen	Analgesic	Relieves bouts of mild pain and fever. Does not cause damage to stomach.	First used by Joseph von Mering, 1893. Large doses can be toxic and an overdose can cause serious damage to liver and kidneys.
Penicillin	Antibiotic	Treats many common infections.	Discovered by Alexander Fleming, 1928. Can cause allergic reactions.
Pethidine	Narcotic analgesic	Used particularly to relieve pain in childbirth. Effect short-lasting.	Introduced by Hoechst, 1939. Habit-forming if taken over long period of time.
Phenylpropan-olamine	Decongestant	Relieves nasal congestion in colds and hay fever.	Can raise the heart rate and cause palpitations.
Quinidine	Anti-arrhythmic drug	Treats abnormal heart rhythms.	Can cause allergic reactions.

Common name	Drug type	Use	Comments
Quinine	Antimalarial drug	Treats malaria and leg cramps.	Discovered by P J Pelletier, J B Caventou, 1818. Now rarely prescribed due to side-effects of headaches, nausea, hearing loss and blurred vision.
Ranitidine	Anti-ulcer drug	Prevents gastric and duodenal ulcers. Reduces amount of acid produced by stomach.	Prescribed only when possibility of stomach cancer has been ruled out.
Salbutamol/ albuterol	Bronchodilator	Treats asthma, bronchitis, and emphysema.	Little stimulant effect on heart rate and blood pressure. Gives rapid relief and is more effective if inhaled rather than taken by mouth.
Sodium bicarbonate	Antacid	Relieves indigestion and discomfort caused by peptic ulcers. Relieves pain from urinary tract infections.	If given by injection, can also be effective in treatment of acidity of the blood.
Temazepam	Benzodiazepine sleeping drug	Short-term treatment of insomnia.	Can be habit-forming.
Terfenadine	Antihistamine	Treats allergic rhinitis, particularly hay fever.	Little or no sedative effect on the nervous system.
Testosterone	Male sex hormone	Increases fertility in men with testicular disorders. Also used to induce puberty in cases of hormone deficiency.	Can interfere with growth or cause over-rapid sexual development.
Tetracycline	Antibiotic	Treats pneumonia, bronchitis, and chest infections.	Common side-effects are nausea and vomiting.

Commonly abused drugs

Name	Common name	Effects	Comments
Alcohol	Booze, drink	Acts as central-nervous-system depressant, so reduces anxiety, impairs concentration, slows reactions.	Long-term effects include liver disease (cirrhosis, liver cancer, hepatitis), heart disease, and inflammation of stomach. Alcoholics have above-average chance of developing dementia.
Amphetamines	Uppers, speed, bennies	Promote feelings of alertness; increases speech and physical activity.	Can produce toxic effects, mood swings, circulatory and cardiac disturbances, feelings of paranoia, hallucinations, and convulsions.
Barbiturates (Nembutal, Seconal, Amytal)	Barbs, reds, downers	Calm the nerves; induce sleep; have hypnotic effect.	Highly addictive; overdose is lethal; can induce state of coma. Often fatal if taken with alcohol.
Benzodiazepines	Tranquillizers	Reduce mental activity and anxiety; slow body's reactions; reduce alertness.	Can cause dependency. Withdrawal symptoms occur on stopping the drug – anxiety, insomnia, panic attacks, headaches, and palpitations.
Cocaine	Coke, crack, ice, snow (crack is a blend of cocaine, baking powder, and water)	Increases blood pressure, heart rate, breathing, and body temperature; gives feelings of euphoria, illusions of increased sensory awareness and mental and physical strength, decreased hunger, pain, and need for sleep.	Regular use can cause anxiety, insomnia, weight loss, increased paranoia, and psychosis. Crack is highly addictive and has more intense effects than cocaine. Increased risk of abnormal heart rhythms, high blood pressure, stroke, and death. Long-term consequences include mental deterioration, personality changes, paranoia, or violent behaviour.
Heroin	Junk, smack	Induces euphoria; relieves pain; often induces sleep.	Highly addictive; overdose can result in death; serum hepatitis is common; as are skin abscesses, inflammation of the veins, constipation, and respiratory depression.
Lysergic acid diethylamide	LSD, acid	Causes hallucinations, alters vision, raises temperature and heart-beat; evokes flashbacks.	Long-term use causes anxiety and depression, impaired memory and attention span, difficulty with abstract thinking.

HUMAN BEINGS

Commonly abused drugs (continued)

Name	Common name	Effects	Comments
Marijuana	Grass, pot, weed, dope	Increases heartbeat; heightens senses; gives feelings of euphoria and relaxation.	Reduces the ability to perform tasks requiring concentration; slows reactions; and impairs coordination.
MDMA	Ecstasy, E	Promotes mental relaxation, increased sensitivity to stimuli, and sometimes hallucinations.	High doses have amphetamine-like effects. Can produce severe or fatal reactions, sometimes after only one dose.
Mescaline	Peyote, cactus buttons	Induces hallucinations; affects sensations and perceptions.	Loss of control of normal thought processes; long-term depression and anxiety; can induce 'breaks from reality'.
Methadone		Induces sleep and feeling of relaxation.	Addictive; overdose can result in death.
Nicotine		Stimulates the nervous system; increases concentration; relieves tension and fatigue; increases heart rate and blood pressure.	Taken regularly, can cause increase in fatty acids in bloodstream, increased risk of heart disease, and circulatory problems; can also increase risk of peptic ulcers. Increased risk of lung, throat, and mouth cancers from tobacco smoke.
Nitrites	Poppers	Give the user a rapid high, felt as rush of energy. Heart rate increases; there are feelings of dizziness and nausea. High doses can cause fainting.	Lasting physical damage, in the form of cardiac problems, can occur.
Phencyclidine	PCP, angel dust	Gives feeling of euphoria; floating sensation; numbness; change in user's perception of the body; visual disturbances.	Can produce violent behaviour against the user or others; and schizophrenic-like psychosis which can last for days or weeks.
Solvents		Cause lightheadedness, dizziness, and drowsiness. Large doses can lead to loss of consciousness.	Some products can seriously disrupt heart rhythm or cause heart failure and sometimes death. Aerosols can cause suffocation by coating the lungs. Risk of death also from depression of the breathing mechanism. Long-term misuse leads to kidney and liver damage.

NUTRITION

Ideal weights for men and women over 25 years of age

Women				Men			
Height		Ideal weight		Height		Ideal weight	
(cm)	(in)	(kg)	(lb)	(cm)	(in)	(kg)	(lb)
153	60	46.3–53.9	102.0–118.8	155	61	53.5–63.9	117.9–140.9
155	61	47.6–55.3	104.9–121.9	157	62	54.8–65.3	120.8–143.9
157	62	48.9–57.1	107.8–125.9	160	63	56.2–67.1	143.7–147.9
160	63	50.3–58.9	110.9–129.8	162	64	57.6–68.9	127.0–151.9
162	64	51.7–61.2	114.0–134.9	165	65	58.9–70.8	129.9–156.1
165	65	53.5–63.0	117.9–138.9	168	66	60.8–73.0	134.0–160.9
168	66	55.3–64.8	121.9–142.8	170	67	62.6–75.3	138.0–166.0
170	67	57.1–66.7	125.9–147.0	173	68	65.4–77.1	144.2–170.0
173	68	58.9–68.5	129.9–151.0	175	69	66.2–78.9	145.9–173.9
175	69	60.8–70.3	134.0–155.0	178	70	68.0–81.2	149.9–179.0
178	70	62.6–72.1	138.0–158.9	180	71	69.8–83.5	153.9–184.1
180	71	64.4–73.9	142.0–162.9	183	72	71.6–86.7	157.8–191.1
183	72	66.2–75.7	145.9–166.9	185	73	73.5–87.9	162.0–193.8
185	73	68.0–77.6	149.9–171.0	188	74	75.7–90.2	166.9–198.8
188	74	69.8–79.3	153.9–174.8	190	75	78.0–92.5	171.9–203.9
				193	76	80.3–94.8	177.0–209.0

Composition of foods

Figures (approximate) per 100 g of food.

Food	Protein (g)	Carbohydrates (g)	Fat (g)	Fibre (g)	Energy value (calories[a])
Meat, poultry, fish					
Bacon, back, grilled	15	2	24	0	271
Bacon, streaky, grilled	16	2	27	0	308
Beef, minced	31	0	16	0	221
Beef, rump steak, grilled	30	0	12	0	218
Chicken, meat only, roast	19	0	4	0	142
Cod, cooked	19	0	1	0	94
Crab, cooked	18	1	5	0	129
Haddock, cooked	19	0	1	0	96
Ham, lean	22	0	5	0	168
Lamb chop, boned, grilled	24	0	29	0	353
Liver, cooked	20	6	13	0	254
Lobster, cooked	20	trace	3	0	119
Mackerel, cooked	25	0	11	0	188
Mussels, cooked	17	0	1	0	86
Pork chop, boned, grilled	28	0	24	0	328
Prawns, cooked	18	0	1	0	107
Salmon, cooked	20	0	13	0	196
Tuna, canned in brine	28	0	1	0	118
Turkey, meat only, roast	36	0	3	0	140
Vegetables					
Asparagus, cooked	2	4	trace	1	18
Aubergine/egg-plant, cooked	1	4	trace	2	14
Beans, broad, cooked	4	66	1	4	46
Beans, dried white, cooked	8	21	7	25	118
Beans, green, cooked	2	5	trace	4	25
Beetroot, cooked	1	7	trace	2	43
Broccoli, cooked	3	5	trace	4	26
Brussel sprouts, cooked	4	6	trace	3	18
Cabbage, cooked	2	trace	trace	2	11
Cabbage, raw	2	5	trace	3	25
Carrots, cooked	1	5	trace	3	20
Carrots, raw	1	6	trace	3	25
Cauliflower, cooked	2	4	trace	2	22
Celery, raw	1	2	trace	2	36
Chick peas, dry	20	50	6	15	320
Corn (on the cob)	3	21	1	5	91
Courgettes/zucchini, cooked	1	3	trace	1	14
Cucumber, raw	1	3	trace	trace	15
Leeks, cooked	1	7	0	4	25
Lentils, cooked	8	19	trace	4	106
Lettuce, raw	1	3	trace	1	12
Mushrooms, raw	3	4	trace	2	14
Onions, raw	2	9	trace	1	38
Parsnip, cooked	1	17	trace	4	50
Peas, fresh, cooked	5	4	trace	5	54
Pepper, green, raw	1	5	trace	1	14
Pepper, red, raw	1	7	trace	1	20
Potatoes, baked in skin	3	21	trace	2	86
Potatoes, boiled in skin	2	17	trace	2	75
Spinach, cooked	3	4	trace	6	23
Swede, cooked	1	4	trace	3	18
Turnip, cooked	1	5	trace	2	14
Fruit					
Apples	trace	15	trace	2	38
Apricots, dried	5	67	1	24	182
Apricots, raw	1	13	trace	2	25
Avocados	2	6	16	2	221
Bananas	1	22	trace	2	85

[a]Multiply calories by 4·187 to convert to kilojoules.

Composition of foods (continued)

Food	Protein (g)	Carbohydrates (g)	Fat (g)	Fibre (g)	Energy value (calories[a])
Blackberries	1	13	1	7	29
Blackcurrants	2	14	trace	9	29
Cherries	1	17	trace	1	70
Dates	2	73	1	7	214
Figs, dried	4	69	1	19	214
Grapefruit	1	11	trace	trace	41
Grapes	1	16	1	1	69
Melon, honeydew	1	5	trace	1	21
Melon, water	trace	5	trace	1	21
Nectarines	1	17	trace	2	64
Oranges, peeled	1	12	trace	2	49
Peaches	1	8	trace	1	38
Pears	1	15	trace	2	61
Pineapple	trace	14	trace	1	46
Prunes	1	77	trace	14	136
Raisins	3	77	trace	7	246
Raspberries	1	14	1	7	25
Strawberries	1	8	1	2	37
Tomatoes	1	5	trace	1	14
Dairy products					
Butter, salted	1	trace	82	0	740
Cheese, Brie	19	2	23	0	314
Cheese, Cheddar	25	2	32	0	414
Cheese, cottage	17	2	4	0	96
Cheese, Edam	30	trace	23	0	314
Cream, double	2	3	48	0	446
Milk, cow's, skimmed	4	5	trace	0	36
Milk, cow's, whole	4	5	4	0	65
Yogurt, skimmed milk	3	5	2	0	50
Yogurt, whole milk	3	5	3	0	62
Grain products					
Flour, white	9	80	1	4	350
Flour, wholemeal	13	56	2	10	318
Oatmeal, cooked	2	10	1	7	399
Oats, porridge	10	70	7	7	377
Pasta, dry	12	71	2	4	353
Rice, brown, cooked	3	26	1	1	129
Rice, white, cooked	3	33	trace	1	121
Legumes, nuts, and seeds					
Almonds	19	20	54	15	564
Brazil nuts	14	11	67	9	618
Peanuts, fresh	26	19	48	8	571
Walnuts	15	16	64	5	525
Miscellaneous					
Biscuit, chocolate digestive	6	64	25	4	506
Biscuit, digestive	7	62	23	5	486
Chocolate bar, plain	4	63	29	0	510
Crisps	6	40	37	11	517
Egg, boiled	13	1	12	0	163
Honey	trace	82	0	0	289
Jam	1	79	trace	1	261
Margarine	trace	1	80	0	730
Oil, vegetable	0	0	100	0	900
Orange juice	1	10	trace	0	45
Sugar	0	100	0	0	394

[a]Multiply calories by 4.187 to convert to kilojoules.

Main types of vitamin

Fat-soluble vitamins

Vitamin	Chemical name	Precursor	Main symptom of deficiency	Dietary source
A	Retinol	Beta-carotene	Xerophthalmia (eye disease)	Retinol: milk, butter, cheese; egg yolk; liver; fatty fish Carotene: green vegetables; yellow and red fruits and vegetables, especially carrots
D	Cholecalciferol	UV-activated 7-dehydro-cholesterol	Rickets; osteomalacia	Fatty fish; margarine; some fortified milks
K	Phytomenadione		Haemorrhagic problems	Green leafy vegetables; liver
E	Tocopherols		Multiple effects	Vegetable oils

Water-soluble vitamins

Vitamin	Chemical name	Main symptom of deficiency	Dietary source
C	Ascorbic acid	Scurvy	Citrus fruits; potatoes; green leafy vegetables
B-vitamins			
B_1	Thiamine	Beri-beri	Seeds and grains: widely distributed
B_2	Riboflavin	Failure to thrive	Liver; milk; cheese; yeast
–	Nicotinic acid	Pellagra	Meat; fish; cereals; pulses
B_6	Pyridoxine	Dermatitis; neurological disorders	Cereals; liver; meat; fruits; leafy vegetables
B_{12}	Cyanocobalamin	Anaemia	Meat; milk; liver
–	Folic acid	Anaemia	Liver; green vegetables
–	Pantothenic acid	Dermatitis	Widespread
–	Biotin	Dermatitis	Liver; kidney; yeast extracts

Main trace minerals

Mineral	Main symptom of deficiency	Dietary source	Proportion of total body weight (%)
Calcium	Rickets in children; osteoporosis in adults	Milk: butter; cheese; sardines; green leafy vegetables; citrus fruits	2.5
Chromium	Adult-onset diabetes	Brewer's yeast; black pepper; liver; wholemeal bread; beer	<0.01
Copper	Anaemia; Menkes' syndrome	Green vegetables; fish; oysters; liver	<0.01
Fluorine	Tooth decay; possibly osteoporosis	Fluoridated drinking water; seafood; tea	<0.01
Iodine	Goitre; cretinism in new-born children	Seafood; salt-water fish; seaweed; iodized salt; table salt	<0.01
Iron	Anaemia	Liver; kidney; green leafy vegetables; egg yolk; dried fruit; potatoes; molasses	0.01
Magnesium	Irregular heartbeat; muscular weakness; insomnia	Green leafy vegetables (eaten raw); nuts; whole grains	0.07
Manganese	Not known in humans	Legumes; cereals; green leafy vegetables; tea	<0.01
Molybdenum	Not known in humans	Legumes; cereals; liver; kidney; some dark-green vegetables	<0.01
Phosphorus	Muscular weakness; bone pain; loss of appetite	Meat; poultry; fish; eggs; dried beans and peas; milk products	1.1
Potassium	Irregular heartbeat; muscular weakness; fatigue; kidney and lung failure	Fresh vegetables; meat; orange juice; bananas; bran	0.10
Selenium	Not known in humans	Seafood; cereals; meat; egg yolk; garlic	<0.01
Sodium	Impaired acid-base balance in body fluids (very rare)	Table salt; other naturally occurring salts	0.10
Zinc	Impaired wound healing; loss of appetite; impaired sexual development	Meat; whole grains; legumes; oysters; milk	<0.01

HUMAN BEINGS

Food additives

The prefix 'E' stands for European and indicates that an additive is accepted as safe throughout the European Community. It was introduced by the Food Labelling Regulations of 1984 and is used by food manufacturers in member states of the EC.
Any number without the prefix 'E' has been approved by the UK, but not yet by the European Community.
Also listed (without numbers) are additives with a long history of use in the food industry for which formal EC approval is either pending or deemed unnecessary.
In the United States, additives require approval by the US Food and Drug Administration (FDA).

Antioxidants
Stop fatty foods from going rancid and protect fat-soluble vitamins from the harmful effects of oxidation.

E300	L-ascorbic acid – *fruit drinks; also used to improve flour and bread dough*
E301	Sodium L–ascorbate
E302	Calcium L-ascorbate
E304	6-0-Palmitoyl-L-ascorbic acid (ascorbyl palmitate) – *Scotch eggs*
E306	Extracts of natural origin rich in tocopherols – *vegetable oils*
E307	Synthetic alpha-tocopherol – *cereal-based baby foods*
E308	Synthetic gamma-tocopherol
E309	Synthetic delta-tocopherol
E310	Propyl gallate – *vegetable oils; chewing gum*
E311	Octyl gallate
E312	Dodecyl gallate
E320	Butylated hydroxyanisole (BHA) – *soup mixes; cheese spread*
E321	Butylated hydroxytoluene (BHT) – *chewing gum*
E322	Lecithins – *low-fat spreads; also used as an emulsifier in chocolate*
	Diphenylamine
	Ethoxyquin – *used to prevent 'scald' (a discoloration) on apples and pears*

Preservatives
Protect against microbes which cause spoilage and food poisoning. They also increase storage life of foods.

E200	Sorbic acid – *soft drinks; fruit yoghurt; processed cheese slices*
E201	Sodium sorbate
E202	Potassium sorbate
E203	Calcium sorbate – *frozen pizza; flour confectionery*
E210	Benzoic acid
E211	Sodium benzoate
E212	Potassium benzoate
E213	Calcium benzoate
E214	Ethyl 4-hydroxybenzoate (ethyl para-hydroxybenzoate)
E215	Ethyl 4-hydroxybenzoate, sodium salt (sodium ethyl para-hydroxybenzoate)
E216	Propyl 4-hydroxybenzoate (propyl para-hydroxybenzoate).
E217	Propyl 4-hydroxybenzoate, sodium salt (sodium propyl para-hydroxybenzoate)
E218	Methyl 4-hydroxybenzoate (methyl para-hydroxybenzoate)
E219	Methyl 4-hydroxybenzoate, sodium salt (sodium methyl para-hydroxybenzoate) – *beer; jam; salad cream; soft drinks; fruit pulp; fruit-based pie fillings; marinated herring and mackerel*
E220	Sulphur dioxide
E221	Sodium sulphite

E222	Sodium hydrogen sulphite (sodium bisulphite)
E223	Sodium metabisulphite
E224	Potassium metabisulphite
E226	Calcium sulphite
E227	Calcium hydrogen sulphite (calcium bisulphite) – *dried fruit; dehydrated vegetables; fruit juices and syrups; sausages; fruit-based dairy desserts; cider, beer, and wine; also used to prevent browning of raw peeled potatoes and to condition biscuit doughs*
E228	Potassium bisulphite – *wines*
E230	Biphenyl (diphenyl)
E231	2-Hydroxybiphenyl (orthophenylphenol)
E232	Sodium biphenyl-2-yl oxide (sodium orthophenylphenate) – *surface treatment of citrus fruit*
E233	2-(Thiazol-4-yl) benzimidazole (thiabendazole) – *surface treatment of bananas*
234	Nisin – *cheese; clotted cream*
E239	Hexamine (hexamethylenetetramine) – *marinated herring and mackerel*
E249	Potassium nitrite
E250	Sodium nitrite
E251	Sodium nitrate
E252	Potassium nitrate – *bacon; ham; cured meats; corned beef; some cheeses*
E280	Propionic acid
E281	Sodium propionate
E282	Calcium propionate
E283	Potassium propionate – *bread and flour confectionery; Christmas pudding*

Colours
Make food more colourful, compensate for colour lost in processing.

E100	Curcumin – *flour confectionery; margarine*
E101	Riboflavin – *sauces*
101(a)	Riboflavin-5$_,$-phosphate
E102	Tartrazine – *soft drinks*
E104	Quinoline yellow
E110	Sunset Yellow FCF – *biscuits*
E120	Cochineal – *alcoholic drinks*
E122	Carmoisine – *jams and preserves*
E123	Amaranth
E124	Ponceau 4R – *dessert mixes*
E127	Erythrosine BS – *glacé cherries*
128	Red 2G – *sausages*
E131	Patent Blue V
E132	Indigo Carmine
133	Brilliant Blue FCF – *canned vegetables*
E140	Chlorophyll
E141	Copper complexes of chlorophyll and chlorophyllins
E142	Green S – *pastilles*
E150	Caramel – *beer; soft drinks; sauces; gravy browning*
E151	Black PN

E153 Carbon Black (vegetable carbon) – *liquorice*
154 Brown FK – *kippers*
155 Brown HT – *chocolate cake*
E160(a) Alpha-carotene; *beta*-carotene; *gamma*-carotene – *margarine; soft drinks*
E160(b) Annatto; bixin; norbixin – *crisps/potato chips*
E160(c) Capsanthin; capsorubin
E160(d) Lycopene
E160(e) *Beta*-apo-8'-carotenal
E160(f) Ethyl ester of beta-apo-8'-carotenoic acid
E161(a) Flavoxanthin
E161(b) Lutein
E161(c) Cryptoxanthin
E161(d) Rubixanthin
E161(e) Violaxanthin
E161(f) Rhodoxanthin
E161(g) Canthaxanthin
E162 Beetroot Red (betanin) – *ice-cream; liquorice*
E163 Anthocyanins – *yogurt*
E171 Titanium dioxide – *sweets*
E172 Iron oxides; iron hydroxides
E173 Aluminium
E174 Silver
E175 Gold – *cake decorations*
E180 Pigment Rubine (lithol rubine BK)
Methyl violet – *used for the surface marking of raw or unprocessed meat*
Paprika – *canned vegetables*
Turmeric – *soup*

Sweeteners
There are two types of sweeteners; intense sweeteners and bulk sweeteners. Intense sweeteners have a sweetness many times that of sugar and are therefore used at very low levels. They are marked with * in the following list. Bulk sweeteners have about the same sweetness as sugar and are used at the same sort of levels as sugar.

*Acesulfame potassium – *canned foods; soft drinks; table-top sweeteners*
*Aspartame – *soft drinks; yogurts; dessert and drink mixes; sweetening tablets*
Hydrogenated glucose syrup
Isomalt
Lactitol
E421 Mannitol – *sugar-free confectionery*
*Saccharin
*Sodium saccharin
*Calcium saccharin – *soft drinks; cider; sweetening tablets; table-top sweeteners*
E420 Sorbitol; sorbitol syrup – *sugar-free confectionery; jams for diabetics*
*Thaumatin – *table-top sweeteners; yogurt*
Xylitol – *sugar-free chewing gum*

Emulsifiers and stabilizers
Enable oils and fats to mix with water in foods; add to smoothness and creaminess of texture; retard baked goods going stale.

E400 Alginic acid – *ice-cream; soft cheese*
E401 Sodium alginate – *cake mixes*
E402 Potassium alginate
E403 Ammonium alginate
E404 Calcium alginate
E405 Propane-1,2-diol alginate (propylene glycol alginate) – *salad dressings; cottage cheese*
E406 Agar – *ice-cream*

E407 Carrageenan – *quick-setting jelly mixes; milk shakes*
E410 Locust bean gum (carob gum) – *salad cream*
E412 Guar gum – *packet soups and meringue mixes*
E413 Tragacanth – *salad dressings; processed cheese*
E414 Gum arabic (acacia) – *confectionery*
E415 Xanthan gum – *sweet pickle; coleslaw*
416 Karaya gum – *soft cheese; brown sauce*
432 Polyoxyethylene (20) sorbitan monolaurate (Polysorbate 20)
433 Polyoxyethylene (20) sorbitan mono-oleate (Polysorbate 80)
434 Polyoxyethylene (20) sorbitan monopalmitate (Polysorbate 40)
435 Polyoxyethylene (20) sorbitan monostearate (Polysorbate 60)
436 Polyoxyethylene (20) sorbitan tristearate (Polysorbate 65) – *bakery products; confectionery creams*
E440 (i) Pectin
E440 (ii) Amidated pectin
Pectin extract – *jams and preserves*
442 Ammonium phosphatides – *cocoa and chocolate products*
E460 Microcrystalline cellulose – *grated cheese*
Alpha-cellulose (powdered cellulose) – *slimming bread*
E461 Methylcellulose – *low-fat spreads*
E463 Hydroxypropylcellulose
E464 Hydroxypropylmethylcellulose – *edible ices*
E465 Ethylmethylcellulose – *gateaux*
E466 Carboxymethylcellulose, sodium salt (CMC) – *jelly; gateaux*
E470 Sodium, potassium and calcium salts of fatty acids – *cake mixes*
E471 Mono- and di-glycerides of fatty acids – *frozen desserts*
E472(a) Acetic acid esters of mono- and di-glycerides of fatty acids – *mousse mixes*
E472(b) Lactic acid esters of mono- and di-glycerides of fatty acids – *dessert toppings*
E472(c) Citric acid esters of mono- and di-glycerides of fatty acids – *continental sausages*
E472(d) Tartaric acid esters of mono- and di-glycerides of fatty acids
E472(e) Mono- and di-acetyltartaric acid esters of mono- and di-glycerides of fatty acids – *bread; frozen pizza*
E472(f) Mixed acetic and tartaric acid esters of mono- and di-glycerides of fatty acids
E473 Sucrose esters of fatty acids
E474 Sucroglycerides – *edible ices*
E475 Polyglycerol esters of fatty acids – *cakes and gateaux*
E476 Polyglycerol esters of polycondensed fatty acids of castor oil (polyglycerol polyricinoleate) – *chocolate-flavour coatings for cakes*
E477 Propane-1,2-diol esters of fatty acids – *instant desserts*
E481 Sodium stearoyl-1-2-lactylate – *bread; cakes; biscuits*
E482 Calcium stearoyl-1-2-lactylate – *gravy granules*
E483 Stearyl tartrate
491 Sorbitan monostearate
492 Sorbitan tristearate
493 Sorbitan monolaurate
494 Sorbitan mono-oleate

Food additives (continued)

495 Sorbitan monopalmitate – *cake mixes*
Extract of quillaia – *used in soft drinks to promote foam*
Oxidatively polymerized soya-bean oil
Polyglycerol esters of dimerized fatty acids of soya-bean oil – *emulsions used to grease bakery tins*

Others

Acids, anti-caking agents, anti-foaming agents, bases, buffers, bulking agents, firming agents, flavour modifiers, flour improvers, glazing agents, humectants, liquid freezants, packaging gases, propellants, release agents, sequestrants, and solvents.

E170 Calcium carbonate – *base, firming agent, release agent, diluent; nutrient in flour*
E260 Acetic acid
E261 Potassium acetate
E262 Sodium hydrogen diacetate
262 Sodium acetate – *acid/acidity regulators (buffers) used in pickles, salad cream and bread; they contribute to flavour and provide protection against mould growth*
E263 Calcium acetate – *firming agent; also provides calcium which is useful in quick-set jelly mix*
E270 Lactic acid – *acid/flavouring protects against mould growth; salad dressings; soft margarines*
E290 Carbon dioxide – *carbonating agent/packaging gas and propellant; used in fizzy drinks*
296 DL-malic acid; L-malic acid
297 Fumaric acid – *acid/flavouring; used in soft drinks, sweets, biscuits, dessert mixes, and pie fillings*
E325 Sodium lactate – *buffer, humectant; used in jams, preserves, sweets, flour confectionery*
E326 Potassium lactate – *buffer; jams, preserves and jellies*
E327 Calcium lactate – *buffer, firming agent; canned fruit, pie filling*
E330 Citric acid
E331 Sodium dihydrogen citrate (monosodium citrate); disodium citrate; trisodium citrate
E332 Potassium dihydrogen citrate (monopotassium citrate); tripotassium citrate
E333 Monocalcium citrate; dicalcium citrate; tricalcium citrate – *acid/flavouring, buffers, sequestrants, emulsifying salts (calcium salts are firming agents); used in soft drinks, jams, preserves, sweets, UHT cream, processed cheese, canned fruit, dessert mixes, ice cream*
E334 L-(+)-tartaric acid
E335 Monosodium L-(+)-tartrate; disodium L-(+)-tartrate
E336 Monopotassium L-(+)-tartrate (cream of tartar); dipotassium L-(+)-tartrate
E337 Potassium sodium L-(+)-tartrate – *acid/flavourings, buffers, emulsifying salts, sequestrants; used in soft drinks, biscuit creams and fillings, sweets, jams, dessert mixes and processed cheese*
E338 Orthophosphoric acid (phosphoric acid) – *acid/flavourings; soft drinks, cocoa*
E339 Sodium dihydrogen orthophosphate; disodium hydrogen orthophosphate; trisodium orthophosphate

E340 Potassium dihydrogen orthophosphate; dipotassium hydrogen orthophosphate; tripotassium orthophosphate – *buffers, sequestrants, emulsifying salts; used in dessert mixes, non-dairy creamers, processed cheese*
E341 Calcium tetrahydrogen diorthophosphate; calcium hydrogen orthophosphate; tricalcium diorthophosphate – *firming agent, anti-caking agent, raising agent; cake mixes, baking powder, dessert mixes*
350 Sodium malate; sodium hydrogen malate
351 Potassium malate – *buffers, humectants; used in jams, sweets, cakes, biscuits*
352 Calcium malate; calcium hydrogen malate – *firming agent in processed fruit and vegetables*
353 Metatartaric acid – *sequestrant used in wine*
355 Adipic acid – *buffer/flavouring; sweets, synthetic cream desserts*
363 Succinic acid – *buffer/flavouring; dry foods and beverage mixes*
370 1,4-heptonolactone – *acid, sequestrant; dried soups, instant desserts*
375 Nicotinic acid – *colour stabilizer and nutrient; bread, flour, breakfast cereals*
380 Triammonium citrate – *buffer, emulsifying salt; processed cheese*
381 Ammonium ferric citrate – *dietary iron supplement; bread*
385 Calcium disodium ethylenediamine-NNN'N'-tetra-acetate (calcium disodium EDTA) – *sequestrant; canned shellfish*
E422 Glycerol – *humectant, solvent; cake icing, confectionery*
E450(a) Disodium dihydrogen diphosphate; trisodium diphosphate; tetrasodium diphosphate; tetrapotassium diphosphate
E450(b) Pentasodium triphosphate; pentapotassium triphosphate
E450(c) Sodium polyphosphates, potassium polyphosphates – *buffers, sequestrants, emulsifying salts, stabilizers, texturizers, raising agents; used in whipping cream, fish and meat products, bread, processed cheese, canned vegetables*
500 Sodium carbonate; sodium hydrogen carbonate (bicarbonate of soda); sodium sesquicarbonate
501 Potassium carbonate; potassium hydrogen carbonate – *bases, aerating agents, diluents; used in jams, jellies, self-raising flour, wine, cocoa*
503 Ammonium carbonate; ammonium hydrogen carbonate – *buffer, aerating agent; cocoa, biscuits*
504 Magnesium carbonate – *base, anti-caking agent; wafer biscuits, icing sugar*
507 Hydrochloric acid
508 Potassium chloride – *gelling agent, salt substitute; table-salt replacement*
509 Calcium chloride – *firming agent in canned fruit and vegetables*
510 Ammonium chloride – *yeast food in bread*
513 Sulphuric acid
514 Sodium sulphate – *diluent for colours*
515 Potassium sulphate – *salt substitute*
516 Calcium sulphate – *firming agent and yeast food; bread*
518 Magnesium sulphate – *firming agent*
524 Sodium hydroxide – *base; cocoa, jams and sweets*

525	Potassium hydroxide – *base; sweets*
526	Calcium hydroxide – *firming agent, neutralizing agent; sweets*
527	Ammonium hydroxide – *diluent and solvent for food colours, base; cocoa*
528	Magnesium hydroxide – *base; sweets*
529	Calcium oxide – *base; sweets*
530	Magnesium oxide – *anti-caking agent; cocoa products*
535	Sodium ferrocyanide
536	Potassium ferrocyanide – *anti-caking agents in salt; crystallization aids in wine*
540	Dicalcium diphosphate – *buffer, neutralizing agent; cheese*
541	Sodium aluminium phosphate – *acid, raising agent; cake mixes, self-raising flour, biscuits*
542	Edible bone phosphate – *anti-caking agent*
544	Calcium polyphosphates – *emulsifying salt; processed cheese*
545	Ammonium polyphosphates – *emulsifier, texturizer; frozen chicken*
551	Silicon dioxide (silica) – *anti-caking agent; skimmed milk powder, sweeteners*
552	Calcium silicate – *anti-caking agent, release agent; icing sugar, sweets*
553(a)	Magnesium silicate, and synthetic magnesium trisilicate – *anti-caking agent; sugar confectionery*
553(b)	Talc – *release agent; tabletted confectionery*
554	Aluminium sodium silicate
556	Aluminium calcium silicate
558	Bentonite
559	Kaolin
570	Stearic acid – *anti-caking agents*
572	Magnesium stearate – *emulsifier, release agent; confectionery*
575	D-glucono-1,5-lactone (glucono delta-lactone) – *acid, sequestrant; cake mixes, continental sausages*
576	Sodium gluconate
577	Potassium gluconate – *sequestrants*
578	Calcium gluconate – *buffer, firming agent, sequestrant; jams, dessert mixes*
620	L-glutamic acid
621	Sodium hydrogen L-glutamate (monosodium glutamate; MSG)
622	Potassium hydrogen L-glutamate (monopotassium glutamate)
623	Calcium dihydrogen di-L-glutamate (calcium glutamate)
627	Guanosine 5'-disodium phosphate (sodium guanylate)
631	Inosine 5'-disodium phosphate (sodium inosinate)
635	Sodium 5'-ribonucleotide – *flavour enhancers used in savoury foods and snacks, soups, sauces and meat products*
636	Maltol
637	Ethyl maltol – *flavourings/flavour enhancers used in cakes and biscuits*
900	Dimethylpolysiloxane – *anti-foaming agent*
901	Beeswax
903	Carnauba wax – *glazing agents used in sugar and chocolate confectionery*
904	Shellac – *glazing agent used to wax apples*
905	Mineral hydrocarbons – *glazing/coating agent used to prevent dried fruit sticking together*
907	Refined microcrystalline wax – *release agent; chewing gum*
920	L-cysteine hydrochloride
925	Chlorine
926	Chlorine dioxide
927	Azodicarbonamide – *flour-treatment agents used to improve the texture of bread, cake, and biscuit doughs*

Aluminium potassium sulphate – *firming agent; chocolate-coated cherries*

2-Aminoethanol – *base; caustic lye used to peel vegetables*

Ammonium dihydrogen orthophosphate; diammonium hydrogen othophosphate – *buffer, yeast food*

Ammonium sulphate – *yeast food*

Benzoyl peroxide – *bleaching agent in flour*

Butyl stearate – *release agent*

Calcium heptonate – *firming agent, sequestrant; prepared fruit and vegetables*

Calcium phytate – *sequestrant; wine*

Dichlorodifluoromethane – *propellant and liquid freezant used to freeze food by immersion*

Diethyl ether – *solvent*

Disodium dihydrogen ethylenediamine-NNN'N'-tetra-acetate (disodium dihydrogen EDTA) – *sequestrant; brandy*

Ethanol (ethylalcohol)

Ethyl acetate

Glycerol mono-acetate (monoacetin)

Glycerol di-acetate (diacetin)

Glycerol tri-acetate (triacetin) – *solvents used to dilute and carry food colours and flavourings*

Glycine – *sequestrant, buffer, nutrient*

Hydrogen

Nitrogen – *packaging gases*

Nitrous oxide – *propellant used in aerosol packs of whipped cream*

Octadecylammonium acetate – *anti-caking agent in yeast foods used in bread*

Oxygen – *packaging gas*

Oxystearin – *sequestrant, fat crystallization inhibitor; salad cream*

Polydextrose – *bulking agent; reduced- and low-calorie foods*

Propan-1,2-diol (propylene glycol)

Propan-2-diol (isopropyl alcohol) – *solvents used to dilute colours and flavourings*

Sodium heptonate – *sequestrant; edible oils*

Spermaceti

Sperm oil – *release agents*

Tannic acid – *flavouring, clarifying agent; beer wine and cider*

HUMAN BEINGS

Top wine-producing nations, 2001

Country	Wine production[a] ML	Share of world consumption %
France	5330	19.92
Italy	5090	19.02
Spain	3050	11.40
USA	1980	7.40
Argentina	1580	5.90
Australia	1020	3.81
Germany	900	3.36
Portugal	770	2.88
South Africa	650	2.43
Chile	570	2.13
World	27491	

[a] Does not include juice and musts.

Top wine-consuming nations, 2001

Country	Wine consumption ML	Share of world consumption %
France	3370	15.4
Italy	3050	13.9
USA	2133	9.7
Germany	1966	9.0
Spain	1400	6.4
Argentina	1204	5.5
United Kingdom	1010	4.6
China	580	2.6
Russia	550	2.5
Romania	470	2.1
World	21892	

Source: G Dutruc-Rosset, Extract of the Report on World Vitiviniculture, 2002

Grape varieties

Although there are now over 4000 named varieties of grape, only a small number have a truly distinctive flavour and are capable of producing great wine. These *classic grapes* form the basis of an international category of wine. The *major varieties* are those grapes which are also fairly widespread across the international wine market but which are considered less distinctive than the classic grapes.

Australia

Classic grapes
RED
Cabernet Sauvignon
Pinot Noir
Syrah
WHITE
Riesling
Chardonnay
Sémillon

Major varieties
Muscat de Frontignan
Muscadelle

Areas
Adelaide Hills
Barossa Valley
Clare Valley
Coonawarra
Corowa-Rutherglen
Upper Hunter Valley
Lower Hunter Valley
Margaret River
Mount Barker
Mount Frankland
Padthaway
Yarra Valley

Central Europe

Classic grapes
RED
Cabernet Sauvignon
Pinot Noir
Merlot
WHITE
Riesling
Chardonnay
Sauvignon Blanc

Major varieties
Austria
Gewürztraminer

Müller-Thurgau
Muscat Ottonel
Pinot Gris
Pinot Blanc
Silvaner
Welschriesling

Bulgaria
Aligoté
Gewürztraminer

Czechoslovakia
Gewürztraminer
Pinot Blanc
Silvaner
Welschriesling

Hungary
Cabernet Franc
Gewürztraminer
Pinot Gris
Pinot Blanc
Silvaner
Welschriesling

Romania
Aligoté
Cabernet Franc
Gewürztraminer
Muscat Ottonel
Pinot Gris
Welschriesling

Russian Federation
Aligoté
Gewürztraminer
Muscat Ottonel

Yugoslavia (formerly)
Cabernet Franc
Gewürztraminer
Malvasia
Muscat Ottonel
Pinot Blanc
Pinot Gris
Welschriesling

France

Alsace
Classic grapes
RED
Pinot Noir
WHITE
Riesling

Major varieties
Gewürztraminer
Muscat
Pinot Gris

Areas
Brand
Eichberg
Geisberg
Gloeckelberg
Goldert Hatschbourg
Hengst
Kastelberg
Kessler
Kirchberg de Barr
Kirchberg de Ribeauville
Kitterle
Moenchberg
Saering
Schloss Rosacker
Sommerberg
Spiegel
Wiebelsberg

Bordeaux
Classic grapes
RED
Cabernet Sauvignon
Merlot
WHITE
Sémillon
Sauvignon Blanc

Major varieties
Cabernet Franc
Colombard

Merlot Blanc
Muscadelle
Trebbiano (Ugni Blanc)

Areas
Côtes de Blaye
Côtes de Bourg
Entre-deux-mers
Fronsac
Graves
Médoc
Pomerol
Sauternes
St-Emilion

Burgundy
Classic grapes
RED
Pinot Noir
WHITE
Chardonnay
Sauvignon Blanc

Major varieties
Gamay
Aligoté

Areas
Beaujolais
Chablis
Côte de Beaune
Côte Chalonnaise
Côte de Nuits
Hautes Côtes de Beaune
Hautes Côtes de Nuits
Maconnais

Champagne
Classic grapes
RED
Pinot Noir
WHITE
Chardonnay

Major varieties
Meunier

Areas
Ambonnay
Avize
Ay
Beaumont-sur-Vesle
Bisseuil
Bouzy
Champillon
Chigny-les-Roses
Chouilly
Cramant
Cuis
Cumieres
Dizy-Magenta
Grauves
Hautvillers
Le Mesnil-sur-Oger
Louvois
Mailly
Mareuil-sur-Ay
Montbre
Mutigny
Oger

Pierry
Puisieulx
Rilly-la-Montagne
Sillery
Tauxieres-Mutry
Tours-sur-Marne
Trepail
Vertus
Verzenay
Verzy
Villers-Marmery

Loire
Classic grapes
RED
Cabernet Sauvignon
Pinot Noir
WHITE
Chardonnay
Sauvignon Blanc
Chenin Blanc

Areas
Anjou
Anjou-Côteaux de la Loire
Anjou Gamay
Bonnezeaux
Bourgueil
Champigny
Côteaux de L'Aubance
Côteaux du Layon
Côteaux de Saumur
Jasnières
Menetou-Salon
Muscadet
Muscadet des Coteaux de la Loire
Muscadet de Sèvre-et-Maine
Pouilly Fumé
Pouilly-sur-Loire
Quarts de Chaume
Quincy
Reuilly
Rose d'Anjou
Sancerre
Saumur
Savennieres
Touraine
Vouvray-Montlouis

The Midi
Classic grapes
RED
Cabernet Sauvignon
Syrah
Merlot
WHITE
Chardonnay
Sauvignon Blanc
Chenin Blanc

Major varieties
Garnacha
Carignan
Cinsaut
Garnacha Blanca

Areas
Aude
Bouches-du-Rhone

Gard
Herault
Pyrenees-Orientales
Var
Vaucluse

Germany

Around 80 per cent of German vineyard produce is white wine. The predominant grape is the Riesling but listed below are also major local varieties which are significant in terms of both quantity and quality. They are listed in the order of the most widely planted variety per region.

Ahr
Pinot Noir
Blauer Portugieser
Riesling
Müller-Thurgau
Kerner

Baden
Pinot Noir
Pinot Gris
Chasselas
Riesling
Silvaner
Pinot Blanc
Blauer Portugieser

Franken
Müller-Thurgau
Silvaner
Riesling
Pinot Noir
Blauer Portugieser
Perle
Rieslaner

Hessische Bergstrasse
Riesling
Müller-Thurgau
Silvaner
Pinot Noir
Blauer Portugieser

Mittelrhein
Riesling
Müller-Thurgau
Kerner
Silvaner
Pinot Noir
Blauer Portugieser

Mosel-Saar-Ruwer
Riesling
Müller-Thurgau
Wiesser Elbling
Kerner

Nahe
Müller-Thurgau
Riesling
Silvaner
Kerner
Blauer Portugieser
Pinot Noir

HUMAN BEINGS

Grape varieties (continued)

Rheingau
Riesling
Müller-Thurgau
Pinot Noir
Silvaner
Blauer Portugieser

Rheinhessen
Müller-Thurgau
Silvaner
Scheurebe
Kerner
Riesling
Morio-Muscat
Blauer Portugieser
Pinot Noir

Rheinpfalz
Müller-Thurgau
Riesling
Kerner
Silvaner
Morio-Muscat
Blauer Portugieser
Scheurebe
Pinot Noir
Gewürztraminer

Württemberg
Riesling
Blauer Trollinger
Müller-Thurgau
Kerner
Silvaner
Blauer Portugieser
Schwarzriesling
Pinot Noir
Pinot Gris

Italy

Classic grapes
RED
Cabernet Sauvignon
Pinot Noir
Merlot
WHITE
Riesling
Chardonnay
Sauvignon Blanc

Major varieties
Barbera
Cabernet Franc
Carignan
Cinsaut
Garnacha
Muscat of Alexandria
Muscat Blanc
Muscat Blanc à Petits Grains
Nebbiolo
Pinot Blanc
Pinot Gris
Sangiovese
Trebbiano
Welschriesling

Areas
Friuli-Venezia Giulia
Lombardia
Piemonte
Trentino/Alto Adige
Veneto

New Zealand

Classic grapes
RED
Cabernet Sauvignon
Pinot Noir
WHITE
Riesling
Chardonnay
Sauvignon Blanc
Chenin Blanc

Major varieties
Gamay
Gewürztraminer
Müller-Thurgau
Palomino
Silvaner

Areas
Auckland
Canterbury
Hawke's Bay
Marlborough
Nelson
Northland
Poverty Bay
Waikato

South Africa

Classic grapes
RED
Cabernet Sauvignon
Pinot Noir
Syrah
Merlot
WHITE
Riesling
Chardonnay
Sémillon
Sauvignon Blanc
Chenin Blanc

Major varieties
Cinsaut
Colombard
Muscat of Alexandria
Muscat Blanc
Muscat Blanc à Petits Grains
Palomino
Trebbiano

Areas
Malmesbury
Montagu
Olifants River
Paarl
Robertson
Stellenbosch
Worcester

South America

Classic grapes
RED
Cabernet Sauvignon
Pinot Noir
Syrah
Merlot
WHITE
Riesling
Chardonnay
Sémillon
Sauvignon Blanc
Chenin Blanc

Major varieties
Argentina
Barbera
Cabernet Franc
Gewürztraminer
Muscat à Petits Grains
Tempranillo
Trebbiano

Brasil
Trebbiano

Chile
Cabernet Franc
Carignan
Gewürztraminer
Muscat of Alexandria
Muscat à Petits Grains
Pinot Blanc

Mexico
Carignan
Colombard
Gamay
Garnacha
Palomino
Pinot Gris
Tempranillo
Trebbiano

Uruguay
Barbera
Nebbiolo
Pinot Blanc

Spain and Portugal

Spain and Portugal grow few of the international classic grapes and are better known as exporters of their own locally grown grape varieties, such as the Palomino, Tempranillo, and Carignan.

Major varieties
Carignan
Garnacha
Malvasia
Palomino
Tempranillo

Areas
Algarve
Alicante

Bairrada
Bucelas
Carcavelos
Carineria
Colares
Dao
Douro
Jumilla
La Mancha
Malaga
Montilla-Moriles
Navarra
Penedes
Rioja (Alta, Alavesa, Baja)
Setubal
Tarragona
Valdepenas
Vinho Verde

USA

California
Major varieties grown in the region

Central Valley
Barbera
Carignan
Cinsaut
Emerald Riesling*
Flora
Garnacha

Muscat Blanc à Petits Grains
Palomino
Trebbiano
Zinfandel*

Mendocino, Lake
Carignan
Gamay Beaujolais
Garnacha
Gewürztraminer
Trousseau Gris
Zinfandel

Monterey, San Benito
Carignan
Colombard
Emerald Riesling
Folle Blanche
Gamay Beaujolais
Garnacha
Gewürztraminer
Melon de Bourgogne
Muscat Blanc à Petits Grains
Silvaner
Zinfandel

Napa
Cabernet Franc
Gamay Beaujolais
Gewürztraminer
Trousseau Gris
Zinfandel

San Luis Obispo, Santa Barbara
Gewürztraminer
Silvaner
Zinfandel

Sonoma
Carignan
Gamay Beaujolais
Gewürztraminer
Melon de Bourgogne
Muscadelle
Zinfandel

S California
Garnacha
Palomino
Zinfandel

*denotes quality grape varieties bred in California

Idaho
Major varieties
Gewürztraminer

Washington
Major varieties
Cabernet Franc
Garnacha
Gewürztraminer
Muscat Blanc à Petits Grains

HUMAN BEINGS

PART SIX

History

THE CALENDAR

Perpetual calendar 1821–2020

The calendar for each year is given under the corresponding letter below.

1821 C	1841 K	1861 E	1881 M	1901 E	1921 M	1941 G	1961 A	1981 I	2001 C
1822 E	1842 G	1862 G	1882 A	1902 G	1922 A	1942 I	1962 C	1982 K	2002 E
1823 G	1843 A	1863 I	1883 C	1903 I	1923 C	1943 K	1963 E	1983 M	2003 G
1824 J	1844 D	1864 L	1884 F	1904 L	1924 F	1944 N	1964 H	1984 B	2004 J
1825 M	1845 G	1865 A	1885 I	1905 A	1925 I	1945 C	1965 K	1985 E	2005 M
1826 A	1846 I	1866 C	1886 K	1906 C	1926 K	1946 E	1966 M	1986 G	2006 A
1827 C	1847 K	1867 E	1887 M	1907 E	1927 M	1947 G	1967 A	1987 I	2007 C
1828 F	1848 N	1868 H	1888 B	1908 H	1928 B	1948 J	1968 D	1988 L	2008 F
1829 I	1849 C	1869 K	1889 E	1909 K	1929 E	1949 M	1969 G	1989 A	2009 I
1830 K	1850 E	1870 M	1890 G	1910 M	1930 G	1950 A	1970 I	1990 C	2010 K
1831 M	1851 G	1871 A	1891 I	1911 A	1931 I	1951 C	1971 K	1991 E	2011 M
1832 B	1852 J	1872 D	1892 L	1912 D	1932 L	1952 F	1972 N	1992 H	2012 B
1833 E	1853 M	1873 G	1893 A	1913 G	1933 A	1953 I	1973 C	1993 K	2013 E
1834 G	1854 A	1874 I	1894 C	1914 I	1934 C	1954 K	1974 E	1994 M	2014 G
1835 I	1855 C	1875 K	1895 E	1915 K	1935 E	1955 M	1975 G	1995 A	2015 I
1836 L	1856 F	1876 N	1896 H	1916 N	1936 H	1956 B	1976 J	1996 D	2016 L
1837 A	1857 I	1877 C	1897 K	1917 C	1937 K	1957 E	1977 M	1997 G	2017 A
1838 C	1858 K	1878 E	1898 M	1918 E	1938 M	1958 G	1978 A	1998 I	2018 C
1839 E	1859 M	1879 G	1899 A	1919 G	1939 A	1959 I	1979 C	1999 K	2019 E
1840 H	1860 B	1880 J	1900 C	1920 J	1940 D	1960 L	1980 F	2000 N	2020 H

A

January
S M T W T F S
    1 2 3 4 5 6 7
8 9 10 11 12 13 14
15 16 17 18 19 20 21
22 23 24 25 26 27 28
29 30 31

February
S M T W T F S
            1 2 3 4
5 6 7 8 9 10 11
12 13 14 15 16 17 18
19 20 21 22 23 24 25
26 27 28

March
S M T W T F S
            1 2 3 4
5 6 7 8 9 10 11
12 13 14 15 16 17 18
19 20 21 22 23 24 25
26 27 28 29 30 31

April
                        1
2 3 4 5 6 7 8
9 10 11 12 13 14 15
16 17 18 19 20 21 22
23 24 25 26 27 28 29
30

May
    1 2 3 4 5 6
7 8 9 10 11 12 13
14 15 16 17 18 19 20
21 22 23 24 25 26 27
28 29 30 31

June
                  1 2 3
4 5 6 7 8 9 10
11 12 13 14 15 16 17
18 19 20 21 22 23 24
25 26 27 28 29 30

July
                        1
2 3 4 5 6 7 8
9 10 11 12 13 14 15
16 17 18 19 20 21 22
23 24 25 26 27 28 29
30 31

August
        1 2 3 4 5
6 7 8 9 10 11 12
13 14 15 16 17 18 19
20 21 22 23 24 25 26
27 28 29 30 31

September
                        1 2
3 4 5 6 7 8 9
10 11 12 13 14 15 16
17 18 19 20 21 22 23
24 25 26 27 28 29 30

October
1 2 3 4 5 6 7
8 9 10 11 12 13 14
15 16 17 18 19 20 21
22 23 24 25 26 27 28
29 30 31

November
            1 2 3 4
5 6 7 8 9 10 11
12 13 14 15 16 17 18
19 20 21 22 23 24 25
26 27 28 29 30

December
                        1 2
3 4 5 6 7 8 9
10 11 12 13 14 15 16
17 18 19 20 21 22 23
24 25 26 27 28 29 30
31

B (leap year)

January
S M T W T F S
    1 2 3 4 5 6 7
8 9 10 11 12 13 14
15 16 17 18 19 20 21
22 23 24 25 26 27 28
29 30 31

February
S M T W T F S
            1 2 3 4
5 6 7 8 9 10 11
12 13 14 15 16 17 18
19 20 21 22 23 24 25
26 27 28 29

March
S M T W T F S
                  1 2 3
4 5 6 7 8 9 10
11 12 13 14 15 16 17
18 19 20 21 22 23 24
25 26 27 28 29 30 31

April
1 2 3 4 5 6 7
8 9 10 11 12 13 14
15 16 17 18 19 20 21
22 23 24 25 26 27 28
29 30

May
        1 2 3 4 5
6 7 8 9 10 11 12
13 14 15 16 17 18 19
20 21 22 23 24 25 26
27 28 29 30 31

June
                        1 2
3 4 5 6 7 8 9
10 11 12 13 14 15 16
17 18 19 20 21 22 23
24 25 26 27 28 29 30

July
1 2 3 4 5 6 7
8 9 10 11 12 13 14
15 16 17 18 19 20 21
22 23 24 25 26 27 28
29 30 31

August
            1 2 3 4
5 6 7 8 9 10 11
12 13 14 15 16 17 18
19 20 21 22 23 24 25
26 27 28 29 30 31

September
                              1
2 3 4 5 6 7 8
9 10 11 12 13 14 15
16 17 18 19 20 21 22
23 24 25 26 27 28 29
30

October
    1 2 3 4 5 6
7 8 9 10 11 12 13
14 15 16 17 18 19 20
21 22 23 24 25 26 27
28 29 30 31

November
                  1 2 3
4 5 6 7 8 9 10
11 12 13 14 15 16 17
18 19 20 21 22 23 24
25 26 27 28 29 30

December
                              1
2 3 4 5 6 7 8
9 10 11 12 13 14 15
16 17 18 19 20 21 22
23 24 25 26 27 28 29
30 31

Perpetual calendar 1821–2020 (continued)

C

January

S	M	T	W	T	F	S
	1	2	3	4	5	6
7	8	9	10	11	12	13
14	15	16	17	18	19	20
21	22	23	24	25	26	27
28	29	30	31			

February

S	M	T	W	T	F	S
				1	2	3
4	5	6	7	8	9	10
11	12	13	14	15	16	17
18	19	20	21	22	23	24
25	26	27	28			

March

S	M	T	W	T	F	S
				1	2	3
4	5	6	7	8	9	10
11	12	13	14	15	16	17
18	19	20	21	22	23	24
25	26	27	28	29	30	31

April

S	M	T	W	T	F	S
1	2	3	4	5	6	7
8	9	10	11	12	13	14
15	16	17	18	19	20	21
22	23	24	25	26	27	28
29	30					

May

S	M	T	W	T	F	S
		1	2	3	4	5
6	7	8	9	10	11	12
13	14	15	16	17	18	19
20	21	22	23	24	25	26
27	28	29	30	31		

June

S	M	T	W	T	F	S
					1	2
3	4	5	6	7	8	9
10	11	12	13	14	15	16
17	18	19	20	21	22	23
24	25	26	27	28	29	30

July

S	M	T	W	T	F	S
1	2	3	4	5	6	7
8	9	10	11	12	13	14
15	16	17	18	19	20	21
22	23	24	25	26	27	28
29	30	31				

August

S	M	T	W	T	F	S
			1	2	3	4
5	6	7	8	9	10	11
12	13	14	15	16	17	18
19	20	21	22	23	24	25
26	27	28	29	30	31	

September

S	M	T	W	T	F	S
						1
2	3	4	5	6	7	8
9	10	11	12	13	14	15
16	17	18	19	20	21	22
23	24	25	26	27	28	29
30						

October

S	M	T	W	T	F	S
	1	2	3	4	5	6
7	8	9	10	11	12	13
14	15	16	17	18	19	20
21	22	23	24	25	26	27
28	29	30	31			

November

S	M	T	W	T	F	S
				1	2	3
4	5	6	7	8	9	10
11	12	13	14	15	16	17
18	19	20	21	22	23	24
25	26	27	28	29	30	

December

S	M	T	W	T	F	S
						1
2	3	4	5	6	7	8
9	10	11	12	13	14	15
16	17	18	19	20	21	22
23	24	25	26	27	28	29
30	31					

D (leap year)

January

S	M	T	W	T	F	S
	1	2	3	4	5	6
7	8	9	10	11	12	13
14	15	16	17	18	19	20
21	22	23	24	25	26	27
28	29	30	31			

February

S	M	T	W	T	F	S
				1	2	3
4	5	6	7	8	9	10
11	12	13	14	15	16	17
18	19	20	21	22	23	24
25	26	27	28	29		

March

S	M	T	W	T	F	S
					1	2
3	4	5	6	7	8	9
10	11	12	13	14	15	16
17	18	19	20	21	22	23
24	25	26	27	28	29	30
31						

April

S	M	T	W	T	F	S
	1	2	3	4	5	6
7	8	9	10	11	12	13
14	15	16	17	18	19	20
21	22	23	24	25	26	27
28	29	30				

May

S	M	T	W	T	F	S
			1	2	3	4
5	6	7	8	9	10	11
12	13	14	15	16	17	18
19	20	21	22	23	24	25
26	27	28	29	30	31	

June

S	M	T	W	T	F	S
						1
2	3	4	5	6	7	8
9	10	11	12	13	14	15
16	17	18	19	20	21	22
23	24	25	26	27	28	29
30						

July

S	M	T	W	T	F	S
	1	2	3	4	5	6
7	8	9	10	11	12	13
14	15	16	17	18	19	20
21	22	23	24	25	26	27
28	29	30	31			

August

S	M	T	W	T	F	S
				1	2	3
4	5	6	7	8	9	10
11	12	13	14	15	16	17
18	19	20	21	22	23	24
25	26	27	28	29	30	31

September

S	M	T	W	T	F	S
1	2	3	4	5	6	7
8	9	10	11	12	13	14
15	16	17	18	19	20	21
22	23	24	25	26	27	28
29	30					

October

S	M	T	W	T	F	S
		1	2	3	4	5
6	7	8	9	10	11	12
13	14	15	16	17	18	19
20	21	22	23	24	25	26
27	28	29	30	31		

November

S	M	T	W	T	F	S
					1	2
3	4	5	6	7	8	9
10	11	12	13	14	15	16
17	18	19	20	21	22	23
24	25	26	27	28	29	30

December

S	M	T	W	T	F	S
1	2	3	4	5	6	7
8	9	10	11	12	13	14
15	16	17	18	19	20	21
22	23	24	25	26	27	28
29	30	31				

E

January

S	M	T	W	T	F	S
		1	2	3	4	5
6	7	8	9	10	11	12
13	14	15	16	17	18	19
20	21	22	23	24	25	26
27	28	29	30	31		

February

S	M	T	W	T	F	S
					1	2
3	4	5	6	7	8	9
10	11	12	13	14	15	16
17	18	19	20	21	22	23
24	25	26	27	28		

March

S	M	T	W	T	F	S
					1	2
3	4	5	6	7	8	9
10	11	12	13	14	15	16
17	18	19	20	21	22	23
24	25	26	27	28	29	30
31						

April

S	M	T	W	T	F	S
	1	2	3	4	5	6
7	8	9	10	11	12	13
14	15	16	17	18	19	20
21	22	23	24	25	26	27
28	29	30				

May

S	M	T	W	T	F	S
			1	2	3	4
5	6	7	8	9	10	11
12	13	14	15	16	17	18
19	20	21	22	23	24	25
26	27	28	29	30	31	

June

S	M	T	W	T	F	S
						1
2	3	4	5	6	7	8
9	10	11	12	13	14	15
16	17	18	19	20	21	22
23	24	25	26	27	28	29
30						

July

S	M	T	W	T	F	S
	1	2	3	4	5	6
7	8	9	10	11	12	13
14	15	16	17	18	19	20
21	22	23	24	25	26	27
28	29	30	31			

August

S	M	T	W	T	F	S
				1	2	3
4	5	6	7	8	9	10
11	12	13	14	15	16	17
18	19	20	21	22	23	24
25	26	27	28	29	30	31

September

S	M	T	W	T	F	S
1	2	3	4	5	6	7
8	9	10	11	12	13	14
15	16	17	18	19	20	21
22	23	24	25	26	27	28
29	30					

October

S	M	T	W	T	F	S
		1	2	3	4	5
6	7	8	9	10	11	12
13	14	15	16	17	18	19
20	21	22	23	24	25	26
27	28	29	30	31		

November

S	M	T	W	T	F	S
					1	2
3	4	5	6	7	8	9
10	11	12	13	14	15	16
17	18	19	20	21	22	23
24	25	26	27	28	29	30

December

S	M	T	W	T	F	S
1	2	3	4	5	6	7
8	9	10	11	12	13	14
15	16	17	18	19	20	21
22	23	24	25	26	27	28
29	30	31				

F (leap year)

January

S	M	T	W	T	F	S
		1	2	3	4	5
6	7	8	9	10	11	12
13	14	15	16	17	18	19
20	21	22	23	24	25	26
27	28	29	30	31		

February

S	M	T	W	T	F	S
					1	2
3	4	5	6	7	8	9
10	11	12	13	14	15	16
17	18	19	20	21	22	23
24	25	26	27	28	29	

March

S	M	T	W	T	F	S
						1
2	3	4	5	6	7	8
9	10	11	12	13	14	15
16	17	18	19	20	21	22
23	24	25	26	27	28	29
30	31					

April

S	M	T	W	T	F	S
		1	2	3	4	5
6	7	8	9	10	11	12
13	14	15	16	17	18	19
20	21	22	23	24	25	26
27	28	29	30			

May

S	M	T	W	T	F	S
				1	2	3
4	5	6	7	8	9	10
11	12	13	14	15	16	17
18	19	20	21	22	23	24
25	26	27	28	29	30	31

June

S	M	T	W	T	F	S
1	2	3	4	5	6	7
8	9	10	11	12	13	14
15	16	17	18	19	20	21
22	23	24	25	26	27	28
29	30					

July

S	M	T	W	T	F	S
		1	2	3	4	5
6	7	8	9	10	11	12
13	14	15	16	17	18	19
20	21	22	23	24	25	26
27	28	29	30	31		

August

S	M	T	W	T	F	S
					1	2
3	4	5	6	7	8	9
10	11	12	13	14	15	16
17	18	19	20	21	22	23
24	25	26	27	28	29	30
31						

September

S	M	T	W	T	F	S
	1	2	3	4	5	6
7	8	9	10	11	12	13
14	15	16	17	18	19	20
21	22	23	24	25	26	27
28	29	30				

October

S	M	T	W	T	F	S
			1	2	3	4
5	6	7	8	9	10	11
12	13	14	15	16	17	18
19	20	21	22	23	24	25
26	27	28	29	30	31	

November

S	M	T	W	T	F	S
						1
2	3	4	5	6	7	8
9	10	11	12	13	14	15
16	17	18	19	20	21	22
23	24	25	26	27	28	29
30						

December

S	M	T	W	T	F	S
	1	2	3	4	5	6
7	8	9	10	11	12	13
14	15	16	17	18	19	20
21	22	23	24	25	26	27
28	29	30	31			

HISTORY

G

January
S	M	T	W	T	F	S
			1	2	3	4
5	6	7	8	9	10	11
12	13	14	15	16	17	18
19	20	21	22	23	24	25
26	27	28	29	30	31	

February
S	M	T	W	T	F	S
						1
2	3	4	5	6	7	8
9	10	11	12	13	14	15
16	17	18	19	20	21	22
23	24	25	26	27	28	

March
S	M	T	W	T	F	S
						1
2	3	4	5	6	7	8
9	10	11	12	13	14	15
16	17	18	19	20	21	22
23	24	25	26	27	28	29
30	31					

April
S	M	T	W	T	F	S
		1	2	3	4	5
6	7	8	9	10	11	12
13	14	15	16	17	18	19
20	21	22	23	24	25	26
27	28	29	30			

May
S	M	T	W	T	F	S
				1	2	3
4	5	6	7	8	9	10
11	12	13	14	15	16	17
18	19	20	21	22	23	24
25	26	27	28	29	30	31

June
S	M	T	W	T	F	S
1	2	3	4	5	6	7
8	9	10	11	12	13	14
15	16	17	18	19	20	21
22	23	24	25	26	27	28
29	30					

July
S	M	T	W	T	F	S
		1	2	3	4	5
6	7	8	9	10	11	12
13	14	15	16	17	18	19
20	21	22	23	24	25	26
27	28	29	30	31		

August
S	M	T	W	T	F	S
					1	2
3	4	5	6	7	8	9
10	11	12	13	14	15	16
17	18	19	20	21	22	23
24	25	26	27	28	29	30
31						

September
S	M	T	W	T	F	S
	1	2	3	4	5	6
7	8	9	10	11	12	13
14	15	16	17	18	19	20
21	22	23	24	25	26	27
28	29	30				

October
S	M	T	W	T	F	S
			1	2	3	4
5	6	7	8	9	10	11
12	13	14	15	16	17	18
19	20	21	22	23	24	25
26	27	28	29	30	31	

November
S	M	T	W	T	F	S
						1
2	3	4	5	6	7	8
9	10	11	12	13	14	15
16	17	18	19	20	21	22
23	24	25	26	27	28	29
30						

December
S	M	T	W	T	F	S
	1	2	3	4	5	6
7	8	9	10	11	12	13
14	15	16	17	18	19	20
21	22	23	24	25	26	27
28	29	30	31			

H (leap year)

January
S	M	T	W	T	F	S
			1	2	3	4
5	6	7	8	9	10	11
12	13	14	15	16	17	18
19	20	21	22	23	24	25
26	27	28	29	30	31	

February
S	M	T	W	T	F	S
						1
2	3	4	5	6	7	8
9	10	11	12	13	14	15
16	17	18	19	20	21	22
23	24	25	26	27	28	29

March
S	M	T	W	T	F	S
1	2	3	4	5	6	7
8	9	10	11	12	13	14
15	16	17	18	19	20	21
22	23	24	25	26	27	28
29	30	31				

April
S	M	T	W	T	F	S
		1	2	3	4	
5	6	7	8	9	10	11
12	13	14	15	16	17	18
19	20	21	22	23	24	25
26	27	28	29	30		

May
S	M	T	W	T	F	S
					1	2
3	4	5	6	7	8	9
10	11	12	13	14	15	16
17	18	19	20	21	22	23
24	25	26	27	28	29	30
31						

June
S	M	T	W	T	F	S
	1	2	3	4	5	6
7	8	9	10	11	12	13
14	15	16	17	18	19	20
21	22	23	24	25	26	27
28	29	30				

July
S	M	T	W	T	F	S
		1	2	3	4	
5	6	7	8	9	10	11
12	13	14	15	16	17	18
19	20	21	22	23	24	25
26	27	28	29	30	31	

August
S	M	T	W	T	F	S
					1	
2	3	4	5	6	7	8
9	10	11	12	13	14	15
16	17	18	19	20	21	22
23	24	25	26	27	28	29
30	31					

September
S	M	T	W	T	F	S
		1	2	3	4	5
6	7	8	9	10	11	12
13	14	15	16	17	18	19
20	21	22	23	24	25	26
27	28	29	30			

October
S	M	T	W	T	F	S
				1	2	3
4	5	6	7	8	9	10
11	12	13	14	15	16	17
18	19	20	21	22	23	24
25	26	27	28	29	30	31

November
S	M	T	W	T	F	S
1	2	3	4	5	6	7
8	9	10	11	12	13	14
15	16	17	18	19	20	21
22	23	24	25	26	27	28
29	30					

December
S	M	T	W	T	F	S
		1	2	3	4	5
6	7	8	9	10	11	12
13	14	15	16	17	18	19
20	21	22	23	24	25	26
27	28	29	30	31		

I

January
S	M	T	W	T	F	S
				1	2	3
4	5	6	7	8	9	10
11	12	13	14	15	16	17
18	19	20	21	22	23	24
25	26	27	28	29	30	31

February
S	M	T	W	T	F	S
1	2	3	4	5	6	7
8	9	10	11	12	13	14
15	16	17	18	19	20	21
22	23	24	25	26	27	28

March
S	M	T	W	T	F	S
1	2	3	4	5	6	7
8	9	10	11	12	13	14
15	16	17	18	19	20	21
22	23	24	25	26	27	28
29	30	31				

April
S	M	T	W	T	F	S
			1	2	3	4
5	6	7	8	9	10	11
12	13	14	15	16	17	18
19	20	21	22	23	24	25
26	27	28	29	30		

May
S	M	T	W	T	F	S
					1	2
3	4	5	6	7	8	9
10	11	12	13	14	15	16
17	18	19	20	21	22	23
24	25	26	27	28	29	30
31						

June
S	M	T	W	T	F	S
	1	2	3	4	5	6
7	8	9	10	11	12	13
14	15	16	17	18	19	20
21	22	23	24	25	26	27
28	29	30				

July
S	M	T	W	T	F	S
			1	2	3	4
5	6	7	8	9	10	11
12	13	14	15	16	17	18
19	20	21	22	23	24	25
26	27	28	29	30	31	

August
S	M	T	W	T	F	S
						1
2	3	4	5	6	7	8
9	10	11	12	13	14	15
16	17	18	19	20	21	22
23	24	25	26	27	28	29
30	31					

September
S	M	T	W	T	F	S
		1	2	3	4	5
6	7	8	9	10	11	12
13	14	15	16	17	18	19
20	21	22	23	24	25	26
27	28	29	30			

October
S	M	T	W	T	F	S
				1	2	3
4	5	6	7	8	9	10
11	12	13	14	15	16	17
18	19	20	21	22	23	24
25	26	27	28	29	30	31

November
S	M	T	W	T	F	S
1	2	3	4	5	6	7
8	9	10	11	12	13	14
15	16	17	18	19	20	21
22	23	24	25	26	27	28
29	30					

December
S	M	T	W	T	F	S
		1	2	3	4	5
6	7	8	9	10	11	12
13	14	15	16	17	18	19
20	21	22	23	24	25	26
27	28	29	30	31		

J (leap year)

January
S	M	T	W	T	F	S
				1	2	3
4	5	6	7	8	9	10
11	12	13	14	15	16	17
18	19	20	21	22	23	24
25	26	27	28	29	30	31

February
S	M	T	W	T	F	S
1	2	3	4	5	6	7
8	9	10	11	12	13	14
15	16	17	18	19	20	21
22	23	24	25	26	27	28
29						

March
S	M	T	W	T	F	S
	1	2	3	4	5	6
7	8	9	10	11	12	13
14	15	16	17	18	19	20
21	22	23	24	25	26	27
28	29	30	31			

April
S	M	T	W	T	F	S
			1	2	3	
4	5	6	7	8	9	10
11	12	13	14	15	16	17
18	19	20	21	22	23	24
25	26	27	28	29	30	

May
S	M	T	W	T	F	S
					1	
2	3	4	5	6	7	8
9	10	11	12	13	14	15
16	17	18	19	20	21	22
23	24	25	26	27	28	29
30	31					

June
S	M	T	W	T	F	S
		1	2	3	4	5
6	7	8	9	10	11	12
13	14	15	16	17	18	19
20	21	22	23	24	25	26
27	28	29	30			

July
S	M	T	W	T	F	S
			1	2	3	
4	5	6	7	8	9	10
11	12	13	14	15	16	17
18	19	20	21	22	23	24
25	26	27	28	29	30	31

August
S	M	T	W	T	F	S
1	2	3	4	5	6	7
8	9	10	11	12	13	14
15	16	17	18	19	20	21
22	23	24	25	26	27	28
29	30	31				

September
S	M	T	W	T	F	S
			1	2	3	4
5	6	7	8	9	10	11
12	13	14	15	16	17	18
19	20	21	22	23	24	25
26	27	28	29	30		

October
S	M	T	W	T	F	S
					1	2
3	4	5	6	7	8	9
10	11	12	13	14	15	16
17	18	19	20	21	22	23
24	25	26	27	28	29	30
31						

November
S	M	T	W	T	F	S
	1	2	3	4	5	6
7	8	9	10	11	12	13
14	15	16	17	18	19	20
21	22	23	24	25	26	27
28	29	30				

December
S	M	T	W	T	F	S
			1	2	3	4
5	6	7	8	9	10	11
12	13	14	15	16	17	18
19	20	21	22	23	24	25
26	27	28	29	30	31	

HISTORY

Perpetual calendar 1821–2020 (continued)

K

```
January               February              March
S  M  T  W  T  F  S   S  M  T  W  T  F  S   S  M  T  W  T  F  S
         1  2             1  2  3  4  5  6             1  2  3  4  5  6
 3  4  5  6  7  8  9    7  8  9 10 11 12 13    7  8  9 10 11 12 13
10 11 12 13 14 15 16   14 15 16 17 18 19 20   14 15 16 17 18 19 20
17 18 19 20 21 22 23   21 22 23 24 25 26 27   21 22 23 24 25 26 27
24 25 26 27 28 29 30   28                     28 29 30 31
31

April                 May                   June
S  M  T  W  T  F  S    S  M  T  W  T  F  S   S  M  T  W  T  F  S
             1  2  3                     1             1  2  3  4  5
 4  5  6  7  8  9 10    2  3  4  5  6  7  8    6  7  8  9 10 11 12
11 12 13 14 15 16 17    9 10 11 12 13 14 15   13 14 15 16 17 18 19
18 19 20 21 22 23 24   16 17 18 19 20 21 22   20 21 22 23 24 25 26
25 26 27 28 29 30      23 24 25 26 27 28 29   27 28 29 30
                       30 31

July                  August                September
S  M  T  W  T  F  S    S  M  T  W  T  F  S   S  M  T  W  T  F  S
             1  2  3    1  2  3  4  5  6  7             1  2  3  4
 4  5  6  7  8  9 10    8  9 10 11 12 13 14    5  6  7  8  9 10 11
11 12 13 14 15 16 17   15 16 17 18 19 20 21   12 13 14 15 16 17 18
18 19 20 21 22 23 24   22 23 24 25 26 27 28   19 20 21 22 23 24 25
25 26 27 28 29 30 31   29 30 31              26 27 28 29 30

October               November              December
S  M  T  W  T  F  S    S  M  T  W  T  F  S   S  M  T  W  T  F  S
                1  2       1  2  3  4  5  6             1  2  3  4
 3  4  5  6  7  8  9    7  8  9 10 11 12 13    5  6  7  8  9 10 11
10 11 12 13 14 15 16   14 15 16 17 18 19 20   12 13 14 15 16 17 18
17 18 19 20 21 22 23   21 22 23 24 25 26 27   19 20 21 22 23 24 25
24 25 26 27 28 29 30   28 29 30              26 27 28 29 30 31
31
```

L (leap year)

```
January               February              March
S  M  T  W  T  F  S    S  M  T  W  T  F  S   S  M  T  W  T  F  S
         1  2             1  2  3  4  5  6          1  2  3  4  5
 3  4  5  6  7  8  9    7  8  9 10 11 12 13    6  7  8  9 10 11 12
10 11 12 13 14 15 16   14 15 16 17 18 19 20   13 14 15 16 17 18 19
17 18 19 20 21 22 23   21 22 23 24 25 26 27   20 21 22 23 24 25 26
24 25 26 27 28 29 30   28 29                 27 28 29 30 31
31

April                 May                   June
S  M  T  W  T  F  S    S  M  T  W  T  F  S   S  M  T  W  T  F  S
             1  2     1  2  3  4  5  6  7           1  2  3  4
 3  4  5  6  7  8  9    8  9 10 11 12 13 14    5  6  7  8  9 10 11
10 11 12 13 14 15 16   15 16 17 18 19 20 21   12 13 14 15 16 17 18
17 18 19 20 21 22 23   22 23 24 25 26 27 28   19 20 21 22 23 24 25
24 25 26 27 28 29 30   29 30 31              26 27 28 29 30

July                  August                September
S  M  T  W  T  F  S    S  M  T  W  T  F  S   S  M  T  W  T  F  S
                1  2       1  2  3  4  5  6             1  2  3
 3  4  5  6  7  8  9    7  8  9 10 11 12 13    4  5  6  7  8  9 10
10 11 12 13 14 15 16   14 15 16 17 18 19 20   11 12 13 14 15 16 17
17 18 19 20 21 22 23   21 22 23 24 25 26 27   18 19 20 21 22 23 24
24 25 26 27 28 29 30   28 29 30 31           25 26 27 28 29 30
31

October               November              December
S  M  T  W  T  F  S    S  M  T  W  T  F  S   S  M  T  W  T  F  S
                   1      1  2  3  4  5             1  2  3
 2  3  4  5  6  7  8    6  7  8  9 10 11 12    4  5  6  7  8  9 10
 9 10 11 12 13 14 15   13 14 15 16 17 18 19   11 12 13 14 15 16 17
16 17 18 19 20 21 22   20 21 22 23 24 25 26   18 19 20 21 22 23 24
23 24 25 26 27 28 29   27 28 29 30           25 26 27 28 29 30 31
30 31
```

M

```
January               February              March
S  M  T  W  T  F  S    S  M  T  W  T  F  S   S  M  T  W  T  F  S
                   1       1  2  3  4  5             1  2  3  4  5
 2  3  4  5  6  7  8    6  7  8  9 10 11 12    6  7  8  9 10 11 12
 9 10 11 12 13 14 15   13 14 15 16 17 18 19   13 14 15 16 17 18 19
16 17 18 19 20 21 22   20 21 22 23 24 25 26   20 21 22 23 24 25 26
23 24 25 26 27 28 29   27 28                 27 28 29 30 31
30 31

April                 May                   June
S  M  T  W  T  F  S    S  M  T  W  T  F  S   S  M  T  W  T  F  S
             1  2     1  2  3  4  5  6  7           1  2  3  4
 3  4  5  6  7  8  9    8  9 10 11 12 13 14    5  6  7  8  9 10 11
10 11 12 13 14 15 16   15 16 17 18 19 20 21   12 13 14 15 16 17 18
17 18 19 20 21 22 23   22 23 24 25 26 27 28   19 20 21 22 23 24 25
24 25 26 27 28 29 30   29 30 31              26 27 28 29 30

July                  August                September
S  M  T  W  T  F  S    S  M  T  W  T  F  S   S  M  T  W  T  F  S
             1  2         1  2  3  4  5  6             1  2  3
 3  4  5  6  7  8  9    7  8  9 10 11 12 13    4  5  6  7  8  9 10
10 11 12 13 14 15 16   14 15 16 17 18 19 20   11 12 13 14 15 16 17
17 18 19 20 21 22 23   21 22 23 24 25 26 27   18 19 20 21 22 23 24
24 25 26 27 28 29 30   28 29 30 31           25 26 27 28 29 30
31

October               November              December
S  M  T  W  T  F  S    S  M  T  W  T  F  S   S  M  T  W  T  F  S
                   1      1  2  3  4  5             1  2  3
 2  3  4  5  6  7  8    6  7  8  9 10 11 12    4  5  6  7  8  9 10
 9 10 11 12 13 14 15   13 14 15 16 17 18 19   11 12 13 14 15 16 17
16 17 18 19 20 21 22   20 21 22 23 24 25 26   18 19 20 21 22 23 24
23 24 25 26 27 28 29   27 28 29 30           25 26 27 28 29 30 31
30 31
```

N (leap year)

```
January               February              March
S  M  T  W  T  F  S    S  M  T  W  T  F  S   S  M  T  W  T  F  S
                   1       1  2  3  4  5           1  2  3  4
 2  3  4  5  6  7  8    6  7  8  9 10 11 12    5  6  7  8  9 10 11
 9 10 11 12 13 14 15   13 14 15 16 17 18 19   12 13 14 15 16 17 18
16 17 18 19 20 21 22   20 21 22 23 24 25 26   19 20 21 22 23 24 25
23 24 25 26 27 28 29   27 28 29              26 27 28 29 30 31
30 31

April                 May                   June
S  M  T  W  T  F  S    S  M  T  W  T  F  S   S  M  T  W  T  F  S
                   1      1  2  3  4  5  6             1  2  3
 2  3  4  5  6  7  8    7  8  9 10 11 12 13    4  5  6  7  8  9 10
 9 10 11 12 13 14 15   14 15 16 17 18 19 20   11 12 13 14 15 16 17
16 17 18 19 20 21 22   21 22 23 24 25 26 27   18 19 20 21 22 23 24
23 24 25 26 27 28 29   28 29 30 31           25 26 27 28 29 30
30

July                  August                September
S  M  T  W  T  F  S    S  M  T  W  T  F  S   S  M  T  W  T  F  S
                   1       1  2  3  4  5                1  2
 2  3  4  5  6  7  8    6  7  8  9 10 11 12    3  4  5  6  7  8  9
 9 10 11 12 13 14 15   13 14 15 16 17 18 19   10 11 12 13 14 15 16
16 17 18 19 20 21 22   20 21 22 23 24 25 26   17 18 19 20 21 22 23
23 24 25 26 27 28 29   27 28 29 30 31        24 25 26 27 28 29 30
30 31

October               November              December
S  M  T  W  T  F  S    S  M  T  W  T  F  S   S  M  T  W  T  F  S
 1  2  3  4  5  6  7          1  2  3  4             1  2
 8  9 10 11 12 13 14    5  6  7  8  9 10 11    3  4  5  6  7  8  9
15 16 17 18 19 20 21   12 13 14 15 16 17 18   10 11 12 13 14 15 16
22 23 24 25 26 27 28   19 20 21 22 23 24 25   17 18 19 20 21 22 23
29 30 31              26 27 28 29 30         24 25 26 27 28 29 30
                                            31
```

The seasons

N hemisphere	S hemisphere	Duration
Spring	Autumn	From vernal/autumnal equinox (c. 21 Mar) to summer/winter solstice (c. 21 Jun)
Summer	Winter	From summer/winter solstice (c. 21 Jun) to autumnal/spring equinox (c. 23 Sept)
Autumn	Spring	From autumnal/spring equinox (c. 23 Sept) to winter/summer solstice (c. 21 Dec)
Winter	Summer	From winter/summer solstice (c. 21 Dec) to vernal/autumnal equinox (c. 21 Mar)

Wedding anniversaries

In many Western countries, different wedding anniversaries have become associated with gifts of different materials. There is some variation between countries.

1st	Cotton	14th	Ivory
2nd	Paper	15th	Crystal
3rd	Leather	20th	China
4th	Fruit; flowers	25th	Silver
5th	Wood	30th	Pearl
6th	Sugar	35th	Coral
7th	Copper; wool	40th	Ruby
8th	Bronze; pottery	45th	Sapphire
9th	Pottery; willow	50th	Gold
10th	Tin	55th	Emerald
11th	Steel	60th	Diamond
12th	Silk; linen	70th	Platinum
13th	Lace		

Year equivalents

Jewish[a] (AM)		Islamic[b] (H)		Hindu[c] (SE)	
5756	(25 Sep 1995–13 Sep 1996)	1416	(31 May 1995–18 May 1996)	1917	(22 Mar 1995–20 Mar 1996)
5757	(14 Sep 1996–1 Oct 1997)	1417	(19 May 1996–8 May 1997)	1918	(21 Mar 1996–21 Mar 1997)
5758	(2 Oct 1997–20 Sep 1998)	1418	(9 May 1997–27 Apr 1998)	1919	(22 Mar 1997–21 Mar 1998)
5759	(21 Sep 1998–10 Sep 1999)	1419	(28 Apr 1998–16 Apr 1999)	1920	(22 Mar 1998–21 Mar 1999)
5760	(11 Sep 1999–29 Sep 2000)	1420	(17 Apr 1999–5 Apr 2000)	1921	(22 Mar 1999–21 Mar 2000)
5761	(30 Sep 2000–17 Sep 2001)	1421	(6 Apr 2000–25 Mar 2001)	1922	(21 Mar 2000–21 Mar 2001)
5762	(18 Sep 2001–6 Sep 2002)	1422	(26 Mar 2001–14 Mar 2002)	1923	(22 Mar 2001–21 Mar 2002)
5763	(7 Sep 2002–26 Sep 2003)	1423	(15 Mar 2002–4 Mar 2003)	1924	(22 Mar 2002–21 Mar 2003)
5764	(27 Sep 2003–15 Sep 2004)	1424	(5 Mar 2003–21 Feb 2004)	1925	(22 Mar 2003– 20 Mar 2004)
5765	(16 Sep 2004–3 Oct 2005)	1425	(22 Feb 2004–9 Feb 2005)	1926	(21 Mar 2004–21 Mar 2005)
5766	(4 Oct 2005–22 Sep 2006)	1426	(10 Feb 2005–30 Jan 2006)	1927	(22 Mar 2005–21 Mar 2006)

Gregorian equivalents are given in parentheses and are AD (= Anno Domini).
[a] Calculated from 3761 BC, said to be the year of the creation of the world. AM = Anno Mundi.
[b] Calculated from AD 622, the year in which the Prophet went from Mecca to Medina. H = Hegira.
[c] Calculated from AD 78, the beginning of the Saka era (SE), used alongside Gregorian dates in Government of India publications since 22 Mar 1957. Other important Hindu eras include: Vikrama era (58 BC), Kalacuri era (AD 248), Gupta era (AD 320), and Harsa era (AD 606).

Month equivalents

Gregorian equivalents to other calendars are given in parentheses; the figures refer to the number of solar days in each month. The Islamic calendar, being purely lunar, is shorter than the Gregorian by 11 days; its months therefore regress through the seasons, and the same Gregorian equivalents recur only every 33 years.

Gregorian	Jewish	Islamic	Hindu
(Basis: Sun)	(Basis: Moon)	(Basis: Moon)	(Basis: Moon)
January (31)	Tishri (Sep–Oct) (30)	Muharram (30)	Caitra (Mar–Apr) (29 or 30)
February (28 or 29)	Heshvan (Oct–Nov) (29 or 30)	Safar (29)	Vaisakha (Apr–May) (29 or 30)
March (31)	Kislev (Nov–Dec) (29 or 30)	Rabi I (30)	Jyaistha (May–Jun) (29 or 30)
April (30)	Tevet (Dec–Jan) (29)	Rabi II (29)	Asadha (Jun–Jul) (29 or 30)
May (31)	Shevat (Jan–Feb) (30)	Jumada I (30)	Dvitiya Asadha certain leap years
June (30)	Adar (Feb–Mar) (29 or 30)	Jumada II (29)	Svrana (Jul–Aug) (29 or 30)
July (31)	Adar Sheni leap years only	Rajab (30)	Dvitiya Sravana certain leap years
August (31)	Nisan (Mar–Apr) (30)	Shaban (29)	Bhadrapada (Aug–Sep) (29 or 30)
September (30)	Iyar (Apr–May) (29)	Ramadan (30)	Asvina (Sep–Oct) (29 or 30)
October (31)	Sivan (May–Jun) (30)	Shawwal (29)	Karttika (Oct–Nov) (29 or 30)
November (30)	Tammuz (Jun–Jul) (29)	Dhu al-Qadah (30)	Margasirsa (Nov–Dec) (29 or 30)
December (31)	Av (Jul–Aug) (30)	Dhu al-Hijjah (29 or 30)	Pausa (Dec–Jan) (29 or 30)
	Elul (Aug–Sep) (29)		Magha (Jan–Feb) (29 or 30)
			Phalguna (Feb–Mar) (29 or 30)

HISTORY

Names of the months

Month	Name origin
January	Janus, the two-faced god of gates
February	Februa, day of purification (February 15)
March	Mars, god of War
April	Apru, Etruscan goddess of love
May	Maia, eldest daughter of Atlas
June	Juno, wife of Jupiter
July	Julius Caesar
August	Augustus, adopted son of Julius Caesar
September	The seventh month of the earlier Roman calendar
October	The eighth month of the earlier Roman calendar
November	The ninth month of the earlier Roman calendar
December	The tenth month of the earlier Roman calendar

Months: associations

In many Western countries, the months are traditionally associated with gemstones and flowers. There is considerable variation between countries. The following combinations are widely recognized in North America and the UK.

Month	Gemstone	Flower
January	Garnet	Carnation, snowdrop
February	Amethyst	Primrose, violet
March	Aquamarine, bloodstone	Jonquil, violet
April	Diamond	Daisy, sweet pea
May	Emerald	Hawthorn, lily of the valley
June	Alexandrite, moonstone, pearl	Honeysuckle, rose
July	Ruby	Larkspur, water lily
August	Peridot, sardonyx	Gladiolus, poppy
September	Sapphire	Aster, morning glory
October	Opal, tourmaline	Calendula, cosmos
November	Topaz	Chrysanthemum
December	Turquoise, zircon	Holly, narcissus, poinsettia

Names of the days

Day	Name origin
Sunday	Sun day
Monday	Moon day
Tuesday	Tiw's day (God of battle)
Wednesday	Woden's or Odin's day (God of poetry and the dead)
Thursday	Thor's day (God of thunder)
Friday	Frigg's day (Goddess of married love)
Saturday	Saturn's day (God of fertility and agriculture)

Chinese animal years and times 1987–2010

Chinese	English	Years		Time of day (hours)
T'u	Hare	1987	1999	0500–0700
Lung	Dragon	1988	2000	0700–0900
She	Serpent	1989	2001	0900–1100
Ma	Horse	1990	2002	1100–1300
Yang	Sheep	1991	2003	1300–1500
Hou	Monkey	1992	2004	1500–1700
Chi	Cock	1993	2005	1700–1900
Kou	Dog	1994	2006	1900–2100
Chu	Boar	1995	2007	2100–2300
Shu	Rat	1996	2008	2300–0100
Niu	Ox	1997	2009	0100–0300
Hu	Tiger	1998	2010	0300–0500

Chinese agricultural calendar

(Basis: Sun and Moon)

Fortnight

Li Chun ('Spring Begins')
Yu Shui ('Rain Water')
Jing Zhe ('Excited Insects')
Chun Fen ('Vernal Equinox')
Qing Ming ('Clear and Bright')
Gu Yu ('Grain Rains')
Li Xia ('Summer Begins')
Xiao Man ('Grain Fills')
Mang Zhong ('Grain in Ear')
Xia Zhi ('Summer Solstice')
Xiao Shu ('Slight Heat')
Da Shu ('Great Heat')
Li Qiu ('Autumn Begins')
Chu Shu ('Limit of Heat')
Bai Lu ('White Dew')
Qui Fen ('Autumn Equinox')
Han Lu ('Cold Dew')
Shuang Jiang ('Frost Descends')
Li Dong ('Winter Begins')
Xiao Xue ('Little Snow')
Da Xue ('Heavy Snow')
Dong Zhi ('Winter Solstice')
Xiao Han ('Little Cold')
Da Han ('Severe Cold')

Zodiac

Spring signs

Aries, the Ram
(Mar 21–Apr 19)

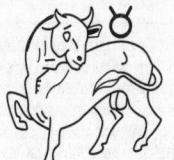

Taurus, the Bull
(Apr 20–May 20)

Gemini, the Twins
(May 21–Jun 20)

Summer signs

Cancer, the Crab
(Jun 21–Jul 22)

Leo, the Lion
(Jul 23–Aug 22)

Virgo, the Virgin
(Aug 23–Sep 22)

Autumn signs

Libra, the Balance
(Sep 23–Oct 22)

Scorpio, the Scorpion
(Oct 23–Nov21)

Sagittarius, the Archer
(Nov 22–Dec 21)

Winter signs

Capricorn, the Goat
(Dec 22–Jan 29)

Aquarius, the
Water Bearer
(Jan 20–Feb 18)

Pisces, the Fishes
(Feb19–Mar 20)

HISTORY

WORLD CHRONOLOGY

World events

There are remarkably few events that have an obligatory place in any summary of world affairs. Judgements about the significance of an event are inevitably bound up with a country's cultural and social history, and are affected by a person's interests and tastes – all of which are inherent in any selection. The chief purpose of a chronological summary, however, is not to make authoritative decisions about significance (even if that were possible), but to present a series of events in such a way that interesting or informative relationships emerge. When a wide range of contexts is surveyed, including science and the arts alongside political history and world exploration, the (sometimes unexpected) contemporaneous juxtapositions can add a fresh dimension to our awareness of historical facts.

BC
c.9000	First walled city founded at Jericho.
c.6000	Çatal Hüyük flourishes in Anatolia.
c.3500	Sumerian civilization flourishes.
c.3500	Pictographic writing in Sumer.
c.3500	Earliest Chinese cities.
c.3500	Megalithic tombs in north-west Europe.
c.3500	Flax used for textiles in Middle East.
c.3100	Dynastic period begins in Egypt.
c.3000	Temple constructed at Uruk.
c.2670	Beginning of Old Kingdom in Egypt.
c.2590	Cheops begins Great Pyramid in Egypt.
c.2500	Beginning of Indus Valley civilization (to c.1500).
c.2500	Canaanite tribes settle in Palestine.
c.2500	Use of papyrus by Egyptians.
c.2300	Mesopotamian empire established.
c.2200	Beginning of Xia dynasty in China.
c.2100	Construction of ziggurat at Ur.
c.2000	Hittites invade Anatolia.
c.2000	Construction of Babylon.
c.2000	Beginning of Minoan civilization in Crete (to c.1450).
c.2000	Completion of Stonehenge.
1991	Beginning of Middle Kingdom in Egypt.
c.1860	Development of early Semitic alphabet.
c.1780	Hammurabi of Babylon promulgates legal code.
c.1650	Hyksos invasion of Egypt.
c.1600	Beginning of Mycenaean civilization in Greece.
1567	Beginning of New Kingdom in Egypt.
c.1500	Composition of the Vedas begun in India.
c.1360	Amenhotep IV (Akhenaton) establishes worship of Sun God.
c.1300	Construction of Temple of Abu Simbel for Rameses II.
c.1260	Archaeological dating of Trojan War.
c.1200	Olmec civilization begins to flourish in Mexico.
1085	Egypt divided into Upper and Lower Kingdoms.
c.1100	Phoenicians develop alphabetic script.
c.1066	Zhou dynasty in China.
c.1000	Israelite kingdoms established by David and Solomon.
c.1000	Building of the Temple in Jerusalem begins.
c.850	Homer writes *Iliad* and *Odyssey*.
814	Traditional year of the foundation of Carthage.
c.800	Beginning of period of composition of the Upanishads.
776	First Olympic Games in Greece.
753	Traditional year of the foundation of Rome.
671	Assyrian conquest of Egypt.
c.650	Iron technology in China.
c.650	Earliest Latin inscriptions.
621	Laws of Draco in Athens.
c.600	Age of Greek lyric poetry.

586	Babylonian captivity of the Jews.
581	First Phythian Games.
581	Building of Shwe Dagon Pagoda, Myanmar.
c.550	Cyrus the Great begins expansion of Persian Empire.
c.550	Abacus developed by Chinese.
c.530	Pythagoras founds school in Greece.
c.530	Temple of Apollo built at Corinth.
521	Darius the Great divides Persian Empire into satrapies.
c.520	Death of Lao Zi, founder of Taoism.
509	Foundation of Roman Republic.
490	Persians defeated by Athenians at Marathon.
c.483	Death of Siddhartha Gautama, founder of Buddhism.
480	Persians defeat Greeks at Thermopylae.
480	Greeks destroy Persian fleet at Salamis.
479	Death of Confucius.
462	Pericles' reforms in Athens.
c.460	Construction of Temple of Zeus at Olympia.
456	Death of Aeschylus.
450	Codification of Roman law (the Twelve Tables).
433	Completion of Parthenon at Athens.
431	Beginning of Peloponnesian War (until 404).
425	Death of Herodotus.
406	Death of Sophocles.
403	Overthrow of the Thirty Tyrants in Athens.
c.377	Death of Hippocrates.
c.370	Plato opens Academy in Athens.
359	Philip of Macedon becomes King of Macedonia.
c.350	Tomb of Mausolus completed.
c.350	Hill fort constructed at Maiden Castle, England.
347	Death of Plato.
336	Assassination of Philip of Macedon.
329	Alexander the Great reaches India.
322	Death of Aristotle.
310	Epicurus opens school of philosophy at Mitylene.
304	Foundation of Ptolemaic dynasty in Egypt.
c.300	Euclid teaching in Alexandria.
c.290	Foundation of library at Alexandria.
264	First Punic War begins (to 241).
c.250	Writing of the Septuagint.
238	Hamilcar begins conquest of Spain.
221	Qin dynasty unifies China.
221	Beginning of Great Wall of China.
218	Second Punic War begins (to 201).
218	Hannibal invades Italy from the north.
212	Death of Archimedes.
206	Early or Western Han dynasty in China.
206	Scipio completes conquest of Spain.
168	Revolt of the Maccabees against Antiochus IV.
146	Romans destroy Corinth.
c.110	Opening of Silk Road across Central Asia.

c.100	Dionysius Thrax writes first Greek grammar.
51	Cleopatra becomes Queen of Egypt.
c.50	Julius Caesar writes account of Gallic Wars.
46	Adoption of Julian calendar.
44	Assassination of Julius Caesar.
43	Death of Cicero.
31	Beginning of Roman Empire.
30	Death of Antony and Cleopatra.
19	Death of Virgil.
6	Annexation of Judaea by Rome.
c.5	Birth of Jesus of Nazareth.

AD

5	Cunobelinus recognized by Romans as King of Britain.
14	Death of Augustus.
25	Later or Eastern Han dynasty in China.
26	Pontius Pilate made procurator of Judaea.
27	Baptism of Jesus Christ.
c.30	Jesus of Nazareth crucified in Jerusalem.
c.34	Conversion of Saul of Tarsus.
43	Roman invasion of Britain.
46	St Paul begins missionary journeys.
54	Nero made emperor in Rome.
61	Defeat of British revolt under Boudicca.
64	Great Fire of Rome.
c.64	Saints Peter and Paul martyred at Rome.
c.65	Foundation of Glastonbury Abbey.
70	Jewish revolt, and destruction of Temple at Jerusalem.
79	Destruction of Pompeii by Vesuvius eruption.
80	Colosseum completed at Rome.
96	Persecution of Christians by Domitian.
c.100	Roman Empire at its peak.
c.105	Paper manufacture begins in China.
120	Earliest Chinese dictionary, by Hsu Shen.
122	Hadrian begins building of wall in Britain.
132	Jewish rebellion and dispersion.
c.150	Buddhism reaches China.
c.150	Ptolemy devises his theory of astronomy.
c.200	Compilation of Mahabharata.
c.200	Codification of Mishnah completed.
220	End of Han dynasty in China.
224	Beginning of Sassanid dynasty in Persia.
238	Gothic invasions of Roman Empire.
265	Six Dynasties in China (to 581).
285	Confucianism reaches Japan.
286	Diocletian divides Empire into West and East.
c.300	Rise of Mayan civilization in Mesoamerica.
312	Constantine unites Roman Empire.
315	Christianity recognized in Roman Empire.
319	Development of Arianism.
320	Chandragupta I founds Gupta Empire in N India.
325	Council of Nicaea formulates Nicene Creed.
330	Capital of Roman Empire moves to Constantinople.
c.350	Gothic Bible produced.
c.350	Fortification of London.
367	Picts and Scots attack Britain.
c.375	Hunnish invasions in Europe.
393	Last Olympic Games of classical times.
405	Latin translation of the Bible by St Jerome (Vulgate).
410	Visigoths sack Rome.
432	St Patrick begins mission to Ireland.
438	Theodosian Code of Roman law.
449	Angles, Saxons, and Jutes invade Britain.

455	Vandals sack Rome.
476	Last Western Roman emperor deposed.
480	End of Gupta Empire in N India.
481	Accession of Clovis I, founder of the Frankish kingdom.
c.515	St Benedict devises monastic rule.
534	Justinian introduces legal code.
552	Buddism introduced into Japan.
c.563	St Columba founds monastery at Iona.
597	St Augustine lands in Britain.
602	Foundation of Archbishopric of Canterbury.
618	Beginning of Tang dynasty in China.
622	Hegira of Mohammed.
625	Mohammed begins dictation of Koran.
632	Death of Mohammed.
641	Arabs begin conquest of North Africa.
664	Synod of Whitby decides date of Easter.
691	Dome of the Rock completed in Jerusalem.
710	Nara becomes capital of Japan.
711	Muslim invasion of Spain.
c.730	Printing begins in China.
732	Arab expansion in Europe stopped by Battle of Poitiers.
735	Death of St Bede.
749	Beginning of Abbasid caliphate.
762	Death of Li Bo, Chinese poet.
762	Foundation of Baghdad.
771	Accession of Charlemagne as King of the Franks.
774	Charlemagne conquers north Italy.
787	Beginning of Viking raids in Britain.
800	Charlemagne crowned Emperor in Rome.
828	Egbert of Wessex recognized as overlord of England.
c.860	Newspaper printed in China.
866	Danish kingdom established in England.
871	Accession of King Alfred the Great in England.
878	Alfred defeats Danes at Edington.
c.900	School of medicine founded at Salerno.
907	Five Dynasties era in China.
910	Foundation of Cluny Abbey.
960	Sung dynasty in China.
967	Fujiwara period begins in Japan.
987	Accession of Capetians in France.
990	Completion of Great Mosque at Córdoba.
c.1000	Inca Empire expands in Peru.
c.1000	Vikings reach America (Vinland).
c.1000	Iron Age settlement in Zimbabwe.
1014	Vikings defeated in Ireland at Clontarf.
1016	Canute made King of England.
1037	Death of Avicenna.
1040	Duncan, King of Scots, killed by Macbeth.
c.1050	Invention of movable type in China.
1054	Schism between Western and Eastern Christianity.
1065	Consecration of Westminster Abbey.
1066	Norman Conquest of England.
1086	Domesday Book completed.
1094	El Cid defeats the Moors at Valencia.
1096	First Crusade begins (to 1099).
1099	Church of Holy Sepulchre built in Jerusalem.
c.1100	Toltec capital built in Mexico.
1113	Foundation of the Knights Hospitallers of St John of Jerusalem.
1147	Second Crusade begins (to 1148)
c.1150	Angkor Wat temple built in Cambodia.
c.1150	Yoruba city states in Nigeria.
1154	Angevins rule in England and France.

World events (continued)

c.1155 Beginnings of Paris University.
1156 Foundation of Moscow.
1163 Building of Notre Dame Cathedral, Paris, begins.
1170 Assassination of Thomas à Becket at Canterbury.
1175 Muslim Empire founded in India.
1187 Saladin captures Jerusalem.
1189 Third Crusade begins (to 1192).
1191 Crusaders capture Acre.
1195 Building of Chartres Cathedral begins.
c.1200 Rise of Mali Empire in West Africa.
1202 Fourth Crusade begins (to 1204)
1204 Crusaders capture Constantinople.
1206 Genghis Khan begins Mongol invasion of Asia.
1211 Delhi Sultanate begins under Iltutmish.
1212 The Children's Crusade.
1215 Magna Carta issued at Runnymede.
1215 Dominican Order of friars founded.
1217 Fifth Crusade begins (to 1221).
1228 Sixth Crusade begins (to 1229).
1236 Mongols conquer Russia.
1242 Alexander Nevsky defeats Teutonic Order.
1248 Seventh Crusade begins (to 1254).
1250 Beginning of Mamluk rule in Egypt.
1260 Ghibellines defeat Guelphs at Montaperti.
1261 Greek rule restored in Constantinople.
1264 Kublai Khan founds Yuan dynasty in China.
1270 Eighth Crusade begins (to 1272).
1271 Marco Polo first visits China.
1274 Death of St Thomas Aquinas.
1276 Edward I begins Welsh wars.
1280 Death of Albertus Magnus.
c.1290 Invention of spectacles.
1291 Knights of St John driven from Acre to Cyprus.
1291 Swiss Confederation begins.
1292 Death of Roger Bacon.
1294 Death of Kublai Khan.
c.1300 Foundation of Ottoman Empire.
1300 Rise of Benin Empire in Nigeria.
1302 First meeting of French estates general.
1306 Scots revolt under Robert Bruce.
1309 Papacy moves to Avignon (to 1377).
1311 Guild of Mastersingers founded at Mainz.
c.1313 Invention of cannon.
1314 Scots defeat English at Bannockburn.
1321 Death of Alighieri Dante.
1337 Hundred Years War begins between France and England.
1339 Building of Kremlin in Moscow.
c.1344 Aztecs build capital at Tenochtitlan.
1346 Edward III defeats French at Crécy.
1347 Black Death arrives in Europe (to 1351).
1353 Ottoman invasion of Europe begins.
1356 English defeat French at Poitiers.
1368 Ming dynasty in China.
1369 Timur (Tamerlane) begins conquest of Asia.
1371 House of Stewart ascends to Scottish throne.
1374 Death of Francesco Petrarch.
1377 Poll tax first introduced in England.
1378 Great Schism begins in West.
1380 John Wycliffe's translation of the Bible into English appears.
1381 Peasants' Revolt in England.
1389 Union of Denmark, Norway, and Sweden.
1399 Death of John of Gaunt.
1399 Henry IV deposes Richard II.

1400 Death of Geoffrey Chaucer.
1403 Henry IV defeats Percys at Shrewsbury.
1411 Foundation of the Guildhall in London.
1415 Defeat of French by Henry V at Agincourt.
1417 End of Great Schism.
1427 Defeat of Hussites in Bohemia.
1431 Joan of Arc burned at Rouen.
c.1445 Johannes Gutenberg introduces printing in Europe.
1450 Jack Cade's rebellion in England.
1453 End of Hundred Years War.
1453 Turks capture Constantinople.
1455 Wars of the Roses begin (to 1485).
1460 Death of Henry the Navigator.
1471 First European observatory at Nürnberg.
1475 William Caxton prints first book in English.
1479 Union of Aragon and Castile under Ferdinand and Isabella.
1485 Henry Tudor defeats Richard III at Bosworth.
1486 Portuguese reach Angola.
1487 Bartolomeu Diaz sails around Cape of Storms (Good Hope).
1492 Christopher Columbus reaches America.
1492 Jews expelled from Spain.
1492 Revolt of Perkin Warbeck in England (to 1499).
1497 John Cabot reaches Newfoundland.
1498 Christopher Columbus reaches South America.
1498 Vasco da Gama reaches India.
1499 Amerigo Vespucci reaches Venezuela.
1500 Pedro Álvarez Cabral reaches Brazil.
1506 Rebuilding of St Peter's, Rome, begins.
1508 Michelangelo Buonarroti begins painting of Sistine Chapel, Vatican (to 1512).
1509 Accession of Henry VIII.
1509 Watch invented in Nuremberg.
1513 Vasco Núñez de Balboa reaches Pacific Ocean.
1513 Juan Ponce de León reaches Florida.
1517 Martin Luther nails theses to church door at Wittenberg.
1517 Coffee introduced to Europe.
1519 Hernán Cortés begins conquest of Aztecs.
1519 Death of Leonardo da Vinci.
1520 Ferdinand Magellan reaches Pacific Ocean.
1520 Death of Raphael.
1521 Books begin to be printed at Cambridge.
1525 William Tyndale's English translation of New Testament published.
1526 Foundation of Mughal dynasty in India.
1531 Francisco Pizarro captures Inca capital.
1534 Henry VIII breaks with Rome.
1534 Ignatius Loyola founds Society of Jesus (Jesuits).
1535 Miles Coverdale publishes first complete Bible in English.
1536 Statute of Union between England and Wales.
1536 Suppression of monasteries begins in England.
1536 Jacques Cartier claims Canada for France.
1536 Akbar the Great defeats Hindus at Panipat.
1536 Death of Desiderius Erasmus.
1539 Death of Nanak, founder of Sikhism.
1539 Publication of the Great Bible in England.
1539 Word *encylopaedia* first used by Thomas Elyot.
1541 John Calvin founds church at Geneva.
1543 Nicolas Copernicus publishes *Of the Revolution of Celestial Bodies*.
1545 Council of Trent begins (to 1563), initiating the Counter-Reformation.
1546 Georgius Agricola makes first scientific

classification of minerals.
1549 Book of Common Prayer issued.
1558 England loses Calais to the French.
1558 Accession of Elizabeth I of England.
1559 Acts of Supremacy and Uniformity in England.
1560 Jacques Nicot brings tobacco into France.
1562 Netherlands revolt against Spain.
1562 Wars of Religion begin in France (to 1598).
1564 Death of Michelangelo Buonarroti.
1564 Birth of William Shakespeare.
1569 Union of Lublin unites Lithuania to Poland.
1569 James Fitzmaurice's rebellion in Ireland.
1569 Mercator Chart introduced.
1571 Turks defeated at Lepanto.
1571 Thirty-Nine Articles adopted in England.
1572 St Bartholomew's Day massacre in France.
1572 Beginning of Dutch rebellion against Spain.
1576 First theatre opens in England, at Shoreditch.
1577 Francis Drake leaves on world voyage.
1581 Independence of United Provinces
     (Netherlands).
1582 Introduction of Gregorian Calendar in Italy.
1584 Walter Raleigh sends first expedition to
     Virginia.
1587 Execution of Mary, Queen of Scots.
1587 First European Academy, in Italy.
1588 Defeat of Spanish Armada by England.
1589 Foundation of Bourbon dynasty in France.
1594 Death of Giovanni Pierluigi da Palestrina.
1600 British and Dutch East India companies
     founded.
1600 William Gilbert writes on electricity and
     magnetism.
1603 Accession of James VI of Scotland as James I of
     England.
1603 Tokugawa shogunate begins in Japan (to 1868).
1605 Discovery of Gunpowder Plot in London.
1607 Jamestown settlement in America.
1608 French found Quebec.
1610 Galileo Galilei records rings of Saturn and
     moons of Jupiter.
1610 Arrival of tea in Europe from China.
1611 Authorized Version of the Bible issued.
1614 Publication of John Napier's book on
     logarithms.
1615 Inigo Jones becomes surveyor-general in
     England.
1616 Death of William Shakespeare.
1616 Baffin explores Baffin Bay.
1617 Ben Jonson made first poet laureate.
1618 Thirty Years War begins (to 1648).
1620 Puritans reach New England in *Mayflower*.
1622 Invention of the slide rule.
1624 Armand Jean du Plessis Richelieu becomes First
     Minister in France.
1625 Dutch found New Amsterdam.
1627 Maratha kingdom founded in India.
1628 William Harvey publishes treatise on
     circulation of the blood.
1629 Capture of Quebec by English from French.
1629 Colony of Massachusetts founded.
1632 Shah Jahan begins building of Taj Mahal (to
     1654).
1635 Death of Lope de Vega.
1636 Foundation of Harvard University.
1638 Scottish Covenant drawn up.
1638 First printing press set up in America.
1640 English Long Parliament assembles.

1640 Stage-coaches introduced into England.
1641 Grand Remonstrance passed against Charles I.
1642 Abel Tasman sights Tasmania (Van Dieman's
     Land).
1642 Beginning of English Civil War.
1643 Death of Claudio Monteverdi.
1643 Evangelista Torricelli invents barometer.
1643 New England Confederation of colonies
     formed.
1644 Qing dynasty founded in China.
1645 Charles I defeated at Naseby.
1645 Abel Tasman circumnavigates Australia.
1647 Blaise Pascal constructs first calculating
     machine.
1648 Peace of Westphalia ends Thirty Years War.
1648 Wars of the Frondes begin in France (to 1653).
1649 Execution of Charles I of England.
1650 Otto von Guericke invents air pump.
1652 First Anglo-Dutch War.
1652 Dutch found Cape Colony.
1653 Oliver Cromwell appointed Lord Protector in
     England.
1660 Restoration of monarchy in England.
1660 Royal Society founded in London.
1660 Samuel Pepys begins his diary (1669).
1661 Louis XIV assumes absolute power in France.
1661 Bank of Sweden issues world's first banknotes.
1662 Robert Boyle states gas law.
1662 Death of Blaise Pascal.
1664 English rename New Amsterdam as New York.
1665 Great Plague of London at its height.
1666 Great Fire of London.
1669 Death of Rembrandt.
1670 Hudson's Bay Trading Company given Royal
     Charter.
1673 Death of Molière.
1674 Death of John Milton.
1675 Christopher Wren begins new St Paul's
     Cathedral (finished 1710).
1678 Popish Plot in England.
1679 Discovery of Niagara Falls.
1681 William Penn granted patent for land in North
     America.
1681 La Salle explores Mississippi.
1681 First (oil) street lamps in London.
1682 Edmond Halley observes 'his' comet.
1687 Isaac Newton publishes his *Principia*.
1688 William of Orange invited to England.
1688 Lloyd's coffee-house in London begins to be
     used as insurance centre.
1689 Grand Alliance against Louis XIV.
1690 James II defeated by William III at the Boyne.
1690 Foundation of Calcutta.
1694 Establishment of Bank of England.
1696 Accession of Peter I (the Great) as sole Tsar of
     Russia.
1699 Death of Jean Racine.
1700 Beginning of Great Northern War (to 1721).
1701 Tull invents horse-drawn seeding drill.
1701 Foundation of Yale University.
1702 War of Spanish Succession begins (to 1713).
1702 England's first daily newspaper issued, *The Daily
     Courant*.
1703 Foundation of St Petersburg.
1704 French defeated by Marlborough at Blenheim.
1705 Introduction of ship's wheel to replace tiller.
1707 Act of Union unites England and Scotland.
1707 Death of Aurangzeb.

World events (continued)

1709 Swedes defeated by Peter the Great at Poltava.
1714 Beginning of Hanoverian dynasty in England (George I).
1714 Gabriel Fahrenheit invents mercury thermometer.
1715 Jacobite rebellion in Britain.
1721 Rifle introduced into America.
1735 Carolus Linnaeus publishes *Systema naturae*.
1738 Daniel Bernoulli states law of hydrodynamics.
1739 War of Jenkins's Ear between Britain and Spain.
1739 Founding of Methodism by John and Charles Wesley.
1740 War of Austrian Succession (to 1748).
1741 Wrought iron first used in bridge construction.
1742 First performance of George Frideric Handel's *Messiah*.
1743 French explorers reach Rocky Mountains.
1745 Jacobite rebellion in Britain.
1746 Benjamin Franklin begins his research into electricity.
1747 Foundation of Afghanistan.
1750 Death of Johann Sebastian Bach.
1750 Nicolas Louis de Lacaille draws up star catalogue.
1751 Denis Diderot begins work on *Encyclopédie* (to 1776).
1752 Gregorian Calendar adopted in Britain.
1755 Publication of Samuel Johnson's *Dictionary*.
1756 Black identifies carbon dioxide.
1756 Beginning of Seven Years War (to 1763).
1756 Black Hole of Calcutta.
1757 British defeat French at Plassey.
1759 Quebec captured by James Wolfe.
1759 Death of George Frideric Handel.
1760 Identification of hydrogen by Henry Cavendish.
1762 Publication of Jean Jacques Rousseau's *Social Contract*.
1764 James Watt invents separate condenser for steam engine.
1767 Mason–Dixon line established.
1768 James Cook's first voyage to the Pacific.
1768 Richard Arkwright introduces spinning frame in England.
1769 Birth of Napoleon Bonaparte.
1770 James Bruce finds source of Blue Nile.
1770 James Cook arrives in Botany Bay.
1771 Carl Scheele discovers oxygen.
1772 First partition of Poland between Russia and Austria.
1772 Bridgewater Canal finished in England.
1773 Boston Tea Party.
1774 Accession of Louis XVI of France.
1774 Formulation of the rules of cricket.
1774 First commercial steam engine produced by James Watt and Matthew Boulton.
1775 US War of Independence begins (to 1783).
1776 American Declaration of Independence.
1776 Publication of Adam Smith's *Wealth of Nations*.
1778 Joseph Bramah invents water-closet.
1778 Death of Voltaire.
1779 Samuel Crompton produces spinning mule.
1781 British surrender to Washington at Yorktown.
1781 Publication of Emmanuel Kant's *Critique of Pure Reason*.
1781 William Herschel discovers Uranus.
1781 Charles Messier produces star catalogue.
1783 Britain recognizes independence of American colonies.

1783 United Empire Loyalists settle in Canada.
1783 Montgolfier brothers ascend in a balloon.
1784 Henry Cort introduces puddling process for iron.
1784 First official mail coach, Bristol–London.
1785 Edmund Cartwright patents power loom.
1786 Martin Klaproth discovers uranium.
1788 British found colony in Australia.
1788 Antoine Lavoisier shows air to be a mixture of oxygen and nitrogen.
1789 French Revolution begins.
1789 George Washington becomes first president of USA.
1789 Mutiny on the *Bounty*.
1789 US Post Office established.
1790 Luigi Galvani carries out electrical experiments.
1790 First table of chemical elements presented by Antoine Lavoisier.
1790 Foundation of Washington.
1790 Edmund Cartwright introduces steam-powered loom.
1791 Bill of Rights ratified by US Congress.
1791 Unsuccessful flight of Louis XVI.
1791 Death of Mozart.
1791 Publication of the first part of Thomas Paine's *The Rights of Man*.
1792 Foundation of French Republic.
1792 First settlements in New Zealand.
1793 French Revolutionary Wars begin (to 1799).
1793 Execution of Louis XVI.
1793 Whitney patents cotton gin.
1794 End of 'Reign of Terror' in France.
1795 Park explores Niger River.
1795 Directory established in France.
1796 Edward Jenner discovers smallpox vaccine.
1796 Aloys Senefelder invents lithography.
1797 MacArthur introduces merino sheep to Australia.
1798 Napoleon Bonaparte invades Egypt.
1798 Irish rebellion suppressed.
1798 Horatio Nelson defeats French at Aboukir Bay.
1798 Publication of William Wordsworth's and Samuel Taylor Coleridge's *Lyrical Ballads*.
1798 Publication of Thomas Malthus's *Essay on the Principle of Population*.
1799 Death of George Washington.
1799 Napoleon Bonaparte becomes First Consul.
1799 Ludwig van Beethoven writes first symphony.
1800 Act of Union between England and Ireland.
1800 Alessandro Volta makes first battery.
1800 Beginning of Napoleonic Wars (to 1815).
1801 Richard Trevithick builds steam carriage.
1802 First paddle steamer used in Scotland.
1802 Peace of Amiens between England and France.
1803 Louisiana Purchase in USA.
1804 Napoleon made Emperor.
1805 British defeat French and Spanish at Trafalgar.
1807 Abolition of slave trade in British Empire.
1808 Independence movements begin in South America.
1808 Peninsular War begins (to 1814).
1809 Death of Joseph Haydn.
1810 Chile and Mexico declare independence from Spain.
c.1810 John Dalton presents basis of atomic theory.

1811 Amedeo Avogadro formulates hypothesis on gas molecules.
1811 Alfried Krupp founds ironworks at Essen.
1812 Napoleon Bonaparte invades Russia.
1812 War between Britain and USA (to 1814).
1812 Luddite riots in England.
1812 Invention of cylinder printing press.
1815 Defeat of Napoleon Bonaparte at Battle of Waterloo.
1815 Congress of Vienna.
1816 Argentina declares independence from Spain.
1816 René-Théophile-Hyacinthe Laennec invents stethoscope.
1817–18 Defeat of Marathas by British in India.
1819 Florida Purchase in USA.
1819 Foundation of Singapore.
1819 Peterloo Massacre at Manchester.
1820 War of Greek Independence begins (to 1828).
1822 Foundation of Liberia for freed slaves.
1822 First photographic image made by Nicéphore Niépce.
1823 Monroe Doctrine formulated.
1824 First Ashanti War (to 1866).
1824 Death of Byron.
1825 First passenger steam railway in England.
1825 Opening of the Erie Canal.
1827 Michael Faraday becomes professor at Royal Institution.
1827 Death of Ludwig van Beethoven.
1828 Publication of Noah Webster's *Dictionary* in USA.
1829 Catholic Emancipation Act in Britain.
1829 Braille invents system of touch-reading for blind.
1829 Joseph Henry invents electromagnetic motor.
1829 First Oxford and Cambridge Boat Race.
1829 George Stephenson constructs the 'Rocket'.
1830 July Revolution in France.
1830 Independence of Belgium.
1831 Charles Darwin begins voyage on the *Beagle*.
1832 First Reform Act in Britain.
1832 First railway constructed in USA.
1832 Death of Johann Wolfgang von Goethe.
1834 German customs union (*Zollverein*) officially founded.
1834 Cyrus McCormick patents harvesting machine.
1835 Samuel Colt patents revolver.
1835 Beginning of construction of Great Western Railway in England.
1835 Foundation of Melbourne.
1835 Samuel Morse develops telegraph in USA.
1836 Boer Great Trek in South Africa.
1836 Siege of the Alamo in Texas.
1837 Isaac Pitman introduces his shorthand system.
1838 Anti-Corn Law League founded in Manchester.
1838 First continuous steam crossing of Atlantic by *Sirius*.
1839 First Opium War between Britain and China (to 1842).
1839 First Grand National steeplechase in Liverpool.
1840 Marriage of Queen Victoria and Prince Albert.
1840 Introduction of penny postage stamps in Britain.
1840 Bicycle invented in Scotland.
1841 Act of Union joins Upper and Lower Canada.
1841 British annexation of New Zealand.
1841 David Livingstone begins explorations in Africa.
1842 British annexation of Hong Kong.
1842 Khyber Pass massacre.

1843 Opening of Marc Isambard Brunel's tunnel under the Thames.
1845 US annexation of Texas.
1846 Britain repeals Corn Laws.
1846 Mexican War begins (to 1848).
1846 Oregon Treaty defines US–Canadian boundary.
1846 Foundation of Smithsonian Institution in Washington, DC.
1846 Elias Howe invents sewing machine.
1847 Mormons emigrate to Utah.
1848 Revolutionary movements throughout Europe.
1848 Abdication of Louis Philippe in France.
1848 Communist Manifesto published.
1848 Linus Yale invents cylinder lock.
1848 Gold discovered in California.
1849 Death of Frédéric Chopin.
1849 Punjab annexed by Britain.
1850 Taiping rebellion in China (to 1864).
1851 Great Exhibition in London.
1851 First publication of *New York Times*.
1852 Louis Napoleon becomes Emperor of France.
1852 Elisha Otis invents lift with automatic brake.
1852 Wells Fargo & Co founded in USA.
1854 Beginning of Crimean War (to 1856).
1854 Georges Haussmann begins reconstruction of Paris.
1855 David Livingstone reaches Victoria Falls.
1856 Introduction of Bessemer process for steel.
1857 Indian Mutiny.
1858 Laying of first Atlantic cable.
1858 John Speke and Richard Burton reach Lake Tanganyika.
1859 Movement for unification of Italy begins (to 1870).
1859 Publication of Charles Darwin's *The Origin of Species*.
1859 Ferdinand de Lesseps begins work on Suez Canal.
1859 First American oil-wells drilled in Pennsylvania.
1860 Giuseppe Garibaldi's Expedition of the Thousand.
1861 American Civil War begins (to 1865).
1861 Emancipation of Russian serfs.
1861 Germ theory of disease proposed by Louis Pasteur.
1862 Otto von Bismarck appointed Prime Minister of Prussia.
1862 Gatling patents machine gun.
1863 Abraham Lincoln's Gettysburg Address.
1863 Beginning of underground railway in London.
1864 Paraguayan War begins (to 1870).
1864 Foundation of Red Cross in Geneva.
1865 American Civil War ends.
1865 Assassination of Abraham Lincoln.
1865 Publication of Lewis Carroll's *Alice in Wonderland*.
1866 Prussia defeats Austria in Seven-Weeks War.
1866 Nobel produces dynamite.
1866 Winchester introduces repeating rifle.
1866 Gregor Mendel proposes laws of inheritance.
1867 US purchase of Alaska from Russia.
1867 Establishment of Dominion of Canada.
1867 Dual Monarchy established in Austria–Hungary.
1867 Publication of Karl Marx's *Das Kapital*.
1867 South African diamond fields discovered.
1867 Christopher Sholes and Carlos Glidden design first commercial typewriter.
1868 Meiji Restoration in Japan.

World events (continued)

1869 Opening of Suez Canal.
1869 Completion of first trans-continental railway in USA.
1869 Dmitri Mendeleyev draws up table of elements.
1870 Franco-Prussian War begins (to 1871).
1870 Papal infallibility declared.
1870 Death of Charles Dickens.
1871 German Empire proclaimed.
1871 Third Republic begins in France.
1872 Claude Monet's 'Impression: Sunrise' gives name to Impressionists.
1873 James Clerk Maxwell publishes treatise on electricity and magnetism.
1875 William Gilbert and Arthur Sullivan produce their first operetta.
1876 Mary Baker Eddy founds Christian Science movement.
1876 George Custer defeated at Battle of Little Big Horn.
1876 Alexander Bell invents telephone.
1876 Nikolaus Otto devises four-stroke-cycle gas engine.
1876 Queen Victoria proclaimed Empress of India.
1877 Thomas Edison invents the phonograph.
1879 War of the Pacific begins (to 1883).
1879 Zulu War in South Africa.
1879 Woolworths opens first store.
1880 First Boer War (to 1881).
1881 Death of Fyodor Dostoevsky.
1881 Louis Pasteur develops immunization against anthrax.
1882 Phoenix Park murders in Dublin.
1882 Robert Koch discovers tuberculosis bacillus.
1882 Mahdi proclaimed as Messiah in Sudan.
1883 Opening of Brooklyn Bridge, New York.
1883 Death of Richard Wagner.
1883 Krakatoa volcanic explosion.
1884 Germany acquires South-West Africa.
1884 Discovery of gold in Transvaal.
1885 Belgium acquires Congo.
1885 Death of Charles Gordon at Khartoum.
1885 Foundation of Indian National Congress.
1885 Karl Benz builds his first motor cars in Germany.
1885 Completion of Canadian Pacific Railway.
1886 Partition of East Africa by Germany and Britain.
1886 Foundation of Johannesburg.
1886 Gottlieb Daimler produces motorcycle.
1886 Statue of Liberty erected in the USA.
1887 French establish Indo-Chinese Union.
1887 Michelson–Morley experiment on relative velocity of light.
1887 Goodwin invents celluloid film.
1887 Invention of pneumatic tyre by Dunlop.
1887 Heinrich Hertz discovers electromagnetic waves.
1887 First book on Esperanto published.
1888 Tesla makes alternating-current motor.
1888 Eastman produces Kodak camera.
1889 Foundation of British South Africa Company.
1889 Gustave Eiffel completes Tower in Paris.
1889 First skyscraper in America (in Chicago).
1890 Dismissal of Bismarck.
1890 Death of Vincent van Gogh.
1891 Beginning of Trans-Siberian Railway.
1893 Death of Piotr Ilyich Tchaikovsky.
1893 Lumière brothers invent cinematograph.

1894 Beginning of Sino-Japanese War (to 1895).
1894 Opening of Blackpool Tower.
1894 Opening of Manchester Ship Canal.
1895 Wilhelm Röntgen discovers X-rays.
1895 Guglielmo Marconi invents wireless telegraphy.
1895 Henry Wood begins Promenade Concerts in London.
1896 Italians defeated by Ethiopians at Battle of Adowa.
1896 Jameson Raid in South Africa.
1896 Henri Becquerel discovers radioactivity.
1897 Launch of first steam-turbine ship (*Turbinia*).
1897 Death of Johannes Brahms.
1897 First Women's Institute, in Canada.
1897 Joseph Thomson discovers the electron.
1897 Diesel demonstrates compression-ignition engine.
1898 The Curies isolate radium.
1898 Spanish–American War.
1898 Hundred Days of Reform in China.
1898 USA annexes Hawaii.
1898 Ebenezer Howard proposes 'garden city' concept.
1899 Second Boer War begins (to 1902).
1899 Permanent Court of Arbitration established in The Hague.
1900 Boxer uprising in China.
1900 Max Planck proposes quantum theory.
1900 Publication of Sigmund Freud's *The Interpretation of Dreams*.
1901 Discovery of principal blood groups.
1901 Establishment of Commonwealth of Australia.
1901 Guglielmo Marconi transmits wireless signals across the Atlantic.
1901 Nobel Prize first awarded.
1902 Enrico Caruso makes first gramophone record.
1903 Panama Canal Zone leased to USA.
1903 Wright brothers make their first flight.
1903 Henry Ford founds motor company.
1903 Publication of Bertrand Russell's *Principles of Mathematics*.
1904 Beginning of Russo–Japanese War (to 1905).
1904 Construction of first engine-powered lifeboat.
1905 Revolution in Russia against Tsar.
1905 Albert Einstein presents special theory of relativity.
1906 Major earthquake in San Francisco.
1906 Foundation of Rolls-Royce Ltd in England.
1906 Death of Henrik Ibsen.
1907 Dominion of New Zealand established.
1907 Cubist exhibition in Paris.
1908 Young Turks revolution.
1908 Robert Baden-Powell founds Boy Scout movement.
1908 First Model T Ford made.
1908 Great meteorite falls in Siberia.
1909 Sergei Diaghilev launches Ballets Russes.
1909 Robert Peary reaches North Pole.
1909 Louis Blériot makes first cross-Channel flight.
1910 Foundation of Union of South Africa.
1910 Beginning of Mexican revolution (to 1917).
1910 Annexation of Korea by Japan.
1910 Constitutional Crisis in Britain.
1910 Paul Ehrlich invents salvarsan as cure for syphilis.
1910 Death of Leo Tolstoy.
1911 Chinese Revolution.

1911 Ernest Rutherford propounds theory of atomic structure.
1911 Roald Amundsen first to reach South Pole.
1912 Beginning of Balkan Wars (to 1913).
1912 Sinking of SS *Titanic*.
1912 Republic of China established under Sun Yat-sen.
1912 Victor Hess discovers cosmic rays.
1914 First Charlie Chaplin films.
1914 Opening of Panama Canal.
1914 First World War begins (to 1918).
1916 Albert Einstein presents general theory of relativity.
1916 Battle of the Somme.
1916 Irish rebellion (to 1921).
1917 US Expeditionary Force in Europe.
1917 Russian Revolution.
1917 Civil war in Russia (to 1922).
1917 Balfour Declaration promises Jews a home in Palestine.
1918 Fourteen Points statement by President Wilson.
1918 End of First World War.
1918 Women over 30 given right to vote in Britain.
1919 May 4th movement in China.
1919 Foundation of Soviet Republic.
1919 Amritsar massacre in India.
1919 Bauhaus movement established in Germany.
1919 John Alcock and Arthur Brown make first Atlantic air crossing.
1919 First woman MP in House of Commons (Lady Astor).
1919 Adolf Hitler founds National Socialist German Workers' Party.
1919 Spartacist rising in Berlin crushed.
1919 League of Nations established.
1920 Radio broadcasting begins.
1921 Treaty partitions Ireland.
1922 USSR established.
1922 Benito Mussolini in power in Italy.
1922 Frederick Banting and Charles Best isolate insulin.
1922 BBC makes first regular broadcasts.
1922 Tomb of Tutankhamun discovered in Egypt.
1923 Munich putsch by Adolf Hitler.
1923 Republic proclaimed in Turkey.
1923 Major earthquake in Japan.
1924 Death of Vladimir Ilyich Lenin.
1925 Publication of Adolf Hitler's *Mein Kampf*.
1926 General Strike in Britain.
1926 Jiang Jieshi (Chiang Kai-shek) leads movement for reunification of China.
1926 John Logie Baird demonstrates television.
1927 Talking pictures begin.
1927 Charles Lindbergh's first solo flight across Atlantic.
1927 Duke Ellington begins playing at the Cotton Club.
1928 Alexander Fleming discovers penicillin.
1928 Walt Disney introduces Mickey Mouse.
1929 Wall Street crash.
1929 Lateran Treaty establishes Vatican as state.
1930 Amy Johnson's solo flight, England to Australia.
1931 Creation of republic in Spain.
1931 Japanese occupy Manchuria.
1931 Empire State Building built in New York.
1932 Foundation of Kingdom of Saudi Arabia.
1932 Chaco War between Paraguay and Bolivia (to 1935).

1933 Franklin Roosevelt introduces New Deal.
1933 Adolf Hitler becomes Chancellor of Germany.
1933 Reichstag Fire in Berlin.
1933 Prohibition repealed in the USA.
1933 Discovery of polythene.
1934 Long March of Chinese Communists begins (to 1935).
1934 Discovery of nuclear fission.
1935 Italian invasion of Abyssinia (Ethiopia).
1936 Beginning of Spanish Civil War (to 1939).
1936 Anti-Comintern Pact between Japan and Germany.
1936 Arab revolt in Palestine.
1936 British constitutional crisis over Edward VIII.
1936 John Maynard Keynes publishes his economic theory.
1936 First public television transmissions in Britain.
1936 *Queen Mary*'s maiden voyage.
1936 Crystal Palace destroyed by fire.
1937 War between Japan and China begins.
1937 Pablo Picasso paints 'Guernica'.
1937 Golden Gate Bridge completed in San Francisco.
1937 *Hindenburg* zeppelin destroyed by fire in USA.
1937 Jet engine tested.
1938 Germany occupies Austria.
1938 Munich Agreement.
1938 Discovery of nylon.
1938 Chester F Carlson makes first xerographic print.
1939 Germany invades Czechoslovakia and Poland.
1939 Second World War begins.
1940 Evacuation of Dunkirk.
1940 Battle of Britain.
1940 Plutonium obtained by bombardment of uranium.
1941 Germany invades Russia.
1941 Japanese attack Pearl Harbor.
1941 Death of James Joyce.
1941 Orson Welles makes *Citizen Kane*.
1942 Construction of first nuclear reactor.
1942 Defeat of Germany at El Alamein.
1942 American defeat of Japan at Midway.
1942 Anglo-American landings in North Africa.
1943 Surrender of German army at Stalingrad.
1943 Capitulation of Italy.
1944 D-Day landing in Normandy.
1944 Education Act in Britain.
1945 Atom bombs dropped on Japan.
1945 Second World War ends.
1945 Yalta Conference.
1945 Nuremberg War Crimes Tribunal opens.
1945 United Nations established.
1945 Republic of Yugoslavia established under Tito.
1946 Perón in power in Argentina.
1946 Civil War in China (to 1949).
1946 Civil War in Indo-China (to 1954).
1946 Construction of first electronic digital computer.
1947 First supersonic flight.
1947 Independence of India and Pakistan.
1947 Greek Civil War (to 1949).
1947 Marshall Plan for European reconstruction.
1947 Dead Sea Scrolls found in Palestine.
1947 Christian Dior introduces 'New Look'.
1947 Invention of the transistor
1948 Creation of State of Israel.
1948 Communist rule established in Czechoslovakia.
1948 Berlin airlift.
1948 Formation of Organization of American States.

HISTORY

World events (continued)

1948 First Arab–Israeli War.
1948 Creation of World Council of Churches.
1948 Assassination of Mahatma Gandhi.
1948 Apartheid policy begins in South Africa.
1948 Creation of World Health Organization.
1948 Kinsey report on sexual behaviour published.
1949 Formation of NATO.
1949 Communist victory in China.
1949 Creation of West and East Germany.
1949 Communist rule established in Hungary.
1950 Beginning of Korean War (to 1953).
1951 Nuclear power stations introduced.
1951 Festival of Britain.
1951 First turbo-jet airliner (*Comet*).
1952 Mau Mau rebellion begins in Kenya.
1952 Military revolt in Egypt.
1952 Accession of Elizabeth II of Britain.
1952 Detonation of first hydrogen bomb.
1953 Death of Josef Stalin.
1953 Edmund Hillary and Sherpa Tenzing conquer Everest.
1953 James Watson and Francis Crick show DNA molecule structure.
1954 Independence of Cambodia and Laos.
1954 Nationalist revolt in Algeria.
1954 Nasser in power in Egypt.
1954 Vietnam divided into North and South.
1954 Independent Television Authority set up in Britain.
1955 Formation of Warsaw Pact.
1955 Enosis (Greek unity) crisis in Cyprus (to 1959).
1956 Władysław Gomułka in power in Poland.
1956 Soviet forces crush Hungarian revolt.
1956 Contraceptive pill introduced.
1956 Second Arab–Israeli War.
1956 Suez Crisis.
1956 Neutrino experimentally observed.
1956 Rock-and-roll music era begins.
1957 Independence of Ghana.
1957 Treaty of Rome forms European Economic Community.
1957 Launch of first space satellite (*Sputnik 1*).
1957 Civil Rights violence at Little Rock, Arkansas.
1958 Fifth Republic formed in France under Charles de Gaulle.
1958 Introduction of stereo recordings.
1959 Formation of European Free Trade Association.
1959 Fidel Castro in power after Cuban revolution.
1959 First photograph of dark side of the Moon (*Luna 3*).
1959 First section of Britain's first motorway opened.
1960 Independence of many African states.
1960 Sharpeville massacre in South Africa.
1960 Development of the laser.
1961 John F Kennedy becomes US president.
1961 Berlin Wall built.
1961 South Africa becomes republic.
1961 Yuri Gagarin becomes first man in space (*Vostok 1*).
1962 Second Vatican Council begins (to 1965).
1962 Independence of Algeria.
1962 Cuban missile crisis.
1963 Assassination of John F Kennedy.
1963 Valentina Tereshkova is first woman in orbit.
1963 Beatles become internationally known.

1964 Publication of *Thoughts of Chairman Mao*.
1964 Civil Rights Bill in USA.
1964 Foundation of Palestine Liberation Organization.
1965 War between India and Pakistan.
1965 Unilateral declaration of independence by Rhodesia (Zimbabwe).
1966 Cultural Revolution in China.
1966 First lunar soft landing (*Luna 9*).
1966 Assassination of Hendrik Verwoerd in Cape Town, South Africa.
1967 Civil war in Nigeria, and secession of Biafra (to 1970).
1967 Third Arab–Israeli War ('Six-Day War').
1967 Oil tanker *Torrey Canyon* disaster.
1967 Christiaan Barnard carries out first heart transplant operation.
1967 Discovery of pulsars.
1968 Soviet invasion of Czechoslovakia.
1968 Student protest movement in many countries.
1968 Assassination of Martin Luther King, Jr.
1968 First manned lunar orbit (*Apollo 8*).
1969 First man on the moon (Neil Armstrong).
1969 Richard Nixon becomes US president.
1969 Outbreak of troubles in Northern Ireland.
1970 Boeing 747 'jumbo' jets introduced.
1971 East Pakistan becomes Bangladesh.
1971 Policy of détente introduced by USA with USSR and China.
1971 Decimal currency introduced into UK.
1972 Pocket calculators introduced.
1973 Fourth Arab–Israeli War.
1973 Britain joins European Economic Community.
1973 US forces withdraw from South Vietnam.
1973 Major famine in Ethiopia.
1973 Death of Pablo Picasso.
1974 Turkish invasion of Cyprus.
1974 Haile Selassie deposed in Ethiopia.
1974 Strategic Arms Limitation Treaty signed.
1974 Resignation of Richard Nixon after Watergate scandal.
1974 First 'test-tube babies'.
1975 End of Vietnam War.
1975 Civil war begins in Lebanon.
1975 Death of Francisco Franco.
1975 Dutch Elm disease widespread.
1975 *Apollo–Soyuz* space project.
1975 Domestic videorecorders introduced.
1975 Floppy disks introduced.
1976 Death of Mao Zedong.
1976 *Concorde* supersonic airliner begins transatlantic flights.
1976 First Bantustan established in South Africa (Transkei).
1977 Military coup in Pakistan.
1977 Jimmy Carter becomes US president.
1977 Death of Elvis Presley.
1977 Launch of *Voyager* missions to outer planets.
1978 Camp David Treaty between Egypt and Israel.
1978 John Paul II becomes Pope.
1979 Former President Bhutto executed in Pakistan.
1979 Idi Amin expelled from Uganda.
1979 Civil war in Nicaragua.
1979 Islamic Republic established in Iran under Ayatollah Khomeini.

HISTORY

1979 Invasion of Afghanistan by USSR.
1979 Vietnam invades Cambodia.
1979 Saddam Hussein becomes president of Iraq.
1979 Margaret Thatcher becomes British prime minister.
1980 Walkman portable cassette player introduced.
1980 Death of Marshal Tito.
1980 Black majority rule in Zimbabwe.
1980 Major famine in East Africa.
1980 Creation of Solidarity union in Poland.
1980 Beginning of Iran–Iraq War (to 1988).
1980 Humber Bridge completed.
1980 Introduction of videodisk.
1980 Growth of Green movement in Europe.
1980 Assassination of John Lennon in New York.
1980 Björn Borg wins Wimbledon for fifth successive year.
1980 Eruption of Mt St Helens in USA.
1981 Ronald Reagan becomes US president.
1981 Martial law in Poland.
1981 Assassination of President Sadat of Egypt.
1981 Hunger strikers die in Northern Ireland.
1981 First re-usable space shuttle flight.
1981 Race riots in British cities.
1981 First reports of AIDS.
1982 War between Britain and Argentina over Falkland Islands.
1982 PLO expelled from Beirut.
1982 Israel withdraws from Sinai Peninsula.
1982 Draft treaty to control CFCs.
1982 Introduction of compact discs.
1983 IBM personal computer system launched.
1983 Global warming effect demonstrated.
1983 US proposes 'star wars' missile programme.
1984 Assassination of Indira Gandhi.
1985 Mikhail Gorbachev in power in USSR.
1986 Halley's comet intercepted.
1986 Chernobyl nuclear power disaster.
1986 State of emergency in South Africa.
1986 US bombing of Libya.
1986 Kurt Waldheim becomes president of Austria.
1986 *Glasnost* and *perestroika* advocated by Gorbachev.
1986 *Challenger* space shuttle disaster.
1986 Hole in ozone layer reported.
1986 Iran–*Contra* scandal in USA.
1987 World population passes 5 thousand million.
1989 George Bush becomes US president.
1989 Soviet army withdraws from Afghanistan.
1989 Solidarity prime minister elected in Poland.
1989 Tiananmen Square demonstration and massacre in Beijing.
1989 Death of Ayatollah Khomeini in Iran.
1989 Opening of Berlin Wall.
1989 End of Communist rule in Czechoslovakia.
1989 Invasion of Panama by USA.
1989 Execution of Nicolae Ceausescu in Romania.
1989 Death of Emperor Hirohito of Japan.
1989 F W de Klerk becomes president of South Africa.
1990 Reunification of Germany.
1990 Resignation of Margaret Thatcher in Britain.
1990 Lech Walesa becomes president of Poland.
1990 Independence of Lithuania.
1990 Release of Nelson Mandela from prison.
1990 Invasion of Kuwait by Iraq.
1990 F W de Klerk begins dismantling of South African apartheid system.
1991 Independence of Armenia.

1991 Gulf War (Operation Desert Storm).
1991 Civil war begins in Yugoslavia.
1991 Nelson Mandela elected President of African National Congress.
1991 Independence of Croatia, Macedonia, Slovenia.
1991 Independence of former Soviet republics.
1991 Formation of Commonwealth of Independent States.
1991 Resignation of Mikhail Gorbachev in Russia.
1991 Boris Yeltsin becomes Russian president.
1992 Independence of Bosnia and Herzegovina.
1993 Division of Czechoslovakia into Czech and Slovak Republics.
1993 Bill Clinton becomes US president.
1993 Israel peace agreement with PLO.
1994 Nelson Mandela becomes South African president.
1994 Opening of Channel Tunnel.
1994 Russian forces invade Chechnya.
1994 Ceasefire agreed in Northern Ireland.
1995 Jacques Chirac becomes President of France.
1995 Assassination of Israeli prime minister Yitzhak Rabin.
1995 Peace agreed in Bosnia.
1996 IRA resume campaign in Northern Ireland.
1997 Cloning of 'Dolly' the sheep.
1997 Hong Kong returned to China.
1997 Death of Diana, Princess of Wales.
1997 Death of Mother Teresa of Calcutta.
1997 Ceasefire resumed in Northern Ireland.
1997 Tony Blair becomes British prime minister.
1997 Emergence in Hong Kong of the deadly H5N1 strain of avian flu.
1998 77 year old John Glenn becomes oldest astronaut to fly in space.
1998 Good Friday Agreement, N. Ireland.
1998 Impeachment of US President Bill Clinton.
1999 US President Bill Clinton acquitted.
1999 Devolved Scottish parliament, Welsh Assembly.
1999 War in Kosovo.
1999 Death of King Hussein of Jordan.
1999 Breitling Orbiter 3 is first balloon to circle the world.
1999 President Mandela retires as president of South Africa.
1999 Resignation of Boris Yeltsin in Russia.
1999 Population of India pass 1000 million.
2000 Macáu returned to China.
2000 Decoding of 90% of human genome completed.
2000 First crew arrives aboard International Space Station.
2000 Crash of Air France Concorde in Paris.
2001 George W Bush becomes US president.
2001 King Birendra of Nepal assassinated by his son.
2001 African Union established.
2001 Dennis Tito becomes world's first space tourist.
2001 Buddhas of Bamian destroyed by Taliban.
2001 Ariel Sharon becomes prime minister of Israel.
2001 IRA announces decommissioning of arms.
2001 World Trade Center, New York, destroyed by terrorist attack (11 Sep).
2001 Foot-and-mouth disease devastates UK livestock farming industry.
2002 Death of Queen Elizabeth, the Queen Mother, of Great Britain.
2002 Queen Elizabeth II of Great Britain celebrates her Golden Jubilee.

HISTORY

World events (continued)

2002 Euro launched as new currency in most European Union countries.
2002 Commonwealth Games held in Manchester.
2002 Steve Fossett is first to fly a balloon solo around the world.
2002 SARS virus first recorded.
2003 US space shuttle *Columbia* breaks up on re-entry with loss of all crew.
2003 Iraq War (Mar–Apr) between Iraq and US-led coalition forces.
2003 Mother Teresa of Calcutta beatified.
2003 Pope John Paul II celebrates his silver jubilee.
2003 China sends first astronaut into space.
2003 Saddam Hussein captured.
2004 NASA's exploration rover, *Spirit*, lands on Mars.
2004 European Union increases to 25 members.
2004 Death of Juliana, former queen of The Netherlands.
2004 Death of former US president Ronald Reagan.
2004 US Coalition in Iraq hands power to interim Iraqi government.
2004 SpaceShipOne, first private spacecraft, flies to the edge of space and back.
2004 Tsunami in Indian Ocean devastates regions in S and E Asia, and E Africa.
2005 Britain's Ellen MacArthur sails solo around the world in record time.

2005 Marriage of Charles, Prince of Wales, to Camilla Parker Bowles.
2005 Benedict XVI becomes pope.
2005 Terrorist bomb attack on London Underground.
2005 New Orleans, LA, devastated by H Katrina.
2005 Trial of Saddam Hussein begins.
2005 Death of Prince Rainier III of Monaco.
2005 Angela Merkel becomes Germany's first woman chancellor.
2005 Iraqis vote for first full-term government since 2003 invasion.
2006 Israel prime minster Ariel Sharon suffers stroke.
2006 Serbia and Montenegro become independent states.
2006 Pluto downgraded to dwarf planet status.
2006 Birth of Prince Hisahito of Japan, first male heir for 50 years.
2006 North Korea conducts first nuclear test.
2006 Saddam Hussein executed for crimes against humanity.
2007 Bulgaria and Romania join European Union.

Dynasties of China

Name	Date	History
Xia	c.2200–c.1523 BC	Emperor Yu
		Land reclaimed, bronze weapons made, grain cultivated, first use of written symbols
Shang or Yin	c.1480–1050 BC	First historic dynasty
		Agricultural society with class system
		First Chinese calendar
		Age of bronze casting
Zhou	c.1066–221 BC	Classical age
		Laws in place
		Money economy
Qin (Ch'in)	221–206 BC	Rule by Shi Huang-ti
		Unification of country begun
		Feudalism replaced by bureaucratic government
		Large part of Great Wall built
Han	206 BC–AD 220	Bureaucratic state based on Confucianism
		Buddhism introduced
Three Kingdoms (San-kuo)	AD 220–65	Divided into three states, Wei, Shu, and Wu
		Increased importance of Buddhism and Taoism
Tsin	265–420	Founded by Wei general
		N China ruled by series of barbarian dynasties
Sui	581–618	Country reunified and central government established
		Canal system constructed
Tang	618–907	Period of territorial expansion
		Buddhism suppressed
		Age of great poets, sculptors, and painters
Five Dynasties and Ten Kingdoms	907–60	Period of hardship with wars and official corruption
		First printing of paper money
Song (Sung)	960–1279	Great changes socially and intellectually
		Confucianism superceeds Taoism and Buddhism
		Central bureaucracy reformed
		Cultivation of tea and cotton on a large scale

Name	Date	History
Yuan	1279–1368	Founding of Mongol dynasty by Kublai Khan Confucianism out of favour End of dynasty in S China Riots in Mongolia
Ming	1368–1644	Mongols expelled Confucianism reinstated Porcelain production flourishes Developments in architecture, the novel, and drama
Ch'ing (Manchu)	1644–1912	Decline of central authority Increase in European trade China divided into spheres of influence by foreign powers Last Chinese monarchy

Dynasties of Ancient Egypt

Period	Dynasty	Date	Major rulers	History
Early Dynastic Period	I	3110–2884 BC	Menes	Unification of Upper and Lower Egypt
	II	2884–2780 BC		Memphis founded
Old Kingdom	III	2780–2680 BC	Snefru	Step Pyramid built
	IV	2680–2565 BC	Khufu (Cheops); Khafre; Menkaure	Age of the great pyramids
	V	2565–2420 BC		
	VI	2420–2258 BC	Pepi I; Pepi II	
First Intermediate Period	VII, VIII	2258–2225 BC		Egypt divided politically Control by local monarchs
	IX, X	2225–2134 BC		Capital at Heracleopolis
	XI	2134–c.2000 BC	Mentuhotep II	Capital at Thebes Reunification
Middle Kingdom	XII	2000–1786 BC	Amenemhet I; Sesostris I; Amenemhet II; Sesostris II; Amenemhet III; Amenemhet IV	Conquest of Nubia
Second Intermediate Period	XIII–XVII	1786–1570 BC	Hyksos	Egypt liberated by Theban dynasty
New Kingdom	XVIII	1570–c.1342 BC	Amenhotep I; Thutmose I, II, Hatshepsut, Thutmose III, IV, Akhenaton; Tutankhamun	Period of empire building – extended from Syria to Southern Sudan Capital city Thebes Extensive building programme
	XIX	c.1342–1200 BC	Ramses I; Ramses II	
	XX	1200–1085 BC	Ramses III	New Kingdom declines
	XXI	1085–945 BC		Egypt divided – Amun rule in Thebes and pharaohs in Tanis
	XXII	945–745 BC	Sheshonk I	Libyan dynasty
	XXIII	745–718 BC		Nubian dynasty with invasion of Piankhi
	XXIV	718–712 BC		
	XXV	712–663 BC	Taharka	Invasion by Assyria – foreign domination follows
	XXVI	663–525 BC	Necho	
	XXVII	525–405 BC	Achaemenids of Persia; Darius II	Egypt revolts
	XXVIII, XXIX, XXX	405–332 BC	Nekhtnebf I	Last native dynasties, ending with conquest of Alexander the Great Capital at Sais, Mendes, then Sebennytos

HISTORY

Seven wonders of the Ancient World

Name	Date built	History
Egyptian Pyramids	more than 4000 years ago	Oldest of the ancient wonders and the only one surviving today. Served as tombs for Egyptian pharoahs.
Colossus of Rhodes	c.305–292 BC	32 m (105 ft) high bronze statue of the sun god Helius. Destroyed by an earthquake in 224 BC.
Hanging Gardens of Babylon	6th century BC	Series of terraces of trees and flowers along the banks of the Euphrates. Built by Nebuchadnezzar II (also known in the Book of Daniel as Nebuchadrezzar).
Mausoleum at Halicarnassus	4th century BC	Tomb of Mausolus built by his widow. Destroyed by an earthquake before the 15th century.
Pharos of Alexandria	c.270 BC	The world's first known lighthouse, at the entrance of Alexandria harbour in Egypt. 122 m/400 ft high. In ruins by 15th century.
Statue of Zeus at Olympia	5th century BC	9 m/30 ft high wooden statue covered with gold and ivory. Designed by Athens sculptor Phidias. Destroyed by fire AD 475.
Temple of Artemis at Ephesus, Asia Minor	6th century BC	Marble temple in honour of goddess of hunting and the moon. Rebuilt in 4th century BC but destroyed by Goths in 3rd century AD.

Rulers of the Roman Empire

Name	Dates	History
Augustus	27 BC–AD 14	Grandnephew of Julius Caesar
Tiberius	AD 14–37	Stepson of Augustus
Gaius Caesar (Caligula)	37–41	Grandnephew of Tiberius
Claudius I	41–54	Uncle of Caligula
Nero	54–68	Stepson of Claudius
Galba	68–9	Proclaimed by soldiers
Otho	69	Military commander
Vespasian	69–79	Military commander
Titus	79–81	Son of Vespasian
Domitian	81–96	Son of Vespasian
Nerva	96–8	Elected interim ruler
Trajan	98–117	Adopted son of Nerva
Hadrian	117–38	Ward of Trajan
Antoninus Pius	138–61	Adopted by Hadrian
Marcus Aurelius	161–80	Adopted by Antoninus Pius
Lucius Verus	161–9	Adopted by Antoninus Pius and ruled together with Marcus Aurelius
Commodus	180–92	Son of Marcus Aurelius
Pertinax	193	Proclaimed emperor by the Praetorian guard
Didius Julianus	193	Bought office from the Praetorian guard
Septimus Severus	193–211	Proclaimed emperor
Caracalla	211–17	Son of Severus
Geta	211–12	Son of Severus and ruled together with Caracalla
Macrinus	217–18	Proclaimed by soldiers
Heliogabalus	218–22	Cousin of Caracalla
Alexander Severus	222–35	Cousin of Heliogabalus
Maximin	235–8	Proclaimed by soldiers
Gordian I and Gordian II, Balbinus, Pupienus	238	Proclaimed by senate and all ruled together
Gordian III	238–44	Son of Gordian II
Philip	244–9	Assassin of Gordian III
Decius	249–51	Proclaimed by soldiers
Hostilianus	251	Son of Decius
Gallus	251–3	Military commander
Aemilianus	253	Military commander
Valerian	253–60	Military commander
Gallienus	253–68	Son of Valerian; co-emperor with his father, then emperor
Claudius II	268–70	Military commander
Aurelian	270–5	Chosen by Claudius as successor
Tacitus	275–6	Chosen by senate
Florianus	276	Half-brother of Tacitus
Probus	276–82	Military commander
Carus	282–3	Proclaimed by the Praetorian guard
Carinus	283–5	Son of Carus
Numerianus	283–4	Son of Carus and ruled together with Carinus
Diocletian	284–305	Military commander; ruled with Maximian and Constantius; Empire divided
Maximian	286–305	Appointed by Diocletian
Constantius I	305–6	Successor of Diocletian
Galerius	305–10	Ruled with Constantius
Maximin	308–13	Nephew of Galerius
Licinius	308–24	Appointed emperor in West by Galerius
Maxentius	306–12	Son of Maximin
Constantine I	306–37	Son of Constantius
Constantine II	337–40	Son of Constantine I
Constans	337–50	Son of Constantine I
Constantius II	337–61	Son of Constantine I
Magnentius	350–3	Usurped Constans
Julian	361–3	Nephew of Constantine I
Jovian	363–4	Elected by the army

Name	Dates	History	Name	Dates	History
Valentinian I	364–75	Proclaimed by the army; ruled in the West	Constantius III	421[b]	Named joint emperor by Honorius
Valens	364–78	Brother of Valentinian I; ruled in the East	Valentinian III	425–55[b]	Nephew of Honorius and son of Constantius III
Grantian	375–83	Son of Valentinian I; co-ruler in West with Valentinian II	Petronius Maximus	455[b]	Bribed his way into office
Maximus	383–8	Usurper in the West	Avitus	455–6[b]	Placed in office by Goths
Valentinian II	375–92	Son of Valentinian I	Majorian	457–61[b]	Puppet emperor of Ricimer
Eugenius	392–4	Usurper in West	Libius Severus	461–5[b]	Puppet emperor of Ricimer
Theodosius I (the Great)	375–95	Appointed ruler in the East by Gratian; last ruler of united empire	Anthemius	467–72[b]	Appointed by Ricimer and Leo I
Arcadius	395–408[a]	Son of Theodosius I	Olybrius	472[b]	Appointed by Ricimer
Theodosius II	408–50[a]	Son of Arcadius	Glycerius	473–4[b]	Appointed by Leo I
Marcian	450–7[a]	Brother-in-law of Theodosius II	Julius Nepos	474–5[b]	Appointed by Leo I
Leo I	457–74[a]	Chosen by senate	Romulus Augustus	475–6[b]	Placed in office by his father Orestes
Leo II	474[a]	Grandson of Leo I			
Honorius	395–423[b]	Son of Theodosius I			
Maximus	409–11[b]	Usurper in Spain			

[a]Emperor in the East
[b]Emperor in the West

The Roman Empire in the 1st century AD

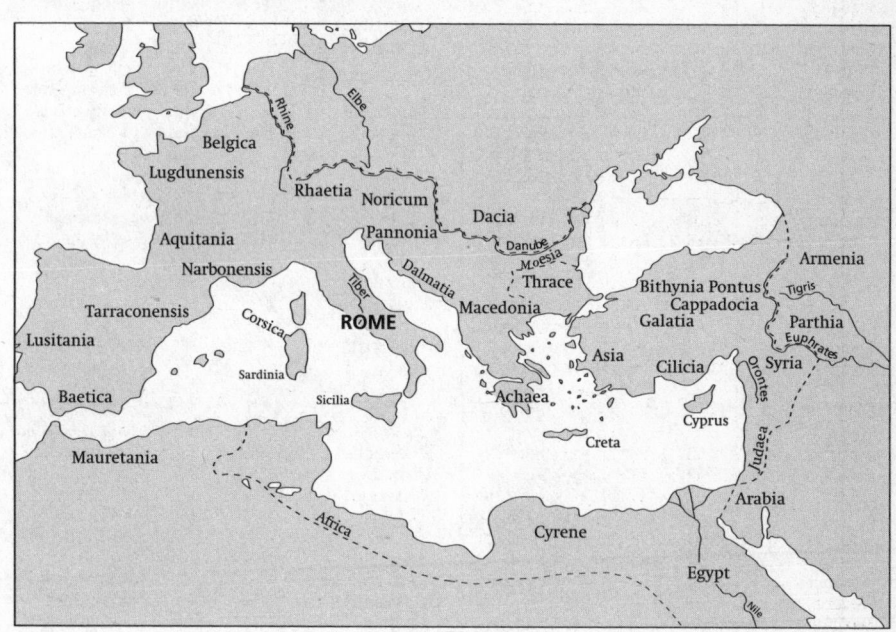

HISTORY

British royal family tree

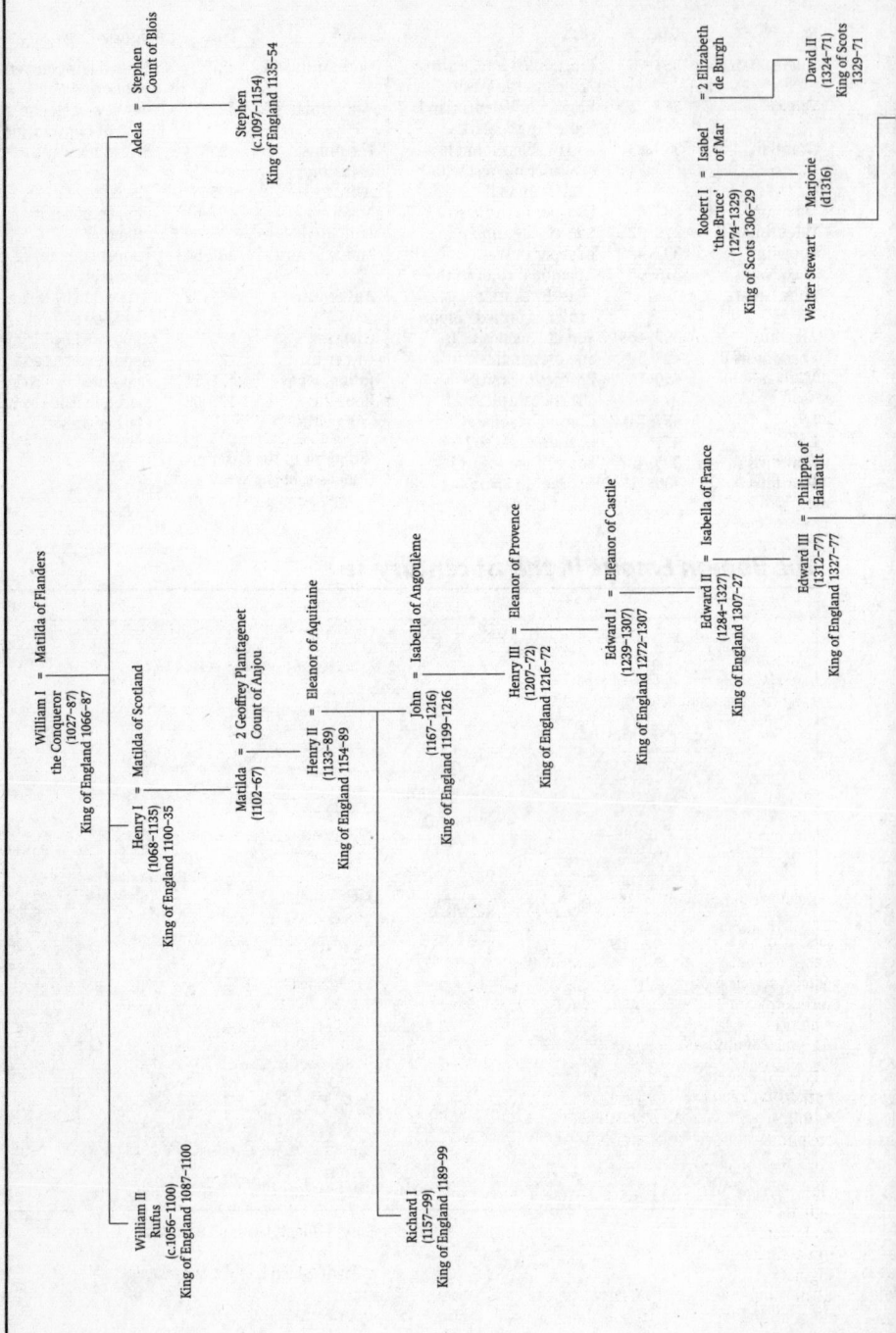

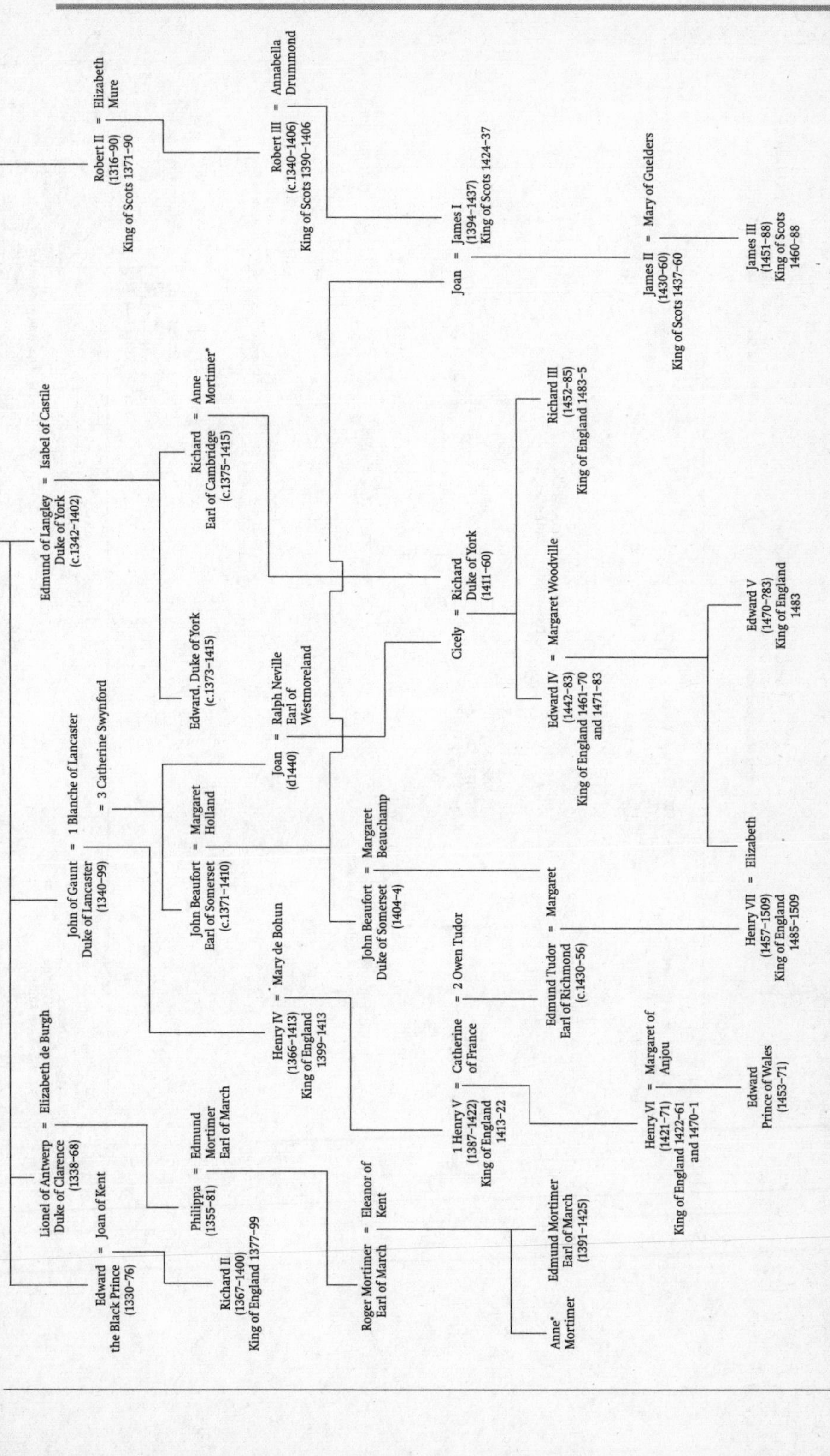

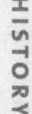

HISTORY

Edward the Black Prince (1330–76) = Joan of Kent

Lionel of Antwerp Duke of Clarence (1338–68) = Elizabeth de Burgh

Edmund of Langley Duke of York (c.1342–1402) = Isabel of Castile

Robert II (1316–90) King of Scots 1371–90 = Elizabeth Mure

Richard II (1367–1400) King of England 1377–99

Philippa (1355–81) = Edmund Mortimer Earl of March

John of Gaunt Duke of Lancaster (1340–99) = 1 Blanche of Lancaster = 3 Catherine Swynford

Edward, Duke of York (c.1373–1415)

Richard Earl of Cambridge (c.1375–1415) = Anne Mortimer*

Robert III (c.1340–1406) King of Scots 1390–1406 = Annabella Drummond

Roger Mortimer Earl of March = Eleanor of Kent

Henry IV (1366–1413) King of England 1399–1413 = Mary de Bohun

John Beaufort Earl of Somerset (c.1371–1410) = Margaret Holland

Joan (d1440) = Ralph Neville Earl of Westmoreland

Joan = James I (1394–1437) King of Scots 1424–37

Anne* Mortimer

Edmund Mortimer Earl of March (1391–1425)

1 Henry V (1387–1422) King of England 1413–22 = Catherine of France = 2 Owen Tudor

John Beaufort Duke of Somerset (1404–4) = Margaret Beauchamp

Richard Duke of York (1411–60) = Cicely

Richard III (1452–85) King of England 1483–5

James II (1430–60) King of Scots 1437–60 = Mary of Guelders

Henry VI (1421–71) King of England 1422–61 and 1470–1 = Margaret of Anjou

Edmund Tudor Earl of Richmond (c.1430–56) = Margaret

Edward IV (1442–83) King of England 1461–70 and 1471–83 = Margaret Woodville

James III (1451–88) King of Scots 1460–88

Edward Prince of Wales (1453–71)

Henry VII (1457–1509) King of England 1485–1509 = Elizabeth

Edward V (1470–?83) King of England 1483

*denotes the same person occurring in a different part of the tree

1 denotes first marriage; 2, second marriage; 3, third marriage

HISTORY

British royal family tree (continued)

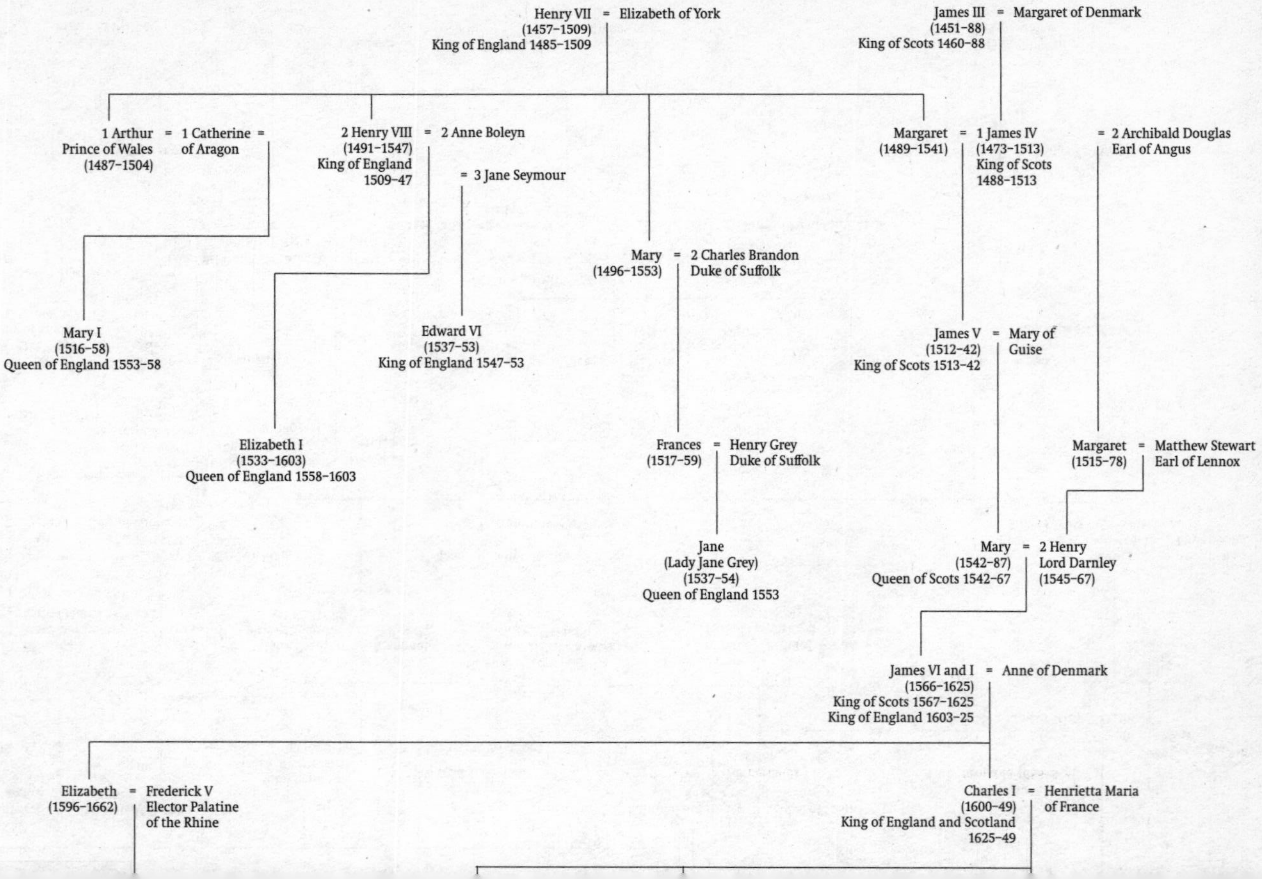

James III = Margaret of Denmark
(1451–88)
King of Scots 1460–88

Margaret = 1 James IV
(1489–1541) (1473–1513)
King of Scots
1488–1513

= 2 Archibald Douglas
Earl of Angus

James V = Mary of
(1512–42) Guise
King of Scots 1513–42

Margaret = Matthew Stewart
(1515–78) Earl of Lennox

Mary = 2 Henry
(1542–87) Lord Darnley
Queen of Scots 1542–67 (1545–67)

James VI and I = Anne of Denmark
(1566–1625)
King of Scots 1567–1625
King of England 1603–25

Charles I = Henrietta Maria
(1600–49) of France
King of England and Scotland
1625–49

Henry VII = Elizabeth of York
(1457–1509)
King of England 1485–1509

1 Arthur = 1 Catherine =
Prince of Wales of Aragon
(1487–1504)

2 Henry VIII = 2 Anne Boleyn
(1491–1547)
King of England
1509–47

= 3 Jane Seymour

Mary = 2 Charles Brandon
(1496–1553) Duke of Suffolk

Frances = Henry Grey
(1517–59) Duke of Suffolk

Jane
(Lady Jane Grey)
(1537–54)
Queen of England 1553

Mary I
(1516–58)
Queen of England 1553–58

Elizabeth I
(1533–1603)
Queen of England 1558–1603

Edward VI
(1537–53)
King of England 1547–53

Elizabeth = Frederick V
(1596–1662) Elector Palatine
of the Rhine

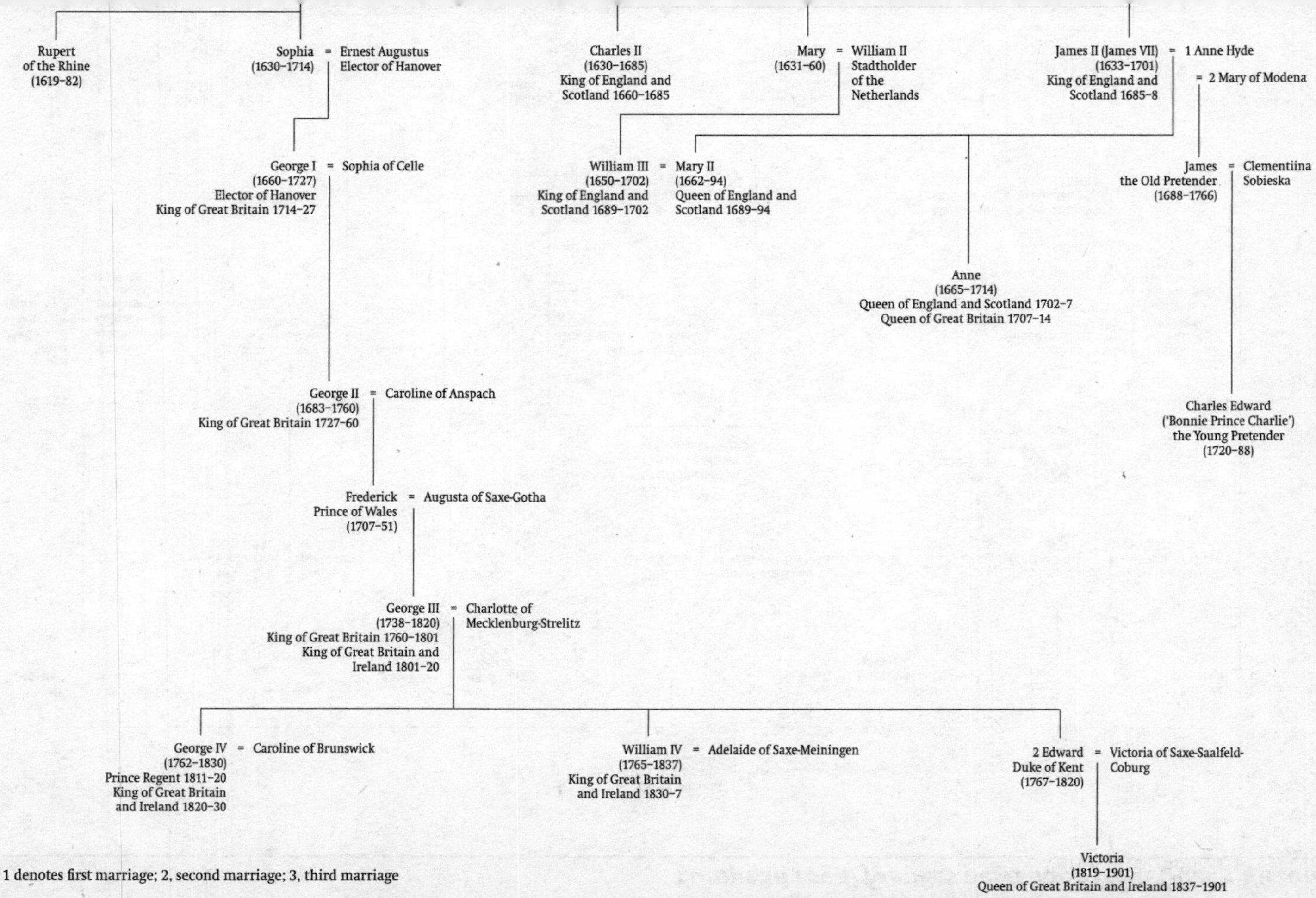

Rupert
of the Rhine
(1619–82)

Sophia = Ernest Augustus
(1630–1714) Elector of Hanover

George I
(1660–1727)
Elector of Hanover
King of Great Britain 1714–27

= Sophia of Celle

Charles II
(1630–1685)
King of England and
Scotland 1660–1685

Mary = William II
(1631–60) Stadtholder
of the
Netherlands

James II (James VII) = 1 Anne Hyde
(1633–1701)   = 2 Mary of Modena
King of England and
Scotland 1685–8

William III = Mary II
(1650–1702) (1662–94)
King of England and   Queen of England and
Scotland 1689–1702   Scotland 1689–94

Anne
(1665–1714)
Queen of England and Scotland 1702–7
Queen of Great Britain 1707–14

James
the Old Pretender
(1688–1766)

= Clementina
Sobieska

Charles Edward
('Bonnie Prince Charlie')
the Young Pretender
(1720–88)

George II = Caroline of Anspach
(1683–1760)
King of Great Britain 1727–60

Frederick = Augusta of Saxe-Gotha
Prince of Wales
(1707–51)

George III = Charlotte of
(1738–1820) Mecklenburg-Strelitz
King of Great Britain 1760–1801
King of Great Britain and
Ireland 1801–20

George IV = Caroline of Brunswick
(1762–1830)
Prince Regent 1811–20
King of Great Britain
and Ireland 1820–30

William IV = Adelaide of Saxe-Meiningen
(1765–1837)
King of Great Britain
and Ireland 1830–7

2 Edward = Victoria of Saxe-Saalfeld-
Duke of Kent   Coburg
(1767–1820)

Victoria
(1819–1901)
Queen of Great Britain and Ireland 1837–1901

1 denotes first marriage; 2, second marriage; 3, third marriage

HISTORY

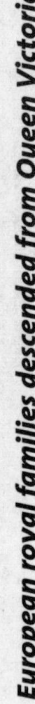

European royal families descended from Queen Victoria

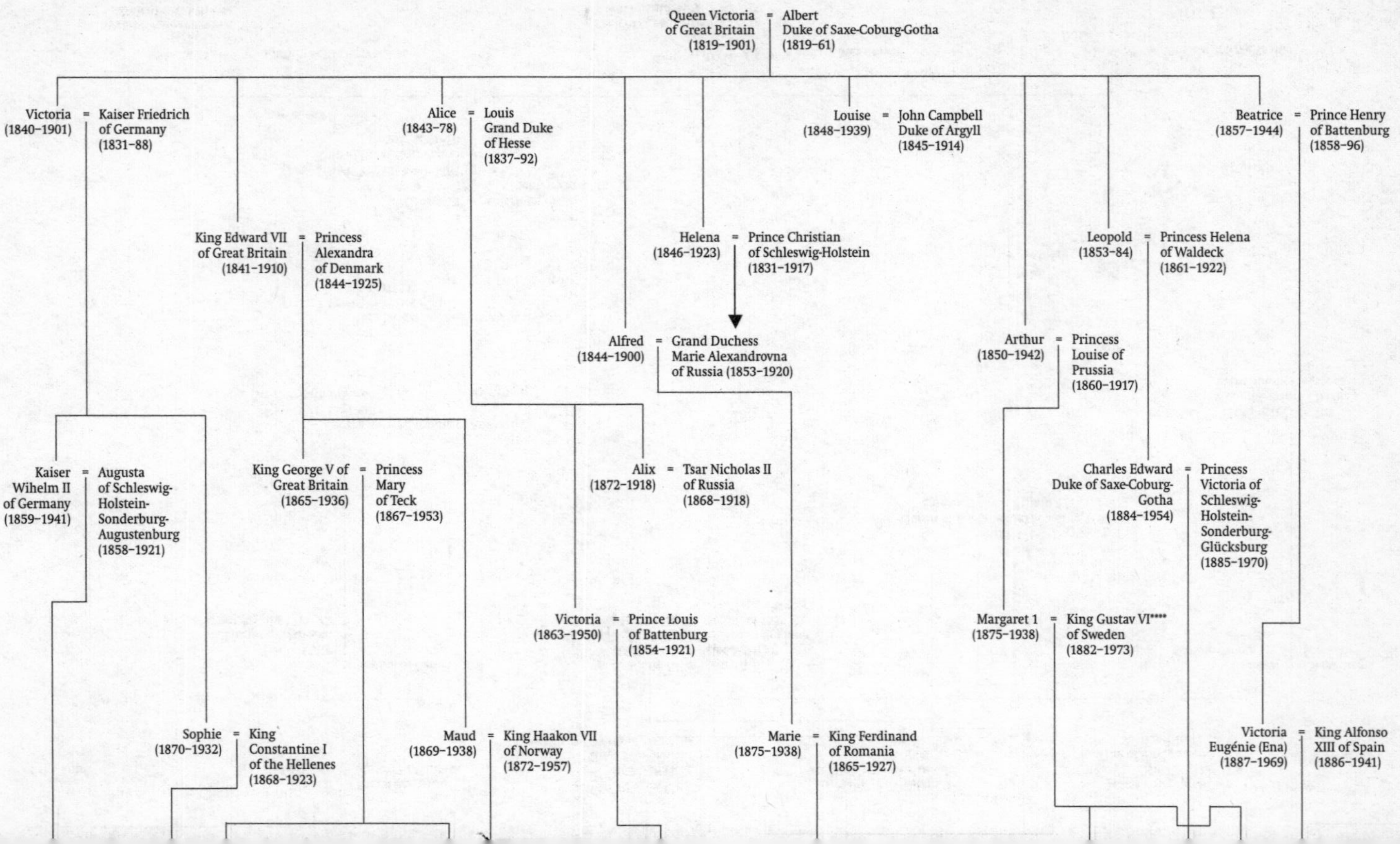

Queen Victoria of Great Britain (1819–1901) = Albert Duke of Saxe-Coburg-Gotha (1819–61)

Victoria (1840–1901) = Kaiser Friedrich of Germany (1831–88)

King Edward VII of Great Britain (1841–1910) = Princess Alexandra of Denmark (1844–1925)

Alice (1843–78) = Louis Grand Duke of Hesse (1837–92)

Alfred (1844–1900)

Helena (1846–1923) = Prince Christian of Schleswig-Holstein (1831–1917)

Louise (1848–1939) = John Campbell Duke of Argyll (1845–1914)

Arthur (1850–1942) = Princess Louise of Prussia (1860–1917)

Leopold (1853–84) = Princess Helena of Waldeck (1861–1922)

Beatrice (1857–1944) = Prince Henry of Battenburg (1858–96)

Kaiser Wilhelm II of Germany (1859–1941) = Augusta of Schleswig-Holstein-Sonderburg-Augustenburg (1858–1921)

Sophie (1870–1932) = King Constantine I of the Hellenes (1868–1923)

King George V of Great Britain (1865–1936) = Princess Mary of Teck (1867–1953)

Maud (1869–1938) = King Haakon VII of Norway (1872–1957)

Victoria (1863–1950) = Prince Louis of Battenburg (1854–1921)

Alix (1872–1918) = Tsar Nicholas II of Russia (1868–1918)

Marie (1875–1938) = King Ferdinand of Romania (1865–1927)

Grand Duchess Marie Alexandrovna of Russia (1853–1920)

Charles Edward Duke of Saxe-Coburg-Gotha (1884–1954)

Princess Victoria of Schleswig-Holstein-Sonderburg-Glücksburg (1885–1970)

Margaret 1 (1875–1938) = King Gustav VI**** of Sweden (1882–1973)

Victoria Eugénie (Ena) (1887–1969) = King Alfonso XIII of Spain (1886–1941)

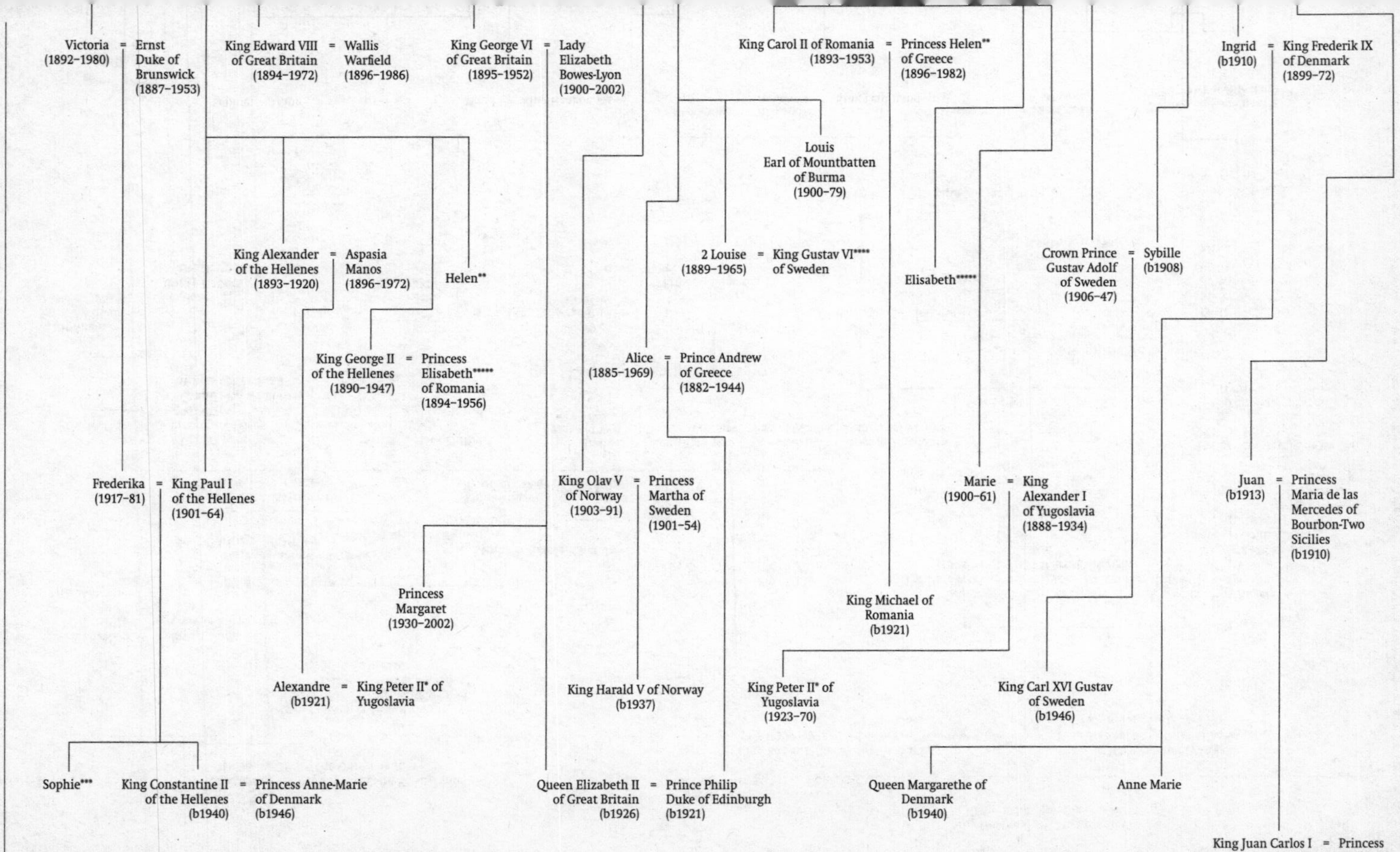

Victoria (1892–1980) = Ernst Duke of Brunswick (1887–1953)

King Edward VIII of Great Britain (1894–1972) = Wallis Warfield (1896–1986)

King George VI of Great Britain (1895–1952) = Lady Elizabeth Bowes-Lyon (1900–2002)

King Carol II of Romania (1893–1953) = Princess Helen** of Greece (1896–1982)

Louis Earl of Mountbatten of Burma (1900–79)

2 Louise (1889–1965) = King Gustav VI***** of Sweden

Elisabeth*****

Crown Prince Gustav Adolf of Sweden (1906–47) = Sybille (b1908)

Ingrid (b1910) = King Frederik IX of Denmark (1899–72)

Juan (b1913) = Princess Maria de las Mercedes of Bourbon-Two Sicilies (b1910)

King Juan Carlos I of Spain (b1938) = Princess Sophie*** of Greece (b1938)

Marie (1900–61) = King Alexander I of Yugoslavia (1888–1934)

Alice (1885–1969) = Prince Andrew of Greece (1882–1944)

King Michael of Romania (b1921)

King Peter II of Yugoslavia (1923–70)

Princess Martha of Sweden (1901–54) = King Olav V of Norway (1903–91)

King Harald V of Norway (b1937)

Queen Elizabeth II of Great Britain (b1926) = Prince Philip Duke of Edinburgh (b1921)

King Carl XVI Gustav of Sweden (b1946)

Anne Marie

Queen Margarethe of Denmark (b1940)

Frederika (1917–81) = King Paul I of the Hellenes (1901–64)

Sophie***

King Alexander of the Hellenes (1893–1920) = Aspasia Manos (1896–1972)

Helen**

King George II of the Hellenes (1890–1947) = Princess Elisabeth***** of Romania (1894–1956)

Princess Margaret (1930–2002)

Alexandre (b1921) = King Peter II* of Yugoslavia

King Constantine II of the Hellenes (b1940) = Princess Anne-Marie of Denmark (b1946)

*denotes the same person occurring more than once in the tree
1 denotes first marriage; 2, second marriage; 3, third marriage

The British Royal Family today

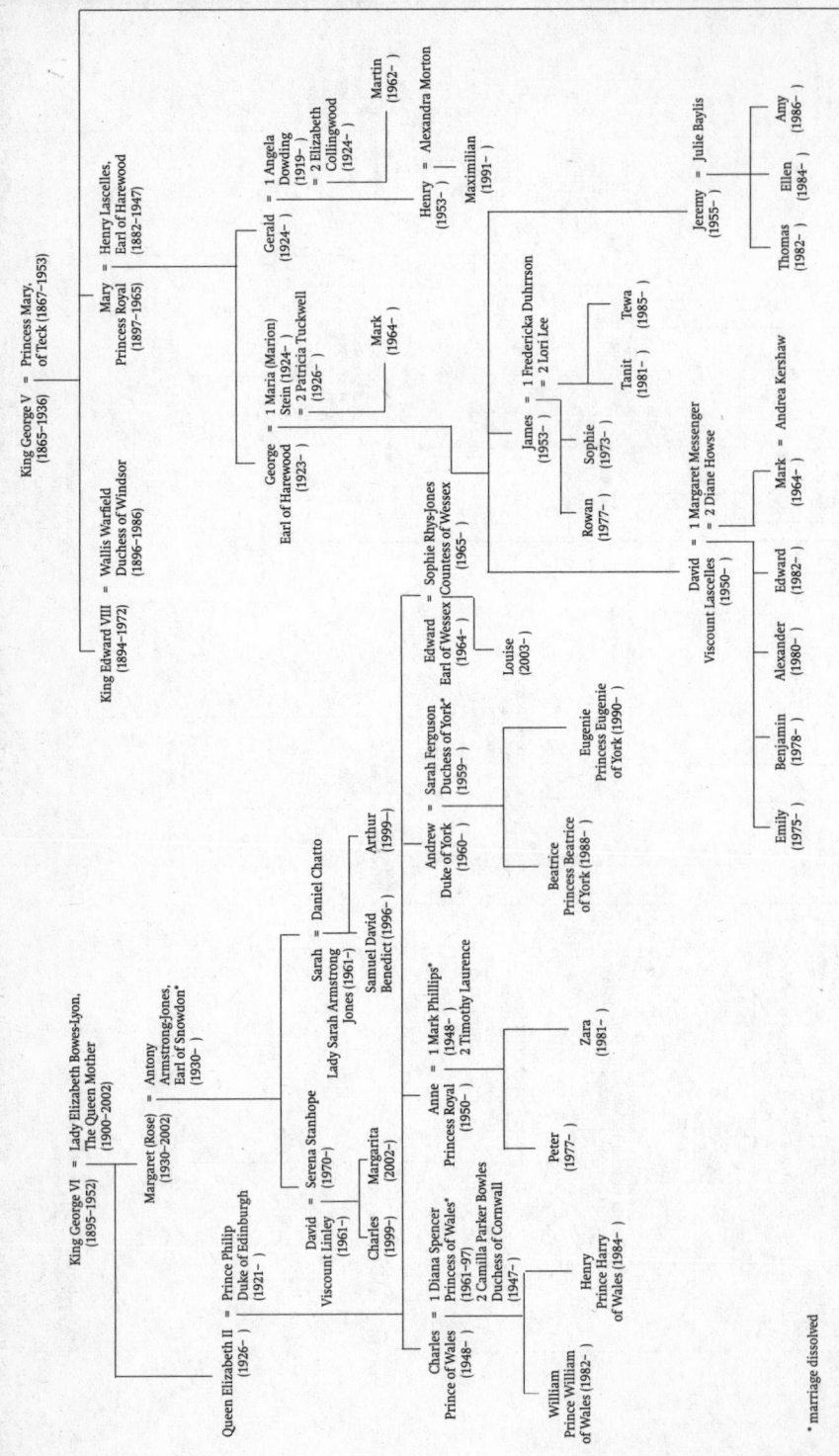

* marriage dissolved

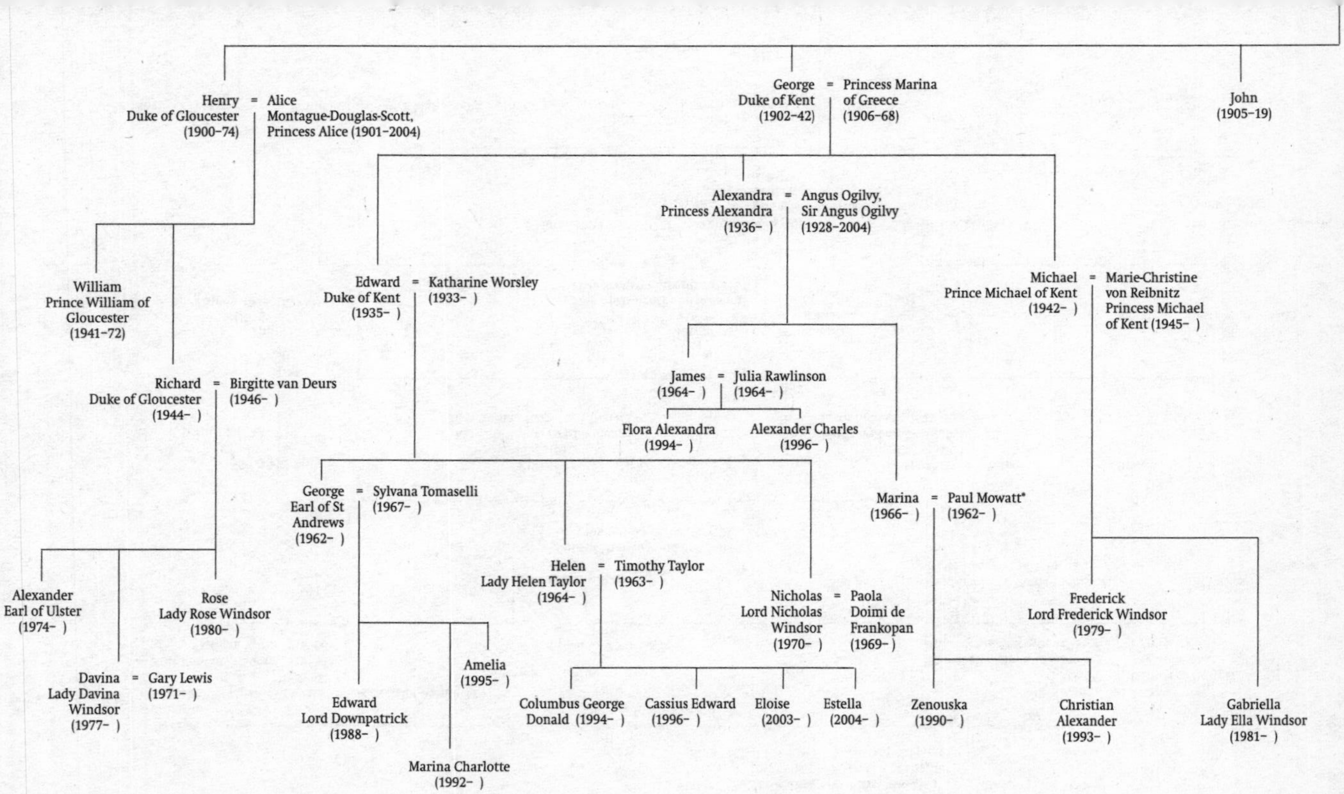

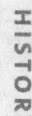

HISTORY

John (1905–19)

George = Princess Marina
Duke of Kent   of Greece
(1902–42)   (1906–68)

Marie-Christine
von Reibnitz
Princess Michael
of Kent (1945–)

Michael =
Prince Michael of Kent
(1942–)

Frederick
Lord Frederick Windsor
(1979–)

Gabriella
Lady Ella Windsor
(1981–)

Christian
Alexander
(1993–)

Alexandra = Angus Ogilvy,
Princess Alexandra   Sir Angus Ogilvy
(1936–)   (1928–2004)

James = Julia Rawlinson
(1964–)   (1964–)

Flora Alexandra
(1994–)

Alexander Charles
(1996–)

Marina =   Paul Mowatt*
(1966–)   (1962–)

Zenouska
(1990–)

Henry = Alice
Duke of Gloucester   Montague-Douglas-Scott,
(1900–74)   Princess Alice (1901–2004)

Edward = Katharine Worsley
Duke of Kent   (1933–)
(1935–)

Nicholas =   Paola
Lord Nicholas   Doimi de
Windsor   Frankopan
(1970–)   (1969–)

Eloise
(2003–)

Estella
(2004–)

Lady Helen Taylor
(1964–)

Helen =   Timothy Taylor
(1964–)   (1963–)

Columbus George
Donald (1994–)

Cassius Edward
(1996–)

George = Sylvana Tomaselli
Earl of St   (1967–)
Andrews
(1962–)

Amelia
(1995–)

Edward
Lord Downpatrick
(1988–)

Marina Charlotte
(1992–)

William
Prince William of
Gloucester
(1941–72)

Richard = Birgitte van Deurs
Duke of Gloucester   (1946–)
(1944–)

Rose
Lady Rose Windsor
(1980–)

Alexander
Earl of Ulster
(1974–)

Davina = Gary Lewis
Lady Davina   (1971–)
Windsor
(1977–)

*marriages dissolved

Order of succession

1 The Prince of Wales
2 Prince William of Wales
3 Prince Henry (Harry) of Wales
4 The Duke of York
5 Princess Beatrice of York
6 Princess Eugenie of York
7 Prince Edward
8 Lady Louise Windsor
9 The Princess Royal
10 Peter Phillips
11 Miss Zara Phillips
12 Viscount Linley
13 Charles Armstrong-Jones
14 Margarita Armstrong-Jones
15 Lady Sarah Chatto
16 Master Samuel Chattô
17 Master Arthur Chatto
18 The Duke of Gloucester
19 The Earl of Ulster
20 Lady Davina Windsor
21 Lady Rose Windsor
22 The Duke of Kent
23 Lady Marina Charlotte Windsor
24 Lady Amelia Windsor
25 Lady Helen Taylor

Habsburgs, Bourbons, and the thrones of Spain, France, and the Holy Roman Empire

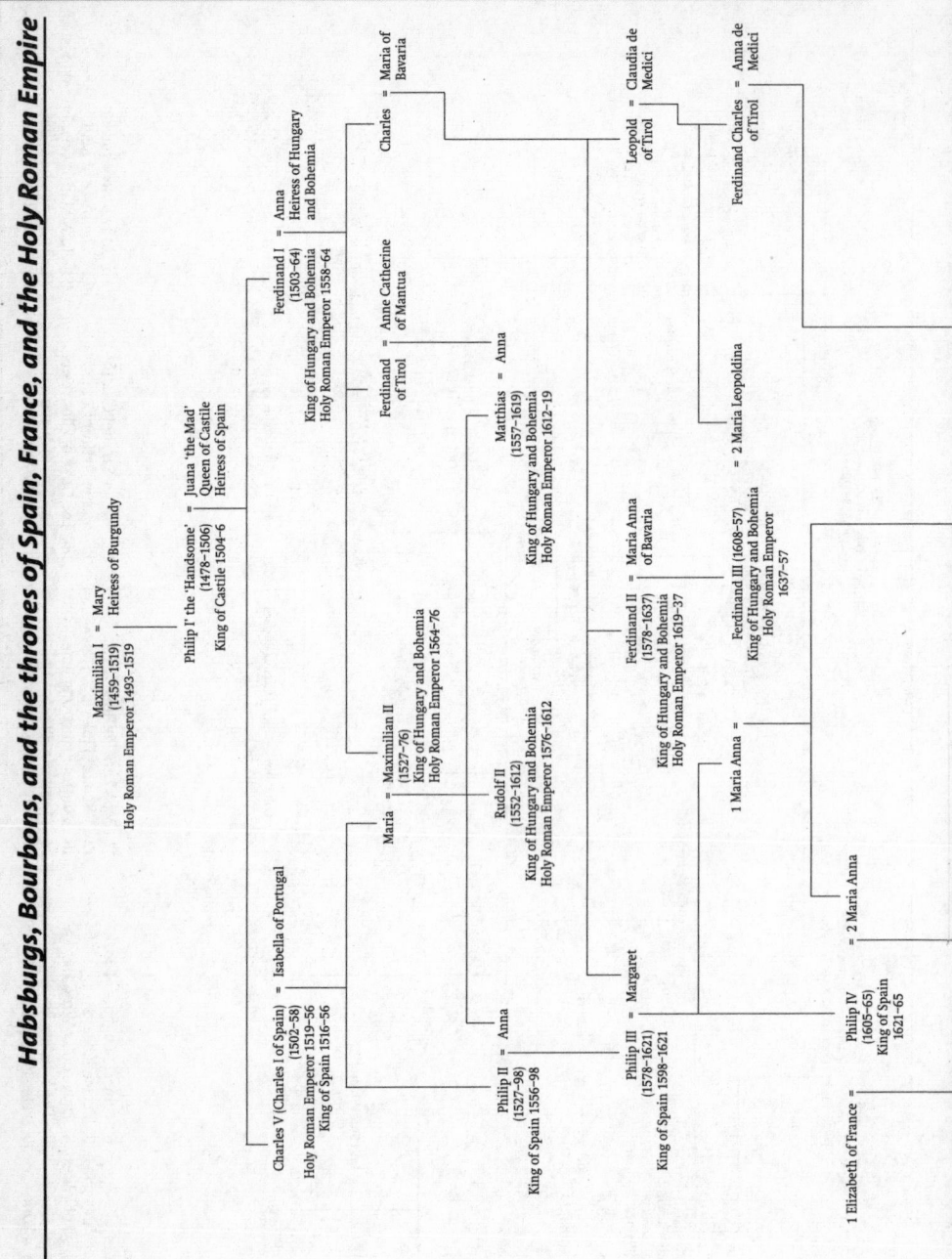

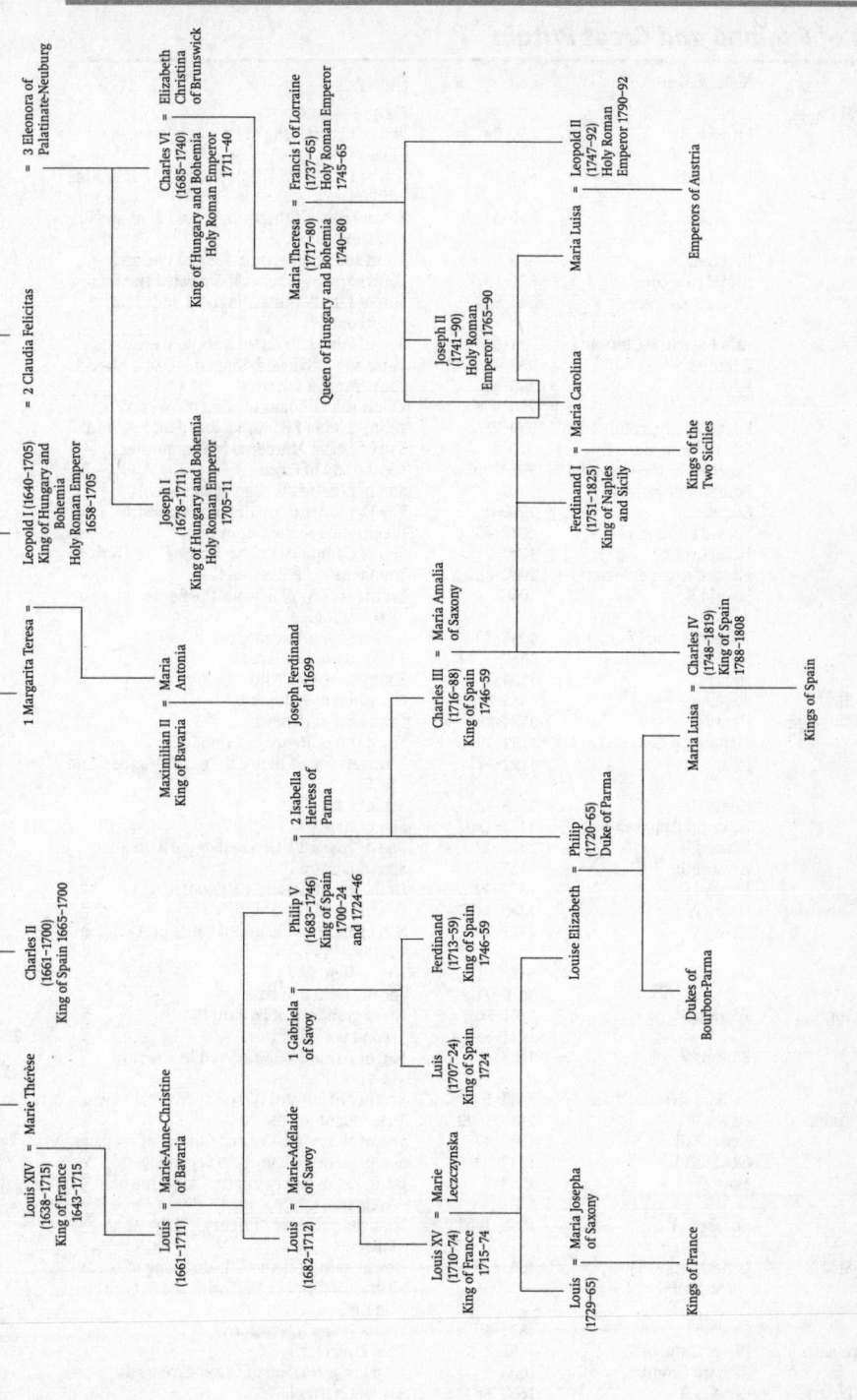

1 denotes first marriage; 2, second marriage; 3, third marriage

Rulers of England and Great Britain

Period	Name of ruler	Dates of rule	History
Saxons and Danes	Egbert	802–39	King of Essex.
	Ethelwulf	839–58	Son of Egbert. King of Wessex, Sussex, Kent, Essex.
	Ethelbald	858–60	Son of Ethelwulf. Displaced his father as King of Wessex.
	Ethelbert	860–5	Second son of Ethelwulf. United Kent and Wessex.
	Ethelred	865–71	Third son of Ethelwulf. King of Wessex.
	Alfred (the Great)	871–99	Fourth son of Ethelwulf. Defeated the Danes.
	Edward (the Elder)	899–924	Son of Alfred. United England and claimed Scotland.
	Athelstan (the Glorious)	924–39	Son of Edward. King of Mercia, Wessex.
	Edmund	939–46	Third son of Edward. King of Wessex, Mercia.
	Edred	946–55	Fourth son of Edward.
	Edwy (the Fair)	955–9	Eldest son of Edmund. King of Wessex.
	Edgar (the Peaceful)	959–75	Younger son of Edmund. Ruled all England.
	Edward (the Martyr)	975–8	Son of Edgar. Murdered by stepmother.
	Ethelred II (the Unready)	978–1016	Second son of Edgar.
	Edmund (Ironside)	1016	Son of Ethelred II. King of London.
	Canute	1016–35	The Dane. Became ruler by conquest.
	Harold I (Harefoot)	1037–40	Illegitimate son of Canute.
	Hardecanute	1040–2	Son of Canute by Emma. King of Denmark.
	Edward (the Confessor)	1042–66	Younger son of Ethelred II.
	Harold II	1066	Brother-in-law of Edward the Confessor. Last Saxon King.
House of Normandy	William I (the Conqueror)	1066–87	Became ruler by conquest.
	William II (Rufus)	1087–1100	Third son of William I.
	Henry I	1100–35	Youngest son of William I.
House of Blois	Stephen	1135–54	Grandson of William I.
House of Plantagenet	Henry II	1154–89	Grandson of Henry I.
	Richard I (Coeur de Lion)	1189–99	Third son of Henry II. Crusader.
	John	1199–1216	Youngest son of Henry II. Signed Magna Carta 1215.
	Henry III	1216–72	Son of John.
	Edward I (Longshanks)	1272–1307	Son of Henry III.
	Edward II	1307–27	Son of Edward I. Deposed by parliament.
	Edward III	1327–77	Son of Edward II.
	Richard II	1377–99	Grandson of Edward III. Deposed.
House of Lancaster	Henry IV	1399–1413	Grandson of Edward III.
	Henry V	1413–22	Son of Henry IV. Victor of Battle of Agincourt 1415.
	Henry VI	1422–61	Son of Henry V.
		1470–71	Second period of rule.
House of York	Edward IV	1461–70	Great-grandson of Edward III.
		1471–83	Second period of rule.
	Edward V	1483	Son of Edward IV. Murdered in Tower of London.
	Richard III (Crookback)	1483–5	Brother of Edward IV. Fell at Bosworth Field.
House of Tudor	Henry VII	1485–1509	Descendant of Edward III.
	Henry VIII	1509–47	Son of Henry VII. Created Church of England.
	Edward VI	1547–53	Son of Henry VIII (by Jane Seymour).
	Mary I	1553–8	Daughter of Henry VIII (by Catherine of Aragon).
	Elizabeth I	1558–1603	Younger daughter of Henry VIII (by Anne Boleyn).
House of Stuart	James I/James VI of Scotland	1603–25	Descendant of Henry VII. First King of Great Britain (official in 1607 with the Act of the Union).
	Charles I	1625–49	Son of James I. Beheaded.
Commonwealth	Oliver Cromwell	1653–8	Lord Protector.
	Richard Cromwell	1658–9	Lord Protector. Son of Oliver Cromwell.
House of Stuart	Charles II	1660–85	Son of Charles I.
	James II	1685–8	Younger son of Charles I. Deposed.
	William III	1689–1702	Son of Mary, daughter of Charles 1.

Period	Name of ruler	Dates of rule	History
	Mary II	1689–94	Daughter of James II. Ruled together with William III.
	Anne	1702–14	Younger daughter of James II.
House of Hanover	George I	1714–27	Great-grandson of James I.
	George II	1727–60	Only son of George I.
	George III	1760–1820	Grandson of George II.
	George IV	1820–30	Eldest son of George III.
	William IV	1830–7	Third son of George III.
	Victoria	1837–1901	Granddaughter of George III.
House of Saxe-Coburg	Edward VII	1901–10	Son of Victoria.
House of Windsor	George V	1910–36	Son of Edward VII.
	Edward VIII	1936	Eldest son of George V. Abdicated.
	George VI	1936–52	Second son of George V.
	Elizabeth II	1952–	Daughter of George VI.

MILITARY WARS AND CAMPAIGNS

Major wars of mediaeval and modern times

War	Dates	History
Norman Conquest of England	1066	France (William the Conqueror)–England (Harold II). Battle of Hastings (14 Oct 1066). Most decisive battle on English soil which led to the successful conquest by the Normans. Harold II died in battle. Began rule of a dynasty of Norman Kings and almost complete replacement of English nobility by Normans, Bretons, and Flemings.
The Crusades	1095–1272	Christians–Turks. Holy Wars authorized by the Pope; fought against infidels in the East, heretics who threatened Catholic unity, and against Christian lay powers who opposed the Papacy.
Conquests of Genghis Khan	1190–1227	Mongols–N China, Kara–Chitai Empire. Subjugation of hostile tribes – Naimans, Tanguts, and Turkish Uigurs.
War of the Sicilian Vespers	1282–1302	Sicily–France. Massacre of the French in Sicily marked the beginning of revolt of Sicilians against Charles of Anjou. War of Sicilian Vespers ensued. Angevins supported by papacy, Italian Guelphs, and Philip II of France, while Aragonese helped by Italian Ghibellines. James II ascended to throne, made peace with papacy, France, and Angevins (to whom he renounced Sicily) by Treaty of Anagni.
Hundred Years War	1337–1453	England–France. Edward III claimed French throne in 1340 and styled himself 'King of England and France'. Traditional rivalries exploded into a dynastic struggle. 1415 Battle of Agincourt – Henry V led overwhelming victory over French. 1417 English then began systematic conquest of Normandy, a task beyond their resources. Evicted from Guyenne (1453) which reduced England's French territories to Calais (lost in 1558) and the Channel Islands. However, the title of King of France was not relinquished until 1801.
Fall of Constantinople	1453	Turks–Byzantine Empire. Collapse of the Byzantine Empire. Since 1261, when Constantinople had been retaken from Latin rule by Michael VII Paleologus, the Byzantine Empire had been threatened by growing power of Ottoman Turks in Asia Minor. 1422 Ottoman Sultan of Turkey Murad II laid siege to the city. This failed but attempt thirty years later by Mehmed II succeeded. Constantinople fell 1453. Last Byzantine emperor Constantine XI Paleologus died in battle.
Wars of the Roses	1455–85	Civil wars in England. Between two rival factions of the House of Plantagenet – York (white rose) and Lancaster (red rose). Began when Richard, Duke of York, claimed protectorship of crown after King Henry VI's mental breakdown and ended with Henry Tudor's defeat of Richard III in Battle of Bosworth. Wars escalated by gentry and by aristocratic feuds.

Major wars of mediaeval and modern times (continued)

War	Dates	History
French Wars of Religion	1562–98	Catholics–Huguenots. Caused by growth of Calvinism, noble factionalism, and weak royal government. From 1550s Calvinist or Huguenot numbers increased, fostered by missionary activities of Geneva. Noble factions of Bourbons, Guise, and Montmorency were split by religion as well as by family interests. Civil wars were encouraged by Philip II's support of Catholic Guise faction and by Elizabeth I's aid to Huguenots. They ended when Henry of Navarre returned to Catholicism and crushed the Guise Catholic League.
Thirty Years' War	1618–48	France–Habsburg rulers. Power struggle between Kings of France and Habsburg rulers of Holy Roman Empire and Spain. War fuelled by conflict between Calvinism and Catholicism, and also by the underlying constitutional conflict between Holy Roman Emperor and the German Princes. With Frederick V's defeat (1620) and intervention by other powers (such as Sweden, Denmark, and France), the conflict intensified and spread. Spain collapsed and left the emperor isolated. Peace negotiations opened and ended German war at the Peace of Westphalia.
Bishops' Wars	1639–40	Scotland–England. Two wars between Charles I and Scotland caused by Charles I's unpopular policies towards the Scottish kirk. Resulted in English defeats and bankruptcy for Charles who was then forced to call the Short and Long Parliaments in 1640, bringing to an end his personal rule.
English Civil Wars	1642–51	Charles I–Parliamentarians. Parliamentary opposition to Royal policies. First battle at Edgehill (Oct 1642), but neither side victorious. Royalists then threatened London, the Parliamentarians' stronghold. By autumn the North and West were in their hands. Crucial event was 1643 alliance of Parliament with the Scots. This increased military strength helped the parliamentarians, led by Oliver Cromwell, defeat the Royalists at Marston Moor. 1646 saw end of first civil war with Charles' surrender to the Scots at Newark in May. 1646–8 negotiations between parliament and King began. Aug 1647 army presented King with Head of Proposals asking for religious tolerance and parliamentary control of the armed forces. Charles made secret pact with the Scots, promising to establish Presbyterianism in England. Scots invaded England and were only repulsed in Battle of Preston. Around 100 000 men died in the two wars (1 in 10 of the adult male population). Charles brought to trial by Cromwell (who was also signatory of his death warrant) and executed Jan 1649.
War of League of Augsburg	1688–97	Louis XIV–European Alliance. The third major war of Louis XIV of France in which his expansionist plans were blocked by the alliance led by England, United Provinces (of the Netherlands), and Austrian Habsburgs. The issue underlying the war was the balance of power between Bourbon and Habsburg dynasties. War began when French marched into the Palatinate while Austria was defeating Turks in the East. Grand alliance of United Provinces, England, Saxony, Bavaria, and Spain, all fearful of French annexations, joined together against France. The war was costly and lengthy. Louis XIV opened negotiations for peace 1696 and in 1697 Treaty of Rijswijk drawn up. This did not resolve conflict between Habsburgs and Bourbons, nor English and French, both of which erupted again only four years later in the War of Spanish Succession.
War of Spanish Succession	1701–14	Alliance–Louis XIV. Alliance of British, Dutch, and Habsburg Emperor against French, supported by Spanish. War arose out of conflict as to succession to throne of Spain following death of childless Charles II. Claimants were England, United Provinces, and France. When alliance collapsed the war was concluded by Treaties of Utrecht which divided inheritance among the powers. Britain's imperial power grew at the expense of France and Spain.
War of Jenkin's Ear	1739–43	Britain–Spain. Began in 1739 but then merged into the War of Austrian Succession. Anti-Spanish feeling in Britain provoked war as Captain Robert Jenkins claimed Spanish coastguards in the Caribbean cut off his ear.

War	Dates	History
War of Austrian Succession	1740–8	Prussia–Austria. Struggle for mastery of German states. Hostilities prompted by Frederick II of Prussia's seizure of Habsburg province of Silesia. French allied with Bavaria and Spain and later Saxony and Prussia. Austria was supported by Britain who feared France's hegemony in Europe which would threaten Britain's colonial and commercial empire. After 1744 this developed into a colonial conflict between Britain and the Franco-Spanish bloc. Peace concluded only by Treaty of Aix-la-Chapelle (1748) which preserved Austrian inheritance but also confirmed Prussian inheritance of Silesia.
Seven Years' War	1756–63	A major European conflict rooted in the rivalry between Austria and Prussia and the imminent colonial struggle between Britain and France in the New World and the Far East. Hostilities in N America (1754) pre-dated the Diplomatic Revolution in Europe (1756), which created two opposing power blocs: Austria, France, Russia, Sweden, and Saxony against Prussia, Britain, and Portugal. British maritime superiority countered Franco-Spanish naval power and prevented an invasion by the French. The European war, precipitated by Prussia's seizure of Saxony, was marked by many notable pitched land battles. Saved from total defeat when Russia switched sides, Frederick II of Prussia retained Silesia in 1763.
US War of Independence	1775–83	American settlers–Britain. Insurrection of thirteen of Britain's N American colonies. Began as civil war but America was later joined by France (1778), Spain (1779), and Netherlands (1780). America rejected Britain's offer of peace in the civil war conflicts and declared independence. Britain ultimately defeated.
French Revolutionary Wars	1792–1802	A series of campaigns between France and neighbouring European states hostile to the Revolution and to French hegemony, merging ultimately with the Napoleonic Wars.
Napoleonic Wars	1800–15	Fought to preserve French hegemony in Europe. Initially a guarantee for political, social, and economic changes of the Revolution, but increasingly became manifestation of Napoleon's territorial ambitions. War began with Napoleon's destruction of the Second Coalition (1800). Britain resumed hostilities (1803), prompting Napoleon to prepare for invasion and encouraging the formation of a Third Coalition. Britain retained naval superiority but Napoleon established territorial domination with the invasions of Spain (1808) and Russia (1812). French finally overwhelmed by the Fourth Coalition and war ended with the Battle of Waterloo (1815).
Peninsular War	1808–14	France–Britain. Struggle for the Iberian peninsula which began as Spanish revolt against imposition of Napoleon's brother, Joseph, as King of Spain, but developed into bitter conflict, with British forces under Wellington liberating Spain (1811). Following Napoleon's Moscow campaign (1812), French resources were overextended, enabling Wellington's army to invade SW France (1813–14).
Greek War of Independence	1821–8	Greece–Turkey. Greece fought alone until 1825 when her cause was seconded by Britain, Russia, and later France. Turks defeated and Greece's independence guaranteed by her allies.
Crimean War	1853–6	Britain and France – Russia. Fought in Crimean Peninsula by Britain and France against Russia. Origins lay in the Russian successes against the Turks in the Black Sea area, and the British and French desire to prevent further Russian expansion westward which threatened the Mediterranean and overland routes to India. Major battles were fought at the River Alma (Sep 1854), Balaclava (1854), and Inkermann (Nov 1854). Fall of Russian fortress at Sebastopol (Sep 1855) led to negotiations for peace. Finally agreed in Paris 1856 that Russia would cede South Bessarabia to Moldavia.
American Civil War	1861–5	Unionists – Confederates. Conflict between Unionists and Confederates. Dealt with two great issues: the nature of the Federal Union and the relative power of the states and central government; and the existence of Black slavery. When Lincoln and the Republican Party's election demonstrated that the South could no longer expect to control the high offices of state, eleven Southern states withdrew from the Union and established the Confederate States

HISTORY

Major wars of mediaeval and modern times (continued)

War	Dates	History
		of America. War broke out (12 Apr 1861) when the Southern batteries opened fire on a Union emplacement in the harbour of Charleston, SC. Lincoln at first defined the issue as preservation of the Union, without any reference to slavery, but he broadened the war aims (Jan 1861), proclaiming the emancipation of all slaves in areas then under arms against the government. The winning strategy began in 1863 when the Unionist General Grant won control of the whole Mississippi valley, isolating the western Confederate states from the rest. After several fierce battles (Gettysburg, Fredericksburg, and the Chattanooga campaign), the South's position became untenable and General Lee, leader of the Confederate forces, abandoned the Confederate capital in Apr 1865 and finally capitulated at Appomattox Court House. The last surrender took place on 26 May.
Franco-Prussian War	1870	France – Prussia. Marked the end of French hegemony in Europe and the foundation of a German empire. In Napoleon III's ambition to conquer Prussia, Bismarck saw an opportunity to bring the S German states into unity with the Prussian-led N German states and build a strong German empire. Conflict was sparked off by disputed candidature for the Spanish throne. The Ems Telegram, sent by Wilhelm I of Prussia refusing the French conditions, succeeded in provoking the French to declare war five days later. After only four weeks the French found themselves trapped at Metz. Main French army tried to relieve them but were surrounded and trapped by Germans at Sedan. French army, with Napoleon III and Macmahon, surrendered. French resistance continued with the new government, and the Germans then began to besiege Paris. Paris surrendered Jan 1871. Treaty of Frankfurt drawn up. Germany annexed Alsace and Lorraine, imposed a high war indemnity on France, and occupied northern territory until indemnity paid.
Boer Wars	1880–1, 1899–1902	Britain – Boers. Wars fought by Britain for the mastery of South Africa. British had made several attempts to re-incorporate the Boers into a South African confederation. First war ended with defeat of British at Majuba Hill and the signing of the Pretoria and London conventions in 1881 and 1884. Second Boer War (1899–1902) can be divided into three phrases – series of Boer successes; counter-offensives by British which captured Pretoria; period of guerilla warfare. Boers effectively won the peace. Retained control of 'native affairs', won back representative government in 1907, and federated South Africa on their own terms (1910). Nevertheless, British interests in South Africa remained protected.
World War 1	1914–18	Allies (Britain, France, Russia, Japan, and Italy) – Central Powers (Germany, Austria-Hungary, Turkey, and Bulgaria). Origins lay in reaction of other great powers to ambitions of German Empire. The political tensions divided Europe into two camps – the Triple Alliance (Britain, France, and Russia) and the Triple Entente (Germany, Austria-Hungary, and Italy). Catalyst to war was the assassination of heir to Habsburg throne, Franz Ferdinand, in Bosnia. Austria declared war on Serbia. Germany then declared war on Russia and France and invaded neutral Belgium. This brought the British into the war on the side of the French. Japan joined Britain, as did Italy in 1915. Germany was joined by Turkey (1914) and Bulgaria (1915). Military campaigns centre on France and Belgium in W Europe. First battle of Ypres prevented the Germans from reaching the ports. By end 1914 static line of defence had been established from Belgian coast to Switzerland. Position of stalemate reached. 1916 allies launched offensive for the W front but stopped by Germans who attacked French at Verdun. To relieve situation Battle of the Somme was launched but proved indecisive. Spring 1918 Germany launched major offensive on West but was driven back by the allies with help from USA. By November armistice was signed with allies having recaptured Belgium and nearly all French territory. Treaty of Versailles drawn up 1919 assigning responsibility for causing the war to Germany and establishing her liability for reparations payments. Germany lost all overseas territories and considerable territory in Poland. Rhineland demilitarized and occupied by allied forces. Germany called treaty a

War	Dates	History
		'Diktat' and its harshness was bitterly resented throughout the interwar years.
Spanish Civil War	1936–9	Republicans–Nationalists (led by General Franco).
		Both sides attracted foreign assistance; Republic from the USSR and the International Brigades and the Nationalists from Fascist Italy and Nazi Germany. Nationalist victory due to balance of foreign aid, to nonintervention on part of the Western democracies and to greater internal unity in the Nationalist army under Franco.
World War 2	1939–45	Allies (Britain and British Commonwealth, China, France, USA, USSR)–Axis Powers (Germany, Italy, Japan).
		Origins lay in three different conflicts which merged after 1941: Germany's desire for expansion, Japan's struggle against China, conflict between Japanese and US interests in the Pacific. War in Europe caused by German unwillingness to accept Treaty of Versailles, which was systematically dismantled aided by the allied policy of appeasement. Increased German aggression finally resulted in the invasion of Czechoslovakia, after which Britain and France abandoned policy of appeasement and pledged support to Poland which was now threatened. Germany signed alliance with Russia and invaded Poland. Britain and France then declared war on Germany. Little fighting took place but Germany proceeded to occupy Norway and Denmark. German Blitzkrieg tactics (a combination of tank warfare and airpower) brought about the surrender of Holland in four days, Belgium in three weeks, and France in seven weeks. After failed attempt to gain air supremacy over Britain (Battle of Britain) the invasion of Britain was postponed. Germany then moved east into Greece and Yugoslavia. British military efforts were concentrated against Italy in Mediterranean and N Africa. Allied forces finally ejected German and Italian forces in mid-1943, invaded Sicily and Italy itself, and forced Italy to make a separate peace. June 1941 Germany invaded her ally Russia and advanced towards Moscow, Leningrad, and the Volga. After two years of occupation and the Battle of Stalingrad in winter 1942–3 (a major turning point in the allied campaign), they were driven out. Allies launched a second front through invasion of Normandy and Paris was liberated in August. Allies advanced into Germany and linked with the Russians on the River Elbe. Germans surrendered unconditionally at Rheims 7 May 1945. Japan's desire for expansion led to her attack on Pearl Harbor, Hawaii, and US declared war on Japan next day (8 Dec 1941). In reply, Germany and Italy declared war on US. Not until June 1942 did naval victories halt Japanese advance. Fighting continued until 1945 when US dropped two atomic bombs on Hiroshima and Nagasaki (6 and 9 Aug). Japan then surrendered.
First Indochinese War	1946–54	Vietnam–France.
		Vietnam controlled by France as colony 1883–1939 and then as a possession 1940–45. Ho Chi Minh proclaimed its independence on 2 Sep 1945 and French opposed the move. Ho Chi Minh led guerrilla warfare against French which ended in Vietnamese victory at Dien Bien Phu in May 1954. Agreement signed in Geneva providing temporary division of the country at the 17th parallel of latitude between the communist-dominated North and the US-supported South. Activities of procommunist rebels would lead to the second Vietnam War.
Korean War	1950–3	Communists and non-Communists.
		Communist North invaded South after series of border clashes. UN forces intervened driving the invaders back to Chinese frontier. China entered conflict and with N Koreans occupied Seoul. UN forces counterattacked and retook territory south of 38th parallel.
Suez War	1956	Britain, France, Israel–Egypt.
		In July 1956 Egyptian President Abdel Nasser nationalized the Suez Canal following American and British decision not to finance construction of the Aswan Dam. When diplomacy failed France and Britain planned military action to regain control of the canal, allied with Israel. In Oct Israel invaded Egypt. Britain and France ordered Israel to leave and also landed at Port Said, apparently to enforce the UN ceasefire. Growing opposition at home, hostile position of USA, and the threatened intervention of the Soviets forced them to withdraw. The outcome of the incident was Israel regaining shipping rights to the canal, though

Major wars of mediaeval and modern times (continued)

War	Dates	History
		France and Britain lost influence in the area.
Vietnam War	1956–75	The war between communist North Vietnam and non-communist South Vietnam, also known as the Second Indochinese War. The Geneva settlement had left North Vietnam under communist rule, and the South ruled first by the emperor Bao Dai (until 1955) and then by Ngo Dinh Diem's dictatorial regime. From 1961, US aid and numbers of 'military advisers' increased considerably. From 1964, US aircraft bombarded the North, and by 1968 over 500 000 troops were involved. These troops were withdrawn in 1973, and hostilities ceased in 1975 when the North's victory was completed with the capture of Saigon (renamed Ho Chi Minh City).
Six Day War	1967	Syrian bombings of Israeli villages intensified early 1967. Israeli air force shot down six Syrian planes. In retaliation Abdel Nasser mobilized Egyptian forces near Sinai border. Israel defeated Egyptian forces and established air superiority. War cost Arabs Old City of Jerusalem, Sinai and Gaza Strip, West Bank, and the Golan Heights.
Cambodian War	1970–5	Cambodia, S Vietnam, US–N Vietnam, Viet Cong, Khmer Rouge. Cambodia had achieved independence in 1953, under Prince Norodom Sihanouk. He assumed position of neutrality in Vietnam war and allowed Vietnamese communists sanctuary in Cambodia. In 1970 he was deposed by coup and US and S Vietnam forces invaded Cambodia to destroy communist sanctuaries. New Cambodian government faced growing threat from Cambodian communists (Khmer Rouge). US launched series of raids by which it hoped to halt Khmer activity but, after five years of civil war, Phnom Penh fell to Khmer Rouge. In 1979 Vietnamese forces invaded and installed a puppet government.
Iran–Iraq War	1980–8	Iran–Iraq. After the Islamic Revolution in Iran, the Iranians accused Baghdad of encouraging the Arabs of Iran's Khuzestan province to demand autonomy. Iraq also feared Iranian provocation of its own large Shi'ite population. Border fighting followed and Iraqi forces advanced into Iran (Sep 1980). Peace finally agreed in 1988 after deaths of around half a million on each side. Iraq accepted Iran's terms in 1990.
Falklands War	1982	Britain–Argentina. Argentinian invasion of the islands ruled by Britain since 1833. War ended after three months in Argentinian surrender.
Gulf War	1991	Iraq–US led allies (29 member coalition). War caused by Iraqi invasion of Kuwait and failure to comply with UN resolution calling for withdrawal. Hostilities suspended after 43 days of fighting when Iraq accepted the UN resolution.
Yugoslavian Civil War	1991–5	Declaration of independence by Slovenia, Macedonia, and Croatia considered illegal by central Yugoslav government. Confrontation between Croatia and Serb-dominated national army developed into civil war. Croatian independence internationally recognized in 1991, but fighting continued throughout 1992–3, despite several rounds of negotiations, and peace proposal. Serb attacks on Sarajevo, 1994–5, resulted in NATO air strikes and hostage-taking. Serbs captured Muslim safe-area enclave of Srebrenica, which brought reports of major atrocities. Successful Croatian offensive in NW Bosnia restored territorial balance in the area. Serb attack on Sarajevo led to NATO/UN attacks on Bosnian Serb targets, and Serb withdrawal. A peace agreement was signed in Dayton, Ohio (Nov). Bosnia was to stay a single state, made up of the Bosnian-Croat Federation and the Bosnian Serb Republic, with a united Sarajevo, and the establishment of a NATO peace implementation force.
Iraq War	2003	A war (Mar–Apr) between Iraq and US-led coalition forces, brought about by Iraq's apparent continued failure to comply with UN Security Council Resolution 1441 to disarm itself of weapons of mass destruction. US President George Bush and UK Prime Minister Tony Blair set a deadline for Iraqi cooperation. No positive response was received from Iraqi leader Saddam Hussein, and the conflict began with air missile strikes on the capital, Baghdad, launched from warships in The Gulf in a "shock and awe" campaign. The port of Umm Qasr was surrounded and US troops marched towards Baghdad, took control of the

War	Dates	History

international airport and entered the city. British troops surrounded Basra. A large US force advanced through Kurdish N Iraq to secure oilfields around Kirkuk and Mosul. Saddam Hussein was captured by US forces near Tikrit, put on trial, and (Dec 2006) executed. A US Coalition Provisional Authority was established, which handed power over to an interim Iraqi government in 2004. An Iraqi coalition government was formed in 2006. Fighting continued into 2007 between Sunni and Shia militias and between local militias and occupying forces.

The main crusades to the East

	Background	Leader(s)	Outcome
First Crusade (1096–9)	Proclaimed by Urban II to aid the Greeks against the Seljuk Turks in Asia Minor, liberate Jerusalem and the Holy Land from Seljuk domination, and safeguard pilgrim routes to the Holy Sepulchre.	Bohemond I Godfrey of Bouillon Raymond, Count of Toulouse Robert, Count of Flanders Robert Curthose, Duke of Normandy Stephen, Count of Blois	Capture of Nicaea in Anatolia (Jun 1097); Turks vanquished at Battle of Dorylaeum (Jul 1097); capture of Antioch in Syria (Jun 1098), Jerusalem (Jul 1099). Godfrey of Bouillon became ruler of the new Latin kingdom of Jerusalem, and defeated the Fatimids of Egypt near Ascalon in Palestine (Aug 1099). Three other crusader states were founded: Antioch, Edessa, Tripoli.
Second Crusade (1147–8)	Proclaimed by Eugenius III to aid the crusader states after the Muslim reconquest of Edessa (1144).	Conrad III of Germany Louis VII of France	German army heavily defeated by Turks near Dorylaeum (Oct 1147), and the French at Laodicea (Jan 1148); Damascus in Syria invested, but siege abandoned after four days (Jul 1148). The crusaders' military reputation was destroyed, and the Syrian Muslims united against the Latins.
Third Crusade (1189–92)	Proclaimed by Gregory VIII after Saladin's defeat of the Latins at the Battle of Hattin (Jul 1187) and his conquest of Jerusalem (Oct 1187). (By 1189 all that remained of the kingdom of Jerusalem was the port of Tyre.)	Frederick I Barbarossa Philip II Augustus of France Richard I of England	Cyprus conquered from Greeks (May 1191), and established as new crusader kingdom (survived until 1489); capture of Acre in Palestine (Jul 1191); Saladin defeated near Arsuf (Sep 1191); three-year truce guaranteeing safe conduct of Christian pilgrims to Jerusalem. Most cities and castles of the Holy Land remained in Muslim hands.
Fourth Crusade (1202–4)	Proclaimed by Innocent III to recover the Holy Places	Boniface of Montferrat	Despite papal objections, crusade diverted from Egypt or Palestine: (1) to Zara, a Christian town in Dalmatia, conquered for Venetians (Nov 1202); (2) to Byzantium, where embroilment in dynastic struggles led to sack of Constantinople (Apr 1204) and foundation of Latin Empire of Constantinople (survived until 1261). The crusading movement was discredited; the Latins in Palestine and Syria were hardly helped at all; the Byzantine empire never fully recovered; and the opportunity was lost of a united front between the Latins and Greeks against the Muslims.

HISTORY

HISTORY

The main crusades to the East (continued)

	Background	Leader(s)	Outcome
Fifth Crusade (1217–21)	Proclaimed by Innocent III when a six-year truce between the kingdom of Jerusalem and Egypt expired.	Andrew II of Hungary John of Brienne, King of Jerusalem Leopold, Duke of Austria	Three indecisive expeditions against Muslims in Palestine (1217); capture of Damietta in Egypt after protracted siege (May 1218–Nov 1219), further conquests attempted, but crusaders forced to relinquish Damietta (Aug 1221) and withdrew.
Sixth Crusade (1228–9)	Emperor Frederick II, who first took the Cross in 1215, married the heiress to the kingdom of Jerusalem in 1225. Excommunicated by Gregory IX for delaying his departure, he finally arrived at Acre in Sep 1228.	Frederick II	Negotiations with Egyptians secured Jerusalem and other places, including Bethlehem and Nazareth (Feb 1229); Frederick crowned King of Jerusalem in church of Holy Sepulchre (Mar 1229). Jerusalem was held until recaptured by the Khorezmian Turks in 1244.
Seventh Crusade (1248–54)	Proclaimed by Innocent IV after the fall of Jerusalem and defeat of the Latin army near Gaza by the Egyptians and Khorezmians (1244).	Louis IX of France	Capture of Damietta (June 1249); defeat at Mansurah (Feb 1250); surrender of crusaders during attempted withdrawal. Damietta relinquished and large ransoms paid (May 1250). Louis spent four years in Palestine, refortifying Acre, Caesarea, Joppa, and Sidon, and fruitlessly attempting to regain Jerusalem by alliances with the Mameluks and Mongols.
Eighth Crusade (1270–2)	Proclaimed after the Mameluk conquest of Arsuf, Caesarea, Haifa (1265). Antioch and Joppa (1268).	Charles of Anjou, King of Naples-Sicily Edward of England (later Edward I) Louis IX of France	Attacked Tunisia in N Africa (Jul 1270); Louis died in Aug; Charles concluded treaty with Tunis and withdrew; Edward negotiated 11 years' truce with Mameluks in Palestine. By 1291 the Latins had been driven from the Holy Land.

The American Civil War

1859
16 Oct — John Brown's raid on Harper's Ferry

1860
6 Nov — Abraham Lincoln elected President
20 Dec — Secession of first Southern states

1861
4 Feb — Announcement of the Confederated States of America – Jefferson Davis named as President
4 Mar — Inauguration of Lincoln as President
12 Apr — Southern Bombardment of Fort Sumter
21 Jul — First Battle of Bull Run

1862
6 Apr — Battle of Shiloh
29–30 Aug — Second Battle of Bull Run
17 Sep — Battle of Antietam
22 Sep — Preliminary Emancipation Proclamation
13 Dec — Battle of Fredericksburg

1863
1 Jan — Emancipation Proclamation
2 May — Battle of Chancellorsville – death of Stonewall Jackson
3 Jul — Battle of Gettysburg
4 Jul — Fall of Vicksburg
19–20 Sep — Battle of Chickamauga
24–25 Nov — Battle of Chattanooga

1864
1 Sep — Fall of Atlanta
15–16 Dec — Battle of Nashville

1865
9 Apr — Surrender of Confederate forces at Appomattox
14 Apr — Assassination of Lincoln

EXPLORATION AND DISCOVERY

Journeys of exploration

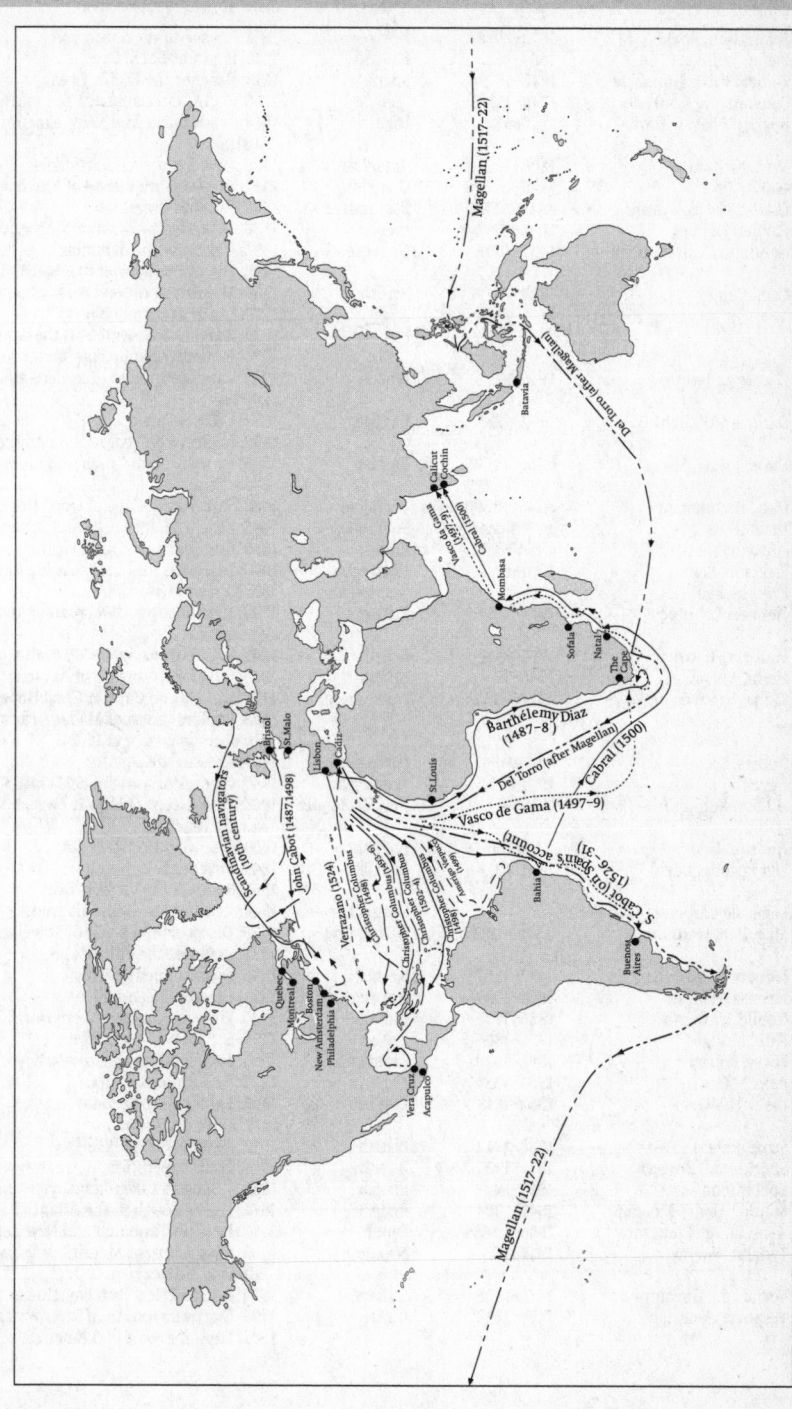

HISTORY

Great explorers

Name	Dates	Nationality	Major voyages of exploration
Amundsen, Roald	1872–1928	Norwegian	1911: Voyage to the South Pole.
Baffin, William	1584–1622	English	1616: Explores Baffin Bay.
Balboa, Vasco Núñez de	1475–1519	Spanish	1513: Reaches the Pacific Ocean.
Bougainville, Louis de	1729–1811	French	1766: Begins circumnavigation of the globe.
Burke, Robert O'Hara	1820–61	Irish	1860: Leads Burke and Wills expedition across Australia.
Byrd, Richard	1888–1957	American	1926: First flight over North Pole.
Cabot, John	1425–c.1500	Genoese	1497: Discovers mainland of North America.
Cabral, Pedro Álvarez	c.1467–1520	Portuguese	1500: Reaches Brazil.
Cartier, Jacques	1491–1557	French	1534: Explores the coast of N America.
Columbus, Christopher	1451–1506	Genoese	1492: Discovers the Bahamas.
			1498: Discovers mainland of South America.
Cook, James	1728–79	British	1769: Maps coast of New Zealand and Australia.
			1770: Lands at Botany Bay.
			1775: Reaches S Georgia and the Sandwich Is.
			1778: Explores islands now known as Hawaii.
Cousteau, Jacques	1910–97	French	1950: Takes command of underwater ship *Calypso*.
Dampier, William	1652–1715	English	1683: Crosses Pacific.
			1699: Explores NW coast of Australia.
Davis, John	c.1550–1605	English	1585: Expedition to Greenland; discovers the Davis Strait.
Diaz, Bartolomeu	c.1450–1500	Portuguese	1488: Sails round Cape of Good Hope.
Diaz, Dinís	c.15th century	Portuguese	1446: Reaches Cape Verde and Senegal.
Drake, Francis	c.1540–96	English	1580: Completes circumnavigation of the globe.
Eriksson, Leif	10th–c.	Norwegian	1000: Discovers Vinland (possibly America).
Erik the Red	10th–c.	Norwegian	985: Explores Greenland coast.
Fiennes, Ranulph	1944–	British	1993: First unsupported crossing on foot of Antarctica.
Flinders, Matthew	1774–1814	British	1801–3: Circumnavigates Australia.
Fuchs, Vivian	1908–99	British	1958: First land crossing of Antarctica.
Gama, Vasco da	c.1469–1525	Portuguese	1497: Sails round Cape of Good Hope.
			1498: Explores coast of Madagascar and discovers sea route to India.
Gomes, Diogo	c.1440–84	Portuguese	1469: Crosses the equator.
Heyerdahl, Thor	1914–	Norwegian	1947: Crosses Atlantic in balsa raft *Kon-Tiki*.
Hillary, Edmund	1919–	New Zealander	1953: First ascent of Mount Everest, with Norgay Tenzing.
Hudson, Henry	c.1565–1611	English	1610: Discovers Hudson's Bay.
Livingstone, David	1813–73	British	1849: Reaches Lake Ngami.
			1855: Reaches the Victoria Falls.
López de Cárdenas, García		Spanish	1540: Reaches the Grand Canyon.
Magellan, Ferdinand	c.1480–1521	Portuguese	1520: Discovers the Strait of Magellan.
			1521: Explores the Philippines.
Mendoza, Pedro de	1487–1537	Spanish	1536: Founds Buenos Aires.
Nansen, Fridtjof	1861–1930	Norwegian	1888: Crosses Greenland.
Nobile, Umberto	1885–1978	Italian	1926: First airship crossing of North Pole.
Park, Mungo	1771–1806	British	1795–6: Explores Niger River.
Peary, Robert	1856–1920	American	1909: Successful voyage to reach North Pole.
Polo, Marco	1254–1324	Italian	1275–92: Explores China.
Raleigh, Walter	1552–1618	English	1595: Explores Orinoco River.
			1617: Explores Guiana.
Scott, Robert Falcon	1868–1912	British	1912: Reaches South Pole.
Shackleton, Ernest	1874–1922	British	1914: Leads expedition to Antarctica.
Speke, John	1827–64	British	1858: Discovers Lakes Tanganyika and Victoria.
Stanley, Henry Morton	1841–1904	British	1874: Traces Congo to the Atlantic.
Tasman, Abel Janszoon	1603–c.1659	Dutch	1642: Reaches Tasmania and New Zealand.
Tenzing Norgay	1914–86	Nepalese	1953: First ascent of Mount Everest, with Edmund Hillary.
Verrazano, Giovanni da	1485–1528	Italian	1524: Reaches New York Bay, Hudson River.
Vespucci, Amerigo	1454–1512	Italian	1499: Discovers mouth of River Amazon.
			1501: Explores coast of S America.

Colonialism (imperialism)

The main era of imperialism was the period 1880–1914, when many European powers sought to gain territories in Africa and Asia. The motivation was, many suggest, economic, and territories were taken normally by force and subjected to rule by the imperial power. It is only in the twentieth century that colonialism has become generally regarded as illegitimate.

Colonial powers in 1914

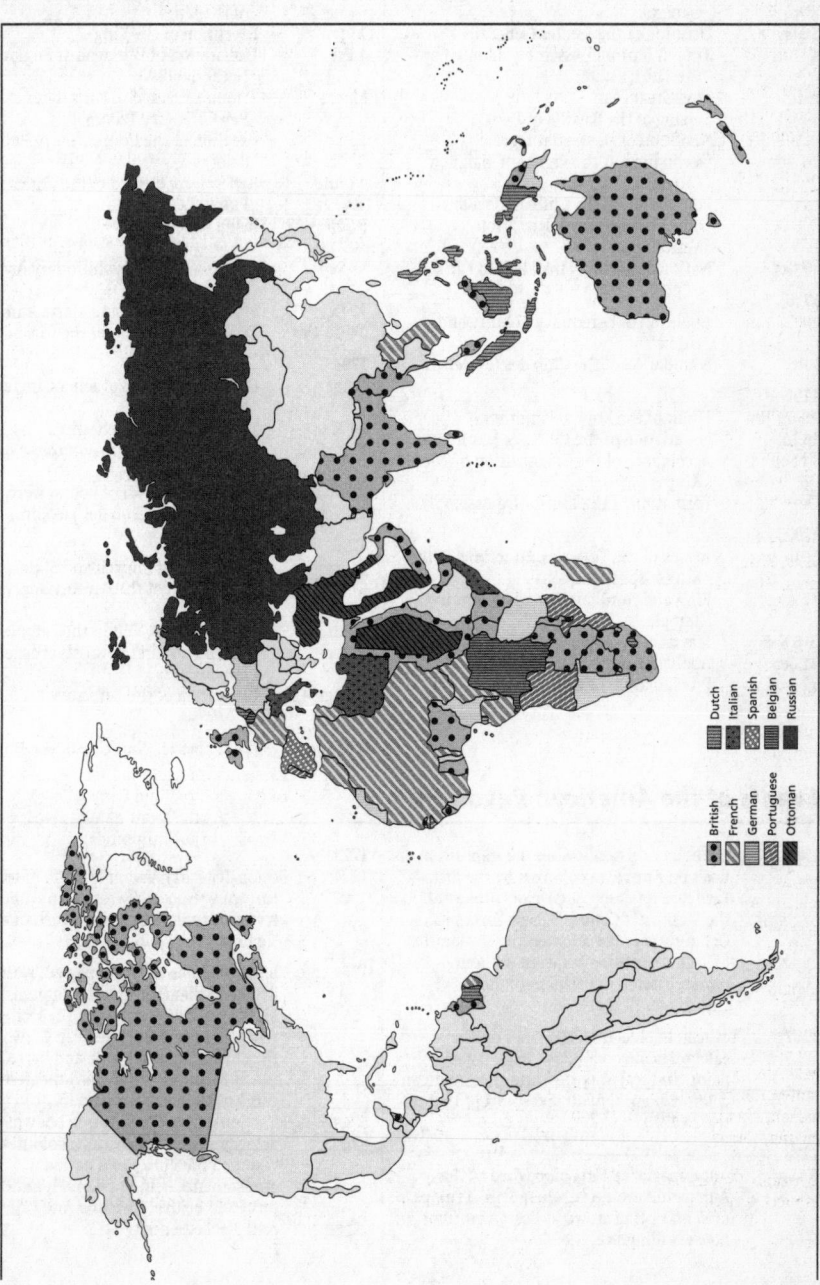

Legend:

British · French · German · Portuguese · Ottoman
Dutch · Italian · Spanish · Belgian · Russian

REVOLUTIONS

Events of the French Revolution

1789

Mar–May	Election of deputies to the Estates General.
5 May	Opening of the Estates General.
17 Jun	Title of National Assembly adopted by the Third Estate.
Jul	The 'Great Fear'.
14 Jul	Seizing of the Bastille in Paris.
4 Aug	Abolition of the feudal regime.
26 Aug	Declaration of the Rights of Man and Citizens.
Oct	Foundation of the Club des Jacobins.
5–6 Oct	Louis XVI brought to Paris from Versailles.
19 Oct	National Assembly installed in Paris.

1790

19–23 Jun	Abolition of hereditary nobility and titles.
July	Foundation of the Club des Cordeliers.

1791

20–21 Jun	Flight of the King to Varennes.
16 Jul	Foundation of the Club des Feuillants.
13 Sep	Acceptance of the Constitution by the King.
Oct	Formation of the Legislative Assembly.

1792

9–10 Aug	Attack of the Tuileries. Functions of the King suspended.
12 Aug	King and royal family imprisoned in the Temple.
2–6 Sep	Massacre of nobles and clergy in prisons.
21 Sep	Abolition of the monarchy.
22 Sep	Proclamation of the Republic.

1793

17 Jan	National Convention votes for the death of the King.
21 Jan	Execution of the King.
1 Feb	Declaration of war against England and Netherlands.
Mar	Tribunal created in Paris (later called the Revolutionary Tribunal).
6 Apr	Creation of the Committee of Public Safety.
27 Jul	Robespierre elected to the Committee of Public Safety.
5 Sep–27 Jul 1794	Reign of Terror.
11 Sep	Creation of the Revolutionary Army of Paris.
16 Oct	Trial and execution of Marie Antoinette.
24–31 Oct	Trial and execution of the Girondins.

1794

5 Apr	Execution of the Cordeliers, including Danton.
24 Mar	Execution of the Hébertists.
8 Jun	Inaugural Feast of the Supreme Being and of Nature.
27 Jul	(9 Thermidor) Fall of Robespierre.
19 Nov	Closure of the Club des Jacobins.

1795

21 Feb	Separation of Church and State.
31 May	Suppression of the Revolutionary Tribunal.
8 Jun	Death of Louis XVII in the Temple.
5 Oct	(13 Vendémiaire) Royalists crushed by Bonaparte.
27 Oct–4 Nov	Institution of the Directory.

1799

9 Nov	(18 Brumaire) Abolition of the Directory.

Events of the American Revolution

1765 Stamp Act crisis. Following the imposition of taxes on American colonists by the British Parliament (Stamp Acts), riots broke out. At the Stamp Act Congress, New York, 7–25 Oct, nine colonies adopted the Declaration of Rights opposing taxation without representation in Parliament. Acts withdrawn 17 Mar 1766.

1767 Townshend Acts imposed taxes on five categories of goods (glass, lead, paper, paint, and tea) imported into the American colonies. Repeal of all taxes, except that on tea, in 1770.

1770

5 Mar Boston massacre. First bloodshed of the American Revolution when British troops fired on rioting crowd at Boston customs house, killing five.

1773

16 Dec Boston Tea Party. Valuable cargo of tea thrown overboard by rebellious American colonists protesting British Parliament's 'Tea Act' (Apr 1773).

1774 The 'Intolerable Acts' are passed by the British Parliament in order to punish Massachusetts, considered the leader of rebels, for the Boston Tea Party. Involved the curtailing of self-rule and barred the use of Boston harbour until the destroyed cargo of tea had been paid for.

5 Sep–26 Oct First Continental Congress (a body of delegates from the thirteen colonies which assumed the duties of a national government), held in Philadelphia, protested British measures and called for civil disobedience.

1775

18 Apr Advance of British on Concord to destroy military stores of rebel American patriots.

19 Apr Beginning of fighting at Lexington and Concord.

17 Jun Battle of Bunker Hill, Massachusetts; technically an American defeat though British suffered high casualties.

1776

7 Jun Proposal in Continental Congress to declare independence from Britain.

2 Jul Resolution adopted.

4 Jul Approval of Declaration of Independence.

27 Aug British defeat of Washington in Battle of Long Island.

15 Sep British occupation of New York City.

1777

3 Jan Defeat of Lord Cornwallis by Washington at Battle of Princeton. Continental Congress adopted Stars and Stripes as flag of the United States.

11 Sep Battle of Brandywine. American retreat enabled British to occupy Philadelphia.

17 Oct Battle of Saratoga. British, under General John Burgoyne, forced to surrender.

15 Nov Articles of Confederation and Perpetual Union adopted by Continental Congress.

1778

6 Feb Assistance of the American patriots by French fleet after France and US sign treaty of aid.

18 Jun British evacuation from Philadelphia.

1781

26 Sep Arrival of joint American and French forces in Williamsburg near Yorktown where British forces, under Cornwallis, had retreated.

6–19 Oct Battle of Yorktown. Beginning of siege of Yorktown, Virginia. British troops heavily outnumbered by joint American and French forces. Eventual surrender of Cornwallis on 19 Oct.

1782

Mar Agreement by new British Cabinet to recognize independence of United States of America.

30 Nov Preliminary agreement signed in Paris.

Events of the Russian Revolution

1916

end Internal state of Russia precarious. Tsar politically isolated and universally unpopular.

1917

beginning Bolsheviks, under Lenin's leadership, cultivate feelings of discontent and organize strikes. February Revolution: On 8 March government of Tsar Nicholas II introduces bread and flour rationing in Petrograd. Mass strike begins. On third day of protest police begin firing on striking workers.

12 Mar The Petrograd Soviet of workers and the Duma form a 'Provisional Committee', later to become a 'Provisional Government'.

15 Mar Tsar Nicholas II abdicates.

Mar–May Conflict in the dual power begins to emerge. Disagreement on whether to continue the war (WWI) and war aims.

Apr Lenin returns from exile in Switzerland. Change of Bolshevik policy in supporting the provisional government. April Theses: Lenin advocates overthrow of provisional government and government by the soviets for the working class. Also advocates redistribution of land to peasants and signature of peace treaty with Germany. Policy of 'All Power to the Soviet'.

Jun Demonstrations called by the Petrograd Soviet to outmanoeuvre the Bolsheviks. Bolshevik support still strong. The July Days: Kronstadt sailors supporting Bolsheviks demonstrate in Petrograd. Demonstrators fired on and chaos follows. Prime Minister Lvov forced to resign and replaced by Kerensky (links to the Soviet). Bolsheviks held responsible for bloodshed and their newspapers closed and warrants for arrest of leaders issued. Lenin and Stalin flee. Trotsky and Kamenev imprisoned.

Sep Kornilov Affair: General Kornilov tries to move on Petrograd with his troops, under pretext of restoring order. Kerensky appeals to Bolsheviks for help in defeating Kornilov. Lenin recognizes the opportunity and forms a Red Guard of Bolshevik soldiers and workers, sets up Military Revolutionary Committee. Most of Kornilov's troops deserte, Kornilov arrested and Bolsheviks support increased further.

26 Oct October Revolution: Bolsheviks agree to make seizure of power 'the order of the day'. Kerensky mobilizes troops too late and they are defeated by troops loyal to the Bolsheviks. Insurrection, led by Trotsky, now begins. All main public buildings occupied. Kerensky flees. Bolsheviks assume power and effect series of radical reforms.

POLITICAL LEADERS AND RULERS

Australia

Head of State: British monarch, represented by Governor-General.

Prime Minister

1901–3	Edmund Barton *Prot*
1903–4	Alfred Deakin *Prot*
1904	John Christian Watson *Lab*
1904–5	George Houstoun Reid *Free*
1905–8	Alfred Deakin *Prot*
1908–9	Andrew Fisher *Lab*
1909–10	Alfred Deakin *Fusion*
1910–13	Andrew Fisher *Lab*
1913–14	Joseph Cook *Lib*
1914–15	Andrew Fisher *Lab*
1915–17	William Morris Hughes *Nat Lab*
1917–23	William Morris Hughes *Nat*
1923–9	Stanley Melbourne Bruce *Nat*
1929–32	James Henry Scullin *Lab*
1932–9	Joseph Aloyslus Lyons *Un*
1939	Earle Christmas Grafton Page *Co*
1939–40	Robert Gordon Menzies *Un*
1941	Arthur William Fadden *Co*
1941–5	John Joseph Curtin *Lab*
1945	Francis Michael Forde *Lab*
1945–9	Joseph Benedict Chifley *Lab*
1949–66	Robert Gordon Menzies *Lib*
1966–7	Harold Edward Holt *Lib*
1967–8	John McEwen *Co*
1968–71	John Grey Gorton *Lib*
1971–2	William McMahon *Lib*
1972–5	(Edward) Gough Whitlam *Lab*
1975–83	John Malcolm Fraser *Lib*
1983–91	Robert James Lee Hawke *Lab*
1991–6	Paul Keating *Lab*
1996–	John Howard *Lib*

Co Country; *Free* Free Trade; *Lab* Labor; *Lib* Liberal; *Nat* Nationalist; *Nat Lab* National Labor; *Prot* Protectionist; *Un* United.

Canada

Head of State: British monarch, represented by Governor-General.

Prime Minister

1867–73	John Alexander MacDonald *Con*
1873–8	Alexander Mackenzie *Lib*
1878–91	John Alexander MacDonald *Con*
1891–2	John J C Abbot *Con*
1892–4	John Sparrow David Thompson *Con*
1894–6	Mackenzie Bowell *Con*
1896	Charles Tupper *Con*
1896–1911	Wilfrid Laurier *Lib*
1911–20	Robert Laird Borden *Con*
1920–1	Arthur Meighen *Con*
1921–6	William Lyon Mackenzie King *Lib*
1926	Arthur Meighen *Con*
1926–30	William Lyon Mackenzie King *Lib*
1930–5	Richard Bedford Bennett *Con*
1935–48	William Lyon Mackenzie King *Lib*
1948–57	Louis Stephen St Laurent *Lib*
1957–63	John George Diefenbaker *Con*
1963–8	Lester Bowles Pearson *Lib*
1968–79	Pierre Elliott Trudeau *Lib*
1979–80	Joseph Clark *Con*
1980–4	Pierre Elliott Trudeau *Lib*
1984	John Napier Turner *Lib*
1984–93	(Martin) Brian Mulroney *Con*
1993	Kim Campbell *Con*
1993–2003	Jean Chrétien *Lib*
2003–	Paul Martin *Lib*

Con Conservative; *Lib* Liberal.

France

Prime Minister

1815	Charles-Maurice, Prince de Talleyrand-Perigord
1815–18	Armand-Emmanuel Vignerot-Duplessis, Duc de Richelieu
1818–19	Jean Joseph, Marquis Dessolle
1819–20	Duc Élie Decazes
1820–1	Armand-Emmanuel Vignerot-Duplessis, Duc de Richelieu
1821–9	Guillaume-Aubin, Comte de Villèle
1829–30	Auguste, Prince de Polignac
1830–1	Jacques Lafitte
1831–2	Casimir Périer
1832–4	Nicolas Soult
1834	Etienne, Comte Gérard
1834	Napoléon Joseph Maret, Duc de Bassano
1834–5	Étienne Mortier, Duc de Trévise
1835–6	Achille, Duc de Broglie
1836	Adolphe Thiers
1836–9	Louis, Comte Molé
1839–40	Nicolas Soult
1840	Adolphe Thiers
1840–7	Nicolas Soult
1847–8	François Guyzot
1848	Jacques Charles Dupont de L'Eure
1848	Louis-Eugène Cavaignac
1848–9	Odilon Barrot
1849–70	*No Prime Minister*

Third Republic

1870–1	Jules Favre
1871–3	Jules Dufaure
1873–4	Albert, Duc de Broglie
1874–5	Ernest Louis Courtot de Cissey
1875–6	Louis Buffet
1876	Jules Dufaure
1876–7	Jules Simon
1877	Albert, Duc de Broglie
1877	Gaetan de Grimaudet de Rochebouét
1877–9	Jules Dufaure
1879	William H Waddington
1879–80	Louis de Freycinet
1880–1	Jules Ferry
1881–2	Léon Gambetta
1882	Louis de Freycinet
1882–3	Eugène Duclerc
1883	Armand Fallières
1883–5	Jules Ferry
1885–6	Henri Brisson
1886	Louis de Freycinet
1886–7	René Goblet
1887	Maurice Rouvier
1887–8	Pierre Tirard
1888–9	Charles Floquet
1889–90	Pierre Tirard
1890–2	Louis de Freycinet
1892	Émile Loubet
1892–3	Alexandre Ribot
1893	Charles Dupuy
1893–4	Jean Casimir-Périer
1894–5	Charles Dupuy
1895	Alexandre Ribot
1895–6	Léon Bourgeois
1896–8	Jules Méline
1898	Henri Brisson
1898–9	Charles Dupuy
1899–1902	Pierre Waldeck-Rousseau
1902–5	Emile Combes
1905–6	Maurice Rouvier
1906	Jean Sarrien
1906–9	Georges Clemenceau
1909–11	Aristide Briand
1911	Ernest Monis
1911–12	Joseph Caillaux
1912–13	Raymond Poincaré
1913	Aristide Briand
1913	Jean Louis Barthou
1913–14	Gaston Doumergue
1914	Alexandre Ribot
1914–15	René Viviani
1915–17	Aristide Briand
1917	Alexandre Ribot
1917	Paul Painlevé

Political leaders and rulers (continued)

1917–20	Georges Clemenceau
1920	Alexandre Millerand
1920–1	Georges Leygues
1921–2	Aristide Briand
1922–4	Raymond Poincaré
1924	Frédéric François-Marsal
1924–5	Édouard Herriot
1925	Paul Painlevé
1925–6	Aristide Briand
1926	Édouard Herriot
1926–9	Raymond Poincaré
1929	Aristide Briand
1929–30	André Tardieu
1930	Camille Chautemps
1930	André Tardieu
1930–1	Théodore Steeg
1931–2	Pierre Laval
1932	André Tardieu
1932	Édouard Herriot
1932–3	Joseph Paul-Boncour
1933	Édouard Daladier
1933	Albert Sarrault
1933–4	Camille Chautemps
1934	Édouard Daladier
1934	Gaston Doumergue
1934–5	Pierre Étienne Flandin
1935	Fernand Bouisson
1935–6	Pierre Laval
1936	Albert Sarrault
1936–7	Léon Blum
1937–8	Camille Chautemps
1938	Léon Blum
1938–40	Édouard Daladier
1940	Paul Reynaud
1940	Philippe Pétain

Vichy Government

1940–4	Philippe Pétain

Provisional Government of the French Republic

1944–6	Charles de Gaulle
1946	Félix Gouin
1946	Georges Bidault

Fourth Republic

1946–7	Léon Blum
1947	Paul Ramadier
1947–8	Robert Schuman
1948	André Marie
1948	Robert Schuman
1948–9	Henri Queuille
1949–50	Georges Bidault
1950	Henri Queuille
1950–1	René Pleven
1951	Henri Queuille
1951–2	René Pleven
1952	Edgar Faure
1952–3	Antoine Pinay
1953	René Mayer
1953–4	Joseph Laniel
1954–5	Pierre Mendès France
1955–6	Edgar Faure
1956–7	Guy Mollet
1957	Maurice Bourgès-Maunoury
1957–8	Félix Gaillard
1958	Pierre Pflimlin

1958–9	Charles de Gaulle

Fifth Republic

1959–62	Michel Debré
1962–8	Georges Pompidou
1968–9	Maurice Couve de Murville
1969–72	Jacques Chaban Delmas
1972–4	Pierre Messmer
1974–6	Jacques Chirac
1976–81	Raymond Barre
1981–4	Pierre Mauroy
1984–6	Laurent Fabius
1986–8	Jacques Chirac
1988–91	Michael Rocard
1991–2	Edith Cresson
1992–3	Pierre Bérégovoy
1993–5	Édouard Balladur
1995–7	Alain Juppé
1997–2002	Lionel Jospin
2002–5	Jean-Pierre Raffarin
2005–	Dominique de Villepin

President

Third Republic

1870–1	*Commune*
1871–3	Louis Adolphe Thiers
1873–9	Marie Edmé de Mac-Mahon
1879–87	Jules Grévy
1887–94	Sadi Carnot
1894–5	Jean Paul Pierre Casimir-Périer
1895–9	François Félix Faure
1899–1906	Émile Loubet
1906–13	Armand Fallières
1913–20	Raymond Poincaré
1920	Paul Deschanel
1920–4	Alexandre Millerand
1924–31	Gaston Doumergue
1931–2	Paul Doumer
1932–40	Albert Lebrun
1940–5	*German occupation*
1945–7	*No President*

Fourth Republic

1947–54	Vincent Auriol
1954–8	René Coty

Fifth Republic

1958–69	Charles de Gaulle
1969–74	Georges Pompidou
1974–81	Valéry Giscard d'Estaing
1981–5	François Mitterrand
1995–	Jacques Chirac

Germany

Chancellor

1871–90	Otto von Bismarck
1890–4	Georg Leo, Graf von Caprivi
1894–1900	Chlodwic, Fürst zu Hohenlohe-Schillingfürst
1900–9	Bernard Heinrich, Prince von Bülow
1909–17	Theobald von Bethmann Hollweg

1917–18	Georg von Herfling
1918	Prince Max of Baden
1918	Friedrich Ebert
1919–20	Philipp Scheidemann
1920	Hermann Müller
1920–1	Konstantin Fehrenbach
1921–2	Karl Joseph Wirth
1922–3	Wilhelm Cuno
1923	Gustav Stresemann
1923–5	Wilhelm Marx
1925–6	Hans Luther
1926–8	Wilhelm Marx
1928–9	Hermann Müller
1929–32	Heinrich Brüning
1932	Franz von Papen
1932–3	Kurt von Schleicher
1933–45	Adolf Hitler (from 1934 *Führer*)

German Democratic Republic (East Germany)

President

1949–60	Wilhelm Pieck

Chairman of the Council of State

1960–73	Walter Ulbricht
1973–6	Willi Stoph
1976–89	Erich Honecker
1989	Egon Krenz
1989–90	Gregor Gysi

Premier

1949–64	Otto Grotewohl
1964–73	Willi Stoph
1973–6	Horst Sindermann
1976–89	Willi Stoph
1989–90	Hans Modrow
1990	Lothar de Maizière

The German Democratic Republic ceased to exist as a separate state and East Germany became part of the German Federal Republic in 1990.

German Federal Republic (until 1990 West Germany)

President

1949–59	Theodor Heuss
1959–69	Heinrich Lübke
1969–74	Gustav Heinemann
1974–9	Walter Scheel
1979–84	Karl Carstens
1984–94	Richard, Baron von Weizsäcker
1994–9	Roman Hertzog
1999–	Johannes Rau

Chancellor

1949–63	Konrad Adenauer
1963–6	Ludwig Erhard
1966–9	Kurt Georg Kiesinger
1969–74	Willy Brandt
1974–82	Helmut Schmidt
1982–98	Helmut Kohl
1998–2005	Gerhard Schröder
2005–	Angela Merkel

HISTORY

Russia and the Union of Soviet Socialist Republics

RUSSIA
Grand Duke of Moscow
House of Riurik
1283–1303	Daniel
1303–25	Yuri
1325–41	Ivan I Kalita
1341–53	Semeon
1353–9	Ivan II
1359–89	Dmitri I Donskoy
1389–1425	Vasily I
1425–62	Vasily II
1462–72	Ivan II 'the Great'

Ruler of all Russia
House of Riurik
1472–1505	Ivan III 'the Great'
1505–33	Vasily III
1533–47	Ivan IV 'the Terrible'

Tsar of Russia
House of Riurik
1547–84	Ivan IV 'the Terrible'
1584–98	Fedor I
1598–1605	Boris Godunov
1605	Fedor II
1605–6	Dmitri II (the 'false Dmitri')
1606–10	Vasily IV Shuisky
1610–13	*Civil war*

House of Romanov
1613–45	Mikhail (Michael Romanov)
1645–76	Alexey I Mihailovitch
1676–82	Fedor III
1682–1725	Peter I 'the Great' *Joint ruler to 1696*
1682–96	Ivan V *Joint ruler*
1725–7	Catherine I
1727–30	Peter II
1730–40	Anna Ivanovna
1740–1	Ivan VI
1741–62	Elizabeth Petrovna
1762	Peter III
1762–96	Catherine II 'the Great'
1796–1801	Paul
1801–25	Alexander I
1825–55	Nicholas I
1855–81	Alexander II 'the Liberator'
1881–94	Alexander III
1894–1917	Nicholas II

SOVIET UNION
President
1917	Lev Borisovich Kamenev
1917–19	Yakov Mikhailovich Sverlov
1919–46	Mikhail Ivanovich Kalinin
1946–53	Nikolai Mikhailovich Shvernik
1953–60	Kliment Yefremovich Voroshilov
1960–4	Leonid Ilyich Brezhnev
1964–5	Anastas Ivanovich Mikoyan
1965–77	Nikolai Viktorovich Podgorny
1977–82	Leonid Ilyich Brezhnev
1982–3	Vasily Vasiliyevich Kuznetsov *Acting*
1983–4	Yuri Vladimirovich Andropov
1984	Vasily Vasiliyevich Kuznetsov *Acting*
1984–5	Konstantin Ustinovich Chernenko
1985	Vasily Vasiliyevich Kuznetsov *Acting*
1985–8	Andrei Andreevich Gromyko
1988–90	Mikhail Sergeyevich Gorbachev

Executive President
1990–1	Mikhail Sergeyevich Gorbachev

RUSSIAN FEDERATION
President
1991–9	Boris Nikolayevich Yeltsin
1999–	Vladimir Putin

Prime Minister
1991–2	Yegor Gaidar
1992–8	Viktor Chernomyrdin
1998	Sergey Kiriyenko
1998–9	Yevgeny Primakov
1999	Sergey Stepashin
1999–2000	Vladimir Putin
2000–4	Mikhail Kasyanov
2004	Viktor Khristenko *Acting*
2004–	Mikhail Fradkov

United Kingdom

Prime Minister
1721–42	Robert Walpole, Earl of Orford *Whig*
1742–3	Spencer Compton, Earl of Wilmington *Whig*
1743–54	Henry Pelham *Whig*
1754–6	Thomas Pelham (Pelham-Hollies), Duke of Newcastle *Whig*
1756–7	William Cavendish, 1st Duke of Devonshire *Whig*
1757–62	Thomas Pelham (Pelham-Hollies), Duke of Newcastle *Whig*
1762–3	John Stuart, 3rd Earl of Bute *Tory*
1763–5	George Grenville *Whig*
1765–6	Charles Watson Wentworth, 2nd Marquis of Rockingham *Whig*
1766–8	William Pitt, 1st Earl of Chatham *Whig*
1768–70	Augustus Henry Fitzroy, 3rd Duke of Grafton *Whig*
1770–82	Frederick, 8th Lord North *Tory*
1782	Charles Watson Wentworth, 2nd Marquis of Rockingham *Whig*
1782–3	William Petty, 2nd Earl of Shelburne *Whig*
1783	William Henry Cavendish, Duke of Portland *Coal*
1783–1801	William Pitt *Tory*
1801–4	Henry Addington *Tory*
1804–6	William Pitt *Tory*
1806–7	William Wyndham Grenville, 1st Baron Grenville *Whig*
1807–9	William Henry Cavendish, Duke of Portland *Coal*
1809–12	Spencer Perceval *Tory*
1812–27	Robert Banks Jenkinson, 2nd Earl of Liverpool *Tory*
1827	George Canning *Tory*
1827–8	Frederick John Robinson, 1st Earl of Ripon *Tory*
1828–30	Arthur Wellesley, 1st Duke of Wellington *Tory*
1830–4	Charles Grey, 2nd Earl Grey *Whig*
1834	William Lamb, 2nd Viscount Melbourne *Whig*
1834–5	Robert Peel *Con*
1835–41	William Lamb, 2nd Viscount Melbourne *Whig*
1841–6	Robert Peel *Con*
1846–52	Lord John Russell, 1st Earl Russell *Lib*
1852	Edward Geoffrey Smith Stanley, 14th Earl of Derby *Con*
1852–5	George Hamilton-Gordon, 4th Earl of Aberdeen *Peelite*
1855–8	Henry John Temple, 3rd Viscount Palmerston *Lib*
1858–9	Edward Geoffrey Smith Stanley, 14th Earl of Derby *Con*
1859–65	Henry John Temple, 3rd Viscount Palmerston *Lib*
1865–6	Lord John Russell, 1st Earl Russell *Lib*
1866–8	Edward Geoffrey Smith Stanley, 14th Earl of Derby *Con*
1868	Benjamin Disraeli *Con*
1868–74	William Ewart Gladstone *Lib*
1874–80	Benjamin Disraeli *Con*
1880–5	William Ewart Gladstone *Lib*
1885–6	Robert Arthur Talbot Gascoyne-Cecil, 3rd Marquis of Salisbury *Con*
1886	William Ewart Gladstone *Lib*
1886–92	Robert Arthur Talbot

Political leaders and rulers (continued)

	Gascoyne-Cecil, 3rd Marquis of Salisbury *Con*
1892–4	William Ewart Gladstone *Lib*
1894–5	Archibald Philip Primrose, 5th Earl of Rosebery *Lib*
1895–1902	Robert Arthur Talbot Gascoyne-Cecil, 3rd Marquis of Salisbury *Con*
1902–5	Arthur James Balfour *Con*
1905–8	Henry Campbell-Bannerman *Lib*
1908–15	Herbert Henry Asquith *Lib*
1915–16	Herbert Henry Asquith *Coal*
1916–22	David Lloyd–George *Coal*
1922–3	Andrew Bonar Law *Con*
1923–4	Stanley Baldwin *Con*
1924	James Ramsay MacDonald *Lab*
1924–9	Stanley Baldwin *Con*
1929–31	James Ramsay MacDonald *Lab*
1931–5	James Ramsay MacDonald *Nat*
1935–7	Stanley Baldwin *Nat*
1937–40	(Arthur) Neville Chamberlain *Nat*
1940–5	Winston Leonard Spencer Churchill *Coal*
1945–51	Clement Richard Attlee *Lab*
1951–5	Winston Leonard Spencer Churchill *Con*
1955–7	(Robert) Anthony Eden, 1st Earl of Avon *Con*
1957–63	(Maurice) Harold Macmillan *Con*
1963–4	Alexander Frederick (Alec) Douglas-Home *Con*
1964–70	(James) Harold Wilson *Lab*
1970–4	Edward Richard George Heath *Con*
1974–6	(James) Harold Wilson *Lab*
1976–9	(Leonard) James Callaghan *Lab*
1979–90	Margaret Hilda Thatcher *Con*
1990–7	John Major *Con*
1997–	Tony Blair *Lab*

Coal Coalition; *Con* Conservative; *Lab* Labour; *Lib* Liberal; *Nat* Nationalist.

United States of America

President

Vice President in parentheses

1789–97	George Washington (1st) (John Adams)
1797–1801	John Adams (2nd) *Fed* (Thomas Jefferson)
1801–9	Thomas Jefferson (3rd) *Dem-Rep* (Aaron Burr, 1801–5) (George Clinton, 1805–9)
1809–17	James Madison (4th) *Dem-Rep* (George Clinton, 1809–12) *No Vice President 1812–13* (Elbridge Gerry, 1813–14) *No Vice President 1814–17*
1817–25	James Monroe (5th) *Dem-Rep* (Daniel D Tompkins)
1825–9	John Quincy Adams (6th) *Dem-Rep* (John Caldwell Calhoun)
1829–37	Andrew Jackson (7th) *Dem* (John Caldwell Calhoun, 1829–32) *No Vice President 1832–3* (Martin Van Buren, 1833–7)
1837–41	Martin Van Buren (8th) *Dem* (Richard Mentor Johnson)
1841	William Henry Harrison (9th) *Whig* (John Tyler)
1841–5	John Tyler (10th) *Whig* *No Vice President*
1845–9	James Knox Polk (11th) *Dem* (George Mifflin Dallas)
1849–50	Zachary Taylor (12th) *Whig* (Millard Fillmore)
1850–3	Millard Fillmore (13th) *Whig* *No Vice President*
1853–7	Franklin Pierce (14th) *Dem* (William Rufus King, 1853) *No Vice President 1853–7*
1857–61	James Buchanan (15th) *Dem* (John C Breckinridge)
1861–5	Abraham Lincoln (16th) *Rep* (Hannibal Hamlin, 1861–5) (Andrew Johnson, 1865)
1865–9	Andrew Johnson (17th) *Dem-Nat* *No Vice President*
1869–77	Ulysses Simpson Grant (18th) *Rep* (Schuyler Colfax, 1869–73) (Henry Wilson, 1873–5) *No Vice President 1875*
1877–81	Rutherford Birchard Hayes (19th) *Rep* (William A Wheeler)
1881	James Abram Garfield (20th) *Rep* (Chester Alan Arthur)
1881–5	Chester Alan Arthur (21st) *Rep* *No Vice President*
1885–9	Stephen Grover Cleveland (22nd) *Dem* (Thomas A Hendricks, 1885) *No Vice President 1885–9*
1889–93	Benjamin Harrison (23rd) *Rep* (Levi Parsons Morton)
1893–7	Stephen Grover Cleveland (24th) *Dem* (Adlai Ewing Stevenson)
1897–1901	William McKinley (25th) *Rep* (Garret A Hobart, 1897–9) *No Vice President 1899–1901* (Theodore Roosevelt, 1901)
1901–9	Theodore Roosevelt (26th) *Rep* *No Vice President 1901–5* (Charles W Fairbanks, 1905–9)
1909–13	William Howard Taft (27th) *Rep* (James S Sherman, 1909–12) *No Vice President 1912–13*
1913–21	Thomas Woodrow Wilson (28th) *Dem* (Thomas R Marshall)
1921–3	Warren G Harding (29th) *Rep* (Calvin Coolidge)
1923–9	Calvin Coolidge (30th) *Rep* *No Vice President 1923–5* (Charles Gates Dawes, 1925–9)
1929–33	Herbert Clark Hoover (31st) *Rep* (Charles Curtis)
1933–45	Franklin Delano Roosevelt (32nd) *Dem* (John N Garner, 1933–41) (Henry Agard Wallace, 1941–5) (Harry S Truman, 1945)
1945–53	Harry S Truman (33rd) *Dem* *No Vice President 1945–9* (Alben W Barkley, 1949–53)
1953–61	Dwight David Eisenhower (34th) *Rep* (Richard Milhous Nixon)
1961–3	John Fitzgerald Kennedy (35th) *Dem* (Lyndon Baines Johnson)
1963–9	Lyndon Baines Johnson (36th) *Dem* *No Vice President 1963–5* (Hubert Horatio Humphrey, 1965–9)
1969–74	Richard Milhous Nixon (37th) *Rep* (Spiro Theodore Agnew, 1969–73) *No Vice President Oct–Dec 1973* (Gerald Rudolph Ford, 1973–4)
1974–7	Gerald Rudolph Ford (38th) *Rep*

Political leaders and rulers (continued)

No Vice President Aug–Dec 1974
(Nelson Aldrich Rockefeller 1974–7)

1977–81 James Earl (Jimmy) Carter (39th) *Dem*
(Walter Frederick Mondale)

1981–9 Ronald Wilson Reagan (40th) *Rep*

(George Herbert Walker Bush)

1989–92 George Herbert Walker Bush (41st) *Rep*
(J Danforth (Dan) Quayle)

1992– 2001 William Jefferson (Bill) Clinton (42nd) *Dem*
(Albert Arnold Gore, Jr)

2001– George W(alker) Bush (43rd) *Rep*
(Dick Cheney)

Dem Democrat; *Dem-Rep* Democratic Republican; *Fed* Federalist; *Nat* National Union; *Rep* Republican.

PART SEVEN

Human Geography

The world political map

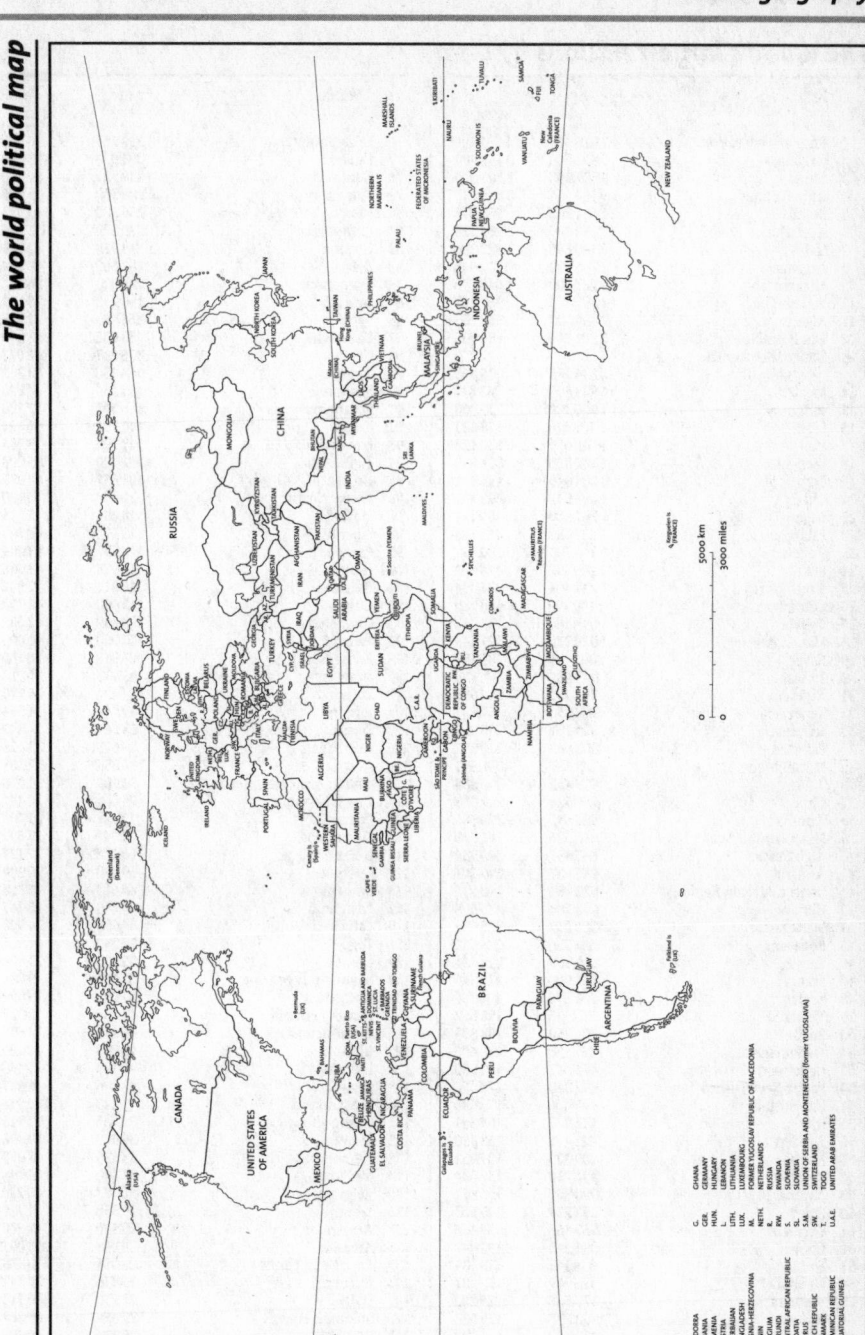

The world's largest nations by area

	Nation	Area km²	sq mi		Nation	Area km²	sq mi
1	Russian Federation	17 075 400	6 591 100	76	United Kingdom	244 755	94 500
2	Canada	9 971 500	3 848 900	77	Uganda	241 038	93 040
3	China	9 597 000	3 704 000	78	Ghana	238 537	92 100
4	United States	9 160 454	3 535 935	79	Romania	237 500	91 675
5	Brazil	8 511 965	3 285 618	80	Laos	236 800	91 405
6	Australia	7 692 300	2 969 228	81	Philippines	229 679	115 676
7	India	3 166 829	1 222 396	82	Guyana	214 969	82 978
8	Argentina	2 780 092	1 073 115	83	Belarus	207 600	80 134
9	Kazakhstan	2 717 300	1 048 878	84	Kyrgyzstan	198 500	76 621
10	Sudan, The	2 505 870	967 243	85	Senegal	196 790	75 729
11	Algeria	2 460 500	949 753	86	Syria	185 180	71 479
12	Saudi Arabia	2 331 000	899 766	87	Cambodia	181 035	68 879
13	Congo, Democratic Republic of	2 234 585	905 365	88	Uruguay	176 215	68 018
14	Mexico	1 978 800	763 817	89	Tunisia	164 150	63 362
15	Indonesia	1 906 200	735 800	90	Suriname	163 265	63 020
16	Libya	1 758 610	678 823	91	Nicaragua	148 000	57 128
17	Iran	1 648 000	636 128	92	Nepal	145 391	56 121
18	Mongolia	1 566 500	604 800	93	Bangladesh	143 998	55 583
19	Peru	1 284 640	495 871	94	Tajikistan	143 100	55 200
20	Chad	1 284 640	495 871	95	Greece	131 957	50 935
21	Niger	1 267 000	489 191	96	Korea, North	122 098	47 130
22	Ethiopia	1 251 282	483 123	97	Malawi	118 484	45 735
23	Angola	1 246 700	480 354	98	Liberia	113 370	43 760
24	Mali	1 240 192	478 841	99	Benin	112 622	43 484
25	South Africa	1 233 404	476 094	100	Honduras	112 088	43 266
26	Colombia	1 140 105	440 080	101	Bulgaria	110 912	42 812
27	Bolivia	1 098 580	424 052	102	Cuba	110 860	42 792
28	Mauritania	1 029 920	397 549	103	Guatemala	108 889	42 031
29	Egypt	1 001 449	386 559	104	Iceland	103 000	40 000
30	Tanzania	945 087	364 900	105	Korea, South	98 913	38 180
31	Nigeria	923 768	356 669	106	Hungary	93 033	35 912
32	Venezuela	912 050	352 051	107	Portugal	91 630	35 370
33	Namibia	824 292	318 261	108	Jordan	89 544	34 564
34	Pakistan	803 943	310 322	109	Serbia	88 361	34 107
35	Mozambique	799 380	308 641	110	Azerbaijan	86 600	33 428
36	Turkey	779 452	300 868	111	Austria	83 854	32 368
37	Chile	756 626	292 058	112	United Arab Emirates	83 600	32 300
38	Zambia	752 613	290 586	113	Czech Republic	78 864	30 441
39	Myanmar (Burma)	678 576	261 930	114	Panama	77 082	29 753
40	Afghanistan	647 497	249 934	115	Sierra Leone	71 740	27 692
41	Somalia	637 357	246 201	116	Ireland	70 282	27 129
42	Central African Republic	622 984	240 535	117	Georgia	69 700	26 900
43	Ukraine	603 700	233 028	118	Sri Lanka	65 610	25 325
44	Madagascar	587 041	226 658	119	Lithuania	65 200	25 167
45	Botswana	581 730	224 711	120	Latvia	64 600	24 900
46	Kenya	580 367	224 081	121	Togo	56 790	21 921
47	France	551 000	212 686	122	Croatia	56 538	21 824
48	Yemen	531 570	205 186	123	Bosnia-Herzegovina	51 129	19 736
49	Thailand	513 115	198 062	124	Costa Rica	51 022	19 694
50	Spain	504 750	194 833	125	Slovak Republic	49 035	18 927
51	Turkmenistan	488 100	188 400	126	Dominican Republic	48 442	18 699
52	Cameroon	475 442	183 569	127	Bhutan	46 600	18 000
53	Papua New Guinea	462 840	178 656	128	Estonia	45 100	17 409
54	Uzbekistan	447 400	172 696	129	Denmark	43 076	16 627
55	Iraq	434 925	167 881	130	Switzerland	41 228	15 914
56	Sweden	411 479	158 830	131	Guinea-Bissau	36 125	13 948
57	Morocco	409 200	157 951	132	Taiwan	36 000	13 896
58	Paraguay	406 750	157 000	133	Netherlands, The	33 929	13 097
59	Zimbabwe	390 759	150 873	134	Moldova	33 700	13 008
60	Japan	377 728	145 803	135	Belgium	30 518	11 780
61	Germany	357 868	138 136	136	Lesotho	30 355	11 720
62	Congo	341 945	132 047	137	Armenia	29 800	11 500
63	Finland	338 145	130 524	138	Albania	28 748	11 097
64	Malaysia	329 749	127 283	139	Equatorial Guinea	28 051	10 828
65	Vietnam	329 566	127 212	140	Burundi	27 834	10 747
66	Norway	323 895	125 023	141	Haiti	27 750	10 712
67	Côte d'Ivoire	322 462	124 503	142	Solomon Islands	27 556	10 637
68	Poland	312 683	120 695	143	Rwanda	26 338	10 169
69	Italy	301 255	116 314	144	Macedonia, former Yugoslav Republic of	25 713	9 925
70	Oman	300 000	115 800	145	Djibouti	23 200	8 958
71	Burkina Faso	274 200	105 870	146	Belize	22 963	8 864
72	Ecuador	270 699	104 490	147	El Salvador	21 476	8 290
73	New Zealand	268 812	103 761	148	Israel	20 770	8 017
74	Gabon	267 667	103 347	149	Slovenia	20 251	7 817
75	Guinea	245 857	94 926	150	Fiji	18 333	7 076

Nation		Area km²	sq mi		Nation		Area km²	sq mi
151	Kuwait	17 818	6878		172	Bahrain	678	262
152	Swaziland	17 363	6702		173	Tonga	646	249
153	East Timor	14 874	5743		174	Singapore	618	238
154	Vanuatu	14 763	5698		175	St Lucia	616	238
155	Bahamas, The	13 934	5378		176	Andorra	453	175
156	Montenegro	13 812	5333		177	Antigua and Barbuda	442	171
157	Qatar	11 437	4415		178	Barbados	430	166
158	Gambia, The	11 295	4361		179	St Vincent and the Grenadines	390	150
159	Jamaica	10 957	4229		180	Grenada	344	133
160	Lebanon	10 452	4034		181	Malta	316	122
161	Cyprus	9251	3571		182	Maldives	300	116
162	Brunei	5765	2225		183	St Kitts and Nevis	269	104
163	Trinidad and Tobago	5128	1979		184	Liechtenstein	160	62
164	Cape Verde	4033	1557		185	San Marino	61	23
165	Samoa	2842	1097		186	Tuvalu	26	10
166	Luxembourg	2586	998		187	Nauru	21.3	8.2
167	Mauritius	1865	720		188	Monaco	1.95	0.75
168	Comoros	1862	719					
169	São Tomé and Príncipe	1001	387					
170	Dominica	751	290					
171	Kiribati	717	277					

This list is not exhaustive, particularly among the smaller nations. Differences of status of many of the 'nations' listed also make direct comparisons difficult.

World population estimates

Date (AD)	Millions	Date (AD)	Millions	Date (AD)	Millions
1	200	1960	3 050	1997	5 880
1000	275	1970	3 700	1998	5 950
1250	375	1980	4 450	1999	6 030
1500	420	1985	4 845	2000	6 100
1700	615	1990	5 246	2050	11 000
1800	900	1991	5 385		
1900	1 625	1992	5 480		
1920	1 860	1993	5 544		
1930	2 070	1994	5 607		
1940	2 295	1995	5 734		
1950	2 500	1996	5 800		

Estimates for 2000 and 2050 are United Nations 'medium' estimates. They should be compared with the 'low' estimates for these years of 5 400 and 8 500 and 'high' estimates of 7 000 and 13 000, respectively.

World population (billions) 1950–2050[a]

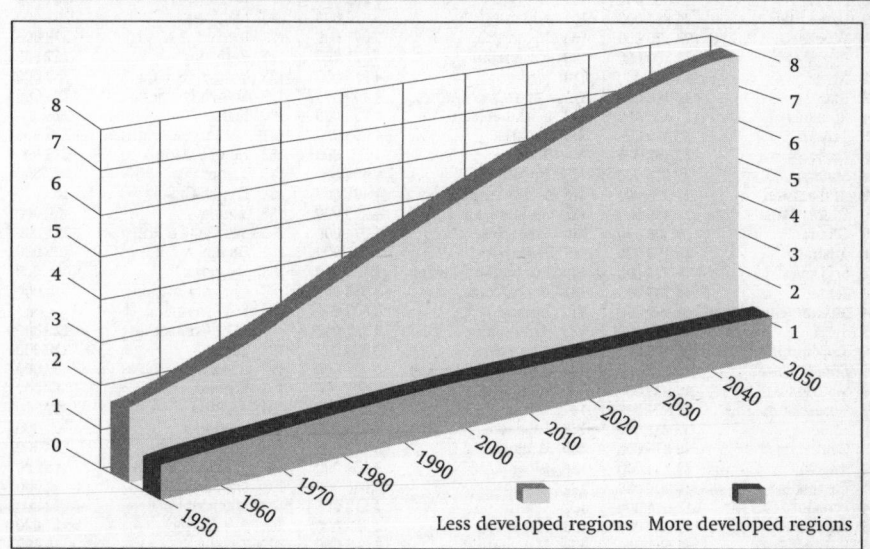

Less developed regions   More developed regions

Source: United Nations publication, ST/ESA/SER.A/176, Copyright (C) United Nations 1999.

[a]1 billion = 1000 million

HUMAN GEOGRAPHY

The world's largest nations by population

Nation	Population total (2000) estimates		Nation	Population total		Nation	Population total
1 China	1 275 133 000		67 Guatemala	11 385 000		135 United Arab Emirates	2 606 000
2 India	1 008 937 000		68 Mali	11 351 000		136 Jamaica	2 576 000
3 United States	283 230 000		69 Malawi	11 308 000		137 Oman	2 538 000
4 Indonesia	212 092 000		70 Cuba	11 199 000		138 Mongolia	2 533 000
5 Brazil	170 406 000		71 Niger	10 832 000		139 Latvia	2 421 000
6 Russia	145 491 000		72 Greece	10 610 000		140 Bhutan	2 085 000
7 Pakistan	141 256 000		73 Zambia	10 421 000		141 Lesotho	2 035 000
8 Bangladesh	137 439 000		74 Czech Republic	10 272 000		142 Macedonia, FYRO	2 034 000
9 Japan	127 096 000		75 Belgium	10 249 000		143 Slovenia	1 988 000
10 Nigeria	113 862 000		76 Belarus	10 187 000		144 Kuwait	1 914 000
11 Mexico	98 872 000		77 Portugal	10 016 000		145 Namibia	1 757 000
12 Germany	82 017 000		78 Hungary	9 968 000		146 Botswana	1 541 000
13 Vietnam	78 137 000		79 Tunisia	9 459 000		147 Estonia	1 393 000
14 Philippines	75 653 000		80 Senegal	9 421 000		148 Gambia, The	1 303 000
15 Iran	70 330 000		81 Sweden	8 842 000		149 Trinidad & Tobago	1 294 000
16 Egypt	67 884 000		82 Somalia	8 778 000		150 Gabon	1 230 000
17 Turkey	66 668 000		83 Dominican Rep.	8 373 000		151 Guinea-Bissau	1 199 000
18 Ethiopia	62 908 000		84 Bolivia	8 329 000		152 Mauritius	1 161 000
19 Thailand	62 806 000		85 Guinea	8 154 000		153 Swaziland	925 000
20 United Kingdom	59 415 000		86 Haiti	8 142 000		154 Fiji	814 000
21 France	59 238 000		87 Austria	8 080 000		155 Cyprus	784 000
22 Italy	57 530 000		88 Azerbaijan	8 041 000		156 Guyana	761 000
23 Congo, Dem. Rep. of	50 948 000		89 Bulgaria	7 949 000		157 East Timor	737 000
24 Ukraine	49 568 000		90 Chad	7 885 000		158 Reunion	721 000
25 Myanmar	47 749 000		91 Rwanda	7 609 000		159 Comoros	706 000
26 Korea, South	46 740 000		92 Serbia	7 500 000		160 Bahrain	640 000
27 South Africa	43 309 000		93 Switzerland	7 170 000		161 Djibouti	632 000
28 Colombia	42 105 000		94 China, Hong Kong (SAR)[1]	6 860 000		162 Montenegro	631 000
29 Spain	39 910 000		95 Honduras	6 417 000		163 Qatar	565 000
30 Poland	38 605 000		96 Burundi	6 356 000		164 Equatorial Guinea	457 000
31 Argentina	37 032 000		97 El Salvador	6 278 000		165 Solomon Islands	447 000
32 Tanzania	35 119 000		98 Benin	6 272 000		166 China, Macao (SAR)[2]	444 000
33 Sudan, The	31 095 000		99 Tajikistan	6 087 000		167 Luxembourg	437 000
34 Canada	30 757 000		100 Israel	6 040 000		168 Guadeloupe	428 000
35 Kenya	30 669 000		101 Paraguay	5 496 000		169 Cape Verde	427 000
36 Algeria	30 291 000		102 Slovak Republic	5 399 000		170 Suriname	417 000
37 Morocco	29 878 000		103 Denmark	5 320 000		171 Malta	390 000
38 Peru	25 662 000		104 Libya	5 290 000		172 Martinique	383 000
39 Uzbekistan	24 881 000		105 Laos	5 279 000		173 Brunei	328 000
40 Venezuela	24 170 000		106 Georgia	5 262 000		174 Bahamas, The	304 000
41 Uganda	23 300 000		107 Finland	5 172 000		175 Maldives	291 000
42 Nepal	23 043 000		108 Nicaragua	5 071 000		176 Iceland	279 000
43 Iraq	22 946 000		109 Kyrgyzstan	4 921 000		177 Barbados	267 000
44 Romania	22 438 000		110 Jordan	4 913 000		178 Western Sahara	252 000
45 Taiwan	22 319 000		111 Papua New Guinea	4 809 000		179 French Polynesia	233 000
46 Korea, North	22 268 000		112 Turkmenistan	4 737 000		180 Belize	226 000
47 Malaysia	22 218 000		113 Croatia	4 654 000		181 Netherlands Antilles	215 000
48 Afghanistan	21 765 000		114 Togo	4 527 000		182 New Caledonia	215 000
49 Saudi Arabia	20 346 000		115 Norway	4 469 000		183 Vanuatu	197 000
50 Ghana	19 306 000		116 Sierra Leone	4 405 000		184 French Guiana	165 000
51 Australia	19 138 000		117 Moldova	4 295 000		185 Samoa	159 000
52 Sri Lanka	18 924 000		118 Costa Rica	4 024 000		186 São Tomé & Principe	159 000
53 Yemen	18 349 000		119 Singapore	4 018 000		187 Guam	155 000
54 Mozambique	18 292 000		120 Bosnia-Herzegovina	3 977 000		188 St Lucia	148 000
55 Syria	16 189 000		121 Puerto Rico	3 915 000		189 Channel Islands	144 000
56 Kazakhstan	16 172 000		122 Ireland	3 803 000		190 St Vincent and The Grenadines	120 000
57 Côte D'Ivoire	16 013 000		123 Armenia	3 787 000		191 Tonga	110 000
58 Madagascar	15 970 000		124 New Zealand	3 778 000		192 Grenada	97 000
59 Netherlands, The	15 864 000		125 Central African Rep.	3 717 000		193 Kiribati	87 000
60 Chile	15 211 000		126 Lithuania	3 696 000		194 Andorra	67 000
61 Cameroon	14 876 000		127 Eritrea	3 659 000		195 Dominica	64 000
62 Angola	13 134 000		128 Lebanon	3 496 000		196 Antigua & Barbuda	64 000
63 Cambodia	13 104 000		129 Uruguay	3 337 000		197 St Kitts and Nevis	43 000
64 Ecuador	12 646 000		130 Albania	3 134 000		198 Liechtenstein	32 000
65 Zimbabwe	12 627 000		131 Congo	3 018 000		199 Monaco	32 000
66 Burkina Faso	11 535 000		132 Liberia	2 913 000		200 San Marino	25 000
			133 Panama	2 856 000		201 Tuvalu	10 000
			134 Mauritania	2 665 000			

1 As of 1 July 1997, Hong Kong became a Special Administrative Region (SAR) of China.
2 As of 20 July 1999, Macao became a Special Administrative Region (SAR) of China.
Source: United Nations Population Division, World Prospects: The 2001 Revision

The world's largest cities by population

Population estimates for cities vary greatly, depending on how the notion of 'city' is defined. The following list gives 2000 estimates for agglomerations. An *agglomeration* consists of a central city (sometimes more than one central city) and neighbouring communities linked to it by continuous built-up areas or by many commuters. The figures in this list are on the high side compared with some other listings: a comparable list from the UN Population Division, gives agglomeration estimates which are usually considerably lower, and a different set of rankings emerges.

Population (millions)	City
34.9	Tokyo, Japan
21.6	New York, USA
21.2	Seoul, South Korea
20.7	Mexico City, Mexico
20.2	São Paulo, Brazil
18.1	Mumbai, India
18.0	Osaka, Japan
17.1	Delhi, India
16.8	Los Angeles, USA
15.8	Jakarta, Indonesia
15.1	Cairo, Egypt
14.1	Calcutta, India
13.7	Buenos Aires, Argentina
13.4	Manila, Philippines
13.2	Moscow, Russia
12.3	Karachi, Pakistan
12.2	Rio de Janeiro
12.2	Shanghai, China
11.8	London, UK
11.1	Tehran, Iran
11.0	Istanbul, Turkey
10.3	Dhaka, Bangladesh
9.8	Paris, France
9.4	Chicago, USA
9.3	Lagos, Nigeria
9.2	Beijing, China
7.9	Lima, Peru
7.8	Washington, DC, USA
7.7	Bogota, Colombia
7.5	Bangkok, Thailand
7.5	Johannesburg, South Africa
7.4	Taipei, Taiwan
7.3	San Francisco, USA
7.2	Chongqing, China
7.1	Madras, India
6.9	Hong Kong, China
6.6	Kinshasa, Dem. Rep. of the Congo
6.5	Lahore, Pakistan
6.3	Bangalore, India
6.3	Philadelphia, USA
6.1	Hyderabad, India
6.0	Ruhr, Germany
5.9	Khartoum, Sudan
5.9	Boston, USA
5.8	Detroit, USA
5.7	Tianjin, China
5.5	St Petersburg, Russia
5.5	Dallas, USA
5.4	Santiago, Chile
5.1	Madrid, Spain
5.1	Nagoya, Japan
5.0	Ahmadabad, India
5.0	Baghdad, Iraq
4.9	Alexandria, Egypt
4.9	Houston, USA
4.9	Toronto, Canada
4.7	Belo Horizonte, Brazil
4.7	Wuhan, China
4.7	Guangzhou, China
4.7	Yangon, Myanmar
4.5	Riyadh, Saudi Arabia
4.5	Harbin, China
4.4	Atlanta, USA
4.4	Caracas, Venezuela
4.4	Shenyang, China
4.2	Sydney, Australia
4.2	Saigon, Vietnam

Population (millions)	City
4.2	Berlin, Germany
4.2	Algiers, Algeria
4.1	Guadalajara, Mexico
4.1	Pune, India
4.0	Miami, USA
4.0	Pusan, South Korea
3.9	Abidjan, Cote d'Ivoire
3.8	Barcelona, Spain
3.8	Kuala Lumpur, Malaysia
3.8	Milan, Italy
3.8	Porto Alegre, Brazil
3.7	Casablanca, Morocco
3.7	Recife, Brazil
3.7	Monterrey, Mexico
3.7	Seattle, USA
3.6	Chengdu, China
3.6	Pyongyang, North Korea
3.5	Montreal, Canada
3.5	Phoenix, USA
3.5	Ankara, Turkey
3.5	Athens, Greece
3.5	Melbourne, Australia
3.4	Medellín, Colombia
3.4	Salvador, Brazil
3.4	Chittagong, Bangladesh
3.3	Kiev, Ukraine
3.3	Jedda, Saudi Arabia
3.3	Rome, Italy
3.3	Singapore, Singapore
3.2	Fortaleza, Brazil
3.1	Surat, India
3.1	Kano, Nigeria
3.1	Minneapolis, USA
3.1	Nanjing, China
3.0	Cape Town, South Africa
3.0	Cleveland, USA
3.0	Naples, Italy
2.9	Addis Ababa, Ethiopia
2.9	Amman, Jordan
2.9	Bandung, Indonesia
2.9	Changchun, China
2.9	Curitiba, Brazil
2.9	Kanpur, India
2.9	Luanda, Angola
2.9	Surabaya, Indonesia
2.9	Lisbon, Portugal
2.9	San Diego, USA
2.9	Xi'an, China
2.8	Dalian, China
2.8	Katowice, Poland
2.8	Santo Domingo, Dominican Republic
2.8	Taegu, South Korea
2.8	Tel Aviv-Yafo, Israel
2.7	Denver, USA
2.7	Ibadan, Nigeria
2.7	Qingdao, China
2.7	Durban, South Africa
2.7	Harare, Zimbabwe
2.7	Nairobi, Kenya
2.7	Stuttgart, Germany
2.6	Kabul, Afghanistan
2.6	Kaohsiung, Taiwan
2.6	St Louis, USA
2.6	Birmingham, UK
2.6	Damascus, Syria
2.6	Hamburg, Germany
2.6	Jaipur, India

Population (millions)	City
2.6	San Juan, Puerto Rico
2.5	Budapest, Hungary
2.5	Cali, Colombia
2.5	Dar es Salaam, Tanzania
2.5	Faisalabad, Pakistan
2.5	Izmir, Turkey
2.5	Brussels, Belgium
2.5	Aleppo, Syria
2.5	Lucknow, India
2.5	Manchester, UK
2.5	Tampa, USA
2.4	Colombo, Sri Lanka
2.4	Havana, Cuba
2.4	Rawalpindi, Pakistan
2.4	Accra, Ghana
2.4	Hangzhou, China
2.4	Pittsburgh, USA
2.4	Portland, USA
2.4	Tashkent, Uzbekistan
2.4	Warsaw, Poland
2.3	Brasília, Brazil
2.3	Guayaquil, Ecuador
2.3	Jinan, China
2.3	Mashhad, Iran
2.3	Bucharest, Romania
2.3	Dakar, Senegal
2.3	Nagpur, India
2.3	Sapporo, Japan
2.3	Zhengzhou, China
2.2	Shijiazhuang, China
2.1	Donetsk, Ukraine
2.1	Irbil, Iraq
2.1	Amsterdam, Netherlands
2.1	Beirut, Lebanon
2.1	Medan, Indonesia
2.1	San Salvador, El Salvador
2.1	Tunis, Tunisia
2.1	Vancouver, Canada
2.0	Belém, Brazil
2.0	Cincinnati, USA
2.0	Fukuoka, Japan
2.0	Leeds, UK
2.0	Taiyuan, China
2.0	Kharkov, Ukraine
2.0	Maracaibo, Venezuela
2.0	Frankfurt, Germany
1.9	Conakry, Guinea
1.9	Kunming, China
1.9	Port-au-Prince, Haiti
1.9	Dammam, Saudi Arabia
1.9	Changsha, China
1.9	Munich, Germany
1.9	Nizhni Novgorod, Russia
1.9	Puebla, Mexico
1.9	Baku, Azerbaijan
1.9	Campinas, Brazil
1.9	Patna, India
1.9	Cologne, Germany
1.9	Rabat, Morocco
1.9	Sacramento, USA
1.9	Vienna, Austria
1.8	Minsk, Belarus
1.8	Kansas City, USA
1.8	Lusaka, Zambia
1.8	Belgrade, Serbia and Montenegro
1.8	Guatemala City, Guatemala

Source: United Nations, Department of Economic and Social Affairs.

HUMAN GEOGRAPHY

World population density

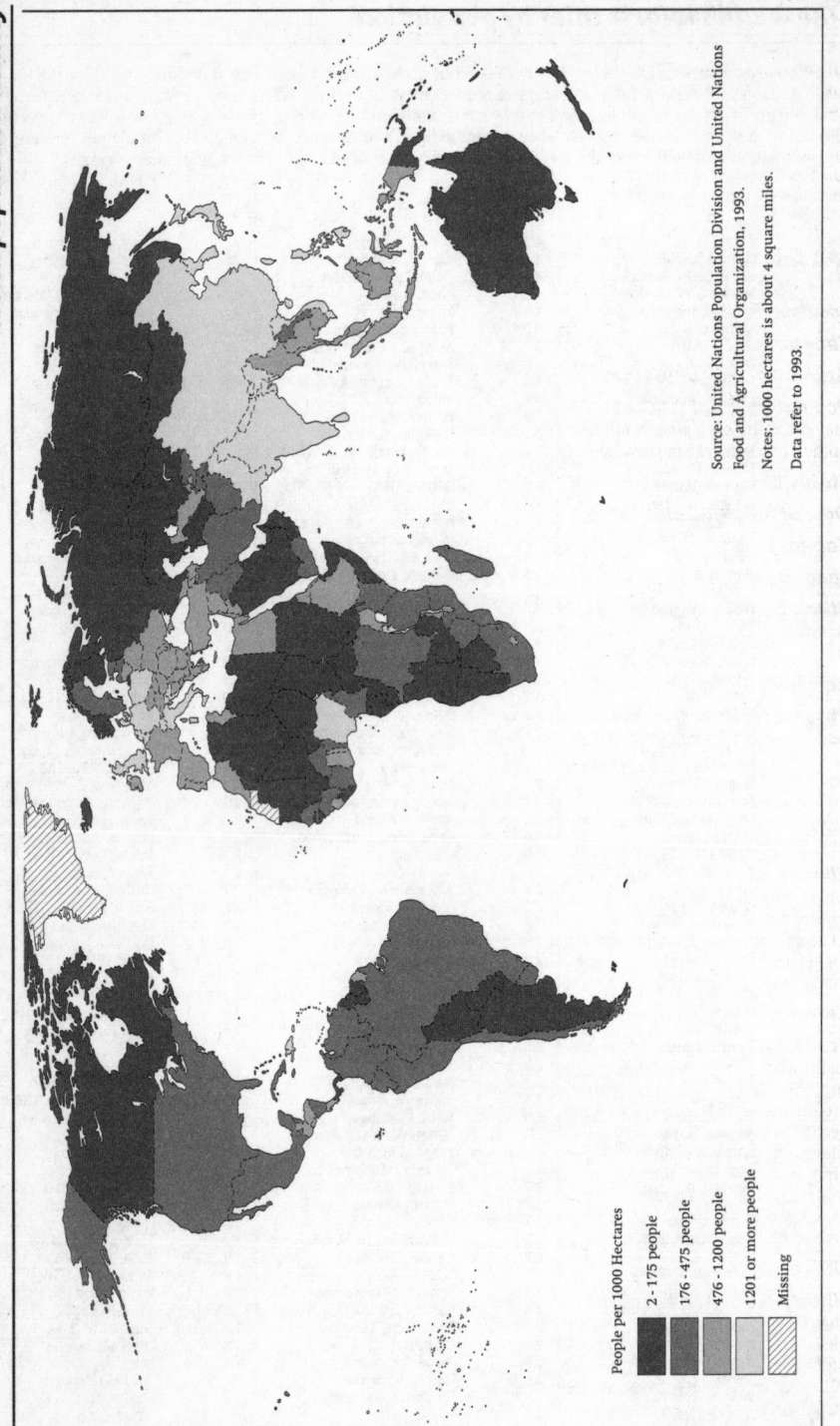

People per 1000 Hectares

- 2 - 175 people
- 176 - 475 people
- 476 - 1200 people
- 1201 or more people
- Missing

Source: United Nations Population Division and United Nations Food and Agricultural Organization, 1993.

Notes: 1000 hectares is about 4 square miles.

Data refer to 1993.

Country summaries

All population figures provided are the latest available authoritative figures. Estimates are indicated using the suffix 'e'. Gross Domestic Product (GDP) and Gross National Product (GNP) figures are provided in US $ in millions (mn) or billions (bn = 1 000 mn). In the majority of cases, the Heads of State/Heads of Government given are those most recently in office. Unless stated, 'Head of State' refers to the president and 'Head of Government' to the prime minister. The UN Human Development Index (HDI) measures average achievements in basic human development (such as life expectancy, literacy, and standard of living) in a single composite index. Currencies are identified using the 150 4217 Currency Abbreviations.

AFGHANISTAN

Local name Afghānestān

Timezone GMT +4.5

Area 647 497 km²/249 934 sq mi

Population total (2002e) 27 756 000, plus an estimated 2.5 million members of nomadic tribes, and c.5 million living in Pakistan and Iran as refugees

Status Democratic republic

Date of independence 1919

Capital Kabul

Languages Pushtu, Dari

Ethnic groups Pathans (50%), Tajik (20%), Uzbek (9%), Hazara (9%), Chahar Aimak (3%), Turkmen (2%), Baluchi (1%)

Religions Muslim (Sunni 84%, Shi'ite 15%)

Physical features Mountainous, landlocked country centred on and divided E–W by the Hindu Kush mountain range which reaches heights of over 7 000 m/24 000 ft. Three distinctive regions: fertile valley of Herat in NW; arid uplands to the S; and 129 495 km²/50 000 sq mi of desert in the SW plateau (including the Rigestan Desert). Amu Darya (Oxus) R forms N border.

Climate Continental climate; summers warm everywhere except on highest peaks; rain mostly during spring and autumn; average annual rainfall 338 mm/13.25 in; winters generally cold, with much snow at higher altitudes (central highlands have a sub-polar climate); at lower levels desert or semi-arid climate.

Currency 1 Afghani (AFA) = 100 puls

Economy Traditionally based on agriculture, especially wheat, fruit, vegetables, maize, barley, cotton, sugar-beet, sugar cane, sheep, cattle, goats; natural-gas production in the N, largely for export; most sectors have been affected by civil war, especially sugar, carpets, textiles; natural resources also include oil, coal, copper, sulphur, lead, zinc, iron, salt, precious and semi-precious stones; many of these resources remain untapped owing to inaccessibility. Main trading partners: Eastern European and CIS countries, Japan, China.

GDP (2002e) $19 bn, per capita $700

History Nation first formed in 1747, under Ahmed Shah Durrani; seen as a bridge between India and the Middle East; Britain failed to gain control during a series of Afghan Wars (the last in 1919); independence declared in 1919 after World War 1; feudal monarchy survived until after World War 2, when constitution became more liberal under several Soviet-influenced five-year economic

□ International Airport

plans; king deposed, 1973, and republic formed; new constitution, 1977; coup (1979) brought to power Hafizullah Amin, which led to invasion by USSR forces and establishment of Babrak Karmal as Head of State; new constitution in 1987 provided for an executive president, bicameral National Assembly, and council of ministers; Soviet withdrawal 1988–9; new regime met with heavy guerrilla resistance from the Mujahadeen (Islamic fighters); resignation of President Najibullah, April 1992; Islamic State of Afghanistan declared, 1992; continuing unrest among Mujahadeen groups, hindering progress of UN-backed peace plans; new conflict, 1994–5, with the *taliban* (army of students), a Muslim force whose military organization emerged in late 1994; Taliban seized Kabul and drove out government forces, imposition of strict Islamic regime, and execution of Najibullah, 1996; government of Burhanuddin Rabbani continued to control part of the country in rebellion against the Taliban government under Mohammad Omar Akhondzada; called Islamic Emirate of Afghanistan, 1997; following the attack on the World Trade Center, New York (11 Sep 2001), US-led coalition forces launched aerial bombardment of Taliban-controlled military installations linked to Osama bin Laden, Oct 2001; Afghan delegations set up interim administration under the UN, Dec 2001; International Security Assistance Force (ISAF) established; US-led ongoing operations against remaining Taliban resistance, 2002; ISAF taken over by NATO, Aug 2003; interim president Hamid Karzai elected, Nov 2004; renewed fighting between Taliban and coalition forces, 2006.

Head of State

2002–   Hamid Karzai

Afghanistan (continued)

Head of Government
1996   Gulbardin Hekmatyar

Interim Council
1996–2001 Mohammad Rabbani (Chairman)

Interim government
2001–2   Hamid Karzai

ALBANIA

Local name Shqïpëri

Timezone GMT +1

Area 28 748 km²/11 097 sq mi

Population total (2002e) 3 108 000

Status Republic

Date of independence 1912

Capital Tiranë

Languages Albanian (official) (Gheg and Tosk, the main dialects), Greek

Ethnic groups Albanian (96%), Greek (2%), Macedonian, Vlach, Gypsy, Bulgarian

Religions Muslim (Sunni 70%), Roman Catholic (5%), Greek Orthodox (2%) (before April 1991, Albania was constitutionally atheist)

Physical features Mountainous country, relatively inaccessible and untravelled; geologically active – earthquakes severe and relatively frequent; N Albanian Alps rise to 2692 m/8832 ft; mountainous highlands (N, S, and E) account for c.70% of the land; coastal lowland in the W is agricultural; rivers include the Drin i zi, Shkumbin, Seman, Vijosë; 45% of land is forested; 25% is arable, mostly grain-producing; c.20% is permanent pasture land.

Climate Mediterranean climate, hot and dry on the plains in summer; average annual temperatures, 8–9°C (Jan), 24–5°C (Jul); thunderstorms frequent; mild, damp, cyclonic winters.

Currency 1 Lek (ALL) = 100 qintars

Economy Seventh five-year plan (1981–5) focused on industrial expansion, especially in oil (new sources were located), mining, chemicals, natural gas; hydroelectric power plans for several rivers (eg the Koman hydroelectric complex on the Drin i zi R); agricultural product processing, textiles, oil products, cement; main crops are wheat, sugar-beet, maize, potatoes, fruit, grapes, oats; all industry is nationalized; progressive transformation of farm cooperatives into state farms; chromate, low-grade iron ore, and soft coal are exported; other natural resources: crude petroleum, asphalt, lignite (brown coal), phosphorus, bauxite, precious metals.

GDP (2002e) $15.69 bn, per capita $440

HDI (2002) 0.733

History Albanians descended from Illyrians, who occupied W Balkan peninsula c.1000 BC; King Argon and, after him, his wife Teuta conquered many territories, provoking the military might of Rome; despite Roman occupation and invasions by Visigoths, Slavs, and Huns, the Albanians were one of the few peoples to retain their Illyrian language and customs; Turkish invasions, 14th-

☐ International Airport   ∴ World heritage site

c; independence after the end of Turkish rule, 1912; occupied by Italian forces, 1914–20; became a republic in 1925, and a monarchy in 1928, under King Zog I; occupied by Germany and Italy during World War 2; new republic instigated in 1946, headed by Enver Hoxha (until 1985); dispute with the Soviet Union in 1961 led to withdrawal from Warsaw Pact in 1968, but close links with China maintained; People's Socialist Republic instituted, 1976; renamed Republic of Albania, 1991; first free elections, 1991, giving a decisive majority to the communists; however general strike and demonstrations forced government to resign; Communist Party renamed itself the Socialist Party; Democratic Party elected in 1992 elections; collapse of fraudulent pyramid finance schemes, 1997, leading to rebellion in the S, arrival of UN protection force, and early elections, with unrest continuing in 1998; new constitution, 1998; People's Assembly (supreme legislative body) elects the president and Council of Ministers.

Head of State
1997–2002 Rexhep Mejdani
2002–   Alfred Moisiu

Head of Government
2002   Pandeli Majko
2002–5   Fatos Nano
2005–   Sali Berisha

HUMAN GEOGRAPHY

ALGERIA

Local name(s) Al-Jazā'ir (Arabic), Algérie (French)

Timezone GMT +1

Area 2 460 500 km²/949 753 sq mi

Population total (2002e) 31 261 000

Status Democratic republic

Date of independence 1962

Capital Algiers (Alger)

Languages Arabic (official), Berber, French

Ethnic groups Arab (75%), Berber (25%)

Religions Muslim (Sunni 99%), Roman Catholic (0.5%)

Physical features Mountainous area in N Africa: mountains rise in a series of ridges and plateaux to the Atlas Saharien; Ahaggar Mts in the far S, rising to 2918 m/ 9573 ft at Mt Tahat; 85% of land is Saharan desert.

Climate Mediterranean in N, with cool, rainy winters and hot dry summers; average annual temperatures 12°C (Jan), 25°C (Jul); average annual rainfall 400– 800 mm/15.8–31.5 in (mostly Nov–Mar); essentially rainless Saharan climate in S.

Currency 1 Algerian Dinar (DZD) = 100 centimes

Economy Petroleum products account for about 30% of national income; natural-gas liquification; jointly built with Italy first trans-Mediterranean gas pipeline; agriculture mainly on N coast: wheat, barley, oats, grapes, citrus fruits, vegetables; also food processing, textiles, clothing.

GDP (2002e) $173.8 bn, per capita $5400

HDI (2002) 0.697

History Islamic Berber empires followed collapse of Numidian, Roman, Vandal, and Byzantine rule; Turkish invasion; 16th-c; French colonial campaign in 19th-c led to French control from 1902; guerrilla war (1954–62) with French forces by the National Liberation Front (FLN) led to independence, 1962; first President of the republic, Ahmed Ben Bella, replaced after coup, 1965; new con-

stitution, 1976; military took control of government in 1992, and a state of emergency declared; continuing violence involving Islamic fundamentalists, including attacks on foreigners, from 1993; legislative power shared by the president and National Assembly.

Head of State
1999–   Abdelaziz Bouteflika

Head of Government
2006–   Abdelaziz Belkhadem

☐ International Airport   ∴ World heritage site

AMERICAN SAMOA >> UNITED STATES OF AMERICA

ANDORRA

Local name Vallée d'Andorre (French), Valls d'Andorra (Spanish)

Timezone GMT +1

Area 453 km²/175 sq mi

Population total (2002e) 66 500

Status Independent State

Capital Andorra la Vella

Languages Catalan (official), French, Spanish

Ethnic groups Catalan (50%), Andorran (29%), French (8%), Portuguese (7%)

Religion Roman Catholic (94%)

Physical features Mountainous country, located on the S slopes of the C Pyrénées between France and Spain, peaks reaching 2946 m/9665 ft at Coma Pedrosa; two valleys (del Norte and del Orient) of the R Valira.

Climate Alpine climate: heavy snow in winter, warm summers; average annual temperature 2°C (Jan), 19°C (Jul); lowest average monthly rainfall, 34 mm/1.34 in (Jan).

Currency 1 Euro (EUR) = 100 cents (previous to February 2002, 1 French Franc (FRF) = 100 centimes, 1 peseta (ESA, ESB) = 100 céntimos)

HUMAN GEOGRAPHY

Andorra (continued)

Economy No restriction on currency exchange, and no direct value-added taxes, therefore a marketing centre for goods imported from Europe and Asia; commerce, agriculture; skiing at five mountain resorts; in recent years, textiles, publishing, leather, mineral water, tourism.

GDP (2000e) $1.3 bn, per capita $19 000

History One of the oldest states in Europe, under the joint protection of France and Spain since 1278; Co-Princes of Principality are the President of France and the Bishop of Urgel; General Council of the Valley appoints the head of the government; independent state since 1993.

Heads of State (Co-Princes)
President of France
Bishop of Urgel, Spain

Head of Government (chief executive)
1994–2005 Marc Forné Molné
2005–   Albert Pintat

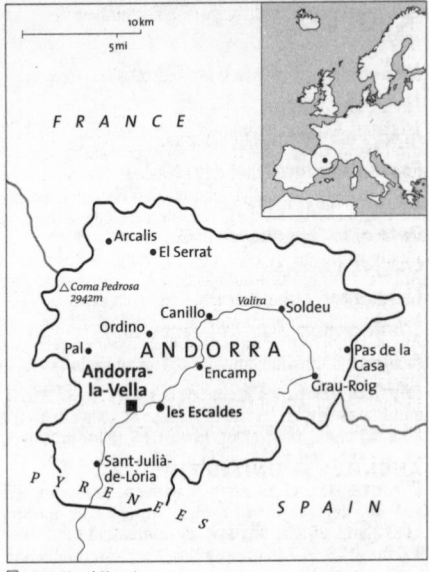

☐ International Airport

ANGOLA

Local name Angola

Timezone GMT +1

Area 1 245 790 km²/480 875 sq mi

Population total (2002e) 10 593 000

Status Republic

Date of independence 1975

Capital Luanda

Languages Portuguese (official), Bantu languages, including: Ovimbundu, Kimbundu, Bakongo, Chokwe

Ethnic groups Ovimbundu (37%), Mbundu (22%), Bakongo (13%), Lunda-Tchokwe (5%); also Nganguela, Nyaneka-Humbe, Herero, Ambo, Portuguese

Religions Traditional religions (12%), Roman Catholic (68%), Protestant (20%)

Physical features Located in SW Africa; narrow coastal plain; in S and E the planalto central (central plateau, continuation of great SW African plateau), covers c.60% of the country; in N, highland plateau, mean elevation 1200 m/4000 ft; highest point, Serro Môco 2619 m/8592 ft; coastal desert in W; in E, upland escarpments; c.40% of land forested.

Climate tropical plateau climate; at Huambo, on the plateau, average annual rainfall 1450 mm/57 in; rainfall varies greatly from SW to NE (negligible rainfall on SW coastal desert caused by Benguela current); average daily temperatures 24–9°C; temperature much reduced on the coast, which is semi-desert as far N as Luanda.

Currency 1 New Kwanza (AOK) = 100 Iweis

Economy Reserves of several minerals; extraction and refining of oil (mainly off the coast of Cabinda Province)

☐ International Airport

provides over 90% of current export earnings; diamond exporter; large producer of honey; principal livestock are cattle, goats, pigs, sheep; agriculture and fishing (mackerel and sardines) industries small; several airfields and railways.

GDP (2002e) $18.36 bn, per capita $1700

HDI (2002) 0.403

History Angola became a Portuguese colony in 1482 after exploration; slave trade flourished, causing friction and war (in early 17th-c, c.10 000 slaves were exported from Luanda annually); boundaries formally defined during the Berlin West Africa Congress (1884–5); became an overseas province of Portugal; 1951; Portuguese finally withdrew in 1975, and the People's Republic of Angola achieved full independence; civil war followed independence, involving three internal factions – the Marxist MPLA (Popular Movement for the Liberation of Angola), UNITA (the National Union for the Total Independence of Angola), and the FNLA (National Front for the Liberation of Angola); Cuban combat troops arrived in 1976, at request of MPLA; at the end of 1988, Geneva agreement linked arrangements for independence of Namibia with withdrawal of Cuban troops, and the cessation of South African attacks and support for UNITA; peace agreement in 1991 established a one-party state, governed by a president, Council of Ministers, and National People's Assembly; adopted the name Republic of Angola; first multi-party legislative elections held in 1992; MPLA victory rejected by UNITA led to resumption of conflict in 1993; Lusaka peace protocol, October 1994; withdrawal of UN peace-keeping force (Jan 1999) as fighting resumed between government and UNITA forces; peace agreement signed, 2002; lifting of UN economic sanctions against UNITA (Dec 2002).

Head of State
1979–   José Eduardo dos Santos

Head of Government
1999–2002 José Eduardo dos Santos
2002–   Fernando da Piedade Dias dos Santos

ANGUILLA >> UNITED KINGDOM

ANTIGUA AND BARBUDA

Local name Antigua and Barbuda

Timezone GMT –4

Area 442 km²/171 sq mi; (Antigua: 280 km²/108 sq mi; Barbuda: 161 km²/62 sq mi; Redonda: 1 km²/0.4 sq mi)

Population total (2002e) 76 400

Status Independent republic within the Commonwealth

Date of independence 1981

Capital St John's (on Antigua)

Language English (official)

Ethnic groups African descent (92%), Portuguese, Lebanese, British (4%)

Religions Anglican (80%), Roman Catholic (10%)

Physical features Group of three islands in the Leeward group of the Lesser Antilles, E Caribbean; W part of Antigua rises to 470 m/1542 ft at Boggy Peak; Barbuda is a flat coral island reaching only 44 m/144 ft at its highest point, with a large lagoon on its W side; Redonda is an uninhabited, volcanic island, rising to 305 m/1000 ft at its highest point.

Climate Tropical; temperatures range from 24°C (Jan) to 27°C (Aug–Sep); mean annual rainfall 1000 mm/40 in.

Currency 1 East Caribbean Dollar (XCD) = 100 cents

Economy Tourism; sugar (40% of national income, marked decline in 1960s, now recovering); cotton.

GDP (2002e) $750 mn, per capita $11 000

HDI (2002) 0.800

History Antigua claimed for Spain by Columbus, 1493; colonized by British, 1632; ceded to Britain, 1667; Barbuda colonized from Antigua, 1661; administered as part of the Leeward Is Federation, 1871–1956; associated state of the

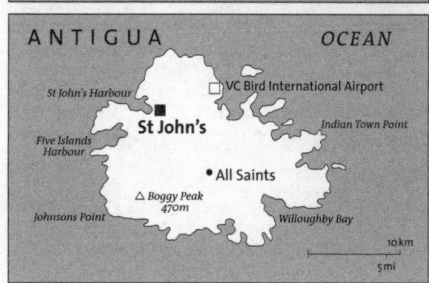

□ International Airport

UK, 1967; independence achieved, 1981; legislative power is vested in a bicameral parliament; Governor-General appoints the Prime Minister and Cabinet.

Head of State
(British monarch represented by Governor-General)
1993–   Sir James Carlisle

Head of Government
1994–2004 Lester Bird
2004–   Baldwin Spencer

ANTILLES, NETHERLANDS >> NETHERLANDS

HUMAN GEOGRAPHY

ARGENTINA

Local name Argentina

Timezone GMT –3

Area American continent: 2780092 km²/1073115 sq mi on Antarctic continent: 964250 km²/372200 sq mi

Population total (2002e) 36446000

Status Republic

Date of independence 1816

Capital Buenos Aires

Language Spanish (official)

Ethnic groups European origin (c.85%), mestizo European/Indian origin (15%)

Religions Roman Catholic (90%), Protestant and Jewish minorities

Physical features Divided into four regions: subtropical NE plains, the Pampa, Patagonia, and the Andes; Andes stretch the entire length of Argentina (N–S), forming the boundary with Chile; highest peak, Aconcagua 6960 m/22831 ft; uneven, semi-desert, arid steppes in the S (Patagonia); grassy, treeless Pampa to E; N drained by the Paraguay, Paraná, and Uruguay rivers, which join in the R Plate estuary; island of Tierra del Fuego off the S tip.

Climate Moderately humid sub-tropical climate in the NE; average annual temperature 16°C; average annual rainfall 500–1000 mm/20–40 in; semi-arid in interior S lowlands; Pampa temperate, dry in W and humid in E, with temperatures ranging from tropical to moderately cool; S directly influenced by strong prevailing westerlies; serious flooding in NE (May 2003).

Currency 1 Argentinian Nuevo Peso (ARS) = 100 centavos (formerly the austral (ARA))

Economy Major contribution to economy from agricultural produce and meat processing; deposits of oil and natural gas, chiefly off the coast of Patagonia; important reserves of iron ore, coal, copper, lead, zinc, gold, silver, uranium, manganese.

GDP (2002) $403.8 bn, per capita $10500

HDI (2002) 0.844

History Pre-colonially, nomadic Indian hunters lived in S and Inca farmers in NW; after long battle, settled in the 16th-c by Spanish; independence as federal Republic

□ International Airport   ∴ World heritage site

of Argentina, 1816, and United Provinces of Río de la Plata established; dictatorship of Juan Manuel de Rosas during 1829–52; federal constitution, 1853; ranchers' oligarchy of 1916 ended by military coup, 1930; acquisition of Gran Chaco after war with Paraguay, 1865–70; considerable European settlement since opening up of the Pampas in 19th-c; Juan Perón elected president (1946, 1973); succeeded by his wife Isabel (Martínez de Perón) who was deposed in 1976; attempt to control Falkland Is (1982) failed following war with UK; successive military governments, until federal constitution re-established in 1983; governed by a President and a bicameral National Congress, with a Chamber of Deputies and a Senate; four presidents resigned amid riots and lootings in protests over stringent economic sanctions (2001–2).

Head of State/Government
2002–3   Eduardo Duhalde
2003–   Néstor Kirchner

ARMENIA

Local name Hayastan

Timezone GMT +3

Area 29800 km²/11500 sq mi

Population total (2002e) 3800000

Status Republic

Date of independence 1991

Capital Yerevan

Language Armenian (official)

Ethnic groups (1991) Armenian (90%), Azer (3%), Kurd (2%), Russian (2%) (ethnic conflict since 1990 makes accurate statistical analysis impossible)

Religions Christian (Armenian Church), Russian Orthodox

Physical features Mountainous region in S Transcaucasia, rising to 4090 m/13418 ft at Mt Aragats (W); rivers include Razdan and Vorotan; largest mountain lake is the Sevan, 1401 km²/541 sq mi – the main source of irrigation system and hydroelectric power.

Climate Varies with elevation; chiefly dry and continental with considerable regional variation.

Currency 1 Dram (AMD) = 100 loumas

Economy Large mineral resources, chiefly copper; also molybdenum, gold, silver; electrical equipment and machinery, chemicals, textiles, cognac; agriculture based on fruits, wheat, wine grapes, cotton, tobacco.

GDP (2002e) $12.13 bn, per capita $3600

HDI (2002) 0.754

History Proclaimed a Soviet Socialist Republic in 1920; constituent republic of the USSR from 1936; civil war over Nagorno-Karabakh began in 1989; declaration of independence, 1990; independence recognized and joined CIS, 1991; ongoing conflict with Azerbaijan over disputed enclave of Nagorno-Karabakh.

Head of State
1998–   Robert Kocharyan

Head of Government
2000–   Andranik Margarian

ARUBA >> NETHERLANDS, THE

☐ International Airport

AUSTRALIA

Local name Australia

Timezone GMT +8 (Western Australia); GMT +10 (New South Wales, Queensland, Tasmania, Victoria, Australian Capital Territory); GMT +9.5 (South Australia, Northern Territory)

Area 7 692 300 km²/2 969 228 sq mi

Population total (2002e) 19 702 000

Status Independent state within the Commonwealth

Date of independence 1901

Capital Canberra

Language English (official)

Ethnic groups European descent (95%), Asian and Pacific (2%), Aboriginal (1%)

Religions Christian (74%, including Roman Catholic 27%, Anglican 24%)

Physical features Smallest continent; consists largely of plains and plateaux, most of which average 600 m/ 2000 ft above sea level; four main regions: Western Craton (or Western Shield), the Great Artesian Basin, the Great Dividing Range (or Eastern Uplands), and the Flinders-Mt Lofty ranges; W Australian Plateau occupies nearly half of the country; MacDonnell Ranges lie in the centre, highest point Mt Liebig, 1525 m/5000 ft; most of the plateau is dry, barren desert; Nullarbor Plain in the S is crossed by the Trans-Australian Railway; Great Dividing Range parallel to the Great Barrier Reef, rising to 2 228 m/7310 ft at Mt Kosciuszko, Australia's highest point; Great Barrier Reef off NE coast stretches for over 1900 km/ 1200 mi; island of Tasmania rises to 1617 m/5305 ft at Mt Ossa; separated from the mainland by the Bass Strait; longest river is the Darling, a tributary of the Murray;

other chief tributaries, the Murrumbidgee, Lachlan; Lake Eyre occupies 8800 km²/3400 sq mi; c.18% of area forested; c.6% arable.

Climate More than a third of Australia receives under 260 mm/10 in mean annual rainfall; less than a third receives over 500 mm/20 in; prolonged drought and frequent heatwaves in many areas; average daily temperature 26–34°C (Nov) and 19–31°C (Jul) in N; rainfall varies from 286 mm/15.2 in (Jan) to zero (Jul); fertile land with a temperate climate and reliable rainfall only in the lowlands and valleys near the E and SE coast, and a small part of the SW corner; Tasmania and Mt Kosciuszko have snowfields in winter.

Currency 1 Australian Dollar (AUD) = 100 cents

Economy Free-enterprise economy; world's largest wool producer, and a top exporter of veal and beef; most important crop is wheat; major mineral producer; petroleum reserves, coal, bauxite, nickel, lead, zinc, copper, tin, uranium, iron ore, and other minerals in early 1960s; manufacturing industry expanded rapidly since 1945, especially engineering, shipbuilding, car manufacture, metals, textiles, clothing, chemicals, food processing, wine; self-sufficient in lumber; marine fishing (especially tuna) important, as are tourism and winter sports.

GDP (2002e) $525.5 bn, per capita $26 900

HDI (2002) 0.939

History Aboriginal people thought to have arrived in Australia from SE Asia c.40 000 years ago; first European visitors were the Dutch, who explored the Gulf of Carpentaria in 1606 and settled in 1616; became known as New Holland in 1644; Captain James Cook arrived in Botany Bay in 1770, and claimed the E coast for Britain; New South Wales established as a penal colony in 1788; gold discov-

Australia (continued)

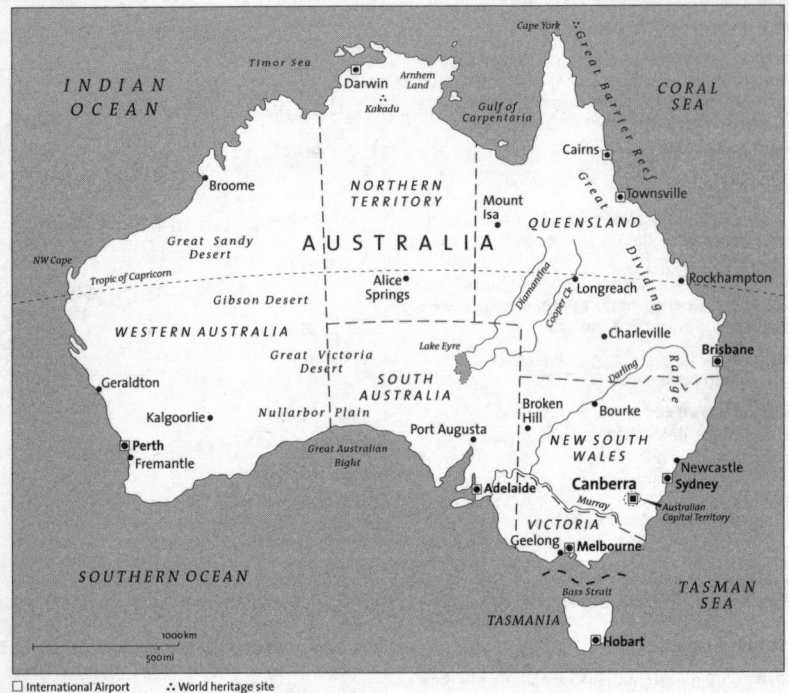

□ International Airport   ∴ World heritage site

ered in New South Wales and Victoria in 1851, and in Western Australia in 1892; transportation of convicts to E Australia ended in 1840, but continued until 1853 in Tasmania and 1868 in Western Australia; during this period the colonies drafted their own constitutions and set up governments: New South Wales (1855), Tasmania and Victoria (1856), South Australia (1857), Queensland (1860), and Western Australia (1890); Commonwealth of Australia established in 1901, with Canberra subsequently chosen as capital (1901); policy of preventing immigration by non-whites remained in force from the end of the 19th-c until 1974; issue of Aboriginal civil rights a major issue since the 1960s; Northern Territory self-governing since 1978; divided into six states and two territories: each state has its own legislature, government, and constitution; legislature comprises a bicameral Federal Parliament with a Prime Minister and Cabinet; British monarch is Head of State, represented by a Governor-General; republican movement growing since the late 1980s; proposal on the issue rejected by referendum, late 1999.

Head of State
(British monarch represented by Governor-General)
2003–   Michael Jeffery

Head of Government
1991–6   Paul Keating
1996–   John Howard

>> *Political leaders and rulers, p.196*

Australian States

Name	Area		State capital
	km²	sq mi	
Australian Capital Territory	2 400	930	Canberra
New South Wales	801 400	309 400	Sydney
Northern Territory	1 346 200	519 800	Darwin
Queensland	1 727 200	666 900	Brisbane
South Australia	984 000	379 900	Adelaide
Tasmania	67 800	26 200	Hobart
Victoria	227 600	87 900	Melbourne
Western Australia	2 525 500	975 000	Perth

External territories

Name	Area		Population total	Date under Australian administration
	km²	sq mi		
The Ashmore and Cartier Islands	3.0	2.0	Uninhabited	1931
Australian Antarctic Territory	6 043 852.0	2 332 927.0	Uninhabited	1936
Christmas Island	155.0	60.0	(2000e) 2700	1958
Cocos (Keeling) Islands	14.2	5.5	(2000e) 780	1955
Coral Sea Island	2.0*	0.8*	Uninhabited	1969
Heard Island and McDonald Islands	412.0	159.0	Uninhabited	1947
Norfolk Island	35.0	13.0	(2000e) 2200	1913

* Land figure only. Islands cover 1 000 000 km²/286 000 sq mi of ocean.

HUMAN GEOGRAPHY

AUSTRIA

Local name Österreich

Timezone GMT +1

Area 83 854 km²/32 368 sq mi

Population total (2002e) 8 077 000

Status Republic

Date of independence 1955

Capital Vienna (Wien)

Languages German (official), Croatian, Slovene

Ethnic groups Austrian (99%), Croatian, Slovakian, Turkish, German

Religions Roman Catholic (85%), Protestant (12%), Muslim (1%), Jewish (1%)

Physical features One of the most mountainous countries in Europe; lies at E end of the Alps; highest point, Grossglockner, 3797 m/12 457 ft; largest lake, Neusiedler See; divided into three regions: Alpine; the highland Bohemian Massif; and the hilly lowland region, including the Vienna basin; R Danube drains whole country; most densely forested country in central Europe (40% of land is forested).

Climate Three climatic regions: the Alps (often sunny in winter, but cloudy in summer); the Danube valley and Vienna basin (driest region); and the SE, a region of often severe winters but warmer summers; average annual temperature: 2°C (Jan), 20°C (Jul) in Vienna; most rain in summer months; average annual rainfall 868 mm/ 34 in; winters cold, especially with winds from the E or NE; humid, continental climate in NE.

Currency 1 Euro (EUR) = 100 cents (previous to February 2002, 1 Schilling (ATS) = 100 Groschen)

Economy Mixed free market; principal agricultural areas to the N of the Alps, and along both sides of the Danube; principal crops: cereals; dairy cattle and pigs; wine industry; wide range of metal and mineral resources; tourism (summer and winter); well-developed transportation networks; river ports at Linz and Vienna; airports at Vienna, Graz, Linz, Klagenfurt, Salzburg, Innsbruck; much power produced hydroelectrically.

GDP (2002e) $227.7 bn, per capita $27 900

☐ International Airport

HDI (2002) 0.926

History Early Iron-Age settlement at Hallstatt; later Illyrian settlers driven out by the Celts; part of Roman Empire until 5th-c, then occupied by Germanic tribes, most significantly Bavarians; Charlemagne drove out the Slavic Avars who also settled in the region; area became a duchy and passed to the Habsburg family in 1282, who made it the foundation of their Empire; Hungarian nationalism and Habsburg defeats in 19th-c led to the dual monarchy of Austria–Hungary from 1867; Nationalist protest resulted in assassination of Archduke Ferdinand in 1914 and World War 1, which ended the Austrian Empire; republic established, 1918; annexed by the German Reich in 1938 (the Anschluss) and named Ostmark; occupied by British, American, French, and Russian troops from 1945; obtained independence, 1955; neutrality declared, since when Austria has been a haven for many refugees; governed by a Federal Assembly; Federal President appoints a Federal Chancellor.

Head of State (Federal President)
1992–2004 Thomas Klestil
2004– Heinz Fischer

Head of Government (Federal Chancellor)
2000– Wolfgang Schüssel

AZERBAIJAN

Local name Azerbaijan

Timezone GMT +3

Area 86 600 km²/33 428 sq mi

Population total (2002e) 8 176 000

Status Republic

Date of independence 1991

Capital Baku

Languages Azeri (official), Russian

Ethnic groups Azeri (83%), Russian (6%), Armenian

(6%) (ethnic conflict since 1990 makes accurate statistical analysis impossible)

Religion Shi'ite Muslim

Physical features Mountainous country in E Transcaucasia: 10% of country is above 1494 m/4900 ft; 40% of land is lowland, 396–1494 m/1300–4900 ft; Bazar-Dyuzi rises to 4480 m/14 698 ft; rivers include the Kara and Araks.

Climate Central and eastern Azerbaijan dry and subtropical with mild winters and long, hot summers (often as hot as 43°C); SE is humid with annual rainfall of 1193–1396 mm/47–55 in.

HUMAN GEOGRAPHY

Azerbaijan (continued)

Currency 1 Manat (AZM) = 100 gopik

Economy Once the former Soviet Union's most important oil-producing region, but now in decline; manufacturing industries include building materials, chemicals, textiles; mineral resources include natural gas, iron, copper, lead, zinc; exports include cotton, wheat, tobacco.

GDP (2002e) $28.61 bn, per capita $3700

HDI (2002) 0.741

History Proclaimed a Soviet Socialist Republic, 1920; constituent republic of the USSR, 1936; declaration of independence; 1991; became a member of UN, 1992; ongoing conflict with Armenia over disputed enclave of Nagorno-Karabakh; governed by a President, Prime Minister, and National Council.

Head of State
2003–   Ilham Aliyev

Head of Government
2003–   Artur Rasizade

AZORES >> PORTUGAL

☐ International Airport   ⌐ ˙⌐ Nagorno-Karabakh

BAHAMAS

Local name Bahamas

Timezone GMT −5

Area 13 934 km²/5 378 sq mi

Population total (2002e) 309 000

Status Independent state within the Commonwealth

Date of independence 1973

Capital Nassau

Language English (official)

Ethnic groups African (85%), European/N American descent (15%)

Religions Baptist (29%), Anglican (29%), Roman Catholic (23%)

Physical features Coral archipelago of 700 islands and 2400 uninhabited cays, forming a chain extending c.800 km/500 mi SE from the coast of Florida; population centres on the two oceanic banks of Little and Great Bahama; highest point, Mt Alvernia, 120 m/394 ft.

Climate Sub-tropical; average temperatures 21°C (Jan) and 27°C (Jul); mean annual rainfall 750–1500 mm/ 30–60 in; hurricanes frequent (Jun–Nov).

Currency 1 Bahamian Dollar (BSD) = 100 cents

Economy Market economy based on tourism; important financial centre (no income tax); oil refining, fishing, rum and liqueur distilling; cement; pharmaceuticals.

GDP (2002e) $4.59 bn, per capita $15 300

HDI (2002) 0.826

History Visited by Columbus in 1492, but first perma-

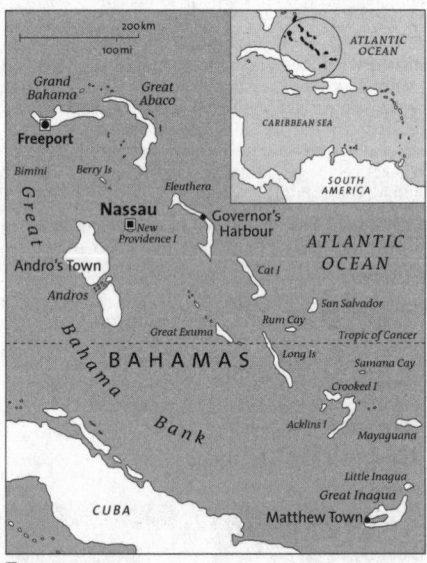

☐ International Airport

nent European settlement not until 1647 by British and Bermudan religious refugees; British Crown Colony from 1717; independence, 1973; governed by a bicameral Parliament.

Head of State
(British monarch represented by Governor-General)
2001–5   Dame Ivy Dumont
2006–   Arthur Dion Hanna

Head of Government
1992–2002 Hubert Alexander Ingraham
2002–   Perry Christie

BAHRAIN

Local name al-Bahrayn

Timezone GMT +3

Area 678 km²/262 sq mi

Population total (2002e) 672 000

Status Independent state

Date of independence 1971

Capital Manama

Languages Arabic (official), Farsi, Urdu, and English

Ethnic groups Bahraini Arab (63%), Asian (13%), Arab (10%), Iranian (9%)

Religions Muslim (Shi'ite 65%), Sunni 35%)

Physical features Island of Bahrain c.48 km/30 mi long, 13–16 km/8–10 mi wide, area 562 km²/217 sq mi; highest point Jabal Dukhan, 135 m/443 ft; largely bare and infertile.

Climate Temperate (Dec–Mar); hot and humid (particularly Jun–Sep); cool N/NE winds with a little rain (Dec–Mar); average annual rainfall 35 mm/1.4 in; average annual temperature 19°C (Jan), 36°C (Jul).

Currency 1 Bahrain Dinar (BHD) = 1000 fils

Economy Major centre for oil trading, banking, commerce.

GDP (2002e) $9.91 bn, per capita $15 100

HDI (2002) 0.831

History Flourishing centre of trade during 2000–1800 BC; treaty of protection with the UK, 1861; independence in 1971, with a constitutional monarchy governed by an Emir; National Assembly dissolved in 1975 and not yet revived; historic territorial dispute with Qatar over

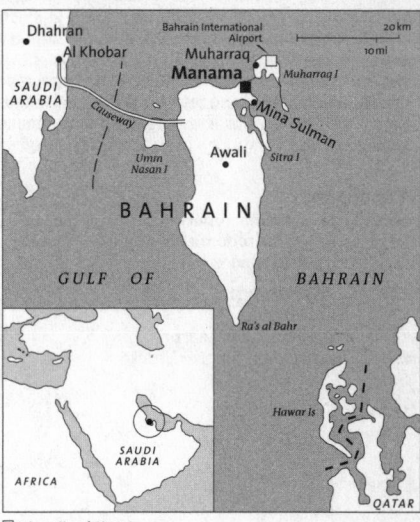

□ International Airport

Hawar Is began with brief occupation of Fasht al-Dibal by Qatari troops, 1986; joined UN coalition during the Iraqi invasion of Kuwait, 1990; became monarchy, 2002.

Head of State (Emir, title changed to King when country officially changed its status from an emirate to a monarchy, 2002)
1999–   Shaikh Hamad II bin Isa al-Khalifa

Head of Government
1971–   Shaikh Khalifa bin Salman al-Khalifa

BALEARIC ISLANDS >> SPAIN

BANGLADESH

Local name Bangladesh

Timezone GMT +6

Area 143 998 km²/55 583 sq mi

Population total (2002e) 133 377 000

Status Republic

Date of independence 1971

Capital Dhaka

Languages Bengali (official), also local dialects and English widely spoken

Ethnic groups Bengali (98%), Bihari (1%), tribal: Garo, Khasi, Santal (1%)

Religions Muslim (86%), Hindu (12%), Buddhist (1%), small Christian majority

Physical features Mainly a vast, low-lying alluvial plain, cut by a network of rivers, canals, swamps, marshes; main rivers the Ganges (Padma), Brahmaputra

(Jamuna), Meghna; joining in the S to form the largest delta in the world, subject to frequent flooding (notably in 1998 and 2004); Chittagong Hill Tracts in the E rise to 1200 m/3900 ft.

Climate Tropical climate; monsoon season (Jun–Oct).

Currency 1 Taka (BDT) = 100 paisa

Economy Agriculture, especially rice (employs 86% of population); and supplies 80% of the world's jute; also paper, aluminium, textiles, glass, shipbuilding, fishing, natural gas.

GDP (2002e) $238.2 bn, per capita $1800

HDI (2002) 0.478

History Part of the State of Bengal until Muslim East Bengal created in 1905, separate from Hindu West Bengal; reunited, 1911; partitioned again in 1947, with West Bengal remaining in India and East Bengal forming East Pakistan; rebellion in 1971 led to independence as the People's Republic of Bangladesh; political unrest led to

HUMAN GEOGRAPHY

Bangladesh (continued)

suspension of constitution, and assassination of first President, Sheikh Mujib, 1975; further coups in 1975, 1977, and 1982; constitution restored, 1986; last military dictator, Hossain Mohammad Ershad, overthrown, 1990; constitutional amendments in 1991 restricted powers of President to ceremonial and restored full powers to unicameral legislature, *Jatiya Sangsad*; further amendment in 2004 reserved 45 seats for women in the 300-member legislature.

Head of State
1996–2001 Shehabuddin Ahmed
2001–2   A.Q.M. Badruddoza Chowdhury
2002–   Iajuddin Ahmed

Head of Government
2001–6   Khaleda Zia
2006–7   Iajuddin Ahmed *Interim*
2007–   Fakhruddin Ahmed *Caretaker*

☐ International Airport   ∴ World heritage site

BARBADOS

Local name Barbados

Timezone GMT –4

Area 430 km²/166 sq mi

Population total (2002e) 270 000

Status Independent state within the Commonwealth

Date of independence 1966

Capital Bridgetown

Language English (official)

Ethnic groups African (80%), mixed race (16%)

Religions Anglican (40%), Protestant (15%), Roman Catholic (4%)

Physical features Small, triangular island in the Atlantic Ocean; length 32 km/20 mi (NW–SE); rising to 340 m/1115 ft at Mt Hillaby; ringed by a coral reef.

Climate Tropical climate, with average annual temperature 27°C; mean annual rainfall 1420 mm/56 in.

Currency 1 Barbados Dollar (BBD) = 100 cents

Economy Market economy based on tourism and sugar cane; cotton, bananas; natural gas; textiles.

GDP (2002e) $4.153 bn, per capita $1500

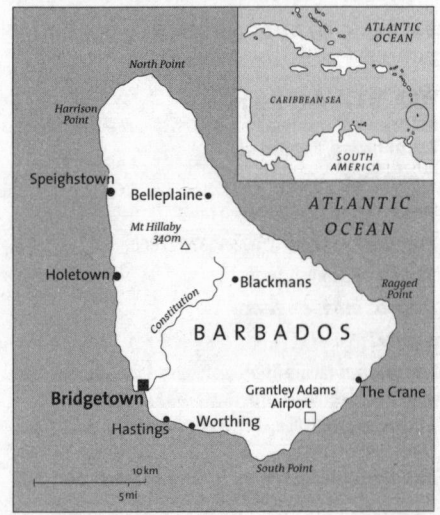

☐ International Airport

HDI (2002) 0.871

History Colonized by the British, 1627; self-government, 1961; independent within the Commonwealth, 1966; executive power rests with the Prime Minister, appointed by a Governor-General, the Senate, and the House of Assembly.

Head of State
(British monarch represented by Governor-General)
1996–   Sir Clifford Husbands

Head of Government
1994–   Owen Seymour Arthur

BELARUS

Local name Belarus

Timezone GMT +3

Area 207 600 km²/80 134 sq mi

Population total (2002e) 9 933 000

Status Republic

Date of independence 1991

Capital Minsk (Mensk)

Languages Belorussian (official), Russian

Ethnic groups (1989) Belorussian (78%), Russian (13%), Polish (4%), Ukrainian (3%), Jewish (1%)

Religions Roman Catholic, Orthodox

Physical features Hilly lowlands with marshes, swamps; Dzyarzhynskaya Mt rises to 346 m/1135 ft; largest lake, Narach; Belaruskaya Hrada, largest glacial ridge, runs NW into Minsk Upland; rivers include the Pripyat and Dnepr; Pripyat marshes in E.

Climate Varies from maritime, near Baltic, to continental and humid; average annual temperatures, 18°C (Jul), –6°C (Jan); average annual rainfall 550–700 mm/22–8 in.

Currency Belorussian Rouble (BYR) = 100 kopec

Economy Main exports include textiles, timber, chemical products, fertilizers, electrical goods; valuable resource: peat marshes.

GDP (2002e) $90.19 bn, per capita $8700

HDI (2002) 0.788

History Neolithic remains widespread; colonized by E Slavic tribes, 5th-c; Mongols conquered Slavs, 13th-c; Catherine the Great of Russia acquired E Belorussia (White Russia) in the first Polish partition in 1772; gained Minsk in 1793 and the remainder in 1795; W Belorussia ceded to Poland in 1921 as part of the Treaty of Riga which ended Soviet–Polish War; regained by Soviet Union as part of Nazi–Soviet Non-aggression Pact of 1939,

☐ International Airport

and Belorussia became Belorussian Soviet Socialist Republic; admitted to UN, 1945; declared independence, 1991; co-founder of Commonwealth of Independent States (CIS), 1991.

Head of State
1994–   Alexander Lukashenko

Head of Government
2003–   Sergey Sidorski

BELAU

Local names Belau, also Pelau, Palau

Timezone GMT +10

Area 494 km²/191 sq mi

Population total (2002e) 19 900

Status Republic

Date of independence 1994

Capital Koror

Languages Palauan, English

Ethnic groups Palauan (83%)

Religions Christianity (66%), traditional beliefs (25%)

Physical features A group of c. 350 small islands and islets, c. 960 km/600 mi E of the Philippines; most W

Belau (continued)

group of the Caroline Is; largest island, Babeldoab (367 km²/142 sq mi).

Climate Warm all year, with high humidity; average annual temperature, 27°C; average annual rainfall, 3810 mm/150 in; typhoons common.

Currency US dollar (USD) = 100 cents

Economy Tourism, taro, pineapple, breadfruit, bananas, yams, citrus fruit, coconuts, pepper, fishing.

GDP (2001e) $174.8 mn, per capita $9000

History The smallest of the four political units to emerge out of the US Trust Territory of the Pacific Islands; organized into 16 states; held by Germany, 1899–1914; mandated to Japan by League of Nations, 1920; invaded by USA, 1944; compact of free association with the USA, signed in 1982, but not confirmed until 1993; independence, 1994; governed by a President and a bicameral National Congress; constitution also provides for an advisory body of chiefs.

Head of State
2001–   Tommy Remengesau

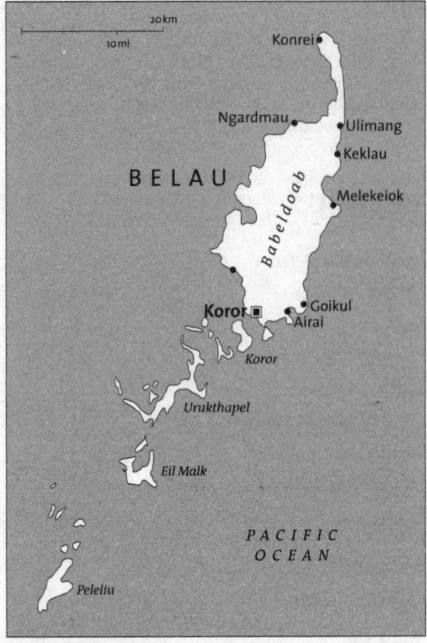

☐ International Airport

BELGIUM

Local names Belgique (French), België (Flemish)

Timezone GMT +1

Area 30 540 km²/11 788 sq mi

Population total (2002e) 10 280 000

Status Kingdom

Date of independence 1830

Capital Brussels

Languages Flemish/Dutch (56%), French (32%), German (1%); (Brussels officially bilingual Flemish/French)

Ethnic groups Flemish (Teutonic origin) (55%), Walloon (French Latin) (33%)

Religions Roman Catholic (90%), Muslim (1%), Protestant (0.4%)

Physical features Mostly low-lying, with some hills in the SE region (Ardennes), average elevation 300–500 m/ 1000–1600 ft; large areas of fertile soil, intensively cultivated for many centuries; main river systems linked by complex network of canals; low-lying, dune-fringed coastline.

Climate Cool and temperate with strong maritime influences; average annual temperatures 2°C (Jan), 18°C (Jul) in Brussels; average annual rainfall 825 mm/35 in.

Currency 1 Euro (EUR) = 100 cents (previous to February 2002, 1 Belgian Franc (BEF) = 100 centimes)

Economy One of the earliest countries in Europe to industrialize, using rich coalfields of the Ardennes;

☐ International Airport

Flanders textile industry; long-standing centre for European trade; major iron and steel industry, with wide range of metallurgical and engineering products; agriculture mainly livestock; full economic union (Benelux Economic Union) between Belgium, Netherlands, and Luxembourg, 1948; Brussels is the headquarters of several major international organizations, including the Commission of the EU.

GDP (2002e) $299.7 bn, per capita $29 200

HDI (2002) 0.939

History Part of the Roman Empire until 2nd-c; then

became part of the Frankish Empire following Celt and Germanic invasions; ruled by the Habsburgs from 1477 until the Peace of Utrecht in 1713, when sovereignty passed to Austria; conquered by the French, 1794; part of the French Republic and Empire until 1815, then united with the Netherlands; Belgian rebellion against Dutch rule in 1830, led to recognition as an independent kingdom under Leopold of Saxe-Coburg; occupied by Germany in both World Wars; became a constitutional monarchy with bicameral Parliament; political tension between Walloons in S and Flemings in N, 1980; federal constitution divided Belgium into the autonomous regions of Flanders, Wallonia, and Brussels, 1989; Constitutional Monarch has limited powers; a Chamber of Deputies and a Senate.

Head of State (Monarch)
1950–93   Baudouin I
1993–   Albert II

Head of Government
1992–9   Jean-Luc Dehaene
1999–   Guy Verhofstadt

BELIZE

Local name Belice (Spanish)

Timezone GMT –6

Area 22963 km²/8864 sq mi

Population total (2002e) 251000

Status Independent state within the Commonwealth

Date of independence 1981

Capital Belmopan

Languages English (official), Spanish, Garifuna, Maya

Ethnic groups Creole (40%), mestizo (33%), Mayan (9.5%), Carib (8%), Garifuna (8%)

Religions Roman Catholic (62%), Protestant (30%)

Physical features Located in Central America; extensive coastal plain; swampy in the N, fertile in the S; Maya Mts extend almost to the E coast, rising to 1120 m/ 3674 ft at Victoria Peak; Belize R flows W–E; inner coastal waters protected by world's second longest barrier reef.

Climate Generally sub-tropical, but tempered by trade winds; average annual temperature 24°C (Jan), 27°C (Jul); variable rainfall; average annual rainfall 1295 mm/51 in (N), 4445 mm/175 in (S); hurricanes frequent.

Currency 1 Belize Dollar (BZD) = 100 cents

Economy Developing free-market economy based on timber and forest products, more recently on agriculture.

GDP (2002e) $1.28 bn, per capita $4900

HDI (2002) 0.784

History Evidence of early Mayan settlement; colonized in the 17th-c by shipwrecked British sailors and disbanded soldiers from Jamaica; created a British colony, 1862; administered from Jamaica until 1884; internal

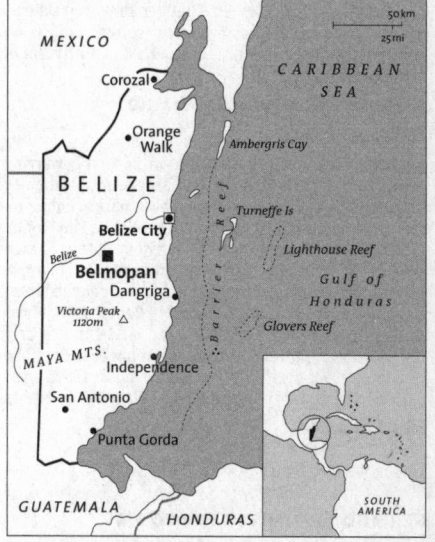

□ International Airport   ∴ World heritage site

self-government, 1964; changed name from British Honduras to Belize, 1973; full independence, 1981; Guatemalan claims over Belize territory have led to a continuing British military presence; Guatemala accord, respecting Belize self-determination, 1991; bicameral National Assembly.

Head of State
(British Monarch represented by Governor-General)
1993–   Colville Norbert Young

Head of Government
1993–8   Manuel Esquivel
1998–   Said Musa

BENIN

Local name Bénin

Timezone GMT +1

Area 112622 km²/43472 sq mi

Population total (2002e) 6788000

Status Republic

Date of independence 1960

Capital Porto Novo (nominal), Cotonou (political and economic)

Languages French (official), Fon (47%), Adja (12%), Bariba (10%), Yoruba (9%), Fulani (6%), Somba (5%), Aizo (5%)

Ethnic groups Fon (40%), Yoruba (10%), Bariba (20%), minority of Fulani nomads

Religions Traditional beliefs (c.70%), Christian (15%), Muslim (13%)

Physical features Located in N Africa; rises from a 100 km/62 mi-long, sandy coast with lagoons to low-lying plains; savannah plateau, c. 400 m/1300 ft, in N; descend

HUMAN GEOGRAPHY

Benin (continued)

to forested lowlands in S fringing the Bight of Benin; Atakora Mts rise to over 500 m/1600 ft in NW; rivers include Ouémé, Alibori, Mekrou; Pendjari National Park in NW.

Climate Tropical climate divided into three zones: in the S, rain throughout the year, especially during the Guinea Monsoon (May–Oct); in C, two rainy seasons (peaks in May–Jun and Oct); in the N, one rainy season (Jul–Sep); dry season in N (Oct–Apr): hot, with low humidity, subject to the dry harmattan wind from the NE.

Currency 1 CFA Franc (XAF) = 100 centimes

Economy Agriculture, especially palm-oil products, cashew nuts, maize, cassava, rice, cotton, coffee; no known natural resources in commercial quantity; small offshore oilfield.

GDP (2002e) $7.38 bn, per capita $1100

HDI (2002) 0.420

History Pre-colonially a collection of small, warring principalities, including the Fon Kingdom of Dahomey (founded 17th-c); Portuguese colonial activities centred on slave trade; subjugated by French, becoming the French Protectorate of Dahomey, 1892; territory within French West Africa from 1904; independent from 1960; Marxist-Leninist regime gained power, 1972; name changed from Dahomey to the People's Republic of Benin, 1975; Marxism-Leninism abandoned, 1989, and a new multi-party constitution approved, 1990; changed name to Republic of Benin, 1990; multi-party elections held, 1991; president elected for five-year term, and a National Assembly.

Head of State
1996–2006 Ahmed Kerekou
2006–   Yayi Boni

□ International Airport

Head of Government
1996–8   Adrien Houngbedji

BERMUDA >> UNITED KINGDOM

BHUTAN

Local name Druk-yul

Timezone GMT +5.5

Area 46 600 km²/18 000 sq mi

Population total (2002e) 1 996 000

Status Kingdom

Capital Thimphu

Languages Dzongkha (official) (60%), Nepalese (25%), English

Ethnic groups Bhote (60%), Nepalese (25%), indigenous or migrant tribes (15%)

Religions Lamaistic Buddhist (75%), Hindu (20%), Muslim (5%)

Physical features High peaks of E Himalayas in the N, over 7000m/23 000 ft; forested mountain ridges with fertile valleys descend to low foothills in the S; rivers include Wong Chu, Manas; permanent snowfields in the mountains; sub-tropical forest in S.

Climate Affected by altitude; snowcapped in glaciated N; average monthly temperatures 4°C (Jan), 17°C (Jul); torrential rain common, average 1000 mm/40 in (C valleys) and 5000 mm/200 in (S).

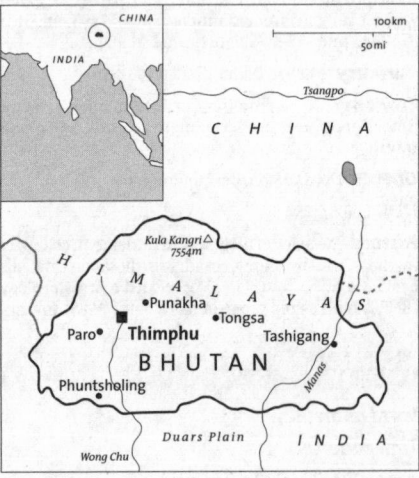

□ International Airport

Currency 1 Ngultrum (BTN) = 100 chetrum

Economy Largely based on agriculture, mainly rice, wheat, maize, mountain barley, potatoes, vegetables, fruit (especially oranges); also timber (large area of plantation forest); sales of tobacco products banned, 2004.

GDP (2002e) $2.7 bn, per capita $1300

HDI (2002) 0.494

History British involvement since treaty of 1774 with the East India Company; S part of the country annexed, 1865; Anglo-Bhutanese Treaty signed, in which Britain agreed not to interfere in internal affairs of Bhutan, 1910; similar treaty (Indo-Bhutan Treaty of Friendship) signed with India, 1949; governed by a maharajah from 1907, now addressed as King of Bhutan; National Assembly (Tsogdu) established, 1953; constitutional monarchy with power shared between the King, the Council of Ministers, the National Assembly, and the monastic head of the kingdom's Buddhist priesthood; King devolved executive powers to to Assembly and royal advisory council, 1998; separatist movements associated with Assam and Bodoland located in the S.

Head of State (Monarch)
1972–   Jigme Singye Wangchuk

Head of Government
2006–   Lyonpo Khandu Wangchuk

BOLIVIA

Local name Bolivia

Timezone GMT –4

Area 1 098 580 km²/424 052 sq mi

Population total (2002e) 8 401 000

Status Republic

Date of independence 1825

Capital La Paz (administrative), Sucre (legal)

Languages Spanish, Quechua, Aymará (all used officially)

Ethnic groups Mestizo (30%), Quechua (30%), Aymará (25%), white (15%)

Religions Roman Catholic (95%), Baha'i (3%)

Physical features Landlocked country, bounded W by the Cordillera Occidental of the Andes, rising to 6542 m/21 463 ft at Sajama; separated from the Cordillera Real to the E by the flat, 400 km/250 mi-long Altiplano plateau, 3600 m/11 800 ft; major lakes, Titicaca and Poopó.

Climate Varies with altitude, ranging from consistently warm (26°C) and damp conditions (1800 mm/71 in of rainfall per year) in NE rainforests of Amazon Basin, to drought conditions in S; over 500 m/16 000 ft, conditions become sub-polar.

Currency 1 Boliviano (BOB) = 100 centavos

Economy Dependent on minerals for foreign exchange; silver largely exhausted, but replaced by tin (a fifth of world supply); oil and natural-gas pipelines to Argentina and Chile; illegally-produced cocaine.

GDP (2002e) $21.15 bn, per capita $2500

HDI (2002) 0.653

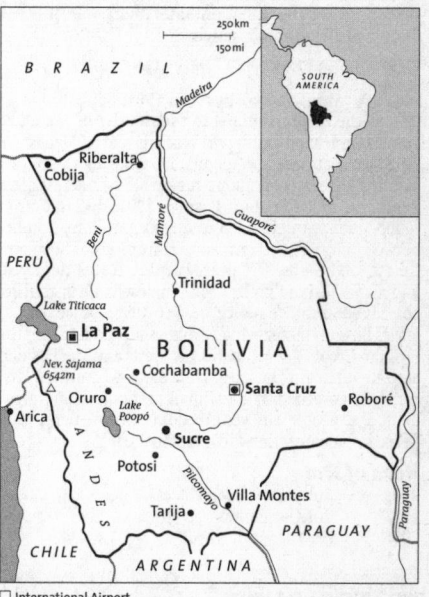

□ International Airport

History Part of Inca Empire, conquered by Spanish in 16th-c; independence after war of liberation, 1825; much territory lost after wars with neighbouring countries; several changes of government and military coups during 1964–82; returned to civilian rule, 1982; governed by a bicameral Congress and an elected President and Cabinet.

Head of State/Government
2003–5   Carlos Mesa
2005–   Evo Morales

BOSNIA–HERZEGOVINA

Local name Bosna-Hercegovina

Timezone GMT +2

Area 51 129 km²/19 736 sq mi

Population total (2002e) 3 964 000

Status Republic

Date of independence 1992

Capital Sarajevo

Language Serbian, Croatian, Bosnian

Ethnic groups (pre-civil war) Slav (44%), Serbian (31%), Croatian (17%)

Religions Muslim (Sunni), Serbian Orthodox, Roman Catholic

Physical features Mountainous region in the Balkan peninsula, noted for its stone gorges, lakes, rivers, mineral springs; reaches heights of 1800 m/6000 ft above

Bosnia-Herzegovina (continued)

sea level; principal rivers are Bosna, Una, Drina, Neretva, Sava; in the SW lies the dry, limestone plateau (karst).

Climate Ranges from Mediterranean to mildly continental; sirocco wind brings rain from SW; strong NE wind (bora) affects coastal area in winter.

Currency 1 Convertible Mark (BAM) = 100 convertible pfennigs

Economy Highly industrialized, particularly iron and steel; large cellulose factory at Banja Luka; forestry strong in Bosnia; inflation rate high; war (1992–3) disrupted all economic activity.

GDP (2002e) $7.3 bn, per capita $1900

History Annexed by Austria in 1908; Serbian opposition to the annexation led to the murder of Archduke Francis Ferdinand and World War 1; ceded to Yugoslavia, 1918; declaration of sovereignty, 1991; Bosnian Serbs proclaimed three autonomous regions (Bosanska Krajina, Romanija, and Northern Bosnia), 1991; declaration of independence in 1992 led to ongoing military conflict between formerly integrated communities of Bosnians, Croats, and Serbs; UN peace-keeping forces deployed, and air-exclusion ('no-fly') zone imposed, 1992; conflict continued until ceasefire in Oct 1995; peace accord leaves Bosnia-Herzegovina a single state, comprising the Bosnian-Croat Federation (in the west) and the Bosnian Serb Republic (in the east), with Sarajevo a united city; centrally governed by a national parliament and president, and people allowed freedom of movement; Nato peace implementation force established.

Head of State[a]
2002–   Sulejman Tihic (*Bosniak*)
2003–   Borislav Paravac (*Serb*)
2005–   Ivo Miro Jovic (*Croat*)

☐ International Airport

Head of Government
2002–   Adnan Terzic

[a]A collective presidency with an 8-month rotating leadership.

BOTSWANA

Local name Botswana

Timezone GMT +2

Area 581 730 km²/224 711 sq mi

Population total (2002e) 1 679 000

Status Independent republic within the Commonwealth

Date of independence 1966

Capital Gaborone

Languages English (official), Tswana

Ethnic groups Tswana (75%), Shona (12%), San (Bushmen) (3%), Khoikhoin (Hottentot) (3%), Ndebele (1%)

Religions Mainly local beliefs; Christian (20%)

Physical features Landlocked S African republic; undulating, sand-filled plateau, part of the S African Plateau; mean elevation c.1000 m/3300 ft; N–S plateau divides country into two regions: hilly grasslands (velt) to E, and Okavango Swamps to W; most of the population lives in fertile, hilly E; SE terrain hilly, 1402 m/4600 ft; dry scrubland, savannah, and the Kalahari Desert in W; salt lakes in N.

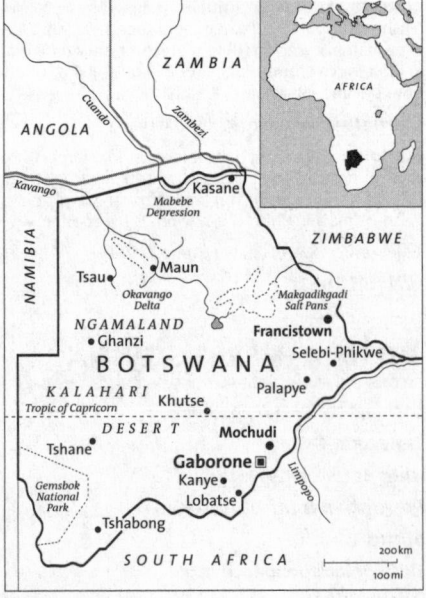

☐ International Airport

Climate Largely sub-tropical; rainfall in N and E almost totally in summer (Oct–Apr); average annual temperature 26°C (Jan), 13°C (Jul) in Gaborone; average annual rainfall 450 mm/17.7 in.

Currency 1 Pula (BWP) = 100 thebes

Economy Mainly subsistence farming, especially livestock; continual problems of drought and disease; some crops, especially sorghum; main minerals, nickel, diamonds (jointly mined by the government and De Beers Consolidated Mines of South Africa), cobalt; tourism, especially wildlife observation; Central Kalahari Game Reserve (54388 km²/21000 sq mi) attracts tourists; Trans-Kalahari Highway completed, 1998; principal trading partners, members of South African Customs Union.

GDP (2002e) $13.48 bn, per capita $8500

BRAZIL

Local name Brasil

Timezone GMT −2 (Atlantic Islands); GMT −3 (E); GMT −4 (mid-W); GMT −5 (extreme W)

Area 8511965 km²/3285618 sq mi

Population total (2002e) 174619000

Status Republic

Date of independence 1822

Capital Brasília

Language Portuguese (official)

Ethnic groups White (53%), mixed (34%), black (6%)

Religions Roman Catholic (80%), Protestant, Spiritualist

Physical features Located in E and C South America; low-lying Amazon basin in the N; where forest canopy cleared, soils susceptible to erosion; Brazilian plateau in the C and S, average height 600–900 m/2000–3000 ft; Guiana Highlands (S) contain Brazil's highest peak, Pico da Neblina, 3014 m/9888 ft; eight river systems, notably Amazon (N), São Francisco (C), Paraguay, Paraná, and Uruguay (S); 30% of population concentrated on a thin coastal strip on the Atlantic, c.100 km/325 mi wide.

Climate Almost entirely tropical, equator passing through the N region, and Tropic of Capricorn through the SE; Amazon basin, annual rainfall 1500–2000 mm/60–80 in; no dry season; average midday temperatures 27–32°C; dry region in the NE, susceptible to long droughts; hot, tropical climate on narrow coastal strip, with rainfall varying greatly N–S; S states have a seasonal temperate climate.

Currency 1 Cruzeiro Real (BRL) = 100 centavos

Economy One of the world's largest farming countries, agriculture employing 35% of population; world's largest exporter of coffee, second largest exporter of cocoa and soya beans; iron-ore reserves (possibly world's largest); timber reserves, third largest in the world, but continuing destruction of Amazon rainforest is causing much concern; road network being extended through Amazon rainforest.

GDP (2002e) $1.376 tn, per capita $7600

HDI (2002) 0.757

HDI (2002) 0.572

History San (Bushmen) were the earliest inhabitants, followed by Sotho peoples who migrated to Botswana c.1600; explored by Europeans, 1801; visited by missionaries during 19th-c; London Missionary Society established a mission on the Kuruman R, 1813; Ndebele raided Botswana; Boers arrived, 1835; gold discovered, 1867; under British protection from 1885; S became a Crown Colony, then part of Cape Colony, 1895; N became the Bechuanaland Protectorate; self-government from 1964; independence and change of name to Botswana, 1966; governed by a legislative National Assembly, President, and Cabinet; House of Chiefs considers chieftaincy matters but has no right of veto.

Head of State/Government
1998–   Festus Mogae

□ International Airport   ∴ World heritage site

History Claimed for the Portuguese by Pedro Alvares Cabral in 1500, first settlement at Salvador da Bahia; King of Portugal moved seat of government to Brazil, 1808; his son, Dom Pedro, declared himself emperor, 1818; independence established, 1822; Dom Pedro forced to abdicate in 1831 and succeeded by his 14-year-old son, Dom Pedro II, 1840; abolition of slavery in 1888, persuaded former slave-owners in declining sugar-plantation areas to join Republican opposition to the king, who was overthrown in the coup of 1889; ruled by dictator, Getúlio Vargas, 1930–45; Vargas deposed by military, and liberal republic restored, 1946; returned to office, 1950, but committed suicide, 1954; capital moved from Rio de Janeiro to Brasília, 1960; another coup in 1964 led to a military-backed presidential regime; President da Costa e Silva resigned and military junta took control, 1969; new elections, 1985; new constitution approved, transferring power from the President to the Congress, 1988; bicameral National Congress.

Head of State/Government
1992–5   Itamar Franco
1995–2002 Fernando Henrique Cardosa
2002–   Luiz Inacio Lula da Silva

BRITISH ANTARCTIC TERRITORY >> UNITED KINGDOM
BRITISH INDIAN OCEAN TERRITORY >> UNITED KINGDOM
BRITISH VIRGIN ISLANDS >> UNITED KINGDOM

HUMAN GEOGRAPHY

BRUNEI

Local name Negara Brunei Darussalam

Timezone GMT +8

Area 5765 km²/2225 sq mi

Population total (2002e) 351 000

Status Independent state

Date of independece 1984

Capital Bandar Seri Begawan

Languages Malay (official), English

Ethnic groups Malay (65%), Chinese (20%)

Religions Muslim (Sunni 65%), Buddhist (12%), Christian (9%)

Physical features Swampy coastal plain; equatorial rainforest covers 75% of land area; rivers include Belait, Tutong Brunei; mountainous tract on Sarawak border, average height 500 m/1640 ft.

Climate Tropical; high temperatures and humidity and no marked seasons; average daily temperature 24–30°C; average annual rainfall 2540 mm/100 in on coast, doubling in the interior.

Currency 1 Brunei Dollar (BND) = 100 cents

Economy Largely dependent on oil (discovered 1929) and gas resources.

GDP (2002e) $6.5 bn, per capita $18 600

HDI (2002) 0.856

History Formerly a powerful Muslim sultanate, with dominion over all of Borneo, its neighbouring islands, and parts of the Philippines by early 16th-c; under British protection from 1888; occupied by Japanese, 1941; liberated and reverted to former status as a British residency, 1945; internal self-government, 1971, and full independence, 1984; a constitutional monarchy with the Sultan as Head of State, who presides over a Council of Cabinet Ministers, a Religious Council, and a Privy Council.

Head of State/Government (Sultan)

1967–   Muda Hassan al Bolkiah Mu'izz-Din-Waddaulah

☐ International Airport

BULGARIA

Local name Bălgarija

Timezone GMT +2

Area 110 912 km²/42 812 sq mi

Population total (2002e) 7 890 000

Status Republic

Date of independence 1908

Capital Sofia

Languages Bulgarian (official), Turkish

Ethnic groups Bulgarian (85%), Turkish (9%)

Religions Bulgarian Orthodox (85%), Muslim (13%)

Physical features Traversed W–E by the Balkan Mts, averaging 2000 m/6500 ft; in the SW, Rhodope Mts, rising to 3000 m/9600 ft; rivers include Maritsa, Iskur, Danube.

Climate Continental climate, with hot summers, cold winters; average annual temperatures –2°C (Jan), 21°C (Jul); average annual rainfall 635 mm/25 in.

Currency 1 Lev (BGL) = 100 stotinki

Economy Mainly agricultural produce; coal, iron ore;

☐ International Airport

offshore oil (Black Sea), natural gas; tourism; tobacco, wine exports.

GDP (2002e) $49.23 bn, per capita $6500

HDI (2002) 0.779

History Bulgars crossed the Danube, 7th-c; their empire continually at war with Byzantines until destroyed by Turks, 14th-c; remained under Turkish rule, 1396–1878; full independence, 1908; became a kingdom, 1908–46; aligned with Germany in both World Wars; occupied by USSR, 1944; Socialist People's Republic founded, 1946; unicameral National Assembly established, 1971; joined proclaimed Republic of Bulgaria, 1990; joined EU 2007; new constitution, 1991, with a directly elected President, and a 250-member National Assembly.

Head of State
2001–   Georgi Parvanov

Head of Government
2005–   Sergei Stanishev

BURKINA FASO

Local name Burkina Faso

Timezone GMT

Area 274 200 km²/105 870 sq mi

Population total (2002e) 12 603 000

Status Republic

Date of independence 1960

Capital Ouagadougou

Languages French (official), with Moré, Mossi, Mande, Fulani, Lobi, and Bobo also spoken

Ethnic groups Mossi (48%), over 50 other groups

Religions Traditional beliefs (45%), Muslim (43%), Christian (12%)

Physical features Landlocked republic in W Africa; low-lying plateau, falling away to the S; tributaries of the Volta and Niger unnavigable in dry season; wooded savannahs in S; semi-desert in N.

Climate Tropical; average annual rainfall 894 mm/35 in; dry season (Dec–May), rainy season (Jun–Oct); average annual temperature 24°C (Jan), 28°C (Jul) in Ouagadougou; violent storms (Aug); subject to drought conditions.

Currency 1 CFA Franc (XAF) = 100 centimes

Economy Based on agriculture, largely at subsistence level; millet, corn, rice, livestock, peanuts, sugar cane, cotton.

GDP (2002e) $14.51 bn, per capita $1100

HDI (2002) 0.325

History Mossi empire in 18th–19th-c; Upper Volta created by French, 1919; abolished in 1932, with most land joined to Ivory Coast; original borders reconstituted,

BURMA >> MYANMAR

□ International Airport

1947; autonomy within French community, 1958; independence, 1960, with several military coups since; changed name from Upper Volta to Burkina Faso ('land of upright men'), 1984; end of military rule, 1991; governed by a president and an appointed Council of Ministers; new constitution, 1991, which promulgated an Assembly of People's Deputies (from 1997, with 111 members).

Head of State
1987–   Blaise Compaoré

Head of Government
2000–   Paramanga Ernest Yonli

BURUNDI

Local name Burundi

Timezone GMT +2

Area 27 834 km²/10 744 sq mi

Population total (2002e) 6 373 000

Status Republic

Date of independence 1962

Capital Bujumbura

Languages French and Kirundi (official), Swahili

Ethnic groups Hutu (82%), Tutsi (14%), Twa Pygmy (1%)

Religions Roman Catholic (62%), traditional beliefs (32%)

Physical features Located in C Africa; lies across Nile–Congo watershed; interior plateau, c.1500 m/5000

HUMAN GEOGRAPHY

Burundi (continued)

ft; highest point, Mt Karonje 2685 m/8809 ft; R Ruzizi forms part of NW frontier with Zaïre and links Lake Kiki in Rwanda, with Lake Tanganyika in S and E; river Malagarasi valley in E.

Climate Equatorial; moderately wet; dry season (Jun–Sep); average annual temperature 23°C; average annual rainfall at Bujumbura, 850 mm/33.5 in.

Currency 1 Burundi Franc (BIF) = 100 centimes

Economy Mainly agriculture; cash crops include coffee, cotton, tea; light consumer goods, shoes, blankets; reserves of rare-earth metals.

GDP (2002e) $3.146 bn, per capita $500

HDI (2002) 0.313

History Ruled by the Tutsi kingdom, 16th-c; occupied by Germany in 1890, and included in German East Africa, 1890; League of Nations mandated territory, administered by Belgians, 1919; joined with Rwanda to become the UN Trust Territory of Ruanda-Urundi, 1946; independent, 1962; full republic following the overthrow of the monarchy, 1966; civil war, 1972; military coup, 1976; new constitution provided a National Assembly, 1981; Assembly dissolved after 1987 coup; Military Council for National Salvation disbanded, 1990; new constitution, 1992; political instability following assassination of president, 1993; major inter-ethnic (Hutu/Tutsi) conflict, 1993–4, followed by periods of transitional governance and ongoing conflict to 2002; peace agreement with Hutu rebels, 2003, and demobilization planned for 2004.

Head of State
2003–   Domitien Ndayizeye
2005–   Pierre Nkurunziza

☐ International Airport

Head of Government
1996–8   Pascal-Firmin Ndimira

CAMBODIA

Local name Cambodia

Timezone GMT +7

Area 181 035 km²/69 879 sq mi

Population total (2002e) 13 414 000

Status Kingdom

Date of independence 1953

Capital Phnom Penh

Languages Khmer (official), French

Ethnic groups Khmer (93%), Chinese (3%), Cham (2%)

Religions Theravada Buddhist (88%), Muslim (2%)

Physical features Kingdom in SE Asia; crossed E by floodplain of Mekong R; Cardamom mountain range 160 km/100 mi across Thailand border, rising to 1813 m/5948 ft at Phnom Aural; Tonlé Sap (Greek Lake) in NW.

Climate Tropical monsoon climate, with a wet season (May–Sep); high temperatures in lowland region throughout the year; average annual temperature 21°C (Jan), 29°C (Jul); average annual rainfall 5000 mm/71 in (SW), 1300 mm/51 in (interior lowlands).

Currency 1 Riel (KHR) = 100 sen

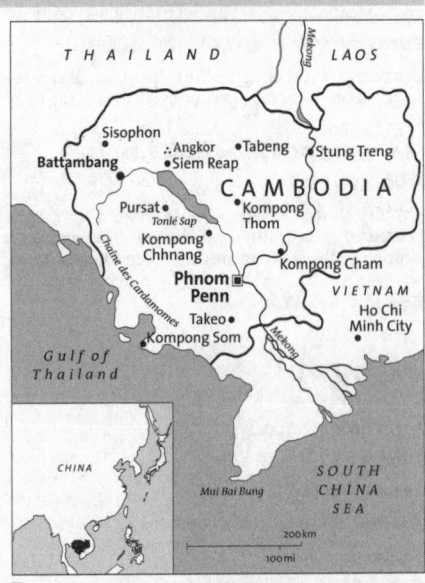

☐ International Airport   ∴ World heritage site

Economy Subsistence agriculture, rice and corn; industrial development disrupted by the civil war.

GNP (2002e) $20.42 bn, per capita $1600

HDI (2002) 0.543

History Originally part of Funan Kingdom, then part of the Khmer Empire, 6th-c; in dispute with Vietnamese and Thais from 15th-c; French Protectorate, 1863; part of Indo-China, 1887; independence, 1953; Prince Sihanouk deposed and Khmer Republic formed, 1970; fighting involved troops from N and S Vietnam and USA; surrender of Phnom Penh to Khmer Rouge, country renamed Kampuchea, 1975; attempt to reform economy by Pol Pot (1975–8) caused deaths of c.3 million people; Phnom Penh captured by Vietnamese, causing Khmer Rouge to flee, 1979; 1981 constitution established Council of State and Council of Ministers; name of Cambodia restored, 1989; Vietnamese troops completed withdrawal, 1989; UN peace plan agreed, with ceasefire and return of Sihanouk as Head of State, 1991; Sihanouk crowned king, 1993; further conflict following Khmer Rouge refusal to take part in 1993 elections; two main parties agreed to form coalition government, 2004; abdication of Sihanouk, Oct 2004.

Head of State (Monarch)
2004   Prince Norodom Ranariddh *Interim*
2004–   Norodom Sihamoni

Head of Government
1998–   Hun Sen

CAMEROON

Local name Cameroun

Timezone GMT +1

Area 475 439 km²/183 519 sq mi

Population total (2002e) 16 185 000

Status Republic

Date of independence 1960

Capital Yaoundé

Languages French and English (official); 24 major African languages including Fang, Bamileke, Luanda, Fulani, Tika, Maka

Ethnic groups Highlanders (31%), Equatorial Bantu (19%), Kirdi (11%), Fulani (10%)

Religions Christian (40%), traditional beliefs (39%), Muslim (21%)

Physical features Located in W Africa; equatorial forest, with low coastal plain. C plateau 1300 m/4200 ft; W forested and mountainous; Mt Cameroon, 4070 m/13 353 ft (active volcano and the highest peak in W Africa); low savannah, semi-desert towards L Chad; rivers include Sanaga and Dja.

Climate Rain all year in equatorial S; daily temperature in Yaoundé 27–30°C; average annual rainfall 4030 mm/159 in.

Currency 1 CFA Franc (XAF) = 100 centimes

Economy Agriculture (employs c.80% of workforce); world's fifth largest producer of cocoa; tourism, especially to national parks.

GNP (2002e) $26.84 bn, per capita $1700

HDI (2002) 0.512

History First explored by Portuguese navigator Fernando Po; later by traders from Spain, Netherlands, Britain; German protectorate of Kamerun, 1884; divided into French and British Cameroon, 1919; confirmed by League of Nations mandate, 1922; UN trusteeships, 1946; French Cameroon independent as Republic of Cameroon, 1960: N sector of British Cameroon voted to become part of Nigeria, S sector part of Cameroon; became Federal Republic of Cameroon, with separate parliaments, 1961; federal system abolished, 1972, and name changed to United Republic of Cameroon; changed name to the Republic of Cameroon, 1984; multiparty legislative and presidential elections, 1992; governed by a President, executive Prime Minister, Cabinet, and National Assembly.

Head of State
1982–   Paul Biya

Head of Government
1996–2004 Peter Mafany Musonge
2004–   Ephraim Inoni

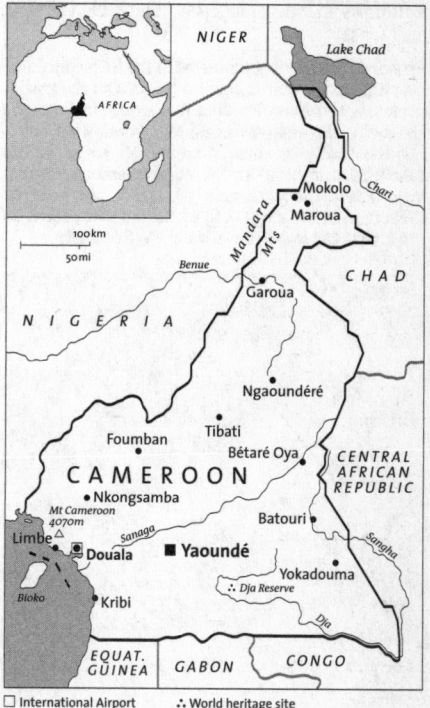

□ International Airport   ∴ World heritage site

CANADA

Local name Canada

Timezone GMT W –9, to E –3

Area 9 971 500 km²/3 848 900 sq mi

Population total (2002e) 31 244 000

Status Independent nation within the Commonwealth

Date of independence 1867 (Dominion of Canada)

Capital Ottawa

Languages English and French (official)

Ethnic groups British origin (45%), French origin (29%), other European, Indian, and Inuit (23%)

Religions Roman Catholic (49%), United Church (18%), Anglican (12%)

Physical features Dominated in the NE by the Canadian Shield; flat prairie country S and W of the Shield, stretching to the Western Cordillera, which includes the Rocky, Cassiar, and Mackenzie Mts; Coast Mts flank a rugged, heavily indented coastline; Mt Logan in the Yukon, 5950 m/19 521 ft, the highest peak in Canada; major rivers; the Mackenzie (W), and St Lawrence (E); Great Bear, 31 330 km²/11 030 sq mi, and Great Slave, 28 570 km²/11 030 sq mi, are lakes in NW Territories.

Climate N coast permanently ice-bound or obstructed by ice floes, but for Hudson Bay (frozen c.9 months each year); mild winters and warm summers on Pacific coast and around Vancouver Is; average annual rainfall from 300 mm/12 in in far N to 2400 mm/90 in in parts of W.

Currency 1 Canadian Dollar (CAD) = 100 cents

Economy Traditionally based on natural resources and agriculture: world's second largest exporter of wheat; world's largest producer of asbestos, zinc, silver, nickel; second largest producer of potash, gypsum, molybdenum, sulphur; hydroelectricity, oil (especially Alberta), natural gas; major industrial development in recent decades.

GDP (2002e) $934.1 bn, per capita $29 300

HDI (2002) 0.940

History Evidence of Viking settlement c.1000; Newfoundland claimed for England, 1583; Champlain founded Quebec, 1608; Hudson's Bay Company founded, 1670; conflict between British and French in late 17th-c; Britain gained large areas from Treaty of Utrecht, 1713; after Seven Years' War, during which British General James Wolfe captured Quebec from Louis Montcalm's forces in 1759, Treaty of Paris gave Britain almost all France's possessions in North America; province of Quebec created, 1774; migration of loyalists from USA after War of Independence led to division of Quebec into

☐ International Airport

Upper and Lower Canada; reunited as Canada, 1841; Dominion of Canada created (1867) by confederation of Quebec, Ontario, Nova Scotia, and New Brunswick; Rupert's Land and Northwest Territories bought from Hudson's Bay Company, 1869–70; joined by Manitoba (1870), British Columbia (1871), Prince Edward I (1873), Alberta and Saskatchewan (1905), and Newfoundland (1949); recurring political tension in recent decades arising from French-Canadian separatist movement in Quebec; Canada Act, 1982, gave Canada full responsibility for constitution; bicameral Federal Parliament includes Senate and a House of Commons; British monarch is Head of State, represented by a Governor-General; referendum on Quebec separation narrowly defeated in 1995.

Head of State
(British monarch represented by Governor-General)
1999–   Adrienne Clarkson

Head of Government
1993–2003 Jean Chrétien
2003–6   Paul Martin
2006–   Stephen Harper

CANARY ISLANDS >> SPAIN

CAPE VERDE

Local name Cabo Verde

Timezone GMT –1

Area 4033 km²/1557 sq mi

Population total (2002e) 453 000

Status Island group

Date of independence 1975

Capital Praia (on São Tiago Island)

Languages Portuguese (official), Crioulo (Portuguese-based creole)

Ethnic groups Creole (mulatto) (60%), African (28%), European (2%)

Religion Roman Catholic (80%), others (20%)

Physical features Island group in the Atlantic Ocean off W Coast of Africa, c.500 km/310 mi W of Dakar, Senegal; Barlavento (windward) group in N, Sotavento (leeward) group in S; mostly mountainous islands of volcanic origin; highest peak, Pico do Cano, 2829 m/9281 ft; active volcano on Fogo I; fine sandy beaches on most islands.

Climate Arid climate; located at N limit of tropical rain belt; low and unreliable rainfall (Aug–Sep); small temperature range throughout year; average annual temperature 23°C; average annual rainfall 250 mm/10 in.

Currency 1 Escudo (CVE) = 100 centavos

Economy Suffering because of drought; substantial emigration in early 1970s; c.70% of workforce are farmers occupying irrigated inland valleys; increase in fishing since 1975.

GDP (2002e) $600 mn, per capita $1400

HDI (2002) 0.715

CAYMAN ISLANDS >> UNITED KINGDOM

>> Political leaders and rulers, p.196

Canadian provinces and territories

Name	Area		Capital
	km²	sq mi	
Alberta	661 190	255 285	Edmonton
British Columbia	947 800	365 945	Victoria
Manitoba	649 950	250 945	Winnipeg
New Brunswick	73 440	28 355	Fredericton
Newfoundland	405 720	156 648	St John's
Northwest Territories	1 346 106	519 597	Yellowknife
Nova Scotia	55 490	21 424	Halifax
Nunavut	2 093 190	807 971	Iqaluit
Ontario	1 068 580	412 578	Toronto
Prince Edward Island	5 660	2 185	Charlottetown
Quebec	1 540 680	594 856	Quebec City
Saskatchewan	652 380	251 883	Regina
Yukon Territory	483 450	186 660	Whitehorse

HUMAN GEOGRAPHY

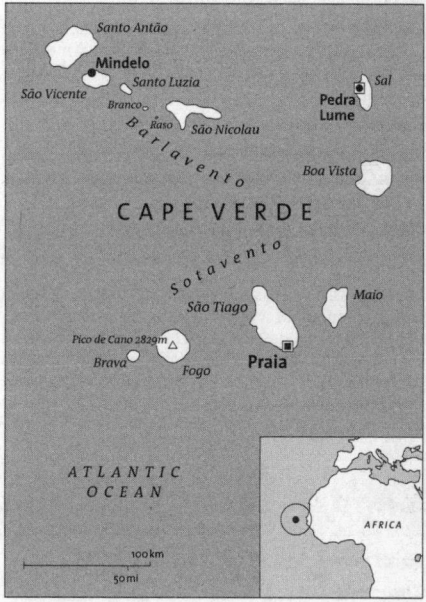

☐ International Airport

History Colonized by Portuguese in 15th-c, also used as a penal colony; administered with Portuguese Guinea until 1879; overseas province of Portugal, 1951; independence, 1975; governed by a President, Council of Ministers, and People's National Assembly; multi-party elections held, 1991.

Head of State
2001–   Pedro Verona Rodrigues Pires

Head of Government
2001–   José Maria Pereira Neves

CENTRAL AFRICAN REPUBLIC

Local name République Centrafricaine

Timezone GMT +1

Area 622 984 km²/240 535 sq mi

Population total (2002e) 3 643 000

Status Republic

Date of independence 1960

Capital Bangui

Languages French (official), Sangho

Ethnic groups Baya (34%), Banda (28%), Sara (10%), over 80 other groups

Religions Christian (50%), (Protestant 25%, Roman Catholic 25%), also Muslim and traditional beliefs

Physical features Located in C Africa; plateau forming a watershed between Chad and Congo river basins; Massif des Bongos rises 1400 m/4593 ft in NW; granite ranges of Mont Karre, 1,220 m/4003 ft in W.

Climate Tropical; single rainy season in N (May–Sep); average annual rainfall 875–1000 mm/34–9 in; more equatorial climate in S; rainfall 1500–2000 mm/60–80 in.

Currency 1 CFA Franc (XAF) = 100 centimes

Economy Agriculture employs c.85% of working population; also sawmilling, brewing, diamond splitting, leather and tobacco processing.

GDP (2002e) $4.296 bn, per capita $1200

HDI (2002) 0.375

History Part of French Equatorial Africa (Ubangi Shari); autonomous republic within the French community, 1958; independence, 1960; coup deposed country's first President, David Dacko, 1965; Jean-Bédel Bokassa declared himself emperor for life, and country's name changed to the Central African Empire, 1976; Bokassa deposed and country reverted to a republic, 1979; mili-

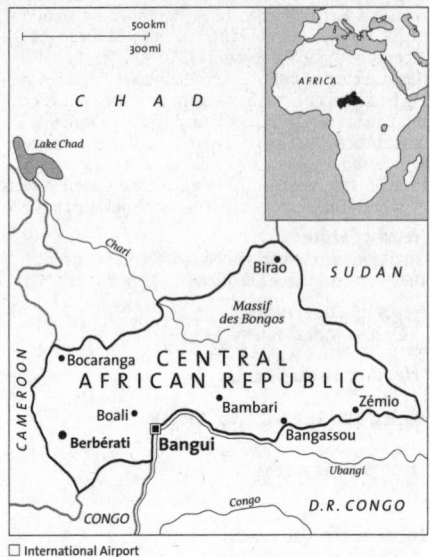

□ International Airport

tary coup established Committee for National Recovery, 1981–5; Committee dissolved and National Assembly established, 1987; movement towards multiparty democracy, 1991; legislative and presidential elections, 1993; President Patasse overthrown in coup by General Bozize, 2003; governed by a president, prime minister, and 85-member National Assembly.

Head of State

2003–   General François Bozize

Head of Government

2005–   Elie Dote

CHAD

Local name Tchad

Timezone GMT +1

Area 1 284 640 km²/495 871 sq mi

Population total (2002e) 8 997 000

Status Republic

Date of independence 1960

Capital N'djamena

Languages Arabic and French (official), many local languages spoken

Ethnic groups Sara, Bagirmi, and Kreish (30%); Sudanic Arab (26%), Teda (17%), Masalit, Maba, Mimi (6%), over 200 groups

Religions Muslim (50%), Christian (Roman Catholic 21%, Protestant 12%), and local religions

Physical features Landlocked in C Africa; mostly arid, semi-desert plateau at edge of Sahara Desert; average altitude of 200–500 m/650–1650 ft; Tibesti Mts (N) rise to 3415 m/11 204 ft at Emi Koussi; rivers in S (Chari and Logne) flow NW to Lake Chad.

Climate Tropical, moderately wet in S (May–Oct); hot, arid N, almost rainless; C plain hot, dry, with brief rainy season (Jun–Sep).

Currency 1 CFA Franc (XAF) = 100 centimes

Economy Severely damaged in recent years by drought, locusts, and civil war; export of cotton, kaolin, animal products; salt mined around L Chad.

HUMAN GEOGRAPHY

GDP (2002e) $9.297 bn, per capita $1000

HDI (2002) 0.365

History Part of French Equatorial Africa, 1908; colonial status, 1920; independence, 1960; Libyan troops occupied the Aozou Strip in extreme N, 1973; fighting between Libyan-supported rebels and French-supported government until cease-fire agreed, 1987; new constitution established a National Assembly, 1989; replaced by a Provisional Council of the Republics, 1991; Chad and Libya presented their individual territorial claims to Aozou Strip, 1990; President Habré ousted by coup and new constitution adopted, 1991; transitional charter, 1993, with elections planned for 1995; Aouzou strip returned to Chad by Libya, 1994; peace agreement, 2001; draft peace agreement signed with the National Resistance Army (ANR), 2003; constitution amended to lift limit on number of presidential terms, May 2004; governed by a president, prime minister, Council of Ministers, and a 57-member Higher Transitional Council.

Head of State
1990–   Idriss Déby

Head of Government
2003–5   Moussa Faki Mahamat
2005–   Pascal Yoadimnadji

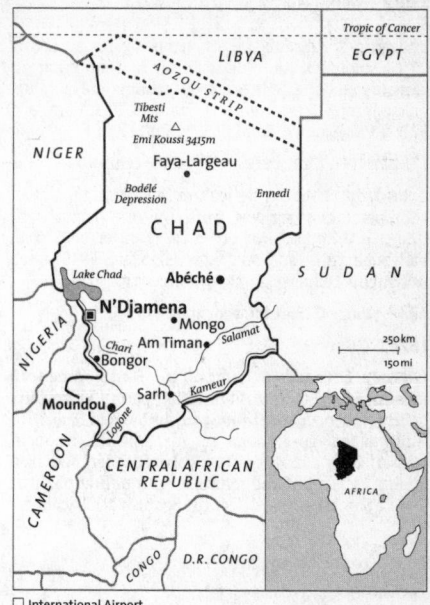

☐ International Airport

CHANNEL ISLANDS >> UNITED KINGDOM

CHILE

Local name Chile

Timezone GMT –4

Area 756 626 km²/292 058 sq mi (excluding territory claimed in Antarctica)

Population total (2002e) 15 082 000

Status Republic

Date of independence 1818

Capital Santiago

Language Spanish (official)

Ethnic groups Mestizo (92%), Indian (6%), European (2%)

Religions Roman Catholic (89%), Protestant (10%), small Jewish and Muslim minority

Physical features Coastal Cordillera, Pampa Central, and the Chilean Andes are parallel regions running almost the entire length of the country; narrow coastal belt, backed by Andean mountain ridges rising in the NW to 6910 m/22 660 ft at Ojos del Salado; Atacama Desert in far NW, rich in minerals; arable land and forest in the S; S Andes still experiences volcanic activity; main river, the Bío-Bío; Punta Arenas located on southern tip of Chile's mainland; Chilean possessions include a rock measuring 424 m/1390 ft on Horn Island in the Wollaston group, and 1 250 000 km²/ 482 628 sq mi of Antarctic territory.

Climate Varied climate (spans 37° of latitude, with altitudes from Andean peaks to coastal plain); extreme

☐ International Airport

Chile (continued)

aridity in N Atacama Desert, temperatures averaging 20°C; cold, wet, and windy in far S; Mediterranean climate in C Chile, with warm wet winters and dry summers; average temperature at Santiago 19°C (Jan), 8°C (Jul); average annual rainfall 375 mm/14.8 in.

Currency 1 Chilean Peso (CLP) = 100 centavos

Economy Based on agriculture and mining; wheat, corn, potatoes, sugar beet, fruit, livestock; fishing in N, timber in S; copper, iron ore, nitrates, silver, gold, coal, molybdenum; oil and gas discovered in far S (1945); steel, wood pulp, cellulose, mineral processing.

GDP (2002e) $156.1 bn, per capita $10 100

HDI (2002) 0.831

History Originally occupied by South American Indians; arrival of Spanish in 16th-c; part of Viceroyalty of Peru; independence from Spain declared in 1810, with a provisional government set up in Santiago; Spain reasserted its authority, 1814; patriot leader, Bernardo O'Higgins, escaped and returned, with military help of José de San Martín, to defeat the Spanish at Chacabuco,

1817; O'Higgins became first president and independence was declared, 1818; border disputes with Bolivia, Peru, and Argentina brought Chilean victory in War of the Pacific, 1879–84; economic unrest in late 1920s led to military dictatorship under Carlos Ibáñez until 1931; Marxist coalition government of Salvador Allende Gossens ousted in 1973, and replaced by military junta under Augusto Pinochet Ugarte, which banned all political activity; constitution providing for eventual return to democracy came into effect, 1981; plebiscite held in 1988 resulted in a defeat for Pinochet's candidacy as President beyond 1990, and limited political reforms; National Congress restored, comprising a Senate and a Chamber of Deputies in 1990; 6-year term for president agreed in 1994.

Head of State/Government
1990–4	Patricio Aylwin Azócar
1994–9	Eduardo Frei Ruíz-Tagle
1999–	Ricardo Lagos Escobar

CHINA

Local name Zhongguo

Timezone GMT +8

Area 9 597 000 km²/3 705 000 sq mi (also claims island of Taiwan)

Population total (2002e) 1 284 211 000

Status People's republic

Capital Beijing (Peking)

Languages Standard Chinese (Putonghua) or Mandarin, also Yue (Cantonese), Wu, Minbei, Minnan, Xiang, Gan and Hakka

Ethnic groups Han Chinese (92%), over 50 minorities, including Chuang, Manchu, Hui, Miao, Uighur, Hani, Kazakh, Tai and Yao

Religions Officially atheist; widespread Confucianism and Taoism (20%), Buddhism (6%)

Physical features Over two-thirds of country are upland hills, mountains, and plateaux; highest mountains in the W, where the Tibetan plateau rises to average altitude of 4000 m/13 000 ft; Mt Everest rises to 8848m/29 028 ft on the Nepal-Tibet border; land descends to desert/semidesert of Xinjiang and Inner Mongolia (NE); broad and fertile plains of Manchuria (NE); further E and S, Sichuan basin, drained by Yangtze R (5980 km/3720 mi in length); Huang He (Yellow) R runs for 4840 km/3010 mi; heavily populated S plains and E coast, with rich, fertile soils.

Climate Varied, with seven zones: (1) NE China: cold winters, with strong N winds, warm and humid summers, unreliable rainfall; (2) C China: warm and humid summers, sometimes typhoons or tropical cyclones on coast; (3) S China: partly within tropics; wettest area in summer, frequent typhoons; (4) SW China: summer temperatures moderated by altitude, winters mild with little rain; (5) Xizang autonomous region: high plateau

surrounded by mountains; winters severe with frequent light snow and hard frost; (6) Xinjiang and W interior: arid desert climate, cold winters; rainfall well distributed throughout year; (7) Inner Mongolia: extreme continental climate; cold winters, warm summers.

Currency 1 Renminbi Yuan (CNY) = 10 jiao = 100 fen

Economy Since 1949, economy largely based on heavy industry; more recently, light industries; special economic zones set up to attract foreign investment; rich mineral deposits; largest oil-producing country in Far East; major subsistence crops include rice, grain, beans, potatoes, tea, sugar, cotton; economy hit by SARS, 2003.

GDP (2002e) $5.989 tn, per capita $4700

HDI (2002) 0.726

History Chinese civilization believed to date from the Xia dynasty (2200–1799 BC); Qin dynasty (221–207 BC) unified warring states and provided system of centralized control; expansion W during Western and Eastern Han dynasties (206 BC–AD 220), and Buddhism introduced from India; split into Three Kingdoms (Wei, Shu, Wu, 220–65); from 4th-c, series of N dynasties set up by invaders, with several dynasties in S; gradually reunited during the Sui (590–618) and Tang (618–906) dynasties; partition into the Five Dynasties (907–60); Song (Sung) dynasty (960–1279), remembered for literature, philosophy, inventions; Kublai Khan established Mongol Yuan dynasty which ruled China 1279–1368; visits by Europeans, such as Marco Polo, 13th–14th-c; Ming dynasty (1368–1644) increased contacts with West; overthrown by Manchus, who ruled China during 1644–1911 under the Qing dynasty, and enlarged empire to include Manchuria, Mongolia, Tibet, Taiwan; opposition to foreign imports led to Opium Wars 1839–42, 1858–60; Sino-Japanese War, 1895; Boxer Rising, 1900; Republic of China founded by Sun Yatsen, 1912; unification under

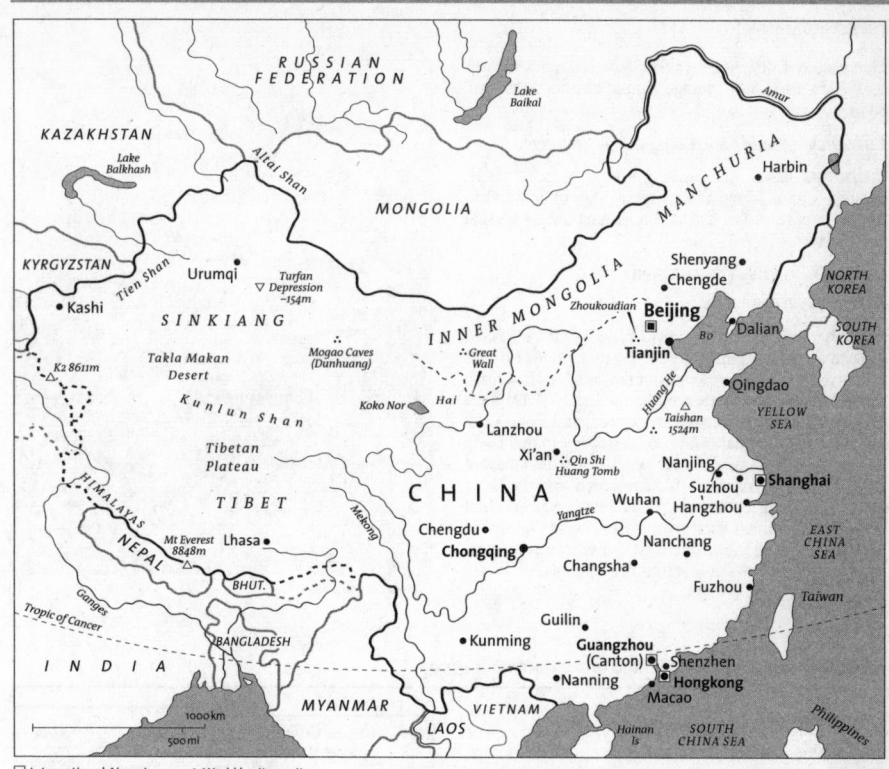

☐ International Airport   ∴ World heritage site

Jiang Jieshi (Chiang Kai-shek), who made Nanjing capital in 1928; conflict between Nationalists and Communists led to the Long March, 1934–5, with Communists moving to NW China under Mao Zedong (Mao Tse-tung); Nationalist defeat by Mao and withdrawal to Taiwan, 1949; People's Republic of China proclaimed, 1949, with capital at Beijing; first Five-Year Plan (1953–7) period of nationalization and collectivization; Great Leap Forward, 1958–9, emphasized local authority and establishment of rural communes; Cultural Revolution initiated by Mao Zedong, 1966; many policies reversed after Mao's death in 1976, and drive towards rapid industrialization and wider trade relations with West; after 1980, Deng Xiaoping became the dominant figure within the ruling Chinese Communist Party, retiring from his last official post in 1990, but remained influential until his death in 1997; governed by elected National People's Congress who elect a State Council; Hong Kong returned to China, 1997; Hu Jintao elected Communist Party chief, 2002.

Head of State
1993–2003 Jiang Zemin
2003–   Hu Jintao

Head of Government
1998–2003 Zhu Rongji
2003–   Wen Jiabao

Hong Kong (Became part of China on 1 July 1997. Because of its special historical interest, details are given below)

Timezone GMT +8

Area 1066 km²/412 sq mi

Population total (2002e) 7 049 000

Capital Hong Kong

Languages English and Cantonese (official), with Mandarin widely spoken

Ethnic groups Chinese (98%), including many illegal immigrants from China and refugees from Vietnam; 59% of population born in Hong Kong, 37% in China

Religions Buddhist, Taoist and Confuncianist majorities, Christian, Muslim, Hindu, Sikh, and Jewish minorities

Physical features Located off the coast of SE China, on the South China Sea; divided into Hong Kong Island, Kowloon, and New Territories (includes most of the colony's 235 islands); highest point, Tai Mo Shan, 957 m/3140 ft; hilly terrain, sharply indented coastline; natural harbour between Kowloon and Hong Kong Island; built-up areas on artificially levelled or reclaimed land.

Climate Subtropical climate, with hot, humid sum-

China (continued)

mers and cool, dry winters; average annual temperatures 16°C (Jan), 29°C (Jul); average annual rainfall 2225 mm/ 88 in.

Currency 1 Hong Kong Dollar (HKD) = 100 cents

Economy Based on banking, import-export trade, tourism, shipbuilding, and a diverse range of light industry; an important freeport acting as a gateway to China for the West.

GDP (2002e) $198.5 bn, per capita $27 200

HDI (2002) 0.888

History Ceded to Britain, 1842, New Territories leased to Britain, 1898; occupied by the Japanese in World War 2; British Crown Colony, Governor represented the British Crown, advised by an Executive Council; in 1997, Britain's 99-year lease of New Territories expired, and Hong Kong was restored to China, 1 July; China has designated Hong Kong a special administrative region; it will remain a freeport, foreign markets will be retained, and the Hong Kong dollar will remain as official currency; new chief executive appointed (first incumbent, Tung Chee-hwa), with new membership of advisory councils; however, anxiety over the colony's political future remains.

Chief Executive
2005–   Donald Tsang

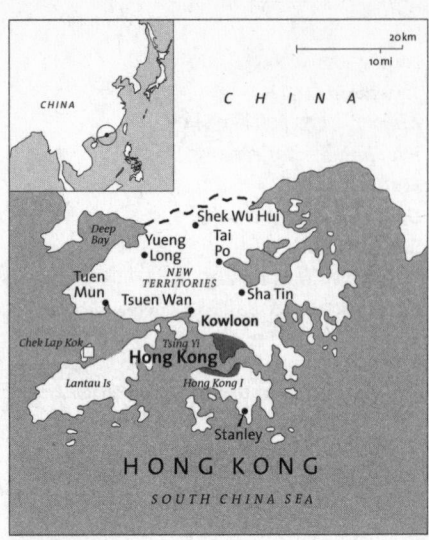
☐ International Airport

Macao *(Became part of China on 20 December 1999)*

Local name Macáu (Port.), Aomen (Chin.)

Timezone GMT +8

Area 16 km²/6 sq mi

Population total (2002e) 464 000

Status Special administrative region of China

Capital Macáu

Languages Portuguese and Cantonese (official), with English generally spoken

Ethnic group Chinese (99%)

Religions Roman Catholic, Buddhist

Physical features Flat, maritime tropical peninsula in SE China; also includes the nearby islands of Taipa and Colôane; on the Pearl R delta, 64 km/40 mi W of Hong Kong; ferry links with Hong Kong.

Climate Subtropical; cool winters, warm summers.

Currency 1 Pataca (MOP) = 100 avos

Economy Textiles, electronics, toys, tourism, fishing.

History Portuguese trade with China began in 16th-c; became Portuguese colony, 1557; right of permanent occupation granted to Portugal by the Sino-Portuguese treaty, 1887; Portugal changed Macao's status from overseas province to a 'territory under Portuguese administration', 1979; Portugal and China agreed that Macao would revert to China in 1999 as a 'special administrative region' governed by a 23-member Legislative Assembly.

Chief Executive
1999–   Edmund Ho

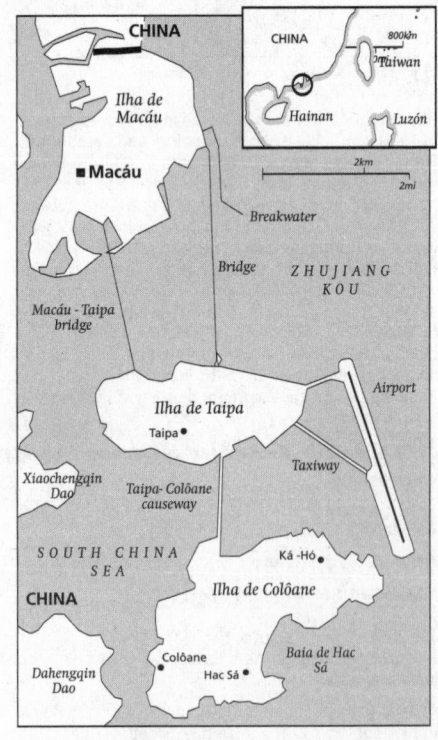

COLOMBIA

Local name Colombia

Timezone GMT –5

Area 1 140 105 km²/440 080 sq mi

Population total (2002e) 41 008 000

Status Republic

Date of independence 1819

Capital Bogotá

Language Spanish (official)

Ethnic groups Mestizo (58%), European descent (20%), mulatto (14%)

Religion Roman Catholic (95%), other (5%)

Physical features Located in NW South America, includes several island possessions (Providencia, San Andrés and Mapelo); Andes run N–S, dividing narrow coastal plains from forested lowlands of Amazon basin; Cordillera Central rises 5000 m/16 000 ft to the high peak of Huila, 5750 m/18 865 ft; rivers include Vaupés, Magdalena, Cauca, and Guaviare.

Climate Hot, humid coastal plains (NW and W); annual rainfall over 2500 mm/100 in; drier period on Caribbean coast (Dec–Apr); hot, humid tropical lowlands in E.

Currency 1 Colombian Peso (COP) = 100 centavos

Economy Virtually self-sufficient in food; major crops include coffee, bananas, cotton; leather; gold, silver, emeralds, coal, oil; widespread illegal cocaine trafficking.

GDP (2002e) $251.6 bn, per capita $6100

HDI (2002) 0.772

History Spanish occupation from early 16th-c, displacing Amerindian peoples; governed by Spain within Viceroyalty of Peru, later Viceroyalty of New Granada; independence in 1819, after the campaigns of Simón Bolívar; union with Ecuador, Venezuela, and Panama as Gran Colombia, 1821–30; civil war in 1950s; considerable political unrest in 1980s; new constitution, 1991; ongoing conflict with FARC (Colombian Revolutionary Armed Forces) led to establishment of a FARC-controlled zone in S Colombia, 1998, as part of peace negotiations, but con-

☐ International Airport

flict continuing into 2004; governed by a President, bicameral Congress and Cabinet.

Head of State/Government

1998–2002 Andrés Pastrana Arango
2002–   Alvaro Uribe

HUMAN GEOGRAPHY

COMMONWEALTH OF INDEPENDENT STATES, THE (CIS)

A multilateral group of independent states which were once members of the USSR; formed in December 1991; membership included all the states that once comprised the USSR, with the exceptions of the Baltic States (Latvia, Lithuania and Estonia) and Georgia; Georgia joined in December 1993.

CIS >> ARMENIA, AZERBAIJAN, BELARUS, GEORGIA, KAZAKHSTAN, KYRGYZSTAN, MOLDOVA, RUSSIA, TAJIKISTAN, TURKMENISTAN, UKRAINE, UZBEKISTAN

>> See map on p.240.

HUMAN GEOGRAPHY

Commonwealth of Independent States, The (CIS) (continued)

☐ International Airport

COMOROS

Local name Comores

Timezone GMT +3

Area 1862 km²/719 sq mi

Population total (2002e) 583 000

Status Federal republic

Date of independence 1975

Capital Moroni (on Njazidja Island)

Languages Arabic, French (official), Kiswahili

Ethnic groups Comorian (97%), Makua (2%)

Religions Sunni Muslim (86%), Roman Catholic (14%)

Physical features Located in the Mozambique Channel between mainland Africa and Madagascar; group of three volcanic islands: Njazidja (Grande Comore), Nzwani (Anjouan), and Mwali (Mohéli); largest island, Njazidja, with an active volcano, Mt Kartala, 2361 m/7746 ft.

Climate Tropical; dry season (May–Oct), hot, humid season (Nov–Apr); average temperatures, 20°C (Jul), 28°C (Nov).

Currency 1 Comorian Franc (KMF) = 100 centimes

Economy Largely agricultural economy: vanilla, copra, cacao, sisal, coffee, cloves, vegetable oils; perfume.

GDP (2002e) $441 mn, per capita $700

HDI (2002) 0.511

History Under French control, 1843–1912; French overseas territory, 1947; internal political autonomy, 1961; unilateral independence declared, 1975; Mayotte, island in the archipelago, remained under French rule; established as Federal Islamic Republic, 1978; a one-party state, governed by a President, Council of Ministers, and unicameral Federal Assembly; new constitution, 2001,

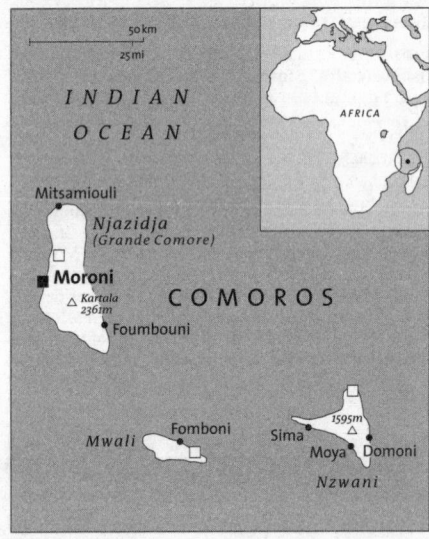

☐ International Airport

provided for creation of a new federation, the Comoros Union, with greater autonomy for the three islands; presidency of the union rotates between the islands; a president, elected for a 4-year term, heads a central government, and a 33-member legislature.

Head of State/Government
2002–6   Azali Assoumani
2006–   Ahmed Abdallah Mohamed Sambi

Prime Minister
2000–2   Hamada Madi

CONGO

Local name Congo

Timezone GMT +1

Area 341 945 km²/132 047 sq mi

Population total (2002e) 2 899 000

Status Republic

Date of independence 1960

Capital Brazzaville

Language French (official), with local languages, including Kongo and Téké

Ethnic groups Kongo (45%), Sangha (15%), Téké (20%)

Religions Roman Catholic (40.5%), Protestant (9.5%), local traditional beliefs

Physical features Niari valley rises to 1040 m/3412 ft at Mont de la Lékéti; mainly covered by dense grassland, mangrove, and tropical rainforest; rivers include Sangha and Alima in N.

Climate Hot, humid equatorial climate; annual rainfall 1250–1750 mm/50–70 in, annual daily temperature 28–33°C in Brazzaville; dry season (Jun–Sep).

Currency 1 CFA Franc (XAF) = 100 centimes

Economy Mainly agriculture and forestry; sugar cane, coffee, cocoa, palm oil, tobacco; oil, timber, diamonds; sugar-refining.

GDP (2002e) $2.5 bn, per capita $512

HDI (2002) 0.512

History Visited by Portuguese, 14th-c; part of French Equatorial Africa, known as 'Middle Congo', 1908–58; independence as Republic of Congo, 1960; military coup created first Marxist state in Africa, renamed People's Republic of the Congo, 1968; Congolese Labour Party (PCT), the single ruling party in Congo, renounced Marxism, 1990; transitional government formed, 1991, and country renamed the Republic of Congo; new constitution, 1992, recognized a multi-party system; violence following disputes over the election process, 1993; new constitution, 2001; executive authority vested in the President, elected for a 7-year term, and a bicameral legislature.

Head of State
1997–   Denis Sassou-Nguesso

Head of Government
1997–2002 Bernard Kolelas

COOK ISLANDS >> NEW ZEALAND

CORSICA >> FRANCE

☐ International Airport

HUMAN GEOGRAPHY

CONGO, THE DEMOCRATIC REPUBLIC OF (from 1997; formerly, ZAIRE)

Local name République Démocratique du Congo

Timezone GMT +1 (W) to +2 (E)

Area 2 234 585 km²/905 365 sq mi

Population total (2002e) 52 557 000

Status Republic

Date of independence 1960

Capital Kinshasa

Languages French (official), English, with various Bantu dialects (including Swahili, Lingala, Ishiluba, and Kikongo) spoken

Ethnic groups Bantu, with Sudanese, Nilotes, Pygmies, Hamite and Angolan minorities

Religions Christian (70%) (Roman Catholic 50%, Protestant 20%), Kimbanguist (10%), Muslim (10%), traditional beliefs (10%)

Physical features Located in C Africa, land rises E from a low-lying basin to a densely forested plateau; Ruwenzori Mts (NE) rise to 5110 m/16 765 ft in the Mt Stanley massif; Mitumba Mts further S; Rift Valley chain of lakes, Albert, Edward, Kivu, and Tanganyika; Congo R.

Climate Equatorial, hot and humid; average annual temperature, 26°C (Jan), 23°C (Jul) in Kinshasa; average

Congo, The Democratic Republic of (continued)

annual rainfall 1125 mm/44 in; dry coastal region; dry season (May–Sep) S of Equator, (Dec–Feb) N of Equator.

Currency 1 Congolese Franc (CDF) = 100 centimes

Economy Subsistence farming employs c.80% of population; palm oil, rubber, quinine, fruit, vegetables, tea, cocoa; extensive mineral reserves; world's biggest producer of cobalt; industrial diamonds, copper; coffee, petroleum, cotton, tobacco processing, chemicals, cement.

GDP (2002) $34 bn, per capita $600

HDI (2002) 0.431

History Visited by Portuguese, 1482; expeditions of Henry Morton Stanley, 1874–7; claimed by Leopold of Belgium, recognized, 1885; Congo Free State ceded to state, 1907, renamed Belgian Congo; independence as Democratic Republic of the Congo, 1960; soon after, mineral-rich Katanga (later, Shaba) province claimed independence, leading to civil war; UN peace-keeping force present to 1964; renamed Republic of Zaïre, 1971; further conflict, 1977–8, as Katangese rebels invaded Shaba province from Angola; ongoing conflict, 1980s; new constitution and period of transition, 1994; further conflict, 1996; Alliance of Democratic Forces for the Liberation of Congo-Zaire took control, led by Laurent Kabila; new transitional government, 1997; further fighting with rebel movements, 1998, with Ugandan and Rwandan troops supporting rebels, and Zimbabwean, Angolan, and Namibian troops supporting government; assassination of Kabila, 2001, succeeded by son Joseph; peace negotiations disrupted by fighting, 2002; power-sharing agreements between government and key rebel groups, 2002; emergency UN peace-keeping force, 2003; interim government, with leaders of main rebel groups as vice-presidents, 2003; tensions

□ International Airport ∴ World heritage site
1 Lake Albert 2 Lake Edward 3 Lake Kivu 4 Lake Tanganyika

with Rwanda after renegade soldiers seized town of Bukavu, 2004; new constitution adopted, 2006; first democratic elections in over 40 years won by President Kabila, Dec 2006.

Head of State
2001– Joseph Kabila

Head of Government
2006– Antoine Gizenga

COSTA RICA

Local name Costa Rica

Timezone GMT –6

Area 51 022 km²/19 694 sq mi

Population total (2002e) 3 960 000

Status Republic

Date of independence 1821

Capital San José

Language Spanish (official)

Ethnic groups European (87%), mestizo (7%), black/mulatto (3%), E Asian (mostly Chinese) (2%), Amerindian (1%)

Religions Roman Catholic (85%), Protestant (15%)

Physical features Second smallest republic in Central America; formed by series of volcanic ridges: Cordillera de Guanacaste (NW), Cordillera Central, and Cordillera de Talamanca; highest peak, Chirripó Grande, 3819 m/12 529 ft. C plateau; swampy land near coast, rising to tropical forest.

Climate Tropical; small temperature range; abundant rainfall; dry season (Dec–May); average annual temperature 26–8°C.

□ International Airport

Currency 1 Costa Rican Colón (CRC) = 100 céntimos

Economy Primarily agriculture, mainly coffee (especially in Meseta Central), bananas, sugar, cattle; silver, bauxite; exploration for oil in collaboration with Mexico.

GDP (2002e) $32 bn, per capita $8300

HDI (2002) 0.820

History Visited by Columbus, 1502; named Costa Rica ('rich coast') in the belief that vast gold treasures existed; independence from Spain, 1821; member of Federation of Central America, 1824–39; new constitution, 1949, established Costa Rica as a democratic state; governed by an executive President, Legislative Assembly, and Cabinet.

Head of State/Government
2002–6   Abel Pacheco
2006–   Oscar Arias

CÔTE D'IVOIRE

Local name Côte d'Ivoire

Timezone GMT

Area 322 462 km²/124 503 sq mi

Population total (2002e) 16 805 000

Status Republic

Date of independence 1960

Capital Yamoussoukro (formerly Abidjan)

Languages French (official), Akan, Kru

Ethnic groups Akan (41%), Kru (17%), Voltaic (16%), Malinke (15%), Southern Mande (10%)

Religions Traditional beliefs (63%), Muslim (25%), Christian (12%)

Physical features Sandy beaches and lagoons backed by broad forest-covered coastal plain; Mt Nimba massif in NW, 1752 m /5748 ft; rivers include Comoé, Sassandra, Bandama.

Climate Tropical, varying with distance from coast; average annual rainfall at Yamoussoukro 2100 mm/ 83 in; average annual temperatures 25–7°C.

Currency 1 CFA Franc (XAF) = 100 centimes

Economy Largely based on agriculture (employs c.82% of the population): palm oil, rice, maize, ground nuts, bananas; world's largest cocoa producer, third largest coffee producer.

GDP (2002e) $24.03 bn, per capita $1400

HDI (2002) 0.428

History Explored by Portuguese, 15th-c; declared a French protectorate, 1889; colony, 1893; territory within French West Africa, 1904; independence, 1960; constitution provides for multi-party system, but opposition parties only allowed since 1990; post of Prime

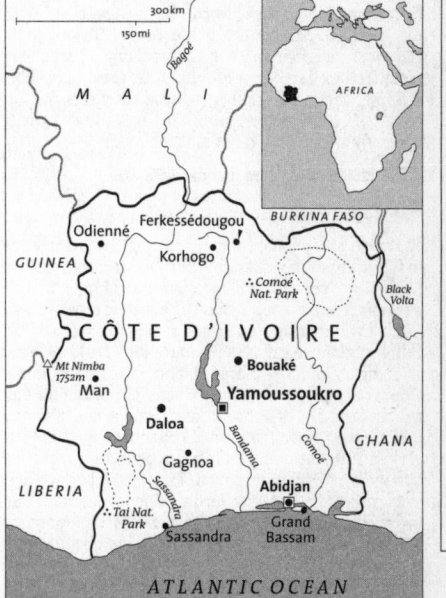

☐ International Airport   ∴ World heritage site

Minister created, 1990; governed by a National Assembly, executive President, Council of Ministers; fighting between rebel groups, 2002; French intervention to support ceasefire, 2002; UN mission to support peace plan, 2003; ceasefire, 2003, broken, 2004; ongoing, 2005.

Head of State
2000–   Laurent Gbagbo

Head of Government
2005–   Charles Konan Banny

CROATIA

Local name Hrvatska

Timezone GMT +1

Area 56 540 km²/21 825 sq mi

Population total (2002e) 4 405 000

Status Republic

Date of independence 1991

Capital Zagreb

Language Croatian

Ethnic groups (1990) Croat (75%), Serb (12%), Slovenes (1%)

Religions Roman Catholic, Eastern Orthodox

Physical features Fertile Pannonian Plain in C and E; mountainous, barren coastal region near Dinaric Alps; Adriatic coast to W; one third of country forested; main rivers: Drava, Danube, Sava; coastal Velebit and Velika

HUMAN GEOGRAPHY

HUMAN GEOGRAPHY

Croatia (continued)

Kapela ranges reach heights of 2200 m/7200 ft; islands include Korčula, Lõsinj, Dugi Otok, Cres, Krk.

Climate Continental in Pannonian Basin: average temperatures 19°C (Jul), –1°C (Jan); average annual rainfall 750 mm/30 in; Mediterranean climate on Adriatic coast: average temperatures 24°C (Jul), 6°C (Jan).

Currency 1 Kuna (HRK) = 100 lipa

Economy Agriculture; corn, oats, sugar-beet, potatoes, meat and dairy products; tourism on Adriatic coast; electrical engineering; metal-working; machinery manufacture; lumber; aluminium, textiles, petroleum refining, chemicals, rubber; natural resources include bauxite, coal, copper, iron; all economic activity adversely affected by war of independence.

GDP (2002e) $43.12 bn, per capita $9800

HDI (2002) 0.809

History Slavic Croat tribes (Chrobati, Hrvati) migrated to White Russia (now Ukraine) during 6th-c; converted to Christianity between 7th and 9th-c and adopted Roman alphabet; Frankish and Byzantine invaders repelled, and Croat kingdom reached its peak during 11th-c; Lázló I of Hungary claimed Croatian throne, 1091; Turkish defeat of Hungary in 1526 placed Pannonian Croatia under Ottoman rule; rest of Croatia elected Ferdinand of Austria as king and fought Turkey; Croatia and Slovenia became part of Hungary until collapse of Austria-Hungary in 1918; formed the Kingdom of Serbs, Croats and Slovenes with Montenegro and Serbia, 1918; became part of Yugoslavia, 1929; proclaimed an independent state during occupation by the Axis Powers, 1941–5; became a republic of Yugoslavia again, 1945; nationalist upsurges during 1950s against Communist rule, culminating in a bloody war with Serbian-dominated Yugoslav army, 1991; declaration of independence, 1991; autonomy claimed by Serb-dominated Krajina area; UN peacekeeping forces deployed, 1992; continued fighting between Croatian forces and Bosnian Serbs in the civil war in

□ International Airport

Bosnia-Herzegovina; 1995 offensive restored territorial balance in Bosnia; ceasefire followed by peace treaty (Nov) recognized Bosnian-Croat Federation in W Bosnia; governed by an Assembly consisting of a Chamber of Deputies and a Chamber of Districts.

Head of State
2000–   Stjepan Mesic

Head of Government
2003–   Ivo Sanader

CUBA

Local name Cuba

Timezone GMT –5

Area 110 860 km²/42 792 sq mi

Population total (2002e) 11 267 000

Status Republic

Date of independence 1902

Capital Havana

Language Spanish (official)

Ethnic groups Mulatto (50%), Spanish (37%), African origin (11%)

Religions Roman Catholic (40%), Protestant (3%), Afro-Cuban syncretist (2%), non-religious (55%): Castro regime discourages religious practice

Physical features Archipelago in the Caribbean Sea, comprising the island of Cuba, Isla de la Juventud, and c.1600 islets and cays; main island of Cuba, 1250 km/

□ International Airport

777 mi; three mountainous regions range E–W, the Oriental, including Cuba's highest peak, Pico Turquino, 2005 m/6578 ft, Central, and Occidental ranges; longest river is Rio Cauto in E.

Climate Subtropical climate, warm and humid; average annual temperature 25°C; dry season (Nov– Apr); mean annual rainfall, 1375 mm/54 in; hurricanes (Jun–Nov).

Currency 1 Cuban Peso (CUP) = 100 centavos

Economy World's second largest sugar producer (accounting for 75% of export earnings); world's fifth largest producer of nickel; fish, coffee, tobacco, citrus fruits, rice.

GDP (2002e) $30.69 bn, per capita $2700

HDI (2002) 0.795

History Visited by Columbus, 1492; Spanish colony until 1898, following revolution under José Martí with support of USA; independence, 1902; struggle against dictatorship of General Batista led by Fidel Castro Ruz, finally successful in 1959, and a Communist state established; invasion of Cuban exiles with US support defeated at Bay of Pigs, 1961; US naval blockade, after Soviet installation of missile bases discovered in Cuba (Cuban Missile Crisis), 1962; Communist Party of Cuba established as the sole legal party, 1965; President of the State Council is Head of State; State Council, appointed by National Assembly of People's Power.

Head of State/Government

1976–   Fidel Castro Ruz

CYPRUS

Local names Kipros (Greek), Kibris (Turkish)

Timezone GMT +2

Area 9251 km²/3571 sq mi

Population total (2002e) 802 000

Status Republic

Date of independence 1960

Capital Nicosia (proposed new name Lefkosia, 1995–)

Languages Greek and Turkish (official), English

Ethnic groups Greek (78%), Turkish (18%), other (4%)

Religions Greek Orthodox (78%), Sunni Muslim (18%), other Christian (4%)

Physical features Third largest island in Mediterranean; Kyrenia Mts extend 150 km/90 mi along N coast, Mt Kyparissovouno, 1024 m/3360 ft; forest-covered Troödos Mts in SW, rising to 1951 m/6401 ft at Mt Olympus; fertile alluvial Mesaoria plain extends across island centre; SE plateau region slopes towards indented coastline, with several long, sandy beaches; major rivers include the Pedios, Karyota, Kouris.

Climate Mediterranean, with hot, dry summers and warm, wet winters; average annual rainfall ranges from 300–400 mm/12–16 in on the Mesaoria Plain to 1200 mm/47 in in the Troödos Mts; mean daily temperatures in Nicosia 10°C (Jan), 28°C (Jul); temperatures range from 22°C on Troödos Mts, to 29°C on Central plain (Jul–Aug); snow on higher land in winter.

Currency Greek Cyprus: 1 Cyprus Pound (CYP) = 100 cents; Turkish Cyprus: 1 Turkish Lira (TRL) = 100 kurus

Economy Main exports include cement, clothing, footwear, citrus, potatoes, grapes, wine; tourism also recovering (now accounting for c.15% of national income); Famagusta (chief port prior to 1974 Turkish invasion) now under Turkish occupation, and declared closed by Cyprus government; Turkish Cypriot economy heavily dependent on agriculture.

GNP (1996) $8.9 bn, per capita $1370

HDI (1998) 0.886

History Recorded history of 4000 years; rulers included

☐ International Airport

Greeks, Ptolemies, Persians, Romans, Byzantines, Arabs, Franks, Venetians, Turks (1571–1878), and British; British Crown Colony from 1925; Greek Cypriot demands for union with Greece (*enosis*) led to guerrilla warfare, under Grivas and Makarios, and four-year state of emergency, 1955–9; independence, 1960, with Britain retaining sovereignty over bases at Akrotiri and Dhekelia; Greek–Turkish fighting through 1960s, with UN peacekeeping force sent in 1964; Greek junta engineered coup d'état, 1974; Turkish invasion in 1974 led to occupation of over a third of the island; island divided into two by the Attila Line, cutting through Nicosia where it is called the Green Line; almost all Turks now live in N sector (37% of island); governed by a President (head of state), elected by the Greek community, and House of Representatives; Turkish members ceased to attend in 1983, when Turkish community declared independence (as 'Turkish Republic of Northern Cyprus' (TRNC), with Raul Denktas as president, recognized only by Turkey); UN peace proposals rejected, 1984; summit meeting between Kyprianou (Greek president of Cyprus) and Denktas failed, 1985; UN-sponsored peace negotiations, 1997; further talks, 2002; Green Line opened for daytime crossings, 2003; UN plan to reunite island rejected by Greek Cypriots, 2004; inter-island trade between TRNC and Greek Cyprus resumed, Aug 2004.

Head of State/Government

2003–   Tassos Papadopoulos

CZECHOSLOVAKIA >> CZECH REPUBLIC; SLOVAK REPUBLIC

HUMAN GEOGRAPHY

HUMAN GEOGRAPHY

CZECH REPUBLIC

Local name Česká republika

Timezone GMT +1

Area 78 864 km²/30 441 sq mi

Population total (2002e) 10 210 000

Status Republic

Date of independence 1993

Capital Prague

Languages Czech (official), with several minorities

Ethnic groups Czech (94%), Slovak (4%), Hungarian, Polish, German, and Ukrainian minorities

Religions Roman Catholic (39%), Protestant (2%)

Physical features Landlocked in C Europe; Bohemian Massif, average height, 900 m/2953 ft, surrounds the Bohemian basin in W; Elbe-Moldau river system flows N into Germany; fertile plains of the Morava River divide Czech from Slovak Republic; c.40% land is arable.

Climate Continental, with warm, humid summers and cold, dry winters; average annual temperatures 2°C (Jan), 19°C (Jul) in Prague; average annual rainfall, 483 mm/19 in.

Currency 1 Koruna (CZK) = 100 halér̆

Economy Steel production around Ostrava coalfields; machinery, iron, glass, chemicals, motor vehicles, cement; wheat, sugar beet, potatoes, rye, corn, barley.

GDP (2002e) $157.1 bn, per capita $15 300

HDI (2002) 0.849

History From 880 ruled by the Premyslid dynasty; rise of Bohemian royal power, 14th-c; ruled by Austrian Habsburgs, early 17th-c; Czech lands united with Slovakia to form separate state of Czechoslovakia, 1918; occupied by

□ International Airport

Germany, 1938; government in exile in London during World War 2; Czechoslovakian independence, with loss of some territory to USSR, 1946; communist rule imposed by Russia following 1948 coup; attempt at liberalization by Dubček terminated by intervention of Warsaw Pact troops, 1968; fall from power of the Communist Party, 1989; 1992 agreement to divide Czechoslovakia into its constituent republics, Czech and Slovak, by Jan 1993; Czech Republic now comprises former provinces of Bohemia, Silesia, Moravia; governed by a Chamber of Deputies and (1996) 81-member Senate.

Head of State
2003–   Václav Klaus

Head of Government
2006–   Mirek Topolanek

DENMARK

Local name Danmark

Timezone GMT +1

Area 43 076 km²/16 627 sq mi (excluding Greenland and Faroe Islands)

Population total (2002e) 5 364 000

Status Kingdom

Capital Copenhagen

Language Danish (official)

Ethnic groups Danish (97%), Turkish (0.5%), other Scandinavian (0.4%)

Religions Evangelical Lutheran (97%), Roman Catholic (0.5%), Jewish (0.1%)

Physical features Consists of most of the Jutland peninsula, several islands in the Baltic Sea, and some of the N Frisian Is in the North Sea; coastline 3400 km/2100 mi; uniformly low-lying; no large rivers and few lakes; shoreline indented by many lagoons and fjords, largest is Lim Fjord.

□ International Airport

Climate Modified by Gulf Stream; cold and cloudy winters, warm and sunny summers; average annual temperatures range from 0.5°C (Jan) to 17°C (Jul); average annual rainfall 800 mm/32 in.

Currency 1 Danish Krone (DKK) = 100 øre

Economy Lack of raw materials has resulted in development of processing industries; intensive agriculture; wide range of food processing; machinery, textiles, furniture, electronics; dairy products.

GDP (2002e) $155.3 bn, per capita $28 900

HDI (2002) 0.926

History Part of Viking kingdoms, 8th–10th-c; Danish Empire under Canute, 11th-c; joined with Sweden and Norway under Queen Margrethe of Denmark, 1389; Sweden separated from union in 16th-c, followed by Norway, 1814; Schleswig-Holstein lost to Germany, 1864; N Schleswig returned after plebiscite, 1920; occupied by Germany during World War 2; Iceland independent, 1944; Greenland and Faroe Is remain dependencies; constitutional monarchy since 1849; unicameral system adopted, 1953; legislative power lies with the Monarch and the Diet jointly.

Head of State (Monarch)
1972–   Margrethe II

Head of Government
1993–2001   Poul Nyrup Rasmussen
2001–   Anders Fogh Rasmussen

Faroe Islands (Faeroe)

Local name Faerøerne (Danish)

Timezone GMT

Area 1400 km²/540 sq mi

Population total (2002e) 47 000

Status Self-governing region of Denmark

Capital Tórshavn

Languages Faroese (official, derived from Old Norse), Danish

Religion Evangelical Lutheran

Physical features Group of 22 sparsely vegetated volcanic islands in the N Atlantic between Iceland and the Shetland Is; 17 inhabited; largest islands: Strømø, Østerø, Vagø, Suderø, Sandø, Bordø.

Greenland (Kalaalit Nunaat)

Local names Kalaalit Nunaat (Greenlandic), Grønland (Danish), Kalâtdlit-Nunât (Inuit)

Timezone GMT 0, –1, –4

Area 2 175 600 km²/839 800 sq mi

Population total (2002e) 57 000

Status Self-governing province of Denmark

Capital Nuuk (Godthåb)

Languages Danish (official), Inuit

Ethnic groups Largely Inuit (Eskimo), with Danish admixtures

Religions Lutheran, Shamanist

Physical features Located in N Atlantic and Arctic Oceans; largely covered by an ice-cap (up to 4300 m/14 000 ft thick); coastal mountains rise to 3702 m/12 145 ft at Gunnbjørn Fjeld (SE); less than 5% of island habitable.

Climate Arctic to subarctic.

Currency 1 Danish Krone (DKK) = 100 Yre

Economy Largely dependent on fishing from ice-free SW ports; hunting for seal and fox furs in N and E; reserves of lead, zinc, molybdenum, uranium, coal, cryolite.

History Settled by seal-hunting Eskimos from North America, c.2500 BC; Norse settlers in SW, 12th–15th-c AD;

Climate Mild winters, overcast cool summers.

Currency 1 Danish Krone (DKK) = 100 øre

Economy Main produce: fish, crafts, potatoes; denmark provides an annual economic subsidy.

History Settled by Norse, 8th-c; part of Norway, 11th-c; passed to Denmark, 1380; parliament restored, 1852; self-governing region of Denmark since 1948; unicameral Parliament (*Lagting*) consists of 34 members.

Head of State (Monarch)
1972–   Margrethe II

Head of Government
2004–   Joannes Eidesgaard

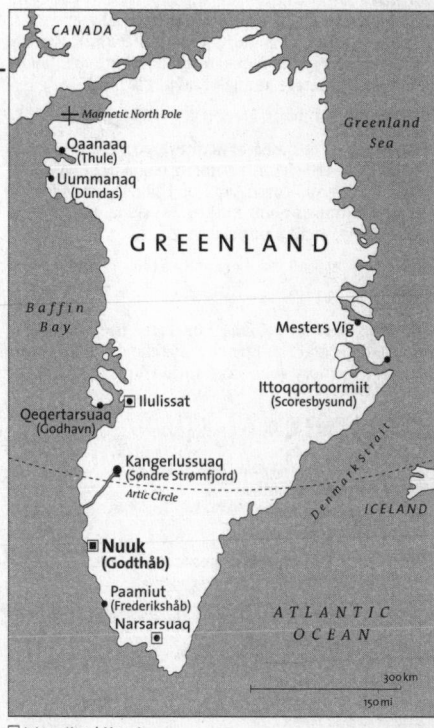

CANADA

✛ *Magnetic North Pole*

Qaanaaq (Thule)
Uummanaq (Dundas)

Greenland Sea

GREENLAND

Baffin Bay

Mesters Vig

Ittoqqortoormiit (Scoresbysund)

Ilulissat
Qeqertarsuaq (Godhavn)

Kangerlussuaq (Søndre Strømfjord)
Artic Circle

Denmark Strait

ICELAND

Nuuk (Godthåb)

Paamiut (Frederikshåb)
Narsarsuaq

ATLANTIC OCEAN

300 km
150 mi

☐ International Airport

HUMAN GEOGRAPHY

Denmark (continued)

explored by Frobisher and Davis, 16th-c; Danish colony from 1721; self-governing province of Denmark, 1979; elected Provincial Council sends two members to the Danish Parliament.

Head of State (Monarch)
1972–   Margrethe II

Head of Government
2002–   Hans Enoksen

DJIBOUTI

Local name Jumhouriyya Djibouti

Timezone GMT +3

Area 23 200 km²/8958 sq mi

Population total (2002e) 473 000

Status Republic

Date of independence 1977

Capital Djibouti

Language Arabic (official)

Ethnic groups Somali (47%), Afar (20%), Arab (mostly Yemeni) (6%), European (4%), other refugees (10%)

Religions Muslim (94%), Christian (Roman Catholic 4%, Protestant 1%, Orthodox 1%)

Physical features Located in NE Africa; series of plateaux dropping down from mountains to flat, low-lying, rocky desert; fertile coastal strip around the Gulf of Tadjoura; highest point, Moussa Ali, rising to 2020 m/ 6627 ft in the N.

Climate Semi-arid climate, with hot season (May–Sep); very high temperatures on coastal plain all year round; average temperatures 26°C (Jan), 36°C (Jul); slightly lower humidity and temperatures in interior highlands; low rainfall; average annual rainfall 130 mm/5 in.

Currency 1 Djibouti Franc (DJF) = 100 centimes

Economy Crop-based agriculture possible only with irrigation; livestock-raising among nomadic population; some fishing on coast; port of Djibouti provides an important transit point for Red Sea trade, particularly for Ethiopia; small industrial sector.

GDP (2002e) $619 mn, per capita $1300

HDI (2002) 0.445

History French colonial interest in mid-19th-c; annexed by France as French Somaliland, 1896; French Overseas Territory, following World War 2; French Terri-

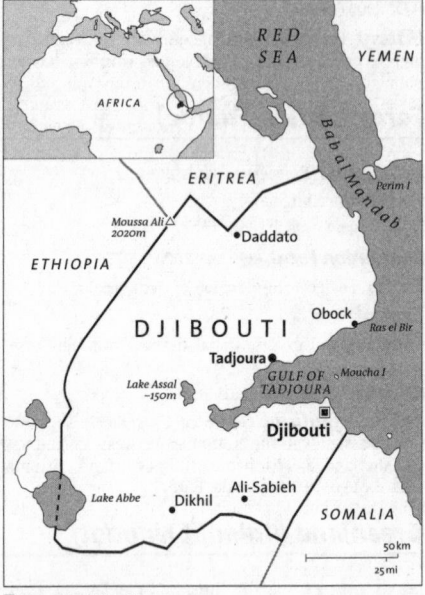

☐ International Airport

tory of the Afars and the Issas, 1967; independence, 1977. Political parties combined in 1979 to form People's Progress Assembly (RPP) as single ruling party; overwhelming majority voted in favour of a multi-party constitution, 1992; governed by a President, a Legislative Chamber, an executive Prime Minister, and a Council.

Head of State
1999–   Ismael Omar Guelleh

Head of Government
2001–   Dileita Mohamed Dileita

DOMINICA

Local name Dominica

Timezone GMT –4

Area 751 km²/290 sq mi

Population total (2002e) 71 700

Status Independent republic within the Commonwealth

Date of independence 1978

Capital Roseau

Languages English (official), with French widely spoken

Ethnic groups African or mixed African-European descent (97%), Amerindian (2%)

Religions Christian (Roman Catholic 77%, Protestant 16%)

Physical features Island in the Windward group of the West Indies; c.50 km/30 mi long and 26 km/16 mi wide; rises to 1447 m/4747 ft at Morne Diablotin; volcanic origin; central ridge, with several rivers; 67% of land area forested.

Climate Warm and humid tropical climate; temperatures ranging 25.6–32.2°C; rainy season (Jun–Oct); heavy rainfall, varies from 1750 mm/70 in average on the coast, to 6250 mm/246 in inland.

Currency 1 East Caribbean Dollar (XCD) = 100 cents

Economy Agriculture; tourism; coconut-based products, cigars, citrus fruits (notably limes), bananas, coconuts, bay oil.

GDP (2002e) $380 mn, per capita $5400

HDI (2002) 0.779

History Visited by Columbus, 1493; colonization attempts by French and British in 18th-c; British Crown Colony from 1805; part of Federation of the West Indies, 1958–62; independent republic within the Commonwealth, 1978; governed by a House of Assembly, President, Prime Minister, and Cabinet.

Head of State
1998–2003 Vernon Shaw
2003–   Dr Nicholas Liverpool

Head of Government
2001–4   Pierre Charles
2004–   Roosevelt Skerrit

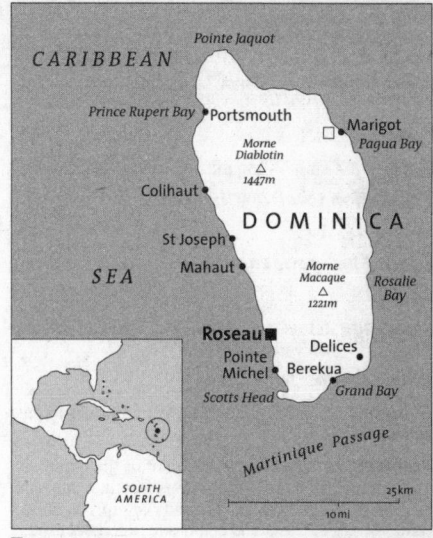
□ International Airport

DOMINICAN REPUBLIC

Local name República Dominicana

Timezone GMT –4

Area 48 442 km²/18 699 sq mi

Population total (2002e) 8 833 000

Status Republic

Date of independence 1844

Capital Santo Domingo

Language Spanish (official)

Ethnic groups Spanish, or mixed Spanish and African descent

Religions Roman Catholic (92%), other (mostly Evangelical Protestant and followers of voodoo) (8%)

Physical features Crossed NW–SE by Cordillera Central, with many peaks over 3000 m/10 000 ft; Pico Duarte, 3175 m/10 416 ft is highest peak in the Caribbean; wide coastal plain in E; main rivers include Yaque del Sur, Yaque del Norte, Yuna (E).

Climate Tropical maritime climate with rainy season (May–Nov); Santo Domingo, average temperature 23.9°C (Jan), 27.2°C (Jul); annual rainfall 1400 mm/55 in; hurricanes (Jun–Nov).

Currency 1 Dominican Peso (DOP) = 100 centavos

Economy Mainly agriculture, especially sugar, cocoa; tourism expanding with new resort complexes on N coast.

GNP (2002e) $53.78 bn, per capita $6300

HDI (2002) 0.727

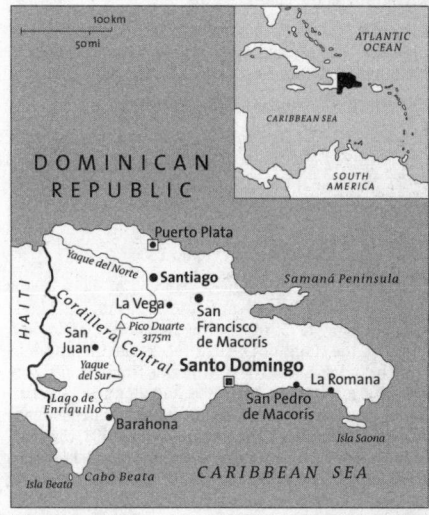
□ International Airport

History Visited by Columbus, 1492; Spanish colony, 16th–17th-c; E province of Santo Domingo remained Spanish after partition of Hispaniola, 1697; taken over by Haiti on several occasions; independence from Haiti, 1844, as Dominican Republic; occupied by USA, 1916–24, 1965; comprises 26 provinces and a National District which contains the capital; governed by a President and National Congress (Senate and Chamber of Deputies).

Head of State/Government
2000–4   Hipólito Mejía
2004–   Leonel Fernandez

EAST TIMOR

Local name (Port.) Timor Leste, (Tetum) Timor Loro Sae

Timezone GMT +8

Area 14 874 km²/5743 sq mi

Population total (2002e) 738 000

Status Republic

Date of independence 2002

Capital Dili

Language Tetum and Portuguese (official), Indonesian and English widely spoken

Ethnic groups Tetum

Religions Roman Catholic (91.4%), traditional animist beliefs

Physical features Occupies E half of the mountainous island of Timor and the enclave of Oecussi (Ambeno) in West Timor, SE Asia, in the Sunda Group, NW of Australia; W half of the island belongs to Indonesia (part of East Nusa Tengarra province); highest peak, Tata Mailau (2950 m/9679 ft); many rivers flowing from the mountains through the coastal plains.

Climate Hot with monsoon rains falling between December and March; average daily temperature 32°C (Oct–Dec), 21°C (Jan–Sep).

Currency 1 US dollar (USD) = 100 cents

Economy 90% of the population live off the land, with one in three households living below the poverty line; coffee is the main export crop, also coconuts, cloves, cacao, and marble; offshore gas and oil to be exploited from 2004.

GDP (2002e) $440 mn, per capita $500

History Former Portuguese colony of East Timor declared itself independent as the Democratic Republic of East Timor, 1975; invaded by Indonesian forces and annexed, the claim not recognized by the UN; administered by Indonesia as the province of Timor Timur; considerable local unrest (1989–90), and mounting international concern over civilian deaths; independence movement (Fretilin) largely supressed by 1993; UN-sponsored talks, 1993; ongoing conflict, mid-1990s; President Habibie grants referendum, 1999, resulting in 78.5% vote in favour of independence, immediately followed by widespread violence and destruction of property by pro-Jakarta militia groups and major refugee movements; growing threat to the UN presence in Dili led to arrival of UN-sponsored, Australian-led intervention force; administered by the UN since 1999, with a transitional administration, 2000; elections for a 38-member Constituent Assembly, 2001; Council of Ministers of the Second Transitional Government, 2001; presidential elections (Apr), followed by full independence, May 2002; UN Mission of Support in East Timor (Unmiset) to remain in place until 2003; parliamentary system of government with a largely ceremonial president; army and police split by internal disputes and gang violence, President Gusmao assumed emergency powers to control looting and unrest (May 2006); José Ramos-Horta appointed prime minister (Jul 2006).

☐ International Airport   1 AMBENO (OECUSSI)

Head of State

2002–   Xanana Gusmao

Head of Government

2001–6   Mari Alkatiri

2006–   José Ramos-Horta

ECUADOR

Local name Ecuador

Timezone GMT –5

Area 270 699 km²/104 490 sq mi (including the Galápagos Islands, 7812 km²/3015 sq mi)

Population total (2002e) 13 095 000

Status Republic

Date of independence 1830

Capital Quito

Languages Spanish (official), with Quechua also spoken

Ethnic groups Quechua (50%), mestizo (40%), white (8.5%), other Amerindian (5%)

Religions Roman Catholic (94%), other (6%)

Physical features Located in NW South America; includes the Galápagos Is, Ecuadorian island group on the equator 970 km/600 mi W of South American mainland; coastal plain in the W, descending from rolling hills (N) to broad lowland basin; Andean uplands in C rising to snow-capped peaks which include Cotopaxi, 5896 m/19343 ft; forested alluvial plains in the E, dissected by rivers flowing from the Andes towards the Amazon (source of the Amazon located in Peru).

Climate Hot and humid, wet equatorial climate on coast; rain throughout year (especially Dec–Apr); average annual rainfall 1115 mm/44 in; average annual temperatures in Quito, 15°C (Jan), 14°C (Jul).

Currency 1 US dollar (USD) = 100 cents (before 2000, the Sucre (ECS))

Economy Agriculture (employs c.35% of population); beans, cereals, livestock; bananas, coffee, fishing (especially shrimps); petrochemicals, steel, cement, pharmaceuticals; oil piped from the Oriente basin in E to refineries at Esmeraldas.

GDP (2002e) $42.65 bn, per capita $3200

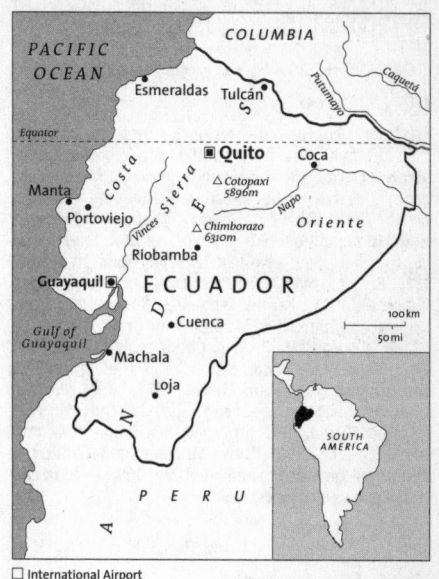

☐ International Airport

HDI (2002) 0.732

History Formerly part of Inca Empire; taken by Spanish, 1534; within Viceroyalty of New Granada; independent, 1822; joined with Panama, Colombia, and Venezuela to form Gran Colombia; left union, to become independent republic, 1830; highly unstable political history; constitution, 1978; comprises 21 provinces, including the Galápagos Is, each administered by a governor; governed by a President and a unicameral National Congress.

Head of State/Government
2002–5   Lucio Gutierrez
2005–6   Alfredo Palacio
2006–   Rafael Correa

EGYPT

Local name Misr

Timezone GMT +2

Area 1 001 449 km²/386 559 sq mi

Population total (2002e) 66 341 000

Status Republic

Date of independence 1922

Capital Cairo

Language Arabic (official)

Ethnic group Population mainly of E Hamitic origin (90%)

Religions Sunni Muslim (c.90%), minority largely Coptic Christian (c.10%)

Physical features R Nile flows N from Sudan, dammed S of Aswan, creating L Nasser; huge delta N of Cairo, 250 km/150 mi across and 160 km/100 mi N–S; narrow Eastern Desert, sparsely inhabited, between Nile and Red Sea; broad Western Desert, covering over two-thirds of the country; Sinai Peninsula (S), desert region with mountains rising to 2637 m/8651 ft at Gebel Katherîna, Egypt's highest point; 90% of population lives on Nile floodplain (c.3% of country's area).

Climate Mainly desert climate, except for 80 km/50 mi wide Mediterranean coastal fringe; very hot on coast where dust-laden khamsin wind blows N from Sahara (Mar-Jun); Alexandria, average maximum daily temperatures 18–30°C; elsewhere rainfall less than 50 mm/2 in.

Currency 1 Egyptian Pound (EGP) = 100 piastres

Economy Agriculture on floodplain of R Nile accounts for about a third of national income; building of Aswan High Dam extended irrigated cultivation; a major tourist area.

HUMAN GEOGRAPHY

Egypt (continued)

GDP (2002e) $289.8 bn, per capita $4000

HDI (2002) 0.642

History Neolithic cultures on R Nile from c.6000 BC; Pharaoh dynasties from c.3100 BC; Egyptian power greatest during the New Empire period, 1576–1085 BC; became Persian province, 6th-c BC; conquered by Alexander the Great, 4th-c BC; Ptolemaic Pharaohs ruled Egypt until 30 BC; conquered by Arabs, AD 672; Suez Canal constructed, 1869; revolt in 1879 put down by British, 1882; British protectorate from 1914; declared independence, 1922; King Farouk deposed by Nasser, 1952; Egypt declared a republic, 1953; attack on Israel followed by Israeli invasion, 1967; Suez Canal remained blocked, 1967–75; changed name to Arab Republic of Egypt, 1971; Yom Kippur War against Israel, 1973; Israel returned disputed Taba Strip, 1989; participated in Gulf War with US-led coalition, 1991; governed by a People's National Assembly, President, Prime Minister, and Council of Ministers; constitution amended (May 2005) to allow contested presidential elections.

Head of State
1981–   Mohammed Hosni Mubarak

Head of Government
2004–   Ahmed Nazif

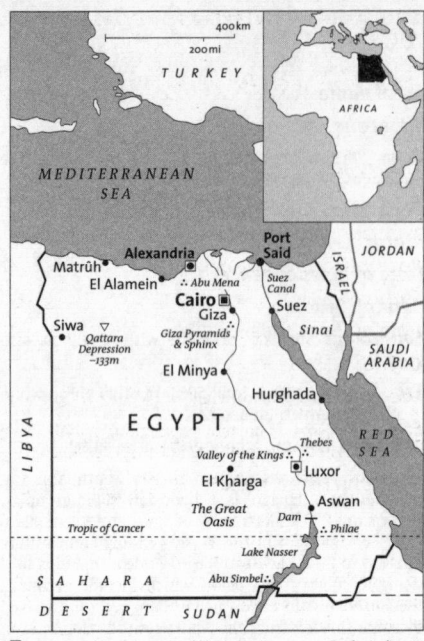

☐ International Airport   ∴ World heritage site   — — Border in dispute

EL SALVADOR

Local name El Salvador

Timezone GMT –6

Area 21 476 km²/8290 sq mi

Population total (2002e) 6 354 000

Status Republic

Date of independence 1841

Capital San Salvador

Language Spanish (official)

Ethnic groups Spanish-Indian (89%), Indian (mostly Pipil) (5%)

Religions Roman Catholic (93%), other (mostly Evangelical Protestant) (7%)

Physical features Smallest of C America republics; two volcanic ranges run E–W; narrow coastal belt in S, rises to mountains in N; highest point, Santa Ana, 2381 m/7812 ft; volcanic lakes; earthquakes common.

Climate Varies greatly with altitude; hot tropical on coastal lowlands; single rainy season (May–Oct); temperate uplands; average annual temperature at San Salvador 23°C (Jul), 22°C (Jan); average annual rainfall 1775 mm/70 in.

Currency 1 US dollar (USD) = 100 cents (before 2001, the Colón (SVC))

Economy Largely based on agriculture; main crops coffee and cotton; sugar, maize, balsam (world's main source); chemicals, rubber, rubber goods, oil products.

☐ International Airport

GDP (2002e) $29.41 bn, per capita $4600

HDI (2002) 0.706

History Originally part of the Aztec kingdom; conquest by Spanish, 1526; independence from Spain, 1821; member of the Central American Federation until its dissolution in 1839; independent republic, 1841; war with Honduras, 1965, 1969; considerable political unrest in 1970s and 80s, with guerrilla activity directed against the US-supported government; civil war, 1979–91; peace plan agreed, 1991; governed by a President and Council of Ministers; unicameral Legislative Assembly.

Head of State/Government
1999–2004 Francisco Flores
2004–   Tony Saca

ENGLAND >> UNITED KINGDOM

EQUATORIAL GUINEA

Local name Guinea Ecuatorial

Timezone GMT +1

Area 26016 km²/10042 sq mi (mainland area)

28051 km²/10828 sq mi (total area)

Population total (2002e) 498000

Status Republic

Date of independence 1968

Capital Malabo

Language Spanish (official)

Ethnic groups Mainland population, mainly Fang (83%), Bubi (10%), Ndowe (4%), Annobonés (2%), Bujeba (1%)

Religions Roman Catholic (80%), traditional beliefs (5%)

Physical features Located in WC Africa; comprises the mainland area (Río Muni) and several islands in the Gulf of Guinea; mainland rises sharply from a narrow coast of mangrove swamps towards the heavily forested African plateau; Bioko, fertile volcanic island in NW, contains Guinea's highest point, Pico de Basilé, 3007 m/ 9865 ft.

Climate Hot and humid equatorial climate; average maximum daily temperature, 29–32°C; average annual rainfall c.2000 mm/80 in.

Currency 1 CFA Franc (XAF) = 100 centimes

Economy Largely based on agriculture; cocoa, coffee, timber, bananas, cassava, palm oil, sweet potatoes.

GDP (2002e) $1.27 bn, per capita $2700

HDI (2002) 0.679

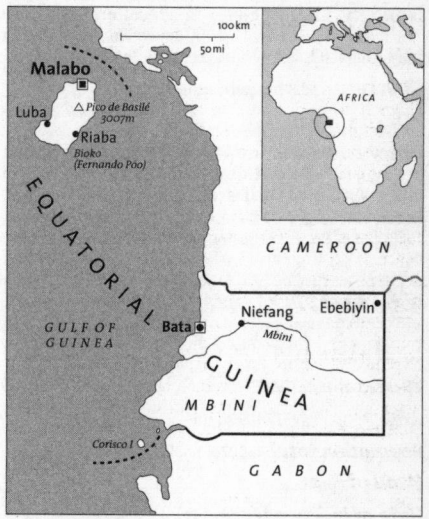

□ International Airport

History First visited by Europeans in 15th-c; island of Fernando Póo claimed by Portugal, 1494–1788; occupied by Britain, 1781–1843; rights to the area acquired by Spain, 1844; independence, 1968; military coup, 1975; governed by Supreme Military Council headed by a President; new constitution, 1991; first multi-party elections, 1993.

Head of State
1968–79   Francisco Macias Nguema
1979–   Teodoro Obiang Nguema Mbasogo

Head of Government
2006–   Ricardo Mangue Obama Nfube

ERITREA

Local name Ertra

Timezone GMT +3

Area 93700 km²/36200 sq mi

Population total (2002e) 3981000

Status Republic

Date of Independence 1993

Capital Asmara

Language Tigrinya, Tigray, Amharic

Ethnic groups Tigray, Amhara

Religions Islam (50%), Coptic Christianity (50%)

Pysical features Ethiopian plateau drops to low plains; E plain includes the Danakil Depression, descending to 116 m/381 ft below sea level.

Climate Tropical climate varied by altitude; annual average temperature at Asmara, 16°C, at Mitsiwa (on coast) 30°C; hot, semi-arid NE and SE lowlands receive

□ International Airport

less than 500 mm/20 in rainfall annually; severe droughts have caused widespread famine.

Currency I Nafka (ERN) = 100 cents (before 1997, the Ethiopian Birr (ETB))

HUMAN GEOGRAPHY

HUMAN GEOGRAPHY

Eritrea (continued)

Economy Largely devoted to agriculture, but badly affected by drought, and heavily dependent on irrigation and foreign aid; textiles, leather, salt, food production.

GDP (2002e) $3.3 bn, per capita $700

HDI (2002) 0.421

History Federated as part of Ethiopia, 1952; province of Ethiopia, 1962, led to political unrest; civil war in 1970s, with major gains for separatists; Soviet- and Cuban-backed government forces regained most areas, 1978; fall of President Mengistu (1991) led to new status as autonomous region, with provisional government established by Eritrean People's Liberation Front; referendum followed by declaration of independence, 1993; transitional government for 4 years, consisting of a National Assembly, which elects the president, and a State Council; escalating conflict with Ethiopia over disputed border territory, 1999–2000; Permanent Court of Arbitration at The Hague issued border ruling, 2002; government accepted ruling 'in principle', Nov 2004.

Head of State
1993–   Isaias Afwerki

ESTONIA

Local name Eesti

Timezone GMT +2

Area 45 100 km²/17 409 sq mi

Population total (2002e) 1 359 000

Status Republic

Date of independence 1991

Capital Tallinn

Languages Estonian (official), also Russian

Ethnic groups Estonian (65%), Russian (28%), Ukrainian (3%), Belorussian (2%)

Religions Evangelical Lutheran, with Orthodox minority

Physical features Consists of mainland area and c.800 islands (including the Baltic island of Saaremaa); S covered with morainal hills, C with elongated glacial hills usually arrayed in the direction of glacial movement; most lakes and rivers drain either E into Lake Peipus, N into the Gulf of Finland; a few W into Gulf of Riga.

Climate Mild climate. Average annual temperatures –6°C (Jan) and 17°C (Jul); average annual rainfall 650 mm/26 in.

Currency 1 Kroon (EEK) = 100 cents

Economy Major industries: agricultural machinery, electric motors; agricultural produce of grain, vegetables; livestock.

GDP (2002e) $15.52 bn, per capita $11 000

HDI (2002) 0.826

History Ceded to Russia, 1721; independence, 1918; proclaimed a Soviet Socialist Republic, 1940; occupied by

□ International Airport

Germany in World War 2; resurgence of nationalist movement in the 1980s; declared independence, 1991; 105-member Parliament; 495-member Congress of Estonia.

Head of State
2001–6   Arnold Rüütel
2006   Toomas Hendrik Ilves

Head of Government
2005–   Andrus Ansip

ETHIOPIA

Local name Ityopiya

Timezone GMT +3

Area 1 251 282 km²/483 123 sq mi

Population total (2002e) 67 673 000

Status Republic

Capital Addis Ababa

Language Amharic (official)

Ethnic groups Oromo (40%), Amhara and Tigray (32%)

Religions Muslim (45%), Ethiopian Orthodox (37%), traditional beliefs (11%)

Physical features Located in NE Africa; dominated by mountainous C plateau, mean elevation 1800–2400 m/ 6–8000 ft; split diagonally by the Great Rift Valley; highest point, Ras Dashan Mt, 4620 m/15 157 ft; crossed E–W by Blue Nile; Danakil Depression (NE) dips to 116 m/ 381 ft below sea level.

Climate Tropical climate, moderated by higher altitudes; distinct wet season (Apr–Sep); hot, semi-arid NE and SE lowlands receive less than 500 mm/20 in of rainfall annually; droughts in 1980s caused widespread famine, deaths, and resettlement; major famine, 2003.

Currency 1 Ethiopian Birr (ETB) = 100 cents

Economy One of the world's poorest countries; over 80% of population employed in agriculture, especially subsistence farming; production severely affected by drought; distribution of foreign aid hindered by internal civil war and poor local organization.

GDP (2002e) $48.53 bn, per capita $700

HDI (2002) 0.327

History Oldest independent country in sub-Saharan Africa; first Christian country in Africa; Eritrea occupied by Italy, 1882; independence of Abyssinia (former name of Ethiopia) recognized by League of Nations, 1923; Haile Selassie became Emperor in 1930, and began programme of modernization and reform; Italian invasion, 1935; annexation as Italian East Africa, 1936–41; Italians forced from Ethiopia by the Allies, and Haile Selassie returned to power, 1941; military coup, 1974; ongoing conflict with Somalia over Ogaden region; internal conflict with regional separatist Eritrean and Tigrean forces; transfer of power to People's Democratic Republic, 1987; government overthrown by separatist forces, 1991; Council of Representatives formed; Eritrea formally recognized as an independent state, 1993; multi-party elections, 1994; new constitution, 1994, recognizing a

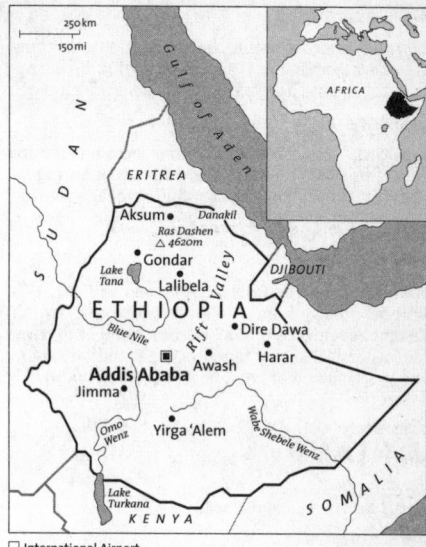

□ International Airport

federal government of nine states, and providing for regional autonomy (allowing the right of secession); new Council of People's Representatives formed, 1995; escalating conflict with Eritrea over disputed border territory, 1999–2000; Permanent Court of Arbitration at The Hague issued a border ruling, 2002.

Head of State
2001– Woldegiorgis Girma

Head of Government
1995– Meles Zenawi

FAROE ISLANDS >> DENMARK

FALKLAND ISLANDS >> UNITED KINGDOM

FIJI

Local name Viti

Timezone GMT +12

Area 18 333 km²/7076 sq mi

Population total (2002e) 824 000

Status Republic

Date of independence 1970

Capital Suva (on Viti Levu Island)

Language English (official)

Ethnic groups Indigenous Fijians (44%), Indian (51%)

Religions Native Fijians, mainly Christian (Methodist c.85%, Roman Catholic 12%); Indo-Fijians, mainly Hindu (c.70%) and Muslim (25%)

Physical features Melanesian group of 844 islands and islets in the SW Pacific Ocean; highest peak, Tomaniivi (Mt Victoria) on Viti Levu, 1324 m/4344 ft; most smaller islands consist of limestone, little vegetation; Great Sea Reef stretches 500 km/300 mi along W

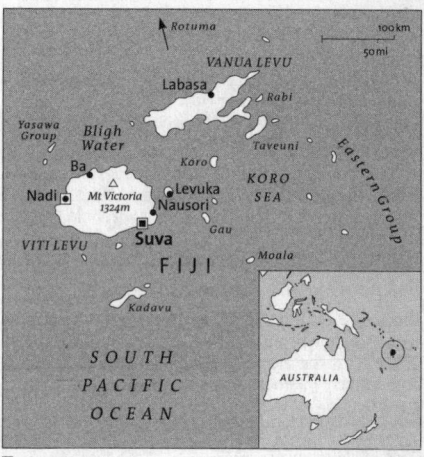

□ International Airport

fringe; dense tropical forest on wet, windward side (SE); mainly treeless on dry, leeward side.

Fiji (continued)

Climate Tropical oceanic climate, high humidity; average annual temperature 27°C, ranging from 35°C (Dec–Apr) to 16°C (Jun–Sep); heavy rainfall; occasional hurricanes.

Currency 1 Fijian Dollar (FJD) = 100 cents

Economy Agriculture; sugar cane (accounts for over two-thirds of export earnings); bananas, ginger; gold, silver, limestone, timber; major tourist area.

GDP (2002e) $4.822 bn, per capita $5600

HDI (2002) 0.758

History Visited by Tasman, 1643, and by Cook, 1774; British colony from 1874; independence within Commonwealth, 1970; 1987 election brought to power Indian-dominated coalition, leading to military coups, and proclamation of republic outside Commonwealth;

civilian government restored, 1987; constitution, 1990 and 1997; readmitted to Commonwealth, 1997; coup, with prime minister and others held as hostages, 2000; suspended from Commonwealth, 2000 (readmitted 2001); parliamentary elections, 2001; military coup dismissed president and prime minister, Dec 2006; Bainimarama named prime minister and President Iloilo reinstated, Jan 2007; bicameral Parliament of a nominated Senate and an elected House of Representatives.

Head of State
2006–7   Frank Bainimarama *Military coup*
2007–   Ratu Josefa Iloilo *Reinstated*

Head of Government
2001–6   Laisenia Qarase
2006   *Military coup*
2007–   Frank Bainimarama *Interim*

FINLAND

Local name Suomi (Finnish)

Timezone GMT +2

Area 338 145 km²/130 524 sq mi

Population total (2002e) 5 201 000

Status Republic

Date of independence 1917

Capital Helsinki

Languages Finnish and Swedish (official), also Saame (Lappish)

Ethnic groups Finnish (92%), Swedish (6%), Lappish, Russian minorities

Religions Lutheran (90%), Finnish/Greek Orthodox

Physical features Low-lying, glaciated plateau, average height 150 m/500 ft; highest peak Haltiatunturi, 1328 m/ 4357 ft, on NW border; over 60 000 shallow lakes in SE, providing a system of inland navigation; over a third of the country located N of the Arctic Circle; Archipelago of Saaristomeri (SW), with over 17 000 islands; including Åland Is (Ahvenanmaa) (SW); forest covers 65% of the country, water covers 10%.

Climate Extreme, N of the Arctic Circle: lowest winter temperatures –45–50°C; half annual precipitation falls as snow; polar night lasts 51 days; sun does not go down beyond the horizon for 73 days during summer; average temperatures –9°C (Jan), 20°C (Jul) at Helsinki; average annual rainfall 618 mm/24 in.

Currency 1 Euro (EUR) = 100 cents (before February 2002, 1 Markka (FIM) = 100 penni)

Economy Traditional focus on forestry, farming; rapid economic growth since 1950s; metals, clothing, chemicals, electronics, electrical equipment, telecommunications (Nokia); hydroelectric and nuclear power.

GDP (2002e) $133.8 bn, per capita $25 800

HDI (2002) 0.930

History Ruled by Sweden from 1157 until ceded to Russia in 1809; Grand Duchy of the Russian Czar, 19th-c; independent republic, 1917; parliamentary system

□ International Airport

created, 1928; invaded by Soviets, 1939–40 (Winter War); lost territory to USSR, including Petsamo and Porkkala peninsula, 1944; signed a friendship treaty with Soviet Union in 1948 (renewed 1955, 1970, 1983), undertaking to resist any attack made on the Soviet Union launched through Finnish territory; Harri Holkeri became Finland's first post-war conservative Prime Minister, 1987; governed by a single-chamber House of Representatives and President assisted by a Council of State; joined the European Union, 1995.

Head of State
1994–2000 Martti Ahtisaarsi
2000–   Tarja Halonen

Head of Government
2003   Anneli Jaatteenmaki
2003–   Matti Vanhanen

FRANCE

Local name France

Timezone GMT +1

Area 551 000 km²/212 686 sq mi

Population total (2002e) 59 440 000

Status Republic

Capital Paris

Languages French (official), Breton, Occitan and Alsatian are also spoken

Ethnic groups Celtic and Latin origin (91%), Breton, Catalan, and large immigrant population (including Portuguese, Algerian, Moroccan, and Arab minorities)

Religions Roman Catholic (90%), Protestant (4%), Muslim (3%), Jewish (1%)

Physical features Bounded S and E by large mountain ranges, notably (interior) the Massif Central, Jura, and Alps (E), rising to 4807 m/15 771 ft at Mont Blanc, and the Pyrénées (S); chief rivers include Loire (longest at 1020 km/633 mi), Rhône, Seine, Garonne; 60% of land arable.

Climate Mediterranean climate in S, with warm, moist winters and hot, dry summers; average temperatures, 3°C (Jan), 18°C (Jul); continental climate in E; average annual rainfall 786 mm/31 in; heatwave in August 2003 caused deaths of many elderly people.

Currency 1 Euro (EUR) = 100 cents (before February 2002, 1 French Franc (FRF) = 100 centimes)

Economy Main industries include wine, fruit, cheese; perfume, textiles, clothing; steel, chemicals, machinery, cars, aircraft; natural resources of coal, iron ore, bauxite, timber; tourism important.

GDP (2002e) $1.558 tn, per capita $26 000

HDI (2002) 0.928

History Celtic-speaking Gauls dominant by 5th-c BC; part of Roman Empire, 125 BC to 5th-c AD; feudal monarchy founded by Hugh Capet, 987; Plantagenets of England acquired several territories, 12th-c; lands gradually recovered in Hundred Years' War, 1337–1453, apart from Calais (regained in 1558); Capetian dynasty followed by the Valois, from 1328, and the Bourbons, from 1589; Wars of Religion, 1562–95; monarchy overthrown by the French Revolution, 1789; First Republic declared, 1792; First Empire, ruled by Napoleon, 1804–14; monarchy restored, 1814–48; Second Republic, 1848–52, and Second Empire, 1852–70, ruled by Louis Napoleon. Third Republic, 1870–1940; great political instability between World Wars, with several governments holding office for short periods; occupied by Germany 1940–4, with pro-German government at Vichy, and Free French in London under de Gaulle; Fourth Republic, 1946; war with Indo-China, 1946–54; conflict in Algeria, 1954–62. Fifth Republic, 1958; referendum on EU constitution rejected, May 2005; governed by a President, an appointed Prime Minster, a Council of Ministers, bicameral National Assembly, and Senate.

Head of State
Fifth Republic
1981–95 François Mitterrand
1995– Jacques Chirac

☐ International Airport

Head of Government
Fifth Republic
2002–5 Jean-Pierre Raffarin
2005– Dominique de Villepin

>> Political leaders and rulers, p.196

Internal Collective Territory
Island of Corsica in the Mediterranean Sea: area 8680 km²/3350 sq mi; capital, Ajaccio; GMT +1

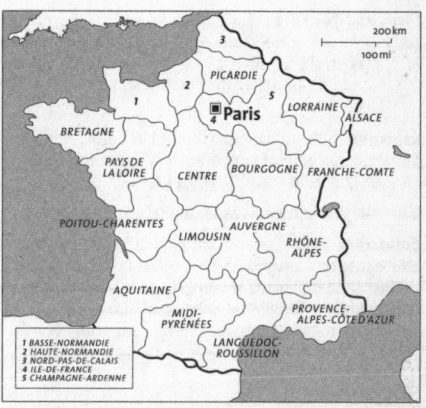
☐ International Airport

France (continued)

Overseas departments

Name	Area		Capital	GMT
	km²	sq mi		
Guadeloupe	1779	687	Basse-Terre	−4
Guiana	90909	35091	Cayenne	−3
Martinique	1079	416	Fort-de-France	−4
Mayotte	374	144	Dzaoudzi	+3
Réunion	2512	970	St Denis	+4
St Pierre et Miquelon	240	93	St Pierre	−3

Overseas territories

Name	Area		Capital/ chief centre	GMT
	km²	sq mi		
French Polynesia	3941	1521	Papeete	−6
New Caledonia	18575	7170	Nouméa	+11
Southern and Antarctic Territories	10100	3900	Port-aux-Français	
Wallis and Futuna	274	106	Matu Utu	+12

GABON

Local name Gabon

Timezone GMT +1

Area 267667 km2/103347 sq mi

Population total (2002e) 1300000

Status Republic

Date of independence 1960

Capital Libreville

Languages French (official), Fang, Myene, Bateke, and other Bantu dialects spoken

Ethnic groups c.40 Bantu tribes (Fang 30%, Eshira 25%, Bateke and Bapounou 10%) and c.10% expatriate Africans and Europeans

Religions Christian (96%) (Roman Catholic 65%, Protestant 19%, other 12%), traditional beliefs

Physical features Located in W Africa; lies on the equator for 880 km/550 mi W–E; land rises towards the African central plateau, cut by several rivers, notably the Ogooué and N'Gounié; highest point, Mont Ibounoji, 980 m/3215 ft.

Climate Typical equatorial climate: hot, wet, and humid; mean annual temperature 27°C; annual average rainfall 1250–2000 mm/50–80 in inland.

Currency 1 CFA Franc (XAF) = 100 centimes

Economy Small area of land under cultivation, but employing 65% of population; coffee, cocoa, palm oil, rubber; timber extraction; rapid economic growth since independence, largely because of offshore oil, natural gas, and minerals; manganese, uranium, iron ore.

GDP (2002e) $8.354 bn, per capita $6500

HDI (2002) 0.637

History Visited by Portuguese, 15th-c; under French control from mid-19th-c; slave ship captured by the French in 1849, the liberated slaves forming the settle-

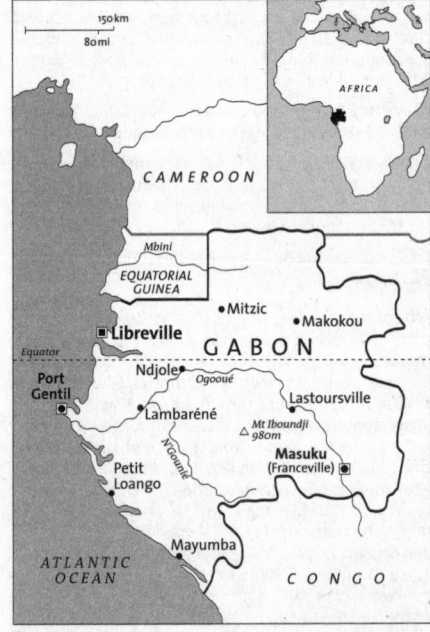

□ International Airport

ment of Libreville; occupied by France, 1885; one of four territories of French West Africa, 1910; independence, 1960; multi-party elections held, 1990; new constitution, 1991; governed by a President, an appointed Council of Ministers, and a legislative National Assembly.

Head of State
1967–   Omar (Albert-Bernard, to 1973) Bongo

Head of Government
2006–   Jean Eyeghe Ndong

GAMBIA, THE

Local name Gambia

Timezone GMT

Area 11 295 km²/4361 sq mi

Population total (2002e) 1 418 000

Status Independent republic within the Commonwealth

Date of independence 1965

Capital Banjul

Languages English (official), also Madinka, Wolof and Fula

Ethnic groups Madinka (40%), Fula (19%), Wolof (15%), Dyola (10%), Sonike (8%)

Religions Muslim (85%), Christian (14%), traditional local beliefs (1%)

Physical features Located in W Africa; surrounded, except for coastline, by Senegal; strip of land 322 km/200 mi E–W along R Gambia; flat country, not rising above 90 m/295 ft; c.25% of land arable.

Climate Tropical climate; average temperatures 23°C (Jan), 27°C (Jul), rising upland to over 40°C; rainy season (Jun–Sep) with high humidity and high night temperatures; rainfall decreasing inland.

Currency 1 Dalasi (GMD) = 100 butut

Economy Agriculture, especially groundnuts; cotton, rice, millet, sorghum, fruit, vegetables, livestock; groundnut processing, brewing, soft drinks, agricultural machinery assembly, metal working, clothing, tourism.

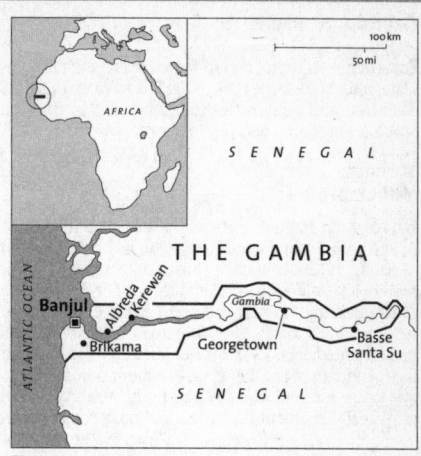

☐ International Airport

GDP (2002e) $2.582 bn, per capita $1800

HDI (2002) 0.405

History Visited by Portuguese, 1455; settled by English in 17th-c; independent British Crown Colony from 1843; independent member of Commonwealth, 1965; republic, 1970; joined Confederation of Senegambia, 1982–9; signed treaty of friendship with Senegal, 1991; military coup, 1994; governed by a House of Representatives, President and Cabinet.

Head of State/Government
1996–   Yayeh Jameh

HUMAN GEOGRAPHY

GEORGIA

Local name Georgia

Timezone GMT +4

Area 69 700 km²/26 900 sq mi

Population total (2002e) 4 961 000

Status Republic

Date of independence 1991

Capital Tbilisi

Languages Georgian (official), also Russian

Ethnic groups Georgian (69%), Armenian (9%), Russian (7%), Azerbaijani (5%), Ossetian (3%), Abkhazian (2%)

Religion Georgian Church, independent of the Russian Orthodox Church since 1917

Physical features Mountainous country in C and W Transcaucasia; contains the Greater Caucasus (N) and Lesser Caucasus (S); highest point in the republic, Mt Shkhara, 5203 m/17 070 ft; chief rivers, Kura and Rioni; c.39% of land forested.

Climate Greater Caucasus in N borders temperate and subtropical climatic zones; average temperatures 1–3°C (Jan), 25°C (Jul) in E Transcaucasia; humid, sub-

☐ International Airport

tropical climate with mild winters in W; Mediterranean climate with humid winters, dry summers in N Black Sea region.

Currency 1 Lari (GEL) - 100 tetri

HUMAN GEOGRAPHY

Georgia (continued)

Economy Kakhetia region famed for its orchards and wines; holiday resorts, spas on the Black Sea; manganese, coal, iron and steel, oil refining; tea, fruits, tung oil, tobacco, vines, silk, textiles, food processing.

GDP (2002e) $16.5 bn, per capita $3200

HDI (2002) 0.748

History Proclaimed a Soviet Socialist Republic, 1921; linked with Armenia and Azerbaijan as Transcaucasian Republic, 1922–36; made a constituent republic within the Soviet Union, 1936; declaration of independence, 1991; quest for regional autonomy led to declaration of secession by S Ossetia, 1991, and declaration of independence by Abkhazia, 1992; did not join Commonwealth of Independent States (CIS), 1991; President Gamsakhurdia overthrown in civil war, 1992, bringing military council to power; Parliament dismissed and powers transferred to a State Council headed by Shevardnadze, 1992; joined CIS, 1993; head of State holds executive power, advised by Cabinet of Ministers; new constitution, 1995; Shevardnadze resigned following people's revolution, replaced by leader of the opposition Mikhail Saakashvili (Jan 2004); post of prime minister reintroduced, 2004.

Head of State
1992–2003	Eduard Shevardnadze
2003–4	Nino Burjanadze *Acting*
2004–	Mikhail Saakashvili

Head of Government
2004–5	Zurab Zhvania
2005–	Zurab Noghaideli

Minister of State
2000–3	Gia Arsenishvili
2003–4	Zurab Zhvania

GERMANY

Local name Bundesrepublik Deutschland

Timezone GMT +1

Area 357 868 km²/138 136 sq mi

Population total (2002e) 82 506 000

Status Federal republic

Capital Berlin

Languages German (official)

Ethnic groups German (93%), Turkish (2%), Yugoslav (1%), Italian (1%), other European Community (3%)

Religions Lutheran (55%), Roman Catholic (38%), Muslim (3%)

Physical features Lowland plains rise SW through C uplands and Alpine foothills to the Bavarian Alps; highest peak, the Zugspitze, 2962 m/9718 ft; C uplands include the Rhenish Slate Mts, Black Forest, and Harz Mts; Rhine crosses the country S–N; complex canal system links chief rivers, Elbe, Weser, Danube, Rhine, Main.

Climate Oceanic climatic influences strongest in NW, where winters are mild, stormy; elsewhere continental climate; lower winter temperatures in E and S, with considerable snowfall; average annual temperatures –0.5°C (Jan) to 19°C (Jul); average annual rainfall 600–700 mm/23–7 in.

Currency 1 Euro (EUR) = 100 cents (before February 2002, 1 Deutsche Mark (DEM) = 100 Pfennige)

Economy Economically powerful member of EC (accounts for 30% of European Community output): substantial heavy industry in NW, wine in Rhine and Moselle valleys; increasing tourism, especially in the S; leading manufacturer of vehicles, electrical and electronic goods; much less development in the E, after the period of socialist economy; following unification, a major socio-economic division emerged between W and E, leading to demonstrations in the E provinces, 1991.

GDP (2002e) $2.16 tn, per capita $26 200

HDI (2002) 0.925

☐ International Airport

History Ancient Germanic tribes united in 8th-c within the Frankish Empire of Charlemagne; elective monarchy after 918 under Otto 1, with Holy Roman Empire divided into several hundred states; after Congress of Vienna, 1814–15, a confederation of 39 states under Austria; under Bismarck, Prussia succeeded

Austria as the leading German power; union of Germany and foundation of Second Reich, 1871, with King of Prussia as hereditary German Emperor; aggressive foreign policy, eventually leading to World War 1; after German defeat, second Reich replaced by democratic Weimar Republic; world economic crisis led to collapse of Weimar Republic and rise of National Socialist movement, 1929; Adolph Hitler became dictator of the totalitarian Third Reich, 1933; acts of aggression led to World War 2 and a second defeat for Germany, with collapse of the German political regime; partition of Germany in 1945, with occupation zones given to UK, USA, France, and USSR, who formed a Control Council; USSR withdrew from the Control Council in 1948, dividing Germany into W and E: W Germany controlled by the three remaining powers, UK, USA and France; E administered by USSR.

West Germany (former Federal Republic of Germany) Area 249 535 km²/96 320 sq mi; population total (1990) 62 679 035; including West Berlin; established, 1949; gained full sovereignty, 1954; entered NATO, 1955; founder member of the European Economic Community, 1957; federal system of government, built around 10 provinces (*Länder*) with considerable powers; two-chamber legislature, consisting of Federal Diet (*Bundestag*) and Federal Council (*Bundesrat*).

East Germany (former German Democratic Republic) Area 108 333 km²/41 816 sq mi; population total (1990) 16 433 796; administered by USSR after 1945 partition, andSoviet model of government established, 1949; anti-Soviet demonstrations put down, 1953; recognized by USSR as an independent republic, 1954; flow of refugees to West Germany continued until 1961, largely stopped by the Berlin Wall built along zonal boundary, dividingwestern sectors of Berlin from eastern; governed by the People's Chamber, a single-chamber parliament (*Volkskammer*) which elected a Council of State, a Council of Ministers, and a National Defence Council; movement for democratic reform culminated in Nov 1989 in the opening and removal of the Wall and other border crossings to the West, and a more open government policy; first free all-German elections since 1932, held in Mar 1990, paving the way for a currency union with West Germany, Jul 1990, and full political unification, Oct 1990.

United Germany The 10 provinces of West Germany joined by the 5 former East German provinces abolished after World War 2 (Brandenburg, Mecklenburg-West, Pomerania, Saxony, Saxony-Anhalt, Thuringia), along with uni-

□ International Airport

Länder of Germany

fied Berlin; West German electoral system adopted in East Germany; first national elections, Dec 1990.

Head of State
2004–   Horst Koehler

Head of Government (Federal Chancellor)
2005–   Angela Merkel

>> Political leaders and rulers, p.197

HUMAN GEOGRAPHY

GHANA

Local name Ghana

Timezone GMT

Area 238 537 km²/92 100 sq mi

Population total (2002e) 20 244 000

Status Republic

Date of independence 1960

Capital Accra

Languages English (official), Akan, Ewe, Ga, several minority languages

Ethnic groups c.75 tribal groups, including Akan (44%), Mole-Dagbani (16%), Ewe (13%), and Ga (8%)

Religions Christian (43%), traditional local beliefs (38%), Muslim (12%)

Physical features Located in W Africa; low-lying plains inland, leading to the Ashanti plateau (W) and R Volta basin (E), dammed to form L Volta; mountains (E) rise to 885 m/2903 ft at Mt Afadjado; Ashanti plateau in Wand Akwapin Toto Mts in E.

Climate Tropical climate, including a warm dry coastal belt (SE); a hot, humid SW corner; and a hot, dry savannah (N); average temperatures 27°C (Jan), 25°C (Jul) in Accra.

Currency 1 Cedi (GHC) = 100 pesewas

Ghana (continued)

Economy Agriculture; cocoa (world's leading producer) provides two-thirds of export revenue; tourism; commercial reserves of oil, diamonds, gold, manganese, bauxite, timber.

GDP (2002e) $41.25 bn, per capita $2000

HDI (2002) 0.548

History Visited by Europeans in 15th-c; centre of slave trade, 18th-c; modern state created by union of two former British territories, British Gold Coast (Crown Colony, 1874) and British Togoland, merging to form Ghana and declaring independence, 1957; independent republic within the Commonwealth, 1960; constitution provides for a Parliament, executive President, Cabinet, and Council of State; series of military coups (1966, 1972, 1979,1982) led to the creation of a Provisional National Defence Council, which rules by decree; new multi-party constitution, 1992, allowing for a directly elected executive President and legislature.

Head of State/Government
(Chairman of the Provisional National Defence Council)
1981–92   Jerry John Rawlings

President
1992–2001 Jerry John Rawlings
2001–   John Kufuor

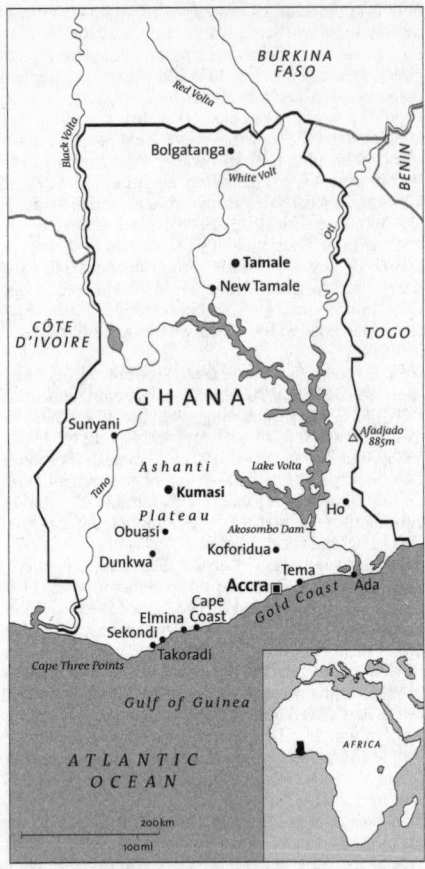

□ International Airport

GIBRALTAR >> UNITED KINGDOM

HUMAN GEOGRAPHY

GREECE

Local name Ellás

Timezone GMT +2

Area 131957 km²/50935 sq mi

Population total (2002e) 10994000

Status Republic

Date of independence 1830

Capital Athens (Athínai)

Languages Greek (official), English and French widely spoken

Ethnic groups Greek (98%), Albanian, Slav, Turkish minorities, and others (2%)

Religions Christian (98%) (Greek Orthodox 97.5%, Roman Catholic 0.4%, Protestant 0.1%), Muslim, Judaism, and others (2%)

Physical features Located in SE Europe, occupying the S part of the Balkan peninsula and numerous islands in the Aegean and Ionian seas: mainland includes the Peloponnese (S), connected via the narrow Isthmus of Corinth; over 1400 islands (only 169 inhabited), including Crete, the largest, 8336 km²/3218 sq mi, Rhodes, Milos, Corfu, Lesbos, Kos: nearly 80% of Greece mountainous or hilly; Pindus Mts run N to S; highest point, Mt Olympus, 2917 m/9570 ft; principal rivers include the Néstos, Strimon, Arakhthos: c.30% of land arable or under permanent cultivation; c.20% forested.

Climate Mediterranean climate for coast and islands, with mild, rainy winters and hot, dry summers; rainfall almost entirely in winter; island of Corfu receives maximum rainfall 1320 mm/52 in; severe winters in mountains; average annual temperatures 9°C (Jan), 28°C (Jul) in Athens.

Currency 1 Euro (EUR) = 100 cents (before February 2002, 1 Drachma (GRD) = 100 lepta)

Economy Strong service sector accounts for c.60% of national income; agriculture based on cereals, cotton, tobacco, fruit, figs, raisins, wine, olive oil, vegetables; major tourist area, especially on islands; world's largest shipping fleet (under own and other flags); member of the EC from 1981.

GDP (2002e) $203.3 bn, per capita $19 100

HDI (2002) 0.885

History Prehistoric civilization culminated in Minoan-Mycenean culture of Crete; Dorians invaded from N, 12th-c BC; Greek colonies established along N and S Mediterranean and on Black Sea; many city-states on mainland, notably Sparta and Athens; Persian invasions, 5th-c BC, repelled at Marathon, Salamis, Plataea, Mycale; Greek literature and art flourished, 5th-c BC; conflict between Sparta and Athens (Peloponnesian War) weakened both, and hegemony passed to Thebes, and then Macedon under Philip II, 4th-c BC; his son, Alexander the Great, conquered Persian Empire; Macedonian power broken by Romans, 197 BC; part of Eastern Roman and Byzantine empires; ruled by Ottoman Turks from 15th-c until 19th-c; national reawakening led to independence as kingdom, 1830; territorial gains after Balkan War and World War 1; absorbed over 100000 refugees after defeat in Asia Minor, 1922; republic established, 1924–35; German occupation, 1941–4; civil war, 1944–9; military coup, 1967; abolition of monarchy, 1969; democracy restored, 1974; Athens hosted 2004 Olympic Games; governed by a Prime Minister; Cabinet, unicameral Parliament, and President.

Head of State
1995–2005 Konstantinos Stephanopoulos
2005–   Karolos Papoulias

Head of Government
1996–2004 Kostas Simitis
2004–   Kostas Karamanlis

GREENLAND >> DENMARK

☐ International Airport

HUMAN GEOGRAPHY

GRENADA

Local name Grenada

Timezone GMT –4

Area 344 km²/133 sq mi

Population total (2002e) 101 900

Status Independent state within the Commonwealth

Date of independence 1974

Capital St George's

Languages English (official), French patois

Ethnic groups African descent (84%), mixed (12%), E Indian (3%) European (1%)

Religions Roman Catholic (64%), Protestant (21%)

Physical features Most southerly of the Windward Is, E Caribbean; comprises the main island of Grenada, 34 km/21 mi long, 19 km/12 mi wide, and the S Grenadines; Grenada volcanic in origin, with a ridge of mountains along its entire length, the highest point, Mt St Catherine, rising to 843 m/2766 ft; many rivers and lakes, including Grand Étang.

Climate Sub-tropical climate; average annual temperature 23°C; wet season (Jun–Dec); annual rainfall varies from 1270 mm/150 in (coast) to 5000 mm/200 in (interior); lies within Caribbean hurricane zone.

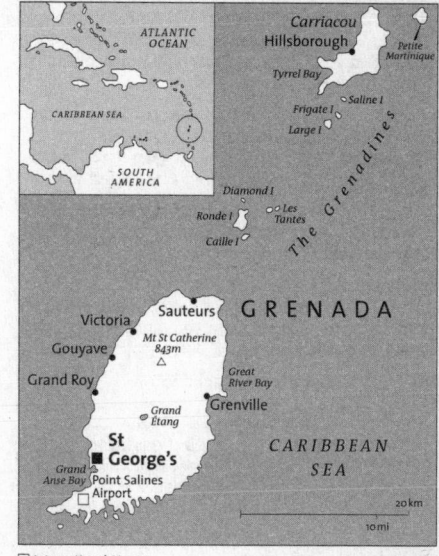
☐ International Airport

Grenada (continued)

Currency 1 East Caribbean Dollar (XCD) = 100 cents
Economy Economy based on agriculture, notably fruit, vegetables, cocoa, nutmegs, bananas, mace; processing of agricultural products and their derivatives; cocoa and nutmeg crops destroyed by H Ivan, Sep 2004.

GDP (2002e) $440 mn, per capita $5000

HDI (2002) 0.747

History Visited by Columbus and named Concepción, 1498; settled by French, mid-17th-c; ceded to Britain, 1763; retaken by France, 1779; ceded to Britain, 1783; British Crown Colony, 1877; independence, 1974; peo-ple's revolution, 1979; Prime Minister Maurice Bishop killed in uprising, 1983; group of Caribbean countries requested US involvement, and troops restored stable government, Oct 1983; governed by a Senate, House of Representatives, Prime Minister, and Cabinet.

Head of State
(British monarch represented by Governor-General)
1996– Daniel Charles Williams

Head of Government
1995– Keith Mitchell

GUADELOUPE >> FRANCE

GUAM >> UNITED STATES OF AMERICA

GUATEMALA

Local name Guatemala

Timezone GMT –6

Area 108 889 km²/42 031 sq mi

Population total (2002e) 11 987 000

Status Republic

Date of independence 1838

Capital Guatemala City

Languages Spanish (official), c.40% speak Indian dialects, including Quiche, Cakchiquel, Kekchi

Ethnic groups Indian (41%) and mestizo

Religions Roman Catholic (75%), Protestant (25%)

Physical features Northernmost of the Central American republics; over two-thirds mountainous, with large forested areas; narrow Pacific coastal plain, rising steeply to highlands of 2500–3000 m/8000–10000 ft; many volcanoes on S edge of highlands; low undulating tableland of El Petén to the N.

Climate Humid tropical climate on lowlands and coast; average annual temperatures 17°C (Jan), 21°C (Jul) in Guatemala City; rainy season (May–Oct); average annual rainfall 1316 mm l51.8 in; area subject to hurricanes and earthquakes.

Currency 1 Quetzal (GTQ) = 100 centavos; also 1 US dollar (USD) = 100 cents

Economy Agricultural products account for c.65% of exports, chiefly coffee, bananas, cotton, sugar; on higher ground, wheat, maize, beans; on the Pacific coastal plain, cotton, sugar cane, rice, beans.

GDP (2002e) $53.2 bn, per capita $3900

HDI (2002) 0.631

History Mayan and Aztec civilizations before Spanish conquest, 1523–4; independence as part of the Federation of Central America, 1821; independence as the Republic of Guatemala, 1838; 1985 constitution provides for the election of a President (who appoints a Cabinet), and a National Assembly; long-standing claim over Belize resolved in 1991.

☐ International Airport   ∴ World heritage site

Head of State/Government
1999–2003 Alfonso Portillo Cabrera
2003– Oscar Berger

GUIANA >> FRANCE

GUINEA

Local name Guinée

Timezone GMT

Area 246 048 km²/94 974 sq mi

Population total (2002e) 7 775 000

Status Republic

Date of independence 1958

Capital Conakry

Languages French (official), Fulani, Malinké, Susu, Kissi, Kpelle

Ethnic groups Fulani (40%), Malinké (25%), Susu (11%), Kissi (6%), Kpelle (5%)

Religions Muslim (75%), traditional beliefs (24%)

Physical features Located in W Africa; coast characterized by mangrove forests, rising to a forested and widely cultivated narrow coastal plain; Fouta Djallon massif beyond, c.900 m/3000 ft; higher peaks near Senegal frontier include Mt Tangue, 1537 m/5043 ft. savannah plains in E; forested Guinea Highlands in S.

Climate Tropical climate; wet season (May–Oct); annual rainfall 4923 mm/194 in at Conakry; average temperature 32°C (dry season) on coast, 23°C (wet season).

Currency 1 Guinean Franc (GNF) = 100 cauris

Economy Agriculture (employs 75% of population); rich in minerals, with a third of the world's bauxite reserves; gold, diamonds; independence brought fall in production as a result of withdrawal of French expertise and investment.

GDP (2002e) $18.69 bn, per capita $2100

HDI (2002) 0.414

History Part of Mali empire, 16th-c; French protec-

☐ International Airport

torate, 1849; governed with Senegal as Rivières du Sud; separate colony, 1893; constituent territory within French West Africa, 1904; overseas territory, 1946; independent republic, 1958; death of Sékou Touré, Guinea's first President (1961–84); coup in 1984 established a Military Committee for National Recovery (CMRN); CMRN replaced by a mixed military and civilian Transitional Committee of National Recovery (CTRN), 1991; governed by a President and Council of Ministers; new constitution, 1990.

Head of State
1984–   Lansana Conté

Head of Government
2004–6   Cellou Dalein Diallo

GUINEA-BISSAU

Local name Guiné-Bissau

Timezone GMT

Area 36 125 km²/13 948 sq mi

Population total (2002e) 1 345 000

Status Republic

Date of independence 1973

Capital Bissau

Languages Portuguese (official), Criolo, Balante

Ethnic groups Balanta (32%), Fula (22%), Mandyako (14%), Mandingo (13%), Pepel (10%)

Religions Traditional beliefs (54%), Muslim (38%), Christian (5%)

Physical features Located in W Africa. indented coast backed by forested coastal plains; main rivers, Geba and Cacheu; low-lying, with savannah-covered plateaux (S, E), rising to 310 m/1017 ft on the Guinea border; includes the heavily-forested Bijagós archipelago in the

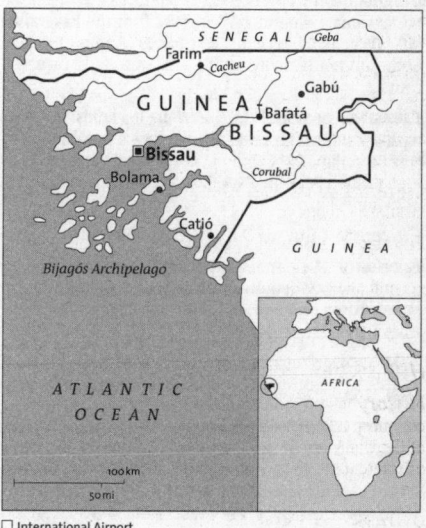

☐ International Airport

HUMAN GEOGRAPHY

HUMAN GEOGRAPHY

Guinea-Bissau (continued)

Atlantic Ocean off the shores of the mainland.

Climate Tropical climate, hot and humid; wet season (Jun–Oct); average annual rainfall at Bissau, 1950 mm/76.8 in; average annual temperature 24°C (Jan), 27°C (Jul) in Bissau.

Currency 1CFA Franc (XAF) = 100 centimes

Economy Based on agriculture, especially rice, maize, beans, peanuts, coconuts, palm oil, groundnuts, shrimps, fish, timber; reserves of petroleum, bauxite, phosphate.

GDP (2002e) $901.4 mn, per capita $700

HDI (2002) 0.349

History Visited by the Portuguese, 1446; Portuguese colony, 1879; overseas territory of Portugal, 1952; independence, 1973; military coup, 1980; new constitution, 1984; National Assembly elects Council of State; President of the Council of State also the Head of Government; introduction of a multi-party system, 1991; governed by a president, prime minister, and a 100-seat National People's Assembly; President Yala deposed in military coup after repeatedly cancelling elections, 2003; transitional government formed; fresh elections planned, Mar 2005.

Head of State
2003–5   Henrique Rosa *Interim*
2005–   Joao Bernardo Vieira

Head of Government
2004–   Carlos Gomes Junior

GUYANA

Local name Guyana

Timezone GMT –3

Area 214 969 km²/82 978 sq mi

Population total (2002e) 775 000

Status Co-operative republic

Date of independence 1966

Capital Georgetown

Languages English (official), Hindi, Urdu, Amerindian dialects

Ethnic groups E Indian (51%), black (30.5%), Amerindian (5%) (Carib 4%, Arawak 1%)

Religions Christian (42%), Hindu (37%), Muslim (9%)

Physical features Located on N coast of South America; inland forest covers c.83% of land area; highest peak; Mt Roraima, rising to 2875 m/9432 ft in the Pakaraima Mts (W); main rivers, Essequibo, Rupununi, and Corantijn, with many rapids and waterfalls in upper courses.

Climate Equatorial climate in the lowlands; hot, wet, with constant high humidity; average annual temperature 26°C (Jan), 27°C (Jul) in Georgetown; two seasons of high rainfall (May–Jul, Nov–Jan); average annual rainfall 2175 mm/87 in.

Currency 1 Guyana Dollar (GYD) = 100 cents

Economy High unemployment, influenced by labour unrest, low productivity, and high foreign debt; economy largely based on sugar, rice, bauxite, shrimps, livestock, cotton, molasses, timber.

GDP (2002e) $2.628 bn, per capita $3800

HDI (2002) 0.708

History Sighted by Columbus, 1498; settled by the Dutch, late 16th-c; several areas ceded to Britain, 1814; consolidated as British Guiana, 1831; independence, 1966; cooperative republic within the Commonwealth, 1970; governed by a President who holds executive

☐ International Airport

power, and appoints a Prime Minister and National Assembly, elected every five years.

Head of State/Government
1997–9   Janet Jagan
1999–   Bharrat Jagdeo

Prime Minister
1999–   Samuel Hinds

HAITI

Local name Haïti

Timezone GMT -5

Area 27750 km²/10712 sq mi

Population total (2002e) 7064000

Status Republic

Date of independence 1804

Capital Port-au-Prince

Languages French (official), with Creole French widely spoken

Ethnic groups African descent (95%), European (mulatto) (5%)

Religions Roman Catholic (80%), Voodoo

Physical features Consists of two mountainous peninsulas, Massif du Nord (N) and Massif de la Hotte (S), separated by a deep structural depression, the Plaine du Cul-de-Sac; highest peak, La Selle, 2680 m/8793 ft: includes islands of Gonâve (W) and Tortue (N).

Climate Tropical climate; average annual temperatures 25°C (Jan) 29°C (Jul) in Port-au-Prince; wet season (May–Sep); average annual rainfall for N coast and mountains 1475–1950 mm/58–77 in, but only 500 mm/20 in on W side; hurricanes common; 2000+ deaths from Hurricane Jeanne, Sep 2004.

Currency 1 Gourde (HTG) = 100 centimes

Economy Based on agriculture; large plantations grow coffee, sugar, sisal, rice, bananas, corn, sorghum, cocoa; sugar refining, textiles, flour milling; cement, bauxite; tourism; light assembly industries.

GDP (2002e) $10.6 bn, per capita $1400

HDI (2002) 0.471

History Visited by Columbus, 1492; created when W third of island ceded to France as Saint-Domingue, 1697; slave rebellion followed by independence as Haiti, 1804; united with Santo Domingo (Dominican Rep.), 1822–44; US occupation, 1915–34; Duvalier family had absolute power, 1957–86; after 1986 coup, new constitution provided for a bicameral National Congress consisting of a Senate and National Assembly; military coup, 1992, forced Jean-Bertrand Aristide to flee the country, provisional government created; Marc Bazin resigned as head of army-backed coalition government, 1993; talks deadlock between deposed President Aristide and coup leader Cedras, 1993; peaceful US invasion restored democratic government, 1994; Aristide re-elected, 2000, amid claims of fraudulent practice; conflict escalated early 2004 with failure of Aristide's political opposition to agree to US-backed power-sharing plan; rebel uprising forced Aristide into exile, Mar 2004 .

Head of State
2006–   René Préval

Head of Government
2006–   Jacques-Edouard Aléxis§

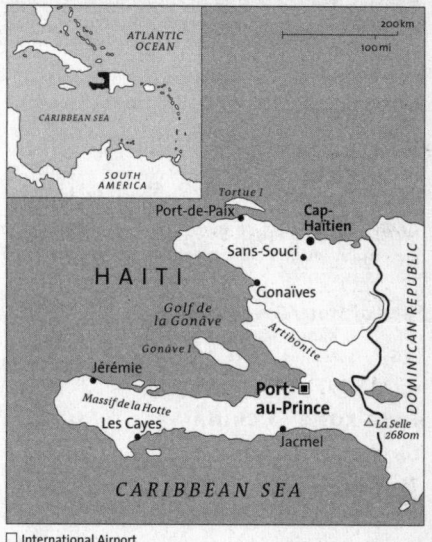

□ International Airport

HUMAN GEOGRAPHY

HONDURAS

Local name Honduras

Timezone GMT -6

Area 112088 km²/43266 sq mi

Population total (2002e) 6561000

Status Republic

Date of independence 1821

Capital Tegucigalpa

Languages Spanish (official), a number of Indian dialects also spoken by aboriginal population

Ethnic groups Spanish-Indian origin (90%), Indian (7%), black (2%)

Religions Roman Catholic (85%), Protestant (mainly Fundamentalist, Moravian, and Methodist) (10%)

Physical features Coastal lands (S) separated from Caribbean coastlands by mountains running NW–SE; S plateau rises to 2849 m/9347 ft at Cerro de las Minas; also includes Bay Is in the Caribbean Sea and nearly 300 islands in the Gulf of Fonseca.

Climate Tropical climate in coastal areas, temperate in C and W; average annual temperatures 19°C (Jan), 23°C (Jul) in Tegucigalpa; two wet seasons in upland areas (May–Jul, Sep–Oct); country devastated by Hurricane Mitch, 1998.

Currency 1 Lempira (HNL) = 100 centavos

Honduras (continued)

Economy Agriculture (provides a third of national income), forestry, mining, cattle raising; bananas, coffee, beef, cotton, tobacco, sugar; exports of silver, lead and zinc; offshore oil exploration in the Caribbean.

GDP (2002e) $16.29 bn, per capita $2500

HDI (2002) 0.638

History Centre of Mayan culture, 4th–9th-c; settled by the Spanish in early 16th-c, and became province of Guatemala; independence from Spain, 1821; joined Federation of Central America; independence, 1838; several military coups in 1970s; since 1980, a democratic constitutional republic, governed by a president and National Assembly.

Head of State/Government
2001–5   Ricardo Maduro
2005–   Manuel Zelaya

HONG KONG >> CHINA

HUNGARY

Local name Magyarország

Timezone GMT +1

Area 93 033 km²/35 912 sq mi

Population total (2002e) 10 162 000

Status Republic

Date of independence 1918

Capital Budapest

Language Hungarian (Magyar) (official)

Ethnic groups Magyar (92%), German (2%), Slovak (1%), Romanian and Yugoslav minorities

Religions Roman Catholic (67%), Calvinist (20%), Lutheran (5%)

Physical features Drained by the R Danube (flows N–S) and its tributaries; crossed (W) by a low spur of the Alps; highest peak, Kékestetö, 1014 m/3327 ft; frequent flooding, especially in the Great Plains (E). 54% of land is arable; 18% forested.

Climate Fairly extreme continental climate, due to landlocked position; average annual temperature 0°C (Jan), 21 °C (Jul) in Budapest; wettest in spring and early summer; average annual rainfall 600 mm/23.6 in; cold winters; R Danube sometimes frozen over for long periods; frequent fogs.

Currency 1 Forint (HUF) = 100 fillér

Economy Large-scale nationalization as part of centralized planning strategy of the new republic, 1946–9; greater independence to individual factories and farms, from 1968; grain, potatoes, sugar beet, fruit, wine; coal, bauxite, lignite; metallurgy, engineering, chemicals, textiles, food processing.

GDP (2002e) $134 bn, per capita $13 300

HDI (2002) 0.835

☐ International Airport   ∴ World heritage site

☐ International Airport

History Kingdom formed under St Stephen 1, 11th-c; conquered by Turks, 1526; part of Habsburg Empire, 17th-c; Austria and Hungary reconstituted as a dual monarchy, 1867; republic, 1918; communist revolt led by Béla Kun, 1919; monarchical constitution restored, 1920; new republic with communist government, 1949; uprising crushed by Soviet forces, 1956; during 1989, pressure for political change towards a multi-party system; multi-party elections in 1990 saw an end to communist rule; governed by a National Assembly which elects a Presidential Council and Council of Ministers.

Head of State
2005–   László Sólyom

Head of Government
2004–   Ferenc Gyurcsany

ICELAND

Local name Ísland

Timezone GMT

Area 103 000 km²/40 000 sq mi

Population total (2002e) 288 000

Status Republic

Date of independence 1944

Capital Reykjavík

Language Icelandic (official)

Ethnic groups Homogeneous (96%), with European minorities

Religions Protestant (95%) (Evangelical Lutheran 93%, other Lutheran 2%), Roman Catholic (1%), non-religious (1%)

Physical features Several active volcanoes, including Hekla, 1491 m/4920 ft; Helgafell, 215 m/706 ft; and Surtsey, 174 m/570 ft; famous for its geysers; many towns heated by subterranean hot water; heavily indented coastline with many long fjords; high ridges rise to 2119 m/6952 ft at Hvannadalshnjukur (SE); several large snowfields and glaciers.

Climate Changeable; summers cool and cloudy, mild winters; average annual temperature 1°C (Jan), 11°C (Jul); Reykjavik generally ice-free throughout year; average monthly rainfall reaches 94 mm/3.7 in (Oct).

Currency 1 Króna (ISK) = 100 aurar

Economy Based on inshore and deep-water fishing (75% of national income); stock and dairy farming, potatoes, greenhouse vegetables; aluminium, diatomite; tourism.

GDP (2002e) $8.444 bn, per capita $30 200

HDI (2002) 0.936

History Settled by the Norse, 9th-c; world's oldest

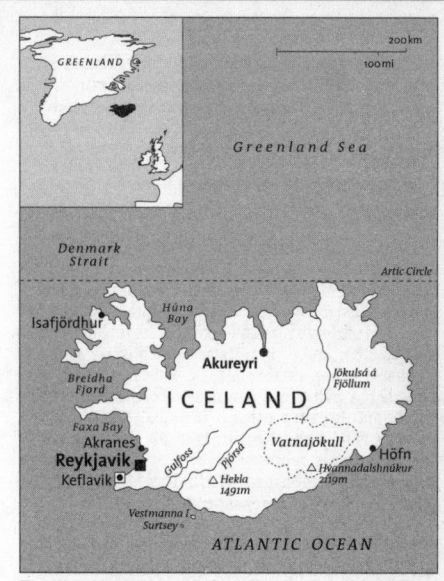

□ International Airport

Parliament (*Althing*), 10th-c; union with Norway, 1262; union with Denmark, 1380; independent kingdom in personal union with Denmark, 1918; independent republic, 1944; extension of the fishing limit around Iceland in 1958 and 1975 precipitated the 'Cod War' disputes with the UK; governed by a bicameral Parliament (*Althing*), President, Prime Minister, and Cabinet.

Head of State
1996– Olafur Ragnar Grimsson

Head of Government
2004–6 Halldor Asgrimsson
2006– Geir Haarde

INDIA

Local name Bharat (Hindi)

Timezone CMT +5.5

Area 3 166 829 km²/1 222 396 sq mi

Population total (2002e) 1 047 671 000

Status Republic

Date of independence 1947

Capital New Delhi

Languages Hindi and English (official); others include Urdu, Panjabi, Gujarati, Marathi, Bengali, Oriya, Kashmiri, Assamese, Kannada, Malayalam, Sindhi, Tamil and Telugu

Ethnic groups Indo-Aryan (72%), Dravidian (25%), with Mongoloid and other minorities

Religions Hindu (83%), Muslim (11%), Christian (2%), Sikh (2%), Buddhist (1%)

Physical features Seventh largest country in the world, located in S Asia; includes Andaman and Nicobar

Is in the Bay of Bengal, and Laccadive Is in the Indian Ocean; folded mountain ridges and valleys in N, highest peaks over 7000 m/23 000 ft; C river plains of the Ganges, Yamuna, Ghaghari, and Brahmaputra to the S, with control measures needed to prevent flooding; Thar Desert in NW bordered by semi-desert areas; Deccan Plateau in the S peninsula, with hills and wide valleys, bounded by the Western and Eastern Ghats; the coastal plains are important areas of rice cultivation.

Climate Dominated by the Asiatic monsoon; rains come from the SW (Jun–Oct); rainfall decreases E–W on the N plains, with desert conditions in extreme W; tropical in S even in cool season; average annual temperature 14°C (Jan), 31°C (Jul) in New Delhi; average annual rainfall 640 mm/25.2 in; cyclones and storms on SE coast (especially Oct–Dec).

Currency 1 Indian Rupee (INR) = 100 paisa

Economy Agriculture employs over two-thirds of the labour force, tea, rice, wheat, coffee, sugar cane, cotton

HUMAN GEOGRAPHY

India (continued)

jute, oil seed, maize, pulses, milk; floods and drought cause major problems; considerable increase in industrial production since independence; iron, steel, oil products, chemicals, fertilizers, chromite, barytes, oil, natural gas; tourism.

GDP (2002e) $2.644 tn, per capita $2600

HDI (2002) 0.577

History Indus civilization emerged c.2500 BC, destroyed 1500 BC by Aryans, who developed Brahmanic caste system; Mauryan Emperor Asoka unified most of India, and established Buddhism as state religion, 3rd-c BC; spread of Hinduism, 2nd-c BC; Muslim influences during 7th-8th-c AD, with sultanate established at Delhi; Mughal Empire established by Babur in 1526 and extended by Akbar and Aurangzeb; Portuguese, French, Dutch, and British footholds in India, 18th-c; conflict between France and Britain, 1746–63; development of British interests represented by East India Company; British power established after Indian Mutiny crushed, 1857; movement for independence from late 19th-c; Government of India Act of 1919 allowed election of Indian ministers to share power with appointed British governors; further Act in 1935 allowed election of independent provincial governments; passive-resistance campaigns of Mahatma Gandhi from 1920s (assassinated, 1948); independence granted in 1947, on condition that Muslim state be established (Pakistan); Indian states later reorganized on linguistic basis; Pakistan–India war over disputed territory in Kashmir and Jammu, 1948; federal democratic republic within Commonwealth, 1950; Hindu–Muslim hostility, notably in 1978, and further India–Pakistan conflict, 1965 and 1971; separatist movements continue, especially relating to Sikh interests in the Punjab; suppression of militant Sikh movement in 1984 led to assassination of Indira Gandhi; Rajiv Gandhi assassinated, 1991; ongoing tension with Pakistan over Kashmir, 2002; SE coast devastated by tsunami, 2004; earthquake hit Java, 2006, with over 6000 deaths; each of 27 states administered by a governor through an Assem-

☐ International Airport ••••Disputed boundary J&K Jammu & Kashmir
--- India/Pakistan line of control

bly; the president, advised by a Council of Ministers, appoints a prime minister; Parliament comprises the president, an Upper House, and a House of the People.

Head of State
1997–2002 K(ocheril) R(aman) Narayanan
2002–   Avul Pakir Jainulabdeen Abdul Kalam

Head of Government
2004–   Manmohan Singh

INDONESIA

Local name Indonesia

Timezone GMT +7 to +9

Area 1 906 200 km²/735 800 sq mi

Population total (2002e) 211 023 000

Status Republic

Date of independence 1945

Capital Jakarta

Languages Bahasa Indonesia (official), English, Dutch, and Javanese widely spoken

Ethnic groups Madurese (40%), Javanese (33%), Sudanese (15%), Bahasa Indonesian (12%)

Religions Muslim (88%), Christian (9%) (Roman Catholic 6%, Protestant 2%), Hindu (2%), Buddhist (1%)

Physical features World's largest island group of 13 677 islands and islets, c.6000 inhabited; five main islands: Sumatra, Java, Kalimantan (two-thirds of Borneo

I), Sulawesi, Irian Jaya (W half of New Guinea I); mountainous volcanic landscape and equatorial rainforest; many volcanic peaks – over 100 on Java, 15 active.

Climate Hot and humid equatorial climate; dry season (Jun–Sep), rainy season (Dec–Mar); average annual temperature 26°C (Jan), 27°C (Jul) in Jakarta; average annual rainfall 1775 mm/69 in.

Currency 1 Indonesian Rupiah (IDR) = 100 sen

Economy Mainly agrarian, notably rice; oil, natural gas, and petroleum products from Borneo and Sumatra account for nearly 60% of national income; small manufacturing industry.

GDP (2002e) $714.2 bn, per capita $3100

HDI (2002) 0.684

History Settled by Hindus and Buddhists; Islam introduced, 14th–15th-c; Portuguese settlers, early 16th-c; Dutch East India Company established, 1602; Japanese occupation in World War 2; independence proclaimed

☐ International Airport

with Sukarno as President, 1945; changed name from Netherlands East Indies to the Republic of the United States of Indonesia, 1949: federal system replaced by unified control, 1950, and unitary Republic of Indonesia proclaimed (W New Guinea remained under Dutch control until 1963, now called Irian Jaya): military coup, 1966; governed by a President elected by a 700-member People's Consultative Assembly, and advised by a Cabinet and several advisory agencies; separatist movements in Irian Jaya, East Timor, and Aceh; East Timor achieved independence, 2002 (>>East Timor); terrorist bomb in Kuta, Bali, 180 killed, 2002; military offensive launched in Aceh after failed peace talks with rebel Free Aceh Movement, 2003; truce signed, 2005; NW devastated by tsunami after earthquake off coast of Sumatra, 2004; earthquake hit Java with over 6000 deaths, 2006.

Head of State/Government
2004–   Susilo Bambang Yudhoyono

IRAN

Local name Īrān

Timezone GMT +3.5

Area 1648 000 km²/636 128 sq mi

Population total (2002e) 65 457 000

Status Islamic Republic

Date of independence 1925

Capital Teheran

Languages Farsi (Persian) (official), several minority languages including Kurdish, Baluchi, Luri, and Turkic (including Afshari, Shahsavani, and Turkish)

Ethnic groups Persian (63%), Turkic (18%), other Iranian (13%), Kurdish (3%), Arab, and other Semitic (3%)

Religions Muslim (Shi'ite 93%, Sunni 5%), Zoroastrian (2%), Jewish, Baha'i, and Christian (1%)

Physical features Largely composed of a vast arid C plateau, average elevation 1200 m/4000 ft bounded N by the Elburz Mts, rising to 5670 m/18 602 ft at Mt Damavand Zagros Mts in W and S.

Climate Mainly a desert climate, hot and humid on Persian Gulf: average annual temperatures 2.2°C (Jan), 29.4°C (Jul) in Teheran; average annual rainfall 246 mm/9.7 in; frequent earthquakes.

Currency 1 Iranian Rial (IRR) = 100 dinars

Economy World's fourth largest oil producer, but production severely disrupted by 1978 revolution, and Gulf War, 1991: agriculture and forestry (employs a third of population); natural gas, iron ore, copper, coal, salt; textiles, sugar refining, petrochemicals; traditional handicrafts (especially carpets).

☐ International Airport   ∴ World heritage site

GDP (2002e) $458.3 bn, per capita $6800

HDI (2002) 0.721

History Early centre of civilization, dynasties including the Achaemenids and Sassanids; ruled by Arabs, Turks, and Mongols until the Sasavid dynasty in the 16th-18th-c, and the Qajar dynasty in the 19th–20th-c; military coup,

Iran (continued)

1921, with independence under Reza Shah Pahlavi, 1925; changed name from Persia to Iran, 1935; protests against Shah's regime in 1970s led to revolution, 1978; exile of Shah, and proclamation of Islamic Republic under Ayatollah Khomeini, 1979; Islamic Cultural Revolution under Khomeini saw a return to strict observance of Muslim principles and traditions; occupation of US Embassy in Teheran, 1979–81; Gulf War following invasion of Iraq, 1980–8; overall authority exercised by appointed spiritual leader: post of Prime Minister abolished, 1989; governed by a President and a Consultative Assembly (*Majlis*).

Leader of the Islamic Revolution
1979–89   Ayatollah Khomeini
1989–   Ayatollah Sayed Ali Khamenei

Head of State/Government
1997–2005 Sayed Mohammad Khatami
2005–   Mahmoud Ahmadinejad

IRAQ

Local name Al'Īrāq

Timezone GMT +3

Area 434 925 km²/167 881 sq mi

Population total (2002e) 24 002 000

Status Republic

Date of independence 1932

Capital Baghdad

Languages Arabic (official), also English, Kurdish, Persian, Turkish, and Assyrian spoken

Ethnic groups Arab (79%), Kurd (largely in NE) (16%), Persian (3%), Turkish (2%)

Religions Muslim (95%) (Shi'ite 63%, Sunni 32%), Christian (3%)

Physical features Comprises the vast alluvial tract of the Tigris–Euphrates lowland (ancient Mesopotamia); Tharthar and Euphrates rivers, divided by al-Jazirah plain, flow over dense swampland and join to form the navigable Shatt al-Arab; mountains (NE) rise to over 3000 m/9800 ft; desert in other areas.

Climate Mainly arid climate; summers very hot and dry; winters often cold; average annual temperature 10°C (Jan), 35°C (Jul) in Baghdad; average annual rainfall 140 mm/5.5 in.

Currency 1 New Iraqi Dinar (NID) = 1000 fils

Economy World's second largest producer of oil, but production severely disrupted during both Gulf Wars; natural gas, oil refining, petrochemicals, cement, textiles; dates, cotton, winter wheat, rice, sheep, cattle.

GDP (2002e) $58 bn, per capita $2400

HDI (1998) 0.583

History Part of Ottoman Empire from 16th-c until World War 1; captured by British forces, 1916; British-mandated territory, 1921; independence under Hashemite dynasty, 1932; monarchy replaced by military rule, and Iraq declared republic, 1958; since 1960s, Kurdish nationalists in NE fighting to establish separate state; invasion of Iran led to Iran–Iraq War (1980–88); invasion and annexation of Kuwait led to Gulf War 1991: UN imposed no-fly zone over S Iraq to protect Shi'ites, and security zone in N Iraq to protect Kurdish refugees, 1992; Iraq War, 2003 (>> p.188); interim constitution, March 2004; handover of power to interim Iraqi government, Jun 2004; US and Iraqi forces launch assault against insurgents.in Fallujah and Mosul, Nov 2004; elections held, Jan

☐ International Airport ∴ World heritage site

2005, Shia United Iraqi Alliance (UIA) form coalition government; voting in referendum on Iraq's constitution to make country an Islamic federal democracy (Oct 2005); constitution approved; UIA gained victory (Jan 2006) but failed to achieve absolute majority; US, British, and other forces in Iraq under increasing attack, 2006; trial and execution of Saddam Hussein, 2006; ongoing Shia/Sunni conflict, 2007.

Head of State/Government
1979–2003 Saddam Hussein at-Takriti
2003–5   Coalition Provisional Authority (CPA)

President
2005–   Jalal Talabani

Prime Minister
2005–6   Ibrahim Jaafari
2006–   Jawad al-Maliki

IRELAND, REPUBLIC OF

Local name Éire (Gaelic)

Timezone GMT

Area 70 282 km²/27 129 sq mi

Population total (2002e) 3 926 000

Status Republic (occupying S, C, and NW Ireland; bounded NE by Northern Ireland, part of the UK)

Capital Dublin

Languages Irish Gaelic and English (official)

Ethnic groups Celtic (94%), small English minority

Religions Roman Catholic (95%), Anglican (Church of Ireland) (3%), Presbyterian (1%)

Physical features Mountainous landscapes in W, part of Caledonian system of Scandinavia and Scotland with quartzite peaks weathered into conical mountains such as Croagh Patrick, 765 m/2510 ft: landscape of ridges and valleys in SW, rising towards Macgillycuddy's Reek Mts; lowlands in E drained by slow-moving rivers such as the Shannon (S), Liffey (E), and Slaney (SE).

Climate Mild and equable climate. Average annual temperature 5°C (Jan), 15°C (Jul); rainfall heaviest in W, often over 3000 mm/10 in.

Currency 1 Euro (EUR) = 100 cents (before February 2002, 1 Irish Pound/Punt (IEP) = 100 new pence)

Economy Primarily agriculture (two-thirds of country covered by improved agricultural land); forestry developed since 1950s; fishing; food, drink, tobacco, textiles; recent growth in light engineering; synthetic fibres, electronics, pharmaceuticals; major tourist area; member of the EC, 1973.

GDP (2002e) $113.7 bn, per capita $29 300

HDI (2002) 0.925

History Occupied by Goidelic-speaking Celts during the Iron Age; conversion to Christianity by St Patrick, 5th-c; SE attacked by Vikings, c.800; Henry II of England declared himself lord of Ireland, 1171; Catholic rebellion during English Civil War suppressed by Oliver Cromwell, 1649–50; supporters of deposed Catholic King James II defeated by William III at Battle of the Boyne, 1690; struggle for Irish freedom developed in 18th-19th-c; Act of Union, 1801; population reduced by half during famine, 1846; Land Acts, 1870–1903; Home Rule Bills introduced by Gladstone, 1886,1893; third Home Rule Bill passed in 1914, but never came into effect because of World War l; armed rebellion, 1916; republic proclaimed by Sinn Fein, 1919; partition proposed by Britain, 1920; treaty signed, giving dominion status, 1921; right of Northern Ireland to opt out exercised, 1925; renamed Éire, 1937; left Commonwealth, 1949; Anglo-Irish Agreement, 1985; governed by a president (*Uachtarán na h'Éireann*), elected for seven years, and a prime minister (*Taoiseach*); National Parliament (*Oireachtas*) includes a House of Representatives (*Dail Éireann*) and a Senate (*Seanad Éireann*).

Head of State
1997– Mary McAleese

Head of Government
1997– (Patrick) Bertie Ahern

□ International Airport

Counties of Ireland

County	Area		Population	Admin. centre
	sq km	sq mi	(2000e)	
Carlow	896	346	41 000	Carlow
Cavan	1891	730	53 000	Cavan
Clare	3188	1231	92 000	Ennis
Cork	7459	2880	415 000	Cork
Donegal	4830	1865	130 000	Lifford
Dublin	922	356	1 038 000	Dublin
Galway	5939	2293	183 000	Galway
Kerry	4701	1815	123 000	Tralee
Kildare	1694	654	124 000	Naas
Kilkenny	2062	796	75 000	Kilkenny
Laoighis (Leix)	1720	664	53 000	Portlaoise
Leitrim	1526	589	24 000	Carrick
Limerick	2686	1037	164 000	Limerick
Longford	1044	403	31 000	Longford
Louth	821	317	92 000	Dundalk
Mayo	5398	2084	112 000	Castlebar
Meath	2339	903	107 000	Trim
Monaghan	1290	498	52 000	Monaghan
Offaly	1997	771	59 000	Tullamore
Roscommon	2463	951	53 000	Roscommon
Sligo	1795	693	55 000	Sligo
Tipperary	4254	1642	134 500	Clonmel
Waterford	1869	710	92 000	Waterford
Westmeath	1764	681	63 000	Mullingar
Wexford	2352	908	103 000	Wexford
Wicklow	2025	782	98 000	Wicklow

HUMAN GEOGRAPHY

ISLE OF MAN >> UNITED KINGDOM

ISRAEL

Local names Yisra'el (Hebrew), Isrā'il (Arabic)

Timezone GMT +2

Area 20 770 km²/8017 sq mi (within boundaries defined by 1949 armistice agreements)

Population total (2002e) 6 394 000 (excluding E Jerusalem and Israeli settlers in occupied territories)

Status Republic

Date of independence 1948

Capital Jerusalem

Languages Hebrew and Arabic (official), also European languages spoken

Ethnic groups Jewish (83%), Arab (11%)

Religions Jewish (85%), Muslim (11%), Christian and others (4%)

Physical features Extends 420 km/261 mi N–S; width varies from 20 km/12 mi to 116 km/72 mi; mountainous interior, rising to 1208 m/3963 ft at Mt Meron; mountains near Galilee (Lake Tiberias) and Samaria in the West Bank, dropping E to below sea-level in the Jordan–Red Sea rift valley: R Jordan forms part of E border; Dead Sea, between Israel and Jordan, 400 m/1286 ft below sea level, is the largest lake and has no outlet; Negev desert (S) occupies c.60% of the country's area.

Climate Mediterranean climate in N and C, with hot, dry summers and warm, wet winters; average annual temperature 9°C (Jan), 23°C (Jul) in Jerusalem; rainfall 528 mm/21 in.

Currency 1 New Israeli Shekel (ILS/NIS) = 100 agorot

Economy Over 90% of exports are industrial products; major tourist area, primarily to the religious centres; copper, potash, phosphates, citrus fruits, cotton, sugar beet, bananas, beef and dairy products; a world leader in agrotechnology, with areas of intensive cultivation; the kibbutz system produces c.40% of food output, but in recent years has turned increasingly towards industry.

GDP (2002e) $117.4 bn, per capita $19 500

HDI (2002) 0.896

History Zionist movement founded by Theodor Herzl, end of 19th-c; thousands of Jews returned to Palestine, then part of the Ottoman Empire: Britain given League of Nations mandate to govern Palestine and establish Jewish national home there, 1922; British evacuated Palestine, and Israel proclaimed independence, 1948; invasion by Arab nations, resulting in armistice, 1949. Israel gained control of the Gaza Strip, Sinai Peninsula (as far as the Suez Canal), West Bank of the R Jordan (including E sector of Jerusalem), and the Golan Heights in Syria, during the Six-Day War, 1967; Camp David conference between Egypt and Israel, 1978; Israeli withdrawal from Sinai, 1979; invasion of Lebanon, forcing the PLO to leave Beirut, 1982–5; renewed tension with uprising of Arabs in occupied territories (the *intifada*), 1988; peace agreement with PLO, and planned recognition of Palestine, 1993; withdrawal from Gaza and Jeri-

☐ International Airport ••••Palestinian National Authority

cho, 1994: conflict with Jordan formally ended, 1994: assassination of Yitzhak Rabin, 1995; Arafat elected president in first Palestine general election, 1996; withdrawal from S Lebanon, 2000; escalating reprisal attacks on Palestinian targets, 2001; siege of Bethlehem, 2002; US-initiated 'road map' and Geneva Accord peace plan proposed, 2003; ongoing conflict, 2003–4; fresh talks with new Palestinian government following death of Arafat, 2005; Jewish settlers left Gaza Strip (Aug–Sep 2005); Islamic military group HAMAS won Palestine election (Jan 2006); President Sharon suffered severe stroke, 2005, power transferred to vice premier Olmert; Olmert won election for Kadima party, Mar 2006; hostile action by Hezbollah militants led to air and sea blockade on Lebanon, Jul 2006; air blockade lifted (Nov 2006); a parliamentary democracy, with a prime minister, a Cabinet, and a unicameral Parliament (Knesset); president elected for a maximum of two five-year terms.

Head of State
2000– Moshe Katzav

Head of Government
1999–2001 Ehud Barak
2001–6 Ariel Sharon
2006– Ehud Olmert

ITALY

Local name Italia

Timezone GMT +1

Area 301 255 km²/116 314 sq mi

Population total (2002e) 57 988 000

Status Republic

Capital Rome

Languages Italian (official), with German spoken in the Trentino-Alto Adige, French in Valle d'Aosta, and Slovene in Trieste-Gorizia

Ethnic groups Homogeneous (98%), with German–Italian, French–Italian, and Slovene–Italian minorities

Religions Roman Catholic (83%), non-religious (14%)

Physical features Comprises the boot-shaped peninsula extending south into the Mediterranean Sea, as well as Sicily, Sardinia, and some smaller islands; Italian peninsula extends c.960 km/600 mi SE from the Lombardy plains; Apennines rise to peaks above 2 900 m/9000 ft; Alps form a border in N; broad, fertile Lombardo-Venetian plain in basin of R Po; several lakes at foot of the Alps, including Maggiore, Como, Garda; flat and marshy on Adriatic coast (N); coastal mountains descend steeply to the Ligurian Sea on the Riviera (W); Mt Vesuvius, 1289 m/4230 ft, and Vulcano, 502 m/1650 ft, are active volcanoes; island of Sicily separated from the mainland by the 4 km/2.5 mi wide Strait of Messina; the island includes the volcanic cone of Mt Etna, 3390 m/11 122 ft.

Climate Warm and temperate in S; hot and sunny summers, short cold winters; average annual temperatures 7°C (Jan), 25°C (Jul); average annual rainfall 657 mm/26 in; cold, wet, often snowy in higher peninsular areas; Mediterranean climate in coastal regions; Adriatic coast colder than the W coast, and receives less rainfall.

Currency 1 Euro (EUR) = 100 cents (before February 2002, 1 Italian Lira (ITL) = 100 centesimi)

Economy Industry largely concentrated in N; machinery, iron and steel; tourism; poorer agricultural region in S; Po valley a major agricultural region, with wheat, maize, sugar, potatoes, rice, beef, dairy farming; foothills of the Alps produce apples, peaches, walnuts, wine; further S, citrus fruits, vines, olives, tobacco.

GDP (2002e) $1.455 tn, per capita $25 100

HDI (2002) 0.913

History Inhabited by the Etruscans (N), Latins (C), and Greeks (S) in pre-Roman times; most regions part of the Roman Empire by 3rd-c BC; invaded by barbarian tribes, 4th-c AD; last Roman emperor deposed, 476; ruled by the Lombards and by the Franks under Charlemagne, crowned Emperor of the Romans, 800; part of the Holy Roman Empire under Otto, 962; conflict between popes and emperors throughout Middle Ages; dispute between Guelphs and Ghibellines, 12th-c; divided among five powers, 14th–15th-c (Kingdom of Naples, Duchy of Milan, republics of Florence and Venice, the papacy); major contribution to European culture through the Renaissance; numerous republics set up after the French Revolution; Napoleon crowned King of Italy, 1804; upsurge of liber-

□ International Airport   ∴ World heritage site

Regions of Italy

alism and nationalism (*Risorgimento*) in 19th-c; unification achieved under Victor Emmanuel II of Sardinia, aided by Cavour and Garibaldi, by 1870; fought alongside Allies in World War I; Fascist movement brought Mussolini to power, 1922; conquest of Abyssinia, 1935–6, and

Italy (continued)

Albania, 1939; alliance with Hitler in World War 2 led to the end of the Italian Empire; monarchy abolished and institution of a democratic republic, 1946; Parliament consists of a Chamber of Deputies and a Senate; the President of the Republic is Head of State and appoints a Prime Minister; continued political instability, with some 50 governments in power since the formation of the republic.

Head of State
1999–2006 Carlo Ciampi
2006–   Giorgio Napolitano

Head of Government
2001–6 Silvio Berlusconi
2006–   Romano Prodi

JAMAICA

Local name Jamaica

Timezone GMT –5

Area 10957 km²/4229 sq mi

Population total (2002e) 2630000

Status Independent state within the Commonwealth

Date of independence 1962

Capital Kingston

Languages English (official), with Jamaican Creole widely spoken

Ethnic groups African (76%), Afro-European (15%), East Indian and Afro-Indian (3%), white (3%), Chinese and Afro-Chinese (1%)

Religions Christian (Protestant 56%, Roman Catholic 5%), non-religious (17%)

Physical features Third largest island in the Caribbean; maximum length, 234 km/145 mi; width, 35–82 km/22–51 mi; mountainous and rugged, particularly in the E, where the Blue Mt Peak rises to 2256 m/ 7401 ft; over 100 small rivers, several used for hydroelectric power.

Climate Humid, tropical climate at sea-level; more temperate at higher altitudes; average annual temperature 24°C (Jan), 27°C (Jul); mean annual rainfall 1980 mm/ 70 in; virtually no rainfall on S and SW plain; lies within the hurricane belt.

Currency 1 Jamaican Dollar (JMD) = 100 cents

Economy Plantation agriculture (still employs about a third of workforce); sugar, bananas, citrus fruits, coffee, cocoa, ginger, coconuts; bauxite (world's second largest producer); cement, fertilizer, textiles, rum, chemical products; tourism.

GNP (2002e) $10.08 bn, per capita $3800

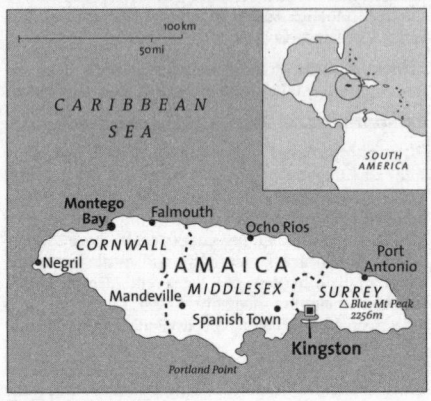

□ International Airport

HDI (2002) 0.742

History Visited by Columbus, 1494; settled by Spanish, 1509; West African slave labour imported for work on sugar plantations from 1640; British occupation, 1655; self-government, 1944; independence, 1962; Governor-General appoints Prime Minister and Cabinet; bicameral Parliament consists of a House of Representatives and a Senate.

Head of State
(British monarch represented by Governor-General)
2006–   Kenneth Octavius Hall

Head of Government
1992–2006 Percival Patterson
2006–   Portia Simpson Miller

JAPAN

Local name Nihon (Nippon)

Timezone GMT +9

Area 377728 km²/145803 sq mi

Population total (2002e) 127347000

Status Monarchy

Capital Tokyo

Language Japanese (official)

Ethnic groups Japanese (99%), with Korean minorities

Religions Shintoist (40%), Buddhist (39%), Christian (4%)

Physical features Island state comprising four large islands (Hokkaido, Honshu, Kyushu, Shikoku) and several small islands; consists mainly of steep mountains with many volcanoes; Hokkaido (N) central range runs N–S, rising to over 2000 m/6500 ft, falling to coastal uplands and plains; Honshu, the largest island, comprises parallel arcs of mountains bounded by narrow coastal plains, and includes Mt Fuji, 3776 m/12388 ft; heavily populated Kanto plain in E; Shikoku and Kyushu (SW) consist of clusters of low cones and rolling hills, mostly 1000–2000 m/3000–6000 ft; Ryukyu chain of volcanic islands to the S, largest Okinawa; frequent earthquakes, notably in Kanto (1993), Kobe (1995).

Climate Oceanic climate, influenced by the Asian monsoon; heavy winter rainfall on W coasts of Honshu and in Hokkaido; short, warm summers in N, and severe winters, with heavy snow; variable winter weather throughout Japan, especially in N and W; typhoons in summer and early autumn; mild and almost subtropical winters in S Honshu, Shikoku, and Kyushu; average annual temperatures 5°C (Jan), 25°C (Jul) in Tokyo.

Currency 1 Yen (JPY) = 100 sen

Economy Limited natural resources (less than 20% of land under cultivation); intensive crop production (principally of rice); timber, fishing, engineering, ship-building, textiles, chemicals; major industrial developments since 1960s, especially in computing, electronics, and vehicles.

GDP (2002e) $3.651 tn, per capita $28700

HDI (2002) 0.933

History Originally occupied by the Ainu; developed into small states, 4th-c; culture strongly influenced by China, 7th–9th-c; ruled by feudal shoguns until power passed to the emperor, 1867; limited contact with the West until the Meiji Restoration, 1868; successful war with China, 1894–5; gained Formosa (Taiwan) and S Manchuria; formed alliance with Britain, 1902; war with Russia, 1904–5; Russia ceded southern half of Sakhalin; Korea annexed, 1910; joined allies in World War 1, 1914; received German Pacific islands as mandates, 1919; war with China; occupied Manchuria, 1931–2; renewed fighting, 1937; entered World War 2 with surprise attack on the US fleet at Pearl Harbor, Hawaii, 1941; occupied British and Dutch possessions in SE Asia, 1941–2; pushed back during 1943–5; atomic bombs dropped on Hiroshima and Nagasaki by allied forces in 1945, ending World War 2 with Japanese surrender; allied control

Key
1. Yokohama
2. Nagoya
3. Kyoto
4. Kobe
5. Osaka
6. Hiroshima
7. Kitakyushu
8. Fukuoka
9. Takamatsu
10. Nagasaki

□ International Airport

commission took power, and Formosa and Manchuria returned to China; Emperor Hirohito became figurehead ruler, 1946; full sovereignty regained, 1952; joined United Nations, 1958; strong economic growth in 1960s; regained Bonin, Okinawa, and Volcano Islands, 1972; a constitutional monarchy with Emperor as Head of State; government consists of a Prime Minister, Cabinet, and bicameral Diet (*Kokkai*), with a House of Representatives and a House of Councillors; co-location (with South Korea) of the 2002 FIFA World Cup.

Head of State (Emperor)
1989–   Akihito (Heisei)

Head of Government (Prime Minister)
2006–   Shinzo Abe

JORDAN

Local name al'Urdun

Timezone GMT +2

Area 89544 km²/34564 sq mi

Population total (2002e) 5260000

Status Hashemite kingdom

Date of independence 1946

Capital Amman

Language Arabic (official)

Ethnic groups Arab (99%), Circassian, Armenian, Turkish, Kurd minorities

Religions Muslim (Sunni 95%), Christian (including Roman Catholic, Anglican, Coptic, Greek Orthodox, and Evangelical Lutheran) (5%)

Physical features Located in Middle East; divided N–S by Red Sea–Jordan rift valley, much lying below sea level; lowest point, –400 m/–1312 ft at the Dead Sea; highest point, Jebel Ram, 1754 m/5754 ft; land levels out to the Syrian desert (E); c.90% of Jordan is desert.

Climate Mediterranean; hot, dry summers, cool, wet winters; desert area uniformly hot, sunny; rainfall below 200 mm/8 in; average annual temperatures 7.5°C (Jan), 24.9°C (Jul) in Amman.

Currency 1 Jordan Dinar (JOD) = 1000 fils

Economy Oil, cement, potash, phosphate (world's third largest exporter), light manufacturing; cereals, vegetables, citrus fruits, olives.

GDP (2002e) $22.63 bn, per capita $4300

HDI (2002) 0.717

HUMAN GEOGRAPHY

Jordan (continued)

History Part of Roman Empire; Arab control, 7th-c; part of Turkish Empire, 16th-c until World War 1; area divided into Palestine (W of R Jordan) and Transjordan (E of R Jordan), administered by Britain; independence as Transjordan, 1946; British mandate over Palestine ended, 1948; renamed Jordan, 1949; Israeli control of West Bank after Six-Day War, 1967; civil war, following attempts by Jordanian army to expel Palestinian guerrillas from West Bank, 1970-1; claims to the West Bank ceded to the Palestine Liberation Organization, 1974; links with the West Bank cut, and PLO established a government in exile, 1988; martial law formally abolished by King Hussein in 1992, and ban on political parties lifted; conflict with Israel formally ended, 1994; Monarch is Head of State and appoints a Prime Minister, who selects a Council of Ministers; Parliament consists of a Senate and a House of Representatives.

Head of State (Monarch)
1952–99   Hussein II
1999–   Abdullah II

Head of Government
2003–5   Faisal al-Fayez
2005   Adnan Badran
2005–   Marouf Bakhet

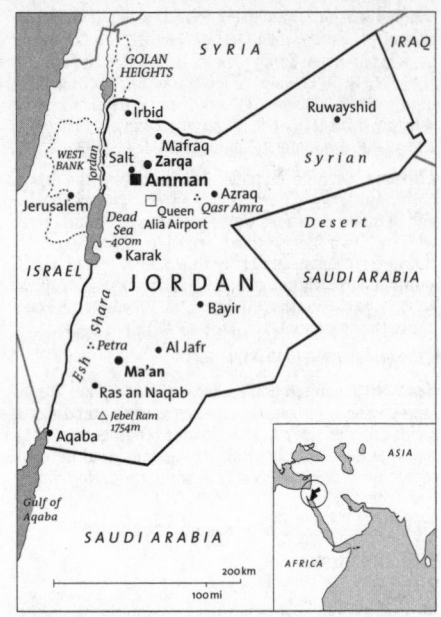

☐ International Airport   ∴ World heritage site

KAZAKHSTAN

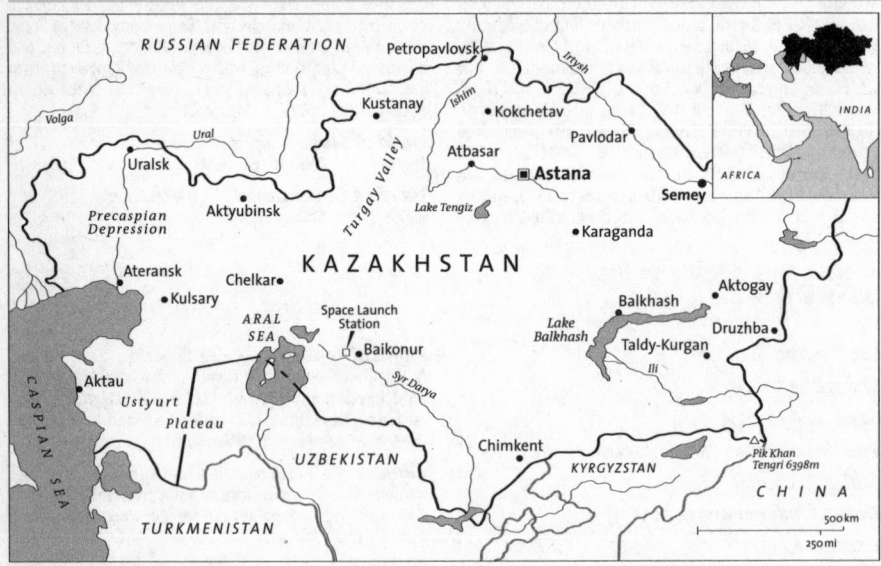

☐ International Airport

Local name Kazakstan

Timezone GMT +5/6

Area 2 717 300 km²/1 048 878 sq mi

Population total (2002e) 14 888 000

Status Republic

Date of independence 1991

Capital Astana (from 1998), formerly Akmola (1997–8) and previously located at Almaty (Alma-Ata)

Languages Kazakh (official), Russian, German

Ethnic groups Kazakh (53.4%), Russian (30%), Ukrainian (3.7%), Uzbek (2.5%), German (2.4%)

Religions Muslim (Sunni), Christian (Russian Orthodox, Protestant)

Physical features Bounded E by China and W by Caspian Sea; second largest republic in former USSR; mountain ranges in E and SE; steppeland (N) gives way to desert (S); lowest elevation near E shore of the Caspian Sea, 132 m/433 ft below sea-level; main rivers, Irtysh, Syr Darya, Ural, Ili; largest lake, L Balkhash; space launch centre at Tyuratam, near Baikonur.

Climate Continental; hot summers, extreme winters; wide range of temperatures, from –17°C in N and C ranges, to –3°C in S (Jan), 20°C in N, 29°C in S (Jul); strong, dry winds common in NW.

Currency 1 Tenge (KZT) = 100 kopecks

Economy Petroleum, natural gas, coal, iron ore, bauxite, zinc, gold, uranium; oil refining, metallurgy, heavy engineering, chemicals, leatherwork, footwear, food processing; cotton, fruit, grain, sheep.

GDP (2002e) $120 bn, per capita $7200

HDI (2002) 0.750

History Under the control of the Mongols, 13th-c; gradually under Russian rule, 1730–1853; became constituent republic of USSR, 1936; independence movement, 1990–1; independence declared in 1991, and joined Commonwealth of Independent States; governed by a President, Prime Minister, and Supreme Soviet.

Head of State
1991–   Nursultan A Nazarbayev

Head of Government
2003–   Karim Masimov *Interim*

KENYA

Local name Kenya

Timezone GMT +3

Area 580 367 km²/224 081 sq mi

Population total (2002e) 31 139 000

Status Republic

Date of independence 1963

Capital Nairobi

Languages English and Swahili (official), with many local languages spoken

Ethnic groups Kikuyu (21%), Luhya (13%), Luo (11%), Kamba (11%), Kalejin (6%), Kisii (6%), Meru (6%)

Religions Christian (66%) (Roman Catholic 28%, Protestant 38%), local beliefs (26%), Muslim (6%)

Physical features Crossed by the Equator; SW plateau rises to 600–3000 m/2000–10 000 ft, includes Mt Kenya, 5200 m/17 058 ft; Great Rift Valley (W) runs N–S; dry, arid semi-desert in the N, generally under 600 m/2000 ft; rivers include Tana and Athi; L Turkana in NW.

Climate Tropical climate on coast, with high temperatures and humidity; average annual temperature 18°C (Jan), 16°C (Jul) in Nairobi; average annual rainfall 958 mm/38 in.

Currency 1 Kenyan shilling (KES) = 100 cents

Economy Agriculture (accounts for c.35% of national income); coffee, tea, cashew nuts, rice, wheat, maize, sugar cane; textiles, chemicals, cement, oil refining, tobacco, rubber; reserves of soda ash, salt, limestone, lead, gemstones, silver, gold; 14 national parks attract large numbers of tourists.

GDP (2002e) $32.89 bn, per capita $1100

HDI (2002) 0.513

History Very early fossil hominids found in the region by anthropologists; coast settled by Arabs, 7th-c; Portuguese control, 16th–17th-c; British control as East African Protectorate, 1895; British colony, 1920; independence movement led to Mau Mau rebellion, 1952–60;

□ International Airport   – – Border dispute

independence within Commonwealth, 1963; Republic of Kenya, 1964; first leader, Jomo Kenyatta; multi-party elections, 1992, gave Arap Moi fourth term of office; result condemned by opposition parties; Moi defeated (Dec 2002) after 24 years' rule; coast hit by Indian Ocean tsunami, 2004; proposed change to constitution, including new post of prime minister, rejected 2005; governed by a President elected for a 5-year term, with a unicameral National Assembly of 224 members.

Head of State/Government
2002–   Mwai Kibaki

KIRIBATI

Local name Kiribati

Timezone GMT –12

Area 717 km²/277 sq mi

Population total (2002e) 90 600

Status Republic

Date of independence 1979

Capital Bairiki (on Tarawa Atoll)

Languages English (official) and Gilbertese

Ethnic groups Micronesian, small Polynesian and non-Pacific minorities

Religions Roman Catholic (54%), Kiribati Protestant (39%), Baha'i (2%), Seventh-day Adventist (2%), Mormon (2%)

Physical features Group of 33 low-lying islands scattered over c.3 000 000 km²/1 200 000 sq mi of the C Pacific Ocean; comprises the Gilbert Is Group, Phoenix Is, and 8 of the 11 Line Islands, including Christmas I; islands seldom rise to more than 4 m/13 ft and usually consist of a reef enclosing a lagoon.

Climate Maritime equatorial climate in central islands, tropical further N and S; periodic drought in some islands; wet season (Nov–Apr); subject to typhoons; average annual temperatures 28°C (Jan), 27°C (July) in Tarawa; average annual rainfall 1977 mm/78 in.

Currency 1 Australian Dollar (AUD) = 100 cents

Economy 50% of land under permanent cultivation; main exports include fish, particularly tuna; phosphates; copra, coconuts, bananas, pandanus, breadfruit, papaya; sea fishing.

GDP (2001e) $79 mn, per capita $800

History Gilbert and Ellice Is proclaimed a British protectorate, 1892; became a Crown Colony, 1916; occupied by Japan during World War 2, but driven out by US forces; Ellice Is severed links with Gilbert Is to form separate dependency of Tuvalu, 1975; Gilbert Is independence as Kiribati, 1979; a sovereign and democratic republic, with a President and an elected House of Assembly.

Head of State/Government
1994–2003   Teburoro Tito
2003–   Anote Tong

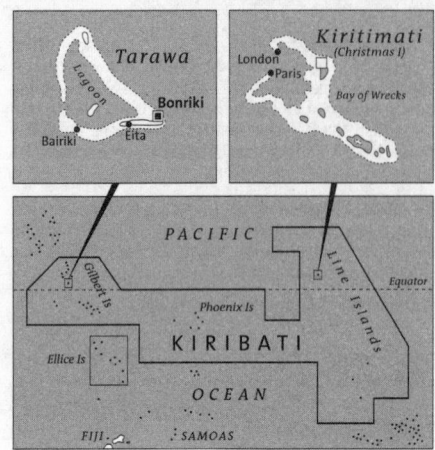

□ International Airport

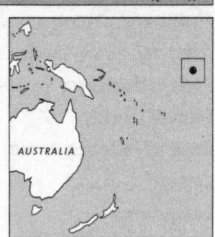

KOREA, NORTH

Local name Chōson Minjujuüi In'min Konghwaguk

Timezone GMT +9

Area 122 098 km²/47 130 sq mi

Population total (2002e) 22 224 000

Status Democratic people's republic

Date of independence 1948

Capital Pyongyang

Language Korean (official)

Ethnic groups Korean (99.8%), Chinese (0.2%)

Religions Atheist or non-religious (68%), Buddhist (2%), Christian (1%)

Physical features Located in E Asia, in the N half of the Korean peninsula; separated from South Korea to the S by a demilitarized zone of 1262 km²/487 sq mi; volcanic peak of Mount Paek-tu rises 2744 m/9003 ft in NE; Yalu river valley marks Korean–Chinese border in NW; fertile Chaeryong and Pyongyang plains in SW; 74% of land forested, 18% arable.

Climate Temperate; warm summers, severely cold winters; often rivers freeze for up to 3–4 months in winter; average annual temperatures –8°C (Jan), 24°C (Jul); average annual rainfall 916 mm/26 in.

Currency 1 North Korean Won (KPW) = 100 chon

Economy Agriculture (employs c.48% of workforce, generally on large-scale collective farms); rice, maize, vegetables, livestock, wheat, barley, beans, tobacco; timber, fishing; severely affected during the Korean War, but rapid recovery with Soviet and Chinese aid; machine building, mining, chemicals, textiles.

GDP (2002e) $22.26 bn, per capita $1000

History (>> KOREA, SOUTH history); formally annexed by Japan, 1910; N area occupied by Soviet troops following invasion by US and Russian troops and the dividing of the country into N and S, 1945; Democratic People's Republic of Korea declared, 1948; Korean War, 1950–3; demilitarized zone established, 1953; friendship and mutual-assistance treaty signed with China, 1961; unsuccessful reunification talks, 1980; member of UN, 1991; non-aggression agreement signed with S Korea, 1991; death of Kim Il-sung, 1994; withdrawal from 1970 Non-Proliferation treaty (2003); first road link between North and South Korea since Korean War, 2003; governed by a President and a Supreme People's Assembly.

Head of State
1972–4   Kim Il-sung
1994–   Kim Jong-il

Head of Government
1997–2003   Hong Song-nam
2003–   Pak Pong-ju

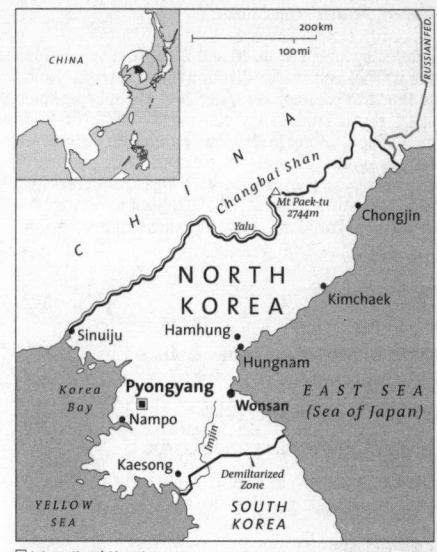

☐ International Airport

KOREA, SOUTH

Local name Taehan-Min'guk

Timezone GMT +9

Area 98 913 km²/38 180 sq mi

Population total (2002e) 47 640 000

Status Republic

Date of independence 1948

Capital Seoul

Language Korean (official)

Ethnic groups Korean (99.9%), Chinese (0.1%)

Religions Buddhist (18%), Christian (Protestant 41%, Roman Catholic 3%), Confucianist (1%)

Physical features Occupies the S half of the Korean peninsula; bordered N by North Korea, from which it is separated by a demilitarized zone at 38°N; Taebaek Sanmaek Mt range runs N–S along the E coast; descends to broad, undulating coastal lowlands; rivers include Naktong and Han; c.3000 islands off the W and S coasts; largest island is Cheju do, which contains Korea's highest peak, Hallasan, 1950 m/6398 ft.

Climate Extreme continental climate, cold winters, hot summers; average annual temperatures –5°C (Jan), 25°C (Jul); average annual rainfall 1250 mm/49 in.

Currency 1 South Korean Won (KRW) = 100 chon

Economy Light consumer goods, with a shift towards heavy industries; petrochemicals, textiles, electrical machinery, steel, ships, fish; one of the world's largest deposits of tungsten; only a fifth of land suitable for cultivation; rice, wheat, barley, grain, pulses, tobacco.

GDP (2002e) $941.5 bn, per capita $19 600

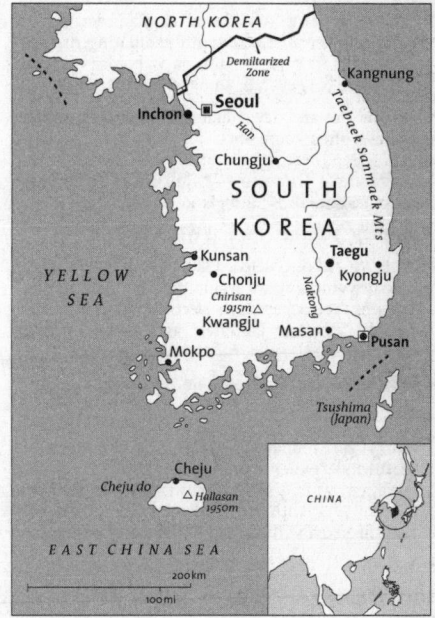

☐ International Airport

HDI (2002) 0.882

History Originally split into three rival kingdoms, united in 668 by the Silla dynasty; succeeded by the Koryo dynasty, 935; Yi dynasty, 1392–1910; independence recognized by China, 1895; annexation by Japan, 1910;

HUMAN GEOGRAPHY

Korea, South (continued)

entered by Russia (from N) and USA (from S) to enforce the Japanese surrender, dividing the country in N and S at the 38th parallel, 1945; declared Republic of Korea, 1948; North Korean forces invaded, 1950; UN forces assisted South Korea in stopping the advance, 1950–3; military coup, 1961; assassination of Park Chung Hee, 1979; non-aggression pact signed with N Korea, 1991; President Roh Moo-hyun impeached (Mar 2004) but reinstated; governed by a President, a State Council, and a National Assembly; co-location (with Japan) of the 2002 FIFA World Cup; first road link between North and South Korea since Korean War, 2003.

Head of State
2003–   Roh Moo-hyun

Head of Government
2006   Han Duk Soo *Acting*
2006–   Han Myung-sook

KUWAIT

Local name Dowlat al-Kuwait (Arabic)

Timezone GMT +3

Area 17 818 km²/6878 sq mi

Population total (2002e) 2 253 000

Status Independent state

Date of independence 1961

Capital Kuwait City

Language Arabic (official)

Ethnic groups Kuwaiti (52%), non-Kuwaiti Arab (45%), Asian (3%)

Religions Muslim (90%), Christian (8%), Hindu (2%)

Physical features Consists of mainland and nine offshore islands; terrain flat or gently undulating, rising SW to 271 m/889 ft; Wadi al Batin on W border with Iraq; low ridges in NE generally stony with sparse vegetation.

Climate Hot and dry climate; summer temperatures very high, often above 45°C (Jul–Aug); humidity often over 90%; sandstorms common all year; average annual temperature 14°C (Jan) to 37°C (Jul) in Kuwait City; average annual rainfall 111 mm/4 in.

Currency 1 Kuwaiti Dinar (KWD) = 1000 fils

Economy Oil discovered, 1938, providing 95% of government revenue; active programme of economic diversification; petrochemicals, fertilizers, construction materials, asbestos, batteries; agriculture gradually expanding; dates, citrus fruits, timber, livestock.

GDP (2002e) $36.85 bn, per capita $17 500

HDI (2002) 0.813

History Port founded in 18th-c; British protectorate, 1914; full independence from Britain, 1961; invasion and annexation by Iraq (Aug 1990), leading to Gulf War (Jan–Feb 1991), with severe damage to Kuwait City; Kuwait liberated with the aid of UN forces in 1991, and

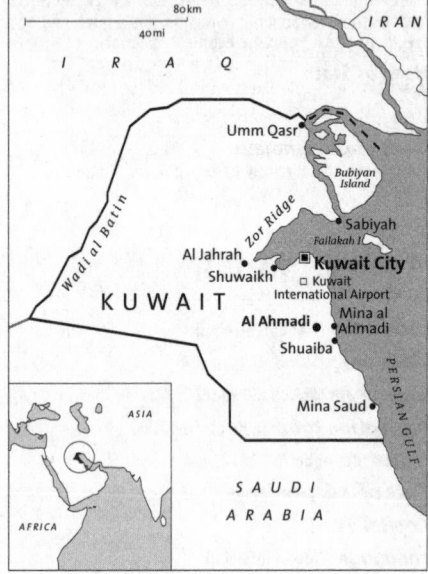

□ International Airport

government returned from exile; large refugee emigration; major post-war problems, including burning of Kuwaiti oil wells by Iraq and pollution of Gulf waters by oil; Emir is Head of State, governing through an appointed Prime Minister and a Council of Ministers.

Head of State (Emir)
2006–   Sabah al-Ahmad al-Jaber al-Sabah

Head of Government (Prime Minister)
2006–   Nasser Muhammad al-Ahmad

KYRGYZSTAN

Local name Kyrgyzstan

Timezone GMT +5

Area 198 500 km²/76 621 sq mi

Population total (2002e) 5 002 000

Status Republic

Date of independence 1991

Capital Bishkek (formerly Frunze)

Language Russian (official), Kyrgyz

Ethnic groups Kyrgyz (52%), Russian (21%), other (27%)

Religion Sunni Muslim (chief religion)

Physical features Located in C Asia, bounded SE and E by China; largely occupied by the Tien Shan Mts; highest point within the republic at Pik Pobedy, 7439 m/24 406 ft; chief river, the Naryn; largest lake, L Issyk-Kul.

Climate Typical desert climate in N, W, and SE; hot, dry summers in valleys; mean annual temperature –18°C (Jan), 28°C (Jul).

Currency 1 Kyrgyzstani Som (KGS) = 100 tyiyn

Economy Metallurgy; machines; coal; natural gas; textiles, food processing, gold; wheat, cotton, tobacco, animal husbandry.

GDP (2002e) $13.88 bn, per capita $2900

HDI (2002) 0.712

History Part of Turkestan republic, 1917–24; constituent republic of USSR, 1936; independence, and joined Commonwealth of Independent States, 1991; governed by a President, Prime Minister, and Supreme Soviet; President Akayev deposed in coup, Mar 2005.

☐ International Airport

Head of State
2005–   Kurmanbek Bakiev

Head of Government
2005–   Kurmanbek Bakiev *Interim*

LAOS

Local name Lao

Timezone GMT +7

Area 236 800 km²/91 405 sq mi

Population total (2002e) 5 777 000

Status Republic

Date of independence 1949

Capital Vientiane

Languages Lao (official), French, and tribal languages

Ethnic groups Laotian (60%), hill tribes (35%)

Religions Buddhist (58%), animist (largely the Lao-Theung) (34%), Christian (2%)

Physical features Landlocked country on the Indo-Chinese peninsula; dense jungle and rugged mountains (E), rising to 2751 m/9025 ft on Vietnamese border, and 2820 m/9252 ft at Phou Bia on the Xieng Khouang plateau; Mekong R flows NW–SE, fertile Mekong floodplains in W; 4% of land arable, 58% forested.

Climate Monsoonal climate; average annual rainfall 1715 mm/67.5 in; (heaviest, May–Sep); average annual temperature 14°C (Jan), 34°C (Jul) in Vientiane.

Currency (1992) 1 Kip (LAK) = 100 at

Economy Agricultural economy suffered severely in the civil war; rice, coffee, tobacco, cotton, spices, opium; tin, iron ore, potash; forestry (1991 logging ban to halt deforestation), rubber, cigarettes, matches; textiles.

GDP (2002e) $10.4 bn, per capita $1800

HDI (2002) 0.485

History Visited by Europeans, 17th-c; French protectorate, 1893; occupied by Japanese in World War 2; independence from France, 1949; civil war, 1953–75,

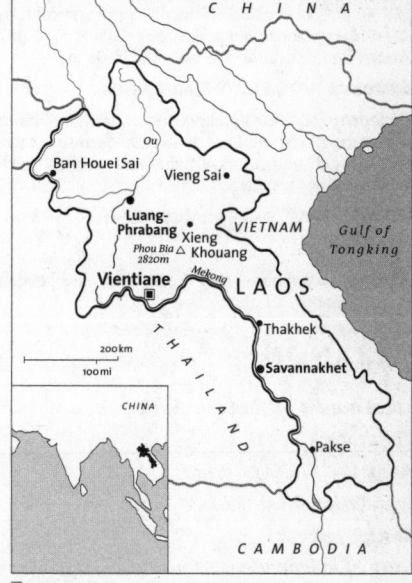

☐ International Airport

between the Lao government, supported by the USA, and the communist-led Patriotic Front *(Pathet Lao)*, supported by North Vietnam; monarchy abolished and communist republic established, 1975 draft constitution approved, 1991, provides for a directly elected National Assembly and executive President.

Head of State
2006–   Choummaly Sayasone

Head of Government
2006–   Bouasone Bouphavanh

LATVIA

Local name Latvija (Latvian)

Timezone GMT +2

Area 64 600 km²/24 900 sq mi

Population total (2002e) 2 331 000

Status Republic

Date of independence 1991

Capital Riga

Language Latvian (official)

Ethnic groups Latvian (52%), Russian (34%), Belorussian (5%), Ukrainian (4%), Polish (2%), Lithuanian (1%)

Religions Predominantly Evangelical Lutheran, with Orthodox and Roman Catholic minorities

Physical features Flat, glaciated region; highest point, central Vidzeme (Livonia) elevation, 312 m/1024 ft; over 40% forested; coastline ranges over 472 km/293 mi; wooded lowland, marshes, lakes; NW coast indented by the Gulf of Riga; chief river, Daugava.

Climate Mild climate, with high humidity; only c.30–40 days of sunshine annually; summers cool and rainy; average mean temperature −2°C (Jan), 17°C (Jul); average annual rainfall 700–800 mm/28–31 in.

Currency (1991) 1 Lat (LVL) = 100 santims

Economy Machine-building, metalworking, electrical engineering, electronics, chemicals, furniture, food processing, fishing, timber, paper and woollen goods, meat and dairy products.

GDP (2002e) $20.99 bn, per capita $8900

HDI (2002) 0.800

History Incorporated into Russia, 1721; independent

□ International Airport

state, 1918–40; proclaimed a Soviet Socialist Republic, 1940; occupied by Germany in World War 2; USSR regained control, 1944; coalition government elected, 1989; declared independence, 1991; governed by a President, Prime Minister, and Congress of Latvia.

Head of State
1999–   Vaira Vike-Freiberga

Head of Government
2004   Indulis Emsis
2004–   Aigars Kalvitis

LEBANON

Local names al-Lubnān (Arab), Liban (French)

Timezone GMT +2

Area 10 452 km²/4034 sq mi

Population total (2002e) 3 678 000

Status Republic

Date of independence 1943

Capital Beirut

Languages Arabic (official), French, English, and Armenian also spoken

Ethnic groups Arab (93%), with several minorities

Religions Muslim (c.75%), Christian (c.25%), also many religious sects including Armenian, Greek, Roman Catholic, Alawite, Druze, and Jewish

Physical features Narrow coastal plain rises gradually E to the Lebanon Mts (Jebel Liban), reaching 3087 m/10 128 ft at Qornet es Saouda; arid E slopes fall abruptly to the fertile Beqaa plateau, average elevation 1000 m/

3 300 ft; Anti-Lebanon range (Jebel esh Sharqi) in the E; R Litani flows S between the two ranges.

Climate Mediterranean climate, varying with altitude; hot, dry summers, warm, moist winters; average annual temperatures 13°C (Jan), 27°C (Jul); average annual rainfall 920 mm/36 in; much drier and cooler in the Bekaa valley.

Currency 1 Lebanese Pound/Livre (LBP) = 100 piastres

Economy Commercial and financial centre of the Middle East until the civil war, which severely damaged economic infrastructure and reduced industrial and agricultural production; oil refining, textiles, chemicals, food processing; citrus fruits, apples, grapes, bananas, sugar beet, olives, wheat; tourism has virtually collapsed, but signs of revival in 1993.

GDP (2002e) $17.61 bn, per capita $4800

HDI (2002) 0.755

History Part of Ottoman Empire from 16th-c; after massacre of (Catholic) Maronites by (Muslim) Druzes,

1860, Maronite area around Jabal Lubnan granted special autonomous status; Greater Lebanon, based on this area, created under French mandate, 1920; Muslim coastal regions incorporated, despite great opposition; constitutional republic, 1926; independence, 1943; Palestinian resistance units established in Lebanon by late 1960s despite government opposition, including the Palestine Liberation Organization (PLO); several militia groups developed in mid-1970s; following terrorist attacks Israel invaded S Lebanon, 1978 and 1982; heavy Israeli bombardment of Beirut forced withdrawal of Palestinian forces, 1982; unilateral withdrawal of Israeli and Syrian forces from Lebanon brought clashes between the Druze (backed by Syria) and Christian Lebanese militia; Syrian troops entered Beirut in attempt to restore order, 1988; release of Western hostages began, 1990; timetable for militia disarmament introduced, 1991; Israeli withdrawal from South Lebanon border area, 2000; Syrian troops withdrawn in line with UN demands, 2005; air and sea blockade imposed by Israel after hostile action by Hezbollah, Jul 2006; invasion by Israel, followed by UN-brokered ceasefire, Jul–Aug 2006; constitution provides for a Council of Ministers, a President (a Maronite Christian), Prime Minister (a Sunni Muslim), a Cabinet, and a Parliament, equally divided between Christians and Muslims.

Head of State
1998–   Emile Lahoud

Head of Government
2005–   Najib Mikati

□ International Airport

LESOTHO

Local name Lesotho

Timezone GMT +2

Area 30 355 km²/11 720 sq mi

Population total (2002e) 2 208 000

Status Independent kingdom within Commonwealth

Date of independence 1960

Capital Maseru

Languages Lesotho (Sesotho) and English (official), Zulu, Afrikaans, French, Xhosa also spoken

Ethnic groups Basotho (99%), Zulu, Tembu, and Fingo tribes, European and Asian minorities

Religions Roman Catholic (44%), Protestant (mostly Lesotho Evangelical) (30%), Anglican (12%), other Christian (8%), traditional beliefs (6%)

Physical features S African kingdom completely bounded by South Africa; Drakensberg Mts in NE and E, highest peak Thabana-Ntlenyana, 3482 m/11 424 ft; serious soil erosion, especially in W; main rivers, the Orange and the Caledon; mountainous land, particularly in SW with the Maloti Mountain range.

Climate Mild, dry winters; warm summer season (Oct–Apr); average annual temperatures 15°C (Jan), 25°C (Jul); average annual rainfall 725 mm/28.5 in (Oct–Apr).

Currency 1 Loti (*plural* Maloti) (LSl) = 100 lisente; 1 South African Rand (ZAR) = 100 cents

□ International Airport

Economy Economy based on intensive agriculture and contract labour working in South Africa; wheat, peas, beans, barley, cattle; diamonds, textiles, pharmaceuticals; jewellery, crafts, wool, mohair.

GDP (2002e) $5.106 bn, per capita $2700

HDI (2002) 0.535

HUMAN GEOGRAPHY

Lesotho (continued)

History Originally inhabited by hunting and gathering bushmen; Bantu arrived 16th-c, and Basotho nation established; incorporated in Orange Free State, 1854; under British protection as Basutoland, 1869; independence, 1960; declared Kingdom of Lesotho in 1966, as a hereditary monarchy within the Commonwealth; constitution suspended and country ruled by Council of Ministers, 1970–86; Prime Minister deposed by coup and political activity banned, 1986, with Military Council as effective ruling body; King Moshoeshoe dethroned by military council in 1990, and replaced by eldest son; elections (first since 1970) to restore civilian rule, 1993; Moshoeshoe returned to the throne, 1994, but died in a car accident, 1996; status of the monarchy a continuing issue; new electoral system introduced, 2002.

Head of State (Monarch)
1966–90	Moshoeshoe II
1990–4	Letsie III *Abdicated*
1994–6	Moshoeshoe II
1996–	Letsie III

Head of Government
1998–	Bethuel Pakalitha Mosisili

LIBERIA

Local name Liberia

Timezone GMT

Area 111 370 km²/42 989 sq mi

Population total (2002e) 3 288 000

Status Republic

Date of independence 1847

Capital Monrovia

Languages English (official) with many dialects/languages of Niger-Congo spoken

Ethnic groups Indigenous tribes (including Kpelle, Bassa, Gio, Kru, Gola, Kissi, Vai, and Bella) (95%), Americo-Liberians (repatriated slaves from the USA) (5%)

Religions Traditional animist beliefs (70%), Muslim (20%), Christian (10%)

Physical features Low coastal belt with lagoons, beaches, and mangrove marshes; land rises inland to mountains, reaching 1752 m/5748 ft at Mt Nimba; rivers include Mano, Moro, St Paul, St John, Cess, Duoubé, Cavalla.

Climate Equatorial climate; high temperatures, abundant rainfall; high humidity during rainy season (Apr–Sep), especially on coast; average annual temperatures 26°C (Jan), 24°C (Jul); average annual rainfall 5138 mm/202 in.

Currency 1 Liberian Dollar (LRD) = 100 cents

Economy Based on minerals, especially iron ore; two-thirds of the population rely on subsistence agriculture; rubber, timber, palm oil, rice, cassava, coffee, cocoa, coconuts; large merchant fleet, including the registration of many foreign ships.

GDP (2002e) $3.116 bn, per capita $1000

History Mapped by the Portuguese in 15th-c; created by US philanthropic societies, wishing to establish a homeland for former slaves; founded in 1822; consti-

☐ International Airport

tuted as the Free and Independent Republic of Liberia 1847; military coup and assassination of President, 1980; new constitution, 1986, with an elected Senate and a House of Representatives; civil war, followed by arrival of West African peacekeeping force, 1990; transitional governments in early 1990s; peace accord signed, 1995; elections held, 1997; new rebel offensive, leading to exile of President Taylor, 2003; power-sharing government established, 2003; UN peace-keeping mission, 2003–4; first woman president elected, Nov 2005.

Head of State/Government
2005–	Ellen Johnson-Sirleaf

LIBYA

Local name Lībiyā

Timezone GMT +1

Area 1 758 610 km²/678 823 sq mi

Population total (2002e) 5 369 000

Status Republic

Date of independence 1951

Capital Tripoli

Languages Arabic (official), with English and French widely spoken

Ethnic groups Berber and Arab (97%), Greek, Maltese, Italian, Egyptian, Pakistani, Turk, Indian, and Tunisian minorities (3%)

Religions Sunni Muslim (96%), Christian (Roman Catholic, Anglican, Coptic Orthodox) (3%), Jewish (1%)

Physical features Mainly low-lying Saharan desert or semi-desert; 93% of land is contained in the arid Saharan plateau; land rises (S) to over 2000 m/6500 ft in the Tibesti massif; highest point, Pic Bette, 2286 m/7500 ft; comparatively fertile region in Gefara plain and Jabal Nafusah plateau in Tripolitania region.

Climate Mediterranean climate on coast; rainy season (Oct–Mar) in NW and NE upland regions; average annual temperature 11°C (Jan), 27°C (Jul) in Tripoli; average annual rainfall 385 mm/15 in.

Currency 1 Libyan Dinar (LYD) = 1000 dirhams

Economy Former agricultural economy; barley, olives, fruit, dates, almonds, tobacco; relatively poor until economy transformed by discovery of oil and natural gas, 1959; petroleum processing; iron, steel, aluminium; textiles; nomadic farming in S.

GDP (2002e) $33.36 bn, per capita $6200

HDI (2002) 0.773

History Controlled by Phoenicians, Carthaginians, Greeks, Vandals, and Byzantines; Arab domination during 7th-c; Turkish rule from 16th-c; Italians gained control, 1911; named Libya by Italians, 1934; heavy fighting during World War 2, followed by British and French control; independent Kingdom of Libya, 1951; military coup established a republic under Muammar al-Gaddafi, 1969; Libyan troops occupied Aozou Strip, 1973 (returned to Chad, 1994); strained relations with other countries over alleged organization of international terrorism; diplomatic relations cut by UK after murder of a policewoman in London, 1984; Tripoli and Benghazi bombed by US Air Force in response to alleged terrorist

□ International Airport　　∴ World heritage site

activity, 1986; alleged base of terrorist operation which caused Lockerbie air disaster (1988), suspects extradited to Netherlands for trial, 1999, followed by suspension of international sanctions; responsibility for the disaster accepted, 2003; international inspection of nuclear sites permitted, 2003; partial US relations resumed and trade embargo lifted, 2004; EU arms embargo lifted, 2004; full US diplomatic relations restored, 2006; a socialist state, governed by a chief-of-state, a General People's Committee, and a 750-member General People's Congress.

Head of State/Government
1969–　　Muammar al-Gaddafi

LIECHTENSTEIN

Local name Liechtenstein

Timezone GMT +1

Area 160 km²/62 sq mi

Population total (2002e) 33 300

Status Independent principality

Date of independence 1719

Capital Vaduz

Language German (official)

Ethnic groups Liechtensteiner (64%), Swiss (16%), Austrian (8%), German (4%)

Religions Roman Catholic (87%), Protestant (9%)

Physical features Alpine principality, located in C Europe; fourth smallest country in the world; land

□ International Airport

Liechtenstein (continued)

boundary 76 km/47 mi; bounded W by the R Rhine; mean altitude, 450 m/1 475 ft; forested mountains rise to 2 599 m/8 527 ft in the Grauspitz; Samina River flows N.

Climate Mild, equable climate; temperatures range from −15°C (Jan), 20–8°C (Jul); average annual rainfall 1050–1200 mm/41–47 in.

Currency 1 Swiss Franc (CHF) = 100 centimes

Economy Industrial sector developing since 1950s; export-based, centred on specialized and high-tech production; metal-working, engineering, chemicals, pharmaceuticals; international banking and finance; tourism.

GDP (1999e) $825 mn, per capita $25 000

History Became a sovereign state in 1342; independent principality within Holy Roman Empire, 1719; part of Holy Roman Empire until 1806; adopted Swiss currency, 1921; united with Switzerland in a customs union, 1923; became a member of UN, 1990; constitutional referendum approved, 2003; constitutional monarchy ruled by hereditary princes of the House of Liechtenstein; governed by a Prime Minister, four Councillors, and a unicameral Parliament.

Head of State (Monarch)
1989–   Hans Adam II

Head of Government
2001–   Otmar Hasler

LITHUANIA

Local name Lietuva

Timezone GMT +2

Area 65 200 km²/25 167 sq mi

Population total (2002e) 3 473 000

Status Republic

Date of independence 1991

Capital Vilnius

Language Lithuanian (official)

Ethnic groups Lithuanian (80%), Russian (9%), Polish (7%), Belorussian (2%)

Religions Roman Catholic, small minority of Evangelical Lutherans and Evangelical Reformists

Physical features Glaciated plains cover much of the area; central lowlands with gentle hills in W and higher terrain in SE; highest point, Jouzapine in the Asmenos Hills, 294 m/964 ft; 25% forested; some 3000 small lakes mostly in E and SE; complex sandy dunes on Kursiu Marios lagoon; chief river, the Nemunas.

Climate Continental climate, affected by maritime weather of W Europe and continental E; Baltic Sea influences a narrow coastal zone; average annual temperatures −5°C (Jan), 16°C (Jul); average annual rainfall 630 mm/25 in.

Currency 1 Litas (LTL) = 100 centai

Economy Electrical engineering, computer hardware, instruments, machine tools, ship building; synthetic fibres, fertilizers, plastics, food processing, oil refining; cattle, pigs, poultry, grain, potatoes, vegetables.

GDP (2002e) $30.08 bn, per capita $8400

☐ International Airport

HDI (2002) 0.808

History United with Poland, 1385–1795; intensive russification led to revolts in 1905 and 1917; occupied by Germany in both World Wars; proclaimed republic, 1918; annexed by USSR, 1940; growth of nationalist movement in late 1980s; declared independence in 1990, not recognized until 1991; President Paskas impeached for violating constitution (Apr 2004, later reinstated); governed by a President, Prime Minister, and Supreme Council.

Head of State
2004–   Valdas Adamkus

Head of Government
2006–   Gediminas Kirkilas

LUXEMBOURG

Local names Lëtzebuerg (Letz), Luxembourg (French), Luxemburg (German)

Timezone GMT +1

Area 2 586 km²/998 sq mi

Population total (2002e) 447 000

Status Grand Duchy

Date of independence 1867

Capital Luxembourg

Languages French, German, Letzeburgish

Ethnic groups Luxemburger (73%), Portuguese (9%), Italian (5%), French (3%), Belgian (3%), German (2%)

Religions Roman Catholic (97%), Protestant (2%), Jewish (1%)

Physical features Divided into the two natural regions of Ardennes (Ösling) (N); forest in N, and Gutland in S, flatter, average height 250 m/820 ft; principal rivers include the Sûre, Our, Moselle.

Climate Mild climate, influenced by warm S wind (*Fröhn*); average annual temperatures 0.7°C (Jan), 18°C (Jul) in Luxembourg; average annual rainfall, 1050–1200 mm/41–7 in.

Currency 1 Euro (EUR) = 100 cents (before February 2002, 1 Luxembourg Franc (LUF) = 100 centimes)

Economy Important international centre based in city of Luxembourg; iron and steel, food processing; chemicals, tyres, metal products; mixed farming, dairy farming; wine; forestry; tourism.

GDP (2002e) $21.94 bn, per capita $48 900

HDI (2002) 0.925

History Made Grand Duchy by the Congress of Vienna, 1815; granted political autonomy, 1838; recognized as neutral independent state, 1867; occupied by Germany in both World Wars; joined Benelux economic union, 1948; neutrality abandoned on joining NATO, 1949; a hereditary monarchy with Grand Duke as Head of State; Parliament consists of Chamber of Deputies and State Council; Head of Government is the Minister of State.

☐ International Airport

Head of State (Grand Dukes and Duchesses)	
1964–2000	Jean
2000–	Henri

Head of Government	
1984–95	Jacques Santer
1995–	Jean-Claude Juncker

MACAO >> CHINA

MACEDONIA, FORMER YUGOSLAV REPUBLIC OF

Local name Makedonija

Timezone GMT +2

Area 25 713 km²/9925 sq mi

Population total (2002e) 2 036 000

Status Republic

Date of independence 1991

Capital Skopje

Language Macedonian (status as language or dialect is a political issue with Greece) and Albanian

Ethnic groups Macedonian Slav (66%), Albanian (23%), with Turk (4%), Serb (3%), and other minorities (but minority totals disputed as underestimates by Albanians and Serbs)

Religions Macedonian Orthodox Christian (autocephalous), Muslim

Physical features Landlocked, mountainous region, bordered by Serbia, Bulgaria, Greece, Albania; divided from Greek Macedonia by the Kožuf and Nidže ranges, highest point, Korab, 2764 m/9068 ft; main rivers, Struma and Vardar.

☐ International Airport

Macedonia (continued)

Climate Continental; average annual temperatures 0°C (Jan), 24°C (Jul); often heavy winter snowfalls; average annual rainfall 500 mm/20 in.

Currency (1994) 1 Denar (MKD) = 100 paras

Economy Agriculture; wheat, barley, corn, rice, tobacco; sheep, cattle; mining of minerals, iron ore, lead, zinc, nickel; steel, chemicals, textiles.

GDP (2002e) $10.57 bn, per capita $5100

HDI (2002) 0.772

History Part of Macedonian, Roman, and Byzantine Empires; settled by Slavs, 6th-c; conquered by Bulgars, 7th-c, and by Serbia, 14th-c; incorporated into Serbia after the Balkan Wars; united in 1918, in what later became Yugoslavia, but continuous demands for autonomy per-

sisted; occupied by Bulgaria during World War 2, 1941–44; declaration of independence, 1991; international discussions continue over the name under which the country will be accorded international recognition (the adjacent province of Greece bears the name Macedonia); received large numbers of refugees during the Kosovo crisis, 1999; peace agreement signed and NATO task force deployed, 2001; EU took over operations, 2003; governed by a President, Prime Minister, and Assembly.

Head of State
2004–   Branko Crvenkovski

Head of Government
2004   Hari Kostov
2004–6   Vlado Buckovski
2006–   Nikola Gruevski

MADAGASCAR

Local name Madagasikara

Timezone GMT +3

Area 587 041 km²/228 658 sq mi

Population total (2002e) 16 473 000

Status Republic

Date of independence 1960

Capital Antananarivo

Languages Malagasy (official), with French widely spoken

Ethnic groups Malagasy (99%) (including Merina 26%, Betsimisaraka 15%, Betsileo 12%)

Religions Traditional animist beliefs (47%), Christian (48%) (Roman Catholic 26%, Protestant 23%), Muslim (5%)

Physical features World's fourth largest island, length (N–S) 1580 km/982 mi; dissected N–S by a ridge of mountains (Tsaratananan Range), rising to 2876 m/9436 ft at Maromokotra; cliffs (E) drop down to a coastal plain through tropical forest; terraced descent (W) through savannah to coast, heavily indented in N.

Climate Tropical, variable rainfall; average annual rainfall 1000–1500 mm/40–60 in, higher in tropical coastal region; average annual temperatures 21°C (Jan), 15°C (Jul).

Currency 1 Ariary (MGA) = 5 iraimbilanja (before 2005, 1 Malagasy Franc (MGF) = 100 centimes

Economy Chiefly agricultural economy; rice, manioc, coffee, sugar, vanilla, cotton, peanuts, tobacco, livestock; food processing, tanning, cement, soap, paper, textiles, oil products; graphite, chrome, coal, ilmenite.

GDP (2002e) $12.59 bn, per capita $800

HDI (2002) 0.469

History Settled by Indonesians in 1st-c AD and by African traders in 8th-c; visited by Portuguese, 16th-c; French established trading posts in late 18th-c; claimed as a protectorate by the French, 1895; autonomous over-

□ International Airport

seas French territory (Malagasy Republic), 1958; independence, 1960; became Madagascar, 1977; new multiparty constitution, 1992; new constitution, 1998; governed by a President, who appoints a Council of Ministers and is guided by a Supreme Revolutionary Council; National People's Assembly is elected every five years; ongoing crisis following elections, 2001, with Didier Ratsiraka refusing to yield power to opposition leader Marc Ravalomanana, eventually appointed president (2002); legislative elections (Dec) followed by new cabinet, 2003.

Head of State
1997–2002   Didier Ratsiraka
2002–   Marc Ravalomanana

Head of Government
1998–2002   Tantely Andrianarivo

MADEIRA (ISLANDS) ≫ PORTUGAL

MALAWI

Local name Malawi (Malaêi)

Timezone GMT +2

Area 118 484 km²/47 747 sq mi

Population total (2002e) 10 520 000

Status Republic

Date of independence 1964

Capital Lilongwe

Languages English and Chichewa (official)

Ethnic groups Maravi (including Nyanja, Chewa, Tonga, Tumbuka) (60%), Lomwe (18%), Yao (13%), Ngoni (7%), also Asian and European minorities

Religions Protestant (55%), Roman Catholic (20%), Muslim (20%), traditional animist beliefs (3%)

Physical features Crossed N–S by the Great Rift Valley; contains Africa's third largest lake, L Malawi; main river, Shire; Shire highlands (S) rise to nearly 3000 m/ 10 000 ft at Mt Mulanje.

Climate Tropical climate in S; high year-round temperatures, 28–37°C; average annual temperatures 23°C (Jan), 16°C (Jul) in Lilongwe; average annual rainfall, 740 mm/30 in; more moderate temperatures in central areas.

Currency 1 Kwacha (MWK) = 100 tambala

Economy Based on agriculture (employs 90% of population); tobacco, sugar, tea, cotton, groundnuts, maize; textiles, matches, cigarettes, beer, spirits, shoes, cement.

GDP (2002e) $6.811 bn, per capita $600

HDI (2002) 0.400

History Visited by the Portuguese, 17th-c; European contact established by David Livingstone, 1859; Scottish church missions in the area; claimed as the British Protectorate of Nyasaland, 1891; British colony, 1907; in

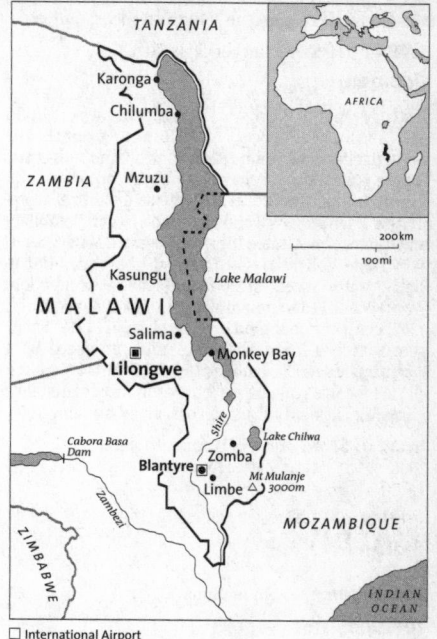

□ International Airport

the 1950s joined with N and S Rhodesia to form the Federation of Rhodesia and Nyasaland; independence, 1964; republic, 1966; governed by a President, Cabinet, and National Assembly.

Head of State/Government

1966–94	Hastings Kamuzu Banda
1994–2004	Bakili Muluzi
2004–	Bingu wa Mutharika

MALAYSIA

Local name Malaysia

Timezone GMT +8

Area 329 749 km²/127 283 sq mi

Population total (2002e) 24 437 000

Status Republic

Date of independence 1957

Capital Kuala Lumpur

Languages Bahasa Malaysia (Malay) (official), also Chinese, English, and Tamil widely spoken

Ethnic groups Malay (59%), Chinese (32%), Indian (9%)

Religions Muslim (53%), Buddhist (17%), Chinese folk-religionist (12%), Hindu (7%), Christian (6%)

Physical features Independent federation of states located in SE Asia, comprising 11 states and a federal territory in Peninsular Malaysia, and the E States of Sabah and Sarawak on the island of Borneo; mountain chain of granite and limestone running N–S, rising to Mt Tahan, 2189 m/7182 ft; peninsula length 700 km/435 mi, width up to 320 km/200 mi; mostly tropical rainforest and mangrove swamp; Mt Kinabalu on Sabah, Malaysia's highest peak, 4094 m/13 432 ft.

Climate Tropical climate strongly influenced by monsoon winds; high humidity; average annual rainfall in the peninsula, 260 mm/10 in (S), 800 mm/32 in (N); average daily temperatures, 21–32°C in coastal areas, 12–25°C in mountains.

Currency 1 Malaysian Dollar/Ringgit (MYR) = 100 cents

Economy Discovery of tin in the late 19th-c brought

Malaysia (continued)

European investment; rubber trees introduced from Brazil; minerals including iron ore, bauxite; oil, natural gas; electronic components, electrical goods; tourism.

GNP (2002e) $198.4 bn, per capita $8800

HDI (2002) 0.772

History Part of Srivijaya Empire, 9th–13th-c; Hindu and Muslim influences, 14th–15th-c; Portugal, the Netherlands, and Britain vied for control from 16th-c; Singapore, Malacca, and Penang formally incorporated into British Colony of the Straits Settlements, 1826; British protection extended over Perak, Selangor, Negeri Sembilan, and Pahang, constituted into the Federated Malay States, 1895; protection treaties with several other states (Unfederated Malay States), 1885–1930; Japanese occupation, World War 2; Federation of Malaya, 1948; independence, 1957; constitutional monarchy of Malaysia, 1963; Singapore withdrew from Federation, 1965; governed by a bicameral Federal Parliament; Head of State is a Monarch elected for five years by his fellow sultans; advised by a Prime Minister and a Cabinet; coast hit by tsunami, 2004.

Head of State (Yang di-Pertuan Agong)
2006–   Mizan Zainal Abidin

1. Langkawi
2. Pinang State
3. Cameron Highlands
4. Mt Tahan 2189m
5. Kuala Terengganu
6. Petaling Jaya
7. Melaka
8. Johor Baharu
9. Kuching
10. Bintulu
11. Labuan
12. Kota Kinabalu
13. Sandakan

☐ International Airport

Head of Government
2003–   Abdullah Ahmad Badawi

MALDIVES

Local name Dhivehi Jumhuriya

Timezone GMT +5

Area 300 km²/116 sq mi

Population total (2002e) 281 500

Status Independent republic within the Commonwealth

Date of independence 1968

Capital Malé

Languages Dhivehi (official), Arabic, Hindi, and English widely spoken

Ethnic groups Sinhalese (Dravidian extraction mainly), also Arab, Negrito, African influences

Religion Almost 100% Sunni Muslim

Physical features Island archipelago in the Indian Ocean; comprises c.1 190 islands (202 inhabited) in chain of 20 coral atolls; none of the islands rising above 1.8 m/5 ft; 10% of land arable, 3% forested.

Climate Generally warm and humid; wet season created by SW monsoons (Apr–Oct), dry season by NE monsoon (Dec–Mar); average annual rainfall, 2100 mm/83 in; average daily temperature 22°C.

Currency 1 Rufiyaa (MVR) = 100 laaris

Economy Agriculture; breadfruit, banana, mango, cassava, sweet potato, millet; fishing, shipping, tourism.

GDP (2002e) $1.25 bn, per capita $3900

HDI (2002) 0.743

History Former dependency of Ceylon (Sri Lanka); British protectorate, 1887–1965; became Republic within the Commonwealth, 1953; Sultan restored, 1954; inde-

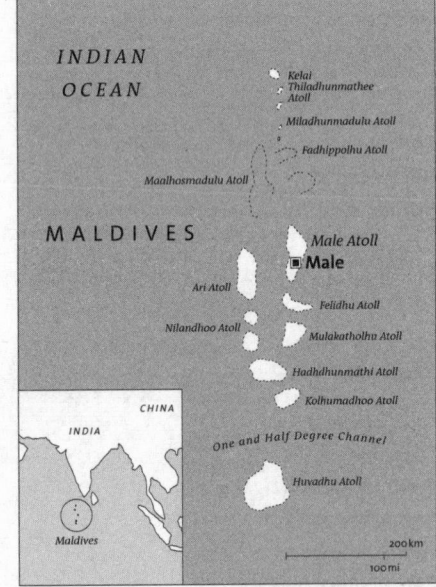

☐ International Airport

pendence, 1965; rejoined Commonwealth, 1982; state of emergency following pro-democracy protests, 2004; governed by a president, a ministers' *Majlis* (cabinet), and a citizens' *Majlis* of 48 members elected for five years; several areas destroyed by tsunami, 2004.

Head of State/Government
1978–   Maumoon Abdul Gayoom

MALI

Local name Mali

Timezone GMT

Area 1 240 192 km²/478 714 sq mi

Population total (2002e) 11 340 000

Status Republic

Date of independence 1960

Capital Bamako

Languages French (official), local languages (including Bambara) widely spoken

Ethnic groups Mande (Bambara, Malinke, Sarakole) (50%), Peul (Fulani nomads) (17%), Voltaic (including Senufo, Bura, Senouto, Minianka) (12%), Songhai (6%), Tuareg and Moor (5%)

Religions Muslim (90%), traditional animist beliefs (9%), Christian (1%) (Roman Catholic 0.5%, Protestant 0.5%)

Physical features Landlocked country on the fringe of the Sahara; lower part of the Hoggar massif (N); arid plains 300–500 m/1000–1600 ft; mainly savannah land in the S; main rivers, Niger, Bani Sénégal; featureless desert land (N).

Climate Subtropical in S and SW, with rainy season (Jun–Oct). Average rainfall c.1 000 mm/40 in; average annual temperatures 24°C (Jan), 27°C (Jul) in Bamako.

Currency 1 CFA Franc (XAF) = 100 centimes

Economy Mainly subsistence agriculture; crops severely affected by drought conditions; fishing, livestock, food processing, textiles, leather, cement; some tourism.

GDP (2002e) $9.775 bn, per capita $900

HDI (2002) 0.386

☐ International Airport

History Mediaeval state controlling the trade routes between savannah and Sahara, reaching its peak in the 14th-c; governed by France, 1881–95; territory of French Sudan (part of French West Africa) until 1959; partnership with Senegal as the Federation of Mali, 1959; separate independence, 1960; under 1979 constitution (suspended, 1991) governed by a President elected every six years, and a National Assembly.

Head of State

1992–2002	Alpha Oumar Konaré
2002–	Amadou Toumani Touré

Head of Government

2002–4	Mohammed Ag Amani
2004–	Ousmane Issoufi Maïga

MALTA

Local name Malta

Timezone GMT +1

Area 316 km²/122 sq mi

Population total (2002e) 386 000

Status Independent republic within the Commonwealth

Date of independence 1964

Capital Valletta

Languages English and Maltese (official)

Ethnic groups Maltese (mixed Arabic, Sicilian, Norman, Spanish, English, Italian racial origin) (95%), English (2%)

Religions Roman Catholic Apostolic (97%), Anglican Communion (2%)

Physical features Archipelago, comprising the islands of Malta (246 km²/95 sq mi), Gozo (67 km²/26 sq mi), and Comino (2.7 km²/1 sq mi), with the uninhabited islets of Cominotto, Filfla, and St Paul; highest point, 252

☐ International Airport

Malta (continued)

m/830 ft, on island of Malta; well-indented coastline with natural harbours, rocky coves; no rivers.

Climate Mediterranean, hot, dry summers, cool, rainy winters; rainy season (Oct–Mar); average annual rainfall 400 mm/16 in; average annual temperatures 13°C (Jan), 26°C (Jul) in Valletta.

Currency 1 Maltese Lira (MTL) = 100 cents

Economy Tourism; ship repair (naval dockyards now converted to commercial use); developing as a trans-shipment centre for the Mediterranean; tobacco, plastic and steel goods, paints, detergents; potatoes, tomatoes, oranges, grapes.

GDP (2002e) $6.818 bn, per capita $17 200

HDI (2002) 0.875

History Controlled at various times by Phoenicia, Greece, Carthage, and Rome; conquered by Arabs, 9th-c; given to the Knights Hospitallers, 1530; British Crown Colony, 1815; important strategic base in both World Wars; for its resistance to heavy air attacks, the island was awarded the George Cross, 1942; achieved independence, 1964; republic, 1974; British military base closed, 1979; governed by a President, Prime Minister, Cabinet and House of Representatives.

Head of State
2004–   Edward Fenech-Adami

Head of Government
2004–   Lawrence Gonzi

MARIANA ISLANDS, NORTHERN >> UNITED STATES OF AMERICA

MARSHALL ISLANDS

Timezone GMT +12

Area c.180 km²/70 sq mi

Population total (2002e) 56 600

Status Republic

Date of independence 1986

Capital Dalap-Uliga-Darrit (municipality on Majuro Atoll)

Languages Marshallese (Kajin-Majol) (official), English and Japanese also spoken

Ethnic group Micronesian (99%)

Religions Christian (Protestant 90%, Roman Catholic 8%)

Physical features Archipelago in C Pacific Ocean; comprising 34 islands, including Kwajalein and Jaluit, and 870 reefs; two parallel chains of coral atolls, Ratik (E) and Ralik (W), extending c.925 km/800 mi in length; volcanic islands, rise no more than a few metres above sea level.

Climate Hot and humid; wet season (May–Nov); typhoon season (Dec–Mar); average annual temperature 27°C.

Currency 1 US Dollar (USD) = 100 cents

Economy Farming; fishing; tropical agriculture; coconuts, tomatoes, melons, breadfruit.

GDP (2001e) $115 mn, per capita $1600

History Explored by the Spanish, 1529; part of UN Trust Territory of the Pacific, 1949–78, administered by the USA; US nuclear weapon tests held on Bikini and Eniwetak atolls, 1946–62; self-governing republic, 1979; compact of free association with the USA in 1986 with US recognizing independence; trusteeship ended, 1990; governed by a President elected by a Parliament.

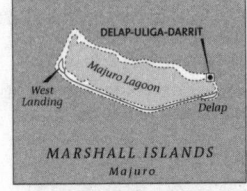
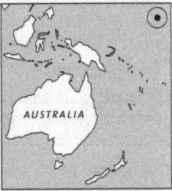
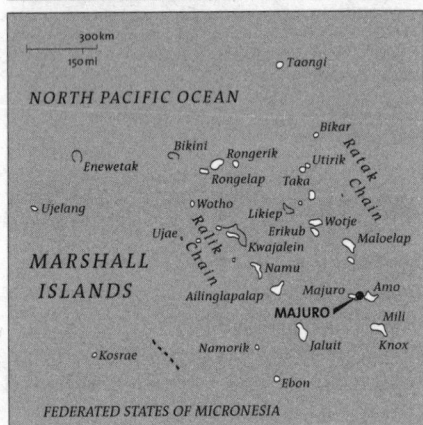

☐ International Airport

Head of State/Government
1996–7   Kunio Lemari *Acting*
1997–2000   Imata Kabua
2000–   Kessia Note

MARTINIQUE >> FRANCE

MAURITANIA

Local names Mūritāniyā (Arabic), Mauritanie (French)

Timezone GMT

Area 1 029 920 km²/397 549 sq mi

Population total (2002e) 2 656 000

Status Islamic republic

Date of independence 1960

Capital Nouakchott

Languages Arabic (official), French and local languages also spoken

Ethnic groups Moor (30%), black (30%), mixed (40%)

Religions Sunni Muslim (99%), Roman Catholic (1%)

Physical features Saharan zone in N comprises two-thirds of the country; coastal zone has minimal rainfall; Sahelian zone, with savannah grasslands; Sénégal R zone, the chief agricultural region; highest point, Kediet Ijill, 915 m/3002 ft in the NW.

Climate Dry, tropical climate, with sparse rainfall; average annual temperatures 22°C (Jan), 28°C (Jul) in Nouakchott; rainy season (May–Sep) in S, with occasional tornadoes; average annual rainfall 158 mm/6.2 in.

Currency 1 Ouguija (MRO) = 5 khoums

Economy Subsistence agriculture (employs 80% of population); crops under constant threat from drought; crops ravaged by locusts, 2004; livestock, cereals, vegetables, dates; mining of iron ore, copper, gypsum.

GDP (2002e) $4.891 bn, per capita $1700

HDI (2002) 0.438

History Visited by Portuguese, 15th-c. French protectorate within French West Africa, 1903; French colony, 1920; independence, 1960; military coup, 1979; new constitution, 1991; republic, 1992; bloodless military

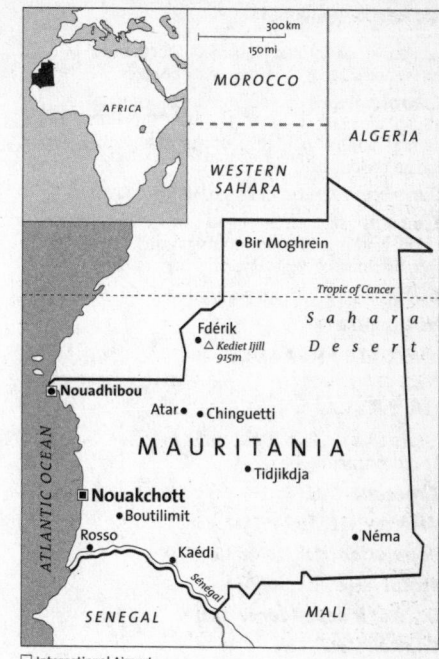

☐ International Airport

coup, Aug 2005; governed by executive President (6-year term), Prime Minister, National Assembly, and Senate.

Head of State

2005   Ely Ould Mohammed Vall *Military Council*

Head of Government

2005–   Sidy Mohamed Ould Boubacar *Military Council*

MAURITIUS

Local name Mauritius

Timeone GMT +4

Area 1865 km²/720 sq mi

Population total (2002e) 1 211 000

Status Republic within the Commonwealth

Date of independence 1968

Capital Port Louis

Languages English (creole-English) (official), French, Hindi, Urdu, Bojpoori, and Hakka also spoken

Ethnic groups Indo-Mauritian (68%), Creole (27%), Sino-Mauritian (3%), Franco-Mauritian (2%)

Religions Hindu (53%), Roman Catholic (26%), Muslim (13%), Protestant (4%)

Physical features Comprises the main island, 20 adjacent islets and the dependencies of Rodrigues I, Agalega I, and Cargados Carajos Is (St Brandon Is); volcanic main island; highest peak, 826 m/2710 ft, Piton de la Petite Rivière Noire; dry, lowland coast with wooded savannah,

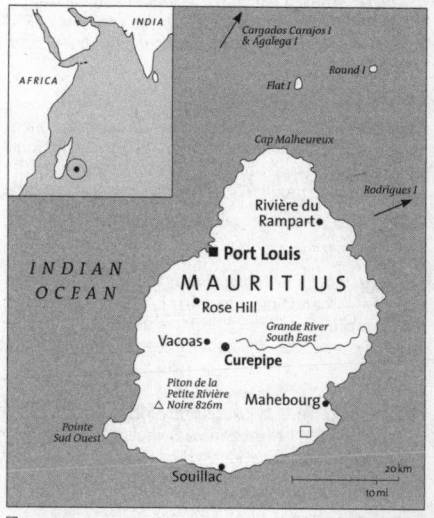

☐ International Airport

Mauritius (continued)

mangrove swamp, and (E) bamboo; surrounded by coral reefs enclosing lagoons and sandy beaches.

Climate Humid tropical-maritime climate; average annual temperatures 23°C (Jan), 27°C (Jul) in Port Louis; average annual rainfall 1000 mm/39 in; lies within Indian cyclone belt.

Currency 1 Mauritian Rupee (MUR) = 100 cents

Economy Sugar-cane (employs over 25% of the workforce); clothing; diamond-cutting, watches, rum, fertilizer; tea, tobacco, vegetables; fishing; tourism.

GDP (2002e) $12.15 bn, per capita $10 100

HDI (2002) 0.772

MAYOTTE >> FRANCE

MEXICO

Local name México

Timezone GMT −8 to −6

Area 1 978 800 km²/763 817 sq mi

Population total (2002e) 100 977 000

Status Republic

Date of independence 1821

Capital Mexico City

Languages Spanish (official), indigenous languages

Ethnic groups Indian-Spanish (mestizo) (60%), Amerindian (30%), white (9%)

Religions Roman Catholic (80%), Protestant (3%)

Physical features Narrow coastal plains; land rises steeply to C plateau, c.2400 m/7800 ft; volcanic peaks to S, notably Citlaltépetl, 5699 m/18 697 ft; limestone lowlands of the Yucatán peninsula stretch into the Gulf of Mexico (SE); region subject to earthquakes.

Climate Tropical climate in S; severe, arid conditions N and W; average annual temperatures 13°C (Jan), 16°C (Jul) in Mexico City; average annual rainfall 747 mm /29.4 in.

Currency 1 Mexican Peso (MXN) = 100 centavos

Economy Wide range of mineral exports; major discoveries of oil and natural gas in the 1970s (now world's fourth largest producer); fluorite and graphite (world's leading producer); large petrochemical industry.

GDP (2002e) $924.4 bn, per capita $8900

HDI (2002) 0.796

History Centre of Indian civilizations for over 2500 years; Gulf Coast Olmecs based at La Venta, Zapotecs at Monte Albán near Oaxaca, Mixtecs at Mitla, Toltecs at Tula, Maya in the Yucatán, Aztecs at Tenochtitlán;

History Visited by the Portuguese and Dutch, 16th-c; settled by the French, 1715; ceded to Britain, 1814; governed jointly with Seychelles as a single colony until 1903; independent sovereign state within the Commonwealth, 1968; links with British monarchy broken, 1992, became a republic, remaining within the Commonwealth; President (ceremonial post) is elected by the National Assembly; Prime Minister appoints the Council of Ministers; a unicameral National Assembly.

Head of State
2003–   Anerood Jugnauth

Head of Government
2005–   Navin Ramgoolam

☐ International Airport

Spanish arrival in 1516; Vice-royalty of New Spain established; struggle for independence from 1810; federal republic, 1824; lost territory to the USA, 1836, and after the Mexican War, 1846–8; civil war, 1858–61; occupation of Mexico City by French forces, 1863–7; revolution, 1910–17; major earthquake in Mexico City, 1985; revolt in S state of Chiapas by Zapatista National Liberation Army, 1994; negotiations over Indian rights in late 1990s, ongoing in 2002; major economic crises, 1994, followed by a package of loan guarantees from USA, 1995; governed by a President, Cabinet, and bicameral Congress with a Senate and a Chamber of Deputies.

Head of State/Government

2000–2006 Vincente Fox
2006–   Felipe Calderón

MICRONESIA, FEDERATED STATES OF

Timezone GMT +11

Area 700 km²/270 sq mi

Population total (2002e) 109 000

Status Republic

Date of independence 1991

Capital Palikir (on Pohnpei Island)

Languages English (official), with several indigenous languages also spoken

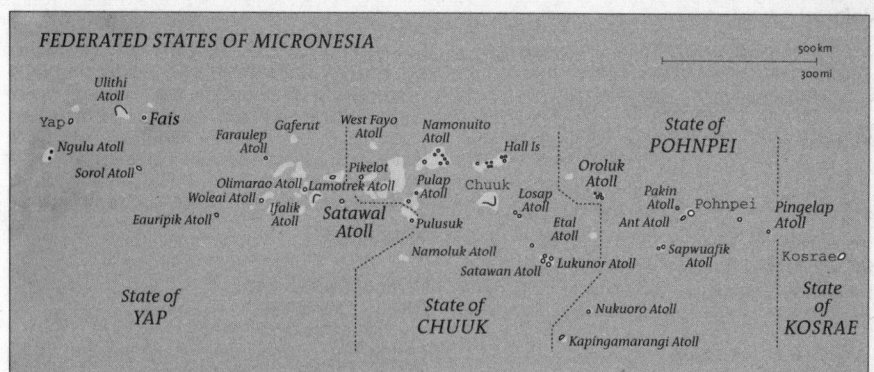

FEDERATED STATES OF MICRONESIA

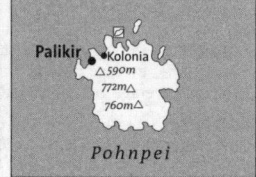

Pohnpei

Ethnic groups Trukese (41%), Pohnpeian (26%)

Religions Roman Catholic, Protestant

Physical features Group of four states in the W Pacific Ocean (Yap, Truk, Pohnpei, Kosrae); comprises all the Caroline I except Belau; islands vary from high mountainous terrain to low coral atolls.

Climate Tropical climate, with occasional typhoons; heavy rainfall all year.

Currency 1 US Dollar (USD) = 100 cents

Economy Agriculture; farming and fishing; tropical fruits, coconuts, vegetables; few mineral resources.

GDP (2002e) $277 mn, per capita $2000

History Settled by Spanish seafarers, 1565; formally annexed by Spain, 1874; sold to Germany, 1899; control mandated to Japan by League of Nations, 1920; American Navy took control following Japan's defeat in World War 2, 1945; part of UN Trust Territory of the Pacific, 1947; compact of free association with the US, 1982; trusteeship ended, 1990; independent state, 1991; under Compact of Free Association, the US continues to control its defence and foreign relations; governed by a President and a National Congress.

Head of State/Government
2003–   Joseph Urusemal

MOLDOVA

Local name Moldova

Timezone GMT +2

Area 33 700 km²/13 008 sq mi

Population total (2002e) 4 231 000

Status Republic

Date of independence 1991

Capital Chisinau (formerly Kishinev)

Languages Moldovan (official), Ukrainian also spoken

Ethnic groups Moldovan (64%), Ukrainian (14%), Russian (13%), Gagauzi (4%), Jewish (2%)

Religions Christian (mainly Russian Orthodox, also Baptist and Roman Catholic)

Physical features Landlocked area consisting of hilly plains, average elevation of 147 m/482 ft, cut by river valleys, ravines, and gullies; uplands in C, Kodry Hills, reach highest point, Mt Balaneshty, 429 m/1409 ft; chief rivers, the Dnestr and Prut; level plain of Bel'tsy Steppe and uplands (N); eroded Medobory-Toltry limestone ridges border R Prut (N).

Climate Warm, moderately continental; long dry periods in S; average annual temperatures –5°C (N), –3°C

☐ International Airport

HUMAN GEOGRAPHY

Moldova (continued)

(S) (Jan), 20°C (N), 23°C (S) (Jul); average annual rainfall 450–550 mm/18–22 in.

Currency 1 Moldovan Leu (MDL) = 100 bani

Economy Main exports include wine, tobacco, food-canning, machinery, electrical engineering, knitwear, textiles, fruit.

GDP (2002e) $11.51 bn, per capita $2600

HDI (2002) 0.701

History Formerly part of Romania (the region known as Bessarabia); W part remained in Romania, Bessarabia in E became the Moldavian Soviet Socialist Republic in 1940; occupied by Romania, who allied with Germany in World War 2; recaptured by USSR, 1944; Moldavian language granted official status, 1989, leading to tension between ethnic Russians and Moldovans; declaration of independence, 1991, joined Commonwealth of Independent States; tension due to separatist pressure from Gagauz and Dnestr Russian minorities, 1990–1; new constitution, 1994; governed by a President, Prime Minister and Supreme Soviet.

Head of State
2001–   Vladimir Voronin

Head of Government
2001–   Vasile Tarlev

MONACO

Local name Monaco

Timezone GMT +1

Area 1.95 km²/0.75 sq mi

Population total (2002e) 32 000

Status Principality

Capital Monaco

Languages French (official), English, Italian, and Monegasque also spoken

Ethnic groups French (58%), Italian (16%), Monegasque (16%)

Religion Roman Catholic (95%)

Physical features Located on Mediterranean Riviera, close to Italian frontier with France; surrounded landward by the French department of Alpes-Maritimes; steep and rugged landscape; area available for commercial development has been extended by land reclaimed from sea.

Climate Mediterranean; warm, dry summers, mild, wet winters; average annual temperatures 10°C (Jan), 23°C (Jul); average annual rainfall 758 mm/30 in.

Currency 1 Euro (EUR) = 100 cents (before February 2002, 1 French Franc (FRF) = 100 centimes)

Economy Tourism; chemicals, printing, textiles, plastics.

GDP (1999e) $870 mn, per capita $27 000

History Under protection of France since 17th-c, except period under Sardinia, 1815–61; 1911 constitution ended power of Prince as absolute ruler; constitution of 1911 suspended, 1959; new constitution adopted, 1962; governed by Prince as Head of State, a Minister of State, heading a Council of Government, and a National Council.

Head of State (Prince)
1949–2005 Rainier III
2005–   Albert II

Head of Government (Minister of State)
2000–   Patrick Leclerq

MAP >> FRANCE

MONGOLIA

Local name Mongol Ard Uls

Timezone GMT +7 (W), +8 (C), +9 (E)

Area 1 566 500 km²/604 800 sq mi

Population total (2002e) 2 457 000

Status State

Date of independence 1911

Capital Ulaanbaatar

Languages Khalka (official), Russian and Chinese spoken by respective minorities

Ethnic groups Mongol (Khalka, Dorbed, Buryat, Dariganga) (90%), Kazakh (4%), Russian (2%), other (4%)

Religions Formerly Tibetan Buddhist (now only a single monastery remains in Ulaanbaatar); unreliable data on current situation as a result of religious suppression in 20th-c.

□ International Airport

Physical features Landlocked mountainous country; highest point, Tavan-Bogdo-Uli, 4373 m/14 347 ft; high ground mainly in W, with mountains lying NW–SE to form Mongolian Altai chain; lower SE area runs into the Gobi Desert; lowland plains; mainly arid grasslands.

Climate Extreme continental climate, with hard and long-lasting frosts in winter; arid desert conditions prevail in the S; average annual temperatures –26°C (Jan), 16°C (Jul); average annual rainfall 208 mm/18.2 in.

Currency 1 Tugrik (MNT) = 100 möngö

Economy Traditionally a pastoral nomadic economy; series of 5-year plans aiming for an agricultural-industrial economy; 70% of agricultural production derived from cattle raising; foodstuffs, animal products; coal, gold, uranium, lead.

GDP (2002e) $5.06 bn, per capita $1900

HDI (2002) 0.655

History Originally the homeland of nomadic tribes, which united under Genghis Khan in the 13th-c to become part of the great Mongol Empire; assimilated into China, and divided into Inner and Outer Mongolia. Outer Mongolia declared itself an independent monarchy, 1911; changed name to Mongolian People's Republic, 1924, not recognized by China until 1946; governed by a Great People's Khural (parliament), a Council of Ministers, and a Presidium; chairman of Presidium is Head of State; changed name to State of Mongolia, 1992, and new constitution established.

Head of State

2005– Nambaryn Enkhbayar

Head of Government

2004–6 Tsakhiagiin Elbegdorj
2006– Miyeegombo Enkhbold

MONTENEGRO

Local name Crna Gora

Timezone GMT +1

Area 13 812 km²/5333 sq mi

Population total (2004e) 631 000

Status Republic

Capital Podgorica (administrative), Cetinje (state)

Languages Serbian (official), Albanian

Ethnic groups Montenegrin (43%), Serbian (32%), Bosniak (8%), Albanian (5%), other (12%)

Religions Orthodox Christian, Muslim, Roman Catholic

Physical features Highly indented coastline with narrow coastal plain, high limestone mountains and plateaus; highest peak Mt Durmitor 2522 m/8274 ft; Lake Skadar 391 km²/151 sq mi; Durmitor National Park, Tara River Gorge, and old city of Kotor are world heritage sites.

Climate Mediterranean climate on coast, winter snow in mountains; average temperatures 5°C (Jan), 25°C (Jul)

Currency 1 Euro (EUR) = 100 cents

Economy Aluminium, bauxite, coal, sea salt, hydroelectricity, steel-making, engineering, wood-processing, textiles, chemicals, leather, household appliances, construction and forestry machinery; grain, tobacco, potatoes, citrus fruits, olives, grapes; tourism.

GDP (2002e) $23·15 bn, per capita $2200 (former Serbia and Montenegro)

History Use of name Montenegro began in 15th-c when the Crnojevic dynasty began to rule the Serbian principality of Zeta; maintained independence from the Ottoman Empire; theocratic state ruled by a series of bishop princes, 16th-c–19th-c; transformed into a secular principality, 1852; independent monarchy until 1918;

☐ International Airport

became constituent republic of Yugoslavia, 1946; federated with Serbia as the Federal Republic of Yugoslavia, 1992; confrontation with Croatia over disputed border areas and status of Serbian minority led to civil war, 1991 (for history of civil war >> Serbia); focus of NATO airstrikes, along with Serbia, in Kosovo crisis, 1999; Union of Serbia and Montenegro, 2003; referendum voted for independence from Serbia, 2006.

Head of State

2006– Filip Vujanovic

Head of Government

2006– Zeljko Sturanovic

MOROCCO

Local name al-Magrib

Timezone GMT

Area 409 200 km²/157 951 sq mi

Population total (2002e) 29 632 000

Status Kingdom

Date of independence 1956

Capital Rabat

Languages Arabic (official), Berber, Spanish, and French also widely spoken

Ethnic groups Arab-Berber (99%), non-Moroccan (0.7%), Jewish (0.2%)

Religions Sunni Muslim (98%), Christian (1%), Jewish (0.2%)

Physical features Dominated by a series of mountain ranges, rising in the Atlas Mts (S) to 4165 m/13 664 ft at Jebel Toubkal; broad coastal plain; main rivers, Drâ'ar (S and SW) and Moulouya (N) draining into the Mediterranean.

Climate Mediterranean climate on N coast; semi-arid in S; Sahara virtually rainless; average annual temperatures 13°C (Jan), 22°C (Jul) in Rabat; average annual rainfall 564 mm/22.2 in.

Currency 1 Moroccan Dirham (MAD) = 100 Moroccan francs

Economy Agriculture (employs over 50% of population); largest known reserves of phosphate in world; fishing, textiles, cement, soap, tobacco, chemicals, paper, timber products; tourism centred on the four imperial cities and the warm Atlantic resorts.

GDP (2002e) $121.8 bn, per capita $3900

HDI (2002) 0.602

History N coast occupied by Phoenicians, Carthaginians, and Romans since 12th-c BC; invasion by Arabs in 7th-c AD; conflicting French and Spanish interest in the region in 19th-c; Treaty of Fez in 1912, established Spanish Morocco (capital, Tétouan) and French Morocco (capital, Rabat); Tangier became an international zone,

□ International Airport

1923–56; protectorates gained independence, 1956; became Kingdom of Morocco, 1957; Spanish withdrew from former Spanish Sahara (Western Sahara), 1975; Morocco laid claim to this area using the 'Green March' as a gesture of peaceful occupation; Mauritania withdrew from southern third of territory in 1979, leaving Morocco fighting with the Polisario for the whole of Western Sahara; ceasefire agreement signed, 1990; a 'constitutional' monarchy, but the King presides over his appointed Cabinet, which is led by a Prime Minister; a unicameral Chamber of Representatives. >> WESTERN SAHARA

Head of State (Monarch)
1999– Mohammed VI

Head of Government
2002– Driss Jettou

MOZAMBIQUE

Local name Moçambique

Timezone GMT +2

Area 799 380 km²/308 641 sq mi

Population total (2002e) 18 083 000

Status Republic

Date of independence 1975

Capital Maputo

Languages Portuguese (official), Swahili and Bantu dialects widely spoken

Ethnic groups Makua/Lomwe (52%), Thonga (24%), Malawi (12%), Shona (6%), Yao (3%)

Religions Local animist beliefs (60%), Christian (majority Roman Catholic) (30%), Muslim (10%)

Physical features Located in SE Africa; main rivers, the Zambezi and Limpopo, provide irrigation and hydroelectricity; savannah plateau inland, mean elevation 800–1000 m/2700–4000 ft; highest peak, Mt Binga, 2436 m/7992 ft. S of Zambezi is low-lying coast with sandy beaches and mangroves; low hills of volcanic origin inland, Zimbabwe plateau further N.

Climate Tropical with high humidity; rainy season (Dec–Mar); drought conditions in S; average annual temperatures 26°C (Jan), 18°C (Jul) in Maputo; average annual rainfall 560 mm/30 in; major flood disaster in S, Feb 2000.

Currency 1 Metical (MZM) = 100 centavos

Economy Badly affected by drought (1981–4), internal strife, and lack of foreign exchange; agriculture (employs 85% of population); cashew nuts, tea, cotton, sugar cane, copra, sisal, groundnuts, fruit, rice, cereals, tobacco; forestry; livestock; reserves of gemstones and minerals.

GDP (2002e) $19.52 bn, per capita $1100

HDI (2002) 0.322

History Originally inhabited by Bantu peoples from the N, 1st–4th-c AD; coast settled by Arab traders; visited by Portuguese explorers by late 15th-c; part of Portuguese Africa since 1751; Mozambique Portuguese East Africa in late 19th-c; overseas province of Portugal, 1951; independence movement, 1962, the Frente de Libertação de Moçambique (FRELIMO), with armed resistance to colonial rule; independence as the People's Republic of Mozambique, 1975; continuing civil war, with first peace talks in 1990; socialist one-party state, 1975–90; new constitution and change of name to Republic of Mozambique, 1990; peace accord signed between Chissanó (President of Mozambique) and Dhlakama (leader of the Renamo-Mozambique National Resistance), 1992; President (term of 5 years) rules with an Assembly of the Republic; new constitution adopted (Nov 2004).

Head of State
2005–   Armando Emilio Guebuza

Head of Government
2004   Luisa Diogo

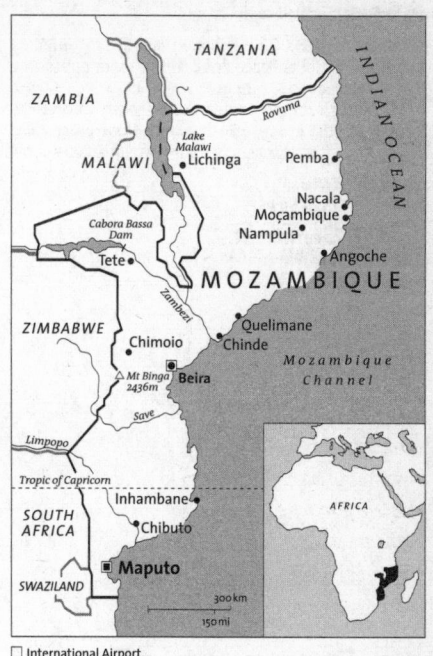

☐ International Airport

MYANMAR (BURMA)

Local name Pyidaungsu Myanma Naingngandaw

Timezone GMT +6.5

Area 678 576 km²/261 930 sq mi

Population total (2002e) 42 238 000

Status Union

Date of independence 1948

Capital Pyinmana (from 2005, formerly Yangon (Rangoon)

Languages Burmese (official), also tribal languages spoken

Ethnic groups Burman (Tibeto-Chinese) (72%), Shan (9%), Karen (7%), Chinese (3%), Indian (2%)

Religions Theravada Buddhist (85%), animist, Muslim, Hindu, Christian minorities (15%)

Physical features Bordered in the N, E, and W by mountains rising (N) to Hkakabo Razi, 5881 m/19 294 ft; located on Chinese frontier, forming part of Kumon Range; Chin Hills (W) descend into upland forests of the Arakan-Yoma range (S); principal rivers, Ayeyarwady (Irrawaddy), Thanlwin (Salween), and Sittang.

Climate Tropical monsoon climate; equatorial on coast; humid temperate in extreme N; SW monsoon season (Jun–Sep); cool, dry season (Nov–Apr); hot, dry season (May–Sep); average annual temperatures 23°C (Jan), 27°C (Jul) in Yangon; average annual rainfall 2616 mm/103 in.

Currency 1 Kyat (MMK) = 100 pyas

Economy Largely agriculture; rice, pulses, sugar cane; forestry (hardwoods); textiles, pharmaceuticals, petroleum refining, and mining of minerals.

GDP (2002e) $73.69 bn, per capita $1700

HDI (2002) 0.552

History First unified 11th-c by King Anawrahta; invasion by Kubla Khan, 1287; second dynasty under King Tabinshweti, 1486, but internal disunity and wars with Siam from 16th-c; new dynasty under King Alaungpaya, 1752; annexed to British India after Anglo-Burmese wars (1824–86); separated from India, 1937; occupied by Japanese in World War 2; independence as Union of Burma under Prime Minister U Nu, 1948; military coup under U Ne Win, 1962; single-party socialist republic, 1974; army coup in 1988, State Law and Order Restoration Council formed, headed by a Chairman; name changed to Union

Myanmar (continued)

of Myanmar in 1989 and renamed capital Yangon; Aung San Sun Kyi (Nobel Peace Prize, 1991), main opposition leader, placed under house arrest 1989–95, 2000–2, 2003–; constitutional conference ongoing since 1992; rebel separatist groups causing unrest but peace talks held Jan 2004; coast severely hit by tsunami, 2004.

Head of State
1992–   Than Shwe

Head of Government
2004–   Soe Win

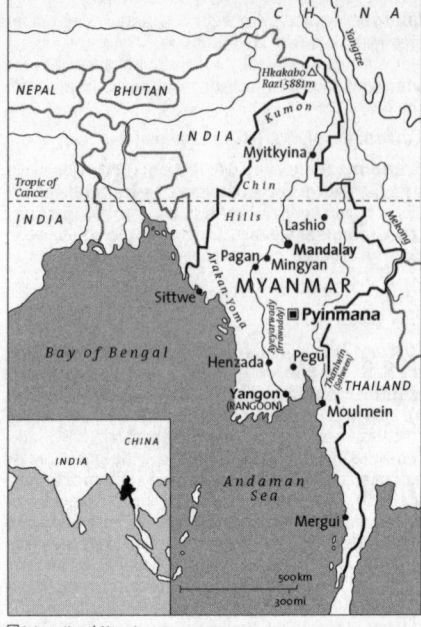

☐ International Airport

NAMIBIA

Local name Namibia

Timezone GMT +2

Area 824 292 km²/318 261 sq mi

Population total (2002e) 1 837 000

Status Republic

Date of independence 1990

Capital Windhoek

Languages English (official), Afrikaans, German, local languages

Ethnic groups African (chiefly Ovambo) (85%), white (7%), mixed (8%)

Religions Christian (Lutheran, Roman Catholic, Dutch Reformed, and Anglican) (90%), traditional animist beliefs (10%)

Physical features Located in SW Africa; Namib Desert runs parallel along the Atlantic Ocean coast; inland plateau, mean elevation 1500 m/5000 ft; highest point, Brandberg, 2606 m/8550 ft; Kalahari Desert to the E and S; Orange R forms S frontier with South Africa.

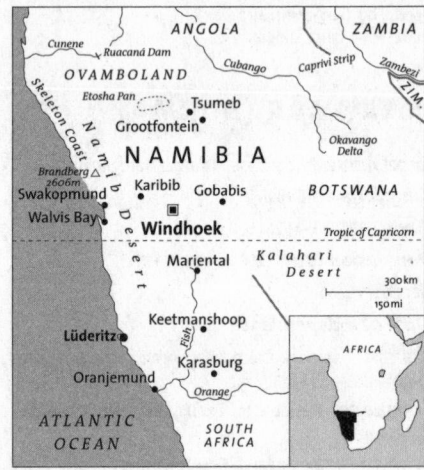

☐ International Airport

Climate Arid, continental tropical climate; average maximum daily temperature, 20–30°C; 49°C (Nov–Apr) in coastal desert (Namib); average annual rainfall 360 mm/14 in at Windhoek.

Currency 1 Namibian Dollar (NAD); 1 South African Rand (ZAR) = 100 cents

Economy Agriculture (employs c.60% of population); indigenous subsistence farming in N; major world producer of diamonds and uranium; fishing; brewing; textiles; plastics.

GDP (2002e) $13.15 bn, per capita $6900

HDI (2002) 0.610

History Visited by British and Dutch from late 18th-c; German protectorate, 1884; mandated to South Africa by League of Nations, 1920; UN assumed direct responsibility, 1966, changing name to Namibia, 1968, and recognizing Southwest Africa People's Organization (SWAPO), 1973; area administered by South Africa as Southwest Africa; SWAPO guerrilla activities, 1966; bases established in S Angola, involving Cuban troops in 1970s; interim administration installed by South Africa, 1985; full independence, 1990; governed by a President, Prime Minister and Cabinet, and an elected National Assembly.

Head of State
2004–   Hifikepunye Pohamba

Head of Government
2005–   Nahas Angula

NAURU

Local name Naeoro (Nauruan)

Timezone GMT +12

Area 21.3 km²/8.2 sq mi

Population total (2002e) 12 300

Status Republic

Date of independence 1968

Capital Yaren District (No official capital)

Languages Nauruan (official), English

Ethnic groups Nauruans (62%), Pacific islanders (26%), Asian (9%), Caucasian (3%)

Religions Christian (Nauruan Protestant, Roman Catholic)

Physical features Small isolated island in WC Pacific Ocean, 4000 km/2 500 mi NE of Sydney, Australia; ground rises from sandy beaches to give fertile coastal belt, c.100–300 m/300–1000 ft wide, the only cultivable soil; central plateau inland, highest point 65 m/213 ft; mainly phosphate-bearing rocks.

Climate Tropical, hot, and humid; average annual temperatures 27°C (Jan), 28°C (Jul); average annual rainfall 1520 mm/60 in; monsoon season (Nov–Feb).

Currency 1 Australian Dollar (AUD) = 100 cents

Economy Based on phosphate mining, now limited reserves; coconuts, some vegetables; tourism; tax haven.

GDP (2001e) $60 mn, per capita $5000

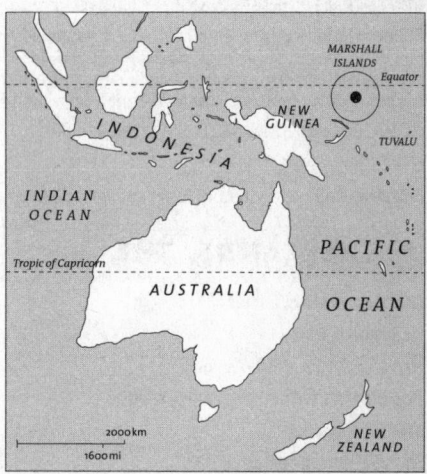

History Under German administration 1880s to 1914; after 1919, League of Nations mandate, administered by Australia; occupied by Japan, 1942–5; independence movement, 1960s; self-government, 1966; full independence, 1968; unicameral Parliament elects a President, who appoints a Cabinet.

Head of State/Government
2001–4   René Harris
2004–   Ludwig Scotty

NEPAL

Local name Nepāl

Timezone GMT +5³/₄

Area 145 391 km²/56 121 sq mi

Population total (2002e) 23 692 000

Status Kingdom

Capital Kathmandu

Languages Nepali (official), Maithir, Bhojpuri

Ethnic groups Nepalese (58%), Bihari (19%), Tamang (4%), Tharu (3%), Newar (3%)

Religions Only official Hindu state in the world: Hindu (90%), Buddhist (5%), Muslim (3%), Christian (0.2%)

Physical features Landlocked, rises steeply from the Ganges basin in India; high fertile valleys in the 'hill country' at 1300 m/4300 ft, notably the Vale of Kathmandu (a world heritage site); dominated by the

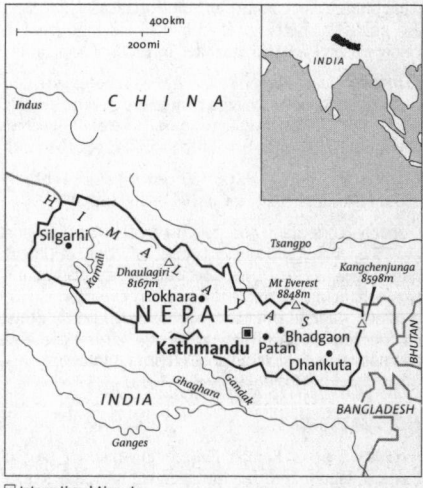

□ International Airport

Nepal (continued)

Himalayas (glaciated), highest peak, Mt Everest, 8848 m/29 028 ft.

Climate Varies from subtropical lowland with hot, humid summers and mild winters, to an alpine climate over 3300 m/10 800 ft, with permanently snow-covered peaks; average annual temperatures 0°C (Jan), 24°C (Jul) in Kathmandu; monsoon season (Jun–Sep); average annual rainfall 1428 mm/56 in.

Currency 1 Nepalese Rupee (NPR) = 100 paise/pice

Economy Agriculture (employs 90% of population); rice, jute, cereals, sugar cane; agricultural and forest-based goods; carpets; garments, handicrafts; hydroelectric power developing; tourism increasingly important.

GDP (2002e) $37.32 bn, per capita $1400

HDI (2002) 0.490

History Originally group of independent hill states, united in 18th-c; parliamentary system introduced, 1959; replaced by village councils (*panchayats*), 1960; a constitutional monarchy ruled by hereditary king; unrest, 1990, followed by reduction of king's powers, new constitution and elections, 1991; king ruled with Council of Ministers, bicameral Parliament consisting of elected House of Representatives and National Council; Crown Prince Dipendra allegedly murdered 10 of his family, including his parents, before killing himself, 2001; state of emergency after new conflict with Maoist rebels, king sacked cabinet and assumed direct power, 2005; parliament reinstated after period of unrest, curtailing king's powers, 2006; peace agreement with rebels, 2006.

Head of State (Monarch)
2001– Gyanendra Bir Bikram Shah

Head of Government
2006– Girija Prasad Koirala

NETHERLANDS, THE

Local name Nederland

Timezone GMT +1

Area 33 929 km²/13 097 sq mi

Population total (2002e) 16 142 000

Status Kingdom

Date of independence 1830

Capital Amsterdam

Language Dutch (official)

Ethnic groups Dutch (Germanic/Gallo-Celtic descent) (99%), Indonesian/Surinamese (1%)

Religions Roman Catholic (38%), Protestant (Dutch Reformed Church and other Protestant churches) (30%)

Physical features Generally low and flat, except SE where hills rise to 321 m/1053 ft. Much of coastal area below sea-level, reaching lowest point –6.7 m/–19.7 ft N of Rotterdam; protected by coastal dunes and artificial dykes; highest point, Vaalserberg, in SE; 27% of land area is below sea level, an area inhabited by c.60% of population.

Climate Cool, temperate maritime climate, with continental influences. Average annual temperatures 1.7°C (Jan), 17°C (Jul); average annual rainfall exceeds 700 mm/27 in, evenly distributed throughout the year.

Currency 1 Euro (EUR) = 100 cents (before February 2002, 1 Guilder (NLG)/ Florin (DFL) = 100 cents)

Economy Rotterdam and newly-constructed Europort are the major European ports of transshipment, handling goods for EC member countries; Amsterdam a world diamond centre; world's largest exporter of dairy produce; highly intensive agriculture; horticulture; engineering, chemicals, oil products, natural gas, high technology and electrical goods; fishing; tourism.

GDP (2002e) $437.8 bn, per capita $27 200

HDI (2002) 0.935

History Part of Roman Empire to 4th-c AD; part of Frankish Empire by 8th-c; incorporated into Holy Roman Empire; lands passed to Philip II, who succeeded to Spain

□ International Airport

and the Netherlands, 1555; attempts to stamp out Protestantism led to rebellion, 1572; seven N provinces united against Spain, 1579; United Provinces independence, 1581; overrun by French, 1795–1813, who established Batavian Republic; united with Belgium as Kingdom of the United Netherlands until Belgian withdrawal, 1830; neutral in World War 1; occupied by Germany, World War 2, with strong Dutch resistance; joined Belgium and Luxembourg to form Benelux economic union, 1948; conflict over independence of Dutch colonies in SE Asia, late 1940s; joined NATO, 1949; independence granted to former colonies,

Indonesia, 1949, with addition of W New Guinea, 1963, and Suriname, 1975; parliamentary democracy under constitutional monarchy; government led by Prime Minister; States General (*Staten-Generaal*) consists of 75-member First Chamber, and 150-member Second Chamber; resignation of entire cabinet, 2002, following critical report on Dutch peace-keeping role in Bosnia in 1995; referendum on proposed EU constitution rejected (Jun 2005).

Head of State (Monarch)
1980–   Beatrix

Head of Government
1994–2002 Wim Kok
2002–   Jan-Peter Balkenende

Aruba

Timezone GMT

Area 193 km²/74.5 sq mi

Population total (2002e) 100 000

Status Self-governing region of The Netherlands

Date of independence 1996

Capital Oranjestad

Languages Dutch (official) with Papiamento, English, and Spanish widely spoken

Ethnic groups Large majority of mixed European/ Caribbean Indian descent

Religions Christian (Roman Catholic and Protestant), small Hindu, Muslim, Confucian, and Jewish minorities

Physical features Island in the Caribbean, the westernmost of the Lesser Antilles, N of Venezuela; flat, rocky terrain, dry, with little vegetation.

Climate Dry, tropical, with little seasonal temperature variation; average annual temperature 27°C; annual rainfall often falls to below 488 mm/19 in; lies just outside the Caribbean hurricane belt.

Currency 1 Aruban Guilder/Florin (AWG) = 100 cents

Economy Lack of natural resources limits agriculture and manufacturing; depends heavily on thriving tourist industry.

GDP (2002e) $1.94 bn, per capita $28 000

History Claimed by Dutch in 1634, but remained undeveloped; construction of an oil refinery brought employment and prosperity, 1929; acquired full internal self-government within kingdom of the Netherlands, 1954, as part of the Netherlands Antilles; growing resentment led to a campaign for Aruba's independence; closure of oil refinery, 1985; obtained separate status from the Netherlands Antilles with full internal autonomy in 1986; full independence in 1996; Sovereign of the Netherlands is Head of State, represented by a

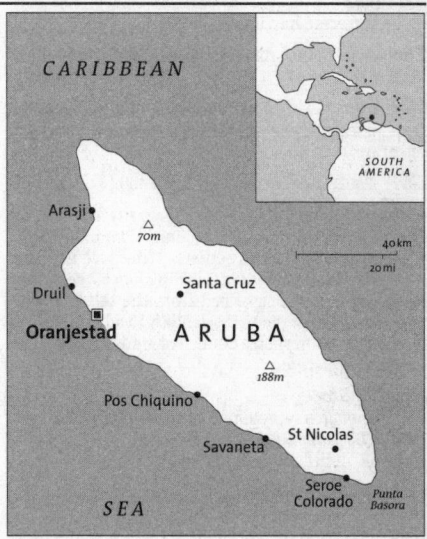

□ International Airport

Governor-General, a prime minister, Council of Ministers and a unicameral legislature.

Head of State
(Dutch monarch represented by Governor-General)
1992–2004 Olindo Koolman
2004–   Fredis Refunjol

Head of Government
1994–2001 Henry Eman
2001–   Nelson Oduber

Netherlands Antilles

Local name Nederlandse Antillen

Timezone GMT –4

Area 993 km²/383 sq mi

Population total (2002e) 221 000

Status Self-governing region of the Netherlands

Capital Willemstad (on Curaçao Island)

Languages Dutch (official), Papiamento, English, and Spanish widely spoken

Ethnic groups Large majority of mixed European/ Caribbean Indian descent

Netherlands Antilles (continued)

Religions Christian (mainly Roman Catholic)

Physical features Islands in the Caribbean Sea, comprising the Southern group (Leeward Is) of Curaçao and Bonaire, 60–110 km/37–68 mi N of the Venezuelan coast, and the Northern group (Windward Is) of St Maarten, St Eustatius, and Saba; terrain generally hilly, with volcanic interiors.

Climate Tropical maritime climate; average annual temperature 27.5°C. Average annual rainfall varies from 500 mm/20 in (S) to 1000 mm/40 in (N); Northern group subject to hurricanes (Jul–Oct).

Currency 1 Netherland Antilles Guilder/Florin (ANG) = 100 cents

Economy Based on refining of crude oil imported from Venezuela; aim of industrial diversification; ship repairing; tourism.

GDP (2002e) $2.4 bn, per capita $11 400

History Visited by Columbus, initially claimed for Spain; small-scale Spanish colonization in Curaçao, 1511; occupied by Dutch settlers, 17th-c; acquired full internal self-government within Kingdom of the Netherlands, 1954; Aruba separated from the other islands, 1986; Sovereign of the Netherlands is Head of State, represented by a Governor, a Council of Ministers and a unicameral legislature.

Head of State
(Dutch monarch represented by Governor-General)
1990–2002   Jaime Saleh
2002–   Fritz Goedgedrag

Head of Government
2004–6   Etienne Ys
2006–   Emily de Jongh-Elhage

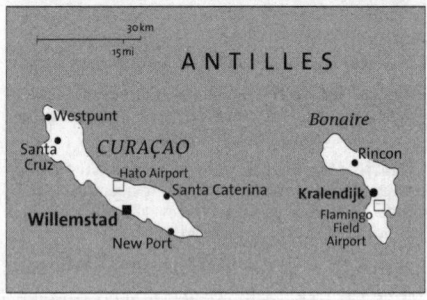

NEW CALEDONIA >> FRANCE

NEW ZEALAND

Local name Aotearoa (Maori)

Timezone GMT +12

Area 268 812 km²/103 761 sq mi

Population total (2002e) 3 893 000

Status Independent member of the Commonwealth

Date of independence 1947

Capital Wellington

Languages English and Maori (official)

Ethnic groups European (mainly British, Australian and Dutch) (87%), Maori (9%)

Religions Christian (59%) (Anglican 25%, Presbyterian 18%, Roman Catholic 16%)

Physical features Consists of two principal islands (North and South) separated by the Cook Strait, and several minor islands; North Island mountainous in the centre with many hot springs; peaks rise to 2797 m/ 9176 ft at Mt Ruapehu; South Island mountainous for its whole length, rising in the Southern Alps to 3753 m/ 12 313 ft at Mt Cook, New Zealand's highest point; many glaciers and mountain lakes; largest area of level lowland is the Canterbury Plain, E side of South Island; L Taupo, largest natural lake, occupies an ancient volcanic crater; major lakes include Te Anau and Wakatipu.

Climate Cool, temperate climate, almost subtropical in extreme N; mean temperature range, 18°C in N, 9°C in S; lower temperatures in South Island; highly changeable weather, all months moderately wet; average daily temperature 16–23°C (Jan), 8–13°C (Jul) in Auckland; average annual rainfall 1053 mm/41 in; subject to periodic subtropical cyclones.

Currency 1 New Zealand Dollar (NZD) = 100 cents

Economy Farming, especially sheep and cattle; one of the world's major exporters of dairy produce; third largest exporter of wool; Kiwi fruit, venison; textiles; timber, food processing; substantial coal and natural gas reserves; hydroelectric power; tourism.

GDP (2002e) $78.4 bn, per capita $20 100

HDI (2002) 0.917

History Settled by Maoris from E Polynesia by c.1000 AD; first European sighting by Abel Tasman in 1642, named Staten Landt; later known as Nieuw Zeeland, after the Dutch Province; visited by Captain Cook, 1769; first European settlement, 1792; dependency of New South Wales until 1840; outbreaks of war between immigrants and Maoris, 1860–70; Dominion of New Zealand, 1907; independent within the Commonwealth, 1947; governed by a Prime Minister, a Cabinet and a unicameral, 97-member House of Representatives; elections every 3 years.

Head of State
(British monarch represented by Governor-General)
2006–   Anand Satyanand

Head of Government
1990–7   James Brendan Bolger
1997–9   Jenny Shipley
1999–   Helen Clark

Overseas territories

Name	Area		Capital	Population total
	km²	sq mi		
Cook Islands	238	92	Avarua	(2002e) 18 000
Niue	263	101	Alofi	(2002e) 2000
Ross Dependency	413 550	159 600	–	uninhabited
Tokelau	10	4	Nukunonu	(2002e) 2000

☐ International Airport

☐ International Airport

NICARAGUA

Local name Nicaragua

Timezone GMT –6

Area 148 000 km²/57 128 sq mi

Population total (2002e) 5 024 000

Status Republic

Date of independence 1821

Capital Managua

Languages Spanish (official), indigenous Indian languages and English (creole-English)

Ethnic groups Mestizo (69%), white (17%), black (9%), Indian (Sumu, Mikito, Ramaguie peoples) (5%)

Religions Roman Catholic (95%), Protestant (5%)

Physical features Mountainous W half, with volcanic ranges rising to over 2000 m/6500 ft (NW); two large lakes, L Nicaragua and L Managua, behind the coastal mountain range; rolling uplands and forested plains to the E; many short rivers flow into the Pacific Ocean and the lakes.

Climate Tropical climate; average annual temperatures, 26°C (Jan), 30°C (Jul) at Managua; rainy season (May–Nov), high humidity; average annual rainfall 1140 mm/45 in; country devastated by hurricane Mitch in 1998.

Currency 1 Córdoba (NIC) = 100 centavos

Economy Agriculture (accounts for over two-thirds of total exports); cotton, coffee, sugar cane, rice, corn, tobacco; oil, natural gas; gold, silver, chemicals, textiles.

GDP (2002e) $11.16 bn, per capita $2200

HDI (2002) 0.635

History Colonized by Spaniards, early 16th-c; independence from Spain, 1821; left the Federation of Central America, 1838; dictatorship under Anastasio Somoza, 1938; Sandinista National Liberation Front seized power in 1979, and established a socialist junta of national reconstruction; under the 1987 constitution, a

Nicaragua (continued)

President and Constituent Assembly are elected for 6-year terms; former supporters of the Somoza government (the Contras), based in Honduras and supported by the USA, carried out guerrilla activities against the junta from 1979; ceasefire and disarmament agreed in 1990.

Head of State/Government
2001–6   Enrique Bolaños Geyer
2006–   Daniel Ortega

NIGER

Local name Niger

Timezone GMT +1

Area 1 267 000 km²/489 191 sq mi

Population total (2002e) 10 640 000

Status Republic

Date of independence 1960

Capital Niamey

Languages French (official) with Hausa, Songhai, Fulfulde, Tamashek, and Arabic widely spoken

Ethnic groups Hausa (54%), Djerma and Songhai (22%), Fulani (9%), Tuareg (8%), Beriberi (4%), Arab (2%)

Religions Muslim (80%), traditional beliefs and small Christian minority (primarily Roman Catholic) (20%)

Physical features Occupies S fringe of Sahara Desert, on a high plateau; Hamada Mangueni plateau (far N); Aïr Massif (C); Ténéré du Tafassasset desert (E); W Talk desert (C and N); water in quantity found only in the SW (R Niger) and SE (L Chad).

Climate One of the hottest countries in the world; average annual temperature 16°C (Jun–Oct), 41°C (Feb–May); rainy season in S (Jun–Oct); rainfall decreases N to almost negligible levels in desert areas; average annual rainfall at Niamey, 554 mm/22 in.

Currency 1 CFA Franc (XAF) = 100 cents

Economy Dominated by agriculture and mining; production badly affected by severe drought conditions in 1970s; uranium, tin, phosphates, coal, salt, natron; building materials, textiles, food processing.

GDP (2002e) $8.713 bn, per capita $800

HDI (2002) 0.277

History Occupied by the French, 1883–99; territory

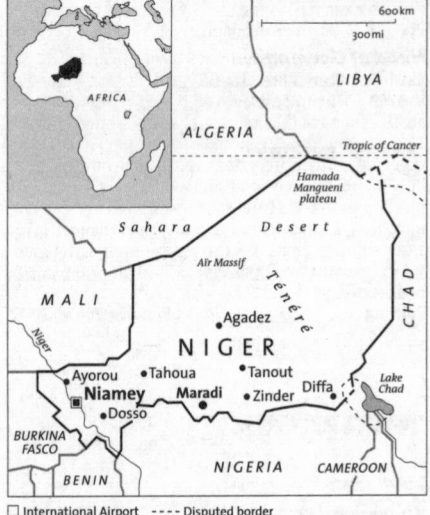

□ International Airport   ---- Disputed border

within French West Africa, 1904; independence, 1960; military coup, 1974; governed by a Higher Council for National Orientation led by a President who appoints a Council of Ministers; elected National Assembly, 1989; constitution suspended, 1991; multi-party constitution adopted, 1992; international aid effort begun for 2.5 million affected by famine in S.

Head of State
1999–   Mamadou Tandjo

Head of Government
2000–   Hama Amadou

NIGERIA

Local name Nigeria

Timezone GMT +1

Area 923 768 km²/356 574 sq mi

Population total (2002e) 129 935 000

Status Republic

Date of independence 1960

Capital Abuja

Languages English (official), Hausa, Yoruba, Ibo, and other Niger-Congo dialects widely used

Ethnic groups Over 250 tribal groups, notably Hausa

and Fulani, Yoruba and Ibo (65%); Kanuri, Tiv, Edo, Nupe, and Ibidio (25%)

Religions Muslim (50%), Christian (34%), indigenous animist beliefs (10%)

Physical features Long, sandy shoreline with mangrove swamp, dominated by R Niger delta; undulating area of tropical rainforest and oil palm bush behind a coastal strip; open woodland and savannah further N; numerous rivers, notably the Niger and the Benue; Gotel Mts on SE frontier, highest point, Mt Vogel, 2024 m/6640 ft.

Climate Tropical; uniformly high temperatures; average annual temperatures 21–7°C (Jan), 25–6°C (Jul); dry season in the N (Oct–Apr); average annual rainfall

1836–2497 mm/54–98 in; subject to influence of the Saharan Harmattan in N.

Currency 1 Naira (NGN) = 100 kobos

Economy Oil (provides c.90% of exports); agriculture (employs 50% of population); palm oil, groundnuts, cotton, cassava, rice, sugar cane, tobacco; fishing, livestock, forestry; natural gas, tin, iron ore, columbite, tantalite, limestone; pulp, paper, textiles, rubber; crops in N devasted by locusts swarms, Aug 2004.

GDP (2002e) $112.5 bn, per capita $900

HDI (2002) 0.462

History Centre of the Nok culture, 500 BC–AD 200; Muslim immigrants, 15th–16th-c; British colony at Lagos, 1861; protectorates of N and S Nigeria, 1900; amalgamated as the Colony and Protectorate of Nigeria, 1914; federation, 1954; independence, 1960; federal republic, 1963; military coup, 1966; E area formed Republic of Biafra, 1967; civil war, and surrender of Biafra, 1970; military coups, 1983 and 1985; major civil and religious unrest, 1992; presidential elections held then annulled, 1993; military coup, 1993; restoration of civilian rule, 1999; governed by a president, a 360-seat House of Representatives, and a 109-seat senate.

Head of State/Government
1999–   Olusegun Obasanjo

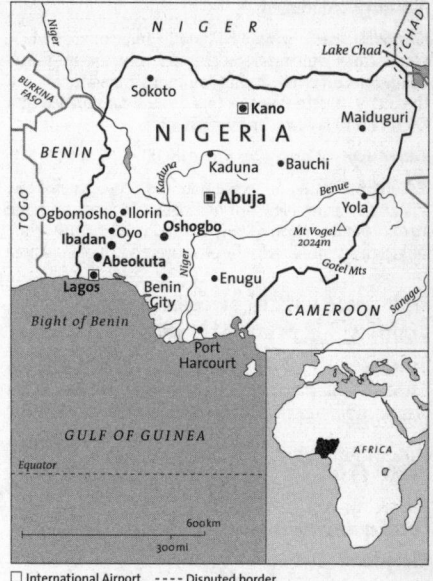

☐ International Airport   ---- Disputed border

NIUE >> NEW ZEALAND

NORTHERN IRELAND >> UNITED KINGDOM

NORTH KOREA >> KOREA, NORTH

NORTHERN MARIANA ISLANDS >> UNITED STATES OF AMERICA

NORWAY

Local name Norge

Timezone GMT +1

Area 323 895 km²/125 023 sq mi

Population total (2002e) 4 537 000

Status Kingdom

Date of independence 1905

Capital Oslo

Languages Norwegian (official) (in the varieties of Bokmål and Nynorsk), Lappish- and Finnish-speaking minorities

Ethnic groups Germanic (Nordic, Alpine, Baltic descent) (97%), Sami/Lapp minority in far N

Religions Evangelical Lutheran (95%), Baptist, Pentecostalist, Methodist, and Roman Catholic

Physical features Mountainous country; Kjölen Mts form the N part of the boundary with Sweden; Jotunheimen range in SC Norway; much of the interior over 1500 m/5000 ft; numerous lakes, the largest being L Mjøsa, 368 km²/142 sq mi; irregular coastline with many small islands and long deep fjords.

☐ International Airport

HUMAN GEOGRAPHY

Norway (continued)

Climate Arctic winter climate in interior highlands, snow, strong winds and severe frosts; comparatively mild conditions on coast; average annual temperatures −4°C (Jan), 17°C (Jul) in Oslo; average annual rainfall 683 mm /27 in; rainfall heavy on W coast.

Currency 1 Norwegian Krone (NOK) = 100 øre

Economy Based on extraction and processing of raw materials, using plentiful hydroelectric power; oil and natural gas from North Sea fields; land under cultivation, less than 3%; productive forests covered 21% of land area in 1985.

GDP (2002e) $149.1 bn, per capita $33 000

HDI (2002) 0.942

History A united kingdom achieved by St Olaf in the 11th-c, whose successor, Cnut, brought Norway under Danish rule; united with Sweden and Denmark, 1389;

annexed by Sweden as a reward for assistance against Napoleon, 1814; growing nationalism resulted in independence, 1905; declared neutrality in both World Wars, but occupied by Germany, 1940–5, after heavy resistance; Free Norwegian government based in London; joined NATO, 1949; joined European Free Trade Association, 1960; a limited, hereditary monarchy; government led by a Prime Minister; Parliament (*Storting*) comprises upper (*Lagting*) and lower (*Odelsting*) chambers.

Head of State (Monarch)
1957–91   Olav V
1991–   Harald V

Head of Government
2000–1   Jens Stoltenberg
2001–5   Kjell Magne Bondevik
2005–   Jens Stoltenberg

OMAN

Local name 'Umān

Timezone GMT +4

Area 300 000 km²/115 800 sq mi

Population total (2002e) 2 522 000

Status Sultanate

Date of independence 1951

Capital Muscat

Languages Arabic (official), English, Baluchi (and other Mahri languages), Urdu and Indian dialects also spoken

Ethnic groups Arab, with small Baluchi, Iranian, Indian, Pakistani, and W European minorities

Religions Ibadhi Muslim (75%), Sunni Muslim, Shi'a Muslim and Hindu (25%)

Physical features Located on the SE corner of the Arabian peninsula; the tip of the Musandam peninsula in the Strait of Hormuz is separated from the rest of the country by an 80 km/50 mi strip belonging to the United Arab Emirates; several peaks in the Hajjar Mt range; Jabal Akhdar ridge rises to 3000 m/10 000 ft; vast sand desert in NE; Dhofar uplands in SW.

Climate Desert climate, hot and arid; hot, humid on coast (Apr–Oct); average annual temperature 22°C (Jan), 33°C (Jul); light monsoon rains in S (Jun–Sep); average annual rainfall 99 mm/3.9 in.

Currency 1 Rial Omani (OMR) = 1000 baizas

Economy Oil discovered, 1964, now provides over 90% of government revenue; natural gas an important source of industrial power; c.70% of the population relies on agriculture; alfalfa, wheat, tobacco, fruit, vegetables, fishing.

GDP (2002e) $22.4 bn, per capita $8300

HDI (2002) 0.751

History Dominant maritime power of the W Indian Ocean in 16th-c; independent from UK, 1951; separatist

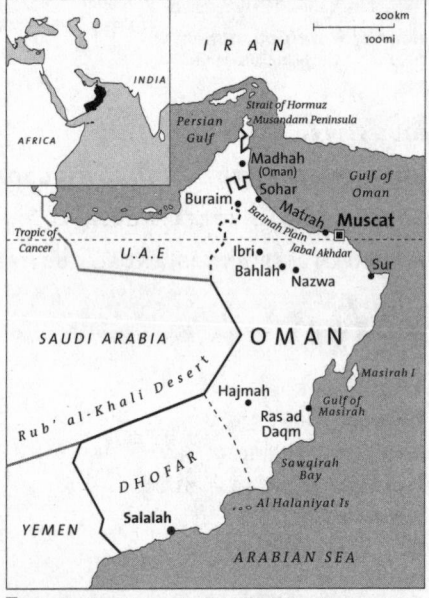

□ International Airport   ---- Border awaiting demarcation

tribal revolt, 1964, led to a palace coup that installed the present Sultan in 1970; opened airbases to Western forces, following Iraqi invasion of Kuwait, 1990; independent state ruled by a Sultan who is both Head of State and Premier, and who appoints a Cabinet and a 59-member Consultative Council.

Head of State/Government (Sultan)
1932–70   Said bin Taimur
1970–   Qaboos bin Said

PAKISTAN

Local name Pākistān

Timezone GMT +5

Area 803 943 km²/310 322 sq mi

Population total (2002e) 145 960 000

Status Republic

Date of independence 1947

Capital Islamabad

Languages Urdu (official), Punjabi, Sindhi, Pashto, Urdu, Baluchi, and Brahvi mainly spoken

Ethnic groups Punjabi (66%), Sindhi (13%), Baluchi (3%), Pathan and Muhajir minorities, also Afghan refugees in W Pakistan

Religions Muslim (97%) (Sunni 77%, Shi'a 20%), Christian, Hindu, Parsee, Buddhist minorities

Physical features R Indus flows from Himalayas to Karachi, forming a vast, fertile, densely populated alluvial floodplain in E; bounded N and W by mountains rising to 8611 m/28 250 ft at K2, and 8126 m/26 660 ft at Nanga Parbat; mostly flat plateau, low-lying plains and arid desert to the S; major rivers include Jhelum, Chenab, Indus, Sutlej.

Climate Continental, with many temperature and rainfall variations; dominated by the Asiatic monsoon; severe winters in mountainous regions; average annual temperatures 10°C (Jan), 32°C (Jul) in Islamabad; average annual rainfall in Punjab, 250 mm/10 in in SW, 635 mm/25 in in NE; rainy season (Jun–Oct).

Currency 1 Pakistan Rupee (PKR) = 100 paisa

Economy Agriculture (employs 55% of labour force); cotton production important, supporting major spinning, weaving, and processing industries; sugar cane; textiles; natural gas; tobacco; salt; uranium.

GDP (2002e) $295.3 bn, per capita $2000

HDI (2002) 0.499

History Remains of Indus Valley civilization over 4000 years ago; Muslim rule under the Mughal Empire, 1526–1761; British rule over most areas, 1840s; separated from India to form a state for the Muslim minority, 1947; consisted of West Pakistan (Baluchistan, North-West Frontier, West Punjab, Sind) and East Pakistan (East Bengal), physically separated by 1 610 km/1 000 mi; occupied Jammu and Kashmir, 1949 (disputed territory with India, and the cause of wars in 1965 and 1971); pro-

☐ International Airport   ∴ World heritage site

1 Peshawar
2 Rawalpindi

claimed an Islamic republic, 1956; differences between E and W Pakistan developed into civil war, 1971; E Pakistan became an independent state (Bangladesh); military coup by General Zia ul-Haq, 1977, with execution of former prime minister Bhutto in 1979; new constitution (1985) strengthened Zia's powers; Benazir Bhutto elected prime minister, 1988, deposed 1990, re-elected 1993; deposed 1996; ethnic (Muslim/Sindh) violence, especially in Karachi, 1994, and ongoing; military coup, 1999; coup leader, General Musharraf, declared president in 2001; sensitive border area with Afghanistan, following the US-led anti-Taliban campaign, 2001, focusing on Afghan refugees, Pakistan pro-Taliban fighters, and Taliban escapees; ongoing tension with India over Kashmir, with some fighting, 2001, escalating into a major crisis, mid-2002; ceasefire announced (Nov 2003) and diplomatic ties and transport links resumed; governed by an elected President and a bicameral Federal Parliament.

Head of State
1997–2001 Muhammad Rafiq Tarar
2001–   Pervez Musharraf

Head of Government
2004–   Shaukat Aziz

PALAU >> BELAU

PANAMA

Local name Panamá

Timezone GMT –5

Area 77 082 km²/29 753 sq mi

Population total (2002e) 2 915 000

Status Republic

Date of independence 1903

Capital Panama City

Languages Spanish (official), English and indigenous languages (including Cuna, Chibchan, Choco)

Panama (continued)

Ethnic groups Mestizo (mixed Spanish-Indian) (70%), West Indian (14%), white (10%), Indian (6%)

Religions Christian (Roman Catholic 93%, Protestant 6%), Jewish, Muslim, and Baha'i minorities

Physical features Mostly mountainous; Serranía de Tabasará (W) rises to 3475 m/11 401 ft at Volcán Baru; Azuero peninsula (Peninsula de Azuero) in the S; lake-studded lowland cuts across the isthmus; dense tropical forests on the Caribbean coast; Panama Canal, 82 km/51 mi long, connects Pacific and Atlantic oceans.

Climate Tropical, with uniformly high temperatures; average annual temperature 26°C (Jan), 27°C (Jul) in Panama City; dry season (Jan–Apr) only; average annual rainfall 1770 mm/69.7 in.

Currency 1 Balboa (PAB); 1 US dollar (USA) = 100 cents

Economy Canal revenue (accounts for 80% of country's wealth); great increase in banking sector since 1970; attempts to diversify include oil refining, cigarettes, paper products; tourism; copper, gold, silver; bananas, coffee, cacao, sugar cane.

GDP (2002e) $18.06 bn, per capita $6200

HDI (2002) 0.787

History Visited by Columbus, 1502; under Spanish colonial rule until 1821; joined the Republic of Greater Colombia; separation from Colombia after a US-inspired revolution, 1903; assumed sovereignty of the 8 km/5 mi-wide Canal zone, previously administered by the

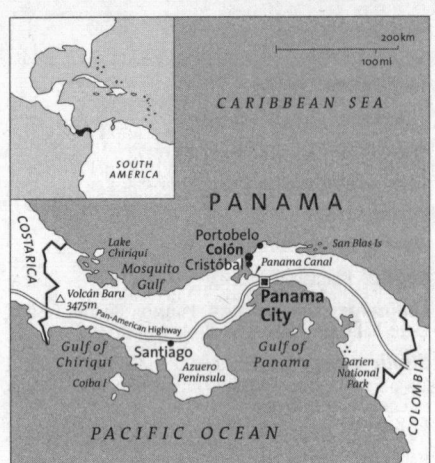

International Airport   ∴ World heritage site

USA, 1979; military rule under Manuel Noriega, 1983–9; US invasion in 1989 deposed Noriega; governed by a President, a Cabinet, and a unicameral Legislative Assembly.

Head of State/Government
1999–2004 Mireya Moscoso
2004–   Martin Torrijos

PAPUA NEW GUINEA

Local name Papua New Guinea

Timezone GMT +10

Area 462 840 km²/178 656 sq mi

Population total (2002e) 5 426 000

Status Independent state within the Commonwealth

Date of independence 1975

Capital Port Moresby

Languages Pidgin English and Hiri Motu (official parliamentary languages), Tok Pisin, and c.750 indigenous languages spoken

Ethnic groups Papuan (80%), Melanesian (15%), Polynesian, Chinese, and European minorities

Religions Christian (Protestant 64%, Roman Catholic 33%), local beliefs

Physical features Island group in SW Pacific Ocean, comprising E half of the island of New Guinea, the Bismarck and Louisiade archipelagos, the Trobriand and D'Entrecasteaux Is, and other off-lying groups; complex system of mountains, highest point, Mt Wilhelm, 4509 m /14 793 ft; mainly covered with tropical rainforest; vast mangrove swamps along coast; archipelago islands are mountainous, mostly volcanic and fringed with coral reefs; many previously unknown plants and animals discovered in the Foja Mts region, 2006.

Climate Typical monsoon, with temperatures and humidity constantly high; average annual temperature

International Airport

28°C (Jan), 26°C (Jul); average annual rainfall 2000–2500 mm /80–100 in.

Currency 1 Kina (PGK) = 100 toea

Economy Farming, fishing, and forestry (engages c.75% of workforce); vegetables, sugar, peanuts; natural gas; brewing; tourism.

GDP (2002e) $10.86 bn, per capita $2100

HDI (2002) 0.535

History British protectorate in SE New Guinea, 1884; some of the islands under German protectorate, 1884; German New Guinea in NE, 1899; German colony annexed by Australia in World War 1; Australia mandated to govern both British and German areas, 1920; combined as the United Nations Trust Territory of Papua and New Guinea, 1949; independence within the Commonwealth, 1975; a Governor-General represents the British Crown; governed by a Prime Minister and Cabinet, with a unicameral National Parliament.

Head of State
(British monarch represented by Governor-General)
2004–   Sir Paulias Matane

Head of Government
1999–2002 Mekere Morauta
2002–   Michael Thomas Somare

PARAGUAY

Local name Paraguay

Timezone GMT –4

Area 406 750 km²/157 000 sq mi

Population total (2002e) 5 774 000

Status Republic

Date of independence 1811

Capital Asunción

Languages Spanish (official), but Guaraní also spoken

Ethnic groups Mestizo (mixed Spanish-Guaraní Indian) (91%), Amerindian, black, European, and Asian minorities

Religions Roman Catholic (96%), Mennonite, Baptist/Anglican minorities

Physical features Landlocked, in C South America; divided into two regions by the R Paraguay; Gran Chaco in the W, mostly cattle country or scrub forest; more fertile land in the E; Paraná plateau at 300–600 m/1000–2000 ft, mainly wet, treeless savannah.

Climate Tropical NW, with hot summers, warm winters; temperate in SE; average annual temperatures 27°C (Jan), 18°C (Jul) in Asunción; average annual rainfall 1316 mm/52 in.

Currency 1 Guaraní (PYG) = 100 céntimos

Economy Agriculture (employs 43% of the labour force); oilseed, cotton, wheat, tobacco, corn, rice, sugar cane; pulp, timber, textiles, cement, glass.

GDP (2002e) $25.19 bn, per capita $4300

HDI (2002) 0.740

History Originally inhabited by Guaraní Indians; arrival of the Spanish, 1537; arrival of Jesuit missionaries,

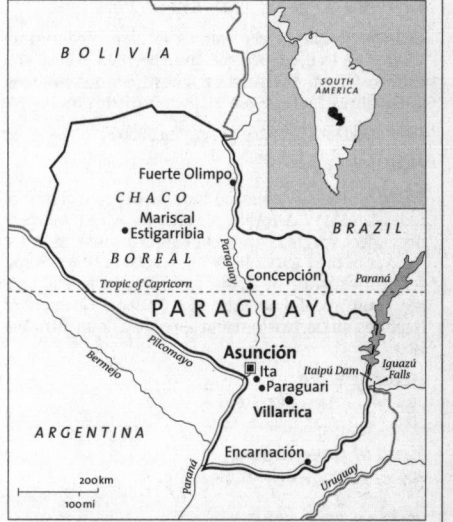

☐ International Airport

1609; independence from Spain, 1811; War of the Triple Alliance against Brazil, Argentina, and Uruguay, 1865–70; Chaco War with Bolivia, 1932–5; civil war, 1947; General Alfredo Stroessner seized power, 1954, forced to stand down following a coup in 1989; new constitution, creating post of Vice-President, 1992; governed by a President, an appointed Council of Ministers, and a bicameral National Congress.

Head of State/Government
1999–2003 Luis Gonzalez Macchi
2003–   Nicanor Duarte Frutos

PERU

Local name Perú

Timezone GMT –5

Area 1 284 640 km²/495 871 sq mi

Population total (2002e) 26 749 000

Status Republic

Date of independence 1821

Capital Lima

Languages Spanish and Quechua (official), Aymará also spoken

Ethnic groups South American Indian (47%), mestizo (mixed Indian and European) (33%), white (12%), black, Japanese, and Chinese (3%)

Religions Roman Catholic (90%), Anglican, Methodist, Peruvian Baha'i minorities

Physical features Arid plains and foothills on the

HUMAN GEOGRAPHY

Peru (continued)

coast, with areas of desert and fertile river valleys; Central Sierra, average altitude 3000 m/10 000 ft, contains 50% of the population; highest peak, Mt Huascarán, 6768 m/22 204 ft, in W; forested Andes and Amazon basin (E), with major rivers flowing to the Amazon.

Climate Mild temperatures all year on coast; dry, arid desert in the S; typically wet, tropical climate in Amazon basin; average annual temperatures 23°C (Jan), 17°C (Jul) in Lima; average annual rainfall 48 mm/1.9 in.

Currency 1 New Sol (PEN) = 100 céntimos

Economy One of the world's leading producers of silver, zinc, lead, copper, gold, iron ore; 80% of Peru's oil extracted from the Amazon forest; cotton, potatoes, sugar, olives; tourism, especially to ancient sites.

GDP (2002e) $138.8 bn, per capita $5000

HDI (2002) 0.747

History Highly developed Inca civilization; arrival of Spanish, 1531; Vice-royalty of Peru established; independence declared, 1821; frequent border disputes in 19th-c (eg War of the Pacific, 1879–83); several military coups; terrorist activities by Maoist guerrillas; bicameral Congress consists of a Senate and a National Chamber of Deputies; an elected President appoints a Council of Ministers.

Head of State
2001–6   Alejandro Toledo
2006–   Alan García Pérez

Head of Government
2006–   Jorge del Castillo Gálvez

☐ International Airport   ∴ World heritage site

PHILIPPINES

Local name Filipinas

Timezone GMT +8

Area 299 679 km²/115 676 sq mi

Population total (2002e) 80 000 000

Status Republic

Date of independence 1946

Capital Manila

Languages Tagalog (Pilipino), and English (official), over 87 local languages, including Cebuano, Ilocano, Bicol, and Samar-Leyte

Ethnic groups Filipino, with Chinese, Spanish, and American minorities

Religions Roman Catholic (83%), Protestant (9%), Muslim (5%), Buddhist (3%)

Physical features An archipelago of more than 7100 islands and islets, NE of Borneo; largest island, Luzon 108 172 km²/41 754 sq mi; Mindanao, 94 227 km²/36 372 sq mi, has active volcano Apo, 2954 m/9690 ft, and mountainous rainforest; Mount Pinatubo volcano, 1758 m/5770 ft, situated 90 km/56 mi NW of Manila; largely mountainous islands.

Climate Tropical, maritime; warm and humid throughout year; average annual temperature 25°C (Jan), 28°C (Jul) in Manila; average annual rainfall 2083 mm/82

☐ International Airport

in; frequent typhoons and occasional earth tremors and tsunamis (tidal waves).

Currency 1 Philippine Peso (PHP) = 100 centavos

Economy Farming (employs c.50% of workforce); rice, pineapples, mangos, vegetables, livestock, sugar, tobacco, rubber, coffee; oil, copper, gold; textiles; vehicles; tourism.

GDP (2002e) $379.7 bn, per capita $4600

HDI (2002) 0.754

History Claimed for Spain by Magellan, 1521; ceded to the USA after the Spanish-American War, 1898; became a self-governing Commonwealth, 1935; occupied by the

PITCAIRN ISLANDS >> UNITED KINGDOM

POLAND

Local name Polska

Timezone GMT +1

Area 312 683 km²/120 695 sq mi

Population total (2002e) 38 644 000

Status Republic

Date of independence 1918

Capital Warsaw

Language Polish (official)

Ethnic groups Polish (99%), Ukrainian, Belorussian, and Jewish minorities

Religions Roman Catholic (94%), small Jewish and Muslim minorities

Physical features Part of the great European plain, with the Carpathian and Sudetes Mts (S) rising in the High Tatra to 2499 m/8199 ft at Mt Rysy; Polish plateau in N, cut by the Bug, San, and Wisła (Vistula) rivers; richest coal basin in Europe in the W (Silesia); flat Baltic coastal area; forests cover 20% of land.

Climate Continental climate, with severe winters, hot summers; average annual temperatures −4°C (Jan), 19°C (Jul) in Warsaw; average annual rainfall 550 mm/22 in.

Currency 1 Złoty (PLN) = 100 groszy

Economy Nearly 50% of the land under cultivation; major producer of coal; zinc, lead, sulphur; shipbuilding, machinery, vehicles, electrical equipment; textiles.

GDP (2002e) $373.2 bn, per capita $9700

HDI (2002) 0.833

History Emergence as a powerful Slavic group in 11th-c; united with Lithuania, 1569; divided between Prussia, Russia, and Austria, 1772, 1793, 1795; semi-independent state after Congress of Vienna, 1815; incorporated into the Russian Empire; after World War 1, declared an independent Polish state, 1918; partition between Germany and the USSR, 1939; invasion by Germany, 1939; major resistance movement, and a government in exile during World War 2; People's Democracy established under

POLYNESIA, FRENCH >> FRANCE

Japanese in World War 2; independence, 1946; Communist guerrilla activity in N; Muslim separatist movement in S; martial law following political unrest, 1972–81; exiled political leader Benigno Aquino assassinated on returning to Manila, 1983; coup in 1986 ended the 20-year rule of President Ferdinand Marcos; new constitution, 1987; attempted coup, 1989, with continuing political unrest; eruption of Mount Pinatubo, 1991; governed by a President and a bicameral legislature, comprising a Senate and a House of Representatives.

Head of State/Government
1998–2001 Joseph Arap Estrada
2001–   Gloria Macapagal Arroyo

□ International Airport   ∴ World heritage site

Soviet influence, 1944; rise of independent trade union, Solidarity, 1980; state of martial law imposed, 1981–3; loss of support for communist government and major success for Solidarity in 1989 elections; proclaimed Polish Republic, 1989, and constitution amended to provide for a bicameral National Assembly.

Head of State
1990–5   Lech Wałęsa
1995–2005 Alexander Kwasniewski
2005–   Lech Kaczynski

Head of Government
2005–6   Kazimierz Marcinkiewicz
2006–   Jaroslaw Kaczynski

PORTUGAL

Local name Portugal
Timezone GMT
Area 91 630 km²/35 370 sq mi
Population total (2002e) 10 384 000
Status Republic
Capital Lisbon
Languages Portuguese (official), with many dialectal variations
Ethnic groups Homogeneous (Mediterranean stock), with small African minority
Religions Roman Catholic (97%), Protestant (1%), Muslim minority
Physical features Located on W side of Iberian peninsula; includes semi-autonomous Azores and Madeira Is; chief mountain range, the Serra da Estrêla (N), rising to 1991 m/6532 ft; main rivers, Douro, Tagus, Guadiana, are the lower courses of rivers beginning in Spain.
Climate Cool, maritime climate in N; warmer Mediterranean type in S; most rainfall in winter; average annual temperature 11°C (Jan), 22°C (Jul) in Lisbon; average annual rainfall 686 mm/27 in; forest fires, C region, 2006.
Currency 1 Euro (EUR) = 100 cents (before February 2002, 1 Escudo (PTE) = 100 centavos)
Economy Several labour-intensive areas, including textiles, leather, wood products, cork, ceramics; timber; wine, fish; chemicals, electrical machinery, steel, shipbuilding; minerals, cereals, pulses, fruit, olive oil; c.20% of land is forested.
GDP (2002e) $195.2 bn, per capita $19 400
HDI (2002) 0.880
History Became a kingdom under Alfonso Henriques in 1140; major period of world exploration and beginning of Portuguese Empire in 15th-c; under Spanish domination, 1580–1640; invaded by the French, 1807; island of Azores granted semi-autonomy, 1895; monarchy overthrown and republic established, 1910; dictatorship of Dr Salazar, 1928–68; military coup in 1974, followed by 10 years of political unrest under 15 governments; island

☐ International Airport

of Madeira gained partial autonomy, 1980; Macao still administered by Portugal; joined EC, 1986; governed by a President, elected for five years, a Prime Minister and Council of Ministers, and a unicameral Assembly of the Republic.

Head of State
2006–   Anibal Cavaco Silva

Head of Government
2004–5   Pedro Santana Lopes
2005–   José Socrates

Azores

Local name Ilhas dos Açôres
Timezone GMT –1
Area 2 300 km²/900 sq mi
Population total (2002e) 245 000
Status Semi-autonomous region of Portugal
Capital Ponta Delgada (on São Miguel Island)
Physical features Island archipelago of volcanic origin, 1400–1800 km/870–1100 mi W of mainland Portugal; three widely separated groups of nine islands; Flores and Corvo (NW), Terceira, Graciosa, São Jorge, Faial (Fayal), Pico (C), and Santa Maria with the Formigas Islands and São Miguel, the principal island (E); highest point, Pico, 2351 m/7713 ft; volcanic terrain.
Economy Agriculture; grain, fruit, tea, tobacco, wine.
History Settled by the Portuguese in 1439; under Spanish rule, 1580–1640; new constitution established in 1832, when islands were grouped into three administra-

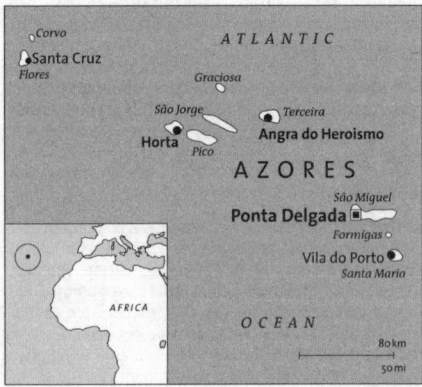

☐ International Airport

tive districts; given limited autonomous administration, 1895; has no central government, but a General Council.

Madeira (islands)

Local name Ilha de Madeira

Timezone GMT

Area 796 km²/307 sq mi

Population total (2002e) 265 000

Status Semi-autonomous region of Portugal

Capital Funchal (on Madeira Island)

Physical features Main island in an archipelago off the coast of N Africa, 980 km/610 mi SW of Lisbon; consists of Madeira, Porto Santo and three uninhabited islands; highest point, Pico Ruivo de Santana, 1862 m/6111 ft on Madeira.

Economy Agriculture; sugar cane, fruit, fishing, Madeira (a fortified wine); embroidery, crafts; tourism.

History Occupied by the Portuguese, 15th-c; occupied by Britain, 1801, and 1807–14; gained partial autonomy, 1980, but remains a Portuguese overseas territory; locally-elected government, and Assembly.

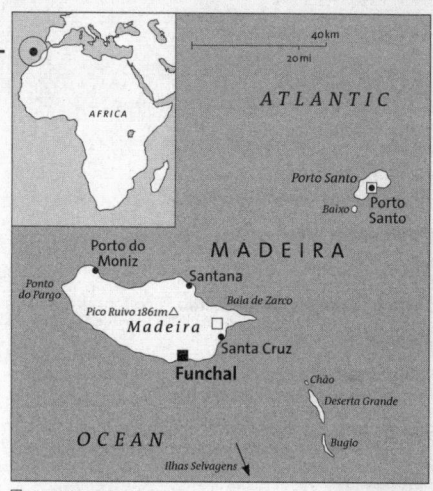

☐ International Airport

QATAR

Local name Qatar

Timezone GMT +3

Area 11 437 km²/4 415 sq mi

Population total (2002e) 606 000

Status Independent state

Date of independence 1971

Capital Doha

Languages Arabic (official), English

Ethnic groups Arab (40%), Pakistani (18%), Indian (18%), Iranian (10%)

Religion Sunni Muslim (95%)

Physical features Low-lying state on the E coast of the Arabian Peninsula, comprising the Qatar Peninsula and numerous small offshore islands; peninsula, 160 km/100 mi long and 55–80 km/34–50 mi wide, slopes gently from the Dukhan Heights 98 m/321 ft, to the E shore; barren terrain, mainly sand and gravel; coral reefs offshore.

Climate Desert climate; average temperatures 23°C (Jan), 35°C (Jul); high humidity; sparse rainfall; average annual rainfall 62 mm/2.4 in.

Currency 1 Qatar Riyal (QAR) = 100 dirhams

Economy Based on oil. Offshore gas reserves thought to be an eighth of known world reserves; oil refineries, petrochemicals, liquefied natural gas, fertilizers, steel, cement, ship repairing, engineering; fishing.

GDP (2002e) $15.91 bn, per capita $20 100

HDI (2002) 0.803

History British protectorate after Turkish withdrawal, 1916; independence, 1971; palace coup brought Khalifah bin Hamad to power, 1972; long-standing territorial dispute with Bahrain over Hawar Is, awarded to Bahrain,

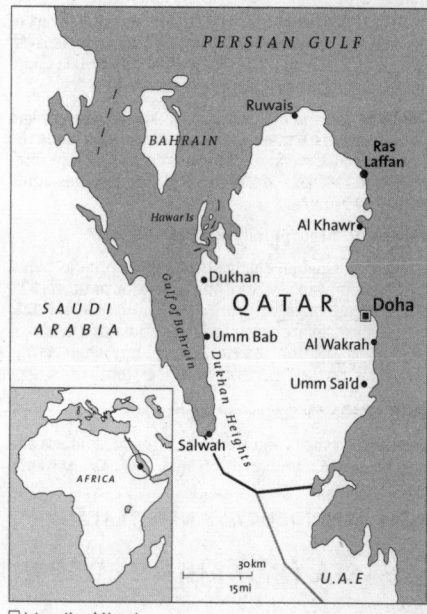

☐ International Airport

2001; hereditary monarchy, the Emir is both Head of State and Prime Minister; Council of Ministers is assisted by a Consultative Council; 2003 national referendum approved first constitution, with 45-member Advisory Council: 30 elected by citizens; 15 appointed by the Emir.

Head of State (Emir)
Family name: al-Thani
1995–ㅤHamad bin Khalifa

Head of Government
1996–ㅤAbdulla bin Khalifa

HUMAN GEOGRAPHY

RÉUNION >> FRANCE

ROMANIA

Local name Romănia

Timezone GMT +2

Area 237 500 km²/91 675 sq mi

Population total (2002e) 21 667 000

Status Republic

Date of independence 1918

Capital Bucharest

Languages Romanian (official), with French, Hungarian, and German widely spoken

Ethnic groups Romanian (89%), Hungarian (7%), German (2%), Ukrainian, Serb, Croat, Russian, Turk, and Gypsy (2%)

Religions Eastern Orthodox Christian (80%), Roman Catholic (6%), Calvinist, Lutheran, Baptist (4%)

Physical features Carpathian Mts form the heart of the country; highest peak, Negoiul, 2548 m/8359 ft; crossed by many rivers; c.3500 glacial ponds, lakes, and coastal lagoons; over 25% of land forested.

Climate Continental, with cold, snowy winters and warm summers; winters can be severe; mildest along the Black Sea coast; average annual temperatures range from 7°C (N), to 11°C (S), –3°C (Jan), 24°C (Jul); average annual rainfall 579 mm/22.8 in.

Currency 1 Leu (plural lei) (ROL) = 100 bani

Economy Gradual change from agricultural to industrial economy (since World War 2); state owns nearly 37% of farm land, mainly organized as collectives and state farms; wheat, maize, sugar beet, fruit, potatoes; livestock; oil, natural gas; iron and steel, metallurgy, engineering, chemicals, textiles, electronics, timber; tourism.

GDP (2002e) $169.3 bn, per capita $7600

History Formed from the unification of Moldavia and Wallachia, 1862; monarchy created, 1866; Transylvania,

□ International Airport   ∴ World heritage site

Bessarabia, and Bucovina united with Romania, 1918; support given to Germany in World War 2; occupied by Soviet forces, 1944; monarchy abolished and People's Republic declared, 1947. Socialist Republic declared, 1965; increasingly independent from the USSR from the 1960s; leading political force was the Romanian Communist Party, led by dictator Nicolae Ceauşescu; popular uprising due to violent repression of protest led to the overthrow of the Ceauşescu regime, 1989; new constitution, 1991; joined EU 2007; governed by a President, Prime Minister, Chamber of Deputies, and Senate.

Head of State
2004–   Traian Basescu

Head of Government
2004–   Calin Tariceanu

ROSS DEPENDENCY >> NEW ZEALAND

RUSSIA (RUSSIAN FEDERATION)

Local name Rossiyskaya (Rossiyskaya Federatsiya)

Timezone GMT ranges from +2 to +12

Area 17 075 400 km²/6 591 100 sq mi

Population total (2002e) 143 673 000

Status Republic

Date of independence 1991

Capital Moscow

Languages Russian (official), and c.100 different languages

Ethnic groups Russian (82%), Tatar (3%), Ukrainian (3%)

Religions Christian (Russian Orthodox 25%), non-religious (60%), Muslim

Physical features Occupying much of E Europe and N Asia; consists of c.75% of the area of the former USSR and over 50% of its population; vast plains dominate the W half; Ural Mts separate the E European Plain (W) from the W Siberian Lowlands (E); E of the R Yenisey lies the C Siberian Plateau; N Siberian Plain further E; Caucasus on S frontier. Lena, Ob, Severnaya Dvina, Pechora, Yenisey, Indigirka, and Kolyma rivers flow to the Arctic Ocean; Amur, Argun, and rivers of the Kamchatka Peninsula flow to the Pacific Ocean; Caspian Sea basin

HUMAN GEOGRAPHY

☐ International Airport ∴ World heritage site

includes the Volga and Ural rivers; over 20 000 lakes, the largest being the Caspian Sea, L Taymyr, L Baikal.

Climate Half of country covered by snow for 6 months of year; coldest region, NE Siberia, average annual temperature −46°C (Jan), 16°C (Jul); summers in rest of country generally short and hot; average annual temperature −18–9°C (Jan), 16–24°C (Jul) in Moscow; average annual rainfall 500–750 mm/20–30 in.

Currency 1 Rouble (RUR) = 100 kopeks

Economy Oil fields in W Siberia (provide 50% of country's petroleum); series of 5-year plans since 1928 promoted industry; heavy-industry products include chemicals, construction materials, machine tools, and steel-making; mining, major producer of iron ore, manganese, natural gas, nickel, and platinum, also coal, copper, gold, zinc, tin, lead; agriculture, primarily wheat, fruit, vegetables, tobacco, cotton, sugar beet; textiles; timber.

GDP (2002e) $1.409 tn, per capita $9700

HDI (2002) 0.781

History Conquered by Mongols in 13th-c; Ivan IV (the Terrible) was first ruler to be crowned Tsar, 1547; Time of Trouble, 1604–13; under Peter the Great, territory expanded to Baltic Sea and St Petersburg founded as capital, 1703; Napoleon invasion failed, 1812; Crimean War, 1853–6; emancipation of serfs, 1861; assassination of Alexander II, 1881; Balkan War with Turkey, 1877–8; Russo-Japanese War, 1904–5; establishment of a parliament (*Duma*) with limited powers, 1906; Russia allied with Britain and France, World War I; revolution overthrew Nicholas II, Bolsheviks (Communists) seized power under dictatorship of Lenin, 1917; Russia forced to withdraw from War; renamed the Russian Soviet Federated Socialist Republic, 1918, and Moscow reinstated as capital; Russia became part of the Union of Soviet Socialist Republics (USSR), 1922; death of Lenin, 1924; Trotsky deported in 1928, by which time Stalin acquiring dictatorial power; USSR fought with the Allies against Germany in World War 2; development of Cold War between East and West from 1946; troops intervened in Afghanistan, 1979; radical reform of the system under the leadership of Gorbachev, 1985–91; first contested elections in Soviet history held, and the end of Cold War announced, 1989; troops withdrawn from Afghanistan, 1989; USSR dissolved, 1991; Russian Republic became independent and a founder member of the Commonwealth of Independent States, 1991; war in Chechnya, 1994–6; further invasion of Chechnya, 1999–; governed by a President, Prime Minister, and Federal Assembly, consisting of a State *Duma* and a Federation Council.

Head of State
1991–9   Boris Yeltsin
1999–   Vladimir Putin

Head of Government
2004   Viktor Khristenko *Acting*
2004–   Mikhail Fradkov

>> Political leaders and rulers, p.197–8

RWANDA

Local name Rwanda

Timezone GMT +2

Area 26 338 km²/10 169 sq mi

Population total (2002e) 7 398 000

Status Republic

Date of independence 1962

Capital Kigali

Languages French, Kinyarwanda, and English (official), with Kiswahili widely used in commerce

Rwanda (continued)

Ethnic groups Hutu (84%), Tutsi (14%), Pygmoid Twa (1%)

Religions Christian (65%), local indigenous beliefs (25%), Muslim (9%)

Physical features Landlocked in C Africa; mountainous, with many of the highest mountains formed by volcanoes; highest point Karisimbi, 4507 m/14 787 ft, in the Virunga range; W third drains into L Kivu and then the R Congo, remainder drains towards the R Nile; L Kivu and R Ruzizi form W border as part of Africa's Great Rift Valley.

Climate Tropical climate, influenced by high altitude; average annual temperature 19°C (Jan), 21°C (Jul) in Kigali; average annual rainfall 1000 mm/40 in in Kigali; two wet seasons (Oct–Dec, Mar–May); highest rainfall in the W, decreasing in the C uplands and to the N and E.

Currency 1 Rwanda Franc (RWF) = 100 centimes

Economy Based largely on agriculture; coffee, tea, pyrethrum, maize, beans, livestock; minerals; plastic goods, textiles.

GDP (2002e) $8.92 bn, per capita $1200

HDI (2002) 0.403

History In the 16th-c the Tutsi tribe moved into the country and took over from the Hutu, forming a monarchy; German protectorate, 1899; mandated with Burundi to Belgium as the Territory of Ruanda-Urundi, 1919; United Nations Trust Territory administered by Belgium, after World War 2; unrest in 1959 led to a Hutu revolt and the overthrow of Tutsi rule; independence, 1962; military coup, 1973; return to civilian rule, 1980; rebellion by (mainly Tutsi) Rwandan Patriotic Front, 1990; new constitution, 1991; peace accord with rebels, 1993; unprecedented outbreak of inter-ethnic violence, with over half a million deaths, 1994; governed by a President,

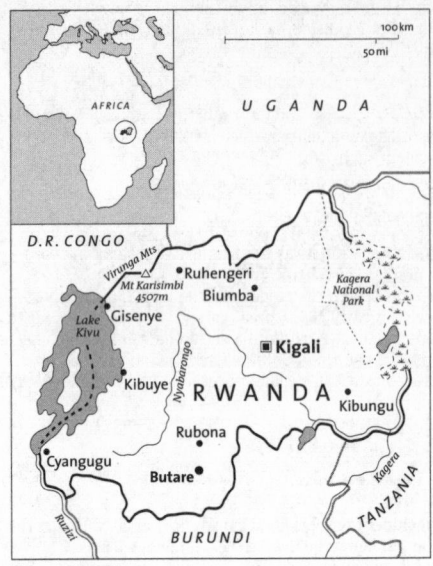

☐ International Airport

Prime Minister, Council of Ministers, and National Development Council; elections scheduled for 1999, but transitional government rule extended to 2003.

Head of State
2000–   Paul Kagame

Head of Government
2000–   Bernard Makuza

SAINT HELENA AND DEPENDENCIES >> UNITED KINGDOM

SAINT KITTS AND NEVIS

Local name Saint Christopher (Kitts) and Nevis

Timezone GMT –4

Area 269 km²/104 sq mi

Population total (2002e) 46 200

Status Independent state within the Commonwealth

Date of independence 1983

Capital Basseterre

Languages English (official), with creole-English widely spoken

Ethnic groups Black African descent (94%), mulatto (3%), white (1%)

Religions Christian (Anglican 36%, Methodist 32%, other Protestant 8%, Roman Catholic 11%)

Physical features Located in the N Leeward Is, E Caribbean; comprises the islands of St Christopher (St Kitts), Nevis, and Sombrero; volcanic origin with mountain ranges rising to 1156 m/3793 ft at Mt Liamuiga; Nevis dominated by a central peak rising to 985 m/3232 ft.

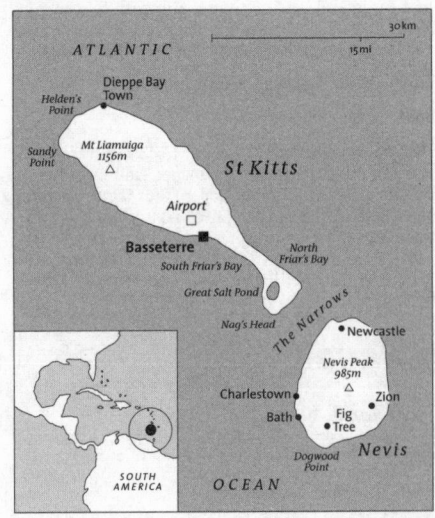

☐ International Airport

Climate Tropical, warm climate; average annual temperature 26°C; average annual rainfall 1375 mm/54 in; low humidity, modified by sea winds; hurricanes possible (Jul–Oct).

Currency 1 East Caribbean Dollar (XCD) = 100 cents

Economy Sugar and its products (supply c.40% of total exports); copra, cotton, electrical appliances, footwear, garments, tourism.

GDP (2002e) $339 mn, per capita $8800

HDI (2002) 0.814

History St Kitts was the first British colony in the W Indies, 1623; control disputed between France and Britain, 17th–18th-c; ceded to Britain, 1783; St Kitts and Nevis united, 1882; area gained full internal self-government, 1967; Anguilla declared itself independent from the control of St Kitts, which led to British troops intervention, 1969; island reverted to British dependent territory, 1971, and was formally separated from St Kitts-Nevis, 1980; independence of St Kitts-Nevis, 1983; British monarch represented by a Governor-General; governed by a Prime Minister and two legislative chambers; island of Nevis has own legislature (the Nevis Island Assembly), and executive, which has exclusive responsibility for the island's internal administration; Nevis I voted in favour of secession, 1997.

Head of State
(British monarch represented by Governor-General)
1996–   Sir Cuthbert Montroville Sebastian

Head of Government
1995–   Denzil Douglas

SAINT LUCIA

Local name Saint Lucia

Timezone GMT –4

Area 616 km²/238 sq mi

Population total (2002e) 160 000

Status Independent state within the Commonwealth

Date of independence 1979

Capital Castries

Languages English (official), with French patois widely spoken

Ethnic groups African descent (90%), mixed (6%), East Indian (3%), Caucasian (1%)

Religions Christian (Roman Catholic 90%, Protestant 7%, Anglican 3%)

Physical features Second largest of the Windward Is, E Caribbean; volcanic island; forested mountainous centre rising to 950 m/3117 ft at Mt Gimie; sulphurous springs of Qualibou and twin peaks of Gros and Petit Pitons (SW).

Climate Tropical climate; average temperature 26°C; wet season (Jun–Dec), dry season (Jan–Apr); average annual rainfall 1500 mm/60 in (lowlands), 3500 mm/138 in (mountainous zone).

Currency 1 East Caribbean Dollar (XCD) = 100 cents

Economy Tourism (fastest-growing sector of the economy); bananas, cocoa, copra, citrus fruits, coconut oil; garments, textiles, electronic components; oil refining and transshipment.

GDP (2002e) $866 mn, per capita $5400

HDI (2002) 0.772

History Reputedly visited by Columbus, 1502; disputed ownership between England and France,

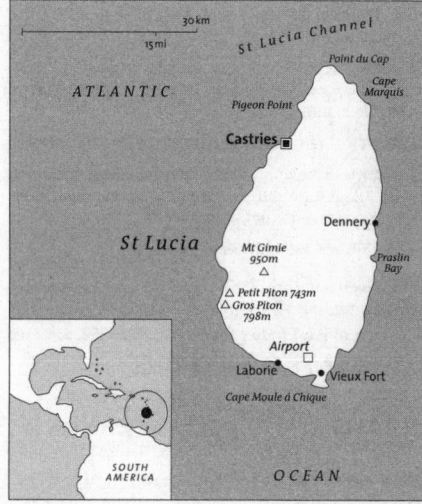

□ International Airport

17th–18th-c; British Crown Colony, 1814; full internal autonomy, 1967; independence, 1979; British monarch represented by a Governor-General; House of Assembly, elected every five years, and a Senate; constitutional amendment (Jul 2003) to replace oath of allegiance to Queen Elizabeth II with oath to St Lucia and its people.

Head of State
(British monarch represented by Governor-General)
1997–   Pearlette Louisy

Head of Government
1997–   Kenny Anthony

SAINT PIERRE AND MIQUELON >> FRANCE

SAINT VINCENT AND THE GRENADINES

Local name Saint Vincent and the Grenadines

Timezone GMT –4

Area 390 km²/150 sq mi

Population total (2002e) 113 100

Status Independent state within the Commonwealth

Date of independence 1979

Capital Kingstown

Languages English (official), with French patois widely spoken

Ethnic groups Black African descent (82%), mixed (14%), white, Asian, and Amerindian minorities

Religions Christian (Anglican 42%, Methodist 21%, Roman Catholic 12%)

Physical features Island group of the Windward Is, E Caribbean, comprising the island of St Vincent and the N Grenadine Is; St Vincent volcanic in origin; highest peak, Soufrière, active volcano 1234 m/4048 ft (N), most recent eruption, 1979.

Climate Tropical climate, average annual temperature, 25°C; average annual rainfall 1500 mm/60 in (coast), 3800 mm/150 in (interior).

Currency 1 East Caribbean Dollar (XCD) = 100 cents

Economy Based on agriculture; bananas, arrowroot (world's largest producer), coconuts, spices, sugar cane; food processing, textiles; tourism.

GDP (2002e) $339 mn, per capita $2900

HDI (2002) 0.733

History Visited by Columbus, 1498; British control, 1763; part of West Indies Federation, 1958–62; achieved

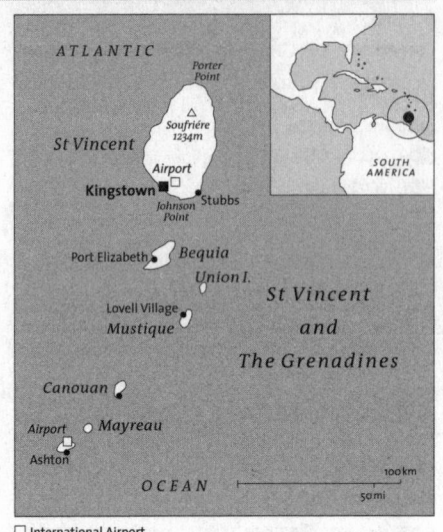

☐ International Airport

internal self-government, 1969; independence, 1979; British sovereign represented by a Governor-General; a Prime Minister leads a unicameral National Assembly.

Head of State
(British monarch represented by Governor-General)
2002–   Sir Freddy Ballantyne

Head of Government
2001–   Ralph Gonsalves

SALVADOR >> EL SALVADOR

SAMOA (formerly WESTERN SAMOA)

Local name Samoa i Sisifo (Samoan)

Timezone GMT –11

Area 2842 km²/1097 sq mi

Population total (2002e) 178 300

Status Independent state within the Commonwealth

Date of independence 1962

Capital Apia

Languages Samoan and English (official)

Ethnic groups Polynesian, with Pacific Islanders, Euronesian, Chinese, and European minorities

Religions Christian (99%) (Protestant 70%, Roman Catholic 20%, other 9%)

Physical features Two large (Upolu, Savai'i) and seven small islands in the South Pacific Ocean, 2600 km/ 1600 mi NE of Auckland, New Zealand; formed from ranges of extinct volcanoes, rising to 1829 m/6001 ft on Savai'i; last volcanic activity, 1905–11; thick tropical vegetation; several coral reefs along coast.

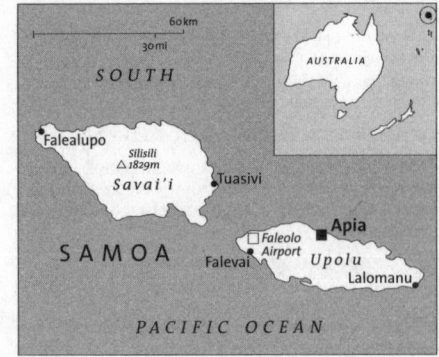

Climate Tropical climate; cool, dry season (May–Nov), average temperature 22°C; rainy season (Dec–Apr) with temperatures reaching 36°C; average annual rainfall, 2775 mm/109 in; frequent hurricanes.

Currency 1 Tala (SAT) = 100 sene

Economy Largely agricultural subsistence economy; taro, yams, breadfruit, pawpaws, coconuts, cocoa, bananas; tourism increasing; internal transportation system depends largely on roads and ferries; charter air service operates between the two main islands.

GDP (2002e) $1 bn, per capita $5600

HDI (2002) 0.715

History Visited by the Dutch, 1772; 1889 commission divided Samoa between Germany (which acquired Western Samoa) and the US (which acquired Tutuila and adjacent small islands, now known as American Samoa); New Zealand granted a League of Nations mandate for Samoa, 1919; UN Trust Territory under New Zealand, 1946; independence, 1962; joined the Commonwealth, 1970; governed by a Monarch as Head of State for life, a Prime Minister, and a 47-member Legislative Assembly (*Fono*).

Head of State (O le Ao O le Malo)
1963–   Malietoa Tanumafili II

Head of Government
1998–   Tuila'epa Sa'ilele Malielegaoi

SAN MARINO

Local name San Marino

Timezone GMT +1

Area 61 km²/23 sq mi

Population total (2002e) 27 700

Status Republic

Capital San Marino

Language Italian (official)

Ethnic groups Sanmarinesi (San Marino citizens) (87%), Italian (12%)

Religion Roman Catholic (95%)

Physical features Landlocked in C Italy; smallest republic in the world, land boundaries, 34 km/21 mi; ruggedly mountainous, centred on the limestone ridges of Monte Titano, 793 m/2602 ft, and the valley of R Ausa.

Climate Temperate climate, with cool winters, warm summers; average annual temperatures –6°C (Jan), 26°C (Jul); moderate rainfall; average annual rainfall 880 mm /35 in.

Currency 1 Euro (EUR) = 100 cents (before February 2002, 1 Italian Lira (ITL)/1 San Marino Lira = 100 centesimi)

Economy Wheat, grapes, cheese, livestock; postage stamps, tourism, textiles, pottery; chemicals, paints, wine.

GDP (2001e) $940 mn, per capita $34 600

History Founded by a 4th-c Christian saint as a refuge against religious persecution; treaty of friendship with the Kingdom of Italy, preserving independence, 1862; in World War 2, followed Italy and declared war on Britain, 1940; declared neutrality shortly before Italian surrender, 1943; governed by an elected unicameral Parliament (the Grand and General Council) and a Congress of State; Parliament elects two of its members every six months to act as Captains-Regent (*Capitani Reggenti*), with the functions of Head of State.

Secretary of State
2003–   Fabio Berardi

MAP >> ITALY

SÃO TOMÉ AND PRÍNCIPE

Local name São Tomé e Príncipe

Timezone GMT

Area 1001 km²/387 sq mi

Population total (2002e) 147 800

Status Democratic republic

Date of independence 1975

Capital São Tomé

Languages Portuguese (official), with a number of creoles spoken

Ethnic groups Portuguese-African descent, African minority

Religions Roman Catholic (80%), Seventh Day Adventist, and Evangelical Protestant

Physical features Equatorial volcanic islands in the Gulf of Guinea, off the coast of Equatorial Guinea, W Africa; comprise São Tomé, Príncipe, and several smaller islands; São Tomé (area 845 km²/326 sq mi),

H U M A N   G E O G R A P H Y

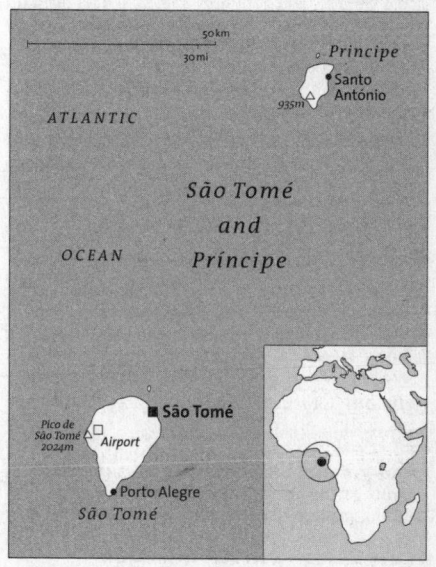

São Tomé and Príncipe (continued)

greatest height, 2024 m/6640 ft, Pico de São Tomé in central volcanic uplands; heavily forested.

Climate Tropical climate; average annual temperature 27°C (coast), 20°C (mountains); rainy season (Oct–May); annual average rainfall 500–1000 mm/20–40 in.

Currency 1 Dobra (STD) = 100 centimos

Economy Based on agriculture (employs c.70% of population); cocoa, copra, palm kernels, coffee, wine, fishing; restructured economy since 1985, with greater involvement in commerce, banking, and tourism.

GDP (2002e) $200 mn, per capita $1200

HDI (2002) 0.632

History Visited by the Portuguese, 1469–72; Portuguese colony, 1522; resistance to Portuguese rule led to riots in 1953, and the formation of an overseas liberation movement based in Gabon; independence, 1975; sole legal party was the Movement for the Liberation of São Tomé and Príncipe, until new constitution in 1990 approved multi-party democratic system; bloodless coup by army rebels (Jul 2003) during President de Menezes' visit to Nigeria; he returned when agreement to restore democratic rule was reached; governed by a President, Prime Minister, and a National Assembly.

Head of State
1991–2001 Miguel Trovoada
2001–   Fradique de Menezes

Head of Government
2005–6 Maria do Carmo Silveira
2006–   Tomé Soares da Vera Cruz

SAUDI ARABIA

Local name al-'Arabīyah as-Sa'ūdīyah (Arabic)

Timezone GMT +3

Area 2 331 000 km²/899 766 sq mi

Population total (2002e) 23 370 000

Status Kingdom

Capital Riyadh (Ar-Riyād)

Language Arabic (official)

Ethnic groups Arab (90%), Afro-Asian (10%)

Religions Muslim (Sunni 85%, Shi'ite 15%), small Christian minority

Physical features Comprises four-fifths of the Arabian peninsula; Red Sea coastal plain bounded E by mountains; highlands in SW contain Jebel Abha, Saudi Arabia's highest peak, 3133m/10279 ft; Arabian peninsula slopes gently N and E towards oil-rich al-Hasa plain on the Persian Gulf; interior comprises two extensive areas of sand desert, the An Nafud (N) and Rub' al-Khali (the Great Sandy Desert) (S); salt flats numerous in E lowlands; large network of wadis drains NE; 95% of land is arid or semi-arid desert.

Climate Hot, dry climate; average temperatures 21°C (N), 26°C (S), rise to 50°C in the interior; night frosts common in N and highlands; Red Sea coast hot and humid; average annual temperatures 14°C (Jan), 33°C (Jul) in Riyadh; average annual rainfall 10 mm/0.4 in.

Currency 1 Saudi Arabian Riyal (SAR) = 100 halalah

Economy Oil discovered in 1930s; now the world's leading oil exporter (reserves account for c.25% of world's known supply); rapidly-developing construction industry; large areas opened up for cultivation in 1980s; agriculture; wheat, dates, livestock; pilgrimage trade.

GDP (2002e) $268.9 bn, per capita $11 400

HDI (2002) 0.759

History Famed as the birthplace of Islam, a centre of pilgrimage to the holy cities of Mecca, Medina, and Jedda(h); modern state founded by Ibn Saud who by

□ International Airport   · – – Boundary awaiting demarcation

1932 united the four tribal provinces of Hejaz (NW), Asir (SW), Najd (C), and al-Hasa (E); governed as an absolute monarchy based on Islamic law and Arab Bedouin tradition; King (official title: Custodian of the Two Holy Mosques (Mecca and Medina)) is Head of State and Prime Minister, assisted by a Council of Ministers; there is no parliament; royal decree, 1992, provided for the creation of a Consultative Council.

Head of State/Government (Monarch)
Family name: al-Saud
2005–   Abdullah Bin-Abd-al-Aziz

SCOTLAND >> UNITED KINGDOM

SENEGAL

Local name Sénégal (French)

Timezone GMT

Area 196 790 km²/75 729 sq mi

Population total (2002e) 9 905 000

Status Republic

Date of independence 1960

Capital Dakar

Languages French (official), with various ethnic languages spoken

Ethnic groups Wolof (36%), Serer (19%), Fulani (13%), Toucouleur (9%), Diola (9%), Mandingo (9%), European and Lebanese (1%)

Religions Sunni Muslim (91%), Roman Catholic (5%), local beliefs (3%)

Physical features Located in W Africa; extensive low-lying basin of savannah and semi-desert vegetation to the N; sand dunes along coastline; dunes and mangrove forests in S, where land rises to around 500 m/1640 ft; lowland savannah and semi-desert regions of N drain into R Sénégal, which forms the N and NE boundary with Mauritania and Mali.

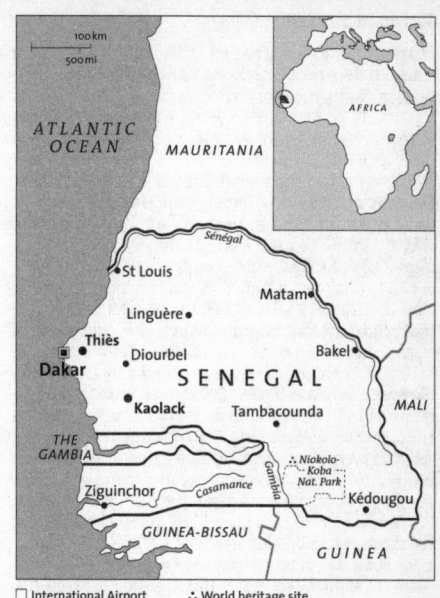

□ International Airport ∴ World heritage site

Climate Tropical climate; rainy season (Jun–Sep); high humidity levels and high night-time temperatures, especially on the coast; average temperature, 22–28°C; average annual rainfall 541 mm/21 in at Dakar.

Currency 1 CFA Franc (XAF) = 100 centimes

Economy Agriculture (employs c.75% of workforce); groundnuts, cotton, sugar, millet, sorghum, maize, livestock; minerals, iron ore, gold; oil, natural gas; fishing; timber; textiles, chemicals; shipbuilding and repairing; tourism.

GDP (2002e) $15.64 bn, per capita $1500

HDI (2002) 0.431

History Part of the Mali Empire, 14th–15th-c; French established a fort at Saint-Louis, 1658; incorporated as a territory within French West Africa, 1902; autonomous state within the French community, 1958; joined with French Sudan as independent Federation of Mali, 1959; withdrew in 1960 to become a separate independent republic; joined with The Gambia to form the Confederation of Senegambia, 1982–9; Confederation collapsed, 1989, following violent clashes between Senegalese and Mauritanians; governed by a President (elected for a 5-year term), Prime Minister, a Senate, and National Assembly.

Head of State
2000–   Abdoulaye Wade

Head of Government
2004–   Macky Sall

SERBIA

Local name Srbija

Timezone GMT +1

Area 88 361 km²/34 107 sq mi

Population total (2002e) 7 500 000 (excluding Kosovo)

Status Republic

Date of independence 2006

Capital Belgrade

Languages Serbian (official)

Ethnic groups Serbian (83%), Hungarian (4%), Bosniak (2%), Roma (1.5%), Yugoslavs (1%), many others under (1%)

Religions 1991: Serbian Orthodox (65%), Muslim (19%), Roman Catholic (4%), Protestant (1%), others (11%); current estimates not available

Physical features Landlocked country located in central Balkan Peninsula; mainly flat in N, mountainous in C and S areas; land rises to Dinaric Alps (W) and Stara Planina (E); fertile Danubian plain in NE; chief river, R Danube, also Morava, Sava, Tisza; linked to Adriatic Sea and Montenegro via Belgrade–Bar railway.

Climate Moderate, continental climate; average annual temperatures 0°C (Jan), 22°C (Jul) in Belgrade; average annual rainfall 610 mm/24 in.

Currency 1 Dinar (CSD) = 100 paras (in Kosovo 1 Euro (EUR) = 100 cents also legal)

Economy Manufactured goods, machinery, transport equipment, food products, wheat, maize, livestock, ore and stone mining.

GDP (2002e) $23.15 bn, per capita $2200 (former Serbia and Montenegro)

HUMAN GEOGRAPHY

HUMAN GEOGRAPHY

Serbia (continued)

History Serbia absorbed by Ottoman Empire during 15th-c–18th-c, became autonomous principality, 1817; Serbian independence recognized by international treaties, 1878; Kingdom of Serbs, Croats, and Slovenes formed 1918, renamed Kingdom of Yugoslavia, 1929; together with Slovenia, Macedonia, Croatia, Bosnia and Montenegro, became a republic in new Socialist Federal Republic of Yugoslavia under Josip Tito, 1945; revised constitution in 1974, instituted a rotating leadership, with the Prime Minister elected annually; governed by a bicameral Federal Assembly, comprising a Federal Chamber and a Chamber of Republics and Provinces; following a break with the USSR in 1948, the country followed an independent form of communism and a general policy of non-alignment; at the end of the 1980s political disagreement between the federal republics increased; ethnic unrest in Serbia (Kosovo); Slovenian unilateral declaration of independence, 1990, followed by Macedonian and Croatian declarations, 1991, considered illegal by central government; inter-republic talks on Yugoslavia's future, but confrontation between Croatia and Serb-dominated National Army developed into civil war, 1991; Serbian support of Serb guerrillas in Bosnia resulted in UN sanctions, mid-1992; arrival of UN Protection Force, 1992; Federal Republic of Yugoslavia declared, 1992, consisting of Montenegro and Serbia; fighting between ethnic groups in Bosnia continued until 1995, when peace accord signed in Dayton, Ohio; conflict in Kosovo between Serbia and ethnic Albanian resistance movement (Kosovo Liberation Army), 1997; escalation of conflict (early 1999) led to Serbian incursions into Kosovo and displacement of Kosovar Albanians; NATO air-strikes campaign against Yugoslav targets; President Milosovic accepted peace terms, with deployment of NATO troops into Kosovo and the departure of Serb forces; Milosevic ousted after elections, 2000, and arrested for crimes against humanity, 2001 (died while awaiting trial, 2006); new accord led to Union of Serbia and Montenegro, 2002, new constitution, 2003; referendum in Montenegro voted for independence from Serbia, 2006; Serbia declared itself an independent sovereign state (5 Jun

☐ International Airport

2006); new constitution (Oct 2006) defined Kosovo as autonomous province.

Head of State
2006–   Boris Tadic

Head of Government
2006–   Vojislav Kostunica

SEYCHELLES

Local name Seychelles

Timezone GMT +4

Area 455 km²/175 sq mi

Population total (2002e) 83 400

Status Republic

Date of independence 1976

Capital Victoria (on Mahé Island)

Languages Creole French (official since 1981), and English

Ethnic groups Seychellois (Asian, African, and European admixtures), Malagasy (3%), Chinese (2%), English (1%)

Religions Roman Catholic (90%)

Physical features Island group in SW Indian Ocean, N of Madagascar, comprising 115 islands; main islands include Mahé (largest), Praslin, and La Digue; islands fall into two main groups, a compact group of 41 mountain-

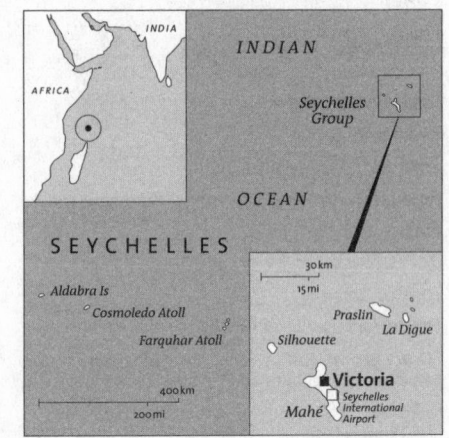

ous islands rising steeply from the sea, highest point 906 m/2972 ft on Mahé; and a group of low-lying coralline islands and atolls to the SW, flat, waterless and mostly uninhabited.

Climate Tropical climate; average annual temperature 27°C (Jan), 26°C (Jul); wet humid season (Dec–May); average annual rainfall 2375 mm/93.5 in.

Currency 1 Seychelles Rupee (SCR) = 100 cents

Economy Agriculture; fruit, vegetables, livestock, cinnamon, copra; brewing, plastics, steel fabricated goods, fishing; tourism.

GDP (2002e) $626 mn, per capita $7800

HDI (2002) 0.811

History Colonized by the French, 1768; captured by Britain, 1794; incorporated as a dependency of Mauritius, 1814; separate Crown Colony, 1903; independent republic within the Commonwealth, 1976; constitution, 1979, established a one-party state; governed by a President, elected for a 5-year term, a Council of Ministers, and a unicameral National Assembly; legislation legalizing the activity of opposition parties adopted, 1991.

Head of State/Government
2004–   James Michel

SIERRA LEONE

Local name Sierra Leone

Timezone GMT

Area 71 740 km²/27 692 sq mi

Population total (2002e) 4 823 000

Status Republic

Date of independence 1961

Capital Freetown

Languages English (official), with Krio widely spoken

Ethnic groups African origin (99%) (including Mendes, Temnes, Limbas, Korankos, and Lokos)

Religions Local beliefs (30%), Sunni Muslim (60%), Christian (Protestant 6%, Roman Catholic 2%)

Physical features Low narrow coastal plain in W Africa; rises to an average height of 500 m/1600 ft in the Loma Mts (E), highest point, Loma Mansa, 1948 m/6391 ft; Tingi Mts rise to 1853 m/6079 ft (SE); principal rivers include the Great Scarcies, Rokel, Gbangbaia, Jong, and Sewa.

Climate Equatorial climate; temperatures uniformly high throughout the year; average annual temperature 27°C; rainy season (May–Oct); highest rainfall on coast; average annual rainfall 3436 mm/135 in at Freetown.

Currency 1 Leone (SLL) = 100 cents

Economy Mining (most important sector of the economy); diamonds (represent c.60% of exports); bauxite, gold, titanium, iron ore, and other mineral and metal ores; subsistence agriculture (employs over 70% of population); rice, coffee, cocoa, citrus fruits; timber; food processing.

GDP (2002e) $2.826 bn, per capita $500

HDI (2002) 0.275

History First visited by Portuguese navigators and British slave traders; land bought from local chiefs by English philanthropists who established settlements for freed slaves, 1780s; British Crown Colony, 1808; hinterland declared a British protectorate, 1896; independence declared within the Commonwealth as a constitutional monarchy, 1961; period of military rule, 1967–8; became a republic, 1971; established as a one-party state, 1978; new constitution, 1991, allowing for multi-party politics, and interim government formed until general elections;

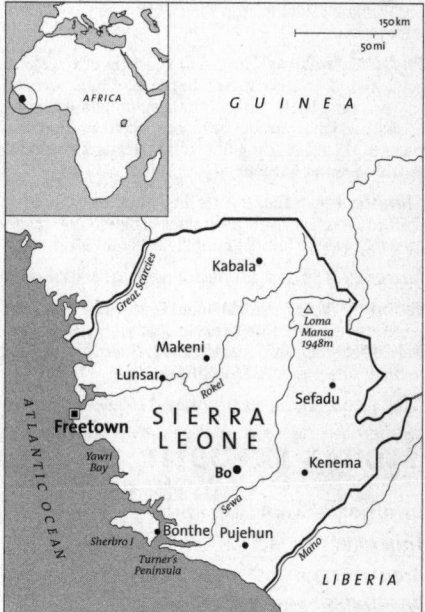

☐ International Airport

interrupted by military coup in 1992, House of Representatives dissolved, and Supreme Council of State (SCS) and Civilian Council of State Secretaries (Cabinet) established; further military coup, 1997; overturned, 1998; renewed fighting in early 1999, followed by Lomé (Togo) peace agreement (Jul) and establishment of UN peacekeeping force; UN troops attacked and abducted by rebels (Apr 2000), leading to a UK-sponsored military assistance plan within the country, and the arrival of UN reinforcements; peace declared, 2002.

Head of State/Government
1998–   Ahmad Tejan Kabbah

SINGAPORE

Local name Singapore

Timezone GMT +8

Area 618 km²/238 sq mi

Population total (2002e) 4 000 000

Status Republic

Date of independence 1965

Capital Singapore City

Languages English, Malay, Chinese, and Tamil (official)

Ethnic groups Chinese (77%), Malay (15%), Indian (6%)

Religions Chinese population mainly Buddhists, Malay mainly Muslim, also Taoist, Christian, and Hindu minorities

Physical features Located at the S tip of the Malay Peninsula, SE Asia; consists of the island of Singapore and c.50 adjacent islets; linked to Malaysia by a causeway across the Johor Strait; Singapore Island is low-lying, rising to 177 m/581 ft at Bukit Timah; Seletar River drains N-E; deep-water harbour (SE).

Climate Equatorial climate; high humidity; no clearly defined seasons; average annual temperature range, 21–34°C; average annual rainfall, 2438 mm/96 in.

Currency 1 Singapore Dollar/Ringgit (SGD) = 100 cents

Economy Major transshipment centre (one of world's largest ports); oil refining; rubber, food processing, chemicals, electronics; ship repair; financial services; fishing; tourism (affected by SARS outbreak, 2003).

GDP (2002e) $112.4 bn, per capita $25 200

HDI (2002) 0.885

History Originally part of the Sumatran Srivijaya kingdom; leased by the British East India Company, on the advice of Sir Stamford Raffles, from the Sultan of Johore, 1819; Singapore, Malacca, and Penang incorporated as the Straits Settlements, 1826; British Crown Colony, 1867; occupied by the Japanese, 1942–5; self-government, 1959; part of the Federation of Malaya from 1963 until its establishment as an independent state in 1965; governed by a President, a Prime Minister, and unicameral Parliament.

Head of State
1999–   Sellapan Ramanathan Nathan

Head of Government
1990–2004 Goh Chok Tong
2004–   Lee Hsien Loong

SLOVAK REPUBLIC

Local name Slovenská republiká

Timezone GMT +1

Area 49 035 km²/18 927 sq mi

Population total (2002e) 5 383 000

Status Republic

Date of independence 1993

Capital Bratislava

Languages Slovak (official), with Czech and Hungarian widely spoken

Ethnic groups Slovak (87%), Hungarian (11%), Czech (1%), with German, Polish, and Ukrainian minorities

Religions Roman Catholic (70%), Protestant (6%)

Physical features Dominated by the Carpathian Mountains, consisting of a system of E–W ranges separated by valleys and basins; ranges include the Low Tatras of the Inner Carpathians, 1829 m/6000 ft, and the highest point, Gerlachovsky, 2655 m/8711 ft in the Tatra Mts (N); main rivers include the Danube, Vah, Hron; national parks at Pieniny, Low and High Tatra.

Climate Continental climate; warm humid summers,

☐ International Airport

cold dry winters; snow remains on the mountains for 130 days of the year; average annual temperature –4°C (Jan), 18°C (Jul) in Bratislava; average annual rainfall 500–650 mm/20–30 in.

Currency 1 Slovak Koruna (SKK) = 100 halers

Economy Agricultural region, especially cereals, wine, fruit; steel production in Košice; heavy industry suffering since previously dependent on state subsidies.

GDP (2002e) $67.34 bn, per capita $12 400

HDI (2002) 0.835

History Settled in 5th–6th-c by Slavs; part of Great Moravia, 9th-c; part of Magyar Empire from 10th-c; became part of Kingdom of Hungary, 11th-c; united with Czech lands to form the separate state of Czechoslovakia, 1918; under German control, 1938–9; Slovakia became a separate republic under German influence, 1939; Czechoslovakia regained its independence, 1945; under Communist rule following 1948 coup; attempt at liberalization by Dubček terminated by intervention of War-

saw Pact troops, 1968; from 1960s, Slovaks revived efforts to gain recognition for Slovak rights; fall from power of Communist party, 1989; 1992 agreement to divide Czechoslovakia into its constituent republics led to declaration of independence of Slovak Republic, 1993; governed by a President, Prime Minister, Council of Ministers, and National Council.

Head of State
2004–   Ivan Gasparovic

Head of Government
1998–2006 Mikuláš Dzurinda
2006–   Robert Fico

SLOVENIA

Local name Slovenija

Timezone GMT +1

Area 20 251 km²/7817 sq mi

Population total (2002e) 1 948 000

Status Republic

Date of independence 1991

Capital Ljubljana

Languages Slovene, Croatian

Ethnic group Slovene (90%)

Religions Roman Catholic, Protestant, some Eastern Orthodox

Physical features Mountainous republic between Austria and Croatia; Slovenian Alps (NW) rise to 2863 m/9393 ft at Triglav in the Julian Alps (Julijske Alpe); rivers include Sava, Savinja, and Drava; chief port, Koper.

Climate Continental climate; more Mediterranean in W; average annual temperature –1°C (Jan), 19°C (Jul) in Ljubljana; average annual rainfall 1600 mm/63 in.

Currency (1991) 1 euro (EUR) = 100 cents (before Jan 2007, 1 Slovene Tolar (SIT) = 100 paras)

Economy Agriculture; maize, wheat, sugar beet, potatoes, livestock, wine, timber, lignite; textiles; large iron and steel plants; vehicles; coal, lead, mercury mining in W.

GDP (2002e) $37.06 bn, per capita $19 200

HDI (2002) 0.879

History Settled by Slovenes, 6th–8th-c; later controlled by Slavs and Franks; part of Austro-Hungarian Empire

☐ International Airport

until 1918; people's republic within Yugoslavia, 1946; declaration of full sovereignty, 1990; declaration of independence from Yugoslavia as Republic of Slovenia, 1991; opposed by central government, brief period of fighting on intervention of federal army who withdrew Aug 1991; tricameral legislature replaced by bicameral National Assembly, consisting of State Assembly and State Council.

Head of State
2002–   Janez Drnovšek

Head of Government
2004–   Janez Jansa

SOLOMON ISLANDS

Local name Solomon Islands

Timezone GMT +11

Land area 27 556 km²/10 637 sq mi

Population total (2002e) 439 000

Status Independent state within the Commonwealth

Date of independence 1978

Capital Honiara

Languages English (official), with pidgin English and c.80 local languages also spoken

Solomon Islands (continued)

Ethnic groups Melanesian (93%), Polynesian (4%), Micronesian (1.5%), European (1%), Chinese (0.5%)

Religions Christian (95%) (Protestant 41%, Anglican 34%, Roman Catholic 19%)

Physical features Archipelago of several hundred islands in the SW Pacific Ocean, stretching c.1400 km/ 870 mi between Papua New Guinea (NW) and Vanuatu (SE); six main islands, Choiseul, Guadalcanal, Malaita, New Georgia, San Cristobal (now Makira), Santa Isabel; highest point, Mt Makarakomburu, 2477 m/8126 ft, on Guadalcanal (largest island); large islands have forested mountain ranges and coastal belts; Anuta, Fataka, and Tikopia islands are volcanic.

Climate Equatorial climate; high humidity; average annual temperature 27°C; maximum rainfall Nov–Apr; average annual rainfall, c.3500 mm/138 in; periodic cyclones.

Currency 1 Solomon Islands Dollar (SBD) = 100 cents

Economy Based on agriculture; forestry, livestock, fisheries, taro, rice, bananas, yams, copra, oil palm; milling, fish processing; crafts.

GDP (2001e) $800 mn, per capita $1700

HDI (2002) 0.622

History Visited by Spanish, 1568; S Solomon Is placed under British protection, 1893; outer islands (Santa Cruz group) added to protectorate, 1899; scene of fierce fighting in World War 2; achieved internal self-government,

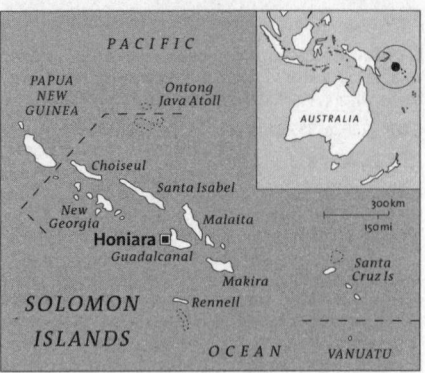

□ International Airport

1976; independence, 1978; British monarch represented by a Governor-General; Prime Minister leads a unicameral National Parliament; fighting between two rival militias led to military coup, 2000; peace treaty brokered by Australia, but continued ethnic unrest; Australian-led peace-keeping force, 2003; further Australian intervention, 2006.

Head of State
(British monarch represented by Governor-General)
2004–   Nathaniel Waena

Head of Government
2006–   Manasseh Sogavare

SOMALIA

Local name Somaliya

Timezone GMT +3

Area 637 357 km²/246 201 sq mi

Population total (2002e) 7 753 000

Status Republic

Date of independence 1960

Capital Mogadishu

Languages Somali, Arabic (official)

Ethnic groups Somali (85%), Bantu (15%), with Arab, European, and Asian minorities

Religions Sunni Muslim (99%), small Christian minority

Physical features Occupies E Horn of Africa, where dry coastal plain broadens to the S, and rises inland to a plateau c.1000 m/3300 ft; forested mountains on the Gulf of Aden coast rise to 2416 m/7926 ft at Mt Shimbiris; main rivers, Jubba and Webi Shabeelle.

Climate Predominantly arid; average daily maximum temperatures 28–32°C in Mogadishu; average annual rainfall 490 mm/19.3 in; heavier rainfall (Apr–Sep) on E coast; serious, persistent threat of drought; coast hit by Indian Ocean tsunami, 2004.

Currency 1 Somali Shilling (SoS) = 100 cents

Economy Agriculture (c.50% nomadic people raising cattle, sheep, goats, camels); bananas, sugar, spices, cotton, rice, citrus fruits, tobacco, iron ore; textiles; fishing.

□ International Airport

GDP (2001e) $4.27 bn, per capita $600

History Settled by Muslims, 7th-c; Italian, French, and British interests after opening of Suez Canal, 1869; after World War 2, Somalia formed by amalgamation of Italian and British protectorates; independence, 1960; from 1960s, territorial conflict with Ethiopia over Ogaden which has large Somali population; military coup, 1969; peace agreement with Ethiopia, 1989; governed by a President, Council of Ministers, and People's Assembly; new constitution approved, 1990; NW region seceded as Somaliland Republic, 1991; civil war, 1991–2, forced UN intervention to safeguard food supplies, 1992; gradual withdrawal of forces, 1993–5; National Salvation Council formed, 1997; transitional government formed, 2000; further peace agreement signed by 42 of the main fac-

tions, 2004; members of first parliament for 13 years sworn in, Aug 2004; conflict between Mogadishu warlords and Islamists, resulting in Islamist control of the S, 2006; Islamists defeated by Ethiopian-backed government forces, Dec 2006.

Head of State
2004–   Abdullahi Yusuf Ahmed

Head of Government
2004–   Ali Mohamed Ghedi

SOUTH AFRICA

Local name South Africa
Timezone GMT +2
Area 1 233 404 km²/476 094 sq mi
Population total (2002e) 45 172 000
Status Republic
Date of independence 1961
Capitals Cape Town (legislative); Pretoria (administrative); Bloemfontein (judicial)
Languages (co-official) Afrikaans, English, Ndebele, Pedi, Sotho, Swazi, Tsonga, Tswana, Venda, Xhosa, Zulu
Ethnic groups Black African (70%), white (18%), Asian (3%), Coloured (9%)
Religions Christian (most whites and Coloureds and c.60% Africans), traditional beliefs, Hindu, Muslim, and Jewish minorities
Physical features Occupies the S extremity of the African plateau; fringed by fold mountains and a lowland coastal margin to the W, E, and S; N interior comprises the Kalahari Basin, scrub grassland, and arid desert; Great Escarpment rises E to 3482 m/11 424 ft at Thabana Ntlenyana; Orange R flows W to meet the Atlantic; chief tributaries, Vaal and Caledon rivers.
Climate Subtropical in E; average annual temperature 4°C (Jan), 17°C (Jul) in Cape Town; average annual rainfall 1008 mm/39.7 in Durban; dry moistureless climate on W coast; desert region further N, annual average rainfall less than 30 mm/1.2 in.
Currency 1 Rand (ZAR) = 100 cents
Economy Industrial growth as a result of 19th-c gold (c.50% of export income) and diamond discoveries; grain, wool, sugar, tobacco, cotton, citrus fruit, dairy products, livestock, fishing; motor vehicles, machinery, chemicals, fertilizers, textiles, clothes, metal products, electronics, computers, tourism.
GDP (2002e) $427.7 bn, per capita $10 000
HDI (2002) 0.695
History Originally inhabited by Khoisan tribes; Portuguese reached the Cape of Good Hope, late 15th-c; settled by Dutch, 1652; arrival of British, 1795; British annexation of the Cape, 1806; Great Trek by Boers NE across the Orange R to Natal, 1836; first Boer republic founded, 1839; Natal annexed by the British in 1843, but the Boer republics of Transvaal (founded 1852) and Orange Free State (1854) were recognized; Zulu War, 1879; South African Wars, 1880–1, 1899–1902; Transvaal, Natal, Orange Free State, and Cape Province joined as the

□ International Airport

Union of South Africa, a dominion of the British Empire, 1910; sovereign state within the Commonwealth, 1931–61; independent republic, 1961; independence granted by South Africa to Transkei (1976), Bophuthatswana (1977), Venda (1979) and Ciskei (1981), not recognized internationally; politics dominated by treatment of non-white majority following the apartheid (racial segregation) policy after 1948; continuing racial violence and strikes led to a state of emergency in 1986, and several countries imposed economic and cultural sanctions; progressive dismantling of apartheid system by F W de Klerk from 1990; black Nationalist leader Nelson Mandela freed after more than 27 years in prison, and the African National Congress unbanned, 1990; readmitted into international sport, USA lifted trade and investment sanctions, 1991; most remaining apartheid legislation abolished, 1991; new constitution, 1996; governed by a President, Cabinet, National Assembly and Senate; elections in May 1994 brought victory to the ANC.

Head of State/Government
1994–9   Nelson Rolihlahla Mandela
1999–   Thabo Mbeki

HUMAN GEOGRAPHY

Spain (continued)

South African Provinces

Name	Area km²	sq mi	Capital
Eastern Cape	170616	65858	Bisho
Mpumalanga	81816	31581	Nelspruit
KwaZulu Natal	91481	35312	Pietermaritzburg/ Ulundi
North-West	118710	45822	Mmabatho
Northern Cape	363389	140268	Kimberley

Name	Area km²	sq mi	Capital
Limpopo (Northern Province)	119606	46168	Pietersburg
Free State	129437	49963	Bloemfontein
Gauteng	18760	7241	Johannesburg/ Pretoria
Western Cape	129386	49943	Cape Town

SOUTH GEORGIA >> UNITED KINGDOM

SOUTH KOREA >> KOREA, SOUTH

SOUTH SANDWICH ISLANDS >> UNITED KINGDOM

SPAIN

Local name España (Spanish)

Timezone GMT +1

Area 504750 km²/194833 sq mi

Population total (2002e) 40998000

Status Kingdom

Capital Madrid

Languages Spanish (official) with Catalan, Galician, and Basque also spoken in their respective regions

Ethnic groups Spanish (Castilian, Valencian, Andalusian, Asturian) (73%), Catalan (16%), Galician (8%), Basque (2%)

Religions Roman Catholic (99%), other Christian (including Anglican, Baptist, Evangelical, Mormon, Jehovah's Witnesses) and Muslim minorities

Physical features Located in SW Europe, occupying four-fifths of the Iberian peninsula; includes the Canary Is, Balearic Is, several islands off the coast of N Africa, as well as the Presidios of Ceuta and Melilla in N Morocco; mostly a furrowed C plateau (the Meseta, average height 700 m/2300 ft) crossed by mountains; Andalusian or Baetic Mts (SE) rise to 3478 m/11 411 ft at Mulhacén; Pyrénées (N) rise to 3404 m/11 168 ft at Pico de Aneto; rivers run E–W, notably the Tagus, Ebro, Guadiana, Miñho, Duero, Guadalquivir, Segura, Júcar.

Climate Continental climate in the Meseta and Ebro Basin, with hot summers, cold winters, low rainfall; highest rainfall in the mountains; S Mediterranean coast has warmest winter temperatures on European mainland; average annual temperatures 5°C (Jan), 25°C (Jul) in Madrid; average annual rainfall 419 mm/16.5 in.

Currency 1 Euro (EUR) = 100 cents (before February 2002, 1 Peseta (ESP) = 100 céntimos)

Economy Traditional agricultural economy gradually being supplemented by varied industries; textiles, iron, steel, shipbuilding, electrical appliances, cars, wine; forestry; fishing; tourism; zinc and other mineral ores; cereals, olives, almonds, pomegranates; member of EC, 1986.

GDP (2002e) $850.7 bn, per capita $21 200

HDI (2002) 0.913

History Early inhabitants included Iberians, Celts, Phoenicians, Greeks, and Romans; Muslim domination

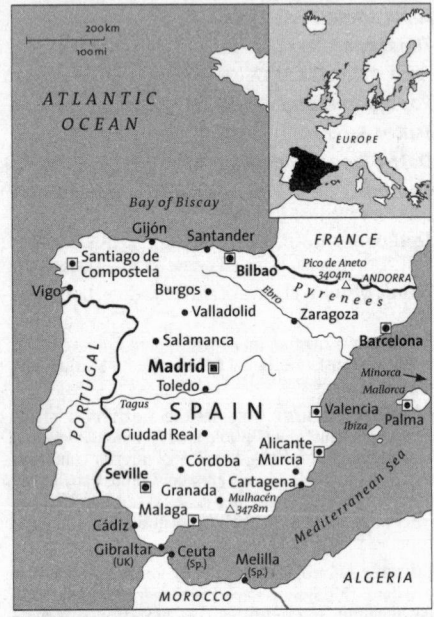

☐ International Airport

1 PRINCIPADO DE ASTURIAS 4 COMUNIDAD FORAL DE NAVARRA
2 CANTABRIA 5 LA RIOJA
3 PAÍS VASCO 6 COMUNIDAD DE MADRID

from the 8th-c; Christian reconquest completed by 1492; a monarchy since unification of Kingdoms of Castile, León, Aragón, and Navarre, largely achieved by 1572; 16th-c exploration of New World, and growth of Spanish Empire; period of decline after Revolt of the Netherlands, 1581, and defeat of Spanish Armada, 1588; War of Spanish Succession, 1701–14; Peninsular War against Napoleon, 1808–14; war with USA in 1898 led to loss of Cuba, Puerto Rico, and remaining Pacific possessions; dictatorship under Primo de Rivera (1923–30), followed by exile of the King and establishment of Second Republic, 1931; military revolt headed by Franco led to civil war and Fascist dictatorship, 1936; Prince Juan Carlos of Bourbon nominated to succeed Franco, 1969; acceded, 1975; terrorist bombs at Madrid railway stations killed over 200 (Mar 2004); under 1978 constitution, the Kingdom of Spain is a constitutional monarchy; Monarch appoints the Prime Minister; governed by a bicameral Parliament (Cortes Generales) comprising a Congress of Deputies and a Senate; move towards local government autonomy with creation of 17 self-governing regions.

Head of State (Monarch)
1975–   Juan Carlos I

Head of Government
2004–   José Luis Rodríguez Zapatero

Balearic islands

Local name Islas Baleares

Area 5014 km²/1935 sq mi

Population total (2000e) 712 000

Status Province of Spain

Capital Palma de Mallorca

Physical features Archipelago of five major islands and 11 islets in the Mediterranean, near the E coast of Spain; E group of islands consists of Mallorca (Majorca), Menorca, Cabrera; Ibiza and Formentera (W group); popular tourist resorts.

Climate Continental; average annual temperatures 11°C (Jan), 25°C (Jul); average annual rainfall 347 mm/14 in.

Currency 1 Euro (EUR) = 100 cents (formerly, 1 Peseta (ESP) = 100 céntimos)

Economy Tourism; fruit, wine, grain, cattle, fishing, textiles, chemicals, cork, timber.

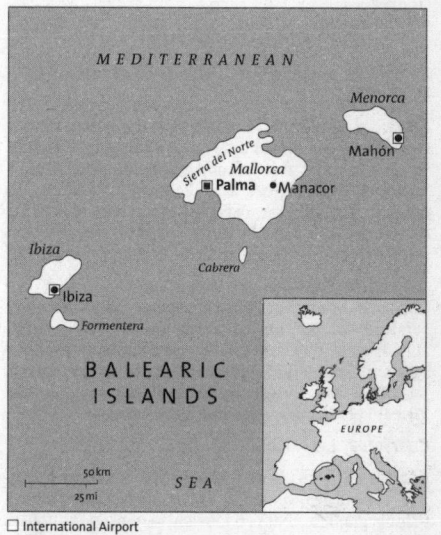

□ International Airport

Canary islands

Local name Islas Canarias

Area 7273 km²/2807 sq mi

Population total (2000e) 1 475 000

Status Forms two provinces of Spain

Chief town Las Palmas

Physical features Island archipelago, located in the Atlantic, 100 km/60 mi off the NW coast of Africa; includes the islands of Tenerife, La Palma, Gomera, Hierro, Grand Canary (Gran Canaria), Fuerteventura, Lanzarote, and several uninhabited islands; major ports, Las Palmas, Santa Cruz; volcanic and mountainous, the Pico de Teide rises to 3718 m/12 198 ft on Tenerife; tourist resorts on main islands.

Climate Continental; average annual temperature 18°C (Jan), 24°C (Jul); average annual rainfall 196 mm/8 in.

Currency 1 Euro (EUR) = 100 cents (before February 2002, 1 Peseta (ESP) = 100 céntimos)

Economy Tourism; agriculture, fishing, canning, textiles, leatherwork, footwear, cork, timber, chemical and metal products.

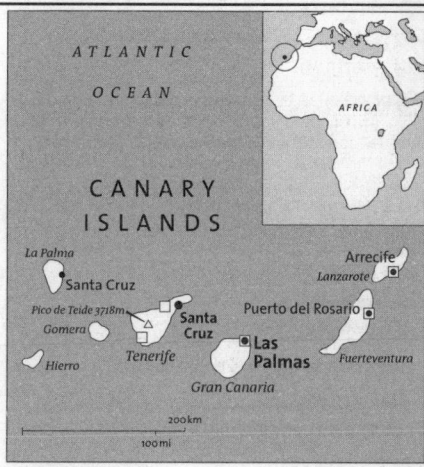

□ International Airport

HUMAN GEOGRAPHY

SRI LANKA

Local name Sri Lanka

Timezone GMT +5.5

Area 65 610 km²/25 sq mi

Population total (2002e) 18 870 000

Status Republic

Date of independence 1972

Capital Sri-Jayawardenapura (since 1983); (former capital, Colombo)

Languages Sinhala, Tamil (official), English also spoken

Ethnic groups Sinhalese (74%), Tamil (18%), Muslim (7%), Burgher, Malay, and Veddha (1%)

Religions Buddhist (69%), Hindu (15%), Christian (8%), Muslim (8%)

Physical features Island state in the Indian Ocean; separated from the Indian sub-continent by the Palk Strait, linked by a series of coral islands known as Adam's Bridge; low-lying areas in N and S, surrounding SC uplands; highest peak, Pidurutalagala, 2524 m/8281 ft; coastal plain fringed by sandy beaches and lagoons; c.50% of land is tropical monsoon forest or open woodland.

Climate Equatorial, tropical climate; modified temperatures in interior according to altitude; average annual temperature 27°C in Sri-Jayawardenapura; average annual rainfall 2527 mm/99.5 in; greatest rainfall on SW coast and in the mountains; monsoon season (Dec–Feb) in NE, dry, semi-arid for rest of year.

Currency 1 Sri Lanka Rupee (LKR) = 100 cents

Economy Agriculture (employs 52% of labour force); rice, rubber, tea, coconuts, spices, sugar cane; timber, fishing; graphite, coal, precious and semi-precious stones; electricity produced largely by water power; textiles, chemicals, paper.

GDP (2002e) $73.7 bn, per capita $3700

HDI (2002) 0.741

History Visited by Portuguese, 1505; taken by Dutch, 1658; British occupation, 1796; British colony, 1802; Tamil labourers brought in from S India during colonial

☐ International Airport

rule, to work on coffee and tea plantations; Dominion status, 1948; changed name of Ceylon and became independent republic of Sri Lanka, 1972; acute political tension between Buddhist Sinhalese majority and Hindu Tamil minority, who want an independent state in N and E (Liberation Tigers of Tamil Eelam, LTTE); state of emergency declared, 1983; ceasefire agreed, 1994, but conflict soon resumed; ceasefire agreed, 2001, but conflict ongoing; power-sharing proposals (Nov 2003); governed by a President, Prime Minister, and National State Assembly; parliament dissolved (Feb 2004), followed by minority government; E coast devastated by tsunami, 2004.

Head of State
2005– Mahinda Rajapakse

Head of Government
2005– Ratnasiri Wickremanayake

SUDAN, THE

Local name As-Sūdān (Arabic)

Timezone GMT +2

Area 2 505 870 km²/967 243 sq mi

Population total (2002e) 37 090 000

Status Republic

Date of independence 1956

Capital Khartoum

Languages Arabic (official), local languages, including Darfurian, Nilotic, and Nilo-Hamitic, are also spoken

Ethnic groups Black (52%), Arab (39%), Beja (6%)

Religions Muslim (Sunni 70%), traditional animist beliefs (20%), Christian (5%)

Physical features Largest country on the African continent, astride the middle reaches of the R Nile; E edge formed by Nubian Highlands and an escarpment rising c.2000 m/6500 ft on the Red Sea; Imatong Mts (S) rise to 3187 m/10 456 ft at Kinyeti, highest point in Sudan; Darfur Massif in the W; White Nile flows N to meet the Blue Nile at Khartoum.

Climate Tropical, continental; desert conditions in

NW, with temperatures rarely falling below 24°C; hottest months (Jul–Aug); sandstorms common; average annual temperature 23°C (Jan), 32°C (Jul) in Khartoum; average annual rainfall 157 mm/6.2 in.

Currency 1 Sudanese dinar (SDD) = 100 piastres

Economy Agriculture (employs c.75% of population); commercial farming (N) and livestock farming (S); large-scale irrigation schemes, fed by dams; major famines, especially 1984–5, 1990–1; gum arabic (80% of world supply); reserves of copper, lead, iron ore, chromite, manganese, gold; hindered by poor transport system.

GDP (2002e) $52.9 bn, per capita $1400

HDI (2002) 0.499

History Christianized in 6th-c; Muslim conversion from 13th-c; Egyptian control of N Sudan, early 19th-c; Mahdi unified W and C tribes in a revolution, 1881; fall of Khartoum, 1885; combined British-Egyptian offensive, 1898, leading to a jointly administered condominium; independence, 1956; military rule following coup in 1985; drought and N–S rivalry contributed to years of instability and several coups; transitional constitution of 1987 provided for a President, Prime Minister, Council of Ministers, and Legislative Assembly; military coup, 1989; civil war between government and rebel Sudanese People's Liberation Army (SPLM); new constitution, 1998; peace talks, 2003; peace accord, 2004; attacks by Janjaweed militia in Darfur region ongoing; peace agreement between government and SPLM, 2005; formation of government of national unity, 2005.

□ International Airport   − − Border in dispute

Head of State/Government

1993–   Omar Hassan Ahmad al-Bashir

SURINAME

Local name Suriname

Timezone GMT –3

Area 163 265 km²/63 020 sq mi

Population total (2002e) 436 000

Status Republic

Date of independence 1975

Capital Paramaribo

Languages Dutch (official), Hindi and Javanese (native languages), Sranan Tongo, Chinese and Spanish also spoken

Ethnic groups Indo-Pakistan (37%), Creole (31%), Javanese (15%), Amerindian (3%), Chinese (2%), European (1%)

Religions Hindu (27%), Protestant (25%), Roman Catholic (23%), Muslim (20%), indigenous beliefs (5%)

Physical features Located in NE South America; N natural regions, range from coastal lowland through savannah to mountainous upland; coastal strip covered by swamp; highland interior (S) overgrown with dense tropical forest; highest point, Juliana Top, 1230 m/4035 ft, in SC; seven major rivers including Marowijne (E), Corantijn (W), Suriname.

Climate Equatorial tropical, uniformly hot and humid; two rainy seasons (May-Jul, Nov-Jan); average annual temperatures 22–33°C in Paramaribo; average monthly rainfall 310 mm/12.2 in (N), 67 mm/2.6 in (S).

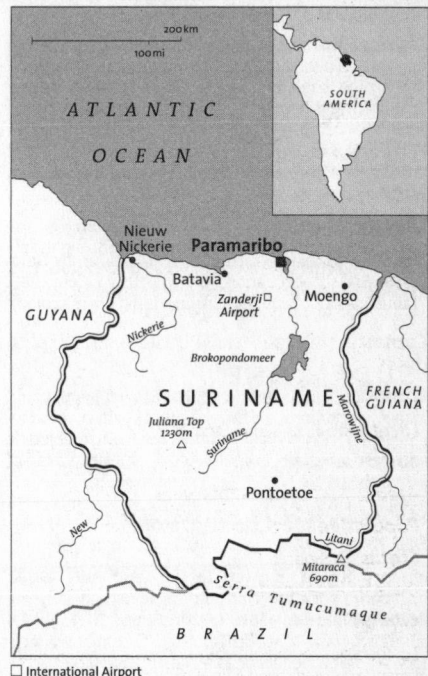

□ International Airport

Suriname (continued)

Currency 1 Suriname dollar (SRD) = 100 cents (before 2004, 1 Suriname guilder (SRG) = 100 cents)

Economy Based on agriculture and mining, but hindered by lack of foreign exchange; bauxite mining (provides c.80% of export income); sugar cane, rice, citrus fruits, coffee, bananas, oil palms, cacao, fishing; vast timber resources.

GDP (2002e) $1.469 bn, per capita $3400

HDI (2002) 0.756

History Sighted by Columbus, 1498; first settled by the British, 1651; taken by the states of Zeeland, 1667; captured by the British, 1799; restored to the Netherlands,

1814 and remained part of Netherland West Indies as Dutch Guiana; independence as the Republic of Suriname, 1975; emigration of c.40% of population to the Netherlands, following independence; military coup, 1980; ban on political activities lifted, 1985; 1987 constitution provides for a National Assembly, and a President elected by the Assembly.

Head of State (President)
2000–   Ronald Ventiaan

Head of Government (Vice-President)
2000–   Jules Ajodhia

SWAZILAND

Local name Swaziland

Timezone GMT +2

Area 17 363 km²/6702 sq mi

Population total (2002e) 1 124 000

Status Kingdom

Date of independence 1968

Capital Mbabane

Languages English and Siswati (official)

Ethnic groups Swazi (97%), European (3%)

Religions Christian (Roman Catholic, Anglican, Methodist, and Evangelical Lutheran) (57%), traditional animist beliefs (40%)

Physical features Landlocked, in SE Africa; divided into four topographical regions: mountainous Highveld (W), highest point Emblembe, 1862 m/6109 ft; heavily populated Middleveld (C), descending to 600–700 m/2000–2300 ft; rolling, bush-covered Lowveld (E), irrigated by river systems; Lubombo escarpment, covering 90% of the territory; main rivers, Komati, Usutu, Mbuluzi, flow W–E.

Climate Temperate; tropical in W, with relatively little rain, 500–890 mm/20–35 in; susceptible to drought; subtropical and drier in C; average annual temperature 15°C (Jul), 22°C (Jan) in Mbabane; average annual rainfall 1402 mm/55 in; rainy season (Nov–Mar).

Currency 1 Lilangeni (plural Emalangeni) (SZL) = 100 cents

Economy Agriculture (employs 70% of population); maize, groundnuts, beans, sorghum, cotton, tobacco, pineapples, citrus; sugar refining, several hydroelectric schemes; asbestos, iron ore, coal, textiles, cement, paper, chemicals.

GDP (2002e) $5.542 bn, per capita $4800

HDI (2002) 0.577

History Arrival of Swazi in the area, early 19th-c; boundaries with the Transvaal decided, and independence guaranteed, 1881; British agreed to Transvaal administration, 1894; British High Commission territory, 1903; independence as a constitutional monarchy

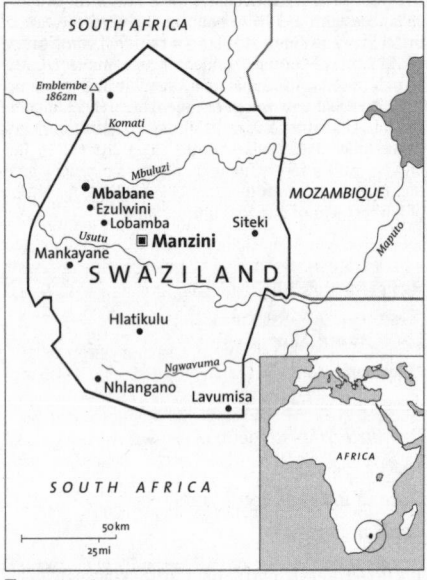

□ International Airport

within the Commonwealth, 1968; all political parties are banned under 1978 constitution; governed by a bicameral Parliament consisting of a National Assembly and a Senate; the King has considerable executive power, appointing a Cabinet and Prime Minister.

Head of State (Monarch)
1986–   Mswati III

Head of Government
2003–   Absalom Themba Dlamini

SWEDEN

Local name Sverige (Swedish)

Timezone GMT +1

Area 411 479 km²/158 830 sq mi

Population total (2002e) 8 925 000

Status Kingdom

Capital Stockholm

Languages Swedish (official), Finnish and Lapp in N

Ethnic groups Swedish (91%), Finns, with Polish, Turkish, W German, Chilean, Iranian, and other minorities

Religions Lutheran Protestant (93%), Roman Catholic (2%), Scandinavian Jewish minorities

Physical features Occupies the E side of the Scandinavian peninsula; 15% of country lies N of the Arctic Circle; large amount of inland water (9%); chief lakes being Vänern, Vättern, and Mälaren; many coastal islands, notably Gotland and Öland; c.57% forested; Kjölen Mts (W) form much of the boundary with Norway; highest peak, Kebnekaise, 2111 m/6926 ft; several rivers flow SE towards the Gulf of Bothnia.

Climate Continental, with cold winters and mild summers; rainfall lowest in SW; winters warmer in SW; enclosed parts of Baltic Sea often freeze in winter and can remain frozen for up to 6 months; continuous daylight in N during Arctic summer produces mean temperatures of −10°C (Jan), 15°C (Jul).

Currency 1 Swedish Krona (SEK) = 100 øre

Economy Gradual shift in the economy from the traditional emphasis on raw materials (timber and iron ore) to advanced technology; transportation equipment, electronics, electrical equipment, chemicals, engineering, steelmaking, non-ferrous metals; hydroelectricity provides 70% of power; wheat, barley, oats, sugar beet, cattle, fishing; tourism.

GDP (2002e) $230.7 bn, per capita $26 000

HDI (2002) 0.941

History Formed from the union of the kingdoms of the Goths and Svears, 7th-c; Danes continued to rule in the extreme S (Skåne) until 1658; united with Denmark and Norway under Danish leadership, 1389; union ended in 1527, following revolt led by Gustavus Vasa; Sweden

□ International Airport

acquired Norway from Denmark, 1814; union with Norway dissolved, 1905; a neutral country since 1814; Social Democratic Party controlled government, 1932–76 and returned to power, 1982; a representative and parliamentary democracy, with a Monarch as Head of State; governed by a Prime Minister and a unicameral Parliament (*Riksdag*) elected every three years.

Head of State (Monarch)
1973–   Carl XVI Gustaf

Head of Government
2006–   Fredrik Reinfeldt

SWITZERLAND

Local names Schweiz (German), La Suisse (French), Svizzera (Italian)

Timezone GMT +1

Area 41 228 km²/15 914 sq mi

Population total (2002e) 7 282 000

Status Confederation

Date of independence 1291

Capital Bern (Berne)

Languages German, French, Italian, Romansch (official), Spanish and Turkish also spoken

Ethnic groups (of Swiss nationals) German (64%), French (20%), Italian (4%), Romansch (1%)

Religions Christian (Roman Catholic 49%, Protestant 48%), Jewish minority

Physical features Landlocked, with Alps running roughly E–W in the S; highest peak, Dufourspitze, 4634 m/15 203 ft; Pre-Alps (NW) average 2000 m/6500 ft;

HUMAN GEOGRAPHY

HUMAN GEOGRAPHY

Switzerland (continued)

sparsely-forested Jura Mts run SW–NW; mean altitude of C plateau, 580 m/1900 ft, fringed with great lakes; chief rivers, Rhine, Rhône, Inn, and tributaries of the Po; c.3000 sq km/1160 sq mi of glaciers, notably the Aletsch.

Climate Temperate climate, subject to Atlantic, Mediterranean and E and C European influences; warm summers, with considerable rainfall; perennial snow cover above 300m/9842 ft; average annual temperature 0°C (Jan), 19°C (Jul) in Bern; average annual rainfall 1000 mm/40 in; the Föhn (warm wind) noticeable late winter and spring in the Alps.

Currency 1 Swiss Franc (CHF) = 100 centimes

Economy Increased specialization and development in high-technology products; machinery, precision instruments, watches, drugs, chemicals, textiles; a major financial centre; headquarters of many international organizations; all-year tourist area; dairy farming, wheat, potatoes, sugar beet, grapes, apples.

GDP (2002e) $230.7 bn, per capita $26 000

HDI (2002) 0.941

History Part of the Holy Roman Empire, 10th-c; Swiss Confederation created, 1291; expanded during 14th-c; centre of the Reformation, 16th-c; Swiss independence and neutrality recognized under the Treaty of Westphalia, 1648; conquered by Napoleon, who instituted the Helvetian Republic, 1798; organized as a confederation of cantons, 1815; federal constitution, 1848; Red Cross founded, 1863; neutral in both World Wars; helped form European Free Trade Association, 1960; Jura became 23rd canton of Switzerland, 1979; became full member of the UN, 2002; bicameral Federal Association comprising a

☐ International Airport

Council of States (*Ständerat*) and a National Council (*Nationalrat*); President elected yearly by Federal Council.

Head of State/Government

2004	Joseph Deiss
2005	Samuel Schmid
2006	Moritz Leuenberger

SYRIA

Local name as-Suriyah (Arabic)

Timezone GMT +2

Area 185 180 km²/71 479 sq mi

Population total (2002e) 17 156 000

Status Republic

Date of independence 1946

Capital Damascus

Languages Arabic (official), Kurdish, Armenian, Aramaic, and Circassian also spoken

Ethnic groups Arab (90%), Kurd, Armenian, Turkish, Circassian, and Assyrian

Religions Muslim (Sunni Muslim 74%, Alawite, Druse, and other sects 16%), Christian (10%)

Physical features Narrow Mediterranean coastal plain; Jabal al Nusayriyah mountain range rises to c.1500 m/ 5000 ft; steep drop (E) to Orontes R valley; Anti-Lebanon range (SW) rises to 2814 m/9232 ft at Mt Hermon; open steppe and desert to the E.

Climate Coastal Mediterranean, hot, dry summers, mild, wet winters; desert or semi-desert climate in 60% of country; annual rainfall below 200 mm/8 in; Khamsin wind causes temperatures to rise to 43–9°C; average annual temperatures 7°C (Jan), 27°C (Jul) in Damascus.

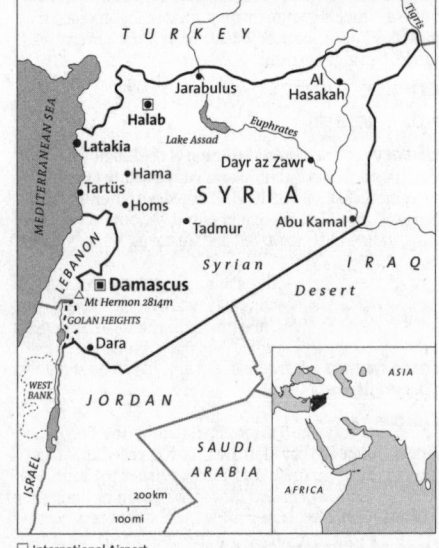

☐ International Airport

Currency 1 Syrian pound (SYP) = 100 piastres

Economy Oil (most important source of export revenue since 1974); Euphrates dam project (begun 1978) presently supplies 97% of domestic electricity; intended to increase arable land by 6400 km²/2500 sq mi; food processing; textiles; tobacco; cement.

GDP (2002e) $63.48 bn, per capita $3700

HDI (2002) 0.691

History Part of Phoenician Empire; Islam introduced in 7th-c; conquered by Turks, 11th-c; part of Ottoman Empire, 1517; brief period of independence in 1920, then made a French mandate; independence, 1946; merged with Egypt and Yemen to form United Arab Republic, 1958; re-established as independent state under present name, 1961; Golan Heights region seized by Israel, 1967;

after outbreak of civil war in Lebanon (1975), Syrian troops sent to restore order and became much involved in the region's power struggle until withdrawn (Apr 2005); breaking of diplomatic relations with Great Britain, 1986; condemned Iraqi invasion of Kuwait and sent allied forces troops in Gulf War in 1990, restoring relations; accepted US proposals for terms of an Arab–Israeli peace conference, 1991; governed by a President, Prime Minister, and 250-member People's Council.

Head of State
2000–   Bashar al-Assad

Head of Government
2003–   Muhammad Naji al-Utri

TAIWAN

Local name T'aiwan

Timezone GMT +8

Area 36 000 km²/13 896 sq mi

Population total (2002e) 22 457 000

Status Republic

Date of independence 1949

Capital Taibei

Languages Mandarin Chinese (official), various dialects including Taiwanese and Hakka also spoken

Ethnic groups Han Chinese (98%), small (Polynesian) aboriginal minority

Religions Taoist, Buddhist, Christian (Protestant and Roman Catholic)

Physical features Consists of Taiwan I and several smaller islands c.130 km/80 mi off the SE coast of mainland China; mountain range runs N–S, covering two-thirds of the island; highest peak, Yu Shan 3997 m/13 113 ft; low-lying land mainly in the W; crossed by the Tropic of Cancer; major earthquake, 1999.

Climate Tropical monsoon-type climate; hot, humid summers, mild, short winters; wet season (May–Sep); typhoons common (Jul–Sep); average daily temperature 12–19°C (Jan), 24–33°C (Jul) in Taibei; average annual rainfall 2500 mm/98 in.

Currency 1 New Taiwan Dollar (TWD) = 100 cents

Economy Progressed from agriculture to industry since 1950s; high technology, textiles, electronics, plastics, petrochemicals, machinery; natural gas, limestone, marble, asbestos; sugar, bananas, pineapples, citrus fruits, vegetables, tea, fish.

GDP (2001e) $386 bn, per capita $17 200

History Taiwan (Formosa) visited by the Portuguese, 1590; conquered by Manchus, 17th-c; ceded to Japan following Sino-Japanese War, 1895; returned to China, 1945; Nationalist government moved to Taiwan by Jiang Jieshi (Chang Kai-shek); government still maintains claim to legal jurisdiction over mainland China and continues to designate itself as the Republic of China; protected by US

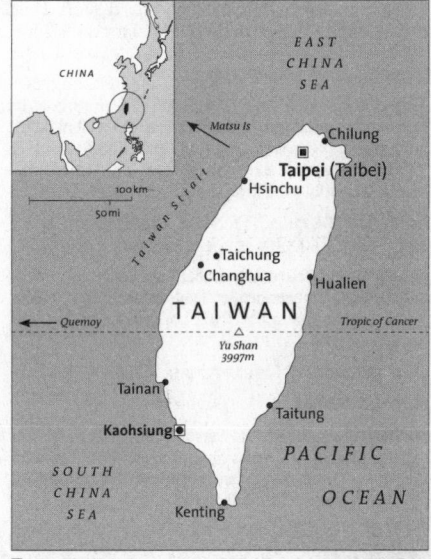

☐ International Airport

naval forces during Korean War, 1950–3; signed mutual defence pact with USA, 1954–79; end of civil war with People's Republic of China declared by President Lee Teng-hui, 1991; governed by President, who appoints premier, National Assembly, and legislative *Yuan*; elections held for reformed National Assembly, 1991; *Yuan* voted in favour of bill for major constitutional change, Aug 2004.

Head of State (President)
2000–   Chen Shui-ban

Head of Government (Premier)
2005–6   Frank Hsieh
2006–   Su Tseng-chang

HUMAN GEOGRAPHY

TAJIKISTAN (TADZHIKISTAN)

Local name Tojikiston

Timezone GMT +3

Area 143 100 km²/55 200 sq mi

Population total (2002e) 6 327 000

Status Republic

Date of independence 1991

Capital Dushanbe

Languages Tajik (official), Russian

Ethnic groups Tajik (59%), Uzbek (23%), Russian (13%)

Religion Sunni Muslim

Physical features Republic in SE Middle Asia; Tien Shan, Gissar-Alai, and Pamir ranges cover over 90% of the area; highest peaks, Communism Peak, 7495 m/ 24 590 ft, and Lenin Peak, 7134 m/23 405 ft, located in N part of Pamirs; R Pyandzh flows E–W along the S border till it is joined by R Valksh to form R Amu Darya; lakes include L Kara-Kul (largest) and L Sarez.

Climate Continental; subtropical valley areas, hot, dry summers; annual mean temperature –0.9°C (Jan), 27°C (Jul); average annual rainfall 150–250 mm/6–10 in; in highlands, average mean temperature –3°C (Jan); average annual rainfall 60–80 mm/2–3 in.

Currency 1 Somoni (TJS) = 100 diram (before 2000, 1 Tajik rouble (TJR) = 100 kopeks)

Economy Oil, natural gas, coal, lead, zinc, machinery, metalworking, chemicals, food processing; cotton, wheat, maize, vegetables, fruit; hot mineral springs and health resorts.

GDP (2002e) $8.476 bn, per capita $1300

HDI (2002) 0.667

History Conquered by Persia, and Alexander the Great; invaded by Arabs in 8th-c; Turkish invasion, 10th-c; until mid 18th-c, part of the emirate of Bukhara,

□ International Airport

which in effect became a protectorate of Russia, 1868; following the Russian Revolution (1917), became part of Turkestan Soviet Socialist Autonomous Republic, 1918; scene of the Basmachi revolt, 1922–3; Tajik Autonomous Soviet Socialist Republic created as part of the Uzbek SSR, 1924; became a Soviet Socialist Republic, 1929; declaration of independence from Soviet Union, 1991; joined Commonwealth of Independent States, 1991; Republican Communist Party remained in power until civil war began, 1992; governed by a President, Prime Minister, and Supreme Assembly.

Head of State
1992–　　Emomali Rahmonov

Head of Government
1999–　　Oqil Oqilov

TANZANIA

Local name Tanzania

Timezone GMT +3

Area 945 087 km²/364 900 sq mi

Population total (2002e) 34 902 000

Status Republic

Date of independence 1961

Capital Dodoma (formerly Dar es Salaam)

Languages Swahili and English (official), various tribal languages

Ethnic groups Bantu (99%) (including Nyamwezi and Sukuma 21%, Swahili 9%, Hehet and Bena 6%, Makonde 6%, Haya 6%, Arab, Asian, and European minorities

Religions Mainland: Christian (34%), Muslim (33%),

traditional animist beliefs (33%); Zanzibar: Muslim (96%), Hindu (4%)

Physical features Largest E African country, just S of the Equator; includes the islands of Zanzibar, Pemba, and Mafia; coast fringed by long sandy beaches protected by coral reefs; rises towards a C plateau, average elevation 1000 m/3300 ft; Rift Valley branches round L Victoria (N), several high volcanic peaks, notably Mt Kilimanjaro, 5895 m/ 19 340 ft; extensive Serengeti Plain to the W; other main lakes, L Tanganyika and L Rukwa.

Climate Tropical; hot, humid climate on coast and off-shore islands; average temperatures 27°C (Jan), 23°C (Jul); average annual rainfall 1000 mm/40 in; hot and dry on C plateau, average annual rainfall 250 mm/10 in; semitemperate conditions above 1500 mm/5000 ft.

Currency 1 Tanzanian Shilling (TZS) = 100 cents

Tanzania (continued)

Economy Agriculture; rice, sorghum, coffee, sugar, cloves (most of world's market), coconuts, tobacco, cotton; reserves of iron, coal, tin, gypsum, salt, phosphate, gold, diamonds, oil; tourism.

GDP (2002e) $20.42 bn, per capita $600

HDI (2002) 0.440

History Swahili culture developed, 10th–15th-c; Zanzibar became the capital of the Omani empire in 1840s; became a British protectorate, 1890; German East Africa established, 1891; British mandate to administer Tanganyika, 1919; first E African country to gain independence and become a member of the Commonwealth, 1961; republic, 1962; Zanzibar given independence as a constitutional monarchy with Sultan as Head of State; Sultan overthrown, 1964, and Act of Union between Zanzibar and Tanganyika led to the United Republic of Tanzania; a one-party state following 1965 constitution; legislation passed allowing for opposition parties, 1991, following a unanimous vote for a multi-party system; governed by a President, Cabinet, and National Assembly; coast hit by Indian Ocean tsunami, 2004.

Head of State
1995–2005 Benjamin Mkapa
2005– Jakaya Kikwete

Head of Government
2005– Edward Lowassa

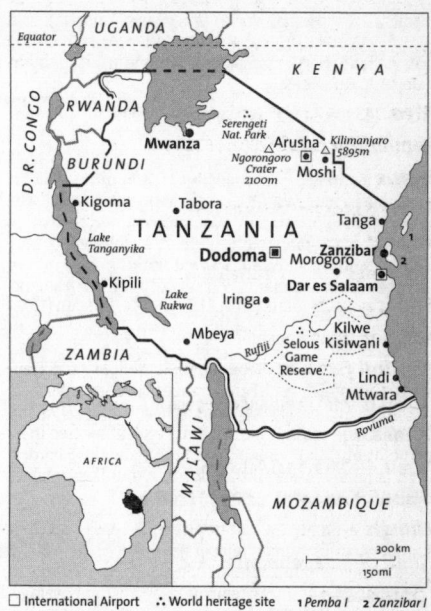

☐ International Airport ∴ World heritage site 1 *Pemba I* 2 *Zanzibar I*

THAILAND

Local name Muang Thai

Timezone GMT +7

Area 513 115 km²/198 062 sq mi

Population total (2002e) 63 430 000

Status Kingdom

Capital Bangkok (Krung Thep)

Languages Thai (official), Malay and English also spoken

Ethnic groups Thai (75%), Chinese (14%), Khmer and Mon minorities

Religions Theravada Buddhist (95%), Muslim, Hindu, Sikh, and Christian (4%)

Physical features Agricultural region dominated by the floodplain of the Chao Phraya R; NE plateau rises above 300 m/1000 ft and covers a third of the country; mountainous N region rising to 2595 m/8514 ft at Doi Inthanon; narrow, low-lying S region separates the Andaman Sea from the Gulf of Thailand; covered in tropical rainforest, except sparsely vegetated Khorat plateau (NE).

Climate Equatorial climate in the S; tropical monsoon climate in the N and C; high temperatures and humidity; wet season (Jun–Oct); average annual temperature 26°C (Jan), 28°C (Jul) in Bangkok; average annual rainfall 1400 mm/55 in; coast devastated by tsunami, 2004.

Currency 1 Baht (THB) = 100 satang

☐ International Airport

Economy Agriculture; rice, maize, bananas, pineapple, sugar cane, rubber, teak; textiles, electronics,

Thailand (continued)

cement, chemicals, food processing, tourism; tin (world's third largest supplier), tungsten (world's second largest supplier), manganese, antimony, lead, zinc, copper, natural gas.

GDP (2002e) $445.8 bn, per capita $7000

HDI (2002) 0.762

History Evidence of Bronze Age communities, 4000 BC; Thai nation founded, 13th-c; only country in S and SE Asia to escape colonization by a European power; revolution ended absolute monarchical rule, 1932; followed by periods of military rule interspersed with brief periods of democratic government; 1991 constitution (with amendments) provides for a National Legislative Assembly comprising a House of Representatives, an elected Senate, and a cabinet headed by a Prime Minister; King is Head of State; Thaksin Shinawatra was first democratically-elected prime minister to win second consecutive term, but was ousted in bloodless military coup (2006).

Head of State (Monarch)
1946–   Bhumibol Adulyadej (Rama IX)

Head of Government
2006   Chidchai Vanasathidya *Acting*
2006   Thaksin Shinawatra
2006–   Surayud Chulanont *Interim*

TOGO

Local name République Togolaise (French)

Timezone GMT

Area 56 790 km²/21 941 sq mi

Population total (2002e) 5 286 000

Status Republic

Date of independence 1960

Capital Lomé

Languages French (official), local languages (Ewe, mostly in S, 47%), Hamitic people in N, mostly Voltaic speaking)

Ethnic groups Ewe (35%), Kabyè (22%), Mina (6%), with c.34 other ethnic groups, European and Syrian-Lebanese minorities

Religions Traditional animist beliefs (50%), Christian (35%), Muslim (10%)

Physical features Located in W Africa; land rises from the lagoon coast of the Gulf of Guinea, past low-lying plains to the Atakora Mts running NE–SW in the N; highest peak, Pic Baumann, 986 m/3235 ft; flat plains in NW. Main rivers, Oti, Mono.

Climate Tropical, high temperatures and humidity; wet seasons (Mar–Jul, Oct–Nov); single rainy season in N (Jul–Sep); average annual temperature 27°C (Jan), 24°C (Jul) in Lomé; average annual rainfall 875 mm/34 in; dry Saharan Harmattan blows from NE (Oct–Apr).

Currency 1 CFA Franc (XAF) = 100 centimes.

Economy Largely agricultural economy; coffee, cocoa, cotton, cassava, maize, rice, timber; phosphates, bauxite, limestone, iron ore, marble; cement, steel, oil refining, food processing, crafts, textiles, beverages.

GDP (2002e) $7.594 bn, per capita $1400

HDI (2002) 0.493

History Formerly part of Kingdom of Togoland; German protectorate, 1884–1914; mandate of League of Nations, 1922, divided between France (French Togo) and Britain (part of British Gold Coast); Trusteeships of United Nations, 1946; French Togo became autonomous republic within French Union, 1956; British Togoland joined Gold Coast (Ghana), 1957; independence, 1960; military coups, 1963, 1967; civilian rule, 1980; riots over slow reforms, 1991; National Assembly dissolved, and Supreme Republican Council established, 1991; parliamentary elections, 1992; governed by a President, Prime Minister, and 81-member National Assembly, elected for five years.

Head of State
2005   Abass Bonfoh *Interim*
2005–   Faure Gnassingbé

Head of Government
2006–   Yawovi Agboyibo

☐ International Airport

TOKELAU >> NEW ZEALAND

TONGA

Local name Tonga

Timezone GMT +13

Area 646 km²/249 sq mi

Population total (2002e) 101 000

Status Independent kingdom within the Commonwealth

Date of independence 1970

Capital Nuku'alofa

Languages Tongan and English (official)

Ethnic groups Tongan (98%), other Polynesian, European minorities

Religions Christian (Free Wesleyan Methodists 47%, Roman Catholic 14%, Mormon 9%, Anglican minorities)

Physical features Island group in the SW Pacific Ocean, 2250 km/1400 mi NE of New Zealand; consists of 169 islands, 36 inhabited, divided into three main groups, Ha'apai, Tongatapu, and Vava'u; Tongatapu, largest island, inhabited by two-thirds of the population; W islands mainly volcanic, some still active; highest point, extinct volcano of Kao, 1014 m/3327 ft.

Climate Semi-tropical; average annual temperature 26°C (Jan), 21°C (Jul) in Nuku'alofa; average annual rainfall 1750 mm/69 in; occasional hurricanes in summer months.

Currency 1 Pa'anga/Tongan Dollar (TOP) = 100 seniti

Economy Largely based on agriculture; copra, coconuts, bananas, watermelons, yams, taro, cassava, groundnuts, rice, maize, tobacco, sugar cane; tourism and cottage handicrafts are small but growing industries.

GDP (2001e) $236 mn, per capita $2200

History Early settlers were Polynesians; visited by Dutch, early 17th-c; visited by the British explorer, James

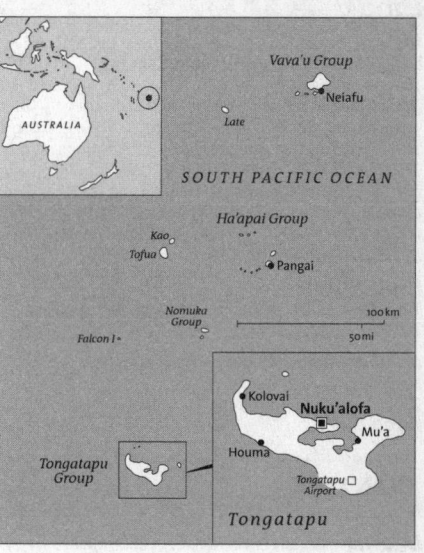

Cook, 1773; Methodist missionaries converted most of population to Christianity during early 19th-c; Chief Taufa'ahau united the islands and declared himself the first Monarch of Tonga, 1845; became a British protectorate, 1900, under its own monarchy; independence, 1970; governed by a Sovereign, a Privy Council, and a unicameral Legislative Assembly of Cabinet members, nobles, and elected people's representatives.

Head of State (Monarch)
1965–   Taufa'ahau Tupou IV

Head of Government (Prime Minister)
2000–6   Ulukalala Lavaka Ata
2006–   Fred Sevele

TRINIDAD AND TOBAGO

Local name Trinidad and Tobago

Timezone GMT –4

Area 5128 km²/1979 sq mi

Population total (2002e) 1 304 000

Status Independent republic within the Commonwealth

Date of independence 1962

Capital Port of Spain

Languages English (official), Hindi, French, Spanish

Ethnic groups African (43%), East Indian (40%), mixed (14%), Chinese (1%)

Religions Christian (Roman Catholic 34%, Protestant 29%), Hindu (25%), Muslim (6%)

Physical features Southernmost islands of the Lesser Antilles, SE Caribbean; Trinidad, area 4828 km²/1864 sq mi, traversed by three mountain ranges (N, C and S), rising to 940 m/3084 ft at El Cerro del Aripo; drained by Caroni, Ortoire and Oropuche rivers; Tobago, area 300 km²/116 sq mi; Main Ridge extends along most of island, rising to 576 m/1890 ft.

Climate Tropical, hot and humid; average annual temperature 29°C; dry season (Jan–May); wet season (Jun–Dec); average annual rainfall 1270 mm/50 in (SW Trinidad), 2540 mm/100 in (Tobago mountains).

Currency 1 Trinidad and Tobago Dollar (TTD) = 100 cents

Economy Oil and gas (main industries); industrial complex, W coast of Trinidad; cement, oil refining, petrochemicals; cocoa, coffee, fruit; tourism.

Trinidad and Tobago (continued)

GDP (2002e) $11.07 bn, per capita $10000

HDI (2002) 0.805

History Trinidad visited by Columbus in 1498; settled by Spain in 16th-c, and acquired by Britain in 1797; Tobago captured by French, 1781, and acquired by Britain, 1802; Tobago became a British colony, 1814; Trinidad and Tobago united as British Crown Colony, 1899; independent member of the Commonwealth, 1962; republic, 1976; governed by a President and bicameral Parliament, comprising a Senate and House of Representatives; also a 15-member Tobago House of Assembly; in 2005 government announced Spanish to become an official language by 2020.

Head of State
1997–2003 Arthur Napoleon Raymond Robinson
2003–   Max Richards

Head of Government
1995–2001 Basdeo Panday
2001–   Patrick Manning

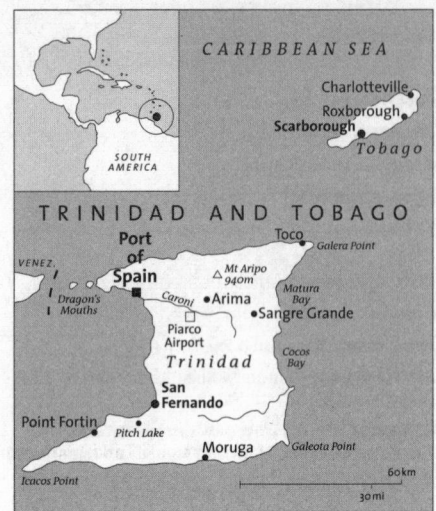

TUNISIA

Local names Tunis (Arabic), Tunisie (French)

Timezone GMT +1

Area 164150 km²/63362 sq mi

Population total (2002e) 9764000

Status Republic

Date of Independence 1956

Capital Tunis

Languages Arabic (official), French and Berber widely spoken

Ethnic groups Arab (98%), European (1%), small Jewish minority

Religions Sunni Muslim (98%), Christian (1%), small Jewish minority

Physical features Located in N Africa, on Mediterranean coast; Atlas Mts (NW) rise to 1544 m/5065 ft at Jebel Chambi; Majardah river valley is the most fertile area (N); from Tabussah range, land descends across a plateau to the Saharan desert (S) and a coastal plain (E).

Climate Mediterranean in N, with hot, dry summers, mild, rainy winters; extreme desert-continental conditions in S, with little rainfall; average annual temperature 9°C (Jan), 26°C (Jul); average annual rainfall 400 mm/15.7 in.

Currency 1 Tunisian Dinar (TND) = 1000 millèmes

Economy Agriculture (employs c.50% of population, but of declining importance); wheat, barley, grapes; olive oil (world's fourth largest producer); phosphates (fifth largest producer).

GDP (2002e) $67.13 bn, per capita $6800

HDI (2002) 0.722

History Ruled by Phoenicians, Carthaginians, Romans, Byzantines, Arabs, Spanish, and Turks; under the control of the Ottoman Empire, 1574; French protectorate, 1883;

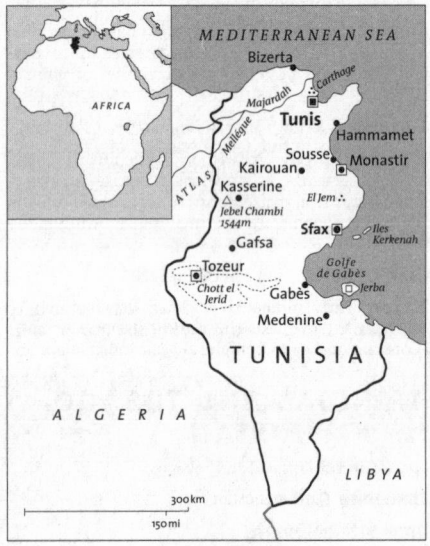

☐ International Airport   ∴ World heritage site

gained internal self-government, 1955; independence, 1956; monarchy abolished and republic declared, 1957; executive power held by President, who appoints the Prime Minister and Council of Ministers; unicameral legislature, National Assembly, elected every five years; new constitution, 2002, removed presidential term limits.

Head of State
1987–   Zine al-Abidine bin Ali

Head of Government
1999–   Mohammed Ghannouchi

TURKEY

Local name Türkiye Cumhuriyeti

Timezone GMT +2

Area 779 452 km²/300 868 sq mi

Population total (2002e) 69 359 000

Status Republic

Capital Ankara

Languages Turkish (Türkçe) (official), Kurdish and Arabic; Greek, Armenian, and Yiddish minorities

Ethnic groups Turkish (85%), Kurd (12%)

Religions Sunni Muslim (98%), Greek Orthodox, Armenian, and Jewish minorities

Physical features Lying partly in Europe and partly in Asia, W area (Thrace), E area (Anatolia); Turkish Straits (Dardanelles, Sea of Marmara, Bosporus) connect the Black Sea (NE) and Mediterranean Sea (SW); mountainous area, Taurus Mts, cover the entire S part of Anatolia; highest peak Mt Ararat, 5165 m/16 945 ft; sources of rivers Euphrates and Tigris in E.

Climate Mediterranean climate on Aegean and Mediterranean coasts, with hot, dry summers, warm, wet winters; mean temperature 19°C (Jul); average annual temperatures 0.3°C (Jan), 23°C (Jul) in Ankara; average annual rainfall 723 mm/28 in.

Currency 1 New Turkish Lira (YTL) = 100 new kurus (before 2005, Turkish Lira (TRL))

Economy Agriculture (employs c.50% of workforce); cotton, tobacco, fruits, nuts, livestock; minerals, textiles, glass, and cement; many Turks find work elsewhere in Europe, especially Germany.

GDP (2002e) $489.7 bn, per capita $7300

HDI (2002) 0.742

History Seljuk sultanate replaced by Ottoman in NW Asia Minor, 13th-c; Turkish invasion of Europe, 1375; fall of Constantinople, 1453; empire at peak under Sulaiman

☐ International Airport

the Magnificent, 16th-c; Young Turks seized power, 1908; Balkan War, 1912–13; allied with Germany during World War 1; Republic followed Young Turk revolution, led by Kemal Atatürk, 1923; policy of westernization and economic development; neutral during most of World War 2, then sided with Allies; military coups, 1960, 1980; strained relations with Greece, invasion of Cyprus, 1974; aided allied forces during Gulf War, 1991; Constitution provides for single-chamber National Assembly; President appoints Prime Minister and Council of Ministers.

Head of State
1993–2000 Süleyman Demirel
2000– Ahmet Necdet Sezer

Head of Government
2003– Recep Tayyip Erdogan

TURKMENISTAN

Local name Turkmenostan

Timezone GMT +5

Area 488 100 km²/188 400 sq mi

Population total (2002e) 4 946 000

Status Republic

Date of independence 1991

Capital Ashkhabad (Ashgabad)

Languages Turkmenian (official), other Turkic languages, Russian

Ethnic groups Turkmen (72%), Russian (10%), Uzbek, Kazakh, Ukrainian minorities

Religion Sunni Muslim

Physical features Kara Kum (Black Sands) desert, area 310 800 km²/120 000 sq mi, covers c.80% of the country; Turan Plain covers four-fifths of Turkmenistan; foothills in the S; Kopet Dag mountain range is volcanic; other foothills are spurs of the Kugitangtau and Pamir-Alay ranges; Rivers Amu Darya and Murghab.

Climate Continental, great variation of temperatures; temperatures range from 50°C (Jul) in Kara Kum, to –33°C (Jan) in the Kushka; average annual rainfall 120–250 mm/5–10 in.

Currency Manat (TMM) = 100 gapik

Economy Mineral resources of oil, natural gas, sulphur, potassium, and salt; oil, gas extraction (main industries); textiles; cotton production; agriculture; raising of Karakul sheep, Turkoman horses, and camels.

HUMAN GEOGRAPHY

Turkmenistan (continued)

GDP (2002e) $31.34 bn, per capita $6700

HDI (2002) 0.741

History Part of the ancient Persian empire; ruled by Seljuk Turks, 11th-c; conquered by Genghis Khan and Mongols, 13th-c; Uzbeks invaded, 15th-c; divided into two: one part belonged to the Khanate of Khiva (which became part of Russian empire), the other to Khanate of Bukhara; Turkistan Autonomous Soviet Socialist Republic formed, 1922; full Soviet Socialist Republic, 1924; declared sovereignty, 1990; independence and membership of Commonwealth of Independent States, 1991; governed by President, who is both head of state and of government, and parliament (*majlis*); parliament made Saparmurad Niyazov president for life (1999), but in 2005 he called for contested elections in 2009; following Niyazov's sudden death (Dec 2006), new acting president installed pending elections (Feb 2007).

Head of State/Government
1990–2006 Saparmurad Niyazov
2006– Kurbanguly Berdymukhamedov *Acting*

TURKS AND CAICOS ISLANDS
>> UNITED KINGDOM

☐ International Airport

TUVALU

Local name Tuvalu

Timezone GMT +12

Area 26 km²/10 sq mi

Population total (2002e) 10 900

Status Independent state within the Commonwealth

Date of independence 1978

Capital Funafuti (Fongafale)

Languages Tuvaluan, English

Ethnic group Polynesian (96%)

Religions Christian (Protestant Church of Tuvalu, Roman Catholic, Baha'i) (97%), small Muslim minority

Physical features Island group in the SW Pacific, 1050 km/650 mi off Fiji; comprises nine low-lying coral atolls, running NW–SE in a chain 580 km/360 mi long; consists of islands of Funafuti, Nukufetau, Nukulailai, Nanumea, Niutao, Nanumanga, Nui, Vaitupu, and Niulakita; all low-lying, highest point, 4.6 m/15 ft, on Niulakita.

Climate Hot, humid climate; average annual temperatures 29°C (Jan), 27°C (Jul) in Funafuti; average annual rainfall 3535 mm/139 in.

Currency 1 Australian Dollar (AUD) = 100 cents; also, a Tuvaluan Dollar (TVD)

Economy Subsistence economy; agriculture, coconuts, copra, tropical fruit; fish; handcrafted products, postage stamps.

GDP (2002e) $12.2 mn, per capita $1100

History Invaded by Samoans, 16th-c; British protectorate as Ellice Is, 1892; administered as colony with Gilbert Is (now Kiribati), 1915; US soldiers occupied Ellice Is during World War 2, countering Japanese advance,

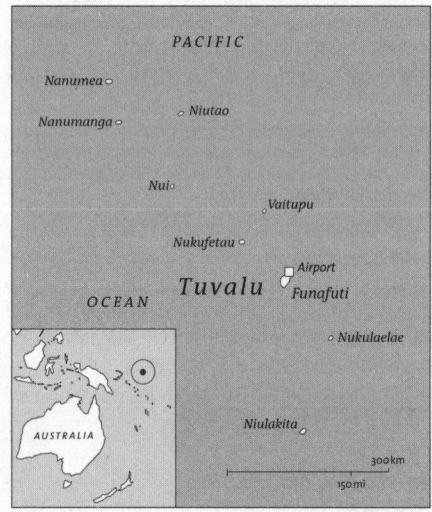

1942; separate constitution, 1974; independence as constitutional monarchy within the Commonwealth, 1978; British monarch represented by a Governor-General; governed by a Prime Minister, Cabinet, and unicameral Parliament; Prime Minister Saufatu Sopoanga lost no-confidence vote, Aug 2004.

Head of State
(British monarch represented by Governor-General)
2005– Filoimea Telito

Head of Government
2004–6 Maati Toafa
2006– Apisai Ielemia

UGANDA

Local name Uganda (Swahili)

Timezone GMT +3

Area 241 038 km²/93 040 sq mi

Population total (2002e) 24 378 000

Status Republic

Date of independence 1962

Capital Kampala

Languages English and Swahili (official), Luganda (Ganda), Ateso, and Luo are also spoken

Ethnic groups Bantu, with Nilotic and Hamitic minorities

Religions Christian (66%) (Roman Catholic 33%, Protestant 33%), traditional animist beliefs (18%), Muslim (6%)

Physical features Landlocked country in E Africa, mainly plateau, height 1200 m/4000 ft; dry savannah or semi-desert in the N; fertile L Victoria basin; highest point in Uganda and Zaïre, Margherita Peak, 5110 m/16 765 ft; main lakes, Victoria (SE), George and Edward (SW), Albert (W), Kwania and Kyoga (C), Bisina (formerly L Salisbury) (E); main rivers are the upper reaches of R Nile, the Victoria Nile, and the Albert Nile.

Climate Tropical climate; temperatures rarely rise above 29°C, or fall below 15°C (S); average annual temperature 23°C (Jan), 21°C (Jul); average annual rainfall 1150 mm/45 in.

Currency 1 Uganda Shilling (UGX) = 100 cents

Economy Agriculture; coffee (over 90% of exports), tea, sugar, cotton; bananas, plantains, cassavas, potatoes, sweet potatoes, maize, sorghum.

GDP (2002e) $30.49 bn, per capita $1200

HDI (2002) 0.444

History Visited by Arab traders, 1840s; explored by Speke, 1860s; granted to the British East Africa Company, 1888; Kingdom of Buganda became British protectorate,

□ International Airport

1893; other territory included by 1903; independence, 1962; Dr Milton Obote assumed all powers, 1966; coup led by General Amin, 1971; Amin overthrown, 1979; further coup overthrew Obote, 1985; National Resistance Movement captured Kampala, 1986, and Museveni became President; governed by a President, Cabinet, Prime Minister, and National Resistance Council; new constitution, 1995; peace agreement with rebels, 2002.

Head of State
1986–   Yoweri Kaguta Museveni

Head of Government
1999–   Apolo Nsibambi

UKRAINE

Local name Ukraina

Timezone GMT +2

Area 603 700 km²/233 028 sq mi

Population total (2002e) 48 120 000

Status Republic

Date of independence 1991

Capital Kiev

Languages Ukrainian (official), Russian

Ethnic groups Ukrainian (73%), Russian (22%), Moldovan, Bulgarian, and Polish minorities

Religions Orthodox (Autocephalous and Russian) (76%), Roman Catholic (14%), Jewish (2%), Baptist, Mennonite, Protestant, and Muslim (8%)

Physical features Most fertile area of former USSR, consisting largely of black soil steppes, forming a substantial part of the East European Plain; borders the Black Sea and Sea of Azov (S); Carpathian Mts, 2061 m/ 6762 ft at Mt Goverla (SW); Crimean Mts (S); main rivers, Dnepr, Yuzhny, Bug; Donets coalfield, area 25 900 km²/10 000 sq mi.

Climate Moderate, mild winters, hot summers (SW); average annual temperatures –3°C (Jan), 23°C (Jul); average annual rainfall in Crimea 400–610 mm/16–24 in.

Currency 1 Hryvna (UAH) = 100 kopijka

Economy Important industrial bases for iron and steel manufacture, chemical and engineering bases; shipbuilding on Black Sea; agriculture (was the USSR's major wheat producer); wheat, corn, rye, potatoes, cotton, flax, sugar beet; coal and salt deposits in Donets basin.

HUMAN GEOGRAPHY

HUMAN GEOGRAPHY

Ukraine (continued)

GDP (2002e) $218 bn, per capita $4500

HDI (2002) 0.748

History Conquered by Mongols, 1240; dominated by Poland, 13–16th-c; applied to Moscow for help fighting Poland, leading to sovereignty, 1654; independence from Russia, 1918, after Russian Revolution; became a member of the USSR, 1922; devastated during World War 2; Chernobyl the site of the world's worst nuclear accident, 1986; declared independence, 1991; ongoing disputes with Russia over control of Black Sea Fleet and status of Crimea; introduction of border controls and new currency, 1993, in contravention of CIS agreements; new constitution, 1996; governed by a President and Supreme Council; Yanukovych elected president (Nov 2004) amid allegations of vote-rigging, public protest supporting opposition leader Yushchenko; poll result suspended by Supreme Court; Yushchenko won poll re-run (Dec 2004), with 52% of vote; Yanukovych approved as prime minister (Aug 2006).

Head of State
1994–2004 Leonid Kuchma
2004– Viktor Yushchenko

Head of Government
2006– Viktor Yanukovych

□ International Airport

UNITED ARAB EMIRATES

Local name Ittihād al-Imārat al-'Arabīyah

Timezone GMT +4

Area 83 600 km²/32 300 sq mi

Population total (2002e) 3 550 000

Status Federation of autonomous emirates

Date of independence 1971

Capital Abu Dhabi

Languages Arabic (official), English, Farsi, Urdu, and Hindi also spoken

Ethnic groups Emirian (19%), other Arab (23%), S Asian (50%)

Religions Muslim (Sunni 80%, Shi'ite 16%), Christian (4%), small Hindu minority

Physical features Seven states in EC Arabian peninsula on S shore (Trucial Coast) of the Persian Gulf; al-Fujairah has a coastline along the Gulf of Oman; salt marshes predominate on coast; barren desert and gravel plain inland; Hajar Mts in al-Fujairah rise to over 1000 m/3000 ft in E.

Climate Hot, dry desert climate, extreme summer temperatures over 40°C and limited rainfall; frequent sandstorms; average annual temperatures 23°C (Jan), 42°C (Jul) in Dubai; average annual rainfall 60 mm/2.4 in.

Currency 1 United Arab Emirates Dirham (AED) = 100 fils

Economy Based on oil and gas (main producers, Abu Dhabi, Dubai); important commercial and trading centre; saline water supplies have restricted agriculture to oases and irrigated valleys of Hajar Mts; vegetables, fruits, dates, dairy farming; tourism.

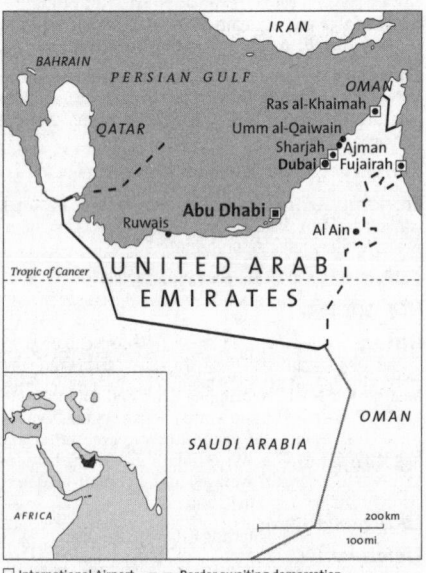

□ International Airport — — Border awaiting demarcation

GDP (2002e) $53.97 bn, per capita $22 100

HDI (2002) 0.812

History Originally peopled by sea-faring tribes, converted to Islam, 7th-c; Mecca conquered by sheikdom of Carmathians; upon its collapse piracy common, area known as Pirate Coast; Portuguese explorers arrived, 16th-c; British East India Company arrived, 17th-c; British attacked coastal ports, 1819–20, exacted pledge to renounce piracy in General Treaty, 1820; known as Trucial Coast after Treaty of Maritime Peace in Perpetuity, 1853; administered by British India, 1873–1947, thereafter by London Foreign Office; Trucial States Council formed, 1960; federated and became United Arab Emirates, 1971, comprising seven emirates: Abu Dhabi, Ajman, Dubai, al-Fujairah, Ras al-Khaimah, Sharjah, and Umm al-Qaiwain; Ras al-Khaimah joined federation, 1972; governed by Supreme Council of the seven emirate rulers (each is an absolute Monarch in own state).

Head of State
1971–2004 Zayed bin Sultan al-Nahyan
2004–   Khalifa bin Zayed al-Nahyan

Head of Government
2006–   Mohammed bin Rashid al-Maktoum

UNITED KINGDOM (UK)

Local names United Kingdom of Great Britain and Northern Ireland, Great Britain, Britain

Timezone GMT

Area 244 755 km²/94 500 sq mi

Population total (2002e) 60 178 000

Status Kingdom

Capital London

Languages English, Irish Gaelic, Scots Gaelic (Gallic), Welsh

Ethnic groups English (81.5%), Scottish (9.5%), Irish (2.4%), Welsh (1.9%), West Indian, Asian, and African (2%), Arabic, Turkish, and Greek minorities

Religions Christian (90%) (Anglican 63%, Roman Catholic 14%, Presbyterian 4%, Methodist 3%, Baptist 1%, Orthodox 1%, other 6%), Muslim (3%), Sikh (1%), Hindu (1%), Jewish (1%), other (1%)

Physical features Varied landscape, comprising the mountainous Lake District in NW, rocky moors in SW, hilly downs of S and SE, and the low, marshy fenlands of C and E; Cheviot Hills separate Scotland and England; highest point, Ben Nevis in Scotland, 1342 m/4406 ft; The Pennines form a ridge down the middle of England, from Lake District to C; highest point in England and Wales, Mt Snowdon in Wales, 1085 m/3560 ft; in N Ireland, the Sperrin Mts and the granite Mourne Mts rise to heights over 610 m/2000 ft.

Climate Temperate maritime climate; SW airstream determines weather, bringing depressions (causing wet weather) or N winds (bringing drier and colder); some regional diversity, but no world climate systems' boundaries pass through the islands; on average, wetter and slightly warmer in W; rainfall evenly distributed throughout the year; average annual rainfall 1600 mm/ 60 in (W), 800 mm/30 in (C and E).

Currency 1 Pound Sterling (GBP) = 100 pence

Economy Service industries; agriculture, potatoes, wheat, barley, and sugar beets; livestock; large fishing industry; deposits of iron ore; oil and gas from N Sea; coal industry declining; highly developed financial systems; London the commercial and financial centre of Western world. UK one of the world's largest trading nations, relying heavily on imports; exports include machinery, transport equipment, petroleum, chemicals, textiles.

GDP (2002e) $1528 bn, per capita $25 500

HDI (2002) 0.928

History Migrations and settlements resulted in the insular Celtic nation; invaded by Rome, 1 AD; Romans

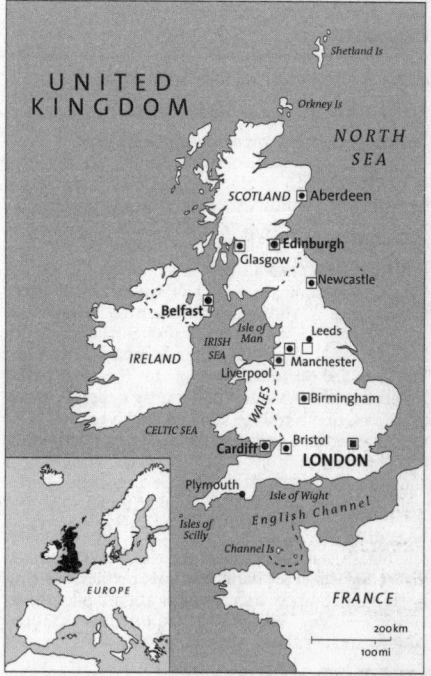

☐ International Airport

withdrew, 5th-c; constantly attacked by Scandinavian tribes, defeated by Alfred, 878; united under the kings of Wessex, 10th-c; Edward the Confessor died, 1066, leaving a disputed succession; Norman invasion under William, Duke of Normandy, 1066; Edward I conquered Wales, 1301; Hundred Years' War with France, 1337–1453; recurring plagues of Black Death, 1347–1400, wiped out one-third of population; Wars of the Roses, 1455–85, resulted in victory for House of Lancaster; establishment of Church of England and split from Church of Rome, 1533; union with Wales, 1536; coronation of Elizabeth I, 1558; execution of Mary Queen of Scots, 1587; defeat of the Spanish Armada, 1588; English Civil War, 1642–6 and 1648–9; execution of Charles I, 1649; England and Scotland joined by the Act of Union, 1707; 1714–60, development of parliamentary government under Hanoverian kings; revolt of the American colonies, 1775–81; Ireland officially joined to Great Britain, 1801; World War 1, 1914–18; became the United Kingdom of Great Britain and Northern Ireland following the establishment of the Irish Free State, 1922; General Strike, 1926; abdication of Edward VIII, 1936; World War 2, 1939–45; National Health system implemented, 1948; Indian independence, 1947; joined EC, 1973; Falklands War with Argentina, 1982; involvement in Gulf War, 1991; involve-

HUMAN GEOGRAPHY

United Kingdom (continued)

ment in Iraq War, 2003, and occupying presence into 2004; a kingdom with the Monarch as Head of State; governed by a bicameral Parliament, comprising an elected 659-member House of Commons and a House of Lords; a Cabinet is appointed by the Prime Minister.

>> *Political leaders and rulers, pp. 198–9*

Head of State (Monarch)
1952– Elizabeth II

Head of Government
1990–97 John Major
1997– Tony Blair

England

Area 130 357 km²/50 318 sq mi

Population total (2000e) 49 392 000

Status Constituent part of the United Kingdom

Capital London

Languages English, with c.300 minority languages

Ethnic groups & Religions >> UNITED KINGDOM

Physical features Largest area within the United Kingdom, forming the S part of the island of Great Britain; since 1974 divided into 46 counties; includes the Isles of Scilly, Lundy, and the Isle of Wight; largely undulating lowland, rising (S) to the Mendips, Cotswolds, Chilterns, and North Downs, (N) to the N–S ridge of the Pennines, and (NW) to the Cumbria Mts; drained E by the Tyne, Tees, Humber, Ouse, and Thames Rivers, and W by the Eden, Ribble, Mersey, and Severn Rivers; Lake District (NW) includes Derwent Water, Ullswater, Windermere and Bassenthwaite; linked to Europe by ferry and hovercraft, and (from 1994) by the Channel Tunnel.

Economy North Sea oil and gas, coal, tin, china clay, salt, potash, lead ore, iron ore; vehicles, heavy engineering, petrochemicals, pharmaceuticals, textiles, food processing, electronics, telecommunications, publishing, brewing, fishing, livestock, agriculture, horticulture, pottery and tourism.

☐ International Airport

History >> **UNITED KINGDOM**

Local Government in England

Local authorities	Area km²	sq mi	Administrative Centre	New Unitary Authorities (introduced 1996-8)	Population (2000e)
Bedfordshire (2-tier)	1235	477	Bedford		555 000
				Luton	176 000
Berkshire (replaced by unitary authorities)	1259	486			765 000
				Bracknell Forest	102 000
				Reading	141 000
				Slough	106 000
				West Berkshire	137 000
				Windsor & Maidenhead	137 000
				Wokingham	142 000
Bristol				Bristol	397 000
Buckinghamshire (2-tier)	1883	727	Aylesbury		672 000
				Milton Keynes	181 000
Cambridgeshire (2-tier)	3409	1316	Cambridge		711 000
				Peterborough	156 000
Cheshire (2-tier)	2328	899	Chester		980 000
				Halton	123 000
				Warrington	189 000
Cornwall & Scilly	3564	1376	Truro		485 000
Cumbria	6810	2629	Carlisle		498 000
Derbyshire (2-tier)	2631	1016	Matlock		969 000
				Derby	227 000
Devon (2-tier)	6711	2591	Exeter		1 075 000
				Plymouth	258 000
				Torbay	122 000

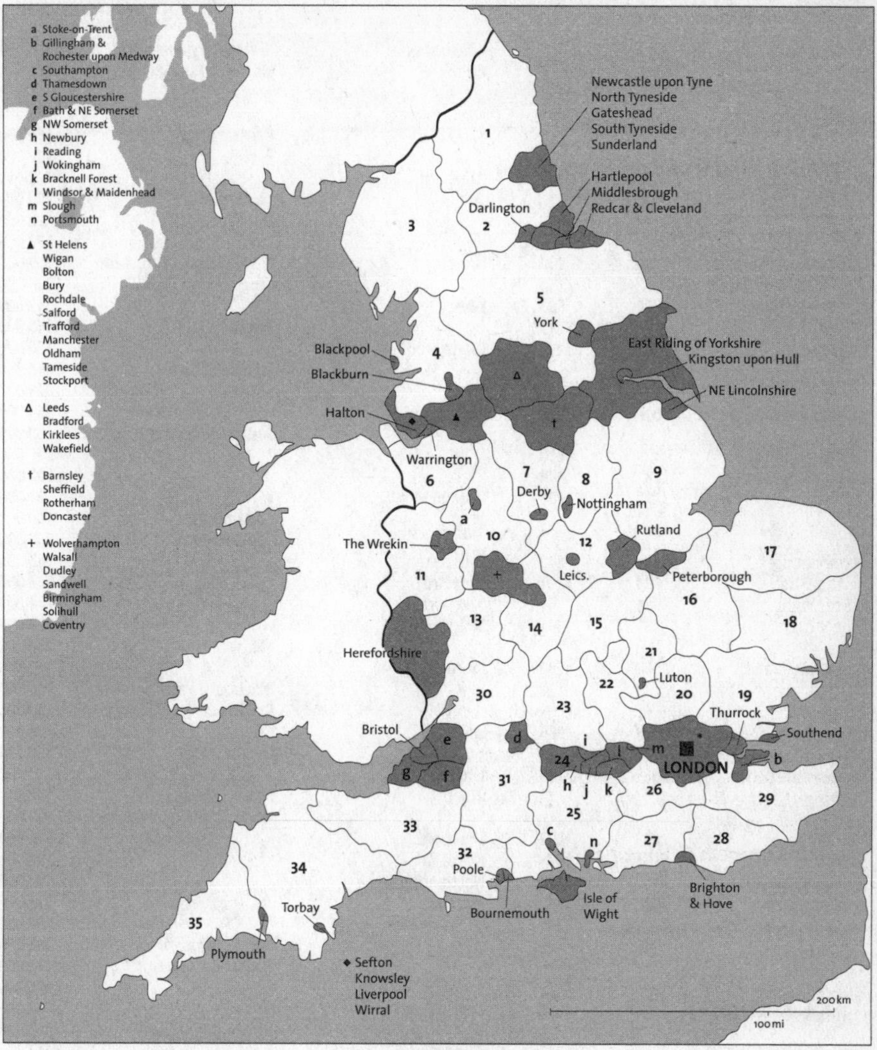

HUMAN GEOGRAPHY

a Stoke-on-Trent
b Gillingham &
  Rochester upon Medway
c Southampton
d Thamesdown
e S Gloucestershire
f Bath & NE Somerset
g NW Somerset
h Newbury
i Reading
j Wokingham
k Bracknell Forest
l Windsor & Maidenhead
m Slough
n Portsmouth

▲ St Helens
  Wigan
  Bolton
  Bury
  Rochdale
  Salford
  Trafford
  Manchester
  Oldham
  Tameside
  Stockport

Δ Leeds
  Bradford
  Kirklees
  Wakefield

† Barnsley
  Sheffield
  Rotherham
  Doncaster

+ Wolverhampton
  Walsall
  Dudley
  Sandwell
  Birmingham
  Solihull
  Coventry

Newcastle upon Tyne
North Tyneside
Gateshead
South Tyneside
Sunderland

Hartlepool
Middlesbrough
Redcar & Cleveland

Darlington

York

East Riding of Yorkshire
Kingston upon Hull

NE Lincolnshire

Blackpool
Blackburn
Halton

Warrington

The Wrekin

Derby
Nottingham
Rutland

Leics.
Peterborough

Herefordshire

Bristol

Luton
Thurrock
Southend

LONDON

Brighton
& Hove

Poole

Bournemouth
Isle of
Wight

Torbay

Plymouth

◆ Sefton
  Knowsley
  Liverpool
  Wirral

200 km
100 mi

Two-tier authority areas

1	NORTHUMBERLAND
2	DURHAM
3	CUMBRIA
4	LANCASHIRE
5	NORTH YORKSHIRE
6	CHESHIRE
7	DERBYSHIRE
8	NOTTINGHAMSHIRE
9	LINCOLNSHIRE
10	STAFFORDSHIRE
11	SHROPSHIRE
12	LEICESTERSHIRE
13	WORCESTERSHIRE
14	WARWICKSHIRE
15	NORTHAMPTONSHIRE
16	CAMBRIDGESHIRE
17	NORFOLK
18	SUFFOLK
19	ESSEX
20	HERTFORDSHIRE
21	BEDFORDSHIRE
22	BUCKINGHAMSHIRE
23	OXFORDSHIRE
24	BERKSHIRE
25	HAMPSHIRE
26	SURREY
27	WEST SUSSEX
28	EAST SUSSEX
29	KENT
30	GLOUCESTERSHIRE
31	WILTSHIRE
32	DORSET
33	SOMERSET
34	DEVON
35	CORNWALL & ISLES OF SCILLY

*Unitary authorities of London

City of London
Barking &
  Dagenham
Barnet
Bexley
Brent
Bromley
Camden
Croydon
Ealing
Enfield
Greenwich
Hackney

Hammersmith
  & Fulham
Haringey
Harrow
Havering
Hillingdon
Hounslow
Islington
Kensington
  & Chelsea
Kingston-
  upon-Thames

Lambeth
Lewisham
Merton
Newham
Redbridge
  upon Thames
Southwark
Sutton
Tower Hamlets
Waltham Forest
Wandsworth
Westminster

Unitary authority
areas

— County
  boundary

United Kingdom (continued)

Local authorities	Area km²	sq mi	Administrative Centre	New Unitary Authorities (introduced 1996-8)	Population (2000e)
Dorset (2-tier)	2654	1025	Dorchester		683 000
				Bournemouth	159 000
				Poole	136 000
Durham (2-tier)	2436	941	Durham		617 000
				Darlington	100 000
				Hartlepool	92 000
				Stockton-on-Tees	178 000
East Riding of Yorkshire	2416	933	Beverley	East Riding of Yorkshire	319 000
				Kingston-upon-Hull	268 000
East Sussex (2-tier)	1795	693	Lewes		743 000
				Brighton and Hove	245 000
Essex (2-tier)	3672	1418	Chelmsford		160 000
				Southend-on-Sea	165 000
				Thurrock	131 000
Gloucestershire (2-tier)	2643	1020	Gloucester		554 000
				South Gloucestershire	230 000
Greater London	1579	610			7 077 000
Greater Manchester	1287	497			2 607 000
Hampshire (2-tier)	3777	1458	Winchester		1 623 000
				Portsmouth	190 000
				Southampton	208 000
Herefordshire	2181	842	Hereford		162 000
Hertfordshire	1634	631	Hertford		1 022 000
Isle of Wight	381	147	Newport		124 000
Kent (2-tier)	3731	1441	Maidstone		1 558 000
				Medway	250 000
Lancashire (2-tier)	3063	1183	Preston		1 440 000
				Blackburn with Darwen	140 000
				Blackpool	153 000
Leicestershire (2-tier)	2553	986	Leicester		926 000
				Leicester City	285 000
Lincolnshire (2-tier)	5915	2284	Lincoln		621 000
				North Lincolnshire	152 000
				North East Lincolnshire	162 000
Merseyside	652	252	Liverpool		1 447 000
Norfolk	5368	2073	Norwich		782 000
Northamptonshire	2367	914	Northampton		607 000
Northumberland	5032	1943	Morpeth		312 000
North Yorkshire (2-tier)	8309	3208	Northallerton		738 000
				Middlesbrough	145 000
				Redcar & Cleveland	143 000
				York	175 000
Nottinghamshire (2-tier)	2164	836	Nottingham		1 051 000
				Nottingham City	283 000
Oxfordshire	2608	1007	Oxford		613 000
Rutland	394	152	Oakham		35 000
Shropshire (2-tier)	3490	1347	Shrewsbury		421 000
				Telford and Wrekin	143 000
Somerset (2-tier)	3451	1332	Taunton		490 000
				Bath & NE Somerset	163 000
				NW Somerset	182 000
South Yorkshire	1560	602	Barnsley		1 325 000
Staffordshire (2-tier)	2716	1049	Stafford		1 069 000
				Stoke-on-Trent	253 000
Suffolk	3797	1466	Ipswich		637 000
Surrey	1679	648	Kingston-upon-Thames		1 057 000
Tyne and Wear	540	208	Newcastle-upon-Tyne		1 160 000
Warwickshire	1981	765	Warwick		506 000
West Midlands	899	347	Birmingham		2 657 000
West Sussex	1989	768	Chichester		721 000
West Yorkshire	2039	787	Wakefield		2 141 000
Wiltshire (2-tier)	3481	1344	Trowbridge		608 000
				Swindon	150 000
Worcestershire	1813	700	Worcester		550 000

Scotland

Area 78 742 km²/30 394 sq mi

Population total (2000e) 5 728 000

Status Constituent part of the United Kingdom

Capital Edinburgh

Languages English, Scots Gaelic (Gallic) (known or used by c.80 000 residents)

Physical features Comprises the N part of the UK, and includes the island groups of Outer and Inner Hebrides, Orkney and Shetland; divided into Southern Uplands, rising to 843 m/2766 ft at Merrick; Central Lowlands (most densely populated area); and Northern Highlands, divided by the fault line following the Great Glen, and rising to 1344 m/4409 ft at Ben Nevis; W coast heavily indented; several wide estuaries on E coast, primarily Firths of Forth, Tay and Moray; many freshwater lochs in the interior, largest being Loch Lomond, 70 km²/27 sq mi, and deepest Loch Morar, 310 m/1020 ft.

Economy Based on coal, but all heavy industry declined through the 1980s, with closure of many pits; oil services on E coast; tourism, especially in Highlands; shipbuilding, steel, whisky, textiles, agriculture, forestry.

History Roman attempts to limit incursions of N tribes marked by Antonine Wall and Hadrian's Wall; beginnings of unification, 9th-c; wars between England and Scotland in Middle Ages; Scottish independence declared by Robert Bruce, recognized 1328; Stuart succession, 14th-c; crowns of Scotland and England united, 1603; parliaments united under Act of Union, 1707; unsuccessful Jacobite rebellions, 1715 and 1745; devolution proposal rejected, 1979; vote for Scottish parliament, 1997; in 1974, divided into 12 regions (including three islands councils); local government reorganization, 1996, replaced this two-tier system by a single tier of 29 mainland councils plus the three islands councils; successful referendum for Scottish parliament, 1997; devolved Scottish parliament, 1999.

Scottish councils

Name	Area		Population total (2000e)	Admin centre
	km²	sq mi		
Aberdeen City	186	72	221 000	Aberdeen
Aberdeenshire	6318	2439	227 000	Aberdeen
Angus	2181	842	113 000	Forfar
Argyll and Bute	6930	2675	92 000	Lochgilphead
Clackmannanshire	157	61	49 000	Alloa
Dumfries and Galloway	6439	2485	150 000	Dumfries
Dundee City	65	25	156 000	Dundee
East Ayrshire	1252	483	126 000	Kilmarnock
East Dunbartonshire	172	66	112 000	Kirkintilloch
East Lothian	6778	2616	87 000	Haddington
East Renfrewshire	173	67	88 000	Giffnock
Edinburgh, City of	262	101	448 000	Edinburgh
Falkirk	299	115	145 000	Falkirk
Fife	1323	511	134 000	Glenrothes
Glasgow, City of	175	68	633 000	Glasgow
Highland	25 784	9953	210 000	Inverness
Inverclyde	162	63	91 000	Greenock
Midlothian	356	137	81 000	Dalkeith
Moray	2238	864	87 000	Elgin

□ International Airport

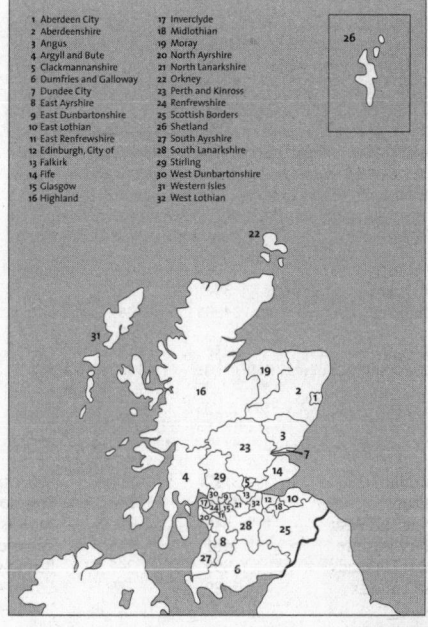

1 Aberdeen City
2 Aberdeenshire
3 Angus
4 Argyll and Bute
5 Clackmannanshire
6 Dumfries and Galloway
7 Dundee City
8 East Ayrshire
9 East Dunbartonshire
10 East Lothian
11 East Renfrewshire
12 Edinburgh, City of
13 Falkirk
14 Fife
15 Glasgow
16 Highland
17 Inverclyde
18 Midlothian
19 Moray
20 North Ayrshire
21 North Lanarkshire
22 Orkney
23 Perth and Kinross
24 Renfrewshire
25 Scottish Borders
26 Shetland
27 South Ayrshire
28 South Lanarkshire
29 Stirling
30 West Dunbartonshire
31 Western Isles
32 West Lothian

United Kingdom (continued)

Name	Area		Population total (2000e)	Admin centre
	km²	sq mi		
North Ayrshire	884	341	141 000	Irvine
North Lanarkshire	474	183	331 000	Motherwell
Orkney	992	383	20 000	Kirkwall
Perth and Kinross	5311	2050	132 000	Perth
Renfrewshire	261	101	179 000	Paisley
Scottish Borders	4734	1827	107 000	Newtown St Boswells

Name	Area		Population total (2000e)	Admin centre
	km²	sq mi		
Shetland	1438	555	23 000	Lerwick
South Ayrshire	1202	464	116 000	Ayr
South Lanarkshire	1771	684	311 000	Hamilton
Stirling	2196	848	83 000	Stirling
West Dunbartonshire	162	63	99 000	Dunbarton
Western Isles	3133	1209	30 000	Stornoway
West Lothian	425	164	149 000	Livingston

Wales

Local name Cymru (Welsh)

Area 20 761 km²/8014 sq mi

Population total (2000e) 2 946 000

Status Principality (Constituent part of the United Kingdom)

Capital Cardiff

Languages English, Welsh

Physical features Situated on the W coast of the UK, divided into 8 counties since 1974; includes the island of Anglesey off the NW coast; land rises to 1085 m/3560 ft at Snowdon (NW), also Cambrian Mts (C); Brecon Beacons (S); drained by the Severn, Clwyd, Dee, Conwy, Dovey, Taff, Towy, and Wye rivers.

Economy Coal; slate, lead, steel; industrialized S valleys and coastal plain; tourism in N and NW; ferries to Ireland at Holyhead, Fishguard; important source of water for England.

History Rhodri Mawr united Wales against Saxons, Norse, and Danes, 9th-c; Edward I of England established authority over Wales, building several castles, 12th–13th-c; Edward I's son created first Prince of Wales, 1301; 14th-c revolt under Owen Glendower; politically united with England by Act of Union, 1535; centre of Nonconformist religion since 18th-c; University of Wales, 1893, with constituent colleges; political nationalist movement (Plaid Cymru) returned first MP, 1966; Welsh television channel, 1982; 1979 referendum opposed devolution; successful referendum for devolved Welsh Assembly, 1997; Welsh Assembly, 1999.

☐ International Airport

Counties of Wales

Name	Area		Population total (2000e)	Admin centre
	km²	sq mi		
Aberconwy and Colwyn	1130	436	111 800	Colwyn Bay
Anglesey	719	277	67 900	Llangefni
Blaenau Gwent	109	42	74 000	Ebbw Vale
Bridgend	246	95	132 200	Bridgend
Caerphilly	279	108	172 700	Hengoed
Cardiff	139	54	312 100	Cardiff
Cardiganshire	1797	694	70 400	Aberystwyth
Carmarthenshire	2398	926	170 700	Carmarthen
Denbighshire	844	326	92 200	Ruthin
Flintshire	437	169	146 800	Mold
Gwynedd	2548	983	119 200	Caernarfon
Merthyr Tydfil	111	43	60 100	Merthyr Tydfil

Name	Area		Population	Admin
	km²	sq mi	total (2000e)	centre
Monmouthshire	851	328	85 000	Cwmbran
Neath and Port Talbot	442	171	141 500	Port Talbot
Newport	191	74	138 800	Newport
Pembrokeshire	1590	614	114 700	Haverfordwest
Powys	5204	2009	123 200	Llandrindod Wells
Rhondda, Cynon Taff	424	164	241 400	Cardiff (temporary)
Swansea	378	146	233 000	Swansea
Torfaen	126	49	91 500	Pontypool
Vale of Glamorgan	337	130	120 300	Barry
Wrexham	499	193	124 600	Wrexham

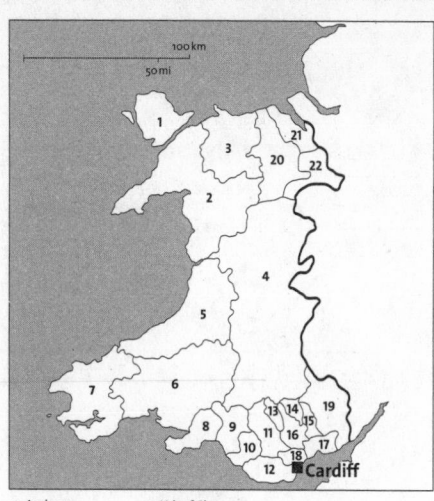

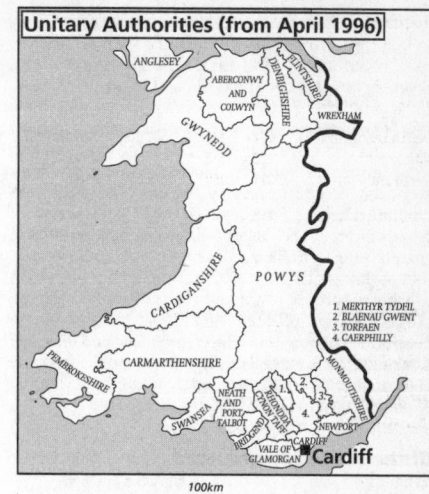

Unitary Authorities (from April 1996)

1 Anglesey	12 Vale of Glamorgan
2 Gwynedd	13 Merthyr Tydfil
3 Aberconwy & Colwyn	14 Blaenau Gwent
4 Powys	15 Torfaen
5 Cardiganshire	16 Caerphilly
6 Carmarthenshire	17 Newport
7 Pembrokeshire	18 Cardiff
8 Swansea	19 Monmouthshire
9 Neath & Port Talbot	20 Denbighshire
10 Bridgend	21 Flintshire
11 Rhondda Cynon Taff	22 Wrexham

Northern Ireland (Ulster)

Area 14120 km²/5450 sq mi

Population total (2000e) 1664000

Status Constituent division of the United Kingdom

Capital Belfast

Languages English, Irish Gaelic

Religions Christian (Roman Catholic 28%, Presbyterian 23%, Church of Ireland 19%)

Physical features Occupies the NE part of Ireland, centred on Lough Neagh; Mourne Mts in SE; highest point, Slieve Donard, 847 m/2786 ft, in the former Co. Down; R Mourne, 82 km/51 mi in length.

Economy Agriculture; service industries, shipbuilding, engineering, chemicals; linen, textiles; economy badly affected by the sectarian troubles since 1969.

History Separate Parliament established in 1920, with a 52-member House of Commons and a 26-member Senate; Protestant majority in the population, generally supporting political union with Great Britain; many of the Roman Catholic minority look for union with the Republic of Ireland; violent conflict between the communities broke out in 1969, leading to the establishment of a British army peace-keeping force; sectarian murders and bombings continued both within and outside the province; as a result of the disturbances, Parliament was abolished in 1972; powers are now vested in the UK Secretary of State for Northern Ireland; formation of a 78-member Assembly, 1973; replaced by a Constitutional Convention, 1975; Assembly re-formed in 1982, but Nationalist members did not take their seats; under the

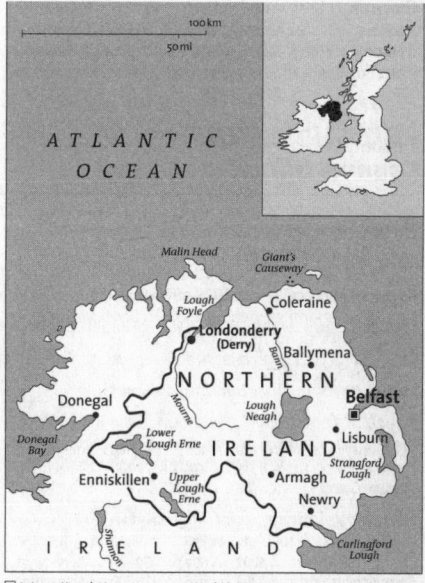

1985 Anglo-Irish agreement, the Republic of Ireland was given a consultative role in the government of Northern Ireland; all Northern Ireland MPs in the British Parlia-

HUMAN GEOGRAPHY

ment resigned in protest, 1986; continuing controversy in late 1980s; fresh talks between all main parties and Irish government, 1992; breakthrough in 1993 with Downing Street Declaration; IRA and loyalist ceasefires, 1994; joint Irish/British Framework Document, 1995; new IRA campaign, 1996; start of all-party talks (initially with Sinn Féin excluded), 1996; Good Friday agreement, 1998, introduces Northern Ireland Assembly; problems over arms decommissioning by the IRA hindered implementation of the agreement through 1999; review of peace process by US senator George Mitchell, resulted in compromise formula and inauguration of Assembly; reimposition of UK rule, 2000; Sinn Féin announced IRA to begin the process of arms decommissioning, 2001; further suspension of devolution, 2002; talks to restore devolution ongoing, 2004; IRA announced end to armed campaign, 2005; emergency legislation published early 2006, to recall Assembly and set deadline for formation of power-sharing executive.

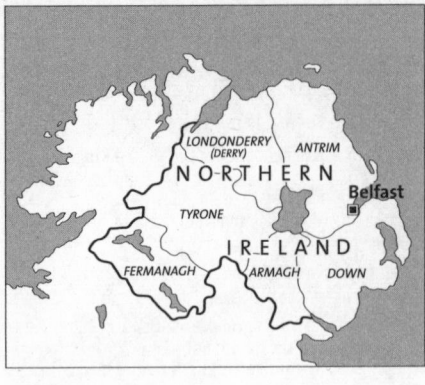

Districts of Northern Ireland

Name	Area		Population total (2000e)	Admin centre
	km²	sq mi		
Antrim	563	217	44700	Antrim
Ards	369	142	67900	Newtownards
Armagh	672	259	52100	Armagh
Ballymena	638	246	57800	Ballymena
Ballymoney	419	162	25500	Ballymoney
Banbridge	444	171	34600	Banbridge
Belfast	140	54	285800	Belfast
Carrickfergus	87	34	35500	Carrickfergus
Castlereagh	85	33	53600	Belfast
Coleraine	485	187	52100	Coleraine
Cookstown	623	240	31800	Cookstown
Craigavon	383	147	77800	Craigavon
Down	646	249	63000	Downpatrick
Dungannon	779	301	49900	Dungannon
Fermanagh	1876	715	54100	Enniskillen
Larne	338	131	30400	Larne
Limavady	587	227	23700	Limavady
Lisburn	444	171	103000	Lisburn
Londonderry/ Derry	382	147	102000	Londonderry/ Derry
Magherafelt	573	221	37500	Magherafelt
Moyle	495	191	15000	Ballycastle
Newry and Mourne	895	346	75600	Newry
Newtownabbey	152	59	77900	Newtownabbey
North Down	73	28	74500	Bangor
Omagh	1129	436	47900	Omagh
Strabane	870	336	37400	Strabane

BRITISH ISLANDS
Channel Islands

Timezone GMT

Area 194 km²/75 sq mi

Population total (2002e) 145000

Status Crown dependency of the United Kingdom

Capital St Helier (on Jersey), St Peter Port (on Guernsey)

Languages English and Norman-French

Physical features Island group of the British Isles in the English Channel, W of Normandy; comprises the islands of Guernsey, Jersey, Alderney, Sark, Herm, Jethou, Brechou, and Lihou.

Economy Tourism, fruit, vegetables, flowers, dairy produce, Jersey and Guernsey cattle; used as a tax haven; not part of the European Community.

History Granted to the Dukes of Normandy, 10th-c; only British possession to have been occupied by Germany during World War 2; a dependent territory of the British Crown, with individual legislative assemblies and legal system; divided into the Bailiwick of Guernsey and the Bailiwick of Jersey; Bailiff presides over the Royal Court and the Representative Assembly (the States).

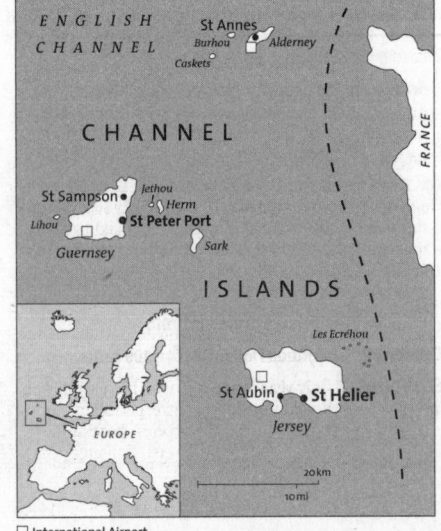

☐ International Airport

Isle of Man

Timezone GMT

Area 572 km²/221 sq mi

Population total (2002e) 75 000

Status Crown dependency of the United Kingdom

Capital Douglas

Languages English (Manx survived as an everyday language until 19th-c)

Physical features Island in the Irish Sea; rises to 620 m/ 2036 ft at Snaefell.

Economy Tourism, agriculture, fishing, light engineering; used as a tax haven; not part of European Community; annual Tourist Trophy motorcycle races held here.

History Ruled by the Welsh, 6th–9th-c; then by the Scandinavians, Scots, and English; purchased by the British Government between 1765 and 1828; the island has its own Parliament, the bicameral Court of Tynwald, which consists of the elected House of Keys and the Legislative Council; Acts of the British Parliament do not generally apply to Man.

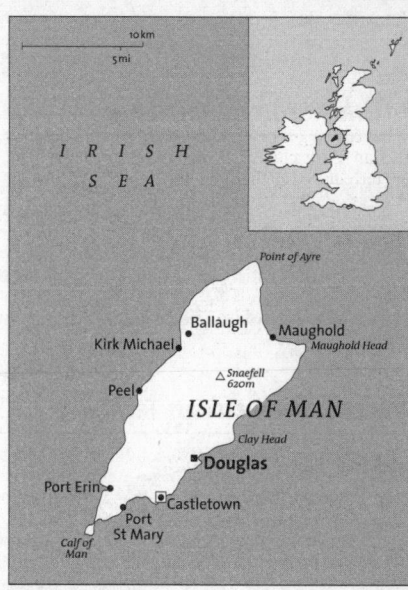

☐ International Airport

BRITISH OVERSEAS TERRITORIES
Anguilla

Timezone GMT –4

Area 155 km²/60 sq mi

Population total (2002e) 12 000

Capital The Valley

Physical features Most northerly of the Leeward Is, E Caribbean; also includes Sombrero I and several other offshore islets and cays; low-lying coral island, covered in low scrub and fringed with white coral-sand beaches.

Climate Tropical climate; average annual temperature ranges from 24–30°C; low and erratic annual rainfall, 550–1250 mm/22–50 in; hurricane season (Jul–Oct).

Currency 1 East Caribbean Dollar (XCD) = 100 cents

Economy Tourism, fishing, peas, corn, sweet potatoes, salt, boatbuilding.

History Colonized by English settlers from St Kitts, 1650; ultimately incorporated in the colony of St Kitts-Nevis-Anguilla; separated, 1980; governor appointed by the British sovereign; Legislative Assembly.

Bermuda

Timezone GMT –4

Area 53 km²/20 sq mi

Population total (2002e) 82 000

Capital Hamilton

Physical features Archipelago in W Atlantic, c.900 km/ 560 mi E of Cape Hatteras, N Carolina; c.150 low-lying coral islands and islets, 20 inhabited, 7 linked by causeways and bridges; largest island, (Great) Bermuda; highest point, Gibb's Hill, 78 m/256 ft.

Climate Subtropical climate; generally humid; rain throughout year; warm summers, mild winters.

Currency 1 Bermuda Dollar (BMD) = 100 cents

Economy Mainly year-round tourism; increasingly an international company business centre; petroleum products, pharmaceuticals, aircraft supplies, boatbuilding, ship repair, vegetables, citrus fruits; fish-processing centre.

History Formerly called Somers Is, discovered by Span-

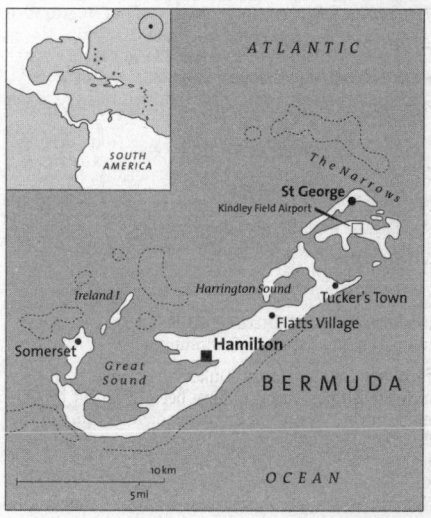

ish mariner, Juan Bermudez, in early 16th-c; colonized by English settlers, 1612; important naval station, and (to 1862) penal settlement; internal self-government, 1968;

British Antarctic Territory

British colonial territory, designated 1962; 20°–80°W and S of 60°S; includes South Orkney Is, South Shetland Is, Antarctic Graham Land Peninsula, and the land mass extending to the South Pole; area, 5.7 million km²/2.2 million sq mi; land area (660 000 km²/170 000 sq mi) covered by ice and fringed by floating ice shelves; population solely of scientists of the British Antarctic Survey; Territory administered by a High Commissioner in the Falkland Is.

British Indian Ocean Territory

British territory, 1900 km/1180 mi NE of Mauritius, c.2300 islands, comprising the Chagos Archipelago; area, 60 km²/23 sq mi; covering c.54 400 km²/21 000 sq mi of Indian Ocean; tropical maritime climate, hot and humid; acquired by France, 18th-c; annexed by Britain, 1814; bought by the Crown, 1967; population working on copra plantations resettled in Mauritius or the Seychelles, 1967–73; construction of a naval and air base by Britain and US started on Diego Garcia, the largest island; population total (2000e) 2900; no permanent civilian population.

movement for independence caused tension in the 1970s, including assassination of the Governor-General; bicameral legislature.

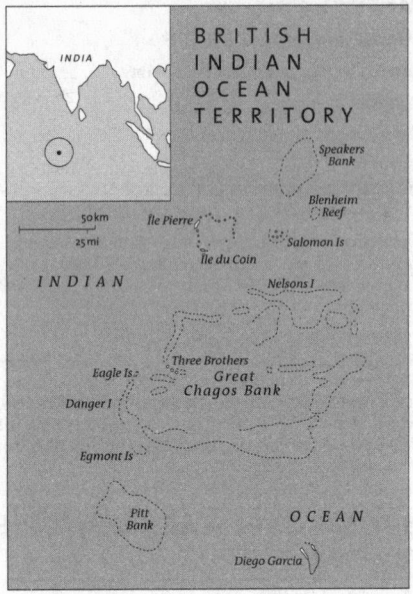

British Virgin Islands

Timezone GMT –4

Area 153 km²/59 sq mi

Population total (2002e) 21 000

Capital Road Town (on Tortola Island)

Physical features Island group at the NW end of the Lesser Antilles chain, E Caribbean, NE of Puerto Rico; comprises 4 large islands (Tortola, Virgin Gorda, Anegada, Jost Van Dyke) and over 30 islets and cays; only 16 inhabited; hilly terrain, except for flat coral island of Anegada; highest point, Sage Mt, 540 m/1 772 ft, on Tortola I.

MAP >> US VIRGIN ISLANDS, p. 365

Climate Subtropical climate; average annual temperatures 17–28°C (Jan), 26–31°C (Jul); average annual rainfall 1270 mm/50 in.

Currency 1 US Dollar (USD) = 100 cents

Economy Tourism (accounts for 50% of national income); construction and stone extraction; rum, paint, gravel, livestock, coconuts, sugar cane, fruit and vegetables, fish.

History Tortola colonized by British planters, 1666; constitutional government, 1774; part of the Leeward Is, 1872; separate Crown Colony, 1956; governor represents the British sovereign; Executive Council and Legislative Council.

Cayman Islands

Timezone GMT –5

Area 260 km²/100 sq mi

Population total (2002e) 40 000

Capital George Town

Physical features Located in W Caribbean, comprising the islands of Grand Cayman, Cayman Brac, and Little Cayman, c.240 km/150 mi S of Cuba; low-lying, rising to 42 m/138 ft on Cayman Brac plateau; ringed by coral reefs.

Climate Tropical climate; average temperatures

24–32°C (May–Oct), 16–24°C (Nov–Apr); average annual rainfall 1420 mm/56 in; hurricane season (Jul–Nov).

Currency 1 Cayman Island Dollar (KYD) = 100 cents

Economy Tourism; international finance, property development; over 450 banks and trust companies established on the islands; oil transshipment; crafts, jewellery, vegetables, tropical fish.

History Visited by Columbus, 1503; ceded to Britain, 1670; colonized by British settlers from Jamaica; British Crown Colony, 1962; a Governor represents the British sovereign, and presides over a Legislative Assembly.

HUMAN GEOGRAPHY

Falkland Islands

Timezone GMT –4

Area c.12 200 km²/4 700 sq mi

Population total (2002e) 3000

Capital Stanley (on East Falkland)

Physical features Located in the S Atlantic, c.650 km/400 mi NE of the Magellan Strait; consists of East Falkland and West Falkland, separated by the Falkland Sound, with over 200 small islands; hilly terrain, rising to 705 m/2313 ft at Mt Usborne (East Falkland) and 700 m/2297 ft at Mt Adam (West Falkland).

Climate Cold, strong westerly winds; low rainfall; narrow temperature range 19°C (Jan), 2°C (Jul); average annual rainfall 635 mm/25 in.

Currency 1 Falkland Pound (FKP) = 100 pence

Economy Agriculture; oats, sheep; service industries to the continuing military presence in the islands.

History Seen by several early navigators, including Capt John Strong in 1689–90, who named the islands; French settlement, 1764; British base established, 1765; French yielded their settlement to the Spanish, 1767; occupied in the name of the Republic of Buenos Aires, 1820; Britain asserted possession, became a British Crown Colony, 1833; formal annexation, 1908 and 1917; the whole island claimed since independence by Argentina; Falklands War, precipitated by the Argentine

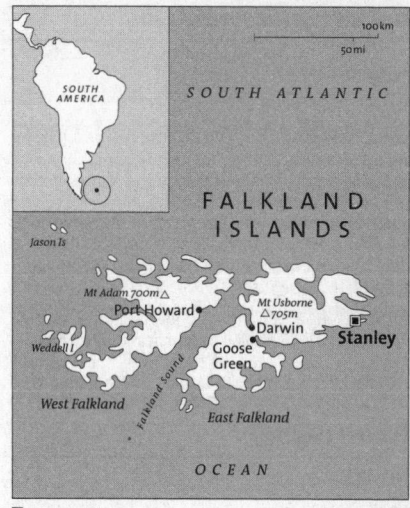

□ International Airport

invasion of the islands in April 1982, led to the dispatch of the British Task Force and the return of the islands to British rule in June 1982; external affairs and defence are the responsibility of the British government, which appoints civil and military commissioners; internal affairs are governed by executive and legislative councils.

South Georgia

British Overseas Territory, located in the S Atlantic, c.500 km/300 mi E of the Falkland Islands; area, c.3750 km²/1450 sq mi; barren, mountainous, snow-covered island; length, 160 km/100 mi; discovered by the London merchant De la Roche, 1675; landing by Captain Cook, 1775; British annexation, 1908 and 1917; burial place of Ernest Shackleton, the British explorer, who died at S Georgia in 1922; sealing and whaling centre until 1965; invaded by Argentina and recaptured by Britain, April 1982; territory administered from the Falkland Islands.

South Sandwich Islands

British Overseas Territory; group of small, uninhabited islands in the S Atlantic, c.720 km/450 mi SE of South Georgia; 56°18–59°25S 26°15W; discovered by Captain Cook, 1775; annexed by Britain, 1908 and 1917; administered from the Falkland Islands.

Gibraltar

Timezone GMT +1

Area 6.5 sq km/2.5 sq mi

Population total (2002e) 27 000

Capital Gibraltar

Physical features Narrow rocky peninsula rising steeply from the low-lying coast of SW Spain at the E end of the Strait of Gibraltar, 8 km/5 mi from Algeciras; narrows to limestone massif, 'The Rock', height 426 m/1398 ft, connected to the Spanish mainland by a sandy plain; home of the Barbary apes, the only native monkeys in Europe.

Climate Mediterranean climate, with mild winters, warm summers; average annual temperature range 13–29°C.

Currency 1 Gibraltar Pound (GIP) = 100 pence

Economy Largely dependent on the presence of British forces; Royal Naval Dockyard converted to a commercial yard, 1985; transshipment trade; fuel supplies to shipping; tourism.

History Settled by Moors, 711; taken by Spain, 1462; ceded to Britain, 1713; Crown Colony, 1830; played a key role in Allied naval operations during both World Wars; proposal to end British rule defeated by referendum, 1967; Spanish closure of frontier, 1969–85; Spain continues to claim sovereignty; British–Spanish talks ongoing, with a backdrop of inhabitants' demonstrations against shared sovereignty, 2002; British Monarch represented by a Governor and House of Assembly; military base; important strategic point of control for the W Mediterranean.

MAP >> SPAIN

HUMAN GEOGRAPHY

Montserrat (Emerald Isle)

Timezone GMT −4

Area 106 km²/41 sq mi

Population total (1997e) 11 000 (pre-disaster); (2002e) 4000

Capital Plymouth

Physical features Volcanic island in the Leeward Is, E Caribbean; mountainous, heavily forested; highest point, Chance's Peak, 914 m/3000 ft; seven active volcanoes.

Climate Tropical climate, with low humidity; average annual rainfall 1500 mm/60 in; hurricanes (Jun–Nov).

Currency 1 East Caribbean Dollar (XCD) = 100 cents

Economy Tourism (accounts for 25% of national income); cotton, peppers, livestock, electronic assembly, crafts, rum distilling, postage stamps.

GDP (2002e) $29 mn, per capita $3400

History Visited by Colombus, 1493; colonized by English and Irish settlers, 1632; plantation economy based on slave labour; British Crown Colony, 1871; joined Federation of the West Indies, 1958–62; island severely damaged by hurricane Hugo, 1989; most of the island, including the capital, destroyed by eruption of Soufriere Hills volcano (Jun 1997), followed by gradual resettlement of the population; British sovereign represented by a Governor, with an Executive Council and a Legislative Council.

Pitcairn Islands

Timezone GMT −9

Area 27 km²/10 sq mi

Population total (2000e) 50

Capital Adamstown

Physical features Volcanic island group in the SE Pacific Ocean, E of French Polynesia; comprises Pitcairn Island, 4.5 km²/1.7 sq mi, and the uninhabited islands of Ducie, Henderson, and Oeno; Pitcairn Island rises to 335 m/1099 ft.

Climate Equable climate; average annual tempera-

tures 24°C (Jan), 19°C (Jul); average annual rainfall 2000 mm/80 in.

Currency 1 New Zealand Dollar (NZD) = 100 cents

Economy Postage stamps; tropical and subtropical crops; crafts, forestry.

History Visited by the British, 1767; occupied by nine mutineers from HMS *Bounty*, 1790; overpopulation led to emigration to Norfolk I, 1856; some returning in 1864; transferred to Fiji, 1952; now a UK Overseas Territory, governed by the High Commissioner in New Zealand.

Saint Helena and Dependencies

Timezone GMT

Area 122 km²/47 sq mi

Population total (2002e) 5000

Capital Jamestown (on St Helena Island)

Physical features Volcanic group of islands in the S Atlantic, 1920 km/1200 mi from the SW coast of Africa; includes St Helena, Ascension, Gough I, Inaccessible I, Nightingale I, and Tristan da Cunha; rugged, volcanic terrain; highest point, Diana's Peak, 823 m/2700 ft.

Climate Tropical marine; mild, tempered by SE 'trade' winds.

Currency 1 St Helena Pound (SHP) = 100 pence

Economy Fish (mostly tuna); agriculture, coffee; postage stamps; heavily subsidized by the UK.

GDP (1998e) $18 mn, per capita $2500

History Discovered by the Portuguese on St Helena's feast day, 1502; annexed by the Dutch, 1633; annexed by the East India Company, 1659; Napoleon exiled here, 1815–21; Ascension and Tristan da Cunha made dependencies, 1922; evacuated between 1961–3, following volcanic eruption; governed by an executive council and 12-member elected Legislative Council.

Turks and Caicos islands

Timezone GMT −5

Area 500 km²/200 sq mi

Population total (2002e) 21 000

Capital Cockburn Town

Physical features Two island groups comprising c.30 islands and cays, forming the SE archipelago of the Bahamas chain, W Atlantic Ocean; Turk I and Caicos I are separated by 35 km/22 mi; only 6 of the other islands are inhabited.

Climate Subtropical climate; average annual tempera-

tures 24–7°C (Jan), 29–32°C (Jul); average annual rainfall 525 mm/21 in; occasional hurricanes.

Currency 1 US Dollar (USD) = 100 cents

Economy Tourism is a rapidly expanding industry; corn, beans, fishing, fish processing.

GDP (2000e) $231 mn, per capita $9600

History Visited by the Spanish, 1512; linked formally to the Bahamas, 1765; transferred to Jamaica, 1848; British Crown Colony, 1972; internal self-government, 1976; British sovereign represented by a Governor, who presides over a Council.

HUMAN GEOGRAPHY

UNITED STATES OF AMERICA (USA)

Local names United States, America

Timezone GMT −5 (E coast) to −8 (Pacific Coast)

Area 9 160 454 km²/3 535 935 sq mi

Population total (2002e) 287 602 000

Status Federal republic

Date of independence 1776

Capital Washington, DC.

Languages English, large Spanish-speaking minority

Ethnic groups European origin (including 9% Hispanic) (89.3%), African American (12.1%), Asian and Pacific (2.9%), Native American, Aleut, and Inuit (0.8%)

Religions Christian (86%) (Protestant 53%, Roman Catholic 26%), Jewish (2%), atheist (7%), other (5%)

Physical features Includes the separate states of Alaska (GMT − 9) and Hawaii (GMT − 10); E Atlantic coastal plain is backed by the Appalachian Mts from the Great Lakes to Alabama, a series of parallel ranges including the Allegheny, Blue Ridge, and Catskill Mts; plain broadens out (S) towards the Gulf of Mexico and into the Florida peninsula; Gulf Plains stretch N to meet the Great Plains from which they are separated by the Ozark Mts; further W, Rocky Mts rise to over 4500 m/14 750 ft; highest point in US, Mt McKinley, Alaska, 6194 m/20 321 ft; Death Valley, −86 m/−282 ft, is the lowest point; drainage N is into the St Lawrence R or the Great Lakes; in the E, the Hudson, Delaware, Potomac, and other rivers flow E to the Atlantic Ocean; central plains drained by the great Red River-Missouri-Mississippi system and by other rivers flowing into the Gulf of Mexico; main rivers in W,

Columbia and Colorado; deserts cover much of Texas, New Mexico, Arizona, Utah, Nevada.

Climate Climate varies from conditions found in hot, tropical deserts (SW), to those typical of Arctic continental regions on the northern Pacific Coast; continental climate on High Plains, with summer dust storms and winter blizzards; temperate continental on Central Plains; continental Mid West and the Great Lakes, with very cold winters; cool temperate in N Appalachians, warm temperate in S; subtropical to warm temperate on the Gulf Coast, with plentiful rainfall and frequent hurricanes and tornadoes; temperate maritime on the Atlantic coast, with heavy snowfall in N; cool temperate in New England, with warm summers and severe winters; mean annual temperatures range from 29°C in Florida, to −13°C in Alaska; average annual temperatures in Chicago, −3°C (Jan), 24°C (Jul); in Arizona, 11°C (Jan), 32°C (Jul); average annual rainfall in Alabama, 1640 mm/65 in, in Arizona, 180 mm/7 in; hot and humid in

1 VERMONT
2 NEW HAMPSHIRE
3 MASSACHUSETTS
4 CONNECTICUT
5 RHODE ISLAND
6 DELAWARE
7 MARYLAND
8 WEST VIRGINIA

Hawaii, with average annual rainfall 1524–5080 mm/ 60–200 in.

Currency 1 US Dollar (USD) = 100 cents

Economy One of the world's most productive industrial nations; highly diversified economy; vast mineral and agricultural resources; major exporter of grains, cereals, potatoes, sugar, fruit; livestock farming of beef, veal, pork; chief exports include aircraft, cars, machinery, chemicals, military equipment, non-fuel minerals; advanced system of communications and transportation; leader in space-exploration programme of the 1970s.

GDP (2002e) $10.45 tn, per capita $36 300

HDI (2002) 0.939

History First settled by groups who migrated from Asia across the Bering Straits over 25 000 years ago; explored by the Norse in 9th-c and by the Spanish in 16th-c, who settled in Florida and Mexico; in the 17th-c, settlements by the British, French, Dutch, Germans, and Swedes; many Black Africans introduced as slaves to work on the plantations; British control during 18th-c after defeat of French in Seven Years' war; revolt of the English-speaking colonies in the War of Independence, 1775–83, resulted in the creation of the United States of America; Louisiana sold to the USA by France in 1803 (the Louisiana Purchase) and the westward movement of settlers began; Florida ceded by Spain in 1819, and further Spanish states joined the Union, 1821–53; 11 Southern states left the Union over the slavery issue and formed the Confederacy, 1860–1; Civil War, 1861–5, ended in victory for the North, and the Southern states later rejoined the Union; Alaska purchased from Russia, 1867; Hawaiian islands annexed, 1898; several other islands formally associated with the USA, such as Puerto Rico, American Samoa, and Guam; in the 19th-c, arrival of millions of immigrants from Europe and the Far East; more recent arrival of large numbers of Spanish-speaking people, mainly from Mexico and the West Indies; entered World War 1 on the side of the Allies, 1917, and again in World War 2 in 1941; became the chief world power opposed to communism, a policy which led to involvement in the Korean War (1950–3) and Vietnam (1956–75); campaign for Black civil rights developed, 1960s, and eventually led to Civil Rights Act (1964); invasion of Grenada, 1983; mid 1980s rapprochement of US and USSR; invasion of Panama, 1989; involvement in Gulf War, 1991; military intervention in Somalia, 1993; ongoing concern over the ability of Iraq to pose a threat through its alleged development of weapons of mass destruction; following Al-Qaeda attack on the World Trade Center in New York (11 Sep 2001), and earlier terrorist attacks (notably, the 1998 bomb attacks on US embassies in Kenya and Tanzania, and the bombing of the USS *Cole* warship in the port of Aden, Yemen in 2000), the USA led the successful campaign to remove the Taliban from power in Afghanistan; further campaign against international terrorism, 2002 and ongoing; invasion of Iraq and removal of Saddam Hussein (2003), with US presence in Iraq scheduled to remain until mid-2004; ongoing terrorist threats against the USA, both within the country and abroad, brought unprecedented levels of security throughout 2003–6; Congress consists of 435-member House of Representatives, and a 100-member Senate; a President elected every 4 years by a college of state representatives, appoints an executive Cabinet responsible to Congress; divided into 50 federal states and the District of Columbia, each state having its own two-body legislature and governor.

Head of State/Government (President)
1993–2001 William Jefferson Clinton
2001–   George W(alker) Bush

>> Political leaders and rulers pp.199–200

American States

(Timezones: two sets of figures indicate that different zones operate in a state. The second figure refers to Summer Time (Apr–Oct, approximately)
2 Aleutian/Hawaii Standard Time : 3 Alaska Standard Time : 4 Pacific Standard Time : 5 Mountain Standard Time : 6 Central Standard Time : 7 Eastern Standard Time

Name	Area km²	Area sq mi	Capital	Time zone	Population figures (2000e)	Nickname(s)
Alabama (AL)	133 911	51 705	Montgomery	7/8	4 387 000	Camellia State, Heart of Dixie
Alaska (AK)	1 518 748	586 412	Juneau	3/4	6 24 000	Mainland State, The Last Frontier
Arizona (AZ)	295 249	114 000	Phoenix	5	4 893 000	Apache State, Grand Canyon State
Arkansas (AR)	137 403	53 187	Little Rock	6/7	2 564 000	Bear State, Land of Opportunity
California (CA)	411 033	158 706	Sacramento	4/5	33 609 000	Golden State
Colorado (CO)	269 585	104 091	Denver	5/6	4 145 000	Centennial State
Connecticut (CT)	12 996	5018	Hartford	7/8	3 292 000	Nutmeg State, Constitution State
Delaware (DE)	5296	2045	Dover	7/8	763 000	Diamond State, First State
District of Columbia (DC)	173.5	67.0	Washington	7/8	516 000	
Florida (FL)	151 934	58 664	Tallahassee	6/7, 7/8	15 323 000	Everglade State, Sunshine State
Georgia (GA)	152 571	58 910	Atlanta	7/8	7 944 000	Empire State of the South, Peach State
Hawaii (HI)	16 759	6471	Honolulu	2	1 181 000	Aloha State
Idaho (ID)	216 422	83 564	Boise	4/5, 5/6	1 273 000	Gem State
Illinois (IL)	145 928	56 345	Springfield	6/7	12 189 000	Prairie State, Land of Lincoln
Indiana (IN)	93 715.5	36 185	Indianapolis	6/7, 7/8	5 979 000	Hoosier State
Iowa (IA)	145 747	56 275	Des Moines	6/7	2 878 000	Hawkeye State, Corn State
Kansas (KS)	213 089	82 277	Topeka	5/6, 6/7	2 670 000	Sunflower State, Jayhawker State
Kentucky (KY)	104 658	40 410	Frankfort	6/7, 7/8	3 989 000	Bluegrass State
Louisiana (LA)	123 673	47 752	Baton Rouge	6/7	4 381 000	Pelican State, Sugar State, Creole State
Maine (ME)	86 153	33 265	Augusta	7/8	1 258 000	Pine Tree State
Maryland (MD)	27 090	10 460	Annapolis	7/8	5 213 000	Old Line State, Free State
Massachusetts (MA)	21 455	8284	Boston	7/8	6 206 000	Bay State, Old Colony
Michigan (MI)	151 579	58 527	Lansing	6/7, 7/8	9 903 000	Wolverine State, Great Lake State
Minnesota (MN)	218 593	84 402	St Paul	6/7	4 823 000	Gopher State, North Star State
Mississippi (MS)	123 510	47 689	Jackson	6/7	2 785 000	Magnolia State
Missouri (MO)	180 508	69 697	Jefferson City	6/7	5 501 000	Bullion State, Show Me State
Montana (MT)	380 834	147 046	Helena	5/6	886 000	Treasure State, Big Sky Country
Nebraska (NE)	200 342	77 352	Lincoln	5/6, 6/7	1 671 000	Cornhusker State, Beef State
Nevada (NV)	286 341	110 561	Carson City	4/5	1 878 000	Silver State, Sagebrush State
New Hampshire (NH)	24 032	9279	Concord	7/8	1 217 000	Granite State
New Jersey (NJ)	20 167	7787	Trenton	7/8	8 192 000	Garden State
New Mexico (NM)	314 914	121 593	Santa Fe	5/6	1 747 000	Sunshine State, Land of Enchantment
New York (NY)	127 185	49 108	Albany	7/8	18 233 000	Empire State

American States (continued)

Name	Area		Capital	Time zone	Population figures (2000e)	Nickname(s)
	km²	sq mi				
North Carolina (NC)	136407	52699	Raleigh	7/8	7758000	Old North State, Tar Heel State
North Dakota (ND)	180180	69567	Bismarck	5/6, 6/7	630000	Flickertail State, Sioux State
Ohio (OH)	107040	41330	Columbus	7/8	11279000	Buckeye State
Oklahoma (OK)	181083	69919	Oklahoma City	6/7	3378000	Sooner State
Oregon(OR)	251409	97073	Salem	4/5	3349000	Sunset State, Beaver State
Pennsylvania (PA)	117343	45308	Harrisburg	7/8	11982000	Keystone State
Rhode Island (RI)	3139	1212	Providence	7/8	994000	Little Rhody, Plantation State
South Carolina (SC)	80579	31113	Columbia	7/8	3932000	Palmetto State
South Dakota (SD)	199723	77116	Pierre	5/6, 6/7	735000	Sunshine State, Coyote State
Tennessee (TN)	109149	42144	Nashville	6/7, 7/8	5533000	Volunteer State
Texas (TX)	691003	266807	Austin	5/6, 6/7	20385000	Lone Star State
Utah (UT)	219880	84899	Salt Lake City	5/6	2160000	Mormon State, Beehive State
Vermont (VT)	24899	9614	Montpelier	7/8	597000	Green Mountain State
Virginia (VA)	105582	40767	Richmond	7/8	6955000	Old Dominion State, Mother of Presidents
Washington (WA)	176473	68139	Olympia	4/5	5825000	Evergreen State, Chinook State
West Virginia (WV)	62758	24232	Charleston	7/8	1802000	Panhandle State, Mountain State
Wisconsin (WI)	145431	56153	Madison	6/7	5277000	Badger State, America's Dairyland
Wyoming (WY)	253315	97809	Cheyenne	5/6	479000	Equality State

UNITED STATES FORMAL DEPENDENCIES
American Samoa

Local name São Paulo de Loanda (Portuguese)

Timezone GMT –11

Area 197 km²/76 sq mi

Population total (2002e) 62000

Capital Fagatogo

Languages English (official), Samoan

Physical features Located in the CS Pacific Ocean, some 3500 km/2175 mi N of New Zealand; five principal volcanic islands (including Tutuila, Aunu'u, Ofu, Olosega, Ta'u, Rose, Swains I) and two coral atolls; main island, Tutuila, 109 km²/42 sq mi, rises to 653 m/2142 ft; islands mostly hilly, with large areas of thick bush and forest.

Climate Tropical maritime climate; average annual temperatures 28°C (Jan), 27°C (Jul) in Fagatogo; plentiful rainfall; rainy season (Nov–Apr); dry season (May–Oct); average annual rainfall 5000 mm/200 in.

Currency 1 US Dollar (USD) = 100 cents

Economy Principal crops, taro, breadfruit, yams, bananas, coconuts; tuna fishing; local inshore fishing, handicrafts.

GDP (2000e) $500 mn, per capita $8000

History US acquired rights to American Samoa, 1899;

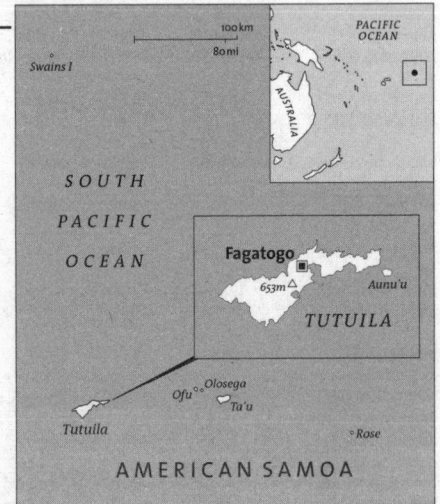

☐ International Airport

islands ceded to US by their chiefs, 1900–25; now unincorporated territory of USA, administered by Department of the Interior; bicameral legislature established, 1948, comprising a Senate and House of Representatives.

Guam

Local name Guam

Timezone GMT +10

Area 541 km²/209 sq mi

Population total (2002e) 163 000

Status Unincorporated territory of the United States of America

Capital Hagåtña (Agana)

Languages Chamorro and English (official), Japanese is also spoken

Ethnic groups Chamorro (37%), Filipino (29%), Caucasian (18%), Micronesian (13%)

Religion Roman Catholic

Physical features Largest and southernmost of the Mariana Islands, covering c.48 km/30 mi in the Pacific Ocean; volcanic island fringed by a coral reef; relatively flat limestone plateau, with narrow coastal plains in N, low rising hills in C and mountains in S; highest point, 406 m/1332 ft at Mt Lamlam.

Climate Tropical maritime climate; average annual temperature 24–30°C; average annual rainfall 2125 mm/84 in; wet season (Jul–Dec).

Currency 1 US Dollar (USD) = 100 cents

Economy Economy highly dependent on government activities; military installations cover 35% of the island; diversifying industrial and commercial projects; oil refining, dairy products, furniture, watches, copra, processed fish; rapidly growing tourist industry.

□ International Airport

History Originally settled by Malay-Filipino peoples; Ferdinand Magellan landed on the island, 1521; claimed for Spain, 1565; rebellion against Spanish missionaries, 1670–95; US consulate established, 1855; ceded to US by Spain after defeat in Spanish-American War, 1898; occupied by Japan, 1941–4; unincorporated territory of the US, Organic Act, 1950; elected Governor and a unicameral legislature.

Puerto Rico, The Commonwealth of

Local name Puerto Rico

Timezone GMT –4

Area 8897 km²/3434 sq mi

Population total (2002e) 3 879 000

Status Commonwealth

Capital San Juan

Languages Spanish (official), with English widely spoken

Religion Roman Catholic

Physical features Easternmost island of the Greater Antilles; almost rectangular in shape; crossed W–E by mountains, rising to 1338 m/4389 ft at Cerro de Punta; coastal plain belt in N; islands of Vieques and Culebra also belong to Puerto Rico.

Climate Tropical maritime climate; average annnual temperature 25°C; high humidity.

Currency 1 US Dollar (USD) = 100 cents

Economy Manufacturing is the most important sector of the economy; food processing, petrochemicals, electrical equipment, pharmaceuticals; textiles, clothing; livestock, tobacco, sugar, pineapples, coconuts; tourism.

GDP (2002e) $43.01 bn, per capita $11 100

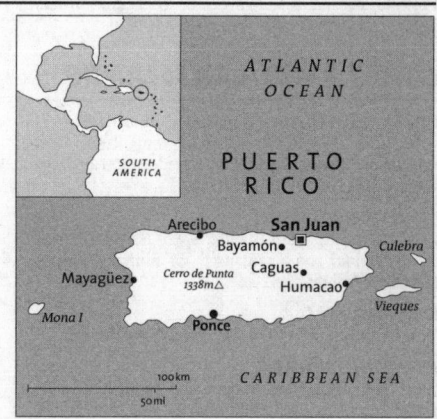

□ International Airport

History Originally occupied by Carib and Arawak Indians; visited by Columbus, 1493; Spanish colony until ceded to the US, 1898; high levels of emigration to the US from 1940s–50s; semi-autonomous Commonwealth in association with US, 1952; executive power exercised by a Governor; a bicameral Legislative Assembly consists of a Senate and House of Representatives.

HUMAN GEOGRAPHY

Virgin Islands, United States

Local name US Virgin Islands

Timezone GMT −4

Area 342 km²/132 sq mi

Population total (2002e) 121 000 (St Croix 53 900, St Thomas 51 400, St John 2900)

Status Territory

Capital Charlotte Amalie (on St Thomas Island)

Languages English (official), with Spanish and Creole widely spoken

Ethnic groups West Indian, French, Hispanic

Religion Protestant

Physical features Nine islands and 75 islets in the Lesser Antilles, Caribbean Sea; three main inhabited islands, St Croix, St Thomas, and St John; volcanic origin, mostly hilly or rugged and mountainous; highest peak, Crown Mt, 474 m/1555 ft on St Thomas.

Climate Subtropical climate; average annual temperatures 21–9°C (Dec–Mar), 24–31°C (Jun–Sep); low humidity; rainy season (May–Nov); subject to severe droughts, floods and earthquakes.

Currency 1 US Dollar (USD) = 100 cents

Economy Tourism (chief industry); St Croix industries include oil and alumina products, clocks and watches,

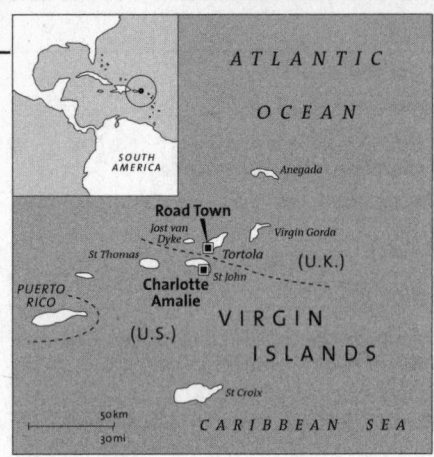

☐ International Airport

textiles, rum, fragrances, petrochemicals; vegetables, fruit, sorghum.

GDP (2002e) $2.4 bn, per capita $19 000

History Originally inhabited by Ciboney Indians, followed by Arawak Indians, then Caribs; discovered by Columbus, 1493; Denmark colonized St Thomas and St John, 1665 and 1718, and bought St Croix from France, 1733; purchased by US, 1917; now an unincorporated territory of the US; Governor heads unicameral legislature.

Mariana Islands, Northern

Located in N Pacific Ocean, area 471 km²/182 sq mi; limestone southern islands, volcanic northern islands; capital, Saipan; population total (2000e) 72 000; tropical marine climate; part of UN Trust Territory of the Pacific, 1947–78; became a self-governing US Commonwealth Territory, 1978–90; trusteeship ended, 1990.

OTHER AMERICAN ISLANDS

BAKER, HOWLAND, AND JARVIS ISLANDS
1500–1650 mi SW of the Hawaiian group, Pacific Ocean; uninhabited since World War 2; under Interior Department.

JOHNSTON ATOLL
Consists of four small islands, SW of Hawaii: Johnston, Sand, Hikina, and Akau; used for military purposes, otherwise uninhabited.

KINGMAN REEF
Uninhabited reef S of Hawaii, under Navy control.

MIDWAY ISLANDS
Atoll and two islands, Eastern and Sand, lying NW of Hawaii, in N Pacific; unpopulated apart from US naval personnel.

PALMYRA
Atoll 1000 mi S of Hawaii; privately owned; under Interior Department.

WAKE ISLAND
Uninhabited but for US naval personnel, Wake I lies between Guam and Midway I; sister islands, Wilkes and Peale.

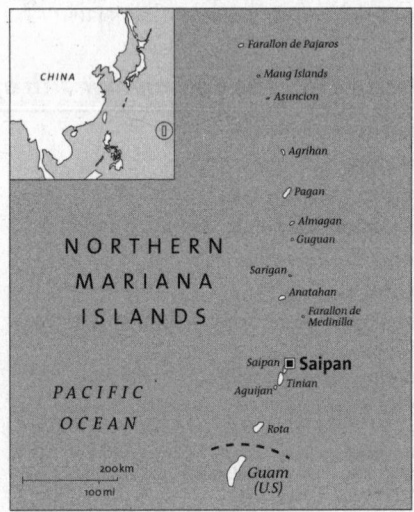

☐ International Airport

NAVASSA
Caribbean island between Jamaica and Haiti, 100 mi S of Guantánamo Bay, Cuba; covers c.3 sq mi and is reserved by US for a lighthouse, administered by US Coast Guard; uninhabited. Guantánamo Bay is an inlet in SE Cuba, c. 19 km (12 mi) by 10 km (6 mi); US marines landed in 1898 during the Spanish-American War; US naval base since 1903.

URUGUAY

Local name Uruguay

Timezone GMT –3

Area 176 215 km²/68 018 sq mi

Population total (2002e) 3 383 000

Status Republic

Date of independence 1828

Capital Montevideo

Language Spanish (official)

Ethnic groups European (mainly Spanish, Italian) (90%), mestizo (8%)

Religions Roman Catholic (60%), Protestant (2%), Jewish (2%), unaffiliated (30%)

Physical features Located in E South America; grass covered plains (S) rise to a high, sandy plateau, traversed SE and NW by the Cuchilla Grande and Cuchilla de Haedo, rising to 501 m/1644 ft at Cerro Mirados; R Negro flows SW to meet the R Uruguay on the Argentine frontier.

Climate Temperate, with warm summers, mild winters; average annual temperature 10°C (Jul), 22°C (Jan) in Montevideo; average annual rainfall 978 mm/38 in; rainy season (Apr–May), occasional droughts.

Currency 1 New Uruguayan Peso (UYU) = 100 centésimos

Economy Traditionally based on livestock and agriculture; meat, wool, fish, wheat, barley, maize, rice; naturally-occurring minerals include granite and marble; hydroelectric power, food processing and packing, light engineering, cement, textiles, leather, steel.

GDP (2002e) $26.82 bn, per capita $7900

HDI (2002) 0.831

☐ International Airport

History Originally occupied by Charrúas Indians; visited by the Spanish, 1516; part of the Spanish Viceroyalty of Río de la Plata, 1726; province of Brazil, 1814–25; independence as the Eastern Republic of Uruguay, 1828; unrest caused by Tupamaro guerrillas in late 1960s and early 1970s; military rule until 1985; a President is advised by a Council of Ministers; bicameral legislature consists of a Senate and Chamber of Deputies.

Head of State/Government
2000–5   Jorge Luis Ibáñez
2005–   Tabare Vazquez

USSR (FORMER) >> CIS, LATVIA, LITHUANIA, ESTONIA

UZBEKISTAN

Local name Ozbekiston Republikasy

Timezone GMT +5

Area 447 400 km²/172 696 sq mi

Population total (2002e) 25 484 000

Status Republic

Date of independence 1991

Capital Tashkent

Language Uzbek

Ethnic groups Uzbek (71%), Russian (8%), Tajik (5%), Kazakh (4%)

Religion Sunni Muslim

Physical features Located in C and N Middle Asia;

four-fifths of area is flat, sandy plain/desert (W); Turan Plain (NW) rises near the Aral Sea to 90 m/300 ft above sea level; delta of major river R Amu Darya forms alluvial plain over C Kara-Kalpak. Sultan-Uizdag Mts rise to 500 m/1600 ft; Kyzyl Kum broken by hills in SE; lowest point, Mynbulak, –12 m/–39 ft; Pskem Mts in E rise to 4299 m/14 104 ft at Beshtor Peak.

Climate Dry and continental; average annual temperatures in S, –12°C (Jan), 32–40°C (Jul); low rainfall.

Currency 1 Som (UZS) = 100 tiyin

Economy Deposits of coal, natural gas, oil, gold, lead, copper, and zinc; third largest cotton-growing area in the world; silk, wool; agriculture dependent on irrigated land; abundant orchards and vineyards; industry powered hydroelectrically.

GDP (2002e) $66.06 bn, per capita $2600

HUMAN GEOGRAPHY

HDI (2002) 0.727

History Conquered by Alexander the Great, 4th-c BC; invaded by Mongols under Genghis Khan, 13th-c; Genghis Khan's grandson, Shibaqan, inherited the area; converted to Islam in 14th-c, under the ruler of Kipchak, Uzbek; became part of Tamerlane the Great's empire, 14th-c; conquered by Russia, mid-19th-c; became the Uzbek Republic in 1924, and Uzbekistan Soviet Socialist Republic in 1925; declared independence, 1991; joined CIS in 1991; governed by a President, Prime Minister, and 250-member Supreme Assembly; new constitution adopted, 1992; proposal for a bicameral legislature approved, 2002.

Head of State
1991–   Islam A Karimov

Head of Government
1995–2003 Otkir Sultonov
2003–   Shavkat Mirziyoev

☐ International Airport

VANUATU

Local name Ripablik Blong Vanuatu

Timezone GMT +11

Area 14 763 km²/5698 sq mi

Population total (2002e) 207 000

Status Independent republic within the Commonwealth

Date of independence 1980

Capital Port Vila (on Efate Island)

Languages Bislama, English, and French (official)

Ethnic groups Melanesian (95%), Micronesian, Polynesian, and European minorities

Religions Christian (70%) (Presbyterian 40%, Roman Catholic 15%, Anglican 15%), indigenous (8%), other (15%)

Physical features Mountainous, volcanic Y-shaped island chain in SW Pacific Ocean, 400 km/250 mi NE of New Caledonia; consisting of 12 islands and 60 islets; two-thirds of population occupy the 4 main islands of Efate, Espiritu Santo, Malekula, and Tanna; highest peak, rises to 1888 m/6194 ft, on Espiritu Santo; raised coral beaches fringed by reefs; several active volcanoes.

Climate Tropical, high temperatures; hot and rainy season (Nov–Apr) when cyclones may occur; average annual temperatures, 27°C (Jan), 22°C (Jul) in Vila; average annual rainfall 2310 mm/91 in.

Currency 1 Vatu (VUV) = 100 centimes

Economy Agriculture; subsistence farming and plantations; yams, breadfruit, taro, copra, beef, cocoa, coffee, timber; manganese, fish processing, foodstuffs, crafts; tourism rapidly increasing, especially from cruise ships.

GDP (2002e) $563 mn, per capita $2900

HDI (2002) 0.542

History Visited by Spanish, 1606; named New Hebrides by James Cook, 1774; Anglo-French administration as condominium of the New Hebrides, 1906; escaped Japanese occupation during World War 2; independence as Republic of Vanuatu, 1980; governed by a President, Prime Minister, Cabinet, and representative Assembly.

Head of State
2004–   Kalkot Mataskelekele

Head of Government
2004–   Ham Lini

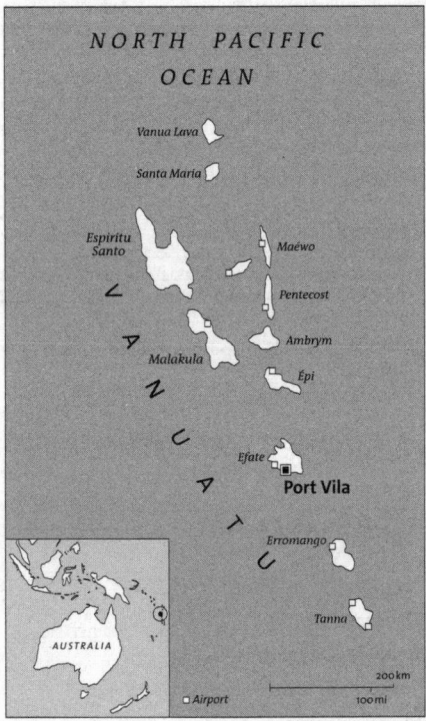

VATICAN CITY STATE

Local name Stato della Città del Vaticano

Timezone GMT +1

Area 0.44 km²/0.17 sq mi

Population total 1000

Status Papal sovereign state

Date of independence 1929

Capital The Holy See, Vatican City

Languages Latin and Italian

Ethnic groups Italian, European, and various minorities

Religion Roman Catholic

Physical features The world's smallest state, situated on the Vatican hill in Rome, on W bank of R Tiber; architectural features include the Vatican Palace and Museum, St Peter's, the Pope's summer villa at Castel Gandolfo, and the Sistine Chapel; three entrances to the city in the care of the Pontifical Swiss Guard, 'The Bronze Doors', the Arch of Charlemagne, or the 'Arch of Bells', and the Via di Porta Angelica.

Climate Mediterranean; average annual temperature 7°C (Jan), 25°C (Jul); average annual rainfall 657 mm/26 in.

Currency 1 Euro (EUR) = 100 cents (before 2002, 1 Vatican Lira (ITL) = 100 centesimi)

Economy The state is supported by special collections and donations from Catholic congregations around the world; issues its own stamps and coinage, and has its own communications and banking systems; tourism; pilgrimages.

Income (1991) income $109 m, expenses $196 m

History Papacy's temporal authority exercised from a palace built on Rome's Vatican hill in 1377; extended to much of central Italy by 16th-c; incorporated into the emerging Italian state during the fight to unite Italy, 1860–70; the Lateran Treaty of 1929 recognized the Holy See's sovereignty in the Vatican City State and Catholicism became Italy's state religion; Karol Wojtyla became the first non-Italian pontiff since the 16th-c, 1978; in 1985, a concordat, replacing the Lateran Treaty, affirmed independence of the Vatican, but ended some of its privileges, Roman Catholicism ceased to be the state religion, and Rome lost its status as a 'sacred city'; sovereignty exercised by Pope, who is elected for life by a conclave of the College of Cardinals.

Head of State (Sovereign Pontiff/Pope)
1978–2005 Pope John Paul II (Karol Wojtyla)
2005–   Pope Benedict XVI (Joseph Ratzinger)

Head of Government (Secretary of State)
1990–   Cardinal Angelo Sodano

MAP >> ITALY

VENEZUELA

Local name República de Venezuela

Timezone GMT –4

Area 912 050 km²/352 051 sq mi

Population total (2002e) 25 093 000

Status Republic

Date of independence 1830

Capital Caracas

Languages Spanish (official), Italian, c.25 Indian languages also spoken in the interior

Ethnic groups Mestizo (69%), European (20%), African origin (9%), Indian (2%)

Religions Roman Catholic (92%), Protestant (2%)

Physical features Occupies most of the N coast of South America; Guiana Highlands (SE) cover almost half the country; Venezuelan Highlands in the W and along the coast, highest point, Pico Bolívar 5007 m/16 411 ft; vast grasslands (*llanos*) in the Orinoco basin; chief river, Orinoco; largest lake in South America, L Maracaibo, 21 486 km²/8296 sq mi; highest waterfall in the world, Angel Falls 979 m/3212 ft.

Climate Tropical, generally hot and humid; average annual temperatures 18°C (Jan), 21°C (Jul) in Caracas; one rainy season (Apr–Oct); average annual rainfall 833 mm/33 in.

Currency 1 Bolívar (VEB) = 100 céntimos

□ International Airport ····Disputed border

Economy Since 1920s, based on oil from Maracaibo (now provides over 90% of export revenue); aluminium (second-highest source of revenue); iron ore, gold, diamonds; only

4% of the land under permanent cultivation; beef and dairy farming; coffee, cocoa, cotton, rice, tobacco, sugar.

GDP (2002e) $131.7 bn, per capita $5400

HDI (2002) 0.770

History Originally inhabited by Caribs and Arawaks; seen by Columbus, 1498; Spanish settlers, 1520; frequent revolts against Spanish colonial rule; independence movement under Simón Bolívar, leading to the establishment of the State of Gran Colombia (Colombia, Ecuador, Venezuela), 1821; independent republic, 1830; short-lived military coup, April 2002; governed by an elected bicameral National Congress, comprising a Senate and a Chamber of Deputies; a President is advised by a Council of Ministers.

Head of State/Government
1998–2002 Hugo Chávez Fríaz
2002 Pedro Carmona *Transitional*
2002– Hugo Chávez Fríaz

VIETNAM

Local name Công Hòa Xã Hôi Chu Nghĩa Việt Nam

Timezone GMT +7

Area 329 566 km²/127 212 sq mi

Population total (2002e) 79 939 000

Status Socialist republic

Date of independence 1976

Capital Hanoi

Languages Vietnamese (official), French, Chinese, English, Khmer

Ethnic groups Vietnamese (85–90%), Chinese (3%), minorities include Khmer, Cham, Hmong, Nung, Tay

Religions Buddhist (principal), Taoist, Confucian, Muslim, Roman Catholic, Hoa Hoa, Cao Dai, Protestant, and animist beliefs

Physical features Occupies a narrow strip along the coast of the Gulf of Tongking and the S China Sea on Indochinese peninsula in SE Asia; highest peak Fan si Pan, 3143 m/10 312 ft; Mekong R delta (S) and Red R delta (N) linked by narrow coastal plain; heavily forested mountains and plateaux.

Climate Tropical, monsoon climate; sub-tropical in N; average annual temperatures 17°C (Jan), 29°C (Jul) in Hanoi; average annual rainfall 1830 mm/72 in; typhoons and flooding frequent in N and SW.

Currency 1 Dông (VND) = 10 hao = 100 xu

Economy Agriculture (employs over 70% of the workforce); natural disasters, war, and political unrest adversely affected economy; Vietnam War brought depopulation, destruction of forest and farmland; exports include coal, minerals, rice, rubber, sugar cane.

GDP (2002e) $183.8 bn, per capita $2300

HDI (2002) 0.688

History Under the influence of China for many centuries; regions of Tongking (N), Annam (C), and Cochin-China (S) united as Vietnamese Empire, 1802; French protectorates established in Cochin-China, 1867, and in Annam and Tongking, 1884; formed the French Indo-Chinese Union with Cambodia and Laos, 1887; occupied by the Japanese in World War 2; communist Viet-Minh League under Ho Chi-minh formed after the War, not recognized by France; Indo-Chinese war, resulting in French withdrawal, 1946–54; 1954 armistice divided the coun-

☐ International Airport

try between the communist 'Democratic Republic' in the N, and the 'State' of Vietnam in the S; civil war led to US intervention on the side of S Vietnam, 1965; fall of Saigon, 1975; reunification as the Socialist Republic of Vietnam, 1976; large numbers of refugees tried to find homes in the W in the late 1970s; Hanoi invaded neighbouring Cambodia, overthrowing hostile Khmer Rouge government, 1978; Chinese responded with invasion of Vietnam in 1979 - greatly increased the number trying to leave the country by sea (Vietnamese boat people); limited troop withdrawals from Laos and Cambodia, 1989; Vietnam supported Cambodian peace agreement, 1991; new constitution, 1992, replaced Council of Ministers with a Prime Minister and a cabinet.

Head of State
1997– Tran Duc Luong

Head of Government
2006– Nguyen Tan Dung

General Secretary
2001– Nong Duc Manh

WESTERN SAHARA

Timezone GMT

Area 252 126 km²/97 321 sq mi

Population total (2002e) 308 000

Status Under dispute, still officially part of Morocco

Capital al-Aioun

Languages Arabic (Hassaniya and Moroccan), French, Berber dialects, Spanish

Ethnic groups Mainly of Arab and Berber descent

Religion Sunni Muslim

Physical features Located in NW Africa, between Morocco (N), Mauritania (S), and Atlantic Ocean (E); low, flat terrain rising to small mountains in S and NE.

Climate Hot, dry desert; limited rainfall; fog and heavy dew produced by cold offshore currents.

Currency 1 Moroccan Dirham (MAD) = 100 Moroccan francs

Economy Limited by low rainfall and few natural resources; fishing and phosphate mining are main sources of income.

History Spanish province known as Spanish Sahara (Western Sahara) since 1884; partitioned by Morocco and Mauritania after its Spanish status ended in 1975; independence proclaimed in 1976, as Saharan Arab Democratic Republic (SADR); Morocco refused to withdraw its claim to the region, resulting in fighting between Morocco and Polisario guerrillas; Mauritania withdrew its claim after signing a peace treaty with the Polisario Front, 1979; SADR admitted to the Organization of African Unity, 1982; UN-supervised talks to decide the region's future, 1990; Polisario guerrilla warfare stopped

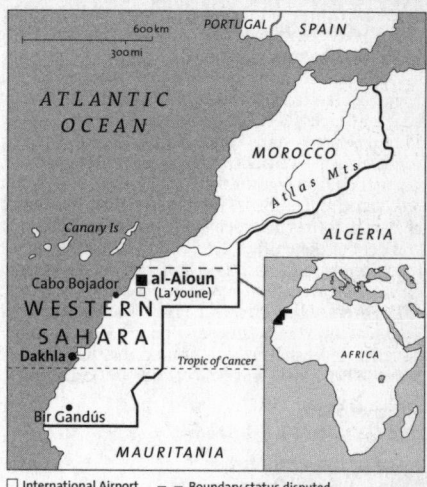

□ International Airport — — Boundary status disputed

under UN ceasefire, 1991; renewed fighting, 1993; agreement to UN proposal for a referendum, 1994, but implementation postponed, 1996.

Main SADR government leaders [a]

Head of State
1982– Mohammed Abdelazziz

Head of Government
1999– Bouchraya Hamoudi Bayoune

[a]Officially administered by Morocco and the Moroccan government.

YEMEN

Local name al-Yaman (Arabic)

Timezone GMT +3

Area 531 570 km²/205 186 sq mi

Population total (2002e) 19 495 000

Status Republic

Date of independence 1967

Capitals Sana (political), Aden (commercial)

Languages Arabic (official), English

Ethnic groups Arab (96%), with Indo-Pakistani, Somali, Amhara and Swahili, Persian, Jewish, and European minorities

Religions Muslim (Sunni 53%, Shiite 47%), small Christian, Hindu, and Yemeni Jew minorities

Physical features Occupies the SW corner of the Arabian peninsula; narrow coastal plain, backed by mountains rising to 3000–3500 m/10 000–11 500 ft; highlands, central plateau and maritime range of former South Yemen form the most fertile part of the country; former North Yemen is largely desert and mountainous.

Climate Hot and humid climate; lowland and desert regions in NE receive an average annual rainfall of 100 mm/4 in; hot and humid on Tihamat coastal strip with mean temperature of 29°C; mild and temperate in interior highlands, with cool winters; average annual temperatures 24°C (Jan), 32°C (Jul) in Aden; average annual rainfall, 46 mm/1.8 in.

Currency 1 Yemeni Riyal (YER) = 100 fils (former N Yemen)

Economy Based on agriculture (largely subsistence) and light industry; cotton has overtaken coffee as chief cash crop; irrigation schemes likely to increase area under cultivation; qat, a narcotic leaf, now a major enterprise; hides, vegetables, dried fish; crude- and refined-oil industry; textiles, cement, aluminium, salt.

GDP (2002e) $15.07 bn, per capita $800

HDI (2002) 0.479

History Part of the Minaean kingdom, 1200–650 BC; converted to Islam, 7th-c; Turkish occupation, 1538–1630 and 1872–1918; between and after Turkish rule, Yemen under the rule of the Hamid al-Din dynasty; sovereignty

Yemen (continued)

of Yemen acknowledged by Saudi Arabia and Britain, 1934; joined Arab League, 1945; Egypt-backed revolution in 1962, resulting in civil war; Yemen Arab Republic (North Yemen) declared, 1962; royalists defeated, 1969; neighbouring People's Republic of South Yemen established, 1967, when Britain ended 129 years of rule in Aden and the Marxist National Liberation Front took over; the People's Republic comprised Aden and 16 of the 20 protectorate states once under British control; renamed People's Democratic Republic of Yemen, 1970; negotiations to merge the two Yemens, 1979; unification proclaimed and ratified, 1990; new state called Republic of Yemen; former President of North Yemen declared President of the unified state, and former President of South Yemen became Prime Minister; supported Iraq during Gulf War, 1991; coalition government formed, 1993, governed by a President, Prime Minister, House of Representatives and Advisory Council; South Yemen declared independence as Democratic Republic of Yemen, 1994; subsequent civil war won by North Yemen.

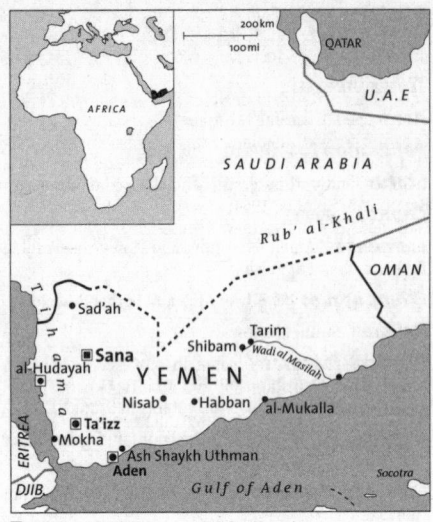

☐ International Airport   - - - - No defined boundary

Head of State
1990–   Ali Abdullah Saleh

Head of Government
2001–   Abd al-Qadir Ba Jammal

YUGOSLAVIA >> SERBIA AND MONTENEGRO

ZAMBIA

Local name Zambia

Timezone GMT +2

Area 752 613 km²/290 586 sq mi

Population total (2002e) 9 959 000

Status Independent republic within the Commonwealth

Date of independence 1964

Capital Lusaka

Languages English (official), with c.70 local languages (including Tonga, Kaonde, Lunda, and Luvale) also spoken

Ethnic groups Bantu (99%), including Bemba, Nyanja, Barotse, Mambwe, and Swahili peoples

Religions Christian (75%), local beliefs (23%), Muslim and Hindu (1%)

Physical features High plateau in SC Africa, altitude 1000–1400 m/3300–4600 ft; highest point, 2067 m/6781 ft, SE of Mbala; a number of rivers drain southwards to join Zambezi R in N, including R Luangwa; highest waterfall, Kalambo Falls, 221 m/726 ft; Victoria Falls on Zambia–Zimbabwe frontier; artificial L Kariba in S, 440 km²/170 sq mi.

Climate Warm temperate climate on plateau; tropical in lower valleys; although in C Africa and subequatorial, protected from very high temperatures by altitude; three distinct seasons, hot, dry (Aug–Oct), warm, wet (Nov–Apr), dry, cool (May–Jul); average annual temperatures, 21°C (Jan), 16°C (Jul) in Lusaka; average annual rainfall 840 mm/33 in.

Currency 1 Kwacha (ZMK) = 100 ngwee

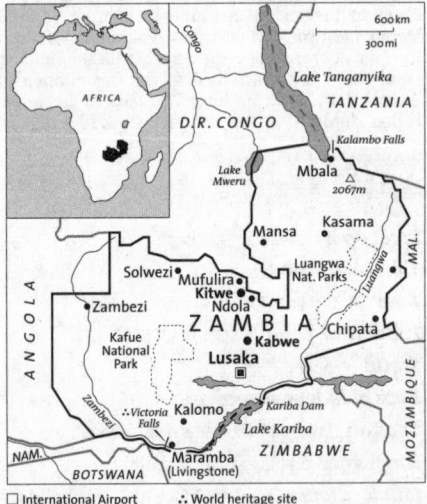

☐ International Airport   ∴ World heritage site

Economy Based on copper and cobalt, (provide over 50% of national income); lead, zinc, coal; corn, tobacco, rice, sugar cane, groundnuts, cotton; sugar refining, glassware, tyres, brewing, oil refining.

GDP (2002e) $8.24 bn, per capita $800

HDI (2002) 0.433

History European influence followed Livingstone's

Zambia (continued)

discovery of the Victoria Falls, 1855; administered by the British South Africa Company under Rhodes; Northern and Southern Rhodesia declared a British sphere of influence, 1889–90; became Northern Rhodesia, 1911; British Crown Colony, 1924; joined with Southern Rhodesia and Nyasaland as the Federation of Rhodesia and Nyasaland, 1953; Federation dissolved, 1963; independence as the Republic of Zambia, 1964; governed by a President and National Assembly; new multi-party constitution adopted in 1991.

Head of State (President)
1991–2002 Frederick Chiluba
2002–   Levy Mwanawasa

Head of Government (Vice-President)
2004–6 Lupando Mwape
2006–   Rupiah Banda

ZIMBABWE

Local name Zimbabwe

Timezone GMT +2

Area 390 759 km²/150 873 sq mi

Population total (2002e) 11 377 000

Status Independent republic within the Commonwealth

Date of independence 1980

Capital Harare

Languages English (official), Ndebele and Shona widely spoken

Ethnic groups Bantu (97%) (including Shona 71%, Ndebele 16%), European (2%)

Religions Syncretic Christian/local beliefs (50%), Christian (25%), traditional animist beliefs (24%), small Muslim minority

Physical features Landlocked country in SC Africa; mostly savannah (tropical grassland); Highveld ridge crosses SW to NE to join the Inyanga Mts on Mozambique border, highest point, Mt Inyangani, 2592 m/8504 ft; Highveld flanked by lower plateau, Middleveld; Lowveld, altitude, 300 m/1000 ft, lies NE; tropical hardwood forests (SE); chief rivers, Zambezi, Limpopo, and Sabi.

Climate Subtropical climate, strongly influenced by altitude; average annual temperature 21°C (Jan), 14°C (Jul) in Harare; average annual rainfall 828 mm/33 in; rainfall increases from SW to NE; wet season (Nov–Mar).

Currency 1 Zimbabwe Dollar (ZWD) = 100 cents

Economy Agriculture (involves 70% of population), manufacturing and mining; sugar, cotton, livestock; natural resources, gold, copper, chrome, nickel, tin, asbestos; tourism to national parks; major industries in steel, textiles, vehicles, and chemicals.

GDP (2002e) $26.07 bn, per capita $2100

HDI (2002) 0.551

History Mediaeval Bantu kingdom during 12–16th-c, with capital at Great Zimbabwe; visited by Livingstone in the 1850s; Southern Rhodesia under British influence in the 1880s as British South Africa Company under Cecil Rhodes; divided into Northern and Southern Rhodesia, 1911; Southern Rhodesia became self-governing British colony, 1923; Northern and Southern Rhodesia and Nyasaland formed multi-racial federation, 1953; independence of Nyasaland and Northern Rhodesia, 1963;

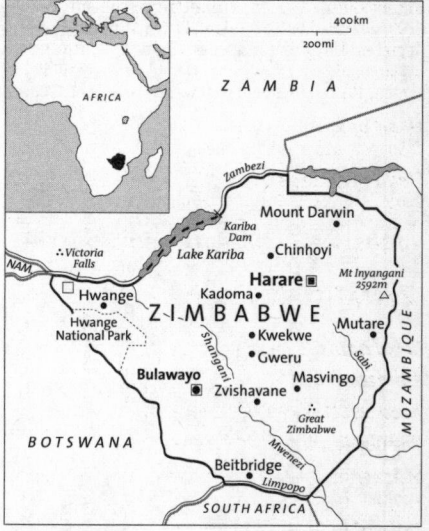

□ International Airport   ∴ World heritage site

opposition to independence of Southern Rhodesia under African rule resulted in Unilateral Declaration of Independence (UDI) by white-dominated government, 1965; economic sanctions and internal guerrilla activity forced government to negotiate with main African groups: Zimbabwe African People's Union (ZAPU), led by Joshua Nkomo, Zimbabwe African National Union (ZANU), led by Robert Mugabe, and United African National Council (UANC), led by Bishop Abel Muzorewa; independence as Republic of Zimbabwe, 1980; since 1987, post of executive President combined posts of Head of State and Head of Government; bicameral legislature replaced, 1990, by new single-chamber Parliament, the House of Assembly; political crisis over land redistribution, focused on white farmers, 2000 and ongoing; increasing international concern over internal democracy, especially in relation to election process, 2002; suspended from Commonwealth for one year, 2002; reaffirmed, 2003, after which Mugabe withdrew Zimbabwe from the organization; Mugabe re-elected, Mar 2005.

Head of State/Government
1987–   Robert Gabriel Mugabe

The nations of the world: general data

In the case of countries that do not use the Roman alphabet (such as the Arabic countries), there is variation in the spelling of names and currencies, depending on the system of transliteration used.

Where more than one language is shown with a country, the status of the languages may not be equal. Some languages have a 'semi-official' status, or are used for a restricted set of purposes, such as trade or tourism.

Population estimates are for 2002.

English name	Local name	Official name (in English)	Capital (English name in parentheses)	Language(s)	Currency	Population
Afghanistan	Afghānestān	Islamic Emirate of Afghanistan	Kābul	Dari, Pushtu	1 Afghani (AFA) = 100 puls	27 756 000
Albania	Shqipëri	Republic of Albania	Tiranë (Tirana)	Albanian	1 Lek (ALL) = 100 qintars	3 108 000
Algeria	Al-Jazā'ir (Arabic); Algérie (French)	Democratic and Popular Republic of Algeria	El Djazair (Algiers)	Arabic	1 Algerian Dinar (DZD) = 100 centimes	31 261 000
Andorra	Andorra	Principality of Andorra; the Valleys of Andorra	Andorra La Vella	Catalan	1 Euro (EUR) = 100 cents	66 500
Angola	Angola	Republic of Angola	Luanda	Portuguese	1 New Kwanza (AOK) = 100 lweis	10 593 000
Antigua and Barbuda	Antigua and Barbuda	Antigua and Barbuda	St John's	English	1 East Caribbean Dollar (XCD) = 100 cents	76 400
Argentina	Argentina	Argentine Republic	Buenos Aires	Spanish	1 Nuevo Peso (ARS) = 100 centavos	36 446 000
Armenia	Hayastan	Republic of Armenia	Yerevan	Armenian	1 Dram (AMD) = 100 joumas	3 800 000
Australia	Australia	Commonwealth of Australia	Canberra	English	1 Australian Dollar (AUD) = 100 cents	19 702 000
Austria	Österreich	Republic of Austria	Vienna	German	1 Euro (EUR) = 100 cents	8 077 000
Azerbaijan	Azerbaijan	Republic of Azerbaijan	Baku	Azerbaijani	1 Manat (AZM) = 100 gopik	8 176 000
Bahamas	Bahamas	Commonwealth of the Bahamas	Nassau	English	1 Bahamian Dollar (BSD) = 100 cents	3 090 500
Bahrain	Al-Bahrayn	State of Bahrain	Al-Manāmah (Manama)	Arabic	1 Bahrain Dinar (BHD) = 1000 fils	672 000
Bangladesh	Bangladesh	People's Republic of Bangladesh	Dhaka (Dacca)	Bengali	1 Taka (BDT) = 100 paisa	133 377 000
Barbados	Barbados	Barbados	Bridgetown	English	1 Barbados Dollar (BBD) = 100 cents	270 000
Belarus	Belarus	Republic of Belarus	Mensk (Minsk)	Belorussian, Russian	1 Belorussian rouble (BYR) = 100 kopecks	9 933 000
Belau	Palau	Republic of Belau	Koror	Palauan, English	1 US Dollar (USD) = 100 cents	19 900
Belgium	Belgique (French); België (Flemish)	Kingdom of Belgium	Bruxelles (Brussels)	Flemish, French, German	1 Euro (EUR) = 100 cents	10 280 000
Belize	Belize	Belize	Belmopan	English	1 Belize Dollar (BZD) = 100 cents	251 000
Benin	Bénin	Republic of Benin	Porto-Novo	French	1 CFA Franc (XAF) = 100 centimes	6 788 000
Bhutan	DrukYul	Kingdom of Bhutan	Thimbu/Thimphu	Dzongkha	1 Ngultrum (BTN) = 100 chetrum	1 996 000
Bolivia	Bolivia	Republic of Bolivia	La Paz/Sucre	Spanish, Aymara, Quechua	1 Boliviano (BOB) = 100 centavos	8 401 000
Bosnia and Herzegovina	Bosna-Hercegovina	Republic of Bosnia-Herzegovina	Sarajevo	Bosnian, Serbian, Croatian	1 Convertible Mark (BAM) = 100 convertible pfennigs	3 964 000

Botswana	Botswana	Republic of Botswana	Gaborone	English, Setswana	1 Pula (BWP) = 100 thebes	1679000
Bosnia and Herzegovina	Bosna-Hercegovina	Republic of Bosnia-Herzegovina	Sarajevo	Bosnian, Serbian, Croatian	1 Convertible Mark (BAM) = 100 convertible pfennigs	3964000
Botswana	Botswana	Republic of Botswana	Gaborone	English, Setswana	1 Pula (BWP) = 100 thebes	1679000
Brazil	Brasil	Federative Republic of Brazil	Brasilia	Portuguese	1 Cruzeiro Real (BRL) = 100 centavos	17619000
Brunei	Brunei Darussalam	State of Brunei, Abode of Peace	Bandar Seri Begawan	Malay, English	1 Brunei Dollar (BND) = 100 cents	351000
Bulgaria	Bâlgarija	Republic of Bulgaria	Sofija (Sofia)	Bulgarian	1 Lev (BGL) = 100 stotinki	7890000
Burkina Faso	Burkina Faso	Burkina Faso	Ouagadougou	French	1 CFA Franc (XAF) = 100 centimes	12603000
Burma see Myanmar						
Burundi	Burundi	Republic of Burundi	Bujumbura	French, (Ki) Rundi	1 Burundi Franc (BIF) = 100 centimes	6373000
Cambodia	Cambodia	Kingdom of Cambodia	Phnum Pénh (Phnom Penh)	Khmer	1 Riel (KHR) = 100 sen	13414000
Cameroon	Cameroun	Republic of Cameroon	Yaoundé	English, French	1 CFA Franc (XAF) = 100 centimes	16185000
Canada	Canada	Canada	Ottawa	English, French	1 Canadian Dollar (CAD) = 100 cents	31244000
Cape Verde	Cabo Verde	Republic of Cape Verde	Praia	Portuguese	1 Escudo (CVE) = 100 centavos	453000
Central African Republic	République Centrafricaine	Central African Republic	Bangui	French	1 CFA Franc (XAF) = 100 centimes	3643000
Chad	Tchad	Republic of Chad	N'djamena	Arabic, French	1 CFA Franc (XAF) = 100 centimes	8997000
Chile	Chile	Republic of Chile	Santiago	Spanish	1 Chilean Peso (CLP) = 100 centavos	15082000
China	Zhongguo	People's Republic of China	Beijing/Peking	Mandarin Chinese	1 Renminbi Yuan (CNY) = 10 jiao = 100 fen	1284211000
Colombia	Colombia	Republic of Colombia	Bogotá	Spanish	1 Colombian Peso (COP) = 100 centavos	41008000
Comoros	Comores	Federal Islamic Republic of the Comoros	Moroni	Arabic, French	1 Comorian Franc (KMF) = 100 centimes	583000
Congo	Congo	Republic of Congo	Brazzaville	French	1 CFA Franc (XAF) = 100 centimes	2899000
Congo, Democratic Republic of	Congo	Democratic Republic of Congo	Kinshasa	French	1 Congolese Franc (CDF) = 100 centimes	52557000
Costa Rica	Costa Rica	Republic of Costa Rica	San José	Spanish	1 Costa Rican Colón (CRC) = 100 céntimos	3960000
Côte d'Ivoire (Ivory Coast)	Côte d'Ivoire	Republic of Côte d'Ivoire	Yamoussoukro	French	1 CFA Franc (XAF) = 100 centimes	16805000
Croatia	Croatia	Republic of Croatia	Zagreb	Croatian	1 Kuna (HRK) = 100 lipa	4405000
Cuba	Cuba	Republic of Cuba	La Habana (Havana)	Spanish	1 Cuban Peso (CUP) = 100 centavos	11267000
Cyprus	Kypros (Greek); Kibris (Turkish)	Republic of Cyprus	Lavkosia (Nicosia)	Greek, Turkish	1 Cyprus Pound (CYP) = 100 cents; 1 Turkish Lira (TRL) = 100 kurus	802000
Czech Republic	Česká republika	Czech Republic	Praha (Prague)	Czech	1 Koruna (CZK) = 100 haléř	10210000
Denmark	Danmark	Kingdom of Denmark	København (Copenhagen)	Danish	1 Danish Krone (DKK) = 100 øre	5377000

HUMAN GEOGRAPHY

HUMAN GEOGRAPHY

The nations of the world: general data (continued)

English name	Local name	Official name (in English)	Capital (English name in parentheses)	Language(s)	Currency	Population
Djibouti	Djibouti	Republic of Djibouti	Djibouti	Arabic, French	1 Djibouti Franc (DJF) = 100 centimes	473 000
Dominica	Dominica	Commonwealth of Dominica	Roseau	English	1 East Caribbean Dollar (XCD) = 100 cents	71 700
Dominican Republic	República Dominicana	Dominican Republic	Santo Domingo	Spanish	1 Dominican Peso (DOP) = 100 centavos	8 833 000
Ecuador	Ecuador	Republic of Ecuador	Quito	Spanish	1 US Dollar (USD) = 100 cents (before 2000, the sucre (ECS))	13 095 000
Egypt	Misr	Arab Republic of Egypt	Al-Qāhirah (Cairo)	Arabic	1 Egyptian Pound (EGP) = 100 piastres	66 341 000
El Salvador	El Salvador	Republic of El Salvador	San Salvador	Spanish	1 US Dollar (USD) = 100 cents before 2001, the Colón (SVC)	6 354 000
Equatorial Guinea	Guinea Ecuatorial	Republic of Equatorial Guinea	Malabo	Spanish	1 CFA Franc (XAF) = 100 centimes	498 000
Eritrea	Ertra	Eritrea	Asmara	Arabic, English	1 Nakfa (ERN) = 100 cents (before 1997, the birr)	3 981 000
Estonia	Eesti	Republic of Estonia	Tallinn	Estonian, Russian	1 Kroon (EEK) = 100 cents	1 359 000
Ethiopia	Ityopiya	Federal Democratic Republic of Ethiopia	Adis Abeba (Addis Ababa)	Amharic	1 Ethiopian Birr (ETB) = 100 cents	67 673 000
Federated states of Micronesia	Federated States of Micronesia	Federated States of Micronesia	Palikir, on Ponape	English	1 US Dollar (USD) = 100 cents	109 000
Fiji	Fiji	Sovereign Democratic Republic of Fiji	Suva	English	1 Fijian Dollar (FJD) = 100 cents	824 000
Finland	Suomi (Finnish); Finland (Swedish)	Republic of Finland	Helsingfors (Helsinki)	Finnish, Swedish	1 Euro (EUR)= 100 cents	5 201 000
France	France	Republic of France	Paris	French	1 Euro (EUR)= 100 cents	59 440 000
Gabon	Gabon	Gabonese Republic	Libreville	French	1 CFA Franc (XAF) = 100 centimes	1 300 000
Gambia, The	Gambia	Republic of the Gambia	Banjul	English	1 Dalasi (GMD) = 100 butut	1 418 000
Georgia	Sakartvelos	Republic of Georgia	Tbilisi	Georgian, Armenian, Russian	1 Lari (GEL) = 100 tetri	4 961 000
Germany	Bundesrepublik Deutschland	Federal Republic of Germany	Berlin	German	1 Euro (EUR) = 100 cents	82 506 000
Ghana	Ghana	Republic of Ghana	Accra	English	1 Cedi (GHC) = 100 pesewas	20 244 000
Greece	Ellás	Hellenic Republic	Athínai (Athens)	Greek	1 Euro (EUR) = 100 cents	10 944 000
Greenland	Kalâtdlit-Nunât Grønland (Danish)	Greenland	Nuuk	Greenlandic, Danish	1 Danish Krone (GRD) = 100 øre	57 000
Grenada	Grenada	Grenada	St George's	English	1 East Caribbean Dollar (XCD) = 100 cents	101 900
Guatemala	Guatemala	Republic of Guatemala	Guatemala City	Spanish	1 Quetzal (GTQ) = 100 centavos; also 1 US Dollar (USD) = 100 cents	11 987 000
Guinea	Guinée	Republic of Guinea	Conakry	French	1 Guinea Franc (GNF) = 100 cauris	7 775 000

Guinea-Bissau	Guiné-Bissau	Republic of Guinea-Bissau	Bissau	Portuguese	1 CFA Franc (XAF) = 100 centimes	1 345 000
Guyana	Guyana	Cooperative Republic of Guyana	Georgetown	English	1 Guyana Dollar (GYD) = 100 cents	775 000
Haiti	Haïti	Republic of Haiti	Port-au-Prince	Hatian Creole, French	1 Gourde (HTG) = 100 centimes	7 064 000
Holland *see* Netherlands, The						
Honduras	Honduras	Republic of Honduras	Tegucigalpa	Spanish	1 Lempira (HNL) = 100 centavos	6 561 000
Hungary	Magyarország	Republic of Hungary	Budapest	Magyar	1 Forint (HUF) = 100 fillér	10 162 000
Iceland	Ísland	Republic of Iceland	Reykjavik	Icelandic	1 Króna (ISK) = 100 aurar	288 000
India	Bhárat (Hindi)	Republic of India	New Delhi	Hindi; English	1 Indian Rupee (INR) = 100 paisa	1 047 671 200
Indonesia	Indonesia	Republic of Indonesia	Jakarta	Bahasa Indonesia	1 Rupiah (IDR) = 100 sen	211 023 000
Iran	Írán	Islamic Republic of Iran	Tehrān (Tehran)	Farsi	1 Iranian Rial (IRR) = 100 dinars	65 457 000
Iraq	Al-'Iráq	Republic of Iraq	Baghdād (Baghdad)	Arabic	1 New Iraqi Dinar (NID) = 1000 fils	24 002 000
Ireland	Éire (Gaelic); Ireland (English)	Republic of Ireland	Baile Átha Cliath (Dublin)	Irish, English	1 Euro (EUR) = 100 cents	3 926 000
Israel	Yisra'el (Hebrew); Isrā'íl (Arabic)	State of Israel	Yerushalayim (Jerusalem)	Hebrew, Arabic	1 New Israeli Shekel (ILS/NIS) = 100 agorot	6 394 000
Italy	Italia	Italian Republic	Roma (Rome)	Italian	1 Euro (EUR) = 100 cents	57 988 000
Ivory Coast *see* Côte d'Ivoire						
Jamaica	Jamaica	Jamaica	Kingston	English	1 Jamaican Dollar (JMD) = 100 cents	2 630 000
Japan	Nippon	Japan	Tōkyō (Tokyo)	Japanese	1 Yen (JPY) = 100 sen	127 347 000
Jordan	Al'Urdunn	Hashemite Kingdom of Jordan	'Ammān (Amman)	Arabic	1 Jordanian Dinar (JOD) = 1000 fils	5 260 000
Kampuchea *see* Cambodia						
Kazakhstan	Kazakhstan	Republic of Kazakhstan	Astana	Kazakh, Russian	1 Tenge (KZT) = 100 Kopecs	14 888 000
Kenya	Kenya	Republic of Kenya	Nairobi	Swahili, English	1 Kenyan shilling (KES) = 100 cents	31 139 000
Kiribati	Kiribati	Republic of Kiribati	Bairiki	English, Gilbertese	1 Australian Dollar (AUD) = 100 cents	90 600
Korea, North	Choson Minjujuui In'min Konghwaguk	Democratic People's Republic of Korea	P'yongyang (Pyongyang)	Korean	1 North Korean Won (KPW) = 100 chon	22 224 000
Korea, South	Taehan-Min'guk	Republic of Korea	Soul (Seoul)	Korean	1 South Korean Won (KRW) = 100 chon	47 640 000
Kuwait	al-Kuwayt	State of Kuwait	al-Kuwayt (Kuwait City)	Arabic	1 Kuwaiti Dinar (KWD) = 1000 fils	2 253 000
Kyrgyzstan	Kirgizstan	Republic of Kyrgyzstan	Bishkek	Kyrgyz, Russian	1 Kyrgyzstani Som (KGS) = 100 tyiyn	5 002 000
Laos	Lao	Lao People's Deomocratic Republic	Viangchan (Vientiane)	Lao	1 Kip (LAK) = 100 at	5 777 000
Latvia	Latvija	Republic of Latvia	Riga	Latvian, Russian	1 Latvian Lat (LVL) = 100 santims	2 331 000
Lebanon	al-Lubnán	Republic of Lebanon	Bayrút (Beirut)	Arabic	1 Lebanese Pound/Livre (LBP) = 100 piastres	3 678 000
Lesotho	Lesoto	Kingdom of Lesotho	Maseru	Sesotho, English,	1 Loti (pl Maloti) (LSL) = 100 lisente; 1 South African Rand (ZAR) = 100 cents	2 208 000

The nations of the world: general data (continued)

English name	Local name	Official name (in English)	Capital (English name in parentheses)	Language(s)	Currency	Population
Liberia	Liberia	Republic of Liberia	Monrovia	English	1 Liberian Dollar (LRD) = 100 cents	3 288 000
Libya	Libiyā	Socialist People's Libyan Arab Jamahiriya	Tarabulus (Tripoli)	Arabic	1 Libyan Dinar (LYD) = 1000 dirhams	5 369 000
Liechtenstein	Liechtenstein	Principality of Liechtenstein	Vaduz	German	1 Swiss Franc (CHF) = 100 centimes	33 300
Lithuania	Lietuva	Republic of Lithuania	Vilnius	Lithuanian, Russian	1 Litas (LTL) = 100 centas	3 473 000
Luxembourg	Lëtzebuerg; Luxembourg (French); Luxembourg (German)	Grand Duchy of Luxembourg	Luxembourg	French, German, Luxembourgish	1 Euro (EUR) = 100 cents (before 2002, 1 Luxembourg Franc (LUF) = 100 centimes)	447 000
Macedonia	Makedonija	(Former Yugoslav) Republic of Macedonia	Skopje	Macedonian	1 Macedonian Denar (MKD) = 100 paras	2 036 000
Madagascar	Madagasikara	Republic of Madagascar	Antananarivo	Malagasy, French	1 Ariary (MGA) = 5 iraimbilanja (before 2005, 1 Franc (MGF = 100 centimes)	16 473 000
Malawi	Malaŵi	Republic of Malawi	Lilongwe	Chichewa, English	1 Kwacha (MWK) = 100 tambala	10 520 000
Malaysia	Malaysia	Malaysia	Kuala Lumpur	Malay	1 Malaysian Dollar/Ringgit (MYR) = 100 cents	24 370 000
Maldives	Maldive; Dhivehi Jumhuriya	Republic of Maldives	Malé	Dhivehi	1 Rufiyaa (MVR) = 100 laaris	281 000
Mali	Mali	Republic of Mali	Bamako	French	1 CFA Franc (XAF) = 100 centimes	11 340 000
Malta	Malta	Republic of Malta	Valletta	Maltese, English	1 Maltese Lira (MTL) = 100 cents	386 000
Marshall Islands		Republic of the Marshall Islands	Dalap-Uliga-Darrit, on Majuro	Marshallese, (Kahjin-Majol) English	1 US Dollar (USD) = 100 cents	56 600
Mauritania	Mauritanie (French); Muritaniya (Arabic)	Islamic Republic of Mauritania	Nouakchott	Arabic	1 Ouguija (MRO) = 5 khoums	2 656 000
Mauritius	Mauritius	Republic of Mauritius	Port Louis	English	1 Mauritian Rupee (MUR) = 100 cents	1 211 000
Mexico	México	United Mexican States	Ciudad de México (Mexico City)	Spanish	1 Mexican Peso (MXN) = 100 centavos	100 977 000
Moldova	Moldova	Republic of Moldova	Chisinau (Kishinev)	Romanian, Moldovan	1 Moldovan Leu (MDL) = 100 bani	4 231 000
Monaco	Monaco	Principality of Monaco	Monaco	French	1 Euro (EUR) = 100 cents	32 000
Mongolia	Mongol Uls	Mongolia	Ulaanbaatar (Ulan Bator)	Khalkha	1 Tugrik (MNT) = 100 möngös	2 457 000
Montenegro	Crna Gora	Republic of Montenegro	Podgorica/Cetinje	Serbian, Albanian	1 Euro (EUR) = 100 cents	
Morocco	al-Magrib	Kingdom of Morocco	Rabat	Arabic	1 Moroccan Dirham (MAD) = 100 Moroccan francs	29 632 000
Mozambique	Moçambique	Republic of Mozambique	Maputo	Portuguese	1 Metical (MZM) = 100 centavos	18 083 000
Myanmar	Pyidaungsu; Myanma Naingngandaw	Union of Myanmar	Yangon (Rangoon)	Burmese	1 Kyat (MMK) = 100 pyas	42 238 000
Namibia	Namibia	Republic of Namibia	Windhoek	English	1 Namibian Dollar (NAD) = 100 cents; 1 South African Rand (ZAR) = 100 cents	1 837 000
Nauru	Naeoro (Nauruan); Nauru (English)	Republic of Nauru	Yaren District	Nauruan, English	1 Australian Dollar (AUD) = 100 cents	12 300

Country	Native name	Official name	Capital	Language	Currency	Population
Nepal	Nepāl	Kingdom of Nepal	Kathmandu	Nepali	1 Nepalese Rupee (NPR) = 100 paise/pice	23 692 000
Netherlands, The	Nederland	Kingdom of the Netherlands	Amsterdam/'s-Gravenhage (The Hague)	Dutch	1 Euro (EUR) = 100 cents	16 142 000
New Zealand	New Zealand (English); Aotearoa (Maori)	New Zealand	Wellington	English, Maori	1 New Zealand Dollar (NZD) = 100 cents	3 893 000
Nicaragua	Nicaragua	Republic of Nicaragua	Managua	Spanish	1 New Córdoba (NIC) = 100 centavos	5 024 000
Niger	Niger	Republic of Niger	Niamey	French	1 CFA Franc (XAF) = 100 centimes	10 640 000
Nigeria	Nigeria	Federal Republic of Nigeria	Abuja	English	1 Naira (NGN) = 100 kobos	129 935 000
Norway	Norge	Kingdom of Norway	Oslo	Norwegian	1 Norwegian Krone (NOK) = 100 øre	4 537 000
Oman	'Umān	Sultanate of Oman	Masqat (Muscat)	Arabic	1 Omani Rial (OMR) = 1000 baizas	2 522 000
Pakistan	Pākistān	Islamic Republic of Pakistan	Islāmābād (Islamabad)	Urdu	1 Pakistan Rupee (PKR) = 100 paisas	145 960 000
Panama	Panamá	Republic of Panama	Panamá (Panama City)	Spanish	1 Balboa (PAB) = 100 cents; 1 US dollar (USD) = 100 cents	2 915 000
Papua New Guinea	Papua New Guinea	Independent State of Papua New Guinea	Port Moresby	English, Tok Pisin	1 Kina (PGK) = 100 toea	5 426 000
Paraguay	Paraguay	Republic of Paraguay	Asunción	Spanish	1 Guarani (PYG) = 100 céntimos	5 774 000
Peru	Perú	Republic of Peru	Lima	Spanish, Quechua	1 New Sol (PEN) = 100 céntimos	26 749 000
Philippines	Filipinas	Republic of the Philippines	Manila	English, Pilipino	1 Philippine peso (PHP) = 100 centavos	80 000 000
Poland	Polska	Republic of Poland	Warszawa (Warsaw)	Polish	1 Zloty (PLN) = 100 groszy	38 644 000
Portugal	Portugal	Republic of Portugal	Lisboa (Lisbon)	Portuguese	1 Euro (EUR) = 100 cents	10 384 000
Puerto Rico	Puerto Rico	Commonwealth of Puerto Rico	San Juan	Spanish, English	1 US Dollar (USD) = 100 cents	3 879 000
Qatar	Qatar	State of Qatar	Ad-Dawhah (Doha)	Arabic	1 Qatar Riyal (QAR) = 100 dirhams	606 000
Romania	România	Republic of Romania	Bucuresti (Bucharest)	Romanian	1 Leu (pl lei) (ROL) = 100 bani	21 667 000
Russia	Rossiyskaya	Russian Federation	Moskva (Moscow)	Russian	1 Rouble (R) (AUR) = 100 kopecks	143 673 000
Rwanda	Rwanda	Republic of Rwanda	Kigali	Kinyarwanda, French	1 Rwanda Franc (RWF) = 100 centimes	7 398 000
Saint Kitts and Nevis	Saint Christopher/Kitts and Nevis	Federation of Saint Kitts and Nevis	Basseterre	English	1 East Caribbean Dollar (XCD) = 100 cents	46 200
Saint Lucia	Saint Lucia	Saint Lucia	Castries	English	1 East Caribbean Dollar (XCD) = 100 cents	160 000
Saint Vincent and the Grenadines	Saint Vincent and the Grenadines	Saint Vincent and the Grenadines	Kingstown	English	1 East Caribbean Dollar (XCD) = 100 cents	113 000
Samoa	Samoa (English); Samoa i Sisifo (Samoan)	Independent State of Samoa	Apia	English, Samoan	1 Tala (SAT) = 100 sene	178 000

Capital (English

HUMAN GEOGRAPHY

The nations of the world: general data (continued)

English name	Local name	Official name (in English)	name in parentheses	Language(s)	Currency	Population
San Marino	San Marino	Most Serene Republic of San Marino	San Marino	Italian	1 Euro (EUR) = 100 cents	27700
São Tomé and Príncipe	São Tomé e Príncipe	Democratic Republic of São Tomé and Príncipe	São Tomé	Portuguese	1 Dobra (STD) = 100 centimos	147000
Saudi Arabia	al-'Arabiyah as-Sa'ūdiyah	Kingdom of Saudi Arabia	Ar-Riyād (Riyādh)	Arabic	1 Saudi Arabian Riyal (SAR) = 100 halalah	23370000
Senegal	Sénégal	Republic of Senegal	Dakar	French	1 CFA Franc (XAF) = 100 centimes	9905000
Serbia	Srbija	Republic of Serbia	Beograd (Belgrade)	Serbian	Serbia: 1 Dinar (CSD) = 100 paras; Kosovo: both currencies legal	10600000
Seychelles	Seychelles	Republic of Seychelles	Victoria	Creole French, English, French	1 Seychelles Rupee (SCR) = 100 cents	83400
Sierra Leone	Sierra Leone	Republic of Sierra Leone	Freetown	English	1 Leone (SLL) = 100 cents	4823000
Singapore	Singapore	Republic of Singapore	Singapore City	Chinese, English, Malay, Tamil	1 Singapore Dollar/Ringgit (SGD) = 100 cents	4000000
Slovak Republic	Slovenská Republika	Slovak Republic	Bratislava	Slovak	1 Slovak Koruna (SKK) = 100 halers	5383000
Slovenia	Slovenija	Republic of Slovenia	Ljubljana	Slovene	1 Euro (EUR) = 100 cents	1948000
Solomon Islands	Solomon Islands	Solomon Islands	Honiara	English	1 Solomon Islands Dollar (SBD) = 100 cents	439000
Somalia	Somaliya	Somali Democratic Republic	Muqdisho (Mogadishu)	Arabic, Somali	1 Somali Shilling (SoS) = 100 cents	7753000
South Africa	South Africa (English); Suid-Afrika (Afrikaans)	Republic of South Africa	Pretoria/Cape Town	Afrikaans, English	1 Rand (ZAR) = 100 cents	45172000
Spain	España	Kingdom of Spain	Madrid	Spanish	1 Euro (EUR) = 100 cents	40998000
Sri Lanka	Sri Lanka	Democratic Socialist Republic of Sri Lanka	Sri Jayawardenapura	Sinhala, Tamil	1 Sri Lanka Rupee (LKR) = 100 cents	18870000
Sudan	As-Sūdān	Republic of the Sudan	Al-Khar tum (Khartoum)	Arabic	1 Sudanese dinar (SDD) = 100 piastres	37090000
Suriname	Suriname	Republic of Suriname	Paramaribo	Dutch	1 Suriname Dollar (SRD) = 100 cents; (before 2004, 1 Suriname Guilder (SRG) = 100 cents)	436000
Swaziland	Swatini	Kingdom of Swaziland	Mbabane	English, Siswati	1 Lilangeni (pl Emalangeni) (SZL) = 100 cents	1124000
Sweden	Sverige	Kingdom of Sweden	Stockholm	Swedish	1 Swedish Krona (SEK) = 100 öre	8925000
Switzerland	Schweiz (German); Suisse (French); Svizzera (Italian)	Swiss Confederation	Bern (Berne)	French, German, Italian, Romansch	1 Swiss Franc (CHF) = 100 centimes	7282000
Syria	As-Sūriyah	Syrian Arab Republic	Dimashq (Damascus)	Arabic	1 Syrian pound (SYP) = 100 piastres	17156000
Taiwan	T'aiWan	Republic of China	T'aipei (Taipei)	Mandarin Chinese	1 New Taiwan Dollar (TWD) = 100 cents	22457000
Tajikistan	Tojikiston	Republic of Tajikistan	Dushanbe Taibei	Tajik, Uzbek, Russian	1 Somoni (TJS) = 100 diram (before 2000, 1 Tajik rouble (TJR) = 100 kopecks)	6327000
Tanzania	Tanzania	United Republic of Tanzania	Dodoma (formerly Dar es Salaam)	Swahili, English	1 Tanzanian Shilling (TZS) = 100 cents	34902000

Country	Local name	Official name	Capital	Language	Currency	Population
Thailand	Muang Thai	Kingdom of Thailand	Krung Thep (Bangkok)	Thai	1 Baht (THB) = 100 satang	63 430 000
Togo	Togo	Republic of Togo	Lomé	French	1 CFA Franc (XAF) = 100 centimes	5 286 000
Tonga	Tonga	Kingdom of Tonga	Nuku'alofa	English, Tongan	1 Pa'anga/Tongan Dollar (TOP) = 100 seniti	101 000
Trinidad and Tobago	Trinidad and Tobago	Republic of Trinidad and Tobago	Port of Spain	English	1 Trinidad and Tobago Dollar (TTD) = 100 cents	1 304 000
Tunisia	Tunis (Arabic); Tunisie (French)	Republic of Tunisia	Tunis	Arabic	1 Tunisian Dinar (TND) = 1000 millimes	9 764 000
Turkey	Türkiye	Republic of Turkey	Ankara	Turkish	1 New Turkish Lira (YTL) = 100 new kurus (before 2005, Turkish Lira (TRL))	69 359 000
Turkmenistan	Turkmenistan	Republic of Turkmenistan	Ashkhabad	Turkmenian, Russian	1 Manat (TMM) = 100 gapik	4 946 000
Tuvalu	Tuvalu	Tuvalu	Funafuti	English	1 Australian Dollar (AUD) = 100 cents; also, a Tuvaluan Dollar (TVD)	10 900
Uganda	Uganda	Republic of Uganda	Kampala	English, Swahili	1 Uganda Shilling (UGX) = 100 cents	24 378 000
Ukraine	Ukraine	Republic of Ukraine	Kiev	Ukrainian, Russian	1 Hryvna (UAH) = 100 kopijka	48 120 000
United Arab Emirates	Ittihād al-Imārāt al-'Arabiyah	United Arab Emirates	Abū Zabi (Abu Dhabi)	Arabic	1 Dirham (AED) = 100 fils	3 550 000
United Kingdom	United Kingdom/ (Great) Britain	United Kingdom of Great Britain and Northern Ireland	London	English	1 Pound Sterling (GBP) = 100 new pence	60 178 000
United States of America	United States of America (USA)	United States of America	Washington, DC	English	1 US Dollar (USD) = 100 cents	287 602 000
Uruguay	Uruguay	Oriental Republic of Uruguay	Montevideo	Spanish	1 Uruguayan New Peso (UYU) = 100 centésimos	3 383 000
Uzbekistan	Ozbekiston	Republic of Uzbekistan	Tashkent	Uzbek, Russian	1 Som (UZS) = 100 tiyin	25 484 000
Vanuatu	Vanuatu	Republic of Vanuatu	Port Vila	English, French, Bislama	1 Vatu (VUV) = 100 centésimes	207 900
Venezuela	Venezuela	Republic of Venezuela	Caracas	Spanish	1 Bolívar (VEB) = 100 céntimos	23 093 000
Vietnam	Viêt-nam	Socialist Republic of Vietnam	Ha-noi (Hanoi)	Vietnamese	1 Dông (VND) = 10 hao = 100 xu	79 939 000
Western Samoa see Samoa						
Yemen	al-Yaman	Republic of Yemen	Sana/Aden	Arabic	1 Yemeni Riyal (YER) = 100 fils	19 495 000
Yugoslavia see Serbia and Montenegro See also Croatia, Bosnia and Herzegovina, Macedonia, Slovenia						
Zaire see Congo, Democratic Republic of						
Zambia	Zambia	Republic of Zambia	Lusaka	English	1 Kwacha (ZMK) = 100 ngwee	9 959 000
Zimbabwe	Zimbabwe	Republic of Zimbabwe	Harare	English	1 Zimbabwe Dollar (ZWD) = 100 cents	11 377 000

HUMAN GEOGRAPHY

Population

Growth of world population
by billion and year.

World population	Year	Elapsed years
1 billion	1805	indefinite
2 billion	1926	121
3 billion	1960	34
4 billion	1974	14
5 billion	1987	13
6 billion	1999	12
7 billion	2010	11
8 billion	2023	13
9 billion	2040	17
10 billion	2070	30

The projected slowing down of world population growth to a peak of 10 billion in 2070 is based on the following assumptions: increased use of contraception in developing countries, and an ageing of the global population (with fertile adults making up a smaller percentage of the whole).

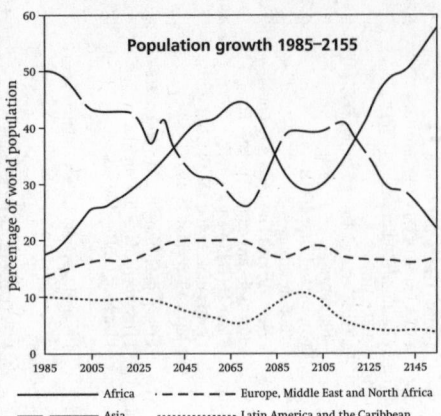

Population growth 1985–2155

Africa ——— Europe, Middle East and North Africa - - - - - Asia ——— Latin America and the Caribbean ···········

Projected population growth, by geographic region

Region	Population (millions)		Growth rate (%)		Birth rate (per 1000)		Death rate (per 1000)	
	1995	2025	1990–5	2020–5	1990–5	2020–5	1990–5	2020–5
World	5734	8188	1.65	0.94	25.7	17.6	9.2	8.2
Africa	878	1495	2.87	1.74	42.3	24.1	13.8	6.7
Asia	3247	4758	1.73	0.89	25.9	17.0	8.5	8.1
America	773	1035	1.49	0.72	21.9	15.3	7.3	8.2
Europe	807	863	0.45	0.15	14.4	13.0	9.8	11.5
Oceania	29	36	1.57	0.59	19.3	15.0	7.8	9.1

UK population summary

	United Kingdom			England and Wales			Wales	Scotland			Northern Ireland		
	Persons	Males	Females	Persons	Males	Females	Persons	Persons	Males	Females	Persons	Males	Females
Enumerated population: census figures (thousands)													
1801	–	–	–	8893	4255	4638	587	1608	739	869	–	–	–
1851	22259	10855	11404	17928	8781	9146	1163	2889	1376	1513	1442	698	745
1901	38237	18492	19745	32528	15729	16799	2013	4472	2174	2298	1237	590	647
1911	42082	20357	21725	36070	17446	18625	2421	4761	2309	2452	1251	603	648
1921[a]	44027	21033	22994	37887	18075	19811	2656	4882	2348	2535	1258	610	648
1931[a]	46038	22060	23978	39952	19133	20819	2593	4843	2326	2517	1243	601	642
1951	50225	24118	26107	43758	21016	22742	2599	5096	2434	2662	1371	668	703
1961	52709	25481	27228	46105	22304	23801	2644	5179	2483	2697	1425	694	731
1966[b]	53788	26044	27745	47136	22841	24295	2663	5168	2479	2689	1485	724	761
1971	55515	26952	28562	48750	23683	25067	2731	5229	2515	2714	1536	755	781
1981	55848	27104	28742	49155	23873	25281	2792	5131	2466	2664	1533	750	783
1991	56467	27344	29123	49890	24182	25707	2891	5107	2470	2637	1601	781	820
2001	58789	28581	30208	52042	25327	26715	2903	5062	2432	2630	1685	821	864

Notes:
[a] Figures for Northern Ireland are estimated. The population at the census of 1926 was 1257000 (608000 males and 649000 females).
[b] Except for Northern Ireland, where a full census was taken, figures are based on the 10 per cent samples census.

Sources: Office for National Statistics, General Register Office for Scotland, and Northern Ireland Statistics and Research Agency.

PART EIGHT

Society

SOCIAL INSTITUTIONS

Honours

Country	Name of honour	Date instituted	History
Denmark	Order of the Dannebrog	1219	One of the most ancient orders in existence and awarded for general merit.
France	Croix de Guerre	1915	Military decoration created in 1915 and 1939 to reward bravery in the two world wars.
	Légion d'Honneur	1802	First order of the French Republic created by Napoleon I as a reward for distinguished civil and military service. Open to all citizens regardless of birth or religion.
Germany	Iron Cross	1813	Instituted first by Prussia and then reinstated by Hitler in 1939. Military decoration awarded for bravery in war time.
	Pour le Mérite	1740	Established by Frederick II the Great. There was a class for military achievement and one for scientific and artistic achievement.
Japan	Chrysanthemum, Order of the	1877	Japan's highest order. Instituted by the Emperor and awarded mainly to members of the Japanese Royal Family, foreign royals, and heads of state. Award exclusive to males.
	Paulownia Sun, Order of the	1888	Founded by the Emperor to reward outstanding military and civil merit. Only awarded to men.
	Rising Sun, Order of the	1875	This was originally the Order of Merit awarded for exceptional civil or military merit.
Netherlands	Order of the House of Orange	1905	The equivalent of the Royal Victorian Order and rewards services to the Royal House.
	Military Order of William	1815	The highest military decoration to military of all ranks and civilians for courageous acts and devotion to duty. Founded by William I.
	Netherlands Lion	1815	An award for patriotism and outstanding devotion to duty, also for scientific/artistic achievements.
United Kingdom	Bath, The Most Honourable Order of the	1725	Order of chivalry formally created by George I in 1725, but traditionally instituted by Henry IV in 1399. The motto of the order is *Tria juncta in uno* (Three joined in one).
	British Empire, The Most Noble Order of the Knight/Dame of the Grand Cross (GBE), Knight/Dame Commander (K/DBE), Commander (CBE), Officer (OBE), Member (MBE)	1917	Founded by George V and the first order of knighthood to be presented to members of both sexes. Appointments made on the recommendations of Government ministers. There are five orders.
	Companions of Honour, Order of the (CH)	1917	Founded by George V to reward men and women for national services. Motto *In action faithful and in honour clear*.
	Distinguished Service Order (DSO)	1886	Military service order in recognition of special services by army and navy officers.
	Garter, The Most Noble Order of the	c.1344–51	The most ancient order of chivalry, founded by Edward III. Motto *Honi soit qui mal y pense* (Shamed be he who thinks badly of it).
	George Cross (GC)	1940	Named after George VI and awarded 'For Gallantry' (acts of great heroism).
	Merit, Order of (OM)	1902	Founded by Edward VII for eminent service in the military or for distinguished performances in science, the arts, and the promotion of culture.
	Royal Victorian Order (RVO) Knight/Dame Grand Cross (GCVO) Knight/Dame Commander (K/DCVO) Commander (CVO), Lieutenant (LVO), Member (MVO)	1896	Knighthood instituted by Queen Victoria to reward distinguished service to the sovereign. There are five orders.
	Thistle, The Most Ancient and Noble Order of the	c.1460–88	Scottish order of chivalry, probably instituted by James III. Motto *Nemo me impune lacessit* (No-one provokes me with impunity).

Honours (continued)

Country	Name of honour	Date instituted	History
	Victoria Cross (VC)	1856	Instituted by Queen Victoria. The highest military award in honour of great bravery.
United States	Congressional Medal of Honor	1862	Established by the US Congress and awarded in its name. The country's highest military decoration. Awarded to members of the armed services who, during a military action, risk their lives in acts of bravery beyond the call of duty.
	Legion of Merit, The	1942	Awarded to native American officers and foreigners for exceptional service in peace and war.
	Medal for Merit	1942	Awarded to civilians who have performed an outstanding service in peace or wartime.
	Presidential Medal of Freedom	1963	The highest decoration awarded to civilians in peacetime. The medal is presented in recognition of outstanding achievement in any of a variety of fields, including the arts.
	Purple Heart, The	1782	Originally an award for gallantry. Revived in 1932 and awarded in recognition of wounds received in action.

Forms of address

In the formulae given below, *F* stands for forename and *S* for surname.

Very formal ceremonial styles for closing letters are now seldom used: 'Yours faithfully' is assumed below, unless otherwise indicated.

Forms of spoken address are given only where a special style is followed.

Holders of courtesy titles are addressed according to their rank, but without 'The', 'The Right Hon.' or 'The Most Hon.'

Ranks in the armed forces, and ecclesiastical and ambassadorial ranks, precede titles in the peerage, eg 'Colonel the Earl of –' or 'The Rev the Marquess of –'.

Although the correct forms of address are given below for members of the British Royal Family, it is more normal practice for letters to be addressed to their private secretary, equerry, or lady-in-waiting.

More detailed information about forms of address in the UK is to be found in Debrett's *Correct Form* and Black's *Titles and Forms of Address*.

Ambassadors (foreign)
Address on envelope: 'His/Her Excellency the Ambassador of –' or 'His/Her Excellency the – Ambassador'. (The wife of an ambassador is not entitled to the style 'Her Excellency'.) *Begin*: 'Your Excellency'. (Within the letter, refer to 'Your Excellency' once, thereafter as 'you'.) *Close*: 'I have the honour to be, Sir/Madam (or according to rank), Your Excellency's obedient servant'. *Spoken address*: 'Your Excellency' at least once, and then 'Sir' or 'Madam', or by name.

Archbishop (Anglican communion)
Address on envelope: 'The Most Reverend Lord Archbishop of –'. (The Archbishops of Canterbury and York are Privy Counsellors, and should be addressed as 'The Most Reverend and Right Hon, the Lord Archbishop of –'.) *Begin*: 'Dear Archbishop' or 'My Lord Archbishop'. *Spoken address*: 'Your Grace'. *Begin an official speech*: 'My Lord Archbishop.'

Archbishop (any, US form)
Address on envelope: 'The Most Reverend [F– S–], Archbishop of–'. *Begin*: 'Your Excellency'.

Archbishop (Roman Catholic)
Address on envelope: 'His Grace the Archbishop of –'. *Begin*: 'My Lord Archbishop'. *Close*: 'I remain, Your Grace, Yours faithfully' or 'Yours faithfully'. *Spoken address*: 'Your Grace'.

Archdeacon
Address on envelope: 'The Venerable the Archdeacon of –'. *Begin*: 'Dear Archdeacon' or 'Venerable Sir'. *Spoken address*: 'Archdeacon'. *Begin an official speech*: 'Venerable Sir'.

Baron
Address on envelope: 'The Right Hon. the Lord–'. *Begin*: 'My Lord'. *Spoken address*: 'My Lord'.

Baron's wife (Baroness)
Address on envelope: 'The Right Hon. the Lady [S–]'. *Begin*: 'Dear Madam'. *Spoken address*: 'Madam'.

Baroness (in her own right)
Address on envelope: either as for Baron's wife, or 'The Right Hon. the Baroness [S–]'. Otherwise, as for Baron's wife.

Baronet
Address on envelope: 'Sir [F– S–], Bt'. *Begin*: 'Dear Sir'. *Spoken address*: 'Sir [F–]'.

Baronet's wife
Address on envelope: 'Lady [S–]'. If she has the title 'Lady' by courtesy, 'Lady [F– S–]'. If she has the courtesy style 'The Hon.', this precedes 'Lady'. *Begin*: 'Dear Madam'. *Spoken address*: 'Madam'.

Bishop (Anglican communion)
Address on envelope: 'The Right Reverend the Lord Bishop of –'. (The Bishop of London is a Privy Counsellor, so is addressed as 'The Right Rev. and Right Hon. the Lord Bishop of London'. The Bishop of Meath is styled 'The Most Reverend'.) *Begin*: 'Dear Bishop' or 'My Lord'. *Spoken address*: 'Bishop'. *Begin an official speech*: 'My Lord'.

Bishop (Episcopal Church in Scotland)
Address on envelope: 'The Right Reverend [F– S–], Bishop of –'. Otherwise as for a bishop of the Anglican communion. The bishop who holds the position of Primus is addressed as 'The Most Reverend the Primus'. *Begin*: 'Dear Primus'. *Spoken address*: 'Primus'.

SOCIETY

Bishop (Episcopal, US form)
Address on envelope: 'The Right Reverend [*F– S–*], Bishop of –'. *Begin*: 'Right Reverend Sir'.

Bishop (Roman Catholic)
Address on envelope: 'His Lordship the Bishop of –' or 'The Right Reverend [*F– S–*] Bishop of –'. In Ireland, 'The Most Reverend' is used instead of 'The Right Reverend'. If an auxiliary bishop, address as 'The Right Reverend [*F– S–*], Auxiliary Bishop of –'. *Begin*: 'My Lord' or (more rarely) 'My Lord Bishop'. *Close*: 'I remain, my Lord' or (more rarely), 'my Lord Bishop', 'Yours faithfully', or simply 'Yours faithfully'. *Spoken address*: 'My Lord' or (more rarely) 'My Lord Bishop'.

Bishop (Roman Catholic, US form)
Address on envelope: 'The Most Reverend [*F– S–*], Bishop of –'. *Begin*: 'Most Reverend Sir' or 'Your Excellency'.

Bishop (Other churches, US form)
Address on envelope: 'The Reverend [*F– S–*]'. *Begin*: 'Reverend Sir'.

Cabinet Minister *see* **Secretary of State**

Canon (Anglican communion)
Address on envelope: 'The Reverend Canon [*F– S–*]. *Begin*: 'Dear Canon' or 'Dear Canon [*S–*]'. *Spoken address*: 'Canon' or 'Canon [*S–*]'.

Canon (Roman Catholic)
Address on envelope: 'The Very Reverend Canon [*F– S–*]'. *Begin*: 'Very Reverend Sir'. *Spoken address*: 'Canon [*S–*]'.

Cardinal
Address on envelope: 'His Eminence Cardinal [*S–*]'. If an archbishop, 'His Eminence the Cardinal Archbishop of –'. *Begin*: 'Your Eminence' or (more rarely) 'My Lord Cardinal'. *Close*: 'I remain, Your Eminence' (or 'My Lord Cardinal'), 'Yours faithfully'. *Spoken address*: 'Your Eminence'.

Cardinal (US form)
Address on envelope: 'His Eminence [*F–*] Cardinal [*S–*]'. *Begin*: 'Your Eminence'.

Clergy (Anglican communion)
Address on envelope: 'The Reverend [*F– S–*]'. *Begin*: 'Dear Sir' or 'Dear Mr [*S–*]'.

Clergy (Roman Catholic)
Address on envelope: 'The Reverend [*F– S–*]'. If a member of a religious order, the initials of the order should be added after the name. *Begin*: 'Dear Reverend Father'.

Clergy (Other churches)
Address on envelope: 'The Reverend [*F– S–*]'. *Begin*: 'Dear Sir/Madam' or 'Dear Mr/Mrs/etc. [*S–*]'.

Congressman/woman
Address on enelope: 'The Honorable *F– S–*' or 'Honorable *F– S–*'. *Begin*: 'Dear Sir' or 'Dear Mr [*S–*]'.

Countess
Address on envelope: 'The Right Hon. the Countess of –'. *Begin*: 'Dear Madam'. *Spoken address*: 'Madam'.

Dean (Anglican)
Address on envelope: 'The Very Reverend the Dean of –'. *Begin*: 'Dear Dean' or 'Very Reverend Sir'. *Spoken address*: 'Dean'. *Begin an official speech*: 'Very Reverend Sir'.

Doctor
Physicians, anaesthetists, pathologists, and radiologists are addressed as 'Doctor'. In the UK, surgeons, whether they hold the degree of Doctor of Medicine or not, are known as 'Mr/Mrs'. In England and Wales, obstetricians and gynaecologists are addressed as 'Mr/Mrs', but in Scotland, Ireland, and elsewhere as 'Doctor'. In addressing a letter to the holder of a doctorate, the initials DD, MD, etc. are placed after the ordinary form of address, eg 'The Rev John Smith, DD'. The 'Rev Dr Smith' and 'Dr John Brown' are also used.

Duchess
Address on envelope: 'Her Grace the Duchess of –'. *Begin*: 'Dear Madam'. *Spoken address*: 'Your Grace'. (For Royal Duchess, *see* Princess.)

Duke
Address on envelope: 'His Grace the Duke of –'. *Begin*: 'My Lord Duke'. *Spoken address*: 'Your Grace'. (For Royal Duke, *see* Prince.)

Earl
Address on envelope: 'The Right Hon. the Earl of –'. *Begin*: 'My Lord'. *Spoken address*: 'My Lord'. (For Earl's wife, *see* Countess.)

Governor of a colony or **Governor-General**
Address on envelope: 'His Excellency (ordinary designation), Governor(-General) of –'. (The Governor-General of Canada has the rank of 'Right Honourable', which he retains for life.) The wife of a Governor-General is styled 'Her Excellency' within the country her husband administers. *Begin*: according to rank. *Close*: 'I have the honour to be, Sir (or 'My Lord', if a peer), Your Excellency's obedient servant'. *Spoken address*: 'Your Excellency'.

Governor (US, state)
Address on envelope: 'The Honorable [*F– S–*], Governor of –'. *Begin*: 'Sir/Madam'. *Spoken address*: 'Governor [*S–*]'.

Judge, High Court
Address on envelope: 'The Hon. Mr/Mrs Justice [*S–*]. *Begin*: 'Dear Sir/Madam'; if on judicial matters, 'My Lord/Lady'. *Spoken address*: 'Sir/Madam'; only on the bench or when dealing with judicial matters should a High Court Judge be addressed as 'My Lord/Lady' or referred to as 'Your Lordship/Ladyship'.

Judge, Circuit
Address on envelope: 'His/Her Honour Judge [*S–*]'. If a Knight, 'His Honour Judge Sir [*F– S–*]'. *Begin*: 'Dear Sir/Madam'. *Spoken address*: 'Sir/Madam'; address as 'Your Honour' only when on the bench or dealing with judicial matters.

Judge (US, federal)
Address on envelope: 'The Honorable [*F– S–*], Judge of the United States District Court of the – District of –'. *Begin*: 'Sir/Madam'. *Spoken address*: 'Judge [*S–*]'.

Justice of the Peace (England and Wales)
When on the bench, refer to and address as 'Your Worship'; otherwise according to rank. The letters 'JP' may be added after the person's name in addressing a letter, if desired.

Knight Bachelor
As Baronet, except that 'Bt' is omitted. Knight of the Bath, of St Michael and St George, etc. *Address on envelope*: 'Sir [*F– S–*], with the initials 'GCB', 'KCB', etc. added. *Begin*: 'Dear Sir'.

Forms of address (continued)

Knight's wife
As Baronet's wife, or according to rank.

Lady Mayoress
Address on envelope: 'The Lady Mayoress of –'. *Begin*: 'My Lady Mayoress'. *Spoken address*: '(My) Lady Mayoress'.

Lord Mayor
Address on envelope: The Lord Mayors of London, York, Belfast, Cardiff, and Dublin, and also Melbourne, Sydney, Adelaide, Perth, Brisbane, and Hobart, are styled 'The Right Hon. the Lord Mayor of –'. Other Lord Mayors are styled 'The Right Worshipful the Lord Mayor of –'. *Begin*: 'My Lord Mayor', even if the holder of the office is a woman. *Spoken address*: '(My) Lord Mayor'.

Marchioness
Address on envelope: 'The Most Hon. the Marchioness of –'. *Begin*: 'Dear Madam'. *Spoken address*: 'Madam'.

Marquess
Address on envelope: 'The Most Hon. the Marquess of –'. *Begin*: 'My Lord'. *Spoken address*: 'My Lord'.

Mayor
Address on envelope: 'The Worshipful the Mayor of –'; in the case of cities and certain towns, 'The Right Worshipful' (UK); 'The Honorable' (US). *Begin*: 'Mr Mayor' or 'Dear Sir'. *Spoken address*: 'Mr Mayor'.

Mayoress
Address on envelope: 'The Mayoress of –'. *Begin*: 'Madam Mayoress' is traditional, but some now prefer 'Madam Mayor'. *Spoken address*: 'Mayoress' (or 'Madam Mayor').

Member of Parliament
Address on envelope: Add 'MP' to the usual form of address. *Begin*: according to rank.

Monsignor
Address on envelope: 'The Reverend Monsignor [*F– S–*]'. If a canon, 'The Very Reverend Monsignor (Canon) [*F– S–*]'. *Begin*: 'Reverend Sir'. *Spoken address*: 'Monsignor [*S–*]'.

Officers in the Armed Forces
Address on envelope: The professional rank is prefixed to any other rank, eg 'Admiral the Right Hon. the Earl of –', 'Lieut.-Col. Sir [*F– S–*], KCB'. Officers below the rank of Rear-Admiral, and Marshal of the Royal Air Force, are entitled to 'RN' (or 'Royal Navy') and 'RAF' respectively after their name. Army officers of the rank of Colonel or below may follow their name with the name of their regiment or corps (which may be abbreviated). Officers in the women's services add 'WRNS', 'WRAF', 'WRAC'. *Begin*: according to social rank.

Officers (retired and former)
Address on envelope: Officers above the rank of Lieutenant (in the Royal Navy), Captain (in the Army), and Flight Lieutenant may continue to use and be addressed by their armed forces rank after being placed on the retired list. The word 'retired' (or in an abbreviated form) should not normally be placed after the person's name. Former officers in the women's services do not normally continue to use their ranks.

Pope
Address on envelope: 'His Holiness, the Pope'. *Begin*: 'Your Holiness' or 'Most Holy Father'. *Close*: if a Roman Catholic, 'I have the honour to be your Holiness's most devoted and obedient child' (or 'most humble child'); if not Roman Catholic, 'I have the honour to be (or 'remain') Your Holiness's obedient servant'. *Spoken address*: 'Your Holiness'.

President of the United States
Address on envelope: 'The President'. *Begin*: 'Mr President'. *Spoken address*: 'Mr President'

Prime Minister, UK
Address on envelope: according to rank. The Prime Minister is a Privy Counsellor (see separate entry) and the letter should be addressed accordingly. *Begin*: according to rank.

Prince
Address on envelope: If a Duke, 'His Royal Highness the Duke of –'; if not a Duke, 'His Royal Highness the Prince [*F–*]', if a child of the sovereign; otherwise 'His Royal Highness Prince [*F–*] of [Kent or Gloucester]'. *Begin*: 'Sir'. Refer to as 'Your Royal Highness'. *Close*: 'I have the honour to remain (or be) Sir, Your Royal Highness's most humble and obedient servant'. *Spoken address*: 'Your Royal Highness' once, thereafter 'Sir'.

Princess
Address on envelope: If a Duchess, 'Her Royal Highness the Duchess of –'; if not a Duchess, the daughter of a sovereign is addressed as 'Her Royal Highness the Princess [*F–*]', followed by any title she holds by marriage. 'The' is omitted in addressing a princess who is not the daughter of a sovereign. A Princess by marriage is addressed 'HRH Princess [husband's *F–*] of –'. *Begin*: 'Madam'. Refer to as 'Your Royal Highness'. *Close*: as for Prince, substituting 'Madam' for 'Sir'. *Spoken address*: 'Your Royal Highness' once, thereafter 'Ma'am'.

Privy Counsellor
Address on envelope: If a peer, 'The Right Hon. the Earl of –, PC'; if not a peer, 'The Right Hon. [*F– S–*]', without the 'PC'. *Begin*: according to rank.

Professor
Address on envelope: 'Professor [*F– S–*]'; in the UK the styles 'Professor Lord [*S–*]' and 'Professor Sir [*F– S–*]' are often used, but are deprecated by some people. If the professor is in holy orders, 'The Reverend Professor'. *Begin*: 'Dear Sir/Madam', or according to rank. *Spoken address*: according to rank.

Queen
Address on envelope: 'Her Majesty the Queen'. *Begin*: 'Madam, with my humble duty'. Refer to as 'Your Majesty'. *Close*: 'I have the honour to remain (or 'be'). Madam, Your Majesty's most humble and obedient servant'. *Spoken address*: 'Your Majesty' once, thereafter 'Ma'am'. *Begin an official speech*: 'May it please Your Majesty'.

Rabbi
Address on envelope: 'Rabbi [initial and *S–*]' or, if a doctor, 'Rabbi Doctor [initial and *S–*]'. *Begin*: 'Dear Sir'. *Spoken address*: 'Rabbi [*S–*]' or '[Doctor *S–*]'.

Secretary of State
Address on envelope: (UK) The Right Hon. [*F– S–*], MP. Secretary of State for –', or 'The Secretary of State for –'. Otherwise according to rank. (US) 'The Honorable the Secretary of State' (or 'Defense' etc). *Begin*: 'Dear Sir/Madam'.

Senator
Address on envelope: 'The Honorable *F– S–*'. *Begin*: 'Dear Sir' or 'Dear Senator'. *Spoken address*: 'Senator'.

Viscount
Address on envelope: 'The Right Hon. the Viscount –'. *Begin*: 'My Lord'. *Spoken address*: 'My Lord'.

Viscountess
Address on envelope: 'The Right Hon. the Viscountess –'. *Begin*: 'Dear Madam'. *Spoken address*: 'Madam'.

Heraldry

Heraldry is the granting and devising of pictorial devices (arms) used originally on the shields of knights in armour to distinguish different sides in battle. In the early 12th-c these devices became hereditary in Europe through the male line of descent.

A glossary of terms

Armorial bearings	Hereditary symbols used to distinguish individuals, institutions and corporations.
Billet	Oblong figure.
Billette	Field with ten or more billets irregularly arranged.
Blazonry	The science of describing pictorial signs used in heraldry.
Charges	Heraldic signs or symbols.
Chevron	Inverted v-shaped stripe.
Chief	Top third of the shield.
Compartment	Ground or foundation on which supporters stand.
Crest	Object placed on top of helmet and bound to it by the wreath of colours (which shows the two main colours used in the shield).
Dexter side	Right-hand side.
Escutcheon	The shield on which a coat of arms is represented.
Field	Basic colour (tincture) or background of the shield.
Helmet	Placed on top of the shield.
Inescutcheon	Small figure shaped like shield in the middle of the shield.
Lozenge	Parallelogram.
Lozengy	Field divided transversely by diagonal lines.
Mascle	Lozenge voided.
Mantling or lambrequin	This is hung from the helmet and is designed to act as a shield for the wearer. It is painted with the principle colour of the shield.
Ordinaries	Basic charges.
Orle	Inner border not touching the edge of the shield.
Pile	Inverted pyramid.
Roundel	Circular symbol.
Shield	Coat of arms.
Sinister side	Left-hand side.
Supporters	Animals or human figures on either side of the shield.
Tressure	Smaller version of orle.

Metals
Argent	Silver.
Or	Gold.

Furs
Ermine	White field with black spots.
Ermines	Black field with white spots.
Erminois	Gold field with black spots.
Pean	Black field with gold spots.
Vair	Blue and white.

Colours
Azure	Blue.
Gules	Red.
Murrey	Tint between gules and purpure.
Purpure	Purple.
Sable	Black.
Tenne	Orange-tawny.
Vert	Green.

Partition lines

Impalement or dimidation – shield divided by straight line (top to bottom) into two parts.
Party per pale – division of field into two equal parts by perpendicular line.
Party per fess – field divided by horizontal line into two equal parts.
Party per bend.
Party per chevron.
Party per saltire.
Gyronny of eight.

Pale   Bend   Fess   Chief

Chevron   Saltire   Gyronny of eight

Heraldic descriptions of animals and their posture
Addorsed	Creatures placed back to back.
Combattant	Two animals fighting on hindlegs.
Couchant	Lying down.
Displayed	Birds with wings extended.
Dormant	Sleeping.
At gaze	Looking full face.
Passant	Walking.
Rampant	On hind legs.
Rampant guardant	On hind legs but full-faced.
Reguardant	Looking back.
Statant	Standing.
Trippant	At a trot (one foot raised).

Aristocratic ranks

England	France	Holy Roman Empire (Germany)	Italy	Spain
king	roi	Kaiser	re	rey
prince	prince	Pfalzgraf	principe	principe
duke	duc	Herzog	duca	duque
marquess	marquis	Markgraf	marchese	marques
earl	comte	Landgraf	conde	conde
viscount	vicomte		visconte	vizconde
baron			barone	
baronet				
knight	chevalier	Ritter	cavaliere	caballero

Law and crime

Courts of Great Britain

England and Wales

CRIMINAL

House of Lords — The final Court of Appeal from all courts in Great Britain and Northern Ireland (except criminal courts in Scotland) for all cases except those concerning European Community Law. Judges are known as Law Lords or Lords of Appeal in Ordinary. Head is the Lord High Chancellor (the only judge who is a political figure), with 12 Law Lords. Normally five judges hear appeals.

Court of Appeal — Established by the Criminal Appeal Act 1966 to replace the now defunct Court of Criminal Appeal. Appeals are heard by one, two or three judges. Headed by the Lord Chief Justice. Judges are the Master of the Rolls, Lords Justices of Appeal and Judges of the High Court.

Crown Court — Established by the Courts Act 1971 to replace the Assizes and Quarter Sessions. Currently around 90 venues in England and Wales where the Court sits. Organized in six circuits – Midland and Oxford, North Eastern, Northern, South Eastern, Wales and Chester, Western.

Magistrates' Court — Tries around 97% of all criminal cases. c. 30000 lay magistrates. Stipendiary magistrates are paid full-time lawyers who preside alone in busier courts. Magistrates' Courts also have youth jurisdiction.

CIVIL

European Court of Justice

House of Lords — See above.

Court of Appeal — Headed by the Master of the Rolls. Judges are known as Lords Justices of Appeal. Cases are heard by one, two or three judges. Ex officio judges are the Lord Chancellor, the Lord Chief Justice, the Master of the Rolls, the President of the Family Division of the High Court and the Vice Chancellor, with 33 Lords Justices of Appeal.

High Court — Established as part of the Supreme Court by the Judicature Acts 1873–5. It has three Divisions. The Chancery Division, headed by the Lord High Chancellor in name, but effectively the Vice Chancellor with 17 puisne judges: deals mainly with trust and probate matters, bankruptcy and partnerships. The Queen's Bench Division (the largest, with the widest jurisdiction), headed by the Lord Chief Justice, with 64 puisne judges: deals with large areas of the law including tort and most contract cases, commercial and admiralty actions and judicial review. Also has some appeal jurisdiction. The Family Division: deals with matrimonial cases and certain cases affecting children (President and 16 puisne judges).

Scotland

CRIMINAL

High Court of Justiciary in Edinburgh
High Court of Justice
Sheriff Court
District Court

CIVIL

House of Lords
Court of Session (Inner House)
Court of Session (Outer House)
Sheriff Principal Court
Sheriff Court

Northern Ireland

CRIMINAL

House of Lords
N Ireland Court of Appeal
Crown Court

CIVIL

House of Lords
N Ireland Court of Appeal
High Court of Justice
County Court
Magistrates Court

Courts of Great Britain (continued)

County Court   Civil courts forming a system covering England and Wales, established in 1846. In 1991 many of the former financial limits on the jurisdiction of the County Court were abolished and new rules for the allocation of cases between the High Court and the County Court were formulated. Each court has a Circuit Judge and a District Judge.

SPECIALIZED CIVIL COURTS

Small Claims Court   Deals with low-value debt enforcement.

Bankruptcy Court   Deals with bankruptcy.

Restrictive Practices Court   Deals with commercial disputes.

Courts Martial Appeal Court

Technology and Construction Court

The judiciary and legal representatives

	1990	1994	1999[j]
England & Wales			
The Judiciary			
Judges[a,b]			
Lords of Appeal in Ordinary			12
Lord Justices	27	32	35
High Court Judges	83	93	99
Circuit Judges	427	534	554
Recorders	752	904	912
Assistant Recorders	421	338	399
District Judges[b]	223	315	355
District Judges Family Division			19
Stipendiary Magistrates			94
Acting Stipendiary Magistrates			88
Lay Magistrates[c]	27011[g]	30088	30239
Legal representatives			
Barristers[d,h]	6645	8498	9698
Solicitors[e,h]	55685	66123	75072
Scotland[b]			
The Judiciary			
Judges	24	26	27
Sheriffs	101	111	116
Stipendiary Magistrates	4	4	8
Justices of the Peace	904	4200	4000[i]
	1990	1994	1999[j]

	1990	1994	1999[j]
Legal representatives[f]			
Advocates	276	368	404
Solicitors	7087	9404	8362
Northern Ireland			
The Judiciary			
Judges			
High Court Judges	10	10	7
County Court Judges	13	10	14
Circuit Judges	4	2	4
Resident Magistrates	17	17	17
Legal representatives			
Barristers	308	380	456
Solicitors	1295	1630	1869

[a]Excludes deputy judges and assistant recorders. [b]Figures relate to 31 Dec each year. [c]Figures relate to 1 Jan each year. [d]Figures relate to 1 Oct each year. [e]Number who applied for a practising certificate in year ending 31 Oct. [f]Practising. [g]Figures are for 1989. [h]Figures are for 1998. [i]Approximate figure. [j]As at 1st July.

Source: Lord Chancellor's Department, London. Bar Council, Belfast. Law Society of Scotland. Faculty of Advocates. The Keeper of the Rolls. Scottish Executive Justice Department.

Courts of Australia

Australia

HIGH COURT   Chief Justice and six other Justices appointed by the Governor-General in Council. Has jurisdiction over cases in which the State is a party, chiefly those involving constitutional issues, over disputes between states and residents of different states, and over matters concerning treaties and foreign representatives in Australia. Has discretionary power to hear appeals from the Federal Court, Family Court, and Supreme Courts of Australian states and territories.

FEDERAL COURT   Established 1977. Chief Justice and 49 Judges. Deals with cases involving industrial and trade practices, intellectual property, administrative law, taxation disputes, bankruptcy, and other civil proceedings. Also hears appeals from the Australian Territory Supreme Court and state Supreme Courts.

STATE COURTS   Each state has a Supreme Court headed by a Chief Justice, as well as lesser courts dealing with civil and criminal cases.

     The right of appeal from Australian courts to the Queen's Privy Council in the UK was abolished by the Australia Act, 1986.

Courts of Canada

SUPREME COURT   Chief Justice and eight puisne judges, holding three sessions per year. Hears appeals in civil and criminal cases if a question of public importance is involved. Advises on constitutional matters and issues raised by the Governor-General in Council.

SOCIETY

Law and crime (continued)

Courts of Canada (continued)

FEDERAL COURT	Chief Justice, Associate Chief Justice and not more than 29 other judges: has two Divisions, The Federal Court of Appeal and the Federal Court (Trial Division). Hears appeals on cases, including those from the Federal Court (Trial Division), involving the Crown and its agents and appeals from federal tribunals. Also reviews decisions made by federal boards and commissions. In addition, the Federal Court (Trial Division) deals with inter-provincial and federal-provincial disputes.
PROVINCIAL COURTS	Each province has a Court of Appeal, which hears appeals from lesser courts within the province concerned, and a Supreme Court or Court of Queen's Bench which deals with civil or criminal matters arising within the jurisdiction.
	Judges in superior, county, and district courts appointed by the Governor-General. Judges in lesser courts are appointed by Lieutenant-Governors of the provinces.

Courts of South Africa

CONSTITUTIONAL COURT	Established under the 1996 Constitution, the President, Deputy President and nine other Justices interpret, protect, and enforce the Constitution, and adjudicate in disputes between tiers of government.
SUPREME COURT OF APPEAL	Shares the postition of highest Court in the country with the Constitutional Court. Hears appeals on all cases other than Constitutional decisions from the High Courts. Headed by the Chief Justice.
HIGH COURTS	Pending decisions currently being made about the court structures and jurisdictions of the High Court, there are at present 10 High Courts. Each is composed of a Judge President, one or more Deputy Judges President, and as many judges as the President may from time to time determine.
MAGISTRATES' COURTS	Organized on district and regional basis, with power of appeal to High Court. Under the Magistrates' Court Act 1993 all Magistrates' Courts fall outside the ambit of the Public Service, with the object of strengthening independence of the judiciary.
	The Judicial Service Commission advises the government on issues concerning the judiciary, and makes representations about the appointment of judges.

Courts of United States

SUPREME COURT	Chief Justice and eight Associate Justices, appointed by the President, with the consent of the Senate. Deals with cases in which the state is a party to the suit. Also hears appeals from lesser federal courts and from the superior state courts.
COURT OF APPEAL	168 Circuit Judges within 13 circuits. Hears appeals from the District Courts and from various federal administrative agencies.
DISTRICT COURT	94 Courts, served by 575 District Court Judges.
TERRITORIAL COURT	Deals with cases arising in Guam, Puerto Rico, and the Virgin Islands. Lesser courts include the Court of International Trade, Court of Federal Claims, Court of Military Appeals, Tax Court, and Court of Veterans Appeals. The courts are further served by the Administrative Office of the Courts, the Federal Judicial Center, and the Sentencing Commission.

Lord Chancellors

Year appointed	Office holder	Year appointed	Office holder	Year appointed	Office holder	Year appointed	Office holder
605	Angmendus	1088	Bloct	1162	John	1227	Ralph de Neville
?	Cenmora	1090	Flambard	?	Ralph de Warnailla	1240	Simon the Norman
?	Bosa	1100	Giffard	?	Walter de	1242	Ralph de Neville
?	Swithulplus	?	Weldric		Constantis	1244	Silvester de Everden
827	St Swithin	?	Godfrey	1181	Geoffrey son of	1246	John Maunsel
920	Turketel	?	Herbert		Rosand	1249	John de Laxington
959	Adolphus	?	Geoffrey Rufus	?	Nigel Bishop of Ely	1253	Queen Eleanour
978	Alfric	?	Ranulfus	?	Walter de Bidem	1254	William de Kilkenny
1043	Lesfric	1135	Alexander, Bishop	1189	William Longchamp	1255	Henry de Wangham
1050	Reinhildus		of Lincoln	1192	Geoffrey son of	1260	Nicholas de Ely
1067	Maurice	?	Roger Pauper		Rosand	1261	Walter de Merton
?	Osmund	?	Philip	1195	William Longchamp	1263	Nicholas de Ely
1073	Augustus	?	Roger de Gant	1196	Eustace Bishop of Ely	1265	Thomas de Cantiluse
1075	Baldrick	?	Reginald	1199	Walter Herbert	1265	Walter Giffard
1075	Herman	1142	William Fitzgibert	1206	Walter de Grey	1266	Godfrey Giffard
1086	Giffard	1155	St Thomas Becket	1214	Richard de Marisco	1268	John de Chrishull

SOCIETY

Year appointed	Office holder	Year appointed	Office holder	Year appointed	Office holder	Year appointed	Office holder
1269	Richard de Middleton	1401	Edmund Stafford	1617	V. Bruckley	1827	Lord Lyndhurst
1272	Walter de Merton	1403	Cardinal Beaufort	1618	Lord Bacon	1830	Lord Brougham
1274	Robert Burnal	1405	Thomas Langley	1621	Lord Keeper Williams	1833	Lord Lyndhurst
1292	John de Langton	1407	Thomas de Arundel			1836	Lord Cottenham
1302	William de Grenefield	1410	Sir Thomas Beaufort	1625	Lord Keeper Coventry	1841	Lord Lyndhurst
		1412	Thomas de Arundel			1846	Lord Cottenham
1304	William de Hamilton	1413	Cardinal Beaufort	1640	Lord Keeper Finch	1850	Great Seal in Commission
		1417	Thomas Langley	1641	Lord Keeper Littleton		
1307	Ralph de Baldock	1424	Cardinal Beaufort	1645	Lord Keeper Lane	1850	Lord Truro
1307	John de Langton	1426	Cardinal Kempe	1645	Earl of Kent	1852	Lord St Leonards
1310	Walter Reynolds	1432	John Stafford	1646	Earl of Salisbury	1852	Lord Cranworth
1314	John de Sandale	1450	Cardinal Kempe	1646	Earl of Manchester	1858	Lord Chelmsford
1318	John de Hottram	1454	Richard Neville, Earl of Salisbury	1648	Earl of Kent	1859	Lord Campbell
1320	John de Salmon			1649	Whitelock	1862	Lord Westbury
1323	Robert de Baldock	1455	Cardinal Bonchier	1653	Sir E. Herbert	1864	Lord Carnworth
1327	John de Hottram	1456	William Waynflete	1654	Whitelock	1866	Lord Chelmsford
1327	Henry de Bungash	1460	George Neville	1655	Colonel Fiennes	1868	Lord Cairns
1330	John de Stratford		Sir George Fortescue	1658	Sir E. Hyde	1868	Lord Hatherley
1334	Richard de Bury			1659	Colonel Fiennes	1871	Lord Selborne
1337	Robert de Stratford	1461	George Neville	1659	Speaker Lenthall	1874	Lord Cairns
1338	Richard de Bynkworth	1467	Robert Stillington	1659	Bradshaw Tyrell	1880	Lord Selbourne
		1473	Henry Bonchier, Earl of Essex	1659	Whitelock	1885	Lord Halsbury
1340	John de Stratford		Lawrence Booth	1660	Lord Clarendon	1886	Lord Herschell
1340	Robert de Stratford	1475	Thomas Rotheram	1667	Sir Orlando Bridgernaw	1886	Lord Helsbury
1340	Sir Robert Bonchier	1483	John Russell			1892	Lord Herschell
1341	Sir Robert Parnage	1485	John Alcock	1672	Lord Shaftesbury	1895	Lord Halsbury
1343	Robert de Sandyngton	1487	Cardinal Morton	1673	Lord Nottingham	1905	Lord Loreburn
		1500	Henry Deane	1682	Lord Keeper Guildford	1912	Lord Haldane
1345	John de Offord	1502	Archbishop Worham			1915	Lord Buckmaster
1349	John de Thoresby	1509	Archbishop Worham	1685	Lord Jeffreys	1916	Lord Finlay
1356	William de Edington	1515	Cardinal Wolsey	1687	Lord Maynard and Others	1919	Lord Birkenhead
1363	Simon de Langham	1529	Sir Thomas More			1922	Lord Cave
1367	William de Wickham	1533	Lord Audley	1690	Lord Trevor and Others	1924	Lord Haldane
		1544	Thomas Wriomosley			1924	Lord Cave
1371	Sir Robert Thorpe	1547	Earl of Southampton	1693	Lord Somers	1928	Lord Hailsham
1372	Sir John Knynet	1547	Lord Wrottesley	1700	Lord K. Wright	1929	Lord Sankey
1377	Adam de Haughton	1547	William Poulet	1705	Lord Cowper	1935	Lord Hailsham
1378	Lord Le Scrope	1547	Lord Rich	1710	Lord Harcourt	1938	Lord Maugham
1380	Simon de Sudbury	1552	Thomas Goodrich, Bishop of Ely	1714	Lord Cowper	1939	Lord Caldecote
1381	William Courtenay			1718	Lord Macclesfield	1940	Lord Simon
?	Lord le Scrope	1553	Bishop Gardyner	1725	Lord King	1945	Lord Jowitt
1382	Robert de Braybrooke	1556	Archbishop Heath	1733	Lord Talbot	1951	Lord Simonds
?	Sir Michael de la Pole	1558	Sir Nicholas Bacon	1737	Lord Hardwicke	1954	Lord Kilmuir
		1579	Sir Thomas Bromley	1757	Lord K. Henley	1962	Lord Dilhorne
1383	Thomas de Arundel	1587	Sir Christopher Hatten	1760	Lord Northington	1964	Lord Gardiner
1389	William de Wickham			1766	Lord Camden	1970	Lord Hailsham of St Marylebone
1391	Thomas de Arundel	1591	Lord Burghley (William Lecit)	1770	Charles Yorke		
1396	Edmund Stafford	1592	Sir John Puckering	1771	Lord Bathurst	1974	Lord Elwyn-Jones
1399	Thomas de Arundel John Scarle	1596	Lord Ellesmere	1778	Lord Thurlow	1979	Lord Hailsham of St Marylebone
		1603	Thomas Eggerton	1793	Lord Loughborough		
				1801	Lord Eldon	1987	Lord Havers
				1806	Lord Erskine	1987	Lord Mackay
				1807	Lord Eldon	1997	Lord Irvine of Lairg
						2003	Lord Falconer

Members of the Supreme Court of the United States[a]

Name: State apptd. from	Term of service	Date of birth	Date of death	Name: State apptd. from	Term of service	Date of birth	Date of death
CHIEF JUSTICES				Harlan F. Stone, NY	1941–46	1872	1946
John Jay, NY	1789–95	1745	1829	Frederick M. Vinson, KY	1946–53	1890	1953
John Rutledge, SC	1795	1739	1800	Earl Warren, CA	1953–69	1891	1974
Oliver Ellsworth, CT	1796–1800	1745	1807	Warren E. Burger, VA	1969–86	1907	1995
John Marshall, VA	1801–35	1755	1835	William H. Rehnquist, AZ	1986–2005	1924	2005
Roger B. Taney, MD	1836–64	1777	1864	John G Roberts, DC	2006–	1955	–
Salmon P. Chase, OH	1864–73	1808	1873				
Morrison R. Waite, OH	1874–88	1816	1888				
Melville W. Fuller, IL	1888–1910	1833	1910				
Edward D. White, LA	1910–21	1845	1921				
William H. Taft, CT	1921–30	1857	1930				
Charles E. Hughes, NY	1930–41	1862	1948				

SOCIETY

Law and crime (continued)

Members of the Supreme Court of the United States[a] (continued)

Name: State apptd. from	Term of service	Date of birth	Date of death	Name: State apptd. from	Term of service	Date of birth	Date of death
ASSOCIATE JUSTICES				Mahlon Pitney, NJ	1912–22	1858	1924
James Wilson, PA	1789–98	1742	1798	James C. McReynolds, TN	1914–41	1862	1946
John Rutledge, SC	1789–91	1739	1800	Louis D. Brandeis, MA	1916–39	1856	1941
William Cushing, MA	1789–1810	1732	1810	John H. Clarke, OH	1916–22	1857	1945
John Blair, VA	1789–96	1732	1800	George Sutherland, UT	1922–38	1862	1942
James Iredell, NC	1790–9	1751	1799	Pierce Butler, MN	1923–39	1866	1939
Thomas Johnson, MD	1791–3	1732	1819	Edward T. Sanford, TN	1923–30	1865	1930
William Paterson, NJ	1793–1806	1745	1806	Harlan F. Stone, NY	1925–41	1872	1946
Samuel Chase, MD	1796–1811	1741	1811	Owen J. Roberts, PA	1930–45	1875	1955
Bushrod Washington, VA	1798–1829	1762	1829	Benjamin N. Cardozo, NY	1932–38	1870	1938
Alfred Moore, NC	1799–1804	1755	1810	Hugo L. Black, AL	1937–71	1886	1971
William Johnson, SC	1804–34	1771	1834	Stanley F. Reed, KY	1938–57	1884	1980
Henry B. Livingston, NY	1806–23	1757	1823	Felix Frankfurter, MA	1939–62	1882	1965
Thomas Todd, KY	1807–26	1765	1826	William O. Douglas, CT	1939–75	1898	1980
Gabriel Duval, MD	1811–35	1752	1844	Frank Murphy, MI	1940–9	1890	1949
Joseph Story, MA	1811–45	1779	1845	James F. Byrnes, SC	1941–2	1879	1972
Smith Thompson, NY	1823–43	1768	1843	Robert H. Jackson, PA	1941–54	1892	1954
Robert Trimble, KY	1826–28	1777	1828	Wiley B. Rutledge, IA	1943–9	1894	1949
John McLean, OH	1830–61	1785	1861	Harold H. Burton, OH	1945–58	1888	1964
Henry Baldwin, PA	1830–44	1780	1844	Tom C. Clark, TX	1949–67	1899	1977
James M. Wayne, GA	1835–67	1790	1867	Sherman Minton, IN	1949–56	1890	1965
Philip P. Barbour, VA	1836–41	1783	1841	John M. Harlan, NY	1955–71	1899	1971
John Catron, TN	1837–65	1786	1865	William J. Brennan, Jr, NJ	1956–90	1906	1997
John McKinley, AL	1837–52	1780	1852	Charles E. Whittaker, MO	1957–62	1901	1973
Peter V. Daniel, VA	1841–60	1784	1860	Potter Stewart, OH	1958–81	1915	1985
Samuel Nelson, NY	1845–72	1792	1873	Byron R. White, CO	1962–93	1917	2002
Levi Woodbury, NH	1845–51	1789	1851	Arthur J. Goldberg, IL	1962–5	1908	1990
Robert C. Grier, PA	1846–70	1794	1870	Abe Fortas, TN	1965–9	1910	1982
Benjamin R. Curtis, MA	1851–57	1809	1874	Thurgood Marshall, NY	1967–91	1908	1993
John A. Campbell, AL	1853–61	1811	1889	Harry A. Blackmun, MN	1970–94	1908	1999
Nathan Clifford, ME	1858–81	1803	1881	Lewis F. Powell, Jr, VA	1972–87	1907	1998
Noah H. Swayne, OH	1862–81	1804	1884	William H. Rehnquist, AZ	1972–86	1924	2005
Samuel F. Miller, IA	1862–90	1816	1890	John Paul Stevens, IL	1975–	1920	–
David Davis, IL	1862–77	1815	1886	Sandra Day O'Connor, AZ	1981–2005	1930	–
Stephen J. Field, CA	1863–97	1816	1899	Antonin Scalia, DC	1986–	1936	–
William Strong, PA	1870–80	1808	1895	Anthony M. Kennedy, CA	1988–	1936	–
Joseph P. Bradley, NJ	1870–92	1813	1892	David H. Souter, NH	1990–	1939	–
Ward Hunt, NY	1873–82	1810	1886	Clarence Thomas, VA	1991–	1948	–
John M. Harlan, KY	1877–1911	1833	1911	Ruth Bader Ginsburg, DC	1993–	1933	–
William B. Woods, GA	1880–87	1824	1887	Stephen Breyer, MA	1994–	1938	–
Stanley Matthews, OH	1881–9	1824	1889	John G. Roberts, DC	2005–	1955	–
Horace Gray, MA	1882–1902	1828	1902	Samuel Alito, NJ	2006–	1950	–
Samuel Blatchford, NY	1882–93	1820	1893				
Lucius Q. C. Lamar, MS	1888–93	1825	1893				
David J. Brewer, KS	1889–1910	1837	1910				
Henry B. Brown, MI	1890–1906	1836	1913				
George Shiras, Jr., PA	1892–1903	1832	1924				
Howell E. Jackson, TN	1893–5	1832	1895				
Edward D. White, LA	1894–1910	1845	1921				
Rufus W. Peckham, NY	1896–1909	1838	1909				
Joseph McKenna, CA	1898–1925	1843	1926				
Oliver W. Holmes, MA	1902–32	1841	1935				
William R. Day, OH	1903–22	1849	1923				
William H. Moody, MA	1906–10	1853	1917				
Horace H. Lurton, TN	1910–14	1844	1914				
Charles E. Hughes, NY	1910–16	1862	1948				
Willis Van Devanter, WY	1910–37	1859	1941				
Joseph R. Lamar, GA	1910–16	1857	1916				

[a]The Supreme Court has nine members – a chief justice and eight associate justices – appointed by the President with the advice and consent of the Senate. It is the highest federal court and, in addition to its jurisdiction relating to appeals, it exercises oversight of the constitution through the power of judicial review of the acts of state and federal legislatures, and the executive.

ARMED FORCES

Defence forces and expenditure

Approximate strengths of selected regular armed forces of the world at 2002

Country	Total	Military personnel				Defence expenditure as % of GNP*
		Army %	Navy %	Air Force %	Other %	
Algeria	136 700	87.8	4.9	7.3	–	4.0
Angola	100 000	90.0	4.0	6.0	–	21.2
Argentina	69 000	59.2	22.9	17.9	–	1.6
Armenia	44 610	87.0	13.0	13.0	–	5.8
Australia	50 920	49.4	24.7	25.9	–	1.8
Austria	34 600	80.2	–	19.8	–	0.8
Azerbaijan	72 100	86.0	3.0	11.0	–	6.6
Bangladesh	137 000	87.6	7.7	4.7	–	1.4
Belarus	79 800	51.8	–	27.6	20.6	1.3
Belgium	39 260	67.0	6.5	21.8	4.7	1.4
Bosnia & Herzegovina[a]	13 000	–	–	–	–	4.5
Brazil	287 600	65.7	16.9	17.4	–	1.9
Bulgaria	68 450	45.3	6.4	26.0	22.3	3.0
Cambodia[b]	125 000	60.0	2.4	1.6[g]	–	4.0
Canada	52 300	36.9	17.2	25.8	–	1.4
Chile	80 500	55.9	28.6	15.5	–	3.0
China	2 270 000	70.5	11.0	18.5	–	2.3
Colombia	158 000	86.1	9.5	4.4	–	3.2
Congo, Dem. Rep. of[c]	6 800	–	–	–	–	14.4[d]
Croatia	51 000	88.2	5.9	5.9	–	6.4
Cuba	46 000	76.1	6.5	17.4	–	1.9
Czech Republic	49 450	73.5	–	22.9	–	2.3
Denmark	22 700	62.6	17.6	19.8	–	1.6
Ecuador	59 500	84.0	9.3	6.7	–	3.7
Egypt	443 000	72.2	4.3	23.5	–	2.7
El Salvador	15 000	89.3	4.2	6.5	–	0.9
Ethiopia	252 500	99.0	–	1.0	–	8.8
Finland	31 850	77.1	14.4	8.5	–	1.4
France	260 400	52.6	17.5	24.6	–	2.7
Georgia	17 500	49.3	7.1	10.5	–	1.2
Germany	296 000	68.0	8.6	22.8	–	1.6
Greece	177 600	70.7	10.7	18.6	–	4.7
Guatemala	31 400	93.0	4.8	2.2	–	0.7
Hungary	33 400	70.7	–	23.1	–	1.7
India[a]	1 326 000	83.0	4.2	12.8	–	2.5
Indonesia	297 000	77.4	13.5	9.1	–	1.1
Iran	520 000	62.5	3.5	10.0	–	2.9
Iraq[e]	–	–	–	–	–	5.5
Israel	161 500	74.3	4.0	21.7	–	8.8
Italy	216 800	59.0	17.5	23.4	–	2.0
Japan	239 900	61.8	18.5	19.0	–	1.0
Jordan	100 240	84.5	0.5	15.0	–	9.2
Kazakhstan	60 000	68.3	–	31.7	–	0.9
Kenya[b]	24 400	82.0	5.7	12.3	–	1.9
Korea, North	1 082 000	87.8	4.2	8.0	–	18.8
Korea, South	686 000	81.6	9.2	9.2	–	2.9
Laos	29 100	88.0	–	12.0	–	2.0
Lebanon	71 830	97.5	1.1	1.4	–	4.0
Libya	76 000	59.2	10.5	30.3	–	6.1[f]
Malaysia	100 000	80.0	12.0	8.0	–	2.3
Mexico	192 770	74.7	19.2	6.1	–	0.6
Morocco	196 300	89.1	4.0	6.9	–	4.3
Myanmar (Burma)	444 000	95.7	2.3	2.0	–	7.8
Netherlands, The	47 430	48.8	25.6	18.5	–	1.8
Nigeria	78 500	79.0	8.9	12.1	–	1.7
Norway	25 800	57.0	23.6	19.4	–	2.2
Oman	41 700	60.0	10.1	9.8	20.1[h]	15.3
Pakistan	620 000	88.7	4.0	7.3	–	5.9
Peru	110 000	63.6	22.7	13.6	–	2.4
Poland	163 000	63.8	8.8	22.4	5.0	2.1
Portugal[a]	44 900	59.5	24.4	16.1	–	2.1
Romania	99 200	66.5	6.3	17.1	10.1	1.6[a]
Russia	988 100	23.5	17.4	18.7	21.3	5.6
Saudi Arabia	124 500	60.2	12.4	27.4	–	14.9
Serbia & Montenegro[a]	74 200	84.1	10.8	5.1	–	3.9
Singapore	60 500	82.7	7.4	9.9	–	4.8
Slovakia	26 200	49.6	–	38.9	–	1.8
South Africa	60 000	67.1	8.3	15.4	–	1.5

Defences forces and expenditure (continued)

Country	Total	Military personnel				Defence expenditure as % of GNP*
		Army %	Navy %	Air Force %	Other %	
Spain[a]	150 700	63.4	15.2	15.1	6.3	1.3
Sri Lanka	157 900	74.7	13.0	12.2	–	4.7
Sudan, The[a]	104 500	95.7	1.4	2.9	–	4.8
Sweden	33 900	56.3	20.9	22.7	–	2.3
Syria	319 000	67.4	1.3	12.5	–	7.0
Taiwan	370 000	64.8	16.8	18.4	–	5.2
Tanzania	27 000	85.2	3.7	11.1	–	1.4
Thailand	306 000	62.1	22.2	15.7	–	1.7
Tunisia	35 000	77.1	12.9	10.0	–	1.8
Turkey	514 850	78.1	10.2	11.7	–	5.3
Uganda	50 000/60 000	–	–	–	–	2.3
Ukraine	302 300	49.9	16.2	4.5	–	3.0
United Arab Emirates	41 500	84.3	6.0	9.7	–	4.1
United Kingdom	210 450	54.5	20.1	25.4	–	2.5
United States[a]	1 427 000	34.0	28.0	25.8	12.2[i]	3.0
Uruguay	23 900	63.6	23.8	12.6	–	1.3
Uzbekistan	50 000/55 000	75.0	–	25.0	–	1.7
Venezuela	82 300	69.3	22.2	8.5	–	1.4
Vietnam	484 000	85.1	8.7	6.2	–	2.5[d]
Yemen	66 500	90.2	2.3	7.5	–	6.1
Zambia	21 600	92.6	–	7.4	–	1.0
Zimbabwe	36 000	88.9	–	11.1	–	5.0

Notes:
* Gross National Product (1999).
[a] 2003
[b] 2001
[c] UN Peacekeepers at July 2003. New national army being created from August 2003.
[d] 1997
[e] US/Allied Coalition forces (Aug 2003) 146 000/30 000
[f] 1995
[g] provincial 36.0
[h] Royal household
[i] Marines

Source: Britannica Year Book, 2004.

Ranks in the UK armed forces

Army

1 Field Marshal
2 General (Gen.)
3 Lieutenant-General (Lt.-Gen.)
4 Major-General (Maj.-Gen.)
5 Brigadier (Brig.)
6 Colonel (Col.)
7 Lieutenant-Colonel (Lt.-Col.)
8 Major (Maj.)
9 Captain (Capt.)
10 Lieutenant (Lt.)
11 Second Lieutenant (2nd Lt.)

Royal Air Force

1 Marshal of the RAF
2 Air Chief Marshal
3 Air Marshal
4 Air Vice-Marshal
5 Air Commodore (Air Cdre)
6 Group Captain (Gp Capt.)
7 Wing Commander (Wg Cdr.)
8 Squadron Leader (Sqn. Ldr.)
9 Flight Lieutenant (Flt. Lt.)
10 Flying Officer (FO)
11 Pilot Officer (PO)

Navy

1 Admiral of the Fleet
2 Admiral (Adm.)
3 Vice-Admiral (Vice-Adm.)
4 Rear-Admiral (Rear-Adm.)
5 Commodore (1st & 2nd Class) (Cdre)
6 Captain (Capt.)
7 Commander (Cdr.)
8 Lieutenant-Commander (Lt.-Cdr.)
9 Lieutenant (Lt.)
10 Sub-Lieutenant (Sub-Lt.)
11 Acting Sub-Lieutenant (Acting Sub-Lt.)

Comparable ranks in the US armed forces

Army

1 General of the Army
2 General (Gen.)
3 Lieutenant-General (Lt.-Gen)
4 Major-General (Maj.-Gen)
5 Brigadier-General (Brig.-Gen)
6 Colonel (Col.)
7 Lieutenant-Colonel (Lt.-Col)
8 Major (Maj.)
9 Captain (Capt.)
10 First Lieutenant (1st Lt.)
11 Second Lieutenant (2nd Lt.)

Air Force

1 General of the Air Force
2 General (Gen.)
3 Lieutenant-General (Lt.-Gen)
4 Major-General (Maj.-Gen)
5 Brigadier-General (Brig.-Gen)
6 Colonel (Col.)
7 Lieutenant-Colonel (Lt.-Col)
8 Major (Maj.)
9 Captain (Capt.)
10 First Lieutenant (1st Lt.)
11 Second Lieutenant (2nd Lt.)

Navy

1 Fleet Admiral
2 Admiral (Adm.)
3 Vice-Admiral (Vice-Adm.)
4 Rear-Admiral (upper half) (Rear-Adm.)
5 Rear-Admiral (lower half) (Rear-Adm.)
6 Captain (Capt.)
7 Commander (Cdr.)
8 Lieutenant-Commander (Lt.-Cdr.)
9 Lieutenant (Lt.)
10 Lieutenant Junior Grade
11 Ensign

SOCIETY

POLITICS

United Nations membership

Grouped according to year of entry. 192 members (as of Sep 2006).

1945	Argentina, Australia, Belgium, Belorussian SSR (Belarus, 1991), Bolivia, Brazil, Canada, Chile, China (Taiwan to 1971), Colombia, Costa Rica, Cuba, Czechoslovakia (to 1993), Denmark, Dominican Republic, Ecuador, Egypt, El Salvador, Ethiopia, France, Greece, Guatemala, Haiti, Honduras, India, Iran, Iraq, Lebanon, Liberia, Luxembourg, Mexico, Netherlands, New Zealand, Nicaragua, Norway, Panama, Paraguay, Peru, Philippines, Poland, Saudi Arabia, South Africa, Syria, Turkey, Ukranian SSR (Ukraine, 1991), USSR (Russia, 1991), UK, USA, Uruguay, Venezuela, Yugoslavia[a] (to 1992)
1946	Afghanistan, Iceland, Sweden, Thailand
1947	Pakistan, Yemen (N, to 1990)
1948	Burma (Myanmar, 1989)
1949	Israel
1950	Indonesia
1955	Albania, Austria, Bulgaria, Cambodia, Ceylon(Sri Lanka, 1970), Finland, Hungary, Ireland, Italy, Jordan, Laos, Libya, Nepal, Portugal, Romania, Spain
1956	Japan, Morocco, Sudan, Tunisia
1957	Ghana, Malaya (Malaysia, 1963)
1958	Guinea
1960	Cameroon, Central African Republic, Chad, Congo, Côted'Ivoire, Cyprus, Dahoney (Benin, 1975), Gabon, Madagascar, Mali, Niger, Nigeria, Senegal, Somalia, Togo, Upper Volta (Burkina Faso, 1984), Democratic Republic of Congo (formerly Zaire)
1961	Mauritania, Mongolia, Sierra Leone, Tanganyika (within Tanzania, 1964)
1962	Algeria, Burundi, Jamaica, Rwanda, Trinidad and Tobago, Uganda
1963	Kenya, Kuwait, Zanzibar (within Tanzania, 1964)
1964	Malawi, Malta, Tanzania, Zambia

1965	Maldives, Singapore, The Gambia
1966	Barbados, Botswana, Guyana, Lesotho
1967	Yemen (S, to 1990)
1968	Equatorial Guinea, Mauritius, Swaziland
1970	Fiji
1971	Bahrain, Bhutan, China (People's Republic), Oman, Qatar, United Arab Emirates
1973	Bahamas, German Democratic Republic (within GFR, 1990), German Federal Republic
1974	Bangladesh, Grenada, Guinea-Bissau
1975	Cape Verde, Comoros, Mozambique, Papua New Guinea, São Tomé and Principe, Suriname
1976	Angola, Seychelles, Samoa (formerly Western Samoa)
1977	Djibouti, Vietnam
1978	Dominica, Solomon Islands
1979	St Lucia
1980	St Vincent and the Grenadines, Zimbabwe
1981	Antigua and Barbuda, Belize, Vanuatu
1983	St Christopher and Nevis
1984	Brunei
1990	Liechtenstein, Namibia, Yemen (formerly N Yemen and S Yemen)
1991	Estonia, Federated States of Micronesia, Latvia, Lithuania, Marshall Islands, N Korea, S Korea
1992	Armenia, Azerbaijan, Bosnia-Herzegovina, Croatia, Georgia, Kazakhstan, Kyrgysztan, Moldova, San Marino, Slovenia, Tajikistan, Turkmenistan, Uzbekistan
1993	Andorra, Czech Republic, Eritrea, Former Yugoslav Republic of Macedonia, Monaco, Slovak Republic
1995	Belau
1999	Nauru, Tonga, Kiribati
2000	Tuvalu
2002	East Timor, Switzerland
2006	Montenegro

[a] Yugoslavia was excluded from UN membership in 1992 and asked to reapply; Federal Republic of Yugoslavia admitted in 2000 (from 2002, Union of Serbia and Montenegro. Following separation of countries (2006) Serbia retained membership, Montenegro joined as new member).

Main bodies of the United Nations

General Assembly	Plenary body which controls much of the UN's work, supervises the subsidiary organs, sets priorities, and debates major issues of international affairs.
Security Council	Has fifteen members, but is dominated by five permanent members (China, France, Russia, UK, USA). Primary role is to maintain international peace and security. Empowered to order mandatory sanctions, call for ceasefires, and establish peace-keeping forces.
Secretariat	Headed by Secretary General. Staff of 66 000 worldwide answerable to UN only and are engaged in considerable diplomatic work.
International Court of Justice	Consists of fifteen judges appointed by the Council and the Assembly. Jurisdiction depends on consent of the states who are parties to a dispute. Also offers advisory opinions to various organs of UN.
Economic and Social Council	Elected by the General Assembly. It supervises the work of various committees, commissions and expert bodies in the economic and social area, and coordinates the work of UN specialized agencies.
Trusteeship Council	Oversees the transition of Trust territories to self-government.

SOCIETY

SOCIETY

Specialized agencies of the United Nations

Abbreviated form	Full title and location	Area of concern
ILO	International Labour Organization, Geneva	Social justice.
FAO	Food and Agriculture, Rome	Improvement of the production and distribution of agricultural products.
UNESCO	United Nations Educational, Scientific and Cultural Organization, Paris	Stimulation of popular education and the spread of culture.
ICAO	International Civil Aviation Organization, Montreal	Encouragement of safety measures in international flight.
IBRD	International Bank for Reconstruction and Development, Washington	Aid of development through investment.
IMF	International Monetary Fund, Washington	Promotion of international monetary cooperation.
UPU	Universal Postal Union, Berne	Uniting members within a single postal territory.
WHO	World Health Organization, Geneva	Promotion of the highest standards of health for all people.
ITU	International Telecommunication Union, Geneva	Allocation of frequencies and regulation of procedures.
WMO	World Meteorological Organization, Geneva	Standardization and utilization of meteorological observations.
IFC	International Finance Corporation, Washington	Promotion of the international flow of private capital.
IMCO	Inter-governmental Maritime Consultative Organization, London	The coordination of safety at sea.
IDA	International Development Association, Washington	Credit on special terms to provide assistance for less-developed countries.
WIPO	World Intellectual Property Organization, Geneva	Protection of copyright, designs, inventions, etc.
IFAD	International Fund for Agricultural Development, Rome	Increase of food production in developing countries by the generation of grants or loans.
UNIDO	United Nations Industrial Development Organization, Vienna	Promotion of industrialization of developing countries, with special emphasis on manufacturing sector. Provides technical assistance and advice, as well as help with planning.
IAEA[a]	International Atomic Energy Association, Vienna	Promotes research and development into peaceful uses of nuclear energy, and oversees system of safeguards and controls governing misuse of nuclear materials for military purposes.
UNICEF[b]	United Nations Children's Fund, New York	Provides primary healthcare and education in developing countries.
UNHCR[b]	United Nations High Commissioner for Refugees, Geneva	Protects rights and interests of refugees; organizes emergency relief and longer-term solutions, eg local integration, resettlement, or voluntary repatriation

[a]Linked to UN but not specialized agency. [b]Specialized bodies established by the General Assembly and supervised jointly with the Economic and Social Council.

United Nations Secretaries General

1946–53	Trygve Lie *Norway*
1953–61	Dag Hammarskjöld *Sweden*
1962–71	U Thant *Burma*
1972–81	Kurt Waldheim *Austria*
1982–92	Javier Pérez de Cuéllar *Peru*
1992–7	Boutros Boutros Ghali *Egypt*
1997–2006	Kofi Annan *Ghana*
2007–	Ban Ki-moon *South Korea*

Commonwealth Secretaries General

1965–75	Arnold Smith *Canada*
1975–90	Shridath S Ramphal *Guyana*
1990–9	Emeka Anyaoku *Nigeria*
1999–	Don McKinnon *New Zealand*

Commonwealth members

The 'Commonwealth' is a free association of independent nations formerly subject to British imperial government, and maintaining friendly and practical links with the UK. In 1931 the Statute of Westminster established the British Commonwealth of Nations; the adjective 'British' was deleted after World War 2. Most of the states granted independence, beginning with India in 1947, chose to be members of the Commonwealth.

Name of country	Year of joining	Name of country	Year of joining	Name of country	Year of joining
Antigua & Barbuda[a]	1981	Kenya	1963	St Vincent & the Grenadines[a]	1979
Australia[a]	1931	Kiribati	1979	Samoa	1970
Bahamas[a]	1973	Lesotho	1966	Seychelles	1976
Bangladesh	1972	Malawi	1964	Sierra Leone	1961
Barbados[a]	1966	Malaysia	1957	Singapore	1965
Belize[a]	1981	Maldives	1982	Solomon Islands[a]	1978
Botswana	1966	Malta	1964	South Africa	left 1961
Brunei	1984	Mauritius	1968		rejoined 1994
Cameroon	1995	Mozambique	1995	Sri Lanka	1948
Canada[a]	1931	Namibia	1990	Swaziland	1968
Cyprus	1961	Nauru	1968	Tanzania	1961
Dominica	1978	New Zealand[a]	1931	Tonga	1970
Fiji	1970	Nigeria	1960	Trinidad & Tobago	1962
	left 1987, readmitted 1997		suspended 1995, readmitted 1999	Tuvalu[a]	1978
Gambia, The	1965	Pakistan	1947	Uganda	1962
Ghana	1957		left 1972, rejoined 1989, left 1999	United Kingdom	1931
Grenada[a]	1974		readmitted 2004	Vanuatu	1980
Guyana	1966	Papua New Guinea[a]	1975	Zambia	1964
India	1947	St Kitts & Nevis[a]	1983	Zimbabwe	1980
Jamaica[a]	1962	St Lucia[a]	1979		suspended 2002, withdrew 2003

[a] Member states recognizing the Queen, represented by a Governor-General, as their Head of State.   Ireland resigned in 1949.

The European Union

Name of country and year of joining

Austria (1995)
Belgium (1958)
Bulgaria (2007)
Cyprus (2004)
Czech Republic (2004)
Denmark (1973)
Estonia (2004)
Finland (1995)
France (1958)
Germany (1958)
Greece (1981)
Hungary (2004)
Ireland (1973)
Italy (1958)
Latvia (2004)
Lithuania (2004)
Luxembourg (1958)
Malta (2004)
Netherlands (1958)
Poland (2004)
Portugal (1986)
Romania (2007)
Slovakia (2004)
Slovenia (2004)
Spain (1986)
Sweden (1995)
United Kingdom (1973)

Negotiations are ongoing with Turkey for future entry.

Representation of political parties in the European Parliament[a]

	EPP-ED	PES	ELDR	GREENS/ EFA	EUL/ NGL	UEN	EDD	Others	Total
Austria	6	7	–	2	–	–	–	3	18
Belgium	7	7	5	2	–	–	–	3	24
Cyprus	2	–	1	–	2	–	–	1	6
Czech Rep	11	2	–	–	6	–	–	5	24
Denmark	1	5	4	–	1	1	1	1	14
Estonia	1	3	2	–	–	–	–	–	6
Finland	4	3	5	1	1	–	–	–	14
France	28	31	–	6	3	–	–	10	78
Germany	49	23	7	13	7	–	–	–	99
Greece	11	8	–	–	4	–	–	1	24
Hungary	13	9	2	–	–	–	–	–	24
Ireland	5	1	–	–	–	4	–	3	13
Italy	26	14	9	2	7	9	–	11	78
Latvia	3	–	1	1	–	4	–	–	9
Lithuania	3	2	3	–	–	–	–	5	13
Luxemb'g	3	1	1	1	–	–	–	–	6
Malta	2	3	–	–	–	–	–	–	5
Neth'lands	7	7	5	2	2	–	2	2	27
Poland	19	8	4	–	–	7	–	16	54
Portugal	7	12	–	–	2	2	–	1	24
Slovakia	8	3	–	–	–	–	–	3	14
Slovenia	4	1	2	–	–	–	–	–	7
Spain	24	24	2	2	2	–	–	–	54
Sweden	5	5	3	1	2	–	–	3	19
UK	28	19	12	5	–	–	12	2	78
Total	**277**	**198**	**68**	**38**	**39**	**27**	**15**	**70**	**732**

[a] The figures represent the political groupings in the parliament in 2004.

EPP-ED European People's Party; PES Party of European Socialists; ELDR European Liberal Democrat and Reform Party; GREENS/EFA European Greens; EUL/NGL European United Left – Nordic Green Left; UEN Union For A Europe of Nations; EDD Europe of Democracies and Diversities   Source: European Parliament.

SOCIETY

SOCIETY

European Union policies and policy makers

	Date established	Role
Common Agricultural Policy (CAP)	1962	Basic principles are free trade within the community for agricultural goods; preference for domestic production; control of imports from the rest of the world. Objectives are increased agricultural productivity; reasonable prices for consumers; stability of markets and food supplies.
Council of Ministers, Brussels	1974	Composed of foreign ministers from each member state, representing national interests within the context of the Community. It is the main body within the Community influencing legislation. Decisions are now taken on the basis of unanimity rather than majority voting.
European Atomic Energy Commission (EURATOM)	1957	Objective is to promote peaceful ways of using atomic energy.
European Coal and Steel Community (ECSC)	1952	Created common framework of laws and institutions to regulate coal and steel industries. Has powers to set quotas and minimum prices. Has abolished currency restrictions, border charges, and discrimination in transport rates.
European Commission, Brussels	1967	This is the bureaucracy of the EU, conducting both administrative and political business. Its functions are to uphold the European ideal, propose new policy initiatives, and ensure that existing policies are implemented. Comprises seventeen members elected by the member countries. The Commission makes decisions by a majority vote and is directly responsible to the European parliament.
European Court of Justice, Luxembourg	1958	Judges cases involving member states; interprets Community treaties and legislation; decides on whether Community law has been breached by any member states.
European Investment Bank, Luxembourg	1958	Finances capital investment projects to help development of the Community. Each member country appoints a minister to the Board of Governors. Bank's capital is made up from the member states' subscriptions. It is a non-profit-making organization.
European Monetary System (EMS)	1979	Financial system set up by EU members with the aim of stabilizing and harmonizing currencies. Member states used a special currency – the European Currency Unit (ECU), later replaced by the Euro. A new European Central Bank was established in 1998 to control monetary policy.
European Parliament, Brussels	1979 (start of direct elections)	The representative assembly of the EU. It has no legislative power but is able to dismiss the Commission if deemed necessary and to reject or amend the EU budget. Directly elected since 1979, and elections are held every five years.

International alliances

Name of organization	Function
African Union (AU)	Founded in 1963 as the Organization of African Unity by representatives of 32 African governments and dedicated to the eradication of all forms of colonialism in Africa, changing its name in 2001. It had 53 members in 2006.
Arab League	Founded in 1945 with the aim of encouraging Arab unity. In 2006 the League had 22 member states.
Association of South-East Asian Nations (ASEAN)	Formed in 1967 to promote economic cooperation between Indonesia, Malaysia, the Philippines, Thailand, and Singapore. Brunei joined, 1984; Vietnam, 1995; Laos, Myanmar formally admitted, 1997; Cambodia, 1999.
Caribbean Community and Common Market (CARICOM)	Established in 1973 with three objectives: coordination of foreign policy among member states; provision of common services; cooperation in matters of health, education, culture, and industrial relations. In 2006 there were 15 full member states.
Commonwealth, The	Free association of independent states formerly subject to British rule and maintaining friendly and practical links with the UK (>> see p. 399).
Council for Mutual Economic Assistance (COMECON)	A body founded by Stalin in 1949 and dominated by the Soviet Union. Its purpose was ostensibly economic integration of the Eastern Bloc as a counterbalance to the economic powers of the EC and EFTA. The ten member states were the USSR, Bulgaria, Cuba, Czechoslovakia, East

Name of organization	Function
	Germany, Hungary, Mongolia, Poland, Romania, and Vietnam. Disbanded in 1991 and replaced by the Organization for International Economic Cooperation.
Council of Europe	Established in 1949, an association of European states which has a Committee of Foreign Ministers and a representative Parliamentary Assembly meeting at Strasbourg to discuss matters of concern. There were 46 members in 2006.
Economic Community of West African States (ECOWAS)	Founded in Lagos in 1975 to promote cultural, economic, and social development of West Africa through mutual cooperation. Measures include gradual elimination of trade barriers and improvement of communication and transportation. Supreme authority is invested in the annual summit of all member states' (15) heads of government.
European Free Trade Association (EFTA)	Established in 1959 with the aim of securing free trade of industrial goods between members. Also aimed to create single market in N Europe. Relations expanded with non-EC states in recent years, particularly E Europe. Formed European Economic Area in cooperation with EC, 1994.
European Union (EU)	An association, established in 1958 essentially as a customs union, with a common external tariff and common market with the removal of barriers to trade among the members. Formerly known as the European Economic Community, or European Community, it became known as the European Union in 1994.
League of Nations	An international organization formed in 1919. Main aims were to preserve international peace and security by speedy settlement of disputes and promotion of disarmament. After World War 2 it transferred its functions to the United Nations.
Mercusor	Common market agreement between Argentina, Brazil, Paraguay, and Uruguay, inaugurated 1995, to promote free movement of goods and services. Venezuela joined, 2006, Chile and Bolivia joined as associate members, 1996.
Nordic Council	Established in 1952 as advisory body on economic and social cooperation, comprising parliamentary delegates from Denmark, Iceland, Norway, Sweden, Finland, Greenland, and Faroe and Åland Is.
North Atlantic Treaty Organization (NATO)	Established in 1949, it is a permanent military alliance established originally to defend W Europe against Soviet aggression. Treaty commits members to regard an armed attack on one of them as an attack on all of them, and for all to assist the country attacked by such actions as are deemed necessary.
Organization for Economic Cooperation and Development (OECD)	Set up in 1961 to assist member states to develop economic and social policies aimed at high sustained economic growth with financial stability. It had 30 members in 2006.
Organization for European Economic Cooperation (OEEC)	Established in 1948 by sixteen European countries and by the occupying forces on behalf of W Germany. Formal aims were to promote trade, stability, and expansion. Replaced in 1961 by the OECD.
Organization of Arab Petroleum Exporting Countries (OAPEC)	Founded in 1968, under the umbrella of OPEC, by Saudi Arabia, Kuwait, and Libya. By 1972 all Arab oil producers had joined.
Organization of Central American States	Established in 1951 by Costa Rica, El Salvador, Guatemala, Honduras, and Nicaragua to promote economic, social, and cultural cooperation. In 1965 this was extended to include political and educational cooperation.
Organization of the Petroleum Exporting Countries (OPEC)	Created in 1960 as a permanent inter-governmental organization which aimed to unify and coordinate the policies of members and to determine the best means of protecting their interests.
Warsaw Pact	Consisted of the countries which signed the East European Mutual Assistance Treaty in Warsaw in 1955 – Albania, Bulgaria, Czechoslovakia, East Germany, Hungary, Poland, Romania, and the USSR. Formally dissolved, 1991.
Western European Union (WEU)	Founded in 1954 to coordinate defence and other policies, replacing the European Defence Community. Members are Belgium, France, Germany, Greece (1995), Italy, Luxembourg, Netherlands, Portugal (1990), Spain (1990) and the UK. Consists of a Council of Ministers, a representative assembly in the Consultative Assembly of the Council of Europe, and a Standing Armaments Committee which works in cooperation with NATO. Reformed as defence organization of the EU, 1992. In 2006 there were six associate members, five observers, and seven associate partners.

SOCIETY

Some political systems

Country	Form of government	System of voting
Argentina	Federal republic Two chambers – Senate and Chamber of Deputies	Simple plurality
Australia	Federal commonwealth Two chambers – Senate and House of Representatives	Alternative vote
Austria	Federal republic Two chambers – Federal Council and National Council	Proportional representation (party list)
Belgium	Parliamentary state and constitutional monarchy Two chambers – Senate and House of Representatives	Proportional representation (party list)
Botswana	Unitary republic One chamber – National Assembly	Simple plurality
Brazil	Federal republic Two chambers – Senate and Chamber of Deputies	Proportional representation (party list)
Canada	Federal commonwealth Two chambers – Senate and House of Commons	Simple plurality
China	People's republic One chamber – National People's Congress	–
Cyprus	Unitary republic One chamber – House of Representatives	Proportional representation (second ballot)
Denmark	Parliamentary state and constitutional monarchy One chamber – Folketing	Proportional representation (party list)
Egypt	Unitary republic One chamber – People's Assembly	Proportional representation (second ballot)
Ethiopia	Unitary republic One chamber – National Assembly	Simple plurality
Finland	Constitutional republic One chamber – Eduskunta	Proportional representation (party list)
France	Constitutional republic Two chambers – Senate and National Assembly	Proportional representation (second ballot)
Germany	Federal republic Two chambers – Bundestag and Bundesrat	Proportional representation (additional member)
Greece	Unitary republic One chamber – Greek Chamber of Deputies	Proportional representation (party list)
India	Federal republic Two chambers – Council of States and House of the People	Simple plurality
Indonesia	Unitary republic One chamber – People's Consultative Assembly	Proportional representation (party list)
Iran	Islamic republic One chamber – Islamic Consultative Assembly	Proportional representation (second ballot)
Iraq	Republic One chamber – National Assembly	Simple plurality
Ireland	Republic Two chambers – Senate and House of Representatives	Proportional representation (single transferable vote)
Israel	Republic One chamber – Knesset	Proportional representation (party list)
Italy	Republic Two chambers – Senate and Chamber of Deputies	Proportional representation (party list)
Jamaica	Parliamentary State Two chambers – Senate and House of Representatives	Simple plurality
Japan	Parliamentary state and monarchy Two chambers – House of Councillors and House of Representatives	Mixed proportional representation Simple plurality
Luxembourg	Parliamentary state and constitutional monarchy One chamber – Chamber of Deputies	Proportional representation (party list)
Malaysia	Federation Two chambers – Senate and House of Representatives	Simple plurality
Malta	Unitary republic One chamber – House of Representatives	Proportional representation (single transferable vote)
Mexico	Federal state Two chambers – Senate and Chamber of Deputies	Proportional representation (additional member)
Netherlands	Parliamentary state and constitutional monarchy Two chambers – First Chamber and Second Chamber	Proportional representation (party list)

Country	Form of government	System of voting
New Zealand	Parliamentary state One chamber – House of Representatives	Proportional representation (party list)
Norway	Parliamentary state and constitutional monarchy Two chambers – Storting	Proportional representation (party list)
Pakistan	Federal republic Two chambers – Senate and National Assembly	Simple plurality
Peru	Unitary republic Two chambers – Senate and Chamber of Deputies	Proportional representation (party list)
Philippines	Unitary republic Two chambers – Senate and House of Representatives	Simple plurality
Portugal	Republic One chamber – Assembly of the Republic	Proportional representation (party list)
Russia	Parliamentary state Two chambers – Supreme Soviet and Congress of People's Deputies	Proportional representation (second ballot)
Singapore	Unitary republic One chamber – Parliament	Simple plurality
South Africa	Republic Two chambers – National Assembly and Senate	Proportional representation (party list)
Spain	Parliamentary state and constitutional monarchy Two chambers – Senate and Congress of Deputies	Proportional representation (party list)
Sri Lanka	Unitary republic One chamber – National State Assembly	Proportional representation (party list)
Sweden	Parliamentary state and constitutional monarchy One chamber – Riksdag	Proportional representation (party list)
Switzerland	Federal state Two chambers – Nationalrat and Ständerat	Proportional representation (party list)
Turkey	Republic One chamber – Turkish Grand National Assembly	Proportional representation (party list)
Uganda	Unitary republic One chamber – National Assembly	Simple plurality
United Kingdom	Parliamentary state and constitutional monarchy Two chambers – House of Lords and House of Commons Welsh and Scottish Assemblies	Simple plurality Proportional representation (party list)
United States of America	Federal state Two chambers – Senate and House of Representatives	Simple plurality
Venezuela	Federal republic Two chambers – Senate and Chamber of Deputies	Proportional representation (party list)
Zimbabwe	Unitary republic Two chambers – Senate and House of Assembly	One party state

Proportional representation Any system of voting designed to ensure that the representation of voters is in proportion to their numbers.

Alternative vote Uses single-member constituencies, each voter choosing a candidate by marking 1 against his/her name. First-preference votes are counted and if one candidate obtains more than 50 per cent of all votes, he/she is elected.

Second ballot Simple majority election is held and if no one gets more than 50 per cent of total vote, the candidate with the fewest votes is eliminated and a second election is held.

Party list Political parties fighting the election produce a list of candidates, presented in descending order of preference. In many cases, the elector votes for the party of his/her choice and seats are then allocated to each party according to the total number of votes received. Names are taken from the lists to fill the seats.

Additional member This system also uses party lists but allows the voter to cast two votes, one for the party and one for the candidate. Half the assembly is elected on simple plurality basis; the other half, using party lists, is chosen so that chamber membership accurately reflects the national vote.

Single transferable vote Uses multi-member constituencies. All candidates are listed on the ballot paper and the voter states his/her order of preference. All votes cast are counted and the 'electoral quota' (the minimum number of votes needed to be elected) is calculated. Any candidates with this quota or more is automatically elected.

Limited vote Multi-member constituencies each return members, but voters are allowed only one non-transferable vote. The three, four or five candidates winning most votes in each constituency are then returned on a simple plurality basis.

Simple plurality Also known as the 'first-past-the-post' system. The party that gains the majority of votes cast secures all the available assembly seats.

SOCIETY

SOCIETY

ECONOMY

Agricultural production

	Agricultural production index (1989–91 = 100)		Cereals Production		Cereals Yield		Pulses production		Roots and tubers production		Meat production (metric tons) 2001
	Total 2002	Per capita 2002	Total (000 metric tons) 2002	% change since 1992	kg per hectare 2002	% change since 1992	Total (000 metric tons) 2002	% change since 1992	Total (000 metric tons) 2002	% change since 1992	
World	127	108	2 029 386	2.8	3 083	10.8	55 165	8.8	684 729	13.6	236 991 142
Asia (excl. Middle East)	–	–	922 018	6.0	3 529	23.1	23 140	23.8	285 587	20.8	89 312 093
Europe	88	87	434 433	10.1	–	–	8 330	(34.3)	127 764	(15.2)	49 796 566
Middle East & N. Africa	–	–	91 439	8.3	–	–	3 396	(8.1)	16 567	22.6	8 144 354
Sub-Saharan Africa	135	98	88 156	34.4	962	7.9	8 296	45.2	169 110	33.4	8 196 212
North America	120	106	334 184	(17.0)	4 833	3.3	3 993	78.6	26 227	11.8	41 916 827
C. America & Caribbean	–	–	33 427	2.1	2 604	4.9	2 650	75.0	4 861	15.4	6 988 588
South America	149	123	104 341	22.2	3 011	24.3	3 953	7.0	48 306	22.6	25 393 700
Oceania	115	97	18 648	(27.9)	1 134	(41.0)	1 393	(33.5)	3 469	13.3	5 285 178
Developed	99	94	840 806	(4.4)	3 591	10.7	14 063	(18.9)	168 439	(9.7)	103 564 712
Developing	150	123	1 185 842	9.6	2 801	12.5	41 089	24.6	513 453	24.9	131 468 806

Notes:

Agricultural production index presents net production (after deduction for feed and seed) of a country's agriculture sector relative to the base period 1989–91. The agricultural production index includes all crop and livestock products originating in each country. Intermediate agricultural inputs, including fodder crops, are not counted.

Cereal production refers to the mass of cereals produced in a given country or region each year, including wheat, barley, maize, rye, oats, millet, sorghum, rice, buckwheat, alpiste/canary seed, fonio, quinoa, triticale, wheat flour, and the cereal component of blended foods. Cereal crops harvested for hay or harvested green for food, feed, or silage or used for grazing are excluded, although mixed grains and buckwheat are included.

Cereal crop yields refers to the amount of grain produced per unit of harvested area of cereals in a given country or region each year.

Pulses production includes beans, lentils, pigeon peas, cowpeas, and vetches harvested for dry grain only. Pulses used for feed are included.

Roots and tubers production covers all root crops grown principally for human consumption, such as cassava, yucca, taro, and yams. Root crops grown principally for feed such as turnips, mangels, and swedes are not included.

Meat production describes total meat production, from both commercial and farm slaughter, in terms of dressed carcass weight, excluding offal and slaughter fats. Total meat production comprises horse meat, poultry meat, and meat from all other domestic or wild animals such as camels, rabbits, reindeer, and game animals.

Source: Food and Agriculture Organization of the United Nations (FAO).

Industrial production[a]

	Weight in 2000	2001	2002	2003	2004 Q1	2004 Q2	12-month rate of change
Canada	4.1	96.1	97.5	98.3	99.8	101.3	7.1
Mexico[b]	3.3	96.6	96.3	95.6	97.6	99.1	4.7
United States	31.5	96.6	96.1	96.3	99.1	100.3	4.6
Australia	1.6	100.8	103.6	104.5	104.6	105.4	1.0
Japan[c]	14.5	93.7	92.6	95.4	99.0	101.5	7.8
Korea[c]	4.4	100.7	108.8	114.4	124.3	125.8	9.0
New Zealand	0.3	100.0	104.0	105.0	111.0	109.0	5.3
Austria	0.9	102.8	103.6	105.6	107.1	111.2	12.1
Belgium	1.0	99.0	100.3	101.0	103.1	103.7	3.6
Czech Rep.[c]	0.7	106.5	116.6	123.4	129.6	137.5	13.3
Denmark[d]	0.5	101.6	103.0	103.4	103.4	104.6	−1.1
Finland	0.6	100.1	102.2	103.0	102.9	107.0	5.2
France	5.0	101.1	99.7	99.3	100.2	100.9	0.7
Germany	8.3	100.2	99.2	99.6	101.2	102.8	4.4
Greece	0.4	101.4	101.8	103.1	102.3	105.6	0.4
Hungary[c]	0.5	103.6	106.4	113.2	120.0	121.2	3.9
Ireland	0.6	110.2	118.8	126.3	127.3	124.9	7.1
Italy	5.4	99.0	97.5	96.9	97.0	97.2	−1.5
Luxembourg	0.0	101.8	102.8	105.4	–	–	–
Netherlands	1.4	100.4	100.1	97.7	100.6	98.8	−0.2
Norway	1.0	98.7	99.7	95.6	98.8	100.5	−5.1
Poland	1.5	100.4	101.8	110.7	123.6	127.5	9.3
Portugal	0.6	103.1	102.7	102.6	99.2	100.0	−3.6
Slovak Rep.	0.3	107.3	114.5	120.8	126.8	125.4	5.7
Spain	2.8	98.6	98.7	100.1	101.1	102.0	1.7
Sweden[e, f]	0.9	99.6	99.9	102.7	105.3	107.5	4.0
Switzerland	0.7	99.0	94.0	94.0	98.0	98.0	4.2
Turkey	1.9	91.3	100.0	108.7	116.5	122.2	10.0
United Kingdom	5.4	98.4	96.0	95.8	95.7	96.8	−0.1
OECD Total[g]	100.0	97.7	97.8	99.0	101.7	103.2	4.7
Major seven[g]	74.2	97.0	96.2	96.8	99.0	100.4	4.5
OECD Europe[g]	40.4	99.8	99.7	100.9	102.5	104.1	2.6
EU15[g]	35.3	100.0	99.2	99.4	100.3	101.3	1.7
Euro area[g, h]	28.5	100.3	99.7	100.0	101.0	101.9	2.0

Notes:
[a] Industrial production refers to the goods produced by establishments engaged in mining (including oil extraction), manufacturing, and production of electricity, gas, and water.
[b] Including construction.
[c] Not adjusted for unequal number of working days in the month.
[d] The series is compiled using data for production in manufacturing before 2000.
[e] Mining and manufacturing.
[f] Annual figures correspond to official annual figures and differ from the average of the monthly figures.
[g] Weights for calculating aggregate indices are derived from gross domestic product originating in industry and the GDP purchasing power parity for 2000.
[h] OECD calculation.

Source: OECD, Main Economic Indicators, 2004.

Solid fuel production and consumption

	Production		Consumption	
	(1000 Metric TOE[a]) 1999	Percent change since 1989	(1000 Metric TOE[a]) 1999	Percent change since 1989
World	2 273 262	2.9	2 278 524	2.5
Asia	947 639	39.2	1 013 218	30.8
Europe	391 517	–	480 313	–
Middle East & North Africa	14 229	4.5	30 956	46.9
Sub-Saharan Africa	–	–	–	–
North America	600 275	8.6	567 286	16.2
Central America & Caribbean	4 868	60.8	6 773	95.1
South America	29 025	61.1	20 749	15.0
Oceania	–	–	–	–
Developed	1 302 566	–	1 292 603	–
Developing	969 806	36.0	959 543	28.7

Notes:
[a] TOE = Tons of Oil Equivalent.

Source: International Energy Agency (IEA), 2001.

Liquid fuel production and consumption[b]

	Production		Consumption	
	(1000 Metric TOE[a]) 1999	Percent change since 1989	(1000 Metric TOE[a]) 1999	Percent change since 1989
World	3 526 390	10.9	3 563 084	9.0
Asia	400 017	36.2	829 930	64.5
Europe	648 678	–	906 066	–
Middle East & North Africa	1 240 170	26.5	412 549	17.1
Sub-Saharan Africa	–	–	–	–
North America	489 867	(9.2)	962 164	11.6
Central America & Caribbean	179 261	9.7	113 220	2.1
South America	345 297	65.0	217 212	26.3
Oceania	–	–	–	–
Developed	1 227 279	–	2 194 548	–
Developing	2 290 314	28.2	1 328 884	35.7

Notes:
[a] TOE = Tons of Oil Equivalent.
[b] Crude oil and natural gas liquids constitute liquid fuels.

Source: International Energy Agency (IEA), 2001.

Gaseous fuel production and consumption[c]

	Production		Consumption	
	(1000 Metric TOE[a]) 1999	Percent change since 1989	(1000 Metric TOE[a]) 1999	Percent change since 1989
World	2 014 696	21.4	2 012 559	22.4
Asia	272 284	168.2	277 374	166.7
Europe	741 413	–	786 787	–
Middle East & North Africa	260 613	95.3	205 143	95.8
Sub-Saharan Africa	–	–	–	–
North America	585 206	18.7	592 290	18.4
Central America & Caribbean	40 297	60.0	39 308	53.7
South America	72 900	57.7	74 583	62.3
Oceania	–	–	–	–
Developed	1 439 576	–	1 531 532	–
Developing	574 213	86.3	475 546	95.4

Notes:
[a] TOE = Tons of Oil Equivalent.
[c] Natural gas constitutes gaseous fuels.

Source: International Energy Agency (IEA), 2001.

SOCIETY

Nuclear fuel production and consumption

	Production		Consumption	
	(1000 Metric TOE[a]) 1999	*Percent change since 1989*	*(1000 Metric TOE[a]) 1999*	*Percent change since 1989*
World	660 051	30.4	661 901	30.8
Asia	117 365	91.7	117 291	91.6
Europe	303 542	–	303 885	–
Middle East & North Africa	0	–	0	–
Sub-Saharan Africa	–	–	–	–
North America	220 291	31.5	221 874	32.4
Central America & Caribbean	2 607	–	2 607	–
South America	2 888	61.3	2 888	61.3
Oceania	–	–	–	–
Developed	610 232	–	612 157	–
Developing	39 807	157.8	39 733	157.3

Notes:
[a] TOE = Tons of Oil Equivalent.

Source: International Energy Agency (IEA), 2001.

Hydroelectric fuel production and consumption

	Production		Consumption	
	(1000 Metric TOE[a]) 1999	*Percent change since 1989*	*(1000 Metric TOE[a]) 1999*	*Percent change since 1989*
World	222 992	23.6	222 223	23.6
Asia	44 165	40.2	44 424	43.9
Europe	61 526	–	60 847	–
Middle East & North Africa	5 653	47.1	5 694	48.1
Sub-Saharan Africa	–	–	–	–
North America	54 923	16.6	54 524	15.8
Central America & Caribbean	4 199	34.1	4 236	33.9
South America	43 298	50.4	43 346	50.6
Oceania	–	–	–	–
Developed	131 578	–	130 499	–
Developing	89 946	43.6	90 276	45.5

Notes:
[a] TOE = Tons of Oil Equivalent.

Source: International Energy Agency (IEA), 2001.

Other fuel production and consumption

	Production		Consumption	
	(1000 Metric TOE[a]) 1999	*Percent change since 1989*	*(1000 Metric TOE[a]) 1999*	*Percent change since 1989*
World	1 095 519	20.1	1 097 889	25.3
Asia	577 942	11.3	578 643	12.8
Europe	67 725	–	64 845	–
Middle East & North Africa	12 124	3.5	11 939	2.0
Sub-Saharan Africa	–	–	–	–
North America	91 945	76.4	94 243	334.4
Central America & Caribbean	29 201	5.1	28 821	4.2
South America	62 553	(0.4)	65 288	0.9
Oceania	–	–	–	–
Developed	189 834	–	189 254	–
Developing	855 791	12.3	860 609	14.4

Notes:
[a] TOE = Tons of Oil Equivalent.

Source: International Energy Agency (IEA), 2001.

All sources of fuel production and consumption

	Production		Consumption	
	(1000 Metric TOE[a]) 1999	Percent change since 1989	(1000 Metric TOE[a]) 1999	Percent change since 1989
World	9 820 862	12.8	9 702 786	12.7
Asia	2 362 223	40.5	2 919 333	43.1
Europe	2 228 407	103.8	2 559 701	–
Middle East & North Africa	1 532 806	34.1	518 436	46.1
Sub-Saharan Africa	528 894	29.4	–	–
North America	2 053 057	8.6	2 511 765	15.2
Central America & Caribbean	260 434	17.0	205 471	22.9
South America	555 962	51.6	383 514	34.4
Oceania	227 112	44.9	–	–
Developed	4 927 331	48.1	5 962 100	–
Developing	4 821 563	32.6	3 597 314	38.5

Notes:

[a] TOE = Tons of Oil Equivalent.

Source: International Energy Agency (IEA), 2001.

Standardized unemployment rates in 26 OECD countries

	As a percentage of total labour force											
	1990	1991	1992	1993	1994	1995	1996	1997	1998	1999	2000	2001
Australia	6.7	9.3	10.5	10.6	9.5	8.2	8.2	8.3	7.7	7.0	6.3	6.7
Austria	–	–	–	4.0	3.8	3.9	4.4	4.4	4.5	4.0	3.7	3.6
Belgium	6.6	6.4	7.1	8.6	9.8	9.7	9.5	9.2	9.3	8.6	6.9	6.6
Canada	8.1	10.3	11.2	11.4	10.4	9.4	9.6	9.1	8.3	7.6	6.8	7.2
Czech Republic	–	–	–	4.4	4.4	4.1	3.9	4.8	6.5	8.8	8.9	8.2
Denmark	7.2	7.9	8.6	9.6	7.7	6.8	6.3	5.3	4.9	4.8	4.4	4.3
Finland	3.2	6.6	11.6	16.4	16.7	15.2	14.5	12.6	11.4	10.2	9.7	9.1
France	8.6	9.1	10.0	11.3	11.8	11.4	11.9	11.8	11.4	10.7	9.3	8.6
Greece	–	–	–	10.5	10.9	10.5	10.6	10.4	9.8	9.0	8.1	7.6
Germany[a]	4.8	4.2	6.6	7.9	8.4	8.2	8.9	9.9	9.3	8.6	7.9	7.9
Hungary	–	–	9.9	12.1	11.0	10.4	10.1	8.9	8.0	7.1	6.5	5.8
Ireland	13.4	14.7	15.4	15.6	14.3	12.3	11.7	9.9	7.5	5.6	4.2	3.8
Italy	8.9	8.5	8.7	10.1	11.0	11.5	11.5	11.6	11.7	11.2	10.4	9.5
Japan	2.1	2.1	2.2	2.5	2.9	3.1	3.4	3.4	4.1	4.7	4.7	5.0
Korea	–	–	–	–	–	–	–	–	–	–	4.3	3.9
Luxembourg	1.7	1.7	2.1	2.6	3.2	2.9	3.0	2.7	2.7	2.4	2.4	2.4
Netherlands	5.9	5.5	5.3	6.2	6.8	6.6	6.0	4.9	3.8	3.2	2.8	2.4
New Zealand	7.8	10.3	10.3	9.5	8.1	6.3	6.1	6.6	7.5	6.8	6.0	5.3
Norway	5.3	5.6	6.0	6.1	5.5	5.0	4.9	4.1	3.3	3.2	3.5	3.6
Poland	–	–	–	14.0	14.4	13.3	12.3	11.2	10.6	–	16.1	18.2
Portugal	4.8	4.2	4.3	5.6	6.9	7.3	7.3	6.8	5.2	4.5	4.1	4.1
Spain	16.1	16.2	18.3	22.5	23.9	22.7	22.0	20.6	18.6	15.8	14.0	13.0
Sweden	1.7	3.1	5.6	9.1	9.4	8.8	9.6	9.9	8.3	7.2	5.9	5.1
Switzerland	–	2.0	3.1	4.0	3.8	3.5	3.9	4.2	3.5	3.0	2.6	–
United Kingdom	6.9	8.6	9.8	10.2	9.4	8.5	8.0	6.9	6.2	5.9	5.4	5.0
United States	5.6	6.8	7.5	6.9	6.1	5.6	5.4	4.9	4.5	4.2	4.0	4.8
European Union[b]	–	8.1	9.0	10.5	10.9	10.5	10.6	10.4	9.8	9.0	8.1	7.6
OECD Europe[b]	–	–	–	10.5	10.8	10.4	10.4	10.1	9.5	9.1	8.6	8.3
Total OECD[b]	–	–	–	7.9	7.8	7.4	7.4	7.1	7.0	6.8	6.3	6.5

Notes:

[a] Up to and including 1992, western Germany; subsequent data concern the whole of Germany.

[b] For above countries only.

Source: OECD Employment Outlook, 2002.

Employment/population ratios, activity, and unemployment rates[a]

| | | Both sexes (percentages) | | | | | | | | |
| | | 15 to 24 | | | 25 to 54 | | | 55 to 64 | | |
		2001	2002	2003	2001	2002	2003	2001	2002	2003
Australia	Unemployment rates	12.9	12.7	11.6	5.3	4.8	4.5	4.8	3.7	3.9
	Labour force participation rates	69.0	68.2	67.7	80.6	80.9	80.6	48.6	50.0	52.2
	Employment/population ratios	60.1	59.6	59.9	76.3	77.1	76.9	46.3	48.2	50.1
Austria	Unemployment rates	6.0	7.2	7.5	3.6	4.5	4.2	5.6	5.8	6.2
	Labour force participation rates	54.7	55.7	54.8	85.2	86.6	87.0	29.0	29.8	30.8
	Employment/population ratios	51.4	51.7	50.7	82.2	82.7	83.4	27.4	28.1	28.9
Belgium	Unemployment rates	15.3	15.7	19.0	5.4	6.2	7.0	3.0	3.5	1.7
	Labour force participation rates	33.6	33.8	33.5	80.9	81.7	81.8	26.0	26.7	28.5
	Employment/population ratios	28.5	28.5	27.1	76.6	76.6	76.1	25.2	25.8	28.1
Canada	Unemployment rates	12.8	13.7	13.8	6.2	6.6	6.5	5.9	6.2	6.3
	Labour force participation rates	64.7	66.3	67.0	85.1	85.9	86.3	51.3	53.7	56.6
	Employment/population ratios	56.4	57.3	57.8	79.8	80.2	80.6	48.3	50.4	53.0
Czech Republic	Unemployment rates	16.6	16.0	17.6	7.2	6.5	7.0	4.9	4.0	4.4
	Labour force participation rates	43.2	40.1	38.1	88.4	88.2	87.8	39.0	42.5	44.2
	Employment/population ratios	36.1	33.7	31.4	82.1	82.5	81.7	37.1	40.8	42.3
Denmark	Unemployment rates	8.3	7.1	9.8	3.5	3.7	5.0	4.0	4.7	3.9
	Labour force participation rates	67.2	68.8	65.9	87.5	88.0	87.8	58.9	60.1	63.1
	Employment/population ratios	61.7	64.0	59.4	84.5	84.7	83.5	56.5	57.3	60.7
Finland	Unemployment rates	19.9	20.7	21.6	7.4	7.3	7.3	8.9	8.1	7.7
	Labour force participation rates	50.4	49.6	49.1	88.0	88.1	87.5	50.3	52.0	54.1
	Employment/population ratios	40.3	39.4	38.5	81.5	81.6	81.1	45.9	47.8	49.9
France	Unemployment rates	18.7	20.2	–	8.1	8.1	–	6.1	5.8	–
	Labour force participation rates	29.9	30.2	–	86.3	86.4	–	38.8	41.7	–
	Employment/population ratios	24.3	24.1	–	79.3	79.4	–	36.5	39.3	–
Germany	Unemployment rates	8.3	9.8	10.6	7.3	8.1	9.1	11.7	10.8	9.7
	Labour force participation rates	51.3	49.7	47.4	85.5	85.8	86.0	42.9	43.3	43.1
	Employment/population ratios	47.0	44.8	42.4	79.3	78.8	78.2	37.9	38.6	39.0
Greece	Unemployment rates	28.0	25.7	25.1	8.8	8.6	8.0	4.1	3.6	3.0
	Labour force participation rates	36.2	36.3	35.1	77.2	78.2	78.9	39.6	40.7	43.2
	Employment/population ratios	26.0	27.0	26.3	70.4	71.5	72.6	38.0	39.2	41.9
Hungary	Unemployment rates	11.2	12.6	13.4	5.1	5.2	5.3	2.9	3.1	2.8
	Labour force participation rates	34.6	32.6	30.8	77.1	77.0	77.8	24.2	26.4	29.8
	Employment/population ratios	30.7	28.5	26.7	73.1	73.0	73.7	23.5	25.6	29.0
Iceland[b]	Unemployment rates	4.8	7.2	–	1.7	2.7	–	2.0	1.4	–
	Labour force participation rates	70.2	64.0	–	92.3	92.5	–	87.3	88.4	–
	Employment/population ratios	66.8	59.4	–	90.7	90.0	–	85.6	87.2	–
Ireland	Unemployment rates	6.2	7.7	7.6	3.2	3.7	3.9	2.6	2.4	2.4
	Labour force participation rates	50.1	49.1	49.6	78.9	79.5	79.1	47.9	49.2	50.5
	Employment/population ratios	47.0	45.3	45.8	76.4	76.6	76.0	46.6	48.0	49.3
Italy	Unemployment rates	27.0	26.3	26.3	7.9	7.5	7.2	4.3	4.1	3.8
	Labour force participation rates	37.6	36.3	35.3	75.1	75.8	76.3	29.2	30.1	31.5
	Employment/population ratios	27.4	26.7	26.0	69.2	70.1	70.8	28.0	28.9	30.3
Japan	Unemployment rates	9.7	10.0	10.2	4.4	4.9	4.7	5.7	5.8	5.5
	Labour force participation rates	46.5	45.6	44.8	82.2	82.0	82.1	65.8	65.4	65.8
	Employment/population ratios	42.0	41.0	40.3	78.6	78.0	78.3	62.0	61.6	62.1
Korea	Unemployment rates	9.7	8.1	9.6	3.4	2.8	3.0	2.1	1.6	1.9
	Labour force participation rates	33.3	34.2	34.0	75.1	75.5	75.3	59.5	60.4	58.9
	Employment/population ratios	30.1	31.5	30.8	72.6	73.4	73.1	58.3	59.5	57.8
Luxembourg	Unemployment rates	6.3	7.0	–	1.4	2.4	–	0.3	0.2	–
	Labour force participation rates	34.5	34.7	–	79.8	81.0	–	24.9	27.9	–
	Employment/population ratios	32.3	32.3	–	78.7	79.1	–	24.8	27.9	–
Mexico	Unemployment rates	4.1	4.9	5.3	1.6	1.8	1.9	1.0	1.3	1.0
	Labour force participation rates	49.7	48.4	47.2	68.9	69.6	69.5	52.6	53.8	54.4
	Employment/population ratios	47.7	46.0	44.7	67.8	68.4	68.1	52.1	53.1	53.8
Netherlands	Unemployment rates	4.4	4.6	6.6	1.7	2.2	3.1	1.5	2.1	2.2
	Labour force participation rates	73.6	73.9	73.2	84.2	84.7	85.1	39.9	42.9	45.9
	Employment/population ratios	70.4	70.5	68.4	82.8	82.9	82.4	39.3	42.0	44.9
New Zealand	Unemployment rates	11.8	11.4	10.2	4.1	4.0	3.5	3.5	3.2	3.6
	Labour force participation rates	63.5	64.2	63.0	82.7	83.0	82.8	62.9	65.5	66.8
	Employment/population ratios	56.0	56.8	56.6	79.3	79.7	79.8	60.7	63.4	64.4

SOCIETY

Employment/population ratios, activity, and unemployment rates (continued)

		Both sexes (percentages)								
		15 to 24			25 to 54			55 to 64		
		2001	2002	2003	2001	2002	2003	2001	2002	2003
Norway[b]	Unemployment rates	10.5	11.5	11.7	2.6	3.0	3.8	1.6	1.8	1.4
	Labour force participation rates	63.1	64.2	62.6	87.4	87.1	86.3	68.5	69.7	69.7
	Employment/population ratios	56.5	56.9	55.3	85.1	84.4	83.0	67.4	68.4	68.8
Poland	Unemployment rates	41.0	43.9	43.0	15.8	17.5	17.3	9.7	10.5	11.2
	Labour force participation rates	37.4	35.6	34.4	82.2	81.8	81.7	32.1	31.2	32.2
	Employment/population ratios	22.1	20.0	19.6	69.3	67.5	67.6	29.0	27.9	28.6
Portugal	Unemployment rates	9.4	11.5	14.6	3.5	4.5	5.7	3.2	3.7	4.3
	Labour force participation rates	47.1	47.3	45.0	85.2	85.4	85.9	51.7	52.9	53.4
	Employment/population ratios	42.7	41.9	38.4	82.2	81.5	81.0	50.0	50.9	51.1
Slovak Republic	Unemployment rates	39.1	37.4	33.1	15.9	15.3	15.1	12.3	15.3	13.6
	Labour force participation rates	45.8	43.5	41.2	88.9	88.6	89.5	25.4	27.0	28.5
	Employment/population ratios	27.9	27.2	27.6	74.8	75.1	76.0	22.3	22.9	24.6
Spain[b]	Unemployment rates	20.8	22.2	22.7	9.3	10.2	10.2	6.3	7.1	6.9
	Labour force participation rates	46.8	47.0	47.6	76.5	78.1	79.4	41.9	42.7	43.8
	Employment/population ratios	37.1	36.6	36.8	69.5	70.1	71.3	39.2	39.7	40.8
Sweden[b]	Unemployment rates	11.8	12.8	13.8	4.1	4.2	4.9	4.9	4.7	4.8
	Labour force participation rates	54.3	53.3	52.3	88.2	87.9	87.8	70.4	71.7	72.5
	Employment/population ratios	47.9	46.5	45.0	84.6	84.2	83.5	67.0	68.3	69.0
Switzerland	Unemployment rates	5.6	5.7	8.6	2.1	2.7	3.6	1.7	2.0	2.5
	Labour force participation rates	67.8	69.2	69.2	87.9	88.4	87.9	68.2	66.1	67.3
	Employment/population ratios	64.0	65.3	63.2	86.1	86.0	84.8	67.1	64.8	65.6
Turkey	Unemployment rates	16.2	19.2	20.5	6.7	8.7	8.7	2.3	3.5	3.7
	Labour force participation rates	42.1	40.9	38.4	59.5	59.8	59.1	36.8	36.6	34.0
	Employment/population ratios	35.3	33.0	30.5	55.5	54.6	54.0	35.9	35.3	32.7
United Kingdom	Unemployment rates	10.5	11.0	11.5	3.9	4.1	3.8	3.3	3.5	3.3
	Labour force participation rates	68.2	68.6	67.6	83.9	84.0	84.1	54.0	55.2	57.5
	Employment/population ratios	61.1	61.0	59.8	80.7	80.6	80.9	52.2	53.3	55.5
United States[b]	Unemployment rates	10.6	12.0	12.4	3.8	4.8	5.0	3.0	3.9	4.1
	Labour force participation rates	64.5	63.3	61.6	83.7	83.3	83.0	60.4	61.9	62.4
	Employment/population ratios	57.7	55.7	53.9	80.5	79.3	78.8	58.6	59.5	59.9
EU-15[c]	Unemployment rates	14.0	14.7	14.7	6.5	6.9	7.0	6.4	6.2	5.7
	Labour force participation rates	47.7	47.4	50.0	82.4	82.9	82.6	42.0	43.3	44.9
	Employment/population ratios	41.0	40.5	42.6	77.1	77.1	76.9	39.3	40.6	42.3
EU-19[c]	Unemployment rates	16.8	17.5	17.7	7.4	7.9	8.1	6.5	6.4	6.0
	Labour force participation rates	46.1	45.5	47.0	82.5	82.8	82.7	40.7	41.9	43.2
	Employment/population ratios	38.4	37.6	38.7	76.4	76.3	76.0	38.0	39.2	40.7
OECD Europe[c]	Unemployment rates	16.4	17.5	17.9	7.2	7.8	8.0	6.1	6.0	5.7
	Labour force participation rates	45.8	45.1	45.6	79.9	80.1	79.4	41.1	42.1	43.1
	Employment/population ratios	38.2	37.2	37.5	74.1	73.8	73.0	38.6	39.6	40.7
Total OECD[c]	Unemployment rates	12.2	13.1	13.3	5.4	6.0	6.0	4.7	4.9	4.7
	Labour force participation rates	51.1	50.4	50.3	80.2	80.3	79.9	50.9	52.0	53.4
	Employment/population ratios	44.9	43.8	43.6	75.9	75.5	75.1	48.5	49.4	50.8

Notes:

[a] by selected age groups.

[b] For these countries, age group 15 to 24 is replaced by 16 to 24.

[c] For above countries only.

Source: OECD Employment Outlook, 2004.

Interest rates

Short-term interest rates

	2001	2002	2003	2004 Q1	2004 Q2
				per cent per annum	
Canada[a]	4.00	2.62	2.97	2.32	2.08
Mexico	12.24	7.46	6.51	5.65	6.77
United States	3.69	1.73	1.15	1.05	1.25
Australia	4.90	4.75	4.90	5.54	5.51
Japan	0.12	0.06	0.04	0.03	0.03
Korea	5.32	4.80	4.30	4.10	3.90
New Zealand	5.74	5.67	5.42	5.49	5.85
Czech Republic	5.17	3.55	2.28	2.06	2.18
Denmark	4.62	3.48	2.36	2.12	2.14
Hungary	10.80	8.91	8.22	12.44	11.49
Iceland[b]	10.98	8.0	5.01	5.12	5.63
Norway	7.23	6.91	4.10	2.04	2.00
Poland[c]	14.85	8.42	5.38	5.27	5.51
Sweden	4.01	4.07	3.03	2.47	2.00
Switzerland	2.86	1.13	0.33	0.25	0.34
United Kingdom	4.97	3.99	3.67	4.11	4.51
Euro area	4.26	3.32	2.34	2.06	2.08

Notes:
Short-term rates generally refer to 3-month interbank rates on 3-month Certificates of deposit or Treasury bills, with the exception of Korea and Hungary for which figures refer to yields. Annual and quarterly data are averages of monthly figures. Unless otherwise specified monthly data are averages of daily rates.
[a] Averages of Wednesdays.
[b] End of month rates.
[c] No issues in November 2003 and February, May 2004. The respective quarterly and annual figures are the average of the available months.

Source: OECD, Main Economic Indicators, September 2004.

Long-term interest rates

	2001	2002	2003	2004 Q1	2004 Q2
				per cent per annum	
Canada[a]	5.48	5.30	4.80	4.43	4.78
United States[b]	5.58	5.32	4.79	4.69	5.20
Australia[b]	5.64	5.83	5.36	5.62	5.89
Japan[b]	1.32	1.26	1.00	1.32	1.61
Korea	6.7	6.5	5.0	5.1	4.9
New Zealand[b]	6.39	6.53	5.87	5.86	6.20
Austria	5.08	4.97	4.15	4.20	4.33
Belgium	5.06	4.89	4.15	4.10	4.26
Denmark	5.09	5.06	4.31	4.25	4.43
Finland	5.04	4.98	4.14	4.06	4.28
France[c]	4.94	4.86	4.13	4.11	4.31
Germany	4.8	4.8	4.1	4.1	4.2
Greece	5.30	5.03	4.27	4.30	4.46
Iceland[b]	10.4	8.0	6.7	7.0	7.3
Ireland[b]	5.02	4.99	4.13	4.12	4.29
Italy	5.19	5.03	4.30	4.28	4.46
Luxembourg	4.86	4.68	3.32	2.88	–
Netherlands	4.96	4.89	4.12	4.08	4.31
Norway	6.24	6.38	5.05	4.32	4.77
Portugal	5.16	5.02	4.19	4.17	4.37
Spain	4.87	4.62	3.52	3.59	3.78
Sweden	5.11	5.30	4.64	4.50	4.65
Switzerland[b]	3.38	3.20	2.66	2.72	2.91
United Kingdom	4.94	4.91	4.52	4.77	5.08
Euro area	5.03	4.92	4.16	4.15	4.36

Notes:
Long-term rates refer to secondary market yields on long-term bonds. Annual and quarterly data are averages of monthly figures. Unless otherwise specified monthly data are averages of daily rates.
[a] Data refer to the last Wednesday of the period.   [b] From July 2003, end of month rates.   [c] Last Friday of month.

Source: OECD, Main Economic Indicators, September 2004.

PART NINE

Religion and Mythology

GODS OF MYTHOLOGY

Principal Greek gods

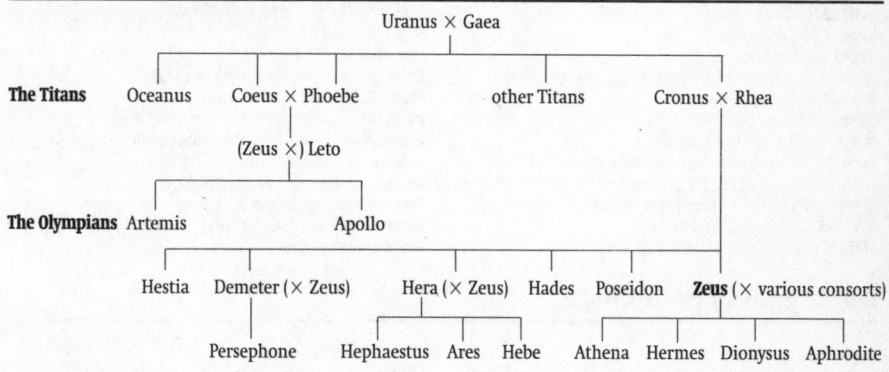

Greek gods of mythology

Aeolus God of the winds
Aphrodite Goddess of love, beauty, and procreation
Apollo God of prophecy, poetry, music, archery, and healing
Ares God of war
Artemis Goddess of the moon, hunting, and fertility
Athene Goddess of wisdom; protectress of Athens
Boreas God of the north wind
Cronus Father of Zeus
Cybele Goddess of fertility and the mountains
Demeter Goddess of fruit, crops, and vegetation
Dionysus God of wine
Eros God of love
Gaea Goddess of the earth
Hades God of the underworld
Hebe Goddess of youth
Hecate Goddess of magic, ghosts, and witchcraft
Helios God of the sun
Hephaestus God of fire

Hera Goddess of marriage and women; queen of heaven
Hermes God of science and commerce; messenger of the gods
Hestia Goddess of the hearth
Iris Goddess of the rainbow; messenger of the gods
Morpheus God of dreams
Nemesis Goddess of vengeance
Nereus Sea god
Nike Goddess of victory
Oceanus Sea god
Pan God of pastures, forests, flocks, and herds
Persephone Goddess of the underworld
Poseidon God of the sea
Rhea Mother of the gods
Selene Moon goddess
Uranus God of the sky
Zeus Overlord of the Olympian gods and goddesses; lord of heaven

RELIGION AND MYTHOLOGY

Principal Roman gods

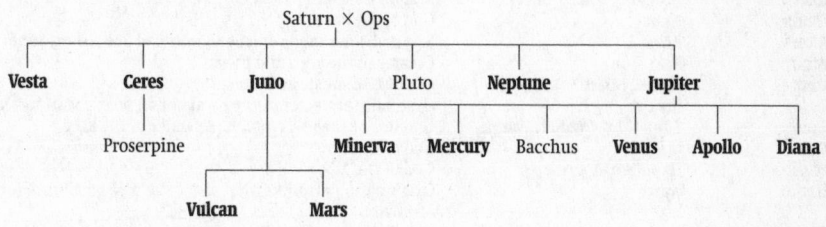

The twelve major gods of Olympus are shown in **bold** type. Bacchus in some accounts supplants Vesta. Pluto and Proserpine are gods of the Underworld.

Roman gods of mythology

Apollo God of the sun, music, poetry, prophecy, and healing
Bacchus God of wine
Bellona Goddess of war
Ceres Corn goddess
Cupid God of love
Diana Goddess of fertility, hunting, and the moon
Faunus God of prophecy
Flora Goddess of flowers
Janus God of gates and doors
Juno Goddess of marriage and women
Jupiter Supreme god; lord of heaven
Lares Gods of the household and state
Libitina Goddess of funerals
Maia Goddess of growth and increase

Mars God of war
Mercury Messenger god; also god of commerce
Minerva Goddess of wisdom, the arts, and trades
Mithras The sun god; god of light
Neptune God of the sea
Ops Goddess of fertility
Pales Goddess of flocks and shepherds
Pluto God of the underworld
Pomona Goddess of fruit trees and fruit
Proserpine Goddess of the underworld
Saturn God of seed time and harvest
Venus Goddess of beauty and love
Vertumnus God of the seasons
Vesta Goddess of the hearth
Vulcan God of fire

Norse gods of mythology

Aegir God of the sea
Aesir Race of warlike gods, including Odin, Thor, Tyr
Alcis Twin gods of the sky
Balder Son of Odin and favourite of the gods
Bor Father of Odin
Bragi God of poetry
Eir Goddess of medicine
Fafnir Dragon god
Fjorgynn Mother of Thor
Freya Goddess of love and fertility
Frey God of fertility, sun, and rain
Frigg Goddess of married love; wife of Odin
Gefion Goddess who received virgins after death
Heimdall Warden of the gods
Hel Goddess of death; Queen of Niflheim, the land of mists
Hermod Son of Odin
Hoenir Companion to Odin and Loki
Hoder Blind god who killed Balder
Idunn Guardian goddess of the golden apples of youth; wife of Bragi
Kvasir God of wise utterances
Logi Fire god

Loki God of mischief
Mimir God of wisdom
Nanna Goddess wife of Balder
Nehallenia Goddess of plenty
Nerthus Goddess of earth
Njord God of ships and the sea
Norns Goddesses of destiny
Odin (Woden, Wotan) Chief of the Aesir family of gods, the 'father' god; the god of war, learning, and poetry
Otr Otter god
Ran Goddess of the sea
Sif Goddess wife of Thor
Sigyn Goddess wife of Loki
Thor (Donar) God of thunder and sky, and good crops
Tyr God of battle, and victory
Ull God of the hunt
Valkyries Female helpers of the gods of war
Vanir Race of benevolent gods, including Njord, Frey, and Freya
Vidar Slayer of the wolf, Fenir
Vor Goddess of truth
Weland (Volundr, Weiland, Wayland) Craftsman god

Egyptian gods

	Alternative names	
Amun	Ammon, Amen, Amon	King of the gods
Anubis	Anpu	God of the dead
Aton	Aten	Sun god, later made chief and only god (for a short time)
Atum	Tem, Tum	Creator of the gods and men
Bast	Bastet, Ubasti	Goddess of music and dance
Bes	Bisu	Originally protector of the royal house, later god of recreation
Buto	Edjo, Udjo, Wadjet, Wadjit	Goddess of Lower Egypt and defender of the King
Geb	Keb, Seb	God of the earth
Hapi	Hap, Hep, Apis	God of the Nile
Hathor	Athyr	Originally a personification of the sky, also goddess of love and festivity
Horus	Hor	Originally the god of Lower Egypt, later identified with the reigning King
Isis	Aset, Eset	Queen of the gods
Khenty-Imentiu	Khenti-Amentiu	Warrior god, god of the underworld before Osiris
Khnum	Khnemu	God of the cataract region, earlier associated with the underworld
Khons	Khensu, Khonsu, Chons	Moon god

	Alternative names	
Ma'at	Mayet	Goddess of law, truth, and justice
Min		God of fertility and harvest
Mont	Mentu, Month	War god of Upper Egypt, also lord of the sky with Re
Nefertum	Nefertem, Nefertemu	God of the lotus
Neith	Neit	Goddess of the loom and war
Nekhbet	Nekhebet	Protectress of childbirth
Nut	Neuth, Nuit	Goddess of the sky
Osiris	Usire	Originally fertility god, later supreme god, king of the underworld
Ptah	Phtah	God of fertility, creator of the universe
Re	Phra, Ra	King of the gods, chief state god
Sati	Satet, Satis	Goddess of the inundation and of fertility
Seker	Sokar, Sokaris	God of darkness and decay
Seshat	Sesheta	Goddess of writing and history
Shu		God of light and supporter of the sky
Taurt	Apet, Opet, Tawaret, Thoueris	Goddess of maternity
Thoth	Djhowtey	Moon god

MODERN RELIGIONS

Religion	Branch/ denomination	Sacred texts	State religion in	Estimated no. of adherents (worldwide), mid-2003
Baha'ism		Kitabal-Aqdas, Haft Wadi, Bayan, al-Kalimat al-Maknnah		7 503 000
Buddhism	Therevada Mahayana Tantrism	Tripitaka	Bhutan, Cambodia, Thailand	372 974 000
Christianity	Anglican Baptist Church of Christ Lutheran Methodist Mormon Orthodox Pentecostal Presbyterian Roman Catholic	Bible

Book of Mormon | UK (England)

Denmark, Iceland, Norway, Sweden

Greece

UK (Scotland) Argentina, Bolivia, Costa Rica, Dominican Republic, Malta, Paraguay, Peru | 2 069 883 000 |
Confucianism		The Analects, Su Ching, Shi Ching, Li Chi, I Ching, Lu		6 425 300
Hinduism	Vishnu Shiva Shakti	Rigveda, Yajurveda, Samaveda, Atharveda	Nepal	837 262 000
Islam (Muslim)	Sunni Shi'a Sufi Ismaili	Koran, Hadith	Afghanistan, Algeria, Bahrain, Bangladesh, Comoros, Egypt, Iran, Iraq, Jordan, Kuwait, Libya, Malaysia, Maldives, Mauritania, Morocco, Oman, Pakistan, Qatar, Saudi Arabia, Somalia, Sudan, Tunisia, United Arab Emirates, Yemen	1 254 222 000
Jainism	Digambara Swetambara	Siddhanta, Pakrit texts		4 413 700
Judaism		Torah, Talmud		14 551 000
Sikhism		Guru Granth Sahib (Adi Granth)		24 295 200
Shintoism		Kojiki, Nohon Shoki		2 680 300

Books of the Bible

Old Testament
Law (Pentateuch)
Genesis
Exodus
Leviticus
Numbers
Deuteronomy

Prophets
(FORMER)
Joshua
Judges
Samuel 1 & 2
Kings 1& 2

(LATTER)
Isaiah
Jeremiah
Ezekiel
Book of twelve prophets (Hosea,
Joel, Amos, Obadiah, Jonah,
Micah, Nahum, Habakkuk,
Zephaniah, Haggai, Zechariah,
Malachi)

Writings
Psalms
Proverbs
Job
Song of Songs
Ruth
Lamentations
Ecclesiastes
Esther
Daniel
Ezra
Nehemiah
Chronicles 1 & 2

New Testament
Gospels (Matthew, Mark, Luke,
John)
Acts of the Apostles
13 Letters attributed to Paul
(Romans, Corinthians 1 & 2,
Galatians, Ephesians, Philippians,
Colossians, Thessalonians 1 & 2,
Timothy 1 & 2, Titus, Philemon)
Letter to the Hebrews
7 General or 'Catholic' letters
(James, Peter 1 & 2, John 1, 2 & 3,
Jude)
Book of Revelation

Apocrypha
Baruch
Additions to the Book of Daniel
Book of Ecclesiasticus
Additions to the Book of Esther
Books of Esdras
Letter of Jeremiah
Book of Judith
Books of the Maccabees
Book of Tobit (Tobias)
Wisdom of Solomon

The Old Testament Apocrypha are a collection of Jewish writings found in the Greek version of the Hebrew Bible, but not found in the Hebrew Bible itself. Roman Catholics consider them as inspired and authoritative, and deuterocanonical, while Protestants attribute less authority to them.

New Testament Apocrypha are Christian documents similar in title, form, or content to many New Testament works, being called Gospels, Acts, Epistles, or Apocalypses, but are not widely accepted as canonical.

Christian religious vestments

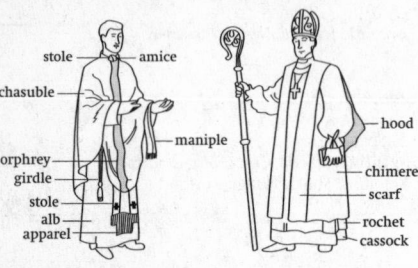

stole — amice
chasuble
orphrey
girdle
stole
alb
apparel
maniple
hood
chimere
scarf
rochet
cassock

chimere Worn by bishops over the rochet; of black or scarlet, open at the front.

cope In the pre-Christian era, a long cloak; now a costly embroidered vestment, semi-circular in shape, worn by bishops and priests on special occasions.

cotta Similar to the surplice, but shorter, especially in the sleeves; sometimes used by clergy and servers in place of the surplice.

girdle Cord worn about the waist.

hood Worn by clergy at choir offices, a mediaeval headdress, now worn hanging down the back; it denotes a university degree.

maniple Worn over the left arm by bishops, priests, and deacons at the Eucharist; originally a napkin.

orphreys The embroidered strips, customarily cross-shaped, on a chasuble.

rochet Worn by bishops, similar to an alb, but used without girdle or apparels.

stole Once a napkin or towel carried by servants on the left shoulder; now folded and narrow, worn over both shoulders.

surplice Of white linen, reaching to the knees; worn by choir and servers as well as clergy.

alb A long white garment reaching to the ankles; derived from an ancient tunic.

amice A linen square worn round the back to protect the other vestments; formerly a neckcloth.

apparels Ornamental panels at the foot of the alb, front and back, and on the amice.

cassock The long black gown worn under other vestments; formerly, the daily working costume of the clergy.

chasuble The outer sleeveless vestment worn by a priest or bishop when celebrating Holy Communion; derived from the commonest outdoor garment of classical times.

Holy orders

Major orders Bishop, Priest, Deacon, (Sub-deacon)
Minor orders Porter, Lector, Exorcist, Acolyte

In the Roman Catholic church there are now only the orders of Bishop, Priest, Deacon and the ministries of acolyte and lector, following the *motu proprio* of Pope Paul VI, 1973.

Movable Christian feasts

Dates for the years 2000–2010.

Year	Ash Wednesday	Easter	Ascension	Whit Sunday[a]	Trinity Sunday	Corpus Christi	First Sunday in Advent
2000	8 Mar	23 Apr	1 Jun	11 Jun	18 Jun	22 Jun	3 Dec
2001	28 Feb	15 Apr	24 May	3 Jun	10 Jun	14 Jun	2 Dec
2002	13 Feb	31 Mar	9 May	19 May	26 May	30 May	1 Dec
2003	5 Mar	20 Apr	29 May	8 Jun	15 Jun	19 Jun	30 Nov
2004	25 Feb	11 Apr	20 May	30 May	6 June	10 Jun	28 Nov
2005	9 Feb	27 Mar	5 May	15 May	22 May	26 May	27 Nov
2006	1 Mar	16 Apr	25 May	4 Jun	11 Jun	15 Jun	3 Dec
2007	21 Feb	8 Apr	17 May	27 May	2 Dec	3 Jun	7 Jun
2008	6 Feb	23 Mar	1 May	11 May	30 Nov	18 May	22 May
2009	25 Feb	12 Apr	21 May	31 May	29 Nov	7 Jun	11 Jun
2010	17 Feb	4 Apr	13 May	23 May	28 Nov	30 May	3 Jun

Ash Wednesday, the first day of Lent, can fall at the earliest on 4 Feb and at the latest on 10 Mar.

Palm (Passion) Sunday is the Sunday before Easter; Good Friday is the Friday before Easter; Holy Saturday (often referred to as Easter Saturday) is the Saturday before Easter; Easter Saturday, in traditional usage, is the Saturday following Easter.

Easter Day can fall at the earliest on 22 Mar and at the latest on 25 Apr. Ascension Day can fall at the earliest on 30 Apr and at the latest on 3 Jun. Whit Sunday can fall at the earliest on 10 May and at the latest on 13 Jun. There are not fewer than 22 and not more than 27 Sundays after Trinity. The first Sunday of Advent is the Sunday nearest to 30 Nov.

[a]Whit Sunday commemorates the day of Pentecost.

Major immovable Christian feasts

Jan 1	Solemenity of Mary, Mother of God
Jan 6	Epiphany
Jan 7	Christmas Day (Eastern Orthodox)[a]
Jan 11	Baptism of Jesus
Jan 25	Conversion of Apostle Paul
Feb 2	Presentation of Jesus (Candlemas Day)
Feb 22	The Chair of Peter, Apostle
Mar 25	Annunciation of the Virgin Mary
Jun 24	Birth of John the Baptist
Aug 6	Transfiguration
Aug 15	Assumption of the Virgin Mary
Aug 22	Queenship of Mary
Sep 8	Birthday of the Virgin Mary
Sep 14	Exaltation of the Holy Cross
Oct 2	Guardian Angels
Nov 1	All Saints
Nov 2	All Souls
Nov 9	Dedication of the Lateran Basilica
Nov 21	Presentation of the Virgin Mary
Dec 8	Immaculate Conception
Dec 25	Christmas Day
Dec 28	Holy Innocents

[a]Fixed feasts in the Julian Calendar fall 13 days later than the Gregorian Calendar date.

The dates of Easter

Dates for the years 1900–2099.

	0	- - - 1	- - - 2	- - - 3	- - - 4	- - - 5	- - - 6	- - - 7	- - - 8	- - - 9
1900	15 Apr	7 Apr	30 Mar	12 Apr	3 Apr	23 Apr	15 Apr	31 Mar	19 Apr	11 Apr
1910	27 Mar	16 Apr	7 Apr	23 Mar	12 Apr	4 Apr	23 Apr	8 Apr	31 Mar	20 Apr
1920	4 Apr	27 Mar	16 Apr	1 Apr	20 Apr	12 Apr	4 Apr	17 Apr	8 Apr	31 Mar
1930	20 Apr	5 Apr	27 Mar	16 Apr	1 Apr	21 Apr	12 Apr	28 Mar	17 Apr	9 Apr
1940	24 Mar	13 Apr	5 Apr	25 Apr	9 Apr	1 Apr	21 Apr	6 Apr	28 Mar	17 Apr
1950	9 Apr	25 Mar	13 Apr	5 Apr	18 Apr	10 Apr	1 Apr	21 Apr	6 Apr	29 Mar
1960	17 Apr	2 Apr	22 Apr	14 Apr	29 Mar	18 Apr	10 Apr	26 Mar	14 Apr	6 Apr
1970	29 Mar	11 Apr	2 Apr	22 Apr	14 Apr	30 Mar	18 Apr	10 Apr	26 Mar	15 Apr
1980	6 Apr	19 Apr	11 Apr	3 Apr	22 Apr	7 Apr	30 Mar	19 Apr	3 Apr	26 Mar
1990	15 Apr	31 Mar	19 Apr	11 Apr	3 Apr	16 Apr	7 Apr	30 Mar	12 Apr	4 Apr
2000	23 Apr	15 Apr	31 Mar	20 Apr	11 Apr	27 Mar	16 Apr	8 Apr	23 Mar	12 Apr
2010	4 Apr	24 Apr	8 Apr	31 Mar	20 Apr	5 Apr	27 Mar	16 Apr	1 Apr	21 Apr
2020	12 Apr	4 Apr	17 Apr	9 Apr	31 Mar	20 Apr	5 Apr	28 Mar	16 Apr	1 Apr
2030	21 Apr	13 Apr	28 Mar	17 Apr	9 Apr	25 Mar	13 Apr	5 Apr	25 Apr	10 Apr
2040	1 Apr	21 Apr	6 Apr	29 Mar	17 Apr	9 Apr	25 Mar	14 Apr	5 Apr	18 Apr
2050	10 Apr	2 Apr	21 Apr	6 Apr	29 Mar	18 Apr	2 Apr	22 Apr	14 Apr	30 Mar
2060	18 Apr	10 Apr	26 Mar	15 Apr	6 Apr	29 Mar	11 Apr	3 Apr	22 Apr	14 Apr
2070	30 Mar	19 Apr	10 Apr	26 Mar	15 Apr	7 Apr	19 Apr	11 Apr	3 Apr	23 Apr
2080	7 Apr	30 Mar	19 Apr	4 Apr	26 Mar	15 Apr	31 Mar	20 Apr	11 Apr	3 Apr
2090	16 Apr	8 Apr	30 Mar	12 Apr	4 Apr	24 Apr	15 Apr	31 Mar	20 Apr	12 Apr

RELIGION AND MYTHOLOGY

Saints' days

The official recognition of Saints, and the choice of a Saint's Day, varies greatly between different branches of Christianity, calendars, and localities. Only major variations are included below, using the following abbreviations:

C Coptic   G Greek
E Eastern   W Western

January
1 Basil (E); Fulgentius; Telemachus
2 Basil and Gregory of Nazianzus (W); Macarius of Alexandria; Seraphim of Sarov
3 Geneviève
4 Angela of Foligno
5 Simeon Stylites (W)
7 Cedda; Lucian of Antioch (W); Raymond of Penyafort
8 Atticus (E); Gudule; Severinus
9 Hadrian the African
10 Agatho; Marcian
12 Ailred; Benedict Biscop
13 Hilary of Poitiers
14 Kentigern
15 Macarius of Egypt; Maurus; Paul of Thebes
16 Honoratus
17 Antony of Egypt
19 Wulfstan
20 Euthymius; Fabian; Sebastian
21 Agnes; Fructuosus; Maximus (E); Meinrad
22 Timothy (G); Vincent
23 Ildefonsus
24 Babylas (W); Francis de Sales
25 Gregory of Nazianzus (E)
26 Paula; Timothy and Titus; Xenophon (E)
27 Angela Merici
28 Ephraem Syrus (E); Paulinus of Nola; Thomas Aquinas
29 Gildas
31 John Bosco; Marcella

February
1 Bride; Pionius
3 Anskar; Blaise (W); Werburga; Simeon (E)
4 Gilbert of Sempringham; Isidore of Pelusium; Phileas
5 Agatha; Avitus
6 Dorothy; Paul Miki and companions; Vedast
8 Theodore (G); Jerome Emiliani
9 Teilo
10 Scholastica
11 Benedict of Aniane; Blaise (E); Caedmon; Gregory II
12 Meletius
13 Agabus (W); Catherine dei Ricci; Priscilla (E)
14 Cyril and Methodius (W); Valentine (W)

16 Flavian (E); Pamphilus (E); Valentine (G)
18 Bernadette (France); Colman; Flavian (W); Leo I (E)
20 Wulfric
21 Peter Damian
23 Polycarp
25 Ethelbert; Tarasius; Walburga
26 Alexander (W); Porphyrius
27 Leander
28 Oswald of York

March
1 David
2 Chad; Simplicius
3 Ailred
4 Casimir
6 Chrodegang
7 Perpetua and Felicity
8 Felix; John of God; Pontius
9 Frances of Rome; Gregory of Nyssa; Pacian
10 John Ogilvie; Macarius of Jerusalem; Simplicius
11 Constantine; Oengus; Sophronius
12 Gregory (the Great)
13 Nicephorus
14 Benedict (E)
15 Clement Hofbauer
17 Gertrude; Joseph of Arimathea (W); Patrick
18 Anselm of Lucca; Cyril of Jerusalem; Edward
19 Joseph (W)
20 Cuthbert; John of Parma; Martin of Braga
21 Serapion of Thmuis
22 Catherine of Sweden; Nicholas of Fluë
23 Turibius de Mongrovejo
30 John Climacus

April
1 Hugh of Grenoble; Mary of Egypt (E); Melito
2 Francis of Paola; Mary of Egypt (W)
3 Richard of Chichester
4 Isidore of Seville
5 Juliana of Liège; Vincent Ferrer
7 Hegesippus; John Baptist de la Salle
8 Agabus (E)
10 Fulbert
11 Gemma Galgani; Guthlac; Stanislaus
12 Julius I; Zeno
13 Martin I
15 Aristarchus; Pudus (E); Trophimus of Ephesus
17 Agapetus (E); Stephen Harding
18 Mme Acarie
19 Alphege; Leo IX
21 Anastasius (E); Anselm; Beuno; Januarius (E)

22 Alexander (C)
23 George
24 Egbert; Fidelis of Sigmaringen; Mellitus
25 Mark; Phaebadius
27 Zita
28 Peter Chanel; Vitalis and Valeria
29 Catherine of Siena; Hugh of Cluny; Peter Martyr; Robert
30 James (the Great) (E); Pius V

May
1 Asaph; Joseph the Worker; Walburga
2 Athanasius
3 Phillip and James (the Less) (W)
4 Gotthard
5 Hilary of Arles
7 John of Beverley
8 John (E); Peter of Tarantaise
10 Antoninus; Comgall; John of Avila; Simon (E)
11 Cyril and Methodius (E); Mamertus
12 Epiphanius; Nereus and Achilleus; Pancras
14 Matthias (W)
16 Brendan; John of Nepomuk; Simon Stock
17 Robert Bellarmine; Paschal Baylon
18 John I
19 Dunstan; Ivo; Pudens (W); Pudentiana (W)
20 Bernardino of Siena
21 Helena (E)
22 Rita of Cascia
23 Ivo of Chartres
24 Vincent of Lérins
25 Aldhelm; Bede; Gregory VII; Mary Magdalene de Pazzi
26 Philip Neri; Quadratus
27 Augustine of Canterbury
30 Joan of Arc

June
1 Justin Martyr; Pamphilus
2 Erasmus; Marcellinus and Peter; Nicephorus (G); Pothinus
3 Charles Lwanga and companions; Clotilde; Kevin
4 Optatus; Petrock
5 Boniface
6 Martha (E); Norbert
7 Paul of Constantinople (W); Willibald
8 William of York
9 Columba; Cyril of Alexandria (E); Ephraem (W)
11 Barnabas; Bartholomew (E)
12 Leo III
13 Anthony of Padua
15 Orsisius; Vitus
17 Alban; Botulph

19 Gervasius and Protasius; Jude (*E*); Romuald
20 Alban
21 Alban of Mainz; Aloysius Gonzaga
22 John Fisher and Thomas More; Niceta; Pantaenus (*C*); Paulinus of Nola
23 Etheldreda
24 Birth of John the Baptist
25 Prosper of Aquitaine
27 Cyril of Alexandria (*W*); Ladislaus
28 Irenaeus
29 Peter and Paul
30 First Martyrs of the Church of Rome

July
1 Cosmas and Damian (*E*); Oliver Plunket
3 Anatolius; Thomas
4 Andrew of Crete (*E*); Elizabeth of Portugal; Ulrich
5 Anthony Zaccaria
6 Maria Goretti
7 Palladius; Pantaenus
8 Kilian; Aquila and Prisca (*W*)
11 Benedict (*W*); Pius I
12 John Gualbert; Veronica
13 Henry II; Mildred; Silas
14 Camillus of Lellis; Deusdedit; Nicholas of the Holy Mountain (*E*)
15 Bonaventure; Jacob of Nisibis; Swithin; Vladimir
16 Eustathius; Our Lady of Mt Carmel
17 Ennodius; Leo IV; Marcellina; Margaret (*E*); Scillitan Martyrs
18 Arnulf; Philastrius
19 Marcrina; Symmachus
20 Aurelius; Margaret (*W*)
21 Lawrence of Brindisi; Praxedes
22 Mary Magdalene
23 Apollinaris; Bridget of Sweden
25 Anne and Joachim (*E*); Christopher; James (the Great) (*W*)
26 Anne and Joachim (*W*)
27 Pantaleon
28 Innocent I; Samson; Victor I
29 Lupus; Martha (*W*); Olave
30 Peter Chrysologus; Silas (*G*)
31 Giovanni Colombini; Germanus; Joseph of Arimathea (*E*); Ignatius of Loyola

August
1 Alphonsus Liguori; Ethelwold
2 Eusebius of Vercelli; Stephen I
4 Jean-Baptiste Vianney
6 Hormisdas
7 Cajetan; Sixtus II and companions
8 Dominic

9 Matthias (*G*)
10 Laurence; Oswald of Northumbria
11 Clare; Susanna
13 Maximus (*W*); Pontian and Hippolytus; Radegunde
14 Maximilian Kolbe
15 Arnulf; Tarsicius
16 Roch; Simplicianus; Stephen of Hungary
17 Hyacinth
19 John Eudes; Sebaldus
20 Bernard; Oswin; Philibert
21 Jane Frances de Chantal; Pius X
23 Rose of Lima; Sidonius Apollinaris
24 Bartholomew (*W*); Ouen
25 Joseph Calasanctius; Louis IX; Menas of Constantinople
26 Blessed Dominic of the Mother of God; Zephyrinus
27 Caesarius; Monica
28 Augustine of Hippo
29 Beheading of John the Baptist; Sabina
30 Pammachius
31 Aidan; Paulinus of Trier

September
1 Giles; Simeon Stylites (*E*)
2 John the Faster (*E*)
3 Gregory (the Great)
4 Babylas (*E*); Boniface I
5 Zacharias (*E*)
9 Peter Claver; Sergius of Antioch
10 Finnian; Nicholas of Tolentino; Pulcheria
11 Deiniol; Ethelburga; Paphnutius
13 John Chrysostom (*W*)
15 Catherine of Genoa; Our Lady of Sorrows
16 Cornelius; Cyprian of Carthage; Euphemia; Ninian
17 Robert Bellarmine; Hildegard; Lambert; Satyrus
19 Januarius (*W*); Theodore of Tarsus
20 Agapetus or Eustace (*W*)
21 Matthew (*W*)
23 Adamnan; Linus; Padre Pio
25 Sergius of Rostov
26 Cosmas and Damian (*W*); Cyprian of Carthage; John (*E*)
27 Frumentius (*W*); Vincent de Paul
28 Exuperius; Wenceslaus
29 Michael (*Michaelmas Day*); Gabriel and Raphael
30 Jerome; Otto

October
1 Remigius; Romanos; Teresa of the Child Jesus
2 Leodegar (Leger)
3 Thérèse de Lisieux; Thomas de Cantilupe

4 Ammon; Francis of Assisi; Petronius
6 Bruno; Thomas (*G*)
9 Demetrius (*W*); Denis and companions; Dionysius of Paris; James (the Less) (*E*); John Leonardi
10 Francis Borgia; Paulinus of York
11 Atticus (*E*); Bruno; Nectarius
12 Wilfrid
13 Edward the Confessor
14 Callistus I; Cosmas Melodus (*E*)
15 Lucian of Antioch (*E*); Teresa of Avila
16 Gall; Hedwig; Lullus; Margaret Mary Alacoque
17 Ignatius of Antioch; Victor
18 Luke
19 John de Bréboeuf and Isaac Jogues and companions; Paul of the Cross; Peter of Alcántara
21 Hilarion; Ursula
22 Abercius
23 John of Capistrano; James
24 Anthony Claret
25 Crispin and Crispinian; Forty Martyrs of England and Wales; Gaudentius
26 Demetrius (*E*)
28 Firmilian (*E*); Simon and Jude
30 Serapion of Antioch
31 Wolfgang

November
1 All Saints; Cosmas and Damian (*E*)
2 Eustace (*E*); Victorinus
3 Hubert; Malachy; Martin de Porres; Pirminius; Winifred
4 Charles Borromeo; Vitalis and Agricola
5 Elizabeth (*W*)
6 Illtyd; Leonard; Paul of Constantinople (*E*)
7 Willibrord
8 Elizabeth (*E*); Willehad
9 Simeon Metaphrastes (*E*)
10 Justus; Leo I (*W*)
11 Martin of Tours (*W*); Menas of Egypt; Theodore of Studios
12 Josaphat; Martin of Tours (*E*); Nilus the Ascetic
13 Abbo; John Chrysostom (*E*); Nicholas I
14 Dubricius; Gregory Palamas (*E*)
15 Albert the Great; Machutus
16 Edmund of Abingdon; Eucherius; Gertrude (the Great); Margaret of Scotland; Matthew (*E*)
17 Elizabeth of Hungary; Gregory Thaumaturgus; Gregory of Tours; Hugh of Lincoln
18 Odo; Romanus
19 Mechthild; Nerses
20 Edmund the Martyr

RELIGION AND MYTHOLOGY

Saints' days (continued)

21 Gelasius
22 Cecilia
23 Amphilochius; Clement I (*W*); Columban; Felicity; Gregory of Agrigentum
25 Clement I (*E*); Mercurius; Mesrob
26 Siricius
27 Barlam and Josaphat
28 Simeon Metaphrastes
29 Cuthbert Mayne
30 Andrew; Frumentius (*G*)

December
1 Eligius
2 Chromatius
3 Francis Xavier
4 Barbara; John Damascene; Osmund
5 Clement of Alexandria; Sabas
6 Nicholas
7 Ambrose
10 Miltiades
11 Damasus; Daniel
12 Jane Frances de Chantal; Spyridon (*E*); Vicelin

13 Lucy; Odilia
14 John of the Cross; Spyridon (*W*)
16 Eusebius
18 Frumentius (*C*)
20 Ignatius of Antioch (*G*)
21 Peter Canisius; Thomas
22 Anastasia (*E*); Chrysogonus (*E*)
23 John of Kanty
26 Stephen (*W*)
27 John (*W*); Fabiola; Stephen (*E*)
29 Thomas Becket; Trophimus of Arles
31 Sylvester

Popes

Antipope refers to a pontiff set up in opposition to one asserted to be canonically chosen.

until c.64	Peter
c.64–c.76	Linus
c.76–c.90	Anacletus
c.90–c.99	Clement I
c.99–c.105	Evaristus
c.105–c.117	Alexander I
c.117–c.127	Sixtus I
c.127–c.137	Telesphorus
c.137–c.140	Hyginus
c.140–c.154	Pius I
c.154–c.166	Anicetus
c.166–c.175	Soter
175–89	Eleutherius
189–98	Victor I
198–217	Zephyrinus
217–22	Callistus I
217–c.235	Hippolytus *Antipope*
222–30	Urban I
230–5	Pontian
235–6	Anterus
236–50	Fabian
251–3	Cornelius
251–c.258	Novatian *Antipope*
253–4	Lucius I
254–7	Stephen I
257–8	Sixtus II
259–68	Dionysius
269–74	Felix I
275–83	Eutychianus
283–96	Caius
296–304	Marcellinus
308–9	Marcellus I
310	Eusebius
311–14	Miltiades
314–35	Sylvester I
336	Mark
337–52	Julius I
352–66	Liberius
355–65	Felix II *Antipope*
366–84	Damasus I
366–7	Ursinus *Antipope*
384–99	Siricius
399–401	Anastasius I
402–17	Innocent I
417–18	Zosimus
418–22	Boniface I
418–19	Eulalius *Antipope*

422–32	Celestine I
432–40	Sixtus III
440–61	Leo I 'the Great'
461–8	Hilarus
468–83	Simplicius
483–92	Felix III (II)
492–6	Gelasius I
496–8	Anastasius II
498–514	Symmachus
498	Laurentius *Antipope*
501–5	Laurentius *Antipope*
514–23	Hormisdas
523–6	John I
526–30	Felix IV (III)
530–2	Boniface II
530	Dioscorus *Antipope*
533–5	John II
535–6	Agapetus I
536–7	Silverius
537–55	Vigilius
556–61	Pelagius I
561–74	John III
575–9	Benedict I
579–90	Pelagius II
590–604	Gregory I 'the Great'
604–6	Sabinianus
607	Boniface III
608–15	Boniface IV
615–18	Deusdedit (Adeodatus I)
619–25	Boniface V
625–38	Honorius I
640	Severinus
640–2	John IV
642–9	Theodore I
649–55	Martin I
654–7	Eugenius I[a]
657–72	Vitalian
672–6	Adeodatus II
676–8	Donus
678–81	Agatho
682–3	Leo II
684–5	Benedict II
685–6	John V
686–7	Cono
687	Theodore *Antipope*
687–92	Paschal *Antipope*
687–701	Sergius I

701–5	John VI
705–7	John VII
708	Sisinnius
708–15	Constantine
715–31	Gregory II
731–41	Gregory III
741–52	Zacharias
752	Stephen II (not consecrated)
752–7	Stephen II (III)
757–67	Paul I
767–9	Constantine II *Antipope*
768	Philip *Antipope*
768–72	Stephen III (IV)
772–95	Adrian I
795–816	Leo III
816–17	Stephen IV (V)
817–24	Paschal I
824–7	Eugenius II
827	Valentine
827–44	Gregory IV
844	John *Antipope*
844–7	Sergius II
847–55	Leo IV
855–8	Benedict III
855	Anastasius Bibliothecarius *Antipope*
858–67	Nicholas I 'the Great'
867–72	Adrian II
872–82	John VIII
882–4	Marinus I
884–5	Adrian III
885–91	Stephen V (VI)
891–6	Formosus
896	Boniface VI
896–7	Stephen VI (VII)
897	Romanus
897	Theodore II
898–900	John IX
900–3	Benedict IV
903	Leo V
903–4	Christopher *Antipope*
904–11	Sergius III
911–13	Anastasius III
913–14	Lando
914–28	John X
928	Leo VI

928–31	Stephen VII (VIII)		Parareschi)	1303	Castani)
931–5	John XI	1130–8	Anacletus II *Antipope*	1303–4	Benedict XI (Niccolo
936–9	Leo VII	1138	Victor IV[b] *Antipope*		Boccasini)
939–42	Stephen IX	1143–4	Celestine II (Guido di	1305–14	Clement V (Raymond
942–6	Marinus II		Castello)		Bertrand de Got)
946–55	Agapetus II	1144–5	Lucius II (Gherardo	1316–34	John XXII (Jacques
955–64	John XII		Caccianemici)		Duèse)
963–5	Leo VIII	1145–53	Eugenius III (Bernardo	1328–30	Nicholas V (Pietro
964–6	Benedict V		Paganelli)		Rainalducci) *Antipope*
965–72	John XIII	1153–4	Anastasius IV (Corrado	1334–42	Benedict XII (Jacques
973–4	Benedict VI		della Subarra)		Fournier)
974	Boniface VII *Antipope*	1154–9	Adrian IV (Nicholas	1342–52	Clement VI (Pierre Roger
984–5	Boniface VII *Antipope*		Breakspear)		de Beaufort)
974–83	Benedict VII	1159–81	Alexander III (Orlando	1352–62	Innocent VI (Étienne
983–4	John XIV		Bandinelli)		Aubert)
985–96	John XV	1159–64	Victor IV[b] (Ottaviano di	1362–70	Urban V (Guillaume de
996–9	Gregory V		Monticelli) *Antipope*		Grimoard)
997–8	John XVI *Antipope*	1164–8	Paschal III (Guido of	1370–8	Gregory XI (Pierre Roger
999–1003	Sylvester II		Crema) *Antipope*		de Beaufort)
1003	John XVII	1168–78	Callistus III (John of	1378–89	Urban VI (Bartolomeo
1004–9	John XVIII		Struma) *Antipope*		Prignano)
1009–12	Sergius IV	1179–80	Innocent III (Lando da	1378–94	Clement VII (Robert of
1012–24	Benedict VIII		Sessa)		Geneva) *Antipope*
1012	Gregory *Antipope*	1181–5	Lucius III (Ubaldo	1389–	Boniface IX (Pietro
1024–32	John XIX		Allucingoli)	1404	Tomacelli)
1032–44	Benedict IX	1185–7	Urban III (Uberto	1394–	Benedict XIII (Pedro de
1045	Sylvester III		Crivelli)	1423	Luna) *Antipope*
1045	Benedict IX (second	1187	Gregory VIII (Alberto di	1404–6	Innocent VII (Cosmato
	reign)		Morra)		de' Migliorati)
1045–6	Gregory VI	1187–91	Clement III (Paolo	1406–15	Gregory XII (Angelo
1046–7	Clement II		Scolari)		Correr)
1047–8	Benedict IX (third reign)	1191–8	Celestine III (Giacinto	1409–10	Alexander V (Petros
1048	Damasus II (Poppo)		Boboni-Orsini)		Philargi) *Antipope*
1048–54	Leo IX (Bruno of Toul)	1198–	Innocent III (Lotario	1410–15	John XXIII (Baldassare
1055–7	Victor II (Gebhard of	1216	de'Conti)		Cossa) *Antipope*
	Hirschberg)	1216–27	Honorius III (Cancio	1417–31	Martin V (Oddone
1057–8	Stephen IX (X) (Frederick		Savelli)		Colonna)
	of Lorraine)	1227–41	Gregory IX (Ugolino di	1423–9	Clement VIII (Gil
1058–9	Benedict X (John of		Segni)		Sanchez Muñoz)
	Tusculum) *Antipope*	1241	Celestine IV (Goffredo		*Antipope*
1059–61	Nicholas II (Gerard of		Castiglione)	1425–30	Benedict XIV (Bernard
	Burgundy)	1243–54	Innocent IV (Sinibaldo		Garnier) *Antipope*
1061–73	Alexander II (Anselm of		de' Fieschi)	1431–47	Eugenius IV (Gabriele
	Lucca)	1254–61	Alexander IV (Rinaldo di		Condulmer)
1061–72	Honorius II (Peter		Segni)	1439–49	Felix V (Amadeus VIII of
	Cadalus) *Antipope*	1261–4	Urban IV (Jacques		Savoy) *Antipope*
1073–85	Gregory VII (St		Pantaléon)	1447–55	Nicholas V (Tommaso
	Hilderbrand)	1265–8	Clement IV (Guy le Gros		Parentuce III)
1080,	Clement III (Guibert of		Foulques)	1455–8	Callistus III (Alfonso de
1084–1100	Ravenna) *Antipope*	1271–6	Gregory X (Tebaldo		Borja)
1086–7	Victor III (Desidenus)		Visconti)	1458–64	Pius II (Enea Silvio de
1088–99	Urban II (Odo of	1276	Innocent V (Pierre de		Piccolomini)
	Chatillon)		Champagni)	1464–71	Paul II (Pietro Barbo)
1099–	Paschal II (Raneiro da	1276	Adrian V (Ottobono	1471–84	Sixtus IV (Francesco della
1118	Bieda)		Fieschi)		Rovere)
1100–2	Theodoric *Antipope*	1276–7	John XXI[c] (Pietro Rebuli-	1484–92	Innocent VIII (Giovanni
1102	Albert *Antipope*		Giuliani)		Battista Cibo)
1105–11	Sylvester IV *Antipope*	1277–80	Nicholas III (Giovanni	1492–	Alexander VI (Rodrigo
1118–19	Gelasius II (John of		Gaetano Orsini)	1503	Borgia)
	Gaeta)	1281–5	Martin IV (Simon de	1503	Pius III (Francesco
1118–21	Gregory VIII (Maurice of		Brie)		Todoeschini-Piccolomini)
	Braga) *Antipope*	1285–7	Honorius IV (Giacomo	1503–13	Julius II (Giuliano della
1119–24	Callistus II (Guy of		Savelli)		Rovere)
	Burgundy)	1288–92	Nicholas IV (Girolamo	1513–21	Leo X (Giovanni de'
1124–30	Honorius II (Lamberto		Masci)		Medici)
	dei Fagnani)	1294	Celestine V (Pietro di	1522–3	Adrian VI (Adrian Dedel)
1124	Celestine II *Antipope*		Morrone)	1523–34	Clement VII (Giulio de'
1130–43	Innocent II (Gregory	1294–	Boniface VIII (Benedetto		Medici)

RELIGION AND MYTHOLOGY

Popes (continued)

1534–49	Paul III (Allessandro Farnese)	1644–55	Innocent X (Giambattista Pamfili)	1800–23	Pius VII (Luigi Barnaba Chiaramonti)
1550–5	Julius III (Gianmaria del Monte)	1655–67	Alexander VII (Fabio Chigi)	1823–9	Leo XII (Annibale della Genga)
1555	Marcellus II (Marcello Cervini)	1667–9	Clement IX (Guilio Rospigliosi)	1829–30	Pius VIII (Francesco Saveno Castiglioni)
1555–9	Paul IV (Giovanni Pietro Caraffa)	1670–6	Clement X (Emilio Altieri)	1831–46	Gregory XVI (Bartolomeo Alberto Cappellari)
1559–65	Pius IV (Giovanni Angelo Medici)	1676–89	Innocent XI (Benedetto Odescalchi)	1846–78	Pius IX (Giovanni Maria Mastai Ferretti)
1566–72	Pius V (Michele Ghislieri)	1689–91	Alexander VIII (Pietro Vito Ottoboni)	1878–1903	Leo XIII (Vincenzo Gioacchino Pecci)
1572–85	Gregory XIII (Ugo Buoncompagni)	1691–1700	Innocent XII (Antonio Pignatelli)	1903–14	Pius X (Giuseppe Sarto)
1585–90	Sixtus V (Felice Peretti)	1700–21	Clement XI (Gian Francesco Albani)	1914–22	Benedict XV (Giacomo della Chiesa)
1590	Urban VII (Giambattista Castagna)	1721–4	Innocent XIII (Michelangelo dei Conti)	1922–39	Pius XI (Achille Ratti)
1590–1	Gregory XIV (Niccolo Sfondrati)	1724–30	Benedict XIII (Pietro Francesco Orsini)	1939–58	Pius XII (Eugenio Pacelli)
1591	Innocent IX (Gian Antonio Facchinetti)	1730–40	Clement XII (Lorenzo Corsini)	1958–63	John XXIII (Angelo Giuseppe Roncalli)
1592–1605	Clement VIII (Ippolito Aldobrandini)	1740–58	Benedict XIV (Prospero Lambertini)	1963–78	Paul VI (Giovanni Battista Montini)
1605	Leo XI (Alessandro de' Medici-Ottaiano)	1758–69	Clement XIII (Carlo Rezzonico)	1978–2005	John Paul II (Karol Jozef Wojtyla)
1605–21	Paul V (Camillo Borghese)	1769–74	Clement XIV (Lorenzo Ganganelli)	2005–	Benedict XVI (Joseph Ratzinger)
1621–3	Gregory XV (Alessandro Ludovisi)	1775–99	Pius VI (Giovanni Angelo Braschi)		
1623–44	Urban VIII (Maffeo Barberini)				

[a]Elected during the banishment of Martin I.   [b]Different individuals.   [c]There was no John XX.

Archbishops of Canterbury

597–604	St Augustine	1020–38	Æthelnoth	1397–9	Roger Walden
604–19	Laurentius	1038–50	Eadsige	1399–1414	Thomas Arundel (*restored*)
619–24	Mellitus	1051–2	Robert of Jumièges	1414–43	Henry Chichele
624–7	Justus	1052–70	Stigand	1443–52	John Stafford
627–53	Honorius	1070–89	Lanfranc	1452–4	John Kemp
655–64	Deusdedit (Frithona)	1093–1109	Anselm	1454–86	Thomas Bourgchier
668–90	Theodore	1114–22	Ralph d'Escures	1486–1500	John Morton
693–731	Beorhtweald	1123–36	William of Corbeil	1501–3	Henry Deane
731–4	Tatwine	1138–61	Theobald (Tebaldus)	1504–32	William Warham
735–9	Nothelm	1162–70	Thomas à Becket	1532–55	Thomas Cranmer
740–60	Cuthbert	1174–84	Richard of Dover	1555–8	Reginald Pole
761–4	Breguwine	1184–90	Baldwin	1559–75	Matthew Parker
765–92	Jaenbeorht	1193–1205	Hubert Walter	1575–83	Edmund Grindal
793–805	Ethelheard	1206–28	Stephen Langton	1583–1604	John Whitgift
805–32	Wulfred	1229–31	Richard le Grant	1604–10	Richard Bancroft
832	Feologild	1233–40	St Edmund (Rich)	1611–33	George Abbot
833–70	Ceolnoth	1241–70	Boniface of Savoy	1633–45	William Laud
870–89	Æthelred	1272–8	Robert Kilwardby	1645–60	No Archbishop of Canterbury
890–914	Plegmund	1279–92	John Pecham	1660–3	William Juxon
914–23	Æthelhelm	1293–1313	Robert Winchelsey	1663–77	Gilbert Sheldon
923–42	Wulfhelm	1313–27	Walter Reynolds	1677–90	William Sancroft
942–58	Oda	1327–33	Simon Mepham	1691–4	John Tillotson
959	Ælfsige	1333–48	John de Stratford	1694–1715	Thomas Tenison
959	Beorhthelm	1348–9	Thomas Bradwardine	1715–37	William Wake
960–88	St Dunstan	1349–66	Simon Islip	1737–47	John Potter
988–90	Æthelgar	1366–8	Simon Langham	1747–57	Thomas Herring
990–4	Sigeric Serio	1368–74	William Whittlesey	1757–8	Matthew Hutton
995–1005	Ælfric	1375–81	Simon Sudbury	1758–68	Thomas Secker
1005–12	Ælfheah	1381–96	William Courtenay	1768–83	Frederick Cornwallis
1013–20	Lyfing	1396–7	Thomas Arundel		

1783–1805	John Moore	1883–96	Edward White Benson	1961–74	Arthur Michael Ramsey
1805–28	Charles Manners Sutton	1896–1902	Frederick Temple	1974–80	Donald Coggan
1828–48	William Howley	1903–28	Randall Thomas Davidson	1980–91	Robert Alexander
1848–62	John Bird Sumner	1928–42	Cosmo Gordon Lang		Kennedy Runcie
1862–8	Charles Thomas Longley	1942–4	William Temple	1991–2002	George Leonard Carey
1868–82	Archibald Campbell Tait	1945–61	Geoffrey Francis Fisher	2002–	Rowan Williams

Dalai Lamas

1391–1475	Gedun Truppa	1683–1706	Tsang–yang Gyatso	1856–75	Trinle Gyatso
1475–1542	Gedun Gyatso	1708–57	Kezang Gyatso	1876–1933	Thupten Gyatso
1543–88	Sonam Gyatso	1758–1804	Jampel Gyatso	1935–	Tenzin Gyatso *in exile*
1589–1617	Yonten Gyatso	1806–15	Luntok Gyatso		1959–
1617–82	Ngawang Lobzang	1816–37	Tshultrim Gyatso		
	Gyatso	1838–56	Khedrup Gyatso		

Buddhism

Founder
Prince Siddhartha Gautama (Buddha), c.563–483 BC

Date founded
c.500 BC, India

Beliefs
'Four Noble Truths':
  All life is permeated by suffering
  Source of suffering is desire for existence
  This cause can be eliminated
  Way of doing this is by treading 'The Eightfold Path'
'The Eightfold Path' leads to 'nirvana' – ultimate state of peace

Major festivals[a]
Buddha's birth
Buddha's enlightenment
Buddha's first sermon
Buddha's death

[a]These take place on different dates in the countries in which Buddhism is practised.

Christianity

Founder
Jesus of Nazareth (Jesus Christ), c.4 BC–AD 30

Date founded
1st-c AD

Beliefs
Trinity – God as three in one (Father, Son, Holy Spirit)
God as creator of universe
Original sin and the forgiveness of sins
God is love
Incarnation of Jesus as Son of God
Redemption/Salvation
Resurrection
Sacramental identity, through baptism and the Eucharist
Old and New Testaments of the Bible

Confucianism

Founder
K'ung Fu-tzu, 551–479 BC

Date founded
6th-c BC, China

Beliefs
Human beings are teachable, improvable, and perfectible
Person can shape his/her own destiny
Self-knowledge and self-realization are attainable through learning
Sense of humanity should infuse society and politics (social participation)
Ritual and tradition

Major Chinese festivals

January/February	Chinese New Year
February/March	Lantern Festival
March/April	Festival of Pure Brightness
May/June	Dragon Boat Festival
July/August	Herd Boy and Weaving Maid
August	All Souls' Festival
September	Mid-Autumn Festival
September/October	Double Ninth Festival
November/December	Winter Solstice

Hinduism

Founder
Aryan invaders of India of Vedic religion

Date founded
c.1500 BC, India

Beliefs
Sacred power (Brahman) is sole reality, the creator, transformer, and preserver of everything
Hindu Trinity of Brahma, Vishnu, and Shiva
Authority of the Veda
Respect for life
Rebirth
Soul emancipated by the Three Margas – duty, knowledge, devotion

Major festivals
S = Sukla, 'waxing fortnight'.
K = Krishna 'waning fortnight'.

Caitra	S9	Ramanavami (Birthday of Lord Rama)
Asadha	S2	Rathayatra (Pilgrimage of the Chariot at Jagannath)
Sravana	S11–15	Jhulanayatra ('Swinging the Lord Krishna')
Sravana	S15	Rakshabandhana ('Tying on lucky threads')

RELIGION AND MYTHOLOGY

Hinduism (continued)

Bhadrapada	K8	Janamashtami (Birthday of Lord Krishna)
Asvina	S7–10	Durga-puja (Homage to Goddess Durga) (*Bengal*)
Asvina	S1–10	Navaratri (Festival of 'Nine Nights')
Asvina	S15	Lakshmi-puja (Homage to Goddess Lakshmi)
Asvina	K15	Diwali, Dipavali ('String of Lights')
Kartikka	S15	Guru Nanak Jananti (Birthday of Guru Nanak)
Magha	K5	Sarasvati-puja (Homage to Goddess Sarasvati)
Magha	K13	Maha-sivaratri (Great Night of Lord Shiva)
Phalguna	S14	Holi (Festival of Fire)
Phalguna	S15	Dolayatra (Swing Festival) (*Bengal*)

Islam

Founder
Mohammed, AD c.570–632

Date founded
7th-C AD, Arabian peninsula

Beliefs
Unity of God
God as creator and sustainer of the universe
Man superior to nature but still servant of God
Pride is cardinal sin
God always ready to pardon – repentance and redemption possible
Prophets are recipients of revelations from God – they, with God, show a person the 'right way'

Major festivals

1	Muharram	New Year's Day; starts on the day which celebrates Mohammed's departure from Mecca to Medina in AD 622
12	Rabi I	Birthday of Mohammed (Mawlid al-Nabi) AD 572; celebrated throughout month of Rabi I
27	Rajab	'Night of Ascent' (Laylat al-Mi'raj) of Mohammed to Heaven
1	Ramadan	Beginning of month of fasting during daylight hours
27	Ramadan	'Night of Power' (Laylat al-Qadr); sending down of the Koran to Mohammed
1	Shawwal	'Feast of breaking the Fast' ('Id al-Fitr); marks the end of Ramadan
8–13	Dhu-l-Hijja	Annual pilgrimage ceremonies at and around Mecca; month during which the great pilgrimage (Hajj) should be made
10	Dhu-l-Hijja	Feast of the Sacrifice ('Id al-Adha)

Jainism

Founder
Vardhamana Mahavira, 599–527 BC

Date founded
c.600 BC, India

Beliefs
World eternal and uncreated
All phenomena linked by chain of cause and effect
Nonviolence to other living creatures (Ahimsa)
Perfection and purification of soul leads to its emancipation and the ultimate attribute of omniscience
Soul has to pass through various stages of spiritual development before freeing itself of karmic bondages
Right conduct, right knowledge, right belief

Judaism

Founders
Abraham, c.2000 BC, and Moses, c.1200 BC

Date founded
c.2000 BC

Beliefs
Unity of God
God as teacher through instruction of Torah
God as redeemer
Resurrection
Coming of the 'Mashiah' who will establish new age in Israel

Major festivals

1–2	Tishri	Rosh Hashanah (New Year)
3	Tishri	Tzom Gedaliahu (Fast of Gedaliah)
10	Tishri	Yom Kippur (Day of Atonement)
15–21	Tishri	Sukkoth (Feast of Tabernacles)
22	Tishri	Shemini Atzeret (8th Day of the Solemn Assembly)
23	Tishri	Simhat Torah (Rejoicing of the Law)
25	Kislev–2–3 Tevet	Hanukkah (Feast of Dedication)
10	Tevet	Asara be-Tevet (Fast of 10th Tevet)
13	Adar	Taanit Esther (Fast of Esther)
14–15	Adar	Purim (Feast of Lots)
15–22	Nisan	Pesach (Passover)
5	Iyar	Israel Independence Day
6–7	Sivan	Shavuoth (Feast of Weeks)
17	Tammuz	Shiva Asar be-Tammuz (Fast of 17th Tammuz)
9	Av	Tisha be-Av (Fast of 9th Av)

The ancient tribes of Israel

Asher Descended from Jacob's eighth son (Z).
Benjamin Descended from Jacob's twelfth and youngest son (R).
Dan Descended from Jacob's fifth son (B).
Issachar Descended from Jacob's ninth son (L).
Joseph Descended from Jacob's eleventh son (R).
Ephraim Descended from Joseph's younger son.
Manasseh Descended from Joseph's elder son.
Judah Descended from Jacob's fourth son (L).
Levi Descended from Jacob's third son (L). (No territory, as it was a priestly caste.)

Naphtali Descended from Jacob's sixth son (B).
Reuben Descended from Jacob's first son (L).
Simeon Descended from Jacob's second son (L).
Zebulun Descended from Jacob's tenth son (L).
Gad Descended from Jacob's seventh son (Z).

B = borne by Bilhah
L = borne by Leah
R = borne by Rachel
Z = borne by Zilpah

Israel during the period of the Judges – approximate tribal areas

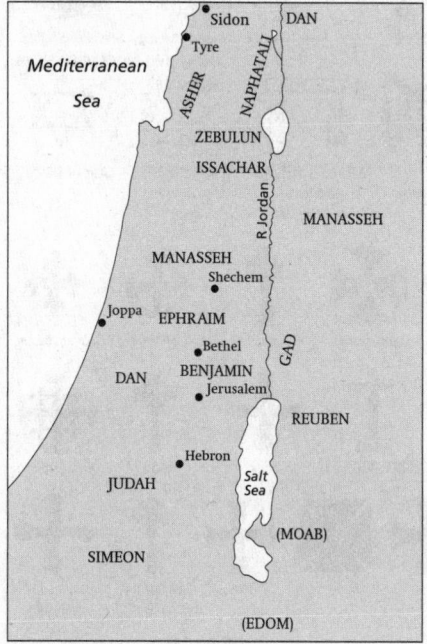

Shintoism

Founder
No founder

Date originated
6th-c AD, Japan

Beliefs
Polytheistic – belief in 'kami' (deities)
Sincerity arising from awareness of the divine
Spiritual and physical purification
Continuity/communion with ancestry

Major Japanese festivals

1–3	Jan	Oshogatsu (New Year)
3	Feb	Setsubun
3	Mar	Ohinamatsuri (Doll *or* Girls' Festival)
5	May	Tango no Sekku (Boys' Festival)
7	Jul	Hoshi matsuri *or* Tanabata (Star Festival)
13–15	Jul	Obon (Buddhist All Souls)
15	Nov	Shichi-go-San (Seven-five-three age celebrations for 7-year-old girls, 5-year-old boys, and 3-year-old girls)

Sikhism

Founder
Guru Nanak, AD 1469–1539

Date founded
c.15th-c AD, India

Beliefs
Unity of God; Birth, death, and rebirth; Guidance of the Guru to 'moksa' (release) and the way of God; Worship of the Adi Granth

Taoism

Founder
Lao Zi, 6th-c BC

Date founded
600 BC, China

Beliefs
Interaction of human society and the universe; Divine nature of sovereign; Cult of Heaven; Law of return; State of original purity; Worship of ancestors

The Templeton Prize for Progress in Religion

1973	Mother Teresa of Calcutta, India
1974	Brother Roger of Taizé France
1975	Dr Sarvepalli Radhakrishnan, India
1976	Leon Joseph Suenens, Cardinal, Belgium
1977	Chiara Lubich, Italy
1978	Rev Prof Thomas F Torrance, UK
1979	Nikkyo Niwano, Japan
1980	Prof Ralph Wendell Burhoe, USA
1981	Dame Cecily Saunders, UK
1982	Rev Dr Billy Graham, USA
1983	Alexander Solzhenitsyn, USSR
1984	Rev Michael Bourdeaux, UK
1985	Sir Alister Hardy, UK
1986	Rev Dr James I McCord, USA
1987	Rev Prof Stanley L Jaki, Hungary/USA
1988	Dr Inamullah Khan, Pakistan
1989	Very Rev Lord Macleod of Fiunary, UK; Prof Carl Friedrich von Weizsäcker, Germany
1990	Baba Amte, India Prof L Charles Birch, Australia
1991	Rt Hon Lord Jakobovits, UK
1992	Dr Kyung-Chik Han, South Korea
1993	Charles W Colson, USA
1994	Michael Novak, USA
1995	Paul Davies, UK
1996	William R(ohl) Bright, USA
1997	Pandurang Shastri Athavale, India
1998	Sir Sigmund Sternberg, Hungary
1999	Prof Ian Graeme Barbour, USA
2000	Prof Freeman Dyson, USA
2001	Rev Canon Dr Arthur Peacocke, USA
2002	Rev Dr John Polkinghorne, UK
2003	Holmes Rolston III, USA
2004	George F R Ellis, South Africa
2005	Charles H(ard) Townes, USA
2006	Prof John D Barrow, UK

RELIGION AND MYTHOLOGY

Religious symbols

The Trinity

 Equilateral triangle

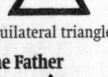 Triangle in circle

 Circle within triangle

 Trefoil

 Triquetra

 Triquetra and circle

 Interwoven circles

God the Father

 All-seeing eye

 Hand of God

 Hand of God

God the Son

 Lamb of God

 Fish

God the Holy Spirit

 Dove descending

 Sevenfold flame

Old Testament

 Menorah (seven branch candlestick)

 Abraham

 The Ten Commandments

 Pentateuch (The Law)

 Marked doorposts and lintel (Passover)

 Twelve tribes of Israel

Modern Judaism

 Star of David

Crosses

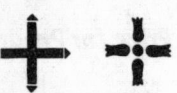

| Aiguisée | Avellane | Barbée | Trefly | Canterbury | Celtic | Cercelée | Cross crosslet |

| Crux ansata | Entrailed | Fleurée | Globical | Graded (Calvary) | Greek | Iona | Jerusalem |

| Latin | Maltese | Millvine | Papal | Patée | Patée formée | Patonce | Patriarchal (or Lorraine) | Pommel or Pommée |

   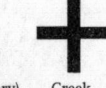

| Potent | Raguly or Ragulée | Russian Orthodox | St Andrew's (Saltire) | St Peter's | Tau (St Anthony's) |

Monograms

IHC (Latin form) (from Gk IHCOYC 'Jesus')

Chi Rho (from Gk XPICTOC 'Christ')

The Christian Church Year

| Advent | Christmas | Epiphany | Lent | Maundy Thursday | Good Friday | Easter Day | Ascension | Pentecost |

Other symbols

           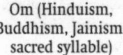

| Ankh (Egyptian) | Yin-yang Tao symbol of harmony | Torii (Shinto) | Om (Hinduism, Buddhism, Jainism; sacred syllable) | Ik-onkar (Sikhism; symbol of God) | Swastika (originally symbol of the Sun) | Yantra: Sri Cakra (wheel of fortune) |

PART TEN

Communications

TRANSPORTATION

Road

Main USA Interstate highways

Odd-number Interstates run South–North; even-number, West–East.

I5	San Diego–Los Angeles–Sacramento–Seattle–Vancouver
I8	San Diego–Tucson
I10	Los Angeles–Phoenix–San Antonio–Houston–New Orleans–Jacksonville
I15	San Diego–Las Vegas–Salt Lake City–Great Falls
I20	Fort Worth–Dallas–Jackson–Birmingham–Atlanta–Columbia
I25	Albuquerque–Colorado Springs–Denver–Buffalo
I30	Dallas–Little Rock
I35	San Antonio–Austin–Fort Worth–Oklahoma City–Wichita–Kansas City–Des Moines–Minneapolis/St Paul–Duluth
I40	Flagstaff–Albuquerque–Oklahoma City–Little Rock–Memphis–Nashville–Greensboro
I45	Dallas–Houston
I55	New Orleans–Jackson–Memphis–St Louis–Chicago
I59	New Orleans–Birmingham–Chattanooga
I64	St Louis–Louisville–Lexington–Charleston
I65	Mobile–Birmingham–Nashville–Louisville–Indianapolis–Chicago
I70	Denver–Kansas City–St Louis–Indianapolis–Columbus–Philadelphia–Baltimore
I71	Louisville–Cincinatti–Columbus
I74	Davenport–Indianapolis–Cincinatti
I75	Tampa–Atlanta–Cincinatti–Toledo–Detroit
I78	Harrisburg–New York
I80	San Francisco–Salt Lake City–Des Moines–Cleveland–New York
I81	Knoxville–Roanoake–Syracuse
I85	Montgomery–Atlanta–Greensboro–Petersburg
I90	Seattle–Billings–Sioux Falls–Chicago–Cleveland–Boston
I94	Billings–Bismarck–Minneapolis/St Paul–Madison–Milwaukee–Chicago–Detroit
I95	Miami–Jacksonville–Richmond–Washington, DC–Baltimore–New York–Boston–Augusta

British motorways

M1	Belfast–Dungannon (N Ireland)
M1	London–Northampton–Leicester–Nottingham–Sheffield–Leeds
M2	Belfast–Randalstown (N Ireland)
M2	Strood–Faversham (Medway)
M3	London–Basingstoke–Winchester
M4	London–Reading–Newport–Cardiff–Swansea
M5	Birmingham–Bristol–Exeter
M6	Birmingham–Wolverhampton–Stoke-on-Trent–Preston–Lancaster–Carlisle
M8	Edinburgh–Glasgow–Langbank
M9	Edinburgh–Stirling
M10	M1–St Albans spur
M11	London–Cambridge
M18	Rotherham–M62 junction 35 (Goole)
M20	Swanley (London)–Folkestone
M23	Redhill–Crawley
M25	London orbital motorway
M26	Chipstead–M20 junction 3
M27	Portsmouth–Southampton–Cadnam
M32	M4–Bristol spur
M40	London–Oxford–Birmingham
M42	Birmingham–Solihull–Tamworth–Appleby Magna
M45	Watford–Dunchurch
M50	Ross-on-Wye–M5 junction 8
M53	Chester–Wallasey
M54	Telford–M6 junction 10a
M55	Fulwood–Blackpool
M56	Chester–Altrincham (N Cheshire)
M57	Liverpool–Aintree
M58	Aintree–Wigan
M61	Manchester–Preston
M62	Liverpool–Manchester–Leeds–North Cave (N Humberside)
M63	Salford–Stockport
M65	Blackburn–Burnley–Colne
M66	Middleton–Ramsbottom
M67	Denton–Mottram in Langendale (Manchester ring)
M69	Leicester–Coventry
M73	M74–Glasgow spur (Maryville–Mollisburn)
M74	Millbank–Maryville
M74	Carlisle–Gretna Green
M80	Longcroft–M9 junction 9 (Haggs)
M85	M90–Perth spur (Perth–Friarton Bridge)
M90	Perth–Inverkeithing
M180	Stainforth–Elsham (S Humberside)
M181	M180–Scunthorpe spur
M271	M27–Totton spur
M275	M27–Portsmouth spur
M606	M62–Bradford spur
M621	M62–Leeds spur
M876	M80–Kincardine Bridge (Banknock–Stenhousemuir)

International E-routes (Euroroutes)

Reference and intermediate roads (class A roads) have two-digit numbers; branch, link, and connecting roads (class B roads, not listed here), have three-digit numbers.

North–South orientated reference roads have two-digit odd numbers ending in the figure 5, and increasing from west to east. East–West orientated reference roads have two-digit even numbers ending in the figure 0, and increasing from north to south.

Intermediate roads have two-digit odd numbers (for N–S roads) or two-digit even numbers (for E–W roads) falling within the numbers of the reference roads between which they are located.

Only a selection of the towns and cities linked by E-roads given.

[···] indicates a sea crossing.

West–East orientation

Reference roads

E10	Narvik–Kiruna–Luleå
E20	Shannon–Dublin ··· Liverpool–Hull ··· Esbjerg–Nyborg ··· Korsør-Køge–Copenhagen ··· Malmö–Stockholm ··· Tallin–St Petersburg

COMMUNICATIONS

COMMUNICATIONS

Road (continued)

E30   Cork–Rosslare ··· Fishguard–London–Felixstowe
      ··· Hook of Holland–Utrecht–Hanover–
      Berlin–Warsaw–Smolensk–Moscow
E40   Calais–Brussels–Aachen–Cologne–Dresden–
      Krakow–Kiev–Rostov na Donu
E50   Brest–Paris–Metz–Nurenberg–Prague–
      Mukačevo
E60   Brest–Tours–Besançon–Basle–Innsbruck–
      Vienna–Budapest–Bucharest–Constanţ
E70   La Coruña–Bilbao–Bordeaux–Lyon–Torino–
      Verona–Trieste–Zagreb–Belgrade–
      Bucharest–Varna
E80   Lisbon–Coimbra–Salamanca–Pau–Toulouse–
      Nice–Genoa–Rome–Pescara ··· Dubrovnik–
      Sofia–Istanbul–Erzincan–Iran
E90   Lisbon–Madrid–Barcelona ··· Mazara del
      Vallo–Messina ··· Reggio di Calabria–Brindisi
      ··· Igoumenitsa–Thessaloniki–Gelibolu ···
      Lapseki–Ankara–Iraq

Intermediate roads
E06   Olderfjord–Kirkenes
E12   Mo i Rana–Umeå ··· Vaasa–Helsinki
E14   Trondheim–Sundsvall
E16   Londonderry–Belfast ··· Glasgow–Edinburgh
E18   Craigavon–Larne ··· Stranraer–Newcastle ···
      Stavanger–Oslo–Stockholm–Kappelskär ···
      Mariehamnţ Turku–Helsinki–Leningrad
E22   Holyhead–Manchester–Immingham ···
      Amsterdam–Hamburg–Sassnitz ···
      Trelleborg–Norrköping
E24   Birmingham–Ipswich
E26   Hamburg–Berlin
E28   Berlin–Gdańsk
E32   Colchester–Harwich
E34   Antwerp–Bad Oeynhausen
E36   Berlin–Legnica
E42   Dunkirk–Aschaffenburg
E44   Le Havre–Luxembourg–Giessen
E46   Cherbourg–Liège
E48   Schweinfurt–Prague
E52   Strasbourg–Salzburg
E54   Paris–Basle–Munich
E56   Nuremberg–Sattledt
E58   Vienna–Bratislava
E62   Nantes–Geneva–Tortona
E64   Turin–Brescia
E66   Fortezza–Székesfehérvár
E68   Szeged–Braşov
E72   Bordeaux–Toulouse
E74   Nice–Alessandria
E76   Migliarino–Florence
E78   Grosseto–Fano
E82   Porto–Tordesillas
E84   Keşan–Silivri
E86   Krystalopigi–Yefira
E88   Ankara–Refahiye
E92   Igoumenitsa–Volos
E94   Corinth–Athens
E96   Izmir–Sivrihisar
E98   Topbogazi–Syria

North–South orientation

Reference roads
E05   Greenock–Birmingham–Southampton ···
      Le Havre–Paris–Bordeaux–Madrid–Algeciras
E15   Inverness–Edinburgh–London–Dover ···
      Calais–Paris–Lyon–Barcelona–Algeciras
E25   Hook of Holland–Luxembourg–Strasbourg–
      Basle–Geneva–Turin–Genoa
E35   Amsterdam–Cologne–Basle–Milan–Rome
E45   Gothenburg ··· Frederikshavn–Hamburg–
      Munich–Innsbruck–Bologna–Rome–Naples–
      Villa S Giovanni ··· Messina–Gela
E55   Kemi-Tornio–Stockholm–Helsingborg ···
      Helsinger–Copenhagen–Gedser ··· Rostock–
      Berlin–Prague–Salzburg–Rimini–Brindisi ···
      Igoumenitsa–Kalamata
E65   Malmö–Ystrad–Świnoujście–Prague–Zagreb–
      Dubrovnik–Bitolj–Antirrion ··· Rion–
      Kalamata – Kissamos–Chania
E75   Karasjok–Helsinki ··· Gdańsk–Budapest–
      Belgrade–Athens ··· Chania–Sitia
E85   Černovcy–Bucharest–Alexandropouli
E95   St Petersburg–Moscow–Yalta

Intermediate roads
E01   Larne–Dublin–Rosslare ··· La Coruña–Lisbon–
      Seville
E03   Cherbourg–La Rochelle
E07   Pau–Zaragoza
E09   Orléans–Barcelona
E11   Vierzon–Montpellier
E13   Doncaster–London
E17   Antwerp–Beaune
E19   Amsterdam–Brussels–Paris
E21   Metz–Geneva
E23   Metz–Lausanne
E27   Belfort–Aosta
E29   Cologne–Sarreguemines
E31   Rotterdam–Ludwigshafen
E33   Parma–La Spezia
E37   Bremen–Cologne
E39   Kristiansand–Aalborg
E41   Dortmund–Altdorf
E43   Würzburg–Bellinzona
E47   Nordkap–Oslo–Copenhagen–Rødby ···
      Puttgarden–Lübeck
E49   Magdeburg–Vienna
E51   Berlin–Nurenberg
E53   Plzeň–Munich
E57   Sattledt–Ljubljana
E59   Prague–Zagreb
E61   Klagenfurt–Rijeka
E63   Sodankylä–Naantali ··· Stockholm–Gothenburg
E67   Warsaw–Prague
E69   Tromsø–Tornio
E71   Košice–Budapest–Split
E73   Budapest–Metkovič
E77   Gdańsk–Budapest
E79   Oradea–Calafat ··· Vidin–Thessaloniki
E81   Halmeu–Piteşti
E83   Bjala–Sofia
E87   Tulcea–Eceabat ··· Çanakkale–Antalya
E89   Gerede–Ankara
E91   Toprakkale–Syria
E93   Orel–Odessa
E97   Trabzon–Aşkale
E99   Doğubeyazit– ŞUrfa

European road distances

Road distances between some cities, given in kilometres. To convert to statute miles, multiply number given by 0.6214.

	Athens	Barcelona	Brussels	Calais	Cherbourg	Cologne	Copenhagen	Geneva	Gibraltar	Hamburg	Hook of Holland	Lisbon	Lyons	Madrid	Marseilles	Milan	Munich	Paris	Rome	Stockholm
Barcelona	3313																			
Brussels	2963	1318																		
Calais	3175	1326	204																	
Cherbourg	3339	1294	583	460																
Cologne	2762	1498	206	409	785															
Copenhagen	3276	2218	966	1136	1545	760														
Geneva	2610	803	677	747	853	1662	1418													
Gibraltar	4485	1172	2256	2224	2047	2436	3196	1975												
Hamburg	2977	2018	597	714	1115	460	460	1118	2897											
Hook of Holland	3030	1490	172	330	731	269	269	895	2428	550										
Lisbon	4532	1304	2084	2052	1827	2290	2971	1936	676	2671	2280									
Lyons	2753	645	690	739	789	714	1458	158	1817	1159	863	1778								
Madrid	3949	636	1558	1550	1347	1764	2498	1439	698	2198	1730	668	1281							
Marseilles	2865	521	1011	1059	1101	1035	1778	425	1693	1479	1183	1762	320	1157						
Milan	2282	1014	925	1077	1209	911	1537	328	2185	1238	1098	2250	328	1724	618					
Munich	2179	1365	747	977	1160	583	1104	591	2565	805	851	2507	724	2010	1109	331				
Paris	3000	1033	285	280	340	465	1176	513	1971	877	457	1799	471	1273	792	856	821			
Rome	817	1460	1511	1662	1794	1497	2050	995	2631	1751	1683	2700	1048	2097	1011	586	946	1476		
Stockholm	3927	2868	1616	1786	2196	1403	650	2068	3886	949	1500	3231	2108	3188	2428	2187	1754	1827	2707	
Vienna	1991	1802	1175	1381	1588	937	1455	1019	2974	1155	1205	2935	1157	2409	1363	898	428	1249	1209	2105

UK road distances

Road distances between British centres are given in statute miles, using routes recommended by the Automobile Association based on the quickest travelling time. To convert to kilometres, multiply number given by 1.6093.

	Aberdeen	Birmingham	Bristol	Cambridge	Cardiff	Dover	Edinburgh	Exeter	Glasgow	Holyhead	Hull	Leeds	Liverpool	Manchester	Newcastle	Norwich	Nottingham	Oxford	Penzance	Plymouth	Shrewsbury	Southampton	Stranraer	York
Birmingham	433																							
Bristol	516	88																						
Cambridge	464	98	171																					
Cardiff	536	108	48	205																				
Dover	589	208	206	124	241																			
Edinburgh	125	298	381	336	401	461																		
Exeter	589	161	83	250	121	244	454																	
Glasgow	148	296	379	356	399	499	46	454																
Holyhead	462	168	251	260	206	370	327	325	325															
Hull	360	141	232	140	252	264	232	306	268	220														
Leeds	328	121	212	148	231	272	200	286	220	165	60													
Liverpool	360	101	184	193	204	303	225	258	223	102	129	74												
Manchester	355	89	172	161	191	291	220	246	218	122	99	44	35											
Newcastle upon Tyne	236	211	302	233	322	357	108	376	153	268	145	97	177	147										
Norwich	488	159	233	63	266	173	360	313	380	305	151	173	241	185	257									
Nottingham	394	54	145	87	165	218	266	219	286	174	93	74	108	71	163	119								
Oxford	505	68	74	100	109	146	370	154	368	239	190	171	173	160	260	143	103							
Penzance	699	271	194	361	231	356	564	109	562	433	415	395	367	355	484	422	328	264						
Plymouth	631	203	125	292	162	287	496	45	494	365	346	327	299	286	416	354	259	195	77					
Shrewsbury	415	48	131	140	110	251	280	205	278	104	163	118	66	70	221	202	86	121	315	246				
Southampton	572	134	76	131	141	152	437	112	434	305	257	237	239	227	327	193	170	66	223	155	187			
Stranraer	240	307	390	367	409	509	132	464	85	335	279	230	233	228	164	391	297	380	573	505	288	446		
York	321	134	226	157	245	281	193	300	213	191	38	24	101	71	90	181	87	184	409	341	145	250	224	
London	548	120	120	60	155	78	413	200	411	282	188	199	216	203	288	115	131	56	310	241	163	80	421	212

COMMUNICATIONS

Road (continued)

International car index marks

A	Austria	ETH	Ethiopia	MW	Malawi[a]	SGP	Singapore[a]
ADN	former Yemen PDR	F	France	N	Norway	SK	Slovakia
AFG	Afghanistan	FJI	Fiji[a]	NA	Netherlands	SL	Slovenia
AL	Albania	FL	Liechtenstein		Antilles	SME	Suriname[a]
AND	Andorra	FR	Faroe Is	NEP	Nepal	SN	Senegal
ARM	Armenia	GB	UK[a]	NIC	Nicaragua	SO	Somalia
AUS	Australia[a]	GBA	Alderney[a]	NL	Netherlands	SU	former USSR
B	Belgium	GBG	Guernsey[a]	NZ	New Zealand[a]	SWA	Namibia[a]
BD	Bangladesh[a]	GBJ	Jersey[a]	P	Portugal	SY	Seychelles[a]
BDS	Barbados[a]	GBM	Isle of Man[a]	PA	Panama	SYR	Syria
BG	Bulgaria	GBZ	Gibraltar	PAK	Pakistan[a]	T	Thailand[a]
BH	Belize	GCA	Guatemala	PE	Peru	TG	Togo
BIH	Bosnia-	GH	Ghana	PL	Poland	TJ	Tajikistan
	Herzegovina	GR	Greece	PNG	Papua New Guinea[a]	TM	Turkmenistan
BR	Brazil	GUY	Guyana[a]	PY	Paraguay	TN	Tunisia
BRN	Bahrain	H	Hungary	RA	Argentina	TR	Turkey
BRU	Brunei[a]	HK	Hong Kong[a]	RB	Botswana[a]	TT	Trinidad and
BS	Bahamas[a]	HKJ	Jordan	RC	Taiwan		Tobago[a]
BUR	Myanmar (Burma)	HR	Croatia	RCA	Central African	USA	USA
C	Cuba	I	Italy		Republic	V	Vatican City
CDN	Canada	IL	Israel	RCB,	Congo, Dem.	VN	Vietnam
CH	Switzerland	IND	India[a]	ZRE	Rep. of	WAG	Gambia
CI	Côte d'Ivoire	IR	Iran		(formerly Zaire)	WAL	Sierra Leone
CL	Sri Lanka[a]	IRL	Ireland[a]	RCH	Chile	WAN	Nigeria
CO	Colombia	IRQ	Iraq	RG	Guinea	WD	Dominica[a]
CR	Costa Rica	IS	Iceland	RH	Haiti	WG	Grenada[a]
CZ	Czech Republic	J	Japan[a]	RI	Indonesia[a]	WL	St Lucia[a]
CY	Cyprus[a]	JA	Jamaica[a]	RIM	Mauritania	WS	W Samoa
D	Germany	KWT	Kuwait	RL	Lebanon	WV	St Vincent and the
DK	Denmark	KZ	Kazakhstan	RM	Madagascar		Grenadines[a]
DOM	Dominican	L	Luxembourg	RMM	Mali	YU	Yugoslavia
	Republic	LAO	Laos PDR	RN	Niger	YV	Venezuela
DY	Benin	LAR	Libya	RO	Romania	Z	Zambia[a]
DZ	Algeria	LB	Liberia	ROK	Korea, Republic of	ZA	South Africa[a]
E	Spain	LR	Latvia	ROU	Uruguay	ZW	Zimbabwe[a]
EAK	Kenya[a]	LS	Lesotho[a]	RP	Philippines		
EAT	Tanzania[a]	M	Malta[a]	RSM	San Marino	[a]Countries in which the rule
EAU	Uganda[a]	MA	Morocco	RU	Burundi	of the road is drive on the
EAZ	Tanzania[a]	MAL	Malaysia[a]	RWA	Rwanda	left; in other countries, drive
EC	Ecuador	MC	Monaco	S	Sweden	on the right.
ES	El Salvador	MEX	Mexico	SD	Swaziland[a]		
ET	Egypt	MS	Mauritius[a]	SF	Finland		

British car index marks (to Sep 2001)

AA	Bournemouth	AX	Cardiff	BT	Leeds	CP	Huddersfield
AB	Worcester	AY	Leicester	BU	Manchester	CR	Portsmouth
AC	Coventry	BA	Manchester	BV	Preston	CS	Glasgow
AD	Gloucester	BB	Newcastle upon	BW	Oxford	CT	Lincoln
AE	Bristol		Tyne	BX	Haverfordwest	CU	Newcastle upon
AF	Truro	BC	Leicester	BY	London NW		Tyne
AG	Hull	BD	Northampton	CA	Chester	CV	Truro
AH	Norwich	BE	Lincoln	CB	Manchester	CW	Preston
AJ	Middlesbrough	BF	Stoke-on-Trent	CC	Bangor	CX	Huddersfield
AK	Sheffield	BG	Liverpool	CD	Brighton	CY	Swansea
AL	Nottingham	BH	Luton	CE	Peterborough	DA	Birmingham
AM	Swindon	BJ	Ipswich	CF	Reading	DB	Manchester
AN	Reading	BK	Portsmouth	CG	Bournemouth	DC	Middlesbrough
AO	Carlisle	BL	Reading	CH	Nottingham	DD	Gloucester
AP	Brighton	BM	Luton	CJ	Gloucester	DE	Haverfordwest
AR	Chelmsford	BN	Manchester	CK	Preston	DF, DG	Gloucester
AS	Inverness	BO	Cardiff	CL	Norwich	DH	Dudley
AT	Hull	BP	Portsmouth	CM	Liverpool	DJ	Liverpool
AU	Nottingham	BR	Newcastle upon	CN	Newcastle upon	DK	Manchester
AV	Peterborough		Tyne		Tyne	DL	Portsmouth
AW	Shrewsbury	BS	Inverness	CO	Exeter	DM	Chester

DN	Leeds	GN–	London SW
DO	Lincoln	GP	
DP	Reading	GR	Newcastle upon Tyne
DR	Exeter	GS	Luton
DS	Glasgow	GT	London SW
DT	Sheffield	GU	London SE
DU	Coventry	GV	Ipswich
DV	Exeter	GW–	London SE
DW	Cardiff	GY	
DX	Ipswich	HA	Dudley
DY	Brighton	HB	Cardiff
EA	Dudley	HC	Brighton
EB	Peterborough	HD	Huddersfield
EC	Preston	HE	Sheffield
ED	Liverpool	HF	Liverpool
EE	Lincoln	HG	Preston
EF	Middlesbrough	HH	Carlisle
EG	Peterborough	HJ, HK	Chelmsford
EH	Stoke-on-Trent	HL	Sheffield
EJ	Haverfordwest	HM	London C
EK	Liverpool	HN	Middlesbrough
EL	Bournemouth	HO	Bournemouth
EM	Liverpool	HP	Coventry
EN	Manchester	HR	Swindon
EO	Preston	HS	Glasgow
EP	Swansea	HT, HU	Bristol
ER	Peterborough	HV	London C
ES	Dundee	HW	Bristol
ET	Sheffield	HX	London C
EU	Bristol	HY	Bristol
EV	Chelmsford	JA	Manchester
EW	Peterborough	JB	Reading
EX	Norwich	JC	Bangor
EY	Bangor	JD	London C
FA	Stoke-on-Trent	JE	Peterborough
FB	Bristol	JF	Leicester
FC	Oxford	JG	Maidstone
FD	Dudley	JH	Reading
FE	Lincoln	JJ	Maidstone
FF	Bangor	JK	Brighton
FG	Brighton	JL	Lincoln
FH	Gloucester	JM	Reading
FJ	Exeter	JN	Chelmsford
FK	Dudley	JO	Oxford
FL	Peterborough	JP	Liverpool
FM	Chester	JR	Newcastle upon Tyne
FN	Maidstone	JS	Inverness
FO	Gloucester	JT	Bournemouth
FP	Leicester	JU	Leicester
FR	Preston	JV	Lincoln
FS	Edinburgh	JW	Birmingham
FT	Newcastle upon Tyne	JX	Huddersfield
FU	Lincoln	JY	Exeter
FV	Preston	KA–	Liverpool
FW	Lincoln	KD	
FX	Bournemouth	KE	Maidstone
FY	Liverpool	KF	Liverpool
GA, GB	Glasgow	KG	Cardiff
GC	London SW	KH	Hull
GD, GE	Glasgow	KJ–	Maidstone
GF	London SW	KR	
GG	Glasgow	KS	Edinburgh
GH–	London SW	KT	Maidstone
GK		KU	Sheffield
GL	Truro	KV	Coventry
GM	Reading		

KW	Sheffield	PP	Luton
KX	Luton	PR	Bournemouth
KY	Sheffield	PS	Aberdeen
LA–LF	London NW	PT	Newcastle upon Tyne
LG	Chester	PU	Chelmsford
LH	London NW	PV	Ipswich
LJ	Bournemouth	PW	Norwich
LK–LR	London NW	PX	Portsmouth
LS	Edinburgh	PY	Middlesbrough
LT, LU	London NW	RA–RC	Nottingham
LV	Liverpool	RD	Reading
LW–LY	London NW	RE, RF	Stoke-on-Trent
MA	Chester	RG	Newcastle upon Tyne
MB	Chester	RH	Hull
MC–	London NE	RJ	Manchester
MH		RK	London NW
MJ	Luton	RL	Truro
MK–	London NE	RM	Carlisle
MM		RN	Preston
MN	*not used*	RO	Luton
MO	Reading	RP	Northampton
MP	London NE	RR	Nottingham
MR	Swindon	RS	Aberdeen
MS	Edinburgh	RT	Ipswich
MT–	London NE	RU	Bournemouth
MV		RV	Portsmouth
MW	Swindon	RW	Coventry
MX–	London SE	RX	Reading
MY		RY	Leicester
NA–	Manchester	SA	Aberdeen
NF		SB	Glasgow
NG	Norwich	SC	Edinburgh
NH	Northampton	SCY	Truro (Isles of Scilly)
NJ	Brighton	SD	Glasgow
NK	Luton	SE	Aberdeen
NL	Newcastle upon Tyne	SF–SH	Edinburgh
NM	Luton	SJ	Glasgow
NN	Nottingham	SK	Inverness
NO	Chelmsford	SL	Dundee
NP	Worcester	SM	Glasgow
NR	Leicester	SN	Dundee
NS	Glasgow	SO	Aberdeen
NT	Shrewsbury	SP–SR	Dundee
NU	Nottingham	SS	Aberdeen
NV	Northampton	ST	Inverness
NW	Leeds	SU	Glasgow
NX	Dudley	SV	*spare*
NY	Cardiff	SW	Glasgow
OA–	Birmingham	SX	Edinburgh
OC		SY	*spare*
OD	Exeter	TA	Exeter
OE–	Birmingham	TB	Liverpool
ON		TC	Bristol
OO	Chelmsford	TD, TE	Manchester
OP	Birmingham	TF	Reading
OR	Portsmouth	TG	Cardiff
OS	Glasgow	TH	Swansea
OT	Portsmouth	TJ	Liverpool
OU	Bristol	TK	Exeter
OV	Birmingham	TL	Lincoln
OW	Portsmouth	TM	Luton
OX	Birmingham	TN	Newcastle upon Tyne
OY	London NW	TO	Nottingham
PA–PM	Guildford		
PN	Brighton		
PO	Portsmouth		

Road (continued)

TP, TR	Portsmouth	UP	Newcastle upon Tyne	VO	Nottingham	WO	Cardiff
TS	Dundee			VP	Birmingham	WP	Worcester
TT	Exeter	UR	Luton	VR	Manchester	WR	Leeds
TU	Chester	US	Glasgow	VS	Luton	WS	Bristol
TV	Nottingham	UT	Leicester	VT	Stoke-on-Trent	WT, WU	Leeds
TW	Chelmsford	UU– UW	London C	VU	Manchester		
TX	Cardiff			VV	Northampton	WV	Brighton
TY	Newcastle upon Tyne	UX	Shrewsbury	VW, VX	Chelmsford	WW– WY	Leeds
UA, UB	Leeds	UY	Worcester				
UC	London C	VA	Peterborough	VY	Leeds	YA–YD	Taunton
UD	Oxford	VB	Maidstone	WA, WB	Sheffield	YE, YF	London C
UE	Dudley	VC	Coventry			YG	Leeds
UF	Brighton	VD	*series withdrawn*	WC	Chelmsford	YH	London C
UG	Leeds	VE	Peterborough	WD	Dudley	YJ	Brighton
UH	Cardiff	VF, VG	Norwich	WE– WG	Sheffield	YK–YR	London C
UJ	Shrewsbury	VH	Huddersfield			YS	Glasgow
UK	Birmingham	VJ	Gloucester	WH	Manchester	YT–YY	London C
UL	London C	VK	Newcastle upon Tyne	WJ	Sheffield		
UM	Leeds			WK	Coventry		
UN, UO	Exeter	VL	Lincoln	WL	Oxford	I, Q, and Z are not used as second elements in the above system.	
		VM	Manchester	WM	Liverpool		
		VN	Middlesbrough	WN	Swansea		

British car index marks (from Sep 2001)

Local memory tags		*Local offices*	*DVLA Local office identifier*
A	Anglia	Peterborough	AA AB AC AD AE AF AG AH AJ AK AL AM AN
		Norwich	AO AP AR AS AT AU
		Ipswich	AV AW AX AY
B	Birmingham	Birmingham	BA–BY
C	Cymru	Cardiff	CA CB CC CD CE CF CG CH CJ CK CL CM CN CO
		Swansea	CP CR CS CT CU CV
		Bangor	CW CX CY
D	Deeside to Shrewsbury	Chester	DA DB DC DD DE DF DG DH DJ DK
		Shrewsbury	DL DM DN DO DP DR DS DT DU DV DW DX DY
E	Essex	Chelmsford	EA–EY
F	Forest & Fens	Nottingham	FA FB FC FD FE FF FG FH FJ FK FL FM FN FP
		Lincoln	FR FS FT FV FW FX FY
G	Garden of England	Maidstone	GA GB GC GD GE GF GG GH GJ GK GL GM GN GO
		Brighton	GP GR GS GT GU GV GW GX GY
	Hampshire & Dorset	Bournemouth	HA HB HC HD HE HF HG HH HJ
		Portsmouth	HK HL HM HN HO HP HR HS HT HU HV HW HX HY
			(HW will be used exclusively for Isle of Wight residents)
K		Luton	KA KB KC KD KE KF KG KH KJ KK KL
		Northampton	KM KN KO KP KR KS KT KU KV KW KX KY
L	London	Wimbledon	LA LB LC LD LE LF LG LH LJ
		Stanmore	LK LL LM LN LO LP LR LS LT
		Sidcup	LU LV LW LX LY
M	Manchester	Manchester & Merseyside	MA–MY
N	North	Newcastle	NA NB NC ND NE NG NH NJ NK NL NM NN NO
		Stockton	NP NR NS NT NU NV NW NX NY
O	Oxford	Oxford	OA–OY
P	Preston	Preston	PA PB PC PD PE PF PG PH PJ PK PL PM PN PO PP PR PS PT
		Carlisle	PU PV PW PX PY
R	Reading	Reading	RA–RY
S	Scotland	Glasgow	SA SB SC SD SE SF SG SH SJ
		Edinburgh	SK SL SM SN SO
		Dundee	SP SR SS ST
		Aberdeen	SU SV SW
		Inverness	SX SY

V	Severn Valley	Worcester	VA–VY
W	West of England	Exeter	WA WB WC WD WE WF WG WH WJ
		Truro	WK WL
		Bristol	WM WN WO WP WR WS WT WU WV WW WX WY
Y	Yorkshire	Leeds	YA YB YC YD YE YF YG YH YJ YK
		Sheffield	YL YM YN YO YP YR YS YT YU
		Beverley	YV YW YX YY

Age identifiers

Date	Code	Date			Code
		Sept	2001–Feb	2002	51
March 2002–Aug 2002	02	Sept	2002–Feb	2003	52
March 2003–Aug 2003	03	Sept	2003–Feb	2004	53
March 2004–Aug 2004	04	Sept	2004–Feb	2005	54
March 2005–Aug 2005	05	Sept	2005–Feb	2006	55
March 2006–Aug 2006	06	Sept	2006–Feb	2007	56
March 2007–Aug 2007	07	Sept	2007–Feb	2008	57
March 2008–Aug 2008	08	Sept	2008–Feb	2009	58
March 2009–Aug 2009	09	Sept	2009–Feb	2010	59
March 2010–Aug 2010	10	Sept	2010–Feb	2011	60
March 2011–Aug 2011	11	Sept	2011–Feb	2012	61

This pattern will continue until all permutations are exhausted.

Fastest cars

Name of car	Speed		Date	Type
	(km/h)	(mph)		
Thrust	1229.775	764.168	1997	Jet-powered
Speed-O-Motive/Spirit 76	696.331	432.692	1991	Single-piston engine
Bluebird	690.909	429.054	1964	Gas-turbine engine
Jaguar XJ 220	341	212.3	1991	Piston-engined
Electric car	111.40	69.21	1991	Electricity-poweredNo.
744 Steamin' Demon	234.33	145.607	1985	Steam-powered
Electric car	111.40	69.21	1991	Electricity-powered

British road signs

Instruction signs

Generally circular. A red border circle indicates a prohibition; blue signs indicate permitted activities.

Entry to
20 mph zone

End of
20 mph zone

School crossing
patrol

Maximum speed

National speed
limit applies

Stop and
give way

Give way to traffic
on major road

No vehicles

No entry for
vehicular traffic

No right turn

No left turn

No U-turns

Instruction signs (continued)

No overtaking

Give priority to vehicles from opposite direction

No motor vehicles

No motor vehicles except solo motorcycles, scooters or mopeds

Manually operated temporary 'STOP' sign

Up to 31.12.96: No vehicles with over 12 seats except regular scheduled, school and works buses. From 1.1.97 No buses (over 8 seats)

No cycling

No pedestrians

No goods vehicles over maximum gross weight shown (in tonnes)

No vehicle or combination of vehicles over length shown

No vehicles over height shown

No vehicles over width shown

No vehicles over maximum gross weight shown (in tonnes)

No horses

No stopping (clearway)

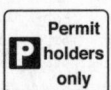
Parking restricted to use by people named on sign

No stopping during times shown except for as long as necessary to set down or pick up passengers

Qualifications

End of restriction

Exception for loading/unloading goods

Exception for regular scheduled, school and work buses

Exception for access to premises and land adjacent to the road where there is no alternative route

Warning signs

Generally triangular.

Distance to 'STOP' line ahead

Crossroads

Junction on bend ahead

T-junction

Staggered junction

Distance to 'GIVE WAY' line ahead

Sharp deviation of route to left (or right if chevrons reversed)

Double bend first to left (symbol may be reversed)

Bend to right (or left if symbol reversed)

Roundabout

Uneven road

Plate below some signs

Dual carriageway ends

Road narrows on right (left if symbol reversed)

Road narrows on both sides

Two-way traffic crosses one-way road

Two-way traffic straight ahead

Traffic signals

 Failure of traffic light signals

 Slippery road

 Steep hill downwards

 Steep hill upwards

Gradients may be shown as a rate eg 20° = 1.5

 School

Children going to or from school

Patrol

School crossing patrol ahead (some signs have amber lights which flash when children are crossing)

 Elderly people

Elderly people (or blind or disabled as shown) crossing road

 No footway for 400 yds

Pedestrians in road ahead

 Pedestrians crossing

 Cycle route ahead

 Side winds

 Hump bridge

Ford

Worded warning sign

Ice

Risk of ice

 Risk of grounding

 STOP when lights show — Light signals ahead at level crossing, airfield or bridge

 Light crossing with barrier or gate ahead

 Light crossing without barrier or gate ahead

 Light crossing without barrier

 Trams crossing ahead

 Cattle

 Wild animals

Wild horses or ponies

Accompanied horses or ponies

Quayside or river bank

 Opening or swing bridge ahead

 Low-flying aircraft or sudden aircraft noise

 Falling or fallen rocks

 14'6" 4.4m — Available width of headroom indicated

 Safe height 16'6" — Overhead electric cable; plate indicates maximum height of vehicles which can pass safely

 1 mile — Distance to tunnel

 Humps for ½ mile — Distance over which road humps extend

 Hidden dip — Other danger; plate indicates nature of danger

 Soft verges for 2 miles — Soft verges

COMMUNICATIONS

Road (continued)

Some European road signs

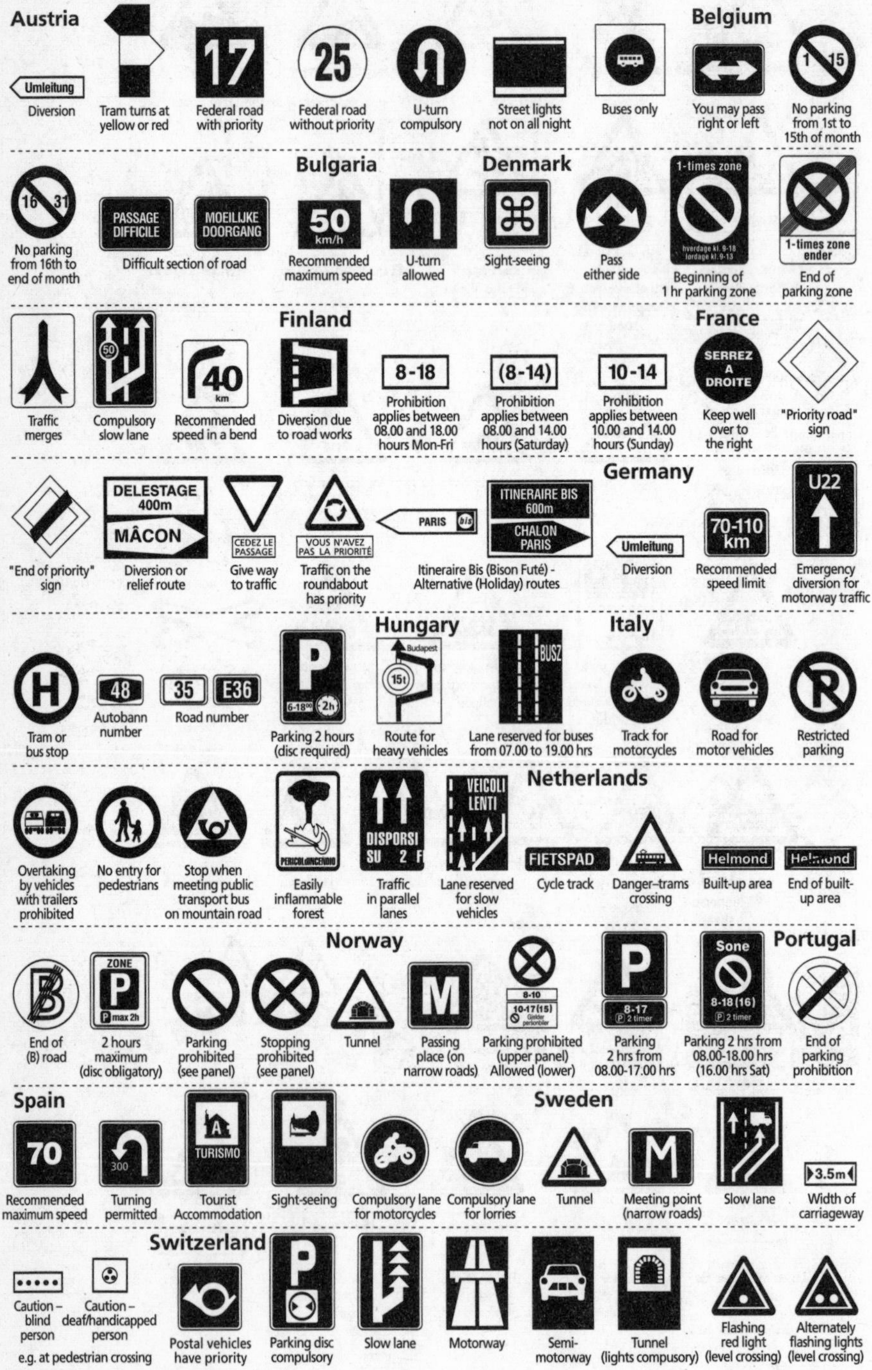

Austria

Diversion — Tram turns at yellow or red — Federal road with priority — Federal road without priority — U-turn compulsory — Street lights not on all night — Buses only

Belgium

You may pass right or left — No parking from 1st to 15th of month

 No parking from 16th to end of month

Bulgaria

 PASSAGE DIFFICILE / MOEILIJKE DOORGANG Difficult section of road
 Recommended maximum speed
 U-turn allowed

Denmark

 Sight-seeing
 Pass either side
 Beginning of 1 hr parking zone
 End of parking zone

Finland

 Traffic merges
 Compulsory slow lane
Recommended speed in a bend
Diversion due to road works
 8-18 Prohibition applies between 08.00 and 18.00 hours Mon-Fri
(8-14) Prohibition applies between 08.00 and 14.00 hours (Saturday)
10-14 Prohibition applies between 10.00 and 14.00 hours (Sunday)

France

 SERREZ A DROITE Keep well over to the right
 "Priority road" sign

 "End of priority" sign
 DELESTAGE 400m MÂCON Diversion or relief route
CEDEZ LE PASSAGE Give way to traffic
 VOUS N'AVEZ PAS LA PRIORITÉ Traffic on the roundabout has priority
 ITINERAIRE BIS 600m CHALON PARIS / PARIS bis — Itineraire Bis (Bison Futé) - Alternative (Holiday) routes

Germany

 Umleitung Diversion
 70-110 km Recommended speed limit
 U22 Emergency diversion for motorway traffic

Hungary

 Tram or bus stop
48 Autobahn number
35 E36 Road number
 Parking 2 hours (disc required)
 Budapest Route for heavy vehicles

Italy

 BUSZ Lane reserved for buses from 07.00 to 19.00 hrs
 Track for motorcycles
Road for motor vehicles
 Restricted parking

 Overtaking by vehicles with trailers prohibited
 No entry for pedestrians
 Stop when meeting public transport bus on mountain road
 PERICOLO INCENDIO Easily inflammable forest
 DISPOSI SU 2 F Traffic in parallel lanes
 VEICOLI LENTI Lane reserved for slow vehicles

Netherlands

 FIETSPAD Cycle track
 Danger–trams crossing
 Helmond Built-up area
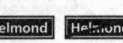 Helmond End of built-up area

Norway

 End of (B) road
 ZONE P max 2h 2 hours maximum (disc obligatory)
 Parking prohibited (see panel)
 Stopping prohibited (see panel)
 Tunnel
 M Passing place (on narrow roads)
 8-10 10-17(15) Parking prohibited (upper panel) Allowed (lower)
 P 8-17 Parking 2 hrs from 08.00-17.00 hrs

Portugal

 Sone 8-18(16) Parking 2 hrs from 08.00-18.00 hrs (16.00 hrs Sat)
 End of parking prohibition

Spain

 70 Recommended maximum speed
 300 Turning permitted
 TURISMO Tourist Accommodation
 Sight-seeing
 Compulsory lane for motorcycles
Compulsory lane for lorries

Sweden

 Tunnel
M Meeting point (narrow roads)
Slow lane
 3.5m Width of carriageway

Switzerland

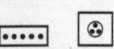 Caution – blind person e.g. at pedestrian crossing
 Caution – deaf/handicapped person
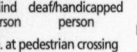 Postal vehicles have priority
 P Parking disc compulsory
 Slow lane
 Motorway
 Semi-motorway
 Tunnel (lights compulsory)
 Flashing red light (level crossing)
 Alternately flashing lights (level crossing)

USA road signs

Instruction signs

 Stop

 4-way stop

 Do not enter

 Yield

 Wrong way

 No right turn

 No U-turn

 One way

 Speed limit

 Speed zone ahead

 Slower traffic keep right

 Speed limit with minimum limit posted

 School speed limit

 Divided highway

 Two-way left-turn lanes

 No turn on red

Warning signs

 Crossroads

 Side road

 Divided highway

 Two-way traffic

 Merge

 Railroad crossing

 No passing zone

 Narrow bridge

 Road curves

 Right reverse turn

 Winding road

 Stop ahead

 Yield ahead

 School crossing

 School zone

 Pedestrian crossing

 Steep downgrade

 Slippery when wet

 Low clearance

 Truck crossing

 Deer crossing

 Cattle crossing

 Farm machinery

 No bicycles

 Road construction

 Flagperson ahead

 Freeway exit ramp speed limit

Services signs

 Rest area

 Telephone

 Hospital

 Campground

 Trailer sites

Rail

UK rail travel times

Intercity routes in the UK; times are given in hours and minutes for typical weekday services (2002).

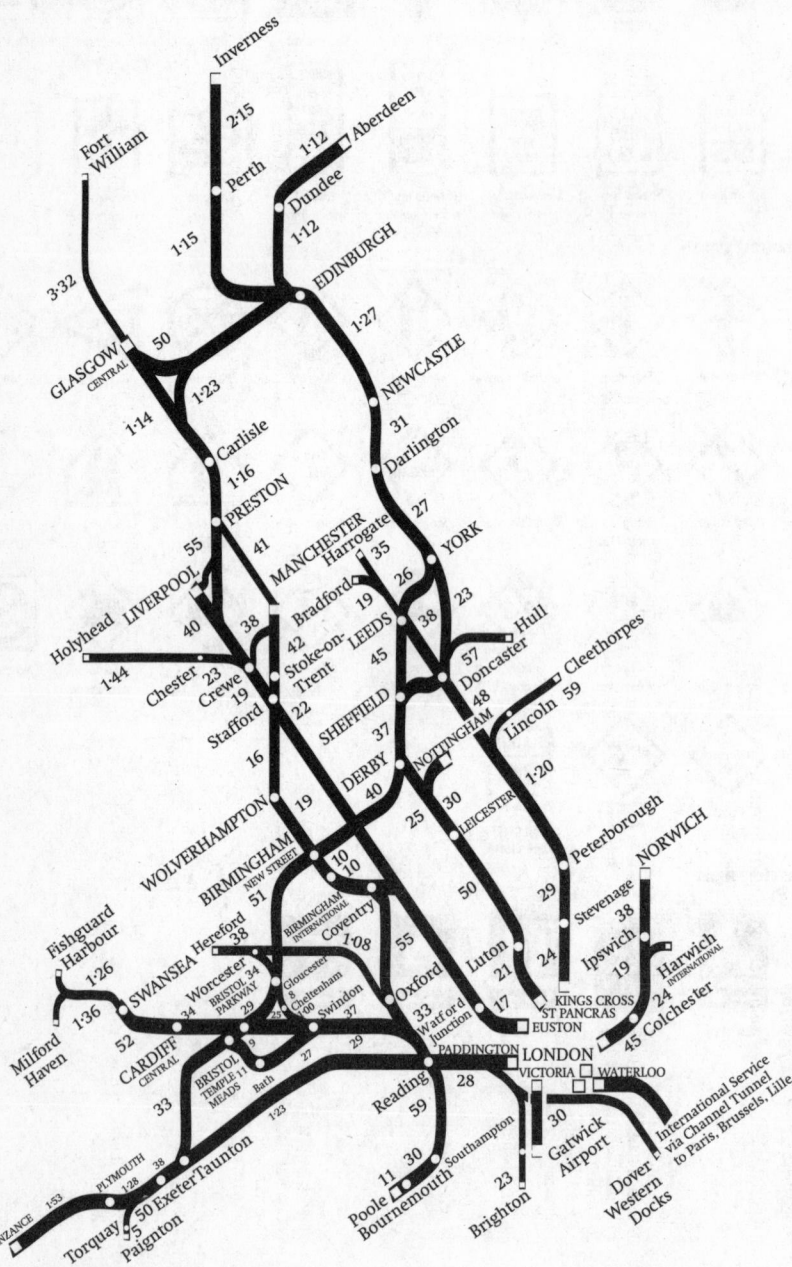

British locomotive classification

This list illustrates the range of diesel and electric locomotives operating on British Railways 1953–92.

Locomotive	Built	Weight (tonnes)	Transmission	Maximum tractive effort (lb)	Maximum speed (mph)	Engine	Wheel diameter
Class 03 British Rail shunter 0-6-0	1958-62	31	Mechanical	15300 lb	28 mph	Gardner 204 hp	3'7"
Class 08 British Rail shunter 0-6-0	1953-62	50	Two English Electric traction motors	35000 lb	15-20 mph	English Electric 400 hp	4'6"
Class 09 British Rail shunter 0-6-0	1959-62	50	Two English Electric traction motors	25000 lb	27 mph	English Electric 350 hp	4'6"
Class 20 English Electric type 1 Bo-Bo	1957-68	73-4	Four English Electric traction motors	42000 lb	60 mph	English Electric 1000 hp	3'7"
Class 26 Birmingham Railway Carriage & Wagon type 2 Bo-Bo	1958-9	75	Four Crompton-Parkinson traction motors	42000 lb	60 mph	Sulzer 1160 hp	3'7"
Class 31 Brush type 2 A1A-A1A	1957-62	107-13	Four Brush traction motors	42800 lb	80-90 mph	English Electric 1470 hp	3'7" (driven) 3'3" (centre)
Class 33 Birmingham Railway Carriage & Wagon type 3 Bo-Bo	1960-2	78-9	Four Crompton-Parkinson traction motors	45000 lb	60-85 mph	Sulzer 1550 hp	3'7"
Class 37 English Electric type 3 Co-Co	1960-5	102-20	Six English Electric traction motors	56000 lb	80 mph	English Electric 1750 hp	3'7"
Class 43 HST Power Cars Bo-Bo	1974-82	70	Four Brush traction motors	17980 lb	125 mph	Paxman Valenta Mirrlees Blackstone	3'4"
Class 47 British Rail and Brush type 4 Co-Co	1963-7	117-25	Six Brush traction motors	60000 lb	75-95 mph	Sulzer 2580 hp	3'9"
Class 50 English Electric type 4 Co-Co	1967-8	117	Six English Electric traction motors	48500 lb	100 mph	English Electric 2700 hp	3'7"
Class 56 British Rail & Brush type 5 Co-Co	1976-84	125	Six Brush traction motors	61800 lb	80 mph	Rushton-Paxman 3250 hp	3'9"
Class 58 BREL type 5 Co-Co	1983-7	129	Six Brush traction motors	61800 lb	80 mph	Rushton-Paxman 3300 hp	3'8"
Class 59 General Motors type 5 Co-Co	1985-9 (USA)	126	General Motors D77B traction motors	113500 lb	60 mph	General Motors 3300 hp	3'4"
Class 59/1 General Motors type 5 Co-Co	1990 (Canada)	126	General Motors D77B traction motors	113500 lb	60 mph	General Motors 3300 hp	3'4"
Class 60 Brush type 5 Co-Co	1989-92	126	Brush traction motors	106500 lb	60 mph	Mirrlees 3100 hp	3'8"
Class 73 British Rail/English Electric electro-diesel Bo-Bo	1962-7	76-7	Four English Electric traction motors	34000-42000 lb	60-90 mph	English Electric 600 hp	3'4"
						Voltage	
Class 86 British Rail Bo-Bo	1965-6	83-7	Four AEI traction motors	46500-58000 lb	75-110 mph	660-750V DC third rail	3'9½"
Class 87 British Rail Bo-Bo	1973-5	83	Four GEC traction motors	58000 lb	110 mph	25 kV AC overhead	3'9½"
Class 89 Brush Co-Co	1986	105	Brush traction motor	46000 lb	125 mph	25 kV AC overhead	3'9¼"
Class 90 BREL General Electric Bo-Bo	1987-90	85	GEC traction motors	46000 lb	110 mph	25 kV AC overhead	3'9¼"
Class 91 BREL General Electric Bo-Bo	1988-91	82	GEC traction motors	43100 lb	140 mph	25 kV AC overhead	3'3¼"

Rail (continued)

Wheel configuration

Basic configurations for steam locomotives operating on British railways 1825–1992.

Tank	Tender	
0-4-0	0-4-0	
0-4-2	0-4-2	
0-4-4	0-6-0	
0-6-0	2-4-0	
0-6-2	2-6-0	'Mogul'
0-6-4	2-6-2	'Prairie'
0-8-0	2-8-0	'Consolidation'
2-4-0	2-8-2	'Mikado'
2-4-2	2-10-0	
2-6-2	4-2-2	'Single'
2-6-4	4-4-0	
4-4-2	4-4-2	'Atlantic'
	4-6-0	
	4-6-2	'Pacific'
	4-6-4	

Fastest trains

	Speed (km/h)	(mph)	
British Rail scheduled train Edinburgh–London *Scottish Pullman*	158.9	98.7 (average)	
Fastest British locomotive Class 91 25kV Electric	260	162	1989
Fastest train on a national rail system TGV (Train à Grande Vitesse), France	515	320	1990
Fastest steam locomotive LNER 4-6-2 No. 4468, *Mallard*, England	201.16	126	1938
Fastest railed vehicle Mach 8 unmanned rocket sled, USA	9851	6121	1982

Air

Aeroplane classification

Executive/Business jets

Type	Range (max. seats)	Capacity	Origin (turbofans)	Engines	Span/length (m)
BAe 125	Medium	14	UK	2 Viper or 2 TFE731	14.33/15.46 (Series 700)
BAe 1000	Medium/long	15	UK	2 PW305	15.66/16.42
Sabreliner	Short	10	US	2 JT12A or 2 CF700 or 2 TFE731	15.37/14.30 (Series 65)
Swearingen SJ30	Short	6	US	2 FJ44	11/12.9
Beechcraft Model 400 Beechjet/Diamond	Medium	8	US Japan	2 JT15D	13.25/13.15 (Beechjet)
Dassault-Breguet Mystère-Falcon 10/100	Medium		France	2 TFE731	13.08/13.85
IAI 1125 Astra	Medium	6	Israel	2 TFE731	16.05/16.94
Dassault-Breguet Mystère-Falcon 20/200	Medium	10	France	2 CF700 or 2 ATF3-6	16.30/17.15
Dassault-Breguet Falcon-50	Medium/long	9	France	3 TFE731	18.86/18.5
Dassault-Breguet Mystère-Falcon 900	Medium/long	19	France	3 TFE731	19.33/19
Dassault Mystère-Falcon 2000	Medium/long	12	France	2 CFE738	19.3/19.23

Passenger jet airliners

Type	Range	Capacity (max. seats)	Origin	Engines (turbofans)	Span/length (m)
Swept-wing, underwing engines					
Boeing 737-100/200	Short/medium	115 (100) 130 (200)	US	2 JT8D	28.35/30.48
Boeing 737-300/400	Short	149 (300) 170 (400)	US	2 CFM56	28.88/33.4 (300) 28.88/36.45 (400)
Boeing 737-500	Medium	108	US	2 CFM56	28.88/36.45
Airbus A320[a]	Short/medium	179	European consortium	2 CFM56 or V2500	33.91/35.75
Tu-204	Medium	214	Russia	2 PS-90 or RB211	42/46.22
Airbus A300[a]	Medium	330	European consortium	2 CF6 or JT9D	44.84/53.62

COMMUNICATIONS

Type	Range	Capacity (max. seats)	Origin	Engines (turbofans)	Span/length (m)
Swept-wing, underwing engines					
Airbus A310[a]	Medium	240	European consortium	2 CF6 or JT9D	43.9/46.6
Type	Range	Capacity (max. seats)	Origin	Engines (turbofans)	Span/length (m)
Boeing 767	Medium	255	US	2 RB211, GE CF6-80 PW JTD9-7R4, or PW4050	47.57/48.51 or 54.94
Boeing 757	Medium	204	US	2 RB 211 or PW2037	37.95/47.32
Airbus A330[a]	Medium/long	335	European consortium	2 CF6 Trent, or PW4000	60.3/63.5
McDonnell Douglas DC-10	Medium/long	380	US	3 CF6 or JT9D	50.41/55.5
McDonnell Douglas MD-11	Medium/long	405	US	3 PW4360, Trent, or CF6	51.66/61.21
Boeing 777	Long	400	US	2 PW4073, GE 90, or Trent	60.25/63.72
Boeing 777-200	Long	320	US	2 GE90 PW4000 or Trent 800	60.90/63.70
Boeing 777-300	Long	386	US	2 GE90 PW4000 or Trent	60.90/73.90
McDonnell Douglas DC8	Medium/long	173	US	4 JT3D	43.41/45.87
DC-8 Super 60		259			45.23/57.12 (Super 63)
Boeing 707	Medium/long	195	US	4 JT3D	44.2/46.61
Ilyushin Il-86 'Camber'	Short	350	Russia	4 Kuznetsov	48.06/59.54
Ilyushin Il-96-300	Medium/long	300	Russia	4 PS-90A	57.66/55.35
Airbus A340[a]	Medium/long	335	European consortium	4 CFM56	60.3/63.65
Airbus 321[a]	Short/medium	185	European consortium	2 CFM56 or V2500	34.10/44.51
Airbus 319[a]	Short/medium	124	European consortium	2 CFM56 V2500	34.10/33.84
Airbus 318[a]	Short/medium	107	European consortium	2 PW 6000	34.10/31.45
Boeing 747	Medium/long	490	US	4 JT9D, CF6 or RB211	59.64/70.51
Boeing 747-400	Long	630	US	4 CF6, RB211, or PW4256	64.92/70.66
BAe 146	Short	93	UK	4 ALF502	26.34/26.16 (Series 100)

[a]The Airbus is built jointly by Aérospatiale in France, MBB (Deutsche Airbus) in Germany, and British Aerospace PLC in UK.

Type	Range	Capacity (max. seats)	Origin	Engines (turbofans)	Span/length (m)
Swept-wing, rear engines					
Aérospatiale Caravelle	Short	139	France	2 Avon or JT8D	34.30/36.24 (Series 12)
BAe One-Eleven	Short	119	UK	2 Spey	28.5/32.61 (Series 500)
Fokker F28 Fellowship	Short	85	Netherlands	2 Spey	25.07/26.76 (Mk 6000)
Fokker 100	Short	110	Netherlands	2 Tay	28.08/35.53
McDonnell Douglas DC-9	Short	125	US	2 JT8D	28.47/38.28 (Series 40)
McDonnell Douglas MD-80	Short/medium	172	US	2 JT8D	32.85/41.3

Air (continued)

Type	Range	Capacity (max. seats)	Origin	Engines (turbofans)	Span/length (m)
McDonnell Douglas MD-90	Short	152	US	2 V2500	32.90/46.50
Tupolev Tu-134 'Crusty'	Short	72	Russia	2 Soloviev	29/34.35
Tupolev Tu-154 'Careless'	Medium	180	Russia	3 Kuznetsov or Soloviev	37.55/47.9
Boeing 727	Medium	189	US	3 JT8D	32.92/46.69 (200)
Ilyushin Il-62 'Classic'	Long	186	Russia	4 Kuznetsov or Soloviev	43.2/53.12
Yakovlev Yak-42 'Clobber'	Short	120	Russia	3 D-36	34.90/36.38
Delta wing Aérospatiale/BAe Concorde[a]	Long	128	France/UK	4 Olympus 593	25.56/61.66

[a]World's only fully operational supersonic airliner

Regional/Commuter Aircraft (20 passengers or more)

Type	Range	Seats	Origin	Engines	Span/length (m)
Jets Canadair Challenger	Medium	28	Canada	2 ALF502 or CF34	18.83/20.82
Canadair Regional Jet	Short	50	Canada	2 CF34	21.44/26.95
Yakovlev Yak-40 'Codling'	Short	32	Russia	3 Ivchenko	25/20.36
Propeller planes Fairchild Metro	Short	20	US	2 TPE331 turboprop	17.37/18.09
Convair CV-240/340/440 Metropolitan	Short	40/44/52	US	2 R-2800 piston	32.12/24.14
Convair 540/580/600/640	Short	56	US	2 Allison 501 or Dart turboprop	32.12/24.14
Martin 4-0-4	Short	40	US	2 R2800 piston	28.44/22.75
Ilyushin Il-14 'Crate'	Short	28	Russia	2 Ash-82 piston	31.69/22.3
Douglas DC-3/Dakota	Short	36	US	2 R-1830 piston	28.96/19.63
Curtiss C-46 Commando	Short	62	US	2 R-2800 piston	32.92/23.26
BAe Jetstream 41	Short	29	UK	2 TPE331 turboprop	18.29/19.25
Gulfstream Aerospace Gulfstream I/I-C	Long	24	US	2 Dart turboprop	23.92/19.43
NAMC YS-11A	Short/medium	60	Japan	2 Dart turboprop	32/26.3
Ilyushin Il-114	Short	60	Russia	2 TV7 turboprop	30/26.31
BAe ATP	Short/medium	64	UK	2 PW126 turboprop	30.63/26
Saab 304A	Short	34	Sweden	2 CT7 turboprop	21.44/19.72
Saab 2000	Short/medium	50	Sweden	2 GMA 2 100A turboprop	24.76/27.93
EMBRAER EMB-110 Bandeirante	Short	21	Brazil	2 PT6A turboprop	15.32/15.08
EMBRAER EMB-120 Brasilia	Short	30	Brazil	2 PW115 turboprop	19.78/20
Aérospatiale N 262/Frégate	Short	26	France	2 Bastan turboprop	21.9/19.28
Fokker F27 Friendship	Short/medium	52	Netherlands	2 Dart turboprop	29/25.06 (Mk 500)
Fokker 50	Short	58	Netherlands	2 PW125 turboprop	29/25.24
Antonov An-24 'Coke'/An-26 'Curl'	Short	50	Ukraine	2 Ivchenko turboprop	29.2/23.53

Type	Range	Seats	Origin	Engines	Span/length (m)
DH DHC-4A Caribou	Short (STOL[a])	30	Canada	2 R-2000 piston	29.15/22.13
DH DHC-5E Transporter	Short	44	Canada	2 CT64 turboprops	29.26/24.08
DH DHC-8 Dash 8	Short	40	Canada	2 PW120 turboprop	25.89/22.25
Airtech CN-235	Short	44	Spain/Indonesia	2 CT7 turboprop	25.81/21.35
Avions de Transport Régional ATR42/72	Short	50/74	France/Italy	2 PW120 turboprop	24.57/22.67 (ATR42)
LET L-610	Short	40	Czechoslovakia	2 M602 or CT-7 turboprop	25.6/21.4
Dornier Do 328	Short	33	Germany	2 PW119 turboprop	20.98/21.22
CASA C-212 Aviocar	Short (STOL[a])	26	Spain	2 TPE331 turboprop	19/15.16
DH DHC-6 Twin Otter	Short	20	Canada	2 PT6 turboprop	19.81/15.77
Shorts 330-200	Short	30	UK	2 PT6A turboprop	22.76/17.69
Shorts 360	Short	36	UK	2 PT6A turboprop	22.75/21.49
Vickers Viscount	Short	65	UK	4 Dart turboprop	28.56/25.04
Ilyushin Il-18/Il-20 'Coot'	Medium	122	Russia	4 Ivchenko turboprop	37.4/35.9
Lockheed L-188 Electra	Medium	98	US	4 Allison 501 turboprop	30.18/31.81
Douglas DC-4	Short	44	US	4 R-2000 piston	35.8/28.6
DH DHC Dash 7 (STOL[a])	Short	50	Canada	4 PT6 turboprop	28.35/24.58

[a]STOL = short take-off and landing.

World air distances

Air distances between some major cities, given in statute miles. To convert to kilometres, multiply number given by 1.6093.

[a]Shortest route.

	Amsterdam	Anchorage	Beijing	Buenos Aires	Cairo	Chicago	Delhi	Hong Kong	Honolulu	Istanbul	Johannesburg	Lagos	London	Los Angeles	Mexico City	Montreal	Moscow	Nairobi	Paris	Perth	Rome	Santiago	Sydney	Tokyo
Anchorage	4475																							
Beijing	6566	4756																						
Buenos Aires	7153	8329	12000																					
Cairo	2042	6059	6685	7468																				
Chicago	4109	2854	7599	5587	6135																			
Delhi	3985	8925	2368	8340	2753	8119																		
Hong Kong	5926	5063	1235	5098	3124	7827	2345																	
Honolulu	8368	2780	6778	8693	9439	4246	7888	5543																
Istanbul	1373	6024	4763	7783	764	5502	2833	5998	9547															
Johannesburg	5606	1042	10108	5725	4012	8705	6765	6728	12892	4776														
Lagos	3161	7587	8030	4832	2443	7065	5196	7541	10367	3207	2854													
London	217	4472	5054	6985	2187	3956	4169	5979	7252	1552	5640	3115												
Los Angeles	5559	2333	6349	6140	7589	1746	8717	7231	2553	6994	10443	7716	5442											
Mexico City	5724	3751	7912	4592	7730	1687	9806	8794	4116	7255	10070	7343	5703	1563										
Montreal	3422	3100	7557	5640	5431	737	7421	8564	4923	4795	8322	5595	3252	2482	2307									
Moscow	1338	4291	3604	8382	1790	5500	2698	4839	8802	1089	6280	4462	1550	6992	6700	4393								
Nairobi	4148	8714	8888	7427	2203	8177	4956	7301	11498	2967	1809	2377	4246	9688	9949	7498	3951							
Paris	261	4683	5108	6892	1995	4140	4089	5987	7463	1394	5422	2922	220	5633	5714	3434	1540	4031						
Perth	9118	8368	4987	9734	7766	11281	5013	3752	7115	7846	5564	10209	9246	9535	11098	12402	8355	7373	12587					
Rome	809	5258	5306	6931	1329	4828	3679	5773	8150	852	4802	2497	898	6340	6601	5431	1478	3349	688	8309				
Santiago	7714	7919	13622	710	8029	5328	12715	3733	8147	10109	5738	6042	8568	5594	4168	5551	10118	7547	461	15129	7548			
Sydney	1039	8522	5689	7760	9196	9324	6495	4586	5078	9883	7601	11700	10565	7498	9061	9980	9425	9410	10150	2037	10149	13092		
Tokyo	6006[a]	3443	1313	13100	6362	6286	3656	1807	3831	5757	9130[a]	5451	6218	6208	7014	6913	4668	8565	6208	4925	6146	11049	4640	
Washington	3854	3430	7930	6097	5859	590	7841	8385	4822	5347	8199	5472	3672	2294	1871	493	4884	7918	3843	11829	4495	5061	9792	6763

COMMUNICATIONS

Air (continued)

World flying times

Approximate flying times between some major cities. Times quoted (in hours and minutes) are flying time only. In many cases, in order to travel between two points, it is necessary to change aircraft one or more times. Time between flights has not been included.

	Amsterdam	Anchorage	Beijing	Buenos Aires	Cairo	Chicago	Delhi	Hong Kong	Honolulu	Istanbul	Johannesburg	Lagos	London	Los Angeles	Mexico City	Montreal	Moscow	Nairobi	Paris	Perth	Rome	Santiago	Sydney	Tokyo
Anchorage	9.00																							
Beijing	16.50	11.45																						
Buenos Aires	17.45	10.48	28.31																					
Cairo	4.20	13.20	13.15	20.40																				
Chicago	8.35	5.44	15.15	15.40	18.40																			
Delhi	8.15	16.50	6.40	26.20	7.00	20.05																		
Hong Kong	15.15	11.40	3.00	29.35	10.55	17.05	6.05																	
Honolulu	16.42	5.44	10.55	19.00	22.50	9.25	16.50	13.05																
Istanbul	3.15	12.15	15.40	18.45	2.00	12.20	7.35	17.35	21.05															
Johannesburg	13.15	19.50	20.10	12.30	8.55	21.40	23.45	14.55	30.25	16.30														
Lagos	6.40	14.55	22.35	9.55	8.20	14.55	14.55	22.30	23.40	8.05	6.55													
London	1.05	8.30	18.05	16.35	5.35	8.30	10.35	16.05	17.15	3.50	13.10	6.25												
Los Angeles	11.15	6.13	15.25	13.45	21.00	5.00	19.30	15.50	5.15	14.50	24.10	17.25	11.00											
Mexico City	12.27	10.49	18.45	10.25	16.47	5.15	20.42	19.10	8.35	15.42	25.42	19.07	14.35	3.20										
Montreal	7.40	7.91	27.30	16.00	12.35	2.20	17.35	23.05	12.50	10.15	20.10	13.25	7.00	6.40	4.45									
Moscow	3.15	12.15	8.40	22.05	5.25	12.15	7.35	18.00	21.00	4.40	13.30	10.10	3.45	14.45	18.10	10.45								
Nairobi	8.15	17.00	16.00	24.55	4.55	17.00	10.45	12.45	25.45	7.15	3.45	6.20	8.30	19.30	20.42	15.30	12.50							
Paris	1.10	9.00	16.35	15.35	5.05	9.00	10.45	16.40	18.05	3.10	15.50	7.45	1.05	12.50	13.25	6.25	4.00	9.20						
Perth	20.35	17.25	11.15	25.20	17.10	23.00	9.30	8.15	17.25	15.20	14.20	25.55	19.30	19.30	22.50	26.30	19.40	23.00	21.40					
Rome	2.20	12.00	16.10	14.40	3.25	11.35	8.50	15.10	19.13	2.35	12.25	6.55	2.25	14.35	5.35	8.10	4.10	7.20	1.55	20.00				
Santiago	20.50	19.13	22.34	2.10	25.10	17.15	29.05	19.15	8.35	21.00	19.55	24.25	21.55	16.00	12.00	14.50	24.05	29.05	19.45	26.00	18.50			
Sydney	23.05	16.35	16.15	20.45	17.20	21.10	13.50	10.35	11.50	18.40	31.50	28.35	21.55	18.10	18.05	24.50	19.40	31.35	25.05	4.35	23.50	24.30		
Tokyo	11.40	7.20	3.50	28.30	19.40	12.55	9.45	4.20	7.05	14.05	25.00	18.40	11.50	11.55	16.25	18.55	9.25	19.55	16.45	10.05	17.40	27.55	9.15	
Washington	8.55	7.25	25.50	11.00	14.20	1.45	20.10	24.15	10.55	11.25	21.20	14.45	8.10	5.25	7.50	2.50	12.30	17.10	9.25	22.45	12.40	17.40	23.35	12.40

US air distances

Air distances between US cities, given in statute miles. To convert to kilometres, multiply number given by 1.6093.

	Atlanta	Boston	Chicago	Dallas	Denver	Detroit	Houston	Kansas City	Los Angeles	Miami	Minneapolis	New Orleans	New York	Oklahoma City	Omaha	Philadelphia	Phoenix	Pittsburgh	Portland	St Louis	Salt Lake City	San Antonio	San Francisco	Seattle
Boston	946																							
Chicago	606	867																						
Dallas	721	1555	796																					
Denver	1208	1767	901	654																				
Detroit	595	632	235	982	1135																			
Houston	689	1603	925	217	864	1095																		
Kansas City	681	1254	403	450	543	630	643																	
Los Angeles	1946	2611	1745	1246	849	1979	1379	1363																
Miami	595	1258	1197	1110	1716	1146	964	1239	2342															
Minneapolis	906	1124	334	853	693	528	1046	394	1536	1501														
New Orleans	425	1367	837	437	1067	936	305	690	1671	674	1040													
New York	760	187	740	1383	1638	509	1417	1113	2475	1090	1028	1182												
Oklahoma City	761	1505	693	181	500	911	395	312	1187	1223	694	567	1345											
Omaha	821	1282	416	585	485	651	793	152	1330	1393	282	841	1155	418										
Philadelphia	665	281	678	1294	1569	453	1324	1039	2401	1013	980	1094	94	1268	1094									
Phoenix	1587	2300	1440	879	589	1681	1015	1043	370	1972	1270	1301	2143	833	1037	2082								
Pittsburgh	526	496	412	1061	1302	201	1124	769	2136	1013	726	918	340	1010	821	267	1814							
Portland	2172	2537	1739	1637	985	1959	1834	1492	834	2700	1426	2050	2454	1484	1368	2411	1009	2148						
St Louis	484	1046	258	546	781	440	667	229	1592	1068	448	604	892	462	342	813	1262	553	1708					
Salt Lake City	1589	2105	1249	1010	381	1489	1204	919	590	2088	991	1428	1989	865	839	1932	507	1659	630	1156				
San Antonio	875	1764	1041	247	793	1215	191	697	1210	1143	1097	495	1587	407	824	1502	843	1277	1714	786	1086			
San Francisco	2139	2704	1846	1476	956	2079	1636	1498	337	2585	1589	1911	2586	1383	1433	2521	651	2253	550	1735	599	1482		
Seattle	2182	2496	1720	1670	1019	1932	1874	1489	954	2725	1399	2087	2421	1520	1368	2383	1109	2124	132	1709	689	1775	678	
Washington, DC	532	414	590	1163	1464	385	1189	927	2288	919	909	969	229	1158	1000	136	1956	184	2339	696	1839	1361	2419	2307

International time zones

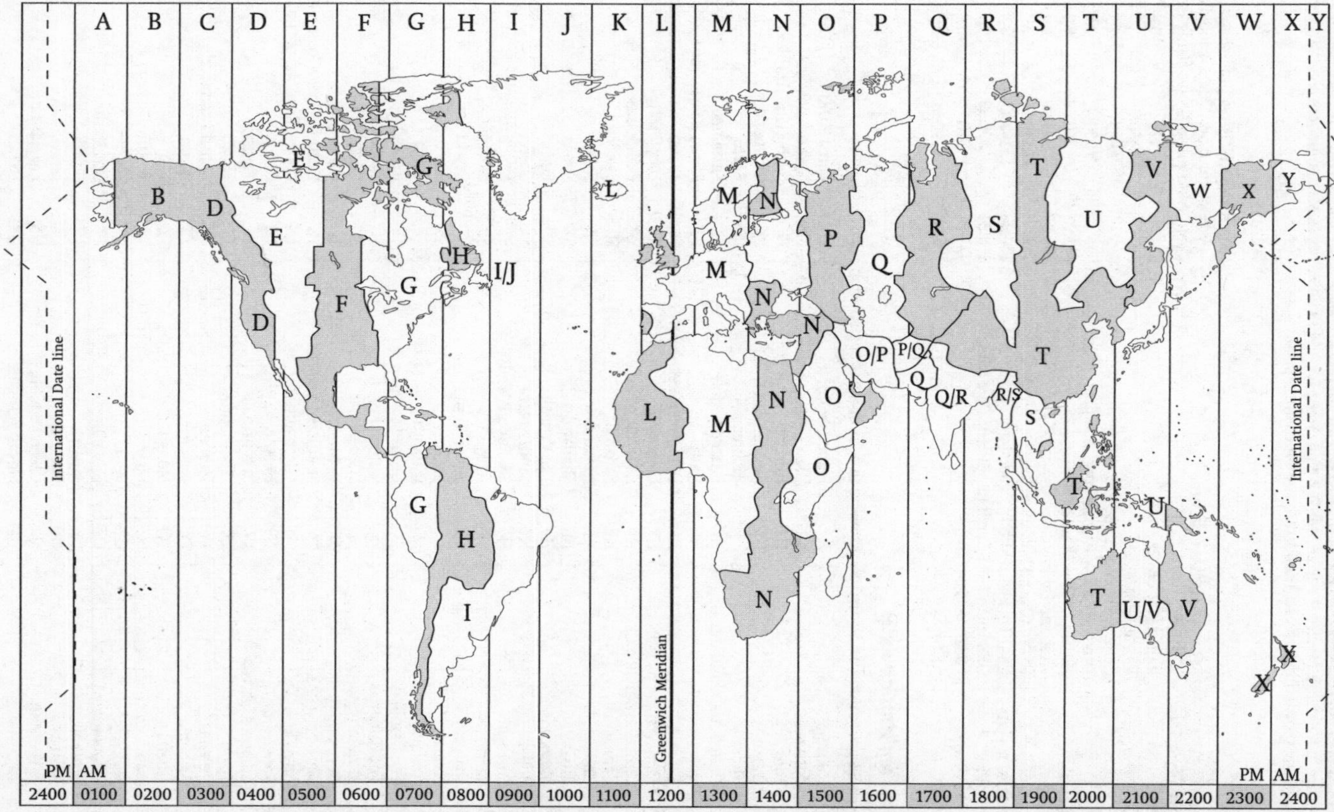

International Date line

PM AM

Greenwich Meridian

International Date line

PM | AM

COMMUNICATIONS

Some countries have adopted half-hour time zones which are indicated on the map as a combination of two coded zones.

Air (continued)

Fastest aeroplanes

A Mach number (Ma) denotes the ratio of the speed of an aircraft to the speed of sound under the same conditions of pressure and density. Mach 1.0 = 1 226 kph/762 mph. Mach 0.5 = 613 kph/381mph. Mach numbers less than 1 indicate subsonic speed, those greater than 1 indicate supersonic speed.

Type	Aircraft	Speed		Mach
		(km/h)	(mph)	
Airliner	Aérospatiale/BAe Concorde	2 333	1450	2
Autogyro/gyroplane	WA-116F	193.9	120.3	0.2
Biplane	Italian Fiat CR42B	520	323	0.4
Bomber	Dassault Mirage IV	2 333	1450	2
	General Dynamics FB-111A (swing-wing)	3 065	1905	2.5
	Tupolev Tu-22M (swing-wing), *Backfire*	3 065	1905	2.5
Flying boat	Martin XP6M-1 Seamaster	911.98	566.69	0.8
Helicopter	Westland Lynx	400.87	249.09	0.3
Combat jet	USSR Mikoyan MiG-25 Foxbat-B	3 395	2 110	3
Reconnaisance jet	USAF Lockheed SR-71A, *Blackbird*	3 529.5	2 193.17	3
Piston-engine	Grumman F8F Bearcat (modified), *Rare Bear*	850.24	528.33	0.7
Propeller-driven	USSR Tu-95/142, *Bear*	925	575	0.8
Ultralight	Gypsy Skycycle	104.6	65	0.1

Aircraft registration codes

These codes are painted on all aircraft, showing their country of registration.

AP	Pakistan	F	France	P	Korea (PDR)
A2	Botswana	G	UK	PH	Netherlands
A3	Tonga	HA	Hungary	PJ	Netherland Antilles
A40	Oman	HB	Switzerland &	PK	Indonesia
A5	Bhutan		Lichtenstein	PP, PT	Brazil
A6	United Arab Emirates	HC	Ecuador	PZ	Suriname
A7	Qatar	HH	Haiti	P2	Papua New Guinea
A9C	Bahrain	HI	Dominican Republic	P4	Aruba
B	China (People's Republic)	HK	Colombia	RDPL	Laos (PDR)
Bt	China/Taiwan (R o C)	HL	Republic of Korea	RP	Philippines
C, CF	Canada	HP	Panama	SE	Sweden
CC	Chile	HR	Honduras	SP	Poland
RA	Russia	HS	Thailand	ST	Sudan
CN	Morocco	HV	The Vatican	SU	Egypt
CP	Bolivia	HZ	Saudi Arabia	SX	Greece
CR, CS	Portugal	H4	Solomon Islands	S2	Bangladesh
CU	Cuba	I	Italy	S5	Slovenia
CX	Uruguay	JA	Japan	S7	Seychelles
C2	Nauru	JY	Jordan	S9	São Tomé
C3	Andorra	J2	Djibouti	TC	Turkey
C5	The Gambia	J3	Grenada	TF	Iceland
C6	The Bahamas	J5	Guinea Bissau	TG	Guatemala
C9	Mozambique	J6	St Lucia	TI	Costa Rica
D	Germany	J7	Dominica	TJ	Cameroon
DQ	Fiji	J8	St Vincent and the	TL	Central African Republic
D2	Angola		Grenadines	TN	Congo, Republic of the
D4	Cape Verde	LN	Norway	TR	Gabon
D6	Comoros Islands	LV	Argentina	TS	Tunisia
EC	Spain	LX	Luxembourg	TT	Chad
EI, EJ	Ireland	LY	Lithuania	TU	Côte d'Ivoire
EK	Armenia	LZ	Bulgaria	TY	Benin
EL	Liberia	MT	Mongolia	TZ	Mali
EP	Iran	N	USA	T2	Tuvalu
ER	Moldova	OB	Peru	T3	Kiribati
ES	Estonia	OD	Lebanon	T7	San Marino
ET	Ethiopia	OE	Austria	T9	Bosnia & Herzegovina
EW	Belarus	OH	Finland	UK	Uzbekistan
EX	Kyrgyzstan	OK	Czech Republic	UN	Kazakhstan
EY	Tajikistan	OM	Slovak Republic	UR	Ukraine
EZ	Turkmenistan	OO	Belgium	VH	Australia
E3	Eritrea	OY	Denmark	VN	Vietnam

VP-F	Falkland Islands	YU	Yugoslavia (Serbia and	5Y	Kenya
VP-LA	Anguilla		Montenegro)	6O	Somalia
VP-LM	Montserrat	YV	Venezuela	6V, 6W	Senegal
VP-LV	British Virgin Islands	Z	Zimbabwe	6Y	Jamaica
VQ-T	Turks and Caicos Islands	ZA	Albania	7O	Yemen
VR-B	Bermuda	ZK, ZL	New Zealand	7P	Lesotho
VR-C	Cayman Islands	ZM		7Q	Malawi
VR-G	Gibraltar	ZP	Paraguay	7T	Algeria
VR-H	Hong Kong	ZS, ZT,	South Africa	8P	Barbados
VT	India	ZU		8Q	Maldives
V2	Antigua and Barbuda	3A	Monaco	8R	Guyana
V3	Belize	3B	Mauritius	9A	Croatia
V4	St Kitts and Nevis	3C	Equatorial Guinea	9G	Ghana
V5	Namibia	3D	Swaziland	9H	Malta
V6	Micronesia, Fed States of	3X	Guinea	9J	Zambia
V7	Marshall Islands	4K	Azerbaijan	9K	Kuwait
V8	Brunei	4L	Georgia	9L	Sierra Leone
XA, XB,	Mexico	4R	Sri Lanka	9M	Malaysia
XC		4U	United Nations	9N	Nepal
XT	Burkina Faso		Organization	9Q , 9T	Democratic Republic of
XU	Cambodia	4X	Israel		Congo
XV	Vietnam, South	5A	Libya	9U	Burundi
XY, XZ	Myanmar (Burma)	5B	Cyprus	9V	Singapore
YA	Afghanistan	5H	Tanzania	9XR	Rwanda
YI	Iraq	5N	Nigeria	9Y	Trinidad and Tobago
YJ	Vanuatu	5R	Madagascar		
YK	Syria	5T	Mauritania		
YL	Latvia	5U	Niger		
YN	Nicaragua	5V	Togo		
YR	Romania	5W	Samoa		*Source*: ICAO
YS	El Salvador	5X	Uganda		

Airline designators

Code[a] Airline		Country	Code[a] Airline		Country
AAA	Ansett Australia	Australia	AUR	Aurigny Air Services	Channel Is
AAH	Aloha Airlines	USA	AUS	Aus-Air	Australia
AAL	American Airlines	USA	AUZ	Australian Airlines	Australia
AAU	Australia Asia Airlines	Australia	AVE	Aerovias Venezolanas (AVENSA)	Venezuela
ABL	Air BC	Canada	AVN	Air Vanuatu	Vanuatu
ACA	Air Canada	Canada	AWE	America West Airlines	USA
ADM	Dominair	Dominica	AZA	Alitalia	Italy
AES	ACES (Aerolineas Centrales	Colombia	AZF	Air Zermatt	Switzerland
	De Colombia)		AZW	Air Zimbabwe	Zimbabwe
AFG	Ariana Afghan Airlines	Afghanistan	BAL	Britannia Airways	UK
AFL	Aeroflot	Russia	BAW	British Airways	UK
AFR	Air France	France	BBC	Biman Bangladesh Airlines	Bangladesh
AGN	Air Gabon	Gabon	BHI	Balkh Airlines	Afghanistan
AHY	Azerbaijan Airlines	Azerbaijan	BHS	Bahamasair	Bahamas
AIC	Air-India	India	BMA	British Midland	UK
AIH	Airtours International	UK	BMI	bmibaby	UK
AJM	Air Jamaica	Jamaica	BOT	Air Botswana	Botswana
ALK	SriLankan Airlines	Sri Lanka	BOU	Bouraq Airlines	Indonesia
AMC	Air Malta	Malta	BRA	Braathens SAFE	Norway
AML	Air Malawi	Malawi	BWA	BWIA West Indies Airways	Trinidad and
AMX	Aeromexico	Mexico			Tobago
ANA	All Nippon Airways	Japan	CAL	China Airlines	China
ANG	Air Niugini	Papua New	CAN	Air Canarias	Spain
		Guinea	CAY	Cayman Airways	Cayman Islands
ANZ	Air New Zealand	New Zealand	CBF	China Northern Airlines	China
AQN	Air Queensland	Australia	CCA	Air China International	China
ARG	Aerolineas Argentinas	Argentina	CEM	Central Mongolia Airways	Mongolia
ARU	Air Aruba	Aruba	CIU	Cielos del Peru	Argentina
ASA	Alaska Airlines	USA	CLT	Air Caribbean	Netherlands
ATC	Air Tanzania	Tanzania			Antilles
ATM	Airlines of Tasmania	Australia	CMP	COPA (Compania Panamena	Panama
AUA	Austrian Airlines	Austria		de Aviación)	
AUI	Ukraine International Airlines	Ukraine	COA	Continental Airlines	USA

Air (continued)

Code[a]	Airline	Country
CPA	Cathay Pacific Airways	Hong Kong
CRQ	Air Creebec	Canada
CRX	Crossair	Switzerland
CSA	Czech Airlines	Czech Republic
CSN	China Southern Airlines	China
CTN	Croatia Airlines	Croatia
CUB	Cubana de Aviación	Cuba
CYP	Cyprus Airways	Cyprus
DAH	Air Algerie	Algeria
DAL	Delta Airlines	USA
DAN	Maersk Air	Denmark
DLH	Deutsche Lufthansa	Germany
DOA	Dominicana de Aviación	Dominica
DSK	Aero Algarve	Portugal
DTA	TAAG Angola Airlines	Angola
DUK	Ducair	Luxembourg
DVN	Dvin-Avia	Armenia
DYA	Alyemda	Yemen
EIN	Air Lingus	Ireland
ELY	El Al Israel Airlines	Israel
ETH	Ethiopian Airlines	Ethiopia
EWA	EastWest Airlines	Australia
EZY	EasyJet	UK
FAJ	Fiji Air Services	Fiji
FDA	African Airlines	Mali
FIN	Finnair	Finland
FJI	Air Pacific	Fiji
FLI	Atlantic Airways	Faroe Islands
FWQ	Flight West Airlines	Australia
FXI	Iceland Air	Iceland
GAW	Gambia Airways	The Gambia
GBL	GB Airways	UK
GCB	Linacongo	Congo
GFA	Gulf Air	Bahrain
GHA	Ghana Airways	Ghana
GIA	Garuda	Indonesia
GIB	Air Guinée	Guinea
GOE	Go Fly	UK
GRL	Greenlandair	Greenland
GYA	Guyana Airways	Guyana
HAL	Hawaiian Airlines	USA
HRH	Royal Tongan Airlines	Tonga
HVN	Vietnam Airlines	Vietnam
IAC	Indian Airlines	India
IBE	Iberia	Spain
ICE	Icelandair	Iceland
IRA	Iran Air	Iran
IRT	Irtysh Avia	Kazakhstan
IYE	Yemenia–Yemen Airways	Yemen
JAL	Japan Airlines	Japan
JAT	JAT (Jugoslovenski Aerotransport)	Yugoslavia (Serbia and Montenegro)
JKK	Spanair	Spain
JND	Air East Africa	Kenya
JPL	Atlas Airlines	Romania
JTU	Zhetsyu	Kazakhstan
KAB	Aviabaltika	Lithuania
KAC	Kuwait Airways	Kuwait
KAL	Korean Airlines	Republic of Korea
KLM	KLM Royal Dutch Airlines	Netherlands
KQA	Kenya Airways	Kenya
KRS	Kyrgyz International Airlines	Kyrgyzstan

Code[a]	Airline	Country
LAA	Jamahiriya Libyan Arab Airlines	Libya
LAI	Air Lesotho	Lesotho
LAL	Labrador Airways	Canada
LAM	LAM (Linhas Aereas de Moçambique)	Mozambique
LAN	Lan-Chile	Chile
LAP	TAM (Transportes Aereos del Mercosur)	Paraguay
LAZ	Balkan–Bulgarian Airlines	Bulgaria
LDA	Lauda Air	Austria
LEI	Leasair International	UK
LGL	Luxair	Luxembourg
LIL	Lithuanian Airlines	Lithuania
LIN	Linair	Hungary
LOG	Loganair	UK
LOT	LOT Polish Airlines	Poland
LRC	Lineas Aereas Costarricenses	Costa Rica
LTL	Latvian Airlines	Latvia
MAH	MALEV Hungarian Airlines	Hungary
MAS	Malaysian	Malaysia
MAU	Air Mauritius	Mauritius
MAY	Maya Airways	Belize
MDG	Air Madagascar	Madagascar
MLD	Air Moldova	Moldova
MNX	Manx Airlines	Isle of Man
MON	Monarch Airways	UK
MRT	Air Mauritanie	Mauritania
MSR	Egyptair	Egypt
MTT	Mastair	Bosnia–Herzegovina
NGA	Nigeria Airways	Nigeria
NMB	Air Namibia	Namibia
NOA	Norontair	Canada
NVR	Nova Airlines	Sweden
NWA	Northwest Airlines	USA
NYA	Noy Avia	Armenia
NZM	Mount Cook Airlines	New Zealand
OAL	Olympic Airways	Greece
OAS	Oman Aviation	Oman
OLY	Olympic Aviation	Greece
OVC	Aerovic	Ecuador
PAL	Philippine Airlines	Philippines
PAO	Polynesian	Samoa
PBU	Air Burundi	Burundi
PIA	Pakistan International Airlines	Pakistan
PIC	Pacific Airlines	Vietnam
PLI	Aeroperu	Peru
PUA	PLUNA (Primeras Lineas Uruguayas de Navigación Aereas)	Uruguay
QFA	Qantas Airways	Australia
QXE	Horizon Air	USA
RAM	Royal Air Maroc	Morocco
RBA	Royal Brunei Airlines	Brunei
RJA	Royal Jordanian	Jordan
RNA	Royal Nepal Airlines	Nepal
RON	Air Nauru	Nauru
ROT	TAROM	Romania
RSN	Royal Swazi National Airways	Swaziland
RWA	Rwanda Airways	Rwanda
RYR	Ryanair	Ireland
RZL	Aero Zambia	Zambia
SAA	South African Airways	South Africa
SAB	SN Brussels Airlines	Belgium

COMMUNICATIONS

SAS	SAS (Scandinavian Air)	Sweden
SAY	ScotAirways	UK
SEY	Air Seychelles	Seychelles
SHA	SAHSA (Servicio Aeero de Honduras)	Honduras
SIA	Singapore Airlines	Singapore
SKW	SkyWest Airlines	USA
SLM	Surinam Airways	Suriname
SUD	Sudan Airways	Sudan
SVA	Saudi Arabian Airlines	Saudi Arabia
SWA	Southwest Airlines	USA
SWR	Swiss Air Transport	Switzerland
SXL	Air Salamis	Cyprus
SYR	Syrian Arab Airlines	Syria
TAP	TAP Air Portugal	Portugal
TAR	Tunisair	Tunisia
TCV	Transportes Aeros de Cabo Verde (TACV)	Cape Verde
TGA	Air Togo	Togo
THA	Thai Airways International	Thailand
THY	Turkish Airlines	Turkey
TRA	Transavia Airlines	Netherlands
TWA	TWA (Trans World Airlines)	USA
TYR	Tyrolean Airways	Austria
TZT	Air Zambezi	Zimbabwe
UAB	United Arabian Airlines	Sudan
UAE	Emirates	United Arab Emirates
UAL	United Airlines	USA
UBA	Myanma Airways	Myanmar (Burma)

UIA	UNI Airways	Taiwan
UKA	KLM UK	UK
UKR	Air Ukraine	Ukraine
USA	US Airways	USA
UYC	Cameroon Airlines	Cameroon
UZB	Uzbekistan Airways	Uzbekistan
VBW	Air Burkina	Burkina Faso
VIR	Virgin Atlantic Airways	UK
VLE	Volare Airlines	Italy
VND	Aviandina	Peru
VRG	Varig	Brazil
VTA	Air Tahiti	French Polynesia
WCB	West Africa Airlines	Ghana
WIA	Windward Islands Airways	Netherlands Antilles
WND	Caribbean Winds Airways	Antigua & Barbuda
WPA	Western Pacific Airservice	Solomon Islands
WTA	Africa West	Togo
XXV	AASANA	Bolivia
ZAK	Zambia Skyways	Zambia
ZAV	Zhetysu Avia	Kazakhstan

[a] The International Civil Aviation Organization (ICAO) switched to three-letter designators in 1987.

Source: ICAO

US local airports

International airports are highlighted in **bold**.

Aberdeen, SD
Abilene, TX
Abingdon, VA
Aiken, SC
Air Park–Dallas
Akron Canton, OH
Akron-Fulton Intl, OH
Akron–Washington County, CO
Alabaster, AL
Alamogordo, NM
Alamosa, CO
Albany County, NY
Albuquerque-Coronado, NM
Albuquerque Intl, NM
Alexandria, MN
Alexandria, IN
Allentown, PA
Allentown–Queen City, PA
Alliance, NE
Alma, GA
Alpine, TX
Alton–St Louis, IL
Altoona, PA
Amarillo Intl, TX
Anchorage Intl, AK
Anchorage–Merrill Field, AK
Anderson, IN
Anderson, SC

Appleton, WI
Ardmore Downtown, OK
Ardmore Municipal, OK
Arlington, TX
Asheboro, NC
Asheville, NC
Ashland, OR
Ashland, WI
Aspen, CO
Astoria, OR
Athens, GA
Atlanta Dekalb-Peachtree, GA
Atlanta Fulton-Brown, GA
Atlantic, IA
Atlantic City, NJ
Atlantic City–Bader, NJ
Auburn, AL
Auburn, ME
Augusta Bush, GA
Augusta Daniel, GA
Augusta State, ME
Aurora, IL
Aurora, CO
Aurora State, OR
Austin, MN
Austin Executive, TX
Austin Mueller, TX
Austin Straubel Intl, WI
Avon Park, FL
Bainbridge, GA

Bakersfield, CA
Ballston Spa, NY
Baltimore-Martin State, MD
Baltimore-Washington Intl, MD
Bangor Intl, ME
Banning, CA
Bardstown, KY
Barre-Montpelier, VT
Barrow, AK
Bartow, FL
Baton Rouge, LA
Battle Creek, MI
Baudette Intl, MN
Beach, ND
Beaufort-Morehead City, NC
Beaumont, TX
Beaumont–Port Arthur, TX
Beaver Falls, PA
Bedford, MA
Bedford, PA
Belfast, ME
Bellingham, WA
Bend Sunriver, OR
Benton Harbor, MI
Bentonville, AR
Berlin, NJ
Bermuda Dunes, CA

Beulah, ND
Beverly, MA
Big Bear City, CA
Big Spring, TX
Big Timber, MT
Billings, MT
Binghamton, NY
Birmingham, AL
Bismarck, ND
Blacksburg, VA
Blanding, UT
Bloomington, IL
Bloomington, IN
Bluefield–Mercer Co, WV
Bluffton, OH
Blytheville Municipal, AR
Boca Raton, FL
Boeing Field/King Co Intl, WA
Boise, ID
Boston–Logan Intl, MA
Bozeman, MT
Bradford, PA
Brainerd, MN
Brandywine, PA
Breckenridge, TX
Bremerton, WA
Bridgeport, CT
Bridgeport, TX
Brooksville, FL
Brownfield, TX

COMMUNICATIONS

Air (continued)

Brownsville, TX
Brunswick, GA
Brunswick McKinnon, GA
Bryan, TX
Buena Vista, CO
Buffalo, NY
Burbank, CA
Burlington, CO
Burlington Intl, VT
Burnet, TX
Butler, PA
Cahokia/St Louis, IL
Calexico Intl, CA
California City, CA
Camden, SC
Canadian, TX
Carbondale
  Murphysboro, IL
Caribou, ME
Carlsbad, CA
Carlsbad, NM
Carrollton, GA
Cartersville, GA
Carthage, MO
Casa Grande, AZ
Casper, WY
Castroville, TX
Cave Junction, OR
Cedar City, UT
Cedar Rapids, IA
Centennial, CO
Central Nebraska
  Regional, NE
Centralia, IL
Challis, ID
Chambersburg, PA
Champaign, IL
Chanute, KS
Charles City, IA
Charleston, WV
Charleston Intl, SC
Charleston-Executive, SC
Charlotte Douglas Intl, NC
Charlottesville, VA
Chattanooga-Lovell, TN
Cherokee, IA
Chesapeake, VA
Cheyenne, WY
Chicago Dupage, IL
Chicago Meigs, IL
Chicago Midway, IL
Chicago O'Hare Intl, IL
Chicago Wheeling, IL
Chickasha, OK
Chicopee, MA
Childress, TX
Chino, CA
Chisholm-Hibbing, MN
Cincinatti Blue Ash, OH
Cincinatti Lunken, OH
Circleville, OH
Clarksburg, WV
Clarksdale, MS
Clarksville, TN
Cleburne, TX

Cleveland, MS
Cleveland, OH
Cleveland Cuyahoga, OH
Cleveland Hopkins Intl, OH
Clinton, IA
Cloverdale, CA
Coatsville, PA
Coeur d'Alene, ID
College Park, MD
Colorado City, TX
Colorado Springs, CO
Columbia, CA
Columbia Metro, SC
Columbia Mt Pleasant, TN
Columbia Owens
  Downtown, SC
Columbia Regional, MO
Columbus, IN
Columbus, NE
Columbus Bolton Fld, OH
Columbus Metro, GA
**Columbus–Port
  Columbus**, OH
Concord, CA
Connersville, IN
Conroe–Montgomery Co,
  TX
Conway, SC
Corpus Christi Intl, TX
Corvallis, OR
Covelo, CA
Covington/Cincinatti, KY
Craig, CO
Crescent City, CA
Crestview, FL
Crete, NE
Cumberland Regional, MD
Cushing, OK
Dalhart, TX
Dallas Addison, TX
Dallas–Fort Worth, TX
Dallas Love, TX
Dallas Redbird, TX
Danbury, CT
Danville, IL
Danville, VA
Davenport, IA
Dayton Cox Intl, OH
Dayton General, OH
Daytona Beach, FL
Decatur, AL
Decatur, IL
Del Rio Intl, TX
Deland, FL
Delano, CA
Delavan, WI
Delaware, OH
Denison, IA
Denton, TX
Denver, CO
Denver Jeffco, CO
Des Moines Intl, IA
Destin, FL
Detroit, MI
Detroit City, MI

Detroit–Grosse Ile, MI
Detroit–Willow Run, MI
Diamond Head, MS
Dickinson, ND
Dodge City, KS
Doersom, PA
Dothan, AL
Douglas, GA
Douglas, WY
Douglas Bisbee, AZ
Downtown Airpark
  Oklahoma City, OK
Driggs, ID
Dublin, GA
Du Bois, PA
Dubuque, IA
Duluth Intl, MN
Duncan Halliburton Fld,
  OK
Durango La Plata, CO
Durhamville, NY
Dyersburg, TN
Eagle, CO
Eagle Pass, TX
El Dorado Downtown, AR
El Monte, CA
El Paso Intl, TX
El Paso–W Texas, TX
Elk, OK
Elkin, NC
Elmira, NY
Ely, MN
Ely, NV
Emporia, KS
Erie, PA
Escanaba, MI
Estherville, IA
Eugene Mahlon Sweet, OR
Eureka Murray Field, CA
Evansville, IN
Everett, WA
Fairbanks Intl, AK
Fairhope Point Clear, AL
Fargo, ND
Farmingdale, NY
Farmington, MO
Fayetteville, AR
Fayetteville, NC
Fergus Falls, MN
Findlay, OH
Fitchburg, MA
Flagstaff Pulliam, AZ
Flora, IL
Fort Collins Loveland, CO
Fort Dodge, IA
Fort Lauderdale, FL
Fort Lauderdale
  Executive, FL
Fort Morgan, CO
Fort Myers, FL
Fort Pierce, FL
Fort Smith, AR
Fort Wayne, IN
Fort Wayne Smith Field, IN
Fort Worth Meacham, TX

Fortuna, CA
Frederick, MD
Frederick, OK
Frenchville, ME
Fresno Air Terminal, CA
Fullerton, CA
Gainesville, FL
Gaithersburg, MD
Galesburg, IL
Gallatin, TN
Galveston, TX
Gary, IN
Gastonia, NC
Georgetown, DE
Gillette, WY
Glendale Municipal, AZ
Glens Falls, NY
Golden Triangle
  Regional, MS
Goodland, KS
Graham, TX
Grand Canyon, AZ
Grand Junction, CO
Grand Prairie, TX
Grand Rapids, MI
Grand Rapids, MN
Grandview, MO
Grayson County, TX
Great Barrington, MA
Great Falls Intl, MT
Green River, UT
Greeneville, TN
Greensboro, NC
Greenville, KY
Greenville, MS
Greenville Donaldson, SC
Greenville Downtown, SC
Greenwood, MS
Greenwood, SC
Greer, SC
Groton, CT
Grove City, PA
Gulfport, MS
Hagerstown, MD
Hailey, ID
Half Moon Bay, CA
Hammond, LA
Hammonton, NJ
Hancock, MI
Hanover, VA
Harbor Springs, MI
Harlingen, TX
Harrison, AR
Hartford, CT
Hartford, KY
Hartford Springfield, CT
Hartsfield–Atlanta Intl, GA
Hastings, NE
Hawesville, KY
Hawthorne, CA
Hawthorne, NV
Hayden Yampa Valley, CO
Hayward, CA
Hebbronville, TX
Helena, MT

Hendersonville, NC
Hickory, NC
Hilo Intl, HI
Hilton Head, SC
Hobbs, NM
Holbrook, AZ
Holland Tulip City, MI
Hollister, CA
Honolulu Intl, HI
Hornell, NY
Horseshoe Bay, TX
Houma, LA
Houston Clover Field, TX
Houston Ellington Field, TX
Houston Gulf, TX
Houston Hobby, TX
Houston Hooks Memorial, TX
Houston Intercontinental, TX
Houston–W Houston, TX
Huntingburg, IN
Huntington Beach, CA
Huntsville, AL
Huron, SD
Hutchinson, KS
Hutchinson County, TX
Hyannis, MA
Immokalee, FL
Indianapolis Brookside, IN
Indianapolis Greenwood, IN
Indianapolis Intl, IN
Indianapolis–Mt Comfort, IN
Indianapolis Terry, IN
Iowa City, IA
Islip, NY
Ithaca Tompkins County, NY
Jackson, MS
Jackson, WY
Jackson Thompson, MS
Jacksonville, IL
Jacksonville, TX
Jacksonville Craig, FL
Jacksonville Intl, FL
Jamestown, ND
Janesville, WI
Jeffersonville, IN
Johnson City, KS
Johnson County Executive, KS
Johnson County Industrial, KS
Joliet, IL
Jonesboro, AR
Joplin, MO
Josephine County, OR
Juneau, AK
Juneau, WI
Kahului, HI
Kailua-Kona, HI
Kalamazoo, MI
Kalispell, MT
Kalispell City, MT

Kankakee, IL
Kansas City Downtown, MO
Kauai, HI
Kearney, NE
Kelso, WA
Kenai, AK
Kendall Tamiami Executive, FL
Kenosha, WI
Keokuk, IA
Kerrville, TX
Ketchikan Intl, AK
Key West Intl, FL
Killeen, TX
Kingston, NY
Kingsville, TX
Kinston, NC
Kirksville, MO
Kissimmee, FL
Klamath Falls, OR
Knoxville, TN
Knoxville Downtown, TN
Kosciusko, MS
La Crosse, WI
La Grange Callaway, GA
La Porte, TX
La Verne, CA
Laconia, NH
Lafayette, IN
Lafayette, LA
Lafayette, TN
Lake Placid, NY
Lake Tahoe, CA
Lake Wales, FL
Lakeland, FL
Lakeport, CA
Lamar, CO
Lambertville, MI
Lampasas, TX
Lancaster, CA
Lancaster, PA
Lancaster, TX
Lansing, IL
Lansing, MI
Laramie, WY
Laredo Intl, TX
Las Cruces, NM
Las Vegas, NM
Las Vegas, NV
Lawrence, MA
Lawrenceville, IL
Lebanon, NH
Lebanon, TN
Leesburg, VA
Lewisburg, WV
Lewistown, MT
Lexington Blue Grass, KY
Lima, OH
Lincoln, CA
Lincoln, NE
Little Falls, MN
Little Rock, AR
Livermore, CA
Lock Haven, PA
Lompoc, CA
Lone Rock, WI
Long Beach, CA

Longview, TX
Lorain-Elyria, OH
Los Angeles Intl, CA
Los Banos, CA
Louisville, KY
Louisville Standiford, KY
Lubbock Intl, TX
Lubbock Town and Country, TX
Lufkin, TX
Lynchburg, VA
Macon, GA
Madera, CA
Madison, WI
Madisonville, KY
Magnolia, AR
Mammoth June Lakes, CA
Manassas, VA
Manchester, NH
Manhattan, KS
Mankato, MN
Mansfield, LA
Mansfield, OH
Manville, NJ
Marathon, FL
Marianna, FL
Marion, OH
Mariposa-Yosemite, CA
Marquette, MI
Marshall, MN
Marshfield, WI
Mason City, IA
Massena Intl, NY
Mattoon Charleston, IL
Maxton, NC
McAlester, OK
McAllen, TX
McCall, ID
McCook, NE
McGregor, TX
McPherson, KS
Medford, OR
Medina, OH
Melbourne, FL
Melfa, VA
Memphis Intl, TN
Meridian, MS
Mesa Falcon Field, AZ
Miami Intl, FL
Miami Opa Locka, FL
Middle Georgia Regional, GA
Midland Intl, TX
Millersburg, OH
Millinocket, ME
Milwaukee Timmerman, WI
Milwaukee–Gen Mitchell, WI
Mineola, TX
Minneapolis, MN
Minneapolis Anoka-Blaine, MN
Minneapolis–Flying Cloud, MN
Minocqua-Woodruff, WI
Minot Intl, ND

Missoula, MT
Mobile, AL
Mobile-Brookley, AL
Modesto City County, CA
Moline, IL
Monahans, TX
Moncks Corner, SC
Monroe, LA
Monroe, NC
Monroeville, AL
Monterey, CA
Montgomery, AL
Montgomery, NY
Montrose, CO
Morganton, NC
Morrilton Municipal, AR
Morristown, NJ
Morristown, TN
Moses Lake, WA
Moultrie, GA
Moundsville, WV
Mount Pleasant, MI
Mount Pleasant, TX
Mount Pocono, PA
Mount Sterling, KY
Mount Vernon, IL
Mountain Home, AR
Muncie, IN
Murfreesboro, TN
Muscatine, IA
Muscle Shoals, AL
Muskegon, MI
Nantucket, MA
Napa, CA
Nashville, TN
Natchez, MS
Nenana, AK
Neosho, MO
New Braunfels, TX
New Castle, IN
New Castle, PA
New Castle County, DE
New Hanover Intl, NC
New Haven, CT
New Iberia, LA
New Kent County, VA
New Orleans Intl, LA
New Orleans Lakefront, LA
New Roads, LA
New York Kennedy Intl, NY
New York La Guardia, NY
Newark, OH
Newark Intl, NJ
Newnan Coweta, GA
Newport News, VA
Newton, KS
Niagara Falls, NY
Nogales Intl, AZ
Norfolk, NE
Norfolk Intl, VA
Norman, OK
North Las Vegas Air Terminal, NV
North Myrtle Beach, SC
North Platte, NE
Norwood, MA
Novato, CA

COMMUNICATIONS

Air (continued)

Oakdale, CA
Oakland, CA
Ogden, UT
Oklahoma City, OK
Oklahoma City
  Expressway, OK
Oklahoma
  City–Sundance, OK
Oklahoma City–Wiley
  Post, OK
Olive Branch, MS
Olney, TX
Olympia, WA
Omaha Eppley, NE
Omaha Millard, NE
Ontario, CA
Ontario, OR
Orangeburg, SC
Orlando Executive, FL
Orlando Intl, FL
Oroville, CA
Oshkosh, WI
Ottumwa, IA
Owatonna, MN
Owensboro, KY
Owosso, MI
Oxford, CT
Oxford, MS
Oxnard, CA
Paducah, KY
Pahokee, FL
Palacios, TX
Palm Beach Intl, FL
Palm Springs, CA
Pampa, TX
Panama City, FL
Paris, TX
Parkersburg Wood
  County, WV
Parsons, KS
Pascagoula, MS
Pasco, WA
Paso Robles, CA
Patterson, LA
Pecos, TX
Pendleton, OR
Pensacola, FL
Peoria, IL
Perkasie, PA
Perry, GA
Perryton, TX
Philadelphia, PA
Philadelphia Intl, PA
Phoenix, AZ
Phoenix–Deer Valley, AZ
Phoenix–Goodyear, AZ
Pierre, SD
Pittsburg, KS
Pittsburgh Allegheny Co,
  PA
Pittsburgh Intl, PA
Pittsburgh Metro, PA
Plainfield, IL
Plainview, TX
Plattsburgh, NY

Plymouth, IN
Plymouth, MA
Pocahontas, IA
Point Lookout, MS
Pompano Beach, FL
Ponca City, OK
Pontiac, MI
Port Angeles, WA
Port Huron, MI
Portland, ME
Portland Hillsboro, OR
Portland Intl, OR
Portland Troutdale, OR
Portsmouth, VA
Prattville, AL
Prescott, AZ
Presque Isle, ME
Price, UT
Princeton, ME
Providence, RI
Provo, UT
Pueblo, CO
Quakertown, PA
Racine, WI
Raleigh County, WV
Raleigh-Durham, NC
Rapid City, SD
Rawlins, WY
Reading, PA
Redding, CA
Redlands, CA
Redmond, OR
Redwood Falls, MN
Reedley, CA
Reidsville, NC
Reno, NV
Reno-Stead, NV
Renton, WA
Rexburg, ID
Rhinelander, WI
Rialto, CA
Richmond Intl, VA
Riverside, CA
Roanoke, VA
Robinson, IL
Rochester, MN
Rochester, NY
Rockford, IL
Rocky Mount, NC
Rolla, ND
Romeoville, IL
Roswell, NM
Roundup, MT
Russell, KS
Russellville, AR
Rutland, VT
Sacramento, CA
Sacramento
  Metropolitan, CA
Saginaw, MI
Saginaw-Browne, MI
Salina, KS
Salinas, CA
Salisbury, MD
Salisbury, NC

Salt Lake City Intl, UT
San Angelo, TX
San Antonio, TX
San Antonio Intl, TX
San Diego, CA
San Diego Brown Field, CA
San Diego Montgomery, CA
San Francisco Intl, CA
San José, CA
San Luis Obispo, CA
Sandusky, OH
Sanford, FL
Sanford, NC
Santa Ana, CA
Santa Barbara, CA
Santa Fe, NM
Santa Maria, CA
Santa Monica, CA
Saranac Lake, NY
Sarasota, FL
Saratoga, WY
Savannah, GA
Scottsbluff, NE
Scottsdale, AZ
Seattle-Tacoma Intl, WA
Sedalia, MO
Selinsgrove, PA
Selma, AL
Selmer, TN
Shamokin, PA
Shawnee, OK
Sheboygan Falls, WI
Sheridan, WY
Shirley, NY
Shreveport, LA
Sidney, MT
Sikeston, MO
Sioux City, IA
Sioux Falls, SD
Slidell, LA
Smyrna, TN
Snyder, TX
Somerset, KY
Somerset, PA
Sonoma County, CA
South Bend, IN
Southern Pines, NC
Southwest Georgia
  Regional, GA
Sparta, MI
Sparta, TN
Spencer, IA
Spokane Felts Field, WA
Spokane Intl, WA
Springfield, IL
Springfield, KY
Springfield, MO
Springhill, LA
St Anthony, GA
St Cloud, MN
St Francis, KS
St John, NB
St Joseph, MO
St Louis, MO
St Paul, MN

St Petersburg, FL
Stanton, TX
Statesboro, GA
Statesville, NC
Stephenville, TX
Stevens Point, WI
Stewart Intl, NY
Stillwater, OK
Stockton, CA
Stuart, FL
Sugar Land Municipal, TX
Sweetwater, TX
Syracuse, NY
Tacoma, WA
Tallahassee, FL
Tampa, FL
Tampa Intl, FL
Taos, NM
Taylorville, IL
Teterboro, NJ
Texarkana, AR
Tifton, GA
Tillamook, OR
Titusville, FL
Toccoa, GA
Toledo, OH
Tonopah, NV
Topeka, KS
Trenton, NJ
Tri-City Regional, TN
Truckee, CA
Tucson, AZ
Tulsa, OK
Tupelo, MS
Tuscaloosa, AL
Tuskegee, AL
Twentynine Palms, CA
Twin Falls, ID
Tyler, TX
Ukiah, CA
Union City, TN
Valdosta, GA
Van Nuys, CA
Vancouver, WA
Vernal, UT
Vero Beach, FL
Victoria, TX
Waco, TX
Wadsworth, OH
Walla Walla, WA
Walnut Ridge, AR
Walterboro, SC
Wapakoneta, OH
Warsaw, IN
Waseca, MN
Washington, DC
Washington Dulles Intl, DC
Waterloo, IA
Watertown, SD
Watertown, WI
Watertown Intl, NY
Waukegan, IL
Waukesha, WI
Wausau, WI
Wasau–Stevens Point, WI

Wellsville, NY	Westfield, MA	Willmar, MN	Xenia, OH
Wenatchee-Pangborn Memorial, WA	Westhampton Beach, NY	Willoughby, OH	Yakima, WA
West Bend, WI	**Wichita**, KS	Wilson Industrial Air Centre, NC	Yankton, SD
West Dover, VT	Wichita Falls, TX		York, PA
West Memphis, AR	Wichita Falls Valley, TX	Winchester, VA	Youngstown, OH
West Palm Beach, FL	Wildwood, NJ	Winslow, AZ	Yuma, AZ
West Plains, MO	Wilkes-Barre, PA	Winston-Salem, NC	Zanesville, OH
Westchester Co White Plains, NY	Willcox Cochise, AZ	Woodward, OK	
	Willimantic, CT	Worcester, MA	
	Williston, ND	Worland, WY	

UK local airports

This list comprises only the airports in Britain which offer passenger services.

Airport	Other name	Location	Type of traffic
England			
Bembridge		Isle of Wight	Charter, IT services
Birmingham	Elmdon	NE of Birmingham	Scheduled, charter, IT, freight services
Blackpool	Squires Gate	S of Blackpool	Scheduled, charter, IT services
Bournemouth	Hurn	NE of Bournemouth	Scheduled, freight services
Bristol	Lulsgate	SW of Bristol	Scheduled, charter, IT services
Cambridge	Teversham	E of Cambridge	Scheduled, charter, IT services
Carlisle	Crosby	NE of Carlisle	Scheduled services; light aircraft
Coventry	Baginton	S of Coventry	Scheduled, charter, IT services; club and private aircraft
East Midlands	Castle Donington	SW of Kegworth	Scheduled, charter, IT, freight services; club and private aircraft
Exeter	Clyst Honiton	E of Exeter	Scheduled, charter, IT services
Gatwick		S of London	Scheduled, charter, IT services
Gloucestershire	Staverton	W of Cheltenham	Charter, IT services
Heathrow		W of London	Scheduled services
Humberside	Kirmington	E of Scunthorpe	Scheduled, charter, IT services
Kent International	Manston	NW of Ramsgate	Non-scheduled, charter, IT, freight services
Land's End	St Just	W of Penzance	Scheduled services; club and private aircraft
Leeds/Bradford	Yeadon	W of Leeds	Scheduled, charter, IT services
Liverpool	John Lennon	SE of Liverpool	Scheduled, charter, IT, mail services; club and private aircraft
London City	STOLport	London	Scheduled services, occasional charter, IT services
Luton		SE of Luton	Scheduled, charter, IT, freight services; club aircraft
Lydd		SW of New Romney	Scheduled, charter, IT services; club and private aircraft
Manchester	Ringway	S of Manchester	Scheduled, charter, IT services; club and private aircraft
Newcastle	Woolsington	NW of Newcastle	Scheduled, charter, IT services
Newquay	St Mawgan	NE of Newquay	Scheduled services; occasional company charter flights
Norwich	Horsham St Faith	N of Norwich	Scheduled, charter, IT services
Penzance		E of Penzance	Scheduled helicopter services
Plymouth City		N of Plymouth	Scheduled services; private and club aircraft
Sheffield		NE of Sheffield	Scheduled services
Shoreham		W of Shoreham	Air taxi, private, club, school flights
Southampton	Eastleigh	NE of Southampton	Scheduled, freight services; private and club aircraft
Southend	Rochford	N of Southend	Scheduled, charter, IT, freight services; private and club aircraft
Stansted		E of Bishop's Stortford	Scheduled, charter, IT, freight services
Teesside	Middleton St George	E of Darlington	Scheduled, charter, IT services; school; air taxi; light aircraft
Alderney		SW Alderney	Passenger services
Guernsey		SW of St Peter Port	Scheduled, charter, freight services

Air (continued)

Airport	Other name	Location	Type of traffic
Isle of Man	Ronaldsway	SW of Douglas	Scheduled services, occasional charter, IT services
Jersey		NW of St Helier	Scheduled services, occasional charter, IT services
Scilly Isles	St Mary's	E of Hugh Town	Scheduled, helicopter, skybus services
Northern Ireland			
Belfast City	Harbour/Sydenham	Belfast	Scheduled services
Belfast International	Aldergrove	NW of Belfast	Scheduled, charter, IT, freight services
Eglinton		N of Londonderry	Scheduled services; light aircraft
Scotland			
Aberdeen	Dyce	NW of Aberdeen	Scheduled, charter, IT, helicopter services
Barra	North Bay	Barra	Scheduled services; air taxi
Benbecula		NW Benbecula	Scheduled services
Colonsay		Colonsay	Scheduled services
Dundee	Riverside	W of Dundee	Business charter service
Eday		W Orkney	Scheduled services
Edinburgh	Turnhouse	W of Edinburgh	Scheduled, charter, IT, freight services; club and private aircraft
Fair Isle		Shetland	Scheduled services
Fetlar		Shetland	Scheduled services
Glasgow	Abbotsinch	W of Glasgow	Scheduled, charter, IT services
Hoy	Longhope	Orkney	Scheduled services
Inverness	Dalcross	NE of Inverness	Scheduled and non-scheduled helicopter services
Islay/Port Ellen	Glenegedale	S Islay	Scheduled services
Kirkwall		Orkney	Scheduled services; oil-industry traffic
Machrihanish	Campbeltown	Kintyre	Scheduled services
North Ronaldsay		SW Orkney	Scheduled services
Oronsay		Oronsay	Scheduled services
Papa Stour		S Shetland	Scheduled services
Papa Westray		W Orkney	Scheduled services
Prestwick		S of Kilmarnock	Charter, IT services
Sanday		C Orkney	Scheduled services
Stornoway		E of Stornoway	Scheduled services; transit stop
Stronsay		NW Orkney	Scheduled services
Sumburgh		Shetland	Scheduled helicopter services; oil-industry traffic
Tingwall	Lerwick	Shetland	Scheduled services
Unst	Baltasound	Shetland	Scheduled services
Westray		N Orkney	Scheduled services
Whalsay		NE Shetland	Scheduled services
Wick		Wick	Scheduled services
Wales			
Cardiff-Wales	Rhoose	SW of Cardiff	Scheduled, charter, IT, freight services

International airports

Abadan	Iran	**Aminu**	Kano, Nigeria
Abu Dhabi	United Arab Emirates	**Anchorage**	Alaska, USA
Adana	Turkey	**Archangel**	Russia
Adelaide	Australia	**Arlanda**	Stockholm, Sweden
Agno	Lugano, Switzerland	**Arnos Vale**	St Vincent
Ain el Bay	Constantine, Algeria	**Arrecife**	Lanzarote, Canary Islands
Albany County	New York, USA	**Arturo Marino Benitez**	Santiago, Chile
Ålborg Roedslet	Nørresundby, Denmark	**Asturias**	Spain
Albuquerque	New Mexico, USA	**Ataturk**	Istanbul, Turkey
Alexandria	Egypt	**Auckland**	New Zealand
Alfonso Bonilla Aragon	Cali, Columbia	**Augusto C Sandino**	Managua, Nicaragua
Alicante	Spain	**Baghdad**	Iraq
Almería	Spain	**Bahrain**	Bahrain
Amarillo	Texas, USA	**Bali/Ngurah Rai**	Denpasar, Indonesia
Amborovy	Majunga, Madagascar	**Balice**	Cracow, Poland
Amilcar Cabral International	Sal Island, Cape Verde	**Bandar Seri Begawan**	Brunei
		Baneasa	Bucharest, Romania

COMMUNICATIONS

Bangkok	Thailand	Cristoforo Colombo	Genoa, Italy
Barajas	Madrid, Spain	Crown Point	Scarborough, Tobago
Barcelona	Spain	Cuscatlán	El Salvador
Basle-Mulhouse	Basle, Switzerland	D F Malan	Cape Town, South Africa
Beijing	China	Dalaman	Turkey
Beira	Mozambique	Dallas/Fort Worth	Texas, USA
Beirut	Khaldeh, Lebanon	Damascus	Syria
Belfast	UK	Dar-es-Salaam	Tanzania
Belgrade	Serbia	Darwin	Australia
Belize City	Belize	Des Moines	Iowa, USA
Ben Gurion	Tel Aviv, Israel	Detroit-Wayne County	Detroit, MI, USA
Benina	Benghazi, Libya	Deurne	Antwerp, Belgium
Benito Juarez	Mexico City, Mexico	Dhahran	Al Khobar, Saudi Arabia
Berlin-Schonefeld	Berlin, Germany	Djibouti	Djibouti
Berlin-Tegel	Berlin, Germany	Doha	Qatar
Berne	Switzerland	Dois de Julho	Salvador, Brazil
Billund	Denmark	Domodedovo	Moscow, Russia
Birmingham	Alabama, USA	Don Miguel Hidalgo	Guadalaraja, Mexico
Blackburne/Plymouth	Montserrat	y Castilla	
Blagnac	Toulouse, France	Dorval	Montreal, Canada
Bole	Addis Ababa, Ethiopia	Douala	Cameroon
Bombay	India	Dresden	Germany
Borispol	Kiev, Ukraine	Dubai	United Arab Emirates
Boukhalef	Tangier, Morocco	Dublin	Ireland
Boulogne	France	Dubrovnik	Croatia
Bourgas	Bulgaria	Dulles	Washington, DC, USA
Bradley	Hartford, CT, USA	Düsseldorf	Germany
Brasília	Brazil	Ecterdingen	Stuttgart, Germany
Bremen	Germany	Edmonton	Canada
Brisbane	Australia	Eduardo Gomes	Manaus, Brazil
Brnik	Ljubljana, Slovenia	Eindhoven	Netherlands
Bromma	Stockholm, Sweden	El Alto	La Paz, Bolivia
Brussels National	Belgium	El Dorado	Bogotá, Colombia
Buffalo	New York, USA	El Paso	Texas, USA
Bujumbura	Burundi	Elat	Israel
Bulawayo	Zimbabwe	Elmas	Cagliari, Italy
Butmir	Sarajevo, Bosnia-Herzegovina	Entebbe	Uganda
Cairns	Queensland, Australia	Entzheim	Strasbourg, France
Cairo	Egypt	Eppley Airfield	Omaha, Nebraska, USA
Calabar	Nigeria	Erie	Pennsylvania, USA
Calcutta	India	Ernestso Cortissoz	Barranquilla, Colombia
Calgary	Canada	Esbjerg	Denmark
Cancún	Mexico	Esenboga	Ankara, Turkey
Cannon	Reno, NV, USA	Faleolo	Apia, Samoa
Canton	Akron, OH, USA	Faro	Portugal
Capodichino	Naples, Italy	Ferihegy	Budapest, Hungary
Carrasco	Montevideo, Uruguay	Findel	Luxembourg
Carthage	Tunis, Tunisia	Fiumicino	Rome, Italy
Cebu	Philippines	(Leonardo da Vinci)	
Changi	Singapore	Flesland	Bergen, Norway
Charleroi (Gossilies)	Belgium	Fontanarossa	Catania, Sicily
Charles de Gaulle	Paris, France	Fort de France	Lamentin, Martinique
Charleston	South Carolina, USA	Fort Lauderdale	Florida, USA
Charleston	West Virginia, USA	Fort Myers	Florida, USA
Charlotte	North Carolina, USA	Frankfurt am Main	Germany
Château Bougon	Nantes, France	Freeport	Bahamas
Chek Lap Kok	Hong Kong	Frejorgues	Montpellier, France
Christchurch	New Zealand	Fuenterrabía	San Sebastián, Spain
Ciampino	Rome, Italy	Fuerteventura	Canary Islands
Cologne-Bonn	Cologne, Germany	Fuhlsbuttel	Hamburg, Germany
Columbus	Ohio, USA	G Marconi	Bologna, Italy
Congonhas	São Paulo, Brazil	Galileo Galilei	Pisa, Italy
Copenhagen	Kastrup, Denmark	Gardermoen	Oslo, Norway
Cork	Ireland	Gatwick	London, UK
Costa Smeralda	Olbia, Sardinia	G'Bessia	Conakry, Guinea Republic
Côte d'Azure	Nice, France	Gen Abelard I.	Tijuana, Mexico
Cotonou	Benin	Rodriguez	

COMMUNICATIONS

Air (continued)

COMMUNICATIONS

Gen Juan N Alvarez	Acapulco, Mexico
Gen Manuel Marquez de Leon	La Paz, Mexico
Gen Mariano Escobedo	Monterrey, Mexico
Gen Mitchell	Milwaukee, WI, USA
Gen Rafael Buelna	Mazatlán, Mexico
Geneva	Switzerland
Gerona/Costa Brava	Gerona, Spain
Gillot	St Denis de la Reunion
Golden Rock	St Kitts
Goleniów	Szczecin, Poland
Glasgow	UK
Granada	Spain
Grantley Adams	Bridgetown, Barbados
Greater Cincinatti	Kentucky, USA
Greater Pittsburgh	Pennsylvania, USA
Guam	Guam
Guararapes	Recife, Brazil
Guarulhos	São Paulo, Brazil
Hahaya	Moroni, Comoros
Halifax	Canada
Halim Perdanakusama	Jakarta, Indonesia
Hamilton Kindley Field	Hamilton, Bermuda
Hancock Field	Syracuse, NY, USA
Haneda	Tokyo, Japan
Hannover-Langenhagen	Hanover, Germany
Hanoi	Vietnam
Harare	Zimbabwe
Harrisburg	Pennsylvania, USA
Hartsfield	Atlanta, Georgia, USA
Hassan	Laayoune, Morocco
Hato	Curaçao, Netherlands Antilles
Heathrow	London, UK
Hellenikon	Athens, Greece
Henderson Field	Honiari, Solomon Islands
Heraklion	Crete, Greece
Hewanorra	St Lucia
Ho Chi Minh City	Vietnam
Hong Kong	Hong Kong
Hongqiao	Shanghai, China
Honolulu	Hawaii, USA
Hopkins	Cleveland, OH, USA
Houari Boumedienne	Dar-el-Beida, Algeria
Houston	Texas, USA
Ibiza	Balearics, Spain
Indianapolis	Indiana, USA
Indira Ghandi	Delhi, India
Inezgane	Agadir, Morocco
Islamabad	Pakistan
Isle Verde	San Juan, Puerto Rico
Itazuke	Fukuoka, Japan
Ivanka	Bratislava, Slovak Republic
Ivato	Antananarivo, Madagascar
Izmir	Turkey
J F Kennedy	New York, USA
Jackson Field	Port Moresby, Papua New Guinea
Jacksonville	Florida, USA
James M Cox	Dayton, OH, USA
Jan Smuts	Johannesburg, South Africa
Jomo Kenyatta	Nairobi, Kenya
Jorge Chavez	Lima, Peru
Jose Marti	Havana, Cuba
Juan Santa Maria	Alajuela, Costa Rica
Kagoshima	Japan
Kalmar	Sweden

Kamazu	Lilongwe, Malawi
Kansai	Osaka, Japan
Kansas City	Missouri, USA
Kaohsiung	Taiwan
Karachi	Pakistan
Karpathos	Karpathos, Greece
Katunayake	Colombo, Sri Lanka
Keflavik	Reykjavík, Iceland
Kent County	Grand Rapids, MI, USA
Kerkyra	Corfu, Greece
Key West	Florida, USA
Khartoum	Sudan
Khoramaksar	Aden, Yemen
Khwaja Rawash	Kabul, Afghanistan
Kigali	Rwanda
Kimpo	Seoul, South Korea
King Abdul Aziz	Jeddah, Saudi Arabia
King Khaled	Riyadh, Saudi Arabia
Kjevik	Kristiansand, Norway
Klagenfurt	Austria
Komaki	Nagoya, Japan
Kos	Greece
Kota Kinabalu	Sabah, Malaysia
Kotoka	Accra, Ghana
Kranebitten	Innsbruck, Austria
Kuching	Sarawak, Malaysia
Kungsangen	Norrköping, Sweden
Kuwait International	Kuwait
La Aurora	Guatemala City, Guatemala
La Coruña	Spain
La Guardia	New York, USA
La Mesa	San Pedro Sula, Honduras
La Parra	Jerez de la Frontera, Spain
Lahore	Pakistan
Landvetter	Gothenburg, Sweden
Larnaca	Cyprus
Las Americas	Santo Domingo, Dominican Republic
Las Palmas	Gran Canaria, Canary Islands
Le Raizet	Point-à-Pitre, Guadeloupe
Leipzig	Germany
Les Angades	Oujda, Morocco
Lesquin	Lille, France
Lester B Pearson	Toronto, Canada
Libreville	Gabon
Lic Gustavo Diaz Ordaz	Puerto Vallarta
Lic Manuel Crecencio Rejon	Mérida, Mexico
Liège (Bierset)	Belgium
Linate	Milan, Italy
Lincoln	Nebraska, USA
Lindbergh	San Diego, USA
Linz	Austria
Lisbon	Portugal
Little Rock	Arkansas, USA
Llabanère	Perpignan, France
Logan	Boston, MA, USA
Lomé	Togo
London Luton	UK
Long Beach	California, USA
Los Angeles	California, USA
Loshitsa	Minsk, Belarus
Louis Botha	Durban, South Africa
Louisville	Kentucky, USA
Lourdes/Tarbes	Juillan, France
Luanda	Angola

Luano	Lubumbashi, D.R. Congo
Lubbock	Texas, USA
Luis Munoz Marin	San Juan, Puerto Rica
Lungi	Freetown, Sierra Leone
Luqa	Malta
Lusaka	Zambia
Luxor	Egypt
Maastricht	Netherlands
McCarran	Las Vegas, NV, USA
McCoy	Orlando, FL, USA
Mactan	Cebu, Philippines
Mahon	Menorca
Mais Gate	Port au Prince, Haiti
Málaga	Spain
Male	Maldives
Malpensa	Milan, Italy
Managua	Nicaragua
Manchester	New Hampshire, USA
Manchester	UK
Maputo	Mozambique
Marco Polo	Venice, Italy
Mariscal Sucre	Quito, Ecuador
Maseru	Lesotho
Matsapha	Manzini, Swaziland
Maupertus	Cherbourg, France
Maxglan	Salzburg, Austria
Maya Maya	Brazzaville, Congo
Medina	Saudi Arabia
Meenambakkam	Madras, India
Mehrabad	Teheran, Iran
Melita	Djerba, Tunisia
Memphis	Tennessee, USA
Menara	Marrakech, Morocco
Merignac	Bordeaux, France
Miami	Florida, USA
Midway	Chicago, IL, USA
Mingaladon Yangon	Myanmar (Burma)
Ministro Pistarini	Buenos Aires, Argentina
Minneapolis/St Paul	Minneapolis, USA
Mirabel	Montreal, Canada
Mogadishu	Somalia
Mohamed V	Casablanca, Morocco
Moi	Mombasa, Kenya
Monroe County	Rochester, NY, USA
Morelos	Mexico City, Mexico
Münster/Osnabrück	Germany
Murmansk	Russia
Murtala Muhammed	Lagos, Nigeria
Nadi	Fiji
Nagasaki	Japan
Narita	Tokyo, Japan
Narssarsuaq	Greenland
Nashville	Tennessee, USA
Nassau	Bahamas
Nauru	Nauru
N'djamena	Chad
N'Djili	Kinshasa, D.R. Congo
Nejrab	Aleppo, Syria
Newcastle	UK
New Orleans	Louisiana, USA
Newark	New Jersey, USA
Niamey	Niger
Ninoy Aquino	Manila, Philippines
Niš	Yugoslavia (Serbia and Montenegro)
Norfolk	Virginia, USA
Norman Manley	Kingston, Jamaica
North Front	Gibraltar

Nouadhibou	Mauritania
Nouakchott	Mauritania
Novo-Alexeyevka	Tblisi, Georgia
Nuremburg	Germany
Oakland	California, USA
Octeville	Le Havrets, France
Odense	Denmark
O'Hare	Chicago, IL, USA
Okecie	Warsaw, Poland
Okinawa	Naha, Japan
Oran	Algeria
Orebro	Sweden
Orlando	Florida, USA
Orly	Paris, France
Osaka	Japan
Osvaldo Veira	Bissau, Guinea Bissau
Otopeni	Bucharest, Romania
Ougadougou	Burkina Faso
Owen Roberts	Grand Cayman
Pago Pago	Samoa
Palese	Bari, Italy
Palma	Majorca
Pamplona	Spain
Panama City	Panama
Paphos	Cyprus
Papola Casale	Brindisi, Italy
Paradisi	Rhodes, Greece
Patenga	Chittagong, Bangladesh
Penang	Malaysia
Peninsula	Monterey, CA, USA
Peretola	Florence, Italy
Perth	Australia
Peshawar	Pakistan
Peterson Field	Colorado Springs, CO, USA
Philadelphia	Pennsylvania, USA
Piarco	Port of Spain, Trinidad
Pleso	Zagreb, Croatia
Pochentong	Phnom Penh, Cambodia
Point Salines	Grenada
Pointe Noire	Congo
Polonia	Medan, Indonesia
Ponta Delgado	São Miguel, Azores
Port Bouet	Abidjan, Côte d'Ivoire
Port Harcourt	Nigeria
Portland	Maine, USA
Portland	Oregon, USA
Port Sudan	Sudan
Porto Pedra Rubras	Oporto, Portugal
Praia	Cape Verde
Prestwick	UK
Princess Beatriz	Aruba
Provence	Marseille, France
Pula	Croatia
Pulkovo	St Petersburg, Russia
Punta Arenas	Chile
Punta Raisi	Palermo, Italy
Queen Alia	Amman, Jordan
Raleigh/Durham	North Carolina, USA
Ras al Khaimah	United Arab Emirates
Rebiechowo	Gdańsk, Poland
Regina	Canada
Reina Sofia	Tenerife
Rejon	Merida, Mexico
Richmond	Virginia, USA
Riem	Munich, Germany
Rio de Janeiro	Brazil
Riyadh	Saudi Arabia
Roberts	Monrovia, Liberia

COMMUNICATIONS

COMMUNICATIONS

Air (continued)

Rochambau	Cayenne, French Guiana
Robert Mueller Municipal	Austin, TX, USA
Ronchi dei Legionari	Trieste, Italy
Rotterdam	Netherlands
Ruzyne	Prague, Czech Republic
Saab	Linköping, Sweden
St Eufemia	Lamezia Terma, Italy
St Louis	Missouri, USA
St Thomas	Virgin Islands
Sainte Foy	Quebec, Canada
Sale	Rabat, Morocco
Salgado Filho	Porto Alegre, Brazil
Salt Lake City	Utah, USA
San Antonio	Texas, USA
San Diego	California, USA
San Francisco	California, USA
San Giusto	Pisa, Italy
San Javier	Murcia, Spain
San José	California, USA
San Pablo	Seville, Spain
San Salvador	El Salvador
Sanaa	Yemen
Sangster	Montego Bay, Jamaica
Santa Caterina	Funchal, Madeira
Santa Cruz	La Palma, Canary Islands
Santa Isabel	Malabo, Guinea
Santander	Spain
Santiago	Spain
Santos Dumont	Rio de Janeiro, Brazil
São Tomé	São Tomé
Satolas	Lyon, France
Schiphol	Amsterdam, Netherlands
Schwechat	Vienna, Austria
Seeb	Muscat, Oman
Senou	Bamako, Mali
Seychelles	Mahe, Seychelles
Sfax	Tunisia
Shannon	Ireland
Sharjah	United Arab Emirates
Sheremetyevo	Moscow, Russia
Silvio Pettirossi	Asuncion, Paraguay
Simon Bolivar	Caracas, Venezuela
Simon Bolivar	Guayaquil, Ecuador
Sir Seewoosagur Ramgoolam	Plaisance, Mauritius
Sir Seretse Khama	Gaborone, Botswana
Skanes	Monastir, Morocco
Skopje	Macedonia
Sky Harbour	Phoenix, AZ, USA
Snilow	Lwow, Ukraine
Sofia	Bulgaria
Sola	Stavanger, Norway
Sondica	Bilbao, Spain
Søndre Strømfjord	Greenland
Spilve	Riga, Latvia
Split	Croatia
Spokane	Washington, USA
Stansted	UK
Stapleton	Denver, CO, USA
Sturup	Malmö, Sweden
Subang	Kuala Lumpur, Malaysia
Sunan	Pyongyang, North Korea
Suvarnabhumi	Thailand
Sydney	Sydney, Australia
Tacoma	Washington, USA

Taiwan Taoyuan	Taipei, Taiwan
Tallahassee	Florida, USA
Tamatve	Madagascar
Tampa	Florida, USA
Tegucigalpa	Toncontin, Honduras
Thalerhof	Graz, Austria
Theodore Francis	Providence, RI, USA
Thessalonika	Greece
Timehri	Georgetown, Guyana
Timis oara	Romania
Tirana	Albania
Tito Menniti	Reggio Calabria, Italy
Tontouta	Noumea, New Caledonia
Townsville	Australia
Tribhuyan	Kathmandu, Nepal
Tripoli	Libya
Trivandrum	India
Truax Field	Madison, WI, USA
Tucson	Arizona, USA
Tullamarine	Melbourne, Australia
Turin	Italy
Turku	Finland
Turnhouse	Edinburgh, UK
Ulemiste	Tallinn, Estonia
Unokovo	Moscow, Russia
Uplands	Ottawa, Canada
V C Bird	Antigua
Vaasa	Finland
Vagar	Faroe Islands
Valencia	Spain
Vancouver	Canada
Vantaa	Helsinki, Finland
Varna	Bulgaria
Verona	Italy
Victoria	British Columbia, Canada
Vigie	St Lucia
Vigo	Spain
Vilnius	Lithuania
Vilo de Porto	Santa Maria, Azores
Viracopos	São Paulo, Brazil
Vitoria	Spain
Washington	Baltimore, MD, USA
Wattay	Vientiane, Laos
Wellington	New Zealand
Wichita	Kansas, USA
Will Rogers	Oklahoma City, OK, USA
Winnipeg	Manitoba, Canada
Yoff	Dakar, Senegal
Yundam	Banjul, Gambia
Zakynthos	Greece
Zia	Dhaka, Bangladesh
Zürich	Switzerland

TELECOMMUNICATIONS

International dialling codes

This table gives the international telephone direct-dialling codes for most countries.

It is not always possible to dial internationally from every country to every other country, and there are sometimes restrictions and special numbers within a country, for which it is necessary to consult the local telephone directory.

Dialling procedure is as follows:

(a) Dial out, using the access code of the country from which you are making the call; you may need to wait for a dialling tone or announcement (shown by + in the table below).

(b) Then dial the code of the country you are calling, followed by any area or city code, and the subscriber number. (When making an international call, it is usually necessary to omit any initial 0 or 9 of an area/city code.)

Country	Dialling-out code	Dialling-in code	Country	Dialling-out code	Dialling-in code
Afghanistan	00	93	Côte d'Ivoire	00	225
Albania	00	355	Croatia	00	385
Algeria	00+	213	Cuba	00	53
Andorra	00	376	Cyprus	00	357
Angola	00	244	Czech Republic	00	420
Anguilla	00	1 264	Denmark	00	45
Antigua and Barbuda	00	1 268	Djibouti	00	253
Antilles (Netherlands)	00	599	Dominica	00	1 767
Argentina	00	54	Dominican	00	1 809
Armenia	00	374	Republic		
Aruba	00	297	Ecuador	00	593
Ascension Island	00	247	Egypt	00	20
Australia	00	61	El Salvador	00	503
Austria	00	43	Equatorial Guinea	00	240
Azerbaijan	00	994	Eritrea	00	291
Azores	00	351	Estonia	00	372
Bahamas	00	1 242	Ethiopia	00	251
Bahrain	00	973	Falkland Islands	00	500
Bangladesh	00	880	Faroe Islands	00	298
Barbados	00	1 246	Fiji	00	679
Belarus	00	375	Finland	00	358
Belgium	00+	32	France	00+	33
Belize	00	501	French Guiana	00	594
Benin	00	229	French Polynesia	00	689
Bermuda	00	1 441	Gabon	00	241
Bhutan	00	975	Gambia	00	220
Bolivia	00	591	Georgia	00	995
Bosnia and Herzegovina	00	387	Germany	00	49
Botswana	00	267	Ghana	00	233
Brazil	00	55	Gibraltar	00	350
Brunei Darussalam	00	673	Greece	00	30
Bulgaria	00	359	Greenland	00	299
Burkina Faso	00	226	Grenada	00	1 473
Burundi	00	257	Guadeloupe	00	590
Cambodia	00	855	Guam	00	671
Cameroon	00	237	Guatemala	00	502
Canada	00	1	Guinea	00	224
Canary Islands	00	34	Guinea-Bissau	00	245
Cape Verde	00	238	Guyana	00	592
Cayman Islands	00	1 345	Haiti	00	509
Central African Republic	00	236	Honduras	00	504
Chad	00	235	Hong Kong	00	852
Chile	00	56	Hungary	00+	36
China	00	86	Iceland	00	354
Christmas Island	00	61	India	00	91
Cocos Island	00	61	Indonesia	00	62
Colombia	00	57	Iran	00	98
Comoros	00	269	Iraq	00	964
Congo	00	242	Ireland, Republic of	00	353
Congo, Democratic Republic of	00	243	Israel	00	972
Cook Islands	00	682	Italy	00	39
Costa Rica	00	506	Jamaica	00	1 876

International dialling codes (continued)

Country	Dialling-out code	Dialling-in code	Country	Dialling-out code	Dialling-in code
Japan	00	81	Puerto Rico	00	1 787
Jordan	00	962	Qatar	00	974
Kazakhstan	00	7	Réunion	00	262
Kenya	00	254	Romania	00	40
Kiribati	00	686	Russian Federation	00	7
Korea, PDR (North)	00	850	Rwanda	00	250
Korea, South	00	82	St Helena	00	290
Kuwait	00	965	St Kitts and Nevis	00+	1 869
Kyrgyzstan	00	996	St Lucia	00	1 758
Laos	00	856	St Pierre and Miquelon	00	508
Latvia	00	371	St Vincent and	00	1 809
Lebanon	00	961	the Grenadines		
Lesotho	00	266	Samoa	00	685
Liberia	00	231	Samoa, American	00	684
Libya	00	218	San Marino	00	378
Liechtenstein	00	41 75	São Tomé and Principe	00	239
Lithuania	00	370	Saudi Arabia	00	966
Luxembourg	00	352	Senegal	00	221
Macao	00	853	Seychelles	00	248
Macedonia	00	389	Sierra Leone	00	232
Madagascar	00	261	Singapore	00	65
Madeira	00	351	Slovak Republic	00	421
Malawi	00	265	Slovenia	00	386
Malaysia	00	60	Solomon Islands	00	677
Maldives	00	960	Somalia	00	252
Mali	00	223	South Africa	00	27
Malta	00	356	Spain	00+	34
Marshall Islands	00	692	Sri Lanka	00	94
Martinique	00	596	Sudan	00	249
Mauritania	00	222	Suriname	00	597
Mauritius	00	230	Swaziland	00	268
Mayotte	00	269	Sweden	00	46
Mexico	00	52	Switzerland	00	41
Micronesia	00	691	Syria	00	963
Moldova	00	373	Taiwan	00	886
Monaco	00+	377	Tajikistan	00	7
Mongolia	00	976	Tanzania	00	255
Montserrat	00	1 664	Thailand	00	66
Morocco	00	212	Togo	00	228
Mozambique	00	258	Tonga	00	676
Myanmar (Burma)	00	95	Trinidad and Tobago	00	1 868
Namibia	00	264	Tunisia	00	216
Nauru	00	674	Turkey	00	90
Nepal	00	977	Turkmenistan	00	993
Netherlands	00+	31	Turks and Caicos Islands	00	1 649
New Caledonia	00	687	Tuvalu	00	688
New Zealand	00	64	Uganda	00	256
Nicaragua	00	505	Ukraine	00	380
Niger	00	227	United Arab Emirates	00	971
Nigeria	00	234	United Kingdom	00	44
Niue	00	683	Uruguay	00	598
Norfolk Island	00	672	USA	00	1
Northern Mariana Islands	00	670	Uzbekistan	00	7
Norway	00	47	Vanuatu	00	678
Oman	00	968	Venezuela	00	58
Pakistan	00	92	Vietnam	00	84
Palau	00	680	Virgin Islands (UK)	00	1 284
Panama	00	507	Virgin Islands (US)	00	1 340
Papua New Guinea	00	675	Yemen	00	967
Paraguay	00	595	Yugoslavia (Serbia and	00	381
Peru	00	51	Montenegro)		
Philippines	00	63	Zambia	00	260
Poland	00	48	Zimbabwe	00	263
Portugal	00	351			

LANGUAGES

Indo-European languages

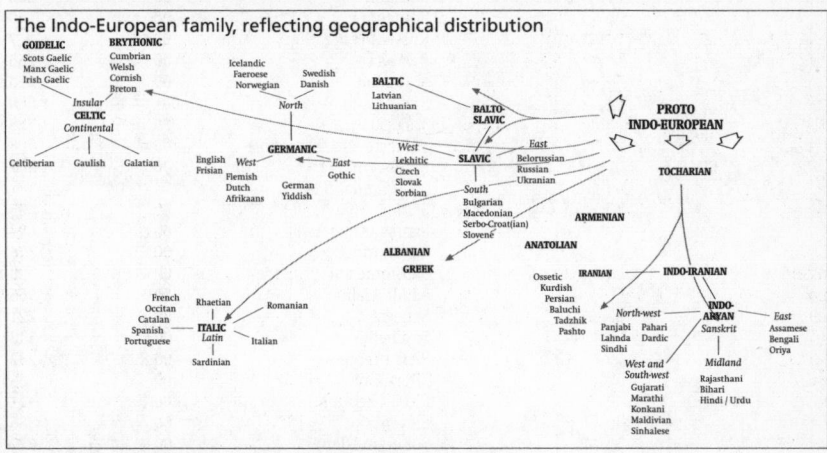

The Indo-European family, reflecting geographical distribution

Language families: numbers of speakers

Estimates of the numbers of speakers in the main language families of the world in the 1990s. The list includes Japanese and Korean, which are not clearly related to any other languages.

Main language families	Speakers
Indo-European	2 500 000 000
Sino-Tibetan	1 088 000 000
Austronesian	269 000 000
Afro-Asiatic	250 000 000
Niger-Congo	206 000 000
Dravidian	165 000 000
Japanese	126 000 000
Altaic	115 000 000

Main language families	Speakers
Austro-Asiatic	75 000 000
Tai	75 000 000
Korean	60 000 000
Nilo-Saharan	28 000 000
Uralic	24 000 000
Amerindian (North, Central, South America)	22 400 000
Caucasian	7 800 000
Miao-Yao	5 600 000
Indo-Pacific	3 500 000
Khoisan	300 000
Australian aborigine	30 000
Palaeosiberian	18 000

The top twenty languages

Speaker estimates for the world's top 20 languages in 2000 (given in millions). The estimates are based on the number of mother tongue (first-language) speakers, and do not include second-language totals, which in many cases are considerably higher (e.g. English > 800 + million).

1	Mandarin Chinese 885	11	Wu Chinese (91)
2	English (400)	12	Javanese (75)
3	Spanish (332)		Korean (75)
4	Hindi (180) (with Urdu, 236)	14	Panjabi (73)
5	Arabic (200)		Telugu (73)
6	Portuguese (175)	16	French (72)
7	Bengali (168)	17	Marathi (65)
8	Russian (170)		Tamil (65)
9	Japanese (125)	19	Italian (57)
10	German (100)	20	Yue Chinese (Cantonese) (55)

COMMUNICATIONS

World language families

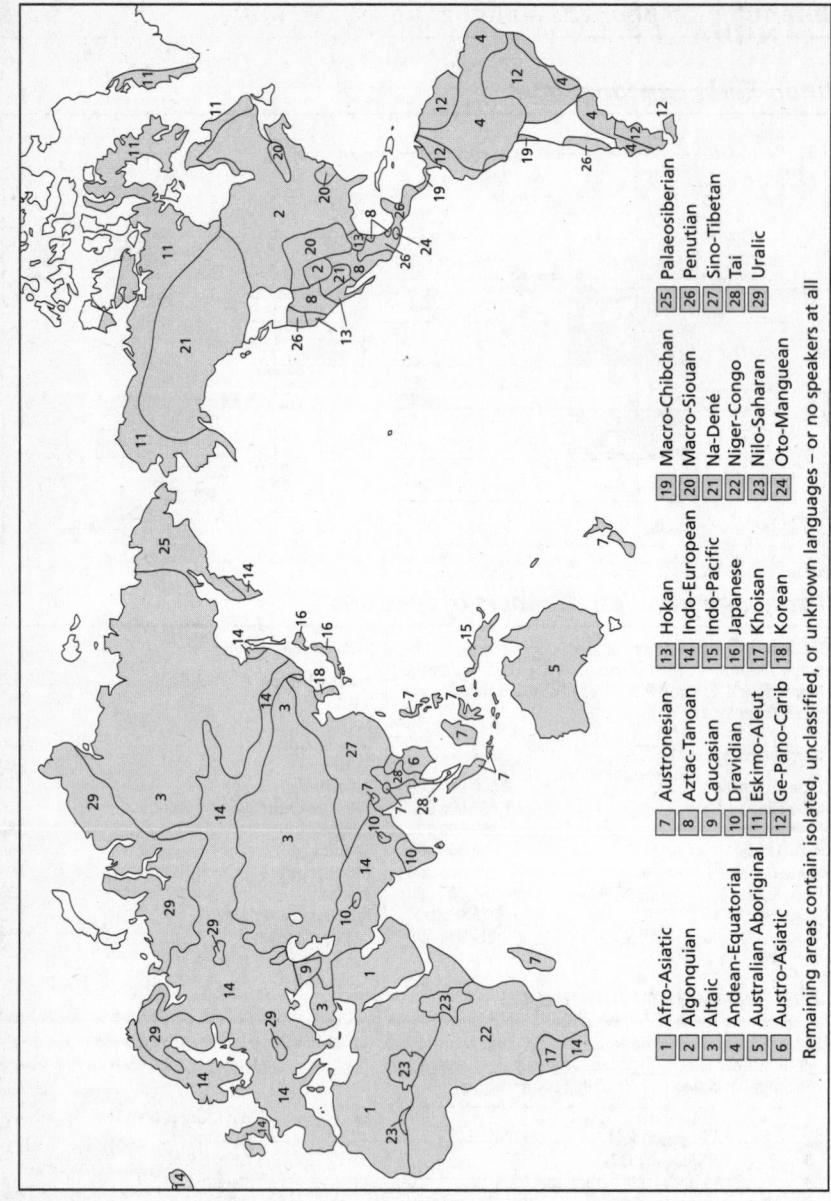

1	Afro-Asiatic	7	Austronesian
2	Algonquian	8	Aztec-Tanoan
3	Altaic	9	Caucasian
4	Andean-Equatorial	10	Dravidian
5	Australian Aboriginal	11	Eskimo-Aleut
6	Austro-Asiatic	12	Ge-Pano-Carib

13	Hokan	19	Macro-Chibchan
14	Indo-European	20	Macro-Siouan
15	Indo-Pacific	21	Na-Dené
16	Japanese	22	Niger-Congo
17	Khoisan	23	Nilo-Saharan
18	Korean	24	Oto-Manguean

25	Palaeosiberian
26	Penutian
27	Sino-Tibetan
28	Tai
29	Uralic

Remaining areas contain isolated, unclassified, or unknown languages – or no speakers at all

International phonetic alphabet (revised to 1989)

Consonants

	Bilabial	Labiodental	Dental	Alveolar	Postalveolar	Retroflex	Palatal	Velar	Uvular	Pharyngeal	Glottal
Plosive	p b			t d		ʈ ɖ	c ɟ	k g	q ɢ		ʔ
Nasal	m	ɱ		n		ɳ	ɲ	ŋ	ɴ		
Trill	ʙ			r					ʀ		
Tap or Flap				ɾ		ɽ					
Fricative	ɸ β	f v	θ ð	s z	ʃ ʒ	ʂ ʐ	ç ʝ	x ɣ	χ ʁ	ħ ʕ	h ɦ
Lateral fricative				ɬ ɮ							
Approximant		ʋ		ɹ		ɻ	j	ɰ			
Lateral approximant				l		ɭ	ʎ	ʟ			
Ejective stop	p'			t'		ʈ'	c'	k'	q'		
Implosive	ɓ ɓ			ƒ ɗ		ƈ ʄ	ƙ ɠ	ʛ ɠ			

Where symbols appear in pairs, the one to the right represents a voiced consonant. Shaded areas denote articulations judged impossible.

Vowels

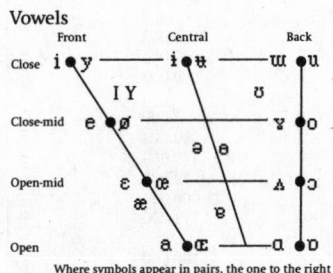

Where symbols appear in pairs, the one to the right represents a rounded vowel.

Suprasegmentals

ˈ	Primary stress	ˌfoʊnəˈtɪʃən
ˌ	Secondary stress	
ː	Long	eː
ˑ	Half-long	eˑ
̆	Extra-short	ĕ
.	Syllable break	ɹi.ækt
|	Minor (foot) group	
‖	Major (intonation group)	
‿	Linking (absence of break)	
↗	Global rise	
↘	Global fall	

Tones & word accents

	Level				Contour	
é	or ˥	Extra high		ě	˄	Rising
é	˦	High		ê	˅	Falling
ē	˧	Mid		é̌	᷄	High rising
è	˨	Low		è̌	᷅	Low rising
è	˩	Extra low		ẽ̌	᷈	Rising-falling etc.
↓	Downstep					
↑	Upstep					

Diacritics

̥	Voiceless	ŋ̥ d̥	̹	More rounded	ɔ̹	ʷ	Labialized	tʷ dʷ
̬	Voiced	s̬ t̬	̜	Less rounded	ɔ̜	ʲ	Palatalized	tʲ dʲ
ʰ	Aspirated	tʰ dʰ	̟	Advanced	u̟	ˠ	Velarized	tˠ dˠ
̈	Breathy voiced	b̤ a̤	̠	Retracted	i̠	ˤ	Pharyngealized	tˤ dˤ
̰	Creaky voiced	b̰ a̰	̈	Centralized	ë	̴	Velarized or pharyngealized	ɫ
̼	Linguolabial	t̼ d̼	̽	Mid-centralized	e̽	̝	Raised	e̝ (ɹ̝ = voiced alveolar fricative)
̪	Dental	t̪ d̪	̩	Syllabic	l̩	̞	Lowered	e̞ (β̞ = voiced bilabial approximant)
̺	Apical	t̺ d̺	̯	Non-syllabic	e̯	̘	Advanced Tongue Root	e̘
̻	Laminal	t̻ d̻	˞	Rhoticity	ɚ	̙	Retracted Tongue Root	e̙

̃	Nasalized	ẽ
ⁿ	Nasal release	dⁿ
ˡ	Lateral release	dˡ
̚	No audible release	d̚

Other symbols

ʍ	Voiceless labial-velar fricative
w	Voiced labial-velar approximant
ɥ	Voiced labial-palatal approximant
ʜ	Voiceless epiglottal fricative
ʢ	Voiced epiglottal fricative
ʡ	Epiglottal plosive
ɕ ʑ	Alveolo-palatal fricatives
ɘ	Additional mid central vowel
ʘ	Bilabial click
ǀ	Dental click
ǃ	(Post)alveolar click
ǂ	Palatoalveolar click
ǁ	Alveolar lateral click
ɺ	Alveolar lateral flap
ɧ	Simultaneous ʃ and x
k͡p	Affricates and double articulations can be represented by two symbols joined by a tie if necessary.
t͡s	

English speakers

This table lists only those countries where English has official or special status. Those who have learned English as a foreign language in countries (eg China, Germany) where it has no such status are not included in the listing.

Areas where English is a creole or creolized pidgin are identified by (c) (eg Sierra Leone).

Figures for English as a second language are often unknown (?) or uncertain. Where a total is preceded by ? (eg Botswana) it has been derived from the numbers of people in the country who have completed their secondary education, and who are thus likely to have achieved a reasonable standard of use. This total excludes any first-language speakers listed for that country.

In first-language countries (eg Canada), no totals are given for second-language use when agreed estimates do not exist; as a result, the world total of second-language speakers is probably a considerable underestimate.

Populations are given for 2001.

Country	Population	First language	Second language
		Total	Total
American Samoa	67 000	2 000	65 000
Antigua and Barbuda (c)	68 000	66 000	2 000
Australia	18 972 000	14 987 000	3 500 000
Bahamas	298 000	260 000	28 000
Bangladesh	131 270 000	?	3 500 000
Barbados (c)	275 000	262 000	13 000
Belize (c)	256 000	190 000	56 000
Bermuda	63 000	63 000	?
Bhutan	2 000 000	?	75 000
Botswana	1 586 000	?	?630 000
British Virgin Is	20 800	20 000	?
Brunei	344 000	10 000	?134 000
Cameroon (c)	15 900 000	?	7 700 000
Canada	31 600 000	20 000 000	?7 000 000
Cayman Islands (c)	36 000	36 000	
Cook Islands	21 000	?1 000	3 000
Dominica (c)	70 000	3 000	60 000
Fiji	850 000	6 000	170 000
Gambia (c)	1 411 000	?	40 000
Ghana (c)	19 894 000	?	?1 400 000
Gibraltar	31 000	28 000	?2 000
Grenada (c)	100 000	100 000	
Guam	160 000	58 000	100 000
Guyana (c)	700 000	650 000	?30 000
Hong Kong	7 210 000	150 000	2 200 000
India	1 029 991 000	?350 000	?200 000 000
Ireland	3 850 000	3 750 000	?100 000
Jamaica (c)	2 665 000	2 600 000	?50 000
Kenya	30 766 000	?	2 700 000
Kiribati	94 000	?	?23 000
Lesotho	2 177 000	?	?500 000
Liberia (c)	3 226 000	?600 000	?2 500 000
Malawi	10 548 000	?	?540 000
Malaysia	22 230 000	380 000	7 000 000
Malta	395 000	13 000	?95 000
Marshall Is	70 000	?	?60 000
Mauritius	1 190 000	2 000	?200 000
Micronesia	135 000	?4 000	?60 000
Montserrat (c)	4 000	4 000	
Namibia	1 800 000	?14 000	?300 000
Nauru	10 700	800	?9 500
New Zealand	3 864 000	3 700 000	?150 000
Nigeria (c)	126 636 000	?	?60 000 000
N. Marianas (c)	75 000	5 000	?65 000
Pakistan	145 000 000	?	?17 000 000
Palau	19 000	?500	?18 000
Papua New Guinea (c)	5 000 000	150 000	?3 000 000
Philippines	83 000 000	?20 000	40 000 000
Puerto Rico	3 937 000	?100 000	1 840 000

Country	Population	First language	Second language
		Total	Total
Rwanda	7 313 000	?	?20 000
Samoa	180 000	?1 000	?93 000
St Kitts and Nevis (c)	39 000	39 000	
St Lucia (c)	158 000	31 000	?40 000
St Vincent and the Grenadines (c)	116 000	114 000	?
Seychelles	80 000	3 000	?30 000
Sierra Leone (c)	5 427 000	?500 000	?4 400 000
Singapore	4 300 000	?350 000	?2 000 000
Solomon Islands (c)	480 000	?10 000	165 000
South Africa	43 586 000	3 700 000	?10 000 000
Suriname (c)	434 000	?260 000	?150 000
Swaziland	1 104 000	?	?50 000
Tanzania	36 232 000	?	?4 000 000
Tonga	104 000	?	?30 000
Trinidad and Tobago (c)	1 170 000	1 245 000	?
Tuvalu	11 000	?	800
Uganda	23 986 000	?	2 500 000
United Kingdom	59 648 000	58 100 000	1 500 000
UK Islands	228 000	227 000	
United States	278 059 000	215 424 000	25 600 000
US Virgin Islands (c)	122 000	98 000	?15 000
Vanuatu (c)	193 000	?60 000	?120 000
Zambia	9 770 000	?110 000	?1 800 000
Zimbabwe	11 365 000	?250 000	?5 300 000
Other dependencies	35 000	20 000	15 000
Totals	2 213 507 500	329 158 300	422 682 300

English sound frequencies

In southern British English (Received Pronunciation) an analysis of the frequency of vowels and consonants in conversation produced the following totals (after D B Fry, 1947).

Consonants

	(%)		(%)
n	7.58	b	1.97
t	6.42	f	1.79
d	5.14	p	1.78
s	4.81	h	1.46
l	3.66	ŋ	1.15
ð	3.56	g	1.05
r	3.51	ʃ	0.96
m	3.22	j	0.88
k	3.09	ʤ	0.60
w	2.81	ʧ	0.41
z	2.46	θ	0.37
v	2.00	ʒ	0.10

Vowels

	(%)		(%)
ə	10.74	ʊ	0.86
ɪ	8.33	ɑː	0.79
e	2.97	aʊ	0.61
aɪ	1.83	ɜː	0.52
ʌ	1.75	ɛə	0.34
eɪ	1.71	ɪə	0.21
iː	1.65	ɔɪ	0.14
əʊ	1.51	ʊə	0.06
æ	1.45		
ɒ	1.37		
ɔː	1.24		
uː	1.13		

The transcription is the one developed by A C Gimson in *An Introduction to the Pronunciation of English* (London, 6th edn, 2001).

The vowel system of Received Pronunciation

/iː/	as in *sea*	/eɪ/	as in *ape*
/ɪ/	as in *him*	/aɪ/	as in *time*
/e/	as in *get*	/ɔɪ/	as in *boy*
/æ/	as in *sat*	/əʊ/	as in *so*
/ʌ/	as in *sun*	/aʊ/	as in *out*
/ɑː/	as in *father*	/ɪə/	as in *deer*
/ɒ/	as in *dog*	/ɛə/	as in *care*
/ɔː/	as in *saw*	/ʊə/	as in *poor*
/ʊ/	as in *put*		
/uː/	as in *soon*		
/ɜː/	as in *bird*		
/ə/	as in *about*		

The consonant system of Received Pronunciation

/p/	as in *pie*	/z/	as in *zoo*
/b/	as in *by*	/ʃ/	as in *shoe*
/t/	as in *tie*	/ʒ/	as in *beige*
/d/	as in *die*	/h/	as in *hi*
/k/	as in *coo*	/m/	as in *my*
/g/	as in *go*	/n/	as in *no*
/ʧ/	as in *chew*	/ŋ/	as in *sing*
/ʤ/	as in *jaw*	/l/	as in *lie*
/f/	as in *fee*	/r/	as in *row*
/v/	as in *view*	/w/	as in *way*
/θ/	as in *thin*	/j/	as in *you*
/ð/	as in *the*		
/s/	as in *so*		

COMMUNICATIONS

English letter frequencies

Here is a selection of frequency orders found in one comparative study of different styles of American English (after A. Zettersten, 1969):

(a) press reporting

(b) religious writing

(c) scientific writing

(d) general fiction

(e) average rank order, based on a description of 15 categories of text totalling over a million words

(f) order used by Samuel Morse (1791–1872) in compiling the Morse Code

(g) quantities of type found in a printer's office, on which Samuel Morse's frequency ordering was based

Rank order by frequency of use

(a)	(b)	(c)	(d)	(e)	(f)	(g)
e	e	e	e	e	e	12 000
t	t	t	t	t	t	9 000
a	i	a	a	a	a	8 000
o	a	i	o	o	i	8 000
n	o	o	h	i	n	8 000
i	n	n	n	n	o	8 000
s	s	s	i	s	s	8 000
r	r	r	s	r	h	6 400
h	h	h	r	h	r	6 200
l	l	l	d	l	d	4 400
d	d	c	l	d	l	4 000
c	c	d	u	c	u	3 400
m	u	u	w	u	c	3 000
u	m	m	m	m	m	3 000
f	f	f	c	f	f	2 500
p	p	p	g	p	w	2 000
g	y	g	f	g	y	2 000
w	w	y	y	w	g	1 700
y	g	b	p	y	p	1 700
b	b	w	b	b	b	1 600
v	v	v	k	v	v	1 200
k	k	k	v	k	k	800
j	x	x	j	x	q	500
x	j	q	x	j	j	400
q	q	j	z	q	x	400
z	z	z	q	z	z	200

Comparative word frequencies

Rank	French	German	Written English	Spoken English	Rank	French	German	Written English	Spoken English
1	de	der	the	the	11	que (p)	auf	on	is
2	le (a)	die	of	and	12	dans	mit	at	yes
3	la (a)	und	to	I	13	il	sich	he	was
4	et	in	in	to	14	à	daß	with	this
5	les	des	and	of	15	en	dem	by	but
6	des	den	a	a	16	ne	sie	be	on
7	est	zu	for	you	17	on	ist	it	well
8	un (a)	das	was	that	18	qui	im	an	he
9	une (a)	von	is	in	19	au	eine	as	have
10	du	für	that	it	20	se	DDR[c]	his	for

a = article *p* = pronoun

[c] This was a study of newspaper text in the 1960s, in which the name of the German Democratic Republic turned up surprisingly often.

Alphabets

The development of the early alphabet

Phoenician	Old Hebrew	Early Greek	Classical Greek	Etruscan	Early Latin	Modern Roman
						Aa
						Bb
						Cc
						Dd
						Ee
						Ff
						Gg
						Hh
						Ii
						Jj
						Kk
						Ll
						Mm
						Nn
						Oo
						Pp
						Qq
						Rr
						Ss
						Tt
						Uu
						Vv
						Ww
						Xx
						Yy
						Zz

A version of the runic alphabet found in Britain

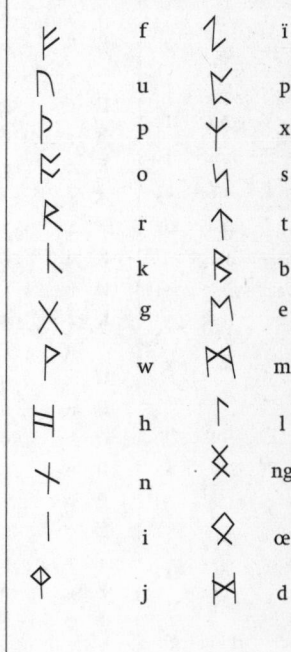

	f		ï
	u		p
	p		x
	o		s
	r		t
	k		b
	g		e
	w		m
	h		l
	n		ng
	i		œ
	j		d

Alphabetic codes

Semaphore	Letters	Morse	Braille
	A	•—	
	B	—•••	
	C	—•—•	
	D	—••	
	E	•	
	F	••—•	
	G	——•	
	H	••••	
	I	••	
	J	•———	
	K	—•—	
	L	•—••	
	M	——	
	N	—•	
	O	———	
	P	•——•	
	Q	——•—	
	R	•—•	
	S	•••	
	T	—	
	U	••—	
	V	•••—	
	W	•——	
	X	—••—	
	Y	—•——	
	Z	——••	

Nato alphabet

Letter	Code name	Pronunciation	Letter	Code name	Pronunciation
A	Alpha	AL-FAH	N	November	NO-VEM-BER
B	Bravo	BRAH-VOH	O	Oscar	OSS-CAH
C	Charlie	CHAR-LEE	P	Papa	PAH-PAH
D	Delta	DELL-TAH	Q	Quebec	KEY-BECK
E	Echo	ECK-OH	R	Romeo	ROW-ME-OH
F	Foxtrot	FOKS-TROT	S	Sierra	SEE-AIR-RAH
G	Golf	GOLF	T	Tango	TAN-GO
H	Hotel	HOH-TELL	U	Uniform	YOU-NEE-FORM
I	India	IN-DEE-AH	V	Victor	VIK-TAH
J	Juliet	JEW-LEE-ETT	W	Whiskey	WISS-KEY
K	Kilo	KEY-LOH	X	Xray	ECKS-RAY
L	Lima	LEE-MAH	Y	Yankee	YANG-KEY
M	Mike	MIKE	Z	Zulu	ZOO-LOO

Transliteration to the Latin alphabet

Arabic

Letter	Name	Trans[a]
ا	'alif	'
ب	ba	b
ت	ta	t
ث	tha	th
ج	jim	j
ح	ha	h
خ	kha	kh
د	dal	d
ذ	dha	th
ر	ra	r
ز	za	z
س	sin	s
ش	shin	sh
ص	sad	s
ض	dad	d
ط	ta	t
ظ	za	z
ع	'ain	'
غ	ghain	gh
ف	fa	f
ق	qaf	q
ك	kaf	k
ل	lam	l
م	mim	m
ن	nun	n
ه	ha	h
و	waw	w
ي	ya	y

Russian

Letter		Trans[a]
А	а	a
Б	б	b
В	в	v
Г	г	g
Д	д	d
Е	е	e
Ж	ж	ž, zh
З	з	z
И	и	i
Й	й	j
К	к	k
Л	л	l
М	м	m
Н	н	n
О	о	o
П	п	p
Р	р	r
С	с	s
Т	т	t
У	у	u
Ф	ф	f
Х	х	h, kh, ch
Ц	ц	c, ts
Ч	ч	č, ch
Ш	ш	š, sh
Щ	щ	šč, shch
Ъ	ъ	"
Ы	ы	y
Ь	ь	'
Э	э	ě
Ю	ю	ju, yu
Я	я	ja, ya

German

Letter		Trans[a]
𝔄	a	a
𝔄̈	ä	ae
𝔅	b	b
ℭ	c	c
𝔇	d	d
𝔈	e	e
𝔉	f	f
𝔊	g	g
𝔥	h	h
ℑ	i	i
𝔍	j	j
𝔎	k	k
𝔏	l	l
𝔐	m	m
𝔑	n	n
𝔒	o	o
𝔒̈	ö	oe
𝔓	p	p
𝔔	q	q
𝔯	r	r
𝔖	s	s
𝔗	t	t
𝔘	u	u
ü	ü	ue
𝔙	v	v
𝔚	w	w
𝔵	x	x
𝔜	y	y
𝔷	z	z

Hebrew

Letter	Name	Trans[a]
א	'aleph	'
ב	beth	b
ג	gimel	g
ד	daleth	d
ה	he	h
ו	waw	w
ז	zayin	z
ח	heth	h
ט	teth	t
י	yodh	y, j
כ ך	kaph	k
ל	lamedh	l
מ ם	mem	m
נ ן	nun	n
ס	samekh	s
ע	'ayin	'
פ ף	pe	p, f
צ ץ	saddhe	s
ק	qoph	q
ר	resh	r
שׁ	shin	sh, ś
שׂ	śin	s
ת	t aw	t

Greek

Letter		Name	Trans[a]
Α	α	alpha	a
Β	β	beta	b
Γ	γ	gamma	g
Δ	δ	delta	d
Ε	ε	epsilon	e
Ζ	ζ	zeta	z
Η	η	eta	e, e
Θ	θ	theta	th
Ι	ι	iota	i
Κ	κ	kappa	k
Λ	λ	lambda	l
Μ	μ	mu	m
Ν	ν	nu	n
Ξ	ξ	xi	x
Ο	ο	omicron	o
Π	π	pi	p
Ρ	ρ	rho	r
Σ	σ	sigma	s
Τ	τ	tau	t
Υ	υ	upsilon	y
Φ	φ	phi	ph
Χ	χ	chi	ch, kh
Ψ	ψ	psi	ps
Ω	ω	omega	o, o

[a]Transliteration.

There is no agreement over the use of a single transliteration system in the case of Arabic, Hebrew, and Russian. The equivalents given here are widely used, but several other possibilities can be found.

Deaf fingerspelling

British

American

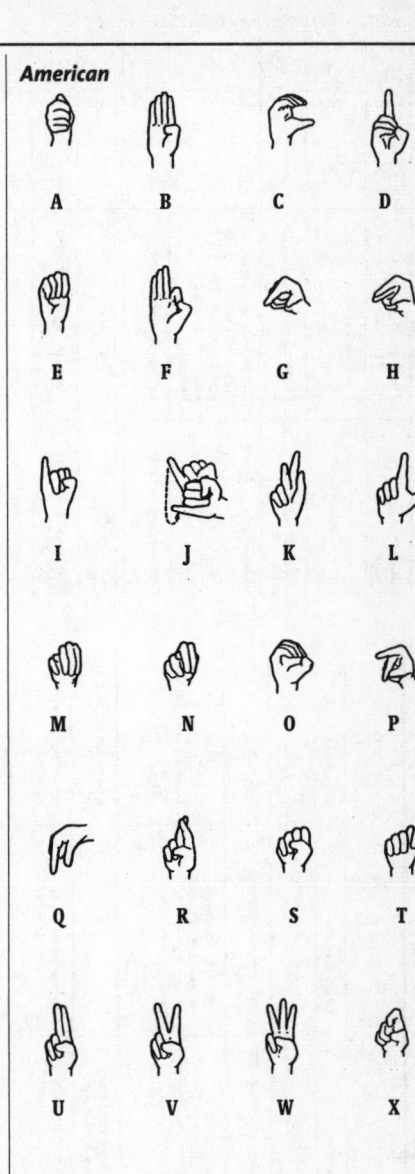

Proof-correction symbols

Instruction	Textual mark	Marginal mark
Substitute or insert oblique	/ through character or λ	⊘
Wrong fount. Replace by character(s) of correct fount	Encircle character(s)	⊗
Change damaged character(s)	Encircle character(s)	×
Set in or change to italic	___ under character(s) Where space does not permit textual marks, encircle the affected area instead	⊟
Change italic to upright type	Encircle character(s)	+
Set in or change to capital letters	≡ under character(s)	≡
Set in or change to small capital letters	═ under character(s)	=
Set in or change to bold type	∼∼∼ under character(s)	∼
Set in or change to bold italic type	∼∼∼ under character(s)	≈
Change capital letters to lower-case letters	Encircle character(s)	≢
Change small capital letters to lower-case letters	Encircle character(s)	≠
Close up. Delete space between characters or words	⌒ linking characters eg a͡scribe	( )
Insert space between characters	| between characters	Y
Insert space between words	Y between words	Y
Reduce space between characters	| between characters	⊤

Give the size of the space when necessary (insert space between characters)

Give the size of the space when necessary (insert space between words)

Give the amount by which the space is to be reduced, when necessary (reduce space)

Instruction	Textual mark	Marginal mark
Leave unchanged	- - - under characters	⟨/⟩
Remove extraneous marks	Encircle marks to be removed	×
Delete	/ through character(s) or ⊢—⊣ through words	♂
Delete and close up	⌢ through character(s) or ⌷	⌢
Insert in text the matter indicated in the margin	λ	New matter followed by λ
Substitute character or substitute part of one or more words	/ through character or ⊢—⊣ through word(s)	New character or new word(s)
Substitute ligature eg æ for separate letters	⊢—⊣ through characters affected	⌒ eg æ
Substitute or insert full stop or decimal point	/ through character or λ	⊙
Substitute or insert comma, semicolon, colon, etc	/ through character or λ	, ; ⊙ ( )
Substitute or insert character in 'superior' position	/ through character or λ	⌄ under character eg ²
Substitute or insert character in 'inferior' position	/ through character or λ	⌃ over character eg ₂
Substitute or insert single or double quotation marks or apostrophe	/ through character or λ	᾿᾿ and/or ῁
Substitute or insert ellipsis	/ through character or λ	…
Substitute or insert hyphen	/ through character or λ	⊢-⊣
Substitute or insert rule	/ through character or λ	Give the size of the rule in the marginal mark 1em ⊢—⊣ 4mm

Instruction	Textual mark	Marginal mark
Reduce space between words	between words	Give the amount by which the space is to be reduced, when necessary
Make space appear equal between characters or words	between characters or words	
Close up to normal interline spacing	(each side of column) linking lines	
Insert space between lines or paragraphs	or	Give the size of the space when necessary
Reduce space between lines or paragraphs	or	Give amount by which the space is to be reduced, when necessary
Start new paragraph		
Run on (no new paragraph)		
Transpose characters or words	between characters or words, numbered when necessary	
Transpose lines		Rules extend from the margin into the text with each line to be transposed numbered in the correct sequence
Transpose a number of lines	3 2 1	
Centre	[enclosing matter to be centred]	
Indent		Give the amount of the indent
Cancel indent		
Move matter specified distance to the right*	enclosing matter to be moved to the right	

Instruction	Textual mark	Marginal mark
Move matter specified distance to the left*	enclosing matter to be moved to the left	
Set line to specified measure*	and/or	
Set column to specified measure*		
Take over character(s), word(s) or line to next line, column or page		The textual mark surrounds the matter to be taken over and extends into the margin
Take back character(s), word(s) or line to previous line, column or page		The textual mark surrounds the matter to be taken back and extends into the margin
Raise matter*	over matter to be raised / under matter to be raised	
Lower matter*	over matter to be lowered / under matter to be lowered	
Move matter to position indicated*	Enclose matter to be moved and indicate new position	
Correct vertical alignment		
Correct horizontal alignment	Single line above and below misaligned matter	placed level with the head and foot of the relevant line

* Give the exact dimensions when necessary.

Typefaces

The typefaces shown are modern versions of the main groups under which most typefaces may be classified. The dates indicating the introduction of each group are approximate. The roman numbers and names refer to categories in the most recent British Standard for the classification of typefaces, BS 2961 : 1967.

𝕭lackletter c.1450 (IX, Graphic) *14pt Monotype Old English Text*

𝕬𝕭𝕮𝕯𝕰𝕱𝕲𝕳𝕴𝕵𝕶𝕷𝕸𝕹𝕺𝕻𝕼𝕽𝕾𝕿𝖀𝖁𝖂𝖃𝖄𝖅
abcdefghijklmnopqrstuvwxyz

Venetian c.1470 (I, Humanist) *14pt Monotype Centaur*

ABCDEFGHIJKLMNOPQRSTUVWXYZ
abcdefghijklmnopqrstuvwxyz & 1234567890

Old Face c.1540 (II, Garalde) *14pt Adobe Garamond*

ABCDEFGHIJKLMNOPQRSTUVWXYZ
abcdefghijklmnopqrstuvwxyz & 1234567890

Transitional c.1757 (III, Transitional) *14pt Monotype Baskerville*

ABCDEFGHIJKLMNOPQRSTUVWXYZ
abcdefghijklmnopqrstuvwxyz & 1234567890

Grotesque c.1816 (VI, Lineale a, b) *14pt Monotype Grotesque*

ABCDEFGHIJKLMNOPQRSTUVWXYZ
abcdefghijklmnopqrstuvwxyz & 1234567890

Slab-serif c.1830 (V, Slab-serif) *14pt Rockwell*

ABCDEFGHIJKLMNOPQRSTUVWXYZ
abcdefghijklmnopqrstuvwxyz & 1234567890

Sans-serif c.1918 (VI, Lineale c, d) *14pt Monotype Gill Sans*

ABCDEFGHIJKLMNOPQRSTUVWXYZ
abcdefghijklmnopqrstuvwxyz & 1234567890

Script c.1557 (VIII, Script) *14pt Englische Schreibschrift*

ABCDEFGHIJKLMNOPQRSTUVWXYZ
abcdefghijklmnopqrstuvwxyz & 1234567890

Symbols in general use

&	Ampersand (and)	✳	Unacceptable form	**In meteorology**	
&c	Et cetera	☠	Poison; danger	▲▲▲	Cold front
@	At; per (in costs)	♂, □	Male	⌒⌒⌒	Warm front
×	By (measuring dimensions, eg 3 × 4)	♀, ○	Female	⌒▲⌒▲	Stationary front
£	Pound			▲▲▲▲	Occluded fron
$	Dollar (also peso, escudo, etc, in certain countries)	✠	Bishop's name follows	**In cards**	
¢	Cent (also centavo, etc, in certain countries)	☎	Telephone number follows	♥	Hearts
©	Copyright	☞ ☞	This way	♦	Diamonds
®	Registered trademark	✂ ✂	Cut here	♠	Spades
¶	New paragraph			♣	Clubs
§	New section	**In astronomy**			
‥	Ditto	●	New moon		
™	Trade mark	☾	Moon, first quarter		
✱	Born (in genealogy)	○	Full moon		
†	Died	☽	Moon, last quarter		

First-name preferences

Boys, England and Wales

	1920s		1960s		1970s		1980s		1990s
1	John	1	Paul	1	Stephen	1	Andrew	1	Daniel
2	William	2	David	2	Mark	2	David	2	Thomas
3	George	3	Andrew	3	Paul	3	Daniel	3	Matthew
4	James	4	Stephen	4	Andrew	4	Christopher	4	Joshua
5	Ronald	5	Mark	5	David	5	Stephen	5	Adam
6	Robert	6	Michael	6	Richard	6	Matthew	6	Luke
7	Kenneth	7	Ian	7	Matthew	7	Paul	7	Michael
8	Frederick	8	Gary	8	Daniel	8	James	8	Christopher
9	Thomas	9	Robert	9	Christopher	9	Mark	9	Ryan
10	Albert	10	Richard	10	Darren	10	Michael	10	Jack

Girls, England and Wales

	1920s		1960s		1970s		1980s		1990s
1	Joan	1	Trac(e)y	1	Claire	1	Sarah	1	Rebecca
2	Mary	2	Deborah	2	Sarah	2	Emma	2	Amy
3	Joyce	3	Julie	3	Nicola	3	Claire	3	Sophie
4	Margaret	4	Karen	4	Emma	4	Kelly	4	Charlotte
5	Dorothy	5	Susan	5	Joanne	5	Rebecca	5	Laura
6	Doris	6	Alison	6	Helen	6	Gemma	6	Lauren
7	Kathleen	7	Jacqueline	7	Rachel	7	Rachel	7	Jessica
8	Irene	8	Helen	8	Lisa	8	Lisa	8	Hannah
9	Betty	9	Amanda	9	Rebecca	9	Victoria	9	Jade
10	Eileen	10	Sharon	10	Karen	10	Laura	10	Emma

Boys, USA

	1920s		1950s		1970s		1990s (white)		1990s (non-white)
1	Robert	1	Robert	1	Michael	1	Michael	1	Christopher
2	John	2	Michael	2	Robert	2	Joshua	2	Michael
3	William	3	James	3	David	3	Matthew	3	Brandon
4	James	4	John	4	James	4	Jacob	4	Joshua
5	Charles	5	David	5	John	5	Zachary	5	James
6	Richard	6	William	6	Jeffrey	6	Christopher	6	Anthony
7	George	7	Thomas	7	Steven	7	Tyler	7	Devonte
8	Donald	8	Richard	8	Christopher	8	Brandon	8	Jonathan
9	Joseph	9	Gary	9	Brian	9	Andrew	9	William
10	Edward	10	Charles	10	Mark	10	Nicholas	10	Justin

COMMUNICATIONS

First-name preferences (continued)

Girls, USA

	1920s		1950s		1970s		1990s (white)		1990s (non-white)
1	Mary	1	Linda	1	Michelle	1	Ashley	1	Jasmine
2	Barbara	2	Mary	2	Jennifer	2	Jessica	2	Brianna
3	Dorothy	3	Patricia	3	Kimberly	3	Sarah	3	Brittany
4	Betty	4	Susan	4	Lisa	4	Brittany	4	Ashley
5	Ruth	5	Deborah	5	Tracy	5	Kaitlyn	5	Alexis
6	Margaret	6	Kathleen	6	Kelly	6	Taylor	6	Jessica
7	Helen	7	Barbara	7	Nicole	7	Emily	7	Chelsea
8	Elizabeth	8	Nancy	8	Angela	8	Megan	8	Courtney
9	Jean	9	Sharon	9	Pamela	9	Samantha	9	Kayla
10	Ann(e)	10	Karen	10	Christine	10	Katherine	10	Sierra

First-name meanings

The meanings of the most popular first names listed above are given here along with a few other well-known names.

Name	Original meaning
Aaron	High mountain (Hebrew)
Adam	Redness (Hebrew)
Alan	?Rock, noble (Celtic)
Albert	Noble bright (Germanic)
Alexander	Defender of men (Greek)
Alison	French diminutive of Alice; of noble kind
Amanda	Fit to be loved (Latin)
Amy	Loved (French)
Andrea	Female form of Andrew
Andrew	Manly (Greek)
Angela	Messenger, angel (Greek)
Ann(e)	English form of Hannah
Anthony	Roman family name
April	Name of the month
Arthur	?Bear, stone (Celtic)
Barbara	Strange, foreign (Greek)
Barry	Spear, javelin (Celtic)
Beatrice	Bringer of joy (Latin)
Benjamin	Son of my right hand (Hebrew)
Bernard	Bear + brave (Germanic)
Beth	Pet form of Elizabeth
Betty	Pet form of Elizabeth
Bill/Billy	Pet form of William
Bob	Pet for of Robert
Brandi	Variant of Brandy, from the common noun
Brandon	Place name; broom-covered hill (Germanic)
Brian	?Hill (?Celtic)
Candice	Meaning unknown
Carl	Man, husbandman (Germanic)
Carol(e)	Form of Caroline, Italian female form of Charles
Catherine	?Pure (Greek)
Charles	Man, husbandman (Germanic)
Christine	French form of Christina ultimately from Christian; anointed
Christopher	Carrier of Christ (Greek)
Claire	Bright, shining (Latin)
Colin	Form of Nicholas
Craig	Rock (Celtic)
Crystal	Female use of the common noun
Daniel	God is my judge (Hebrew)

Name	Original meaning
Danielle	Female form of Daniel
Darren	Irish surname
Darryl	Surname; uncertain origin
David	?Beloved, friend (Hebrew)
Dawn	Female use of the common noun
Dean	Surname; valley or leader
Deborah	Bee (Hebrew)
Dennis	Of Dionysus (Greek), the god of wine
Derek	Form of Theodoric; ruler of the people (Germanic)
Diane	French form of Diana; divine (Latin)
Donald	World mighty (Gaelic)
Donna	Lady (Latin)
Doreen	From Dora, a short form of Dorothy; gift of God
Doris	Woman from Doris (Greek)
Dorothy	Gift of God (Greek)
Ebony	Female use of the common noun
Edward	Property guardian (Germanic)
Eileen	Irish form of ?Helen
Elizabeth	Oath/perfection of God (Hebrew)
Emily	Roman family name
Emma	All-embracing (Germanic)
Eric	Ruler of all (Norse)
Erica	Female form of Eric
Eugenie	French form of Eugene; well-born (Greek)
Frank	Pet form of Francis; Frenchman
Frederick	Peaceful ruler (Germanic)
Gail	Pet form of Abigail; father rejoices (Hebrew)
Gareth	Gentle (Welsh)
Gary	?Surname; US place name
Gavin	Scottish form of Gawain; hawk + white (Welsh)
Gemma	Gem (Italian)
Geoffrey	?Peace (Germanic)
George	Husbandman, farmer (Greek)
Graham	Germanic place name
Hannah	Grace, favour (Hebrew)
Harold	Army power/ruler (Germanic)
Harry	Pet form of Henry; home ruler (Germanic)
Hayley	English place name; hay-meadow

Name	Original meaning
Heather	Plant name
Helen	Bright/shining one (Greek)
Ian	Modern Scottish form of John
Irene	Peace (Greek)
Jacqueline	French female form of Jacques (James)
James	Latin form of Jacob; one who takes by the heel (Hebrew)
Jane	From Latin Johanna, female form of John
Janet	Diminutive form of Jane
Jason	Form of Joshua; Jehovah is salvation (Hebrew)
Jeffrey	US spelling of Geoffrey
Jean	French form of Johanna, from John
Jennifer	Fair/white + yielding/smooth (Celtic)
Jeremy	English form of Jeremiah; Jehova exalts (Hebrew)
Jessica	He beholds (Hebrew)
Joan	Contracted form of Johanna, from John
Joanne	French form of Johanna, from John
John	Jehovah has been gracious (Hebrew)
Jonathan	Jehovah's gift (Hebrew)
Joseph	Jehovah adds (Hebrew)
Joyce	?Joyful (?Latin)
Julie	French female form of Latin Julius; descended from Jove
Karen	Danish form of Katarina (Catherine)
Katherine	US spelling of Catherine
Kathleen	English form of Irish Caitlin (from Catherine)
Kelly	Irish surname; warlike one
Kenneth	English form of Gaelic; fair one or fire-sprung
Kerry	Irish place name
Kevin	Handsome at birth (Irish)
Kimberly	South African place name
Lakisha	La + ?Aisha; woman (Arabic)
Latoya	La + form of Tonya (Antonia)
Laura	Bay, laurel (Latin)
Lauren	Diminutive of Laura
Lee	Germanic place name; wood, clearing
Leslie	Scottish place name
Lilian	Lily (Italian)
Linda	Serpent (symbol of wisdom) (Germanic)
Lindsay	Scottish place name
Lisa	Pet form of Elizabeth
Margaret	Pearl (Greek)
Marjorie	From Marguerite, French form of Margaret
Mark	English form of Marcus, from Mars, god of war
Martin	From Mars, god of war (Latin)
Mary	Greek form of Miriam (Hebrew); unknown meaning

Name	Original meaning
Matthew	Gift of the Lord (Hebrew)
Melissa	Bee (Greek)
Michael	Like the Lord (Hebrew)
Michelle	English spelling of French, Michèle from Michael
Nancy	Pet form of Ann
Natalie	Birthday of the Lord (Latin)
Neil	Champion (Irish)
Nicholas	Victory people (Greek)
Nicola	Italian form of Nicholas used as a female name in the UK
Nicole	French female form of Nicholas
Pamela	?All honey (Greek)
Patricia	Noble (Latin)
Paul	Small (Latin)
Pauline	French female form of Paul
Peter	Stone, rock (Greek)
Philip	Fond of horses (Greek)
Rachel	Ewe (Hebrew)
Rebecca	?Noose (Hebrew)
Richard	Strong ruler (Germanic)
Robert	Fame bright (Germanic)
Ronald	Counsel + power (Germanic)
Ruth	?Companion (Hebrew)
Ryan	Irish surname
Sally	Pet form of Sarah
Samantha	Female form of Samuel; heard/name of God (Hebrew)
Sandra	Pet form from Alexandra
Sarah	Princess (Hebrew)
Scott	Surname from Scotland
Sharon	The plain (Hebrew)
Shaun	English spelling of Irish Sean, from John
Shirley	Bright clearing (Germanic)
Simon	Form of Simeon; listening attentively (Hebrew)
Stephanie	French female form of Stephen
Stephen	Crown (Greek)
Stuart	Steward (Germanic)
Susan	Short form of Susannah; lily (Hebrew)
Teresa	Woman of Theresia (Greek)
Thomas	Twin (Hebrew)
Tiffany	Manifestation of God (Greek)
Timothy	Honouring God (Greek)
Trac(e)y	?Pet form of Teresa
Vera	Faith (Slavic)
Victoria	Victory (Latin)
Vincent	Conquer (Latin)
Virginia	Maiden (Latin)
Walter	Ruling people (Germanic)
Wayne	Surname; wagon-maker
William	Will + helmet (Germanic)
Zoë	Life (Greek)

Common abbreviations

COMMUNICATIONS

AA	Alcoholics Anonymous
AA	Automobile Association
AA(A)	anti-aircraft (artillery)
AAA	Amateur Athletics Association
AAA	American Automobile Association
AAAS	American Association for the Advancement of Science
ABA	Amateur Boxing Association
ABA	American Broadcasting Association
ABA	American Bar Association
ABC	Australian Broadcasting Corporation
ABM	antiballistic missile
ABS	antilock braking system
ABTA	Association of British Travel Agents
AC	air conditioning
AC	alternating current
ACAD	auto computer aided design
ACAS	Advisory, Conciliation, and Arbitration Service
ACC/SCN	ACC Subcommittee on Nutrition
ACLS	American Council of Learned Societies
ACLU	American Civil Liberties Union
ACT	Australian Capital Territory
ACTH	adrenocorticotrophic hormone
ACTU	Australian Council of Trade Unions
AD	anno Domini (in the year of Our Lord)
A-D	analog-to-digital (in computing)
ADH	antidiuretic hormone
ADP	adenosine diphosphate
AEA	Atomic Energy Authority (UK)
AEC	Atomic Energy Commission (USA)
AEF	American Expeditionary Force
AFC	American Football Conference
AFL/CIO	American Federation of Labor/Congress of Industrial Organizations
AFP	Agence France Presse
AFV	armoured fighting vehicle
AGM	annual general meeting
AGR	advanced gas-cooled reactor
AH	anno Hegirae (in the year of Hegira)
AHF	anti-haemophilic factor
AI	artificial intelligence
AID	artificial insemination by donor
AIDS	Acquired Immune Deficiency Syndrome
AIF	Australian Imperial Force
AIH	artificial insemination by husband
aka	also known as
AKC	American Kennel Club
AL	American Legion
ALCM	air-launched cruise missile
ALGOL	algorithmic language
ALP	Australian Labor Party
ALU	arithmetic and logic unit
AM	amplitude modulation
AMA	American Medical Association
AMU	atomic mass unit
ANC	African National Congress
ANS	autonomic nervous system
ANSI	American National Standards Institute
ANZAC	Australian and New Zealand Army Corps
ANZUS	Australia, New Zealand and the United States
AOB	any other business
AONB	Area of Outstanding Natural Beauty
AP	Associated Press
APEX	Association of Professional, Executive, Clerical, and Computer Staff
APL	A Programming Language
APR	annual percentage rate
APT	Advanced Passenger Train
AR	autonomous republic
AR	aspect ratio
ARC	American Red Cross
ARC	Arthritis Research Campaign
ARCIC	Anglican–Roman Catholic International Commission
ARE	European Radical Alliance
ARP	air-raid precautions
A/S	Advanced/Supplementary
ASA	American Standards Association
ASAP	as soon as possible
ASCII	American Standards Code for Information Interchange
ASDIC	Admiralty Submarine Detection Investigation Committee
ASEAN	Association of South-East Asian Nations
ASL	American Sign Language
ASLEF	Associated Society of Locomotive Engineers and Firemen
ASLIB	Association of Special Libraries and Information Bureaux
ASM	air-to-surface missile
ASPCA	American Society for the Prevention of Cruelty to Animals
ASSR	Autonomous Soviet Socialist Republic
ASTMS	Association of Scientific, Technical, and Managerial Staffs
AT	automatic transmission
ATP	adenosine triphosphate
ATS	Auxiliary Territorial Service
ATV	Associated Television
AU	astronomical unit
AV	audio-visual
AWACS	Airborne Warning and Control System
AWOL	absent without leave
AWU	Australian Workers' Union
BA	Bachelor of Arts
B&W	black and white
BAFTA	British Academy of Film and Television Arts
BALPA	British Airline Pilots' Association
BASIC	Beginners All-purpose Symbolic Instruction Code
BASIC	British American Scientific International Commercial (English)
BBC	British Broadcasting Corporation
BC	before Christ
Bcc	blind carbon copy
BCD	binary coded decimal
BCG	bacille (bacillus) Calmette Guérin
Bcm	billion cubic metres
BD	Bachelor of Divinity
BDA	British Diabetic Association
BE, BEd	Bachelor of Education
BEF	British Expeditionary Force
BEV	Black English Vernacular
BHP	Broken Hill Proprietary Company
BIA	Bureau of Indian Affairs
BIS	Bank for International Settlements
BIT	binary digit

BLAISE	British Library Automated Information Service
BLit, BLitt	Bachelor of Literature
BMA	British Medical Association
BMOC	big man on campus
BOSS	Bureau of State Security (South Africa)
BP	blood pressure
BSc	Bachelor of Science
BSA	Boy Scouts of America
BSE	bovine spongiform encephalopathy
BSI	British Standards Institution
BST	British Summer Time
btu	British thermal unit
BUF	British Union of Fascists
BUPA	British United Provident Association
CAB	Citizen's Advice Bureau
CACM	Central American Common Market
CAD	computer-aided design
CAI	computer-aided instruction
CAL	computer-aided learning
CAM	computer-aided manufacture
CAP	Common Agricultural Policy
CARICOM	Caribbean Community
CARIFTA	Caribbean Free Trade Area
CAT	Computerized axial tomography
CATV	cable television
CB	citizen's band (radio)
CBE	Commander of the (Order of the) British Empire
CBI	Confederation of British Industry
CBS	Columbia Broadcasting System
Cc	carbon copy
CCD	charge-coupled device
CCK	cholecystokinin-pancreozymin
CCR	camera cassette recorder
CCTV	closed-circuit television
CD	Civil Defence
CD	compact disc
CDC	Centers for Disease Control
CDROM	compact disc read-only memory
CDU	Christian Democratic Union
CEDEFOP	European Centre for the Development of Vocational training
CENTO	Central Treaty Organization
CERN	Organisation Européene pour la Recherche Nucléaire (formerly, Conseil Européen pour la Recherche Nucléaire)
CFC	chlorofluorocarbon
CGS	centimetre-gram-second
CGT	capital gains tax
CGT	Confédération Générale du Travail
CH	Companion of Honour
CHAPS	Clearing House Automated Clearing System
CHIPS	Clearing House Interbank Payments System
CIA	Central Intelligence Agency
CID	Criminal Investigation Department
CIO	Congress of Industrial Organizations
CJD	Creutzfeldt-Jacob disease
CM	Congregation of the Mission
CMG	Companion of (the Order of) St Michael & St George
CNAA	Council for National Academic Awards
CND	Campaign for Nuclear Disarmament
CNES	Centre National d'Espace
CNN	Cable News Network
CNS	central nervous system

COBOL	Common Business Oriented Language
COED	computer-operated electronic display
COMAL	Common Algorithmic Language
COMECON	Council for Mutual Economic Assistance
CORE	Congress of Racial Equality
CP	Congregation of the Passion
CPI	Consumer Price Index
CP/M	control program monitor
CPR	cardio-pulmonary resuscitation
CPS	characters per second
CPU	central processing unit
CRO	cathode-ray oscilloscope
CRT	cathode-ray tube
CSA	Child Support Agency
CSE	Certificate of Secondary Education
CSF	cerebrospinal fluid
CSIRO	Commonwealth Scientific and Industrial Research Organization
CSO	colour separation overlay
CTT	capital transfer tax
CV	cultivar
CV	curriculum vitae
CVO	Commander of the Royal Victorian Order
CVS	chorionic villus sampling
CWA	County Women's Association
CWS	Cooperative Wholesale Society
D-A	digital-to-analog (in computing)
DALR	dry adiabatic lapse rate
DALY	disability adjusted life year
D&C	dilation and curettage
DBE	Dame Commander of the (Order of the) British Empire
DBMS	database management system
DBS	direct broadcasting from satellite
DC	direct current
DCF	discounted cash flow
DCMG	Dame Commander Grand Cross of (the Order of) St Michael and St George
DCVO	Dame Commander of the Royal Victorian Order
DDT	dichloro-diphenyl-trichloroethane
DERV	diesel-engined road vehicle
DES	Department of Education and Science
DES	diethylstilboestrol
DFC	Distinguished Flying Cross
DHA	District Health Authority
DIA	Defence Intelligence Agency
DIVA	digital images for visual arts
DIY	do-it-yourself
DLL	dynamic link library
DLP	Democratic Labor Party (Australia)
DMS	date management system
DMSO	dimethyl sulphoxide
DNA	deoxyribonucleic acid
DNC	Democratic National Committe
DNS	domain name system
DOA	dead on arrival
DOE	Department of Education
DOS	disk-operating system
DPM	deputy prime minister
DPP	Director of Public Prosecutions
DSBB	Dissemination Standards Bulletin Board
DSN	Deep Space Network
DSO	Distinguished Service Order
DST	daylight-saving time
DTI	Department of Trade and Industry
DTP	desk-top publishing

COMMUNICATIONS

Common abbreviations (continued)

DVD	digital video (versatile) disc
DVLC	Driver and Vehicle Licensing Centre
EAC	European Atomic Commission
EARM	electrically alterable read-only memory
EBCDIC	extended binary-coded decimal interchange code
EBU	European Boxing Union
EBU	European Broadcasting Union
EC	European Community
ECA	Economic Commission for Africa
ECA	European Commission on Agriculture
ECB	European Central Bank
ECE	Economic Commision for Europe
ECF	extracellular fluid
ECG	electrocardiograph
ECLAC	Economic Commission for Latin America and the Caribbean
ECM	European Common Market
ECO	European Coal Organization
ECOSOC	Economic and Social Council (of the United Nations)
ECOWAS	Economic Community of West African States
ECSC	European Coal and Steel Community
ECT	electroconvulsive therapy
ECU	European currency unit
EDC	European Defence Community
EDVAC	Electronic Discrete Variable Automatic Computer
EEA	European Environment Agency
EEG	electroencephalograph
EEOC	Equal Employment Opportunity Commission
EFA	European Fighter Aircraft
EFC	European Forestry Commission
EFTA	European Free Trade Association
EGF	epidermal growth factor
EI	Exposure Index
ELDO	European Launcher Development Organization
ELDR	Liberal, Democratic and Reform Party
ELT	English language teaching
E-MAIL	electronic mail
EMCDDA	European Monitoring Centre for Drugs and Drug Addiction
EMEA	European Agency for the Evaluation of Medicinal Products
EMF	electromotive force
EMS	European Monetary System
EMU	electromagnetic units
ENIAC	Electronic Numeral Indicator and Calculator
EOKA	Ethniki Organosis Kipriakou Agonos (National Organization of Cypriot Struggle)
EP	European Parliament
EPA	Environmental Protection Agency
EPOS	electronic point of sale
EPR	electron paramagnetic resonance
EPROM	electronically programmable read-only memory
ERM	exchange rate mechanism
ERNIE	Electronic Random Number Indicator Equipment
ERW	enhanced radiation weapon

ESA	Environmentally Sensitive Area
ESA	European Space Agency
ESC	electronic stills camera
ESCAP	Economic and Social Commission for Asia and the Pacific
ESCU	European Space Operations Centre
ESO	European Southern Observatory
ESP	extra-sensory perception
ESRO	European Space Research Organization
ESTEC	European Space Research and Technology Centre
ETA	estimated time of arrival
ETU	Electricians Trade Union
EU	European Union
EUFA	European Union Football Associations
EURATOM	European Atomic Energy Community
EUROSTAT	Statistical Office of the European Communities
EXE	executable
FA	Football Association
FAA	Federal Aviation Administration
FAO	Food and Agriculture Organization
FAQ	frequently asked question
FBI	Federal Bureau of Investigation
FCA	Farm Credit Administration
FCC	Federal Communications Commission
FCO	Foreign and Commonwealth Office
FDA	Food and Drug Administration
FDIC	Federal Deposit Insurance Corporation
FDISK	fix disk
FIFA	Fédération Internationale de Football Association (International Association Football Federation)
FILO	first in, last out
FIMBRA	Financial Intermediaries, Managers and Brokers Regulatory Association
FLN	Front de Libération Nationale (National Liberation Front)
FM	frequency modulation
FO	Foreign Office
FORTRAN	formula translation
FPS	foot-pound-second
FRELIMO	Frente de Libertação de Moçambique (liberation Front of Mozambique)
FSH	follicle-stimulating hormone
FT	Financial Times
FTC	Federal Trade Commission
FTP	file transfer protocol
FWA	Federal Works Agency
GAR	Grand Army of the Republic
GATT	General Agreement on Tariffs and Trade
GBE	Knight/Dame Grand Cross of (the Order of the) British Empire
GBH	grievous bodily harm
GC	George Cross
GCC	Gulf Co-operation Council
GCE	General Certificate of Education
GCHQ	Government Communications Headquarters
GCMG	Knight/Dame Grand Cross of (the Order of) St Michael and St George
GCSE	General Certificate of Secondary Education
GCVO	Knight/Dame Grand Cross of the Royal Victorian Order
GDI	gross domestic income

GDP	gross domestic product	ID	identification
GEO	geosynchronous Earth orbit	IDA	International Development Agency
GESP	generalized extra-sensory perception	I-EDN	Independents/Europe of Nations
GH	growth hormone	IFAD	International Fund for Agricultural Development
GHQ	general headquarters
GI	government issue	IFC	International Finance Corporation
GIF	graphics interchange format	ILO	International Labour Organization
GIGO	garbage in, garbage out	IMCO	Intergovernmental Maritime Consultative Organization
GLC	gas-liquid chromatography
GLCM	ground-launched cruise missile	IMF	International Monetary Fund
GM	George Medal	INLA	Irish National Liberation Army
GMC	General Medical Council	INRI	Iesus Nazarenus Rex Iudeorum (Jesus of Nazareth, King of the Jews)
GMT	Greenwich Mean Time
GNP	gross national product
GnRH	gonadotrophin-releasing hormone	INSTRAW	International Research and Training Institute for the Advancement of Women
GP	General Practitioner
GPSS	General Purpose System Simulator	INTELSAT	International Telecommunications Satellite Organization
GSA	Girl Scouts of America
GUE/NGL	European United Left/Nordic Green Left	IOC	International Olympic Committee
GUI	graphical user interface	IPA	International Phonetic Alphabet
GUT	grand unified theory	IQ	intelligence quotient
GW	gigawatt	IR	infrared
HAMAS	Harakat al-Muqawama al-Islamiyya "movement of Islamic Resistance"	IRA	Irish Republican Army
		IRB	Irish Republican Brotherhood
		IRBM	intermediate-range ballistic missile
HCG	human chorionic gonadotrophin	IRC	Internet relay chat
HE	His/Her Excellency	IRS	Internal Revenue Service
HEP	hydro-electric power	ISA	Individual Savings Account
HF	high frequency	ISBN	International Standard Book Number
HGV	heavy goods vehicle	ISCC	Information Systems Coordination Committee
HIH	His/Her Imperial Highness
HIM	His/Her Imperial Majesty	ISDN	intergrated services digital network
HIV	human immunodeficiency virus	ISO	International Organization for Standardization
HLA	human leucocyte antigen
HM	His/Her Majesty	ISP	Internet service provider
HMG	His/Her Majesty's Government	ISSN	International Standard Serial Number
HMI	His/Her Majesty's Inspectorate	IT	information technology
HMO	health maintenance organization	ITA	Initial Teaching Alphabet
HMS	His/Her Majesty's Ship/Service	ITCZ	intertropical convergence zone
HMSO	His/Her Majesty's Stationery Office	ITN	Independent Television News
HNC	Higher National Certificate	ITT	International Telephone and Telegraph Corporation
HND	Higher National Diploma
HOTOL	horizontal take-off and landing	ITU	International Telecommunication Union
HP	horsepower	ITV	Independent Television
HQ	headquarters	IUCN	World Conservation Union
HR	House of Representatives	IUD	intra-uterine device
HRH	His/Her Royal Highness	IUPAC	International Union of Pure and Applied Chemistry
HRT	hormone replacement therapy
HSBC	Hong Kong and Shanghai Banking Corporation	IUPAP	International Union of Pure and Applied Physics
		IVF	in vitro fertilization
HTML	hypertext markup language	IVR	International Vehicle Registration
http	hypertext transfer protocol	IWW	Industrial Workers of the World
IAEA	International Atomic Energy Agency	JCB	Joseph Cyril Bamford (earth-movers)
IATA	International Air Transport Association	JET	Joint European Torus
IBA	Independent Broadcasting Authority	JP	Justice of the Peace
IBM	International Business Machines	JPEG	joint photographic expert group format
IBRD	International Bank for Reconstruction and Development	JPL	Jet Propulsion Laboratory
		KADU	Kenya African Democratic Union
ICAO	International Civil Aviation Organization	KANU	Kenya African National Union
ICBM	intercontinental ballistic missile	KB	Knight Bachelor; Knight of the Bath
ICC	International Computing Centre	KBE	Knight Commander of the (Order of the) British Empire
ICFTU	International Confederation of Free Trade Unions
		KC	King's Counsel
ICI	Imperial Chemical Industries	KCB	Knight Commander of the Bath
ICRF	Imperial Cancer Research Fund	KCMG	Knight Commander Grand Cross of (the Order of) St Michael and St George
ICSC	International civil service commission
ICSID	International Centre for Settlement of Investment Disputes

COMMUNICATIONS

Common abbreviations (continued)

KCVO	Knight Commander of The Royal Victorian Order
KG	Knight of the Order of the Garter
KGB	Komitet Gosudarstvennoye Bezhopaznosti (Committee of State Security)
KKK	Ku Klux Klan
KMT	Kuomintang
KO	knock-out
kPC	kiloparsec
KT	Knight of the Thistle
LA	Los Angeles
LAFTA	Latin American Free Trade Association
LAN	local area network
LAUTRO	Life Assurance and Unit Trust Companies
LCD	liquid-crystal display
LDC	less-developed country
LEA	Local Education Authority
LED	light-emitting diode
LEO	low Earth orbit
LFA	less favoured area
LH	luteinizing hormone
LHRH	luteinizing-hormone-releasing hormone
LIFFE	London International Financial Futures Exchange
LISP	list processing
LMS	London Missionary Society
LPG	liquefied petroleum gas
LSD	lysergic acid diethylamide
LSI	large-scale integration
LV	luncheon voucher
LVO	Lieutenant of the Royal Victorian Order
LW	long wave
MA	Master of Arts
MAC	multiplexed analogue component
MAO	monoamine oxidase
MASH	Mobile Army Surgical Hospital
MASH	multi-stage noise shaping
MATV	Master Antenna Television
MBE	Member of the Order of the British Empire
MC	Master of Ceremonies
MCA	monetary compensation amount
MCC	Marylebone Cricket Club
MCP	male chauvinist pig
MD	Managing Director
MD	Doctor of Medicine
MDMA	methylenedioxymethamphetamine
ME	myalgic encephalomyelitis
MEP	Member of the European Parliament
MH	Medal of Honor
MHD	magnetohydrodynamics
MIA	missing in action
MICR	magnetic ink character recognition
MIGA	Multilateral Investment Guarantee Agency
MIRED	micro reciprocal degrees
MIRV	multiple independently targetted re-entry vehicle
MKSA	metre-kilogram-second-ampere
MLB	Major League Baseball
MLR	minimum lending rate
MMF	magnetomotive force
MMI	man-machine interaction
MNCRS	Mobile network computer reference specification
MO	Medical Officer
MOD	Ministry of Defence

MODEM	modulator/demodulator
MORI	Market and Opinion Research International
MOT	Ministry of Transport (certificate)
MP	Member of Parliament
MOH	Medal of Honor
MPC	megaparsec
MPS	marginal propensity to save
MPTP	methylphenyltetrahydropyridine
MRA	Moral Rearmament
MS	multiple sclerosis
MSC	Manpower Services Commission
MSG	monosodium glutamate
MSH	melanocyte-stimulating hormone
Mt	million tonnes
MVD	Ministerstvo Vnutrennykh Del (Ministry for Internal Affairs)
MVO	Member of the Royal Victorian Order
NAACP	National Association for the Advancement of Coloured People
NAAFI	Navy, Army and Air Force Institutes
NABE	National Association of Business Economists
NACAB	National Association of Citizen Advice Bureaus
NACRO	National Association for the Care and Resettlement of Offenders
NANC	non-adrenergic non-cholinergic
NAPO	National Association of Probation Officers
NASA	National Aeronautics and Space Administration
NASDA	National Space Development Agency
NATO	North Atlantic Treaty Organization
NBA	National Basketball Association
NBC	National Broadcasting Corporation
NC	network computer
NCI	Network Computer, Inc
NCOS	network computer operating system
NCP	network computer profile
NCRP	network computer reference profile
NDE	near-death experience
NEDO	National Economic Development Office
NEP	new economic policy
NF	National Front
NFC	National Football Conference
NFL	National Football League
NGC	new general catalogue
NGF	nerve growth factor
NGO	non-governmental organization
NHL	National Hockey League
NHRBC	National Home Builders' Registration Council
NHS	National Health Service
NICAM	near instantaneously companded audi multiplex
NIH	National Institutes of Health
NIMBY	not in my back yard
NIREX	Nuclear Industry Radioactive Waste Disposal Executive
NKVD	Narodnyi Komissariat Vnutrennikh Del (People's Commissariat of Internal Affairs)
NLRB	National Labor Relations Board
NMR	nuclear magnetic resonance
NOW	National Organization for Women
NPT	Non-Proliferation Treaty
NRA	National Recovery Administration

NRAO	National Radio Astronomy Observatory
NSF	National Science Foundation
NSPCC	National Society for the Prevention of Cruelty to Children
NT	National Trust
NT	new technology
NTSC	National Television System Commission
NUM	National Union of Mineworkers
NUT	National Union of Teachers
NVC	non-verbal communication
NYC	New York City
NYPD	New York Police Department
OAP	old age pensioner
OAPEC	Organization of Arab Petroleum Exporting Countries
OAS	Organisation de l'Armée Secrète (Secret Army Organization)
OAS	Organization of American States
OAU	Organization of African Unity
OB	Order of the Bath
OB	outside broadcast
OBE	Officer of the (Order of the) British Empire
OCARM	Order of the Brothers of the Blessed Virgin Mary of Mount Carmel
OCART	Order of Carthusians
OCR	optical character recognition/reader
OCSO	Order of the Reformed Cistercians of the Strict Observance
OD	ordnance datum
ODC	Order of Discalced Carmelites
ODECA	Organizacion de Estados Centro Americanos (Organization of Central American States)
OECD	Organization for Economic Co-operation and Development
OEEC	Organization for European Economic Co-operation
OEM	Original Equipment Manufacturer
OFM	Order of Friars Minor
OFMCap	Order of Friars Minor Capuchin
OFMConv	Order of Friars Minor Conventual
OFTEL	Office of Telecommunications
OGPU	Otdelenie Gosudarstvenni Politcheskoi Upravi (Special Government Political Administration)
OHMS	On His/Her Majesty's Service
OHP	overhead projector
OM	Order of Merit
OMCap	Order of Friars Minor of St Francis Capuccinorum
OOBE	out-of-body experience
OP	Order of Preachers
OPEC	Organization of Petroleum Exporting Countries
OS	Ordanance Survey
OSA	Order of the Hermit Friars of St Augustine
OSB	Order of St Benedict
OSFC	Order of Friars Minor of St Francis Capuccinorum
OT	Old Testament
OTC	over-the-counter (stocks and shares, drugs)
OTEC	ocean thermal energy conversion
OU	Open University
OXFAM	Oxford Committee for Famine Relief
PA	personal assistant
PAC	Pan-African Congress
PAC	political action committee
PAL	phase alternation line
PAYE	pay as you earn
PC	parsec
PC	personal computer
PC	Poor Clares
pc	politically correct
PCP	phenylcyclohexylpiperidine
PDA	personal digital assistant
PDGF	platelet-derived growth factor
PDR	precision depth recorder
PEN	International Association of Poets, Playwrights, Editors, Essayists, and Novelists
PEP	personal equity plan
PEP	Political and Economic Planning
PF	Patriotic Front
PG	parental guidance (film)
PGA	Professional Golfers' Association
PH	Purple Heart
PhD	Doctor of Philosophy
PIN	personal identification number
PK	psychokinesis
PKU	phenylketonuria
PLA	People's Liberation Army
PLC	public limited company
PLO	Palestine Liberation Organization
PM	Prime Minister
PM of F	Presidential Medal of Freedom
PMT	pre-menstrual tension
PNLM	Palestine National Liberation Movement
POP	Post Office Protocol
POW	prisoner of war
PPE	European People's Party
PPI	plan position indicator
PPP	personal pension plan
PPS	Parliamentary Private Secretary
PR	proportional representation
PRO	Public Record Office
PRO	public relations officer
PROM	programmable read-only memory
PSBR	public sector borrowing requirement
PSE	Party of European Socialists
PTA	parent-teacher association
PTFE	polytetrafluoroethylene
PTO	please turn over
PVA	polyvinyl acetate
PVC	polyvinyl chloride
PWA	Public Works Administration
PWR	pressurized-water reactor
PYO	pick-your-own
QC	Queen's Counsel
QCD	quantum chromodynamics
QED	quantum electrodynamics
RA	Royal Academy
R&A	Royal & Ancient Golf Club of St Andrews
RAAF	Royal Australian Air Force
RAC	Royal Automobile Club
RADA	Royal Academy of Dramatic Art
RAF	Royal Air Force
RAM	random access memory
RAM	Royal Academy of Music
RAN	Royal Australian Navy
RDA	recommended daily allowance
REM	rapid eye movement
RGB	red, green and blue (colour television)
RHA	Regional Health Authority
RIP	raster image processing

COMMUNICATIONS

Common abbreviations (continued)

COMMUNICATIONS

RIP	rest in peace
RISC	Reduced Instruction Set Computer
RKKA	Rabochekrest'yanshi Krasny (Red Army of Workers and Peasants)
RLE	run length encoding
RLL	run length limited
RM	Royal Marines
RMS	root mean square
RN	Royal Navy
RNA	ribonucleic acid
RNIB	Royal National Institute for the Blind
RNID	Royal National Institute for Deaf People
RNLI	Royal National Lifeboat Institution
ROM	read-only memory
RORO	roll-on, roll-off (ferry)
ROSPA	Royal Society for the Prevention of Accidents
RP	received pronunciation
RPG	rocket propelled grenade
RPI	retail price index
RPM	resale price maintenance
RPM	revolutions per minute
RRP	recommended retail price
RS	Royal Society
RSPB	Royal Society for the Protection of Birds
RSC	Royal Shakespeare Company
RSI	repetitive strain injury
RSPCA	Royal Society for the Prevention of Cruelty to Animals
RSVP	please reply (répondez s'il vous plaît)
RTA	road traffic accident
RTG	radio-isotope thermo-electric generator
RUC	Royal Ulster Constabulary
RVO	Royal Victorian Order
SA	Sturm Abteilung (Storm Troopers)
SAE	stamped addressed envelope
SALR	saturated adiabatic lapse rate
SALT	Strategic Arms Limitation Talks
SAM	surface-to-air missile
SAS	Special Air Service
SAT	scholastic aptitude test
SBR	styrene butadiene rubber
SCID	severe combined immuno-deficiency
SCLC	Southern Christian Leadership Conference
SCSI	small computer system interface
SDI	selective dissemination of information
SDI	strategic defence initiative
SDP	Social Democratic Party
SDR	special drawing rights
SDS	Students for a Democratic Society
SDU	Social Democratic Union
SEAQ	Stock Exchange Automated Quotations
SEATO	South-East Asia Treaty Organization
SEC	Securities and Exchange Commission
SECAM	Séquence Electronique Couleur avec Mémoire (Electronic Colour Sequence with Memory)
SERPS	state earnings-related pension scheme
SGML	standard generalized markup language
SHAEF	Supreme Headquarters Allied Expeditionary Force
SHAPE	Supreme Headquarters Allied Powers, Europe
SHF	super-high frequency

SI	Système International (International System)
SIB	Securities and Investments Board
SIOP	single integrated operation plan
SJ	Society of Jesus
SLBM	submarine-launched ballistic missile
SLCM	sea-launched cruise missile
SLDP	Social and Liberal Democratic Party
SLE	systemic lupus erythematosus
SLR	single-lens reflex
SMTP	simple mail transfer protocol
SNCC	Student Non-Violent Co-ordinating Committee
SNOBOL	String-Oriented Symbolic Language
SNP	Scottish National Party
SOCist	Cistercians of Common Observance
SOE	Special Operations Executive
SONAR	sound navigation and ranging
SOR	sale or return
SQUID	superconducting quantum interference device
SRO	self-regulatory organization
SRO	single room occupancy
SS	Schutzstaffel (Protective Squad)
SSR	Soviet Socialist Republic
SSSI	Site of Special Scientific Interest
START	Strategic Arms Reduction Talks
STB	set top box
STD	sexually transmitted disease
STOL	short take-off and landing
SW	short wave
SWAPO	South-West Africa People's Organization
SWF	single white female
SWS	slow-wave sleep
SYS	system file
TA	Territorial Army
TAB	Totalizator Agency Board
TARDIS	time and relative dimensions in space
TASS	Telegrafnoe Agentsvo Sovetskovo Soyuza (Telegraph Agency of the Soviet Union)
TB	tuberculosis
TBA	to be announced
TCDD	tetrachlorodibenzo-p-dioxin
TCP	trichlorophenylmethyliodialicyl
TCP/IP	transmission control protocol/Internet protocol
TEFL	Teaching English as a Foreign Language
TESL	Teaching English as a Second Language
TESSA	Tax Exempt Special Savings Account
TGV	train à grande vitesse (French high-speed train)
TGWU	Transport and General Workers Union
TIF	tagged image format
TNT	trinitrotoluene
TSB	Trustee Savings Bank
TT	Tourist Trophy
TTL	through the lens
TUC	Trades Union Congress
TV	television
TVA	Tennessee Valley Authority
TVP	textured vegetable protein
TWh	Terawatt hours
TWOC	taking without owner's consent
TXT	text file
UAE	United Arab Emirates

UAP	United Australia Party	UPU	Universal Postal Union
UCAR	Union of Central African Republics	URL	uniform resource locator
UCCA	University Central Council on Admissions	USA	United States of America
UDA	Ulster Defence Association	USAF	United States Air Force
UDI	Unilateral Declaration of Independence	USCG	United States Coast Guard
UEFA	Union of European Football Associations	USIS	United States Information Service
UFO	unidentified flying object	USS	United States Ship
UHF	ultra-high frequency	USSR	Union of Soviet Socialist Republics
UHT	ultra-high temperature	UV	ultra-violet
UK	United Kingdom	UBX	unexploded bomb
UKAEA	United Kingdom Atomic Energy Authority		
UN	United Nations	V	The Greens in the European Parliament
UNAIDS	Joint United Nations Programme on HIV/Aids	VA	Veterans Administration
		VAT	value-added tax
UNCC	United Nations Compensation Committee	VC	Victoria Cross
UNCED	United Nations Convention to Combat Desertification	VCR	video cassette recorder
		VD	venereal disease
UNCHS	United Nations Centre for Human Settlements	VDISK	virtual disk
		VDU	visual display unit
UNCITRAL	United Nations Commission on International Trade Law	VGA	video graphics array
		VHF	very high frequency
UNCTAD	United Nations Conference on Trade and Development	VHS	video home system
		VIP	vasoactive intestinal polypeptide
UNDC	United Nations Disarmament Commission	VLF	very low frequency
UNDCP	United Nations International Drug Control Programme	VLSI	very large scale integration
		VOA	Voice of America
UNDP	United Nations Development Programme	VSEPR	valence-shell electron pair repulsion
UNEP	United Nations Environment Programme	VSO	Voluntary Service Overseas
UNESCO	United Nations Economic, Scientific and Cultural Organization	VTOL	vertical take-off and landing
		VTR	video tape recorder
UNFAO	United Nations Food and Agriculture Organization	WAAC	Women's Auxiliary Army Corps
		WAAF	Women's Auxiliary Air Force
UNFCCC	United Nations Framework Convention on Climate Change	WAC	Women's Army Corps
		WASP	White Anglo-Saxon Protestant
UNFPA	United Nations Population Fund	WBA	World Boxing Association
UNGA	United Nations General Assembly	WBC	World Boxing Council
UNHCHR	United Nations High Commissioner for Human Rights	WCC	World Council of Churches
		WCMC	World Conservation Monitoring Centre
UNHCR	United Nations High Commission for Refugees	WEA	Workers' Educational Association
		WEU	Western European Union
UNICEF	United Nations Children's Fund (formerly UN International Children's Emergency Fund)	WFP	World Food Programme
		WFTU	World Federation of Trade Unions
		WHO	World Health Organization
UNICRI	United Nations Interregional Crime and Justice Research Institute	WI	(National Federation of) Women's Institutes
		WIPO	World Intellectual Property Organization
UNIDO	United Nations Industrial Development Organization	WMF	Windows metafile format
		WMO	World Meteorological Organization
UNIFEM	United Nations Development Fund for Women	WPA	Work Projects Administration
		WRAC	Women's Royal Army Corps
UNIS	United Nations International School – New York, USA	WRAF	Women's Royal Air Force
		WRNS	Women's Royal Naval Service
UNITAR	United Nations Institute for Training and Research	WRVS	Women's Royal Voluntary Service
		WTO	World Trade Organization
UNO	United Nations Organization	WVS	Women's Voluntary Service
UNOG	United Nations Office at Geneva	WWF	World Wildlife Fund
UNOPS	United Nations Office for Project Services	www	world wide web
UNOV	United Nations Office at Vienna	WYSIWYG	what you see is what you get
UNRISD	United Nations Research Institute for Social Development	XMS	extended memory specification
UNRWA	United Nations Relief and Works Agency for Palestine Refugees in the Near East	YAHOO	Yet another heirarchical officious oracle
		YHA	Youth Hostels Association
UNSC	United Nations Security Council	YMCA	Young Men's Christian Association
UNSC	United Nations Staff College	YMHA	Young Men's Hebrew Association
UNSG	United Nations Secretary General	YUPPIE	young upwardly mobile professional
UNTT	United Nations Trust Territory	YWCA	Young Women's Christian Association
UPE	Union of Europe	YWHA	Young Women's Hebrew Association

COMMUNICATIONS

MEDIA

News agencies

Agency		Headquartered
AA	Anadol Ajansi	Ankara
AAP	Australian Associated Press	Sydney
AASA	Agence Arabe Syrienne d'Information	Damascus
ADN	Allgemeiner Deutscher Nachrichtendienst	Berlin
AE	Agence Europe	Brussels
AFP	Agence France Presse	Paris
AIO	Agencia Informativa Orbe de Chile	Santiago
AIP	Agence Ivoirienne de Presse	Abidjan
ALD	Agence Los Diarios	Buenos Aires
ALI	Agencia Lusa de Informacao	Lisbon
AM	Agencia Meridional	Rio de Janeiro
AN	Agencia Nacional	Brasilia
ANA	Athenagence	Athens
ANGOP	Angola Agêcia Naticiosa N'gola Press	Luanda
ANP	Algemeen Nederlands Persbureau	The Hague
ANSA	Agenzia Nazionale Stampa Associate	Rome
ANTARA	Indonesian National News Agency	Jakarta
AP	Associated Press	New York
APA	Austria Presse Agentur	Vienna
APP	Agence Parisienne de Presse	Paris
APP	Associated Press of Pakistan	Islamabad
APS	Agence de Presse Senegalaise	Dakar
APS	Algeria Presse Service	Algiers
ATA	Albanian Telegraphic Agency	Tirana
AUP	Australian United Press	Melbourne
BATRA	Jordan News Agency	Amman
BELGA	Agence Belga	Brussels
BERNAMA	Malaysian National News Agency	Kuala Lumpur
BOPA	Botswana Press Agency	Gaborone
BSS	Bangladesh Sangbad Sangstha	Dhaka
BTA	Bulgarska Telegrafitscheka Agentzia	Sofia
CANA	Caribbean News Agency	Bridgetown
CIP	Centre d'Information de Presse	Brussels
CNA	Central News Agency	Taipei
CNA	Cyprus News Agency	Nicosia
CNS	China News Service	Beijing
COLPRENSA	Colprensa	Bogota
CP	Canadian Press	Toronto
CSTK	Ceskoslovenska Tiskova Kancelar	Prague
DPA	Deutsche Presse Agentur	Hamburg
EFE	Agencia EFE	Madrid
ENA	Eastern News Agency	Dhaka
ETA	Eesti Teadate Agentuur	Tallinn
EXTEL	Exchange and Telegraph Company	London

Agency		Headquartered
FIDES	Agenzia Internazionale Fides	Vatican City
GNA	Agence Guinéenne de Presse	Conakry
GNA	Ghana News Agency	Accra
GNA	Guyana News Agency	Georgetown
HHA	Hurriyet Haber Ajasi	Istanbul
HINA	Hrvatska Izvjestajna Novinska Agencija	Zagreb
IC	Inforpress Centroamericana	Guatemala
INA	Iraqi News Agency	Baghdad
IPS	Inter Press Service	Rome
IRNA	Islamic Republic News Agency	Tehran
ITIM	Associated Israel Press	Tel Aviv
JAMPRESS	Jampress	Kingston
JANA	Jamahiriya News Agency	Tripoli
JIJI	Jiji Tsushin-Sha	Tokyo
JTA	Jewish Telegraphic Agency	Jerusalem
KCNA	Korean Central News Agency	Pyongyang
KNA	Kenya News Agency	Nairobi
KPL	Khao San Pathet Lao	Vientiane
KUNA	Kuwait News Agency	Kuwait City
KYODO	Kyodo Tsushin	Tokyo
LAI	Logos Agencia de Informacion	Madrid
LETA	Latvijas Telegrafa Agentura	Riga
MENA	Middle East News Agency	Cairo
MTI	Magyar Tavariti Iroda	Budapest
NA	Noticias Argentinas	Buenos Aires
NAEWOE	Naewoe Press	Seoul
NAN	News Agency of Nigeria	Lagos
NOTIMEX	Noticias Mexicanas	Mexico City
NOVOSTI	Agentstvo Pechati Novosti	Moscow
NPS	Norsk Presse Service	Oslo
NTB	Norsk Telegrambyra	Oslo
NZPA	New Zealand Press Agency	Wellington
OPA	Orbis Press Agency	Prague
OTTFNB	Oy Suomen Tietoimisto Notisbyrån Ab	Helsinki
PA	Press Association	London
PANA	Pan-African News Agency	Dakar
PAP	Polska Agencija Prasowa	Warsaw
PNA	Philippines News Agency	Manila
PPI	Pakistan Press International	Karachi
PRELA	Prensa Latina	Havana
PS	Presse Services	Paris
PTI	Press Trust of India	Bombay
RB	Ritzaus Bureau	Copenhagen
REUTERS	Reuters	London
ROMPRESS	Romanian News Agency	Bucharest
SAPA	South African Press Association	Johannesburg
SDA	Schweizerische Depeschenagentur	Berne
SIP	Svensk Internationella Pressbyrån	Stockholm
SLENA	Sierra Leone News Agency	Freetown

SOFIAPRES	Sofia Press Agency	Sofia
SOPAC-NEWS	South Pacific News Service	Wellington
SPA	Saudi Press Agency	Riyadh
SPK	Saporamean Kampuchea	Phnom Penh
STA	Slovenska Tiskovna Agencija	Ljubljana
TANJUG	Novinska Agencija Tanjug	Belgrade
TAP	Tunis Afrique Presse	Tunis
TASS	Telegraph Agency of the Soviet Union/ Sovereign States	Moscow
TT	Tidningarnes Telegrambyra	Stockholm
UNI	United News of India	New Delhi
UPI	United Press International	New York
UPP	United Press of Pakistan	Karachi
VNA	Vietnam News Agency	Hanoi
XINHUA	Xinhua	Beijing
YONHAP	Yonhap (United) Press Agency	Seoul
ZIANA	Zimbabwe Inter-Africa News Agency	Harare

Publishing

Newspaper publishers' associations

Argentina	Asociación de Editores de Diarios de Buenos Aires
Australia	Australian Newspapers Council; Country Press Australia; Regional Dailies of Australia
Austria	Verband Österreichischer Zeitungsherausgeber und Zeitungsverleger (VÖZZ)
Bangladesh	Bangladesh Council of Newspapers and News Agencies
Belgium	Belgische Vereniging van de Dagbladuitgevers
Brazil	Asociaçio Brasileira de Imprensa
Canada	Canadian Daily Newspaper Publishers' Association
Chile	Asociación Nacional de la Prensa
Colombia	Asociación Nacional de Medios de Communicación
Denmark	Danske Dagblades Forening (DDF)
El Salvador	Asociación Salvadoreña de Empresarios de Radiodifusión (ASDER)
Finland	Sanomalehtien Liitto/Tindningamas Förbund
France	Fédération Nationale de la Presse Française
Germany	Bundesverband Deutscher Zeitungsverleger
Guinea	Guinean Association of Independent Press Publishers (AGEPI)
Hong Kong	Hsiangkang Hua Wenpaoyeh Hsieh-hui; Newspaper Society of Hong Kong/ Hsiangkang Paoyeh Kunghui
India	Indian Languages Newspapers' Association; Indian Newspaper Society
Indonesia	Serikat Penerbit Suratkabar
Israel	Igud Ha'itonim Hayomiyim Beyisra'el
Italy	Federazione Italiana Editori Giornali; Federazione Nazionale della Stampa Italiana
Japan	Nihon Shimbun Kyokai; Nihon Zasshi Kyokai
Korea, South	Han'guk Shinmun Hypuhoe
Lebanon	Niqabat al-Mukhbirun al-Lubnaniyun
Luxembourg	Association Luxembourgeoise des Editeurs de Journaux
Malaysia	Persatuan Penerbit-Penerbit Akhbar Malaysia
Mexico	Asociación de Diarios Independentes; Asociación de Editores de Periódicos Diarios de la República Mexicana
Netherlands	Vereniging De Nederlandse Dagbladpers
New Zealand	Community Newspapers' Association; Newspaper Publishers' Association of New Zealand
Nigeria	Newspaper Proprietors' Organization of Nigeria
Norway	Norsk Presseforbund; Norsk Avisers Landsforbund
Pakistan	All Pakistan Newspapers Society
Philippines	National Press Club of the Philippines
Portugal	Associaçio da Imprensa Diária
South Africa	Newspaper Press Union
Spain	Asociación de Editores de Diarios Españoles (AEDE); Federación de Asociaciones de la Prensa de España (FAPE)
Sri Lanka	Sri Lanka Press Association
Sweden	Svenska Tidningsutgivareföreningen
Switzerland	Schweizerischer Verband der Zeitungs und Zeitschriftenverleger/ Association Suisse des Editeurs de Journaux et Periodiques
Thailand	Samakom Nangsupim Hang Prathet Thai
Uganda	Uganda News Editors' and Proprietors' Association
United Kingdom	Newspaper Society; Newspaper Publishers' Association; Scottish Daily Newspaper Society
USA	American Newspaper Publishers' Association (ANPA); American Society of Newspaper Editors (ASNE); National Newspaper Association (NNA)
Uruguay	Asociación de Diarios del Uruguay
Venezuela	Bloque de Prensa Venezolano

Circulations

In this section, circulation totals are given based on a recent audit. However, as circulations often vary greatly over short periods of time, the figures given should be seen only as approximations.

COMMUNICATIONS

Publishing (continued)

Major British newspapers

Paper	Location	Circulation	Issue
Daily Express	London	763 544	Daily
Daily Mail	London	2 212 727	Daily
Daily Mirror	London	1 495 157	Daily
Daily Record	Glasgow	412 563	Daily
Daily Star	London	661 395	Daily
Daily Telegraph	London	842 274	Daily
Evening Standard	London	289 254	Daily
Financial Times	London	131 739	Daily
Guardian	London	335 317	Daily
Independent	London	223 151	Daily
Independent on Sunday	London	199 367	Sunday
Mail on Sunday	London	2 152 035	Sunday
News of the World	London	3 220 777	Sunday
Observer	London	402 665	Sunday
People	London	741 679	Sunday
Racing Post	London	60 631	Daily
Scotland on Sunday	Edinburgh	74 362	Sunday
Scotsman	Edinburgh	60 088	Daily
Sun	London	3 005 466	Daily
Sunday Express	London	778 183	Sunday
Sunday Mail	Glasgow	511 639	Sunday
Sunday Mirror	London	1 330 549	Sunday
Sunday Sport	London	107 926	Sunday
Sunday Telegraph	London	641 084	Sunday
Sunday Times	London	1 140 467	Sunday
Times	London	638 451	Daily

Daily = Monday through Saturday. Figures are average net circulation for October 2006. UK editions only.
Source: Audit Bureau of Circulations.

Best-selling European newspapers

Included are newspapers with circulations of 250 000 and over.

Austria

Kleine Zeitung	Graz	275 000	Weekly
Die Ganze Woche	Vienna	850 000	2-weekly
Kurier	Vienna	620 000	Daily & Sun
Neue Kronenzeitung	Vienna	1 000 000	Daily

Belgium

Antwerpse Post (Dutch/nederlands)	Antwerp	313 327	Weekly
Die Nieuwe Gazet Antwerp (Dutch/nederlands)	Antwerp	298 882	Daily
Visite (Dutch/nederlands)	Berchem	574 355	Monthly
Belgique No 1 (French)	Brussels	530 000	Weekly
L'Echo (French)	Brussels	380 000	Weekly
Groupe AZ (French)	Brussels	1 625 000	Weekly
Groep AZ (Dutch/nederlands)	Brussels	2 800 000	Weekly
Vlan (French)	Brussels	425 000	Weekly
De Gentenaar (Dutch/nederlands)	Ghent	326 000	Daily

Paper	Location	Circulation	Issue
Het Nieuwsblad (Dutch/nederlands)	Groot-Bijgaarden	382 397	Daily
De Standaard (Dutch/nederlands)	Groot-Bijgaarden	382 397	Daily
Hier Groep (Dutch/nederlands)	Hasselt	350 000	Weekly
Publi-Hebdo	Liege	382 000	Weekly
Deze Week in (Dutch/nederlands)	Roeselare	840 000	Weekly

Bulgaria

Duma	Sofia	300 000	Daily
Otechestven Front (Fatherland Front)	Sofia	280 000	Daily

Czech Republic

MF Dnes	Prague	350 000	Daily
Práce (Labour)	Prague	350 000	Daily
Právo	Prague	200 000	Daily

Éire

Sunday World	Dublin	263 088	Weekly

France

Sud-Ouest	Bordeaux	367 860	Daily
La Montagne	Clermont Ferrand	250 288	Daily
L'Est Républicain	Heillecourt	251 236	Daily
Le Progrès	Lyons	353 608	Daily
Nice Matin	Nice	258 205	Daily
Le Figaro	Paris	428 700	Daily
France-Dimanche	Paris	706 338	Weekly
France-Soir	Paris	334 035	Daily
Ici Paris	Paris	422 796	Weekly
Le Journal Dimanche	Paris	360 029	Weekly
Le Monde	Paris	381 549	Daily
Le Parisien	Paris	365 661	Daily
VSD (Vendredi, Samedi, Dimanche)	Paris	261 612	Weekly
Ouest-France	Rennes	739 047	Daily
La Nouvelle République du Centre-Ouest	Tours	271 504	Daily
Le Dauphiné Libéré	Veurey-Voroize	813 209	Daily

Germany

Augsburger Allgemeine	Augsburg	362 000	Daily
BZ-Berlin	Berlin	279 269	Daily
Berliner Zeitung	Berlin	425 000	Daily
Bild Berlin	Berlin	250 000	Daily
Junge Welt	Berlin	330 000	Daily
Express Köln	Cologne	437 104	Daily
Lausitzer Rundschau	Cottbus	291 000	Daily
Sächsische Zeitung	Dresden	513 000	Daily
Rheinische Post	Düsseldorf	391 489	Daily
Das Volk	Erfurt	401 000	Daily
Westdeutsche Allgemeine Zeitung (WAZ)	Essen	1 236 304	Daily

Paper	Location	Circulation	Issue
Frankfurter Allgemeine Zeitung (FAZ)	Frankfurt/ Main	366 703	Daily
Bild	Hamburg	4 416 240	Daily
Die Zeit	Hamburg	488 212	Weekly
Hannoversche Allgemeine Zeitung (HAZ)	Hannover	511 027	Daily
HNA Hessische/ Niedersäch Allgemeine	Kassel	272 249	Daily
Leipziger Volkszeitung	Leipzig	484 000	Daily
Volksstimme	Magdeburg	379 407	Daily
Süddeutsche Zeitung (SZ)	Magdeburg	386 287	Daily
Super Zeitung	Munich	600 000	Daily
Nürnberger Nachrichten	Nuremburg	325 000	Daily
Nordwest Zeitung	Oldenburg	317 077	Daily
Neue Osnabrücker Zeitung	Osnabruck	299 572	Daily
Ostee Zeitung	Rostock	293 000	Daily
Sonntag Aktuell	Stuttgart	877 140	Weekly
Stuttgarter Zeitung	Stuttgart	509 710	Daily
Südwest Presse	Ulm	367 129	Daily

Hungary

Népsport (People's Sport)	Budapest	250 000	Daily
Népszabadsag (People's Freedom)	Budapest	450 000	Daily
Reform	Budapest	385 000	Weekly
Vasárnapi Hirek	Budapest	270 595	Weekly

Italy

Corriere Della Sera	Milan	644 856	Daily
La Gazzetta Dello Sport	Milan	814 889	Daily
Il Sole 24 Ore	Milan	258 771	Daily
Corriere Dello Sport-Stadio	Rome	542 275	Daily
Il Messaggero	Rome	400 000	Daily
La Repubblica	Rome	826 224	Daily
La Stampa	Turin	406 951	Daily

Netherlands

De Telegraaf	Amsterdam	725 700	Daily
De Volkskrant	Amsterdam	340 038	Daily
Algemeen Dagblad	Rotterdam	417 000	Daily

Norway

Verdens Gang (VG)	Oslo	365 000	Daily
Aftenposten	Oslo	262 892	Daily

Poland

Gazeta Wyborcza	Warsaw	550 000	Daily
Zycie Warszawy (Warsaw Life)	Warsaw	250 000	Daily

Romania

Ardevarul	Bucharest	250 000	Daily
România Liberia	Bucharest	400 000	Daily

Slovakia

Práca	Bratislava	260 300	Daily
Pravda	Bratislava	260 000	Daily

Spain

ABC	Madrid	280 356	Daily
El Pais	Madrid	377 528	Daily

Paper	Location	Circulation	Issue
Sweden			
Göteborg-Posten	Gothenburg	281 000	Daily
Aftonbladet	Stockholm	480 000	Daily
Dagens Nyheter	Stockholm	519 000	Daily
Expressen	Stockholm	575 000	Daily
Turkey			
Milliyet (Nationalism)	Istanbul	250 000	Daily
Sabah (Morning)	Istanbul	506 671	Daily
Russia			
Izvestiya	Moscow	10 130 000	Daily
Komsomolskaya Pravda (Youth Truth)	Moscow	20 354 000	Daily
Moskovskaya Pravda	Moscow	725 000	Daily
Pravda	Moscow	7 700 000	Daily
Rabochaya Tribuna (Worker's Tribune)	Moscow	1 405 000	Daily
Selskaya Zhizn (Country Life)	Moscow	5 772 000	Daily
Sotsialisticheskaya Industriya	Moscow	1 500 000	Daily
Sovetski Sport	Moscow	4 863 000	Daily
Trud (Labour)	Moscow	21 429 000	Daily
Vechernyaya Moskva (Evening News)	Moscow	650 000	Daily

Daily = Monday through Saturday

US newspapers

The highest circulation figures are quoted, whether they be for a paper's Sunday or weekday issue. All papers listed have circulation figures of over 100 000. No free papers are listed.

Alabama			
News	Birmingham	159 823	Daily
Arizona			
New Times	Phoenix	135 000	Weekly
Republic	Phoenix	362 199	Daily
Star	Tucson	159 698	Daily
Arkansas			
Democrat-Gazette	Little Rock	174 883	Daily
California			
Bee	Fresno	150 438	Daily
Press-Telegram	Long Beach	128 750	Daily
Central News	Los Angeles	210 000	Weekly
Daily News (Japanese)	Los Angeles	215 586	Daily
Daily News	Los Angeles	207 011	Daily & Sun
Herald-Examiner	Los Angeles	303 320	Daily & Sun
Investors Daily	Los Angeles	176 740	Daily
L.A. Times	Los Angeles	1 062 202	Daily & Sun
La Opinion (Spanish)	Los Angeles	105 918	Daily & Sun
Tribune	Oakland	121 537	Daily & Sun
Press-Enterprise	Riverside	161 659	Daily & Sun
Sacramento Bee	Sacramento	275 696	Daily & Sun
Sun	San Bernadino	100 688	Daily & Sun

Publishing (continued)

Paper	Location	Circulation	Issue
Union-Tribune	San Diego	372 466	Daily & Sun
San Francisco Chronicle	San Francisco	509 548	Daily
San Francisco Examiner	San Francisco	136 346	Daily
Sun Examiner/ Chronicle	San Francisco	716 339	Weekly
Wall Street Journal, western edition	San Francisco	388 013	Daily
Mercury News	San Jose	283 590	Daily & Sun
Register	Santa Ana	350 387	Daily & Sun
Daily Breeze	Torrance	100 000	Daily & Sun
Colorado			
Gazette Telegraph	Colorado Springs	115 883	Daily
Post	Denver	287 213	Daily & Sun
Rocky Mountain News	Denver	344 585	Daily & Sun
Connecticut			
Hartford Courant	Hartford	226 533	Daily & Sun
Register	New Haven	135 569	Daily & Sun
Delaware			
News Journal	Wilmington	125 742	Daily
District of Columbia			
Washington Post	Washington	810 675	Daily & Sun
Washington Times	Washington	100 000	Weekly
Florida			
News Journal	Daytona Beach	106 169	Daily & Sun
Sun-Sentinel	Fort Lauderdale	263 256	Daily
News Press	Fort Myers	102 016	Daily & Sun
Florida Times-Union	Jacksonville	181 841	Daily & Sun
Florida Today	Melbourne	106 878	Daily
Miami Herald	Miami	393 791	Daily & Sun
State Paper	Miami	140 000	Daily
Suncoast News	New Port Richey	172 000	2-weekly
Sentinel	Orlando	270 970	Daily
Herald-Tribune	Sarasota	130 872	Daily
Times	St Petersburg	354 164	Daily & Sun
Tribune & Times	Tampa	264 400	Daily & Sun
Palm Beach Post	West Palm Beach	172 744	Daily
Georgia			
Atlanta Constitution	Atlanta	309 906	Mon–Fri
Dekalb News/Sun	Decatur	104 000	Weekly
Journal	Atlanta	140 473	Daily
Macon Telegraph & News	Macon	100 488	Daily & Sun
Illinois			
Chicago Sun Times	Chicago	518 094	Daily
Chicago Tribune	Chicago	678 085	Daily & Sun
Daily Herald	Chicago	124 595	Daily
Wall Street Journal, midwest edition	Chicago	513 653	Daily
Journal Star	Peoria	110 115	Daily & Sun
Indiana			
Courier	Evansville	116 962	Daily & Sun
Journal-Gazette	Fort Wayne	139 275	Daily & Sun

Paper	Location	Circulation	Issue
News	Indianapolis	101 091	Daily
Star	Indianapolis	231 423	Daily & Sun
Iowa			
Register	Des Moines	184 591	Daily & Sun
Kansas			
Wichita Eagle	Wichita	198 906	Daily & Sun
Kentucky			
Herald Leader	Lexington	157 908	Daily & Sun
Courier Journal	Louisville	239 595	Daily & Sun
Louisiana			
Times Picayune	New Orleans	267 938	Daily & Sun
Maryland			
Sun	Baltimore	248 520	Daily
Massachusetts			
The Boston Globe	Boston	506 545	Daily & Sun
Boston Herald	Boston	309 935	Daily & Sun
Christian Science Monitor	Boston	104 314	Mon–Fri
Phoenix	Boston	134 000	Weekly
Patriot Ledger	Quincy	101 639	Daily
Union	Springfield	156 880	Daily
Telegram & Gazette	Worcester	135 891	Daily
Michigan			
Free Press	Detroit	554 606	Daily & Sun
News	Detroit	355 970	Daily & Sun
Journal	Flint	107 940	Daily
Press	Grand Rapids	147 530	Daily & Sun
Minnesota			
Star Tribune	Minneapolis	407 504	Daily & Sun
Pioneer Press Dispatch	St Paul	207 802	Daily
Mississippi			
Clarion Ledger	Jackson	123 052	Daily
Missouri			
Star	Kansas City	290 650	Mon–Fri
Post Dispatch	St Louis	333 968	Daily & Sun
Nebraska			
World Herald	Omaha	233 035	Daily & Sun
Nevada			
Las Vegas Review Journal	Las Vegas	137 153	Daily & Sun
New Jersey			
Asbury Park Press	Asbury Park	228 140	Daily
Courier-Post	Camden-Cherry Hill	101 803	Mon–Fri & Sun
Record	Hackensack	159 545	Daily & Sun
Star-Ledger	Newark	455 919	Daily & Sun
North Jersey Herald News	Passaic	140 260	Daily & Sun
Press	Pleasantville	163 282	Daily & Sun
New Mexico			
Journal	Albuquerque	158 078	Daily & Sun
New York			
Times-Union	Albany	173 944	Daily & Sun
News	Buffalo	296 820	Daily & Sun
Newsday	Long Island	693 550	Daily & Sun

Paper	Location	Circulation	Issue
Times-Herald Record	Middletown	101 097	Daily & Sun
Daily News	New York	753 024	Daily & Sun
New York Post	New York	405 318	Daily
The New York Times	New York	1 114 905	Daily & Sun
Village Voice	New York	147 000	Weekly
Wall Street Journal	New York	1 780 442	Mon–Fri
Suffolk Life	Riverhead	468 000	Weekly
Democrat & Chronicle	Rochester	143 392	Daily & Sun
North Carolina			
Observer	Charlotte	236 579	Daily & Sun
News & Record	Greensboro	130 977	Daily & Sun
News & Observer	Raleigh	148 618	Daily & Sun
Journal	Winston-Salem	107 331	Daily & Sun
Ohio			
Beacon Journal	Akron	155 812	Daily & Sun
The Cincinnati Post	Cincinnati	104 264	Daily
Enquirer	Cincinnati	203 118	Daily & Sun
Plain Dealer	Cleveland	394 692	Daily
Dispatch	Columbus	260 355	Daily & Sun
News	Dayton	162 039	Daily
Blade	Toledo	149 760	Daily & Sun
Vindicator	Youngstown	134 931	Daily & Sun
Oklahoma			
Oklahoman	Oklahoma City	207 759	Daily & Sun
World	Tulsa	170 208	Daily
Oregon			
Oregonian	Portland	334 744	Daily & Sun
This Week	Portland	442 000	Weekly
Pennsylvania			
Morning Call	Allentown	136 645	Daily & Sun
Daily News	Philadelphia	196 239	Daily
News Gleaner	Philadelphia	109 000	Weekly
Philadelphia Inquirer[a]	Philadelphia	478 999	Daily & Sun
Times-Northeast	Philadelphia	137 000	Weekly
Post-Gazette	Pittsburgh	248 183	Daily
Rhode Island			
Bulletin	Providence	265 210	Mon–Fri
Journal	Providence	190 876	Daily
South Carolina			
News & Courier	Charleston	125 714	Daily
State	Columbia	130 649	Daily & Sun
Tennessee			
News-Free Press	Chattanooga	107 373	Daily & Sun
Commercial Appeal	Memphis	185 834	Daily & Sun
Tennessean	Nashville	144 331	Daily & Sun
Texas			
American Statesman	Austin	176 696	Daily & Sun
Dallas Morning News	Dallas	491 480	Daily & Sun

Paper	Location	Circulation	Issue
Wall Street Journal, southwest edition	Dallas	187 177	Daily
Star-Telegram	Fort Worth	237 031	Daily & Sun
Houston Chronicle	Houston	409 340	Daily & Sun
Express-News	San Antonio	232 037	Daily & Sun
Utah			
Tribune	Salt Lake City	125 037	Daily & Sun
Virginia			
U.S.A. Today	Arlington	1 465 926	Mon–Fri
News Leader	Richmond	259 093	Daily
Times & World News	Roanoke	126 795	Daily & Sun
Times-Dispatch	Richmond	211 227	Daily
Virginian-Pilot	Norfolk	165 940	Daily
Washington			
Post-Intelligencer	Seattle	203 679	Daily
Times	Seattle	230 286	Daily
Chronicle	Spokane	145 507	Daily
News-Tribune	Tacoma	128 932	Daily & Sun
Wisconsin			
Journal	Milwaukee	214 243	Daily & Sun
Sentinel	Milwaukee	175 330	Daily

Daily = Monday through Saturday
[a]The oldest daily in USA.

Canadian newspapers

All papers listed have circulations of 10 000 or over. In each case the highest circulation figure is given, whether it be for the paper's Sunday or weekly issue.

Paper	Location	Circulation	Issue
Alberta			
Calgary Herald	Calgary	163 206	Daily
Calgary Sun	Calgary	100 466	Daily
Edmonton Journal	Edmonton	155 590	Daily & Sun
Edmonton Sun	Edmonton	125 058	Daily
Daily Herald Tribune	Grand Prairie	11 674	Daily
Lethbridge Herald	Lethbridge	24 720	Daily
News	Medicine Hat	13 942	Daily
Advocate	Red Deer	22 028	Daily
St Albert Gazette	St Albert	10 000	Weekly
British Columbia			
Abbotsford News	Abbotsford	40 700	2-weekly
Chilliwack	Chilliwack	12 700	Weekly
Delta Optimist	Delta	34 500	Weekly
Kamloops Daily News	Kamloops	19 083	Daily
Daily Courier	Kelowna	18 833	Daily
Advance	Langley	10 000	Daily
Daily Free Press	Nanaimo	10 600	Daily
Citizen	Prince George	21 649	Daily
Richmond Review	Richmond	40 000	2-weekly
North Shore News	Vancouver	58 500	3-weekly
Province	Vancouver	161 032	Mon–Fri & Sun
Vancouver Sun	Vancouver	187 984	Daily
Times-Colonist	Victoria	78 796	Daily
Manitoba			
Sun	Brandon	17 748	Daily & Sun
Carillon	Steinbach	13 000	Weekly

Publishing (continued)

Paper	Location	Circulation	Issue
Winnipeg Free Press	Winnipeg	227 290	Daily
New Brunswick			
L'Acadie Nouvelle (French)	Caraquet	14 442	Daily
Le Madawaska (French)	Madawaska	10 000	Weekly
Gleaner	Fredericton	29 775	Daily
Times-Transcript	Moncton	53 344	Daily
Telegraph-Journal	Moncton	61 562	Daily
Newfoundland			
Western Star	Corner Brook	11 240	Daily
Evening Telegram	St John's	57 740	Daily
Nova Scotia			
Chronicle-Herald	Halifax	87 250	Daily
Daily News	Halifax	37 000	Daily & Sun
Mail-Star	Halifax	55 230	Daily
Advertiser	Kentville	10 258	Weekly
Evening News	New Glasgow	11 735	Daily
Cape Breton Post	Sydney	31 741	Daily
Ontario			
Examiner	Barrie	14 742	Daily
Intelligencer	Belleville	19 021	Daily
Expositor	Brantford	32 319	Daily
Recorder & Times	Brockville	16 711	Daily
Burlington Weekend Post	Burlington	40 000	Weekly
Daily Reporter	Cambridge	14 728	Daily
Chatham Daily News	Chatham	16 553	Daily
Standard-Freeholder	Cornwall	18 430	Daily
Daily Mercury	Guelph	19 547	Daily
Hamilton Recorder	Hamilton	20 000	Weekly
Spectator	Hamilton	114 877	Daily
Spectator	Burlington	22 282	Daily
Whig Standard	Kingston	42 007	Daily
Kitchener-Waterloo Record	Kitchener	80 917	Daily
Lindsay Daily Post	Lindsay	10 011	Mon–Fri
London Free Press	London	124 879	Daily
Mississauga News	Mississauga	105 000	Weekly
Review	Niagara Falls	23 000	Daily
Nugget	North Bay	24 109	Daily
Packet	Orillia	11 219	Daily
Oshawa Times	Oshawa	20 905	Daily
This Week	Oshawa	60 000	Weekly
Citizen	Ottawa	161 394	Daily
Le Droit (French)	Ottawa	39 762	Daily
Ottawa Sun	Ottawa	40 790	Mon–Fri & Sun
Sun Times	Owen Sound	24 198	Daily
Examiner	Peterborough	27 089	Mon–Fri
Sarnia Observer	Sarnia	23 979	Daily
Star	Saute Ste Marie	26 757	Daily
Reformer	Simcoe	10 577	Mon–Fri
Standard	St Catharines	43 134	Daily
Times-Journal	St Thomas	10 145	Daily
Beacon Herald	Stratford	13 788	Daily
Sudbury Star	Sudbury	29 483	Daily
Chronicle-Journal	Thunder Bay	38 141	Mon–Fri
Daily Press	Timmins	13 283	Daily

Paper	Location	Circulation	Issue
Canadian Jewish News	Toronto	50 587	Weekly
Corriere Canadese (Italian)	Toronto	22 500	Daily
Daily Racing Form	Toronto	10 357	Daily & Sun
Etobicoke Guardian	Etobicoke	66 000	2-weekly
Financial Post	Toronto	186 358	Tues–Sat
Globe & Mail	Toronto	306 260	Daily
Toronto Star	Toronto	494 719	Daily
Toronto Sun	Toronto	243 334	Daily
Welland-Port Colborne Tribune	Welland	17 937	Daily
Windsor Star	Windsor	85 632	Daily
Woodstock-Ingersoll Sentinel Review	Woodstock	10 170	Daily
Québec			
Progrès-Dimanche	Chicoutimi	50 963	Weekly
Le Quotidien	Chicoutimi	31 140	Daily
La Parole	Drummond-ville	29 000	Weekly
La Voix de l'Est	Granby	15 520	Daily
Le Devoir	Montreal	29 508	Daily
Gazette (English)	Montreal	154 171	Daily
Le Guide de Montreal Nord	Montreal	16 800	Weekly
Le Journal de Montreal	Montreal	273 588	Daily
La Presse	Montreal	186 546	Daily
Le Journal de Québec	Québec	109 353	Daily
Le Soliel	Québec	141 797	Daily
L'Etoile du Lac	Roberval	11 300	Weekly
La Frontière	Rouyn	12 500	Weekly
La Tribune	Sherbrooke	44 590	Daily
L'Eclaireur Progrès -Beauce Nouvelle	St Georges	25 200	Weekly
Le Courrier	St Hyancinthe	13 063	Weekly
Le Canada Français	St Jean	15 417	Weekly
Le Nouvelleiste	Trois Rivieres	49 722	Daily
L'Union des Cantons de l'Est	Victoriaville	12 538	Weekly
Saskatchewan			
Leader-Post	Regina	68 944	Daily
Star-Phoenix	Saskatoon	63 587	Daily
Prince Edward Island			
Guardian	Charlottetown	19 699	Daily
Journal Pioneer	Summerside	11 256	Daily

Daily = Monday through Saturday

Australian newspapers

All papers listed have circulations of over 10 000. Free papers are not listed.

Australian Capital Territory

Canberra Times	Canberra	44 000	Daily

New South Wales

Border Morning Mail	Albury	25 196	Daily

Paper	Location	Circulation	Issue
Richmond River Express Examiner	Casino	13400	Weekly
Newcastle & Lake Macquarie Post	Newcastle	104510	Weekly
Newcastle Herald	Newcastle	52225	Daily
Australian	Sydney[a]	138497	Daily
Australian Financial Review	Sydney[a]	76637	Daily
Daily Telegraph Mirror	Sydney	480000	Daily
Sun-Herald	Sydney	550354	Weekly
Sunday Telegraph	Sydney	562000	Weekly
Sydney Morning Herald	Sydney	378313	Daily
Weekend Australian	Sydney[a]	280000	Weekly
Advertiser	Parramatta	102918	Weekly
Bankstown-Canterbury Express	Bankstown	75000	Weekly
Blacktown Advocate	Blacktown	41371	Weekly
Farm & Garden	Castle Hill	20746	Weekly
Hawkesbury Courier	North Richmond	14700	Weekly
Hornsby & Upper North Shore Advocate	Hornsby	46547	Weekly
Liverpool-Fairfield Champion	Liverpool	67450	Weekly
Macarthur Advertiser	Campbell-town	28369	Weekly
Manly Daily	Manly	80784	Daily
Mosman & Lower North Shore Daily	Manly	21179	Daily
North Shore Times	Manly	103980	2-weekly
Northern District Times	Eastwood	51915	Weekly
Penrith Press	Parramatta	56542	Weekly
St George & Sutherland Shire Leader	Hurstville	118383	Weekly
Western Standard	Druitt	25690	Weekly
Western Suburbs Courier	Waterloo	62624	Weekly
Northern Daily Leader	Tamworth	11600	Daily
Daily Advertiser	Wagga Wagga	16413	Daily
Illawarra Mercury	Wollongong	36680	Daily

[a] National distribution

Northern Territory

Paper	Location	Circulation	Issue
Northern Territory News	Darwin	19500	Daily

Queensland

Paper	Location	Circulation	Issue
Courier-Mail	Brisbane	250918	Daily
Sun	Brisbane	362319	Daily
Sunday Mail	Brisbane	348000	Weekly
Drum	Bundaberg	20000	Weekly
Cairns Post	Cairns	20665	Daily
Queensland Times	Ipswich	17100	Daily
Daily Mercury	Mackay	16670	Daily
Sunshine Coast Daily	Maroochy-dore	20787	Daily
Rockhampton Morning Bulletin	Rockhampton	24000	Daily
Toowoomba Chronicle	Toowoomba	30644	Daily

Paper	Location	Circulation	Issue
Townsville Bulletin	Townsville	25750	Daily

South Australia

Paper	Location	Circulation	Issue
Adelaide Advertiser	Adelaide	213341	Daily
News	Adelaide	129819	Daily
Sunday Mail	Adelaide	268029	Weekly
City Messenger	Adelaide	24573	Weekly
Community Courier	Adelaide	33770	Weekly
Eastern Suburbs Messenger	Adelaide	23170	Weekly
Elizabeth Salisbury News Review	Adelaide	61286	Weekly
Guardian	Adelaide	45640	Weekly
Hills & Valley Gazette	Adelaide	20582	Weekly
North East Leader	Adelaide	32882	Weekly
Payneham Messenger	Adelaide	29570	Weekly
Parkside Messenger	Adelaide	28932	Weekly
Southern Times	Adelaide	48415	Weekly
Standard	Adelaide	29931	Weekly
Weekly Times	Adelaide	41190	Weekly
Westside	Adelaide	23315	Weekly
Mount Barker Courier	Adelaide	13000	Weekly

Tasmania

Paper	Location	Circulation	Issue
Advocate	Burnie	27293	Daily
Mercury	Hobart	53864	Daily
Sunday Tasmanian	Hobart	54753	Weekly
Examiner	Launceton	38500	Daily

Victoria

Paper	Location	Circulation	Issue
Ballarat Courier	Ballarat	23595	Daily
Ballarat News	Ballarat	31000	Weekly
Bendigo Advertiser	Bendigo	16500	Daily
Geelong Advertiser	Geelong	31991	Daily
Geelong News	Geelong	46261	2-weekly
Wimmera Mail-Times	Horsham	10046	3-weekly
Midland Express	Kyneton	19907	Weekly
Age	Melbourne	339905	Daily
Herald-Sun	Melbourne	680000	Daily
Sunday Age	Melbourne	119756	Weekly
Sunday Herald Sun	Melbourne	600000	Weekly
Sunday Observer	Melbourne	90844	Weekly
Truth	Melbourne	240433	2-weekly
Weekly Times	Melbourne	118000	Weekly
Broadmedows Observer	Glenroy	27767	Weekly
Brunswick Sentinel	Northcote	19487	Weekly
Chadstone Progress	Northcote	93863	Weekly
Coburg Courier	Northcote	28078	Weekly
Dandenong Journal	Dandenong	34160	Weekly
Diamond Valley News	Northcote	28065	Weekly
Doncaster Mirror	Cheltenham	26297	Weekly
Doncaster & Templestowe News	Northcote	25974	Weekly
Essendon Gazette	Glenroy	26598	Weekly

Publishing (continued)

Paper	Location	Circulation	Issue
Footsaray & Western Suburbs Advertiser	Dandenong	44108	Weekly
Frankston Peninsula News	Dandenong	11801	Weekly
Frankston Standard	Cheltenham	42273	Weekly
Heidelberger	Northcote	24831	Weekly
Keilor Messenger	Glenroy	27022	Weekly
Knox Sherbrooke News	Boronia	39446	Weekly
Northcote Leader	Northcote	22789	Weekly
Nunawading Gazette	Blackburn	32975	Weekly
Progress Press	Blackburn	79329	Weekly
Ringwood & Croydon Mail	Blackburn	36315	Weekly
Sandringham & Brighton Advertiser	Cheltenham	23098	Weekly
Standard Times	Cheltenham	22836	Weekly
Sunshine Advocate	Dandenong	33004	Weekly
Waverley Gazette	Glenwaverley	42048	Weekly
Whittlesea Post	Northcote	19516	Weekly
Malvern Caulfield Progress	Oakleigh	59355	Weekly
Berwick City News	Packenham	25100	Weekly
Warrnambool Standard	Warrnambool	12900	Daily

Western Australia

Paper	Location	Circulation	Issue
Sunday Times	Perth	324700	Weekly
West Australia	Perth	252503	Daily

Daily = Monday through Saturday

New Zealand newspapers

All papers listed have circulation figures of over 10 000.

Paper	Location	Circulation	Issue
National Business Review	Auckland	19900	Weekly
New Zealand Herald	Auckland	246458	Daily
North Shore Times Advertiser	Auckland	56000	3-weekly
Sunday News	Auckland	154000	Weekly
Sunday Star	Auckland	120000	Weekly

Paper	Location	Circulation	Issue
Marlborough Express	Blenheim	10400	Daily
Press	Christchurch	95933	Daily
Star	Christchurch	57957	Daily
Weekend Star	Christchurch	23502	Weekly
Otago Daily Times	Dunedin	52000	Daily
Gisborne Herald	Gisborne	10582	Daily
Waikato Times	Hamilton	41090	Daily
Hawke's Bay Herald Tribune	Hastings	20349	Daily
Southland Times	Invercargill	34504	Daily
News Gazette	Kawerau	11000	Weekly
Daily Telegraph	Napier	16500	Daily
Nelson Evening Mail	Nelson	19549	Daily
Daily News	New Plymouth	30454	Daily
Taranaki Herald	New Plymouth	10410	Daily
Evening Standard	Palmerston North	25911	Daily
Daily Post	Rotorua	13992	Daily
Bay of Plenty Times	Tauranga	21061	Daily
Timaru Herald	Timaru	16339	Daily
South Waikato News	Tokoroa	10441	2-weekly
Wanganui Chronicle	Wanganui	16549	Daily
Contact	Wellington	130377	Weekly
Dominion	Wellington	87466	Weekly
Eastern News	Wellington	13550	Weekly
Evening Post	Wellington	76770	Daily
Hutt News	Wellington	38550	Weekly
Independent Herald	Wellington	18823	Weekly
New Zealand Times	Wellington	89247	Weekly
Northern Advocate	Whangarei	16654	Daily

Daily = Monday through Saturday

South African newspapers

All papers listed have circulations of over 10000.

Paper	Location	Circulation	Issue
North-West			
Die Echo (English & Afrikaans)	Secunda	12300	Weekly
Mafikeng Mail (English)	Mafikeng	10000	Daily
Mafikeng Mail & Botswana Guardian (English)	Mafikeng	17000	Weekly
Western Transvaal Record (English & Afrikaans)	Klerksdorp	11040	Weekly
Western Cape			
Argus (English)	Cape Town	102060	Daily
Die Burger (Afrikaans)	Cape Town	79113	Daily
Cape Times (English)	Cape Town	60316	Daily
Weekend Argus (English)	Cape Town	113614	Weekly
South (English)	Woodstock	25000	Weekly

COMMUNICATIONS

Paper	Location	Circulation	Issue
Northern Cape			
Diamond Falls Advertiser	Kimberley	10 000	Daily
Eastern Cape			
Daily Dispatch (English)	East London	33 505	Daily
Eastern Province Herald (English)	Port Elizabeth	28 336	Daily
Evening Post (English)	Port Elizabeth	22 596	Daily
Indaba (English)	East London	37 108	Weekly
Weekend Post (English)	Port Elizabeth	39 141	Weekly
KwaZulu-Natal			
Daily News (English)	Durban	100 570	Daily
Ilanga (Zulu)	Durban	142 277	2-weekly
Leader (English)	Durban	15 000	Weekly
Natal Mercury (English)	Durban	62 549	Daily
Post (English)	Durban	47 500	Weekly
Sunday Tribune (English)	Durban	124 547	Weekly
Paper	*Location*	*Circulation*	*Issue*
Newcastle Advertiser (English & Afrikaans)	Newcastle	18 000	Weekly
Natal Witness (English)	Pietermaritzburg	26 927	Daily
Highway Mail (English)	Pinetown	28 920	Weekly
Northglen News (English)	Pinetown	14 136	Weekly
Free State			
Die Volksblad (Afrikaans)	Bloemfontein	27 268	Daily
Vista (English)	Welkom	26 375	2-weekly
Gauteng			
Benoni City Times en Oosrandse Nuus (English & Afrikaans)	Benoni	23 500	Weekly
Brakpan Herald (English & Afrikaans)	Benoni	12 885	Weekly
Germiston City News (English)	Benoni	28 296	Weekly
Beeld (Afrikaans)	Johannesburg	103 887	Daily
Boksburg Advertiser/ (English & Afrikaans) *Boksburg Volksblad*	Johannesburg	24 150	Weekly
Business Day (English)	Johannesburg	32 871	Mon–Fri
Citizen (English)	Johannesburg	138 512	Daily
City Press (English)	Johannesburg	144 416	Weekly
New Nation (English)	Johannesburg	49 538	Weekly
Randfontein Herald (English & Afrikaans)	Johannesburg	12 016	Weekly
Rapport (English)	Johannesburg	370 565	Weekly
Sowetan (English)	Johannesburg	174 043	Daily
Star (English)	Johannesburg	218 405	Daily
Sunday Star (English)	Johannesburg	97 142	Weekly
Sunday Times (English)	Johannesburg	509 888	Weekly
Die Transvaler (Afrikaans)	Johannesburg	49 580	Daily
Vaderland (Afrikaans)	Johannesburg	150 000	Daily
Vrye Weekblad (Afrikaans)	Johannesburg	14 000	Weekly
Weekly Mail (English)	Johannesburg	31 000	Weekly
Heidelberg Nigel Heraut (English & Afrikaans)	Kempton Park	27 500	Weekly
Hoofstad (Afrikaans)	Pretoria	11 855	Daily
Pretoria News (English)	Pretoria	26 880	Daily
Gemsbok Kourier (English & Afrikaans)	Roosevelt Park	10 000	Weekly
Springs & Brakpan Advertiser (English & Afrikaans)	Springs	12 994	Weekly
Vanderbijlpark Vaal Weekblad (English & Afrikaans)	Vanderbijlpark	13 268	Weekly
Limpopo (Northern Province)			
Thohoyuandou (English, Afrikaans, & Venda)	Venda	33 000	Weekly
Mpumalanga			
Highveld Herald/Die Hoevelder (English & Afrikaans)	Ermelo	15 000	Weekly
Die Noord Transvaler (Afrikaans)	Pietersburg	18 000	Weekly
Lebowa, Gazankulu & Venda Times (English & N Sesotho)	Pietersburg	16 500	Weekly

Daily = Monday through Saturday

Broadcasting stations and networks

Main terrestrial television broadcasters and stations

Country	Public service broadcaster	Commercial broadcaster	Military
Albania	Radiotelevisione Shqiptar		
Australia	Australian Broadcasting Corporation (ABC) (satellite) Special Broadcasting Service (SBS) (satellite) Imparja Television Pty Ltd (satellite)	6th Metropolitan TV Channel Seven Network (satellite) Nine Network (satellite) Network Ten Australia (satellite)	
Austria	Österreichischer Rundfunk (ORF): ORF FS 1 & ORF FS 2		
Azores	Radiotelevisão Portuguesa (RTO)		AFRTS (US Air Force)
Belarus	Belaruskaje Telebačanne Ostankino Kanal 1 (OK-1) Rossijskoje Televidenije (RTV)	TV Peterburg (TV-P)	
Belgium	Belgische Radio En Televisie (BRTN): TV1 & TV2 (Dutch) Radio Télévision Belge de la Communaute (French) Culturelle Française (RTBF-TV) Tele-21 (French)	Canal Plus RTL-TVi	
Bosnia & Herzegovina	Televizija Sarajevo		
Bulgaria	Bâlgarska Televizija Russian television relay		
Canada	Canadian Broadcasting Corporation/ Société Radio Canada (satellite) Société de Radio-Télévision du Québec TV Ontario (satellite)	City TV (satellite) Canwest Global System (satellite) CTV Television Network Ltd Le Reseau de Télévision (TVA) Télévision Quatre Saisons	
Croatia	Hrvatska Televisija (HTV)		
Czech Republic	Československá Televize Cesk Televize (CTV)	Nova Prima TV	
Denmark	Danmarks Radio (8 channels)	TV-2	
Estonia	Estonian TV Ostankino TV (Moscow) Russian TV	TV-Petersburg (TV-P)	
Faroe Islands	Sjónvarp Føroya		
Finland	Oy Yleisradio AB: YLE TV1 & YLE TV 2	MTV Oy Channel 3 Finland (MTV 3)	
France	France 2 France 3 (FR3) La Sept Arte Tele Monte Carlo	Télévision Française 1 (TF1) Canal Plus M6 Metropole TV Tele Toulouse Tele Bleue Tele Lyon Metropole 8 Mont Blanc Aqui TV RTL TV	
Germany	ARD (Programmdirektion Deutsches Fernsehen) Zweites Deutsches Fernsehen (ZDF)	RTL Television SAT. 1 PRO 7 RTL 2 Kabel 1	US Forces Television Germany SSVC Television (UK) Belgium Forces Television French Forces Television

Country	Public service broadcaster	Commercial broadcaster	Military
Gibraltar	GBC Television		
Greece	Elliniki Tileorassi-1 (ET-1) Elliniki Tileorassi-2 (ET-2) Elliniki Tileorassi-3 (ET-3) AFN TV	Antenna TV Mega Channel New Channel Kanali 29 7X TeleCity New Television Sky TV	
Hungary	Magyar Televísió		
Iceland	Ríkisútvarpid - Sjónvarp Stöd 2		
Ireland	Radio Telefis Eireann (RTE) Network 2	Ulster TV (overspill) Channel 4 (overspill)	
Italy	Radiotelevisione Italiana: RAI Uno, RAI Due, & TV 3 Rundfunkanstalt SüdTirol (RAS)	Canale 5 Circuito 5 Stelle Italia 1 Italia 7 Italia 9 Junior TV Odeon Rete A Rete Quattro Tele Monte Carlo Tele Più 2 Sport Video Music	
Latvia	Latvijas Televizija (LTV)		
Lithuania	Lietuvos Televisija LRT Kauno Direkcija RYTU Lietuvos Televizija Russian television relays	Panevezio Telestudija Kauno Telestukija Plius	
Luxembourg		Tele Luxembourg (RTL) Hei Elei	
Macedonia	Televizija Makedonije: TV Makedonije, & TV Skopje		
Malta	Xandir Television		
Monaco		Tele Monte Carlo	
Montenegro	TV Montenegro Montenegrin Broadcasting Company (MBC) TV Pink M	TV IN ntv Montena TV Elmag	
Netherlands	Nederlandse Omroepprogrammia Stichting (NOS): NOS 1, 2 & 3		American Forces Network
New Zealand	Television New Zealand Canterbury Television (CTV)	TV3	
Norway	Norsk Rikskringkasting	TV 2 Norway Philips Petroleum 66: TV 1 & 2	
Poland	Telewizja Polska: TP 1 & 2 Tele-9	Top Kanal Independent TV Echo TV	
Portugal	Radiotelevisão Portuguesa (RTP): RTP 1 & 2	SIC Televisão Independente	
Romania	Radioteleviziumea Româna: TV 1 & 2	SOTI Antenna Independenta	
Russia	Rossijskaja Gosudarstvennaja Teleradiokompanija: 'Ostankino' (OK), Ostankino Kanal 1 (OK-1), & Ostankino Kanal 4 (OK-4)	TV-Peterburg (TV-P)	

COMMUNICATIONS

Broadcasting stations and networks (continued)

Country	Public service broadcaster	Commercial broadcaster	Military
	Vserossijskaja Gosudarstvennaja Teleradiokompanija (VGTRK) Rossijskoje Televidenije (RTV)		
Serbia	Radio-TV Serbia (RTS) Studio B TV	B92 TV	
Slovak Republic	Slovak Television (STV)	Markiza TV VTV	
Slovenia	Televizija Slovenia		
South Africa	South African Broadcasting Corporation (SABC-TV) Contemporary Community Value TV Transkei TV	M-Net Television Bophuthatswana Television Trinity Broadcasting – Ciskei MNET Transkei Trinity Broadcasting – Transkei	
Spain	Radiotelevision Española (RTVE) La2 Televisio Valenciana - Canal 9 TV Vasca-Euskal Telebista	Televisio de Catalunya TV3 Canal 33 Television Murciana ETB1 7 ETB2 Tele Madrid TV de Galicia (TVG)	(US Air Force): AFRTS
Sweden	Sveriges Television AB STV 2 Kanal 1 Finnish television relay	TV4 Nordisk Television Co	
Switzerland	Swiss Broadcasting Company (SBC) DRS (German) TSR (French) TSI (Italian)	Telecine Teleclub	
Ukraine	Ukrajinska Telebačennja (UT-1 + 2) Ostankino Kanal 1 (OK-1)		
United Kingdom	British Broadcasting Company (BBC) Independent Television Commission Anglia Television Border Television Carlton Television Ltd Central Independent Telelvision Channel 4 Channel 5 Channel Television Data Broadcasting International Ltd GMTV Ltd Grampian Television Granada Television HTV Group Welsh Fourth Channel Authority (S4C) London Weekend Television Meridian Broadcasting Ltd Scottish Television Teletext UK Ltd Tyne Tees Television Ulster Television Westcountry Television Ltd Yorkshire Television	British Sky Broadcasting Independent Television News (ITN) Independent Television Association (ITVA)	
USA	Public Broadcasting Service (PBS) TV Marti	ABC Television Division CBS Inc. Fox Television Network National Broadcasting Company	

Major European television broadcasts by satellite

Satellite	Program/Programme	Owner	Satellite	Program/Programme	Owner
63° E Intelsat 602	M-Net (Johannesburg)	Inter-		MTV	
	SABC-TV (Johannesburg)	national		SKY Movies Plus	
	Channel 3 (Bangkok		19.2° E Astra 1B	Premiere	
	Entertainment Co)			The Movie Channel	
	Channel 9 (Mass Comms.			Eins Plus	
	Org. of Thailand)			Sky Sports	
	IRIB TV 2			DSF (Deutsches	
	IRIB TV 1			Sportfernsehen)	
	AFRTS-E2			MTV	
	Rete 4 (Italy)			UK Gold	
	Italia 1			JSTV	
	Canale 5 (Italy			NHK (Japanese)	
60° E Intelsat 604	Wir in Bayern	Inter-		TCC (The Children's	
	(Germany)	national		Channel)	
	Bayern Journal			N3	
	AFN-Television			Sky Movies Gold	
	interSTAR			Home Video	
	TRT TV4 (Turkey)			Channel	
	TRT TV3			TV Asia	
	TRT TV1			Scansat TV 3	
	TRT TV2			(Denmark)	
	TV Gap			CNN International	
53° E Gorizont 11	Ostankino TV1	Russia		BSkyB	
	MIR-Station			Scansat TV3 (Norway)	
40° E Gorizont 12	Rossia TV 2	Russia	16° E Eutelsat II f3	Eurostep (Dutch)	European
	TV 5 Europe (French)			Antenna Tres (Spanish)	
	RTP International			RTV Zagreb	
	(Portuguese)			Tele 5 (Spanish)	
28.5° E Kopernikus	Wir in Niedersachsen	Germany		Canal Plus Español	
(DFS-2)	RTL Nord			(Spanish)	
23.5° E Kopernikus	SAT 1	Germany		Polish Television's	
(DFS-1)	3 Sat			Third Program	
	ARTE (French/German)			Hungaria TV	
	VOX			RTP International	
	Eins Plus			HBB-TV/HAS-TV	
	RTL Plus			(Turkish)	
	n-tv			TV 7 Tunisia	
	PRO 7			TV PLUS (Dutch)	
	Premiere		13° E Eutelsat II f1	Eurosport	European
	DSR (16 channels)			Super Channel/	
	West-3			Channel e	
	Deutschlandfunk			Der Kabelkanal	
	DSF (Deutsches Sport-			TV 5 Europe	
	fernsehen)			RTL-2 (German)	
	Bayerisches Fernsehen			Deutsche Welle	
	(regional German TV)			Fernsehen	
19.2° E Astra 1A	Screen Sports	Luxem-		WorldNet	
	RTL Plus (German)	bourg		TRT (Turkish)	
	Scansat TV3 (Swedish)			Red Hot Dutch	
	Eurosport			(Adult)	
	Lifestyle TV			Middle East Broad-	
	Sat-1 (German)			casting Centre	
	TV 1000 Succekanalen			ARD Eins (German)	
	(Scandinavian)			FilmNet Plus (Belgium)	
	SKY One (English)			FilmNet (Dutch)	
	Teleclub			VisEurope	
	3-Sat			BrightStar	
	FilmNet (Scandinavian)			WTN/ITN	
	SKY News (English)			EuroPace	
	RTL-4 (Dutch)			TV Sport (France)	
	Pro 7 (German)		10° E Eutelsat II f1	RAI Uno (Italy)	European
				RAI Due	

Broadcasting stations and networks (continued)

Satellite	Program/Programme	Owner
	TVE-Internaçional (Spain)	
	Show TV (Turkey)	
	Teleon (Turkey)	
	interSTAR (Turkey)	
	SIP Canal Courses	
	TV Campus	
7° E Eutelsat II f4	ET 1 (Greece)	European
	Kanal 6 (Turkish)	
	CYBC (Cyprus)	
	RTV Beograd (Serbia)	
5° E Tele-X	TV4 (Swedish)	Scand-
	NRK (Norwegian TV)	inavian
	TV5 Nordic	
	Kompetenskanalen	
	SSC Tele-X/1	
1° W Intelsat 512	TVN (Norwegian)	Inter-
	Nordisk TV4 (Norway)	national
	SVT-2 (Sweden)	
	SVT-1 (Sweden)	
	IBA TV 1 & 2 & 3	
5° W Télécom 2B	RFO/France 2	France
	Métropole 6	
	ARTE	
	Canal Plus	
	TF 1	
	Canal J(eunesse)	
	Canal Jimmy	
	Cine Cinema	
8° W Télécom 2A	Canal Plus	France
	France 2	
	Cine Cinefil	
	Cine Cinema	
	Canal J	
	Canal Jimmy	
	MCM Euromusique	
	Planette	
	TV Sport	
11° W Gorizont 7	EBU Moscow	CIS

Satellite	Program/Programme	Owner
14° W Gorizont 15	Ostankino TV 1/ Brightside TV	CIS
	Moscow Visnews	

Satellite	Program	Owner
18.5° W Intelsat 515	STV 1	Inter-
	TV Norge	national
	TV-4 Norway	
	STV 2	
	TV 2 (Norway)	
19° W TDF 1A/B	Monte Carlo Music	France
	Canal Plus (French)	
	ARTE (French & German)	
	France 2	
19.2° W TV-Sat 1/2	RTL Plus	Germany
	Sat-1	
	3 Sat	
	DSR (16 channels)	
	Eins Plus	
21.5° W Intelsat K	BrightStar	Inter- national
27.5° W Intelsat 601	BBC World Service TV	Inter-
	WorldNet	national
	Canal France Internationale	
	CNN International	
	TVE (Spain)	
	Bravo	
	The Parliamentary Channel	
	The Children's Channel	
	Discovery Channel	
	KinderNet	
	The Learning Channel	
	Ladbroke Horse Racing	
	Country Music TV Europe	
	Kanal Market (Turkish)	

Major radio broadcasters in Europe and selected countries

Country	Public service	Commercial	Military
Albania	Radiotelevisione Shqiptar Trans World Radio		
Andorra	Servei de Telecomunicacions d'Andorra (STA) Radio Andorra	Radio Valira	
Australia	Australian Broadcasting Corporation (ABC) Domestic Shortwave Service Northern Territory Shortwave Service Public Broadcasting Association of Australia Special Broadcasting Service (SBS)	Federation of Australian Radio Broadcasters	
Austria	Österreichischer Rundfunk (ORF)		
Belarus	Belaruskaje Radyjo		

Country	Public service	Commercial	Military
Belgium	Belgische Radio en Televisie (BRTN) (Dutch) Radio-Télévision Belge de la Communaute Française (RTBF) (French) Belgisches Rundfunk & Fernsehzentrum der Deutschsprachigen Gemeinschaft (BRF)	Radio Contact Radio Nostalgie Network (Dutch) Radio Nostalgie Network (French)	US Forces Network, SHAPE British Forces Broadcasting
Bosnia & Herzegovina	Radiotelevizija Sarajevo		
Bulgaria	Bulgarian National Radio Horizont Christo Botev Orphei Znanie	Radio Express Radio Larik Radio Tanra Radio FM Channel Kom Radio Vesselina Channel TNN Radio Galatea	
Canada	Canadian Broadcasting Corporation/ Société Radio-Canada Radio Canada International CBC Northern Quebec Shortwave Service Sackville Relay Facility		
Croatia	Hrvatska Radio Televizija (HRT) Hrvatski Radio (HR)		
Czech Republic	Radio Praha	Radio Hády	
Denmark	Danmarks Radio		
Estonia	Eesti Raadio		
Faroe Islands	Útvarp Føroya (Danish)		
Finland	Oy Yleisradio AB		
France	Télédiffusion de France (TDF) Radio Télévision Française d'Outre-Mer (RFO) Radio France Internationale Radio France	Sud Radio Europe 1 Radio Monte Carlo NRJ	
Germany	ARD Deutsche Welle Deutschlandsender Kultur Rias Berlin Radio Moscow relay BBC Berlin relay	Antenne Bayern Radio Hamburg Radio FFH OK Radio Europe 1	Voice of America (VOA) Radio Volga (Russian Armed Forces) American Forces Network Europe (AFN) British Forces Broadcasting Service Canadian Forces Network Radio Forces Françaises de Berlin
Gibraltar	Gibraltar Broadcasting Corporation British Forces Broadcasting Service Gibraltar		Armed Forces Radio Service (US Air Force)
Greece	Elliniki Radiophonia (ERA) Voice of America	Antenna Sky Athina 98.4 Radio Athens	
Hungary	Magyar Radio	Radio Danubius Calypso 873 Radio Bridge	
Iceland	Icelandic National Broadcasting Service Ríkisútvarpid		Navy Broadcasting Service (US Navy)

COMMUNICATIONS

Broadcasting stations and networks (continued)

Country	Public service	Commercial	Military
Ireland	Radio Telefís Éireann Radió Na Gaeltachta	Atlantic 252	

Italy	RAI-Radiotelevisione Italiana	Rundfunk Anstalt SüdTirol
		  (RAS)
		Radio Tirol
		Adventist World Radio
		  Europe
		Nexus International
		  Broadcasting Association
			S European
			  Broadcasting (US
			Armed Forces)

Latvia	Latvijas Radio Liepajas Radio	Radio AA Radio Dejas Radio Sigulda	
Lithuania	Lietuvos Radijas Radio Vilnius LRT Kauno Programu Direkcija Majak relay	Radiocentras M-1 Vilniaus Varpas Znad Wilii Titanika	
Luxembourg		Radio-Télé-Luxembourg	
Macedonia	Radiotelevizija Makedonije		
Malta	Malta Broadcasting Authority Voice of the Mediterranean Deutsche Welle Relay Malta		
Moldova	Radioteleviziunea Naţională Radio Moldova International Radio Moscow relay		
Monaco		Radio Monte Carlo Riviera Radio Trans World Radio	

Netherlands	NOS
	Stichting Ether Reclame Ster
	Nozema
	RNW
			US Forces Network
			  (SHAPE)
			British Forces
			  Broadcasting Service
			Canadian Forces
			  Network–Brunssum

New Zealand	Radio New Zealand Radio New Zealand International	RNZ Community Net National Radio Net Independent Broadcasters Association	
Norway	Teledirektoratet Norsk Rikskringkasting Foreign Service Svalbard (Spitsbergen)		
Poland	Polskie Radio I Telewizja Rozglosina Harcerska Radio Mazury		

Portugal	Radiodifusão Portuguesa (RDP)
	RDP International–Radio Portugal
	Rádio Renascença Lda Emissora
	  Católica Portuguesa
	Sociedade de Radioretransmissão Ld
	Radio Trans Europe
	Voice of America relay
		Radio Altitude	American Forces
			  Radio & TV Service

Romania	Radio Romania Radio Romania International RM6	Radio Contact Romania	

Country	Public service	Commercial	Military
Russia	Rossiyskaya Gosudarstvennaya Teleradiokompaniya 'Ostankino' Vserossiyskaya Gosudarsdtvennaya Teleradiokompniya Radio Moscow International Radio Aum Shinrikyo		
Serbia & Montenegro (Yugoslavia)	Radio Crne Gore Radio Methohija Radio Novi Sad1 Radio Novi Sad 2 Radio Srbije One Radio Srbije Two Radio Srbije Three		
Slovak Republic	Rada Slovenskej republiky	Radia Twist	
Slovenia	Radiotelevizija Slovenia		
South Africa	South African Broadcasting Corporation (SABC) Channel Africa Ciskeian Broadcasting Corporation Transkei Broadcasting Corporation Radio Thohoyandou (Venda Radio)	Home Services Bophuthatswana Broadcasting Radio 702 Capital Radio (Transkei)	
Spain	Ente Publico Radiotelvision Española Radio Nacional de España Radio Exterior de España Sociedad Española de Radiodifusion (SER)	Cadena de Ondas Populares Españolas (COPE) Onda Cero Radio Antena 3 de Radio Cadena Dial Radio Minuto Eusko Irrati Telebista (Basque) Radiotelevision Galicia Radiotelevision de Andalucia Radiotelevision Valencia Canal Sur Radio	
Sweden	Svensk Rundradio AB Sveriges Radio AB Sveriges Utbildningsradio AB		
Switzerland	Swiss Broadcasting Corporation Swiss Radio International United Nations Broadcasting from Geneva Broadcasts from the International Committee of the Red Cross, Geneva		
Ukraine	Derzhavna Teleradiomovna Kompaniya Ukrayiny Radio Ukraine International Radio Moscow relay		
United Kingdom	British Broadcasting Corporation Voice of America	Classic FM Virgin Radio Radio Talk UK	British Forces Broadcasting Services
USA	National Public Radio Voice of America VOA Europe Radio Marti United Nations Radio BBC relays	ABC Radio Networks CBS Radio Division NBC Radio Mutual Radio Network National Black Network Sheridan Broadcasting Network C-Span Audio Networks KCBI International International Broadcast Station KGEI Radio Station KJES KTBN	US Armed Forces Radio & Television Service

COMMUNICATIONS

Broadcasting stations and networks (continued)

Country	Public service	Commercial	Military
		KVOH	
		Radio Earth International	
		Radio Miami International	
		WEWN Catholic Radio Service	
		WHRI World Harvest Radio	
		WMLK	
		World International Broadcasters	
		Worldwide Christian Radio	
		WRNO Worldwide	
		World Service of the Christian Science Monitor	
		World Wide Gospel Radio,	
		WYFR–Family Radio Organization of the American States	
Vatican City State	Vatican Radio		

British national radio stations

BBC Radio
Radio 1   Pop and rock music (Radio 1 Xtra – new black music)
Radio 2   Popular music, comedy, arts, entertainment
Radio 3   Classical music, documentaries, arts, cricket (seasonal)
Radio 4   News, documentaries, drama, entertainment
Radio 5   Sport, education, children's programmes (Radio 5 Live Sports Extra)
Radio 6   Music
Asian Network   British Asian communities
Network Z   Comedy and drama

BBC World Service
World Service in English and 42 other languages (in 2002): Albanian, Arabic, Azeri, Bengali, Bulgarian, Burmese, Caribbean English, Chinese, Croatian, Czech, French, Greek, Hausa, Hindi, Hungarian, Indonesian, Kazakh, Kinyarwanda, Kirundi, Kyrgyz, Macedonian, Nepali, Pashto, Persian, Polish, Portuguese (also, in Africa), Romanian, Russian, Serbian, Sinhala, Slovene, Slovak, Somali, Spanish, Swahili, Tamil, Thai, Turkish, Ukrainian, Urdu, Uzbek, Vietnamese
BBC English (broadcasts series of English-language teaching courses worldwide)
BBC Monitoring (overseas and regional radio and television news)
Topical Tapes — provides tapes of programmes for use by overseas radio stations & produces 'Calling the Falklands'
BBC Transcription — produces and sells recorded BBC programmes to overseas radio stations

National regional radio
Radio Scotland
  Radios Aberdeen, Highland & Orkney
Radio Ulster
Radio Wales
Radio Cymru (Welsh)
Radio Foyle
Nan Gaidheal

Independent national radio stations
Classic FM
Virgin Radio
Radio Talk UK

PART ELEVEN

Science and Technology

MATHEMATICS

Signs and symbols

+	plus; positive; underestimate
−	minus; negative; overestimate
±	plus or minus; positive or negative; degree of accuracy
∓	minus or plus; negative or positive
×	multiplies (colloq. 'times') (6×4)
·	multiplies (colloq. 'times') $(6 \cdot 4)$; scalar product of two vectors (**A·B**)
÷	divided by $(6 \div 4)$
/	divided by; ratio of $(6/4)$
——	divided by; ratio of $(\frac{6}{4})$
!	factorial $(4! = 4 \times 3 \times 2 \times 1)$
=	equals
≠,≠	not equal to
≡	identical with
≢, ≢	not identical with
≙	corresponds to
:	ratio of $(6:4)$
::	proportionately equals $(1:2::2:4)$
≈	approximately equal to; equivalent to; similar to
>	greater than
≫	much greater than
≯	not greater than
<	less than
≪	much less than
≮	not less than
⩾,≥,≧	equal to or greater than
⩽,≤,≦	equal to or less than
∝	directly proportional to
( )	parentheses
[ ]	brackets
{ }	braces
—	vinculum: division $(\overline{a-b})$; chord of circle or length of line $(\overline{AB})$; arithmetic mean $(\overline{X})$
∃	there exists
∀	for all
∞	infinity
→	approaches the limit
√	square root
$^3\sqrt{}, ^4\sqrt{}$	cube root, fourth root, etc
%	per cent
′	prime; minute(s) of arc; foot/feet
″	double prime; second(s) of arc; inch(es)
⌒	arc of circle
°	degree of arc
∠, ∠ˢ	angle(s)
⩟	equiangular
⊥	perpendicular
‖	parallel
○,⊙	circle(s)
△,▲	triangle(s)
□	square
▭	rectangle
▱	parallelogram
≅	congruent to
∴	therefore
∵	because
≞	measured by
Δ	increment
Σ	summation
Π	product
∫	integral sign
∇	del: differential operator
∪	union
∩	intersection
∈	is an element of
⊂	strict inclusion
⊃	contains
⇒	implies
⇐	implied by
⇔	implies and is implied by

Important formulae

Circumference, area, and volume

The value of π is approximately $3 \cdot 1416$.

Circle

Circumference = $2\pi r = \pi d$.
Area = $\pi r^2 = \frac{1}{4}\pi d^2$.

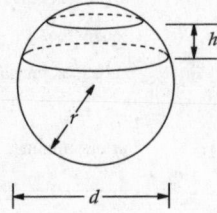

Sphere

Surface area = $4\pi r^2 = \pi d^2$.
Volume = $\frac{4}{3}\pi r^3 = \frac{1}{6}\pi d^3$.
Surface area of zone
  bounded by parallel
  planes = $2\pi rh$.

Prism, including cylinder

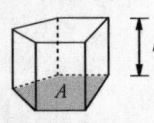

p = perimeter of base

Surface area (excluding ends) = ph.
Volume = Ah.

For the **circular cylinder**:
Surface area (excluding ends) = $2\pi rh$.
Volume = πr^2h.

Pyramid, including cone

Volume = $\frac{1}{3}Ah$.

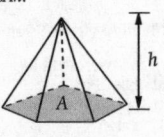 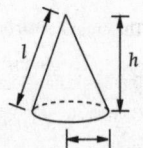

For the **circular cone**:
Surface area (excluding base) = πrl.
Volume = $\frac{1}{3}\pi r^2h$.

Parallelogram
Area = bh.

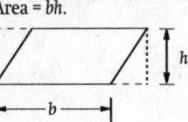

Triangle
Area = $\frac{1}{2}bh$.

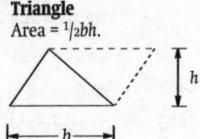

Trapezium
Area = $\frac{1}{2}(a+b)h$.

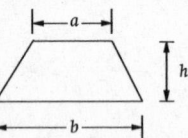

Algebra

Series

$$\sum_{i=1}^{n} i = \frac{1}{2}n(n+1) \text{ (an \textbf{arithmetic progression})}; \quad \sum_{i=1}^{n} i^2 = \frac{1}{6}n(n+1)(2n+1); \quad \sum_{i=1}^{n} i^3 = \frac{1}{4}n^2(n+1)^2.$$

Logarithms

$\log_b x = \log_c x/\log_c b$; in particular, $\log_b x = \ln x/\ln b$.
To any base, $\log 1 = 0$; $\log(xy) = \log x + \log y$; $\log(x/y) = \log x - \log y$; $\log x^k = k\log x$.

Factorials

$0! = 1$, $(i+1)! = (i+1) \times i!$ for $i = 0, 1, 2, \dots$

For large values of n, **Stirling's approximation** is $\ln(n!) \approx \frac{1}{2}\ln(2\pi) + (n + \frac{1}{2})\ln n - n + \frac{1}{12n}$

Binomial coefficients (i denotes a natural number)

For any real n, $\binom{n}{i} = \dfrac{n(n-1)\dots(n-i+1)}{i!}$.

This may be calculated from the inductive definition $\binom{n}{0} = 1$, $\binom{n}{i+1} = \dfrac{n-i}{i+1}\binom{n}{i}$ for $i = 0, 1, 2, \dots$

The 'Pascal triangle' rule: $\binom{n+1}{i} = \binom{n}{i-1} + \binom{n}{i}$.

If n is also a natural number, and if $_nC_i$ denotes the number of subsets of i elements contained in a set of n elements, then $_nC_i = \binom{n}{i} = \dfrac{n!}{i!(n-i)!}$

The binomial theorem: If n is a natural number, $(b+a)^n = \sum\limits_{i=0}^{n} \binom{n}{i} b^{n-i} a^i$.

Quadratic functions and equations

Completing the square: If $a \neq 0$, $ax^2 + bx + c = a\left(x + \dfrac{b}{2a}\right)^2 + \dfrac{4ac - b^2}{4a}$,

so that

$$ax^2 + bx + c = 0 \Leftrightarrow x = \frac{-b \pm \sqrt{(b^2 - 4ac)}}{2a}.$$

Cubic equations

If $a \neq 0$, and the roots of $ax^3 + bx^2 + cx + d = 0$ are α, β, γ, then

$$\alpha + \beta + \gamma = -b/a, \quad \beta\gamma + \gamma\alpha + \alpha\beta = c/a, \quad \alpha\beta\gamma = -d/a.$$

Complex numbers

The **modulus-argument form** of z is $z = [r, \theta] = r(\cos \theta + j \sin \theta) = r \exp(\theta j)$, where r, θ are real.

The **product rule** $[r, \theta] \times [s, \phi] = [rs, \theta + \phi]$.

De Moivre's theorem for integral index: $[1, \theta]^n = [1, n\theta]$, or $(\cos \theta + j \sin \theta)^n = \cos n\theta + j \sin n\theta$.

The roots of $z^n = 1$ are $z = [1, 2\pi k/n] = \exp\{2\pi(k/n)j\}$ for $k = 0, 1, 2, ..., n-1$. In particular, the roots of $z^3 = 1$ are ω, ω^2, where $\omega = \cos \frac{2}{3}\pi + j \sin \frac{2}{3}\pi = -\frac{1}{2} + \left(\frac{1}{2}\sqrt{3}\right)j$, so that $\omega^3 = 1$ and $1 + \omega + \omega^2 = 0$.

Vectors

Products

If the vectors **a**, **b** are represented by column matrices $\begin{bmatrix} a_1 \\ a_2 \\ a_3 \end{bmatrix}$, $\begin{bmatrix} b_1 \\ b_2 \\ b_3 \end{bmatrix}$ of their components with respect to a rectangular system of right-handed axes, or as $a_1\mathbf{i} + a_2\mathbf{j} + a_3\mathbf{k}$, $b_1\mathbf{i} + b_2\mathbf{j} + b_3\mathbf{k}$, then $\mathbf{a} \cdot \mathbf{b} = a_1b_1 + a_2b_2 + a_3b_3$;

$$\mathbf{a} \times \mathbf{b} = \begin{bmatrix} a_2b_3 - a_3b_2 \\ a_3b_1 - a_1b_3 \\ a_1b_2 - a_2b_1 \end{bmatrix} = (a_2b_3 - a_3b_2)\,\mathbf{i} + (a_3b_1 - a_1b_3)\,\mathbf{j} + (a_1b_2 - a_2b_1)\,\mathbf{k}.$$

Scalar triple product: $[\mathbf{a} \cdot \mathbf{b} \cdot \mathbf{c}] = \mathbf{a} \cdot (\mathbf{b} \times \mathbf{c}) = \mathbf{b} \cdot (\mathbf{c} \times \mathbf{a}) = \mathbf{c} \cdot (\mathbf{a} \times \mathbf{b}) = \det \begin{bmatrix} a_1 & b_1 & c_1 \\ a_2 & b_2 & c_2 \\ a_3 & b_3 & c_3 \end{bmatrix}$.

Vector triple product: $\mathbf{a} \times (\mathbf{b} \times \mathbf{c}) = (\mathbf{a} \cdot \mathbf{c})\,\mathbf{b} - (\mathbf{a} \cdot \mathbf{b})\,\mathbf{c}$; $(\mathbf{a} \times \mathbf{b}) \times \mathbf{c} = (\mathbf{a} \cdot \mathbf{c})\,\mathbf{b} - (\mathbf{b} \cdot \mathbf{c})\,\mathbf{a}$.

SCIENCE AND TECHNOLOGY

Important formulae (continued)

Trigonometry

Formulae involving sines

Coordinates: $y = r \sin \theta.$

For any angle θ:

$$\sin (90° - \theta) = \cos \theta,$$
$$\sin (180° - \theta) = \sin \theta,$$
$$\sin (360° - \theta) = - \sin \theta.$$

In a right-angled triangle:

$$\text{sine (angle)} = \frac{\text{opposite side}}{\text{hypotenuse}}.$$

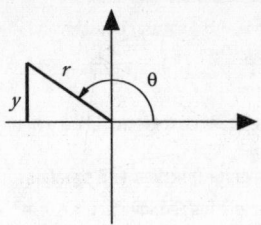

Formulae involving cosines

Coordinates: $x = r \cos \theta.$

For any angle θ:

$$\cos (90° - \theta) = \sin \theta,$$
$$\cos (180° - \theta) = -\cos \theta,$$
$$\cos (360° - \theta) = \cos \theta.$$

In a right-angled triangle:

$$\text{cosine (angle)} = \frac{\text{adjacent side}}{\text{hypotenuse}}.$$

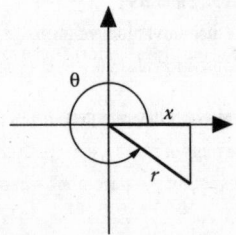

Formulae involving tangents

Coordinates: $y = x \tan \theta.$

For any angle θ:

$$\tan \theta = \frac{\sin \theta}{\cos \theta}$$

$$\tan (90° - \theta) = \frac{1}{\tan \theta}.$$

$$\tan (180° - \theta) = -\tan \theta,$$
$$\tan (360° - \theta) = -\tan \theta.$$

In a right-angled triangle:

$$\text{tangent (angle)} = \frac{\text{opposite side}}{\text{adjacent side}}.$$

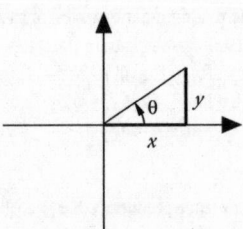

$$\sec \theta = \frac{1}{\cos \theta}, \quad \tan \theta = \frac{\sin \theta}{\cos \theta} \quad [\theta \neq (k + \tfrac{1}{2}) \pi];$$

$$\text{cosec } \theta \text{ (or csc } \theta) = \frac{1}{\sin \theta}, \quad \cot \theta = \frac{1}{\tan \theta} = \frac{\cos \theta}{\sin \theta} \quad [\theta \neq k \pi].$$

Pythagorean formulae: $\cos^2\theta + \sin^2\theta = 1$; $1 + \tan^2\theta = \sec^2\theta$; $\cot^2\theta + 1 = \text{cosec}^2\theta.$

Additional formulae: $\sin (\theta \pm \phi) = \sin \theta \cos \phi \pm \cos \theta \sin \phi$; $\cos (\theta \pm \phi) = \cos \theta \cos \phi \mp \sin \theta \sin \phi$;

$$\tan (\theta \pm \phi) = \frac{\tan \theta \pm \tan \phi}{1 \mp \tan \theta \tan \phi}.$$

Triangle formulae: In the triangle *ABC*,

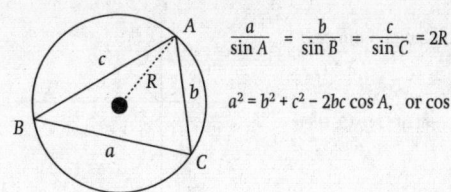

$$\frac{a}{\sin A} = \frac{b}{\sin B} = \frac{c}{\sin C} = 2R \quad \text{(the \textbf{sine rule})};$$

$$a^2 = b^2 + c^2 - 2bc \cos A, \quad \text{or} \cos A = \frac{b^2 + c^2 - a^2}{2bc} \quad \text{(the \textbf{cosine rule})}.$$

Calculus

Chain rule: If $y = f(u)$ and $u = g(x)$, then $\dfrac{dy}{dx} = \dfrac{dy}{du} \times \dfrac{du}{dx}$.

Taylor's polynomial approximation

For small h, $f(a + h) \approx f(a) + f'(a) \cdot h + \dfrac{1}{2!} f''(a) \cdot h^2 + \ldots + \dfrac{1}{n!} f^{(n)}(a) \cdot h^n$.

The remainder (error) can be expressed as $\dfrac{1}{(n+1)!} f^{(n+1)}(\xi) \cdot h^{n+1}$, where ξ is some number between a and $a + h$.

Power series with intervals of validity

$(1 + x)^m = \displaystyle\sum_{i=0}^{\infty} \binom{m}{i} x^i$ for $|x| < 1$. and sometimes also for $x = 1$ and/or $x = -1$.

$\ln(1 + x) = \displaystyle\sum_{i=0}^{\infty} (-1)^{i+1} \dfrac{x^i}{i}$ for $-1 < x \leqslant 1$.

$e^x = \displaystyle\sum_{i=0}^{\infty} \dfrac{x^i}{i!}$ for all x.

Indefinite integrals: In the following we take $a > 0$ and omit the additive constant.

$f(x)$	$\int f(x)\, dx$	$f(x)$	$\int f(x)\, dx$
x^n $(n \neq -1)$	$x^{n+1}/(n+1)$	$\sin x$	$-\cos x$
$1/x$	$\ln|x|,\ x \neq 0$	$\cos x$	$\sin x$
$\dfrac{1}{x^2 + a^2}$	$\dfrac{1}{a}\tan^{-1}\dfrac{x}{a}$	$\tan x$	$\ln|\sec x|$

Integration by parts: $\displaystyle\int u \frac{dv}{dx}\, dx = uv - \int \frac{du}{dx} v\, dx$.

Curvature: $\kappa = \dfrac{d\psi}{ds} = \dfrac{x'y'' - x''y'}{[(x')^2 + (y')^2]^{3/2}}$.

Important formulae (continued)

NUMERICAL METHODS

Simpson's rule, in which n must be *even*, giving an *odd* number of ordinates:

$$\int_{x_0}^{x_n} f(x)\, dx \approx \tfrac{1}{3}h\,[(y_0 + y_n) + 4\,(y_1 + y_3 + \ldots + y_{n-1}) + 2\,(y_2 + y_4 + \ldots + y_{n-2})].$$

Newton–Raphson method: If p_n is an approximation to a root of $f(x) = 0$, then

$$p_{n+1} = p_n - \frac{f(p_n)}{f'(p_n)}$$

is generally a better one. The error is approximately

$$\frac{[f(p_n)]^2 f''(p_n)}{2\,[f'(p_n)]^3}$$

Conics

Name of curve	Standard form of equation	Standard parametric forms	Eccentricity e	Foci F and F'	Directrices d and d'	Asymptotes
Parabola	$y^2 = 4ax$	$(ap^2, 2ap)$	1	$(a, 0)$	$x = -a$	none
Ellipse	$\dfrac{x^2}{a^2} + \dfrac{y^2}{b^2} = 1$	$(a\cos\theta,\, b\sin\theta)$	$\dfrac{\sqrt{(a^2 - b^2)}}{a} < 1$	$(\pm ae, 0)$	$x = \pm\dfrac{a}{e}$	none
Circle	$x^2 + y^2 = a^2$	$(a\cos\theta,\, a\sin\theta)$	0	$(0, 0)$	none	none
Hyperbola	$\dfrac{x^2}{a^2} - \dfrac{y^2}{b^2} = 1$	$(a\sec\phi,\, b\tan\phi)$ or $(\pm a\cosh u,\, b\sinh u)$	$\dfrac{\sqrt{(a^2 + b^2)}}{a} > 1$	$(\pm ae, 0)$	$x = \pm\dfrac{a}{e}$	$\dfrac{x}{a} \pm \dfrac{y}{b} = 0$

Probability

$P(A \text{ and } B) + P(A \text{ and } \sim B) = P(A); \quad P(A \text{ or } B) = P(A) + P(B) - P(A \text{ and } B).$

Conditional probability: $P(A \mid B) = P(A \text{ and } B) / P(B).$

Bayes' theorem: $P(A \mid B) = \dfrac{P(B \mid A) \times P(A)}{P(B \mid A) \times P(A) + P(B \mid \sim A) \times P(\sim A)}.$

Parameters

Mean $\mu = E(X) = \Sigma x_i p(x_i)$ or $\int x\phi(x)\,dx$ (evaluated over the possibility space).
Variance $\sigma^2 = V(X) = E((X - \mu)^2) = E(X^2) - \mu^2 = \Sigma x_i^2 p(x_i) - \mu^2$ or $\int x^2 \phi(x)\,dx - \mu^2.$

Expectation

For a single random variable, $E(aX + b) = aE(X) + b, V(aX+b) = a^2 V(X).$
For two random variables, $E(X \pm Y) = E(X) \pm E(Y), V(X \pm Y) = V(X) + V(Y) \pm 2\text{cov}(X, Y),$
where the covariance $\text{cov}(X,Y) = E((X - \mu_X)(Y - \mu_Y)) = E(XY) - \mu_X\mu_Y.$
If X, Y are independent, $\text{cov}(X, Y) = 0$ so that $V(X \pm Y) = V(X) + V(Y).$

Particular probability models

Discrete

	Parameter	Probability p(i)	Probability generator	Mean	Variance	Meaning of p(i)
Binomial $B(n, a)$	$P(\text{success}) = a$ $P(\text{failure}) = b$	$\dfrac{n!\,a^i b^j}{i!\,j!}$ $[i + j = n]$	$(b + at)^n$	na	nab	probability of i successes in n independent trials
Geometric	$[a + b = 1]$	$ab^{i-1}\ [i \geq 1]$	$at/(1 - bt)$	$1/a$	b/a^2	probability that the first success occurs at the ith trial
Poisson	Mean λ in unit interval	$\dfrac{\lambda^i e^{-\lambda}}{i!}\ [i \geq 0]$	$e^{\lambda(t-1)}$	λ	λ	probability of i occurrences in unit interval

Statistics
Statistical measures

If n is the sample size and $f(x_i)$ the frequency of occurrence of the value x_i in the sample (so that $n = \Sigma f(x_i)$), then:

sample mean m (or $\bar{x}$) $= \dfrac{1}{n}\sum_i x_i f(x_i).$

Conic sections

Cone (sometimes double) cut by a plane in (*a*) a single point; (*b*) a pair of straight lines; (*c*) a hyperbola; (*d*) a parabola; (*e*) a circle; (*f*) an ellipse.

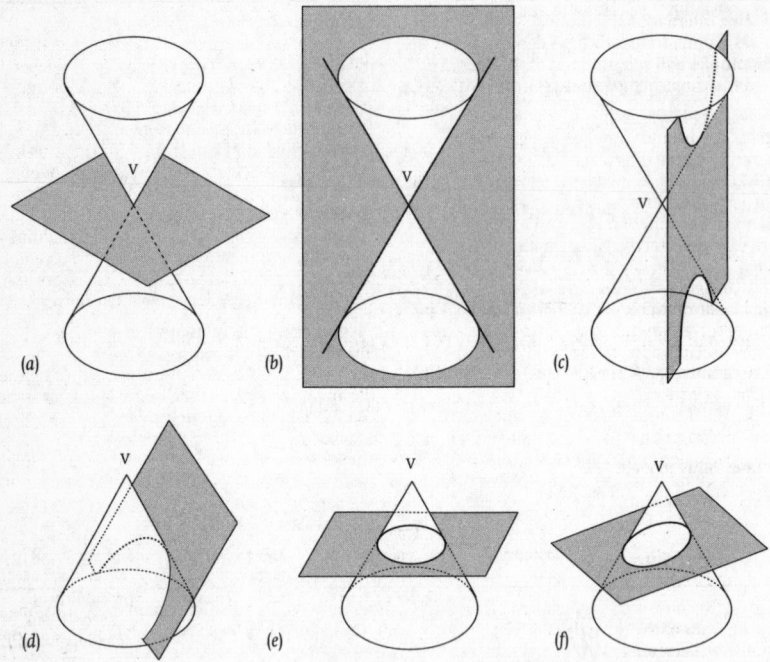

Pythagoras' theorem

A mathematical proposition advanced by Pythagoras, that in any right-angled triangle, the square on the hypotenuse is equal to the sum of the squares on the other two sides. The converse of the theorem is also true: in any triangle in which the square on the longest side is equal to the sum of the squares on the other two sides, the angle opposite the longest side is a right angle. Although known to the Babylonians, tradition ascribes to Pythagoras himself the first proof, probably based on the first diagram. The commoner proof (the second diagram), proving first that the area of square *ABXY* is equal to that of the rectangle *APRS*, was given by Euclid.

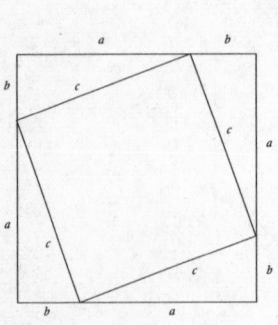

Pythagoras' theorem: $c^2 = a^2 + b^2$

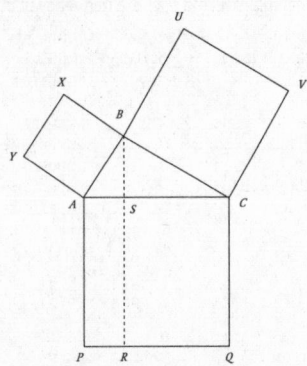

Pythagoras' theorem: $AC^2 = AB^2 + BC^2$

MEASUREMENT

Basic SI units

The SI (Système International d'Unitiés) system of units has seven basic units from which all derived units are obtained. Multiples and submultiples of the basic units may be used with approved prefixes.

1 metre *(unit of length) symbol:* m
The metre is the distance travelled by light in a vacuum during a time interval of 1/299 729 458 seconds.

2 kilogram *(unit of mass) symbol:* kg
The kilogram is the unit of mass equal to the mass of the international prototype kilogram kept at Sèvres, France.

3 second *(unit of time) symbol:* s
The second is the duration of 9 192 631 770 periods of the radiation corresponding to the quantized electron transition between two hyperfine levels of the ground state of the caesium-133 atom.

4 ampere *(unit of electric current) symbol:* A
The ampere is that constant electric current which, if maintained in two straight parallel conductors of infinite length, of negligible cross-section and placed 1 metre apart in vacuum, would produce between these conductors a force equal to 2×10^{-7} newton/ metre.

5 kelvin *(unit of temperature) symbol:* K
The kelvin, unit of thermodynamic temperature is the fraction 1/273.16 of the thermodynamic temperature of the triple point of water.

6 candela *(unit of luminous intensity) symbol:* cd
The candela is the luminous intensity, in a perpendicular direction, of a surface 1/600 000 $metre^2$ of a black body at the freezing point of platinum at a pressure of 101 325 $newton/metre^2$.

7 mole *(unit of amount of substance) symbol:* mol
The mole is the amount of substance containing as many elementary units as there are carbon atoms in 0.012 kilogram of carbon-12. The elementary unit may be an atom, a molecule, an ion or an electron.

Two supplementary units are also used:
radian *(unit of plane angle) symbol:* rad
The radian is the unit of measurement of angle and is the angle subtended at the centre of a circle by an arc equal in length to the circle radius.

steradian *(unit of solid angle) symbol:* sr
The steradian is the unit of measurement of solid angle and is the solid angle subtended at the centre of a circle by a spherical cap equal in area to the square of the circle radius.

SI conversion factors

This table gives the conversion factors for many British and other units which are still in common use, showing their equivalents in terms of the International System of Units (SI). The column labelled 'SI equivalent' gives the SI value of 1 unit of the type named in the first column, e.g. 1 calorie is 4.187 joules. The column labelled 'Reciprocal' allows conversion the other way, eg 1 joule is 0.239 calories. (All values are to three decimal places.) As a second example, 1 dyne is $10 \mu N = 10 \times 10^{-6} N = 10^{-5} N$; so 1 newton is $0.1 \times 10^{+6} = 10^5$ dyne. Finally, 1 torr is 0.133 kPa = 0.133 $\times 10^3$ Pa; so 1 Pa is 7.501×10^{-3} torr.

Unit name	Symbol	Quantity	SI equivalent	Unit	Reciprocal
acre		area	0.405	hm^2	2.471
ångström[a]	Å	length	0.1	nm	10
astronomical unit	AU	length	0.150	Tm	6.684
atomic mass unit	amu	mass	1.661×10^{-27}	kg	6.022×10^{26}
bar	bar	pressure	0.1	MPa	10
barn	b	area	100	fm^2	0.01
barrel (US) = 42 US gal	bbl	volume	0.159	m^3	6.290
British thermal unit	btu	energy	1.055	kJ	0.948
calorie	cal	energy	4.187	J	0.239
cubic foot	cu ft	volume	0.028	m^3	35.315
cubic inch	cu in	volume	16.387	cm^3	0.061
cubic yard	cu yd	volume	0.765	m^3	1.308
curie[a]	Ci	activity of radionuclide	37	GBq	0.027
degree = 1/90 rt angle	°	plane angle	$\pi/180$	rad	57.296
degree Celsius	°C	temperature	1	K	1
degree Centigrade	°C	temperature	1	K	1
degree Fahrenheit	°F	temperature	5/9	K	1.8
degree Rankine	°R	temperature	5/9	K	1.8
dyne	dyn	force	10	μN	0.1
electronvolt	eV	energy	0.160	aJ	6.241
erg	erg	energy	0.1	μJ	10
fathom (6ft)		length	1.829	m	0.547
fermi	fm	length	1	fm	1
foot	ft	length	30.48	cm	0.033
foot per second	ft s^{-1}	velocity	0.305	m s^{-1}	3.281
			1.097	km h^{-1}	0.911
gallon (UK)[a]	gal	volume	4.546	dm^3	0.220

SI conversion factors (continued)

Unit name	Symbol	Quantity	SI equivalent	Unit	Reciprocal
gallon (US)[a] = 231cu in	gal	volume	3.785	dm^3	0.264
gallon (UK) per mile		consumption	2.825	$dm^3\,km^{-1}$	0.354
gauss	Gs, G	magnetic flux density	100	μT	0.01
grade = 0.01 rt angle	rt angle	plane angle	$\pi/200$	rad	63.662
grain	gr	mass	0.065	g	15.432
hectare[a]	ha	area	1	hm^2	1
horsepower	hp	power	0.746	kW	1.341
inch	in	length	2.54	cm	0.394
kilogram-force	kgf	force	9.807	N	0.102
knot[a]		velocity	1.852	$km\,h^{-1}$	0.540
light year	ly	length	9.461×10^{15}	m	1.057×10^{-16}
litre	l	volume	1	dm^3	1
Mach number	Ma	velocity	1193.3	$km\,h^{-1}$	8.380×10^{-4}
maxwell	Mx	magnetic flux	10	nWb	0.1
metric carat		mass	0.2	g	5
micron	μ	length	1	μm	1
mile (nautical)[a]		length	1.852	km	0.540
mile (statute)		length	1.609	km	0.621
miles per hour (mph)	$mile\,h^{-1}$	velocity	1.609	$km\,h^{-1}$	0.621
minute = $(1/60)°$	'	plane angle	$\pi/10\,800$	rad	3437.75
oersted	Oe	magnetic field strength	$1/(4\pi)$	$kA\,m^{-1}$	4π
ounce (avoirdupois)	oz	mass	28.349	g	0.035
ounce (troy) = 480 gr		mass	31.103	g	0.032
parsec	pc	length	30857	Tm	0.0000324
phot	ph	illuminance	10	klx	0.1
pint (UK)	pt	volume	0.568	dm^3	1.760
poise	P	viscosity	0.1	Pa s	10
pound	lb	mass	0.454	kg	2.205
pound force	lbf	force	4.448	N	0.225
pound force/in		pressure	6.895	kPa	0.145
poundal	pdl	force	0.138	N	7.233
pounds per square inch	psi	pressure	6.895×10^3	kPa	0.145
rad[a]	rad	absorbed dose	0.01	Gy	100
rem[a]	rem	dose equivalent	0.01	Sv	100
right angle = $\pi/2$ rad		plane angle	1.571	rad	0.637
röntgen[a]	R	exposure	0.258	$mC\,kg^{-1}$	3.876
second = $(1/60)'$	"	plane angle	$\pi/648$	mrad	206.265
slug		mass	14.594	kg	0.068
solar mass	M	mass	1.989×10^{30}	kg	5.028×10^{-31}
square foot	sq ft	area	9.290	dm^2	0.108
square inch	sq in	area	6.452	cm^2	0.155
square mile (statute)	sq mi	area	2.590	km^2	0.386
square yard	sq yd	area	0.836	m^2	1.196
standard atmosphere	atm	pressure	0.101	MPa	9.869
stere	st	volume	1	m^3	1
stilb	sb	luminance	10	$kcd\,m^{-2}$	0.1
stokes	St	viscosity	1	$cm^2\,s^{-1}$	1
therm = 10^5 btu		energy	0.105	GJ	9.478
ton = 2240 lb		mass	1.016	Mg	0.984
ton-force	tonf	force	9.964	kN	0.100
ton-force/sq in		pressure	15.444	MPa	0.065
tonne	t	mass	1	Mg	1
torr, or mmHg	torr	pressure	0.133	kPa	7.501
X unit		length	0.100	pm	10
yard	yd	length	0.914	m	1.093

[a]In temporary use with SI.

SI prefixes

Factor	Prefix	Symbol	Factor	Prefix	Symbol	Factor	Prefix	Symbol
10^{18}	exa-	E	10^2	hecto-	h	10^{-9}	nano-	n
10^{15}	peta-	P	10^1	deca-	da	10^{-12}	pico-	p
10^{12}	tera-	T	10^{-1}	deci-	d	10^{-15}	femto-	f
10^9	giga-	G	10^{-2}	centi-	c	10^{-18}	atto-	a
10^6	mega-	M	10^{-3}	milli-	m			
10^3	kilo-	k	10^{-6}	micro-	μ			

Common measures

Metric units		Imperial equivalent	Imperial units		Metric equivalent
Length			*Length*		
	1 millimetre (mm)	0.03937 in		1 inch	2.54 cm
10 mm	1 centimetre (cm)	0.39 in	12 in	1 foot	30.48 cm
10 cm	1 decimetre (dm)	3.94 in	3 ft	1 yard	0.9144 m
100 cm	1 metre (m)	39.37 in	1 760 yd	1 mile	1.6093 km
1000 m	1 kilometre (km)	0.62 mi			
			Area		
Area				1 square inch	6.45 cm^2
	1 square millimetre	0.0016 sq in	144 sq in	1 square foot	0.0929 m^2
	1 square centimetre	0.155 sq in	9 sq ft	1 square yard	0.836 m^2
100 cm^2	1 square decimetre	15.5 sq in	4 840 sq yd	1 acre	0.405 ha
10 000 cm^2	1 square metre	10.76 sq ft	640 acres	1 square mile	259 ha
10 000 m^2	1 hectare	2.47 acres			
			Volume		
Volume				1 cubic inch	16.3871 cm^3
	1 cubic centimetre	0.061 cu in	1 728 cu in	1 cubic foot	0.028 m^3
1 000 cm^3	1 cubic decimetre	61.024 cu in	27 cu ft	1 cubic yard	0.765 m^3
1 000 dm^3	1 cubic metre	35.31 cu ft			
		1.308 cu yd	*Liquid volume*		
				1 pint	0.57 l
Liquid volume			2 pt	1 quart	1.14 l
	1 litre	1.76 pt	4 qt	1 gallon	4.55 l
100 l	1 hectolitre	22 gal			
			Weight		
Weight				1 ounce	28.3495 g
	1 gram	0.035 oz	16 oz	1 pound	0.4536 kg
1 000 g	1 kilogram	2.2046 lb	14 lb	1 stone	6.35 kg
1 000 kg	1 tonne	0.0842 ton	8 st	1 hundredweight	50.8 kg
			20 cwt	1 ton	1.016 t

Conversion factors

Imperial to metric			Multiply by
Length			
inches	→	millimetres	25.4
inches	→	centimetres	2.54
feet	→	metres	0.3048
yards	→	metres	0.9144
statute miles	→	kilometres	1.6093
nautical miles	→	kilometres	1.852
Area			
square inches	→	square centimetres	6.4516
square feet	→	square metres	0.0929
square yards	→	square metres	0.8361
acres	→	hectares	0.4047
square miles	→	square kilometres	2.5899
Volume			
cubic inches	→	cubic centimetres	16.3871
cubic feet	→	cubic metres	0.0283
cubic yards	→	cubic metres	0.7646
Capacity			
UK fluid ounces	→	litres	0.0284
US fluid ounces	→	litres	0.0296
UK pints	→	litres	0.5682
US pints	→	litres	0.4732
UK gallons	→	litres	4.546
US gallons	→	litres	3.7854
Weight			
ounces (avoirdupois)	→	grams	28.3495
ounces (troy)	→	grams	31.1035
pounds	→	kilograms	0.4536
tons (long)	→	tonnes	1.016

Metric to imperial			Multiply by
Length			
millimetres	→	inches	0.0394
centimetres	→	inches	0.3937
metres	→	feet	3.2806
metres	→	yards	1.0936
kilometres	→	statute miles	0.6214
kilometres	→	nautical miles	0.54
Area			
square centimetres	→	square inches	0.155
square metres	→	square feet	10.764
square metres	→	square yards	1.196
hectares	→	acres	2.471
square kilometres	→	square miles	0.386

Conversion factors (continued)

Volume		Multiply by
cubic centimetres	→ cubic inches	0.061
cubic metres	→ cubic feet	35.315
cubic metres	→ cubic yards	1.308

Capacity		
litres	→ UK fluid ounces	35.1961
litres	→ US fluid ounces	33.8150
litres	→ UK pints	1.7598

litres	→ US pints	2.1134
litres	→ UK gallons	0.2199
litres	→ US gallons	0.2642

Weight		
grams	→ ounces (avoirdupois)	0.0353
grams	→ ounces (troy)	0.0322
kilograms	→ pounds	2.2046
tonnes	→ tons (long)	0.9842

Conversion tables: length

in	cm
$1/8$	0.3
$1/4$	0.6
$3/8$	1
$1/2$	1.3
$5/8$	1.6
$3/4$	1.9
$7/8$	2.2
1	2.5
2	5.1
3	7.6
4	10.2
5	12.7
6	15.2
7	17.8
8	20.3
9	22.9
10	25.4
11	27.9
12	30.5
13	33
14	35.6
15	38.1
16	40.6
17	43.2
18	45.7
19	48.3
20	50.8
21	53.3
22	55.9
23	58.4
24	61
25	63.5
26	66
27	68.6
28	71.1
29	73.7
30	76.2
40	101.6
50	127
60	152.4
70	177.8
80	203.2
90	228.6
100	254

Exact conversion:
1 in = 2.540 cm

cm	in
1	0.39
2	0.79
3	1.18
4	1.57
5	1.97
6	2.36
7	2.76
8	3.15
9	3.54
10	3.94
11	4.33
12	4.72
13	5.12
14	5.51
15	5.91
16	6.3
17	6.69
18	7.09
19	7.48
20	7.87
21	8.27
22	8.66
23	9.06
24	9.45
25	9.84
26	10.24
27	10.63
28	11.02
29	11.42
30	11.81
31	12.2
32	12.6
33	12.99
34	13.39
35	13.78
36	14.17
37	14.57
38	14.96
39	15.35
40	15.75
50	19.69
60	23.62
70	27.56
80	31.5
90	35.43
100	39.37

Exact conversion:
1 cm = 0.3937 in

in	mm
$1/8$	3.2
$1/4$	6.4
$3/8$	9.5
$1/2$	12.7
$5/8$	15.9
$3/4$	19
$7/8$	22.2
1	25.4
2	50.8
3	76.2
4	101.6
5	127
6	152.4
7	177.8
8	203.2
9	228.6
10	254
11	279.4
12	304.8
13	330.2
14	355.6
15	381

Exact conversion:
1 mm = 0.0394 in

mm	in
1	0.04
2	0.08
3	0.12
4	0.16
5	0.2
6	0.24
7	0.28
8	0.31
9	0.35
10	0.39
11	0.43
12	0.47
13	0.51
14	0.55
15	0.59
16	0.63
17	0.67
18	0.71
19	0.75
20	0.79
25	0.98
50	1.97
100	3.94

Exact conversion:
1 in = 2.540 cm

ft	m
1	0.3
2	0.6
3	0.9
4	1.2
5	1.5
6	1.8
7	2.1
8	2.4
9	2.7
10	3.0
15	4.6
20	6.1
25	7.6
30	9.1
35	10.7
40	12.2
45	13.7
50	15.2
75	22.9
100	30.5
200	61.0
300	91.4
400	121.9
500	152.4
600	182.9
700	213.4
800	243.8
900	274.3
1 000	304.8
1 500	457.2
2 000	609.6
2 500	762.0
3 000	914.4
3 500	1 066.8
4 000	1 219.2
5 000	1 524.0
10 000	3 048.0

Exact conversion:
1 ft = 0.3048 m

m	ft
1	3.3
2	6.6
3	9.8
4	13.1
5	16.4
6	19.7
7	23.0
8	26.2
9	29.5

m	ft
10	32.8
15	49.2
20	65.5
25	22.9
30	98.4
35	114.8
40	131.2
45	147.6
50	164.0
75	246.1
100	328.1
200	656.2
300	984.3
400	1 312.3
500	1 640.4
600	1 968.5
700	2 296.6
800	2 624.7
900	2 952.8
1 000	3 280.8
1 500	4 921.3
2 000	6 561.7
2 500	8 202.1
3 000	9 842.5
3 500	11 482.9
4 000	13 123.4
5 000	16 404.2
10 000	32 808.4

Exact conversion:
1 m = 3.2808 ft

yd	m
1	0.9
2	1.8
3	2.7
4	3.7
5	4.6
6	5.5
7	6.4
8	7.3
9	8.2
10	9.1
15	13.7
20	18.3
25	22.9
30	27.4
35	32.0
40	36.6
45	41.1
50	45.7
75	68.6

yd	m
100	91.4
200	182.9
220	201.2
300	274.3
400	365.8
440	402.3
500	457.2
600	548.6
700	640.1
800	731.5
880	804.7
900	823.0
1 000	914.4
1 500	1 371.6
2 000	1 828.8
2 500	2 286.0
5 000	4 572.0
10 000	9 144.0

Exact conversion:
1 yd = 0.9144 m

m	yd
1	1.1
2	2.2
3	3.3
4	4.4
5	5.5
6	6.6
7	7.7
8	8.7
9	9.8
10	10.9
15	16.4
20	21.9
25	27.3
30	32.8
35	38.3
40	43.7
45	49.2
50	54.7
75	82.0
100	109.4
200	218.7
220	240.6
300	328.1
400	437.4
440	481.2
500	546.8
600	656.2
700	765.5
800	874.9

SCIENCE AND TECHNOLOGY

		mi*	km	mi*	km	km	mi	km	mi	km	mi
880	962.4			80	128.7	1	0.6	50	31.1	2500	1553.4
900	984.2	7	11.3	85	136.8	2	1.2	55	34.2	5000	3106.9
1000	1093.6	8	12.9	90	144.8	3	1.9	60	37.3		
1500	1640.4	9	14.5	95	152.9	4	2.5	65	40.4	Exact conversion:	
2000	2187.2	10	16.1	100	160.9	5	3.1	70	43.5	1 km = 0.6214 mi	
2500	2734.0	15	24.1	200	321.9	6	3.7	75	46.6		
5000	5468.1	20	32.2	300	482.8	7	4.3	80	49.7		
10000	10936.1	25	40.2	400	643.7	8	5.0	85	52.8		
		30	48.3	500	804.7	9	5.6	90	55.9		
Exact conversion:		35	56.3	750	1207.0	10	6.2	95	59.0		
1 m = 1.0936 yd		40	64.4	1000	1609.3	15	9.3	100	62.1		
		45	72.4	2500	4023.4	20	12.4	200	124.3		
mi*	km	50	80.5	5000	8046.7	25	15.5	300	186.4		
1	1.6	55	88.5			30	18.6	400	248.5		
2	3.2	60	96.6	*Statute miles		35	21.7	500	310.7		
3	4.8	65	104.6	Exact conversion:		40	24.9	750	466.0		
4	6.4	70	112.7	1 mi = 1.6093 km		45	28.0	1000	621.4		
5	8.0	75	120.7								
6	9.7										

Conversion tables: area

sq in	cm²	cm²	sq in	sq ft	m²	acre	hectares	hectares	acre	sq mi	km²
1	6.45	13	2.02	250	23.23	1	0.40	9	22.2	17	44.0
2	12.90	14	2.17	500	46.45	2	0.81	10	24.7	18	46.6
3	19.35	15	2.33	750	69.68	3	1.21	11	27.2	19	49.2
4	25.81	16	2.48	1000	92.90	4	1.62	12	29.7	20	51.8
5	32.26	17	2.64			5	2.02	13	32.1	21	54.4
6	38.71	18	2.79	Exact conversion:		6	2.43	14	34.6	22	57.0
7	45.16	19	2.95	1 sq ft = 0.0929 m²		7	2.83	15	37.1	23	59.6
8	51.61	20	3.10			8	3.24	16	39.5	24	62.2
9	58.06	25	3.88	m²	sq ft	9	3.64	17	42	25	64.7
10	64.52	50	7.75	1	10.8	10	4.05	18	44.5	30	77.7
11	70.97	75	11.63	2	21.5	11	4.45	19	46.9	40	103.6
12	77.42	100	15.50	3	32.3	12	4.86	20	49.4	50	129.5
13	83.87	125	19.38	4	43.1	13	5.26	25	61.8	60	155.4
14	90.32	150	23.25	5	53.8	14	5.67	50	123.6	70	181.3
15	96.77			6	64.6	15	6.07	75	185.3	80	207.2
16	103.23	Exact conversion:		7	75.3	16	6.47	100	247.1	90	233.1
17	109.68	1 cm² = 0.155 sq in		8	86.1	17	6.88	250	617.8	100	259.0
18	116.13			9	96.9	18	7.28	500	1235.5	200	518.0
19	122.58	sq ft	m²	10	107.6	19	7.69	750	1853.3	300	777.0
20	129.03	1	0.09	11	118.4	20	8.09	1000	2471.1	400	1036.0
25	161.29	2	0.19	12	129.2	25	10.12	1500	3706.6	500	1295.0
50	322.58	3	0.28	13	139.9	50	20.23			600	1554.0
75	483.87	4	0.37	14	150.7	75	30.35	Exact conversion:		700	1813.0
100	645.16	5	0.46	15	161.5	100	40.47	1 hectare =		800	2072.0
125	806.45	6	0.56	16	172.2	250	101.17	2.471 acres		900	2331.0
150	967.74	7	0.65	17	183	500	202.34			1000	2590.0
		8	0.74	18	193.8	750	303.51	sq mi	km²	1500	3885.0
Exact conversion:		9	0.84	19	204.5	1000	404.69	1	2.6	2000	5180.0
1 sq in = 6.4516 cm²		10	0.93	20	215.3	1500	607.03	2	5.2	2500	6475.0
		11	1.02	25	269.1			3	7.8	3000	7770.0
cm²	sq in	12	1.11	50	538.2	Exact conversion:		4	10.4	3500	9065.0
1	0.16	13	1.21	75	807.3	1 acre =		5	12.9	4000	10360.0
2	0.31	14	1.30	100	1076.4	0.4047 hectare		6	15.5	5000	12950.0
3	0.47	15	1.39	250	2691			7	18.1	7500	19424.9
4	0.62	16	1.49	500	5382	hectares	acre	8	20.7	10000	25899.9
5	0.78	17	1.58	750	8072.9	1	2.5	9	23.3		
6	0.93	18	1.67	1000	10763.9	2	4.9	10	25.9	km²	sq mi
7	1.09	19	1.77			3	7.4	11	28.5	1	0.39
8	1.24	20	1.86	Exact conversion:		4	9.9	12	31.1	2	0.77
9	1.40	25	2.32	1 m² =		5	12.4	13	33.7	3	1.16
10	1.55	50	4.65	10.7639 sq ft		6	14.8	14	36.3	4	1.54
11	1.71	75	6.97			7	17.3	15	38.8	5	1.93
12	1.86	100	9.29			8	19.8	16	41.4	6	2.32

Conversion tables: area (continued)

km²	sq mi	km²	sq mi	km²	sq mi	km²	sq mi	km²	sq mi	km²	sq mi
7	2.70	15	5.79	23	8.88	80	30.89	700	270.27	3 500	1 351.4
8	3.09	16	6.18	24	9.27	90	34.75	800	308.88	4 000	1 544.4
9	3.47	17	6.56	25	9.65	100	38.61	900	347.49	5 000	1 930.5
10	3.86	18	6.95	30	11.58	200	77.22	1 000	386.1	7 500	2 895.8
11	4.25	19	7.34	40	15.44	300	115.83	1 500	579.2	10 000	3 861.0
12	4.63	20	7.72	50	19.31	400	154.44	2 000	772.2		
13	5.02	21	8.11	60	23.17	500	193.05	2 500	965.3		
14	5.41	22	8.49	70	27.03	600	231.66	3 000	1 158.3		

Exact conversions:
1 sq mi = 2.589999 km²
1 km² = 0.3861 sq mi

Conversion tables: volume

cu in	cm³	cm³	cu in	cu ft	m³	m³	cu ft	cu yd	m³	m³	cu yd
1	16.39	1	.061	1	0.03	1	35.3	1	0.76	1	1.31
2	32.77	2	.122	2	0.06	2	70.6	2	1.53	2	2.62
3	49.16	3	.183	3	0.08	3	105.9	3	2.29	3	3.92
4	65.55	4	.244	4	0.11	4	141.3	4	3.06	4	5.23
5	81.93	5	.305	5	0.14	5	176.6	5	3.82	5	6.54
6	93.32	6	.366	6	0.17	6	211.9	6	4.59	6	7.85
7	114.71	7	.427	7	0.20	7	247.2	7	5.35	7	9.16
8	131.10	8	.488	8	0.23	8	282.5	8	6.12	8	10.46
9	147.48	9	.549	9	0.25	9	317.8	9	6.88	9	11.77
10	163.87	10	.610	10	0.28	10	353.1	10	7.65	10	13.08
11	180.26	11	.671	11	0.31	11	388.5	11	8.41	11	14.39
12	196.64	12	.732	12	0.34	12	423.8	12	9.17	12	15.70
13	213.03	13	.793	13	0.37	13	459.1	13	9.94	13	17.00
14	229.42	14	.854	14	0.40	14	494.4	14	10.70	14	18.31
15	245.81	15	.915	15	0.42	15	529.7	15	11.47	15	19.62
20	327.74	20	1.220	20	0.57	20	706.3	20	15.29	20	26.16
50	819.35	50	3.050	50	1.41	50	1 765.7	50	38.23	50	65.40
100	1638.71	100	6.100	100	2.83	100	3 531.5	100	76.46	100	130.80

Exact conversions:
1 cu in = 16.3871 cm³
1 cm³ = 0.061027 cu in
1 cu ft = 0.0283 m³
1 m³ = 35.3147 cu ft
1 cu yd = 0.7646 m³
1 m³ = 1.3080 cu yd

Conversion tables: capacity

Liquid measure

UK fl oz	l	US fl oz	l	l	UK fl oz	US fl oz	UK pt	l	US pt	l	l	UK pt	US pt
1	0.0284	1	0.0296	1	35.2	33.8	1	0.57	1	0.47	1	1.76	2.11
2	0.0568	2	0.0592	2	70.4	67.6	2	1.14	2	0.95	2	3.52	4.23
3	0.0852	3	0.0888	3	105.6	101.4	3	1.70	3	1.42	3	5.28	6.34
4	0.114	4	0.118	4	140.8	135.3	4	2.27	4	1.89	4	7.04	8.45
5	0.142	5	0.148	5	176.0	169.1	5	2.84	5	2.37	5	8.80	10.57
6	0.170	6	0.178	6	211.2	202.9	6	3.41	6	2.84	6	10.56	12.68
7	0.199	7	0.207	7	246.4	236.7	7	3.98	7	3.31	7	12.32	14.79
8	0.227	8	0.237	8	281.6	270.5	8	4.55	8	3.78	8	14.08	16.91
9	0.256	9	0.266	9	316.8	304.3	9	5.11	9	4.26	9	15.84	19.02
10	0.284	10	0.296	10	352.0	338.1	10	5.68	10	4.73	10	17.60	21.13
11	0.312	11	0.326	11	387.2	372.0	11	6.25	11	5.20	11	19.36	23.25
12	0.341	12	0.355	12	422.4	405.8	12	6.82	12	5.68	12	21.12	25.36
13	0.369	13	0.385	13	457.5	439.6	13	7.38	13	6.15	13	22.88	27.47
14	0.397	14	0.414	14	492.7	473.4	14	7.95	14	6.62	14	24.64	29.59
15	0.426	15	0.444	15	527.9	507.2	15	8.52	15	7.10	15	26.40	31.70
20	0.568	20	0.592	20	703.9	676.3	20	11.36	20	9.46	20	35.20	105.67
50	1.42	50	1.48	50	1 759.8	1 690.7	50	28.41	50	23.66	50	87.99	211.34
100	2.84	100	2.96	100	3 519.6	3 381.5	100	56.82	100	47.32	100	175.98	422.68

Exact conversions:
1 fl oz = 0.0284 l
1 fl oz = 0.0296 l
1 l = 35.1961 UK fl oz
1 l = 33.8140 US fl oz
1 UK pt = 0.5682 l
1 UK pt = 1.20 US pt
1 US pt = 0.4732 l
1 US pt = 0.83 UK pt
1 l = 1.7598 UK pt, 2.1134 US pt
1 US cup = 8 US fl oz

Conversion tables: capacity (continued)

UK gall	l	l	UK gall	US gall
1	4.55	1	0.22	0.26
2	9.09	2	0.44	0.53
3	13.64	3	0.66	0.79
4	18.18	4	0.88	1.06
5	22.73	5	1.10	1.32
6	27.28	6	1.32	1.58
7	31.82	7	1.54	1.85
8	36.37	8	1.76	2.11
9	40.91	9	1.98	2.38
10	45.46	10	2.20	2.64
11	50.01	11	2.42	2.91
12	54.55	12	2.64	3.17
13	59.10	13	2.86	3.43
14	63.64	14	3.08	3.70
15	68.19	15	3.30	3.96
16	72.74	16	3.52	4.23
17	77.28	17	3.74	4.49
18	81.83	18	3.96	4.76
19	86.37	19	4.18	5.02
20	90.92	20	4.40	5.28
21	95.47	21	4.62	5.55
22	100.01	22	4.84	5.81
23	104.56	23	5.06	6.08
24	109.10	24	5.28	6.34
25	113.65	25	5.50	6.60
50	227.30	50	11.00	13.20
75	340.96	75	16.50	19.81
100	454.61	100	22.00	26.42

Exact conversion:
1 UK gal = 4.546 l

Exact conversion: 1 l = 0.220 UK gal
1 l = 0.2642 US gal

US gall	l	UK gall	US gall	US gall	UK gall
1	3.78	1	1.2	1	0.8
2	7.57	2	2.4	2	1.7
3	11.36	3	3.6	3	2.5
4	15.14	4	4.8	4	3.3
5	18.93	5	6	5	4.2
6	22.71	6	7.2	6	5
7	26.50	7	8.4	7	5.8
8	30.28	8	9.6	8	6.7
9	34.07	9	10.8	9	7.5
10	37.85	10	12	10	8.3
11	41.64	11	13.2	11	9.2
12	45.42	12	14.4	12	10
13	49.21	13	15.6	13	10.8
14	52.99	14	16.8	14	11.7
15	56.78	15	18	15	12.5
16	60.57	20	24	16	13.3
17	64.35	25	30	17	14.1
18	68.14	50	60	18	15
19	71.92			19	15.8
20	75.71			20	16.6
21	79.49			25	20.8
22	83.28			50	41.6
23	87.06			75	62.4
24	90.85			100	83.3
25	94.63				
50	189.27				
75	283.90				
100	378.54				

Exact conversion:
1 US gal = 3.7854 l

Exact conversion:
1 UK gal = 1.200929 US gal

Exact conversion:
1 US gal = 0.832688 UK gal

Other liquid-capacity measures

UK qt	l	US qt	l
1	1.14	1	0.95
2	2.27	2	1.89
3	3.41	3	2.84
4	4.55	4	3.78
5	5.68	5	4.73
10	11.36	10	9.46

Exact conversion:
1 UK qt = 1.1365 l

Exact conversion:
1 US qt = 0.9463 l

l	US qt	UK qt
1	0.88	1.06
2	1.76	2.11
3	2.64	3.17
4	3.52	4.23
5	4.40	5.28
10	8.80	10.57

Exact conversions: 1 l = 0.220 UK gal
1 l = 1.0567 US qts

cu in	l	cu ft	l
1	0.016	1	28.3
2	0.033	2	56.6
3	0.049	3	84.9
4	0.066	4	4.23
5	0.082	5	5.28
10	0.164	10	283.1

Exact conversion:
1 cu in = 0.0164 l

Exact conversion:
1 cu ft = 28.3161 l

l	cu in	cu ft
1	61	0.03
2	122	0.07
3	183	0.11
4	244	0.14
5	305	0.18
10	610	0.35

Exact conversions: 1 l = 61.0255 cu in
1 l = 0.0353 cu ft

Conversion tables: capacity (continued)

Petrol consumption
Use UK table and US table independently.

per UK gal		per l	
mi	km	mi	km
30	48	6.6	10.61
35	56	7.7	12.38
40	64	8.8	14.15
45	72	9.9	15.92
50	80	11	17.69

per US gal		per l	
mi	km	mi	km
30	48	7.9	12.78
35	56	9.3	14.91
40	64	10.6	17.04
45	72	11.9	19.17
50	80	13.2	21.30

Dry capacity measures

UK bu	m^3	l
1	0.037	36.4
2	0.074	72.7
3	0.111	109.1
4	0.148	145.5
5	0.184	181.8
10	0.369	363.7

Exact conversions:
1 UK bu = 0.0369 m^3
1 UK bu = 36.3677 l

US bu	m^3	l
1	0.035	35.2
2	0.071	70.5
3	0.106	105.7
4	0.141	140.9
5	0.175	176.2
10	0.353	352.4

Exact conversions:
1 US bu = 0.9353 m^3
1 US bu = 35.2381 l

m^3	UK bu	US bu
1	27.5	28.4
2	55.0	56.7
3	82.5	85.1
4	110	113
5	137	142
10	275	284

Exact conversions:
1 m^3 = 27.4962 UK bu
1 m^3 = 28.3776 US bu

l	UK bu	US bu
1	0.027	0.028
2	0.055	0.057
3	0.082	0.085
4	0.110	0.114
5	0.137	0.142
10	0.275	0.284

Exact conversions:
1 l = 0.0275 UK bu
1 l = 0.0284 US bu

UK pecks	l	US pecks	l
1	9.1	1	8.8
2	18.2	2	17.6
3	27.3	3	26.4
4	36.4	4	35.2
5	45.5	5	44
10	90.9	10	88.1

Exact conversion: Exact conversion:
1 UK peck =   1 US peck =
9.0919 l   8.8095 l

l	UK pecks	US pecks
1	0.110	0.113
2	0.220	0.226
3	0.330	0.339
4	0.440	0.454
5	0.550	0.567
10	1.100	1.135

Exact conversions:
1 l = 0.1100 UK pecks
1 l = 0.1135 US pecks

US qt	m^3	l
1	1 101	1.1
2	2 202	2.2
3	3 304	3.3
4	4 405	4.4
5	5 506	5.5
10	11 012	11

Exact conversions:
1 US qt = 1101.2209 cm^3
1 US qt = 1.1012 l

US pt	m^3	l
1	551	0.55
2	1 101	1.10
3	1 652	1.65
4	2 202	2.20
5	2 753	2.75
10	5 506	5.51

Exact conversions:
1 US pt = 550.6105 cm^3
1 US pt = 0.5506 l

Conversion tables: weight

oz[a]	g
1	28.3
2	56.7
3	85
4	113.4
5	141.7
6	170.1
7	198.4
8	226.8
9	255.1
10	283.5
11	311.7
12	340.2
13	368.5
14	396.9
15	425.2
16	453.6

[a] Avoirdupois.
Exact conversion:
1 oz (avdp) = 28.3495 g

g	oz
1	0.04
2	0.07
3	0.11
4	0.14
5	0.18
6	0.21
7	0.25
8	0.28
9	0.32
10	0.35
20	0.71
30	1.06
40	1.41
50	1.76
60	2.12
70	2.47
80	2.82
90	3.18
100	3.53

Exact conversion:
1 g = 0.0353 oz (avdp)

lb	kg
1	0.45
2	0.91
3	1.36
4	1.81
5	2.27
6	2.72
7	3.18
8	3.63
9	4.08
10	4.54
11	4.99
12	5.44
13	5.90
14	6.35
15	6.80
16	7.26
17	7.71
18	8.16
19	8.62
20	9.07
25	11.34
30	13.61
35	15.88
40	18.14
45	20.41
50	22.68
60	27.24
70	31.78
80	36.32
90	40.86
100	45.36
200	90.72
250	113.40
500	226.80
750	340.19
1000	453.59

Exact conversion:
1 lb = 0.454 kg

kg	lb
1	2.2
2	4.4
3	6.6
4	8.8
5	11
6	13.2
7	15.4
8	17.6
9	19.8
10	22
11	24.3
12	26.5
13	28.7
14	30.9
15	33.1
16	35.3
17	37.5
18	39.7
19	41.9
20	44.1
25	55.1
30	66.1
35	77.2
40	88.2
45	99.2
50	110.2
60	132.3
70	154.4
80	176.4
90	198.5
100	220.5
200	440.9
250	551.2
500	1102.3
750	1653.5
1000	2204.6

Exact conversion:
1 kg = 2.205 lb

st	lb
1	14
2	28
3	42
4	56
5	70
6	84
7	98
8	112
9	126
10	140
11	154
12	168

st	lb
13	182
14	196
15	210
16	224
17	238
18	252
19	266
20	280

Exact conversions:
1 st = 14 lb
1 lb = 0.07 st

st	kg
1	6.35
2	12.70
3	19.05
4	25.40
5	31.75
6	38.10
7	44.45
8	50.80
9	57.15
10	63.50

Exact conversions:
1 st = 6.350 kg
1 kg = 0.1575 st

UK cwt[b]	kg
1	50.8
2	102
3	152
4	203
5	254
10	508
15	762
20	1016
50	2540
75	3810
100	5080

Exact conversion:
1 UK cwt = 50.8023 kg

UK cwt[b]	US cwt[b]
1	1.12
2	2.24
3	3.36
4	4.48
5	5.6
10	11.2
15	16.8
20	22.4
50	56
75	84
100	102

Exact conversion:
1 UK cwt = 1.1199 US cwt

US tons	t
1	0.91
2	1.81
3	2.72
4	3.63
5	4.54
10	9.07
15	13.61
20	18.14
50	45.36
75	68.04
100	90.72

Exact conversion:
1 US ton = 0.9072 t

[b] Hundredweights: long, UK 112 lb; short, US 100 lb

US cwt	kg
1	45.4
2	90.7
3	136
4	181
5	227
10	454
15	680
20	907
50	2268
75	3402
100	4536

Exact conversion:
1 US cwt = 45.3592 kg

UK tons	t
1	1.02
2	2.03
3	3.05
4	4.06
5	5.08
10	10.16
15	15.24
20	20.32
50	50.80
75	76.20
100	101.61

Exact conversion:
1 UK ton = 1.0160 t

UK tons	US tons
1	1.12
2	2.24
3	3.36
4	4.48
5	5.6
10	11.2
15	16.8
20	22.4
50	56
75	84
100	102

Exact conversion:
1 UK ton = 1.1199 US tons

SCIENCE AND TECHNOLOGY

Conversion tables: weight (continued)

kg	UK cwt	US cwt	US cwt	UK cwt	t	UK tons[a]	US tons[a]	US tons[a]	UK tons[a]
1	0.0197	0.022	1	0.89	1	0.98	1.10	1	0.89
2	0.039	0.044	2	1.79	2	1.97	2.20	2	1.79
3	0.059	0.066	3	2.68	3	2.95	3.30	3	2.68
4	0.079	0.088	4	3.57	4	3.94	4.40	4	3.57
5	0.098	0.11	5	4.46	5	4.92	5.50	5	4.46
10	0.197	0.22	10	8.93	10	9.84	11.02	10	8.93
15	0.295	0.33	15	13.39	15	14.76	16.53	15	13.39
20	0.394	1.44	20	17.86	20	19.68	22.05	20	17.86
50	0.985	1.10	50	44.64	50	49.21	55.11	50	44.64
75	1.477	1.65	75	66.96	75	73.82	82.67	75	66.96
100	1.970	2.20	100	89.29	100		98.42 110.23	100	89.29

Exact conversions:
1 kg = 0.0197 UK cwt
= 0.0220 US cwt

Exact conversion:
1 US cwt =
0.8929 UK cwt

Exact conversions:
1 t = 0.9842 UK ton
= 1.1023 US ton

Exact conversion:
1 US ton =
0.8929 UK ton

[a]Tons: long, UK 2240 lb; short, US 2000 lb

Conversion table: tyre pressures

lb per sq in	kg/cm²
10	0.7
15	1.1
20	1.4
24	1.7
26	1.8
28	2
30	2.1
40	2.8

Conversion table: oven temperatures

Gas Mark	Electricity		Rating
	°C	°F	
½	120	250	Slow
1	140	275	
2	150	300	
3	170	325	
4	180	350	Moderate
5	190	375	
6	200	400	Hot
7	220	425	
8	230	450	Very hot
9	260	500	

Temperature conversion

To convert	To	Operations
°Fahrenheit	°Celsius	−32, × 5, ÷ 9
°Fahrenheit	°Rankine	+ 459.67
°Fahrenheit	°Réaumur	− 32, × 4, ÷ 9
°Celsius	°Fahrenheit	× 9, ÷ 5, + 32
°Celsius	Kelvin	+ 273.16
°Celsius	°Réaumur	× 4, ÷ 5
Kelvin	°Celsius	− 273.16
°Rankine	°Fahrenheit	−459.67
°Réaumur	°Fahrenheit	× 9, ÷ 4, + 32
°Réaumur	°Celsius	× 5, ÷ 4

Carry out operations in sequence.

Temperature scales

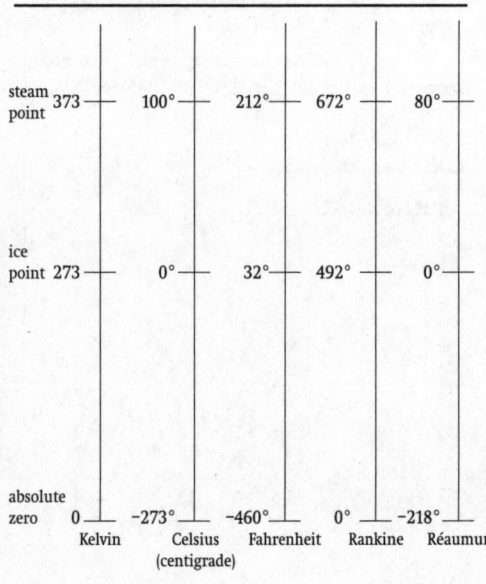

	Kelvin	Celsius (centigrade)	Fahrenheit	Rankine	Réaumur
steam point	373 — 100°	212°	672°	80°	
ice point	273 — 0°	32°	492°	0°	
absolute zero	0 — −273°	−460°	0°	−218°	

Conversion tables: temperature

Degrees Fahrenheit (°F) → degrees Celsius (centigrade) (°C)

°F	°C	°F	°C	°F	°C	°F	°C	°F	°C	°F	°C
1	−17.2	37	2.8	73	22.8	109	42.8	145	62.8	181	82.8
2	−16.7	38	3.3	74	23.3	110	43.3	146	63.3	182	83.3
3	−16.1	39	3.9	75	23.9	111	43.9	147	63.9	183	83.9
4	−15.5	40	4.4	76	24.4	112	44.4	148	64.4	184	84.4
5	−15.0	41	5.0	77	25.0	113	45.0	149	65.0	185	85.0
6	−14.4	42	5.5	78	25.5	114	45.5	150	65.5	186	85.5
7	−13.9	43	6.1	79	26.1	115	46.1	151	66.1	187	86.1
8	−13.3	44	6.7	80	26.7	116	46.7	152	66.7	188	86.7
9	−12.8	45	7.2	81	27.2	117	47.2	153	67.2	189	87.2
10	−12.2	46	7.8	82	27.8	118	47.8	154	67.8	190	87.8
11	−11.6	47	8.3	83	28.3	119	48.3	155	68.3	191	88.3
12	−11.1	48	8.9	84	28.9	120	48.9	156	68.9	192	88.8
13	−10.5	49	9.4	85	29.4	121	49.4	157	69.4	193	89.4
14	−10.0	50	10.0	86	30.0	122	50.0	158	70.0	194	90.0
15	−9.4	51	10.5	87	30.5	123	50.5	159	70.5	195	90.5
16	−8.9	52	11.1	88	31.1	124	51.1	160	71.1	196	91.1
17	−8.3	53	11.7	89	31.7	125	51.7	161	71.7	197	91.7
18	−7.8	54	12.2	90	32.2	126	52.2	162	72.2	198	92.2
19	−7.2	55	12.8	91	32.8	127	52.8	163	72.8	199	92.8
20	−6.7	56	13.3	92	33.3	128	53.3	164	73.3	200	93.3
21	−6.1	57	13.9	93	33.9	129	53.9	165	73.9	201	93.9
22	−5.5	58	14.4	94	34.4	130	54.4	166	74.4	202	94.4
23	−5.0	59	15.0	95	35.0	131	55.0	167	75.0	203	95.0
24	−4.4	60	15.5	96	35.5	132	55.5	168	75.5	204	95.5
25	−3.9	61	16.1	97	36.1	133	56.1	169	76.1	205	96.1
26	−3.3	62	16.7	98	36.7	134	56.7	170	76.7	206	96.7
27	−2.8	63	17.2	99	37.2	135	57.2	171	77.2	207	97.2
28	−2.2	64	17.8	100	37.8	136	57.8	172	77.8	208	97.8
29	−1.7	65	18.3	101	38.3	137	58.3	173	78.3	209	98.3
30	−1.1	66	18.9	102	38.9	138	58.9	174	78.9	210	98.9
31	−0.5	67	19.4	103	39.4	139	59.4	175	79.4	211	99.4
32	0	68	20.0	104	40.0	140	60.0	176	80.0	212	100.0
33	0.5	69	20.5	105	40.5	141	60.5	177	80.5		
34	1.1	70	21.1	106	41.1	142	61.1	178	81.1		
35	1.7	71	21.7	107	41.7	143	61.7	179	81.7		
36	2.2	72	22.2	108	42.2	144	62.2	180	82.2		

Degrees Celsius (centigrade) (°C) → degrees Fahrenheit (°F)

°C	°F	°C	°F	°C	°F	°C	°F	°C	°F	°C	°F
1	33.8	18	64.4	35	95.0	52	125.6	69	156.2	86	186.8
2	35.6	19	66.2	36	96.8	53	127.4	70	158.0	87	188.6
3	37.4	20	68.0	37	98.6	54	129.2	71	159.8	88	190.4
4	39.2	21	69.8	38	100.4	55	131.0	72	161.6	89	192.2
5	41.0	22	71.6	39	102.2	56	132.8	73	163.4	90	194.0
6	42.8	23	73.4	40	104.0	57	134.6	74	165.2	91	195.8
7	44.6	24	75.2	41	105.8	58	136.4	75	167.0	92	197.6
8	46.4	25	77.0	42	107.6	59	138.2	76	168.8	93	199.4
9	48.2	26	78.8	43	109.4	60	140.0	77	170.6	94	201.2
10	50.0	27	80.6	44	111.2	61	141.8	78	172.4	95	203.0
11	51.8	28	82.4	45	113.0	62	143.6	79	174.2	96	204.8
12	53.6	29	84.2	46	114.8	63	145.4	80	176.0	97	206.6
13	55.4	30	86.0	47	116.6	64	147.2	81	177.8	98	208.4
14	57.2	31	87.8	48	118.4	65	149.0	82	179.6	99	210.2
15	59.0	32	89.6	49	120.2	66	150.8	83	181.4	100	212.0
16	60.8	33	91.4	50	122.0	67	152.6	84	183.2		
17	62.6	34	93.2	51	123.8	68	154.4	85	185.0		

SCIENCE AND TECHNOLOGY

Numerical equivalents

Arabic	Roman	Greek	Binary numbers
1	I	α′	1
2	II	β′	10
3	III	γ′	11
4	IV	δ′	100
5	V	ε′	101
6	VI	ϛ′	110
7	VII	ζ′	111
8	VIII	η′	1000
9	IX	θ′	1001
10	X	ι′	1010
11	XI	ια′	1011
12	XII	ιβ′	1100
13	XIII	ιγ′	1101
14	XIV	ιδ′	1110
15	XV	ιε′	1111
16	XVI	ιϛ′	10000
17	XVII	ιζ′	10001
18	XVIII	ιη′	10010
19	XIX	ιθ′	10011
20	XX	κ′	10100
30	XXX	λ′	11110
40	XL	μ′	101000
50	L	ν′	110010
60	LX	ξ′	111100
70	LXX	ο′	1000110
80	LXXX	π′	1010000
90	XC	͵ο′	1011010
100	C	ρ′	1100100
200	CC	σ′	11001000
300	CCC	τ′	100101100
400	CD	υ′	110010000
500	D	φ′	111110100
1000	M	͵α	1111101000
5000	V̅	͵ε	1001110001000
10000	X̅	͵ι	10011100010000
100000	C̅	͵ρ	11000011010100000

Fraction	Decimal	Fraction	Decimal	%	Decimal	Fraction
$1/2$	0.5000	$8/11$	0.7272	1	0.01	$1/100$
$1/3$	0.3333	$9/11$	0.8181	2	0.02	$1/50$
$2/3$	0.6667	$10/11$	0.9090	3	0.03	$3/100$
$1/4$	0.2500	$1/12$	0.0833	4	0.04	$1/25$
$3/4$	0.7500	$5/12$	0.4167	5	0.05	$1/20$
$1/5$	0.2000	$7/12$	0.5833	6	0.06	$3/50$
$2/5$	0.4000	$11/12$	0.9167	7	0.07	$7/100$
$3/5$	0.6000	$1/16$	0.0625	8	0.08	$2/25$
$4/5$	0.8000	$3/16$	0.1875	$8 1/3$	0.083	$1/12$
$1/6$	0.1667	$5/16$	0.3125	9	0.09	$9/100$
$5/6$	0.8333	$7/16$	0.4375	10	0.1	$1/10$
$1/7$	0.1429	$9/16$	0.5625	11	0.11	$11/100$
$2/7$	0.2857	$11/16$	0.6875	12	0.12	$3/25$
$3/7$	0.4286	$13/16$	0.8125	$12 1/2$	0.125	$1/8$
$4/7$	0.5714	$15/16$	0.9375	13	0.13	$13/100$
$5/7$	0.7143	$1/20$	0.0500	14	0.14	$7/50$
$6/7$	0.8571	$3/20$	0.1500	15	0.15	$3/20$
$1/8$	0.1250	$7/20$	0.3500	16	0.16	$4/25$
$3/8$	0.3750	$9/20$	0.4500	$16 2/3$	0.167	$1/6$
$5/8$	0.6250	$11/20$	0.5500	17	0.17	$17/100$
$7/8$	0.8750	$13/20$	0.6500	18	0.18	$9/50$
$1/9$	0.1111	$17/20$	0.8500	19	0.19	$19/100$
$2/9$	0.2222	$19/20$	0.9500	20	0.20	$1/5$
$4/9$	0.4444	$1/32$	0.0312	21	0.21	$21/100$
$5/9$	0.5555	$3/32$	0.0938	22	0.22	$11/50$
$7/9$	0.7778	$5/32$	0.1562	23	0.23	$23/100$
$8/9$	0.8889	$7/32$	0.2187	24	0.24	$6/25$
$1/10$	0.1000	$9/32$	0.2812	25	0.25	$1/4$
$3/10$	0.3000	$11/32$	0.3437	26	0.26	$13/50$
$7/10$	0.7000	$13/32$	0.4062	27	0.27	$27/100$
$9/10$	0.9000	$15/32$	0.4687	28	0.28	$7/25$
$1/11$	0.0909	$17/32$	0.5312	29	0.29	$29/100$
$2/11$	0.1818	$19/32$	0.5937	30	0.30	$3/10$
$3/11$	0.2727	$21/32$	0.6562	31	0.31	$31/100$
$4/11$	0.3636	$23/32$	0.7187	32	0.32	$8/25$
$5/11$	0.4545	$25/32$	0.7812	33	0.33	$33/100$
$6/11$	0.5454	$27/32$	0.8437	$33 1/3$	0.333	$1/3$
$7/11$	0.6363	$29/32$	0.9062	34	0.34	$17/50$
		$31/32$	0.9687	35	0.35	$7/20$
				36	0.36	$9/25$
				37	0.37	$37/100$
				38	0.38	$19/50$
				39	0.39	$39/100$
				40	0.40	$2/5$
				41	0.41	$41/100$
				42	0.42	$21/50$
				43	0.43	$43/100$
				44	0.44	$11/25$
				45	0.45	$9/20$
				46	0.46	$23/50$
				47	0.47	$47/100$
				48	0.48	$12/25$
				49	0.49	$49/100$
				50	0.50	$1/2$
				55	0.55	$11/20$
				60	0.60	$3/5$
				65	0.65	$13/20$
				70	0.70	$7/10$
				75	0.75	$3/4$
				80	0.80	$4/5$
				85	0.85	$17/20$
				90	0.90	$9/10$
				95	0.95	$19/20$
				100	1.00	1

Multiplication table

	2	3	4	5	6	7	8	9	10	11	12	13	14	15	16	17	18	19	20	21	22	23	24	25
2	4	6	8	10	12	14	16	18	20	22	24	26	28	30	32	34	36	38	40	42	44	46	48	50
3	6	9	12	15	18	21	24	27	30	33	36	39	42	45	48	51	54	57	60	63	66	69	72	75
4	8	12	16	20	24	28	32	36	40	44	48	52	56	60	64	68	72	76	80	84	88	92	96	100
5	10	15	20	25	30	35	40	45	50	55	60	65	70	75	80	85	90	95	100	105	110	115	120	125
6	12	18	24	30	36	42	48	54	60	66	72	78	84	90	96	102	108	114	120	126	132	138	144	150
7	14	21	28	35	42	49	56	63	70	77	84	91	98	105	112	119	126	133	140	147	154	161	168	175
8	16	24	32	40	48	56	64	72	80	88	96	104	112	120	128	136	144	152	160	168	176	184	192	200
9	18	27	36	45	54	63	72	81	90	99	108	117	126	135	144	153	162	171	180	189	198	207	216	225
10	20	30	40	50	60	70	80	90	100	110	120	130	140	150	160	170	180	190	200	210	220	230	240	250
11	22	33	44	55	66	77	88	99	110	121	132	143	154	165	176	187	198	209	220	231	242	253	264	275
12	24	36	48	60	72	84	96	108	120	132	144	156	168	180	192	204	216	228	240	252	264	276	288	300
13	26	39	52	65	78	91	104	117	130	143	156	169	182	195	208	221	234	247	260	273	286	299	312	325
14	28	42	56	70	84	98	112	126	140	154	168	182	196	210	224	238	252	266	280	294	308	322	336	350
15	30	45	60	75	90	105	120	135	150	165	180	195	210	225	240	255	270	285	300	315	330	345	360	375
16	32	48	64	80	96	112	128	144	160	176	192	208	224	240	256	272	288	304	320	336	352	368	384	400
17	34	51	68	85	102	119	136	153	170	187	204	221	238	255	272	289	306	323	340	357	374	391	408	425
18	36	54	72	90	108	126	144	162	180	198	216	234	252	270	288	306	324	342	360	378	396	414	432	450
19	38	57	76	95	114	133	152	171	190	209	228	247	266	285	304	323	342	361	380	399	418	437	456	475
20	40	60	80	100	120	140	160	180	200	220	240	260	280	300	320	340	360	380	400	420	440	460	480	500
21	42	63	84	105	126	147	168	189	210	231	252	273	294	315	336	357	378	399	420	441	462	483	504	525
22	44	66	88	110	132	154	176	198	220	242	264	286	308	330	352	374	396	418	440	462	484	506	528	550
23	46	69	92	115	138	161	184	207	230	253	276	299	322	345	368	391	414	437	460	483	506	529	552	575
24	48	72	96	120	144	168	192	216	240	264	288	312	336	360	384	408	432	456	480	501	528	552	576	600
25	50	75	100	125	150	175	200	225	250	275	300	325	350	375	400	425	450	475	500	525	550	575	600	625

Squares, cubes, and roots

No.	Square	Cube	Square root	Cube root	No.	Square	Cube	Square root	Cube root
1	1	1	1.000	1.000	13	169	2 197	3.606	2.351
2	4	8	1.414	1.260	14	196	2 744	3.742	2.410
3	9	27	1.732	1.442	15	225	3 375	3.873	2.466
4	16	64	2.000	1.587	16	256	4 096	4.000	2.520
5	25	125	2.236	1.710	17	289	4 913	4.123	2.571
6	36	216	2.449	1.817	18	324	5 832	4.243	2.621
7	49	343	2.646	1.913	19	361	6 859	4.359	2.668
8	64	512	2.828	2.000	20	400	8 000	4.472	2.714
9	81	729	3.000	2.080	25	625	15 625	5.000	2.924
10	100	1 000	3.162	2.154	30	900	27 000	5.477	3.107
11	121	1 331	3.317	2.224	40	1 600	64 000	6.325	3.420
12	144	1 728	3.464	2.289	50	2 500	125 000	7.071	3.684

International paper sizes

A series

	mm	in			mm	in
A0	841 × 1189	33.11 × 46.81		B5	176 × 250	6.93 × 9.84
A1	594 × 841	23.39 × 33.1		B6	125 × 176	4.92 × 6.93
A2	420 × 594	16.54 × 23.29		B7	88 × 125	3.46 × 4.92
A3	297 × 420	11.69 × 16.54		B8	62 × 88	2.44 × 3.46
A4	210 × 297	8.27 × 11.69		B9	44 × 62	1.73 × 2.44
A5	148 × 210	5.83 × 8.27		B10	31 × 44	1.22 × 1.73
A6	105 × 148	4.13 × 5.83				
A7	74 × 105	2.91 × 4.13		**C series**		
A8	52 × 74	2.05 × 2.91			mm	in
A9	37 × 52	1.46 × 2.05		C0	917 × 1 297	36.00 × 51.20
A10	26 × 37	1.02 × 1.46		C1	648 × 917	25.60 × 36.00
				C2	458 × 648	18.00 × 25.60
B series				C3	324 × 458	12.80 × 18.00
	mm	in		C4	229 × 324	9.00 × 12.80
B0	1 000 × 1414	39.37 × 55.67		C5	162 × 229	6.40 × 9.00
B1	707 × 1000	27.83 × 39.37		C6	114 × 162	4.50 × 6.40
B2	500 × 707	19.68 × 27.83		C7	81 × 114	3.20 × 4.50
B3	353 × 500	13.90 × 19.68		DL	110 × 220	4.33 × 8.66
B4	250 × 353	9.84 × 13.90		C7/6	81 × 162	3.19 × 6.38

All sizes in these series have sides in the proportion of 1: $\sqrt{2}$.
A series is used for writing paper, books and magazines; **B** series for posters; **C** series for envelopes.

PHYSICS

Basic equations

Density
$$\text{density} = \frac{\text{mass}}{\text{volume}} \qquad \text{volume} = \frac{\text{mass}}{\text{density}}$$

mass = volume × density

Velocity
$v = u + at$
where v is the final velocity, u the original velocity, a the acceleration, and t the time taken

Pressure
$$\text{pressure} = \frac{\text{force}}{\text{area}} \qquad P = \frac{F}{A}$$

Energy
potential energy = weight × height above ground
kinetic energy = $\frac{1}{2} mv^2$
where m is the mass and v is the velocity

Waves
speed = frequency × wavelength $\quad v = f\lambda$

Electricity
charge = current × time
(coulombs) (amperes) (seconds)

$$\text{resistance} = \frac{\text{voltage (volts)}}{\text{current (amperes)}} \qquad R = \frac{V}{I}$$
(ohms)

$V = I \times R$

Electrical power
power = voltage × current $\quad P = V \times I$
(watts) (volts) (amperes)

$V = \dfrac{P}{I}$ and $I = \dfrac{P}{V}$

Forces of nature

	Gravity	Electro-magnetism	Weak nuclear force	Strong nuclear force
Range m	Infinite	Infinite	10^{-18} (sub-atomic)	10^{-15} (sub-atomic)
Relative strength	6×10^{-39}	1/137	10^{-5}	1
Examples of application	Orbit of Earth around Sun	Force between electrical charges	Radio-active β-decay	Binds atomic nucleus together

Elementary particles

Fundamental particles (matter particles)
Electrons
Muons
Neutrinos
Quarks
Taus

Force particles
Gluons
Gravitons
Photons
W and Z bosons

Some common physical qualities and their units

Physical quantity	Symbol	SI unit	SI symbol
Acceleration, deceleration	a	metre/second^2	m s^{-2}
		kilometre/hour/second	km h^{-1} s^{-1}
Angular velocity	ω	radian/second	rad s^{-1}; s^{-1}
Capacitance	C	farad	F
		(coulomb/volt)	(CV^{-1})
Coefficient of viscosity	η	poise, decapoise	
		(newton second/metre^2)	N s m^{-2}
		(kilogram/metre/second)	kg m^{-1} s^{-1}
Density	ρ	kilogram/metre^3	kg m^{-3}
		kilogram/millilitre	kg ml^{-1}
Displacement, distance	S	metre	m
Electric charge	Q, q	coulomb	C
Electric current	I, i	ampere	A
		(coulomb/second)	C s^{-1}
Electrical energy	–	megajoule,	MJ
		kilowatt-hour	kWh
Electric intensity, field strength	E ($= -dV/dr$)	newton/coulomb	N C^{-1}
		volt/metre	V m^{-1}
Electric pd	V	volt	V
		(joule/coulomb)	(J C^{-1})
Electrical power	–	watt	W
		(joule/second)	(J s^{-1})
Electromotive force (emf)	E	volt	V
		(watt/ampere)	(W A^{-1})
Electrical conductance	S	siemen	A V^{-1}
		(ohm $^{-1}$)	
Electrical resistance	R	ohm	Ω
		(volt/ampere)	(V A^{-1})
Electric permittivity	ε	farad/metre	F m^{-1}
Frequency	f	hertz	Hz
		(cycles/second)	(s^{-1})
Force	F	newton	N
		(kilogram metre/second^2)	(kg m s^{-2})
Gravitational intensity, field strength	–	newton/kilogram	N kg^{-1}
Heat capacity of a body	ms	joule/kelvin	J K^{-1}

Physical quantity	Symbol	SI unit	SI symbol
Inductance	L	henry	H
		(volt second/ampere)	(V s A^{-1})
		(weber/ampere)	(Wb A^{-1})
Induced emf	e	volt	V
		(weber/second)	(Wb s^{-1})
Magnetic field strength	H	ampere/metre	A m^{-1}
Magnetic flux	ϕ	weber	Wb
Magnetic flux density	B	tesla	T
		(weber/metre^2)	(Wb m^{-2})
Magnetic permeability	μ	henry/metre	H m^{-1}
Mass	m	kilogram	kg
Mechanical power	–	watt	W
		(joule/second)	(J s^{-1})
Moment of inertia	I	kilogram metre^2	kg m^2
Momentum	mv	kilogram metre/second	kg m s^{-1}
Pressure	P	pascal	Pa
		(newton/metre^2)	(N m^{-2})
Quantity of substance	–	mole	mol
Specific heat capacity	s	joule/kilogram/kelvin	J kg^{-1} K^{-1}
Specific latent heats of fusion, vaporization	L	joule/kilogram	J kg^{-1}
Surface tension	T, γ	newton/metre	N m^{-1}
Torque, moment of force, moment of couple	–	newton metre	N m
Velocity gradient	dv/dr	metre/second/metre	(m s^{-1} m^{-1})
Velocity, speed	u, v	metre/second	m s^{-1}
		kilometre/hour	km h^{-1}
Volume	V	metre^3	m^3
		millilitre	ml
Wavelength	λ	metre	m
Weight	W	newton,	N
		kilogram-force	kgf
Work, energy	–	joule	J
		(newton metre)	(N m)

Newton's laws

First law: The velocity of an object does not change unless a force acts on the object.

Second law: A force F applied to an object of mass m causes an acceleration a according to $F = ma$.

Third law: Every action has an equal and opposite reaction.

Newton's law of gravitation

$F = Gm_1m_2/r^2$ where F is the force between objects of mass m_1 and m_2 separated by distance r, and G is the gravitational constant.

Einstein's principle of relativity

All physical laws are the same in all frames of reference in uniform motion with respect to one another.

If the energy of a body changes by amount E then its mass must change by E/c^2 where c is the velocity of light (or, expressed in its better-known form, $E = mc^2$).

Magnetism

A magnetic field is a region of magnetic influence around a magnet, moving charge, or current-carrying wire; denoted by B (unit: tesla), the magnetic flux density, and by H (unit: ampere/metre), the magnetic field strength.

Lines of magnetic field circulate around current-carrying wire.

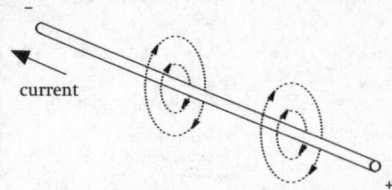

current

Circuit symbols

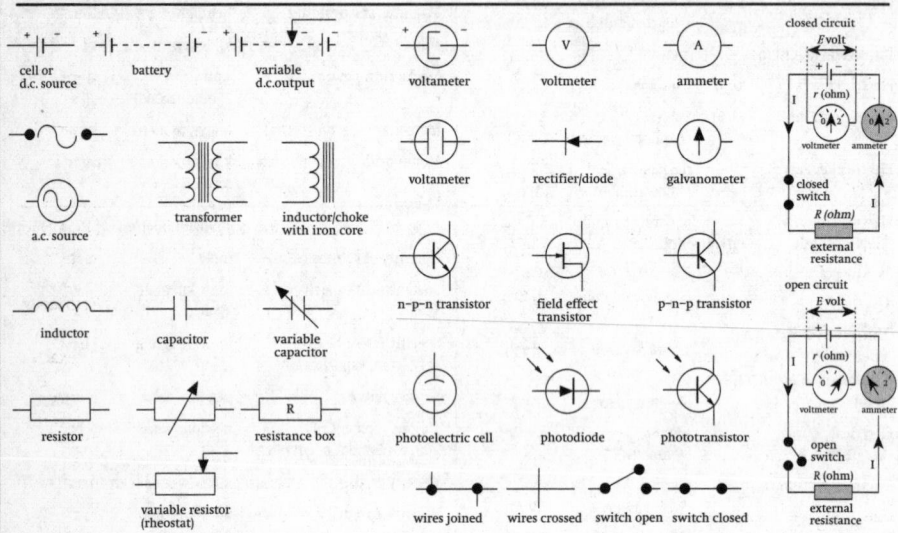

cell or d.c. source   battery   variable d.c. output   voltmeter   voltmeter   ammeter

a.c. source   transformer   inductor/choke with iron core   voltameter   rectifier/diode   galvanometer

closed circuit
E volt

inductor   capacitor   variable capacitor   n-p-n transistor   field effect transistor   p-n-p transistor

r (ohm)
voltmeter   ammeter
closed switch
R (ohm)
external resistance

resistor   resistance box   photoelectric cell   photodiode   phototransistor

open circuit
E volt

variable resistor (rheostat)   wires joined   wires crossed   switch open   switch closed

r (ohm)
voltmeter   ammeter
open switch
R (ohm)
external resistance

Optics

Reflection at a mirror

The law of reflection says that angles A and B are the same.

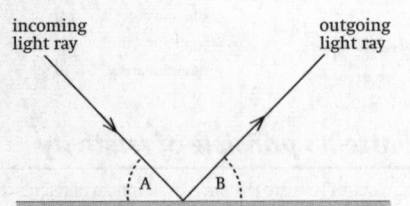

incoming light ray   outgoing light ray

A   B

Double-convex converging lens

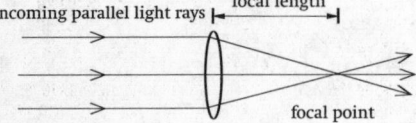

incoming parallel light rays   focal length

focal point

Double-concave diverging lens

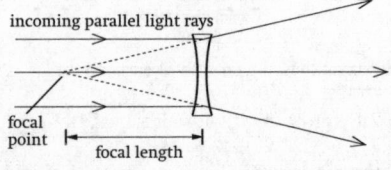

incoming parallel light rays

focal point   focal length

Basic telescope

A long-focal-length objective lens and a short-focal-length eyepiece are required.

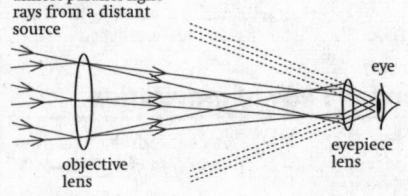

almost parallel light rays from a distant source

eye

objective lens   eyepiece lens

Basic compound microscope

The object lens forms an enlarged real image of the object, which is then viewed via the eyepiece. A short-focal-length objective lens and eyepiece are required. A 'virtual image' is an image which cannot be projected onto a screen.

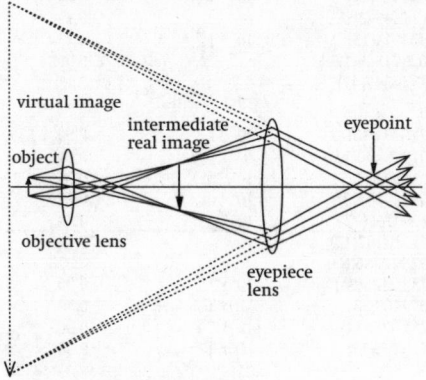

Prism

A beam of white light falling onto a prism splits into constituent colours (wavelengths), since the bending of light at an air–glass surface depends on the light wavelength, and white light comprises a mixture of colours. The white light is *dispersed* into a spectrum: the spectrum is really a continuous range of colours, not simply six as shown. With lenses, the actual bending of light occurs only at air–glass interfaces.

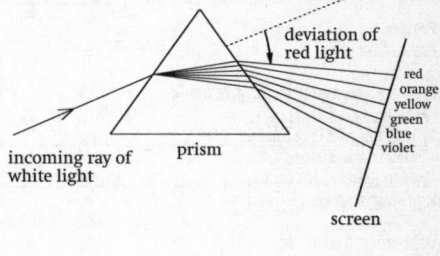

Physical constants

1986 recommended values of the main fundamental physical constants of physics and chemistry, based on a least-squares adjustment with 17 degrees of freedom. The digits in parentheses are the one-standard-deviation uncertainty in the last digits of the given value. (After Cohen and Taylor, 1987)

Quantity	Symbol	Value	Units	Relative uncertainty
Universal constants				
Speed of light in vacuum	c	299 792 458	m s^{-1}	(exact)
Permeability of vacuum	μ_0	$4\pi \times 10^{-7}$	N A^{-2}	
		$= 12.566370614\ldots$	10^{-7} N A^{-2}	(exact)
Permittivity of vacuum $1/\mu_0 c^2$	ε_0	$8.854187187\ldots$	10^{-12} F m^{-1}	(exact)
Newtonian constant of gravitation	G	6.67259(85)	10^{-11} m^3 kg^{-1} s^{-2}	128
Planck constant	h	6.6260755(40)	10^{-34} J s	0.60
	$h/2\pi$	1.05457266(63)	10^{-34} J s	0.60
Electromagnetic constants				
Elementary charge	e	1.60217733(49)	10^{-19} C	0.30
	e/h	2.41798836(72)	10^{14} A J^{-1}	0.30
Magnetic flux quantum, $h/2e$	Φ_0	2.06783461(61)	10^{-15} Wb	0.30
Josephson frequency–voltage quotient	$2e/h$	4.8359767(14)	10^{-14} Hz V^{-1}	0.30
Bohr magneton, $eh/2m_e$	μ_B	9.2740154(31)	10^{-24} J T^{-1}	0.34
Nuclear magneton, $eh/2m_p$	μ_N	5.0507866(17)	10^{-27} J T^{-1}	0.34
Atomic constants				
Fine-structure constant, $\mu_0 c e^2/2h$	α	7.29735308(33)	10^{-3}	0.045
	α^{-1}	137.0359895(61)		0.045
Rydberg constant, $m_e c \alpha^2/2h$	R_∞	10 973 731.534(13)	m^{-1}	0.0012
Bohr radius, $\alpha/4\pi R_\infty$	a_0	0.529177249(24)	10^{-10} m	0.045
Quantum of circulation	$h/2m_e$	3.63694807(33)	10^{-4} m^2 s^{-1}	0.089
	h/m_e	7.27389614(65)	10^{-4} m^2 s^{-1}	0.089
Electron				
Electron mass	m_e	9.1093897(54)	10^{-31} kg	0.59
		5.48579903(13)	10^{-4} u	0.023
Electron–muon mass ratio	m_e/m_μ	4.83633218(71)	10^{-3}	0.15
Electron–proton mass ratio	m_e/m_p	5.44617013(11)	10^{-4}	0.020
Electron specific charge	$-e/m_e$	-1.75881962(53)	10^{11} C kg^{-1}	0.30
Compton wavelength, $h/m_e c$	λ_c	2.42631058(22)	10^{-12} m	0.089
$\lambda_c/2\pi = \alpha a_0 = \alpha^2/4\pi R_\infty$	λ_c	3.86159323(35)	10^{-13} m	0.089
Classical electron radius, $\alpha^2 a_0$	r_e	2.81794092(38)	10^{-15} m	0.13
Electron magnetic moment	μ_e	928.47701(31)	10^{-26} J T^{-1}	0.34
Electron g factor, $2(1+a_e)$	g_e	2.002319304386(20)		1×10^{-5}
Electron–proton magnetic moment ratio	μ_e/μ_p	658.2106881(66)		0.010

Physical constants (continued)

Quantity	Symbol	Value	Units	Relative uncertainty (ppm)
Muon				
Muon mass	m_μ	1.8835327(11)	10^{-28} kg	0.61
		0.113428913(17)	u	0.15
Muon magnetic moment	μ_μ	4.4904514(15)	10^{-26} J T^{-1}	0.33
Muon g factor, $2(1+a_\mu)$	g_μ	2.002331846(17)		0.0084
Muon–proton magnetic moment ratio	μ_μ/μ_p	3.18334547(47)		0.15
Proton				
Proton mass	m_p	1.6726231(10)	10^{-27} kg	0.59
		1.007276470(12)	u	0.012
Proton Compton wavelength, h/m_pc	$\lambda_{C,p}$	1.32141002(12)	10^{-15} m	0.089
$\lambda_{C,p}/2\pi$	$\lambda_{C,p}$	2.10308937(19)	10^{-16} m	0.089
Proton magnetic moment	μ_p	1.41060761(47)	10^{-26} J T^{-1}	0.34
in Bohr magnetons	μ_p/μ_B	1.521032202(15)	10^{-3}	0.010
in nuclear magnetons	μ_p/μ_N	2.792847386(63)		0.023
Proton gyromagnetic ratio	γ_p	26 752.2128(81)	10^4 s^{-1} T^{-1}	0.30
	$\gamma_p/2\pi$	42.577469(13)	MHz T^{-1}	0.30
Uncorrected (H_2O, sph., 25°C)	γ'_p	26 751.525581)	10^4 s^{-1} T^{-1}	0.30
	$\gamma'_p/2\pi$	42.576375(13)	MHz T^{-1}	0.30
Neutron				
Neutron mass	m_n	1.6749286(10)	10^{-27} kg	0.59
		1.008664904(14)	u	0.014
Neutron Compton wavelength, h/m_nc	$\lambda_{C,n}$	1.31959110(12)	10^{-15} m	0.089
$\lambda_{C,n}/2\pi$	$\lambda_{C,n}$	2.10019445(19)	10^{-16} m	0.089
Physico-chemical constants				
Avogadro constant	N_A, L	6.0221367(36)	10^{23} mol^{-1}	0.59
Atomic mass constant, $m_u = {}^1/_{12}m$ (^{12}C)	m_u	1.6605402(10)	10^{-27} kg	0.59
Faraday constant, N_Ae	F	96 485.309(29)	C mol^{-1}	0.30
Molar gas constant	R	8.314510(70)	J mol^{-1} K^{-1}	8.4
Boltzmann constant, R/N_A	k	1.380658(12)	10^{-23} J K^{-1}	8.5
Molar volume (ideal gas), RT/p				
$T = 273.15$ K, $p = 101\,325$ Pa	V_m	0.02241410(19)	m^3 mol^{-1}	8.4
Stefan–Boltzmann constant, $(\pi^2/60)\,k^4/\hbar^3c^2$	σ	5.67051(19)	10^{-8} W m^{-2} K^{-4}	34
First radiation constant, $2\pi hc^2$	c_1	3.7417749(22)	10^{-16} W m^2	0.60
Second radiation constant, hc/k	c_2	0.01438769(12)	m K	8.4

The electromagnetic spectrum

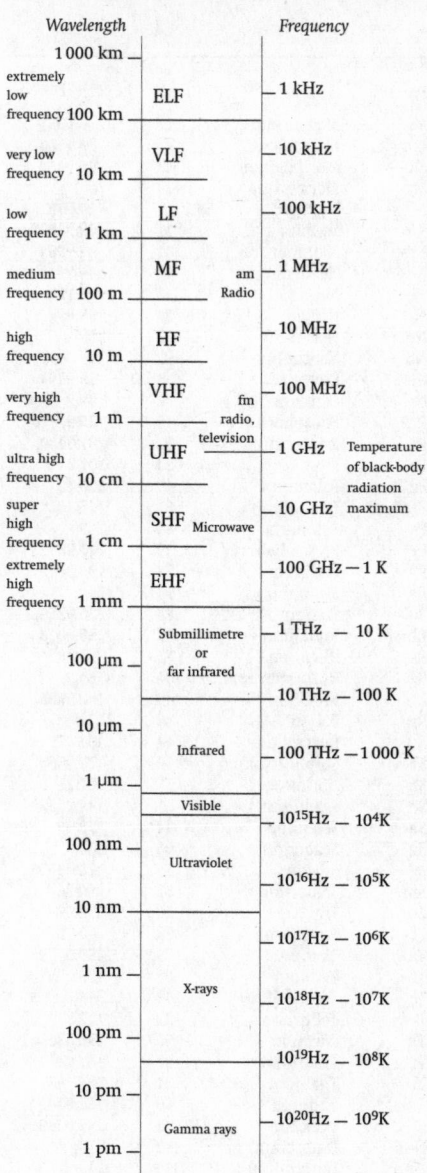

Radioactivity units

The activity of a radioactive source is expressed in *becquerels*, Bq, where 1 Bq is one decay per second. Particles from different substances may be produced in similar numbers but with very different energies. This is taken into account using a second unit, the *gray*, Gy, which measures the energy deposited in some object by the radiation: the *absorbed dose*. Different types of radiation cause different degrees of biological damage, even if the total energy deposited is the same; for example, 1 Gy of alpha radiation causes 20 times as much damage as 1 Gy of beta radiation. This potential for causing harm is expressed as the *dose equivalent* (unit: sievert, Sv), which is the product of the absorbed dose in Gy and a *relative biological effectiveness* (RBE) factor. Radiation limits for working places and the environment are expressed in Sv. Names, definitions, and units are summarized in the table.

Name	Definition	Unit	Old unit
Activity	Rate of disintegrations	Bq	Ci (curie)
Absorbed dose	Energy deposited in object, divided by mass of object	Gy	rad
Dose equivalent	Absorbed dose × RBE	Sv	rem

RBE	Radiation
20	Alpha
10	Neutron
1	Beta, gamma, X-ray

Sound-intensity level

Source	Sound-intensity level (dB)[a]
Jet aircraft	120
Heavy machinery	90
Busy street	70
Conversation	50
Whisper	20

[a]dB = decibels.

CHEMISTRY

Table of elements

Atomic weights are taken from the 1983 list of the International Union of Pure and Applied Chemistry. For radioactive elements, the mass number of the most stable isotope is given in square brackets.

Symbol	Element	Atomic no.	Weight
Ac	Actinium	89	[227.0278]
Ag	Silver	47	107.8682
Al	Aluminium	13	26.98154
Am	Americium	95	[243]
Ar	Argon	18	39.948
As	Arsenic	33	74.9216
At	Astatine	85	[210]
Au	Gold	79	196.9665
B	Boron	5	10.811
Ba	Barium	56	137.33
Be	Beryllium	4	9.01218
Bh	Bohrium	107	[262]
Bi	Bismuth	83	208.9804
Bk	Berkelium	97	[247]
Br	Bromine	35	79.904
C	Carbon	6	12.011
Ca	Calcium	20	40.078
Cd	Cadmium	48	112.41
Ce	Cerium	58	140.12
Cf	Californium	98	[252]
Cl	Chlorine	17	35.453
Cm	Curium	96	[247]
Co	Cobalt	27	58.9332
Cr	Chromium	24	51.9961
Cs	Caesium/Cesium	55	132.9054
Cu	Copper	29	63.546
Db	Dubnium	105	[262]
Dy	Dysprosium	66	162.50
Er	Erbium	68	167.26
Es	Einsteinium	99	[254]
Eu	Europium	63	151.96
F	Fluorine	9	18.998403
Fe	Iron	26	55.847
Fm	Fermium	100	[257]
Fr	Francium	87	[223]
Ga	Gallium	31	69.723
Gd	Gadolinium	64	157.25
Ge	Germanium	32	72.59
H	Hydrogen	1	1.00794
He	Helium	2	4.002602
Hf	Hafnium	72	178.49
Hg	Mercury	80	200.59
Ho	Holmium	67	164.9304
Hs	Hassium	108	[265]
I	Iodine	53	126.9045
In	Indium	49	114.82
Ir	Iridium	77	192.22
K	Potassium	19	39.0983
Kr	Krypton	36	83.80
La	Lanthanum	57	138.9055
Li	Lithium	3	6.941
Lr	Lutetium	71	174.967
Lw	Lawrencium	103	[260]
Md	Mendelevium	101	[258]

Symbol	Element	Atomic no.	Weight
Mg	Magnesium	12	24.305
Mn	Manganese	25	54.9380
Mo	Molybdenum	42	95.94
Mt	Meitnerium	109	[266]
N	Nitrogen	7	14.0067
Na	Sodium	11	22.98977
Nb	Niobium	41	92.9064
Nd	Neodymium	60	144.24
Ne	Neon	10	20.179
Ni	Nickel	28	58.69
No	Nobelium	102	[259]
Np	Neptunium	93	[237.0482]
O	Oxygen	8	15.9994
Os	Osmium	76	190.2
P	Phosphorus	15	30.97376
Pa	Protactinium	91	[231.0359]
Pb	Lead	82	207.2
Pd	Palladium	46	106.42
Pm	Promethium	61	[145]
Po	Polonium	84	[209]
Pr	Praseodymium	59	140.9077
Pt	Platinum	78	195.08
Pu	Plutonium	94	[244]
Ra	Radium	88	[226.0254]
Rb	Rubidium	37	85.4678
Re	Rhenium	75	186.207
Rf	Rutherfordium	104	[261]
Rh	Rhodium	45	102.9055
Rn	Radon	86	[222]
Ru	Ruthenium	44	101.77
S	Sulphur/sulfur	16	32.066
Sb	Antimony	51	121.75
Sc	Scandium	21	44.95591
Se	Selenium	34	78.96
Sg	Seaborgium	106	[263]
Si	Silicon	14	28.0855
Sm	Samarium	62	150.36
Sn	Tin	50	118.69
Sr	Strontium	38	87.62
Ta	Tantalum	73	180.9479
Tb	Terbium	65	158.9254
Tc	Technetium	43	[98]
Te	Tellurium	52	127.60
Th	Thorium	90	232.0381
Ti	Titanium	22	47.88
Tl	Thallium	81	204.383
Tm	Thulium	69	168.9342
U	Uranium	92	238.0289
Uub	Ununbium	112	[277]
Uun	Ununnilium	110	[269]
Uuu	Unununium	111	[272]
V	Vanadium	23	50.9415
W	Tungsten	74	183.85
Xe	Xenon	54	131.29
Y	Yttrium	39	88.9059
Yb	Ytterbium	70	173.04
Zn	Zinc	30	65.38
Zr	Zirconium	40	91.224

Periodic table of elements

1	2	3	4	5	6	7	8	9	10	11	12	13	14	15	16	17	18
1 H Hydrogen 1.00794																	2 He Helium 4.002160
3 Li Lithium 6.941	4 Be Beryllium 24.305											5 B Boron 10.81	6 C Carbon 12.011	7 N Nitrogen 14.0067	8 O Oxygen 15.9994	9 F Flourine 18.998403	10 Ne Neon 20.179
11 Na Sodium 22.98977	12 Mg Magnesium 24.305											13 Al Aluminium 26.98154	14 Si Silicon 28.0855	15 P Phosphorus 30.97376	16 S Sulphur 32.066	17 Cl Chlorine 35.453	18 Ar Argon 39.948
19 K Potassium 39.0983	20 Ca Calcium 40.08	21 Sc Scandium 44.9559	22 Ti Titanium 47.88	23 V Vanadium 50.9415	24 Cr Chromium 51.996	25 Mn Manganese 54.9380	26 Fe Iron 55.847	27 Co Cobalt 58.9332	28 Ni Nickel 58.69	29 Cu Copper 63.546	30 Zn Zinc 65.38	31 Ga Gallium 69.72	32 Ge Germanium 72.59	33 As Arsenic 74.9216	34 Se Selenium 78.96	35 Br Bromine 79.904	36 Kr Krypton 83.80
37 Rb Rubidium 85.4678	38 Sr Strontium 87.62	39 Y Yttrium 88.9059	40 Zr Zirconium 91.22	41 Nb Niobium 92.9064	42 Mo Molybdenum 95.94	43 Tc Technetium (98)	44 Ru Ruthenium 101.9342	45 Rh Rhodium 102.9055	46 Pd Palladium 106.42	47 Ag Silver 107.8682	48 Cd Cadmium 112.41	49 In Indium 114.82	50 Sn Tin 118.69	51 Sb Antimony 121.75	52 Te Tellurium 127.60	53 I Iodine 126.9045	54 Xe Xenon 131.29
55 Cs Caesium 132.9054	56 Ba Barium 137.33	57–71 Lanthanide series (rare earth elements) *	72 Hf Hafnium 178.49	73 Ta Tantalum 180.9479	74 W Tungsten 183.85	75 Re Rhenium 186.207	76 Os Osmium 190.2	77 Ir Iridium 192.2	78 Pt Platinum 195.08	79 Au Gold 196.9665	80 Hg Mercury 200.59	81 Tl Thallium 204.383	82 Pb Lead 207.2	83 Bi Bismuth 208.9804	84 Po Polonium (209)	85 At Astatine (210)	86 Rn Radon (222)
87 Fr Francium (223)	88 Ra Radium 226.0254	89–103 Actinide series (radioactive rare earth elements) ☆	104 Rf Rutherfordium (261)	105 Db Dubnium (262)	106 Sg Seaborgium (263)	107 Bh Bohrium (262)	108 Hs Hassium (265)	109 Mt Meitnerium (266)	110 Uun Ununnilium (269)	111 Uuu Unununium (272)	112 Uub Ununbium (277)						

Transition series

under investigation

*	57 La Lanthanum 138.9055	58 Ce Cerium 140.12	59 Pr Praseodymium 140.9077	60 Nd Neodymium 144.24	61 Pm Promethium (145)	62 Sm Samarium 150.36	63 Eu Europium 151.96	64 Gd Gadolinium 157.25	65 Tb Terbium 158.9254	66 Dy Dysprosium 162.50	67 Ho Holmium 164.9304	68 Er Erbium 167.26	69 Tm Thulium 168.9342	70 Yt Ytterbium 173.04	71 Lu Lutetium 174.967
☆	89 Ac Actinium 227.0278	90 Th Thorium 232.0381	91 Pa Protactinium 231.0359	92 U Uranium 238.0289	93 Np Neptunium 237.0482	94 Pu Plutonium (244)	95 Am Americium (243)	96 Cm Curium (247)	97 Bk Berkelium (247)	98 Cf Californium (251)	99 Es Einsteinium (254)	100 Fm Fermium (257)	101 Md Mendelevium (258)	102 No Nobelium (259)	103 Lr Lawrencium (260)

atomic number — symbol

86 Rn Radon (222)

element name

atomic weight (most stable isotope of radioactive elements in parenthesis)

Physical properties of metals

Metal	Electron structure	Electronegativity	Atomic number	Melting point (°C)	Boiling point (°C)
Aluminium (Al)	$(Ne)3s^23p^1$	1.5	13	659	2447
Barium (Ba)	$(Xe)6s^2$	0.9	56	710	1637
Beryllium (Be)	$(He)2s^2$	1.5	4	1283	2477
Caesium (Cs)	$(Xe)6s'$	0.7	55	29	685
Calcium (Ca)	$(Ar)4s^2$	1.0	20	850	1492
Chromium (Cr)	$(Ar)3d^54s'$	1.6	24	2176	2915
Cobalt (Co)	$(Ar)3d^74s^2$	1.8	27	1768	3150
Copper (Cu)	$(Ar)3d^{10}4s'$	1.9	29	1356	2855
Iron (Fe)	$(Ar)3d^64s^2$	1.8	26	1812	3160
Lead (Pb)	$(Xe)5d^{10}6s^26p^2$	1.8	82	328	1751
Lithium (Li)	$(He)2s^1$	1.0	3	181	1331
Magnesium (Mg)	$(Ne)3s^2$	1.2	12	650	117
Manganese (Mn)	$(Ar)3d^54s^2$	1.5	25	1517	2314
Nickel (Ni)	$(Ar)3d^84s^2$	1.8	28	1728	3110
Potassium (K)	$(Ar)4s^1$	0.8	19	63	766
Rubidium (Rb)	$(Kr)5s^1$	0.8	37	39	701
Sodium (Na)	$(Ne)3s^1$	0.9	11	98	890
Strontium (Sr)	$(Kr)5s^2$	1.0	38	770	1367
Tin (Sn)	$(Kr)4d^{10}5s^25p^2$	1.8	50	232	2690
Titanium (Ti)	$(Ar)3d^24s^2$	1.5	22	1673	2750
Vanadium (V)	$(Ar)3d^34s^2$	1.6	23	2190	3650
Zinc (Zn)	$(Ar)3d^{10}4s^2$	1.6	30	693	1181

Symbols used in chemistry

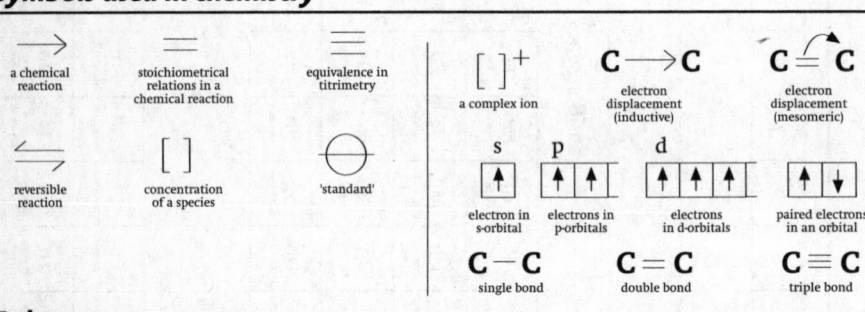

→	a chemical reaction
=	stoichiometrical relations in a chemical reaction
≡	equivalence in titrimetry
⇌	reversible reaction
[ ]	concentration of a species
⊖	'standard'
[ ]$^+$	a complex ion
C → C	electron displacement (inductive)
C ⇋ C	electron displacement (mesomeric)

s — electron in s-orbital
p — electrons in p-orbitals
d — electrons in d-orbitals
paired electrons in an orbital

C — C single bond
C = C double bond
C ≡ C triple bond

Polymers

Polymer	Repeat unit	Properties and uses
Polyamides		
Nylon-6,6	$-N-(CH_2)_6-N-C-(CH_2)_4-C-$ (with H on N, O double bonds on C)	Textile fibre, threads, ropes. Moulded gears and electrical insulation
Nylon-6,10	$-N-(CH_2)_6-N-C-(CH_2)_8-C-$ (with H on N, O double bonds on C)	Sports equipment. Bristles for brushes
Nomex	aromatic amide structure	Heat-resistant polymer in space suits. Also for parachute cords
Polyesters and polycarbonates		
Terylene, Dacron	$-O-CH_2-CH_2-O-C-$ (aromatic, O double bonds)	Textile fibre. Basis for magnetic tape and photographic film

Polymer	Repeat unit	Properties and uses
Lexan		Tough and transparent Bullet-proof windows, safety glass Food containers Car components

Polyethers

Polyglycol 166		Making urethanes and speciality elastomers, eg for oil and fuel hoses, oil-well equipment
Delrin, Celcon		Tough plastic for gears, pipes, pens

Phenol-based

Bakelite		Hard thermosetting polymer Telephones, buttons, electrical insulators
Poly(melamine formaldehyde)		Laminated surfaces, eg table tops, cupboards

Polyurethanes

Polyurethane		Foam rubber, synthetic leather
Lycra		Expanded foam rubber, carpet underlays, clothing

Alkenes

ABS[a] polymers contain these four types of repeat unit		Tough structural plastic or rubber Telephones, pipes, many moulded articles
Polybutadiene (butadiene rubber)		Alternative to natural rubber Footwear, tyres, toys

[a]ABS = acrylonitrile–butadiene–styrene

SCIENCE AND TECHNOLOGY

SCIENCE AND TECHNOLOGY

Polymer	Repeat unit	Properties and uses
Neoprene		Adhesive golf-ball covers, liquid seals
Polythene[a] (polyethene)		Tough plastic Fibres, thin films, extrusion-moulded objects, toys, bottles
Butyl rubber		Tyre inner tubes, raincoats, seals
Natural rubber (poly (cis-1,4-isoprene))		After vulcanization, used in car, and other, tyres
PTFE (poly(tetra-fluoroethene), Teflon)		Highly water-repellent Nonstick cooking ware Industrial uses where very low friction needed
Polystyrene		Transparent, glass-like Wide variety of moulded and expanded objects Packing and insulation
Perspex (poly(methyl methacrylate))		Transparent, glass-like Windows, fibre optics, illuminated signs
PVC (polyvinyl chloride)		Hard inflexible polymer With plasticizer, used in tubing, thin films, car-seat covers, floor tile
Alkynes		
Polyethyne (polyacetylene)	 delocalized electrons	With iodine, an electrically conducting polymer
Inorganic		
Silicone rubber		Seals, hoses, waterproofing, 'silicone grease'
Carbon fibres	Carbon layers with layers parallel to axis of fibre	Very high-strength fibres, eg in aeroplane and boat building
Polythiazyl	$-S \equiv N-$	An electrically conducting polymer Semiconductor at very low temperatures

[a]There are two main types of polyethene; low-density polyethene (LDPE) has considerable branching; high-density polyethene (HDPE) has no branching.

Hazardous substances symbols

  Harmful/ irritant

 Toxic

 Radioactive

 Flammable

 Corrosive

 Oxidizing/ supports fire

 Explosive

TECHNOLOGY

Major technological inventions

Date	Invention	Inventor/discoverer
1752	Lightning conductor	Benjamin Franklin
1764	Spinning jenny	James Hargreaves
1768	Spinning frame	Richard Arkwright
1769	Condenser (steam engine)	James Watt
1774	Telegraph (electric)	Georges Louis Lesage
1775	Steam ship	Jacques Perrier
1776	Submarine	David Bushnell
1779	Spinning mule	Samuel Crompton
1780	Circular saw	Gervinus
1783	Hot-air balloon	Jacques and Joseph Montgolfier
1784	Safety lock	Joseph Bramah
1785	Chemical bleaching	Claude Berthollet
1792	Cotton gin	Eli Whitney
1792	Gas lighting	William Murdock
1795	Preserving jar (foods)	Nicolas Appert
1798	Lithography	Aloys Senefelder
1799	Sheet paper-making machine	Louis Robert
1800	Electric battery	Alessandro Volta
1802	Wood-planing machine	Joseph Bramah
1804	Locomotive	Richard Trevithick
1807	Conveyor belt	Oliver Evans
1810	Canning	Nicolas Appert
1812	Photographic lens	William H Wollaston
1813	Power loom	William Horrocks
1823	Waterproof material	Charles Macintosh
1824	Cement	Joseph Aspdin
1829	Typewriter	William Burt
1831	Electric generator	Michael Faraday
1834	Harvesting machine	Cyrus McCormick
1835	Revolver	Samuel Colt
1835	Computer	Charles Babbage
1838	Photography (on paper)	William Henry Fox Talbot
1839	Bicycle	Kirkpatrick Macmillan
1843	Underground railway	Charles Pearson
1845	Hydraulic crane	W G Armstrong
1846	Sewing machine	Elias Howe
1846	Rotary printing press	Richard Hoe
1850	Synthetic oil	James Young
1850	Refrigerator	James Harrison and Alexander Twining
1851	Mechanical lift	Elisha Otis
1854	Hydraulic lift	Elisha Otis
1855	Celluloid	Alexander Parks
1855	Steel production	Henry Bessemer

Date	Invention	Inventor/discoverer
1856	Synthetic dye	William Henry Perkin
1861	Colour photography	James Clerk Maxwell
1866	Telegraph (transatlantic)	Willliam Thompson (Lord Kelvin)
1867	Pasteurization	Louis Pasteur
1868	Tungsten steel	Robert Mushet
1868	Traffic lights	J P Knight
1871	Pneumatic drill	Samuel Ingersoll
1872	Electric typewriter	Thomas Edison
1873	Barbed wire	Joseph Glidden
1876	Telephone	Alexander Graham Bell
1876	Microphone	Alexander Graham Bell
1877	Electric welding	Elisha Thomson
1877	Gramophone	Thomas Edison
1878	Electric railway	Ernst Werner von Siemens
1879	Electric lamp	Thomas Edison
1880	Pendulum seismograph	James Ewing, Thomas Gray, and Sir John Milne
1882	Electric flat iron	Harry W Seeley
1883	Automatic machine gun	Sir Hiram (Stevens) Maxim
1884	Fountain pen	Lewis Waterman
1884	Car (internal combustion engine)	Gottlieb Daimler
1885	Adding machine	William Burroughs
1885	Petrol engine	Gottlieb Daimler
1885	Motorcycle	Gottlieb Daimler
1886	Car (petrol engine)	Karl Benz
1887	Celluloid film	Goodwin
1888	Pneumatic tyre	John Boyd Dunlop
1888	Alternating-current motor	Nikola Tesla
1888	Gramophone record	Emil Berliner
1889	Photographic film	George Eastman
1892	Escalator	Jesse Reno
1894	Automatic loom	J H Northrop
1894	Cinematograph	Auguste and Louis Lumière
1894	Turbine ship	Charles Parsons
1895	X-ray	Wilhelm Röntgen
1895	Safety razor	King C Gillette
1898	Diesel engine	Rudolf Diesel
1900	Cellophane	J E Brandenburger
1900	Airship	Graf Ferdinand von Zeppelin
1901	Radio	Guglielmo Marconi
1901	Vacuum cleaner (electric)	Hubert Cecil Booth

Major technological inventions (continued)

Date	Invention	Inventor/discoverer
1902	Windscreen wipers	Mary Anderson
1903	Electrocardiograph	Willem Einthoven
1903	Aeroplane	Orville and Wilbur Wright
1906	Freeze-drying	Arsene D'Arsonval and Georges Bordas
1907	Electric washing machine	Hurley Machine Co.
1907	Facsimile machine (fax)	Arthur Korn
1907	Bakelite	Leo Baekeland
1911	Neon light	Georges Claude
1913	Stainless steel	Harry Brearley
1924	Loudspeaker	Rice-Kellogg
1926	Television	John Logie Baird
1926	Liquid-fuel rocket	Robert Goddard
1933	Electron microscope	Max Knoll and Ernst Ruska
1934	Cat's eyes	Percy Shaw
1935	Parking meter	Carlton C Magee
1937	Turbo jet	Frank Whittle
1938	Ball-point pen	Laszlo and Georg Biró
1938	Nylon	Wallace Carrothers
1938	Xerography	Chester F Carlson
1939	Helicopter	Igor Sikorsky
1939	Atom bomb	Otto Frisch, Niels Bohr, and Rudolf Peierls
1941	Terylene	J R Whinfield and J T Dickson
1942	Turbo-prop engine	Max Mueller
1944	Digital computer	Harvard University
1945	Microwave oven	Percy Le Baron Spencer
1948	Transistor	William Shockley, John Bardeen, and Walter Brattain
1950	Gas-turbine powered car	Rover Motor Co.
1954	Solar battery	Bell Telephone Co.
1956	Video recorder	Ampex Co.
1959	Hovercraft	Christopher Cockerell
1959	Microchip	Kilby and Robert Noyce
1960	Laser	Charles Townes
1967	Laser-surgery	Cincinnati, US operating theatre
1969	Concorde supersonic	Britain–France
1969	Test-tube baby	Robert Edwards, Patrick Steptoe
1969	V/STOL Harrier	Hawker Siddeley
1969	Charge-coupled device (CCD)	Bell Labs
1970	747 Jumbo jet	Boeing
1971	Microprocessor	Marcian Hoff

Date	Invention	Inventor/discoverer
1971	First e-mail message	Ray Tomlinson
1972	Pocket calculator	
1976	Industrial robot	
1976	Space shuttle	NASA
1978	TGV high-speed train	France
1979	Walkman	Sony
1979	Compact disc	Philips and Sony
1980	MRI (Magnetic Resonance Imaging)	Damadian, Lauterbur, Mansfield
1981	Personal computer	IBM
1983	Analog Camcorder	Sony
1983	Cell phone	Martin Cooper
1985	Battery-powered vehicle (C5)	Clive Sinclair
1985	Genetic fingerprinting	Alec Jeffreys
1986	Laser instruments for heart and eye surgery	
1986	Pocket telephone	
1987	Digital audio tape	
1988	Video walkman	Sony
1988	Optical microprocessor	
1988	Digital camera	Fuji
1990	INCAT (High speed catamaran car ferry)	INCAT, Tasmania
1991	World Wide Web	Tim Berners-Lee
1991	Bagless vacuum cleaner	James Dyson
1992	Superconducting ceramic microchip	Sanyo Electric
1992	Compact disc-interactive player	Philips
1992	First text message to mobile phone sent in UK	
1993	Pentium 64-bit processor	Intel
1994	Digital camcorder	
1995	Commercial text messaging service	
1996	Fuel-cell powered car	Daimler–Benz
1997	Cloning of "Dolly" the sheep	Roslin Institute
1997	Hybrid petrol-electric motor car	Toyota
1998	Digital TV broadcasting	
1998	Spacecraft using ion-drive	NASA
1999	Wireless networking	
2001	iPod MP3 music player	Apple
2001	Broadband ADSL widespread	
2002	Supersonic Combustion Ramjet (Scramjet)	University of Queensland

The world's tallest structures

Name of structure	Location	Year	Height	
			m	ft
Warszawa Radio Mast	Konstantynow, Poland	1974 *(collapsed 1991)*	646	2120
KTHI-TV mast	North Dakota, US	1963	629	2063
CN Tower	Toronto, Canada	1975	555	1822
Ostankino TV Tower	Nr Moscow, Russia	1967	537	1762
WRBL-TV & WTVM	Georgia, US	1963	533	1749
WBIR-TV	Tennessee, US	1963	533	1749
Chongqing Office Tower	Chongqing, China	1998	516	1692
KFVS-TV	Missouri, US	1960	510	1672
WSPD-TV	Kentucky, US	2004	499	1638
WGAN-TV	Maine, US	1959	493	1619
KSWS-TV	New Mexico, US	1956	490	1610
WKY-TV	Oklahoma, US	1965	487	1600
KW-TV	Oklahoma, US	1954	479	1572
Oriental Pearl Television Tower	Shanghai, China	1995	468	1535
Bren Tower	Nevada, US	1962	465	1527

The world's tallest buildings

This listing is based entirely on the buildings' structural height. TV towers, masts, and other building types are not included.

Name of building	Location	Year	Height	
			m	ft
Taipei 101	Taipei, Taiwan	2004	509	1671
Petronas Twin Towers	Kuala Lumpur, Malaysia	1998	452	1483
Sears Tower	Chicago, US	1974	442	1451
Jin Mao Tower	Shanghai, China	1998	421	1380
Two International Finance	Hong Kong	2003	415	1362
CITIC Plaza	Guangzhou, China	1997	391	1283
Shun Hing Square	Shenzhen, China	1996	384	1260
Empire State Building	New York City, US	1931	381	1250
Central Plaza	Hong Kong	1992	374	1227
Bank of China Tower	Hong Kong	1990	367	1205
Emirates Office Tower	Dubai	2000	355	1163
Tuntex Sky Tower	Kaohsiung, Taiwan	1997	348	1140
Aon Center	Chicago, US	1973	346	1136
The Center	Hong Kong	1998	346	1136
John Hancock Center	Chicago, US	1969	344	1127
Shimao International Plaza	Shanghai, China	2006	333	1093
Minsheng Bank Building	Wuhan, China	2006	331	1087
Ryugyong Hotel	Pyongyang, North Korea	1992	330	1083
Qi Tower	Gold Coast City, Australia	2005	323	1058
Burj Al Arab	Dubai	1999	321	1053
Chrysler Building	New York City, US	1930	319	1046
Nina Tower 1	Hong Kong	2006	319	1046
Bank of America Plaza	Atlanta, US	1992	312	1023
US Bank Tower	Los Angeles, US	1989	310	1018
Menara Telekom	Kuala Lumpur, Malaysia	2001	310	1018
Jumeirah Emirates Towers	Dubai	2000	309	1014
AT&T Corporate Center	Chicago, US	1989	307	1007
JPMorgan Chase Tower	Houston, US	1982	305	1002
Baiyoke Tower II	Bangkok, Thailand	1997	304	997
Two Prudential Plaza	Chicago, US	1990	303	995
Wells Fargo Plaza	Houston, US	1983	302	992
Kingdom Centre	Riyadh, Saudi Arabia	2002	302	992
First Canadian Place	Toronto, Canada	1976	298	978
Eureka Tower	Melbourne, Australia	2006	297	975
Yokohama Landmark Tower	Yokohama, Japan	1993	296	972

Source © Emporis 10/2006

SCIENCE AND TECHNOLOGY

The world's highest dams

Name	Date completed	Place	Height m	ft
Rogun	1985	Tadzhikistan	335	1099
Nurek	1980	Tadzhikistan	300	984
Xiaowan	uncompleted	China	292	958
Grande Dixence	1962	Switzerland	285	935
Longtan	uncompleted	China	285	935
Inguri	1984	Georgia, US	272	892
Boruca	uncompleted	Costa Rica	267	875
Vaiont	1961	Italy	265	869
Chicoasen	1981	Mexico	265	869
Tehri	uncompleted	India	261	856
Kambaratinsk	uncompleted	Kyrgyzstan	255	836
Kinshau	1985	India	253	830
Guavio	1989	Columbia	250	820
Mica	1972	Canada	242	794
Sayano-Shushenk	1980	Russia	242	794
Mihoesti	1983	Romania	242	794
Ertan	1999	China	240	787
Chivor	1975	Columbia	237	778
Mauvoisin	1957	Switzerland	237	778
Oroville	1968	California	235	770
Chirkey	1977	Ukraine	233	764
Bekhme	uncompleted	Iraq	230	754
Bhakra	1963	India	226	741
El Cajon	1984	Honduras	226	741
Hoover	1936	Arizona/Nevada, US	221	726
Contra	1965	Switzerland	220	722
Dabaklamm	uncompleted	Austria	220	722
Three Gorges	uncompleted	China	181	594

The world's longest tunnels

Name	Date completed	Place	Length km	mi
Seikan	1985	Japan	53.9	33.5
Channel	1994	UK/France	49.9	31
Moscow subway	1990	Russia	37.9	23.5
Chesapeake Bay	1964	US	28	17.4
Dai-shimizu	1979	Japan	22.5	14
Simplon I and II	1906, 1922	Switzerland/Italy	19.3	12
Kanmon	1975	Japan	19.3	12
Apennine	1934	Italy	17.7	11
Rokko (rail)	1972	Japan	16	10
St Gotthard (rail)	1882	Switzerland	14.9	9.3
Mount MacDonald	1989	Canada	14.6	9.1
Lotschberg	1913	Switzerland	14.5	9
Cascade	1929	US	14.5	9
Hokuriku	1962	Japan	14.5	9
Fréjus (Mont Cenis)	1871	France/Italy	12.8	8
Shin Shimizu	1961	Japan	12.8	8
Flathead	1970	US	12.8	8
Aki	1975	Japan	12.8	8
Mont Blanc	1965	France/Italy	11.6	7.2
Rove	1927	France	7.1	4.4
San Fransisco Subway	1971	US	5.8	3.6
Mersey	1934	UK	4	2.5

The world's longest bridges[a]

Name	Date completed	Place	Length m	ft
Seto-Ohashi	1988	Japan	3 220	43 374
Akashi-Kaikyo	1998	Japan	1 990	6 529
Great Belt East	1997	Denmark	1 624	5 328
Humber	1981	UK	1 410	4 626
Tsing Ma	1997	Hong Kong	1 377	4 518
Verrazano-Narrows	1964	New York Harbor, US	1 298	4 260
Golden Gate	1937	San Francisco, US	1 280	4 200
Höga Kusten	1997	Sweden	1 210	3 970
Mackinac	1957	Michigan, US	1 158	3 800
Minami-Bisan-Seto	1988	Japan	1 100	3 609
Bosporus II	1988	Istanbul, Turkey	1 090	3 576
Bosporus I	1973	Istanbul, Turkey	1 074	3 524
George Washington Bridge	1931	New York City, US	1 067	3 500
Kurushima	1999	Japan	1 030	3 379
Rio Niteroi	1972	Brazil	1 025	3 363
Salazar/25 April	1966	Lisbon, Portugal	1 013	3 323
Forth Road Bridge	1964	Scotland, UK	1 006	3 300
Severn Bridge	1966	UK	988	3 241
Pierre Laporte	1970	Quebec, Canada	908	2 979
Tatara	1999	Japan	890	2 920
Save Bridge	1970	Mozambique	872	2 860
Tete	1971	Mozambique	872	2 860
Pont de Normandie	1995	France	856	2 808

[a] Figures are for main spans, excluding approach roads, etc.

COMPUTERS

Programming languages

Language	Derivation of name	Applications
Ada		A high-level procedural language designed for programming computers for real-time applications – more specifically, where the computer is controlling the behaviour of military devices.
ALGOL	(ALGOrithmic Language)	One of the first languages developed for mathematical and scientific use. It introduced a number of new concepts and has been very influential in the design of other languages.
Assembly language		A low-level language which is a notation for representing machine code in human-readable form.
BASIC	(Beginners' All-purpose Symbolic Instruction Code)	A simple high-level language that can be used for general-purpose computing, especially on microcomputers. Designed for beginners.
C		Provides all the structure of a high-level language with certain low-level features that do not require the programmer to use assembly language. It is fast and portable and is the language in which the UNIX operating system was developed.
C++		An object-orientated language that is a descendent of C but in the tradition of ALGOL.
COBOL	(COmmon Business Oriented Language)	A high-level language that is the standard for all business data processing.
FORTRAN	(FORmula TRANslation)	A high-level language widely used for scientific computing; current standard is FORTRAN 77, but dates from 1956.
HTML	Hypertext Markup Language	Language adopted in the 1990s for the creation of World Wide Web documents on the Internet.
Hypertalk		A scripting language that is the basis of Hypercard.
LISP	(LISt Processing)	A high-level functional language with the imperative features designed for the processing of non-numeric data. Used for symbolic manipulation and in Artificial Intelligence.
LOGO		A graphics language used mainly for teaching small children.
Machine code		A low-level language into which all high-level languages must be translated before they can run. Machine codes are specific to machines and are in fact a series of machine-readable instructions.
ML	(Meta Language)	A high-level functional language used mainly for research purposes.
Modula 2		A high-level imperative language, derived from Pascal, in which programs may be written in modular form, ie built up from independently-written modules.
Pascal		A high-level imperative language descended from ALGOL, originally designed for teaching purposes.
PROLOG	(PROgramming in LOGic)	A high-level declarative language, designed for use in Artificial Intelligence.
Smalltalk		One of the first object-orientated languages, developed at Xerox Palo Alto Research Center.

The development of computers

Name of instrument	Inventor	Date developed	Comments
Abacus		Middle Ages	Calculations performed by sliding counters
Mechanical adding machine	Blaise Pascal, France	1642	
Stepped reckoner	Gottfried Leibniz, Germany	1673	Mechanical instrument to multiply, divide and extract square roots as well as add
Analytical engine	Charles Babbage, Britain	1830	First automatic computer. Able to combine arithmetic processes with decisions based on own computations
Boolean algebra	George Boole, Britain	mid 19th century	Boole discovered analogy of algebraic symbols and those of logic. Binary logic operations brought about electronic computer switching theory and procedures
Data-processing cards	Hermann Hollerith, US	1890	Introduction of perforated cards with pattern of holes which could be read by machine designed to sort and manipulate the data represented by the holes
Prototype of electromechanical digital computer	John Atanasoff, US	1939	
Calculator	Howard Aiken, US	1939	
Automatic Sequence Controlled calculator (Harvard Mark I)	Howard Aiken, US	1944	Series of instructions coded on punched paper tape entered and output recorded on cards or by electric typewriter
Colossus	Alan Turing, Britain	1943	Special-purpose electronic computer designed to decipher codes
ENIAC (Electronic Numerical integrator and Calculator)	J Presper Eckert and John W Mauchly	1946	Marked the beginning of the first generation of modern computers. This was the first all-purpose electronic digital computer
Transistor	Shockley, Bardeen and Brattain	1948	Reliable with low power consumption
EDSAC	Cambridge University	1949	First working version of a stored-program computer
EDVAC (Electronic Discrete Variable Automatic Computer)	John Neumann	1950	Stored-program computer.
UNIVAC (Universal Automatic Computer)	Eckert and Mauchly	1951	Used memory system made of mercury delay lines which gave access time of 500 microseconds. First computer able to handle numerical and alphabetical data with equal ease
Harvard Mark III		mid 1950s	Magnetic drum memory provided large storage capacity
Integrated circuit (IC)		1960s/70s	Allowed construction of large-scale (mainframe) computers with high operating speeds
LSI (Large-scale Integration)		1960s/70s	Thousands of transistors and related devices could be packed onto a single integrated circuit
RAM (Random Access Memory)		1960s/70s	RAM chip used in constructing semiconductor memory units
PDP-8	DEC (Digital Equipment)	1963	First minicomputer

Name of instrument	Inventor	Date developed	Comments
IBM System/360	IBM	1964	First family of compatible computers launched
Control Data CD6000		1965	First supercomputer developed
Intel 4004	Marcian Hoff, US	1971	First microprocessor. (Integrated circuit with all arithmetic, logic and control circuitry to serve central processing unit (CPU)
Altair 8800		1975	First personal computer
Xerox Start System		1981	First windows, icons, menus, and pointing devices system developed
Osborne		1981	First portable computer
CD Rom		mid-1980s	Data storage up to 640 mbs
MP3	Fraunhofer IIS, Germany	1987	Audiodata compression algorithm; led to personal digital music players in 1990s
Optical microchip		1988	Used light instead of electricity
Wafer-scale silicon memory chip		1989	Able to store 200 million characters
CD-I player	Philips	1992	Provided compact disc interactive multimedia programs for home use
Pentium processor	Intel	1993	Highly integrated semiconductor device with external bus width of 64 bits, almost twice as fast as its predecessor
DVD		1996	Data and video storage up to 17 Gbs
USB (Universal Serial Bus)		1996	Interface standard for connecting devices to computers; permits 'hot-swapping'
Key-chain removable memory	Agaté Technologies	2001	Plugs into USB port and acts as hard drive with up to 2Gb capacity (by 2004)

SCIENCE AND TECHNOLOGY

SCIENTISTS AND INVENTORS

Name	Dates	Nationality	Field of work
Abel, Niels Henrik	1802–29	Norwegian	Mathematics
Abel, Sir Frederick Augustus	1827–1902	British	Chemistry
Abu Al-Wafa	940–98	Persian	Mathematics, astronomy
Achard, Franz Karl	1753–1821	German	Chemistry
Adams, John Couch	1819–92	British	Astronomy
Ader, Clément	1841–1926	French	Engineering; constructed first aeroplane to make a powered take-off
Adrian, Edgar Douglas, Baron	1889–1977	British	Physiology
Agassiz, Jean Louis Rodolphe	1807–73	Swiss	Natural history
Agnesi, Maria Gaetana	1718–99	Italian	Mathematics, philosophy
Agricola, Georgius	1494–1555	German	Medicine, mineralogy
Aiken, Howard Hathaway	1900–73	American	Mathematics
Airy, Sir George Biddell	1801–92	British	Astronomy
Alfven, Hannes Olof Gösta	1908–95	Swedish	Astrophysics
Al-Khwarizmi, Muhammed Ibn Musa	c.780–c.850	Arabic	Mathematics
Alvarez, Luis Walter	1911–88	American	Physics
Ambartsumian, Viktor Amazaspovich	1908–96	Russian	Astrophysics
Amici, Giovanni Battista	1786–1863	Italian	Astronomy, microscopy, optical instruments
Ampère, André Marie	1775–1836	French	Physics; laid foundations of electrodynamics
Anderson, Carl David	1905–91	American	Physics
Ångström, Anders Jonas	1814–74	Swedish	Physics, astronomy
Apollonius of Perga	c.261–c.190–BC	Greek	Mathematics
Appert, Nicolas	1750–1841	French	Inventions; pioneered food preservation
Arago, Dominique François Jean	1786–1853	French	Astronomy, physics
Archer, Frederick Scott	1813–57	British	Inventions
Archimedes	c.287–c.212–BC	Greek	Mathematics, inventions; invented Archimedes' screw for raising water and discovered formulae for areas and volumes of various figures
Aristarchus of Samos	c.310–230–BC	Greek	Astronomy
Arkwright, Sir Richard	1732–92	British	Inventions, devised first cotton-spinning machine, 1768
Armstrong, Edwin Howard	1890–1954	American	Electrical engineering
Armstrong, William George, Baron	1810–1900	British	Engineering
Arrhenius, Svante August	1859–1927	Swedish	Physics, chemistry
Arrowsmith, Aaron	1750–1823	British	Cartography
Aston, Francis William	1877–1945	British	Chemistry
Audubon, John James	1785–1851	American	Natural history
Avery, Oswald Theodore	1877–1955	Canadian	Bacteriology
Avogadro, Amedeo	1776–1856	Italian	Physics
Babbage, Charles	1792–1871	British	Mathematics, inventions; built early calculating machines
Bacon, Roger	c. 1214–c. 1292	English	General science; investigated alchemy, optics, and possibility of flying machines
Baer, Karl Ernst von	1792–1876	Russian	Embryology
Baeyer, Adolf von	1835–1917	German	Chemistry
Baily, Francis	1774–1844	British	Astronomy
Baird, John Logie	1888–1946	British	Electrical engineering; gave first demonstration of television, 1926
Baker, Sir Benjamin	1840–1907	British	Civil engineering
Bakewell, Robert	1725–95	British	Agriculture
Banks, Sir Joseph	1743–1820	British	Botany
Bardeen, John	1908–91	American	Physics; helped develop point-contact transistor, 1947, and published theory of superconductivity, 1972
Barkhausen, Heinrich	1881–1956	German	Physics
Barnard, Edward Emerson	1857–1923	American	Astronomy
Baskerville, John	1706–75	British	Printing
Bates, Henry Walter	1825–92	British	Natural history
Bateson, William	1861–1926	British	Biology
Baylis, Trevor	1937–	British	Engineering; invented clockwork radio

Name	Dates	Nationality	Field of work
Beadle, George Wells	1903–89	American	Genetics
Becquerel, Henri	1852–1908	French	Physics; discovered radioactivity
Beebe, Charles William	1877–1962	American	Natural history
Bell, Alexander Graham	1847–1922	British	Inventions; invented the telephone, 1875
Benz, Karl	1844–1929	German	Engineering
Bergius, Friedrich	1884–1949	German	Chemistry
Berners-Lee, Tim	1955–	British	Computing; invented World Wide Web
Bernoulli, Jacques, Jean, and Daniel	1654–1705 1667–1748 1700–82	Swiss	Mathematics
Berthelot, Marcelin	1827–1907	French	Chemistry
Berthollet Claude Louis Comte	1748–1822	French	Chemistry, physics
Berzelius, Jöns Jakob, Baron	1779–1848	Swedish	Chemistry
Bessemer, Sir Henry	1813–98	British	Engineering, inventions; invented process for turning pig-iron into steel
Bethe, Hans Albrecht	1906–	American	Physics
Bhoskhara II	1114–c. 1185	Indian	Mathematics
Birkhoff, George David	1864–1944	American	Mathematics
Bjerknes, Vilhelm Friman Koren	1862–1951	Norwegian	Meteorology, physics
Black, Joseph	1728–99	British	Physics, chemistry
Blackett, Patrick Maynard Stuart Baron	1897–1974	British	Physics
Blenkinsop, John	1783–1831	British	Engineering
Bloch, Felix	1905–83	American	Physics
Bodoni, Giambattista	1740–1813	Italian	Printing
Bohr, Niels Henrik David	1885–1962	Danish	Physics; extended theory of atomic structure
Boltzmann, Ludwig Eduard	1844–1906	Austrian	Physics; established Boltzmann's law on the equipartition of energy and laid foundation of statistical mechanics
Bolyai, János	1802–60	Hungarian	Mathematics
Bondi, Sir Hermann	1919–2005	British	Cosmology, mathematics
Bonnet, Charles	1720–93	Swiss	Natural history
Boole, George	1815–64	British	Mathematics; wrote pioneering works on modern symbolic logic
Bordet, Jules Jean Baptiste Vincent	1870–1961	Belgian	Bacteriology
Borlaug, Norman	1914–	American	Plant breeding
Born, Max	1882–1970	British	Physics
Bosch, Carl	1874–1940	German	Chemistry
Bose, Sir Jagadis Chandra	1858–1937	Indian	Plant physiology, physics
Bothe, Walther Wilhelm Georg Franz	1891–1957	German	Physics
Boveri, Theodor Heinrich	1862–1915	German	Cell biology
Bovet, Daniel	1907–92	Swiss	Pharmacology
Bowen, Norman Levi	1887–1956	Canadian	Petrology
Bower, Frederick Orpen	1855–1948	British	Botany
Boyd Orr of Brechin Mearns, John, Baron	1880–1971	British	Biology
Boyle, Robert	1627–91	Irish	Physics, chemistry, formulated Boyle's law, stating that the pressure and volume of a gas are inversely proportional, 1662
Bragg, Sir William Henry	1862–1942	British	Physics
Brahe, Tycho	1546–1601	Danish	Astronomy
Braille, Louis	1809–52	French	Inventions; devised system of writing and printing for the blind
Bramah, Joseph	1748–1814	British	Engineering, inventions
Brattain, Walter Houser	1902–87	American	Physics; helped develop point-contact transistor and studied semiconductors
Brewster, Sir David	1781–1868	British	Physics
Bridgman, Percy Williams	1882–1961	American	Physics
Briggs, Henry	1561–1630	English	Mathematics
Brindley, James	1716–72	British	Civil engineering; designed canals
Bronowski, Jacob	1908–74	British	Mathematics
Brouwer, Luitzen Egbertus Jan	1881–1966	Dutch	Mathematics
Brown, Robert	1773–1858	British	Botany
Brunel, Isambard Kingdom	1806–59	British	Engineering; designed steamships, bridges, and worked on the Great Western Railway

SCIENCE AND TECHNOLOGY

Scientists and inventors (continued)

Name	Dates	Nationality	Field of work
Buffon, Georges Louis Leclerc, Comte de	1707–88	French	Natural history
Bunsen, Robert Wilhelm	1811–99	German	Chemistry; invented Bunsen burner
Burbank, Luther	1849–1926	American	Plant breeding
Burge, Joost	1552–1632	Swiss	Mathematics
Bushnell, David	1742–1824	American	Inventions; constructed first submarine
Calmette, Albert Léon Charles	1863–1933	French	Bacteriology
Calvin, Melvin	1911–97	American	Biochemistry
Candela, Felix	1910–	Mexican	Engineering
Cannizzaro, Stanislao	1826–1910	Italian	Chemistry
Cantor, Georg	1845–1918	Russian	Mathematics
Cardano, Girolamo	1501–76	Italian	Mathematics
Carnot, Sadi	1796–1832	French	General science
Carrel, Alexis	1873–1944	French	Surgery
Cartwright, Edmund	1743–1823	British	Inventions; invented power loom, 1785–90
Carver, George Washington	1864–1943	American	Agriculture
Cauchy, Augustin Louis, Baron	1789–1857	French	Mathematics
Cavendish, Henry	1731–1810	British	Physics
Caxton, William	c.1442–91	English	Printing; set up first English press, 1476
Cayley, Arthur	1821–95	British	Mathematics
Cayley, Sir George	1773–1857	British	Engineering; designed early flying machines
Chadwick, Sir James	1891–1974	British	Physics
Chain, Sir Ernst Boris	1906–79	British	Biochemistry
Chamberlain, Owen	1920–	American	Physics
Chandrasekhar, Subrahmanyan	1910–95	American	Astronomy
Chebishev, Pafnuti Lvovich	1821–94	Russian	Mathematics
Cherenkov, Pavel Alekseievich	1904–90	Russian	Physics
Clausius, Rudolf Julius Emanuel	1822–88	German	Physics
Cockcroft, Sir John Douglas	1897–1967	British	Physics; pioneered use of particle accelerators
Cohn, Ferdinand Julius	1839–84	German	Botany
Coke, Thomas William, of Holkham, Earl of Leicester	1752–1842	British	Agriculture
Compton, Arthur Holly	1892–1962	American	Physics
Copernicus, Nicolas	1473–1543	Polish	Astronomy; put forward theory that the Earth rotates about the Sun, 1543
Cornforth, Sir John Warcup	1917–	Australian	Chemistry
Correns, Carl Erich	1864–1933	German	Botany, genetics
Cort, Henry	1740–1800	British	Inventions; devised puddling process for converting pig-iron to wrought iron
Coulomb, Charles Augustin de	1736–1806	French	Physics
Creed, Frederick	1871–1957	Canadian	Inventions
Crick, Francis Harry Compton	1916–2004	British	Biophysics; collaborated in development of molecular model of DNA, 1953
Crompton, Samuel	1753–1827	British	Inventions; invented spinning-mule for yarn, 1779
Crookes, Sir William	1832–1919	British	Physics
Culpeper, Nicholas	1616–54	English	Astrology, herbalism
Curie, Marie	1867–1934	Polish	Chemistry; studied radioactivity, discovering radium and isolating plutonium, 1910
Curie, Pierre	1859–1906	French	Physics
Curtiss, Glenn	1878–1930	American	Aviation, aeronautical engineering
Cuvier, Georges, Baron	1769–1832	French	Zoology; originated system of animal classification and established sciences of palaeontology and comparative anatomy
Daguerre, Louis-Jacques-Mandé	1789–1851	French	Photography
Daimler, Gottlieb	1834–1900	German	Inventions; patented high-speed internal combustion engine, 1885
d'Alembert, Jean Le Rond	1717–83	French	Mathematics
Dalton, John	1766–1844	British	Chemistry
Dam, Carl Peter Henrik	1895–1976	Danish	Biochemistry

Name	Dates	Nationality	Field of work
Daniell, John Frederic	1790–1845	British	Chemistry
Darwin, Charles Robert	1809–82	British	Natural history; developed theory of natural selection to explain the origin of species
Daubenton, Louis Jean Marie	1716–1800	French	Natural history
Davenport, Charles Benedict	1866–1944	American	Zoology
Davy, Sir Humphry	1778–1829	British	Chemistry, inventions; discovered potassium, sodium, barium, strontium, calcium, and magnesium and invented miners' safety lamp, 1815
De Bary, Heinrich Anton	1831–88	German	Botany
Debye, Peter Joseph Wilhelm	1884–1966	Dutch	Physics, chemistry
Dedekind, Richard	1831–1916	German	Mathematics
de Duve, Christian	1917–	Belgian	Biochemistry
De Forest, Lee	1873–1961	American	Electrical engineering
de La Rue, Warren	1815–89	British	Astronomy
De Morgan, Augustus	1806–71	British	Mathematics, logic
de Vries, Hugo Marie	1848–1935	Dutch	Botany
Diels, Otto Paul Hermann	1876–1954	German	Chemistry
Diophantus of Alexandria	3rd century	Greek	Mathematics
Dioscorides Pedanius	c.40–c.90	Greek	Medicine
Dirac, Paul Adrien Maurice	1902–84	British	Physics
Dobzhansky, Theodosius	1900–75	American	Genetics
Doppler, Christian Johann	1803–53	Austrian	Physics; explained Doppler effect concerning perceived frequency variation of sound and light waves
Dreyer, Johan Ludvig Emil	1852–1926	Danish	Astronomy
Driesch, Hans Adolf Eduard	1867–1941	German	Zoology
Du Mont, Allen Balcom	1901–65	American	Engineering
Dunlop, John Boyd	1840–1921	British	Inventions; invented pneumatic tyre, c.1887
Eads, John Buchanan	1820–87	American	Civil engineering
Eckert, John Presper	1919–95	American	Electronics engineering
Eddington, Sir Arthur Stanley	1882–1944	British	Astronomy
Edison, Thomas Alva	1847–1931	American	Inventions, invented phonograph, 1877, carbon-filament light bulb, 1879, and motion picture equipment and discovered thermionic emission, 1883
Eichler, August Wilhelm	1839–87	German	Botany
Einstein, Albert	1879–1955	German	Physics; proposed special theory of relativity, 1905, general theory of relativity, 1916, and sought to prove unified field theory linking the general theory and quantum theory, 1950
Elton, Charles	1900–91	British	Zoology
Enders, John Franklin	1897–1985	American	Microbiology
Endlicher, Stephan Ladislaus	1804–49	Hungarian	Botany
Engler, Gustav Heinrich Adolf	1844–1930	German	Botany
Eratosthenes of Cyrene	c.276–c.194–BC	Greek	Astronomy
Ericsson, John	1803–89	American	Naval engineering
Euclid	c.300–BC	Greek	Mathematics
Eudoxus of Cnidus	c.408–c.355–BC	Greek	Astronomy, mathematics
Euler, Leonhard	1707–83	Swiss	Mathematics, physics, astronomy; wrote standard works on calculus and algebra
Evans, Oliver	1755–1819	American	Engineering
Fabre, Jean Henri	1823–1915	French	Entomology
Fabry, Charles	1867–1945	French	Physics
Faraday, Michael	1791–1867	British	Chemistry, physics; studied electricity, electrolysis, and the relationship between electricity and magnetism
Fermat, Pierre de	1601–65	French	Mathematics; proposed Fermat's principle in optics and laid foundation of probability theory
Fermi, Enrico	1901–54	American	Physics; played prominent role in developing atomic energy
Feynman, Richard Phillips	1918–88	American	Physics

SCIENCE AND TECHNOLOGY

Scientists and inventors (continued)

Name	Dates	Nationality	Field of work
Fibonacci, Leonardo	c.1170–c.1230	Italian	Mathematics
Finsen, Niels Ryberg	1860–1904	Danish	Medicine
Fischer, Emil Hermann	1852–1919	German	Chemistry
Fitzgerald, George Francis	1851–1901	Irish	Physics
Flamsteed, John	1646–1719	English	Astronomy
Fleming, Sir Alexander	1881–1955	British	Bacteriology, discovered penicillin, 1928
Fleming, Sir John Ambrose	1849–1945	British	Electrical engineering
Fokker, Anthony Hermann Gerard	1890–1939	Dutch	Aeronautical engineering
Foucault, Jean Bernard Léon	1819–68	French	Physics; determined the velocity of light, 1850, proved the Earth rotates, 1851, invented the gyroscope, 1852, and improved mirrors for reflecting telescopes, 1858
Fourier, Jean Baptiste Joseph, Baron	1768–1830	French	Mathematics, physics
Fourneyron, Benoît	1802–67	French	Engineering
Franck, James	1882–1964	American	Physics
Fraunhofer, Joseph von	1787–1826	German	Physics
Frege, Gottlob	1848–1925	German	Mathematics, logic
Fresnel, Augustin Jean	1788–1827	French	Physics
Frisch, Karl von	1886–1982	Austrian	Zoology
Fulton, Robert	1765–1815	American	Inventions; invented torpedo and developed paddle-wheel steamboat, 1807
Fust, Johann	1400–66	German	Printing
Gabor, Dennis	1900–79	British	Electrical engineering
Galileo Galilei	1564–1642	Italian	Mathematics, physics, astronomy; improved refracting telescope, 1610, and established laws concerning gravity and weight
Galle, Johann Gottfried	1812–1910	German	Astronomy
Galois, Évariste	1811–32	French	Mathematics
Galton, Sir Francis	1822–1911	British	Eugenics
Galvani, Luigi	1737–98	Italian	Medicine; investigated effects of electrostatic stimuli upon muscles
Gassendi, Pierre	1592–1655	French	Physics
Gauss, Carl Friedrich	1777–1855	German	Mathematics; wrote first modern book on number theory and applied mathematics to gravitation, magnetism, and electricity
Gay-Lussac, Joseph Louis	1778–1850	French	Chemistry, physics; proposed Gay-Lussac law of combining volumes of gases, 1808
Geber	14th century	Spanish	Alchemy
Geiger, Hans	1882–1945	German	Physics; invented Geiger counter to measure radioactivity
Gell-Mann, Murray	1929–	American	Physics
Geoffroy Saint-Hilaire, Étienne	1772–1844	French	Natural history
Gesner, Conrad	1516–65	Swiss	Physics
Gibbs, Josiah Willard	1839–1903	American	Physics
Gilbert, William	1544–1603	English	Physics
Goddard, Robert Hutchings	1882–1945	American	Physics
Gödel, Kurt	1906–78	American	Mathematics
Gold, Thomas	1920–2004	Austrian	Astronomy
Goldschmidt, Richard Benedict	1878–1958	American	Genetics
Graham, Thomas	1805–69	British	Physics
Gray, Asa	1810–88	American	Botany
Gregory, James	1638–75	Scottish	Mathematics, astronomy
Guericke, Otto von	1602–86	German	Physics
Gutenberg, Johannes	c.1400–c.1468	German	Printing
Haber, Fritz	1868–1934	German	Chemistry, inventions
Haeckel, Ernst Heinrich	1834–1919	German	Zoology
Hahn, Otto	1879–1968	German	Chemistry, physics
Halley, Edmond	1656–1742	English	Astronomy
Hamilton, Sir William Rowan	1805–65	Irish	Mathematics
Hardy, Godfrey Harold	1877–1947	British	Mathematics
Hargreaves, James	c.1720–78	British	Inventions; invented spinning jenny, c. 1764

Name	Dates	Nationality	Field of work
Hawking, Stephen	1942–	British	Physics, cosmology; wrote best-selling *A Brief History of Time*, 1988
Haworth, Sir Walter Norman	1883–1950	British	Biochemistry
Heaviside, Oliver	1850–1925	British	Physics; predicted existence of ionosphere
Heisenberg, Werner Karl	1901–76	German	Physics
Helmholtz, Hermann von	1821–94	German	Physics, physiology; proposed law of the conservation of energy
Helmont, Jan Baptist van	1580–1644	Belgian	Alchemy, medicine
Henry, Joseph	1797–1878	American	Physics
Hermite, Charles	1822–1901	French	Mathematics
Hero of Alexandria	1st century	Greek	Engineering, mathematics
Herschel, Sir William	1738–1822	British	Astronomy; discovered Uranus, 1781
Hertz, Heinrich Rudolf	1857–94	German	Physics
Hess, Victor Francis	1883–1964	American	Physics
Hevesy, George Charles de	1885–1966	Hungarian	Chemistry
Hilbert, David	1862–1943	German	Mathematics
Hinshelwood, Sir Cyril Norman	1897–1967	British	Chemistry
Hipparchus	c.190–c.120–BC	Greek	Astronomy
Hodgkin, Sir Alan Lloyd	1914–98	British	Physiology
Hodgkin, Dorothy Mary Crowfoot	1910–94	British	Biochemistry
Hofmeister, Wilhelm Friedrich Benedict	1824–77	German	Botany
Hooke, Robert	1635–1703	English	Physics
Hooker, Sir William Jackson	1785–1865	British	Botany
Hopkins, Sir Frederick Gowland	1861–1947	British	Biochemistry
Hopkinson, John	1849–98	British	Physics, electrical engineering
Howe, Elias	1819–67	American	Inventions; patented first sewing machine, 1846
Hoyle, Sir Fred	1915–2001	British	Astronomy
Hubble, Edwin Powell	1889–1953	American	Astronomy
Huggins, Sir William	1824–1910	British	Astronomy
Hutton, James	1726–97	British	Medicine
Huxley, Thomas Henry	1825–95	British	Biology
Huygens, Christiaan	1629–95	Dutch	Astronomy, physics
Ilyushin, Sergei Vladimirovich	1894–1977	Russian	Aeronautical engineering
Ingenhousz, Jan	1730–99	Dutch	Medicine, plant physiology
Ipatieff, Vladimir Nikolaievich	1867–1952	American	Physics
Jacquard, Joseph-Marie	1752–1834	French	Inventions; Jacquard silk-weaving loom
Jansky, Karl Guthe	1905–50	American	Radio engineering
Jeans, Sir James Hopwood	1877–1946	British	Mathematics, astronomy
Jenson, Nicolas	c.1420–80	French	Printing
Johannsen, Wilhelm Ludvig	1857–1927	Danish	Genetics
Joliot-Curie, Frédéric	1900–59	French	Physics
Joliot-Curie, Irène	1896–1956	French	Physics
Josephson, Brian David	1940–	British	Physics; deduced Josephson effect in superconductivity
Joule, James Prescott	1818–89	British	Physics; established mechanical equivalent of heat and worked on refrigeration
Jussieu, Bernard and Antoine	c.1699–1777 1748–1836	French	Botany
Kapitza, Peter Leonidovich	1894–1984	Russian	Physics
Kay, John	1704–c.1764	British	Inventions; patented flying-shuttle, 1733
Kekulé von Stradonitz, Friedrich August	1829–96	German	Chemistry
Kelvin, William Thomson, Baron	1824–1907	British	Mathematics, physics; helped develop law of the conservation of energy and the absolute temperature (Kelvin) scale
Kendall, Edward Calvin	1886–1972	American	Biochemistry
Kendrew, Sir John Cowdery	1917–97	British	Biochemistry
Kennelly, Arthur Edwin	1861–1939	American	Electrical engineering
Kepler, Johannes	1571–1630	German	Astronomy
Khorana, Har Gobind	1922–	American	Biochemistry
Kidinnu	4th century –BC	Babylonian	Mathematics, astronomy
Kinsey, Alfred	1894–1956	American	Zoology, sociology; produced studies on human sexuality, 1948 and 1953

Scientists and inventors (continued)

Name	Dates	Nationality	Field of work
Kirchhoff, Gustav Robert	1824–87	German	Physics
Klaproth, Martin Heinrich	1743–1817	German	Chemistry
Koch, Robert	1843–1910	German	Bacteriology
Kolbe, Hermann	1818–84	German	Chemistry
Kolmogorov, Andrei Nikolaevich	1903–87	Russian	Mathematics
Koroliov, Sergei Pavlovich	1906–66	Russian	Aeronautical engineering
Krebs, Sir Hans Adolf	1900–81	British	Physiology
Kurchatov, Igor Vasilievich	1903–60	Russian	Physics
Lagrange, Joseph Louis, Comte de	1736–1813	French	Mathematics, astronomy
Lalande, Joseph-Jérôme le Français de	1732–1807	French	Astronomy
Lamarck, Jean-Baptiste de Monet, Chevalier de	1744–1829	French	Natural history; postulated theory of inheritance of acquired characteristics
Lambert, Johann Heinrich	1728–77	German	Mathematics, astronomy
Land, Edwin Herbert	1909–91	American	Inventions; Land Polaroid camera, 1947
Landau, Lev Davidovich	1908–68	Russian	Physics
Langley, Samuel Pierpont	1834–1906	American	Astronomy
Langmuir, Irving	1881–1957	American	Chemistry
Lankester, Sir Edwin Ray	1847–1929	British	Zoology
Laplace, Pierre Simon, Marquis de	1749–1827	French	Mathematics, astronomy
Lartet, Édouard Armand Isidore Hippolyte	1801–71	French	Archaeology
Laue, Max Theodor Felix von	1879–1960	German	Physics
Lavoisier, Antoine Laurent	1743–94	French	Chemistry; showed that air is mixture of oxygen and nitrogen, 1788, now recognized as father of modern chemistry
Lawes, Sir John Bennet	1814–1900	British	Agriculture
Lawrence, Ernest Orlando	1901–58	American	Physics
Le Châtelier, Henri-Louis	1850–1936	French	Chemistry
Lecoq de Boisbaudran, Paul-Émile	1838–1912	French	Chemistry
Lederberg, Joshua	1925–	American	Genetics
Lee, Tsung-Dao	1926–	American	Physics
Leeuwenhoek, Antonie van	1632–1723	Dutch	Microscopy
Legendre, Adrien Marie	1752–1833	French	Mathematics
Lemaître, Georges Édouard, Abbé	1894–1966	Belgian	Astronomy
Lesseps, Ferdinand de	1805–94	French	Civil engineering; constructed Suez Canal, 1860–9, and began Panama Canal, 1881
Leuckart, Karl Georg Friedrich Rudolph	1822–98	German	Zoology
Leverrier, Urbain Jean Joseph	1811–77	French	Astronomy
Libby, Willard Frank	1908–80	American	Chemistry
Liebig, Justus, Baron von	1803–73	German	Chemistry
Lilienthal, Otto	1848–96	German	Aeronautical engineering
Linnaeus, Carolus (Carl von Linné)	1707–78	Swedish	Botany; founder of modern taxonomic botany
Liouville, Joseph	1809–82	French	Mathematics
Lippershey, Hans	c.1570–c.1619	Dutch	optics
Lipscomb, William Nunn	1919–	American	Chemistry
Lobachevski, Nikolai Ivanovich	1793–1856	Russian	Mathematics
Lockyer, Sir Joseph Norman	1836–1920	British	Astronomy
Lodge, Sir Oliver Joseph	1851–1940	British	Physics; pioneered radio-telegraphy
Loeb, Jacques	1859–1924	American	Zoology
Lonsdale, Dame Kathleen	1903–71	Irish	Physics
Lorentz, Hendrick Antoon	1853–1928	Dutch	Physics
Lorenz, Konrad	1903–89	Austrian	Zoology
Lovell, Sir Bernard	1913–	British	Astronomy
Lowell, Percival	1855–1916	American	Astronomy
Lumière, Auguste and Louis	1862–1954 1864–1948	French	Photography
Lyell, Sir Charles	1797–1875	British	Geology
Lysenko, Trofim Denisovich	1898–1976	Russian	Genetics; proposed now discredited theory that heredity can be changed by good husbandry
McAdam, John Loudon	1756–1836	British	Inventions; introduced macadamized roads

Name	Dates	Nationality	Field of work
Mach, Ernst	1838–1916	Austrian	Physics; worked on aeronautical design and the science of projectiles
Macintosh, Charles	1766–1843	British	Chemistry
McMillan, Edwin Mattison	1907–91	American	Physics
Macmillan, Kirkpatrick	1813–78	British	Inventions; constructed the first bicycle
Marconi, Guglielmo	1874–1937	Italian	Electrical engineering; made first successful experiments in wireless telegraphy, 1895
Markov, Andrei Andreevich	1856–1922	Russian	Mathematics
Martin, Archer John Porter	1910–	British	Biochemistry
Martin, Pierre-Émile	1824–1915	French	Engineering
Maudslay, Henry	1771–1831	British	Engineering
Maupertius, Pierre Louis Moreau de	1698–1759	French	Mathematics
Maxim, Sir Hiram Stevens	1840–1916	British	Inventions; perfected Maxim machine-gun, 1883
Maxwell, James Clerk	1831–79	British	Physics; proposed theory of electro-magnetic radiation
Mayer, Julius Robert Von	1814–78	German	Physics
Mayo, Charles Horace and William James	1865–1939 1861–1939	American	Medical research; founders of the Mayo Clinic, 1905
Meitner, Lise	1878–1968	Austrian	Physics
Mendel, Gregor Johann	1822–84	Austrian	Biology, botany; established basis for modern genetics
Mendeleyev, Dimitrii Ivanovich	1834–1907	Russian	Chemistry
Mercator, Gerardus	1512–94	Flemish	Mathematics, geography, cartography; introduced Mercator map projection to aid navigators, 1569
Messier, Charles	1730–1817	French	Astronomy
Metchnikov, Ilya Ilich	1845–1916	Russian	Zoology
Meyerhof, Otto Fritz	1884–1951	American	Biochemistry
Michelson, Albert Abraham	1852–1931	American	Physics
Millikan, Robert Andrews	1868–1953	American	Physics
Mitchell, Reginald Joseph	1895–1937	British	Aeronautical engineering
Monge, Gaspard	1746–1818	French	Mathematics
Monod, Jacques-Lucien	1910–76	French	Biochemistry
Montgolfier, Joseph Michel and Jacques-Étienne	1740–1810 1745–99	French	Inventions; made first manned flight, in a balloon, 1783
Morgan, Thomas Hunt	1866–1945	American	Genetics
Morley, Edward Williams	1838–1923	American	Chemistry
Morris, Desmond John	1928–	British	Zoology
Morse, Samuel Finley Breese	1791–1872	American	Inventions; inaugurated first experimental telegraph line, 1844
Moseley, Henry Gwyn Jeffries	1887–1915	British	Physics
Muller, Hermann Joseph	1890–1967	American	Genetics
Muller, Paul Hermann	1899–1965	Swiss	Chemistry
Mulliken, Robert Sanderson	1896–1986	American	Chemistry, physics
Napier, John	1550–1617	Scottish	Mathematics; invented logarithms and Napier's bones calculating machine
Nernst, Walther Hermann	1864–1941	German	Physical chemistry
Neumann, John von	1903–57	American	Mathematics
Newcomen, Thomas	1663–1729	English	Inventions; designed first steam engine
Newton, Sir Isaac	1642–1727	English	Physics and mathematics; developed theory of gravitation and defined the laws of motion as well as working on optics and calculus
Nicholson, William	1753–1815	British	Chemistry
Nirenberg, Marshall Warren	1927–	American	Biochemistry
Nobel, Alfred Bernhard	1833–96	Swedish	Chemistry; invented dynamite, 1866, and left money for annual Nobel Prizes
Noble, Sir Andrew	1831–1915	British	Physics
Nostradamus	1503–66	French	Medicine, astrology
Oersted, Hans Christian	1777–1851	Danish	Physics
Ohm, Georg Simon	1787–1854	German	Physics
Olbers, Heinrich Wilhelm Matthäus	1758–1840	German	Astronomy
Oliphant, Sir Mark Laurence Elwin	1901–2000	Australian	Physics
Onsager, Lars	1903–76	American	Chemistry

Scientists and inventors (continued)

Name	Dates	Nationality	Field of work
Oppenheimer, J Robert	1904–67	American	Physics; directed Los Alamos atom bomb laboratory, 1943–5
Ostwald, Wilhelm	1853–1932	German	Chemistry
Otis, Elisha Graves	1811–61	American	Inventions; designed elevator, 1853
Otto, Nikolaus August	1832–91	German	Engineering
Pappus of Alexandria	3rd century–BC	Greek	Mathematics
Parsons, Sir Charles Algernon	1854–1931	British	Engineering
Pascal, Blaise	1623–62	French	Mathematics, physics; invented calculating machine, barometer, hydraulic press, and the syringe
Pasteur, Louis	1822–95	French	Chemistry, microbiology; established that putrefaction and fermentation are caused by micro-organisms and developed practice of pasteurization
Pauli, Wolfgang	1900–58	American	Physics; formulated exclusion principle in atomic physics and predicted existence of neutrino
Pauling, Linus Carl	1901–94	American	Chemistry
Pelletier, Pierre Joseph	1788–1842	French	Chemistry
Penney, William George, Baron	1909–91	British	Mathematics
Perkin, Sir William Henry	1838–1907	British	Chemistry
Perrin, Jean-Baptiste	1870–1942	French	Physics
Piccard, Auguste Antoine and Jean Felix	1884–1962 1884–1963	Swiss	Physics, chemistry; explored the stratosphere by balloon and the ocean depths by bathyscaphe
Planck, Max Karl Ernst Ludwig	1858–1947	German	Physics; introduced the quantum theory, 1900
Poincaré, Jules Henri	1854–1912	French	Mathematics
Poisson, Siméon Dénis	1781–1840	French	Mathematics
Popov, Aleksandr Stepanovich	1859–1905	Russian	Physics
Powell, Cecil Frank	1903–69	British	Physics
Prandtl, Ludwig	1875–1953	German	Physics
Priestley, Joseph	1733–1804	British	Chemistry; discovered oxygen
Proust, Joseph-Louis	1754–1826	French	Chemistry
Prout, William	1785–1850	British	Chemistry, physiology
Prusiner, Stanley B	1942–	American	Neurologist; discovered the disease-causing agent known as a prion
Ptolemy (Claudius Ptolemaeus)	2nd century	Egyptian	Mathematics, astronomy, geography
Purcell, Edward Mills	1912–97	American	Physics
Rabi, Isidor Isaac	1898–1988	American	Physics
Raman, Sir Chandrasekhara Venkata	1888–1970	Indian	Physics
Ramsay, Sir William	1852–1916	British	Chemistry; discovered argon, 1894, and identified helium, neon, krypton, and xenon
Ray, John	1627–1705	English	Natural history
Rayleigh, John William Strutt, Baron	1842–1919	British	Physics
Réaumur, René-Antoine Ferchault de	1683–1757	French	Physics
Reber, Grote	1911–	American	Astronomy
Regiomontanus	1436–76	German	Astronomy, mathematics
Rennie, John	1761–1821	British	Civil engineering
Rheticus	1514–76	German	Mathematics
Rhine, Joseph Banks	1895–1980	American	Psychology
Riemann, Georg Friedrich Bernhard	1826–66	German	Mathematics
Robinson, Sir Robert	1886–1975	British	Chemistry
Roebling, John Augustus	1806–69	American	Engineering
Röntgen, Wilhelm Konrad von	1845–1923	German	Physics; discovered X-rays, 1895
Rosse, William Parsons, 3rd Earl of	1800–67	Irish	Astronomy
Rumford, Benjamin Thompson, Count	1753–1814	American	General science
Rutherford, Ernest, Baron	1871–1937	British	Physics; developed modern concept of the atom
Ryle, Sir Martin	1918–84	British	Astronomy
Sabatier, Paul	1854–1941	French	Chemistry
Sakharov, Andrei Dimitrievich	1921–1989	Russian	Physics

Name	Dates	Nationality	Field of work
Salk, Jonas Edward	1914–95	American	Virology; developed first polio vaccine
Sandage, Allan Rex	1926–	American	Astronomy
Sanger, Frederick	1918–	British	Biochemistry
Savery, Thomas	c.1650–1715	English	Engineering; patented first practical steam engine, 1698
Scheele, Carl Wilhelm	1742–86	Swedish	Chemistry
Schleiden, Matthias Jakob	1804–81	German	Botany
Schrödinger, Erwin	1887–1961	Austrian	Physics; proposed wave equation in quantum mechanics, 1926
Schwann, Theodor	1810–82	German	Physiology
Seaborg, Glenn Theodore	1912–99	American	Physics
Segrè, Emilio	1905–89	American	Physics
Sherrington, Sir Charles Scott	1857–1952	British	Physiology
Shockley, William Bradford	1910–89	American	Physics; devised junction transistor
Sholes, Christopher Latham	1819–90	American	Inventions; invented typewriter
Shrapnel, Henry	1761–1842	British	Inventions; invented shrapnel shell
Siemens, Ernst Werner von	1816–92	German	Electrical engineering
Sikorsky, Igor Ivan	1889–1972	American	Aeronautical engineering; developed first successful helicopter, 1939
Simpson, George Gaylord	1902–84	American	Palaeontology
Singer, Isaac Merrit	1811–75	American	Inventions; designed improved sewing machine, 1852
Sloane, Sir Hans	1660–1753	English	Physics, natural history
Soddy, Frederick	1877–1956	British	Chemistry
Sommerfeld, Arnold Johannes Wilhelm	1868–1951	German	Physics
Sosigenes of Alexandria	1st century–BC	Greek	Astronomy
Spallanzani, Lazzaro	1729–99	Italian	Physiology
Stahl, Georg Ernst	1660–1734	German	Physics, chemistry
Staudinger, Hermann	1881–1965	German	Chemistry
Steinmetz, Charles Proteus	1865–1923	American	Electrical engineering
Stephenson, George	1781–1848	British	Engineering; constructed *Rocket* locomotive, 1829
Stirling, James	1692–1770	Scottish	Mathematics
Stokes, Sir George Gabriel	1819–1903	British	Physics, mathematics
Struve, Otto	1897–1963	American	Astronomy
Sutton, Walter Stanborough	1877–1916	American	Genetics
Swammerdam, Jan	1637–80	Dutch	Natural history, microscopy
Swan, Sir Joseph Wilson	1828–1914	British	Physics
Szent-Györgyi, Albert	1893–1986	American	Biochemistry
Szilard, Leo	1898–1964	American	Physics
Talbot, William Henry Fox	1800–77	British	Botany, physics
Tatum, Edward Lawrie	1909–75	American	Genetics
Taylor, Brook	1685–1737	English	Mathematics
Taylor, Frederick Winslow	1856–1915	American	Engineering
Telford, Thomas	1757–1834	British	Civil engineering, constructed canals, bridges, and docks
Teller, Edward	1908–	American	Physics; developed first H-bomb, 1952
Tesla, Nikola	1856–1943	American	Electrical engineering
Thenard, Louis-Jacques	1777–1857	French	Chemistry
Thomson, Sir Joseph John	1856–1940	British	Physics
Tinbergen, Nikolaas	1907–88	Dutch	Zoology, ethology
Todd, Alexander Robertus, Baron	1907–97	British	Biochemistry
Torricelli, Evangelista	1608–47	Italian	Physics; developed barometer
Tournefort, Joseph Pitton de	1656–1708	French	Botany
Townes, Charles Hard	1915–	American	Physics
Trevithick, Richard	1771–1833	British	Engineering; designed early steam trains
Tsiolkovsky, Konstantin Eduardovich	1857–1935	Russian	Aeronautical engineering
Tull, Jethro	1674–1741	English	Agriculture; invented the seed drill
Tupolev, Andrei Niklaievich	1888–1972	Russian	Aeronautical engineering
Tyndall, John	1820–93	Irish	Medicine
Urey, Harold Clayton	1893–1981	American	Physics
Van Allen, James Alfred	1914–	American	Physics; discovered Van Allen radiation belts around the Earth
van der Waals, Johannes Diderik	1837–1923	Dutch	Physics; devised van der Waals equation of state, 1873
van't Hoff, Jacobus Henricus	1852–1911	Dutch	Chemistry

SCIENCE AND TECHNOLOGY

Scientists and inventors (continued)

Name	Dates	Nationality	Field of work
Vauban, Sébastian Le Prestre de	1633–1707	French	Military engineering
Vavilov, Nikolai Ivanovich	1887–1943	Russian	Plant genetics
Volta. Alessandro Giuseppe Antonio Anastasio, Count	1745– 1827	Italian	Physics; developed first electric battery, 1800
Waksman, Selman Abraham	1888–1973	American	Microbiology
Wallace, Alfred Russel	1823–1913	British	Natural history
Wallis, Sir Barnes	1887–1979	British	Aeronautical engineering; designed airships, aeroplanes, and World War II 'bouncing bomb'
Walton, Ernest Thomas Sinton	1903–94	Irish	Physics; collaborated on first successful particle accelerator
Watson, James Dewey	1928–	American	Genetics; helped discover molecular structure of DNA
Watson-Watt, Sir Robert Alexander	1892–1973	British	Physics
Watt, James	1736–1819	British	Engineering; designed early steam engines
Weber, Ernst Heinrich	1795–1878	German	Physiology
Wegener, Alfred Lothar	1880–1930	German	Geology
Weismann, August Friedrich Leopold	1834–1914	German	Biology
Wheatstone, Sir Charles	1802–75	British	Physics
White, Gilbert	1720–93	British	Natural history
Whitney, Eli	1765–1825	American	Inventions; patented cotton-gin machine, 1793
Whittle, Sir Frank	1907–96	British	Aeronautical engineering; invented jet engine
Wiener, Norbert	1894–1964	American	Mathematics
Wigner, Eugene Paul	1902–95	American	Physics
Wilkins, Maurice Hugh Frederick	1916–2004	New Zealand	Physics; helped discover molecular structure of DNA
Wilson, Edmund Beecher	1856–1939	American	Biology
Wöhler, Friedrich	1800–82	German	Chemistry
Woodward, Robert Burns	1917–79	American	Chemistry
Yang, Chen Ning	1922–	American	Physics
Young, Thomas	1773–1829	British	Physics
Yukawa, Hideki	1907–81	Japanese	Physics
Zeeman, Pieter	1865–1943	Dutch	Physics
Zernike, Frits	1888–1966	Dutch	Physics
Ziegler, Karl	1898–1973	German	Chemistry
Zsigmondy, Richard Adolph	1865–1929	Austrian	Chemistry
Zuckerman, Solly, Baron	1904–84	British	Anatomy
Zworykin, Vladimir Kosma	1889–1982	American	Physics

PART TWELVE

Arts and Culture

LITERATURE

Novelists

Name	Dates	Place of birth	Selected works
Achebe, Chinua	1930–	Ogidi, Nigeria	*Things Fall Apart* (1958); *Anthills of the Savannah* (1987); *A Tribute to James Baldwin* (1989)
Ackroyd, Peter	1949–	London	*The Last Days of Oscar Wilde* (1983); *Milton in America* (1996); *The Lambs of London* (2004)
Adams, Douglas	1952–2001	Cambridge	*The Hitch Hiker's Guide to the Galaxy* (1979); *The Illustrated Hitch Hiker's Guide to the Galaxy* (1994)
Adams, Richard	1920–	Newbury, Berkshire	*Watership Down* (1972); *Shardik* (1974); *The Bureaucrats* (1985); *Tales from Watership Down* (1996)
Alcott, Louisa M(ay)	1832–88	Germantown, PA	*Little Women* (1868)
Amis, Kingsley	1922–95	London	*Lucky Jim* (1954); *That Uncertain Feeling* (1956); *Jake's Thing* (1978); *The Old Devils* (1986); *Difficulties with Girls* (1988); *You Can't Do Both* (1994)
Amis, Martin	1949–	Oxford	*The Rachel Papers* (1973); *Time's Arrow* (1991); *The Information* (1995); *Night Train* (1997); *Experience* (2000); *Yellow Dog* (2003); *The Pregnant Widow* (2007)
Angelou, Maya	1928–	St Louis, Missouri	*I Know Why The Caged Bird Sings* (1970); *All God's Children Need Travelling Shoes* (1986); *I Shall Not Be Moved* (1990); *My Painted House, My Friendly Chicken and Me* (1994)
Archer, Jeffrey	1940–	Somerset	*Not a Penny More, Not a Penny Less* (1975); *Kane and Abel* (1979); *First Among Equals* (1984); *The Fourth Estate* (1996); *Sons of Fortune* (2003); *False Impression* (2006)
Asimov, Isaac	1920–92	Petrovichi, USSR	*Foundation* (1951), *The Disappearing Man and other stories* (1985); *Nightfall* (1990)
Atwood, Margaret	1939–	Ottawa, Canada	*The Handmaid's Tale* (1985); *Cat's Eye* (1989); *The Robber Bride* (1994); *Alias Grace* (1996); *Oryx and Crake* (2003)
Austen, Jane	1775–1817	Steventon, Hampshire	*Sense and Sensibility* (1811); *Pride and Prejudice* (1813); *Mansfield Park* (1814); *Emma* (1815); *Persuasion* (1818)
Auster, Paul	1947–	Newark, New Jersey	*The New York Trilogy* (1985–6); *The Leviathan* (1992); *The Brooklyn Follies* (2005); *Travels in the Scriptorium* (2007)
Bainbridge, Beryl	1934–	Liverpool	*The Dressmaker* (1973); *Injury Time* (1977); *An Awfully Big Adventure* (1989); *Master George* (1998); *According to Queeney* (2001); *The Girl in the Polka Dot Dress* (2007)
Baldwin, James	1924–87	Harlem, New York City	*Go Tell It On the Mountain* (1954); *Another Country* (1962); *Just Above My Head* (1979)
Ballard, J(ames) G(raham)	1930–	Shanghai, China	*The Drowned World* (1962); *Empire of the Sun* (1984); *A User's Guide to the Millennium* (1996); *Millennium People* (2003); *Kingdom Come* (2006)
Balzac, Honoré de	1799–1850	Tours	*La Comédie humaine* (1827–47); *Illusions perdues* (1837–43)
Banks, Iain	1954–	Fife, Scotland	*The Wasp Factory* (1984); *Complicity* (1993); *Whit* (1995); *Inversions* (1999); *Dead Air* (2002); *The Algebraist* (2004); *The Steep Approach to Garbadale* (2007)
Banville, John	1945–	Wexford, Ireland	*Mefisto* (1986); *Ghosts* (1993); *Athena* (1994); *The Untouchable* (1997); *Shroud* (2004); *The Sea* (2005)
Barnes, Djuna	1892–1982	New York	*Nightwood* (1936); *Spillway* (1972)
Barnes, Julian	1946–	Leicester	*Flaubert's Parrot* (1984); *A History of the World in 10½ Chapters* (1989); *Love, etc* (2000); *Arthur & George* (2005)
Barstow, Stan(ley)	1928–	Horbury, Yorkshire	*A Kind of Loving* (1960); *Just You Wait and See* (1986); *In My Own Good Time* (Autobiography, 2001)
Bates, H(erbert) E(rnest)	1905–74	Northamptonshire	*The Two Sisters* (1926); *The Jacaranda Tree* (1949); *The Darling Buds of May* (1958); *Oh, To Be in England* (1963)
Bawden, Nina	1925–	London	*The Birds on the Trees* (1970); *The Ice House* (1983); *Nice Change* (1997); *Ruffian on the Stair* (2001)
Beckett, Samuel	1906–89	Dublin	*Murphy* (1938); *Malone Dies* (1951); *The Unnameable* (1953); *Ill Seen Ill Said* (1981)
Bedford, Sybille	1911–	Charlottenburg, Germany	*A Legacy* (1956); *Jigsaw: An Unsentimental Education* (1989)
Bellow, Saul	1915–2005	Quebec, Canada	*Herzog* (1964); *Humboldt's Gift* (1975); *More Die of Heartbreak* (1987); *The Actual* (1997); *Ravelstein* (2000)
Bennett, Arnold	1867–1931	Hanley, Staffordshire	*Anna of the Five Towns* (1902); *Clayhanger* series (1910–18)

Novelists (continued)

Name	Dates	Place of birth	Selected works
Binchy, Maeve	1940–	Dublin	*Light a Penny Candle* (1982); *Echoes* (1985); *Circle of Friends* (1990); *Evening Class* (1996); *Tara Road* (1998); *Nights of Rain and Stars* (2004); *Whitethorn Woods* (2006)
Blackmore, R(ichard) D(oddridge)	1825–1900	Longworth, Oxfordshire	*Lorna Doone* (1869)
Böll, Heinrich	1917–85	Cologne	*The Unguarded House* (1954); *The Bread of Our Early Years* (1955); *The Lost Honour of Katherina Blum* (1974)
Borges, Jorge Luis	1899–1986	Buenos Aires	*Fictions* (1945); *El Aleph* (1949); *Labyrinths* (1953)
Bowen, Elizabeth	1899–1973	Dublin	*The Death of the Heart* (1938); *The Heat of the Day* (1949)
Bowles, Paul	1910–99	New York City	*The Sheltering Sky* (1949); *Up Above the World* (1966)
Boyd, William	1952–	Accra, Ghana	*A Good Man in Africa* (1982); *An Ice Cream War* (1983); *Armadillo* (1998); *Restless* (2006)
Bradbury, Malcolm	1932–2000	Sheffield	*Eating People Is Wrong* (1959); *The History Man* (1975); *Rates of Exchange* (1983); *Dr Criminale* (1992); *To The Hermitage* (2000)
Bradbury, Ray(mond)	1920–	Waukegan, Illinois	*Fahrenheit 451* (1953); *Something Wicked This Way Comes* (1962); *Let's All Kill Constance* (2002)
Bradford, Barbara Taylor	1933–	Leeds	*A Woman of Substance* (1980); *Hold the Dream* (1985); *The Women in his Life* (1990); *Unexpected Blessings* (2004); *Just Rewards* (2005); *The Ravenscar Dynasty* (2006)
Bragg, Melvyn	1939–	Carlisle	*The Maid of Buttermere* (1987); *A Time to Dance* (1990); *Credo* (1996); *Crossing the Lines* (2003)
Brittain, Vera	1893–1970	Stoke-on-Trent	*Testament of Youth* (1933); *Testament of Friendship* (1940)
Brontë, Anne	1820–49	Thornton, Yorkshire	*Agnes Grey* (1845); *The Tenant of Wildfell Hall* (1848)
Brontë, Charlotte	1816–55	Thornton, Yorkshire	*Jane Eyre* (1847); *Shirley* (1849); *Villette* (1853)
Brontë, Emily	1818–48	Thornton, Yorkshire	*Wuthering Heights* (1847)
Brookner, Anita	1928–	London	*Hotel du Lac* (1984); *Brief Lives* (1991); *The Rules of Engagement* (2003); *Leaving Home* (2005)
Brown, Dan	1964–	Exeter, New Hampshire	*The Digital Fortress* (1998); *Angels and Demons* (2000); *Deception Point* (2001); *The Da Vinci Code* (2003)
Buchan, John	1875–1940	Perth, Scotland	*The Thirty-Nine Steps* (1915)
Buck, Pearl	1892–1973	Hillsboro, West Virginia	*The Good Earth* (1931); *Pavilion of Women* (1946)
Bulgakov, Mikhail	1891–1940	Kiev	*The Master and Margarita* (1928–40); *The White Guard* (1925); *Heart of a Dog* (1925)
Bunyan, John	1628–88	Elstow, nr Bedford	*The Pilgrim's Progress* (1678, 1684)
Burgess, Anthony	1917–94	Manchester	*A Clockwork Orange* (1962); *Earthly Powers* (1980); *Kingdom of the Wicked* (1985); *Any Old Iron* (1989); *A Dead Man in Deptford* (1993); *Byrne* (1993)
Burroughs, William S(eward)	1914–97	St Louis, Missouri	*The Naked Lunch* (1959); *The Soft Machine* (1961); *The Wild Boys* (1971); *Exterminator!* (1974); *Cities of the Red Night* (1981); *The Western Lands* (1987); *Interzone* (1989)
Butler, Samuel	1835–1902	Langar Rectory, Nottinghamshire	*Erewhon* (1872); *The Way of All Flesh* (1903)
Byatt, A(ntonia) S(usan)	1936–	Sheffield	*The Shadow of a Sun* (1964); *The Virgin in the Garden* (1978); *Possession* (1989); *Babel Tower* (1996); *Elementals: Stories of Fire and Ice* (1999); *A Whistling Woman* (2002)
Caldwell, Erskine	1903–87	Georgia	*Tobacco Road* (1932); *God's Little Acre* (1933); *Journeyman* (1935); *Close to Home* (1962)
Calvino, Italo	1923–87	Santiago de Las Vegas, Cuba	*Invisible Cities* (1972); *The Castle of Crossed Destinies* (1969); *If on a Winter's Night a Traveller* (1979)
Camus, Albert	1913–60	Mondovi, Algeria	*The Outsider* (1942); *The Plague* (1947); *The Fall* (1956)
Canetti, Elias	1905– 94	Russe, Bulgaria	*Auto da Fé* (1936); *Crowds and Power* (1960); *A Torch in my Ear* (1980); *The Play of the Eyes* (1985)
Capote, Truman	1924–84	New Orleans	*Other Voices; Other Rooms* (1948); *Breakfast at Tiffany's* (1958); *In Cold Blood* (1966)
Carey, Peter	1943–	Bacchus Marsh, Victoria	*Bliss* (1981); *Illywhacker* (1985); *Oscar and Lucinda* (1988); *Jack Maggs* (1997); *The True History of the Kelly Gang* (2001); *My Life as a Fake* (2003); *Theft: A Love Story* (2006)
Carroll, Lewis	1832–98	Daresbury, Cheshire	*Alice's Adventures in Wonderland* (1865); *Through the Looking Glass and What Alice Found There* (1872); *The Hunting of the Snark* (1876)
Carter, Angela	1940–92	London	*The Magic Toyshop* (1967); *The Infernal Desire Machines of Dr Hoffman;* (1972); *Wise Children* (1991)

Name	Dates	Place of birth	Selected works
Cartland, Barbara	1901–2000	Birmingham	*The Husband Hunters* (1976); *Wings on My Heart* (1954); *The Castle Made for Love* (1985); *Beyond the Stars* (1990); *The Little Pretender* (1999)
Cary, Joyce	1888–1957	Londonderry	*The Horse's Mouth* (1944)
Cather, Willa	1876–1947	Winchester, Virginia	*O Pioneers!* (1913); *My Antonia* (1918); *The Professor's House* (1925); *My Mortal Enemy* (1926); *Death Comes for the Archbishop* (1927); *Sapphira and the Slave Girl* (1940)
Chandler, Raymond	1888–1959	Chicago	*The Big Sleep* (1939); *Farewell, My Lovely* (1940); *The Lady in the Lake* (1943); *The Long Goodbye* (1953)
Chatwin, Bruce	1940–89	Sheffield	*In Patagonia* (1977); *On the Black Hill* (1982); *Utz* (1988)
Chesterton, G(ilbert) K(eith)	1874–1936	London	*The Innocence of Father Brown* (1911)
Christie, Agatha	1890–1976	Torquay, Devon	*Murder on the Orient Express* (1934); *Death on the Nile* (1937); *Ten Little Niggers* (1939); *Curtain* (1975)
Clarke, Arthur C(harles)	1917–	Minehead, Somerset	*Childhood's End* (1953); *The Fountains of Paradise* (1979); *The Garden of Rama* (1991); *The Hammer of God* (1993); *The Snows of Olympus* (1994); *3001: the Final Odyssey* (1997)
Cleland, John	1709–89	London	*Fanny Hill* (1750)
Coetzee, J(ohn) M(axwell)	1940–	Cape Town	*Life and Times of Michael K* (1983); *The Master of Petersburg* (1994); *Boyhood: Scenes from Provincial Life* (1997); *Youth: Scenes from Provincial Life* (2002); *Slow Man* (2005)
Collins, Wilkie	1824–89	London	*The Woman in White* (1860); *No Name* (1862); *Armadale* (1866); *The Moonstone* (1868)
Compton-Burnett, Ivy	1892–1969	Pinner, Middlesex	*A House and its Head* (1935); *A Family and a Fortune* (1939); *Manservant and Maidservant* (1947)
Conrad, Joseph	1857–1924	Berdichev, Ukraine	*Lord Jim* (1900); *Heart of Darkness* (1902); *Nostromo* (1904); *The Secret Agent* (1907); *Chance* (1914)
Cookson, Catherine	1906–98	East Jarrow, Tyne and Wear	*The Glass Virgin* (1969); *Tilly Trotter* (1981); *The Parson's Daughter* (1986); *The Gillyvors* (1990); *A Ruthless Need* (1995); *Branded Man* (1997); *The Thursday Friend* (1998)
Cooper, James Fenimore	1789–1851	Burlington, New Jersey	*The Pioneers* (1823); *The Last of the Mohicans* (1826)
Cooper, Jilly	1937–	Yorkshire	*Men and Supermen* (1972); *Riders* (1978); *Rivals* (1988); *Score!* (1999); *Pandora* (2002); *Wicked!* (2006)
Cornwell, Bernard	1944–	London	*Sharpe* series, from *Sharpe's Eagle* (1981) to *Sharpe's Fury* (2006); *The Pale Horseman* (2005); *The Lords of the North* (2006)
Cornwell, Patricia	1957–	Miami	*Body of Evidence* (1991); *Black Notice* (1999); *Isle of Dogs* (2001); *Blow Fly* (2003); *Trace* (2004); *Predator* (2005); *At Risk* (2006)
Crane, Stephen	1871–1900	Newark, New Jersey	*The Red Badge of Courage* (1895)
Davies, Robertson	1913–95	Thamesville, Ontario	*Tempest Tost* (1951); *Leaven of Malice* (1952); *What's Bred In the Bone* (1985); *The Cunning Man* (1995)
De Beauvoir, Simone	1908–86	Paris	*The Second Sex* (1949); *Les Mandarins* (1954); *Memoirs of a Dutiful Daughter* (1959)
Defoe, Daniel	1660–1731	Stoke Newington, London	*Robinson Crusoe* (1719); *Moll Flanders* (1722); *A Journal of the Plague Year* (1722)
Deighton, Len	1929–	London	*The Ipcress File* (1962); *Funeral in Berlin* (1965); *Spy Hook* (1988); *Spy Line* (1989); *Spy Sinker* (1990); *City of Gold* (1992); *Faith* (1994); *Hope* (1995); *Charity* (1997)
DeLillo, Don	1936–	New York City	*End Zone* (1972); *Ratner's Star* (1976); *White Noise* (1985); *Libra* (1988); *Underworld* (1997); *Cosmopolis* (2003)
De Quincey, Thomas	1785–1859	Manchester	*Confessions of an English Opium Eater* (1821)
Desai, Anita	1937–	Mussoorie, N India	*In Custody* (1980); *Journey to Ithaca* (1995); *Fasting, Feasting* (1999); *The Zigzag Way* (2004)
Dibdin, Michael	1947–		*Dirty Tricks* (1991); *Dark Spectre* (1995); *And Then You Die* (2001); *Medusa* (2003); *Back to Bologna* (2005)
Dickens, Charles	1812–70	Landport, Portsmouth	*Oliver Twist* (1837–9); *David Copperfield* (1849–50); *Bleak House* (1852–3); *Great Expectations* (1860–1)
Dinesen, Isak	1885–1962	Rungsted, Denmark	*Seven Gothic Tales* (1934); *Out of Africa* (1937)
Doctorow, E(dgar) L(awrence)	1931–	New York City	*Ragtime* (1975); *Billy Bathgate* (1988); *The Waterworks* (1994); *City of God* (2001); *The March* (2005)
Dos Passos, John	1896–1970	Chicago	*Manhattan Transfer* (1925); *USA* (1930–6)
Dostoevsky, Fyodor Mikhailovich	1821–81	Moscow	*Crime and Punishment* (1866); *The Idiot* (1868–9) *The Brothers Karamazov* (1880)

Novelists (continued)

Name	Dates	Place of birth	Selected works
Doyle, Arthur Conan	1859–1930	Edinburgh	The Memoirs of Sherlock Holmes (1894); The Hound of the Baskervilles (1902); The Lost World (1912)
Doyle, Roddy	1958–	Dublin	The Commitments (1987); Paddy Clarke Ha Ha Ha (1993); A Star Called Henry (1999); Oh, Play That Thing (2004); Paula Spencer (2006)
Drabble, Margaret	1939–	Sheffield	The Millstone (1965); The Witch of Exmoor (1996); The Peppered Moth (2001); The Red Queen (2004); The Sea Lady (2006)
Dreiser, Theodore	1871–1945	Terre Haute, Indiana	Sister Carrie (1900); Jennie Gerhardt (1911)
Du Maurier, Daphne	1907-89	London	Rebecca (1938); My Cousin Rachel (1951)
Dunmore, Helen	1952–	Yorkshire	A Spell of Winter (1995); With Your Crooked Heart (2000); Mourning Ruby (2003); House of Orphans (2006)
Durrell, Gerald	1925–95	Jamshedpur, India	The Overloaded Ark (1953); My Family and Other Animals (1956); The Aye-Aye and I (1992)
Durrell, Lawrence	1912–90	Darjeeling, India	Prospero's Cell (1945); 'Alexandria Quartet' (1957–60)
Eco, Umberto	1932–	Alessandria, Piedmont	The Name of the Rose (1981); Foucault's Pendulum (1989); The Island of the Day Before (1995); The Mysterious Flame of Queen Loana (2005)
Eliot, George	1819–80	Arbury, Warwickshire	Adam Bede (1859); The Mill on the Floss (1860); Silas Marner (1861); Middlemarch (1871-2); Daniel Deronda (1874-6)
Ellis, Alice Thomas	1932–2005	Liverpool	The Sin Eater (1977); The 27th Kingdom (1982); Pillars of Gold (1992); Cat Among the Pigeons (1994); Valentine's Day (2000); Fish, Flesh and Good Red Herring (2004)
Faulkner, William	1897–1962	New Albany, Mississippi	Sartoris (1929); The Sound and the Fury (1929); Absalom, Absalom! (1936)
Fielding, Helen	1958–	Morley, W Yorkshire	Cause Celeb (1994); Bridget Jones's Diary (1996); Bridget Jones: The Edge of Reason (2000)
Fielding, Henry	1707-54	Sharpham Park, nr Glastonbury	Joseph Andrews (1742); Tom Jones (1749)
Fitzgerald, F(rancis) Scott	1896–1940	St Paul, Minnesota	The Great Gatsby (1925); Tender is the Night (1934)
Fitzgerald, Penelope	1916–2000	Lincoln	The Bookshop (1978); Offshore (1979); The Gate of Angels (1990); The Blue Flower (1995)
Flaubert, Gustave	1821–80	Rouen	Madame Bovary (1857); Salammbo (1862); Sentimental Education (1869); Bouvard et Pécuchet (1881)
Fleming, Ian	1908-64	Lancaster	Casino Royale (1953); From Russia with Love (1957); Goldfinger (1959); The Man with the Golden Gun (1965)
Ford, Ford Madox	1873–1939	Merton, Surrey	The Fifth Queen (1906); The Good Soldier (1915); Parade 's End (1924–8)
Forester, C(ecil) S(cott)	1899–1966	Cairo	The Happy Return (1937); The African Queen (1935)
Forster, E(dward) M(organ)	1879–1970	London	A Room with a View (1908); Howards End (1910); A Passage to India (1922–4); Maurice (1913, published 1971)
Forsyth, Frederick	1938–	Ashford, Kent	The Day of the Jackal (1971); The Odessa File (1972); The Fourth Protocol (1984); Icon (1996); Avenger (2003); The Afghan (2006)
Fowles, John	1926–2005	Leigh-on-Sea	The Magus (1966, revised 1977); The French Lieutenant's Woman (1969); Mantissa (1982); Tessera (1993)
France, Anatole	1844–1924	Paris	Le Crime de Sylvestre Bonnard (1881); Les Dieux ont soif (1912)
Fraser, Antonia	1932–	London	Quiet as a Nun (1977); A Splash of Red (1981); Oxford Blood (1985); Jemima Shore's First Case (1986); Your Royal Hostage (1987); Political Death (1994)
French, Marilyn	1929–	New York City	The Women's Room (1977); The Bleeding Heart (1980); Her Mother's Daughter (1987); In the Name of Friendship (2006)
Gaddis, William	1922-98	New York City	JR (1976); Carpenter's Gothic (1985); A Frolic of His Own (1993)
Galsworthy, John	1867-1933	Coombe, Surrey	The Forsyte Saga (1906–28)
García Márquez, Gabriel	1928–	Aracataca, Colombia	Love in the Time of Cholera (1985); Funerals of the Great Matriarch (1999); Memories of My Melancholy Whores (2004)
Gaskell, Mrs Elizabeth	1810–65	London	Cranford (1853); North and South (1855)
Genet, Jean	1910-86	Paris	Our Lady of the Flowers (1944); The Miracle of the Rose (1946)

Name	Dates	Place of birth	Selected works
Gibbons, Stella	1902–89	London	*Cold Comfort Farm* (1932)
Gide, André	1869–1951	Paris	*The Immoralist* (1902); *Strait is the Gate* (1909); *The Vatican Cellars* (1914); *The Pastoral Symphony* (1919); *The Counterfeiters* (1926)
Gilchrist, Ellen	1935–	Vicksburg, Michigan	*The Annunciation* (1983); *I Cannot Get You Close Enough* (1990); *Flight of Angels* (1998); *The Cabal* (2000)
Goethe, Johann Wolfgang von	1749–1832	Frankfurt-am-Main	*The Sorrows of Young Werther* (1774); *Wilhelm Meister's Apprenticeship* (1796); *Elective Affinities* (1809)
Gogol, Nikolai Vasilievich	1809–52	Sorochintsi, Poltava	*The Overcoat* (1835); *Diary of a Madman* (1835); *Dead Souls* (1842); *The Odd Women* (1893)
Golding, William	1911–93	St Columb Minor, Cornwall	*Lord of the Flies* (1954); *The Spire* (1964); *Rites of Passage* (1980); *The Paper Men* (1984); *Close Quarters* (1987); *Fire Down Below* (1989)
Goldsmith, Oliver	1728–74	Kilkenny West, County Kilkenny	*The Vicar of Wakefield* (1766)
Gordimer, Nadine	1923–	Springs, Transvaal	*Occasion for Loving* (1963); *None to Accompany Me* (1994); *The Pickup* (2001); *Get a Life* (2005)
Gorky, Maxim	1868–1936	Nizhny Novgorod (New Gorky)	*The Mother* (1906–7); *Childhood* (1913); *The Life of Klim Samgin* (1925–36)
Grahame, Kenneth	1859–1932	Edinburgh	*The Wind in the Willows* (1908)
Grass, Günter	1927–	Gdánsk (Formerly Danzig)	*The Tin Drum* (1959); *Cat and Mouse* (1961); *The Meeting at Telgte* (1979); *Die Ratte* (1987); *Der Ruf der Kröte* (1992); *A Wide Field* (1995); *Crabwalk* (2003)
Graves, Robert	1895–1985	Wimbledon	*No Decency Left* (1932); *The Real David Copperfield* (1933); *I, Claudius* (1934)
Gray, Alisdair	1934–	Glasgow	*Lanark: A Life in Four Books* (1981); *Janine* (1984); *Poor Things* (1993); *The Ends of our Tethers: Stories* (2003)
Greene, Graham	1904–91	Berkhamstead, Hertfordshire	*Brighton Rock* (1938); *The Power and the Glory* (1940); *The Third Man* (1950); *The Honorary Consul* (1973)
Grisham, John	1955–	Jonesboro, Arkansas	*A Time to Kill* (1988); *The Testament* (1999); *The Summons* (2002); *The Last Juror* (2004); *The Broker* (2005)
Haggard, H(enry) Rider	1856–1925	Buckinghamshire	*King Solomon's Mines* (1885); *She: A History of Adventure* (1887)
Hammett, Dashiell	1894–1961	Maryland	*The Maltese Falcon* (1930); *The Thin Man* (1932)
Hamsun, Knut	1859–1952	Oudsrandsdal, Valley, Norway	*Hunger* (1890); *Mysteries* (1892); *Pan* (1894); *Victoria* (1898); *Growth of the Soil* (1917)
Hardy, Thomas	1840–1928	Higher Bockhampton, Dorset	*Far from the Madding Crowd* (1874); *The Mayor of Casterbridge* (1886); *Tess of the D'Urbervilles* (1891); *Jude the Obscure* (1896)
Harris, Joanne	1964–	Barnsley, S Yorkshire	*Chocolat* (1999); *Blackberry Wine* (2000); *Holy Fools* (2003); *Gentlemen and Players* (2005)
Hartley, L(eslie) P(oles)	1895–1972	Whittlesey, Cambridgeshire	*The Go-Between* (1953)
Heller, Joseph	1923–99	Brooklyn, New York	*Catch 22* (1961); *Something Happened* (1974); *Picture This* (1988); *Now and Then: From Coney Island to Here* (1998)
Hemingway, Ernest	1899–1961	Chicago, Illinois	*A Farewell to Arms* (1929); *For Whom the Bell Tolls* (1940); *The Old Man and the Sea* (1952)
Hesse, Herman	1877–1962	Calw, Württemberg	*Siddhartha* (1922); *Steppenwolf* (1927); *The Glass Bead Game* (1945)
Highsmith, Patricia	1921–95	Fort Worth	*Strangers on a Train* (1949); *The Talented Mr Ripley* (1956); *Ripley Under Ground* (1971); *Ripley Under Water* (1991); *Small g: A Summer Idyll* (1995)
Hoban, Russell	1925–	Lansdale, Pennsylvania	*Turtle Diary* (1975); *Riddley Walker* (1980); *Her Name Was Lola* (2003); *Come Dance With Me* (2005)
Holt, Victoria also as Philippa Carr, Jean Plaidy	1906–93	London	*Catherine de 'Medici* (1969 – as JP); *Will You Love Me in September* (1981 – as PC); *The Captive* (1989 – as VH); *Daughter of Deceit* (1991 – as VH)
Hornby, Nick	1957–	Maidenhead, Berkshire	*Fever Pitch* (1992); *High Fidelity* (1995); *About a Boy* (1998); *A Long Way Down* (2005)
Hugo, Victor	1802–85	Besançon	*Notre Dame de Paris* (1831); *Les Misérables* (1862)
Hulme, Keri	1947–	Christchurch, New Zealand	*The Bone People* (1983); *Lost Possessions* (1984); *The Windeater* (1987); *Bait* (1992)
Hurston, Zora Neale	1903–60	Eatonville, Florida	*Their Eyes Were Watching God* (1937); *Moses: Man of the Mountain* (1939)
Huxley, Aldous	1894–1963	Godalming, Surrey	*Brave New World* (1932); *Eyeless in Gaza* (1936); *Island* (1962)

Novelists (continued)

Name	Dates	Place of birth	Selected works
Irving, John	1942–	Exeter, New Hampshire	*The World According to Garp* (1978); *The Hotel New Hampshire* (1981); *A Widow for One Year* (1998); *The Fourth Hand* (2002); *Until I Find You* (2005)
Isherwood, Christopher	1904–86	Disley, Cheshire	*Mr Norris Changes Trains* (1935); *Goodbye to Berlin* (1939); *Down There on a Visit* (1962)
Ishiguro, Kazuo	1954–	Japan	*The Remains of the Day* (1989); *The Unconsoled* (1995); *When We Were Orphans* (2000); *Never Let Me Go* (2005)
Jacobson, Dan	1929–	Johannesburg	*A Dance in the Sun* (1950); *The Rape of Tamar* (1970); *Her Story* (1987); *The God-Fearer* (1993); *All For Love* (2005)
James, Henry	1843–1916	New York	*The Portrait of a Lady* (1881); *The Bostonians* (1886); *The Turn of the Screw* (1898); *The Awkward Age* (1899); *The Ambassadors* (1903); *The Golden Bowl* (1904)
James, P(hyllis) D(orothy)	1920–	Oxford	*Cover Her Face* (1962); *Death of an Expert Witness* (1977); *A Certain Justice* (1997); *The Murder Room* (2003); *The Lighthouse* (2005)
Jerome, Jerome K(lapka)	1859–1927	Walsall, Staffordshire	*Three Men in a Boat* (1889)
Jhabvala, Ruth Prawer	1927–	Cologne, Germany	*Heat and Dust* (1975); *In Search of Love and Beauty* (1983); *The Nature of Passion* (1986); *Poet and Dancer* (1993); *Shards of Memory* (1995); *My Nine Lives* (1998)
Johnston, Jennifer	1930–	Dublin	*The Captains and the Kings* (1972); *How Many Miles to Babylon* (1974); *The Invisible Worm* (1991); *The Gingerbread Woman* (2000); *Grace and Truth* (2005)
Joyce, James	1882–1941	Dublin	*Dubliners* (1914); *A Portrait of the Artist as a Young Man* (1914–15); *Ulysses* (1922); *Finnegans Wake* (1939)
Kafka, Franz	1883–1924	Prague	*The Metamorphosis* (1916); *The Trial* (1925); *The Castle* (1926); *America* (1927)
Kazantzakis, Nikos	1883–1957	Heraklion, Crete	*Zorba The Greek* (1946)
Keillor, Garrison	1942–	Anoka, Minnesota	*Lake Wobegone Days* (1985); *Leaving Home* (1987); *WLT: A Radio Romance* (1992); *The Wobegone Boy* (1997); *Me: by Jimmy (Big Boy) Valente* (1999); *Love Me* (2003)
Kelman, James	1946–	Glasgow	*The Busconductor Hines* (1984); *A Disaffection* (1989); *How Late it Was, How Late* (1994); *Translated Accounts* (2001); *You Have to be Careful in the Land of the Free* (2004)
Keneally, Thomas	1935–	Sydney	*A Dutiful Daughter* (1971); *Schindler's Ark* (1982); *The Great Shame: And the Triumph of the Irish in the English-Speaking World* (1999); *The Tyrant's Novel* (2003)
Kerouac, Jack	1922–69	Lowell, Massachusetts	*On The Road* (1957)
Kesey, Ken	1935–2001	La Junta, Colorado	*One Flew Over The Cuckoo's Nest* (1962); *Sailor Song* (1993)
Keyes, Marian	1963–	Limerick, Ireland	*Watermelon* (1993); *Lucy Sullivan is Getting Married* (1997); *Angels* (2001); *The Other Side of the Story* (2004); *Magician's Girl* (2006); *Anybody Out There?* (2006)
King, Stephen	1947–	Portland, Maine	*Carrie* (1974); *The Shining* (1977); *Christine* (1983); *Insomnia* (1994); *Rose Madder* (1995); *Bag of Bones* (1998); *Song of Susannah* (2004); *Cell* (2006)
Kingsley, Charles	1819–75	Holne, Devon	*Westward Ho!* (1855); *The Heroes* (1856); *The Water Babies* (1863)
Kipling, Rudyard	1865–1936	Bombay	*The Jungle Book* (1894); *Kim* (1901); *Just So Stories* (1902)
Koestler, Arthur	1905–83	Budapest	*Darkness at Noon* (1940); *Arrival and Departure* (1943)
Kundera, Milan	1929–	Brno	*The Book of Laughter and Forgetting* (1979); *The Unbearable Lightness of Being* (1984); *Immortality* (1991); *Identity* (1998); *La Ignorancia* (2001)
Laclos, Pierre Choderlos de	1741–1803	Amiens	*Les Liaisons Dangereuses* (1782)
La Fayette, Marie Madeleine	1634–93	Paris	*Zaïde* (1670); *La Princesse de Clèves* (1678)
Lampedusa Giuseppe, Tomasi di	1896–1957	Palermo, Sicily	*The Leopard* (1958)
Lawrence, D(avid) H(erbert)	1885–1930	Eastwood, Nottinghamshire	*Sons and Lovers* (1913); *The Rainbow* (1915); *Women in Love* (1920); *Lady Chatterley's Lover* (1928)
Le Carré, John	1931–	Poole, Dorset	*Tinker, Tailor, Soldier, Spy* (1974); *Smiley's People* (1980); *The Little Drummer Girl* (1983); *The Tailor of Panama* (1996); *Absolute Friends* (2003); *The Mission Song* (2006)

Name	Dates	Place of birth	Selected works
Lee, Harper	1926–	Monroeville, Alabama	*To Kill A Mockingbird* (1960)
Lee, Laurie	1914–97	Slad, Gloucestershire	*Cider With Rosie* (1959); *As I Walked Out One Midsummer Morning* (1969); *A Moment of War* (1991)
Lehmann, Rosamond	1901–90	Bourne End, Buckinghamshire	*Dusty Answer* (1927); *An Invitation to the Waltz* (1932); *The Ballad and the Source* (1944); *The Echoing Grove* (1953)
Leroux, Gaston	1868–1927	France	*The Phantom of the Opera* (1911)
Lessing, Doris	1919–	Kermanshah, Iran	*The Grass is Singing* (1950); *The Golden Notebook* (1962); *The Sweetest Dream* (2002); *The Story of General Dann & Mara's Daughter* (2005)
Levi, Primo	1919–87	Turin	*If This is a Man* (1947); *The Periodic Table* (1985)
Lewis, Sinclair	1885–1951	Sauk Center, Minnesota	*Main Street* (1920); *Babbitt* (1922); *Martin Arrowsmith* (1925); *Elmer Gantry* (1927)
Lively, Penelope	1933–	Cairo, Egypt	*The Road to Lichfield* (1977); *Moon Tiger* (1987); *City of the Mind* (1991); *Cleopatra's Sister* (1993); *Spiderweb* (1999); *The Photograph* (2002); *Making It Up* (2005)
Llosa, Mario Vargas	1936–	Arequipa, Peru	*Aunt Julia and the Scriptwriter* (1977); *A Fish in the Water* (1994); *The Notebooks of Don Rigoberto* (1998); *The Feast of the Goat* (2001); *The Way to Paradise* (2003)
Lodge, David	1935–	London	*Changing Places* (1975); *Small World* (1984); *Therapy* (1995); *Thinks* (2001); *Author, Author* (2004)
London, Jack	1876–1916	San Francisco	*The Call of the Wild* (1903); *White Fang* (1907); *Martin Eden* (1909)
Lurie, Alison	1926–	Chicago	*Love and Friendship* (1962); *The War Between the Tates* (1974); *The Truth About Lorin Jones* (1988); *The Last Resort* (1998); *Truth and Consequences* (2005)
Macaulay, Rose	1881–1958	Rugby, Warwickshire	*Dangerous Ages* (1921); *The Towers of Trebizond* (1956)
Mailer, Norman	1923–	Long Branch, New Jersey	*The Naked and the Dead* (1948); *Barbary Shore* (1951); *Tough Guys Don't Dance* (1984); *The Gospel According to the Son* (1997); *The Time of Our Time* (1999)
Malouf, David	1934–	Brisbane	*An Imaginary Life* (1978); *Remembering Babylon* (1993); *Conversation at Curlow Creek* (1997); *Dream Stuff* (2000)
Malraux, André	1901–76	Paris	*La Condition Humaine* (1933)
Mann, Thomas	1875–1955	Lübeck	*Death in Venice* (1913); *The Magic Mountain* (1924); *Dr Faustus* (1947)
Mansfield, Katherine	1888–1923	Wellington, New Zealand	*Prelude* (1918); *Bliss* (1920); *The Garden Party* (1922)
Mars-Jones, Adam	1954–	London	*Lantern Lecture* (1981); *The Darker Proof* (1987); *The Waters of Thirst* (1993); *Blind Bitter Happiness* (1997)
Maugham, Somerset	1874–1965	Paris	*Of Human Bondage* (1915); *The Moon and Sixpence* (1919); *The Razor's Edge* (1945)
Maupassant, Guy de	1850–93	Miromesnil	*Bel-ami* (1885)
Maupin, Armistead	1944–	Washington D.C.	*Tales of the City* (1978); *More Tales of the City* (1980); *Further Tales of the City* (1982); *Significant Others* (1988); *Maybe The Moon* (1992); *Night Listener* (2000)
Mauriac, François	1885–1970	Bordeaux	*Le Baiser au Lepreux* (1922); *Thérèse Desqueyroux* (1927)
McCullers, Carson	1917–67	Columbus, Georgia	*The Heart is a Lonely Hunter* (1940); *The Member of the Wedding* (1940); *The Ballad of the Sad Café* (1951)
McEwan, Ian	1948–	Aldershot, Hampshire	*First Love, Last Rites* (1975); *The Cement Garden* (1978); *The Child in Time* (1987); *The Innocent* (1990); *Amsterdam* (1998); *Atonement* (2001); *Saturday* (2005)
McGahern, John	1934–2006	Dublin	*The Leavetaking* (1975); *The Pornographer* (1979); *Amongst Women* (1990); *That They May Face The Rising Sun* (2003)
Melville, Herman	1819–91	New York	*Typee* (1846); *Omoo* (1847); *Moby Dick* (1851)
Meredith, George	1828–1909	Portsmouth	*The Egoist* (1879); *Diana of the Crossways* (1885)
Miller, Henry Valentine	1891–1980	New York	*Tropic of Cancer* (1934); *Tropic of Capricorn* (1938)
Mishima, Yukio	1925–70	Tokyo	*Confessions of a Mask* (1949); *The Temple of the Golden Pavilion* (1959); *The Sea of Fertility* (1965–70)
Mitchell, Margaret	1900–49	Atlanta, Georgia	*Gone with the Wind* (1936)
Mitford, Nancy	1904–73	London	*Love in a Cold Climate* (1949); *Don't Tell Alfred* (1960)
Montgomery, Lucy Maud	1874–1942	Prince Edward Island, Canada	*Anne of Green Gables* (1908); *Anne of Avonlea* (1909)
Mo, Timothy	1950–	Hong Kong	*The Monkey King* (1978); *Sour Sweet* (1982); *The Redundancy of Courage* (1991); *Brownout on Breadfruit Boulevard* (1995); *Renegade or Halo Squared* (1999)

ARTS AND CULTURE

Novelists (continued)

Name	Dates	Place of birth	Selected works
Moore, Brian	1921–99	Belfast	Judith Hearne (1955; later retitled The Lonely Passion of Judith Hearne); The Mangan Inheritance (1979); Lies of Silence (1990); The Statement (1995); The Magician's Wife (1998)
Morrison, Toni	1931–	Lorain, Ohio	The Bluest Eye (1970); Song of Solomon (1977); Tar Baby (1981); Beloved (1987); Paradise (1998); Love (2003)
Mosley, Nicholas	1923–	London	Spaces of the Dark (1951); Accident (1965); Hopeful Monsters (1991); Children of Darkness and Light (1996); The Hesperides Tree (2001); Look at the Dark (2005)
Munro, Alice	1931–	Wingham, Ontario	Lives of Girls and Women (1971); The Progress of Love (1987); The Love of a Good Woman (1998); Hateship, Friendship, Courtship, Loveship, Marriage (2001); Runaway (2005)
Murdoch, Iris	1919–99	Dublin	The Bell (1958); The Sea,The Sea (1978); The Book and the Brotherhood (1987); The Message to the Planet (1989); The Green Knight (1993); Jackson's Dilemma (1995)
Nabokov, Vladimir	1899–1977	St Petersburg	Lolita (1958)
Naipaul, V(idiadhar) S(urajprasad)	1932–	Trinidad	A House for Mr Biswas (1961); In a Free State (1971); A Bend in the River (1979); The Enigma of Arrival (1987); Half a Life (2001); Magic Seeds (2004)
Nesbit, E(dith)	1858–1924	London	Five Children and It (1902); The Railway Children (1906)
Oates, Joyce Carol	1938–	New York	A Garden of Earthly Delights (1967); Wonderland (1971); Marya: A Life (1986); Broke Heart Blues (1999); The Falls (2004); Missing Mom (2005); Black Girl, White Girl (2006)
O'Brien, Edna	1932–	Tuamgranay, County Clare	The Country Girls (1960); Johnny, I Hardly Knew You (1977); Down by the River (1996); In the Forest (2002); The Light of Evening (2006)
Okri, Ben	1959–	Minna, Nigeria	The Famished Road (1991); A Way of Being Free (1997); Infinite Riches (1998); In Arcadia (2002)
Ondaatje, Michael	1943–	Sri Lanka	Running in the Family (1982); In the Skin of a Lion (1987); The English Patient (1992); Anil's Ghost (2000)
Orczy, Baroness	1865–1947	Tarna-Eörs, Hungary	The Scarlet Pimpernel (1905)
Orwell, George	1903–50	Bengal	Down and Out in Paris and London (1933); Animal Farm (1945); Nineteen Eighty-Four (1949)
Pasternak, Boris	1890–1960	Moscow	Doctor Zhivago (1957)
Paton, Alan	1903–88	Pietermaritzburg, Natal	Cry, the Beloved Country (1948)
Patterson, James	1949–	Newburgh, New York	Along Came a Spider (1993); Kiss the Girls (1995); Pop Goes the Weasel (1999); The Big Bad Wolf (2003); Mary, Mary (2005); Cross (2006)
Peacock, Thomas Love	1785–1866	Weymouth, Dorset	Headlong Hall (1816); Nightmare Abbey (1818); Crotchet Castle (1883)
Peake, Mervyn	1911–68	Kuling, China	Titus Groan (1946); Gormenghast (1950); Titus Alone (1959)
Plath, Sylvia	1932–63	Boston	The Bell Jar (1963)
Powell, Anthony	1905–2000	London	A Dance to the Music of Time (1951–75); The Fisher King (1986)
Pratchett, Terry	1948–	Beaconsfield, Buckinghamshire	The Colour of Magic (1983) and later Discworld novels; Truckers (1989); Only You Can Save Mankind (1992); The Wee Free Men (2003); Thud (2005); Wintersmith (2006)
Priestley, J(ohn) B(oynton)	1894–1984	Bradford	The Good Companions (1929); Angel Pavement (1930)
Proulx, E(dna) Annie	1935–	Norwich, CT	The Shipping News (1994); Accordion Crimes (1996); That Old Ace in the Hole (2002)
Proust, Marcel	1871–1922	Paris	Remembrance of Things Past (1912–27)
Pullman, Philip	1946–	Norwich, Norfolk	Northern Lights (1995); The Subtle Knife (1997); The Amber Spyglass (2000); The Scarecrow and his Servant (2004)
Pushkin, Alexander	1799–1837	Moscow	The Prisoner of the Caucasus (1821); Eugene Onegin (1828); Boris Godunov (1831)
Pynchon, Thomas	1937–	Glen Cove, New York	V (1963); The Crying of Lot 49 (1966); Gravity's Rainbow (1973); Vineland (1992); Mason and Dixon (1997); Against the Day (2006)
Radcliffe, Ann	1764–1823	London	The Mysteries of Udolpho (1794); The Italian (1797)
Rand, Ayn	1905–82	Russia	The Fountainhead (1943); Atlas Shrugged (1957); Anthem (1966)
Rankin, Ian	1960–	Fife, Scotland	Knots and Crosses (1987); Black and Blue (1997); The Falls (2001); Fleshmarket Close (2004); Naming of the Dead (2006)

Name	Dates	Place of birth	Selected works
Rendell, Ruth	1930–	London	*A Judgement in Stone* (1977); *The Killing Doll* (1980); *A Sight for Sore Eyes* (1999); *Thirteen Steps Down* (2004); *The Water's Lovely* (2006)
Rhys, Jean	1894–1979	Dominica, West Indies	*Wide Sargasso Sea* (1966); *Tigers Are Better Looking* (1968)
Richardson, Samuel	1689–1761	Macworth, Derbyshire	*Pamela* (1740); *Clarissa* (1747-8); *Sir Charles Grandison* (1753–4)
Richler, Mordecai	1931–2001	Montreal	*The Apprenticeship of Duddy Kravitz* (1959); *Solomon Gursky Was Here* (1989); *Barney's Version* (1998)
Roth, Philip	1933–	Newark, New Jersey	*Portnoy's Complaint* (1969); *American Pastoral* (1997); *The Human Stain* (2000); *The Plot Against America* (2004); *Everyman* (2006)
Rowling, J(oanne) K(athleen)	1965–	Chipping Sodbury, Gloucestershire	*Harry Potter & the Philosopher's Stone* (1997); ... *Chamber of Secrets* (1999); ... *Prisoner of Azkaban* (1999); ... *Goblet of Fire* (2000); ... *Order of the Phoenix* (2003); *Half Blood Prince* (2005)
Rubens, Bernice	1928–	Cardiff	*The Elected Member* (1970); *Our Father* (1987); *A Solitary Grief* (1991); *I, Dreyfuss* (1998); *The Sergeant's Tale* (2003)
Rushdie, Salman	1947–	Bombay	*Midnight's Children* (1981); *The Satanic Verses* (1988); *The Ground Beneath Her Feet* (1999); *Fury* (2001); *Shalimar the Clown* (2005)
Sackville-West, Vita	1892–1962	Knole, Kent	*The Edwardians* (1930); *All Passion Spent* (1931); *Signposts in the Sea* (1961)
Sade, Marquis de	1740–1814	Paris	*Justine* (1791); *La Philosphie dans le Boudoir* (1795); *Juliette* (1797); *Les Crimes de L'Amour* (1800)
Salinger, J(erome) D(avid)	1919–	New York	*Catcher in the Rye* (1951); *Franny and Zooey* (1961); *Hapworth 16, 1924* (1997)
Sand, George	1804–76	Paris	*Lelia* (1833); *La Petite Fadette* (1849)
Sartre, Jean-Paul	1905–80	Paris	*Nausea* (1949); *The Roads to Freedom* (1945–9)
Schreiner, Olive	1855–1920	Wittebergen, S Africa	*The Story of an African Farm* (1883)
Scott, Paul	1920–78	London	*The Jewel in the Crown* (1965); *Staying On* (1977)
Scott, Walter	1771–1832	Edinburgh	*The Lady of the Lake* (1810); *Waverley* (1814); *Rob Roy* (1817); *The Bride of Lammermoor* (1819)
Seth, Vikram	1952–	Calcutta	*From Heaven Lake* (1983); *The Golden Gate* (1986); *A Suitable Boy* (1993); *An Equal Music* (1999)
Sharpe, Tom	1928–	London	*Blott on the Landscape* (1975); *Porterhouse Blue* (1978); *Wilt* (1976); *The Midden* (1996); *Wilt in Nowhere* (2004)
Shelley, Mary	1797–1851	London	*Frankenstein* (1818))
Shields, Carol	1935–2003	Oak Park, Illinois	*Small Ceremonies* (1976); *The Stone Diaries* (1993); *Larry's Party* (1997); *Unless* (2001)
Shute, Nevil	1899–1960	Ealing	*A Town Like Alice* (1949)
Sillitoe, Alan	1928–	Nottingham	*Saturday Night and Sunday Morning* (1958); *The German Numbers Woman* (1999); *A Man of His Time* (2004)
Sinclair, Upton	1878–1968	Baltimore	*The Jungle* (1906); *Dragon's Teeth* (1942)
Singer, Isaac Bashevis	1904–91	Radzymin, Poland	*The Family Moskat* (1950); *Satan in Goray* (1955); *The Slave* (1962); *Enemies: a Love Story* (1972)
Smollett, Tobias	1721–71	Cardross, Dunbartonshire	*The Adventures of Roderick Random* (1748); *The Adventures of Peregrine Pickle* (1751)
Snicket, Lemony	1970–	San Francisco, California	*The Bad Beginning* (1999); *The Vile Village* (2001); *The Slippery Slope* (2003); *The Penultimate Peril* (2005); *The End* (2006)
Solzhenitsyn, Alexander	1918–	Kislovodsk, Caucasus	*One Day in the Life of Ivan Denisovich* (1962); *The Gulag Archipelago* (1973–8); *Two Hundred Years Together* (2001)
Spark, Muriel	1918–2006	Edinburgh	*The Ballad of Peckham Rye* (1960); *The Prime of Miss Jean Brodie* (1961); *Aiding and Abetting* (2000); *The Finishing School* (2004)
Stead, Christina	1902–83	Sydney, Australia	*Seven Poor Men of Sydney* (1934); *The Man Who Loved Children* (1940); *For Love Alone* (1945)
Stein, Gertrude	1874–1946	Allegheny, PA	*Three Lives* (1908); *Tender Buttons* (1914)
Steinbeck, John	1902–68	Salinas, California	*Of Mice and Men* (1937); *The Grapes of Wrath* (1939); *East of Eden* (1952)
Stendhal	1788–1842	Grenoble	*The Red and The Black* (1830); *The Charterhouse of Parma* (1839)
Sterne, Lawrence	1713–68	Clonmel, Tipperary	*Tristram Shandy* (1759–67); *A Sentimental Journey* (1768)

ARTS AND CULTURE

Novelists (continued)

Name	Dates	Place of birth	Selected works
Stevenson, Robert Louis	1850–94	Edinburgh	*Treasure Island* (1883); *Kidnapped* (1886); *The Strange Case of Dr Jekyll and Mr Hyde* (1886)
Stoker, Bram	1847–1912	Dublin	*Dracula* (1897)
Stowe, Harriet Beecher	1811–96	Litchfield, CT	*Uncle Tom's Cabin* (1852)
Süskind, Patrick	1949–		*Perfume* (1985); *The Story of Mr Sommer* (1993); *Three Stories and A Reflection* (1996)
Swift, Graham	1949–	London	*The Sweet Shop Owner* (1980); *Waterland* (1984); *Ever After* (1992); *Last Orders* (1996); *The Light of Day* (2003)
Swift, Jonathan	1667–1745	Dublin	*Gulliver's Travels* (1726)
Thackeray, William Makepeace	1811–63	Calcutta	*Vanity Fair* (1847–8); *Pendennis* (1848–50); *The History of Henry Esmond* (1852)
Theroux, Paul	1941–	Medford, Massachusetts	*The Mosquito Coast* (1981); *The Pillars of Hercules* (1995); *Kowloon Tong* (1997); *Hotel Honolulu* (2001); *Blinding Light* (2005)
Thomas, D(onald) M(ichael)	1935–	Redruth, Cornwall	*The White Hotel* (1981); *Ararat* (1983); *Eating Pavlova* (1994); *Charlotte: the Final Journey* (2000)
Tolkien, J(ohn) R(onald) R(euel)	1892–1973	Bloemfontein, S Africa	*The Hobbit* (1937); *The Lord of the Rings* (1954–5)
Tolkin, Michael	1950–	New York City	*The Player* (1988); *Among the Dead* (1993); *The Return of the Player* (2006)
Tolstoy, Leo	1828–1910	Yasnaya Polyana, Central Russia	*War and Peace* (1865–9); *Anna Karenina* (1875–7)
Toole, John Kennedy	1937–69	New Orleans	*A Confederacy of Dunces* (1980); *The Neon Bible* (1989)
Townsend, Sue	1946–	Leicester	*The Secret Diary of Adrian Mole* (1982); *Ghost Children* (1997); *The Cappuccino Years* (1999); *Number 10* (2003); *Queen Camilla* (2006)
Trapido, Barbara	1942–	Cape Town, S Africa	*Brother of the More Famous Jack* (1982); *The Travelling Hornplayer* (1999); *Frankie & Stankie* (2003)
Tremain, Rose	1943–	London	*The Cupboard* (1981); *Restoration* (1989); *Evangelista's Fan* (1994); *The Way I Found Her* (1998); *The Colour* (2003)
Trollope, Anthony	1815–82	London	*Barchester Towers* (1857); *The Way We Live Now* (1875)
Trollope, Joanna	1943–	Gloucestershire	*A Village Affair* (1989); *The Rector's Wife* (1991); *Girl From the South* (2002); *Brother and Sister* (2004); *Second Honeymoon* (2006)
Turgenev, Ivan	1818–83	Orel province, Russia	*Fathers and Sons* (1862)
Tutuola, Amos	1920–97	Abeokuta, Nigeria	*The Palm-Wine Drinkard* (1952); *The Wild Hunter in the Bush of Ghosts* (1989)
Twain, Mark	1835–1910	Florida, Missouri	*The Adventures of Tom Sawyer* (1876); *The Prince and the Pauper* (1882); *The Adventures of Huckleberry Finn* (1884); *A Connecticut Yankee in King Arthur's Court* (1889)
Tyler, Anne	1941–	Minneapolis	*The Accidental Tourist* (1985); *A Patchwork Planet* (1998); *The Amateur Marriage* (2004); *Digging to America* (2006)
Unsworth, Barry	1930–	Wingate, Co Durham	*Pascali's Island* (1980); *The Stone Virgin* (1985); *The Songs of the Kings* (2003); *The Ruby in Her Navel* (2006)
Updike, John	1932–	Shillington, Pennsylvania	*Rabbit, Run* (1960); *The Centaur* (1963); *Toward the End of Time* (1997); *Seek My Face* (2003); *Terrorist* (2006)
Uris, Leon	1924–2003	Baltimore, Maryland	*Exodus* (1958); *Trinity* (1976); *Mitla Pass* (1989); *A God in Ruins* (1999); *O'Hara's Choice* (2003)
van der Post, Laurens	1906–96	Philippolis, S Africa	*Flamingo Feather* (1955); *The Lost World of the Kalahari* (1958); *A Walk with a White Bushman* (1986)
Verne, Jules	1828–1905	Nantes	*Voyage to the Centre of the Earth* (1864); *Twenty Thousand Leagues Under the Sea* (1870)
Vidal, Gore	1925–	West Point, New York	*The Season of Comfort* (1949); *Myra Breckenridge* (1968); *Kalki* (1978); *The Smithsonian Institution* (1999)
Vonnegut, Kurt	1922–	Indianapolis, Indiana	*Cat's Cradle* (1963); *Slaughterhouse-Five* (1969); *Hocus Pocus* (1990); *Timequake* (1997)
Walker, Alice	1944–	Eatonville, Georgia	*The Color Purple* (1982); *Possessing the Secret of Joy* (1992); *By the Light of My Father's Smile* (1998); *Now is the Time to Open Your Heart* (2004)
Warner, Marina	1946–	London	*In A Dark Wood* (1977); *The Skating Party* (1982); *The Mermaids in the Basement* (1993); *The Leto Bundle* (2001)
Warner, Rex	1905–86	Birmingham	*The Wild Goose Chase* (1937); *The Professor* (1938); *The Aerodrome* (1941)
Waugh, Evelyn	1903–66	Hampstead	*Decline and Fall* (1928); *A Handful of Dust* (1934); *Brideshead Revisited* (1945)

Name	Dates	Place of birth	Selected works
Weldon, Fay	1931–	Alvechurch, Worcestershire	*Down Among Women* (1971); *Life and Loves of a She-Devil* (1983); *Big Girls Don't Cry* (1998); *Mantrapped* (2004); *She May Not Leave* (2005)
Wells, H(erbert) G(eorge)	1866–1946	Bromley, Kent	*The Time Machine* (1895); *The Invisible Man* (1897); *The War of the Worlds* (1898); *The History of Mr Polly* (1910)
Welty, Eudora	1909–2001	Jackson, Mississippi	*The Robber Bridegroom* (1942); *The Ponder Heart* (1954); *Losing Battles* (1970); *The Optimist's Daughter* (1972)
Wesley, Mary	1912–2002	Englefield Green, Berkshire	*The Camomile Lawn* (1984); *A Sensible Life* (1990); *Part of the Furniture* (1997); *Part of the Scenery* (2001)
Wharton, Edith	1862–1937	New York	*The House of Mirth* (1905); *Ethan Frome* (1911); *The Age of Innocence* (1920)
White, Antonia	1899–1980	London	*Frost in May* (1933)
White, Edmund	1940–	Cincinnati, Ohio	*A Boy's Own Story* (1982); *The Burning Library* (1994); *The Farewell Symphony* (1997); *Fanny: A Fiction* (2003)
White, Patrick	1912–90	London	*Voss* (1957); *The Vivisector* (1970); *A Fringe of Leaves* (1976)
Wilde, Oscar	1854–1900	Dublin	*The Picture of Dorian Gray* (1891)
Wilder, Thornton	1897–1975	Madison, Wisconsin	*The Bridge Of San Luis Rey* (1927); *The Woman of Andros* (1930); *Heaven's My Destination* (1935)
Wilson, A(ndrew) N(orman)	1950–	London	*Kindly Light* (1979); *Wise Virgin* (1982); *Daughters of Albion* (1991); *The Vicar of Sorrows* (1993); *My Name is Legion* (2004); *A Jealous Ghost* (2005)
Wilson, Angus	1913–91	Bexhill, Sussex	*Anglo-Saxon Attitudes* (1956); *The Old Men At The Zoo* (1961)
Wilson, Jacqueline	1945–	Bath	*The Story of Tracy Beaker* (1992); *The Illustrated Mum* (1999); *Best Friends* (2004); *Candy Floss* (2006)
Winterson, Jeanette	1959–	Lancashire	*Oranges Are Not The Only Fruit* (1987); *Sexing The Cherry* (1989); *The Powerbook* (2000); *Lighthousekeeping* (2004); *Tanglewreck* (2006)
Wodehouse, P(elham) G(renville)	1881–1975	Guildford, Surrey	*My Man Jeeves* (1919); *The Inimitable Jeeves* (1923); *Carry On, Jeeves* (1925)
Wolfe, Tom	1931–	Richmond, Virginia	*The Right Stuff* (1979); *The Bonfire of the Vanities* (1988); *The New America* (1989); *A Man in Full* (1998); *I am Charlotte Simmons* (2004)
Woolf, Virginia	1882–1941	London	*Mrs Dalloway* (1925); *To The Lighthouse* (1927); *Orlando* (1928); *A Room of One's Own* (1929); *The Waves* (1931)
Wright, Richard	1908–60	Natchez, Mississippi	*Native Son* (1940)
Wyndham, John	1903–69	Knowle, West Midlands	*The Day of the Triffids* (1951); *The Midwich Cuckoos* (1957)
Zola, Emile	1840–1902	Paris	*Thérèse Raquin* (1867); *Les Rougon-Macquart* (1871–93); *Germinal* (1885)

Prix Goncourt

1903	John-Antoine Nau, *Force ennemie*	1919	Marcel Proust, *A l'ombre des jeunes filles en fleur*
1904	Léon Frapié, *La Maternelle*		
1905	Claude Farrère, *Les Civilisés*	1920	Ernest Pérochon, *Nêne*
1906	Jérôme and Jean Tharaud, *Dingley, l'illustre écrivain*	1921	René Maran, *Batouala*
		1922	Henri Béraud, *Le Vitriol de lune* and *Le Martyre de l'obèse*
1907	Émile Moselly, *Terres lorraines*		
1908	Francis de Miomandre, *Écrit sur de l'eau*	1923	Lucien Fabre, *Rabevel ou Le Mal des ardents*
1909	Marius and Ary Leblond, *En France*	1924	Thierry Sandre, *Le Chèvrefeuille; Le Purgatoire; Le Chapitre XIII d' Athénée*
1910	Louis Pergaud, *De Goupil à Margot*		
1911	Alphonse de Chateaubriant, *Monsieur des Lourdines*	1925	Maurice Genevoix, *Raboliot*
		1926	Henri Deberly, *Le Supplice de Phèdre*
1912	André Savignon, *Les Filles de la pluie*	1927	Maurice Bedel, *Jérôme 60° latitude Nord*
1913	Marc Elder, *Le Peuple de la mer*	1928	Maurice Constantin-Weyer, *Un homme se penche sur son passé*
1914	*Award delayed until 1916*		
1915	René Benjamin, *Gaspard*	1929	Marcel Arland, *L'Ordre*
1916	Henri Babusse, *Le Feu*	1930	Henri Fauconnier, *Malaisie*
	Adrien Bertrand, *L'Appel du sol*	1931	Jean Fayard, *Mal d'amour*
1917	Henri Malherbe, *La Flamme au poing*	1932	Guy Mazeline, *Les Loups*
1918	Georges Duhamel, *Civilisation*	1933	André Malraux, *La Condition humaine*

Prix Goncourt (continued)

1934	Roger Vercel, *Capitaine Conan*
1935	Joseph Peyré, *Sang et lumières*
1936	Maxence Van der Meersch, *L' Empreinte du dieu*
1937	Charles Plisnier, *Faux Passeports*
1938	Henri Troyat, *L'Araigne*
1939	Philippe Hériat, *Les Enfants gatés*
1940	*Prize reserved for a prisoner or political deportee and awarded in 1946 to Francois Ambrière, Les Grandes Vacances*
1941	Henri Pourrat, *Vent de mars*
1942	Marc Bernard, *Pareils à des enfants*
1943	Marius Grout, *Passage de l'homme*
1944	Elsa Triolet, *Le premier accroc coûte deux cents francs*
1945	Jean-Louis Bory, *Mon village a l'heure allemande*
1946	Jean-Jacques Gautier, *Histoire d'un faite divers*
1947	Jean-Louis Curtis, *Les Forêts de la nuit*
1948	Maurice Druon, *Les Grandes Familles*
1949	Robert Merle, *Week-End à Zuydcoote*
1950	Paul Colin, *Les Jeux sauvages*
1951	Julien Gracq, *Le Rivage des Syrtes* (declined)
1952	Béatrice Beck, *Léon Morin, prêtre*
1953	Pierre Gascar, *Les Temps des morts; Les Bêtes*
1954	Simone de Beauvoir, *Les Mandarins*
1955	Roger Ikor, *Les Eaux melées*
1956	Romain Gary, *Les Racines du ciel*
1957	Roger Vailland, *La Loi*
1958	Francis Walder, *Saint-Germain ou La Négociation*
1959	André Schwarz-Bart, *Le Dernier des justes*
1960	Vintila Horia, *Dieu est né en exil* (declined)
1961	Jean Cau, *La Pitié de Dieu*
1962	Anne Langfus, *Les Bagages de sable*
1963	Armand Lanoux, *Quand la mer se retire*
1964	Georges Conchon, *L'État sauvage*
1965	Jacques Borel, *L'Adoration*
1966	Edmonde Charles-Roux, *Oublier Palerme*
1967	André Pieyre de Mandiargues, *La Marge*

1968	Bernard Clavel, *Les Fruits de l'hiver*
1969	Félicien Marceau, *Creezy*
1970	Michel Tournier, *Le Roi des Aulnes*
1971	Jacques Laurent, *Les Bêtises*
1972	Jean Carrière, *L'Epervier de Maheux*
1973	Jacques Chessex, *L'Orgre*
1974	Pascal Lainé, *La Dentellière*
1975	Émile Ajar, *La Vie devant soi*
1976	Patrick Grainville, *Les Flamboyants*
1977	Didier Decoin, *John L'Enfer*
1978	Patrick Modiano, *Rue des boutiques obscures*
1979	Antonine Maillet, *Pélagie la Charrette*
1980	Yves Navarre, *Le Jardin d'acclimatation*
1981	Lucien Bodard, *Anne Marie*
1982	Dominique Fernandez, *Dans la main de l'ange*
1983	Frédérick Tristan, *Les Égarés*
1984	Marguerite Duras, *L'Amant*
1985	Yann Queffelec, *Les Noces barbares*
1986	Michel Host, *Valet de nuit*
1987	Tahar ben Jalloun, *La Nuit sacrée*
1988	Erik Orsenna, *L'Exposition coloniale*
1989	Jean Vautrin, *Un Grand Pas vers le bon Dieu*
1990	Jean Rouaud, *Les Champs d'honneur*
1991	Pierre Combescot, *Les Filles du Calvaire*
1992	Patrick Chamoiseau, *Texaco*
1993	Amin Maalouf, *Le Rocher de Tanois*
1994	Didier van Cauwelaert, *Un Aller simple*
1995	Andrei Makine, *Le Testament français*
1996	Pascale Roze, *Chasseur Zéro*
1997	Patrick Rambaud, *La Bataille*
1998	Paule Constant, *Confidence Pour Confidence*
1999	Jean Echenoz, *Je m'en vais*
2000	Jean-Jacques Schulh, *Ingrid Caven*
2001	John-Christophe Rufin, *Rouge Bresil*
2002	Pascal Quignard, *Les Ombres errantes*
2003	Jacques-Pierre Amette, *La Maitresse de Brecht*
2004	Laurent Gaude, *Le Soleil des Scorta*
2005	François Weyergans, *Trois jours chez ma mère*
2006	Jonathan Littell, *Les Bienveillantes*

Booker Prize

1971	V S Naipaul *In a Free State*
1972	John Berger *G*
1973	J G Farrell *The Siege of Krishnapur*
1974	Nadine Gordimer *The Conservationist*
	Stanley Middleton *Holiday*
1975	Ruth Prawer Jhabvala *Heat and Dust*
1976	David Storey *Saville*
1977	Paul Scott *Staying On*
1978	Iris Murdoch *The Sea, The Sea*
1979	Penelope Fitzgerald *Offshore*
1980	William Golding *Rites of Passage*
1981	Salman Rushdie *Midnight's Children*
1982	Thomas Keneally *Schindler's Ark*
1983	J M Coetzee *Life and Times of Michael K*
1984	Anita Brookner *Hotel du Lac*
1985	Keri Hulme *The Bone People*
1986	Kingsley Amis *The Old Devils*
1987	Penelope Lively *Moon Tiger*
1988	Peter Carey *Oscar and Lucinda*
1989	Kazuo Ishiguro *The Remains of the Day*
1990	A S Byatt *Possession*

1991	Ben Okri *The Famished Road*
1992	Barry Unsworth *Sacred Hunger*
	Michael Ondaatje *The English Patient*
1993	Roddy Doyle *Paddy Clarke–Ha ha ha*
1994	James Kelman *How late it was, how late*
1995	Pat Barker *The Ghost Road*
1996	Graham Swift *Last Orders*
1997	Arundhati Roy *The God of Small Things*
1998	Ian McEwan *Amsterdam*
1999	J M Coetzee *Disgrace*
2000	Margaret Atwood *The Blind Assassin*
2001	Peter Carey *The True History of the Kelly Gang*
2002	Yann Martel *Life of Pi*
2003	D B C Pierre *Vernon God Little*
2004	Alan Hollinghurst *The Line of Beauty*
2005	John Banville *The Sea*
2006	Kiran Desai *The Inheritance of Loss*

Costa Book Awards (from 2006, formerly Whitbread Awards)

1973	Shiva Naipaul, *The Chip Chip Gatherers*[a]
1974	Iris Murdoch, *The Sacred and Profane Love Machine*[a]
1975	William McIlvanney, *Docherty*[a]
1976	William Trevor, *The Children of Dynmouth*[a]
1977	Beryl Bainbridge, *Injury Time*[a]
1978	Paul Theroux, *Picture Palace*[a]
1979	Jennifer Johnston, *The Old Jest*[a]
1980	David Lodge, *How Far Can You Go*[a, f]
1981	Maurice Leitch, *Silver's City*[a]
	William Boyd, *A Good Man in Africa*[b]
1982	John Wain, *Young Shoulders*[a]
	Bruce Chatwin, *On the Black Hill*[b]
1983	William Trevor, *Fools of Fortune*[a]
	John Fuller, *Flying to Nowhere*[b]
1984	Christopher Hope, *Kruger's Alp*[a]
	James Buchan, *A Parish of Rich Women*[b]
1985	Peter Ackroyd, *Hawksmoor*[a]
	Jeannette Winterson, *Oranges Are Not the Only Fruit*[a]
1986	Kazou Ishiguro, *An Artist of the Floating World*[a, f]
	Jim Crace, *Continent*[b]
	Andrew Taylor, *The Coal House*[e]
	Peter Reading, *Stet*[c]
	Richard Mabey, *Gilbert White*[d]
1987	Ian McEwan, *The Child in Time*[a]
	Francis Wyndham, *The Other Garden*[b]
	Geraldine McCaughrean, *A Little Lower Than the Angels*[e]
	Seamus Heaney, *The Haw Lantern*[c]
	Christopher Nolan, *Under the Eye of the Clock*[d, f]
1988	Salman Rushdie, *The Satanic Verses*[a]
	Paul Sayer, *The Comfort of Madness*[b, f]
	Judy Allen, *Awaiting Developments*[e]
	Peter Porter, *The Automatic Oracle*[c]
	A N Wilson, *Tolstoy*[d]
1989	Lindsay Clarke, *The Chymical Wedding*[a]
	James Hamilton-Paterson, *Gerontius*[b]
	Hugh Scott, *Why Weeps the Brogan*[e]
	Michael Donaghy, *Shibboleth*[c]
	Richard Holmes, *Coleridge: Early Visions*[d, f]
1990	Nicholas Mosley, *Hopeful Monsters*[a, f]
	Hanif Kureishi, *The Buddha of Suburbia*[b]
	Peter Dickinson, *AK*[e]
	Paul Durcan, *Daddy Daddy*[c]
	Anne Thwaite, *A. A. Milne: His Life*[d]
1991	Jane Gardham, *The Queen of the Tambourine*[a]
	Gordon Burn, *Alma Cogan*[b]
1992	Alasdair Gray, *Poor Things*[a]
	Jeff Torrington, *Swing Hammer Swing!*[b]
	Tony Harrison, *The Gaze of the Gorgon*[c]
1993	Joan Brady, *Theory of War*[a, f]
	Rachel Cusk, *Saving Agnes*[b]
	Anne Fine, *Flour Babies*[e]
1994	William Trevor, *Felicia's Journey*[a, f]
	Fred D'Aguiar, *The Longest Memory*[b]
1995	Salman Rushdie, *The Moor's Last Sigh*[a]
	Kate Atkinson, *Behind the Scenes at the Museum*[b, f]
	Michael Morpurgo, *The Wreck of the Zanzibar*[e]
	Bernard O'Donoghue, *Gunpowder*[c]
	Roy Jenkins, *Gladstone*[d]

1996	Beryl Bainbridge, *Every Man for Himself*[a]
	John Lanchester, *The Debt to Pleasure*[b]
	Seamus Heaney, *Spirit Level*[c, f]
	Diarmaid McCulloch, *Thomas Cranmer: A Life*[d]
	Anne Fine, *Tulip Touch*[e, g]
1997	Jim Crace, *Quarantine*[a]
	Pauline Melville, *The Ventriloquist's Tale*[b]
	Ted Hughes, *Tales from Ovid*[c]
	Graham Robb, *Victor Hugo: A Biography*[d]
	Andrew Norriss, *Aquila*[g]
1998	Justin Cartwright, *Leading the Cheers*[a]
	Giles Foden, *The Last King of Scotland*[b]
	Ted Hughes, *Birthday Letters*[c]
	Amanda Foreman, *Georgiana, Duchess of Devonshire*[d]
	David Almond, *Skellig*[g]
1999	Rose Tremain, *Music and Silence*[a]
	Tim Lott, *White City Blue*[b]
	Seamus Heaney, *Beowulf*[c, f]
	David Cairns, *Berlioz, Volume 2*[d]
	J K Rowling, *Harry Potter and the Prisoner of Azkaban*[g]
2000	Matthew Kneale, *English Passengers*[a, f]
	Zadie Smith, *White Teeth*[b]
	John Burnside, *The Asylum Dance*[c]
	Lorna Sage, *Bad Blood*[d]
	Jamila Gavin, *Coram Boy*[c]
2001	Patrick Neale, *Twelve Bar Blues*[a]
	Sid Smith, *Something Like a House*[b]
	Selima Hill, *Bunny*[c]
	Diana Souhami, *Selkirk's Island*[d]
	Philip Pullman, *The Amber Spyglass*[e, f]
2002	Michael Frayn, *Spies*[a]
	Norman Lebrecht, *The Song of Names*[b]
	Paul Farley, *The Ice Age*[c]
	Claire Tomalin, *Samuel Pepys*[d, f]
	Hilary McKay, *Saffy's Angel*[e]
2003	Mark Haddon, *The Curious Incident of the Dog in the Night-Time*[a, f]
	D B C Pierre, *Vernon God Little*[b]
	Don Paterson, *Landing Light*[c]
	D J Taylor, *Orwell: The Life*[d]
	David Almond, *The Fire-Eaters*[e]
2004	Andrea Levy, *Small Island*[a, f]
	Susan Fletcher, *Eve Green*[b]
	Michael Symmons Roberts, *Corpus*[c]
	John Guy, *My Heart is My Own: The Life of Mary Queen of Scots*[d]
	Geraldine McCaughrean, *Not the End of the World*[e]
2005	Ali Smith, *The Accidental*[a]
	Tash Aw, *The Harmony Silk Factory*[b]
	Christopher Logue, *Cold Calls*[c]
	Hilary Spurling, *Matisse the Master*[d, f]
	Kate Thompson, *The New Policeman*[e]
2006	William Boyd, *Restless*[a]
	Stef Penney, *The Tenderness of Wolves*[b]
	John Haynes, *Letter to Patience*[c]
	Brian Thompson, *Keeping Mum*[d]
	Linda Newbery, *Set in Stone*[e]

[a]Novel. [b]First novel. [c]Poetry. [d]Biography. [e]Children's novel.
[f]Book of the Year. [g]Children's Book of the Year.

ARTS AND CULTURE

Pulitzer Prize in fiction

1918	Ernest Poole *His Family*
1919	Booth Tarkington *The Magnificent Ambersons*
1921	Edith Wharton *The Age of Innocence*
1922	Booth Tarkington *Alice Adams*
1923	Willa Cather *One of Ours*
1924	Margaret Wilson *The Able McLaughlins*
1925	Edna Ferber *So Big*
1926	Sinclair Lewis *Arrowsmith*
1927	Louis Bromfield *Early Autumn*
1928	Thornton Wilder *The Bridge of San Luis Rey*
1929	Julia Peterkin *Scarlet Sister Mary*
1930	Oliver LaFarge *Laughing Boy*
1931	Margaret Ayer Barnes *Years of Grace*
1932	Pearl S Buck *The Good Earth*
1933	T S Stribling *The Store*
1934	Caroline Miller *Lamb in His Bosom*
1935	Josephine Winslow Johnson *Now in November*
1936	Harold L Davis *Honey in the Horn*
1937	Margaret Mitchell *Gone with the Wind*
1938	John Phillips Marquand *The Late George Apley*
1939	Marjorie Kinnan Rawlings *The Yearling*
1940	John Steinbeck *The Grapes of Wrath*
1942	Ellen Glasgow *In This Our Life*
1943	Upton Sinclair *Dragon's Teeth*
1944	Martin Flavin *Journey in the Dark*
1945	John Hersey *A Bell for Adano*
1947	Robert Penn Warren *All the King's Men*
1948	James Michener *Tales of the South Pacific*
1949	James Gould Cozzens *Guard of Honor*
1950	A B Guthrie Jr *The Way West*
1951	Conrad Richter *The Town*
1952	Herman Wouk *The Caine Mutiny*
1953	Ernest Hemingway *The Old Man and the Sea*
1955	William Faulkner *A Fable*
1956	MacKinlay Kantor *Andersonville*
1958	James Agee *A Death in the Family*
1959	Robert Lewis Taylor *The Travels of Jaime McPheeters*
1960	Allen Drury *Advise and Consent*
1961	Harper Lee *To Kill a Mockingbird*
1962	Edwin O'Connor *The Edge of Sadness*
1963	William Faulkner *The Reivers*
1965	Shirley Ann Grau *The Keepers of the House*
1966	Katherine Anne Porter *The Collected Stories*
1967	Bernard Malamud *The Fixer*
1968	William Styron *The Confessions of Nat Turner*
1969	Navarre Scott Momaday *House Made of Dawn*
1970	Jean Stafford *Collected Stories*

1972	Wallace Stegner *Angle of Repose*
1973	Eudora Welty *The Optimist's Daughter*
1975	Michael Shaara *The Killer Angels*
1976	Saul Bellow *Humboldt's Gift*
1978	James Alan McPherson *Elbow Room*
1979	John Cheever *The Stories of John Cheever*
1980	Norman Mailer *The Executioner's Song*
1981	John Kennedy Toole *A Confederacy of Dunces*
1982	John Updike *Rabbit is Rich*
1983	Alice Walker *The Color Purple*
1984	William Kennedy *Ironweed*
1985	Alison Lurie *Foreign Affairs*
1986	Larry McMurty *Lonesome Dove*
1987	Peter Taylor *A Summons to Memphis*
1988	Toni Morrison *Beloved*
1989	Anne Tyler *Breathing Lessons*
1990	Oscar Hijuelos *The Mambo Kings Play Songs of Love*
1991	John Updike *Rabbit at Rest*
1992	Jane Smiley *A Thousand Acres*
	Art Spiegelmann *Maus* (special award)
1993	Robert Olen Butler *A Good Scent from a Strange Mountain*
1994	E Annie Proulx *The Shipping News*
1995	Carol Sheilds *The Stone Diaries*
1996	Richard Ford *Independence Day*
1997	Steven Millhauser *Martin Dressler: The Tale of an American Dreamer*
1998	Philip Roth *American Pastoral*
1999	Michael Cunningham *The Hours*
2000	Jhumpa Lahiri *Interpreter of Maladies*
2001	Michael Chabon *The Amazing Adventures of Cavalier and Clay*
2002	Richard Russo *Empire Falls*
2003	Jeffrey Eugenides *Middlesex*
2004	Edward P Jones *The Known World*
2005	Marilynne Robinson *Gilead*
2006	Geraldine Brooks *March*

No awards in 1917, 1920, 1941, 1946, 1954, 1957, 1964

The Orange Prize

1996	Helen Dunmore, *A Spell of Winter*
1997	Anne Michaels, *Fugitive Pieces*
1998	Carol Shields, *Larry's Party*
1999	Suzanne Berne, *A Crime in the Neighbourhood*
2000	Linda Grant, *When I Lived in Modern Times*
2001	Kate Grenville, *The Idea of Perfection*

2002	Ann Patchett, *Bel Canto*
2003	Valerie Martin, *Property*
2004	Andrea Levy, *Small Island*
2005	Lionel Shriver, *We Need to Talk about Kevin*
2006	Zadie Smith, *On Beauty*

Poets

Name	Dates	Place of birth	Selected works
Adcock, Fleur	1934–	Papakura, New Zealand	*The Eye of the Hurricane* (1964); *The Incident Book* (1986); *Time-Zones* (1991); *Poems 1960–2000* (2000)
Apollinaire, Guillaume	1880–1918	Rome	*Les Alcools* (1913); *Calligrammes* (1918)
Arnold, Matthew	1822–88	Laleham, Surrey	*The Strayed Reveller* (1849); *Poems: A New Edition* (1853–4); *Merope* (1858); *New Poems* (1867)
Auden, W(ystan) H(ugh)	1907–73	York	*Another Time* (1940); *The Sea and the Mirror* (1944); *The Age of Anxiety* (1947)
Baudelaire, Charles	1821–67	Paris	*Les Fleurs du Mal* (1857)
Belloc, Hilaire	1870–1953	St Cloud, France	*Cautionary Tales* (1907); *Sonnets and Verse* (1923)
Betjeman, John	1906–84	Highgate	*Mount Zion* (1933); *New Bats in Old Belfries* (1945); *A Nip in the Air* (1972)
Blake, William	1757–1827	London	*The Marriage of Heaven and Hell* (1791); *The Vision of the Daughter of Albion* (1793); *Songs of Innocence and Experience* (1794); *Milton* (1810)
Blunden, Edmund	1896–1974	London	*The Waggoner and Other Poems* (1920); *The Shepherd and Other Poems of Peace and War* (1922); *English Poems* (1929); *After the Bombing and Other Short Poems* (1950); *A Hong Kong House* (1962)
Blunt, Wilfrid Scawen	1840–1922	Petworth, Sussex	*Sonnets and Songs by Proteus* (1875); *In Vinculis* (1899)
Boccaccio, Giovanni	1313–75	Florence	*The Decameron; Filostrato*
Brodsky, Joseph	1940–96	St Petersburg	*Ostanovka v pustynie* (1970); *Chast rechi* (1977); *Uraniia* (1984)
Brooke, Rupert	1887–1915	Rugby	*Poems* (1911); *1914 and Other Poems* (1915); *Complete Poems* (1946)
Browning, Elizabeth Barrett	1806–61	Coxhoe Hall, Durham	*Sonnets from the Portuguese* (1850); *Aurora Leigh* (1855)
Browning, Robert	1812–89	Camberwell	*Bells and Pomegranates* (1841–6); *Dramatic Lyrics* (1842); *Men and Women* (1855); *The Ring and the Book* (1868-9)
Burns, Robert	1759–96	Alloway, Ayr	*Poems Chiefly in the Scottish Dialect* (1786); *Tam O'Shanter* (1790)
Byron, George Gordon	1788–1824	London	*Hours of Idleness* (1807); *Childe Harolde* (1817); *Don Juan* (1819–24)
Chaucer, Geoffrey	1343–1400	London	*Troilus and Criseyde* (c.1385); *The Canterbury Tales* (1387–1400)
Coleridge, Samuel Taylor	1722–1834	Ottery St Mary, Devon	*Kubla Khan* (1797); *The Rime of the Ancient Mariner* (1798); *Christabel* (1798); *Sybylline Leaves* (1817); *Collected Poems* (1817)
Cowper, William	1731–1800	Great Berkhampstead, Hertfordshire	*The Task* (1785)
Cummings, E(dward) E(stlin)	1894–1962	Cambridge, Massachusetts	*Tulips and Chimneys* (1923); *XLI Poems* (1925); *is 5* (1926)
Dante, Alighieri	1265–1321	Florence	*Divine Comedy* (1321)
Day Lewis, Cecil	1904–72	Ballintubber, Co Kildare	*Overtures to Death* (1938); *The Aeneid of Virgil* (1952)
De la Mare, Walter	1873–1956	Charlton, Kent	*The Listeners* (1912); *The Burning Glass and Other Poems* (1945)
Dickinson, Emily	1830–86	Amherst, Massachusetts	*Poems* (1891–6)
Donne, John	1572–1631	London	*Satires and Elegies* (1590s); *Holy Sonnets* (1610–11)
Dryden, John	1631–1700	Aldwincle All Saints, Northamptonshire	*Astrea Redux* (1660); *Absalom and Achitophel* (1681); *MacFlecknoe* (1684)
Dunbar, Paul	1872–1906	Dayton, Ohio	*Lyrics of Lowly Life* (1896); *Complete Poems* (1913)
Dunn, Douglas	1942–	Inchinnann, Scotland	*Love or Nothing* (1974); *Elegies* (1985); *Northlight* (1988); *Dante's Drum-kit* (1993); *New Selected Poems 1964–2000* (2003)
Eliot, T(homas) S(tearns)	1888–1965	St Louis, Missouri	*Prufrock and Other Observations* (1917); *The Waste Land* (1922); *Ash Wednesday* (1930); *Four Quartets* (1944)
Éluard, Paul	1895–1952	Saint-Denis	*La Vie Immediate* (1934); *Poesie et Verité* (1942)
Emerson, Ralph Waldo	1803–82	Boston	*Complete Works* (1903–4)
Fitzgerald, Edward	1809–83	Bredfield, Suffolk	*The Rubáiyát of Omar Khayyám* (1859)
Frost, Robert	1874–1963	San Francisco	*North of Boston* (1914); *Mountain Interval* (1916); *New Hampshire* (1923); *In The Clearing* (1962)
Ginsberg, Allen	1926–97	Newark, New Jersey	*Howl and Other Poems* (1956); *Empty Mirror* (1961); *The Fall of America* (1973); *White Shroud: Peoms 1980–1985* (1986)
Goethe, Johann Wolfgang von	1749–1832	Frankfurt	*Römische Elegien* (1795); *Der west-östliche Divan* (1819)

Poets (continued)

Name	Dates	Place of birth	Selected works
Graham, W(illiam) S(ydney)	1918–86	Greenock, Renfrewshire	*Cage Without Grievance* (1942); *The Seven Journeys* (1944), *The White Threshold* (1949); *The Nightfishing* (1955); *Implements in their Place* (1977); *Collected Poems* (1979); *Aimed at Nobody* (1993)
Graves, Robert	1895–1985	London	*Fairies and Fusiliers* (1917)
Hardy, Thomas	1840–1928	Higher Bockhampton, Dorset	*Wessex Poems* (1898); *Poems of the Past and Present* (1902); *Satires of Circumstance, Lyrics and Reveries* (1914); *Moments of Vision and Miscellaneous Verse* (1917); *Human Shows, Far Phantasies, Songs and Trifles* (1925)
Harrison, Tony	1937–	Leeds	*V* (1985); *The Gaze of the Gorgon* (1992); *The Prince's Play* (1996); *Laureate's Block and Other Occasional Poems* (2000); *Under the Clock* (2005)
Heaney, Seamus	1939–	County Londonderry	*Death of a Naturalist* (1966); *Door into the Dark* (1969); *Field Work* (1979); *Station Island* (1984); *Sweeney's Flight* (1992); *Beowulf* (1999); *Electric Light* (2001); *District and Circle* (2006)
Heine, Henrich	1797–1856	Düsseldorf	*Das Buch der Lieder* (1827)
Herbert, George	1593–1633	Montgomery	*The Temple* (1633)
Hopkins, Gerard Manley	1844–89	London	*The Wreck of the Deutschland* (1876)
Hughes, Langston	1902–67	Joplin, Missouri	*Shakespeare of Harlem* (1942); *Ask your Mama* (1961)
Hughes, Ted	1930–98	Mytholmroyd, Yorkshire	*The Hawk in the Rain* (1957); *Lupercal* (1960); *Crow* (1970); *Seasons Songs* (1976); *River* (1983); *Wolfwatching* (1989); *Rain-Charm for the Duchy and Other Laureate Poems* (1992); *Tales from Ovid* (1997); *Birthday Letters* (1998)
Keats, John	1795–1821	London	*Endymion* (1818); *Lamia and Other Poems* (1820)
Lamartine, Alphonse de	1790–1869	Mâcon	*Meditations Poétiques* (1820); *Harmonies Poétiques et Religieuses* (1830); *Recueillements Poétiques* (1839)
Langland, William	1332–1400	Ledbury, Herefordshire	*Piers Plowman* (1362–99)
Larkin, Philip	1922–1985	Coventry	*The North Ship* (1945); *The Whitsun Weddings* (1964); *High Windows* (1974)
Lear, Edward	1812–88	London	*A Book of Nonsense* (1846); *Laughable Lyrics* (1876); *Queery Leary Nonsense* (1911); *Teapots and Quails* (1953)
Longfellow, Henry	1807–82	Portland, Maine	*Voices and the Night* (1839); *Ballads and Other Poems* (1841); *Hiawatha* (1855); *Divina Comedia* (1872)
MacDiarmid, Hugh	1892–1978	Langholm, Dumfriesshire	*A Drunk Man Looks at the Thistle* (1926)
MacNeice, Louis	1907–63	Belfast	*Blind Fireworks* (1929); *Solstices* (1961)
Mallarmé, Stéphane	1842–98	Paris	*Herodiade* (1864); *Prélude à L'Apres-midi d'un Faune* (1865); *Poésies* (1887)
Marvell, Andrew	1621–78	Yorkshire	*Elegy* (1649); *Upon Appleton House* (c. 1652-3); *To His Coy Mistress* (pre–1653)
Masefield, John	1878–1967	Ledbury, Herefordshire	*The Everlasting Mercy* (1911); *Dauber* (1913); *Collected Poems* (1923)
Millay, Edna St Vincent	1892–1950	Rockland, Maine	*Renascence and Other Poems* (1917); *A Few Figs From Thistles* (1920); *The Harp-Weaver and Other Poems* (1923)
Milton, John	1608–74	London	*Paradise Lost* (1667)
Moore, Marianne	1887–1972	St Louis, Missouri	*Poems* (1921); *Observations* (1924); *Collected Poems* (1951); *O, to be a Dragon* (1959); *Tell Me, Tell Me: Granite, Steel and Other Topics* (1966)
Motion, Andrew	1952–	London	*The Pleasure Steamers* (1978); *Natural Causes* (1987); *Love in a Life* (1991); *Selected Poems 1996–1997* (1998); *In a Perfect World* (1999); *Picture This* (2000); *Here to Eternity* (2001); *Public Property* (2002); *Spring Wedding* (2005)
Muir, Edwin	1887–1959	Deerness, Orkney	*First Poems* (1925); *Chorus of the Newly Dead* (1926); *Variations on a Time Theme* (1934); *The Labyrinth* (1949); *New Poems* (1949–51)
Muldoon, Paul	1951–	County Armagh	*New Weather* (1973); *Quoof* (1984); *Madoc: A Mystery* (1990); *Hay* (1998); *Poems 1968–1998* (2001); *Moy Sand and Gravel* (2002); *Horse Latitudes* (2006)
Murray, Les(lie Allen)	1938–	Nabiac, New South Wales	*The Ilex Tree* (1965); *The People's Otherworld* (1983); *Subhuman Redneck Poems* (1996); *Fredy Neptune: A Novel in Verse* (1999); *Collected Poems 1961–2002* (2002); *The Biplane Houses* (2006)
Nash, Ogden	1902–71	New York	*Free Wheeling* (1931)
Nerval, Gérard de	1808–55	Paris	*Les Chimères* (1854)
O'Hara, Frank	1926–66	Baltimore	*A City Winter and Other Poems* (1952); *Lunch Poems* (1964)

Name	Dates	Place of birth	Selected works
Owen, Wilfred	1893–1918	Oswestry, Shropshire	Poems (1920, 1931); Collected Poems (1963)
Parker, Dorothy	1893–1967	New Jersey	Enough Rope (1926); Sunset Gun (1928); Death and Taxes (1931); Not so Deep as a Well (1936)
Paulin, Tom	1949–	Leeds	A Sense of Justice (1977); The Strange Museum (1980); Seize the Fire (1990); Walking a Line (1994); The Invasion Handbook (2002)
Paz, Octavio	1914–98	Mexico City	Salamander (1958–61); Collected Poems (1988)
Petrarch	1304–74	Arezzo	Rime Sparse
Plath, Sylvia	1932–63	Boston	The Colossus and Other Poems (1960); Ariel (1965); Crossing the Water (1971); Winter Trees (1972)
Pound, Ezra	1885–1972	Hailey, Idaho	The Cantos (1917, 1948, 1959)
Pushkin, Aleksandr	1799–1837	Moscow	Eugen Onegin (1828); Ruslan and Lyudmila (1820)
Raine, Craig	1944–	Shildon, Co Durham	The Onion, Memory (1978); A Martian Sends a Postcard Home (1979); Rich (1984); 1953 (1990); A la recherche du temps perdu (2000)
Raine, Kathleen	1908–2003	London	Stone and Flower (1943); Living With Mystery: Poems (1992)
Rilke, Rainer Maria	1875–1926	Prague	Die Sonette an Orpheus (1923)
Rimbaud, Arthur	1854–91	Charleville, Ardennes	Les Illuminations (1872)
Rossetti, Christina	1830–94	London	Goblin Market (1862); The Prince's Progress (1872); A Pageant and Other Poems (1881)
Sassoon, Siegfried	1886–1967	Kent	Counter-Attack and Other Poems (1918); The Road to Ruin (1933)
Schiller, Friedrich	1759–1805	Marbach	Die Künstler (The Artists); An die Freude (Ode to Joy)
Shelley, Percy Bysshe	1792–1822	Sussex	Prometheus Unbound (1820); The Mask of Anarchy (1819); Ode to the West Wind (1819); The Triumph of Life
Sitwell, Dame Edith	1887–1964	Scarborough	Facade (1922); Colonel Fantock (1926)
Smith, Stevie	1902–71	Hull	Not Waving But Drowning (1957)
Spender, Stephen	1909–95	London	Poems (1933); Collected Poems 1928–1953 (1955)
Spenser, Edmund	1552–99	London	The Shepheardes Calender (1579); The Faerie Queene (1590)
Stevens, Wallace	1879–1955	Reading, Pennsylvania	Harmonium (1923); Transport to Summer (1947)
Tate, James	1943–	Kansas City	The Lost Pilot (1967); The Oblivion Ha-Ha (1970); Selected Poems (1991); Shroud of the Gnome: Poems (1997); Memoir of the Hawk (2001); Return to the City of White Donkeys: Poems (2004)
Tennyson, Alfred, Lord	1809–92	Somersby Rectory, Lincolnshire	Poems (1832); The Princess (1847); In Memoriam (1850); Idylls of the King (1859); Maud (1885)
Thomas, Dylan	1914–53	Swansea	Twenty-five Poems (1936); Deaths and Entrances (1946); In Country Sleep and Other Poems (1952); Under Milk Wood (1954)
Valéry, Paul	1871–1945	Sete	La Jeune Parque (1917); Charmes (1922)
Vega, Lope de	1562–1635	Madrid	La Dragentea (1598)
Verlaine, Paul	1844–96	Metz	Fêtes Galantes (1869); Sagesse (1881)
Walcott, Derek	1930–	Castries, St Lucia	In a Green Night (1962); The Castaway (1965); The Gulf (1969); The Odyssey (1989); Omeros (1990); Selected Poetry (1993); The Bounty (1997); Tiepelo's Hound (2000); The Prodigal (2005)
Warren, Robert Penn	1905–89	Guthrie, Kentucky	Brother to Dragons (1953); Promises: Poems 1954-56 (1957); Now and Then: Poems 1976–78 (1978); Portrait of a Father (1988)
Whitman, Walt	1819–92	New York	Leaves of Grass (1855–89)
Williams, William Carlos	1883–1963	New Jersey	The Tempers (1913); Sour Grapes (1921); The Desert Music and Poems (1954); Journey to Love (1955); Pictures from Breughel and Other Poems (1962)
Wordsworth, William	1770–1850	Cockermouth	Lyrical Ballads (1798); The Prelude (1799, 1805, 1850); The Excursion (1814
Yeats W(illiam) B(utler)	1865–1939	County Dublin	The Wanderings of Oisin and Other Poems (1888); The Wind Among the Reeds (1892); The Wild Swans at Coole (1917); Michael Robartes and the Dancer (1921); The Winding Stair and Other Poems (1933)
Yevtushenko, Yevgeny	1933–	Zima, Russia	The Third Snow (1955); Babi Yar (1962); Under the Skin of the Statue of Liberty (1972, play); Pre-morning (1995)
Zephaniah, Benjamin	1958–	Birmingham	Pen Rhythm (1980); City Psalms (1992); Propa Propaganda (1996); Too Black Too Strong (2001); We Are Britain! (2002); J is for Jamaica (2006)

ARTS AND CULTURE

Pulitzer Prize in poetry

1917	No award	1963	William Carlos Williams *Pictures from Breughel*
1918	Sara Teasdale *Love Songs*	1964	Louis Simpson *At the End of the Open Road*
1919	Carl Sandburg *Corn Huskers*	1965	John Berryman *77 Dream Songs*
	Margaret Widdemer *Old Road to Paradise*	1966	Richard Eberhart *Selected Poems*
1920	No award	1967	Ann Sexton *Live or Die*
1921	No award	1968	Anthony Hecht *The Hard Hour*
1922	Edwin Arlington Robinson *Collected Poems*	1969	George Oppen *Of Being Numerous*
1923	Edna St Vincent Millay *The Harp Weaver and Other Poems*	1970	Richard Howard *Untitled Subjects*
		1971	W S Merwin *The Carrier of Ladders*
1924	Robert Frost *New Hampshire: a Poem with Notes and Grace Notes*	1972	James Wright *Collected Poems*
		1973	Maxine Winokur Kumin *Up Country*
1925	Edwin Arlington Robinson *The Man Who Died Twice*	1974	Robert Lowell *The Dolphin*
		1975	Gary Snyder *Turtle Island*
1926	Amy Lowell *What's O'Clock?*	1976	John Ashbery *Self-Portrait in a Convex Mirror*
1927	Leonora Speyer *Fiddler's Farewell*	1977	James Merrill *Divine Comedies*
1928	Edwin Arlington Robinson *Tristram*	1978	Howard Nemerov *Collected Poems*
1929	Stephen Vincent Benét *John Brown's Body*	1979	Robert Penn Warren *Now and Then*
1930	Conrad Aiken *Selected Poems*	1980	Donald Justice *Selected Poems*
1931	Robert Frost *Collected Poems*	1981	James Schuyler *The Morning of the Poem*
1932	George Dillon *The Flowering Stone*	1982	Sylvia Plath *The Collected Poems*
1933	Archibald MacLeish *Conquistador*	1983	Galway Kinnell *Selected Poems*
1934	Robert Hillyer *Collected Verse*	1984	Mary Oliver *American Primitive*
1935	Audrey Wurdemann *Bright Ambush*	1985	Carolyn Kizer *Yin*
1936	R P Tristram Coffin *Strange Holiness*	1986	Henry Taylor *The Flying Change*
1937	Robert Frost *A Further Range*	1987	Rita Dove *Thomas and Beulah*
1938	Marya Zaturenska *Cold Morning Sky*	1988	William Meredith *Partial Accounts; New and Selected Poems*
1939	John Gould Fletcher *Selected Poems*		
1940	Mark Van Doren *Collected Poems*	1989	Richard Wilbur *New and Selected Poems*
1941	Leonard Bacon *Sunderland Capture*	1990	Charles Simic *The World Doesn't End*
1942	William Benét *The Dust Which is God*	1991	Mona van Duyn *Near Changes*
1943	Robert Frost *A Witness Tree*	1992	James Tate *Selected Poems*
1944	Stephen Vincent Benét *Western Star*	1993	Louise Glück *The Wild Iris*
1945	Karl Shapiro *V–Letter and Other Poems*	1994	Yusef Komunyakaa *Neon Vernacular*
1946	No award	1995	Philip Levine *The Simple Truth*
1947	Robert Lowell *Lord Weary's Castle*	1996	Jorie Graham *The Dream of the Unified Field*
1948	W H Auden *The Age of Anxiety*	1997	Lisel Mueller *Alive Together: New and Selected Poems*
1949	Peter Viereck *Terror and Decorum*		
1950	Gwendolyn Brooks *Annie Allen*	1998	Charles Wright *Black Zodiac*
1951	Carl Sandburg *Complete Poems*	1999	Mark Strand *Blizzard of One*
1952	Marianne Moore *Collected Poems*	2000	C K Williams *Repair*
1953	Archibald MacLeish *Collected Poems 1917–1952*	2001	Stephen Dunn *Different Hours*
1954	Theodore Roethke *The Waking*	2002	Carl Dennis *Practical Gods*
1955	Wallace Stevens *Collected Poems*	2003	Paul Muldoon *Moy Sand and Gravel*
1956	Elizabeth Bishop *Poems – North & South*	2004	Franz Wright *Walking to Martha's Vineyard*
1957	Richard Wilbur *Things of This World*	2005	Ted Kooser *Delights and Shadows*
1958	Robert Penn Warren *Promises: Poems 1954–56*	2006	Claudia Emerson *Late Wife*
1959	Stanley Kunitz *Selected Poems 1928–1958*		
1960	W D Snodgrass *Heart's Needle*		
1961	Phyllis McGinley *Times Three: Selected Verse from Three Decades*		
1962	Alan Dugan *Poems*		

UK Poets laureate

1617	Ben Jonson[a]	1730	Colley Cibber	1896	Alfred Austin
1638	William Davenant[a]	1757	William Whitehead	1913	Robert Bridges
1668	John Dryden	1785	Thomas Warton	1930	John Masefield
1689	Thomas Shadwell	1790	Henry Pye	1968	Cecil Day Lewis
1692	Nahum Tate	1813	Robert Southey	1972	John Betjeman
1715	Nicholas Rowe	1843	William Wordsworth	1984	Ted Hughes
1718	Laurence Eusden	1850	Alfred, Lord Tennyson	1999	Andrew Motion

[a]The post was not officially established until 1668.

THEATRE

Playwrights

Name	Dates	Place of birth	Selected works
Aeschylus	c.525–426 BC	Eleusis, nr Athens	*Persians* (c.472 BC); *Seven Against Thebes* (c.467 BC); *Oresteia* (458 BC)
Albee, Edward	1928–	Washington DC	*The American Dream* (1960); *Who's Afraid of Virginia Woolf?* (1962); *Three Tall Women* (1991); *Fragments* (1993); *The Play About the Baby* (1997); *Occupant* (2001); *Peter & Jerry* (2004)
Anouilh, Jean	1910–87	Bordeaux	*Antigone* (1944); *L'Alouette* (1953); *Beckett* (1959)
Arden, John	1930–	Barnsley	*All Fall Down* (1955); *The Waters of Babylon* (1957); *Serjeant Musgrave's Dance* 1959); *The Workhouse Donkey* (1963)
Aristophanes	c.448–380 BC	Athens	*Clouds* (c.423 BC); *Wasps* (c.422 BC); *Birds* (c.414 BC); *Lysistrata* (c.411 BC); *Frogs* (c.405 BC)
Ayckbourn, Alan	1939–	London	*Absurd Person Singular* (1973); *The Norman Conquests* (1974); *A Chorus of Disapproval* (1985); *Communicating Doors* (1995); *My Sister Sadie* (2003); *Private Fears in Public Places* (2004)
Barker, Howard	1946–	London	*Cheek* (1970); *The Love of a Good Man* (1978); *The Possibilities* (1988); *A Hard Heart* (1992); *The Europeans* (1993)
Barnes, Peter	1931–2004	Stroud	*The Bewitched* (1974); *Laughter* (1978); *Red Noses* (1985); *Sunsets and Glories* (1990); *Corpsing* (1996)
Barrie, J(ames) M(atthew)	1860–1937	Kirriemuir, Angus	*Peter Pan* (1904); *What Every Woman Knows* (1908)
Beckett, Samuel	1906–89	Foxrock, Dublin	*Waiting for Godot* (1954); *Endgame* (1956); *Happy Days* (1961)
Behan, Brendan	1923–64	Dublin	*The Quare Fellow* (1954); *The Hostage* (1958)
Bennett, Alan	1934–	Yorkshire	*Beyond the Fringe* (1960); *Forty Years On* (1968); *Getting On* (1971); *Habeas Corpus* (1973); *The Madness of George III* (1991); *The History Boys* (2004)
Berkoff, Steven	1937–	London	*East* (1975); *Greek* (1979); *Decadence* (1981); *Sink the Belgrano!* (1986); *Coriolanus in Deutschland* (1993); *Shakespeare's Villains* (1998); *The Crime of the Twenty-First Century* (1999)
Bleasdale, Alan	1946–	Liverpool	*Boys from the Blackstuff* (1982); *The Monocled Mutineer* (1986)
Bolt, Robert	1924–95	Sale, Manchester	*A Man for All Seasons* (1960); *Vivat! Vivat Regina!* (1970)
Bond, Edward	1934–	London	*Saved* (1965); *Lear* (1971); *The Fool* (1975); *At the Inland Sea* (1996); *The Crime of the Twenty-First Century* (1999)
Brecht, Bertolt	1898–1956	Augsburg	*Galileo* (1938–9); *Mother Courage* (1938); *The Good Person of Setzuan* (1943); *Caucasian Chalk Circle* (1955)
Brenton, Howard	1942–	Portsmouth	*Christie in Love* (1969); *The Romans in Britain* (1980); *Pravda* (with David Hare) (1985); *Moscow Gold* (with Tariq Ali) (1990); *Berlin Bertie* (1992); *Ugly Rumours* (1998, with Ali)
Calderon de la Barca, Pedro	1600–81	Madrid	*Life is a Dream* (1635); *The Mayor of Zalamea* (1643)
Čapek, Karel	1890–1938	Bohemia	*RUR* (1920); *The Makropulos Affair* (1923)
Chekhov, Anton	1860–1904	Taganrog	*The Seagull* (1896); *Uncle Vanya* (1900); *Three Sisters* (1901); *The Cherry Orchard* (1904)
Churchill, Caryl	1938–	London	*Cloud Nine* (1979); *Top Girls* (1982); *Serious Money* (1987); *Mad Forest* (1990); *The Skriker* (1994); *Blue Heart* (1997); *A Number* (2002); *Drunk Enough to Say I Love You?* (2006)
Cocteau, Jean	1889–1963	Maisons-Lafitte, nr Paris	*Orphée* (1926); *La Machine Infernale* (1934)
Congreve, William	1670–1729	Bardsey, nr Leeds	*The Way of the World* (1700)
Cooney, Ray	1932–	London	*Run for Your Wife* (1983); *Wife Begins at Forty* (1986); *Funny Money* (1996); *Caught in the Net* (2001)

ARTS AND CULTURE

Playwrights (continued)

Name	Dates	Place of birth	Selected works
Corneille, Pierre	1606–84	Rouen	*Le Cid* (1636); *Horace* (1639); *Cinna* (1639); *Polyeucte* (1640)
Coward, Noel	1899–1973	London	*Hay Fever* (1925); *Private Lives* (1930); *Blithe Spirit* (1941)
Delaney, Shelagh	1939–	Salford	*A Taste of Honey* (1958)
Dürrenmatt, Friedrich	1921–90	Bern	*The Visit* (1956); *The Physicists* (1962)
Edgar, David	1948–	Birmingham	*Destiny* (1976); *Maydays* (1983); *Pentecost* (1995); *The Prisoner's Dilemma* (2001); *Playing With Fire* (2005)
Eliot, T S	1888–1965	St Louis, Missouri	*Murder in the Cathedral* (1935); *The Cocktail Party* (1950); *The Family Reunion* (1939)
Euripides	c.480–406 BC	Phyla, Attica	*Medea* (c. 431 BC); *Electra* (c. 422–416 BC); *Iphigenia in Tauris* (c.414 BC); *Bacchae* (?, produced posthumously)
Farquhar, George	1678–1707	Dublin	*The Constant Couple* (1699); *The Recruiting Officer* (1706); *The Beaux' Stratagem* (1707)
Feydeau, Georges	1862–1921	Paris	*A Flea in Her Ear* (1907); *Look After Lulu* (1908)
Fo, Dario	1926–	Lombardy	*Accidental Death of an Anarchist* (1970); *Johan Padan and the Discovery of America* (1992); *The Two-headed Anomaly* (2004)
Ford, John	1586–1640	Devonshire	*'Tis Pity She's a Whore* (1633)
Frayn, Michael	1933–	London	*The Two of Us* (1970); *Donkey's Years* (1976); *Noises Off* (1982); *Now You Know* (1995); *Copenhagen* (1999); *Democracy* (2003)
Friel, Brian	1929–	Omagh	*Philadelphia, Here I Come!* (1964); *Lovers* (1967); *Translations* (1980); *Dancing at Lughnasa* (1991); *Molly Sweeney* (1995); *Give Me Your Answer, Do!* (1997); *The Home Place* (2005)
Fry, Christopher	1907–2005		*The Lady's Not for Burning* (1949); *A Yard of Sun* (1970)
Fugard, Athol	1932–	Middleburg, Cape Province	*Sizwe Bansi is Dead* (1972); *A Lesson From Aloes* (1979); *Master Harold ... and the Boys* (1982); *My Children! My Africa!* (1989); *The Captain's Tiger* (1998); *Sorrows and Rejoicings* (2002)
Genet, Jean	1910–86	Paris	*Les Bonnes (The Maids)* (1947); *Le Balcon (The Balcony)* (1956)
Giraudoux, Jean	1882–1944	Bellac	*Amphitryon 38* (1929); *La Guerre de Troie n'aura pas Lieu* (1935)
Goethe, Johann Wolfgang von	1749–1832	Frankfurt	*Faust I* (1808); *Faust II* (1832)
Gogol, Nikolai	1809–52	Polt, Ukraine	*The Government Inspector* (1836)
Goldoni, Carlo	1707–93	Venice	*The Servant of Two Masters* (1746); *Mirandolina* (1753); *The Fan* (1763)
Goldsmith, Oliver	1728–74	Pallas, Ireland	*She Stoops to Conquer* (1773)
Gorky, Maxim	1868–1936	Nizhni Novgorod, Russia	*The Lower Depths* (1902); *Summer Folk* (1904)
Gray, Simon	1936–	Hampshire	*The Common Pursuit* (1984); *Hidden Laughter* (1990); *Simply Disconnected* (1996); *The Smoking Diaries* (2004)
Griffiths, Trevor	1935–	Manchester	*Occupations* (1970); *The Party* (1973); *Comedians* (1975); *Who Shall Be Happy ...?* (1996)
Hampton, Christopher	1946–	Fayal, Azores	*The Philanthropist* (1970), *Savages* (1973); *Tales from Hollywood* (1982); *Les Liaisons Dangereuses* (1985); (1991); *Sunset Boulevard* (1993); *Carrington* (1995); *The Talking Cure* (2002)
Hare, David	1947–	Bexhill	*Teeth 'n' Smiles* (1975); *Plenty* (1978); *The Secret Rapture* (1988); *The Judas Kiss* (1998); *The Breath of Life* (2002); *The Permanent Way* (2003); *Stuff Happens* (2005); *The Vertical Hour* (2006)
Hauptmann, Gerhart	1862–1946	Obersalzbrunn	*Vor Sonnenaufgang (Before Sunrise)* (1889); *The Weavers* (1892)
Hellman, Lillian	1905–84	New Orleans	*The Little Foxes* (1939)
Ibsen, Henrik	1828–1906	Skien, Norway	*Peer Gynt* (1867); *A Doll's House* (1879); *Hedda Gabler* (1890); *The Master Builder* (1892)
Ionesco, Eugène	1912–94	Romania	*La Cantatrice Chauve (The Bald Prima Donna)* (1950); *Rhinoceros* (1960)
Jonson, Ben	1572–1637	Westminster	*Every Man His Humour* (1598); *Sejanus* (1603); *Volpone* (1606); *The Alchemist* (1610); *Bartholomew Fair* (1614)
Lorca, Federico Garcia	1898–1936	Fuente Vaqueros, Spain	*Blood Wedding* (1933); *The House of Bernarda Alba* (1936)
Mamet, David	1947–	Chicago	*Sexual Perversity in Chicago* (1974); *American Buffalo* (1976); *Glengarry Glen Ross* (1983); *The Old Neighborhood* (1990); *Oleanna* (1992); *The Cryptogram* (1994); *Romance* (2005)
Marlowe, Christopher	1564–1593	Canterbury	*Tamburlaine the Great* (1587); *Dr Faustus* (1588); *The Jew of Malta* (1589); *Edward II* (1592)
Middleton, Thomas	c.1580–1627	London	*Women Beware Women* (c.1621); *The Changeling* (1622)

Name	Dates	Place of birth	Selected works
Miller, Arthur	1915–2005	New York	*All My Sons* (1947); *Death of a Salesman* (1949); *The Crucible* (1953); *View From the Bridge* (1955); *The Misfits* (1961); *Broken Glass* (1994); *Finishing the Picture* (2004)
Molière	1622–73	Paris	*Tartuffe* (1664); *Le Misanthrope* (1666); *Le Bourgeois Gentilhomme* (1670); *Le Malade Imaginaire* (1673)
Musset, Alfred de	1810–57	Paris	*Fantasio* (1834); *On Ne Badine Pas Avec L'Amour* (1834); *Lorenzaccio* (1834)
Nichols, Peter	1927–	Bristol	*A Day In the Death of Joe Egg* (1967); *Privates on Parade* (1977); *Passion Play* (1980); *Poppy* (1982); *About Turner* (1991); *Blue Murder* (1995)
O'Casey, Sean	1880–1964	Dublin	*Juno and the Paycock* (1924); *The Plough and the Stars* (1926)
Odets, Clifford	1906–63	Philadelphia	*Awake and Sing* (1935); *Waiting for Lefty* (1935); *Golden Boy* (1937)
O'Neill, Eugene	1888–1953	New York	*Long Day's Journey into Night* (1956)
Orton, Joe	1933–67	Leicester	*Entertaining Mr Sloane* (1964); *Loot* (1965); *What the Butler Saw* (1969)
Osborne, John	1929–94	London	*Look Back in Anger* (1956); *The Entertainer* (1957); *A Patriot for Me* (1965); *Déjàvu* (1991)
Otway, Thomas	1652–85	Milland, Sussex	*The Orphan* (1680); *Venice Preserv'd* (1682)
Pinero, Arthur Wing	1855–1934	London	*The Second Mrs Tanqueray* (1893); *Trelawny of the Wells* (1898)
Pinter, Harold	1930–	London	*The Birthday Party* (1957); *The Caretaker* (1960); *The Homecoming* (1965); *A Kind of Alaska* (1982); *Mountain Language* (1988); *Ashes to Ashes* (1996); *Celebration* (2000)
Pirandello, Luigi	1867–1936	Agrigento, Sicily	*Six Characters in Search of an Author* (1920); *Henry IV* (1922)
Poliakoff, Stephen	1952–	London	*The Carnation Gang* (1973); *Hitting Town* (1975); *Breaking the Silences* (1984); *Playing with Trains* (1989); *Blinded by the Sun* (1996); *Sweet Panic* (2003); *Gideon's Daughter* (2006)
Priestley, J(ohn) B(oynton)	1894–1984	Bradford	*Dangerous Corner* (1932); *Time and the Conways* (1937); *When We Are Married* (1938); *An Inspector Calls* (1947)
Racine, Jean	1639–99	La Ferté-Milon	*Andromaque* (1667); *Bérénice* (1670); *Phèdre* (1677)
Rattigan, Terence	1911–77	London	*French Without Tears* (1936); *The Winslow Boy* (1946); *The Browning Version* (1948); *The Deep Blue Sea* (1952); *Ross* (1960)
Rosenthal, Jack	1931–2004	Manchester	*The Evacuees* (1975); *Barmitzvah Boy* (1976); *Spend, Spend, Spend* (1977); *The Knowledge* (1979)
Rostand, Edmond de	1868–1918	Marseilles	*Cyrano de Bergerac* (1897)
Russell, Willy	1947–	Whiston, Lancashire	*Educating Rita* (1979); *Blood Brothers* (1983); *Shirley Valentine* (1986)
Sartre, Jean-Paul	1905–80	Paris	*Les Mouches (The Flies)* (1943); *Huis Clos* (1944); *Les Séquestrés D'Altona (The Condemned of Altona)* (1961)
Schiller, Friedrich	1759–1805	Marbach	*The Robbers* (1781); *Wallenstein* (1799); *Maria Stuart* (1800)
Shaffer, Peter	1926–	Liverpool	*Five Finger Exercise* (1958); *The Royal Hunt of the Sun* (1964); *Equus* (1973); *Amadeus* (1979); *Yonadab* (1985); *Lettice and Lovage* (1987); *The Gift of the Gorgon* (1992)
Shakespeare, William	1564–1616	Stratford-Upon-Avon	For complete list of plays see pp 582–3.
Shaw, George Bernard	1856–1950	Dublin	*Arms and the Man* (1894); *Man and Superman* (1903); *Pygmalion* (1913); *Heartbreak House* (1919); *Saint Joan* (1923)
Shepard, Sam	1943–	Sheridan, Illinois	*La Turista* (1966); *The Tooth of Crime* (1972); *Fool For Love* (1979); *A Lie of the Mind* (1985); *The States of Shock* (1991); *Eyes for Consuela* (1998); *The God of Hell* (2004)
Sheridan, Richard Brinsley	1751–1816	Dublin	*The Rivals* (1775); *The School for Scandal* (1777)
Sherriff, R(obert) C(edric)	1896–1973	Kingston-upon-Thames	*Journey's End* (1929)
Simon, Neil	1927–	New York	*Barefoot in the Park* (1963); *The Odd Couple* (1965); *Plaza Suite* (1968); *The Last of the Red Hot Lovers* (1969); *California Suite* (1976); *Lost in Yonkers* (1991); *Rose's Dilemma* (2003)
Sophocles	c.496–406 BC	Colonus, nr Athens	*Antigone* (c.442 BC); *Oedipus Tyrannus* (c.420 BC); *Electra* (c.409 BC); *Philoctetes* (c.409 BC)
Soyinka, Wole	1934–	Abeskata, Nigeria	*The Swamp Dwellers* (1958); *The Lion and the Jewel* (1959); *The Bacchae of Euripides* (1973); *A Play of Giants* (1985); *A Scourge of Hyacinths* (1992); *King Baabu* (2001)

ARTS AND CULTURE

Playwrights (continued)

Name	Dates	Place of birth	Selected works
Stoppard, Tom	1937–	Zlin, Czechoslovakia	*Rosencrantz and Guildenstern are Dead* (1966); *Jumpers* (1972); *Travesties* (1974); *Indian Ink* (1995); *The Invention of Love* (1997); *The Coast of Utopia* (2002, trilogy); *Rock 'n' Roll* (2006)
Storey, David	1933–	Wakefield	*The Contractor* (1970); *Home* (1970); *The Changing Room* (1972); *Life Class* (1974); *Sisters* (1978); *The March on Russia* (1989); *Stages* (1992)
Strindberg, August	1849–1912	Stockholm	*Miss Julie* (1888); *Master Olof* (1877); *The Dance of Death* (1901)
Synge J(ohn), M(illington)	1871–1909	Dublin	*The Playboy of the Western World* (1907)
Taylor, Cecil P(hilip)	1928–81	Glasgow	*Good* (1981)
Terson, Peter	1932–	Tyneside	*A Night to Make the Angels Weep* (1964); *Zigger, Zagger* (1967); *Strippers* (1984)
Travers, Ben	1886–1980	Hendon	*Rookery Nook* (1926); *Thark* (1927)
Turgenev, Ivan	1818–83	Orel, Russia	*A Month in the Country* (1850)
Vanbrugh, John	1664–1726	London	*The Relapse* (1696); *The Provoked Wife* (1697)
Webster, John	1578–1632	London	*The White Devil* (1612); *The Duchess of Malfi* (c.1613)
Wedekind, Frank	1864–1918	Hanover, Germany	*Spring Awakening* (1891); *Pandora's Box* (1903)
Wertenbaker, Timberlake	1951–	France	*The Love of the Nightingale* (1988); *Three Birds Alighting in a Field* (1991); *Break of Day* (1995); *Galileo's Daughter* (2004)
Wesker, Arnold	1932–	London	*Chicken Soup With Barley* (1958); *Roots* (1959); *I'm Talking About Jerusalem* (1960); *Chips With Everything* (1962); *Caritas* (1981); *Three Women Talking* (1992); *Longitude* (2002)
Wilde, Oscar	1854–1900	Dublin	*Lady Windermere's Fan* (1892); *The Importance of Being Earnest* (1895); *Salomé* (1896)
Wilder, Thornton	1897–1975	Wisconsin	*Our Town* (1938); *The Merchant of Yonkers* (1938); *The Skin of Our Teeth* (1942)
Williams, Tennessee	1911–83	Mississippi	*The Glass Menagerie* (1944); *A Streetcar Named Desire* (1947); *Cat on a Hot Tin Roof* (1955); *Sweet Bird of Youth* (1959)
Wycherley, William	1641–1716	Clive, nr Shrewsbury	*The Country Wife* (1675); *The Plain Dealer* (1676)

Shakespeare: the plays

Early comedies	Written	Well-known characters
The Comedy of Errors	1590–4	Antipholus, Dromio, Adriana
Love's Labour's Lost	1590–4	Armado, Berowne, Costard
The Two Gentlemen of Verona	1592–3	Proteus, Valentine, Julia, Sylvia
The Taming of the Shrew	1592	Petruchio, Katherina, Sly

Histories		
Henry VI Part I (with others)	1589–90	Henry, Talbot, Joan of Arc
Henry VI Part II	1590–1	Henry, Margaret, Jack Cade
Henry VI Part III	1590–1	Henry, Margaret, Richard of Gloucester
Edward III (with others)	1590–5	Edward, Philippa, Prince Edward, Countess
Richard III	1592–3	Richard, Margaret, Clarence, Anne
King John	1595–7	John, Constance, Arthur, Bastard
Richard II	1595	Richard, John of Gaunt, Bolingbroke
Henry IV Part I	1596	Henry, Hal, Hotspur, Falstaff
Henry IV Part II	1597	Henry, Hal, Falstaff, Mistress Quickly
Henry V	1599	Henry (formerly Hal), Pistol, Nym, Katherine
Henry VIII (with John Fletcher)	1613	Henry, Katherine, Wolsley

Middle comedies		
A Midsummer Night's Dream	1595	Oberon, Titania, Puck, Bottom
The Merchant of Venice	1596–8	Bassanio, Portia, Shylock, Jessica
The Merry Wives of Windsor	1597	Falstaff, Mistress Quickly, Shallow
As You Like It	1599	Rosalind, Orlando, Touchstone, Jaques
Twelfth Night	1600–2	Orsino, Olivia, Viola, Malvolio, Feste, Sir Andrew, Sir Toby

Dark comedies		
Much Ado About Nothing	1598	Beatrice, Benedick, Dogberry, Verges
All's Well That Ends Well	1602–3	Bertram, Helena, Parolles
Measure for Measure	1604–5	Duke, Angelo, Isabella, Mariana

Tragedies

Romeo and Juliet	1595–6	Romeo, Juliet, Mercutio, the Nurse
Hamlet	1600–1	Hamlet, Ophelia, the Ghost, the Grave-Digger
Othello	1604	Othello, Desdemona, Iago, Cassio
King Lear	1605–6	Lear, Cordelia, the Fool, Kent, Edgar/Poor Tom
Macbeth	1605–6	Macbeth, Lady Macbeth, Banquo, the Three Witches

Greek and Roman plays

Titus Andronicus	1590–4	Andronicus, Aaron, Lavinia
Julius Caesar	1599	Caesar, Brutus, Cassius, Antony
Troilus and Cressida	1601–2	Troilus, Cressida, Pandarus
Timon of Athens (with Thomas Middleton)	1605–9	Timon, Apemantus
Antony and Cleopatra	1606–7	Antony, Cleopatra, Enobarbus
Coriolanus	1607–8	Coriolanus, Volumnia, Menenius

Late plays

Pericles (with George Wilkins)	1607–8	Pericles, Marina
Cymbeline	1609–10	Innogen, Iachimo, Posthumus
The Winter's Tale	1611	Leontes, Perdita, Florizel, Autolycus
The Tempest	1613	Prospero, Miranda, Ferdinand, Ariel, Caliban
The Two Noble Kinsmen (with John Fletcher)	1613	Arcite, Palamon, Emilia, Theseus

Theatre personalities

Name	Dates	Place of birth	Occupation
Abbott, George	1887–1995	New York	Director/playwright/producer
Abington, Frances	1737–1815	London	Actress
Ackerman, Robert Allan	1945–	North Yorkshire	Director
Agate, James (Evershed)	1877–1947	Manchester	Critic
Aitken, Maria	1945–	Dublin	Actress/director
Alexander, Bill	1948–	Hunstanton	Actor/director
Alleyn, Edward	1566–1626	London	Actor
Allgood, Sara	1883–1950	Dublin	Actress
Anderson, Judith	1898–1992	Adelaide	Actress
Antoine, André	1858–1943	Limoges	Actor
Appia, Adolphe	1862–1928	Geneva	Designer
Arliss, George	1868–1946	London	Actor
Arnaud, Yvonne Germaine	1892–1958	Bordeaux	Actress
Artaud, Antonin	1896–1948	Marseilles	Dramatist/actor/director/theorist
Ashcroft, Peggy	1907–91	London	Actress
Attenborough, Michael	1950–	London	Director
Attenborough, Richard	1923–	Cambridge	Actor/director
Aylmer, Felix Edward	1889–1979	Corsham, Wiltshire	Actor
Bancroft, Squire	1841–1926	London	Actor/manager
Barba, Eugenio	1936–	Brindisi	Director/theorist
Barber, Frances	1957–	Wolverhampton	Actress
Barrault, Jean-Louis	1910–94	Le Vesinet	Actor/director/manager
Barrymore, Ethel	1879–1959	Philadelphia	Actress
Barton, John	1928–	London	Director
Baylis, Lilian	1874–1937	London	Theatrical manager
Bel Geddes, Norman	1893–1958	Adrian, Michigan	Stage designer
Benson, Frank Robert	1858–1939	Alresford, Hampshire	Actor/manager
Bergman, Ingmar	1918–	Stockholm	Director
Berkoff, Steven	1937–	London	Dramatist/actor/director
Bernhardt, Sarah	1844–1923	Paris	Actress
Berry, Cicely	1926–	Berkhampstead	Voice Director
Betterton, Thomas	1635–1710	London	Actor/manager
Billington, Michael	1939–	Leamington Spa, Warwickshire	Critic
Bjornson, Maria	1949–2002	Paris	Stage designer
Blakely, Colin	1930–87	Bangor, Co Down	Actor
Blin, Roger	1907–84	Neuilly, Paris	Director
Bloom, Claire	1931–	London	Actress
Boal, Augusto	1931–	Brazil	Director/theorist

Theatre personalities (continued)

Name	Dates	Place of birth	Occupation
Bogdanov, Michael	1938–	London	Director
Booth, Edwin Thomas	1833–93	Harford County, Maryland	Actor
Boyd, Michael	1955–	Belfast	Director
Bracegirdle, Anne	c.1663–1748	London	Actress
Branagh, Kenneth	1960–	Belfast	Actor/director
Briers, Richard	1934–	Croydon, Surrey	Actor
Bron, Eleanor	1938–	Stanmore, Middlesex	Actress/director
Brook, Peter	1925–	London	Director
Brustein, Robert	1927–	New York	Critic/director
Bryant, Michael Dennis	1928–2002	London	Actor
Bryden, Bill	1942–	Greenock,WC Scotland	Playwright/director
Burbage, Richard	c.1567–1619	London	Actor; builder of the Globe Theatre, 1599
Bury, John	1925–2000	Aberystwyth	Stage designer
Caird, John	1948–	Edmonton, Canada	Director/writer
Caldwell, Zoe	1933–	Victoria, Australia	Actress/director
Callow, Simon	1949–	London	Actor/director
Campbell, Mrs Patrick	1865–1940	Kensington	Actress
Carte, Richard D'Oyly	1844–1901	London	Impresario
Casson, Lewis	1875–1969	Birkenhead	Actor/manager
Chaikin, Joseph	1935–	Brooklyn	Director/actor/producer
Charleson, Ian	1949–90	Edinburgh	Actor
Cheeseman, Peter	1932–	Portsmouth	Director/artistic director
Chereau, Patrice	1944–	France	Director
Chevalier, Albert	1862–1923	London	Actor
Cibber, Colley	1671–1757	London	Actor /dramatist
Cibber, Mrs	1714–66	London	Actress
Clements, John Selby	1911–88	London	Actor/director
Clurman, Harold Edgar	1901–80	New York City	Director/critic
Cochran, Charles Blake	1872–1951	Lindfield, Sussex	Producer
Compton, Fay	1894–1978	London	Actress
Cooney, Ray	1932–	London	Dramatist/director/producer
Copeau, Jacques	1879–1949	France	Director/manager
Copley, John (Micha	1933–	Birmingham	Producer
Cornell, Katharine	1893–1974	Berlin	Actress/producer/manager
Courtenay, Tom	1937–	Hull	Actor
Courtneidge, Cicely	1893–1980	Sydney	Actress
Coward, Noel	1899–1973	Teddington	Actor/director/dramatist
Cox, Brian	1946–	Dundee	Actor/director
Craig, Edward Gordon	1872–1966	Stevenage	Actor/stage designer
Crawford, Michael	1942–	Salisbury, Wiltshire	Actor
Croft, Michael	1922–86	Manchester	Director
Cronyn, Hume	1911–2003	London, Ontario	Actor/director/producer
Crowley, Bob	1954–	Dublin	Stage designer
Cusack, Cyril	1910–93	Durban	Actor/director
Cusack, Sinead	1948–	Dublin	Actress
Cushman, Robert	1943–	London	Critic/director
Daubeny, Peter	1921–75	na	Impresario/theatre manager
Davies, Howard	1945–	Reading	Director
Debureau, Jean Gaspard	1796–1846	Bohemia	Actor
De La Tour, Frances	1944–	Bovingdon, Hertfordshire	Actress
Dench, Judi	1934–	York	Actress
Devine, George	1910–65	Hendon, London	Actor/stage director
Dewhurst, Colleen	1926–1991	Montreal	Actress
Dexter, John	1925–90	Derby	Director
Doran, Gregory	1958–	Huddersfield	Director
Draper, Ruth	1884–1956	New York	Monologist and diseuse
Drew, John	1853–1927	Philadelphia	Actor
Drew, Mrs John	1820–97	London	Actress/manager
Dudley, William	1947–	London	Stage designer
Dukakis, Olympia	1931–	Lowell, Massachusetts	Actress
Du Maurier, Gerald	1873–1934	London	Actor-manager
Dunlop, Frank	1927–	Leeds	Stage director

Name	Dates	Place of birth	Occupation
Duse, Eleonora	1859–1924	Venice	Actress
Eddington, Paul	1927–95	London	Actor
Egan, Peter	1946–	London	Actor/director
Espert, Nuria	1935–	Spain	Actress/director
Evans, Edith	1888–1976	London	Actress
Eyre, Richard	1943–	Barnstaple	Director
Finlay, Frank	1926–	Farnworth, Lancashire	Actor
Finney, Albert	1936–	Salford	Actor
Forbes-Robertson, Johnston	1853–1937	London	Actor
Forrest, Edwin	1806–72	Philadelphia	Actor
Gambon, Michael	1940–	Dublin	Actor
Garrick, David	1717–79	Hereford	Actor
Gielgud, John	1904–2000	London	Actor
Glover, Julian	1935–	London	Actor
Grimaldi, Joseph	1778–1837	London	Actor
Grotowski, Jerzy	1933–99	Rzeszów, Poland	Stage director
Guinness, Alec	1914–2000	Southborne	Actor
Guthrie, William Tyrone	1900–71	Tunbridge Wells	Producer
Gwyn, Eleanor (known as Nell)	c.1650–87	Hereford	Actress
Hall, Peter	1930–	Bury St Edmund's	Director
Hancock, Sheila	1933–	Blackgang, Isle of Wight	Actress
Hands, Terry	1941–	Aldershot	Stage director
Hardwicke, Cedric	1893–1964	Lye, Worcestershire	Actor
Hare, Robertson	1891–1979	London	Actor
Harewood, George Henry Hubert Lascelles, 7th Earl of	1923–	Harewood, nr Leeds	Arts patron
Harris, Julie	1925–	Michigan	Actress
Harris, Rosemary	1930–	Ashby, Suffolk	Actress
Harvey, John Martin	1863–1944	Wivenhoe, Essex	Actor-manager
Hawthorne, Nigel	1929–2001	Coventry	Actor
Hayes, Helen	1900–93	Washington	Actress
Higgins, Clare	1957–	Yorkshire	Actress
Hijikata, Tatsumi	1928–86	Akita province	Performance artist
Hiller, Wendy	1912–2003	Bramhall, Cheshire	Actress
Holm, Ian	1931–	Ilford, Essex	Actor
Hordern, Michael	1911–95	Berkhampsted	Actor
Horniman, Anne Elizabeth Fredericka	1860–1937	Forest Hall, London	Theatre manager
Houseman, John	1902–89	Bucharest	Actor/stage director
Howard, Alan	1937–	London	Actor
Irving, Henry	1838–1905	Keinton-Mandeville, Somerset	Actor
Izzard, Eddie	1962–	Aden, Yemen	Actor/comedian
Jackson, Glenda	1936–	Birkenhead	Actress
Jacobi, Derek	1938–	London	Actor/director
Jacobs, Sally	1932–	London	Designer
Jefferson, Joseph	1829–1905	Philadelphia	Actor
Johnson, Celia	1908–82	Richmond, Surrey	Actress
Jones, Inigo	1573–1652	London	Stage designer
Jouvet, Louis	1887–1951	Finistère	Director/actor
Kazan, Elia	1909–2003	Constantinople	Director
Kean, Charles	1811–68	Waterford, Ireland	Actor/manager
Kean, Edmund	1789–1833	London	Actor
Kemble, Frances ('Fanny')	1809–93	London	Actress
Kemble, John Philip	1757–1823	Prescott, Lancashire	Actor/manager
Kemp, Lindsay	1939–	Lewis, Hebrides	Mime artist/actor/director
Kemp, Will	c.1560–c.1603	na	Actor
Kendal, Felicity	1946–	Olton, Warwickshire	Actress
Kendal, Madge	1848–1935	Cleethorpes	Actress
Kerr, Walter Francis	1913–96	Evanston, Illinois	Critic
Kingsley, Ben	1943–	Snaiton, Yorkshire	Actor
Langtry, Lilly	1853–1929	Jersey	Actress
Lapotaire, Jane	1944–	Ipswich	Actress
Lawrence, Gertrude	1898–1952	London	Actress

Theatre personalities (continued)

Name	Dates	Place of birth	Occupation
Lecoq, Jacques	1921–99	Paris	Mime artist/director
Lehmann, Beatrix	1903–79	Bourne End, Buckinghamshire	Actress/director-producer
Lemaître, Frédérick	1800–76	Le Havre	Actor
Lenya, Lotte	1900–1981	Hitzing, Vienna	Actress
Littlewood, Joan	1914–2002	London	Stage director
Lloyd, Marie	1870–1922	London	Actress
Lloyd Webber, Andrew	1948–	London	Musicals composer
Lunt, Alfred	1892–1977	Milwaukee	Actor
Lyubimov, Yuri	1917–	Russia	Stage director
Mackintosh, Cameron	1946–	Enfield, Middlesex	Producer
Macrae, John Duncan	1905–67	na	Actor
Macready, William Charles	1793–1873	London	Actor
Marceau, Marcel	1923–	Strasbourg	Mime artist
Massey, Raymond	1896–1983	Toronto	Actor/director
Mathews, Charles James	1803–78	Liverpool	Actor/playwright
McClintic, Guthrie	1893–1961	Seattle	Director/actor/producer
McCowen, Alec	1925–	Tunbridge Wells	Actor
McEwan, Geraldine	1932–	Old Windsor	Actress
McKellen, Ian	1939–	Burnley	Actor
McKenzie, Julia	1941–	Middlesex	Actress
McKern, Leo (	1920–2002	Sydney	Actor
Menken, Adah Isaacs	1835–68	New Orleans	Actress
Merman, Ethel	1909–84	Long Island, New York	Actress
Meyerhold, Vsevolod Emilievich	1874–1940	Penza	Actor/director
Mielziner, Jo	1901–76	Paris	Stage designer/actor
Miles, Bernard	1907–91	Uxbridge	Actor/stage director
Miller, Jonathan Wolfe	1934–	London	Director
Mirren, Helen	1946–	London	Actress
Mnouchkine, Arianne	1938–	France	Stage director
Morley, Sheridan	1941–	Ascot	Critic
Napier, John	1944–	London	Stage designer
Nemirovich-Danchenko, Vladimir	1858–1943	Ozurgety, Georgia	Director/theorist
Neville, John	1925–	London	Actor/director
Noble, Adrian	1950–	Ashford, Middlesex	Director
Nunn, Trevor	1940–	Ipswich	Director
Olivier, Laurence	1907–89	Dorking	Actor/director
Page, Geraldine	1924–87	Kirksville, Missouri	Actress
Papp, Joseph	1921–91	Brooklyn, New York	Stage director/producer
Pennington, Michael	1943–	Cambridge	Actor
Perry, Antoinette	1888–1946	Denver	Actress/director
Pimlott, Steven	1953–	Stockport	Director
Piscator, Erwin	1893–1966	Ulm, Germany	Stage director
Plowright, Joan	1929–	Brigg, Lincolnshire	Actress
Porter, Eric	1928–95	London	Actor
Prince, Hal	1928–	New York City	Stage director/producer
Prowse, Philip	1937–	Worcester	Director
Pryce, Jonathan	1947–	Holywell	Actor
Quayle, Anthony	1913–89	Ainsdale	Actor
Redgrave, Michael	1908–85	Bristol	Actor
Redgrave, Vanessa	1937–	London	Actress
Rees, Roger	1944–	Aberystwyth	Actor
Reinhardt, Max	1873–1943	Baden, nr Vienna	Theatre manager
Richardson, Ian	1934–	Edinburgh	Actor
Richardson, Ralph	1902–83	Cheltenham	Actor
Rix, Brian	1924–	Cottingham	Actor
Robards, Jason	1922–2000	Chicago	Actor
Robeson, Paul	1898–1976	Princeton, New Jersey	Actor/singer
Robson, Flora	1902–84	South Shields	Actress
Rossiter, Leonard	1926–84	Liverpool	Actor
Routledge, Patricia	1929–	Birkenhead	Actress
Rylance, Mark	1960–	Willesborough, Kent	Actor/director
Scales, Prunella	1932–	Abinger, Surrey	Actress

Name	Dates	Place of birth	Occupation
Scofield, Paul	1922–	Hurstpierpoint, Sussex	Actor
Sellars, Peter	1957–	Pittsburgh	Actor
Sheen, Michael	1969–	Wales	Actor
Sher, Antony	1949–	South Africa	Actor
Sherrin, Ned	1931–	Low Ham, Somerset	Producer/director/critic
Siddons, Sarah	1755–1831	Brecon, Wales	Actress
Sinden, Donald	1923–	Sussex	Actor
Smith, Maggie	1934–	Ilford, Essex	Actress
Sondheim, Stephen	1930–	New York City	Musicals composer
Speaight, Robert William	1904–76	na	Actor
Stafford-Clark, Max	1941–	Cambridge	Director
Stanislavsky	1863–1938	Moscow	Actor/producer/teacher
Stapleton, Maureen	1925–	New York	Actress
Steadman, Alison	1946–	Liverpool	Actress
Stein, Peter	1937–	Berlin	Director
Stevenson, Juliet	1956–	London	Actress
Stott, Ken	1955–	Edinburgh	Actor
Strasberg, Lee	1901–82	Budzanow	Actor/director/teacher
Strehler, Giorgio	1921–97	Italy	Director
Stubbs, Imogen	1961–	Northumberland	Actress
Suzman, Janet	1939–	S Africa	Actress
Terry, Ellen	1847–1928	Coventry	Actress
Thacker, David	1950–	na	Actor
Thorndike, Cybil	1882–1976	Gainsborough	Actress
Threlfell, David	1953–	Manchester	Actor
Tinker, Jack	1938–96	Oldham	Critic
Tree, Herbert Beerbohm	1853–1917	London	Actor-manager
Tutin, Dorothy	1931–2001	London	Actress
Tynan, Kenneth	1927–1980	Birmingham	Critic
Vestris, Mme	1797–1856	London	Actress/manager
Wall, Max	1908–90	London	Actor
Walter, Harriet	1950–	na	Actress
Wanamaker, Sam	1919–93	Chicago	Actor/director
Wanamaker, Zoë	1949–	New York City	Actress
Wardle, Irving	1929–	Bolton	Critic
Warner, Deborah	1959–	Avon	Director
Weigel, Helene	1900–71	Austria	Actress; founded the Berliner Ensemble, 1948, with husband Bertolt Brecht
West, Samuel	1966–	London	Actor
West, Timothy	1934–	Bradford	Actor/director
Whitelaw, Billie	1932–	Coventry	Actress
Wilson, Snoo	1948–	Reading	Director
Wilton, Penelope	1946–	Scarborough	Actress
Wolfit, Donald	1902–68	New Balderton, Nottinghamshire	Actor/manager
Wood, Peter Lawrence	1927–	Colyton, Devon	Director
Worth, Irene	1916–2002	Nebraska	Actress
Zeffirelli, Franco	1923–	Florence	Director
Ziegfeld, Florenz	1869–1932	Chicago	Theatre manager/producer

na = not available See also *Film and Television Personalities*, pp. 591–618

Pulitzer Prize in drama

1918	*No award*
1919	Jesse Lynch Williams *Why Marry?*
1920	*No award*
1921	Eugene O'Neill *Beyond the Horizon*
1922	Zona Gale *Miss Lulu Bett*
1923	Eugene O'Neill *Anna Christie*
1924	Owen Davis *Icebound*
1925	Hatcher Hughes *Hell-Bent for Heaven*
1926	Sidney Howard *They Knew What They Wanted*
1927	George Kelly *Craig's Wife*
1928	Paul Green *In Abraham's Bosom*
1929	Eugene O'Neill *Strange Interlude*
1930	Elmer Rice *Street Scene*
1931	Marc Connelly *The Green Pastures*
1932	Susan Glaspell *Alison's House*
1933	George S Kaufman *Morris Ryskind and Ira Gershwin: Of Thee I Sing*
1934	Maxwell Anderson *Both Your Houses*
1935	Sidney Kingsley *Men in White*
1936	Zoë Akins *The Old Maid*
1937	Robert E Sherwood *Idiot's Delight*
1938	George S Kaufman and Moss Hart *You Can't Take It With You*
1939	Thornton Wilder *Our Town*
1940	Robert E Sherwood *Abe Lincoln in Illinois*
1941	William Saroyan *The Time of Your Life*
1942	Robert E Sherwood *There Shall Be No Night*
1943	*No award*
1944	Thornton Wilder *The Skin of Our Teeth*
1945	*No award*
1946	Mary Chase *Harvey*
1947	Russell Crouse and Howard Lindsay *State of the Union*
1948	*No award*
1949	Tennessee Williams *A Streetcar Named Desire*
1950	Arthur Miller *Death of a Salesman*
1951	Richard Rodgers, Oscar Hammerstein II, and Joshua Logan *South Pacific*
1952	*No award*
1953	Joseph Kramm *The Shake*
1954	William Inge *Picnic*
1955	John Patrick *Teahouse of the August Moon*
1956	Tennessee Williams *Cat on a Hot Tin Roof*
1957	Frances Goodrich and Albert Hackett *The Diary of Anne Frank*
1958	Eugene O'Neill *Long Day's Journey into Night*
1959	Ketti Frings *Look Homeward Angel*
1960	Archibald Macleish *JB*
1961	George Abbott, Jerome Weidman, Sheldon Harnick, and Jerry Bock *Fiorello*
1962	Tad Mosel *All the Way Home*
1963	Frank Loesser and Abe Burrows *How to Succeed in Business Without Really Trying*
1964	*No award*
1965	*No award*
1966	Frank D Gilroy *The Subject Was Roses*
1967	*No award*
1968	Edward Albee *A Delicate Balance*
1969	*No award*
1970	Howard Sackler *The Great White Hope*
1971	Charles Gordone *No Place to Be Somebody*
1972	Paul Zindel *The Effect of Gamma Rays on Man-in-the-Moon Marigolds*
1973	*No award*
1974	Jason Miller *The Championship Season*
1975	*No award*
1976	*No award*
1977	Michael Bennett, James Kirkwood, Nicholas Dante, Marvin Hamlisch, and Edward Kleban *A Chorus Line*
1978	Michael Cristofer *The Shadow Box*
1979	Donald L Coburn *The Gin Game*
1980	Sam Shepard *Buried Child*
1981	Lanford Wildon *Talley's Folly*
	Beth Henley *Games of the Heart*
1982	Charles Fuller *A Soldier's Play*
1983	Marsha Norman *'Night, Mother*
1984	David Mamet *Glengarry Glen Ross*
1985	Stephen Sondhiem and James Lapine *Sunday in the Park with George*
1986	*No award*
1987	August Wilson *Fences*
1988	Alfred Uhry *Driving Miss Daisy*
1989	Wendy Wasserstein *The Heidi Chronicles*
1990	August Wilson *The Piano Lesson*
1991	Neil Simon *Lost in Yonkers*
1992	Robert Schenkkan *The Kentucky Cycle*
1993	Tony Kushner *Angels in America: Millennium Approaches*
1994	Edward Albee *Three Tall Women*
1995	Horton Foote *The Young Man from Atlanta*
1996	Jonathan Larson *Rent* (posthumous)
1997	*No award*
1998	Paula Vogel *How I Learned to Drive*
1999	Margaret Edson *Wit*
2000	Donald Margulies *Dinner With Friends*
2001	David Auburn *Proof*
2002	Suzan Lori-Parks *Topdog/Underdog*
2003	Nilo Cruz *Anna in the Tropics*
2004	Doug Wright *I Am My Own Wife*
2005	John Patrick Shanley *Doubt, a parable*
2006	*No award*

Musicals

Show	Date	Composer(s)	Lyricist(s)	Librettist(s)
A Chorus Line	1975	Marvin Hamlisch	Edward Kleban	James Kirkwood & Nicholas Dante
A Funny Thing Happened on the Way to the Forum	1962	Stephen Sondheim	Stephen Sondheim	Bert Shevelove & Larry Gelbart
A Little Night Music	1973	Stephen Sondheim	Stephen Sondheim	Hugh Wheeler
Annie	1976	Charles Strouse	Martin Charnin	Thomas Meehan
Annie Get Your Gun	1946	Irving Berlin	Herbert & Dorothy Fields	Herbert & Dorothy Fields
Anyone Can Whistle	1964	Stephen Sondheim	Stephen Sondheim	Arthur Laurents
Anything Goes	1934	Cole Porter	Cole Porter	Guy Bolton & PG Wodehouse
Aspects of Love	1989	Andrew Lloyd Webber	Don Black & Charles Hart	Don Black & Charles Hart
Beauty and the Beast	1994	Alan Menken	Howard Ashman & Tim Rice	Linda Woolverton
Billy Elliot	2005	Elton John	Lee Hall	Lee Hall
Blood Brothers	1983	Willy Russell	Willy Russell	Willy Russell
Bombay Dreams	2002	A R Raham	Don Black	Meera Syal
Brigadoon	1947	Frederick Loewe	Alan Jay Lerner	Alan Jay Lerner
Cabaret	1966	John Kander	Fred Ebb	Joe Masteroff
Camelot	1960	Frederick Loewe	Alan Jay Lerner	Alan Jay Lerner
Candide	1956	Leonard Bernstein	Richard Wilbur	Lillian Hellman
Carmen Jones	1943	Georges Bizet, adapted by Meilhac & Halevy	Oscar Hammerstein II	Oscar Hammerstein II
Carousel	1945	Richard Rodgers	Oscar Hammerstein II	Oscar Hammerstein II
Cats	1981	Andrew Lloyd Webber	TS Eliot, adapted by Trevor Nunn	TS Eliot, adapted by Trevor Nunn
Chess	1986	Bjorn Ulvaeus & Benny Andersson	Tim Rice	Tim Rice
Chicago	1975	John Kander	Fred Ebb	Fred Ebb & Bob Fosse
City of Angels	1993	Cy Coleman	David Zippel	Larry Gelbart
Company	1970	Stephen Sondheim	Stephen Sondheim	George Furth
Crazy for You	1993	George Gershwin	Ira Gershwin	Ken Ludwig, adapted from Girl Crazy
Do I Hear a Waltz?	1965	Richard Rodgers	Stephen Sondheim	Arthur Laurents
Evita	1978	Andrew Lloyd Webber	Tim Rice	Tim Rice
Fiddler on the Roof	1964	Jerry Bock	Sheldon Harnick	Joseph Stein
Follies	1971	Stephen Sondheim	Stephen Sondheim	James Goldman
42nd Street	1980	Harry Warren	Al Dubin	Michael Stewart & Mark Bramble
Funny Girl	1964	Jule Styne	Bob Merrill	Isobel Lennart
Godspell	1971	Stephen Schwartz	Stephen Schwartz	John-Michael Tebelak
Grease	1972	Jim Jacobs & Warren Casey	Jim Jacobs & Warren Casey	Jim Jacobs & Warren Casey
Guys and Dolls	1950	Frank Loesser	Frank Loesser	Abe Burrows & Jo Swerling
Gypsy	1959	Jule Styne	Stephen Sondheim	Arthur Laurents
Hair	1967	Galt MacDermot	Galt MacDermot	Gerome Ragni & James Rado
Half a Sixpence	1963	David Heneker	David Heneker	Beverley Cross
Hello Dolly	1964	Jerry Herman	Jerry Herman	Michael Stewart
How to Succeed in Business Without Really Trying	1961	Frank Loesser	Frank Loesser	Abe Burrows, Jack Weinstock, & Willie Gilbert
Into the Woods	1987	Stephen Sondheim	Stephen Sondheim	James Lapine
Irma La Douce	1956	Margaret Monnot	Margaret Monnot	Alexandre Breffort
Jesus Christ Superstar	1971	Andrew Lloyd Webber	Tim Rice	Tim Rice
Joseph and the Amazing Technicolor Dreamcoat	1968	Andrew Lloyd Webber	Tim Rice	Tim Rice
Kismet	1953	Aleksandr Borodin, arr Robert Wright & George Forrest	Robert Wright & George Forrest	Charles Lederer & Luther Davis
Kiss Me Kate	1947	Cole Porter	Cole Porter	Samuel & Bella Spewack
Kiss of the Spider Woman	1993	John Kander	Fred Ebb	Terence McNally, adapted from Manuel Puig
La Cage aux Folles	1983	Jerry Herman	Jerry Herman	Harvey Fierstein

Musicals (continued)

Show	Date	Composer(s)	Lyricist(s)	Librettist(s)
Lady Be Good	1924	George Gershwin	Ira Gershwin	Guy Bolton & Fred Thompson
Lady in the Dark	1941	Kurt Weill	Ira Gershwin	Moss Hart
Les Misérables	1980	Claude-Michel Schönburg	Alain Boublil & Jean-Marc Natel (English lyrics: Herbert Kretzmer)	Alain Boublil & Jean-Marc Natel
Little Shop of Horrors	1982	Alan Menken	Howard Ashman	Howard Ashman
Mame	1966	Jerry Herman	Jerry Herman	Jerome Lawrence & Robert E Lee
Mamma Mia!	1999	Benny Andersson Björn Ulvaeus	Benny Andersson & Björn Ulvaeus	Catherine Johnson
Man of La Mancha	1972	Mitch Leigh	Joe Darion	Dale Wassermann
Me and My Girl	1937	Noel Gay	L Arthur Rose & Douglas Farber	L Arthur Rose & Douglas Farber
Miss Saigon	1990	Claude-Michel Schönburg	Alain Boublil & Richard Maltby Jr	Alain Boublil & Richard Maltby Jr
My Fair Lady	1956	Frederick Loewe	Alan Jay Lerner	Alan Jay Lerner
No, No, Nanette	1925	Vincent Youmans	Irving Caesar & Otto Harbach	Burt Shevelove
Of Thee I Sing	1931	George Gershwin	Ira Gershwin	George S Kaufman & Murray Ryskind
Oh, Kay!	1926	George Gershwin	Ira Gershwin	Guy Bolton & PG Wodehouse
Oklahoma!	1943	Richard Rodgers	Oscar Hammerstein II	Oscar Hammerstein II
Oliver!	1960	Lionel Bart	Lionel Bart	Lionel Bart
On The Town	1944	Leonard Bernstein	Betty Comden & Adolph Green	Betty Comden & Adolph Green
On the Twentieth Century	1978	Cy Coleman	Betty Comden & Adolph Green	Betty Comden & Adolph Green
On Your Toes	1936	Richard Rodgers	Lorenz Hart	Richard Rogers, Lorenz Hart, & George Abbott
Paint Your Wagon	1951	Frederick Loewe	Alan Jay Lerner	Alan Jay Lerner
Pal Joey	1940	Richard Rodgers	Lorenz Hart	John O'Hara
Ragtime	1996	Stephen Flaherty	Lynn Ahrens	Terence McNally
Rent	1996	Jonathan Larson	Jonathan Larson	Jonathan Larson
Rose Marie	1924	Rudolf Friml	Oscar Hammerstein II & Otto Harbach	Oscar Hammerstein II & Otto Harbach
Salad Days	1954	Julian Slade	Julian Slade & Dorothy Reynolds	Julian Slade & Dorothy Reynolds
Show Boat	1927	Jerome Kern	Oscar Hammerstein II	Oscar Hammerstein II
South Pacific	1949	Richard Rodgers	Oscar Hammerstein II	Oscar Hammerstein II & Joshua Logan
Starlight Express	1984	Andrew Lloyd Webber	Richard Stilgoe	Andrew Lloyd Webber & Richard Stilgoe
Stop the World – I Want to Get Off	1961	Leslie Bricuse & Anthony Newley	Leslie Bricuse & Anthony Newley	Leslie Bricuse & Anthony Newley
Sunday in the Park with George	1984	Stephen Sondheim	Stephen Sondheim	James Lapine
Sunset Boulevard	1993	Andrew Lloyd Webber	Christopher Hampton & Don Black	Christopher Hampton & Don Black
Sweeney Todd	1979	Stephen Sondheim	Stephen Sondheim	Hugh Wheeler
Sweet Charity	1966	Cy Coleman	Dorothy Fields	Neil Simon
The Boyfriend	1953	Sandy Wilson	Sandy Wilson	Sandy Wilson
The Desert Song	1926	Sigmund Romberg	Oscar Hammerstein II	Oscar Hammerstein II
The King and I	1951	Richard Rodgers	Oscar Hammerstein II	Oscar Hammerstein II
The Most Happy Fella	1956	Frank Loesser	Frank Loesser	Frank Loesser
The Music Man	1957	Meredith Wilson	Meredith Wilson	Meredith Wilson
The Pajama Game	1954	Richard Adler	Jerry Ross	Richard Adler & Jerry Ross
The Phantom of the Opera	1987	Andrew Lloyd Webber	Charles Hart	Andrew Lloyd Webber & Richard Stilgoe
The Producers	2001	Mel Brooks	Mel Brooks	Mel Brooks & Thomas Meehan
The Rocky Horror Show	1973	Richard O'Brien	Richard O'Brien	Richard O'Brien

ARTS AND CULTURE

Musicals (continued)

Show	Date	Composer(s)	Lyricist(s)	Librettist(s)
The Sound of Music	1959	Richard Rodgers	Oscar Hammerstein II	Howard Lindsay & Russell Crouse
The Woman in White	2004	Andrew Lloyd Webber	David Zippel	Charlotte Jones
We Will Rock You	2002	Queen	Queen	Ben Elton
West Side Story	1957	Leonard Bernstein	Stephen Sondheim	Arthur Laurents
Wonderful Town	1953	Leonard Bernstein	Betty Comden & Adolph Green	Joseph Fields & Jerome Chadarov

FILM AND TELEVISION

Film and television personalities

Name	Dates	Place of birth	Selected works
Adjani, Isabelle	1955–	Paris	*The Story of Adele H* (1975); *Nosferatu* (1978); *Possession* (1980); *Quartet* (1981); *One Deadly Summer* (1983); *Ishtar* (1987); *Camille Claudel* (1988); *Diabolique* (1996); *Bon Voyage* (2003)
Affleck, Ben	1972–	Berkeley, California	*Goodwill Hunting* (1997); *Armageddon* (1998); *Shakespeare in Love* (1998); *Changing Lanes*(2002); *Paycheck* (2003); *Jersey Girl* (2004); *Man About Town* (2005); *Hollywoodland* (2006)
Agutter, Jenny	1952–	Taunton, Somerset	*The Railway Children* (1970); *Logan's Run* (1976); *Equus* (1977); *An American Werewolf in London* (1981); *The Alan Clark Diaries* (TV, 2004); *Heroes and Villains* (2006)
Aimée, Anouk	1934–	Paris	*Les Amants de Verone* (1949); *La Dolce Vita* (1960); *Lola* (1961); *Un Homme et Une Femme* (1966); *Prêt à Porter* (1994); *Festival in Cannes* (2002); *De particulier à particulier* (2006)
Alda, Alan	1936–	New York City	*Paper Lion* (1968); *Catch 22* (1970); *M*A*S*H* (TV, 1972–83); *California Suite* (1978); *Crimes and Misdemeanours* (1990); *What Women Want* (2000); *West Wing* (TV, 2004–)
Allen, Woody	1935–	New York City	Director/screenplay writer/actor: *Play it Again Sam* (1972); *Annie Hall* (1977); *Manhattan* (1979); *Hannah and Her Sisters* (1986); *Anything Else* (2003); *Match Point* (2005)
Alley, Kirstie	1955–	Wichita, Kansas	*Cheers* (TV, 1987–92); *Look Who's Talking* (1989); *Village of the Damned* (1995); *Deconstructing Harry* (1997); *Veronica's Closet* (TV, 1997–2000); *Back By Midnight* (2002)
Almodovar, Pedro	1951–	Calzada de Calatrava, Spain	Director: *Women on the Verge of a Nervous Breakdown* (1988); *Tie Me Up! Tie Me Down!* (1990); *High Heels* (1991); *All About My Mother* (1999); *Talk to Her* (2002); *Volver* (2006)
Altman, Robert	1925–2006	Kansas City	Director: *The James Dean Story* (1957); *The Long Goodbye* (1973); *Popeye* (1980); *The Gingerbread Man* (1997); *Gosford Park* (2001);*The Company* (2004); *A Prairie Home Companion* (2006)
Anderson, Gillian	1968–	Chicago, Illinois	*The X-Files* (TV, 1993–2002); *The X-Files Movie* (1998); *The Mighty* (1998); *The House of Mirth* (2000); *Bleak House* (TV, 2005); *The Last King of Scotland* (2006)
Anderson, Lindsay	1923–94	Bangalore, India	*This Sporting Life* (1963); *If... * (1968); *O Lucky Man* (1973); *Britannia Hospital* (1982); *The Whales of August* (1987)
Andress, Ursula	1936–	Berne	*Dr No* (1963); *She* (1965); *What's New Pussycat?* (1965); *Casino Royale* (1967); *The Clash of the Titans* (1981); *The Chinatown Murders* (TV, 1989)

ARTS AND CULTURE

Film and television personalities (continued)

Name	Dates	Place of birth	Selected works
Andrews, Julie	1935–	Walton-on-Thames, Surrey	*Mary Poppins* (1964); *The Sound of Music* (1965); *Star!* (1968); *Victor/Victoria* (1982); *Duet for One* (1987); *A Fine Romance* (1992); *Shrek 2* (2004)
Aniston, Jennifer	1969–	Sherman Oaks, California	*Friends* (TV, 1994–2004); *Picture Perfect* (1997); *Bruce Almighty* (2003); *Along Came Polly* (2004); *Rumor Has It* (2005); *The Break-Up* (2006)
Antonioni, Michelangelo	1912–	Ferrara, Italy	Director: *L'Avventura* (1959); *La Notte* (1961); *Blow-up* (1966); *Zabriskie Point* (1969); *Beyond The Clouds* (1995)
Arquette, David	1972–	Chicago, Illinois	*Buffy the Vampire Slayer* (1992); *Scream* (1996, 99, 2000); *Never Die Alone* (2004); *Slingshot* (2005); *The Darwin Awards* (2006)
Arquette, Patricia	1968–	Chicago, Illinois	*True Romance* (1994); *Secret Agent* (1996); *The Hi-Lo Country* (1998); *Tiptoes* (2003); *Medium* (TV, 2005)
Arquette, Rosanna	1959–	New York City	*Johnny Belinda* (TV, 1982); *Pulp Fiction* (1994); *Big Bad Love* (2001); *Max and Grace* (2004); *Iowa* (2005)
Ashcroft, Peggy	1907–91	Croydon, Surrey	*The Thirty-Nine Steps* (1935); *Quiet Wedding* (1940); *A Passage to India* (1984); *The Jewel in the Crown* (TV, 1984); *Madame Sousatzka* (1988)
Astaire, Fred	1899–1987	Omaha, Nebraska	*Top Hat* (1935); *Follow the Fleet* (1936); *Easter Parade* (1948)
Atkinson, Rowan	1955–	Northumberland	*Blackadder I, II, & III* (TV, 1984–6); *Mr Bean* (TV, 1990); *Four Weddings and a Funeral* (1994); *Bean* (1997); *Johnny English* (2003); *Keeping Mum* (2006)
Attenborough, Richard	1923–	Cambridge	*In Which We Serve* (1942); *Brighton Rock* (1947); *Shakespeare in Love* (1998); Director: *Oh What A Lovely War* (1969); *Gandhi* (1982); *A Chorus Line* (1985); *Shadowlands* (1993); *Grey Owl* (2000)
August, Bille	1948–	Denmark	Director: *Pelle The Conqueror* (1987); *The Best Intentions* (1992); *Jerusalem* (1996); *A Song For Martin* (2001); *Return to Sender* (2004)
Avnet, Jon	1949–	New York City	*Fried Green Tomatoes* (1991); *Up Close and Personal* (1996); *Uprising* (2001); *Land of the Blind* (2006)
Aykroyd, Dan	1952–	Ottawa	*The Blues Brothers* (1980); *Ghostbusters* (1984, 1989); *Driving Miss Daisy* (1989); *Grosse Point Blank* (1997); *Bright Young Things* (2003); *Christmas with the Kranks* (2004)
Bacall, Lauren	1924–	New York City	*The Big Sleep* (1946); *Key Largo* (1948); *The Shootist* (1976); *The Mirror Has Two Faces* (1996); *Dogville* (2004); *Birth* (2004)
Baldwin, Alec	1958–	Amityville, New York	*Working Girl* (1988); *Prelude to a Kiss* (1992); *Malice* (1993); *The Edge* (1997); *Notting Hill* (1999) *Elizabethtown* (2005); *Brooklyn Rules* (2006)
Ball, Lucille	1911–89	Celaron, New York	*Ziegfield Follies* (1946); *I Love Lucy* (TV, 1951–5)
Bancroft, Anne	1931–2005	New York City	*The Miracle Worker* (1962); *The Graduate* (1968); *The Elephant Man* (1980); *84 Charing Cross Road* (1986); *Home for the Holidays* (1995); *G. I. Jane* (1997); *Up at the Villa* (1999)
Banderas, Antonio	1960–	Malaga, Spain	*Interview with the Vampire* (1994); *Desperado* (1995); *Evita* (1996); *The Mask of Zorro* (1998); *Femme Fatale* (2002); *Shrek* (2004); *Bordertown* (2006)
Bankhead, Tallulah	1903–68	Huntsville, Texas	*Tarnished Lady* (1931); *Lifeboat* (1944); *A Royal Scandal* (1945)
Bardot, Brigitte	1934–	Paris	*Et Dieu Créa La Femme* (1956); *Si Don Juan Était Une Femme* (1973)
Barker, Ronnie	1929–2005	Bedford	TV series: *Porridge* (1974–7); *Open All Hours* (1976, 1981–5); *The Two Ronnies* (1971–87); *The Two Ronnies Sketchbook* (2005)

Name	Dates	Place of birth	Selected works
Barrault, Jean-Louis	1910–94	Le Vesinet, France	*Les Enfants du Paradis* (1945); *La Ronde* (1950); *The Longest Day* (1962)
Barrymore, Drew	1975–	Los Angeles	*Far From Home* (1989); *Wayne's World 2* (1993); *Batman Forever* (1995); *Donnie Darko* (2001); *50 First Dates* (2004); *Fever Pitch* (2005)
Barrymore, Ethel	1879–1959	Philadelphia	*Rasputin and the Empress* (1932); *None But the Lonely Heart* (1944)
Barrymore, John	1882–1942	Philadelphia	*Grand Hotel* (1932); *Dinner At Eight* (1933); *Midnight* (1939)
Basinger, Kim	1953–	Athens, Georgia	*Never Say Never Again* (1983); *9^1/$_2$ Weeks* (1985); *Batman* (1989); *Too Hot to Handle* (1991); *LA Confidential* (1997); *Cellular* (2004); *The Sentinel* (2006)
Bates, Alan	1934–2003	Allestree, Derbyshire	*A Kind of Loving* (1962); *Whistle Down the Wind* (1962); *Zorba the Greek* (1965); *Far From the Madding Crowd* (1967); *Women in Love* (1969); *Hamlet* (1990); *Oliver's Travels* (TV, 1995)
Beatty, Warren	1937–	Richmond, Virginia	*Splendour in the Grass* (1961); *All Fall Down* (1962); *Bonnie and Clyde*(1967); *Dick Tracy* (1990); *Bugsy* (1991); *Love Affair* (1994); *Bulworth* (1998); *Town and Country* (2001)
Belmondo, Jean-Paul	1933–	Neuilly-sur-Seine France	*A Bout de Souffle* (*Breathless*, 1959); *That Man From Rio* (1964); *Hold Up* (1985); *Peut Être* (1985); *Amazone* (2000)
Bergman, Ingmar	1918–	Uppsala, Sweden	Director: *Smiles of a Summer Night* (1955); *The Seventh Seal* (1957); *Wild Strawberries* (1957); *Herbsonate* (1978); *Fanny and Alexander* (1983); *Saraband* (2005)
Bergman, Ingrid	1915–82	Stockholm	*Intermezzo* (1939); *Casablanca* (1942); *For Whom The Bell Tolls* (1943); *Gaslight* (1944); *Anastasia* (1956); *Autumn Sonata* (1978); *A Woman Called Golda* (TV, 1982)
Bertolucci, Bernardo	1941–	Parma, Italy	Director: *Last Tango in Paris* (1972); *The Last Emperor* (1987); *Stealing Beauty* (1996); *Besieged* (1998); *Training Day* (2001); *The Dreamers* (2004)
Besson, Luc	1959–	Paris	Director: *Subway* (1985); *The Big Blue* (1988); *Nikita* (1990); *Leon* (1994); *Joan of Arc* (1999); *Angel-A* (2005)
Binoche, Juliette	1964–	Paris	*The Unbearable Lightness of Being* (1988); *Damage* (1992); *The English Patient* (1996); *Chocolat* (2000); *Jet Lag* (2002); *Hidden* (2005); *Breaking and Entering* (2006)
Blanchett, Cate	1970–	Melbourne	*Paradise Road* (1997); *Oscar and Lucinda* (1997); *Elizabeth* (1998); *The Lord ofthe Rings* (2001–3); *Veronica Guerin* (2003); *The Aviator* (2004; *Babel* (2006)
Blethyn, Brenda	1946–	Ramsgate, Kent	*Outside Edge* (TV, 1994); *Secrets and Lies* (1996); *Little Voice* (1998); *Pumpkin* (2002); *Pride & Prejudice* (2005)
Bloom, Claire	1931–	London	*Look Back In Anger* (1959); *The Spy Who Came in From the Cold* (1966); *Crimes and Misdemeanours* (1990); *Wrestling With Alligators* (1990)
Bloom, Orlando	1977–	Canterbury, Kent	*The Lord of the Rings* trilogy (2001–3); *Pirates of the Caribbean* (2003; sequel 2006); *Troy* (2004); *Kingdom of Heaven* (2005)
Bogarde, Dirk	1921–99	London	*Victim* (1961); *The Servant* (1963); *The Damned* (1969); *Death in Venice* (1971); *Providence* (1977); *Daddy Nostalgie* (1990)
Bogart, Humphrey	1899–1957	New York City	*The Maltese Falcon* (1941); *Casablanca* (1942); *The Big Sleep* (1946); *The Treasure of the Sierra Madre* (1948); *The African Queen* (1951)
Bogdanovich, Peter	1939–	Kingston, New York	Director: *The Last Picture Show* (1971); *Paper Moon* (1973); *Nickelodeon* (1976); *Mask* (1985); *Noises Off* (1992); *The Thing Called Love* (1993)

ARTS AND CULTURE

Film and television personalities (continued)

Name	Dates	Place of birth	Selected works
Bonham-Carter, Helena	1966–	London	*A Room With a View* (1985); *Hamlet* (1990); *The Heart of Me* (2003); *Big Fish* (2004); *Charlie and the Chocolate Factory* (2005)
Boorman, John	1933–	London	Director: *Deliverance* (1972); *Hope and Glory* (1987); *Beyond Rangoon* (1995); *The General* (1998); *The Tailor of Panama* (2000); *Country of My Skull* (2004)
Bow, Clara	1905–65	New York City	*Mantrap* (1926); *It* (1927); *Wings* (1927)
Boyer, Charles	1899–1978	Figeac, France	*Mayerling* (1936); *The Garden of Allah* (1936); *The Mad Woman of Chaillot* (1969); *Stavisky* (1974)
Branagh, Kenneth	1960–	Belfast	*Henry V* (1989); *Much Ado About Nothing* (1993); *Mary Shelley's Frankenstein* (1994); *In the Bleak Midwinter* (1995); *Hamlet* (1997); *Rabbit-Proof Fence* (2002); *Five Children and It* (2004)
Brandauer, Klaus Maria von	1944–	Alt Aussee, Austria	*Out of Africa* (1985); *The Russia House* (1990); *Becoming Colette* (1992); *Between Strangers* (2002)
Brando, Marlon	1924–2004	Omaha, Nebraska	*A Streetcar Named Desire* (1951); *On The Waterfront* (1954); *Mutiny on the Bounty* (1962); *The Godfather* (1972); *Last Tango in Paris* (1972); *Apocalypse Now* (1979); *The Score* (2001)
Bresson, Robert	1907–99	Auvergne, France	Director: *Anges du Péché* (1943); *Le Journal d'un Curé de Campagne* (1951); *L'Argent* (1983)
Bridges, Beau	1941–	Los Angeles	*Greased Lightning* (1997); *The Fabulous Baker Boys* (1989); *Losing Chase* (1996); *10.5* (TV 2004); *The Ballad of Jack and Rose* (2005)
Bridges, Jeff	1949–	Los Angeles	*The Last Picture Show* (1971); *Against All Odds* (1983); *The Fabulous Baker Boys* (1989); *The Fisher King* (1991); *The Mirror Has Two Faces* (1996); *The Muse* (1999); *Seabiscuit* (2003); *The Moguls* (2005)
Broderick, Matthew	1963–	New York City	*Biloxi Blues* (1988); *Torch Song Trilogy* (1988); *The Night We Never Met* (1993); *Godzilla* (1998); *The Stepford Wives* (2004); *Strangers with Candy* (2005)
Bronson, Charles	1921–2003	Ehrenfield, Pennsylvania	*The Magnificent Seven* (1960); *This Property is Condemned* (1966); *The Dirty Dozen* (1967); *Death Wish* (1974); *Death Wish V: The Face of Death* (1994)
Brooks, Louise	1906–85	Cherryvale, Kansas	*Pandora's Box* (1929); *Diary of a Lost Girl* (1930)
Brooks, Mel	1926–	New York City	Director: *Blazing Saddles* (1974); *Silent Movie* (1976); *History of the World Part One* (1980); *Spaceballs* (1987); *Dracula: Dead and Loving It* (1995)
Brosnan, Pierce	1953–	County Meath, Ireland	*The Long Good Friday* (1980); *Mrs Doubtfire* (1993); *Goldeneye* (1995); *The Thomas Crown Affair* (1999); *Laws of Attraction* (2004); *The Matador* (2005)
Bruckheimer, Jerry	c. 1945	Detroit, Michigan	Producer: *Farewell My Lovely* (1975); *American Gigolo* (1980); *Armageddon* (1998); *Pirates of the Caribbean* (2003; sequel 2006); *King Arthur* (2004)
Bullock, Sandra	1964–	Arlington, Virginia	*Speed* (1994; sequel 1997); *While You Were Sleeping* (1995); *Practical Magic* (1998); *Miss Congeniality* (2000; sequel 2005); *The Lake House* (2006)
Buñuel, Luis	1900–83	Calanda, Spain	Director: *Un Chien Andalou* (1928); *L'Age D'Or* (1930); *Los Olvidados* (1950); *That Obscure Object of Desire* (1977)
Burton, Richard	1925–84	Pontrhydfen, Wales	*My Cousin Rachel* (1952); *Look Back in Anger* (1959); *Cleopatra* (1962); *The Night of the Iguana* (1964); *Who's Afraid of Virginia Woolf?* (1966); *Where Eagles Dare* (1969); *1984* (1984)
Buscemi, Steve	1957–	Brooklyn, New York	*Fargo* (1996); *Con Air* (1997); *Armageddon* (1998); *Big Fish* (2003); *Romance & Cigarettes* (2005)
Busey, Jake	1972–	Los Angeles	*Barbarosa* (1982); *Twister* (1996); *Starship Troopers* (1997); *Lost Junction* (2002); *The Rain Makers* (2005); *Road House 2: Last Call* (2006)
Byrne, Gabriel	1950–	Dublin	*Excalibur* (1981); *Christopher Columbus* (1991); *Enemy of the State* (1998); *Vanity Fair* (2004); *Wah-Wah* (2005); *Jindabyne* (2006)

Name	Dates	Place of birth	Selected works
Cage, Nicolas	1964–	Long Beach, California	*The Cotton Club* (1984); *Peggy Sue Got Married* (1986); *Leaving Las Vegas* (1995); *Captain Corelli's Mandolin* (2001); *Lord of War* (2005); *The Wicker Man* (2006)
Cagney, James	1899–1986	New York City	*Public Enemy* (1931); *Lady Killer* (1933); *A Midsummer Night's Dream* (1935); *Yankee Doodle Dandee* (1942)
Caine, Michael	1933–	London	*The Ipcress File* (1965); *Alfie* (1966); *Educating Rita* (1983); *Hannah and Her Sisters* (1986); *The Quiet American* (2002); *The Weather Man* (2005); *Children of Men* (2006)
Callow, Simon	1945–	London	*Amadeus* (1984); *A Room With A View* (1985); *Four Weddings and a Funeral* (1994); *Shakespeare in Love* (1998); *The Phantom of the Opera* (2005)
Cameron, James	1954–	Kapuskasing, Ontario	Director: *The Terminator* (1984); *Aliens* (1986); *True Lies* (1994); *Titanic* (1997); *Aliens of the Deep* (2005)
Capra, Frank	1897–1991	Palermo, Italy	Director: *It Happened One Night* (1934); *You Can't Take It With You* (1938); *Arsenic and Old Lace* (1942); *It's A Wonderful Life* (1946)
Carlyle, Robert	1954–	Glasgow	*Hamish Macbeth* (TV, 1995–7); *Trainspotting* (1996); *The Full Monty* (1996); *Angela's Ashes* (1998); *The Mighty Celt* (2005)
Carné, Marcel	1909–96	Paris	Director: *Quai des Brumes* (1938); *Le Jour se Lève* (1939); *Les Enfants du Paradis* (1944)
Cassavetes, John	1929–89	New York City	Director: *The Dirty Dozen* (1967); *Rosemary's Baby* (1969); *The Fury* (1978); *Whose Life is it Anyway?* (1981); *Tempest* (1983)
Chabrol, Claude	1930–	Paris	*Le Beau Serge* (1958); *Le Boucher* (1970); *Les Noces Rouges* (1973); *Rien Ne Va Plus* (1997); *Merci pour le chocolat* (2000); *La Demoiselle d'honneur* (2004); *L'Ivresse du pouvoir* (2006)
Chaney, Lon	1883–1930	Colorado Springs	*The Hunchback of Notre Dame* (1923); *The Phantom of the Opera* (1925)
Chaplin, Charlie	1889–1977	London	*The Kid* (1921); *The Goldrush* (1925); *City Lights* (1931); *Modern Times* (1936); *The Great Dictator* (1940)
Chase, Chevy	1943–	New York City	*National Lampoon's Vacation* (1988); *Cops and Robbersons* (1994); *Vegas Vacation* (1996); *Goose* (2004); *Ellie Parker* (2005); *Funny Money* (2006)
Cher	1946–	El Centro, California	*Silkwood* (1983); *Moonstruck* (1987); *The Witches of Eastwick* (1987); *Tea With Mussolini* (1998)
Chevalier, Maurice	1888–1972	Paris	*The Innocents of Paris* (1929); *One Hour With You* (1932); *Gigi* (1958)
Christie, Julie	1940–	Assam, India	*Billy Liar* (1963); *Doctor Zhivago* (1965); *Far From the Madding Crowd* (1967); *The Go-Between* (1971); *Heat and Dust* (1982); *Hamlet* (1996); *Afterglow* (1997); *Troy* (2004)
Clair, René	1898–1981	Paris	Director: *Sous les Toits de Paris* (1930); *And Then There Were None* (1945); *Les Belles de Nuit* (1952); *Porte des Lilas* (1956)
Cleese, John	1939–	Weston-Super-Mare, Somerset	*Monty Python's Flying Circus* (TV, 1969–74); *Monty Python and the Holy Grail* (1974); *Fawlty Towers* (TV, 1975, 1979); *A Fish Called Wanda* (1988); *Man About Town* (2006)
Clift, Montgomery	1920–66	Omaha, Nebraska	*Red River* (1946); *A Place in the Sun* (1951); *From Here To Eternity* (1953); *Suddenly Last Summer* (1968)
Close, Glenn	1947–	Greenwich, Connecticut	*The World According to Garp* (1982); *Fatal Attraction* (1987); *Hamlet* (1990); *101 Dalmations* (1996); *The Stepford Wives* (2004); *The Chumscrubber* (2005)
Clooney, George	1961	Lexington, Kentucky	*ER* (TV 1994–9); *Batman and Robin* (1997); *Ocean's Eleven* (2001, sequel 2004); *Syriana* (2005). Director: *Confessions of a Dangerous Mind* (2003); *Good Night, and Good Luck* (2005)

Film and television personalities (continued)

Name	Dates	Place of birth	Selected works
Coen, Ethan and Joel	1958– 1955–	St Louis Park, Minnesota	Directors, screenplay writers, and producers: *Blood Simple* (1984); *Barton Fink* (1991); *The Big Lebowski* (1997); *The Man Who Wasn't There* (2001); *The Lady Killers* (2004)
Colbert, Claudette	1903–96	Paris	*It Happened One Night* (1934); *Tovarich* (1937); *The Palm Beach Story* (1942)
Coltrane, Robbie	1950–	Rutherglen, Glasgow	*Flash Gordon* (1980); *Cracker* (TV, 1993–); *Harry Potter and the Philosopher's Stone* (2001; sequels 2004, 2005); *Stormbreaker* (2006)
Connery, Sean	1930–	Edinburgh	*Dr No* (1962); and James Bond films to 1983; *The Name of the Rose* (1986); *Indiana Jones and The Last Crusade* (1989); *The Russia House* (1991); *The League of Extraordinary Gentlemen* (2004)
Cooper, Gary	1901–61	Helena, Montana	*The Winning of Barbara Worth* (1926); *A Farewell to Arms* (1932); *For Whom the Bell Tolls* (1943); *High Noon* (1952)
Coppola, Francis Ford	1939–	Detroit	Director: *The Godfather* (1972; sequels 1974, 1990); *Apocalypse Now* (1979); *The Cotton Club* (1984); *Peggy Sue Got Married* (1987); *Bram Stoker's Dracula* (1992); *Rainmaker* (1998)
Costner, Kevin	1955–	Compton, California	*Field of Dreams* (1989); *Dances with Wolves* (1990); *Robin Hood: Prince of Thieves* (1991); *JFK* (1991); *Open Range* (2003); *The Upside of Anger* (2005); *The Guardian* (2006)
Courtenay, Tom	1937–	Hull, Humberside	*The Loneliness of the Long Distance Runner* (1962); *Billy Liar* (1963); *Dr Zhivago* (1965); *The Dresser* (1983); *Let Him Have It* (1991); *A Rather English Marriage* (TV, 1998); *Last Orders* (2001)
Cox (Arquette), Courtney	1964–	Birmingham, Alabama	*Friends* (TV 1994–2004); *Ace Ventura: Pet Detective* (1994); *Scream* (1996); *Scream 2* (1998); *Alien Love Triangle* (2002); *Zoom* (2006)
Crawford, Joan	1904–77	San Antonio, Texas	*Our Dancing Daughters* (1928); *Mildred Pierce* (1945); *Possessed* (1947); *Whatever Happened to Baby Jane?* (1962)
Cronenberg, David	1943–	Toronto	*The Dead Zone* (1983); *The Fly* (1986); *M. Butterfly* (1993); *Crash* (1996); *eXistenZ* (1998); *Spider* (2002); *A History of Violence* (2005)
Crosby, Bing	1904–77	Tacoma, Washington	*Anything Goes* (1936); *Road to Singapore* (1940), *Road to Morocco* (1942); *A Connecticut Yankee in King Arthur's Court* (1949); *White Christmas* (1954); *High Society* (1956)
Crowe, Russell	1964–	Wellington, New Zealand	*Gladiator* (2000); *A Beautiful Mind* (2001); *Master and Commander* (2003); *Cinderella Man* (2005)
Cruise, Tom	1962–	Syracuse, New York	*Top Gun* (1985); *Rain Man* (1988); *Born on the Fourth of July* (1989); *Mission: Impossible* (1996; sequels 2000, 2006); *Eyes Wide Shut* (1999); *The Last Samurai* (2003); *War of the Worlds* (2005)
Crystal, Billy	1947–	Long Beach, New York	*Throw Momma From the Train* (1987); *When Harry Met Sally* (1989); *City Slickers* (1991); *City Slickers II* (1994); *Forget Paris* (1995); *Fathers' Day* (1997); *Analyze This* (1999); *America's Sweethearts* (2001)
Cukor, George D(ewey)	1899–1983	New York City	Director: *Girls About Town* (1931); *Little Women* (1933); *Gaslight* (1944); *A Star is Born* (1954); *My Fair Lady* (1964)
Curtis, Tony	1925–	New York City	*Some Like it Hot* (1959); *Spartacus* (1960); *The Boston Strangler* (1968); *The Mirror Crack'd* (1980); *The Continued Adventures of Reptile Man* (1996)
Curtiz, Michael	1888–1962	Budapest	Director: *Captain Blood* (1935); *Charge of the Light Brigade* (1936); *The Adventures of Robin Hood* (1938); *Yankee Doodle Dandee* (1942); *Casablanca* (1943); *White Christmas* (1954)

Name	Dates	Place of birth	Selected works
Cushing, Peter	1913–94	Kenley, Surrey	*The Man in the Iron Mask* (1939); *The Curse of Frankenstein* (1956); *Dracula* (1958); *The Hound of the Baskervilles* (1959)
Dafoe, Willem	1955–	Appleton, Wisconsin	*Platoon* (1986); *The Last Temptation of Christ* (1988); *Body of Evidence* (1992); *The English Patient* (1996); *Spider-Man* (2002); *The Reckoning* (2004); *Manderlay* (2005); *Inside Man* (2006)
Dalton, Timothy	1946–	Colwyn Bay, Wales	*Wuthering Heights* (1970); *Mary Queen of Scots* (1971); *Licence to Kill* (1989); *The Beautician and the Beast* (1996); *American Outlaws* (2001)
Damon, Matt	1970–	Cambridge, Massachusetts	*Good Will Hunting* (1997); *Saving Private Ryan* (1998); *The Talented Mr Ripley* (1999); *The Bourne Identity* (2002); *The Bourne Supremacy* (2004); *The Brothers Grimm* (2005)
Dance, Charles	1946–	Rednal, Worcestershire	*The Jewel in the Crown* (TV, 1984); *Plenty* (1985); *White Mischief* (1987); *Pascali's Island* (1988); *Alien 3* (1992); *Michael Collins* (1996); *Hilary and Jackie* (1998); *Bleak House* (TV, 2005)
Danson, Ted	1947–	Flagstaff, Arizona	*Cheers* (TV, 1982–93); *Three Men and a Baby* (1987); *Made in America* (1993); *Gulliver's Travels* (TV, 1996); *Living with the Dead* (2002)
Davis, Bette	1908–89	Lowell, Massachusetts	*Bad Sister* (1931); *Dangerous* (1935); *Jezebel* (1938); *Whatever Happened to Baby Jane?* (1962); *Death on the Nile* (1978); *The Whales of August* (1987)
Davis, Geena	1957–	Wareham, Massachusetts	*Tootsie* (1982); *The Accidental Tourist* (1986); *Earth Girls Are Easy* (1989); *Thelma and Louise* (1991); *Stuart Little* (1999; sequel 2002)
Davis, Judy	1956–	Perth	*My Brilliant Career* (1979); *A Passage To India* (1987); *Husbands and Wives* (1992); *Children of the Revolution* (1996); *Celebrity* (1998); *The Man Who Sued God* (2001); *The Break-Up* (2006)
Day, Doris	1924–	Cincinnati, Ohio	*Calamity Jane* (1953); *Young at Heart* (1954); *The Pyjama Game* (1957); *Pillow Talk* (1959)
Day-Lewis, Daniel	1957–	London	*Gandhi* (1983); *My Beautiful Launderette* (1985); *Room With A View* (1985); *My Left Foot* (1989); *In the Name of the Father* (1994); *Gangs of New York* (2002); *The Ballad of Jack and Rose* (2005)
Dean, James	1931–55	Marion, Indiana	*East of Eden* (1955); *Rebel Without A Cause* (1955); *Giant* (1956)
De Havilland, Olivia	1916–	Tokyo	*A Midsummer Night's Dream* (1935); *The Adventures of Robin Hood* (1938); *Gone With The Wind* (1939); (1939); *The Dark Mirror* (1946); *The Heiress* (1949)
Delon, Alain	1935–	Paris	*The Leopard* (1962); *Swann in Love* (1984); *The Day and the Night* (1997); *The Lion* (TV, 2003)
De Mille, Cecil B(lount)	1881–1959	Ashfield, Massachusetts	Director: *The Squaw Man* (1913); *The Ten Commandments* (1923); *The Plainsman* (1937); *The Greatest Show On Earth* (1952)
Demme, Jonathan	1944–	Long Island, New York	Director: *Married To The Mob* (1988); *The Silence of the Lambs* (1991); *Beloved* (1998); *The Truth About Charlie* (2002); *The Agronomist* (2004)
Dench, Judi	1934–	York	*A Fine Romance* (TV, 1981–4); *A Room With A View* (1985); *Mrs Brown* (1997); *Shakespeare in Love* (1998); *Iris* (2001); *The Chronicles of Riddick* (2004); *Pride & Prejudice* (2005)
Deneuve, Catherine	1943–	Paris	*Repulsion* (1965); *Belle de Jour* (1967); *Tristana* (1970); *The Hunger* (1983); *Indochine* (1992); *Place Vendôme* (1998); *8 femmes* (2002); *Les Temps qui changent* (2004)
De Niro, Robert	1943–	New York City	*Mean Streets* (1973); *Taxi Driver* (1976); *The Deer Hunter* (1978); *Goodfellas* (1990); *Awakenings* (1990); *Sleepers* (1996); *Analyze That* (2002); *Godsend* (2002); *Meet the Fockers* (2004)

ARTS AND CULTURE

Film and television personalities (continued)

Name	Dates	Place of birth	Selected works
Dennehy, Brian	1940–	Bridgeport, Connecticut	*First Blood* (1982); *Gorky Park* (1983); *Belly of An Architect* (1987); *Presumed Innocent* (1990); *Gladiator* (1992); *Nostromo* (TV, 1996); *Stolen Summer* (2002); *Assault on Precinct 13* (2005)
De Palma, Brian	1940–	Newark, New Jersey	Director: *Dressed To Kill* (1980); *Scarface* (1983); *The Untouchables* (1987); *Mission Impossible* (1996); *Snake Eyes* (1998); *Femme Fatale* (2002); *The Black Dahlia* (2006)
Depardieu, Gerard	1948–	Chateauroux	*Loulou* (1980); *The Return of Martin Guerre* (1981); *Jean de Florette* (1986); *Cyrano de Bergerac* (1990); *Green Card* (1990); *The Man in the Iron Mask* (1998); *San Antonio* (2004); *Boudu* (2005)
Depp, Johnny	1963–	Owensboro, Kentucky	*A Nightmare on Elm Street* (1984); *Edward Scissorhands* (1990); *Pirates of the Caribbean* (2003; sequel 2006); *Finding Neverland* (2004); *Charlie and the Chocolate Factory* (2005)
Dern, Laura	1967–	Los Angeles	*Mask* (1985); *Rambling Rose* (1991); *Jurassic Park* (1993); *Damaged Care* (TV, 2002); *Happy Endings* (2005); *Inland Empire* (2006)
Diaz, Cameron	1972–	San Diego, California	*The Mask* (1994); *Feeling Minnesota* (1996); *She's The One* (1996); *My Best Friend's Wedding* (1997); *There's Something About Mary* (1998); *Gangs of New York* (2002); *In Her Shoes* (2005)
DiCaprio, Leonardo	1974–	Los Angeles	*What's Eating Gilbert Grape?* (1993); *Romeo + Juliet* (1996); *Titanic* (1997); *The Man in the Iron Mask* (1998); *The Beach* (1999); *Gangs of New York* (2002); *The Aviator* (2004); *The Departed* (2006)
Dietrich, Marlene	1901–92	Berlin	*Der Blaue Engel* (*The Blue Angel*, 1930); *Blond Venus* (1932); *Shanghai Express* (1932); *The Devil is A Woman* (1935); *Desire* (1936); *Notorious* (1956); *Judgement at Nuremberg* (1961)
Dillon, Matt	1964–	Larchmont, New York	*Rumblefish* (1983); *The Flamingo Kid* (1984); *Target* (1985); *Drugstore Cowboy* (1989); *Wild Things* (1998); *City of Ghosts* (2002); *Loverboy* (2005); *You, Me and Dupree* (2006)
Disney, Walt	1901–66	Chicago	Artist and film producer: *Snow White and the Seven Dwarfs* (1937); *Pinocchio* (1940); *Fantasia* (1940); *Dumbo* (1941)
Donat, Robert	1905–58	Withington Manchester	*The Count of Monte Cristo* (1934); *The Thirty-Nine Steps* (1935); *The Citadel* (1938); *Goodbye Mr Chips* (1939); *Inn of the Sixth Happiness* (1958)
Donner, Richard	1939–	New York City	Director: *The Omen* (1976); *Lethal Weapon* (1987); *Maverick* (1994); *Conspiracy Theory* (1997); *Lethal Weapon 4* (1998); *Timeline* (2003)
Douglas, Kirk	1916–	Amsterdam, New York	*The Strange Love of Martha Ivers* (1946); *Lust for Life* (1956); *Gunfight at the OK Corral* (1957); *Paths of Glory* (1957); *Spartacus* (1960); *The Man From Snowy River* (1982)
Douglas, Michael	1944–	New Jersey	*The China Syndrome* (1980); *Romancing the Stone* (1984); *Fatal Attraction* (1987); *Basic Instinct* (1992); *A Perfect Murder* (1998); *Traffic* (2000); *The In-Laws* (2003); *The Sentinel* (2006)
Dreyfuss, Richard	1947–	New York City	*Jaws* (1975); *Close Encounters of the Third Kind* (1977); *Down and Out in Beverly Hills* (1986); *Postcards From the Edge* (1990); *Krippendorf's Tribe* (1998); *Silver City* (2004); *Poseidon* (2006)
Duchovny, David	1960–	New York City	*Working Girl* (1988); *Beethoven* (1992); *The X-Files* (TV, 1993–); *The X-Files Movie* (1998); *Full Frontal* (2002); *House of D* (2004); *The Secret* (2006)
Dunaway, Faye	1941–	Bascom, Florida	*Bonnie and Clyde* (1967); *The Towering Inferno* (1974); *Mommie Dearest* (1981); *Barfly* (1987); *The Handmaid's Tale* (1990); *Fanny Hill* (1998); *Colored Eggs* (2002); *Jennifer's Shadow* (2004)

Name	Dates	Place of birth	Selected works
Dunst, Kirsten	1982–	New Jersey	*Spider-Man* (2002; sequel 2004); *Mona Lisa Smile* (2003); *Wimbledon* (2004); *Elizabethtown* (2005); *Marie Antoinette* (2006)
Eastwood, Clint	1930–	San Francisco	*A Fistful of Dollars* (1964); *The Good, The Bad and the Ugly* (1966); *Play Misty For Me* (1971), Director: *Bridges of Madison County* (1995); *Mystic River* (2003); *Letters from Iwo Jima* (2006)
Eisenstein, Sergei	1898–1948	Riga, Latvia	Director: *The Battleship Potemkin* (1925); *October* (1927); *Alexander Nevski* (1938); *Ivan The Terrible* (1944)
Elliott, Denholm	1922–92	London	*A Bridge Too Far* (1977); *Raiders of the Lost Ark* (1981); *A Private Function* (1984); *A Room With A View* (1985); *Defence of the Maurice* (1987); *Indiana Jones and the Last Crusade* (1989)
Emmerich, Roland	1955–	Stuttgart	Director: *Hollywood Monster* (1987); *Stargate* (1994); *Independence Day* (1996); *Godzilla* (1998); *The Day After Tomorrow* (2004)
Everett, Rupert	1960–	Norfolk	*Another Country* (1984); *Dance With A Stranger* (1985); *The Comfort of Strangers* (1990); *My Best Friend's Wedding* (1997); *An Ideal Husband* (1999); *The Chronicles of Narnia* (2005)
Fairbanks, Douglas Sr	1883–1939	Denver, Colorado	*The Mark of Zorro* (1920); *The Three Musketeers* (1921); *Robin Hood* (1922); *The Thief of Baghdad* (1924)
Fairbanks, Douglas Jr	1909–2000	New York City	*Catherine the Great* (1934); *The Prisoner of Zenda* (1937); *Sinbad the Sailor* (1947)
Farrell, Colin	1976–	Dublin	*Minority Report* (2002); *The Recruit* (2003); *Veronica Guerin* (2003); *Alexander* (2004); *Miami Vice* (2006)
Farrow, Mia	1945–	Los Angeles	*Rosemary's Baby* (1968); *The Great Gatsby* (1973); *The Purple Rose of Cairo* (1985); *Hannah and Her Sisters* (1986); *Husbands and Wives* (1992); *Miracle at Midnight* (1997); *The Omen* (2006)
Fassbinder, Rainer Werner	1945–82	Bad Wörishofen, Germany	Director: *Die Bitteren Tränen der Petra von Kant* (1972); *Die Ehe der Maria Braun* (1978)
Fellini, Federico	1920–93	Rimini, Italy	Director: *La Strada* (1954); *Fellini's Roma* (1972); *Amarcord* (1974); *La Dolce Vita* (1960)
Fields, W C	1880–1946	Philadelphia	*It's A Gift* (1934); *The Old-Fashioned Way* (1934); *David Copperfield* (1935); *My Little Chickadee* (1940); *Never Give A Sucker An Even Break* (1941)
Fiennes, Joseph	1970–	Salisbury, Wiltshire	*Stealing Beauty* (1996); *Elizabeth* (1998); *Shakespeare in Love* (1998); *Dust* (2001); *Luther* (2003); *The Great Raid* (2005); *The Darwin Awards* (2006)
Fiennes, Ralph	1962–	Suffolk	*Schindler's List* (1993); *Strange Days* (1995); *The English Patient* (1996); *Oscar and Lucinda* (1997); *Onegin* (1999); *Spider* (2002); *The Constant Gardener* (2005)
Finney, Albert	1936–	Salford, Manchester	*Saturday Night and Sunday Morning* (1960); *Tom Jones* (1963); *The Dresser* (1983); *A Rather English Marriage* (TV, 1998); *The Gathering Storm* (TV, 2002); *Big Fish* (2004); *Amazing Grace* (2007)
Firth, Colin	1960–	Grayshott, Hampshire	*Pride and Prejudice* (TV, 1995); *The English Patient* (1996); *Shakespeare in Love* (1998); *Bridget Jones's Diary* (2001); *Love Actually* (2003); *Trauma* (2004); *Nanny McPhee* (2005); *The Last Legion* (2007)
Firth, Peter	1953–	Bradford Yorkshire	*Equus* (1983); *A Letter To Breshnev* (1985); *The Hunt for Red October* (1990); *The Garden of Redemption* (1997); *Spooks* (TV, 2002–)
Fishburne, Lawrence	1961–	Augusta, Georgia	*The Color Purple* (1985); *What's Love Got to Do with It* (1993); *Othello* (1995); *The Matrix* (1999, sequels 2003); *Assault on Precinct 13* (2005)
Flaherty, Robert	1884–1951	Iron Mountain, Michigan	Documentary film-maker: *Nanook of the North* (1922); *Moana* (1924); *Tabu* (1930). Director: *Elephant Boy* (1937); *Louisiana Story* (1948)

Film and television personalities (continued)

Name	Dates	Place of birth	Selected works
Flockhart, Calista	1964–	Freeport, Illinois	*The Birdcage* (1996); *Ally McBeal* (TV, 1997–2000); *A Midsummer Night's Dream* (1999); *The Last Shot* (2004); *Fragile* (2005)
Flynn, Errol	1909–59	Hobart, Tasmania	*In the Wake of the Bounty* (1933); *Captain Blood* (1935); *The Charge of the Light Brigade* (1936); *The Adventures of Robin Hood* (1938)
Fonda, Bridget	1964–	Los Angeles	*Single White Female* (1992); *Jackie Brown* (1997); *Lake Placid* (1999); *Kiss of the Dragon* (2001)
Fonda, Henry	1905–82	Grand Island, Nebraska	*Young Mr Lincoln* (1939); *The Grapes of Wrath* (1940); *Twelve Angry Men* (1957); *On Golden Pond* (1981)
Fonda, Jane	1937–	New York City	*Barbarella* (1968); *They Shoot Horses, Don't They?* (1969); *Coming Home* (1978); *The China Syndrome* (1980); *Nine To Five* (1981); *On Golden Pond* (1981); *Old Gringo* (1989); *Monster-in-Law* (2005)
Fonda, Peter	1939–	New York City	*Easy Rider* (1969); *Canonball Run* (1981); *The Rose Garden* (1989); *Ulee's Gold* (1997); *The Laramie Project* (2002)
Ford, Harrison	1942–	Chicago	*Star Wars* (1977); *Raiders of the Lost Ark* (1981); *Blade Runner* (1982); *Indiana Jones and the Temple of Doom* (1984); *Clear and Present Danger* (1994); *K-19: The Widowmaker* (2002); *Firewall* (2006)
Ford, John	1895–1973	Cape Elizabeth, Maine	Director: *Stagecoach* (1939); *The Grapes of Wrath* (1940); *How Green was my Valley* (1941); *The Quiet Man* (1952)
Forman, Milos	1932–	Cáslav, Czechoslovakia	*Lásky Jedné Plavovlásky* (1965); *Horí Mà Panenko* (1967); *One Flew Over the Cuckoo's Nest* (1975); *Amadeus* (1983); *The People vs. Larry Flynt* (1996); *Man on the Moon* (1999)
Forsyth, Bill	1947–	Glasgow	Director: *That Sinking Feeling* (1979); *Gregory's Girl* (1981); *Local Hero* (1983); *Being Human* (1993); *Gregory's Two Girls* (1999)
Foster, Jodie	1962–	Los Angeles, California	*Alice Doesn't Live Here Anymore* (1974); *Bugsy Malone* (1976); *Taxi Driver* (1976); *The Accused* (1988); *The Silence of the Lambs* (1991); *Contact* (1997); *Panic Room* (2002); *Flightplan* (2005)
Fox, Michael J	1961–	Edmonton, Alberta	*Back to the Future* (1985); *The Secret of My Success* (1987); *Bright Lights, Big City* (1988); *The Hard Way* (1991); *For Love of Money* (1993); *Mars Attacks!* (1996); *Interstate 60* (2002)
Foxx, Jamie	1967–	Terrell, Texas	*Ali* (2001); *Collateral* (2004); *Ray* (2004); *Stealth* (2005)
Frears, Stephen	1931–	Leicester	Director: *Gumshoe* (1971); *My Beautiful Launderette* (1985); *Sammie and Rosie Get Laid* (1987); *The Grifters* (1990); *High Fidelity* (2000); *The Deal* (TV, 2003); *The Queen* (2006)
Freeman, Morgan	1937–	Memphis, Tennessee	*Driving Miss Daisy* (1989); *Se7en* (1995); *Million Dollar Baby* (2004); *Batman Begins* (2005); *An Unfinished Life* (2005)
Gabin, Jean	1904–76	Paris	*Pépé le Moko* (1936); *Quai des Brumes (Port of Shadows*, 1938); *Le Jour Se Lève (Daybreak*, 1939)
Gable, Clark	1901–60	Cadiz, Ohio	*It Happened One Night* (1934); *Mutiny on the Bounty* (1935); *Gone With the Wind* (1939); *The Misfits* (1961)
Gambon, Michael	1940–	Dublin	*The Singing Detective* (TV, 1986); *The Cook, The Thief, His Wife and Her Lover* (1989); *Harry Potter and the Prisoner of Azkaban* (2004; *... Goblet of Fire*, 2005); *Amazing Grace* (2006)
Garbo, Greta	1905–90	Stockholm	*Grand Hotel* (1932), *Anna Karenina* (1935); *Camille* (1936); *Ninotchka* (1939)
Gardner, Ava	1922–90	Smithfield, North Carolina	*The Barefoot Contessa* (1954); *The Sun Also Rises* (1957); *The Night of the Iguana* (1964)
Garland, Judy	1922–69	Grand Rapids, Minnesota	*The Wizard of Oz* (1939); *Babes in Arms* (1939); *Meet Me in St Louis* (1944); *Easter Parade* (1948); *A Star is Born* (1954)

Name	Dates	Place of birth	Selected works
Gere, Richard	1949–	Philadelphia	*An Officer and a Gentleman* (1982); *The Cotton Club* (1984); *Pretty Woman* (1990); *The Jackal* (1997); *Runaway Bride* (1999); *Chicago* (2002); *Shall We Dance?* (2004); *Bee Season* (2005)
Gibson, Mel	1956–	Peekskill, New York	*Mad Max* (1979); *Lethal Weapon* (1987); *Hamlet* (1990); *Forever Young* (1992); *Braveheart* (1995); *Conspiracy* (1997); *We Were Soldiers* (2002). Director: *The Passion of The Christ* (2004)
Gielgud, John	1904–2000	London	*Oh What A Lovely War* (1969); *Brideshead Revisited* (TV, 1981); *Gandhi* (1982); *Prospero's Books* (1991); *Elizabeth* (1998)
Gilliam, Terry	1940–	Minneapolis	Director: *Jabberwocky* (1977); *The Time Bandits* (1980); *The Adventures of Baron Munchausen* (1988); *The Fisher King* (1991); *Fear and Loathing in Las Vegas* (1998); *The Brothers Grimm* (2005)
Gish, Lillian	1896–1993	Springfield, Ohio	*Birth of A Nation* (1915); *Intolerance* (1916); *Orphans of the Storm* (1922)
Godard, Jean-Luc	1930–	Paris	Director: *A Bout de Souffle* (1960); *Vivre Sa Vie* (1962); *Weekend* (1968); *Sauve Qui Peut* (1980); *Nouvelle Vague* (1990); *For Ever Mozart* (1997); *In Praise of Love* (2001); *Our Music* (2004)
Goldberg, Whoopi	1955–	Manhattan, New York	*The Color Purple* (1985); *Jumping Jack Flash* (1986); *Ghost* (1990); *Sister Act* (1992; sequel 1994); *Boys on the Side* (1995); *The Associate* (1996); *The Deep End of the Ocean* (1999); *Homie Spumoni* (2006)
Goldblum, Jeff	1952–	Pittsburgh	*Death Wish* (1974); *Invasion of the Bodysnatchers* (1978); *The Fly* (1985); *The Tall Guy* (1989); *Earth Girls Are Easy* (1989); *Jurassic Park* (1993, 1997); *Mini's First Time* (2005); *Man of the Year* (2006)
Goodman, John	1953–	St Louis, Missouri	*Roseanne* (TV, 1988–97); *Barton Fink* (1991); *Born Yesterday* (1993); *The Flintstones* (1994); *The Borrowers* (1997); *One Night at McCool's* (2001); *Beyond the Sea* (2004)
Grammer, Kelsey	1955–	St Thomas, US Virgin Islands	*Cheers* (TV, 1982–93); *Frasier* (TV, 1994–2004); *Down Periscope* (1996); *The Real Howard Spitz* (1998); *X-Men: The Last Stand* (2006)
Granger, Stewart	1913–93	London	*The Man in Grey* (1943); *Love Story* (1944); *King Solomon's Mines* (1950); *Beau Brummell* (1954); *The Wild Geese* (1977)
Grant, Cary	1904–86	Bristol	*The Awful Truth* (1937); *His Girl Friday* (1940); *Arsenic and Old Lace* (1944); *Notorious* (1946); *To Catch A Thief* (1955); *North by Northwest* (1959)
Grant, Hugh	1960–	London	*Four Weddings and a Funeral* (1994); *Nine Months* (1995); *Notting Hill* (1999); *Bridget Jones's Diary* (2001; sequel 2004); *About a Boy* (2002); *Love Actually* (2003); *American Dreamz* (2006)
Grant, Richard E	1957–	Mbabane, Swaziland	*Withnail and I* (1987); *Bram Stoker's Dracula* (1992); *The Portrait of a Lady* (1996); *The Scarlet Pimpernel* (TV, 1998); *Gosford Park* (2001); *Tooth* (2004); *Wah-Wah* (2005); *Penelope* (2006)
Greenaway, Peter	1942–	London	Director: *The Draughtsman's Contract* (1982); *The Cook, The Thief, His Wife and Her Lover* (1989); *Prospero's Books* (1991); *The Pillow-Book* (1996); *A Life in Suitcases* (2005)
Grenfell, Joyce	1910–79	London	*The Happiest Days of Your Life* (1949); *Laughter in Paradise* (1951); *The Bells of St Trinians* (1954)
Griffith, D(avid) W(ark)	1875–1948	Floydsfork, Kentucky	Director: *The Birth of a Nation* (1915); *Intolerance* (1916)
Griffith, Melanie	1957–	New York City	*Something Wild* (1987); *Working Girl* (1988); *Bonfire of the Vanities* (1990); *Paradise* (1992); *Mulholland Falls* (1995); *Lolita* (1997); *Celebrity* (1998); *Tempo* (2003); *Have Mercy* (2006)
Guinness, Alec	1914–2000	London	*Oliver Twist* (1948); *Kind Hearts and Coronets* (1949); *The Bridge on the River Kwai* (1957); *Lawrence of Arabia* (1962); *Tinker Tailor, Soldier, Spy* (TV, 1979); *Kafka* (1991)

ARTS AND CULTURE

Film and television personalities (continued)

Name	Dates	Place of birth	Selected works
Hackman, Gene	1931–	San Bernardino, California	Bonnie and Clyde (1967); French Connection (1971); The Poseidon Adventure (1972); Postcards From the Edge (1990); Runaway Jury (2003); Welcome to Mooseport (2004); Superman II (2006)
Hancock, Tony	1924–68	Birmingham	Educating Archie (Radio, 1951); Hancock's Half Hour (TV, 1954–61)
Hanks, Tom	1957–	Concord, California	Big (1988); Philadelphia Story (1993); Forrest Gump (1994); Apollo 13 (1995); Saving Private Ryan (1998); Road to Perdition (2002); The Terminal (2004); The Da Vinci Code (2006)
Hannah, John	1962–	Glasgow	Four Weddings and a Funeral (1994); McCallum (TV, 1995); Sliding Doors (1998); The Mummy (1999); Before You Go (2002); I Accuse (2003); Ghost Son (2006)
Harlow, Jean	1911–37	Kansas City	Hell's Angels (1930); Platinum Blonde (1931); Bombshell (1933)
Harrelson, Woody	1961–	Midland, Texas	Cheers (TV, 1985–92); Natural Born Killers (1994); The People vs Larry Flint (1996); Anger Management (2003); North Country (2005); A Scanner Darkly (2006)
Harris, Richard	1930–2002	County Limerick	The Guns of Navarone (1961); Mutiny on the Bounty (1962); This Sporting Life (1963); Camelot (1967); A Man Called Horse (1969); The Wild Geese (1978); The Field (1990); Harry Potter (2001, 2002)
Harrison, Rex	1908–90	Huyton-with-Roby, Lancashire	Storm in a Teacup (1937); Blithe Spirit (1945); The Constant Husband (1958); My Fair Lady (1964); Dr Doolittle (1967)
Hauer, Rutger	1944–	Amsterdam	Blade Runner (1982); The Osterman Weekend (1983); The Hitcher (1985); Fatherland (1994); Hostile Waters (TV, 1997); Simon Magus (1999); Batman Begins (2005); Moving McAllister (2007)
Hawke, Ethan	1970–	Austin, Texas	Waterland (1992); Reality Bites (1994); Great Expectations (1998); The Jimmy Show (2002); Taking Lives (2004); Lord of War (2005); Fast Food Nation (2006)
Hawks, Howard	1896–1977	Goshen, Indiana	Director: The Road to Glory (1926); The Dawn Patrol (1930); The Big Sleep (1946)
Hawn, Goldie	1945–	Washington DC	There's A Girl in my Soup (1970); Private Benjamin (1980); Death Becomes Her (1992); First Wives Club (1996); Everyone Says I Love You (1997); The Out-of-Towners (1999); Town and Country (2001)
Hayek, Salma	1968–	Veracuz, Mexico	Desperado (1995); The Faculty (1998); Wild, Wild West (1999); In the Time of the Butterflies (2001); Frida (2002); After the Sunset (2004); Lonely Hearts (2006)
Hayworth, Rita	1918–87	New York City	Gilda (1946); Separate Tables (1958); The Money Trap (1965); Road to Salina (1971); The Wrath of God (1972)
Hepburn, Audrey	1929–93	Brussels	Roman Holiday (1953); Funny Face (1957); The Nun's Story (1959); Breakfast at Tiffany's (1961); My Fair Lady (1964); Wait Until Dark (1967); Robin and Marian (1976); Always (1991)
Hepburn, Katharine	1909–2003	Hartford, (Connecticut	The Philadelphia Story (1940); The African Queen (1951); Long Day's Journey into Night (1962); Guess Who's Coming to Dinner? (1967); On Golden Pond (1981); Love Affair (1994)
Hershey, Barbara	1948–	Hollywood, California	The Right Stuff (1983); The Natural (1984); Hannah and Her Sisters (1986); Beaches (1988); Naked Lunch (1991); Falling Down (1993); The Pallbearer (1996); Lantana (2001); Riding the Bullet (2004)
Herzog, Werner	1942–	Sachrang, Germany	Director: Aguirre, der Zorn Gottes (1973); Jeder Für Sich und Gott Gegen Alle (1974); Nosferatu, The Vampyre (1979); Scream of Stone (1991); The White Diamond (2004); Rescue Dawn (2006)

Name	Dates	Place of birth	Selected works
Heston, Charlton	1923–	Evanston, Illinois	*Dark City* (1950); *The Greatest Show on Earth* (1951); *The Ten Commandments* (1956); *Ben Hur* (1959); *The Awakening* (1980); *True Lies* (1994); *Alaska* (1996); *The Order* (2001)
Hill, George Roy	1922–	Minneapolis	Director: *Butch Cassidy and the Sundance Kid* (1969); *Slaughterhouse 5* (1972); *The Sting* (1973); *The World According to Garp* (1982); *Funny Farm* (1988)
Hitchcock, Alfred	1899–1980	London	Director: *The Thirty-Nine Steps* (1935); *The Lady Vanishes* (1938); *Rebecca* (1940); *Psycho* (1960); *The Birds* (1963); *Frenzy* (1972)
Hoffman, Dustin	1937–	Los Angeles	*The Graduate* (1967); *Midnight Cowboy* (1969); *Marathon Man* (1976); *All The President's Men* (1976); *Kramer vs Kramer* (1979); *Rain Man* (1988); *Meet the Fockers* (2004); *Perfume* (2006)
Holden, William	1918–82	O'Fallon, Illinois	*Sunset Boulevard* (1950); *The Bridge on the River Kwai* (1957); *Casino Royale* (1967); *The Wild Bunch* (1969)
Hope, Bob	1903–2003	Eltham, London	*Road to Singapore* (1940); *My Favourite Blonde* (1942); *Road to Morocco* (1942); *Road to Hong Kong* (1961)
Hopkins, Anthony	1941–	Port Talbot, Wales	*The Elephant Man* (1980); *84 Charing Cross Road* (1986); *The Silence of the Lambs* (1991); *Remains of the Day* (1993); *Shadowlands* (1994); *The Human Stain* (2003); *Proof* (2005); *Bobby* (2006)
Hopper, Dennis	1936–	Dodge City, Kansas	*Rebel without a Cause* (1955); *Easy Rider* (1969); *Apocalypse Now* (1979); *Blue Velvet* (1986); *Vanished* (1994); *Star Truckers* (1997); *Out of Season* (2004); *Land of the Dead* (2005)
Hordern, Michael	1911–95	Berkhampsted	*The Constant Husband* (1955); *A Funny Thing Happened on the Way to the Forum* (1966); *The Missionary* (1982); *Paradise Postponed* (TV, 1986); *The Fool* (1990)
Hoskins, Bob	1942–	Bury St Edmunds,	*Pennies from Heaven* (TV, 1978); *Mona Lisa* (1986); *Who Framed Roger Rabbit?* (1988); *Hook* (1991); *The Sleeping Dictionary* (2002); *Beyond the Sea* (2004); *Mrs Henderson Presents* (2005)
Howard, Leslie	1893–1943	London	*The Scarlet Pimpernel* (1935); *Gone With The Wind* (1939); *In Which We Serve* (1942)
Howard, Ron(ald)	1954–	Duncan, Oklahoma	Director: *Cocoon* (1985); *Apollo 13* (1995); *How The Grinch Stole Christmas* (2000); *A Beautiful Mind* (2002); *Cinderella Man* (2005); *The Da Vinci Code* (2006)
Howard, Trevor	1916–88	Cliftonville, Kent	*Brief Encounter* (1946); *The Third Man* (1949); *Mutiny on the Bounty* (1962); *The Charge of the Light Brigade* (1968); *Ryan's Daughter* (1970); *Gandhi* (1982); *White Mischief* (1987)
Hudson, Rock	1925–85	Winnetka, Illinois	*Magnificent Obsession* (1954); *Giant* (1956); *Pillow Talk* (1959); *Ice Station Zebra* (1968)
Hunt, Helen	1963–	Culver City, California	*Mad About You* (TV, 1992–9); *Twister* (1996); *As Good As It Gets* (1997); *The Curse of the Jade Scorpion* (2001); *A Good Woman* (2004); *Bobby* (2006)
Hunter, Holly	1958–	Conyers, Georgia	*Broadcast News* (1987); *The Firm* (1993); *The Piano* (1993); *Home For the Holidays* (1995); *O Brother, Where Art Thou?* (2000); *Little Black Book* (2004); *The Big White* (2005)
Hurt, John	1940–	Chesterfield, Derbyshire	*A Man for All Seasons* (1966); *The Naked Civil Servant* (TV, 1975); *Midnight Express* (1978); *The Elephant Man* (1980); *1984* (1984); *The Alan Clark Diaries* (TV, 2004); *Shooting Dogs* (2005)
Hurt, William	1950–	Washington DC	*The Janitor* (1981); *Body Heat* (1981); *The Big Chill* (1983); *Gorky Park* (1983); *Children of a Lesser God* (1986); *Jane Eyre* (1996); *Changing Lanes* (2002); *The Village* (2004); *A History of Violence* (2005)
Huston, Anjelica	1952–	Ireland	*The Last Tycoon* (1976); *Prizzi's Honor* (1985); *The Witches* (1990); *The Grifters* (1990); *The Addams Family* (1991; sequel 1993); *Bitter Moon* (1992); *Blood Work* (2002); *Material Girls* (2006)

ARTS AND CULTURE

Film and television personalities (continued)

Name	Dates	Place of birth	Selected works
Huston, John	1906–87	Nevada, Missouri	Director: *The Maltese Falcon* (1941); *The African Queen* (1951); *Moby Dick* (1956); *The Man Who Would Be King* (1975); *Annie* (1982); *Prizzi's Honor* (1985); *The Dead* (1987)
Irons, Jeremy	1948–	Cowes	*The French Lieutenant's Woman* (1981); *Brideshead Revisited* (TV, 1981); *The Mission* (1985); *Stealing Beauty* (1996); *The Time Machine* (2002); *Kingdom of Heaven* (2005); *Inland Empire* (2006)
Ivory, James	1928–	Berkeley, California	Director: *Heat and Dust* (1982); *The Bostonians* (1984); *A Room With A View* (1985); *Howard's End* (1992); *The Remains of the Day* (1993); *Le Divorce* (2003); *The White Countess* (2006)
Jackson, Glenda	1936–	Liverpool	*Women in Love* (1969); *Sunday Bloody Sunday* (1971); *A Touch of Class* (1973); *Turtle Diary* (1985); *Business As Usual* (1986); *The Rainbow* (1989)
Jackson, Gordon	1923–89	Glasgow	*Whisky Galore* (1948); *The Great Escape* (1962); *The Prime of Miss Jean Brodie* (1969); *Upstairs, Downstairs* (TV, 1970–5); *The Professionals* (TV, 1977–81); *The Shooting Party* (1980)
Jackson, Peter	1961–	Pukerua, New Zealand	Director: *The Lord of the Rings* trilogy: *The Fellowship of the Ring* (2001); *The Two Towers* (2002); *The Return of the King* (2003); *King Kong* (2005)
Jackson, Samuel L	1948–	Washington, DC	*Sea of Love* (1989); *Pulp Fiction* (1992); *Jackie Brown* (1997); *Star Wars* films: *The Phantom Menace* (1999; sequels 2002, 2005); *Basic* (2003); *Twisted* (2004); *Snakes on a Plane* (2006)
Jarman, Derek	1942–94	Northwood, Middlesex	*Jubilee* (1977); *Caravaggio* (1985); *Edward II* (1991); *Wittgenstein* (1993)
Jason, David	1940–	London	TV series: *Open All Hours* (1981–5); *Only Fools and Horses* (several); *The Darling Buds of May* (1990–3); *A Touch of Frost* (1992–)
Johansson, Scarlett	1984–	New York City	*The Horse Whisperer* (1998); *Girl with a Pearl Earring* (2003); *Lost in Translation* (2003); *The Perfect Score* (2004); *The Island* (2005); *The Black Dahlia* (2006)
Johnson, Celia	1908–82	Richmond, Surrey	*In Which We Serve* (1942); *This Happy Breed* (1944); *Brief Encounter* (1945); *The Prime of Miss Jean Brodie* (1968)
Johnson, Don	1949–	Flatt Creek, Missouri	*Miami Vice* (TV, 1985–9); *Paradise* (1991); *Tin Cup* (1996); *Goodbye Lover* (1998); *Word of Honor* (TV, 2003)
Jordan, Neil	1950–	Sligo	Director: *The Company of Wolves* (1985); *Mona Lisa* (1986); *High Spirits* (1988); *The Crying Game* (1992); *Michael Collins* (1996); *The End of the Affair* (1999); *Breakfast on Pluto* (2005)
Kapur, Shekhar	1945–	Bombay	Director: *Bandit Queen* (1994); *Dush Mani* (1995); *Time Machine* (1995); *Elizabeth* (1998); *The Four Feathers* (2004)
Karloff, Boris	1887–1969	London	*Frankenstein* (1931)
Kasdan, Lawrence	1949–	Miami Beach, Florida	Director: *Body Heat* (1981); *The Big Chill* (1983); *The Accidental Tourist* (1989); *Love You to Death* (1990); *The Bodyguard* (1992); *Wyatt Earp* (1996); *Mumford* (1999); *Dreamcatcher* (2003)
Kaufman, Philip	1936–	Chicago	Director: *Invasion of the Body Snatchers* (1978); *The Right Stuff* (1983); *The Unbearable Lightness of Being* (1988); *China: The Wild East* (1995); *Twisted* (2004)
Kaye, Danny	1913–87	New York City	*Up In Arms* (1943); *Wonder Man* (1944); *The Secret Life of Walter Mitty* (1946); *Hans Christian Andersen* (1952)
Kazan, Elia	1909–2003	Constantinople	*Gentleman's Agreement* (1948); *On the Waterfront* (1954); *East of Eden* (1955); *The Last Tycoon* (1976)

Name	Dates	Place of birth	Selected works
Keaton, Buster	1895–1966	Piqua, Kansas	*The Butcher Boy* (1917); *The Navigator* (1924); *The General* (1926); *It's A Mad, Mad, Mad, Mad World* (1963)
Keaton, Diane	1946–	Los Angeles	*The Godfather* (1972); *Sleeper* (1973); *Annie Hall* (1977); *Manhattan* (1979); *The Godfather, Part III* (1990); *First Wives Club* (1996); *Something's Gotta Give* (2003); *The Family Stone* (2005)
Keaton, Michael	1951–	Carapolis, Pennsylvania	*Beetlejuice* (1988); *Batman* (1989; sequel 1992); *The Dream Team* (1989); *Much Ado About Nothing* (1993); *Multiplicity* (1996); *Jack Frost* (1998); *Quicksand* (2001); *First Daughter* (2004)
Keitel, Harvey	1939–	New York City	*Alice Doesn't Live Here Anymore* (1974); *Thelma and Louise* 1991); *Reservoir Dogs* (1991); *The Piano* (1993); *Pulp Fiction* (1994); *Finding Graceland* (1998); *The Shadow Dancer* (2005)
Kelly, Gene	1912–96	Pittsburgh	*For Me and My Gal* (1942); *An American in Paris* (1951); *Singin' in the Rain* (1952)
Kelly, Grace	1929–82	Philadelphia	*High Noon* (1952); *Dial M for Murder* (1954); *Rear Window* (1954); *To Catch a Thief* (1955); *High Society* (1956)
Kerr, Deborah	1921–	Helensburgh, Scotland	*The Life and Death of Colonel Blimp* (1943); *Perfect Strangers* (1945); *Black Narcissus* (1947); *The King and I* (1956); *Separate Tables* (1958); *The Night of the Iguana* (1964); *Casino Royale* (1967)
Kidman, Nicole	1968–	Honolulu, Hawaii	*To Die For* (1995); *Practical Magic* (1998); *Eyes Wide Shut* (1999); *Moulin Rouge* (2001); *The Hours* (2002); *The Stepford Wives* (2004); *The Interpreter* (2005)
Kilmer, Val	1959–	Los Angeles	*Top Gun* (1986); *The Doors* (1991); *Tombstone* (1994); *The Saint* (1997); *The Salton Sea* (2002); *Mindhunters* (2004); *Summer Love* (2006)
Kingsley, Ben	1943–	Snaiton, Yorkshire	*Gandhi* (1982); *Pascali's Island* (1988); *Necessary Love* (1991); *Schindler's List* (1993); *The Triumph of Love* (2001); *Thunderbirds* (2004); *Oliver Twist* (2005); *Lucky Number Slevin* (2006)
Kinski, Klaus	1926–91	Sopot, Gdańsk	*For A Few Dollars More* (1965); *Dr Zhivago* (1965); *Nosferatu* (1979); *Fitzcarraldo* (1982)
Kinski, Natassja	1960–	Berlin	*Tess* (1979); *Cat People* (1982); *Paris Texas* (1984); *Revolution* (1985); *Terminal Velocity* (1995); *My Two Dads* (1997); *Beyond the City Limits* (2002)
Kline, Kevin	1947–	St Louis, Missouri	*Sophie's Choice* (1983); *The Big Chill* (1983); *Cry Freedom* (1987); *A Fish Called Wanda* (1988); *Looking for Richard* (1996); *Life as a House* (2001); *De-Lovely* (2004); *As You Like It* (2006)
Knightley, Keira	1985–	Greater London	*Bend it Like Beckham* (2002); *Pirates of the Caribbean* (2003; sequel 2006); *King Arthur* (2004); *Pride & Prejudice* (2005)
Korda, Alexander	1893–1956	Turkeye, Hungary	Director: *The Private Life of Henry VIII* (1932); *The Thief of Baghdad* (1940); *The Third Man* (1949); *Richard III* (1956)
Kubrick, Stanley	1928–99	New York City	Director: *Spartacus* (1960); *Lolita* (1962); *Dr Strangelove* (1964); *2001: A Space Odyssey* (1968); *A Clockwork Orange* (1971); *The Shining* (1980); *Full Metal Jacket* (1987); *Eyes Wide Shut* (1999)
Kudrow, Lisa	1963–2004	Encino, California	*Friends* (TV, 1994–2004); *Romy and Michele's High School Reunion* (1997); *The Opposite of Sex* (1998); *Hanging Up* (2000); *Wonderland* (2004)
Kurosawa, Akira	1910–98	Tokyo	Director: *Rashomon* (1950); *The Seven Samurai* (1954); *Kagemusha* (1980); *Ran* (1985); *Madadayo* (1993)
Lambert, Christopher	1957–	New York City	*Greystoke* (1984); *Highlander* (1985, 1990); *The Sicilian* (1987); *Knight Moves* (1992); *Arlette* (1997); *Resurrection* (1999); *Absolon* (2003); *Day of Wrath* (2006)

ARTS AND CULTURE

Film and television personalities (continued)

Name	Dates	Place of birth	Selected works
Lancaster, Burt	1913–94	New York City	*From Here To Eternity* (1953); *Gunfight at the OK Corral* (1957); *Birdman of Alcatraz* (1962); *Local Hero* (1983); *Field of Dreams* (1989)
Lang, Fritz	1890–1976	Vienna	Director: *Metropolis* (1926); *Fury* (1936)
Lange, Jessica	1949–	Cloquet, Minnesota	*King Kong* (1976); *The Postman Always Rings Twice* (1981); *Tootsie* (1982); *Music Box* (1989); *Cape Fear* (1991); *Rob Roy* (1995); *Big Fish* (2004); *Broken Flowers* (2005); *Bonneville* (2006)
Laughton, Charles	1899–1962	Scarborough	*The Private Life of Henry VIII* (1932); *Mutiny on the Bounty* (1935); *Hobson's Choice* (1954)
Laurel and Hardy			
Oliver Hardy	1892–1957	Atlanta, Georgia	*Putting Pants on Philip* (1927); *The Battle of the*
Stan Laurel	1890–1965	Ulverston, Lancashire	*Century* (1927); *The Perfect Day* (1929); *The Music Box* (1932); *Babes in Toyland* (1934); *The Flying Deuces* (1939); *Atoll K* (1950)
Laurie, Piper	1932–	Detroit	*The Hustler* (1961); *Carrie* (1976); *Tender is the Night* (TV, 1985); *Children of a Lesser God* (1986); *Twin Peaks* (TV, 1991); *The Grass Harp* (1996); *The Faculty* (1998); *Eulogy* (2004)
Law, Jude	1972–	London	*Wilde* (1997); *AI: Artificial Intelligence* (2001); *Cold Mountain* (2003); *Alfie* (2004); *Breaking and Entering* (2006)
Lean, David	1908–91	Croydon, Greater London	Director: *Blithe Spirit* (1945); *Brief Encounter* (1945); *Great Expectations* (1946); *The Bridge on the River Kwai* (1957); *Lawrence of Arabia* (1962); *Doctor Zhivago* (1965); *A Passage to India* (1984)
LeBlanc, Matt	1967–	Newton, Massachusetts	*Friends* (TV, 1994–2004); *Ed* (1996); *Lost in Space* (1998); *All The Queen's Men* (2001); *Joey* (TV, 2004–)
Lee, Christopher	1922–	London	*The Curse of Frankenstein* (1956); *Dracula* (1958); *The Mummy* (1959); *The Three Musketeers* (1973); (1974); *Howling II* (1985); *Funny Man* (1994); *The Stupids* (1996); *The Lord of the Rings* (2001)
Lee, Spike	1957–	Atlanta, Georgia	Director: *She's Gotta Have it* (1986); *Do the Right Thing* (1989); *Mo Better Blues* (1990); *Malcolm X* (1992); *Clockers* (1995); *Get on the Bus* (1996); *She Hate Me* (2004); *Inside Man* (2006)
Leigh, Vivien	1913–67	Darjeeling, India	*Fire Over England* (1937); *Gone With the Wind* (1939); *Lady Hamilton* (1941); *Anna Karenina* (1941); *A Streetcar Named Desire* (1951)
Lemmon, Jack	1925–2001	Boston	*Some Like it Hot* (1959); *The Great Race* (1965); *The Odd Couple* (1968); *The China Syndrome* (1979); *JFK* (1991); *The Player* (1992); *Glengarry Glen Ross* (1992); *Out to Sea* (1997); *The Odd Couple II* (1998)
Levinson, Barry	1942–	Baltimore	Director: *Diner* (1982); *The Natural* (1984); *Good Morning Vietnam* (1987); *Rain Man* (1988); *Bugsy* (1991); *Sleepers* (1996); *Donnie Brasco* (1997); *Wag the Dog* (1998); *Bandits* (2001); *Envy* (2004)
Lloyd, Harold	1893–1971	Burchard, Nebraska	*High and Dizzy* (1920); *Safety Last* (1923); *The Freshman* (1925); *Welcome Danger* (1929)
Lockwood, Margaret	1916–90	Karachi, India	*Lorna Doone* (1934); *The Lady Vanishes* (1938); *The Wicked Lady* (1945)
Loren, Sophia	1934–	Rome	*The Pride and the Passion* (1957); *Two Women* (1961); *The Cassandra Crossing* (1977); *Prêt à Porter* (1994
Losey, Joseph	1909–84	La Crosse, Wisconsin	Director: *The Boy with the Green Hair* (1945); *The Servant* (1963); *The Go-Between* (1971)
Lubitsch, Ernst	1892–1947	Berlin	Director: *The Love Parade* (1929); *Ninotchka* (1939)
Lucas, George	1944–	Modesto, California	Director: *American Graffiti* (1973); *Star Wars* films: *Star Wars* (1997); *The Empire Strikes Back* (1980); *The Phantom Menace* (1999), *Attack of the Clones* (2002); *Revenge of the Sith* (2005)
Luhrmann, Baz	1962–	Australia	Director: *Strictly Ballroom* (1992); *Romeo + Juliet* (1996); *Moulin Rouge* (2001)

Name	Dates	Place of birth	Selected works
Lynch, David	1946–	Missoula, Montana	Director: *Eraserhead* (1977); *The Elephant Man* (1980); *Blue Velvet* (1986); *Twin Peaks* (TV 1990–1); *Twin Peaks: Fire Walk With Me* (1992); *Mulholland Drive* (2000); *Inland Empire* (2006)
MacDowell, Andie	1958–	Gaffney, South Carolina	*Greystoke* (1984); *Green Card* (1990); *Four Weddings and a Funeral* (1994); *The Muse* (1999); *Tara Road* (2005)
McGregor, Ewan	1971–	Crieff, Perthshire	*Lipstick on Your Collar* (TV, 1993); *Trainspotting* (1996); *Star Wars* films: *The Phantom Menace* (1999; sequels 2002, 2005); *Moulin Rouge* (2001); *Big Fish* (2004); *Stormbreaker* (2006)
MacLachlan, Kyle	1959–	Yakima, Washington	*Dune* (1984); *Blue Velvet* (1986); *Twin Peaks* (TV, 1990); *Twin Peaks: Fire Walk With Me* (1992); *Route 9* (1998); *Touch of Pink* (2004)
MacLaine, Shirley	1934–	Richmond, Virginia	*The Trouble with Harry* (1955); *Sweet Charity* (1969); *Terms of Endearment* (1983); *Postcards From the Edge* (1990); *Salem Witch Trials* (2002); *Bewitched* (2005)
McQueen, Steve	1930–80	Beech Grove, Indiana	*The Magnificent Seven* (1960); *The Great Escape* (1963); *The Cincinnati Kid* (1965); *Getaway* (1972); *Papillon* (1973); *Towering Inferno* (1974)
McTiernan, John	1951–	New York	Director: *Die Hard* (1988); *The Hunt for Red October* (1990); *Die Hard 3* (1995); *The Thomas Crown Affair* (1999); *Austin Powers: The Spy Who Shagged Me* (1999); *Basic* (2003)
Macy, William H	1950–	Miami, Florida	*Fargo* (1996); *Boogie Nights* (1997); *Psycho* (1998) *Welcome to Collinwood* (2002); *Cellular* (2004); *Bobby* (2006)
Maguire, Tobey	1975–	Santa Monica, California	*Wonder Boys* (2000); *Spider-Man* (2002); *Seabiscuit* (2003); *Spider-Man 2* (2004)
Malkovich, John	1953–	Christopher, Illinois	*The Killing Fields* (1984); *Empire of the Sun* (1987); *Dangerous Liaisons* (1988); *Ripley's Game* (2002); *The Hitchhiker's Guide to the Galaxy* (2005); *The Call* (2006)
Malle, Louis	1932–95	Thumeries, France	Director, producer, screenwriter: *Les Amants* (1958); *Zazie dans le Métro* (1960); *Atlantic City* (1990); *My Dinner with André* (1981); *Au revoir, Les enfants* (1987); *Damage* (1993)
Mankiewicz, Joseph Leo	1909–93	Wilkes-Barre, Pennsylvania	Director: *All About Eve* (1950); *The Barefoot Contessa* (1954); *Guys and Dolls* (1954); *Suddenly Last Summer* (1959); *Sleuth* (1972)
Mansfield, Jayne	1933–67	Bryn Mawr, Pennsylvania	*The Girl Can't Help It* (1957); *Too Hot to Handle* (1960)
Mantegna, Joe	1947–	Chicago, Illinois	*Three Amigos!* (1986); *Bugsy* (1991); *Body of Evidence* (1993); *Up Close and Personal* (1996); *Celebrity* (1998); *Off Key* (2001); *Stateside* (2004); *Club Soda* (2006)
Martin, Steve	1945–	Waco, Texas	*The Little Shop of Horrors* (1986); *Planes, Trains and Automobiles* (1987); *Roxanne* (1987); *LA Story* (1991); *Bowfinger* (1999); *Cheaper By the Dozen* (2003); *The Pink Panther* (2006)
Marx Brothers, The			*The Cocoanuts* (1929); *Monkey Business*; (1931); *Horse Feathers* (1932); *Duck Soup* (1933) *A Day at the Races* (1937)
Chico	1886–1961	New York City	
Harpo	1888–1964		
Groucho	1890–1977		
Zeppo	1901–77		
Mason, James	1909–84	Huddersfield	*Fanny by Gaslight* (1944); *The Wicked Lady* (1946); *A Star is Born* (1954); *Lolita* (1962); *Georgy Girl* (1966); *Heaven Can Wait* (1978); *The Boys From Brazil* (1978); *The Shooting Party* (1984)
Mastroianni, Marcello	1924–96	Fontana Liri	*La Dolce Vita* (1960); *Otto e Mezzo* (1963); *Dark Eyes* (1987); *Three Lives and Only One Death* (1996)
Matthau, Walter	1920–2000	New York City	*The Odd Couple* (1968); *Hello Dolly* (1969); *Cactus Flower* (1969); *Pirates* (1986); *I.Q.* (1995); *The Odd Couple II* (1998)

ARTS AND CULTURE

Film and television personalities (continued)

Name	Dates	Place of birth	Selected works
Maura, Carmen	1945–	Madrid	*Dark Habits* (1983); *What Have I Done to Deserve This?* (1964); *Law of Desire* (1987); *Women on the Verge of a Nervous Breakdown* (1988); *Alice and Martin* (1998); *Valentín* (2002); *Volver* (2006)
Midler, Bette	1945–	Honolulu, Hawaii	*Down and Out in Beverly Hills* (1986); *Outrageous Fortune* (1987); *Scenes From the Mall* (1991); *Hocus Pocus* (1993); *The First Wives Club* (1996); *Isn't She Great* (2000); *The Stepford Wives* (2004)
Mercouri, Melina	1923–94	Athens	*Never on Sunday* (1960); *Topkapi* (1964); *Gaily, Gaily* (1969)
Mills, Hayley	1946–	London	*Tiger Bay* (1959); *Whistle Down the Wind* (1961); *Appointment with Death* (1988); *After Midnight* (1990); *Stricken* (2005)
Mills, John	1908–2005	Felixstowe, Suffolk	*In Which We Serve* (1942); *Great Expectations* (1946); *The History of Mr Polly* (1972); *Ryan's Daughter* (1970); *Hamlet* (1996)
Minghella, Anthony	1954–	Ryde, Isle of Wight	*Truly, Madly, Deeply* (1991); *The English Patient* (1996); *The Talented Mr Ripley* (1999); *Cold Mountain* (2003); *Breaking and Entering* (2006)
Minnelli, Liza	1946–	Los Angeles	*Cabaret* (1972); *The West Side Waltz* (TV, 1995); *Arrested Development* (TV, 2003)
Mirren, Helen	1945–	London	*The Cook, The Thief, His Wife and Her Lover* (1989); *Prime Suspect* (TV, from 1991); *The Madness of King George* (1994); *Gosford Park* (2001); *Calendar Girls* (2003); *The Queen* (2006)
Mitchum, Robert	1917–97	Bridgeport, Connecticut	*Cape Fear* (1962); *Ryan's Daughter* (1970); *Farewell My Lovely* (1975); *The Big Sleep* (1978); *War and Remembrance* (TV, 1987); *Cape Fear* (1991); *Dead Man* (1996)
Monroe, Marilyn	1926–62	Los Angeles	*Gentlemen Prefer Blondes* (1953); *The Seven Year Itch* (1955); *Some Like it Hot* (1959); *The Misfits* (1961)
Montand, Yves	1921–91	Monsumagno, Italy	*The Wages of Fear* (1953); *Let's Make Love* (1960); *Jean de Florette* (1986); *Manon des Sources* (1986)
Moore, Demi	1962–	Roswell, New Mexico	*Ghost* (1990); *The Butcher's Wife* (1991); *A Few Good Men* (1992); *Indecent Proposal* (1992); *G.I. Jane* (1997); *Charlie's Angels* (2003); *Bobby* (2006)
Moore, Julianne	1961–	Boston, Massachusetts	*The Hand That Rocks the Cradle* (1992); *Psycho* (1998); *The Shipping News* (2001); *The Hours* (2002); *Laws of Attraction* (2004); *The Forgotten* (2004); *Children of Men* (2006)
Moore, Roger	1927–	London	*The Saint* (TV, 1962–9); *Live and Let Die* (1973); *The Man with the Golden Gun* (1974); *The Spy Who Loved Me* (1977); *For Your Eyes Only* (1981); *Octopussy* (1983); *A View to a Kill* (1985)
Moreau, Jeanne	1928–	Paris	*Les Amants* (1958); *Jules et Jim* (1961); *Journal d'une Femme de Chambre* (1964); *Nikita* (1990); *The Proprietor* (1996); *Juliette et son amour* (2000)
Mortensen, Viggo	1958–	New York City	*Witness* (1985); *Portrait of a Lady* (1996); *The Lord of the Rings* trilogy (2000–3); *Hidalgo* (2004); *A History of Violence* (2005); *Alatriste* (2006)
Murphy, Eddie	1961–	New York City	*Trading Places* (1983); *Beverly Hills Cop* (1985); *Another 48 Hours* (1990); *The Nutty Professor* (1996); *Dr Dolittle* (1998); *Showtime* (2002); *Shrek 2* (2004)
Murray, Bill	1950–	Wilmette, Illinois	*Ghostbusters* (1984); *Groundhog Day* (1993); *Rushmore* (1998); *The Royal Tenenbaums* (2001); *Lost in Translation* (2003); *Garfield* (2004); *Broken Flowers* (2005)
Myers, Mike	1964–	Toronto	*Wayne's World* (1992; sequel 1993); *So I Married an Axe Murderer* (1993); *Austin Powers* films: *International Man of Mystery* (1997), *The Spy Who Shagged Me* (1999); *Shrek 2* (2004)

Name	Dates	Place of birth	Selected works
Neeson, Liam	1952–	Ballymena, N Ireland	*Schindler's List* (1993); *Michael Collins* (1996); *Les Misérables* (1998); *Star Wars: The Phantom Menace* (1999); *Love Actually* (2003); *The Chronicles of Narnia* (2005); *Seraphim Falls* (2006)
Neill, Sam	1948–	Omagh, N Ireland 1983);	*The Final Conflict* (1981); *Reilly Ace of Spies* (TV, A Cry in the Dark (1988); *The Hunt for Red October* (1990); *Jurassic Park* (1993); *The Piano* (1993); *Wimbledon* (2004); *Yes* (2005)
Newman, Paul	1925–	Cleveland, Ohio	*Cat on a Hot Tin Roof* (1958); *Butch Cassidy and the Sundance Kid* (1969); *The Sting* (1973); *The Color of Money* (1986); *Nobody's Fool* (1995); *Twilight* (1998); *Empire Falls* (TV, 2005)
Nicholson, Jack	1937–	Neptune, New Jersey	*One Flew Over the Cuckoo's Nest* (1975); *The Shining* (1980); *The Postman Always Rings Twice* (1981); *The Witches of Eastwick* (1987); *Something's Gotta Give* (2003); *The Departed* (2006)
Niven, David	1910–83	London	*Wuthering Heights* (1939); *Around the World in Eighty Days* (1956); *Separate Tables* (1958); *The Guns of Navarone* (1961); *The Pink Panther* (1964; sequels 1982, 1983); *Casino Royale* (1967)
Nolte, Nick	1940–	Omaha, Nebraska	*48 Hours* (1982); *Down and Out in Beverly Hills* (1986); *The Player* (1992); *Lorenzo's Oil* (1992); *Mulholland Falls* (1996); *Hotel Rwanda* (2004); *Neverwas* (2005); *Off the Black* (2006)
O'Neal, Ryan	1941–	Los Angeles	*Love Story* (1970); *What's Up Doc?* (1972); *Paper Moon* (1973); *Nickelodeon* (1976); *Hacks* (1997); *Malibu's Most Wanted* (2003)
O'Toole, Peter	1932–	Kerry, Connemara	*Lawrence of Arabia* (1962); *Goodbye Mr Chips* (1969); *The Stunt Man* (1980); *The Last Emperor* (1987); *Molokai* (1998); *Troy* (2004); *One Night with the King* (2005)
Oldman, Gary	1959–	New Cross, London	*Sid and Nancy* (1986); *Prick up Your Ears* (1987); *Track 29* (1988); *JFK* (1991); *True Romance* (1993); *Murder in the First* (1995); *Lost in Space* (1998); *Interstate 60* (2002); *Batman Begins* (2005)
Olivier, Laurence	1907–89	Dorking	*Wuthering Heights* (1939); *Rebecca* (1940); *Henry V* (1944); *Hamlet* (1948); *Richard III* (1956); *The Entertainer* (1960); *Marathon Man* (1976); *Brideshead Revisited* (TV, 1982)
Ophuls or Opüls, Max	1902–57	Saarbrücken	Director: *La Ronde* (1950); *Lola Montez* (1955)
Pabst, G(eorg) W(ilhelm)	1895–1967	Raudnitz	Director: *Die Liebe der Jeanne Ney* (The Love of Jeanne Ney, 1927); *Westfront 1918* (1930); *Der Letzte Akt* (The Last Act, 1955)
Pacino, Al(fredo)	1940–	New York City	*The Godfather* (1972); *Scarface* (1983); *Dick Tracy* (1990); *Scent of a Woman* (1992); *Looking for Richard* (1996); *The Merchant of Venice* (2004); *Two for the Money* (2005)
Palin, Michael	1943–	Sheffield	*Monty Python's Flying Circus* (TV, 1969–74); *Monty Python and the Holy Grail* (1974); *The Life of Brian* (1978); *A Fish Called Wanda* (1988); *Around the World in 80 Days* (TV, 1989); *Himalaya* (TV, 2004)
Paltrow, Gwyneth	1973–	Los Angeles	*Emma* (1996); *Sliding Doors* (1998); *A Perfect Murder* (1998); *Shakespeare in Love* (1998); *Possession* (2002); *Sylvia* (2003); *Sky Captain and the World of Tomorrow* (2004); *Proof* (2005)
Parker, Alan	1944–	London	Director: *Bugsy Malone* (1976); *Midnight Express* (1978); *Birdy* (1985); *Angel Heart* (1987); *The Commitments* (1991); *Evita* (1996); *Angela's Ashes* (1998); *The Life of David Gale* (2002)
Pasolini, Pier Paolo	1922–75	Bologna	Director: *The Gospel According to St Matthew* (1964); *The Decameron* (1971); *The Canterbury Tales* (1973)
Paxton, Bill	1955–	Fort Worth, Texas	*The Terminator* (1984); *True Lies* (1994); *Twister* (1996); *Titanic* (1997); *Mighty Joe Young* (1998); *Haven* (2004)

ARTS AND CULTURE

Film and television personalities (continued)

Name	Dates	Place of birth	Selected works
Peck, Gregory	1916–2003	La Jolla, California	Spellbound (1945); The Man in the Grey Flannel Suit (1956); Cape Fear (1962); To Kill a Mockingbird (1962); The Omen (1976); Old Gringo (1989); Cape Fear (1991); Moby Dick (TV, 1998)
Peckinpah, Sam	1925–84	Fresno, California	Director: The Deadly Companions (1961); Major Dundee (1965); The Wild Bunch (1969)
Perry, Matthew	1969–	Williamstown, Massachusetts	Friends (TV, 1994–2004); Fools Rush In (1997); Almost Heroes (1998); The Whole Nine Yards (2000); The Whole Ten Yards (2004); Americano (2005)
Pesci, Joe	1943–	Newark, New Jersey	Raging Bull (1980); Good Fellows (1990); A Bronx Tale (1994); Lethal Weapon 4 (1998); The Good Shepherd (2006)
Pfeiffer, Michelle	1957–	Santa Ana, California	The Witches of Eastwick (1987); Dangerous Liaisons (1988); The Fabulous Baker Boys (1989); The Russia House (1990); White Oleander (2002); I Could Never Be Your Woman (2007)
Phoenix, River	1970–93	Madras, Oregon	Mosquito Coast (1986); Running on Empty (1988); Indiana Jones and the Last Crusade (1989); Love You to Death (1990); My Own Private Idaho (1991)
Pickford, Mary	1893–1979	Toronto	Rebecca of Sunnybrook Farm (1917); Poor Little Rich Girl (1917); Pollyanna (1919); Little Lord Fauntleroy (1921)
Pitt, Brad	1963–	Shawnee, Oklahoma	True Romance (1993); Interview with the Vampire (1994); Meet Joe Black (1998); Ocean's Eleven (2001; sequels 2004, 2007); Troy (2004); Mr & Mrs Smith (2005)
Plowright, Joan	1929–	Scunthorpe Brigg, Lincolnshire	The Entertainer (1960); Drowning By Numbers (1988); Love You to Death (1990); Surviving Picasso (1995); Tea with Mussolini (1998); Goose on the Loose (2006)
Plummer, Christopher	1927–	Toronto	The Sound of Music (1965); The Man Who Would be King (1975); The Return of the Pink Panther (1975); The Clown at Midnight (1998); A Beautiful Mind (2001); The Lake House (2006)
Poitier, Sidney	1924–	Miami, Florida	The Blackboard Jungle (1955); Lilies of the Field (1963); In The Heat of the Night (1967); To Sir With Love (1967); One Man, One Vote (1997); The Last Bricklayer in America (TV, 2001)
Polanski, Roman	1933–	Paris	Director: Nóz w Wodzie (Knife in the Water, 1962); Rosemary's Baby (1968); Tess (1979); Frantic (1988); Bitter Moon (1992); Death and the Maiden (1995); The Pianist (2002); Oliver Twist (2005)
Pollack, Sydney	1934–	South Bend, Indiana	Director: They Shoot Horses Don't They? (1969); The Electric Horseman (1979); Tootsie (1982); Out of Africa (1985); The Firm (1993); Sabrina (1995); Up at the Villa (2000); The Interpreter (2005)
Portman, Natalie	1981–	Jerusalem	Leon (1995); Everyone Says I Love You (1996); Prince of Egypt (voice, 1998); Star Wars films: The Phantom Menace (1999; sequels 2002, 2005)
Powell, Michael	1905–90	Canterbury	Director: The Thief of Baghdad (1940); Black Narcissus (1947); The Tales of Hoffman (1951); Peeping Tom (1960); The Boy Who Turned Yellow (1972)
Powell, Robert	1944–	Salford, Lancashire	Jesus of Nazareth (TV, 1977); The 39 Steps (1978); Pygmalion (TV, 1981); The Detectives (TV, 1992–4)
Preminger, Otto	1906–86	Vienna	Director: Laura (1944); Carmen Jones (1954); Bonjour Tristesse (1959); Porgy and Bess (1959); Exodus (1960); The Human Factor (1979)
Pudovkin, Vsevoled	1893–1953	Penza, Russia	Director: Konets Sankt-Peterburga (1927); Potomok Chingis-Khan (1928); Dezetir (1933)
Pullman, Bill	1954–	Hornell, New York	The Accidental Tourist (1988); Sleepless in Seattle (1993); Independence Day (1996); The Thin Red Line (1998); Igby Goes Down (2002); Dear Wendy (2005); Scary Movie 4 (2006)

Name	Dates	Place of birth	Selected works
Quaid, Dennis	1954–	Houston, Texas	The Big Easy (1986); Suspect (1987); Postcards From the Edge (1990); Wyatt Earp (1994); Going West In America (1996); Playing By Heart (1998); Cold Creek Manor (2004); American Dreamz (2006)
Radcliffe, Daniel	1989–	London	The Taylor of Panama (2001); Harry Potter and the Philosopher's Stone (2001); ... the Chamber of Secrets (2002); ... the Prisoner of Azkaban (2004); ... the Goblet of Fire (2005)
Ramis, Harold	1944–	Chicago, Illinois	Director: National Lampoon's Vacation (1983); Ghostbusters (1984; sequel 1989); Groundhog Day (1993); Multiplicity (1996); Analyze This (1999); Orange County (2002); The Ice Harvest (2005)
Rampling, Charlotte	1946–	Sturmer, Essex	Georgy Girl (1966); Angel Heart (1987); Invasion of Privacy (1996); Great Expectations (TV, 1999); Swimming Pool (2003); I'll Sleep When I'm Dead (2004); Lemming (2005); Basic Instinct 2 (2006)
Rathbone, Basil	1892–1967	Johannesburg	David Copperfield (1935); Anna Karenina (1935); Captain Blood (1935); The Hound of the Baskervilles (1939); The Adventures of Sherlock Holmes (1939)
Ray, Satyajit	1921–92	Calcutta	Director: Pather Panchali (1954); Aparajito (1956); Apu Sansar (1959); The Kingdom of Diamonds (1980); Pickoo (1982); The Home and the World (1984)
Redford, Robert	1937–	Santa Barbara, California	Barefoot in the Park (1968); Butch Cassidy and the Sundance Kid (1969); Indecent Proposal (1993); Up Close and Personal 1996); Director: The Horse Whisperer (1998); The Clearing (2003)
Redgrave, Michael	1908–85	Bristol	The Lady Vanishes (1938); The Dam Busters (1955); The Quiet American (1958); The Innocents (1961); Oh! What a Lovely War (1969)
Redgrave, Vanessa	1937–	London	The Bostonians (1983); Wetherby (1985); The Ballad of the Sad Café (1991); Howard's End (1992); Mission Impossible (1996); Celebrity (1998); The Gathering Storm (TV, 2002)
Reed, Carol	1906–76	London	Director: The Fallen Idol (1948); The Third Man (1949); Our Man in Havana (1959); Oliver! (1968)
Reed, Oliver	1938–99	London	The Damned (1962); Women in Love (1969); Castaway (1987); Parting Shots (1998)
Reeve, Christopher	1952–2004	New York City	Superman (1978); Superman II (1980); Superman III (1983); The Bostonians (1984); Rear Window (TV, 1998)
Reeves, Keanu	1965–	Beirut, Lebanon	Dangerous Liaisons (1988); Bill and Ted's Excellent Adventure (1989); Much Ado About Nothing (1993); Devil's Advocate (1997); The Matrix (1999; sequels 2003); Constantine (2005); The Lake House (2006)
Reiner, Rob	1945–	New York City	Director: This is Spinal Tap (1984); The Princess Bride (1988); When Harry Met Sally (1989); A Few Good Men (1992); North (1994); Ghosts of Mississippi (1997); Alex and Emma (2003)
Réno, Jean	1948–	Casablanca	Nikita (1990); Leon (1994); French Kiss (1995); Mission Impossible (1996); Godzilla (1998); Rollerball (2002); The Tiger and the Snow (2005); The Da Vinci Code (2006)
Renoir, Jean	1894–1979	Paris	Director: La Grande Illusion (1937), La Règle du Jeu (1939); Le Déjeuner sur l'herbe (1959)
Resnais, Alain	1922–	Vannes, France	Van Gogh (1948); Guernica (1950); Hiroshima, Mon Amour (1959); L'Année Dernière à Marienbad (1961); Mon Oncle d'Amérique (1980); La Vie est un Roman (1983); On Connaît la Chanson (1997)
Richardson, Miranda	1958–	Liverpool	Dance With a Stranger (1984); Blackadder II (TV, 1986); Empire of the Sun (1987); A Month in the Country (1988); Tom and Viv (1995); The Hours (2002); Wah-Wah (2005)

ARTS AND CULTURE

Film and television personalities (continued)

Name	Dates	Place of birth	Selected works
Richardson, Ralph	1902–83	Cheltenham	*Anna Karenina* (1948); *The Fallen Idol* (1948); *Richard III* (1956); *Long Day's Journey Into Night* (1962); *Dr Zhivago* (1966)
Riefenstahl, Leni	1902–2003	Berlin	Film-maker: *Triumph des Willens* (*Triumph of the Will*, 1935); *Olympia* (1938)
Robbins, Tim	1958–	New York City	*Bull Durham* (1988); *The Player* (1992); *The Shawshank Redemption* (1994); *Mystic River* (2003); *War of the Worlds* (2005). Writer/director: *Dead Man Walking* (1995); *The Cradle Will Rock* (1999)
Roberts, Julia	1967–	Smyrna, Georgia	*Mystic Pizza* (1988); *Pretty Woman* (1990); *Sleeping With the Enemy* (1991); *Michael Collins* (1996); *My Best Friend's Wedding* (1997); *Notting Hill* (1999); *Erin Brockovich* (2000); *Closer* (2004)
Robinson, Edward G	1893–1973	Bucharest	*Little Caesar* (1930); *Double Indemnity* (1944); *All My Sons* (1948); *The Cincinnati Kid* (1965)
Roeg, Nicolas Jack	1928–	London	Director: *Walkabout* (1971); *Don't Look Now* (1973); *The Man Who Fell to Earth* (1976); *Bad Timing* (1980); *Castaway* (1986); *Black Widow* (1988); *Track 29* (1988); *Two Deaths* (1996)
Rogers, Ginger	1911–95	Missouri	*Flying Down to Rio* (1933); *The Gay Divorcee* (1934); *Top Hat* (1935); *Follow The Fleet* (1936)
Rooney, Mickey	1920–	New York City	*A Midsummer Night's Dream* (1935); *Summer Holiday* (1948); *Breakfast at Tiffany's* (1961); *It's a Mad, Mad, Mad, Mad World* (1963) *Erik the Viking* (1989); *Animals* (1997)
Rossellini, Isabella	1952–	Rome	*White Nights* (1985); *Blue Velvet* (1985); *Cousins* (1989); *Wild at Heart* (1990); *Death Becomes Her* (1992); *Big Night* (1996); *The Imposters* (1998); *King of the Corner* (2004); *Infamous* (2006)
Rossellini, Roberto	1906–77	Rome	Director: *Roma, città aperta* (1945); *Paisà* (1946); *Germania, anno zero* (1947); *Il Generale della Rovere* (1959)
Roth, Tim	1961–	London	*Reservoir Dogs* (1992); *Pulp Fiction* (1994); *Animals* (1998); *Planet of the Apes* (2001); *Dark Water* (2005)
Rourke, Mickey	1956–	Schenectady, New York	*Rumble Fish* (1983); *9½ weeks* (1985); *Angel Heart* (1987); *Wild Orchid* (1990); *White Sands* (1992); *Buffalo 66* (1998); *Animal Factory* (2000); *Sin City* (2005); *Stormbreaker* (2006)
Rush, Geoffrey	1951–	Toowoomba, Queensland	*Shine* (1996); *Les Misérables* (1998); *Elizabeth* (1998); *Shakespeare in Love* (1998); *Ned Kelly* (2003); *Candy* (2005); *Pirates of the Caribbean* (2003; sequel 2006)
Russell, Jane	1921–	Bemidji, Minnesota	*The Outlaw* (1943); *The Paleface* (1948); *Gentlemen Prefer Blondes* (1953); *Johnny Reno* (1966); *The Yellow Rose* (TV, 1984)
Russell, Ken	1927–	Southampton	Director: *Women in Love* (1969); *The Music Lovers* (1971); *The Devils* (1971); *Gothic* (1987); *The Rainbow* (1989); *Lady Chatterley's Lover* (1993); *The Fall of the House of Usher* (2002)
Russell, Kurt	1951–	Springfield, Massachusetts	*Silkwood* (1983); *Tequila Sunrise* (1988); *Backdraft* (1991); *Unlawful Entry* (1992); *Stargate* (1994); *Soldier* (1998); *Dark Blue* (2002); *Miracle* (2004); *Dreamer* (2005); *Poseidon* (2006)
Russo, Rene	1954–	Burbank, California	*Major League* (1989); *Get Shorty* (1995); *Tin Cup* (1996); *Lethal Weapon 4* (1998); *The Thomas Crown Affair* (1999); *Showtime* (2002); *Two for the Money* (2005)
Rutherford, Margaret	1892–1972	London	*Blithe Spirit* (1945); *The Happiest Days of Your Life* (1950); *Murder She Said* (1961); *Murder Most Foul* (1964)
Ryan, Meg	1961–	Fairfield, Connecticut	*Top Gun* (1985); *When Harry Met Sally* (1989); *Sleepless in Seattle* (1993); *French Kiss* (1995); *You've Got Mail* (1998); *Kate and Leopold* (2001); *Against the Ropes* (2004)

Name	Dates	Place of birth	Selected works
Ryder, Winona	1971–	Winona, Michigan	*Beetlejuice* (1988); *Heathers* (1989); *Dracula* (1992); *The Age of Innocence* (1993); *Reality Bites* (1994); *Little Women* (1995); *The Crucible* (1996); *Celebrity* (1998); *Mr Deeds* (2002); *A Scanner Darkly* (2006)
Saint, Eva Marie	1924–	Newark, New Jersey	*On the Waterfront* (1954); *North by Northwest* (1959); *A Talent for Loving* (1969); *My Antonia* (TV, 1995)
Sandler, Adam	1966–	Brooklyn, New York	*Airheads* (1994); *Billy Madison* (1995); *The Waterboy* (1998); *Mr Deeds* (2002); *50 First Dates* (2004); *The Longest Yard* (2005)
Sarandon, Susan	1946–	New York City	*The Hunger* (1983); *The Witches of Eastwick* (1987); *Thelma and Louise* (1991); *Lorenzo's Oil* (1992); *Little Women* (1995); *Dead Man Walking* (1995); *Igby Goes Down* (2002); *Elizabethtown* (2005)
Schlesinger, John	1926–2003	London	Director: *A Kind Of Loving* (1962); *Billy Liar* (1963); *Midnight Cowboy* (1969); *Sunday, Bloody Sunday* (1971); *Marathon Man* (1976); *Pacific Heights* (1990); *The Next Best Thing* (2000)
Schumacher, Joel	1939–	New York City	Director: *The Incredible Shrinking Woman* (1981); *St Elmo's Fire* (1985); *Batman Forever* (1995); *Bad Company* (2002); *Veronica Guerin* (2003); *The Phantom of the Opera* (2004)
Schwarzenegger, Arnold	1947–	Graz, Austria	*Conan the Barbarian* (1982); *Conan the Destroyer* (1984); *The Terminator* (1984, 1991, 2003); *Total Recall* (1990); *Kindergarten Cop* (1990); *Batman and Robin* (1997); *The Kid & I* (2005)
Schwimmer, David	1966–	New York City	*Friends* (TV, 1994–); *The Pallbearer* (1996); *Kissing a Fool* (1998); *Uprising* (2001); *Duane Hopwood* (2005)
Scofield, Paul	1922–	Hurstpierpoint, Sussex	*A Man For All Seasons* (1966); *Hamlet* (1990); *The Crucible* (1996)
Scorsese, Martin	1942–	New York City	Director: *Mean Streets* (1973); *Taxi Driver* (1976); *Raging Bull* (1980); *The Mission* (1986); *The Last Temptation of Christ* (1988); *Goodfellas* (1990); *The Aviator* (2004); *The Departed* (2006)
Scott, George C(ampbell)	1927–99	Wise, Virginia	*Anatomy of a Murder* (1959); *The Hustler* (1962); *Dr Strangelove* (1963); *Patton* (1970); *The Changeling* (1980); *Oliver Twist* (1982); *The Exorcist III* (1990); *Country Justice* (1997)
Scott, Ridley	1937–	South Shields	Director. *Alien* (1979); *Blade Runner* (1982); *Thelma and Louise* (1991); *G.I. Jane* (1997); *Gladiator* (2000); *Matchstick Men* (2003); *Kingdom of Heaven* (2005); *A Good Year* (2006)
Scott Thomas, Kristin	1960–	Redruth, Cornwall	*Four Weddings and a Funeral* (1994); *Richard III* (1995); *The English Patient* (1996); *The Horse Whisperer* (1998); *Gosford Park* (2001); *Chromophobia* (2005)
Segal, George	1934–	New York City	*Who's Afraid of Virginia Woolf?* (1966); *The Owl and the Pussycat* (1979); *The Last Married Couple in America* (1979); *Look Who's Talking* (1989); *The Mirror Has Two Faces* (1996); *Heights* (2004)
Sellers, Peter	1925–80	Southsea	*The Ladykillers* (1955); *I'm Alright Jack* (1959); *Dr Strangelove* (1963); *The Pink Panther* (1963; sequels 1975, 1976, 1978); *A Shot in the Dark* (1964)
Sennett, Mack	1880–1960	Richmond, Quebec	Producer: *The Keystone Cops* (1912); *Sennett Bathing Beauties* (1920)
Sewell, Rufus	1967–	London	*Middlemarch* (TV, 1994); *Carrington* (1995); *Cold Comfort Farm* (TV, 1995); *Dangerous Beauty* (1998); *The Extremists* (2002); *The Legend of Zorro* (2005); *Amazing Grace* (2006)
Sharif, Omar	1932–	Alexandria, Egypt	*Lawrence of Arabia* (1962); *Doctor Zhivago* (1965); *Funny Girl* (1968); *The Tamarind Seed* (1974); *Gulliver's Travels* (TV 1996); *Hidalgo* (2004)

ARTS AND CULTURE

Film and television personalities (continued)

Name	Dates	Place of birth	Selected works
Sheen, Charlie	1965–	Santa Monica, California	*Wall Street* (1987); *Platoon* (1987); *Young Guns* (1988); *The Rookie* (1990); *The Chase* (1994); *Shadow Conspiracy* (1997); *Good Advice* (2001); *The Big Bounce* (2004); *Scary Movie 4* (2006)
Sheen, Martin	1940–	Dayton, Ohio	*Catch 22* (1970); *Apocalypse Now* (1979); *Gandhi* (1982); *The Dead Zone* (1983); *Wall Street* (1987); *Hostile Waters* (TV, 1997); *West Wing* (TV, 1999–); *Duplicity* (2006)
Shepherd, Cybill	1950–	Memphis, Tennessee	*The Last Picture Show* (1971); *Taxi Driver* (1976); *The Lady Vanishes* (1979); *Moonlighting* (TV, 1985–9); *Alice* (1991); *Cybill* (TV series, 1995–8)
Signoret, Simone	1921–85	Wiesbaden	*La Ronde* (1950); *Les Diaboliques* (1954); *Room at the Top* (1959); *Ship of Fools* (1965)
Sim, Alistair	1900–76	Edinburgh	*The Happiest Days of Your Life* (1950); *Scrooge* (1951); *Laughter in Paradise* (1951); *The Belles of St Trinians* (1954)
Simmons, Jean	1929–	London	*Great Expectations* (1946); *Black Narcissus* (1946); *Hamlet* (1948); *The Blue Lagoon* (1948); *Spartacus* (1960); *The Dawning* (1988); *How to Make an American Quilt* (1995)
Sinatra, Frank	1915–98	Hoboken, New Jersey	*From Here to Eternity* (1953); *The Man With the Golden Arm* (1957); *The Manchurian Candidate* (1962)
Sizemore, Tom	1964–	Detroit, Michigan	*Born on the Fourth of July* (1989); *True Romance* (1993); *Natural Born Killers* (1994); *Saving Private Ryan* (1998); *Big Trouble* (2002); *Paparazzi* (2004); *The Flyboys* (2006)
Slater, Christian	1969–	New York City	*The Name of the Rose* (1986); *Robin Hood, Prince of Thieves* (1991); *Bed of Roses* (1996); *Hard Rain* (1998); *Windtalkers* (2002); *Pursued* (2004); *Bobby* (2006)
Smith, Maggie	1934–	Ilford, Essex	*The Prime of Miss Jean Brodie* (1969); *Travels with my Aunt* (1972); *A Room With a View* (1985); *The First Wives Club* (1996); *Gosford Park* (2001); *Harry Potter and the Prisoner of Azkaban* (2004)
Smith, Will	1968–	Philadelphia, Pennsylvania	*Six Degrees of Separation* (1993); *Independence Day* (1996); *Men in Black* (1997; sequel 2002); *Wild Wild West* (1999); *Ali* (2001); *I, Robot* (2004); *Hitch* (2005)
Snipes, Wesley	1962–	Orlando, Florida	*Streets of Gold* (1986); *Demolition Man* (1993); *The Fan* (1996); *Undisputed* (2002); *Unstoppable* (2004); *Hard Luck* (2006)
Sonnenfeld, Barry	1953–	New York City	*Blood Simple* (1984); *When Harry Met Sally* (1989); Director: *Get Shorty* (1995); *Men in Black* (1997; sequel 2002); *Wild, Wild West* (1999); *RV* (2006)
Spacey, Kevin	1959–	South Orange, New Jersey	*Glengarry Glen Ross* (1992); *The Usual Suspects* (1995); *Seven* (1995); *American Beauty* (1999); *The Life of David Gale* (2002); *Beyond the Sea* (2004); *Edison* (2005); *Superman Returns* (2006)
Spader, James	1960–	Boston, Massachusetts	*Sex, Lies and Videotape* (1989); *The Rachel Papers* (1989); *Bad Influence* (1990); *The Music of Chance* (1993); *Crash* (1997); *Secretary* (2002); *Shadow of Fear* (2004)
Spielberg, Steven	1947–	Cincinnati, Ohio	Director: *Jaws* (1975); *Close Encounters of the Third Kind* (1977); *Indiana Jones and the Temple of Doom* (1984); *Jurassic Park* (1993, 1997); *Schindler's List* (1993); *War of the Worlds* (2005)
Springer, Jerry	1944–	London	*The Jerry Springer Show* (TV host, 1991–)
Stallone, Sylvester	1946–	New York City	*Rocky* (1976); *Part II* (1979); *III* (1982); *IV* (1985); *V* (1990); *Rambo* (1985); *Over the Top* (1987); *Rambo III* (1988); *Cliffhanger* (1992); *Demolition Man* (1993); *The Specialist* (1995); *D-Tox* (2002)

Name	Dates	Place of birth	Selected works
Stamp, Terence	1939–	Stepney	*Far From the Madding Crowd* (1967); *Superman* (1978; sequel 1980); *The Company of Wolves* (1985); *Legal Eagles* (1986); *Wall Street* (1987); *Full Frontal* (2002); *These Foolish Things* (2006)
Stanton, Harry Dean	1926–	Kentucky	*Cool Hand Luke* (1967); *The Godfather: Part II* (1974); *Alien* (1979); *The Last Temptation of Christ* (1988); *Fear and Loathing in Las Vegas* (1998); *Inland Empire* (2006)
Steiger, Rod	1925–2002	Westhampton, New York	*On the Waterfront* (1954); *Al Capone* (1958); *Dr Zhivago* (1965); *In the Heat of the Night* (1967); *American Gothic* (1988); *Incognito* (1997)
Sternberg, Josef von	1894–1969	Vienna	*Der Blaue Engel* (1930); *The Devil is a Woman* (1935)
Stewart, James	1908–97	Indiana, Pennsylvania	*You Can't Take it With You* (1938); *The Philadelphia Story* (1940); *Rear Window* (1954); *Vertigo* (1958); *Anatomy of a Murder* (1959)
Stoltz, Eric	1961–	Whittier, California	*Mask* (1985); *Pulp Fiction* (1994); *Rob Roy* (1995); *Hi-Life* (1998); *Happy Hour* (2001); *Childstar* (2004); *The Honeymooners* (2005)
Stone, Oliver	1946–	New York City	Director: *Platoon* (1987); *Born on the Fourth of July* (1989); *JFK* (1991); *Natural Born Killers* (1994); *Nixon* (1995); *U Turn* (1998); *Alexander* (2004); *World Trade Center* (2006)
Streep, Meryl	1949–	Summit, New Jersey	*The Deer Hunter* (1978); *Kramer vs Kramer* (1979); *The French Lieutenant's Woman* (1981); *Bridges of Madison County* (1995); *The Hours* (2002); *Prime* (2005); *The Devil Wears Prada* (2006)
Streisand, Barbra	1942–	New York City	*Funny Girl* (1968); *Hello Dolly* (1969); *What's up Doc?* (1972); *The Way We Were* (1973); *A Star Is Born* (1976); *Yentl* (1983); *Nuts* (1987); *The Mirror Has Two Faces* (1996); *Meet the Fockers* (2004)
Stroheim, Erich von	1886–1957	Vienna	Director: *Blind Husbands* (1919); *Greed* (1923); *La Grande Illusion* (1930); *Sunset Boulevard* (1955)
Sutherland, Donald	1934–	Saint John, New Brunswick	*The Dirty Dozen* (1967); *The Eagle Has Landed* (1977); *Ordinary People* (1980); *Outbreak* (1995); *Shadow Conspiracy* (1997); *Uprising* (2001); *Cold Mountain* (2003); *Pride & Prejudice* (2005)
Sutherland, Kiefer	1966–	London	*The Lost Boys* (1987); *Young Guns* (1988); *Renegades* (1989); *A Few Good Men* (1992); *Behind the Red Door* (2002); *Taking Lives* (2004); *The Sentinel* (2006)
Suzman, Janet	1939–	Johannesburg	*Nicholas and Alexandra* (1972); *Voyage of the Damned* (1976); *The Draughtsman's Contract* (1982); *Leon, the Pig Farmer* (1992); *Max* (2002)
Swanson, Gloria	1897–1983	Chicago	*Male and Female* (1919); *Manhandled* (1924); *The Trespasser* (1929); *Sunset Boulevard* (1950)
Swayze, Patrick	1954–	Houston, Texas	*Dirty Dancing* (1987); *Ghost* (1990); *Desperado* (1993); *Letters from a Killer* (1998); *Donnie Darko* (2001); *George and the Dragon* (2004); *Keeping Mum* (2005)
Tandy, Jessica	1909–94	London	*The Birds* (1963); *The World According to Garp* (1982); *Still of the Night* (1982); *The Bostonians* (1984); *Cocoon* (1985); *The House on Carroll Street* (1988); *Driving Miss Daisy* (1989)
Tarantino, Quentin	1963–	Knoxville, Tennessee	*Reservoir Dogs* (1991); *Pulp Fiction* (1994); *From Dusk Till Dawn* (1996); *Jackie Brown* (1998); *Kill Bill* (2003, 2004)
Tati, Jacques	1908–82	Pecq	Director: *Jour de Fête* (1947); *Les Vacances de Mr Hulot* (1953); *Mon Oncle* (1958)
Taylor, Elizabeth	1932–	London	*The Father of the Bride* (1950); *Cat on a Hot Tin Roof* (1958); *Cleopatra* (1962); *Who's Afraid of Virginia Woolf?* (1966); *Suddenly Last Summer* (1968); *Young Toscanini* (1988)
Temple, Shirley	1928–	Santa Monica, California	*Stand Up and Cheer* (1934); *Bright Eyes* (1934); *Heidi* (1937); *The Little Princess* (1939)

Film and television *personalities* (continued)

Name	Dates	Place of birth	Selected works
Terry-Thomas	1911–90	Finchley, London	*Private's Progress* (1956); *I'm All Right Jack* (1959); *It's a Mad, Mad, Mad, Mad World* (1963); *Those Magnificent Men in Their Flying Machines* (1965); *Don't Look Now* (1968)
Thompson, Emma	1959–	London	*Henry V* (1989); *Howard's End* (1992); *Remains of the Day* (1993); *Sense and Sensibility* (1996); *Judas Kiss* (1998); *Love Actually* (2003); *Nanny McPhee* (2005); *Stranger Than Fiction* (2006)
Thornton, Billy Bob	1955–	Hots Springs, Arkansas	*Indecent Proposal* (1993); *Sling Blade* (1996); *Primary Colors* (1998); *The Alamo* (2004); *School for Scoundrels* (2006)
Thurman, Uma	1970–	Boston, Massachusetts	*Dangerous Liaisons* (1988); *Pulp Fiction* (1994); *Batman and Robin* (1997); *The Avengers* (1998); *Hysterical Blindness* (2002); *Kill Bill* (2003, 2004); *My Super Ex-Girlfriend* (2006)
Tracy, Spencer	1900–67	Milwaukee	*Up The River* (1930); *Captains Courageous* (1937); *Woman of the Year* (1942); *State of the Union* (1948); *Father of the Bride*(1950); *Guess Who's Coming to Dinner* (1967)
Travolta, John	1954–	Englewood, New Jersey	*Saturday Night Fever* (1977); *Grease* (1978); *Staying Alive* (1983); *Perfect* (1985); *Look Who's Talking* (1989); *Pulp Fiction* (1994); *Get Shorty* (1995); *The Punisher* (2004); *Be Cool* (2005)
Truffaut, François	1932–84	Paris	Director: *Les Quatres Cents Coups* (1959); *Tirez sur le Pianiste* (1960); *Jules et Jim* (1962); *La Nuit Américaine* (1973); *L'Enfant Sauvage* (1969); *Le Dernier Metro* (1980); *Vivement Dimanche* (1983)
Tucci, Stanley	1960–	Katonah, New York	*Prizzi's Honor* (1985); *The Pelican Brief* (1993); *A Midsummer Night's Dream* (1999); *Road to Perdition* (2002); *The Terminal* (2004); *The Devil Wears Prada* (2006)
Turner, Kathleen	1954–	Springfield, Missouri	*Romancing the Stone* (1984); *Prizzi's Honor* (1985); *Peggy Sue Got Married* (1986); *The War of the Roses* (1989); *Prince of Central Park* (2000); *Without Love* (2004); *Monster House* (2006)
Turturro, John	1957–	New York City	*Raging Bull* (1980); *Hannah and Her Sisters* (1986); *Miller's Crossing* (1990); *Barton Fink* (1991); *Fearless* (1993); *The Big Lebowski* (1997); *Mr Deeds* (2002); *Secret Window* (2004)
Ustinov, Peter	1921–2004	London	*Quo Vadis* (1951); *Spartacus* (1960); *Topkapi* (1964); *Death on the Nile* (1978); *Appointment with Death* (1988); *Lorenzo's Oil* (1992); *Stiff Upper Lips* (1997)
Vadim, Roger	1928–2000	Paris	Director: *Et Dieu Créa La Femme* (1956); *Les Liaisons Dangereuses* (1959); *Barbarella* (1968); *La Vice et la Vertue* (1962)
Valentino, Rudolph	1895–1926	Castellaneta	*The Four Horsemen of the Apocalypse* (1919); *The Sheik* (1921); *Blood and Sand* (1922)
Van Sant, Gus	1952–	Louisville, Kentucky	Director: *Even Cowgirls Get the Blues* (1993); *To Die For* (1995); *Good Will Hunting* (1997); *Psycho* (1998); *Finding Forrester* (2000); *Elephant* (2003); *Last Days* (2005)
Verhoeven, Paul	1938–	Amsterdam	Director: *Turkish Delight* (1973); *Spetters* (1980); *Robocop* (1987); *Total Recall* (1990); *Basic Instinct* (1992); *Starship Troopers* (1997); *Hollow Man* (2000); *Black Book* (2006)
Vidor, King	1894–1982	Galveston, Texas	Director: *The Turn of the Road* (1919); *The Big Parade* (1925); *Hallelujah* (1929); *Northwest Passage* (1940); *War and Peace* (1956); *Solomon and Sheba* (1959)
Visconti, Luchino	1906–76	Milan	Director: *Ossessione* (1942); *La Terra Trema* (1947); *Il Gattopardo* (1963); *Morte a Venezia* (1971)

Name	Dates	Place of birth	Selected works
Von Sydow, Max	1929–	Lund	*The Greatest Story Ever Told* (1965); *Hannah and Her Sisters* (1986); *Awakenings* (1991); *Private Confessions* (1998); *Minority Report* (2002); *Intacto* (2003); *Heidi* (2005); *The Inquiry* (2006)
Wajda, Andrzej	1926–	Suwalki, Poland	Director: *Pokolenie* (1954); *Czlowiek z marmary* (1977); *Czlowiek z Zelaza* (1981); *Crime and Punishment* (1984); *Miss Nobody* (1997); *Zemsta* (2002)
Walken, Christopher	1943–	Astoria, New York	*The Deer Hunter* (1978); *Heaven's Gate* (1980); *Batman Returns* (1992); *America's Sweethearts* (2001); *Catch Me If You Can* (2002); *The Stepford Wives* (2004); *Domino* (2005); *Click* (2006)
Walters, Julie	1950–	Birmingham	*Educating Rita* (1983); *Personal Services* (1987); *Jake's Progress* (TV, 1995); *Melissa* (TV, 1997); *Billy Elliot* (2000); *Calendar Girls* (2003); *Wah-Wah* (2005); *Driving Lessons* (2006)
Washington, Denzel	1954–	Mt Vernon, New York	*Cry Freedom* (1987); *Malcolm X* (1992); *Much Ado About Nothing* (1993); *The Preacher's Wife* (1996); *The Bone Collector* (1999); *Training Day* (2001); *Man on Fire* (2004); *Inside Man* (2006)
Watson, Emily	1967–	London	*Breaking the Waves* (1996); *Hilary and Jackie* (1998); *Angela's Ashes* (1998); *Punch-Drunk Love* (2002); *Wah-Wah* (2005); *Separate Lies* (2006)
Wayne, John	1907–79	Winterset, Iowa	*Stagecoach* (1939); *Red River* (1948); *She Wore a Yellow Ribbon* (1949); *The Quiet Man* (1952); *True Grit* (1969)
Weaver, Sigourney	1949–	New York City	*Alien* (1979; sequels 1986, 1992, 1997); *The Year of Living Dangerously* (1982); *Ghostbusters* (1984); *Gorillas in the Mist* (1988); *Heartbreakers* (2001); *The Village* (2004); *Infamous* (2006)
Weaving, Hugo	1960	Nigeria	*Reckless Kelly* (1993); *The Adventures of Priscilla, Queen of the Desert* (1994); *The Matrix* (1999); *The Lord of the Rings* (2001); *Peaches* (2004); *Little Fish* (2006)
Weir, Peter	1944–	Sydney	Director: *Picnic at Hanging Rock* (1975); *Gallipoli* (1980); *Witness* (1985); *Dead Poet's Society* (1989); *Green Card* (1990); *The Truman Show* (1998); *Master and Commander* (2004)
Welles, Orson	1915–85	Kenosha, Wisconsin	Director, screenplay writer, actor: *Citizen Kane* (1941); *The Magnificent Ambersons* (1942); *Macbeth* (1948); *The Third Man* (1949); *Othello* (1952); *Chimes at Midnight* (1966)
West, Mae	1893–1980	New York City	*Night After Night* (1932); *I'm No Angel* (1933); *My Little Chickadee* (1940); *Myra Breckinridge* (1970)
Wilder, Billy	1906–2002	Vienna	Director: *The Major and The Minor* (1942); *The Lost Weekend* (1945); *Sunset Boulevard* (1950); *The Apartment* (1960); *The Private Life of Sherlock Holmes* (1970); *Fedora* (1978)
Wilder, Gene	1935–	Milwaukee	*Bonnie and Clyde* (1967); *Blazing Saddles* (1974); *Young Frankenstein* (1974); *Stir Crazy* (1982); *Haunted Honeymoon* (1986); *Another You* (1991); *The Lady in Question* (TV, 1999)
Williams, Robin	1952–	Chicago	*Popeye* (1980); *The World According to Garp* (1982); *Dead Poets Society* (1989); *Awakenings* (1990); *The Fisher King* (1991); *Mrs Doubtfire* (1993); *The Big White* (2005); *RV* (2006)
Willis, Bruce	1955–	West Germany	*Moonlighting* (TV, 1985–9); *Die Hard* (1988, 1990, 1995); *The Fifth Element* (1997); *The Jackal* (1997); *The Sixth Sense* (1999); *The Whole Ten Yards* (2004); *Sin City* (2005); *Fast Food Nation* (2006)
Winfrey, Oprah	1954–	Kosciusko, Missouri	*The Color Purple* (1985); *The Oprah Winfrey Show* (TV host, 1986–); *Beloved* (1998)

ARTS AND CULTURE

Film and television personalities (continued)

Name	Dates	Place of birth	Selected works
Winger, Debra	1955–	Columbus, Ohio	*An Officer and a Gentleman* (1982); *Terms of Endearment* (1983); *Betrayed* (1988); *Shadowlands* (1994); *Forget Paris* (1995); *Big Bad Love* (2001); *Radio* (2003); *Sometimes in April* (TV, 2005)
Winslet, Kate	1975–	Reading, Berkshire	*Sense and Sensibility* (1995); *Hamlet* (1996); *Titanic* (1997); *Hideous Kinky* (1998); *Iris* (2001); *Finding Neverland* (2004); *Romance & Cigarettes* (2005); *All the King's Men* (2006)
Winters, Shelley	1922–2006	St Louis, Missouri	*A Double Life* (1948); *The Night of the Hunter* 1955); *Lolita* (1962); *Heavy* (1995)
Wood, Elijah	1981–	Cedar Rapids, Iowa	*Paradise* (1991); *The Lord of the Rings* (2001–3); *Eternal Sunshine of the Spotless Mind* (2004); *Green Street* (2005); *Bobby* (2006)
Wood, Natalie	1938–81	San Francisco	*Rebel Without a Cause* (1955); *Splendor in the Grass* (1961); *West Side Story* (1961); *This Property is Condemned* (1966); *Bob and Carol and Ted and Alice* (1969)
Woods, James	1947–	Vernal, Utah	*Salvador* (1985); *Chaplin* (1992); *Nixon* (1995); *Ghosts of Mississippi* (1997); *The Virgin Suicides* (1998); *Northfork* (2002); *Be Cool* (2005); *End Game* (2006)
Woodward, Joanne	1930–	Thomasville, Georgia	*The Long Hot Summer* (1958); *The Glass Menagerie* (1987); *Mr and Mrs Bridge* (1990); *Breathing Lessons* (TV, 1994); *Empire Falls* (TV, 2005)
Wyler, William	1902–81	Mulhausen, Alsace	Director: *Mrs Miniver* (1942); *The Best Years of our Lives* (1946); *Friendly Persuasion* (1956); *Ben Hur* (1959); *Funny Girl* (1968)
Zeffirelli, Franco	1923–	Florence	Director: *Romeo and Juliet* (1968); *La Traviata* (1983); *Othello* (1986); *Hamlet* (1990); *Jane Eyre* (1996); *Tea with Mussolini* (1998); *Callas Forever* (2002); *Tre fratelli* (2005)
Zellweger, Renée	1969–	Katy, Texas	*Nurse Betty* (2000); *Bridget Jones's Diary* (2001; sequel 2004); *Chicago* (2002); *Cold Mountain* (2003); *Cinderella Man* (2005); *Miss Potter* (2006)
Zeta-Jones, Catherine	1969–	Swansea	*Splitting Heirs* (1993); *The Mask of Zorro* (1998); *Entrapment* (1999); *America's Sweethearts* (2001); *Chicago* (2002); *Intolerable Cruelty* (2003); *The Terminal* (2004); *The Legend of Zorro* (2005)
Zinnemann, Fred	1907–97	Vienna	Director: *High Noon* (1952); *From Here to Eternity* (1953); *A Man for All Seasons* (1966); *The Day of the Jackal* (1973)

See also **Theatre Personalities**, pp. 583–8

Motion picture Academy Awards (Oscars)

1928
Picture *Wings*, Paramount
Director Frank Borzage, *Seventh Heaven*;
Lewis Milestone, *Two Arabian Nights*
Actress Janet Gaynor, *Seventh Heaven, Street Angel, Sunrise*
Actor Emil Jannings, *The Way of All Flesh, The Last Command*

1929
Picture *The Broadway Melody*, MGM
Director Frank Lloyd, *The Divine Lady*
Actress Mary Pickford, *Coquette*
Actor Warner Baxter, *In Old Arizona*

1930
Picture *All Quiet on the Western Front*, Universal
Director Lewis Milestone, *All Quiet on the Western Front*
Actress Norma Shearer, *The Divorcee*
Actor George Arliss, *Disraeli*

1931
Picture *Cimarron*, RKO Radio
Director Norman Taurog, *Skippy*
Actress Marie Dressler, *Min and Bill*
Actor Lionel Barrymore, *A Free Soul*

1932
Picture *Grand Hotel*, MGM
Director Frank Borzage, *Bad Girl*
Actress Helen Hayes, *The Sin of Madelon Claudet*
Actor Fredric March, *Dr Jekyll and Mr Hyde*,
and Wallace Beery, *The Champ*

1933
Picture *Cavalcade*, Fox
Director Frank Lloyd, *Cavalcade*
Actress Katharine Hepburn, *Morning Glory*
Actor Charles Laughton, *The Private Life of Henry VIII*

1934
Picture *It Happened One Night*, Columbia
Director Frank Capra, *It Happened One Night*
Actress Claudette Colbert, *It Happened One Night*
Actor Clark Gable, *It Happened One Night*

1935
Picture *Mutiny on the Bounty*, MGM
Director John Ford, *The Informer*
Actress Bette Davis, *Dangerous*
Actor Victor McLaglen, *The Informer*

1936
Picture *The Great Ziegfeld*, MGM
Director Frank Capra, *Mr. Deeds Goes to Town*
Actress Luise Rainer, *The Great Ziegfeld*
Actor Paul Muni, *The Story of Louis Pasteur*
Supporting actress Gale Sondergaard, *Anthony Adverse*
Supporting actor Walter Brennan, *Come and Get It*

1937
Picture *The Life of Emile Zola*, Warner Bros
Director Leo McCarey, *The Awful Truth*
Actress Luise Rainer, *The Good Earth*
Actor Spencer Tracy, *Captains Courageous*
Supporting actress Alice Brady, *In Old Chicago*
Supporting actor Joseph Schildkraut, *The Life of Emile Zola*

1938
Picture *You Can't Take it With You*, Columbia
Director Frank Capra, *You Can't Take it With You*

Actress Bette Davis, *Jezebel*
Actor Spencer Tracy, *Boys Town*
Supporting actress Fay Bainter, *Jezebel*
Supporting actor Walter Brennan, *Kentucky*

1939
Picture *Gone with the Wind*, Selznick MGM
Director Victor Fleming, *Gone with the Wind*
Actress Vivien Leigh, *Gone with the Wind*
Actor Robert Donat, *Goodbye Mr Chips*
Supporting actress Hattie McDaniel, *Gone with the Wind*
Supporting actor Thomas Mitchell, *Stagecoach*

1940
Picture *Rebecca*, Selznick UA
Director John Ford, *The Grapes of Wrath*
Actress Ginger Rogers, *Kitty Foyle*
Actor James Stewart, *The Philadelphia Story*
Supporting actress Jane Darwell, *The Grapes of Wrath*
Supporting actor Walter Brennan, *The Westerner*

1941
Picture *How Green Was My Valley*, 20th Century Fox
Director John Ford, *How Green Was My Valley*
Actress Joan Fontaine, *Suspicion*
Actor Gary Cooper, *Sergeant York*
Supporting actress Mary Astor, *The Great Lie*
Supporting actor Donald Crisp, *How Green Was My Valley*

1942
Picture *Mrs Miniver*, MGM
Director William Wyler, *Mrs Miniver*
Actress Greer Garson, *Mrs Miniver*
Actor James Cagney, *Yankee Doodle Dandy*
Supporting actress Teresa Wright, *Mrs Miniver*
Supporting actor Van Heflin, *Johnny Eager*

1943
Picture *Casablanca*, Warner Bros
Director Michael Curtiz, *Casablanca*
Actress Jennifer Jones, *The Song of Bernadette*
Actor Paul Lukas, *Watch on the Rhine*
Supporting actress Katina Paxinou, *For Whom the Bell Tolls*
Supporting actor Charles Coburn, *The More the Merrier*

1944
Picture *Going My Way*, Paramount
Director Leo McCarey, *Going My Way*
Actress Ingrid Bergman, *Gaslight*
Actor Bing Crosby, *Going My Way*
Supporting actress Ethel Barrymore, *None But the Lonely Heart*
Supporting actor Barry Fitzgerald, *Going My Way*

1945
Picture *The Lost Weekend*, Paramount
Director Billy Wilder, *The Lost Weekend*
Actress Joan Crawford, *Mildred Pierce*
Actor Ray Milland, *The Lost Weekend*
Supporting actress Anne Revere, *National Velvet*
Supporting actor James Dunn, *A Tree Grows in Brooklyn*

1946
Picture *The Best Years of Our Lives*, Goldwyn-RKO Radio
Director William Wyler, *The Best Years of Our Lives*
Actress Olivia de Havilland, *To Each His Own*
Actor Fredric March, *The Best Years of Our Lives*
Supporting actress Anne Baxter, *The Razor's Edge*
Supporting actor Harold Russell, *The Best Years of Our Lives*

Motion picture Academy Awards (Oscars) (continued)

1947
Picture *Gentleman's Agreement*, 20th Century Fox
Director Elia Kazan, *Gentleman's Agreement*
Actress Loretta Young, *The Farmer's Daughter*
Actor Ronald Colman, *A Double Life*
Supporting actress Celeste Holm, *Gentleman's Agreement*
Supporting actor Edmund Gwenn, *Miracle on 34th Street*

1948
Picture *Hamlet*, Rank-Two Cities-UI
Director John Huston, *Treasure of the Sierra Madre*
Actress Jane Wyman, *Johnny Belinda*
Actor Laurence Olivier, *Hamlet*
Supporting actress Claire Trevor, *Key Largo*
Supporting actor Walter Huston, *Treasure of the Sierra Madre*

1949
Picture *All the King's Men*, Rossen-Columbia
Director Joseph L Mankiewicz, *A Letter to Three Wives*
Actress Olivia de Havilland, *The Heiress*
Actor Broderick Crawford, *All the King's Men*
Supporting actress Mercedes McCambridge, *All the King's Men*
Supporting actor Dean Jagger, *Twelve O'Clock High*

1950
Picture *All About Eve*, 20th Century Fox
Director Joseph L Mankiewicz, *All About Eve*
Actress Judy Holliday, *Born Yesterday*
Actor José Ferrer, *Cyrano de Bergerac*
Supporting actress Josephine Hull, *Harvey*
Supporting actor George Sanders, *All About Eve*

1951
Picture *An American in Paris*, MGM
Director George Stevens, *A Place in the Sun*
Actress Vivien Leigh, *A Streetcar Named Desire*
Actor Humphrey Bogart, *The African Queen*
Supporting actress Kim Hunter, *A Streetcar Named Desire*
Supporting actor Karl Malden, *A Streetcar Named Desire*

1952
Picture *The Greatest Show on Earth*, DeMille-Paramount
Director John Ford, *The Quiet Man*
Actress Shirley Booth, *Come Back, Little Sheba*
Actor Gary Cooper, High Noon
Supporting actress Gloria Grahame, *The Bad and the Beautiful*
Supporting actor Anthony Quinn, *Viva Zapata*

1953
Picture *From Here to Eternity*, Columbia
Director Fred Zinnemann, *From Here to Eternity*
Actress Audrey Hepburn, *Roman Holiday*
Actor William Holden, *Stalag 17*
Supporting actress Donna Reed, *From Here to Eternity*
Supporting actor Frank Sinatra, *From Here to Eternity*

1954
Picture *On the Waterfront*, Horizon-American Corp, Columbia
Director Elia Kazan, *On the Waterfront*
Actress Grace Kelly, *The Country Girl*
Actor Marlon Brando, *On the Waterfront*
Supporting actress Eva Marie Saint, *On the Waterfront*
Supporting actor Edmond O'Brien, *The Barefoot Contessa*

1955
Picture *Marty*, Hecht and Lancaster, United Artists
Director Delbert Mann, *Marty*
Actress Anna Magnani, *The Rose Tattoo*
Actor Ernest Borgnine, *Marty*
Supporting actress Jo Van Fleet, *East of Eden*
Supporting actor Jack Lemmon, *Mister Roberts*

1956
Picture *Around the World in 80 Days*, Michael Todd Co, Inc-UA
Director George Stevens, *Giant*
Actress Ingrid Bergman, *Anastasia*
Actor Yul Brynner, *The King and I*
Supporting actress Dorothy Malone, *Written on the Wind*
Supporting actor Anthony Quinn, *Lust for Life*

1957
Picture *The Bridge on the River Kwai*, Horizon Picture, Columbia
Director David Lean, *The Bridge on the River Kwai*
Actress Joanne Woodward, *The Three Faces of Eve*
Actor Alec Guinness, *The Bridge on the River Kwai*
Supporting actress Miyoshi Umeki, *Sayonara*
Supporting actor Red Buttons, *Sayonara*

1958
Picture *Gigi*, Arthur Freed Productions Inc, MGM
Director Vincente Minnelli, *Gigi*
Actress Susan Hayward, *I Want to Live!*
Actor David Niven, *Separate Tables*
Supporting actress Wendy Hiller, *Separate Tables*
Supporting actor Burl Ives, *The Big Country*

1959
Picture *Ben Hur*, MGM
Director William Wyler, *Ben Hur*
Actress Simone Signoret, *Room at the Top*
Actor Charlton Heston, *Ben Hur*
Supporting actress Shelley Winters, *The Diary of Anne Frank*
Supporting actor Hugh Griffith, *Ben Hur*

1960
Picture *The Apartment*, Mirisch Co Inc, United Artists
Director Billy Wilder, *The Apartment*
Actress Elizabeth Taylor, *Butterfield 8*
Actor Burt Lancaster, *Elmer Gantry*
Supporting actress Shirley Jones, *Elmer Gantry*
Supporting actor Peter Ustinov, *Spartacus*

1961
Picture *West Side Story*, Mirisch Pictures Inc, and B and P Enterprises Inc, United Artists
Director Robert Wise and Jerome Robbins, *West Side Story*
Actress Sophia Loren, *Two Women*
Actor Maximillian Schell, *Judgment at Nuremberg*
Supporting actress Rita Moreno, *West Side Story*
Supporting actor George Chakiris, *West Side Story*

1962
Picture *Lawrence of Arabia*, Horizon Pictures Ltd, Columbia
Director David Lean, *Lawrence of Arabia*
Actress Anne Bancroft, *The Miracle Worker*
Actor Gregory Peck, *To Kill a Mockingbird*
Supporting actress Patty Duke, *The Miracle Worker*
Supporting actor Ed Begley, *Sweet Bird of Youth*

1963
Picture Tom Jones, A Woodfall Production, UA-Lopert Pictures
Director Tony Richardson, *Tom Jones*
Actress Patricia Neal, *Hud*
Actor Sidney Poitier, *Lilies of the Field*
Supporting actress Margaret Rutherford, *The VIPs*
Supporting actor Melvyn Douglas, *Hud*

1964
Picture My Fair Lady, Warner Bros
Director George Cukor, *My Fair Lady*
Actress Julie Andrews, *Mary Poppins*
Actor Rex Harrison, *My Fair Lady*
Supporting actress Lila Kedrova, *Zorba the Greek*
Supporting actor Peter Ustinov, *Topkapi*

1965
Picture The Sound of Music, Argyle Enterprises Production, 20th Century Fox
Director Robert Wise, *The Sound of Music*
Actress Julie Christie, *Darling*
Actor Lee Marvin, *Cat Ballou*
Supporting actress Shelley Winters, *A Patch of Blue*
Supporting actor Martin Balsam, *A Thousand Clowns*

1966
Picture A Man for All Seasons, Highland Films Ltd Production, Columbia
Director Fred Zinnemann, *A Man for All Seasons*
Actress Elizabeth Taylor, *Who's Afraid of Virginia Woolf?*
Actor Paul Scofield, *A Man for All Seasons*
Supporting actress Sandy Dennis, *Who's Afraid of Virginia Woolf?*
Supporting actor Walter Matthau, *The Fortune Cookie*

1967
Picture In the Heat of the Night, Mirisch Corp Productions, United Artists
Director Mike Nichols, *The Graduate*
Actress Katharine Hepburn, *Guess Who's Coming to Dinner?*
Actor Rod Steiger, *In the Heat of the Night*
Supporting actress Estelle Parsons, *Bonnie and Clyde*
Supporting actor George Kennedy, *Cool Hand Luke*

1968
Picture Oliver! Columbia Pictures
Director Sir Carol Reed, *Oliver!*
Actress Katharine Hepburn, *The Lion in Winter* and Barbra Streisand, *Funny Girl*
Actor Cliff Robertson, *Charly*
Supporting actress Ruth Gordon, *Rosemary's Baby*
Supporting actor Jack Albertson, *The Subject Was Roses*

1969
Picture Midnight Cowboy, Jerome Hellman-John Schlesinger Production, United Artists
Director John Schlesinger, *Midnight Cowboy*
Actress Maggie Smith, *The Prime of Miss Jean Brodie*
Actor John Wayne, *True Grit*
Supporting actress Goldie Hawn, *Cactus Flower*
Supporting actor Gig Young, *They Shoot Horses Don't They?*

1970
Picture Patton, Frank McCarthy-Franklin J Schaffner Production, 20th Century Fox
Director Franklin J Schaffner, *Patton*
Actress Glenda Jackson, *Women in Love*
Actor George C Scott, *Patton*
Supporting actress Helen Hayes, *Airport*
Supporting actor John Mills, *Ryan's Daughter*

1971
Picture The French Connection, D'Antoni Productions, 20th Century Fox
Director William Friedkin, *The French Connection*
Actress Jane Fonda, *Klute*
Actor Gene Hackman, *The French Connection*
Supporting actress Cloris Leachman, *The Last Picture Show*
Supporting actor Ben Johnson, *The Last Picture Show*

1972
Picture The Godfather, Albert S Ruddy Production, Paramount
Director Bob Fosse, *Cabaret*
Actress Liza Minnelli, *Cabaret*
Actor Marlon Brando, *The Godfather*
Supporting actress Eileen Heckart, *Butterflies Are Free*
Supporting actor Joel Grey, *Cabaret*

1973
Picture The Sting, Universal/Bill Phillips/George Roy Hill Production, Universal
Director George Roy Hill, *The Sting*
Actress Glenda Jackson, *A Touch of Class*
Actor Jack Lemmon, *Save the Tiger*
Supporting actress Tatum O'Neal, *Paper Moon*
Supporting actor John Houseman, *The Paper Chase*

1974
Picture The Godfather, Part II, Coppola Co Production, Paramount
Director Francis Ford Coppola, *The Godfather, Part II*
Actress Ellen Burstyn, *Alice Doesn't Live Here Anymore*
Actor Art Carney, *Harry and Tonto*
Supporting actress Ingrid Bergman, *Murder on the Orient Express*
Supporting actor Robert De Niro, *The Godfather, Part II*

1975
Picture One Flew Over the Cuckoo's Nest, Fantasy Films Production, United Artists
Director Milos Forman, *One Flew Over the Cuckoo's Nest*
Actress Louise Fletcher, *One Flew Over the Cuckoo's Nest*
Actor Jack Nicholson, *One Flew Over the Cuckoo's Nest*
Supporting actress Lee Grant, *Shampoo*
Supporting actor George Burns, *The Sunshine Boys*

1976
Picture Rocky, Robert Chartoff-Irwin Winkler Production, United Artists
Director John G Avildsen, *Rocky*
Actress Faye Dunaway, *Network*
Actor Peter Finch, *Network*
Supporting actress Beatrice Straight, *Network*
Supporting actor Jason Robards, *All the President's Men*

1977
Picture Annie Hall, Jack Rollins-Charles H Joffe Production, United Artists
Director Woody Allen, *Annie Hall*
Actress Diane Keaton, *Annie Hall*
Actor Richard Dreyfuss, *The Goodbye Girl*
Supporting actress Vanessa Redgrave, *Julia*
Supporting actor Jason Robards, *Julia*

1978
Picture The Deer Hunter, Michael Cimino Film Production, Universal
Director Michael Cimino, *The Deer Hunter*
Actress Jane Fonda, *Coming Home*
Actor Jon Voight, *Coming Home*

Motion picture Academy Awards (Oscars) (continued)

Supporting actress Maggie Smith, *California Suite*
Supporting actor Christopher Walken, *The Deer Hunter*

1979
Picture *Kramer vs Kramer*, Stanley Jaffe Production, Columbia Pictures
Director Robert Benton, *Kramer vs Kramer*
Actress Sally Field, *Norma Rae*
Actor Dustin Hoffman, *Kramer vs Kramer*
Supporting actress Meryl Streep, *Kramer vs Kramer*
Supporting actor Melvyn Douglas, *Being There*

1980
Picture *Ordinary People*, Wildwood Enterprises Production, Paramount
Director Robert Redford, *Ordinary People*
Actress Sissy Spacek, *Coal Miner's Daughter*
Actor Robert De Niro, *Raging Bull*
Supporting actress Mary Steenburgen, *Melvin and Howard*
Supporting actor Timothy Hutton, *Ordinary People*

1981
Picture *Chariots of Fire*, Enigma Productions, Ladd Company/Warner Bros
Director Warren Beatty, *Reds*
Actress Katharine Hepburn, *On Golden Pond*
Actor Henry Fonda, *On Golden Pond*
Supporting actress Maureen Stapleton, *Reds*
Supporting actor John Gielgud, *Arthur*

1982
Picture *Gandhi*, Indo-British Films Production/Columbia
Director Richard Attenborough, *Gandhi*
Actress Meryl Streep, *Sophie's Choice*
Actor Ben Kingsley, *Gandhi*
Supporting actress Jessica Lange, *Tootsie*
Supporting actor Louis Gossett Jr, *An Officer and a Gentleman*

1983
Picture *Terms of Endearment*, Paramount
Director James L Brooks, *Terms of Endearment*
Actress Shirley MacLaine, *Terms of Endearment*
Actor Robert Duvall, *Tender Mercies*
Supporting actress Linda Hunt, *The Year of Living Dangerously*
Supporting actor Jack Nicholson, *Terms of Endearment*

1984
Picture *Amadeus*, Orion Pictures
Director Milos Forman, *Amadeus*
Actress Sally Field, *Places in the Heart*
Actor F Murray Abraham, *Amadeus*
Supporting actress Dame Peggy Ashcroft, *A Passage to India*
Supporting actor Haing S Ngor, *The Killing Fields*

1985
Picture *Out of Africa*, Universal
Director Sydney Pollack, *Out of Africa*
Actress Geraldine Page, *The Trip to Bountiful*
Actor William Hurt, *Kiss of the Spider Woman*
Supporting actress Anjelica Huston, *Prizzi's Honor*
Supporting actor Don Ameche, *Cocoon*

1986
Picture *Platoon*, Orion Pictures
Director Oliver Stone, *Platoon*

Actress Marlee Matlin, *Children of a Lesser God*
Actor Paul Newman, *The Color of Money*
Supporting actress Dianne Wiest, *Hannah and Her Sisters*
Supporting actor Michael Caine, *Hannah and Her Sisters*

1987
Picture *The Last Emperor*, Columbia Pictures
Director Bernardo Bertolucci, *The Last Emperor*
Actress Cher, *Moonstruck*
Actor Michael Douglas, *Wall Street*
Supporting actress Olympia Dukakis, *Moonstruck*
Supporting actor Sean Connery, *The Untouchables*

1988
Picture *Rain Man*, United Artists
Director Barry Levinson, *Rain Man*
Actress Jodie Foster, *The Accused*
Actor Dustin Hoffman, *Rain Man*
Supporting actress Geena Davis, *The Accidental Tourist*
Supporting actor Kevin Kline, *A Fish Called Wanda*

1989
Picture *Driving Miss Daisy*, Warner Brothers
Director Oliver Stone, *Born on the Fourth of July*
Actress Jessica Tandy, *Driving Miss Daisy*
Actor Daniel Day-Lewis, *My Left Foot*
Supporting actress Brenda Fricker, *My Left Foot*
Supporting actor Denzel Washington, *Glory*

1990
Picture *Dances With Wolves*, Orion
Director Kevin Costner, *Dances With Wolves*
Actress Kathy Bates, *Misery*
Actor Jeremy Irons, *Reversal of Fortune*
Supporting actress Whoopi Goldberg, *Ghost*
Supporting actor Joe Pesci, *Goodfellas*

1991
Picture *The Silence of the Lambs*, Orion
Director Jonathan Demme, *The Silence of the Lambs*
Actress Jodie Foster, *The Silence of the Lambs*
Actor Anthony Hopkins, *The Silence of the Lambs*
Supporting actress Mercedes Ruehl, *The Fisher King*
Supporting actor Jack Palance, *City Slickers*

1992
Picture *Unforgiven*
Director Clint Eastwood, *Unforgiven*
Actress Emma Thompson, *Howard's End*
Actor Al Pacino, *Scent of a Woman*
Supporting actress Marisa Tomei, *My Cousin Vinny*
Supporting actor Gene Hackman, *Unforgiven*

1993
Picture *Schindler's List*
Director Steven Spielberg, *Schindler's List*
Actress Holly Hunter, *The Piano*
Actor Tom Hanks, *Philadelphia*
Supporting actress Anna Paquin, *The Piano*
Supporting actor Tommy Lee Jones, *The Fugitive*

1994
Picture *Forrest Gump*, Paramount
Director Robert Zemeckis, *Forrest Gump*
Actress Jessica Lange, *Blue Sky*
Actor Tom Hanks, *Forrest Gump*
Supporting actress Dianne Wiest, *Bullets over Broadway*
Supporting actor Martin Landau, *Ed Wood*

ARTS AND CULTURE

1995
Picture *Braveheart*, 20th Century Fox
Director Mel Gibson, *Braveheart*
Actress Susan Sarandon, *Dead Man Walking*
Actor Nicholas Cage, *Leaving Las Vegas*
Supporting actress Mira Sorvino, *Mighty Aphrodite*
Supporting actor Kevin Spacey, *The Usual Suspects*

1996
Picture *The English Patient*, Miramax
Director Anthony Minghella, *The English Patient*
Actress Frances McDormand, *Fargo*
Actor Geoffrey Rush, *Shine*
Supporting actress Juliette Binoche, *The English Patient*
Supporting actor Cuba Gooding, *Jerry Maguire*

1997
Picture *Titanic*, Paramount, 20th Century Fox
Director James Cameron, *Titanic*
Actress Helen Hunt, *As Good As it Gets*
Actor Jack Nicholson, *As Good As it Gets*
Supporting actress Kim Basinger, *LA Confidential*
Supporting actor Robin Williams, *Good Will Hunting*

1998
Picture *Shakespeare in Love*, Miramax
Director Steven Spielberg, *Saving Private Ryan*
Actress Gwyneth Paltrow, *Shakespeare in Love*
Actor Roberto Benigni, *Life is Beautiful*
Supporting actress Judi Dench, *Shakespeare in Love*
Supporting actor James Coburn, *Affliction*

1999
Picture *American Beauty*, DreamWorks
Director Sam Mendes, *American Beauty*
Actress Hilary Swank, *Boys Don't Cry*
Actor Kevin Spacey, *American Beauty*
Supporting actress Angelina Jolie, *Girl, Interrupted*
Supporting actor Michael Caine, *The Cider House Rules*

2000
Picture *Gladiator*, Universal Pictures/DreamWorks
Director Steven Soderberg, *Traffic*
Actress Julia Roberts, *Erin Brockovich*
Actor Russell Crowe, *Gladiator*
Supporting actress Marcia Gay Harden, *Pollock*
Supporting actor Benicio Del Toro, *Traffic*

2001
Picture *A Beautiful Mind*, Universal Pictures/Dream Works
Director Ron Howard, *A Beautiful Mind*
Actress Halle Berry, *Monster's Ball*
Actor Denzel Washington, *Training Day*
Supporting actress Jennifer Connelly, *A Beautiful Mind*
Supporting actor Jim Broadbent, *Iris*

2002
Picture *Chicago*, Miramax
Director Roman Polanski, *The Pianist*
Actress Nicole Kidman, *The Hours*
Actor Adrien Brody, *The Pianist*
Supporting actress Catherine Zeta-Jones, *Chicago*
Supporting actor Chris Cooper, *Adaptation*

2003
Picture *The Lord of the Rings: The Return of the King*, New Line Cinema
Director Peter Jackson, *The Lord of the Rings: The Return of the King*

Actress Charlize Theron, *Monster*
Actor Sean Penn, *Mystic River*
Supporting actress Renée Zellweger, *Cold Mountain*
Supporting actor Tim Robbins, *Mystic River*

2004
Picture *Million Dollar Baby*, Warner Brothers Pictures
Director Clint Eastwood, *Million Dollar Baby*
Actress Hilary Swank, *Million Dollar Baby*
Actor Jamie Foxx, *Ray*
Supporting actress Cate Blanchett, *The Aviator*
Supporting actor Morgan Freeman, *Million Dollar Baby*

2005
Picture *Crash*, Lions Gate
Director Ang Lee, *Brokeback Mountain*
Actress Reese Witherspoon, *Walk the Line*
Actor Philip Seymour Hoffman, *Capote*
Supporting actress Rachel Weisz, *The Constant Gardener*
Supporting actor George Clooney, *Syriana*

Cannes Film Festival Awards

1949
Grand Prix *The Third Man*, Carol Reed
Director René Clément, *The Walls of Malapaga*
Actor Edward G. Robinson, *House of Strangers*
Actress Isa Miranda, *The Walls of Malapaga*

1951
Grand Prix *Miracle in Milan*, Vittoria De Sica; *Miss Julie*, Alf Sjöberg
Director Luis Buñuel, *Los Olvidados*
Actor Michael Redgrave, *The Browning Version*
Actress Bette Davis, *All About Eve*

1952
Grand Prix *Two Pennyworth of Hope*, Renato Castellani; *Othello*, Orson Welles
Director Christian-Jaque, *Fanfan la Tulipe*
Actor Marlon Brando, *Viva Zapata*
Actress Lee Grant, *Detective Story*

1953
Grand Prix *The Wages of Fear*, Henri-Georges Clouzot
Actor Charles Vanel, *The Wages of Fear*

1954
Grand Prix *Gate of Hell*, Teinosuke Kinugasa

1955
Palme d'Or *Marty*, Delbert Mann
Director Sergei Vasiliev, *The Heroes of Shipka*; Jules Dassin, *Rififi*
Performance Spencer Tracy

1956
Palme d'Or *The Silent World*, Jacques Yves Cousteau, Louis Malle
Director Sergei Yutkevich, *Othello*
Performance Susan Hayward, *I'll Cry Tomorrow*

1957
Palme d'Or *Friendly Persuasion*, William Wyler
Director Robert Bresson, *A Man Escaped*
Actor John Kitzmiller, *Valley of Peace*
Actress Giulietta Masina, *Nights of Cabiria*

1958
Palme d'Or *The Cranes Are Flying*, Mikhail Kalatozov
Director Ingmar Bergman, *So Close to Life*
Actor Paul Newman, *The Long Hot Summer*
Actress Bibi Andersson, Eva Dahlbeck, Barbro Hiortas-Ornas, Ingrid Thulin, *So Close to Life*

1959
Palme d'Or *Black Orpheus*, Marcel Camus
Director François Truffaut, *The 400 Blows*
Actor Dean Stockwell, Bradford Dillman, Orson Welles, *Compulsion*
Actress Simone Signoret, *Room at the Top*

1960
Palme d'Or *La Dolce Vita*, Federico Fellini
Actress Melina Mercouri, *Never on Sunday*; Jeanne Moreau, *Moderato Cantabile*

1961
Palme d'Or *Vindiana*, Luis Buñuel; *Une Aussi Longue Absence*, Henri Colpi
Director Julia Sointseva, *The Flaming Years*
Actor Anthony Perkins, *Goodbye Again*
Actress Sophia Loren, *Two Women*

1962
Palme d'Or *The Given Word*, Anselmo Duarte
Actor Ralph Richardson, Jason Robards Jnr, Dean Stockwell, *Long Day's Journey into Night*; Murray Melvin, *A Taste of Honey*
Actress Katharine Hepburn, *Long Day's Journey into Night*; Rita Tushingham, *A Taste of Honey*

1963
Palme d'Or *The Leopard*, Luchino Visconti
Actor Richard Harris, *This Sporting Life*
Actress Marina Vlady, *Queen Bee*, aka *The Conjugal Bed*

1964
Palme d'Or *The Umbrellas of Cherbourg*, Jacques Demy
Actor Saro Urzi, *Sedcuced and Abandoned*; Antal Pager, *The Lark*
Actress Anne Bancroft, *The Pumpkin Eater*; Barbara Barrie, *One Potato, Two Potato*

1965
Palme d'Or *The Knack ... And How to Get It*, Richard Lester
Director Liviu Ciulei, *The Forest of the Hanged*
Actor Terence Stamp, *The Collector*
Actress Samantha Eggar, *The Collector*

1966
Palme d'Or *A Man and a Woman*, Claude Lelouch; *The Birds, the Bees, and the Italians*, Pietro Germi
Director Sergei Yutkevich, *Lenin in Poland*
Actor Per Oscarrson, *Hunger*
Actress Vanessa Redgrave, *Morgan!*

1967
Palme d'Or *Blow Up*, Michelangelo Antonioni
Director Ferenc Kósa, *Ten Thousand Suns*
Actor Odded Kotier, *Three Days and a Child*
Actress Pia Degermark, *Elvira Madigan*

1969
Palme d'Or *If ...*, Lindsay Anderson
Director Glauber Rocha, *Antonio das Mortes*; Vojtech Jasn, *All My Good Countrymen*
Actor Jean-Louis Trintignant, *Z*
Actress Vanessa Redgrave, *Isadora*

1970
Palme d'Or *M*A*S*H*, Robert Altman
Director John Boorman, *Leo the Last*
Actor Marcello Mastroianni, *Jealousy, Italian Style*
Actress Ottavia Piccolo, *Metello*

1971
Palme d'Or
Director *The Go-Between*, Joseph Losey
Actor Riccardo Cucciolla, *Sacco e Vanzetti*
Actress Kitty Winn, *Panic in Needle Park*

1972
Palme d'Or *The Mattei Affair*, Francesco Rossi; *The Working Class Go to Heaven*, aka *Lulu the Tool*, Elio Petri
Director Miklós Jancsó, *Red Psalm*
Actor Jean Yanne, *We Will Not Grow Old Together*
Actress Susannah York, *Images*

1973
Palme d'Or *Scarecrow*, Jerry Schatzberg; *The Hireling*, Alan Bridges
Actor Giancarlo Giannini, *Love and Anarchy*

Actress Joanne Woodward, *The Effect of Gamma Rays on Man-in-the-Moon Marigolds*

1974
Palme d'Or *The Conversation*, Francis Ford Coppola
Actor Jack Nicholson, *The Last Detail*
Actress Marie-José Nat, *Les Violons du Bal*

1975
Palme d'Or *Chronicle of the Burning Years*, Mohammed Lakhdar Hamina
Director Michel Brault, *The Orders*; Costa-Gavras, *Special Section*
Actor Vittorio Gassman, *Scent of a Woman*
Actress Valerie Perrine, *Lenny*

1976
Palme d'Or *Taxi Driver*, Martin Scorsese
Director Ettore Scola, *Down and Dirty*
Actor José Luis Gomez, *Pascual Duarte*
Actress Mari Töröcsic, *Where Are You, Mrs Dery?*; Dominique Sanda, *The Inheritance*

1977
Palme d'Or *Padre Padrone*, Paolo and Vittorio Taviani
Actor Fernando Rey, *Elisa, My Life*
Actress Shelley Duvall, *Three Women*; Monique Mercure, *J. A. Martin Photographe*

1978
Palme d'Or *The Tree of Wooden Clogs*, Ermanno Elmi
Director Nagisa Oshima, *The Empire of Passion*
Actor Jon Voight, *Coming Home*
Actress Jill Clayburgh, *An Unmarried Woman*; Isabelle Huppert, *Violette*

1979
Palme d'Or *The Tin Drum*, Volker Schlöndorff; *Apocalypse Now*, Francis Ford Coppola
Director Terrence Malick, *Days of Heaven*
Actor Jack Lemmon, *The China Syndrome*
Actress Sally Field, *Norma Rae*

1980
Palme d'Or *Kagemusha*, Akira Kurosawa; *All That Jazz*, Bob Fosse
Actor Michel Piccoli, *Leap into the Void*
Actress Anouk Aimée, *Leap into the Void*

1981
Palme d'Or *Man of Iron*, Andrzej Wajda
Actor Ugo Tognazzi, *Tragedy of a Ridiculous Man*
Actress Isabelle Adjani, *Quartet*; *Possession*

1982
Palme d'Or *Missing*, Costa-Gavras; *Yol*, Yilmaz Güney, Serif Gören
Director Werner Herzog, *Fitzcarraldo*
Actor Jack Lemmon, *Missing*
Actress Jadwiga Jankowska-Cieslak, *Another Way*

1983
Palme d'Or *The Ballad of Narayama*, Shohei Imamura
Actor Gian Maria Volonte, *The Death of Mario Ricci*
Actress Hanna Schygulla, *Story of Piera*

1984
Palme d'Or *Paris, Texas*, Wim Wenders
Director Bertrand Tavernier, *A Sunday in the Country*
Actor Alfredo Landa, Francisco Rabal, *The Holy Innocents*
Actress Helen Mirren, *Cal*

1985
Palme d'Or *When Father Was Away on Business*, Emir Kusturica
Director André Téchiné, *Rendezvous*
Actor William Hurt, *Kiss of the Spider Woman*
Actress Cher, *Mask*; Norma Aleandro, *The Official Story*

1986
Palme d'Or *The Mission*, Roland Joffe
Director Martin Scorsese, *After Hours*
Actor Michel Blanc, *Menage*; Bob Hoskins, *Mona Lisa*
Actress Barbara Sukowa, *Rosa Luxemburg*; Fernanda Torres, *I Love You*

1987
Palme d'Or *Under Satan's Sun*, Maurice Pialat
Director Wim Wenders, *Wings of Desire*
Actor Marcello Mastroianni, *Dark Eyes*
Actress Barbara Hershey, *Shy People*

1988
Palme d'Or *Pelle the Conqueror*, Bille August
Director Fernando E. Solanas, *South*
Actor Forest Whitaker, *Bird*
Actress Barbara Hersey, Johdi May, Linda Mvusi, *A World Apart*

1989
Palme d'Or *sex, lies and videotape*, Steven Soderbergh
Director Emir Kusturica, *The Time of the Gypsies*
Actor James Spader, *sex, lies and videotape*
Actress Meryl Streep, *A Cry in the Dark*, aka *Evil Angels*

1990
Palme d'Or *Wild at Heart*, David Lynch
Director Pavel Lounguine, *Taxi Blues*
Actor Gérard Depardieu, *Cyrano de Bergerac*
Actress Krystyna Janda, *Interrogation*

1991
Palme d'Or *Barton Fink*, Joel and Ethan Coen
Director Joel Coen, *Barton Fink*
Actor John Turturro, *Barton Fink*
Actress Irene Jacob, *The Double Life of Veronique*

1992
Palme d'Or *Best Intentions*, Bille August
Director Robert Altman, *The Player*
Actor Tim Robbins, *The Player*
Actress Pernilla August, *Best Intentions*

1993
Palme d'Or *Farewell My Concubine*, Chen Kaige; *The Piano*, Jane Campion
Director Mike Leigh, *Naked*
Actor David Thewlis, *Naked*
Actress Holly Hunter, *The Piano*

1994
Palme d'Or *Pulp Fiction*, Quentin Tarantino
Director Nanni Moretti, *Dear Diary*
Actor Ge Yu, *To Live*
Actress Virna Lisi, *Queen Margaret*

1995
Palme d'Or *Underground*, Emir Kusturica
Director Mathieu Kassovitz, *La Haine*
Actor Jonathan Pryce, *Carrington*
Actress Helen Mirren, *The Madness of King George*

Cannnes Film Festival Awards (continued)

1996
Palme d'Or *Secrets and Lies*, Mike Leigh
Director Joel Coen, *Fargo*
Actor Daniel Auteuil, Pascal Duquenne, *The Eighth Day*
Actress Brenda Blethyn, *Secrets and Lies*

1997
Palme d'Or *The Eel*, Shohei Imamura; *The Taste of Cherries*, Abbas Kiorostami
Director Wong Kar-Wai, *Happy Together*
Actor Sean Penn, *She's So Lovely*
Actress Kathy Burke, *Nil by Mouth*

1998
Palme d'Or *Eternity and a Day*, Theo Angelopoulos
Director John Boorman, *The General*
Actor Peter Mullen, *My Name is Joe*
Actress Elodie Bouchez, Natacha Régnier, *Dream Life of Angels*

1999
Palme d'Or *Rosetta*, Luc and Jean-Pierre Dardenne
Director Pedro Almodovar, *All About My Mother*
Actor Emmanuel Schotte, *Humanity*
Actress Emilie Dequenne, *Rosetta*; Severine Caneele, *Humanity*

2000
Palme d'Or *Dancer in the Dark*, Lars von Trier
Director Edward Yang, *Yi Yi*
Actor Tony Leung Chiu-Wai, *In the Mood for Love*
Actress Björk, *Dancer in the Dark*

2001
Palme d'Or *La Stanza del figlio*, Nanni Moretti
Director Joel Coen, *The Man Who Wasn't There*; David Lynch, *Mulholland Drive*
Actor Benoît Magimel, *La Pianiste*
Actress Isabelle Huppert, *La Pianiste*

2002
Palme d'Or *The Pianist*, Roman Polanski
Director Paul Thomas Anderson, *Punch-Drunk Love*; Kwon-Taek Im, *Chiwaseon*
Actor Olivier Gourmet, *Le Fils*
Actress Kati Outinen, *The Man Without a Past*

2003
Palme d'Or *Elephant*, Gus van Sant
Director Gus van Sant, *Elephant*
Actor Muzaffer Ozdemir, Mehmet Emin Toprak, *Uzak*
Actress Marie Josée Croze, *Barbarian Invasions*

2004
Palme d'Or *Fahrenheit 9/11*, Michael Moore
Director Tony Gatlif, *Exils*
Actor Yuya Yagira, *Dare mo shiranai*
Actress Maggie Cheung, *Clean*

2005
Palme d'Or *L'Enfant*, Luc and Jean-Pierre Dardenne
Director Michael Haneke, *Hidden*
Actor Tommy Lee Jones, *The Three Burials of Melquiades Estrada*
Actress Hanna Laslo, *Free Zone*

2006
Palme d'Or *The Wind that Shakes the Barley*, Ken Loach
Director Alejandro Gonzalez Inarritu, *Babel*
Actor Jamel Debbouze (and cast), *Days of Glory*
Actress Penelope Cruz (and cast), *Volver*

BAFTA Awards (British Academy of Film and Television Arts)

1947
Film *The Best Years of Our Lives*, William Wyler
British Film *Odd Man Out*, Carol Reed

1948
Film *Hamlet*, Laurence Olivier
British Film *The Fallen Idol*, Carol Reed

1949
Film *The Bicycle Thief*, Vittorio De Sica
British Film *The Third Man*, Carol Reed

1950
Film *All About Eve*, Joseph L. Mankiewicz
British Film *The Blue Lamp*. Basil Dearden

1951
Film *La Ronde*, Max Ophuls
British Film *The Lavender Hill Mob*, Charles Crichton

1952
Film *The Sound Barrier* (US: *Breaking the Sound Barrier*), David Lean
British Film *The Sound Barrier*, David Lean
Actor Ralph Richardson, *The Sound Barrier*
Actress Vivien Leigh, *A Streetcar Named Desire*

1953
Film *Forbidden Games*, René Clément
British Film *Genevieve*, Henry Cornelius
Actor John Gielgud, *Julius Caesar*
Actress Audrey Hepburn, *Roman Holiday*

1954
Film *The Wages of Fear*, Henri-Georges Clouzot
British Film *Hobson's Choice*, David Lean
Actor Kenneth More, *Doctor in the House*
Actress Yvonne Mitchell, *The Divided Heart*

1955
Film *Richard III*, Laurence Olivier
British Film *Richard III*, Laurence Olivier
Actor Laurence Olivier, *Richard III*
Actress Katie Johnson, *The Ladykillers*

1956
Film *Gervaise*, René Clément
British Film *Reach for the Sky*, Lewis Gilbert
Actor Peter Finch, *A Town Like Alice* aka *The Rape of Malaya*
Actress Virginia McKenna, *A Town Like Alice* aka *The Rape of Malaya*

1957
Film *The Bridge on the River Kwai*, David Lean
British Film *The Bridge on the River Kwai*, David Lean
Actor Alec Guinness, *The Bridge on the River Kwai*
Actress Heather Sears, *The Story of Esther Costello*

1958
Film *Room at the Top*, Jack Clayton
British Film *Room at the Top*, Jack Clayton
Actor Trevor Howard, *The Key*
Actress Irene Worth, *Orders to Kill*

1959
Film *Ben-Hur*, William Wyler
British Film *Sapphire*, Basil Dearden
Actor Peter Sellers, *I'm All Right Jack*
Actress Audrey Hepburn, *The Nun's Story*

1960
Film *The Apartment*, Billy Wilder
British Film *Saturday Night and Sunday Morning*, Karel Reisz
Actor Peter Finch, *The Trials of Oscar Wilde*
Actress Rachel Roberts, *Saturday Night and Sunday Morning*

1961
Film *Ballad of a Soldier*, Grigori Chukrai; *The Hustler*, Robert Rossen
British Film *A Taste of Honey*, Tony Richardson
Actor Peter Finch, *No Love for Johnnie*
Actress Dora Bryan, *A Taste of Honey*

1962
Film *Laurence of Arabia*, David Lean
British Film *Lawrence of Arabia*, David Lean
Actor Peter O'Toole, *Lawrence of Arabia*
Actress Leslie Caron, *The L-Shaped Room*

1963
Film *Tom Jones*, Tony Richardson
British Film *Tom Jones*, Tony Richardson
Actor Dirk Bogarde, *The Servant*
Actress Rachel Roberts, *This Sporting Life*

1964
Film *Dr Strangelove*, Stanley Kubrick
British Film *Dr Strangelove*, Stanley Kubrick
Actor Richard Attenborough, *Séance on a Wet Afternoon*; *Guns at Batasi*
Actress Audrey Hepburn, *Charade*

1965
Film *My Fair Lady*, George Cukor
British Film *The Ipcress File*, Sidney J. Furie
Actor Dirk Bogarde, *Darling*
Actress Julie Christie, *Darling*

1966
Film *Who's Afraid of Virginia Woolf?*, Mike Nichols
British Film *The Spy Who Came in from the Cold*
Actor Richard Burton, *Who's Afraid of Virginia Woolf?*; *The Spy Who Came in from The Cold*
Actress Elizabeth Taylor, *Who's Afraid of Virginia Woolf?*

1967
Film *A Man for All Seasons*, Fred Zinnemann
British Film *A Man for All Seasons*, Fred Zinnemann
Actor Paul Scofield, *A Man for All Seasons*
Actress Edith Evans, *The Whisperers*

1968
Film *The Graduate*, Mike Nichols
Director Mike Nichols, *The Graduate*
Actor Spencer Tracy, *Guess Who's Coming to Dinner?*
Actress Katharine Hepburn, *Guess Who's Coming to Dinner?*
Supporting actor Ian Holm, *The Bofors Gun*
Supporting actress Billie Whitelaw, *The Twisted Nerve*; *Charlie Bubbles*

1969
Film *Midnight Cowboy*, John Schlesinger
Director John Schlesinger, *Midnight Cowboy*
Actor Dustin Hoffman, *Midnight Cowboy*; *John and Mary*
Actress Maggie Smith, *The Prime of Miss Jean Brodie*
Supporting actor Laurence Olivier, *Oh! What a Lovely War*
Supporting actress Celia Johnson, *The Prime of Miss Jean Brodie*

1970
Film *Butch Cassidy and the Sundance Kid*, George Roy Hill
Director George Roy Hill, *Butch Cassidy and the Sundance Kid*
Actor Robert Redford, *Butch Cassidy and the Sundance Kid*; *Tell Them Willie Boy Is Here*; *Downhill Racer*
Actress Katharine Ross, *Butch Cassidy and the Sundance Kid*; *Tell Them Willie Boy Is Here*
Supporting actor Colin Welland, *Kes*
Supporting actress Susannah York, *They Shoot Horses, Don't They?*

1971
Film *Sunday, Bloody Sunday*, John Schlesinger
Director John Schlesinger, *Sunday, Bloody Sunday*
Actor Peter Finch, *Sunday, Bloody Sunday*
Actress Glenda Jackson, *Sunday, Bloody Sunday*
Supporting actor Edward Fox, *The Go-Between*
Supporting actress Margaret Leighton, *The Go-Between*

1972
Film *Cabaret*, Bob Fosse
Director Bob Fosse, *Cabaret*
Actor Gene Hackman, *The French Connection*; *The Poseidon Adventure*
Actress Liza Minnelli, *Cabaret*
Supporting actor Ben Johnson, *The Last Picture Show*
Supporting actress Cloris Leachman, *The Last Picture Show*

1973
Film *Day for Night*, François Truffaut
Director François Truffaut, *Day for Night*
Actor Walter Matthau, *Pete 'n' Tillie*; *Charley Varrick*
Actress Stéphane Audran, *The Discreet Charm of the Bourgeoisie*; *Just before Nightfall*
Supporting actor Arthur Lowe, *O Lucky Man!*
Supporting actress Valentina Cortese, *Day for Night*

1974
Film *Lacombe Lucien*, Louis Malle
Director Roman Polanski, *Chinatown*
Actor Jack Nicholson, *Chinatown*; *The Last Detail*
Actress Joanne Woodward, *Summer Wishes, Winter Dreams*
Supporting actor John Gielgud, *Murder on the Orient Express*
Supporting actress Ingrid Bergman, *Murder on the Orient Express*

1975
Film *Alice Doesn't Live Here Any More*, Martin Scorsese
Director Stanley Kubrick, *Barry Lyndon*
Actor Al Pacino, *The Godfather Part II*; *Dog Day Afternoon*

ARTS AND CULTURE

BAFTA Awards (continued)

Actress Ellen Burstyn, *Alice Doesn't Live Here Any More*
Supporting actor Fred Astaire, *The Towering Inferno*
Supporting actress Diane Ladd, *Alice Doesn't Live Here Any More*

1976
Film *One Flew over the Cuckoo's Nest*, Milos Forman
Director Milos Forman, *One Flew over the Cuckoo's Nest*
Actor Jack Nicholson, *One Flew over the Cuckoo's Nest*
Actress Louise Fletcher, *One Flew over the Cuckoo's Nest*
Supporting actor Brad Dourif, *One Flew over the Cuckoo's Nest*
Supporting actress Jodie Foster, *Taxi Driver; Bugsy Malone*

1977
Film *Annie Hall*, Woody Allen
Director Woody Allen, *Annie Hall*
Actor Peter Finch, *Network*
Actress Diane Keaton, *Annie Hall*
Supporting actor Edward Fox, *A Bridge Too Far*
Supporting actress Jenny Agutter, *Equus*

1978
Film *Julia*, Fred Zinnemann
Director Alan Parker, *Midnight Express*
Actor Richard Dreyfuss, *The Goodbye Girl*
Actress Jane Fonda, *Julia*
Supporting actor John Hurt, *Midnight Express*
Supporting actress Geraldine Page, *Interiors*

1979
Film *Manhattan*, Woody Allen
Director Francis Ford Coppola, *Apocalypse Now*
Actor Jack Lemmon, *The China Syndrome*
Actress Jane Fonda, *The China Syndrome*
Supporting actor Robert Duvall, *Apocalypse Now*
Supporting actress Rachel Roberts, *Yanks*

1980
Film *The Elephant Man*, David Lynch
Director Akira Kurosawa, *Kagemusha*
Actor John Hurt, *The Elephant Man*
Actress Judy Davis, *My Brilliant Career*

1981
Film *Chariots of Fire*, Hugh Hudson
Director Louis Malle, *Atlantic City*
Actor Burt Lancaster, *Atlantic City*
Actress Meryl Streep, *The French Lieutenant's Woman*
Supporting artist Ian Holm, *Chariots of Fire*

1982
Film *Gandhi*, Richard Attenborough
Director Richard Attenborough, *Gandhi*
Actor Ben Kingsley, *Gandhi*
Actress Katharine Hepburn, *On Golden Pond*
Supporting actor Jack Nicholson, *Reds*
Supporting actress Maureen Stapleton, *Reds*; Rohini Hattangadi, *Gandhi*

1983
Film *Educating Rita*, Lewis Gilbert
Director Bill Forsyth, *Local Hero*
Actor Michael Caine, *Educating Rita*
Actress Julie Walters, *Educating Rita*
Supporting actor Denholm Elliott, *Trading Places*
Supporting actress Jamie Lee Curtis, *Trading Places*

1984
Film *The Killing Fields*, Roland Joffe

Director Wim Wenders, *Paris, Texas*
Actor Haing S, Ngor, *The Killing Fields*
Actress Maggie Smith, *A Private Function*
Supporting actor Denholm Elliott, *A Private Function*
Supporting actress Liz Smith, *A Private Function*

1985
Film *The Purple Rose of Cairo*, Woody Allen
Actor William Hurt, *Kiss of the Spider Woman*
Actress Peggy Ashcroft, *A Passage to India*
Supporting actor Denholm Elliott, *Defence of the Realm*
Supporting actress Rosanna Arquette, *Desperately Seeking Susan*

1986
Film *A Room with a View*, James Ivory
Director Woody Allen, *Hannah and Her Sisters*
Actor Bob Hoskins, *Mona Lisa*
Actress Maggie Smith, *A Room with a View*
Supporting actor Ray McAnally, *The Mission*
Supporting actress Judi Dench, *A Room with a View*

1987
Film *Jean de Florette*, Claude Berri
Director Oliver Stone, *Platoon*
Actor Sean Connery, *The Name of the Rose*
Actress Anne Bancroft, *84 Charing Cross Road*
Supporting actor Daniel Auteuil, *Jean de Florette*
Supporting actress Susan Wooldridge, *Hope and Glory*

1988
Film *The Last Emperor*, Bernardo Bertolucci
Director Louis Malle, *Au Revoir les Enfants*
Actor John Cleese, *A Fish Called Wanda*
Actress Maggie Smith, *The Lonely Passion of Judith Hearne*
Supporting actor Michael Palin, *A Fish Called Wanda*
Supporting actress Judi Dench, *A Handful of Dust*

1989
Film *Dead Poets Society*, Peter Weir
Director Kenneth Branagh, *Henry V*
Actor Daniel Day-Lewis, *My Left Foot*
Actress Pauline Collins, *Shirley Valentine*
Supporting actor Ray McAnally, *My Left Foot*
Supporting actress Michelle Pfeiffer, *Dangerous Liaisons*

1990
Film *GoodFellas*, Martin Scorsese
Director Martin Scorsese, *GoodFellas*
Actor Philippe Noiret, *Nuovo Cinema Paradiso*
Actress Jessica Tandy, *Driving Miss Daisy*
Supporting actor Salvatore Cascio, *Nuovo Cinema Paradiso*
Supporting actress Whoopi Goldberg, *Ghost*

1991
Film *The Commitments*, Alan Parker
Director Alan Parker, *The Commitments*
Actor Anthony Hopkins, *The Silence of the Lambs*
Actress Jodie Foster, *The Silence of the Lambs*
Supporting actor Alan Rickman, *Robin Hood: Prince of Thieves*
Supporting actress Kate Nelligan, *Frankie and Johnnie*

1992
Film *Howards End*, James Ivory
Director Robert Altman, *The Player*
Actor Robert Downey Jnr, *Chaplin*
Actress Emma Thompson, *Howards End*
Supporting actor Gene Hackman, *Unforgiven*

Supporting actress Miranda Richardson, *Damage*

1993
Film *Schindler's List*, Steven Spielberg
British Film *Shadowlands*, Richard Attenborough
Director Steven Spielberg, *Schindler's List*
Actor Anthony Hopkins, *The Remains of the Day*
Actress Holly Hunter, *The Piano*
Supporting actor Ralph Fiennes, *Schindler's List*
Supporting actress Miriam Margolyes, *The Age of Innocence*

1994
Film *Four Weddings and a Funeral*, Mike Newell
British Film *Shallow Grave*, Danny Boyle
Director Mike Newell, *Four Weddings and a Funeral*
Actor Hugh Grant, *Four Weddings and a Funeral*
Actress Susan Sarandon, *The Client*
Supporting actor Samuel L Jackson, *Pulp Fiction*
Supporting actress Kristin Scott Thomas, *Four Weddings and a Funeral*

1995
Film *Sense and Sensibility*, Ang Lee
British Film *The Madness of King George*, Nicholas Hytner
Director Michael Radford, *The Postman/Il Postino*
Actor Nigel Hawthorne, *The Madness of King George*
Actress Emma Thompson, *Sense and Sensibility*
Supporting actor Tim Roth, *Rob Roy*
Supporting actress Kate Winslet, *Sense and Sensibility*

1996
Film *The English Patient*, Anthony Minghella
British Film *Secrets and Lies*, Mike Leigh
Director Joel Coen, *Fargo*
Actor Geoffrey Rush, *Shine*
Actress Brenda Blethyn, *Secrets and Lies*
Supporting actor Paul Scofield, *The Crucible*
Supporting actress Juliette Binoche, *The English Patient*

1997
Film *The Full Monty*, Peter Cattaneo
British Film *Nil by Mouth*, Gary Oldman
Director Baz Luhrmann, *William Shakespeare's Romeo & Juliet*
Actor Robert Carlyle, *The Full Monty*
Actress Judi Dench, *Mrs Brown*
Supporting actor Tom Wilkinson, *The Full Monty*
Supporting actress Sigourney Weaver, *The Ice Storm*

1998
Film *Shakespeare in Love*, John Madden
Director Peter Weir, *The Truman Show*
Actor Roberto Benigni, *Life is Beautiful*
Actress Cate Blanchett, *Elizabeth*
Supporting actor Geoffrey Rush, *Shakespeare in Love*
Supporting actress Judi Dench, *Shakespeare in Love*

1999
Film *American Beauty*, Sam Mendes
Director Pedro Almodovar, *All About My Mother*
Actor Kevin Spacey, *American Beauty*
Actress Annette Bening, *American Beauty*
Supporting actor Jude Law, *The Talented Mr Ripley*
Supporting actress Maggie Smith, *Tea With Mussolini*

2000
Film *Gladiator*, Ridley Scott
Director Ang Lee, *Crouching Tiger, Hidden Dragon*
Actor Jamie Bell, *Billy Elliot*

Actress Julia Roberts, *Erin Brockovich*
Supporting actor Benicio Del Toro, *Traffic*
Supporting actress Julie Walters, *Billy Elliot*

2001
Film *The Lord of the Rings: The Fellowship of the Ring*, Peter Jackson, Barrie M Osborne, Tim Sanders, Fran Walsh
Director Peter Jackson, *The Lord of the Rings: The Fellowship of the Ring*
Actor Russell Crowe, *A Beautiful Mind*
Actress Judi Dench, *Iris*
Supporting actor Jim Broadbent, *Moulin Rouge*
Supporting actress Jennifer Connelly, *A Beautiful Mind*

2002
Film *The Pianist*, Roman Polanski
Director Roman Polanski, *The Pianist*
Actor Daniel Day-Lewis, *Gangs of New York*
Actress Nicole Kidman, *The Hours*
Supporting actor Christopher Walken, *Catch Me If You Can*
Supporting actress Catherine Zeta-Jones, *Chicago*

2003
Film *The Lord of the Rings: The Return of the King*, Peter Jackson
Director Peter Weir, *Master and Commander*
Actor Bill Murray, *Lost in Translation*
Actress Scarlett Johansson, *Lost in Translation*
Supporting actor Bill Nighy, *Love Actually*
Supporting actress Renée Zellweger, *Cold Mountain*

2004
Film *The Aviator*, Martin Scorsese
Director Mike Leigh, *Vera Drake*
Actor Jamie Foxx, *Ray*
Actress Imelda Staunton, *Vera Drake*
Supporting actor Clive Owen, *Closer*
Supporting actress Cate Blanchett, *The Aviator*

2005
Film *Brokeback Mountain*, Ang Lee
Director Ang Lee, *Brokeback Mountain*
Actor Philip Seymour Hoffman, *Capote*
Actress Reese Witherspoon, *Walk the Line*
Supporting actor Jake Gyllenhaal, *Brokeback Mountain*
Supporting actress Thandie Newton, *Crash*

ARTS AND CULTURE

International film festivals

Exact dates of these festivals may vary but the months indicated remain generally the same.

*Denotes a festival recognized by the International Federation of Film Producers Association.

Country	Festival	Time of year
Albania	Tirana International Film Festival	Dec
Argentina	Buenos Aires, Mar del Plata	Mar
Australia	Australian International Film Festival	Sept
	Melbourne*	Jul–Aug
	Sydney*	Jun
Austria	Austrian Film Days	Sept
	Viennale (Vienna)	Oct
Belgium	Antwerp	Feb
	Brussels Film Festival	Mar
	Flanders (Ghent)	Oct
Bosnia & Herzegovina	Sarajevo Film Festival*	Aug–Sept
Brazil	Rio de Janeiro	Sept–Oct
	São Paulo	Oct
Bulgaria	Sofia International Film Festival	Mar
	Varna	Jun
Burkina Faso	Pan African Film Festival	Feb–Mar
Canada	Atlantic Film Festival, Halifax	Sept
	Banff TV Festival	Jun
	Global Visions Film Festival, Alberta	Nov
	Montreal World Film Festival	Aug
	Toronto	Sept
	Vancouver	Sept–Oct
China	Shanghai International Film Festival	Jun
Colombia	Bogota	Oct
	Cartagena	Apr
Croatia	Dubrovnik	May
	Pula	Jul
	Split	Jun
	Zagreb*	Jun
Cuba	New Latin American Cinema	Dec
Czech Republic	Karlovy Vary*	Jul
	Prague Television Festival	Jun
Denmark	Odense	Aug
Egypt	Cairo	Dec
England	Birmingham Film & Television Festival	Oct–Nov
	Bristol Film & Television Festival	Sept
	Cambridge	Jul
	London Film Festival	Nov–Dec
Estonia	Black Nights Film Festival, Tallinn	Nov–Dec
Finland	Midnight Sun	Jun
	Tampere Film Festival*	Mar
France	Amiens	Nov
	Annecy (animation)	May–Jun (alternate years)
	Annonay	Feb
	Biarritz (Iberian, Latin American)	September

Country	Festival	Time of year
	Cannes*	May
	Cherbourg	Oct
	Clermont-Ferrand (shorts)	Feb
	Cognac	Apr
	Deauville (American films)	Sept
	Gerardmer (Fantasy)	Jan
	Grenoble (thrillers)	Oct
	Paris	Mar–Apr
	Rouen	Mar
	Strasbourg	Mar
Georgia	Tbilisi	Sept
Germany	Berlin*	Feb
	Frankfurt*	Sept
	Hof	Oct
	Munich	Jun
	Oberhausen*	Nov
	Wiesbaden*	Apr
Greece	Athens	Sept
	Thessaloniki	Nov
Hong Kong	Hong Kong International Film Festival	Apr
Hungary	Györ	Apr–May
India	Indian International Film Festival	Dec
	Kerala	Dec
	Kolkata	Nov
Ireland	Cork*	Sept–Oct
	Dublin	Oct
	Galway	Jul
Israel	Haifa	Oct
	Jerusalem	Jul
Italy	Bergamo	Mar
	Festival dei Popoli, Florence	Nov–Dec
	Milan	Sept
	Noir in Film Festival, Courmayeur*	Dec
	Pesaro International Festival of New Cinema	Jun
	Pordenone (silents)	Oct
	Salerno	Nov
	San Remo	Mar
	Taormina*	Jun
	Torino*	Nov
	Trieste Science-Fiction Festival	Jul
	Venice Film Festival	Sept
Japan	Tokyo*	Oct–Nov
Korea	Pusan	Jul
Malta	Golden Knight Amateur Film & Video Festival	Sept
Mexico	Guadalajara	Mar
Monaco	Monte Carlo Film Festival	Jan–Feb
Netherlands	Dutch Film Days & Film Market	Sept
	Rotterdam Film International	Feb
New Zealand	Wellington	Jul–Nov
Norway	Haugesund	Aug
Pakistan	Karachi	Dec

Country	Festival	Time of year
Poland	Gdańsk	Sept
	Katowice (scientific/technical)	Nov
	Krakow* (shorts)	Jun
	Warsaw*	Oct
Portugal	Cinanima-Espinho International Animation Festival	Jul
	Porto Fantasy Film Festival	Feb
	Setúbal*	May–Jun
Romania	Bucharest	Nov
Russia	Moscow*	Jun
	Teleforum, Moscow	Sept
Scotland	Edinburgh	Aug–Sept
Serbia	Belgrade	Feb–Mar
Singapore	Singapore International Film Festival	Apr
Slovenia	Lubjljana*	Apr
Spain	Barcelona	Nov
	Bilbao*	Nov
	Gijón*	Nov
	Madrid (Imagfic)	Mar–Apr
	San Sebastian*	Sept
	Sitges (horror)	Sept–Oct
	Valencia*	Jun–Jul
Sweden	Gothenburg	Nov
	Malmo	Jul
	Stockholm*	Nov
Switzerland	Fribourg	Oct
	Locarno*	Aug
	Nyon* (documentaries)	Oct
	Vevey	Sept
Taiwan	Taipei	Oct

Country	Festival	Time of year
Tanzania	Zanzibar	Jul
Turkey	Istanbul*	Apr
Ukraine	Kiev*	Oct
United States	AFI/European Community Film Festival, Los Angeles	Jun
	AFI/LA Film Festival	Apr
	American Film Market, Los Angeles	Feb–Mar
	Boston	Sept
	Chicago	Oct
	Cinetex, Las Vegas	Sept
	Filmfest DC, Washington	Apr–May
	Hawaii, Honolulu	Nov
	Miami	Feb
	Mill Valley Film & Video Festival	Oct
	NATPE, New Orleans	Jan
	New York*	Sept–Oct
	Palm Springs	Jan
	Portland	Feb
	Santa Barbara International Film Festival	Mar
	San Francisco International Film Festival*	Apr–May
	Seattle International Film Festival	May–Jun
	Sundance Film Festival, Park City, Utah	Jan
	Women in Film, LA	Oct

MUSIC

Musical symbols, terms, and abbreviations

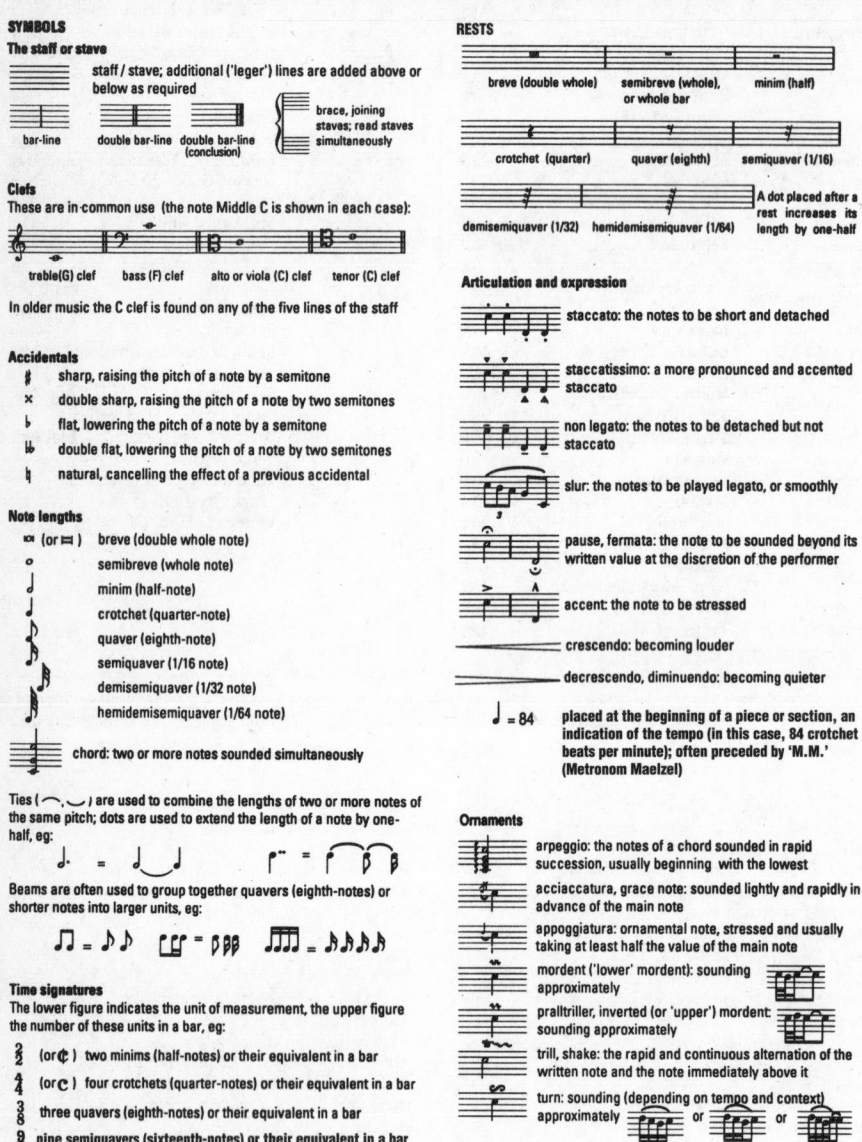

SYMBOLS

The staff or stave

staff / stave; additional ('leger') lines are added above or below as required

bar-line double bar-line double bar-line (conclusion)

brace, joining staves; read staves simultaneously

Clefs

These are in common use (the note Middle C is shown in each case):

treble(G) clef bass (F) clef alto or viola (C) clef tenor (C) clef

In older music the C clef is found on any of the five lines of the staff

Accidentals

♯ sharp, raising the pitch of a note by a semitone

× double sharp, raising the pitch of a note by two semitones

♭ flat, lowering the pitch of a note by a semitone

♭♭ double flat, lowering the pitch of a note by two semitones

♮ natural, cancelling the effect of a previous accidental

Note lengths

breve (double whole note)

semibreve (whole note)

minim (half-note)

crotchet (quarter-note)

quaver (eighth-note)

semiquaver (1/16 note)

demisemiquaver (1/32 note)

hemidemisemiquaver (1/64 note)

chord: two or more notes sounded simultaneously

Ties (⌒, ⌣) are used to combine the lengths of two or more notes of the same pitch; dots are used to extend the length of a note by one-half, eg:

Beams are often used to group together quavers (eighth-notes) or shorter notes into larger units, eg:

Time signatures

The lower figure indicates the unit of measurement, the upper figure the number of these units in a bar, eg:

(or ₵) two minims (half-notes) or their equivalent in a bar

(or C) four crotchets (quarter-notes) or their equivalent in a bar

three quavers (eighth-notes) or their equivalent in a bar

nine semiquavers (sixteenth-notes) or their equivalent in a bar

RESTS

breve (double whole) semibreve (whole), or whole bar minim (half)

crotchet (quarter) quaver (eighth) semiquaver (1/16)

demisemiquaver (1/32) hemidemisemiquaver (1/64)

A dot placed after a rest increases its length by one-half

Articulation and expression

staccato: the notes to be short and detached

staccatissimo: a more pronounced and accented staccato

non legato: the notes to be detached but not staccato

slur: the notes to be played legato, or smoothly

pause, fermata: the note to be sounded beyond its written value at the discretion of the performer

accent: the note to be stressed

crescendo: becoming louder

decrescendo, diminuendo: becoming quieter

♩ = 84 placed at the beginning of a piece or section, an indication of the tempo (in this case, 84 crotchet beats per minute); often preceded by 'M.M.' (Metronom Maelzel)

Ornaments

arpeggio: the notes of a chord sounded in rapid succession, usually beginning with the lowest

acciaccatura, grace note: sounded lightly and rapidly in advance of the main note

appoggiatura: ornamental note, stressed and usually taking at least half the value of the main note

mordent ('lower' mordent): sounding approximately

pralltriller, inverted (or 'upper') mordent: sounding approximately

trill, shake: the rapid and continuous alternation of the written note and the note immediately above it

turn: sounding (depending on tempo and context) approximately or or

Musical scales and keys

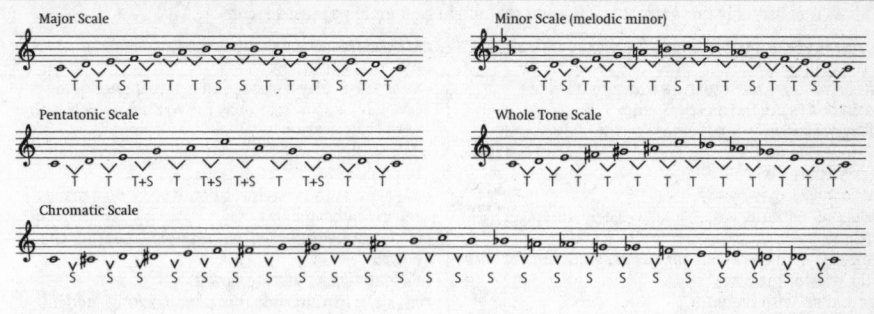

Key signatures
(Major keys: capital letters: minor keys: lower-case letters)

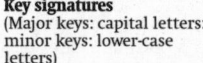

Repetition
In instrumental music repeated notes, figures and even whole sections are often shown in abbreviated form, eg:

repeat signs, indicating that the passage between them is to be performed twice

Tempo and expression marks

Italian terms placed at the head of a piece or section to indicate its tempo and general expression have changed in meaning over the years and are rarely precise. The following list gives some indication of how the more common terms are generally understood today.

adagio slow
agitato agitated
allegro lively, fast
allegretto rather lively
andante 'going'; at a moderate pace
andantino a little quicker than *andante*
animato animated, lively
appassionato impassioned
assai 'very' (*allegro assai* very fast)
brio 'spirit', 'fire' (*allegro con brio* fast energetic)
cantabile in a singing style
dolente sadly
energico energetic, vigorous
espressivo expressive
feroce fierce
fuoco 'fire' (*con fuoco* with fire)
furioso furious
giocoso light, humorous
grave slow, solemn
grazioso graceful
larghetto fairly slow
largo slow, broad
legato smoothly
leggiero light
lento slow

maestoso majestic
marciale in the style of a march
marziale in a military style
meno 'less' (*meno mosso* slower)
moderato moderate, at a moderate pace
molto 'much', 'very' (*molto lento* very slow)
moto 'motion' (*con moto* quickly)
pesante heavy, ponderous
piacevole pleasant, agreeable
più 'more' (*più mosso* faster)
poco 'little' (*poco adagio* rather slowly)
presto very fast
prestissimo faster than *presto*
quasi 'as if', 'almost' (*andante, quasi allegretto*)
risoluto resolute, in a determined manner
scherzando in a jocular style
semplice simple, in an unforced style
sotto voce extremely quiet
strepitoso loud, noisy, boisterous
tanto, troppo 'so much', 'too much' (*allegro non tanto* fast but not very fast; *lento ma non troppo* slow, but not becoming too slow)
veloce rapid
vivace lively, very fast
vivo vigorous, brisk

Other terms and abbreviations

This section lists only those symbols and terms that might be found in a musical score.

a tempo in time (ie reverting to the original speed)
accel (accelerando) getting gradually faster
alla breve in a time signature where minims or semibreves are the metrical units
allarg. (allargando) broadening, getting slower and (usually) louder
arco with the bow
cal. (calando) dying away
colla voce 'with the voice', follow closely the singer's tempo
col legno 'with the wood', play a string instrument with the stick of the bow
con sordino with the mute
cresc. (crescendo) becoming louder
D C, da capo (al fine) return to the start of the piece or movement (and play to the end marked *fine*)
decresc. (decrescendo) becoming quieter
dim. (diminuendo) becoming quieter
dol (dolce) sweetly
D S, dal segno return to and repeat from the sign (usually $)
f (forte) loud; *ff (fortissimo)*, *fff* increasing degrees of loudness
fine see *D C* above
fz (forzato) accented
gliss. (glissando) slide quickly from one note to another
GP 'General pause', a rest for the whole ensemble
MM metronom maelzel
marc. (marcato) stressed, accented
mf (mezzo forte) moderately loud

mp (mezzo piano) moderately quiet
ossia 'or', 'alternatively'
ottava, 8va, 8 play a passage an octave higher or lower, *coll ottava, col 8va, col 8:* play the written notes together with their octaves
p (piano) quiet, soft; *pp (pianissimo)*, *ppp* increasing (but imprecise) degrees of softness
ped. depress the sustaining (loud) pedal on a piano, release indicated by *
pizz. (pizzicato) 'plucked' with the finger, rather than bowed
rall. (rallentando) getting slower
rinf., rfz, rf (rinforcando, sforzando) getting suddenly louder
rit., ritard. (ritardando) getting slower
rubato with a freedom of tempo, but not impairing the overall flow of the music
segno see *D S* above
senza sordino without the mute
sf, sfz (sforzando, sforzato) strongly accented
simile play in the same manner as before
smorz. (smorzando) fading away
sost. (sostenuto) sustained
stacc. (stoccato) short and detached
string. (stringendo) getting much faster
ten. (tenuto) linger slightly on the note
tre. corde see *una corda* below
una corda depress the soft pedal on the piano, release indicated by *tre corde*
V S (volti subito) turn the page quickly

World orchestras

Name	Location	Name	Location	Name	Location
Argentina		Tasmanian Symphony Orchestra	Hobart	Orchestre Philharmonique de Liege et De la Communate Française	Liege
Philharmonic Orchestra of Buenos Aires	*Buenos Aires*	West Australian Symphony Orchestra	*Perth*	Symphony Orchestra of Minnaie	*Brussels*
National Sinfonia Orchestra	*Buenos Aires*	**Austria**		Royal Philharmonic Orchestra of Flanders	*Antwerp*
Armenia		Austrian Hungarian Haydn Orchestra	*Vienna*	**Brazil**	
Armenian Philharmonia Orchestra	*Yerevan*	Bruckner Orchestra Linz	*Linz*	Philharmonic Orchestra of Rio de Janeiro	*Rio de Janeiro*
Armenian State Symphony Orchestra	*Yerevan*	The Haydn Academy	*Korneuburg*	Brazil Sinfonia Orchestra	*Rio de Janeiro*
Australia		Mozarteum Orchester	*Salzburg*	**Bulgaria**	
Adelaide Symphony Orchestra	*Adelaide*	Symphony Orchestra Vorarlberg/Camerata	*Bregenz*	Bulgarian National Radio Symphony Orchestra	*Bulgaria*
Canberra Symphony Orchestra	*Canberra*	Vienna Chamber Orchestra	*Vienna*	Sofia Philharmonic Orchestra	*Sofia*
Melbourne Philharmonic Orchestra	*Melbourne*	Vienna Mozart Orchestra	*Vienna*	Vratza State Philharmonic Orchestra	*Vratza*
Melbourne Symphony Orchestra	*Melbourne*	Vienna Philharmonic	*Vienna*	**Canada**	
Queensland Symphony Orchestra	*Brisbane*	**Belarus**		Calgary Philharmonic Orchestra	*Calgary*
State Orchestra of Victoria	*Melbourne*	State Academic Symphony Orchestra of Byelorussia	*Minsk*	Edmonton Symphony Orchestra	*Edmonton*
Sydney Symphony Orchestra	*Sydney*	**Belgium**		International Symphony Orchestra	*Sarnia*
Symphony Australia	*Sydney*	BRTN-Philharmonic Orchestra	*Brussels*	Kingston Symphony	*Kingston*
		Collegium Instrumentale Brugense	*Bruges*		
		National Orchestra of Belgium	*Brussels*		

Name	Location
Kitchener-Waterloo Symphony	Kitchener
Montreal Chamber Orchestra	Montreal
Montreal Symphony Orchestra	Montreal
National Arts Centre Orchestra of Canada	Ottawa
Newfoundland Symphony Orchestra	St John's
Niagara Symphony Orchestra London	St Catharine's
Canada Inc	London (Ontario)
Ottawa Symphony Orchestra	Ottawa
Quebec Symphony Orchestra	Quebec
Toronto Symphony Orchestra	Toronto
Vancouver Symphony	Vancouver
Victoria Symphony	Victoria
Winnipeg Symphony Orchestra	Winnipeg

Chile

Sinfonia Orchestra of Concepción	Concepción
Santiago Philharmonic Orchestra	Santiago

China

Beijing Central Ensemble of National Radio	Beijing
Hong Kong Philharmonic Orchestra	Kowloon
Pan Asia Symphony Orchestra	Kowloon
Shanghai Symphony Orchestra	Shanghai

Colombia

Bogota Philharmonic Orchestra	Bogota
Sinfonia Orchestra of Colombia	Bogota

Croatia

Dubrovnik Symphony Orchestra	Dubrovnik
Zagreb Philharmonic	Zagreb

Czech Republic

Bohemia Symphony Orchestra	Podebrady
Brno Philharmonic Orchestra	Brno
Czech Philharmonic Orchestra	Prague
Czech Symphony Orchestra FISYO	Prague
Janacek Philharmonic Orchestra	Ostrava
Moravian Philharmonic Orchestra	Olomouc
North Bohemian Philharmonic	Teplice
Prague Symphony Orchestra	Prague
Radio Symphony Orchestra Plzen	Plzen

Name	Location
West Bohemian Symphony Orchestra	Mariannske Lazne

Denmark

Aalborg Symphony Orchestra	Aalborg
Aarhus Symphony Orchestra	Aarhus
Copenhagen Philharmonic Orchestra	Copenhagen
Danish National Radio Symphony Orchestra	Frederiksberg
De Unges Symfoniorkester Dusika	Vanlose
Det Kongelige Kapel	Copenhagen
Foroya Symphony Orchestra	Klaksvik
Odense Symphony Orchestra	Odense
Randers Byorkester	Randers
Royal Danish Orchestra	Copenhagen
Sonderjyllands Symphony Orchestra	Sonderborg
Vestjsk Symphony Orchestra	Esbjerg

Estonia

Estonian National Opera Symphony Orchestra	Tallinn
Estonian National Symphony Orchestra	Tallinn

Finland

Finnish Radio Symphony Orchestra	Finland
Helsinki Philharmonic Orchestra	Helsinki
Orchestra of the Finnish National Opera	Helsinki
Symphony Orchestra Vivo	Riihimaki
Tampere Philharmonic Orchestra	Tampere
Turku Philharmonic Orchestra	Turku
Vaasa City Orchestra	Vaasa

France

The Chapel Royal/Orchestra of the Champs Elysees	Paris
Lorraine Philharmonic	Metz
National Orchestra of Bordeaux-Aquitaine	Bordeaux
National Orchestra of France	Paris
National Orchestra of Lille	Lille
National Orchestra of Lyon	Lyon
Orchestra of Paris	Paris
Orchestra of the Concerts Lamoureux	Paris
Orchestre National du Capitole de Toulouse	Toulouse
Orchestre Philharmonique de Pays de Loire	Angers
Orchestre Symphonique et Lyrique de Nancy	Nancy
Philharmonic Orchestra of Montpellier	Montpellier
Philharmonic Orchestra of Nice	Nice
Philharmonic Orchestra of Radio-France	Paris

Name	Location
Philharmonic Orchestra of Strasbourg	Strasbourg

Germany

Bamberger Symphonic	Bamberg
Bayerische Staatsorchester	Munich
Berlin Philharmonic Orchestra	Berlin
Berlin Symphonic Orchestra	Berlin
Dresden Philharmonic	Dresden
Dusseldorf Symphonic Orchestra	Dusseldorf
Essen Philharmonic Orchestra	Essen
Hamburg Symphony Orchestra	Hamburg
Handerlfestspiel Orchestra	Halle
Kolner Rundfunk-Sinfonia-Orchestra	Cologne
Leipziger Gewandhaus Orchestra	Leipzig
MDR Sinfonia Orchestra	Leipzig
Munich Philharmonic	Munich
Orchestra of the German Opera Berlin	Berlin
Philharmonic Orchestra of the Landeschauptstadt Kiel	Kiel
Philharmonisches Staatsorchester Halle	Halle
Philharmonisches Staatsorchester Hamburg	Hamburg
Radio Sinfonia-Orchestra Frankfurt	Frankfurt-am-Main
Radio-Sinfonia Orchester Suddeutscher Rundfunk Stuttgart	Stuttgart
Robert Schumann Philharmonic	Dresden
Staats Philharmonic Rheinland-Pfalz	Ludwigshafen -am-Rhein
Stadt Augsburg Philharmonic Orchestra	Augsburg
Westphalian Symphony Orchestra	Recklinghausen

Greece

Athens Broadcasting Symphony Orchestra	Athens
La Camerata-Orchestra of the Friends of Music	Athens
Orchestra of the National Opera of Greece	Athens
Thessaloniki State Orchestra	Thessaloniki

Hungary

Budapest Concert Orchestra MAV	Budapest
Budapest Philharmonic Orchestra	Budapest
Budapest Symphony Orchestra	Budapest
Gyor Philharmonic Orchestra	Gyor
Hungarian National Philharmonic Orchestra	Budapest
Hungarian Symphony Orchestra	Budapest

World orchestras (continued)

Name	Location
Israel	
Haifa Symphony Orchestra	Haifa
Israel Chamber Orchestra	Tel Aviv
Israel Chamber Orchestra of Ramat Gam	Ramat Gam
Israel Philharmonic Orchestra	Tel Aviv
The Israel Symphony Orchestra Rishon Le-Zion	Rishon Le-Zion
Jerusalem Symphony Orchestra	Jerusalem
Italy	
Orchestra of Arena	Verona
Orchestra of Tuscany	Firenze
Philharmonic Orchestra of La Scala	Milan
Philharmonic Orchestra of Marchigiana	Ancona
Rome Sinfonia Orchestra for Italian Radio and Television	Rome
Sinfonia Orchestra of Sicily	Palermo
Orchestra Teatro Regio di Torino	Torino
Toscanini Symphony Orchestra	Parma
Japan	
Gunma Symphony Orchestra	Gunma
Hiroshima Symphony Orchestra	Tokyo
Kangawa Philharmonic Orchestra	Yokohama
Kyoto City Symphony Orchestra	Kyoto
Kyushu Symphony Orchestra	Fukuoka
Nagoya Philharmonic Orchestra	Nagoya
New Japan Philharmonic	Tokyo
NHK Symphony Orchestra	Tokyo
Osaka Philharmonic Orchestra	Osaka
Tokyo Metropolitan Symphony Orchestra	Tokyo
Tokyo Philharmonic Orchestra	Tokyo
Korea	
Korean Symphony Orchestra	Seoul
Pusan Philharmonic Orchestra	Pusan
Seoul Philharmonic Orchestra	Seoul
Latvia	
Latvian National Orchestra	Riga
Latvian Philharmonic Chamber Orchestra	Riga
Liepaja Symphony Orchestra	Liepaja
Lithuania	
Lithuanian National Symphony Orchestra	Vilnius
Lithuanian State Symphony Orchestra	Vilnius

Name	Location
Luxembourg	
Philharmonic Orchestra of Luxembourg	Luxembourg
Malaysia	
Malaysian Philharmonic Orchestra	Kuala Lumpur
Mexico	
Estado de Mexico	Toluca
National Symphony Orchestra of Mexico	Mexico City
Philharmonic Orchestra of Jalisco	Jalisco
Philharmonic of Mexico City	Mexico City
Philharmonic of Queretaro	Queretaro
State of Mexico Symphony Orchestra	Toluca
Moldova	
National Orchestra for Radio and Television	Chisinau
Symphony Orchestra of the National Philharmonic of Moldova	Chisinau
Netherlands	
Arnhem Philharmonic Orchestra	Arnhem
Barokrkest van De Nederlands Bachvereniging	Utrecht
Brabant Philharmonic Orchestra	Eindhoven
The Gelders Orchestra	Arnhem
Limburgs Symphony Orchestra/ Symphony Orchestra of Maastricht	Maastricht
Netherlands Ballet Orchestra	Amsterdam
Netherlands Philharmonic Orchestra	Amsterdam
Netherlands Radio Philharmonic	Hilversum
Noordhollands Philharmonic Orchestra	Haarlem
Radio Symphony Orchestra	Hilversum
Resident Orchestra of The Hague	The Hague
Rotterdam Philharmonic Orchestra	Rotterdam
Royal Concertgebouw Orchestra	Amsterdam
New Zealand	
Auckland Philharmonic Orchestra	Auckland
Christchurch Symphony Orchestra	Christchurch
New Zealand Symphony Orchestra	Wellington
Norway	
Bergen Philharmonic Orchestra	Bergen

Name	Location
Kristiansand Symphony Orchestra	Kristiansand
Norwegian Baroque Orchestra	Trondheim
Norwegian Chamber Orchestra	Oslo
Oslo Philharmonic Orchestra	Oslo
Stavanger Symphony Orchestra	Stavanger
Trondheim Symphony Orchestra	Trondheim
Peru	
National Sinfonia Orchestra	Lima
Philippines	
Manila Symphony Orchestra	Manila
National Philharmonic Orchestra	Manila
Philippine Philharmonic Orchestra	Manila
Poland	
Kielce Philharmonic	Kielce
Krakow Philharmonic	Krakow
Lublin Philharmonic	Olsztyn
Orchestra of the National Theatre	Warsaw
Philharmonic Orchestra	Lodz
Polish Chamber Orchestra	Warsaw
Polish Radio National Symphony Orchestra	Katowice
Poznan Philharmonic	Poznan
Silesian State Philharmonic in Katowice	Katowice
State Philharmonic Orchestra	Wroclaw
Szymanowski Philharmonic Orchestra	Krakow
Warsaw Philharmonic	Warsaw
Portugal	
Gulbenkian Orchestra	Lisbon
Lisbon Metropolitan Orchestra	Lisbon
Oporto Classical Orchestra	Oporto
Portuguese Symphony Orchestra	Lisbon
Republic of Georgia	
Chamber Orchestra	Tbilisi
Republic of Ireland	
National Symphony Orchestra of Ireland	Dublin
RTE Concert Orchestra	Dublin
Romania	
Arad State Philharmonic	Arad
Brasov State Philharmonic	Brasov
Iasi Philharmonic	Iasi
Sibiu State Philharmonic	Cluj-Napoca
Russia	
Bolshoi Symphony Orchestra	Moscow
Russian National Symphony Orchestra	Moscow

Name	Location
Russian State Philharmonic Orchestra	Moscow
St Petersburg Philharmonic	St Petersburg

Singapore
Singapore Symphony Orchestra — Singapore

Slovak Republic
Kosice State Philharmonic — Kosice
Slovak Radio Symphony Orchestra — Bratislava

Slovenia
Slovenian Philharmonic — Ljubljana
Slovenian Radio and Television Symphony Orchestra — Ljubljana

South Africa
Cape Town Philharmonic Orchestra — Cape Town
Natal Philharmonic Orchestra — Natal
New Arts Philharmonic Orchestra Pretoria — Pretoria

Spain
Bilbao Symphony Orchestra — Bilbao
City of Palma Symphony Orchestra, Baleares — Palma de Mallorca
Gran Teatre del Liceu Symphony Orchestra — Barcelona
La Capella Reial de Catalunya — Barcelona
Le Concert des Nations — Barcelona
National Orchestra and Chorus of Spain — Madrid
Orchestra of Cadaques — Barcelona
Orchestra of Valencia — Valencia
Orquesta Sinfonica de Barcelona i Nacional — Barcelona
De Catalunya Philharmonic Orchestra of Gran Canaria — Las Palmas de Gran Canaria
Sinfonia Orchestra of Euskadi — San Sebastian
Sinfonia Orchestra of Galicia — La Coruna
Real Sinfonia Orchestra of Seville — Seville
Symphony Orchestra of Castille and Leon — Valladolid
Tenerife Symphony Orchestra — Santa Cruz de Tenerife

Sweden
Goteborgs Opera Orchestra — Goteborg
Royal Stockholm Philharmonic Orchestra — Stockholm
Royal Swedish Opera Orchestra — Stockholm
Swedish National Orchestra — Gothenburg
Swedish Radio Symphony Orchestra — Stockholm

Switzerland
Basel Sinfonia Orchestra — Basel
Basel Sinfonietta — Basel
Berner Symphony Orchestra — Berne
Orchestra of Opera Zurich — Zurich

Name	Location
Orchestra of the Suisse Romande	Geneva
Tonhalle-Orchestra Zurich	Zurich

Taiwan
Taipei Symphony Orchestra — Taipei

Thailand
Bangkok Symphony Orchestra — Bangkok

Turkey
Istanbul State Symphony Orchestra — Istanbul
Izmir State Symphony Orchestra — Izmir
Presidential Symphony Orchestra — Ankara

Ukraine
Crimea State Symphony Orchestra — Yalta
Kharkov Philharmonic Orchestra — Kharkov
National Symphony Orchestra of Ukraine — Kiev
Odessa Philharmonic Orchestra — Odessa
Ukrainian Chamber Orchestra — Kiev
Ukrainian Television and Radio Symphony Orchestra — Kiev

United Kingdom
Academy of Ancient Music — London
Academy of London — London
Academy of St Martin-in-the-Fields — London
Ambache Chamber Orchestra — London
BBC Concert Orchestra — London
BBC National Orchestra of Wales — Cardiff
BBC Philharmonic — Manchester
BBC Scottish Symphony Orchestra — Glasgow
BBC Symphony Orchestra — London
Birmingham Contemporary Music Group — Birmingham
Bournemouth Sinfonietta — Bournemouth
Bournemouth Symphony Orchestra — Bournemouth
The Brandenburg Consort — Bath
Britten Sinfonia — Cambridge
BT Scottish Ensemble — Glasgow
City of Birmingham Symphony Orchestra — Birmingham
City of London Sinfonia — London
City of Oxford Orchestra — Oxford
Corydon Orchestra — London
East of England Orchestra — Derby
English Camerata — Leeds
English Classical Players — London
English Northern Philharmonia — Leeds
English Sinfonia — London
English String Orchestra — Malvern
English Symphony Orchestra — Malvern
Guildford Philharmonic Orchestra — Guildford

Name	Location
Guildhall String Ensemble	London
Hallé Orchestra	Manchester
London Festival Orchestra	London
London Handel Orchestra	London
London Jupiter Orchestra	London
London Mozart Players	London
London Philharmonic Orchestra	London
London Pro Arte Orchestra	London
London Sinfonietta	London
London Soloists Chamber Orchestra	London
London Symphony Orchestra	London
Manchester Camerata	Manchester
Milton Keynes City Orchestra	Milton Keynes
Mozart Orchestra	Birmingham
New London Orchestra	London
New Queens Hall Orchestra	London
Northern Ballet Theatre Orchestra	Leeds
Northern Sinfonia	Newcastle upon Tyne
Orchestra da Camera	Warwick
Orchestra of St John's Square	London
Orchestra of the Age of Enlightenment	London
Orchestra of the Golden Age	Sale
Orchestra of the Royal Opera House	London
Performing Arts Symphony Orchestra	Manchester
Philharmonia Orchestra	London
Philomusica of London	London
Royal Liverpool Philharmonic Society	Liverpool
Royal Philharmonic Orchestra	London
Royal Scottish National Orchestra	Glasgow
Scottish Chamber Orchestra	Edinburgh
Sinfonia 21	London
Ulster Orchestra	Belfast

United States
Huntsville Symphony Orchestra — Alabama
Anchorage Symphony — Alaska
Flagstaff Symphony Orchestra — Arizona
Phoenix Symphony Orchestra — Arizona
Arkansas Symphony Orchestra — Arkansas
North Arkansas Symphony Orchestra — Arkansas
American Jazz Philharmonic — California
Asia America Symphony — California
Bear Valley Music Festival — California
Berkeley Symphony Orchestra — California
Chamber Orchestra of South Bay — California
Claremont Symphony Orchestra — California

Name	Location
Coastside Community Orchestra	California
Fresno Philharmonic	California
Hollywood Bowl Orchestra	California
Livermore-Amador Symphony	California
Long Beach Symphony Orchestra	California
Los Angeles Philharmonic	California
Merced Symphony	California
Modesto Symphony	California
Monterey County Symphony	California
Oakland East Bay Symphony	California
Pasadena Pops	California
Peninsula Symphony North	California
Philharmonic Society of Orange County	California
The Redwood Symphony	California
San Diego Youth Symphony	California
San Luis Obispo Symphony	California
Santa Barbara Chamber Orchestra	California
Santa Barbara Symphony	California
Santa Cruz County Symphony	California
Santa Monica Symphony	California
Santa Rosa Symphony	California
Southwest Chamber Music Society	California
Stockton Symphony	California
San Francisco Symphony Orchestra	California
San Jose Symphony	California
Boulder Philharmonic Orchestra	Colorado
Colorado Springs Symphony Orchestra	Colorado
Colorado Symphony Orchestra	Colorado
Fort Collins Symphony Orchestra	Colorado
Delaware Symphony Orchestra	Delaware
National Symphony Orchestra	District of Columbia
Washington Symphony Orchestra	District of Columbia
Boca Pops	Florida
The Florida Orchestra	Florida
The Florida Philharmonic	Florida
Florida West Coast Symphony Orchestra	Florida
Naples Philharmonic	Florida
New World Symphony	Florida
Atlanta Symphony Orchestra	Georgia
Augusta Symphony Orchestra	Georgia
Savannah Symphony Orchestra	Georgia
Boise Philharmonic Association	Idaho

Name	Location
Chicago Symphony Orchestra	Illinois
Evansville Philharmonic Orchestra	Indiana
The Indianapolis Symphonic Band	Indiana
Indianapolis Symphony Orchestra	Indiana
Muncie Symphony Orchestra	Indiana
Quad City Symphony	Iowa
The Wichita Symphony Orchestra	Kansas
Ownesboro Symphony Orchestra	Kentucky
Paducah Symphony Orchestra	Kentucky
Louisiana Philharmonic Orchestra	Louisiana
Bangor Symphony Orchestra	Maine
Portland Symphony	Maine
Baltimore Symphony Orchestra	Maryland
Maryland Symphony Orchestra	Maryland
Boston Chamber Ensemble	Massachusetts
Boston Modern Orchestra Project	Massachusetts
Boston Symphony Orchestra	Massachusetts
Nashua Symphony	Massachusetts
Pro Arte Chamber Orchestra of Boston	Massachusetts
Detroit Symphony	Michigan
Jackson Symphony Orchestra	Michigan
Kalamazoo Symphony Orchestra	Michigan
Traverse Symphony Orchestra	Michigan
The Minnesota Orchestra	Minnesota
Mississippi Symphony Orchestra	Mississippi
Saint Louis Symphony Orchestra	Missouri
Billings Symphony Orchestra	Montana
Omaha Symphony	Nebraska
Reno Philharmonic	Nevada
New Hampshire Philharmonic	New Hampshire
New Jersey Symphony	New Jersey
Roswell Symphony Orchestra	New Mexico
Albany Symphony Orchestra	New York
Buffalo Philharmonic Orchestra	New York
Chautauqua Symphony Orchestra	New York
Long Island Philharmonic	New York
Manhattan Philharmonic	New York
Nassau Pops Symphony Orchestra	New York
New York Philharmonic	New York

Name	Location
Rochester Philharmonic Orchestra	New York
Charlotte Philharmonic Orchestra	North Carolina
Charlotte Symphony Orchestra	North Carolina
Greensboro Symphony Orchestra	North Carolina
Bismarck-Mandan Symphony Orchestra	North Dakota
The Cleveland Orchestra	Ohio
Columbus Symphony Orchestra	Ohio
Toledo Symphony Orchestra	Ohio
Oklahoma City Philharmonic Orchestra	Oklahoma
Tulsa Philharmonic Orchestra	Oklahoma
Britt Festival	Oregon
Oregon Symphony	Oregon
Seattle Symphony	Oregon
Northeastern Pennsylvania Philharmonic	Pennsylvania
The Philadelphia Orchestra	Pennsylvania
Pittsburg Symphony Orchestra	Pennsylvania
Providence Mandolin Orchestra	Rhode Island
South Carolina Philharmonic	South Carolina
South Dakota Symphony Orchestra	South Dakota
Jackson Symphony Orchestra	Tennessee
Amarillo Symphony Orchestra	Texas
Austin Symphony Orchestra	Texas
Clear Lake Symphony Orchestra	Texas
Dallas Symphony	Texas
Fort Worth Symphony	Texas
Galveston Symphony Orchestra	Texas
The Houston Symphony	Texas
Irving Symphony Orchestra Association	Texas
San Antonio Symphony	Texas
Utah Symphony Orchestra	Utah
Vermont Symphony Orchestra	Vermont
Arlington Philharmonic Orchestra	Virginia
Arlington Symphony	Virginia
Fairfax Symphony Orchestra	Virginia
Richmond Symphony	Virginia
Roanoke Symphony	Virginia
West Virginia Symphony	West Virginia
Wheeling Symphony Orchestra	West Virginia
Green Bay Symphony Orchestra	Wisconsin
Milwaukee Symphony Orchestra	Wisconsin
Wyoming Symphony Orchestra	Wyoming

Brass instruments

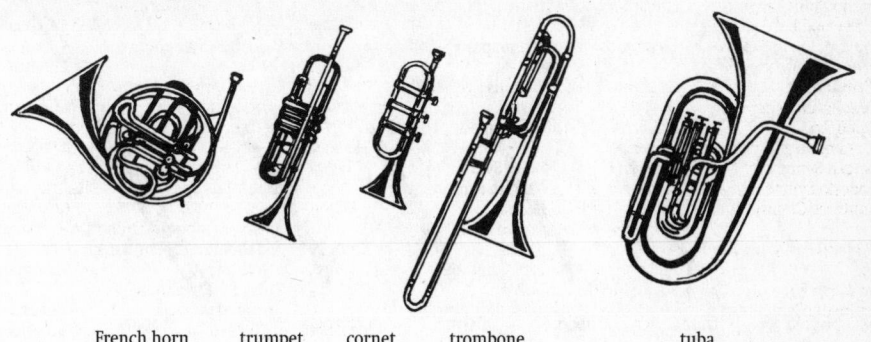

French horn   trumpet   cornet   trombone   tuba

Percussion instruments

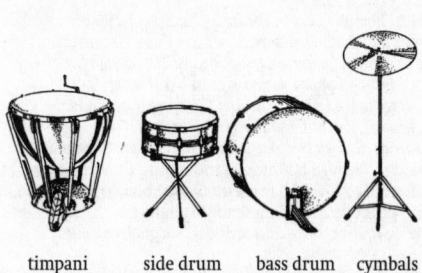

timpani   side drum   bass drum   cymbals

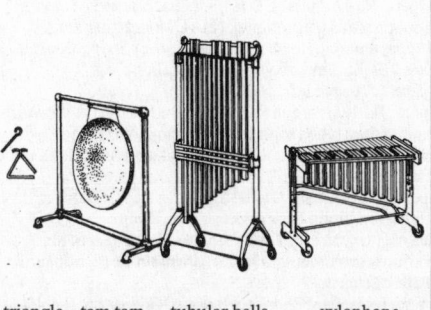

triangle   tam-tam   tubular bells   xylophone

String instruments

violin   viola

violoncello   double bass

Woodwind instruments

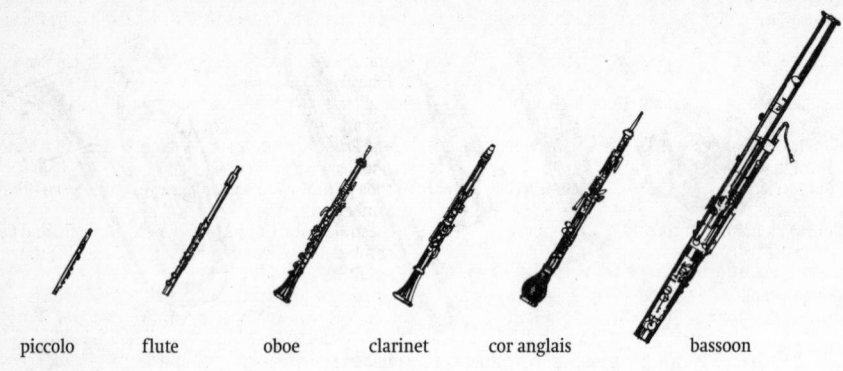

piccolo   flute   oboe   clarinet   cor anglais   bassoon

Composers

Name	Dates	Place of birth	Selected works
Albinoni, Tommaso	1671–1751	Venice	String concertos; concerti grossi; Adagio for organ and strings in G minor.
Arnold, Malcolm	1921–2006	Northampton,	Scores: *Hobson's Choice*; *The Inn of the Sixth Happiness*; *Whistle Down the Wind*; *Bridge over the River Kwai*. Orchestral: *Double Violin Concerto*. Symphonies: *The Seventh Symphony*; *The Ninth Symphony*. Overture: *Tam O'Shanter*. Ballet: *Homage to the Queen*; *Solitaire*; *The Three Musketeers*.
Babbitt, Milton	1916–	Philadelphia	Orchestral: *Relata I and II*; *Ars combinatoria*.
Bach, Johann Sebastian	1685–1750	Eisenach, Germany	Oratorios: *St John Passion*; *St Matthew Passion*; *Christmas Oratorio*. Mass in B Minor. Brandenburg Concertos: Nos.1–6. Keyboard: *The Well-Tempered Clavier*; *Goldberg Variations*. Organ: Toccata and Fugue in D minor.
Barber, Samuel	1910–81	West Chester, Pennsylvania	*Dover Beach* (for voice and strings). *Adagio for Strings*.
Bartók, Béla	1881–1945	Nagyszentmiklos, Hungary (now Sinnicolau Mare, Romania)	Opera: *Duke Bluebeard's Castle*. Ballet: *The Wooden Prince*; *The Miraculous Mandarin*. Orchestral: *Kossuth*; *Dance Suite*; *Concerto for Orchestra*; *Music for Strings, Percussion and Celesta*. Piano concertos: 3. String quartets: 6.
Beethoven, Ludwig van	1770–1827	Bonn	Symphonies: No.3 in E Flat Major (Eroica); No.5 in C Minor; No.6 in F Major (Pastoral); No. 9 in D Minor (Choral). Piano concertos: No.5 in E Flat Major (Emperor). Violin Concerto in D Major. Triple Concerto in C Major. Overtures: *Leonora*, Nos.1,2, and 3; *Egmont*; *Ruins of Athens*. Opera: *Fidelio*. Mass in D Major (*Missa Solemnis*). Piano Sonatas: No.8 (Pathétique); No.14 (Moonlight); No.23: (Appassionata); No.29 (Hammerklavier). String Quartets: Nos.7–9 (Rasumowsky), Nos.12–16; *Grosse Fuge*.
Bellini, Vincenzo	1801–35	Catania, Sicily	Opera: *La Sonnambula*; *Norma*.
Bennett, Richard Rodney	1936–	Broadstairs, Kent	Opera: *The Mines of Sulphur*; *Penny for a Song*. *Spells* (for voice and orchestra). Saxophone Concerto. Concerto for Bassoon and Strings; *Rondel* (for jazz ensemble) Ballet: *Isadora*.
Berg, Alban	1885–1935	Vienna	Opera: *Wozzeck*; *Lulu*. Orchestral: *Three Pieces*. Chamber Concerto. Violin Concerto.
Berio, Luciano	1925–2003	Oneglia, Italy	*Sinfonia* (for voice and orchestra). *Sequenza* (pieces for various instruments). Opera: *La vera storia*; *Un re in ascolto*. Ballet: *Compass*
Berlioz, Hector	1803–69	La Cote-St-André, Isere	Opera: *Les Troyens*; *Béatrice et Benedict*. Orchestral: *Harold in Italy*; *Symphonie Fantastique*. For voice and orchestra: *Requiem*; *Roméo et Juliette*; *La Damnation de Faust*; *Les Nuits d'Été*.

Name	Dates	Place of birth	Selected works
Birtwistle, Harrison	1934–	Accrington, Lancashire	Opera: *Punch and Judy; The Mask of Orpheus; Gawain; The Second Mrs Kong.* Orchestral: *Earth Dances; Exody; The Last Supper.*
Bizet, Georges	1838–75	Paris	Opera: *The Pearl Fishers; The Fair Maid of Perth; Carmen.* Orchestral: *L'Arlésienne.*
Bloch, Ernst	1880–1959	Geneva	Opera: *Macbeth.* Orchestral: *Israel Symphony; Shelomo.* For voice and orchestra: *Sacred Service.*
Borodin, Alexander Porphiryevich	1833–87	St Petersburg	Opera: *Prince Igor.* Orchestral: Symphony No.2 in B Minor; *In the Steppes of Central Asia.*
Boulez, Pierre	1925–	Montbrison, France	*Pli selon pli* (for voice and orchestra). *Éclats; Répons* (for chamber orchestra).
Brahms, Johannes	1833–97	Hamburg	Orchestral: Violin Concerto; Concerto for Violin and Cello; Chamber music: Piano Quintet in F; Clarinet Quintet. Choral: *Ein Deutsches Requiem.*
Bridge, Frank	1879–1941	Brighton	Song: *Love Went a-Riding.* Orchestral: *The Sea; Oration.*
Britten, Benjamin	1913–76	Lowestoft	Opera: *Peter Grimes; Albert Herring; Billy Budd; The Turn of the Screw; A Midsummer Night's Dream; Death in Venice.* Orchestral: *Simple Symphony; Variations on a Theme of Frank Bridge; Sinfonia da Requiem; Young Persons Guide to the Orchestra.* For voice and orchestra: *Cantata Academica; War Requiem; Our Hunting Fathers.*
Bruch, Max	1838–1920	Cologne	Violin concertos: 3. *Scottish Fantasy* (for violin and orchestra).
Bruckner, Anton	1824–96	Ansfelden, Austria	Symphonies: No. 4 in E Flat Major (Romantic); No.7 in E Major; No.8 in C Minor; No.9 in D Minor (unfinished).
Busoni, Ferruccio	1866–1924	Empoli, Italy	Opera: *Arlecchino; Turandot; Doktor Faust.* Orchestral: *Berceuse élégiaque.* Piano: *Indian Diary.*
Byrd, William	1543–1623	Lincoln (probably)	Masses: 3. Keyboard: *My Ladye Nevells Booke.*
Cage, John	1912–92	Los Angeles	*Variations I–VI* (for any number of performers and objects). *4'33"* (silent: for any instrument(s)).
Carter, Elliott	1908–	New York	String quartets: 4. Orchestral: Double Concerto for Harpsichord and Piano; *A Symphony of Three Orchestras; Three Occasions for Orchestra.*
Chopin, Frédéric	1810–49	Zelazowa Wola, Poland	Piano concertos: 2. For solo piano: 3 piano sonatas, numerous Ballades, Scherzos, Études, Nocturnes, Préludes, Valses, Polonaises, Mazurkas.
Copland, Aaron	1900–90	Brooklyn, New York	Ballets: *Billy the Kid; Rodeo; Appalachian Spring.* Orchestral: *A Lincoln Portrait; Fanfare for the Common Man.*
Couperin, François	1668–1733	Paris	For harpsichord: *Pièces de Clavecin* (Books I–IV).
Davies, Peter Maxwell	1934–	Salford	Opera: *Taverner; The Martyrdom of St Magnus.* Theatre: *Eight Songs for a Mad King.* Orchestral: *1st Fantasia on In Nomine of John Taverner; Sinfonia; An Orkney Wedding, with Sunrise.* Symphonies: 4. Ballet: *Maxwell's Reel, with Northern Lights.*
Debussy, Claude	1862–1918	St Germain-en-Laye, France	Opera: *Pelléas et Mélisande.* Ballet: *Jeux.* Orchestral: *Prélude à l'après-midi d'un faune; Nocturnes; La Mer.* Chamber: String quartet; cello sonata; violin sonata. Piano: *Préludes* (Books I and II).
Delibes, Léo	1836–91	St Germain-du-Val, France	Ballet: *Coppélia; Sylvia.* Opera: *Lakmé.*
Delius, Frederick	1862–1934	Bradford, Yorkshire	Opera: *A Village Romeo and Juliette.* Orchestral: *Brigg Fair; In a Summer Garden; On Hearing the First Cuckoo in Spring.* For voice, chorus, and orchestra: *Sea Drift; A Mass of Life.*
Donizetti, Gaetano	1797–1848	Bergamo, Italy	Opera: *L'Elisir d'Amore; Lucia di Lammermoor.*
Dukas, Paul	1865–1935	Paris	Orchestral: *The Sorcerer's Apprentice.*
Dvořák, Antonín	1841–1904	Nelahozeves, Czechoslovakia	Symphonies: (No.6 in D Major; No.8 in G Major; No.9 in E Minor (From the New World). *Slavonic Dances.* Concertos: violin concerto; cello concerto.
Elgar, Edward	1857–1934	Broadheath, nr Worcester	Orchestral: *Variations on an Original Theme (Enigma Variations); Pomp and Circumstance Marches; Cockaigne; Falstaff.* Concertos: violin concerto; cello concerto. Symphony No.1. For voice, chorus, and orchestra: *Dream of Gerontius.*
Falla, Manuel de	1876–1946	Cadiz	Ballet: *The Three-Cornered Hat.* Orchestral: *Nights in the Gardens of Spain.*

Composers (continued)

Name	Dates	Place of birth	Selected works
Fauré, Gabriel	1845–1924	Pamiers	Opera: *Pénélope*. For voice, chorus, and orchestra: *Requiem*. Songs (*Après un rêve*; *Les Roses d'Ispahan*; *Clair de Lune*)
Franck, César	1822–90	Liège	Orchestral: *Symphonic Variations*; *Symphony in D Minor*. For chorus and orchestra: *Psyché*.
Gershwin, George	1898–1937	Brooklyn, New York	Opera: *Porgy and Bess*. Orchestral: *Rhapsody in Blue*; *An American in Paris*.
Glass, Philip	1937–	Baltimore	Opera: *Einstein on the Beach*; *Akhnaten*; *The Making of the Representative for Planet Eight*; *Monsters of Grace*; *Waiting for the Barbarians*. Scores: *Koyaanisqatsi*; *Kundun*; *The Hours*.
Glazunov, Alexander	1865–1936	St Petersburg	Orchestral: *Symphony No.1*; *The Seasons*.
Glinka, Mikhail	1804–57	Smolensk	Opera: *A Life for the Tsar*; *Ruslan and Lyudmila*.
Gluck, Christoph	1714–87	Erasbach	Opera: *Orfeo*; *Alceste*; *Iphigénie en Aulide*; *Iphigénie en Tauride*.
Goehr, Alexander	1932–	Berlin	Opera: *Arden Must Die*; *Behold the Sun*. Orchestral: *The Deluge*; *Sutter's Gold*; *Little Symphony*; *Idées Fixes*.
Górecki, Henryk	1933–	Czernica, Poland	Orchestral: *Symphony No.3 (Symphony of Sorrowful Songs)*. Chamber: *Genesis*; *Kleine Phantasie*.
Gounod, Charles	1818–93	Paris	Opera: *Faust*; *Roméo et Juliette*. Songs: *Ave Maria*.
Grieg, Edvard	1843–1907	Bergen	Orchestral: *Piano Concerto in A Minor*; *Peer Gynt* (Suites 1 and 2).
Handel, George Frideric	1685–1759	Halle	Orchestral: *Water Music*; *Music for Royal Fireworks*. Oratorios: *Saul*; *Messiah*; *Belshazzar*; *Solomon*.
Haydn, Franz Joseph	1732–1809	Rohrau, Austria	Oratorios: *The Creation*; *The Seasons*. Symphonies: Nos.82–7 (Paris); Nos.93–104 (London). String quartets: Nos.50–6 (*Seven Last Words from the Cross*); No.61 (*Razor*).
Henze, Hans Werner	1926–	Gütersloh, Germany	Opera: *The Bassarids*; *We Come to the River*. Orchestral: *Das Floss der 'Medusa'*; *Symphony No. 9*.
Hindemith, Paul	1895–1963	Hanau, Germany	Orchestral: *Mathis der Maler* (symphony); *Trauermusik* (for viola and strings); *Symphonic Metamorphosis of Themes by Carl Maria von Weber*.
Holst, Gustav	1874–1934	Cheltenham	Orchestral: *The Planets* (suite); *Egdon Heath*.
Honegger, Arthur	1892–1955	Le Havre	Oratorio: *Jeanne d'Arc au Bûcher*. Orchestral: *Pacific 231*.
Ives, Charles	1874–1954	Danbury, Connecticut	Orchestral: *Holidays Symphony*; *The Unanswered Question*; *Central Park in the Dark*; *Symphonies 1–3*; *Variations on 'America'*.
Janáček, Leoš	1854–1928	Hukvaldy, Czechoslovakia	Opera: *Jenufa*; *Kata Kabanova*; *The Cunning Little Vixen*; *From the House of the Dead*. Orchestral: *Sinfonietta*; *Taras Bulba*. For voice, chorus, organ, and orchestra: *Glagolitic Mass*. String quartets: 2. Piano sonata (*I.X.1905*).
Khachaturian, Aram	1903–78	Tbilisi	Ballet: *Gayane*; *Spartacus*.
Kodály, Zoltan	1882–1967	Kecskemét, Hungary	Opera: *Háry János*. For voice, chorus, and orchestra: *Psalmus Hungaricus*.
Krenek, Ernst	1900–91	Vienna	Opera: *Johnny spielt auf*; *Karl V*.
Léhar, Franz	1870–1948	Komarom, Hungary	Operetta: *The Merry Widow*; *The Land of Smiles*.
Ligeti, György	1923–2006	Dicsöszent-Márton, Transylvania	Opera: *Le Grand Macabre*. Orchestral: *Atmosphères*; *Melodien*; *Piano Concerto*; *Etude pour Piano No. 14a*.
Liszt, Franz	1811–86	Raiding, Hungary	Orchestral: *A Faust Symphony*; *Mazeppa*. Piano: *Années de Pèlerinages* (Books I–III); *Mephisto Waltz No.2*; *Sonata in B Minor*; *Hungarian Rhapsodies*.
Lully, Jean-Baptiste	1632–87	Florence	*Le Bourgeois Gentilhomme* (comedy-ballet, after Molière). Many operas.
Lutoslawski, Witold	1913–95	Warsaw	Orchestral: *Concerto for Orchestra*; *Symphonic Variations*.
Mahler, Gustav	1860–1911	Kalist, Austria (later Czechoslovakia)	Symphonies: No.2 in C Minor (*Resurrection*); No.3 in D Minor; No.5 in C Sharp Minor; No.6 in A Minor (*Tragic*); No.8 in E Flat Major (*Symphony of a Thousand*); No.9 in D Major. Song symphony: *Das Lied von der Erde*. Song cycles: *Lieder eines fahrenden Gesellen*; *Kindertotenlieder*. Songs: *Des Knaben Wunderhorn*.
Mascagni, Pietro	1863–1945	Livorno, Italy	Opera: *Cavalleria Rusticana*.
Maw, Nicholas	1935–	Grantham, Lincolnshire	Opera: *One Man Show*; *The Rising of the Moon*. Violin Concerto.

Name	Dates	Place of birth	Selected works
Mendelssohn, Felix	1809–47	Hamburg	Symphonies: No.3 in A Minor (*Scottish*); No.4 in A Major (*Italian*). Piano concertos: 2. Violin Concerto in E Minor, Overtures: *A Midsummer Night's Dream*; *Hebrides (Fingal's Cave)*. Piano: *Songs Without Words* (Books I–VIII).
Menotti, Gian Carlo	1911–	Cadegliano, Italy	Opera: *The Medium*; *The Consul*; *Amahl and the Night Visitors*.
Messiaen, Olivier	1908–92	Avignon	Orchestral: *Turangalîla-symphonie*; *Oiseaux Exotiques*. Piano: *Vingt Regards sur l'enfant Jésus*. Organ: *Nativité du Seigneur*. Chamber: *Quatuor pour la fin du temps*.
Milhaud, Darius	1892–1974	Aix-en-Provence	Opera: *Christophe Colomb*. Ballet: *Le Boeuf sur le Toit*; *La Création du Monde*. Orchestral: *Saudades do Brazil*; *Suite Provençal*.
Monteverdi, Claudio	1567–1643	Cremona, Italy	Opera: *Orfeo*. Church Music: *Vespers of 1610 (Vespro della Beata Vergine)*.
Mozart, Wolfgang Amadeus	1756–91	Salzburg	Opera: *Die Entführung aus dem Serail*; *Le Nozze di Figaro*; *Don Giovanni*; *Così fan tutte*; *Die Zauberflöte*. Orchestral: Symphonies (Nos.35–41), Serenades *(Gran Partita, Eine Kleine Nachtmusik)*. Concertos: No.21 for piano: *Elvira Madigan*, for viola and violin: *Sinfonia Concertante*, for clarinet in A major, and flute and harp in C major. Church music: *Coronation Mass*; *Requiem*.
Musgrave, Thea	1928–	Edinburgh	Opera: *Beauty and the Beast*; *The Voice of Ariadne*; *Simon Bolívar*. Orchestral: *The Seasons*; *Rainbow*.
Mussorgsky, Modest	1839–81	Karevo, Russia	Opera: *Boris Godunov*. Orchestral: *Night on the Bare Mountain*. Piano: *Pictures at an Exhibition*
Nielsen, Carl	1865–1931	Norre-Lyndelse, Denmark	Opera: *Saul and David*. Symphonies: No.1 in G Minor, No.3 (*Sinfonia Espansiva*); No.4 (*The Inextinguishable*); No.5.
Nono, Luigi	1924–90	Venice	Opera: *Intolleranza*. Choral: *Canto per il Vietnam*.
Nyman, Michael	1944–	UK	Scores: *The Draughtsman's Contract*; *A Zed & Two Noughts* (and other Peter Greenaway films); *Carrington*. Opera: *The Man Who Mistook His Wife for a Hat*; *Facing Goya*. Orchestral: *Double Concerto for Saxophone and Cello*.
Offenbach, Jacques	1819–80	Cologne	Opera: *Orpheus in the Underworld*; *The Tales of Hoffmann*.
Orff, Carl	1895–1982	Munich	*Carmina Burana* (for voice, boy's choir, chorus, and orchestra).
Palestrina, Giovanni Pierluigi da	c.1525–94	Palestrina, nr Rome	Many masses and motets.
Penderecki, Krzysztof	1933–	Debica, Poland	Opera: *The Devils of Loudon*. Orchestral: *Threnody for the Victims of Hiroshima*; *Passacaglia and Rondo*.
Poulenc, Francis	1899–1963	Paris	Opera: *Les Dialogues des Carmélites*; *La Voix humaine*. Ballet: *Les Biches*. Concerto in G minor for organ, strings and timpani. Chamber: violin sonata; cello sonata. Choral: *4 Motets pour un temps de pénitence*.
Prokofiev, Sergei Sergeyevitch	1891–1953	Sontsovka, Ukraine	Opera: *Love for Three Oranges*. Ballet: *The Age of Steel*, *Romeo and Juliet*; *Cinderella*. Symphonies: No.1 in D Major (Classical); No.5 in B Flat Major; No.7 in C Sharp Minor. *Peter and the Wolf* (for narrator and orchestra). Scores: *Lieutenant Kijé*; *Alexander Nevsky*. Piano concertos: 5.
Puccini, Giacomo	1858–1924	Lucca, Italy	Opera: *Manon Lescaut*; *La Bohème*; *Tosca*; *Madama Butterfly*; *Turandot*
Purcell, Henry	1659–95	London	Opera: *Dido and Aeneas*. Choral: *Come ye sons of art, away*; *Ode on St Cecilia's Day*; *Thou knowest, Lord, the Secrets of our Hearts*.
Rachmaninov, Sergei Vasileyevich	1873–1943	Semyonovo, Russia	Orchestral: 4 piano concertos, 3 symphonies; *The Isle of the Dead*; *Rhapsody on a Theme of Paganini*; *Symphonic Dances*
Rameau, Jean-Philippe	1683–1764	Dijon	Opera: *Castor et Pollux*. Many pieces for harpsichord.
Ravel, Maurice	1875–1937	Ciboure, France	Opera: *L'Heure Espagnole*; *L'Enfant et les Sortilèges*. Ballet: *Daphnis and Chloé*; *Boléro*. Orchestral: *Alborada del gracioso*, *Rapsodie Espagnole*; *Ma Mère l'Oye*; *La Valse*. Piano Concerto for Left Hand; Piano Concerto in G Major. Chamber: Quartet; *Introduction and Allegro* (for harp, flute, clarinet and string quartet). Piano: *Pavane pour une infante défunte*; *Miroirs*; *Valses nobles et sentimentales*; *Le Tombeau de Couperin*.

Composers (continued)

Name	Dates	Place of birth	Selected works
Reich, Steve	1936–	New York	*Drumming* (for percussion and voices). Orchestral: *Four Sections. The Desert Music* (for chorus and orchestra): *Different Trains.* With Beryl Korot: *Hindenburg; City Life; Three Tales.*
Rimsky-Korsakov, Nikolai	1844–1908	Tikhvin-Novgorod, Russia	Opera: *The Golden Cockerel.* Orchestral: *Capriccio Espagnol; Scheherazade.*
Rodrigo, Joáquin	1902–99	Sagunto, Spain	*Concierto de Aranjuez* (for guitar and orchestra); *Concierto Pastorale* (for flute and orchestra).
Rossini, Gioacchino	1792–1868	Pesaro, Italy	Opera: *The Barber of Seville; Otello; William Tell.*
Saint-Saëns, Camille	1835–1921	Paris	Opera: *Samson et Dalila.* Orchestral: Symphony No.3 *(Organ)*; 3 piano concertos; *Carnaval des Animaux* (for piano and orchestra).
Satie, Erik	1866–1925	Honfleur, France	Ballet: *Parade.* Solo piano: 3 *Gymnopédies*; 6 *Gnossiennes*; *Morceaux en forme de poire.*
Scarlatti, Alessandro	1660–1725	Palermo	Many operas, oratorios, and masses.
Schoenberg, Arnold	1874–1951	Vienna	Opera: *Moses und Aron.* Orchestral: 5 *Orchestral Pieces*; *Chamber Symphony No.1.* For voice, chorus, and orchestra: *Gurrelieder* For voice and chamber orchestra: *Pierrot Lunaire.* Chamber: *Verklärte Nacht* (for string sextet).
Schubert, Franz	1797–1828	Vienna	Symphonies: No.5 in B Flat Major; No.8 in B minor (Unfinished); No.9 in C Major (Great). Chamber: String Quartet No.14 in D Minor (Death and the Maiden); Piano Quintet in A Major (Trout); Octet in F Major. Song-cycles: *Winterreise; Schwanengesang.* Many songs.
Schumann, Robert	1810–56	Zwickau, Germany	Orchestral: Symphony No.1 (Spring); No.3 (Rhenish); Piano Concerto in A Minor; Cello Concerto in A Minor. Solo piano: *Fantasiestücke; Études Symphoniques; Kinderscenen; Waldscenen; Albumblätter.*
Shostakovich, Dmitri	1906–75	St Petersburg	Opera: *The Nose; Lady Macbeth of Mtsensk.* Ballet: *The Age of Gold.* Symphonies: No.1 in F Minor; No.4 in C Minor; No.5 in D Minor; No.7 in C Major (Leningrad); No.10 in E Minor; No.13 in B Flat Minor (Babi-Yar); No.15 in A Major. Orchestral: 2 piano concertos; 2 violin concertos; 2 cello concertos. String quartets: No.8 in C Minor; No.10 in A Flat Major. Solo piano: *24 Preludes and Fugues.*
Sibelius, Jean	1865–1957	Hameenlinna, Finland	Symphonies: No.1 in E Minor; No.2 in D Major; No.5 in E Flat Major; *Finlandia* (symphonic piece); *Karelia Overture.*
Smetana, Bedřich	1824–84	Litomyšl, Czechoslovakia	Opera: *The Bartered Bride; Dalibor.* Orchestral: *Má Vlast.*
Sousa, John Philip	1854–1932	Washington DC	Marches: *Stars and Stripes; Liberty Bell; Hands across the Sea.*
Stockhausen, Karlheinz	1928–	Burg Modrath	Opera: *Donnerstag aus Licht; Samstag; Montag.* Orchestral: *Spiel; Punkte; Gruppen.* Instrumental: *Kontra-Punkte; Zeitmasze; Zyklus.* Electronic: *Gesang der Jünglinge.*
Strauss, Johann II	1825–99	Vienna	Opera: *Die Fledermaus.* Many waltzes: *Blue Danube; Roses from the South; Tales from the Vienna Woods.*
Strauss, Richard	1864–1949	Munich	Opera: *Salomé; Elektra; Der Rosenkavalier; Ariadne auf Naxos; Capriccio.* Orchestral: *Symphonia Domestica; An Alpine Symphony.* Symphonic Poems: *Don Juan; Death and Transfiguration; Till Eulenspiegels lustige Streiche; Also Sprach Zarathustra; Don Quixote; Ein Heldenleben; Metamorphosen.* Song-cycle: *Four Last Songs.*
Stravinsky, Igor	1882–1971	Oranienbaum (now Lomonosov, Russia)	Opera: *Oedipus Rex; The Rake's Progress.* Ballet: *The Firebird; Petrushka; The Rite of Spring; Pulcinella; Jeu de cartes; Orpheus.* Theatre: *The Soldier's Tale.* Orchestral: *Symphony in C; Symphony in Three Movements; Symphonies of Wind Instruments*; violin concerto; *Ebony Concerto* (for clarinet). Liturgical: *Symphony of Psalms; Mass; Canticum Sacrum.*
Suk, Joseph	1874–1935	Krecovice, Czechoslovakia	*Asrael Symphony.*
Sullivan, Arthur	1842–1900	London	Operetta: *HMS Pinafore; The Pirates of Penzance; Iolanthe; The Mikado; The Yeomen of the Guard; The Gondoliers.*

Name	Dates	Place of birth	Selected works
Szymanowski, Karol	1882–1937	Tymoshovka, Ukraine	Orchestral: Symphony No.2 in B Flat; Symphony No.3 *(Song of the Night)*; *Symphonie Concertante* (for piano and orchestra); 2 violin concertos; *Stabat Mater* (for voice, women's chorus and orchestra).
Tallis, Thomas	c.1505–85	Greenwich	Liturgical music: *Spem in alium* (40-part motet).
Tavener, John	1944–	London	Cantata: *The Whale*. For soloists, chorus, and orchestra: *Ultimos ritos*. Opera: *Therese*. Chamber: *Svyatuiee*. Funeral Music of Diana, Princess of Wales; *Eternity's Sunrise*; *The Veil of the Temple*.
Tchaikovsky, Peter Ilyich	1840–93	Kamsko-Votkinsk, Russia	Opera: *Eugene Onegin*; *Queen of Spades*. Ballet: *Swan Lake*; *Sleeping Beauty*; *Nutcracker*. Orchestral: Symphony No.4 in F Minor; Symphony No.5 in E Minor; Symphony No.6 in B Minor *(Pathétique)*; *Manfred Symphony*; *Romeo and Juliet* (overture).
Telemann, Georg Philipp	1681–1767	Magdeburg, Germany	c.600 overtures; also many operas, oratorios, and concertos.
Tippett, Michael	1905–98	London	Opera: *The Midsummer Marriage*; *The Ice Break*; *New Year*. Oratorio: *A Child of Our Time*; *The Mask of Time*. Orchestral: *Fantasia Concertante on a Theme of Corelli*. Piano sonatas: 4.
Vaughan Williams, Ralph	1872–1958	Down Ampney, Gloucestershire	Opera: *The Pilgrim's Progress*. Orchestral: *A Sea Symphony*; *A London Symphony*; *A Pastoral Symphony*; Symphony No.4 in F Minor; *Sinfonia Antarctica*; *The Wasps* (overture); *Fantasia on a Theme by Thomas Tallis*; *The Lark Ascending* (for violin and orchestra).
Verdi, Giuseppe	1813–1901	Roncole	Opera: *Nabucco*; *Macbeth*; *Rigoletto*; *Il Trovatore*; *La Traviata*; *Simon Boccanegra*; *A Masked Ball*; *The Force of Destiny*; *Don Carlos*; *Aida*; *Otello*; *Falstaff*. Orchestral: *Requiem*.
Villa-Lobos, Heitor	1887–1959	Rio de Janeiro	*Bachianas Brasilieras* (9 chamber pieces).
Vivaldi, Antonio	1678–1741	Venice	c.230 violin concertos: *Le quattro stagioni (The Four Seasons)*; orchestral concertos; bassoon, cello, oboe and flute concertos. Many operas and cantatas.
Wagner, Richard	1813–83	Leipzig	Opera: *Rienzi*; *Der fliegende Holländer*; *Tannhäuser*; *Lohengrin*; *Der Ring des Nibelungen (Das Rheingold, Die Walküre, Siegfried Götterdämmerung)*; *Tristan und Isolde*; *Die Meistersinger von Nürnberg*; *Parsifal*. Orchestral: *Siegfried Idyll*.
Walton, William	1902–83	Oldham	*Façade* (for reciter and chamber orchestra). Orchestral: Symphony No.1 in B Flat Major; Viola Concerto in B Minor; Coronation marches *(Crown Imperial, Orb and Sceptre)*. For chorus and orchestra: *Belshazzar's Feast*. Scores: *Henry V*; *Hamlet*; *Battle of Britain*; *Richard III*.
Weber, Carl Maria von	1786–1826	Eutin, in Oldenburg, Germany	Opera: *Der Freischütz*; *Euryanthe*; *Die drei Pintos*; *Oberon*.
Webern, Anton von	1883–1945	Vienna	Orchestral: *Passacaglia*; *6 Pieces*; *5 Pieces*. Choral: *Das Augenlicht*.
Weill, Kurt	1900–50	Dessau, Germany	Opera: *The Threepenny Opera*; *Rise and Fall of the City of Mahagonny*; *Happy End*. Ballet: *Seven Deadly Sins*. Orchestral: 2 symphonies; violin concerto; *The Berlin Requiem*.
Williamson, Malcolm	1931–2003	Sydney	Opera: *Our Man in Havana*; *The Red Sea*; *The Brilliant and the Dark*. Orchestral: *Hammarskjöld Portrait*.
Wolf, Hugo	1860–1903	Windischgraz, Austria	Opera: *Der Corregidor*. Orchestral: *Italian Serenade*. Songs: *Spanish Songbook*; *Italian Songbook*.
Xenakis, Iannis	1922–2001	Braila, Romania	Orchestral: *Metastasis*; *Shaar*; *Lichens*; *Thallein*.
Zemlinsky, Alexander von	1871–1942	Vienna	Opera: *Eine florentinische Tragödie*. Ballet: *Das gläserne Herz*. Orchestral: *Lyric Symphony*.

ARTS AND CULTURE

Operatic works

Name of work	Date	Composer	Librettist
Aida	1871	Verdi	Ghislanzoni
Alceste	1767	Gluck	Calzabigi
Arabella	1933	Richard Strauss	Hofmannsthal
Barber of Seville	1816	Rossini	Sterbini
Bartered Bride, The	1866	Smetana	Sabini
Beggar's Opera	1728	Gay	Gay
Billy Budd	1951	Britten	Forster/Crozier
Bohème, La	1896	Puccini	Giacoso/Illica
Boris Godunov	1974	Mussorgsky	Mussorgsky
Carmen	1875	Bizet	Meilhac/Halévy
Cavalleria Rusticana	1890	Mascagni	Menasci/Targioni-Tozetti
Clemenza di Tito, La	1791	Mozart	Mazzolà
Coronation of Poppea	1642	Monteverdi	Busenello
Cosi Fan Tutte	1790	Mozart	Da Ponte
Cunning Little Vixen, The	1924	Janáček	Janáček
Damnation of Faust, The	1846	Berlioz	Berlioz
Death in Venice	1973	Britten	Piper
Dido and Aeneas	1689	Purcell	Tate
Don Giovanni	1787	Mozart	Da Ponte
Duke Bluebeard's Castle	1918	Bartók	Balasz
Elektra	1909	Richard Strauss	Hofmannsthal
Eugene Onegin	1879	Tchaikovsky	Tchaikovsky/Shilovsky
Falstaff	1893	Verdi	Wagner
Faust	1859	Gounod	Barbier/Carré
Fidelio	1805	Beethoven	Sonnleithner
Fledermaus, Die	1874	Johann Strauss II	Haffner/Genée
Flying Dutchman, The	1843	Wagner	Wagner
Freischütz, Der	1821	Weber	Kind
Golden Cockerel, The	1909	Rimsky-Korsakov	Byelsky
Idomeneo	1781	Mozart	Varesco
Jenufa	1904	Janáček	Janáček
Julius Caesar in Egypt	1724	Handel	Haym
Kátya Kabanová	1921	Janáček	Janáček
King Priam	1962	Tippett	Tippett
Les Huguenots	1836	Meyerbeer	Scribe
Lohengrin	1850	Wagner	Wagner
Love for Three Oranges, The	1920	Prokofiev	Prokofiev
Lucia di Lammermoor	1835	Donizetti	Cammarano
Lulu	1937	Berg	Berg
Macbeth	1847	Verdi	Piave
Madame Butterfly	1904	Puccini	Giacoso/Illica
Magic Flute, The	1791	Mozart	Schikaneder
Manon Lescaut	1893	Puccini	Giacoso/Illica
Marriage of Figaro, The	1786	Mozart	Da Ponte
Mask of Orpheus, The	1986	Birtwistle	Zinovieff
Meistersinger, Die	1868	Wagner	Wagner
Midsummer Marriage	1955	Tippett	Duncan
Midsummer Night's Dream, A	1960	Britten	Britten/Pears
Mikado, The	1885	Sullivan	Gilbert
Nabucco	1842	Verdi	Solera
Oedipus Rex	1927	Stravinsky	Cocteau
Orfeo	1607	Monteverdi	Striggio
Orpheus and Eurydice	1762	Gluck	Calzabigi
Orpheus in the Underworld	1858	Offenbach	Cremeux/Halévy
Otello	1887	Verdi	Boito
Pagliacci	1892	Leoncavallo	Leoncavallo
Paradise Lost	1978	Penderecki	Fry
Parsifal	1882	Wagner	Wagner
Pelléas et Mélissande	1902	Debussy	Maeterlinck
Peter Grimes	1945	Britten	Slater
Pilgrim's Progress, The	1951	Vaughan Williams	Vaughan Williams/Wood
Porgy and Bess	1935	Gershwin	Ira Gershwin/Heyward
Prince Igor	1890	Borodin	Borodin
Rake's Progress, The	1951	Stravinsky	Auden/Kallman
Rape of Lucretia, The	1946	Britten	Duncan
Rigoletto	1851	Verdi	Piave
Ring of the Nibelung, The	1876	Wagner	Wagner
Rosenkavalier, Der	1911	Richard Strauss	Hofmannsthal
Rossignol, Le	1914	Stravinsky	Stravinsky/Mitusov
Salomé	1905	Richard Strauss	Wilde/Lachmann
Samson and Delilah	1877	Saint-Saëns	Lemaire
Tales of Hoffmann, The	1881	Offenbach	Barbier
Tannhäuser	1845	Wagner	Wagner
Threepenny Opera, The	1928	Weill	Brecht/Hauptmann
Tosca	1900	Puccini	Giacosa/Illica
Traviata, La	1853	Verdi	Piave
Tristan and Isolde	1865	Wagner	Wagner
Trojans, The (Les Troyens)	1863	Berlioz	Berlioz
Trovatore, Il	1853	Verdi	Cammarano
Turandot	1926	Puccini	Adami/Simoni
Turn of the Screw, The	1954	Britten	Piper
William Tell	1829	Rossini	De Jouy/Bis/Marrast
Wozzeck	1925	Berg	Berg

Opera singers

Name	Dates	Place of birth	Range
Allen, Thomas	1944–	Seaham	Baritone
Ameling, Elly	1938–	Rotterdam	Soprano
Anderson, Marian	1897–1993	Philadelphia	Contralto
Austral, Florence	1894–1968	Richmond, Melbourne	Soprano
Bailey, Norman	1933–	Birmingham	Baritone
Baker, Dame Janet	1933–	Hatfield, Yorkshire	Mezzo-soprano
Barstow, Josephine	1940–	Sheffield	Soprano
Bartoli, Cecilia	1966–	Rome	Mezzo-soprano
Battistini, Mattia	1856–1928	Contigliano, Italy	Baritone
Bergonzi, Carlo	1924–	Polisene, Italy	Tenor
Berganza, Teresa	1935–	Madrid	Mezzo-soprano
Björling, Jussi	1911–60	Stora Tuna, Sweden	Tenor
Borgatti, Giuseppe	1871–1950	Cento, Italy	Tenor
Borgioli, Dino	1891–1960	Florence	Tenor
Bowman, James	1941–	Oxford	Counter-tenor
Bronhill, June	1929–2005	Broken Hill, New South Wales	Soprano
Butt, Dame Clara	1872–1936	Southwick, Sussex	Contralto
Caballé, Montserrat	1933–	Barcelona	Soprano
Callas, Maria (Maria Kalogeropoulos)	1923–77	New York	Soprano
Carreras, José	1946–	Barcelona	Tenor
Caruso, Enrico	1873–1921	Naples	Tenor
Chaliapin, Fyodor	1873–1938	Kazan, Russia	Bass
Deller, Alfred	1912–79	Margate	Counter-tenor
De Los Angeles, Victoria	1923–2005	Barcelona	Soprano
Domingo, Plácido	1941–	Madrid	Tenor
Evans, Sir Geraint	1922–92	Pontypridd, S Wales	Baritone
Ewing, Maria	1950–	Detroit	Mezzo-soprano
Farrar, Geraldine	1882–1967	Ridgefield, Connecticut	Soprano
Ferrier, Kathleen	1912–53	Higher Walton, Lancashire	Contralto
Fischer-Dieskau, Dietrich	1925–	Berlin	Baritone
Flagstad, Kirsten	1895–1962	Hamar, Norway	Soprano
Forrester, Maureen	1930–	Montreal	Contralto
Freni, Mirella	1936–	Modena, Italy	Soprano
Garrett, Lesley	1955–	Doncaster	Soprano
Gedda, Nicolai	1925–	Stockholm	Tenor
Gigli, Beniamino	1890–1957	Recanati, Italy	Tenor
Gobi, Tito	1913–84	Bassano del Grappa, Italy	Baritone
Hendricks, Barbara	1948–	Stephens, Arizona	Soprano
Hotter, Hans	1909–2003	Offenbach-am-Main, Germany	Bass-baritone
Kollo, René	1937–	Berlin	Tenor
Kraus, Alfredo	1927–99	Las Palmas	Tenor
Lehmann, Lotte	1888–1976	Perleberg, Germany	Soprano
Lind, Jenny	1820–87	Stockholm	Soprano
Ludwig, Christa	1924–	Berlin	Mezzo-soprano
Luxon, Benjamin	1937–	Camborne, Cornwall	Baritone
Martinelli, Giovanni	1885–1969	Montagnana, Italy	Tenor
McCormack, John	1884–1945	Athlone, Ireland	Tenor
Melba, Dame Nellie	1861–1931	Richmond, nr Melbourne	Soprano
Melchoir, Lauritz	1890–1973	Copenhagen, Denmark	Tenor
Merrill, Robert	1919–2004	New York City	Baritone
Migenes-Johnson Julia	1945–	New York	Soprano
Milanov, Zinka	1906–89	Zagreb	Soprano
Nilsson, Birgit	1918–2005	Karup, Sweden	Soprano
Norman, Jessye	1945–	Augusta, Georgia	Soprano
Patti, Adelina	1843–1919	Madrid	Soprano
Pavarotti, Luciano	1935–	Modena, Italy	Tenor
Pears, Sir Peter	1910–86	Farnham, Surrey	Tenor
Peerce, Jan	1904–84	New York City	Tenor
Peters, Roberta	1930–	New York City	Soprano
Pinza, Ezio	1892–1957	Rome	Bass
Pons, Lily	1898–1976	Nr Cannes, France	Soprano
Ponselle, Rosa	1897–1981	Meriden, Connecticut	Soprano
Popp, Lucia	1939–93	Lihorska, Czechoslovakia	Soprano
Prey, Hermann	1929–98	Berlin	Baritone
Price, Leontyne	1927–	Laurel, Mississippi	Soprano
Schumann, Elisabeth	1885–1952	Merseburg, Germany	Soprano
Schwarzkopf, Dame Elisabeth	1915–2006	Janotschin, nr Poznań	Soprano
Scotto, Renata	1933–	Savona, Italy	Soprano
Shirley-Quirk, John	1931–	Liverpool	Baritone
Sills, Beverly	1929–	New York City	Soprano
Söderström, Elisabeth	1927–	Stockholm	Soprano
Stratas, Teresa	1938–	Toronto	Soprano
Studer, Cheryl	1955–	Midland, Michigan	Soprano
Sutherland, Dame Joan	1926–	Sydney	Soprano
Tauber, Richard	1892–1948	Linz	Tenor
Tear, Robert	1939–	Barry, Glamorgan	Tenor
Tebaldi, Renata	1922–2004	Pesaro, Italy	Soprano
Te Kanawa, Dame Kiri	1944–	Gisborne, New Zealand	Soprano

Opera singers (continued)

Name	Dates	Place of birth	Range	Name	Dates	Place of birth	Range
Terfel, Bryn	1965–	Pant-glas, N Wales	Bass-baritone	Turner, Dame Eva	1892–1990	Oldham	Soprano
Tetrazzini, Luisa	1871–1938	Milan	Soprano	Van Dam, José	1940–	Brussels	Baritone
Teyte, Dame Maggie	1888–1976	Wolverhampton	Soprano	Vickers, Jon	1926–	Prince Albert, Saskatchewan	Tenor
Tucker, Richard	1913–75	New York City	Tenor	Warren, Leonard	1911–60	New York City	Baritone

Jazz personalities

Name	Dates	Place of birth	Instrument
Armatrading, Joan	1950–	Basseterre, St Kitts	Vocal
Armstrong, Louis	1900–71	New Orleans	Trumpet, cornet, vocal
Baker, Chet	1929–88	Yale, Oklahoma	Trumpet, flugelhorn, vocal
Barber, Chris	1930–	Hertfordshire	Trombone, bass trumpet, vocal
Basie, William 'Count'	1904–84	Red Bank, New Jersey	Piano, organ
Bechet, Sidney	1897–1959	New Orleans	Soprano, tenor, and bass saxophones, clarinet, piano
Beiderbecke, Bix	1903–31	Davenport, Iowa	Cornet
Blakey, Art	1919–90	Pittsburgh	Drums
Bley, Carla	1938–	Oakland, California	Piano
Braxton, Anthony	1945–	Chicago	Alto saxophone, clarinet, flute
Brubeck, Dave	1920–	Concord, California	Piano
Calloway, Cab	1907–94	New York	Vocal
Charles, Ray	1930–2004	Albany	Vocal, piano
Cherry, Don	1936–95	Oklahoma City	Trumpet, flute
Christian, Charlie	1916–42	Dallas	Guitar
Clark, Kenny	1914–85	Pittsburgh	Drums
Coleman, Ornette	1930–	Fort Worth	Alto and soprano saxophones, vocal
Coltrane, John	1926–67	Hamlet, North Carolina	Soprano, alto, and tenor saxophones, flute
Corea, Chick	1941–	Chelsea (US)	Piano, keyboards
Dankworth, John	1927–	London	Alto saxophone
Davis, Miles	1926–91	Alton, Illinois	Trumpet
Desmond, Paul	1924–77	San Francisco	Alto saxophone
Dolphy, Eric	1928–64	Los Angeles	Flute, alto saxophone, bass clarinet, clarinet
Eldridge, Roy	1911–89	Pittsburgh	Trumpet
Ellington, Duke	1899–1974	Washington	Piano
Evans, Bill	1929–80	Plainfield, New Jersey	Piano
Evans, Gil (Ian Ernest Gilmore Green)	1912–88	Toronto	Piano
Fitzgerald, Ella	1918–96	Newport News, Virginia	Vocal
Gaillard, Slim	1916–91	Detroit	Vocal
Garbarek, Jan	1947–	Mysen, Norway	Soprano, tenor, and bass saxophones, flute
Garner, Errol	1923–77	Pittsburgh	Piano
Getz, Stan	1927–91	Philadelphia	Soprano, tenor, and baritone saxophones
Gillespie, Dizzy	1917–93	Cheraw, South Carolina	Trumpet, piano, vocal
Goodman, Benny	1909–86	Chicago	Clarinet
Gordon, Dexter	1923–89	Los Angeles	Soprano and tenor saxophones
Grappelli, Stephane	1908–97	Paris	Violin
Hamilton, Chico	1921–	Los Angeles	Drums
Hamilton, Scott	1954–	Providence, Rhode Island	Tenor saxophone
Hampton, Lionel	1908–2002	Louisville, Kentucky	Vibraphone
Hancock, Herbie	1940–	Chicago	Piano
Hawkins, Coleman	1904–69	Saint Joseph, Missouri	Tenor saxophone, vocal
Herman, Woody	1913–87	Milwaukee	Alto saxophone, clarinet, vocal
Hines, Earl	1903–83	Duquesne, Pennsylvania	Piano, vocal

Name	Dates	Place of birth	Instrument
Hodges, Johnny	1906–70	Cambridge, Massachusetts	Soprano and alto saxophone
Holland, Jools (Julian Miles Holland)	1958–	London	Piano, keyboard, vocal
Holliday, Billie	1915–59	Baltimore	Vocal
Ibrahim, Abdullah (Dollar Brand)	1934–	Cape Town	Piano
Jackson, Milt	1923–99	Detroit	Vibraphone
Jarrett, Keith	1945–	Allentown, Pennsylvania	Piano, organ, soprano saxophone
Johnson, J J	1924–2001	Indianapolis	Trombone
Jones, Elvin	1927–2004	Pontiac, Michigan	Drums
Kenton, Stan	1912–79	Wichita, Kansas	Piano, vocal
Konitz, Lee	1927–	Chicago	Soprano and alto saxophones
Lacy, Steve	1934–2004	New York	Soprano saxophone
Lyttelton, Humphrey	1921–	Windsor, Berkshire	Trumpet, cornet, clarinet
Marsalis, Branford	1960–	Breaux Bridge, Louisiana	Soprano and tenor saxophone
Marsalis, Wynton	1961–	New Orleans	Trumpet
McLaughlin, John	1942–	Yorkshire	Guitar
Merrill, Helen	1930–	New York	Vocal
Metheny, Pat	1954–	Lee's Summit, Missouri	Guitar
Mingus, Charles	1922–79	Nogales, Arizona	Double bass, piano
Monk, Thelonious	1917–82	Rocky Mount, North Carolina	Piano
Montgomery, Wes	1925–68	Indianapolis	Guitar, bass guitar
Morton, Jelly Roll (Frederick LaMenthe)	1885–1941	Gulfport, Louisiana	Piano
Mulligan, Gerry	1927–96	New York	Soprano and baritone saxophone, piano
Navarro, Theodore 'Fats'	1923–50	Key West, Florida	Trumpet
O'Day, Anita	1919–2006	Chicago	Vocal
Oliver, King	1885–1938	Abend, Louisiana	Cornet, trumpet
Parker, Charlie	1920–55	Kansas City	Alto and tenor saxophones
Pepper, Art	1925–82	Gardena, California	Alto and tenor saxophones, clarinet
Peterson, Oscar	1925–	Montreal	Piano
Pettiford, Oscar	1922–60	Okmulgee, Oklahoma	Double bass, cello
Pine, Courtney	1964–	London	Soprano saxophone, bass clarinet
Powell, Bud	1924–66	New York	Piano
Rheinhardt, Django	1910–53	Liverchies, Belgium	Guitar
Rich, Buddy	1917–87	New York	Drums, vocal
Roach, Max	1924–	New York	Drums
Rollins, Sonny	1929–	New York	Soprano and tenor saxophones
Shaw, Artie	1910–2004	New York	Clarinet
Shepp, Archie	1937–	Fort Lauderdale, Florida	Soprano, alto, and tenor saxophones
Sheppard, Andy	1957–	Bristol	Tenor and soprano saxophones
Shorter, Wayne	1933–	Newark, New Jersey	Soprano and tenor saxophones
Simone, Nina	1933–2003	North Carolina	Vocal
Smith, Bessie	1895–1937	Chattanooga, Tennessee	Vocal
Smith, Tommy	1967–	Luton	Tenor saxophone
Solal, Martial	1927–	Algiers	Piano
Surman, John	1944–	Tavistock	Soprano and baritone saxophones, bass clarinet, piano
Tatum, Art	1910–56	Toledo, Ohio	Piano
Taylor, Cecil	1933–	New York	Piano, vocal
Taylor, James	1964–	Rochester, Kent	Organ, clarinet
Terry, Clark	1920–	St Louis	Trumpet, flugelhorn
Thielemans, Jean-Baptiste 'Toots'	1922–	Brussels	Harmonica
Thompson, Barbara	1944–	Oxford	Alto, tenor, and soprano saxophones, flute
Tracey, Stan	1926–	London	Piano
Tristano, Lennie	1919–78	Chicago	Piano
Tyner, McCoy	1938–	Philadelphia	Piano, flute
Vaughan, Sarah	1924–90	Newark, New Jersey	Vocal
Walker, T-Bone	1910–75	Linden, New Jersey	Guitar
Waller, Thomas 'Fats'	1904–43	New York	Piano, organ, vocal

ARTS AND CULTURE

Jazz personalities (continued)

Name	Dates	Place of birth	Instrument
Washington, Dinah	1924–63	Alabama	Vocal
Washington, Grover	1943–99	Buffalo	Saxophones
Weber, Eberhard	1940–	Stuttgart	Double bass
Webster, Ben	1909–73	Missouri	Tenor saxophone
Williams, Tony	1945–	Chicago	Drums
Young, Lester	1909–59	Woodville, Mississippi	Tenor saxophone

Classic pop and rock groups/singers

*Group members are given for the best-known line-up.

Name	Country of origin	Group members*	Period	Major hits
ABBA	Sweden	Benny Andersson (keyboards, vocals) Björn Ulvaeus (guitar, vocals) Agnetha Fältskog (vocals) Anni-Frid Lyngstad (vocals)	1970s–80s	*Waterloo; Mamma Mia; Fernando; Knowing Me Knowing You; Dancing Queen; The Name of the Game; Take a Chance on Me; I Have a Dream; Super Trouper; The Winner Takes it All*
Adams, Bryan	Canada	Bryan Adams (vocals, guitar) Keith Scott (guitar, vocals) Dave Taylor (bass) Mickey Curry (drums) Tommy Mandel (keyboards) Danny Cummings (percussion)	1980s–present	*Thought I'd Died and Gone to Heaven; Everything I Do (I Do It For You); Have You Ever Really Loved a Woman; Please Forgive Me; The Only Thing That Looks Good On Me Is You; Cloud Number Nine; Spirit; When You're gone*
Aerosmith	USA	Steven Tyler (vocals) Joe Perry (guitar) Tom Hamilton (bass) Joey Kramer (drums) Brad Whitford (guitar)	1970s–present	Albums: *Get Your Wings; Toys in the Attic; Rocks; Pump; Get A Grip; Nine Lives; Just Push Play; Honkin' on Bobo; Rockin' the Joint*
Animals, The	Britain	Eric Burden (vocals) Alan Price (keyboards) Hilton Valentine ((guitar) Chas Chandler (bass) John Steel (drums)	1960s	*House of the Rising Sun; I'm Crying; Don't Let Me Be Misunderstood; Bring it on Home to Me; We've Gotta Get Out of This Place; It's My Life; Don't Bring Me Down*
Band, The	Canada	Robbie Robertson (guitar, vocals) Richard Manuel (piano, vocals) Garth Hudson (organ) Rick Danko (bass, vocals) Levon Helm (drums, vocals)	1960s–70s	*Up on Cripple Creek; Rag Mama Rag; Stage Fright.* Albums: *The Band; Cahoots; Before the Flood; The Last Waltz*
Beach Boys, The	USA	Brian Wilson (bass, keyboards, vocals) Mike Love (vocals) Carl Wilson (guitar, vocals) Al Jardine (guitar, vocals) Denis Wilson (drums, vocals)	1960s–70s	*Get Around; When I Grow Up; Do You Wanna Dance; Help Me Rhonda; California Girls; Barbara Ann; Surfin' USA; God Only Knows; Wouldn't It Be Nice; Good Vibrations; Then I Kissed Her; Heroes and Villains; Darlin'; Do It Again; I Can Hear Music; Rock and Roll Music; Lady Lynda*

Name	Country of origin	Group members*	Period	Major hits
Beatles, The	Britain	John Lennon (vocals, rhythm guitar) Paul McCartney (vocals, bass) George Harrison (vocals, lead guitar) Ringo Starr (vocals, drums)	1960s	Please Please Me; From Me to You; She Loves You; I Want to Hold Your Hand; Can't Buy Me Love; A Hard Day's Night; I Feel Fine; Eight Days A Week; Ticket to Ride; Help!; Yesterday; Day Tripper; We Can it Out; Paperback Writer; Yellow Submarine; Eleanor Rigby; Penny Lane; Strawberry Fields Forever; All You Need is Love; Hello Goodbye; Lady Madonna; Hey Jude; Get Back; The Ballad of John and Yoko; Let it Albums: Sergeant Pepper's Lonely Hearts Club Band; issue of previously unreleased recordings, 1995
Bee Gees, The	Britain	Barry Gibb (vocals, guitar) Maurice Gibb (vocals, bass) Robin Gibb (vocals)	1950s–present	To Love Somebody; I've Gotta Get a Message to You; How Deep is Your Love; Stayin' Alive; Saturday Night Fever; Tragedy; You Win Again
Berry, Chuck	USA		1950s–90s	Maybellene; Roll over Beethoven; School Day; Rock and Roll Music; Sweet Little Sixteen; Johnny Be Good; Carol; No Particular Place to Go; My Ding-A-Ling
Black Sabbath	Britain	Tony Iommi (guitar) 'Geezer' Butler (bass) Ozzy Osbourne (vocals) Bill Ward (drums)	1970s	Paranoid; Never Say Die; Neon Knights. Albums: Paranoid; Black Sabbath Vol. 4; Sabbath Bloody Sabbath; Master of Reality; Sabotage; Technical Ecstasy; Heaven and Hell; Mob Rules; Born Again
Blige, Mary J	USA		1990s–present	Albums: What's the 411?; My Life; Share My World; No More Drama; Love and Life; The Breakthrough; Reflections
Blondie	USA	Debbie Harry (vocals) Chris Stein (guitar) Jimmy Destri (keyboards) Gary Valentine (bass) Clem Burke (drums)	1970s–90s	Denis; (I'm Always Touched by Your) Presence Dear; Picture This; Hanging on the Telephone; Heart of Glass Sunday Girl; Dreaming; Atomic; Call Me; The Tide is High; Rapture; French Kissin' in the USA; Maria
Blur	Britain	Damon Albarn (vocals) Graham Coxon (guitar) Alex James (bass) Dave Rowntree (drums)	1990s–present	Albums: Leisure; Modern Life is Rubbish; Parklife; The Great Escape; Blur; 13; Think Tank
Bowie, David	Britain		1970s–present	Space Oddity; Aladdin Sane; The Jean Genie; Time; Sound and Vision; Ashes to Ashes; Fashion; Let's Dance; China Girl; Modern Love; Absolute Beginners; Thursday's Child
Boyzone	Ireland	Ronan Keating (vocals) Stephen Gately (vocals) Shane Lynch (vocals) Keith Duffy (vocals) Michael Graham (vocals)	1990s	Love Me For a Reason; Key To My Life; Father and Son; Words; Isn't It A Wonder; Picture of You; Baby Can I Hold You; All That I Need; No Matter What; When The Going Gets Tough; You Needed Me. Album: Ballads: The Love Songs; Said and Done; A Different Beat; Where We Belong

ARTS AND CULTURE

Classic pop and rock groups/singers (continued)

Name	Country of origin	Group members*	Period	Major hits
Brown, James	USA		1950s–2006	*Papa's Got a Brand New Bag; I Got You (I Feel Good); It's a Man's Man's Man's World; I Got the Feelin'; Say it; Loud – I'm Back and I'm Proud; Give it Up or Turn it Loose; Mother Popcorn; Get Up; I Feel Like Being a Sex Machine; Super Bad; Get on the Good Foot; King of the Mountain*
Bush, Kate	Britain		1980s–	*Wuthering Heights; The Man With the Child in His Eyes; Babooshka; December Will Be Magic Again; Running Up That Hill; King of the Mountain*
Byrds, The	USA	Roger (Jim) McGuinn (vocals, guitar) Gene Clark (vocals, percussion) David Crosby (vocals, guitar) Chris Hillman (vocals, bass) Michael Clarke (drums)	1960s–70s	*Mr Tambourine Man; All I Really Want to Do; Turn! Turn! Turn!; Eight Miles High; Chestnut Mare*
Carey, Mariah	USA		1990s– present	Albums: *Emotions; Music Box; Merry Christmas; Daydream; Butterfly; Charmbracelet; The Emancipation of Mimi*
Carpenters, The	USA	Karen Carpenter (vocals, drums) Richard Carpenter (vocals, keyboards)	1970s–80s	*Close to You; We've Only Just Begun; For All We Know; Rainy Days and Mondays; Hurting Each Other; Goodbye to Love; Sing; Please Mr Postman; Only Yesterday; Calling Occupants of Interplanetary Craft*
Chemical Brothers	Britain	Ed Simons (electronics) Tom Rowlands (electronics)	1990s– present	Albums: *Exit Planet Dust; Dig Your Own Hole; Brothers Gonna Work It Out; Surrender; Push the Button*
Clapton, Eric	Britain		1960s– present	*Layla; I Shot the Sheriff; Lay Down Sally; Wonderful Tonight; Forever Man; Cocaine; Knocking on Heaven's Door; Behind the Mask; Tears in Heaven*
Clash, The	Britain	Joe Strummer (vocals, guitar) Mick Jones (guitar) Paul Simonon (bass) Nicky 'Topper' Headon (drums)	1970s–80s	*Tommy Gun; Bankrobber; Rock the Casbah; Should I Stay or Should I Go?*
Cochran, Eddie	USA		1950s	*Sittin' in the Balcony; Summertime Blues; C'Mon Everybody; Somethin' Else; Three Steps to Heaven; Hallelujah I Love Her So*
Coldplay	Britain	Chris Martin (vocals, guitar) Jonny Buckland (guitar) Guy Berryman (guitar) Will Champion (drums)	1990s– present	Albums: *Parachutes; A Rush of Blood to the Head; X & Y*
Collins, Phil	Britain		1980s– present	*In the Air Tonight; I Missed Again; You Can't Hurry Love; Against All Odds; Easy Lover; Sussudio; One More Night; Separate Lives; Take Me Home; Groovy Kind of Love; Two Hearts; Another Day in Paradise; I Wish it Would Rain; True Colors; Testify*
Commodores, The	USA	Lionel Richie (vocals, keyboards) William King (trumpet) Thomas McClary (lead guitar) Milan Williams (keyboards, trombone, guitar, drums) Ronald LaPread (bass, trumpet) Walter (Clyde) Orange (vocals, drums)	1970s–80s	*Machine Gun; Slippery When Wet; Sweet Love; Just To Be Close To You; Easy; Brickhouse; Three Times A Lady; Sail On; Still; Nightshift*

Name	Country of origin	Group members*	Period	Major hits
Corrs, The	Ireland	Andrea Corr (vocals) Caroline Corr (bodhrán, drums) Jim Corr (keyboards, guitar) Sharon Corr (violin)	1990s–present	Albums: *Forgiven, Not Forgotten; Talk On Corners; In Blue; Borrowed Heaven Home*
Cream	Britain	Eric Clapton (vocals, guitar) Jack Bruce (vocals, bass) Ginger Baker (drums)	1960s	*I Feel Free; Strange Brew; Sunshine of Your Love; White Room; Badge*
Culture Club	Britain	"Boy" George (O'Dowd) (vocals) Roy Hay (guitar, keyboards) Mikey Craig (bass) Jon Moss (drums)	1980s–1990s	*Do You Really Want To Hurt Me?; Time; Church of the Poison Mind; Karma Chameleon; Victims; It's A Miracle; Miss You Blind; Move Away*
Cure, The	Britain	Robert Smith (vocals) Michael Dempsey (bass guitar, vocals) Laurence (Lol) Tolhurst (drums)	1970s–present	Albums: *Boys Don't Cry; Faith; Pornography; Kiss Me Kiss Me Kiss Me; Wish*
Diamond, Neil	USA		1960s–present	*Cherry Cherry; I Got the Feelin'; You Got to Me; Girl You'll Be A Woman Soon; Sweet Caroline; Holly Holy; Cracklin' Rosie; I Am ... I Said; Stones; Song Sung Blue; Longfellow Serenade; Beautiful Noise; You Don't Bring Me Flowers; Forever in Blue Jeans; Love on the Rocks*
Diddley, Bo	USA		1950s–60s	*Bo Diddley; I'm a Man; Who Do You Love; Road Runner; Hey Good Lookin'*
Dion, Celine	Canada		1990s–present	*Falling Into You; It's All Coming Back to Me Now; Our Love Will Go On*
Dire Straits	Britain	Mark Knopfler (guitar, vocals) John Illsley (bass) Hal Lindes (guitar) Pick Withers (drums) Alan Clark (keyboards)	1970s–80s	*Sultans of Swing; Romeo and Juliet; Telegraph Road; Private Investigations; Money for Nothing; Walk of Life*
Doors, The	USA	Jim Morrison (vocals) Ray Manzarek (keyboards) Robbie Krieger (guitar) John Densmore (drums)	1960s–70s	*Light My Fire; Love Me Two Times; Hello I Love You; Touch Me; Love Her Madly; Riders on the Storm*
Duran Duran	Britain	Simon Le Bon (vocals) Nick Rhodes (piano) Andy Taylor (guitar) John Taylor (bass) Roger Taylor (drums)	1980s–90s	*Girls on Film; Hungry Like a Wolf; Say a Prayer; Is There Something I Should Know?; The Reflex; Wild Boys; A View To A Kill; Notorious; Reach Up For the Sunrise*
Dylan, Bob	USA		1960s–present	*Blowin' in the Wind; The Times They Are a-Changin'; Subterranean Homesick Blues; Like a Rollin' Stone; Positively 4th Street; Can You Please Crawl Out Your Window; Rainy Day Woman; Just Like a Woman; Lay Lady Lay; Knockin' on Heaven's Door; Baby*
Eagles, The	USA	Glenn Frey (guitar, vocals) Bernie Leadon (guitar, vocals) Randy Meisner (bass, vocals) Don Henley (drums, vocals)	1970s	*Take it Easy; Witchy Woman; The Best of My Love; One of These Nights; Lyin' Eyes; Hotel California; New Kid in Town; Life in the Fast Lane; Life's Been Good; Heartache Tonight*
Eurythmics, The	Britain	Annie Lennox (vocals) Dave Stewart (keyboards, guitar)	1980s	*Sweet Dreams; Love is a Stranger; Right By Your Side; Here Comes The Rain Again; Who's That Girl; Would I Lie To You? There Must Be An Angel; Sisters Are Doing It For Themselves; It's Alright; Thorn In My Side*

ARTS AND CULTURE

Classic pop and rock groups/singers (continued)

Name	Country of origin	Group members*	Period	Major hits
Everly Brothers, The	USA	Don Everly (vocals, guitar) Phil Everly (vocals, guitar)	1950s–60s	Bye Bye Love; Wake Up Little Susie; All I Have to Do is Dream; Devoted to You; Bird Dog; Problems; A Message to Mary; I Kissed You; Let It Be Me; Cathy's Clown; When Will I Be Loved; Like Strangers; Walk Right Back; Ebony Eyes; Temptation; Crying in the Rain; That's Old-Fashioned; Love is Strange
Fleetwood Mac	UK/USA	Mick Fleetwood (drums) John McVie (bass) Christine McVie (keyboards, vocals) Lindsey Buckingham (guitars, vocals) Stevie Nicks (vocals)	1960s–present	Albatross; Man of the World; Oh Well; The Green Manalishi; Over My Head; Go Your Own Way; Don't Stop; Dreams; You Make Loving Fun; Tusk; Sara; Trouble; Hold Me; Oh Diane; Big Love; Little Lies; Everywhere; Say You Will
Four Tops, The	USA	Levi Stubbs (vocals) Renaldo 'Obie' Benson (vocals) Abdul 'Duke' Fakir (vocals) Lawrence Paynton (vocals)	1960s–80s	I Can't Help Myself; It's the Same Old Song; Loving You is Sweeter Than Ever; Reach Out I'll Be There; Bernadette; Seven Rooms of Gloom; Walk Away Renée; If I Were A Carpenter; What is a Man; Do What You Gotta Do; I Can't Help Myself; River Deep Mountain High; So Deep Within You; Ain't No Woman; When She was My Girl; Don't Walk Away; Loco in Acapulco
Franklin, Aretha	USA		1960s–80s	I Never Loved a Man; Do Right Woman – Do Right Man; Respect; Baby I Love You; Natural Woman; Since You've Been Gone; I Say A Little Prayer; The House That Jack Built; Chain of Fools; Don't Play That Song; Bridge Over Troubled Water; A Brand New Me; Spanish Harlem; Rock Steady; Who's Zoomin' Who; Sisters Are Doing it For Themselves; I Knew You Were Waiting
Gabriel, Peter	Britain		1980s	Games Without Frontiers; Sledge-hammer; In Your Eyes; Don't Give Up
Gaye, Marvin	USA		1960s–80s	How Sweet It Is; Ain't That Peculiar; It Takes Two; You're All I Need To Get By; I Heard It Through The Grapevine; Too Busy Thinking About My Baby; The Onion Song; Abraham; Martin and John; What's Going On? Mercy Mercy Mercy; Let's Get It On; You Are Everything; Sexual Healing
Genesis	Britain	Tony Banks (keyboards) Mike Rutherford (guitars) Phil Collins (drums, vocals)	1960s–present	Follow You; Follow Me; Turn It On Again; Paperlate; Mama; That's All; In Too Deep; Throwing It All Away; Land of Confusion; Tonight Tonight Tonight
Grateful Dead, The	USA	Jerry Garcia (lead guitar) Bob Weir (rhythm guitar) Ron 'Pigpen' McKernan (organ, harmonica) Phil Lesh (bass) Bill Kreutzmann (drums)	1960s–90s	Touch of Grey. Albums: Grateful Dead; Workingman's Dead; Europe '72; Wake of the Flood; Blues for Allah; Terrapin Station; Dead Set; In the Dark

Name	Country of origin	Group members*	Period	Major hits
Guns N' Roses	USA	Axl Rose (vocals) Slash (lead guitar) Izzy Stradlin (lead guitar) Duff McKagen (bass guitar) Steven Adler (drums)	1970–present	Albums: *Appetite for Destruction; G N' R Lies; Use Your Illusion; Use Your Illusion II*
Haley, Bill, and his Comets	USA	Bill Haley (vocals, guitar) Frannie Beecher (lead guitar) Al Pompilli (bass) Rudi Pompilli (saxophone) Ralph Jones (drums)	1950s	*Shake; Rattle and Roll; Rock Around the Clock; Rock-a-Beatin' Boogie; See You Later Alligator; The Saints Rock'n'Roll; Rockin' Through The Rye; Razzle Dazzle; Rip it Up*
Hendrix, Jimi	USA		1960s	*Hey Joe; Purple Haze; The Wind Cries Mary; Burning of the Midnight Lamp; Axis: Bold As Love; All Along The Watchtower; Voodoo Chile*
Hollies, The	Britain	Allan Clarke (vocals) Graham Nash (guitar) Tony Hicks (guitar) Erick Haydock (bass) Bobby Elliott (drums)	1960s–70s	*Just Like Me; Searchin'; Stay; Here I Go Again; We're Through; Yes I Will; I'm Alive; Look Through Any Window; I Can't Let Go; Bus Stop; Stop Stop Stop; On a Carousel; Carrie-Anne; Jennifer Eccles; Listen To Me; Sorry Suza; He Ain't Heavy He's My Brother; I Can't Tell the Bottom From the Top; The Air That I Breathe*
Holly, Buddy, and the Crickets	USA	Buddy Holly (vocals, guitar) Sonny Curtis (guitar) Joe B. Mauldin (bass) Jerry Allison (drums)	1950s	*That'll Be The Day; Peggy Sue; Oh Boy! ; Listen to Me; Maybe Baby*
Houston, Whitney	USA		1980s	*Saving All My Love for You; How Will I Know; Greatest Love of All; I Wanna Dance With Somebody; Didn't We Almost Have It All; So Emotional; One Moment in Time; I'm Your Baby Tonight; I'll Always Love You; I Have Nothing; It's Not Right, But It's OK; My Love Is Your Love*
Iron Maiden	Britain	Bruce Dickinson (vocals) Dave Murray (lead guitar) Dennis Stratton (lead guitar) Steve Harris (bass guitar) Nicko McBrain (drums)	1970s–present	Albums: *Number of the Beast; Piece of Mind; Seventh Son of a Seventh Son; No Prayer for the Dying; Fear of the Dark; Virtual XI; Brave New World; Beast over Hammersmith*
Jackson, Janet	USA		1980s–present	*Say You Do; What Have You Done For Me Lately; Miss You Much; Whoops Now; Again; Runaway; Twenty Foreplay; Together Again*
Jackson, Michael	USA		1970s–present	*Don't Stop 'Til You Get Enough; Rock With You; She's Out of My Life; One Day in Your Life; The Girl is Mine; Billie Jean; Beat It; Wanna Be Startin' Somethin'; Say Say Say; Thriller; PYT; I Just Can't Stop Loving You; Bad; The Way You Make Me Feel; Dirty Diana; Another Part of Me; Smooth Criminal; Leave Me Alone; Earth Song; Blood on the Dance Floor*
Jacksons, The	USA	Jackie Jackson (vocals) Tito Jackson (vocals) Jermaine Jackson (vocals) Marlon Jackson (vocals) Michael Jackson (vocals)	1960s–80s	*I Want You Back; ABC; The Love You Save; I'll Be There; Mama's Pearl; Never Can Say Goodbye; Dancing Machine; Enjoy Yourself; Show You the Way to Go; Blame It on the Boogie; Shake Your Body; Can You Feel It; State of Shock; Torture*

Classic pop and rock groups/singers (continued)

Name	Country of origin	Group members*	Period	Major hits
Jam, The	Britain	Paul Weller (vocals, bass) Bruce Foxton (guitar) Rick Buckler (drums)	1970s–80s	*In the City; All Around the World; Down in the Tube Station at Midnight; Eton Rifles; Going Underground; Start; Funeral Pyre; Absolute Beginners; Town Called Malice; Just Who is the Five O'Clock Hero?; The Bitterest Pill; Beat Surrender*
Jarre, Jean-Michel	France		1970s–present	Albums: *Oxygène; Equinoxe; Magnetic Fields; Rendezvous; Revolutions*
Jefferson Airplane /Starship	USA	Grace Slick (vocals) Marty Balin (vocals) Paul Kantner (guitar) Jorma Kaukonen (guitar) Jack Casady (bass guitar) Spencer Dryden (drums)	1960s–70s	*White Rabbit; Miracles; With Your Love; Count on Me; Runaway; Jane; Hearts*
Jethro Tull	Britain	Ian Anderson (vocals, flute) Mick Abrahams (guitar) Glen Connick (bass) Clive Bunker (drums)	1960s–present	*Living in the Past; The Witch's Promise/Teacher; Life Is A Long Song; Bungle in the Jungle; Thick as a Brick; Too Old To Rock and Roll – Too Young to Die*
Joel, Billy	USA		1970s–present	*New York State of Mind; Say Hollywood; Just The Way You Are; Goodbye to She's Always a Woman; My Life; It's Still Rock'n'Roll to Me; Tell Her About It; Uptown Girl; An Innocent Man; The Longest Time; We Didn't Start the Fire; The River of Dreams*
John, Elton	Britain		1970s–present	*Your Song; Rocket Man; Crocodile Rock Daniel; Saturday Night's Alright for Fighting; Goodbye Yellow Brick Road; Candle in the Wind; Don't Let the Sun Go Down on Me; Don't Go Breaking My Heart; Sorry Seems to be the Hardest Word; Song for Guy; Blue Eyes; I Guess That's Why They Call It The Blues; I'm Still Standing; Sad Songs; Nikita; Sacrifice; Candle in the Wind 1997; Written in the Stars*
Jones, Tom	Britain		1960s–present	*It's Not Unusual; What's New; Pussycat? Green Green Grass of Home Home; Detroit City; Funny Familiar Forgotten Feelings; I'll Never Fall in Love Again; I'm Coming Home; Deliah; Help Yourself; Love Me Tonight; Daughter of Darkness; A Boy From Nowhere; Kiss*
King, B.B.	USA		1950s–80s	*Three O'Clock Blues; You Didn't Want Me; The Thrill is Gone; Hold On*
King, Carole	USA		1960s–80s	*It Might As Well Rain Until September; It's Too Late/I Feel the Earth; Sweet Seasons; Jazzman; Nightingale*
Kinks, The	Britain	Ray Davies (vocals, guitar) Dave Davies (vocals, guitar) Pete Quaire (bass) Mick Avory (drums)	1960s–80s	*You Really Got Me; All Day and All of the Night; Tired of Waiting for You; See My Friend; Till the End of the Day; Sunny Afternoon; Dead End Street; Waterloo Sunset; Autumn Almanac; Lola; Come Dancing*

Name	Country of origin	Group members*	Period	Major hits
Knight, Gladys, and the Pips	USA	Gladys Knight (vocals) Merald 'Bubba' Knight (vocals) William Guest (vocals) Edward Patten (vocals)	1960s–80s	*Every Beat of My Heart; Take Me in Your Arms and Love Me; I Heard It Through the Grapevine; Just Walk in My Shoes; Help Me Make It Through the Night; Neither One of Us; Midnight Train to Georgia; I've Got to Use My Imagination; On and On; The Way We Were; Best Thing That Ever Happened To Me; Come Back and Finish What You Started*
Led Zeppelin	Britain	Robert Plant (vocals) Jimmy Page (guitar) John Paul Jones (bass) John Bonham (drums)	1960s–1980s	*Whole Lotta Love; Stairway to Heaven; Black Dog; Kashmir; Dazed and Confused; Delta Blues*
Lennon, John	Britain		1960s–80s	*Give Peace A Chance; Instant Karma; Power to the People; Imagine; Whatever Gets You Through the Night; Dream; Starting Over; Woman; Jealous Guy*
Lewis, Jerry Lee	USA		1950s–present	*Whole Lotta Shakin'; Great Balls of Fire; Breathless; High School Confidential; What'd I Say; Good Golly Miss Molly; Chantilly Lace*
Little Richard	USA		1950s–present	*Tutti Frutti; Long Tall Sally; Rip it Up; She's Got It; The Girl Can't Help It; Lucille; Jenny Jenny; Keep a-Knockin'; Good Golly Miss Molly; Baby Face; Bama Lama Bama Loo*
McCartney, Paul	Britain		1970s–present	Songs with Wings: *Another Day; Mary Had a Little Lamb; Hi Hi Hi; My Love; Live and Let Die; Helen Wheels; Jet; Band on the Run; Listen to What The Man Said; Silly Love Songs; Let 'Em In; Mull of Kintyre; With a Little Luck.* McCartney's solo songs: *Wonderful Christmastime; Ebony and Ivory; The Girl Is Mine; Say Say Say; Pipes of Peace; No More Lonely Nights; We All Stand Together; My Brave Face; It's a Fine Line*
Madness	Britain	Graham 'Suggs' McPherson (vocals) Mike Barson (keyboards) Chris Foreman (guitar) Mark Bedford (bass) Lee Thompson (saxophone, vocals) Dan Woodgate (drums) Carl 'Chas Smash' Smyth (horns)	1980s	*One Step Beyond; My Girl; Night Train to Cairo; Baggy Trousers; Embarrassment; Return of the Los Palmas Seven; Grey Day; It Must Be Love; House of Fun; Driving in My Car; Our House; Wings of a Dove; The Sun and the Rain*
Madonna	USA		1980s–present	*Like a Virgin; Material Girl; Holiday; Crazy for You; Angel; True Blue; Papa Don't Preach; Open Your Heart; La Isla Bonita; Who's That Girl; Express Yourself; Like a Prayer; Cherish; Dear Jessie; Vogue; Hanky Panky; Justify My Love; Erotica; Don't Cry For Me, Argentina; Frozen; Beautiful Stranger; American Pie; Music; Die Another Day; Hung Up; Sorry*
Mamas and the Papas, The	USA	John Phillips (vocals) Denny Doherty (vocals) Cass Elliot (vocals) Michelle Gilliam (vocals)	1960s	*California Dreamin'; Monday Monday; I Saw Her Again; Dedicated to the One I Love; San Francisco; Dream a Little Dream of Me*

Classic pop and rock groups/singers (continued)

Name	Country of origin	Group members*	Period	Major hits
Manic Street Preachers	Britain	James Dean Bradfield (vocals, guitar) Nicky Wire (bass) Sean Moore (drums)	1990s–present	Albums: *The Holy Bible; Everything Must Go; This Is My Truth, Tell Me Yours; Know Your Enemy; Lifeblood*
Marley, Bob, and the Wailers	Jamaica	Bob Marley (vocals, guitar) Peter Tosh (vocals, guitar) Bunny Wailer (vocals, percussion) Carlton Barrett (drums) Aston 'Family Man' Barrett (bass)	1970s	*No Woman No Cry; Exodus; Jamming; Is This Love; Satisfy My Soul; Could You Be Loved; Buffalo Soldier*
Mavericks, The	USA	Raul Malo (vocals, guitar) Robert Reynolds (bass) Nick Kane (guitar) Paul Deakin (drums)	1990s	Albums: *From Hell to Paradise; What a Crying Shame; Music For All Occasions; Trampoline*
Michael, George	Britain		1980s–present	*Careless Whisper; I Knew You Were Waiting; I Want Your Sex; Faith; Father Figure; One More Try; Praying for Time; Freedom!; Too Funky; Somebody to Love; Jesus to a Child; Fastlove; Outside; Flawless*
Minogue, Kylie	Australia		1980s–present	*I Should Be So Lucky; Especially For You; Better the Devil you Know; Give Me Just a Little More Time; Can't Get You Out Of My Head; Slow*
Monkees, The	USA	Davy Jones (vocals, guitar) Mike Nesmith (vocals, guitar) Peter Tork (vocals, keyboards, bass guitar) Micky Dolenz (drums)	1960s	*Hey Hey We're the Monkees; Last Train to Clarksville; I'm a Believer; A Little Bit of Me; A Little Bit of You; Alternate Title; Pleasant Valley Sunday; Valleri*
Morrison, Van	Ireland		1960s–present	*Brown Eyed Girl; Blue Money; Wild Night; Jackie Wilson Said; Magic Time*
M People	Britain	Heather Small (voice) Mike Pickering (keyboards) Paul Heard (guitar)	1990s	*One Night in Heaven; Moving On Up; Search For the Hero* Albums: *Elegant Slumming; Bizzare Fruit; Fresco; Testify*
Newman, Randy	USA		1960s–present	*Short People.* Albums: *Little Criminals; Born Again; Guilty: 30 Years of Randy Newman*
Nirvana	USA	Kurt Cobain (vocals, lead guitar) Chris Novoselic (bass guitar) Dave Grohl (drums)	1990s	Albums: *Bleach; Nevermind; Incesticide*
Oasis	Britain	Liam Gallagher (vocals) Noel Gallagher (lead guitar, vocals) Paul 'Bonehead' Arthurs (rhythm, left 1999) Paul 'Guigsy' McGuigan (bass, left 1999) Gem Archer (rhythm, joined 1999) Andy Bell (bass, joined 1999) Alan White (drums)	1990s–present	*Supersonic; Shakermaker; Roll With It; Wonderwall; Don't Look Back In Anger; D'You Know What I Mean; All Around the World* Albums: *Standing on the Shoulders of Giants; Heathen Chemistry; Don't Believe the Truth*
O'Connor, Sinead	Ireland		1990s	*Mandinka; Nothing Compares 2 U; Don't Cry For Me Argentina*
Orbison, Roy	USA		1950s–60s, 1980s	*Pretty Woman; Only the Lonely; Blue Angel; I'm Hurtin'; Running Scared; Cryin'; Dream By; Falling; Blue Bayou; It's Over; Pretty Paper; Too Soon To Know; You Got It*
Orbital	Britain	Phil Hartnoll (electronics) Paul Hartnoll (electronics)	1990s–2004	Albums: *Orbital; Orbital 2; Snivilization; In Sides; The Middle of Nowhere*
Osmonds; The	USA	Alan Osmond (vocals) Wayne Osmond (vocals) Merrill Osmond (vocals) Jay Osmond (vocals) Donny Osmond (vocals)	1970s	*One Bad Apple; Yo-Yo; Down By the Lazy River; Let Me In; I Can't Stop; Love Me for a Reason; The Proud One; Crazy Horses*

Name	Country of origin	Group members*	Period	Major hits
Pet Shop Boys	Britain	Neil Tennant (vocals) Chris Lowe (keyboards)	1970s–present	West End Girls; Suburbia; It's A Sin; Always On My Mind; Absolutely Fabulous; Se A Vida É; I Don't Know What You Want (But I Can't Give It Anymore)
Petty, Tom and the Heartbreakers	USA	Tom Petty (vocals, guitar) Mike Campbell (guitar) Benmont Tench (keyboards) Stan Lynch (drums) Ron Blair (bass)	1970s–present	Albums: Damn The Torpedoes; Southern Accents; Into the Great Wide Open; Wildflowers; She's The One; Echo; The Last DJ; Highway Companion
Pink Floyd	Britain	Roger Waters (vocals, bass) Rick Wright (keyboards) David Gilmour (vocals, guitar) Nick Mason (drums)	1960s–present	Arnold Layne; See Emily Play; Another Brick in the Wall; Not Now John. Albums: The Piper at the Gates of Dawn; A Saucerful of Secrets; Ummagumma; Dark Side of the Moon; Wish You Were Here; Animals; The Wall; The Final Cut
Pitney, Gene	USA		1960s–80s	24 Hours From Tulsa; Something's Gotten Hold of My Heart; Backstage; A Town Without Pity; 24 Sycamore; Maria Elena
Pogues, The	Britain	Shane MacGowan (vocals, guitar) Jem Finer (banjo) James Fearnley (accordian) Spider Stacy (tin whistle) Caitlin O'Riordan (bass) Andrew Ranken (drums)	1980s–present	A Pair of Brown Eyes; Dirty Old Town; The Irish Rover; A Fairytale of New York
Police, The	Britain	Sting (vocals, bass) Andy Summers (vocals, guitar) Stewart Copeland (drums, percussion, vocals)	1970s–80s	Roxanne; Can't Stand Losing You; Message In a Bottle; Walking on the Moon; So Lonely; Don't Stand So Close To Me; Invisible Sun; Every Little Thing She Does is Magic; Every Breath You Take
Presley, Elvis	USA		1950s–70s	Baby Let's Play House; Heartbreak Hotel; Blue Suede Shoes; Hound Dog; I Want You I Need You I Love You; Don't Be Cruel; Love Me Tender; All Shook Up; Teddy Bear; Jailhouse Rock; Don't; Hard-Headed Woman; A Big Hunk of Love; Stuck On You; It's Now or Never; Are You Lonesome Tonight? Surrender; His Latest Flame; Can't Help Falling In Love; Good Luck Charm; She's Not You; Return to Sender; Devil in Disguise; Crying in the Chapel; Suspicious Minds; Don't Cry Daddy; The Wonder of You; I Just Can't Help Believing American Trilogy; In the Ghetto
Pretenders, The	Britain	Chrissie Hynde (vocals) Pete Farndon (bass) James Honeyman-Scott (guitar) Martin Chambers (drums)	1970s–present	Stop Your Sobbing; Brass in Pocket (I'm Special); Talk of the Town; Message of Love; I Go to Sleep; Back on the Chain Gang; Don't Get Me Wrong; Learning to Crawl; Packed. Album: Loose Screw
Prince	USA		1980s–present	Little Red Corvette; 1999; When Doves Cry; Purple Rain; Let's Go Crazy; Kiss; Girls and Boys; Sign of the Times; U Got The Look; Alphabet St; Batdance

ARTS AND CULTURE

Classic pop and rock groups/singers (continued)

Name	Country of origin	Group members*	Period	Major hits
Pulp	Britain	Jarvis Cocker (vocals) Russel Senior (violin, guitar left 1999) Mark Webber (guitar, joined 1999) Steve Mackey (bass) Candida Doyle (keyboards, vocals) Nick Banks (drums)	1980s–present	Disco 2000; Common People; Something Changed; Help The Aged; This Is Hardcore; A Little Soul; Party Hard
Queen	Britain	Freddie Mercury (vocals) Brian May (guitar) John Deacon (bass) Roger Taylor (drums)	1970s–90s	Seven Seas of Rye; Killer Queen; Now I'm Here; Bohemian Rhapsody; You're My Best Friend; Somebody To Love; We Are The Champions; We Will Rock You; Fat Bottomed Girls; Don't Stop Me Now; Crazy Little Thing Called Love; Another One Bites the Dust; Flash; Under Pressure; Radio GaGa; I Want To Break Free; A Kind of Magic; The Great Pretender; I Want It All; Innuendo
Redding, Otis	USA		1960s	I've Been Loving You Too Long; Mr Pitiful; Pain in My Heart; My Girl; Try a Little Tenderness; The Dock of the Bay
Reed, Lou	USA		1970s	Walk on the Wild Side; Soul Man
REM	USA	Michael Stipe (vocals) Peter Buck (guitar) Mike Mills (bass) Bill Berry (drums), left 1997	1980s–present	Radio Free Europe; It's the End of the World As We Know It; The One I Love; Stand; Losing My Religion; The Greenhouse Effect. Albums: In Time; Up; Around the Sun
Richard, Cliff	Britain		1950s–present	Move It; Livin' Lovin' Doll; Mean Streak; Living Doll; A Voice in the Wilderness; Fall In Love With You; Please Don't Tease; Nine Times Out of Ten; I Love You; Theme For A Dream; A Girl Like You; When The Girl In Your Arms Is The Girl In Your Heart; It'll Be Me; The Next Time; Batchelor Boy; Summer Holiday; Lucky Lips; Don't Talk To Him; I'm The Lonely One; On The Beach; I Could Easily Fall; The Minute You're Gone; Wind Me Up; Vision; In the Country; The Day I Met Marie; All My Love; Congratulations; Big Ship; Goodbye Sam Hello Samantha; Power To All Our Friends; Devil Woman; We Don't Talk Anymore; Carrie; Dreaming; Wired for Sound; Daddy's Home; Silhouette; Saviour's Day; Millennium Prayer
Richie, Lionel	USA		1980s–present	Endless Love; Truly; All Night Long; Running in the Night; Hello; Stuck On You; Penny Lover; Say You Say Me; Dancing on the Ceiling; Ballerina Girl Albums: Time; Encore; Just for You

Name	Country of origin	Group members*	Period	Major hits
Robinson, Smokey	USA		1950s–present	Smokey Robinson and The Miracles songs: *Sheree Baby; Shop Around; You've Really Got A Hold On Me; I Second That Emotion; Tracks of my Tears; The Tears of a Clown; I Don't Blame You At All.* Smokey Robinson solo songs: *Love Machine; Being with You*
Rolling Stones, The	Britain	Mick Jagger (vocals, harmonica) Keith Richard (rhythm guitar) Brian Jones (lead guitar) Bill Wyman (bass) Charlie Watts (drums) Mick Taylor (lead guitar 1969–74) Ron Wood (lead guitar 1974–present)	1960s–present	*Come On; I Wanna Be Your Man; Not Fade Away; It's All Over Now; Little Red Rooster; Time Is On My Side; The Last Time; Satisfaction; Get Off Of My Cloud; 19th Nervous Breakdown; Paint It Black; Out of Time; Have You Seen Your Mother Baby Standin' In The Shadows?; Let's Spend the Night Together; Jumpin' Jack Flash; Honky Tonk Woman; Brown Sugar; Fool To Cry; Miss You; Emotional Rescue; Start Me Up; Harlem Shuffle; Under Cover of the Night*
Ross, Diana	USA		1970s–present	*Ain't No Mountain High Enough; I'm still Waiting; Touch Me in The Morning; All of My Life; You Are Everything; One Love In My Lifetime; Upside Down; My Old Piano; It's My Turn; Endless Love; Chain Reaction*
Roxy Music	Britain	Bryan Ferry (vocals) Andy MacKay (saxophone, woodwind) Phil Manzanera (guitar) Brian Eno (keyboards) Rik Kenton (bass) Paul Thompson (drums)	1970s–90s	*Virginia Plain; Pyjamarama; Street Life; Love Is The Drug; Dance Away; Angel Eyes; Over You; Oh Yeah; Avalon; The Same Old Scene; The Same Old Scene; Jealous Guy; More Than This*
Sex Pistols, The	Britain	Johnny Rotten (vocals) Steve Jones (guitar) Sid Vicious (bass) Paul Cook (drums)	1970s	*God Save The Queen; Pretty Vacant; Holidays in the Sun; Something Else; C'Mon Everybody; Silly Thing*
Shadows, The	Britain	Hank Marvin (lead guitar) Bruce Welch (rhythm guitar) Brian Bennett (drums) Jet Harris (bass 1958–62, left band) Tony Meehan (drums 1958–61, replaced by Bennett)	1960s–present	*Apache; Man of Mystery; The Stranger; The Frightened City; Kon-Tiki; Wonderful Land; Guitar Tango; Dance On; Foot Tapper; Atlantis; Shindig; Don't Make My My Baby Blue; Riders in the Sky*
Simon and Garfunkel	USA	Paul Simon (vocals, guitar) Art Garfunkel (vocals)	1960s–70s	*The Sound of Silence; Homeward Bound; I am a Rock; Scarborough Fair; 59th Street Bridge Song; Mrs Robinson; The Boxer; Bridge Over Troubled Water*
Simon, Paul	USA		1970s–present	*Kodachrome; Loves Me Like A Rock; Slip Slidin' Away; Late in the Evening; Fifty Ways to Leave Your Lover; American Theme; You Can Call Me Al; Surprise*
Simple Minds	Britain	Jim Kerr (vocals) Charlie Burchill (guitar) Mike McNeil (keyboards) John Giblin (bass) Mel Gaynor (drums)	1980s–present	*Promised You a Miracle; Waterfront; Don't You Forget About Me; Sanctify Yourself; All the Things She Said; Belfast Child*

Classic pop and rock groups/singers (continued)

Name	Country of origin	Group members*	Period	Major hits
Simply Red	Britain	Mick Hucknall (vocals) Sylvan Richardson (guitar) Fritz McIntyre (keyboards) Tony Bowers (bass) Chris Joyce (drums) Tim Kellett (horns)	1980s–present	Holding Back The Years; Money's Too Tight To Mention; The Right Thing; If You Don't Know Me By Now; Life; Something Got Me Started; Remembering the First Time; Say You Love Me
Smiths, The	Britain	Morrissey (vocals) Johnny Marr (guitar) Andy Rourke (bass) Mike Joyce (drums)	1980s	What Difference Does It Make?; Heaven Knows I'm Miserable Now; Panic; Shoplifters of the World Unite; Sheila Take a Bow; Girlfriend in a Coma
Spears, Britney	USA		2000–	Albums: Baby One More Time; Oops!...I Did It Again; Britney; In The Zone
Spice Girls, The	Britain	Victoria Adams (Posh Spice) Melanie Chisholm (Sporty Spice) Melanie Brown (Scary Spice) Emma Bunton (Baby Spice) Geri Halliwell (Ginger Spice, left 1998)	1990s	Wannabe!; Say You'll Be There; 2 Become 1; Who Do You Think You Are; Spice Up Your Life; Viva Forever; Goodbye
Springfield, Dusty	Britain		1960s–90s	I Only Want To Be With You; I Just Don't Know What To Do With Myself; Wishin' and Hopin'; You Don't Have To Say You Love Me; Island of Dreams; Say I Won't Be There; Losing You; In the Middle of Nowhere; Some of Your Lovin'; All I See Is You; I Close My Eyes and Count to Ten; Son of a Preacher Man; What Have I Done To Deserve This; In Private
Springsteen, Bruce	USA		1970s–present	The River; Hungry Heart; Fire; Dancing in the Dark; Cover Me; Born in the USA; I'm On Fire; Born to Run; The Rising; The Essential Bruce Springsteen; Devils and Dust
Status Quo	Britain	Francis Rossi (guitar, vocals) Rick Parfitt (guitar, vocals) Alan Lancaster (bass) John Coghlan (drums)	1960s–90s	Pictures of Matchstick Men; Ice in the Sun; Paper Plane; Caroline; Break the Rules; Down Down; Roll Over Lay Down; Rain; Mystery Song; Wild Side of Life; Again and Again; Whatever You Want; Lies; Somethin' 'Bout You Baby I Like; Dear John; The Wanderer; Rockin' All Over The World; Rollin' Home; In The Army Now; Burning Bridges
Stewart, Rod	Britain		1970s–present	Maggie May; You Wear It Well; Oh No Not My Baby; Sailing; Tonight's The Night; The Killing of Georgie; I Don't Want to Talk About It; You're In My Heart; Hotlegs; D'Ya Think I'm Sexy? Tonight I'm Yours; Young Turks; Baby Jane; What Am I Gonna Do? Infatuation; Some Guys Have All the Luck; Every Beat of My Heart; Downtown Train; It Takes Two; Rhythm of the Heart
Sting	Britain		1980s–present	Spread a Little Happiness; Russians; We'll Be Together; An Englishman in New York; Songs of the Labyrinth Album: Sacred Love

Name	Country of origin	Group members*	Period	Major hits
Stranglers, The	Britain	Hugh Cornwell (vocals, guitar) Dave Greenfield (keyboards) Jean-Jacques Burnel (bass) Jet Black (drums)	1970s–present	*Peaches; Something Better Change; No More Heroes; Five Minutes; Nice'n'Sleazy; Golden Brown; European Female; Skin Deep; All Day and All of the Night*
Suede	Britain	Brett Anderson (vocals) Richard Oaks (guitar) Mat Osman (bass) Simon Gilbert (drums) Neil Codling (keyboards)	1990s–2003	*Albums: Sci Fi; Lullabies; Dog Man Star; Suede; Coming Up; Head Music; A New Morning*
Summer, Donna	USA		1970s–80s	*Love to Love You Baby; I Feel Love; I Remember Yesterday; Down Deep; Last Dance; MacArthur Park; Heaven Knows; Hot Stuff; Bad Girls; Dim All the Lights; No More Tears; On The Radio; The Wanderer; State of Independence; She Works Hard for the Money; This Time I Know It's For Real; I Don't Wanna Get Hurt*
Supremes, The	USA	Diana Ross (vocals) Mary Wilson (vocals) Florence Ballard (vocals)	1960s–70s	*Where Did Our Love Go?; Baby Love; Come See About Me; Stop! In The Name of Love; Back In My Arms Again; I Hear a Symphony; You Can't Hurry Love; You Keep Me Hangin' On; Love Is Here And Now You're Gone; The Happening; In And Out Of Love; Love Child; I'm Gonna Make You Love Me; I Second That Emotion; Someday We'll Be Together; Up The Ladder to the Roof; Stoned Love; Floy Joy; River Deep Mountain High*
T-Rex	Britain	Marc Bolan (vocals, guitar) Steve Peregrine Took (percussion)	1960s–70s	*Ride a White Swan; Hot Love; Get It On; Jeepster; Telegram Sam; Metal Guru; Children of the Revolution; Solid Gold Easy Action; Twentieth Century Boy; The Groover; Truck On; Teenage Dream; I Love to Boogie*
Take That	Britain	Mark Owen (vocals) Gary Barlow (vocals) Jason Orange (vocals) Howard Donald (vocals) Robbie Williams (vocals)	1990s–present	*It Only Takes a Minute; Could It Be Magic; A Million Love Songs; Why Can't I Wake Up With You*
Talking Heads	USA	David Byrne (guitar, vocals) Tina Weymouth (bass) Jerry Harrison (keyboards) Chris Frantz (drums)	1970s–80s	*Psycho Killer; Once in a Lifetime; Burning Down the House; Road to Nowhere; And She Was*
Temptations, The	USA	Eddie Kendricks (vocals) Otis Williams (vocals) Paul Williams (vocals) Melvin Franklin (vocals) David Ruffin (vocals)	1960s–present	*The Way You Do The Things You Do; My Girl; Ain't Too Proud to Beg; Beauty is Only Skin Deep; You're My Everythng; Get Ready; Papa Was a Rollin' Stone; Treat Her Like a Lady*
10CC	Britain	Graham Gouldman (vocals, guitar) Eric Stewart (vocals, guitar) Lol Creme (vocals, guitar) Kevin Godley (vocals, drums)	1970s	*Rubber Bullets; The Dean and I; Wall Street Shuffle; Life Is A Minestrone; I'm Not In Love; Art For Art's Sake; I'm Mandy Fly Me; Things We Do For Love; Good Morning Judge; Dreadlock Holiday*

ARTS AND CULTURE

Classic pop and rock groups/singers (continued)

Name	Country of origin	Group members*	Period	Major hits
Turner, Tina	USA		1960s–present	Ike and Tina Turner songs: *It's Gonna Work Out Fine; River Deep Mountain High; Proud Mary* Tina Turner solo songs: *Let's Stay Together; What's Love Got To Do With It?; Better Be Good To Me; We Don't Need Another Hero; The Best; I Don't Wanna Lose You; Steamy Windows; Private Dancer*
U2	Ireland	Bono (vocals) The Edge (guitar) Adam Clayton (bass) Larry Mullen, Jr (drums)	1980s–present	*New Year's Day; Sunday Bloody Sunday; Two Hearts Beat As One; Pride; The Unforgettable Fire; The Streets Have No Name; With or Without You; I Still Haven't Found What I'm Looking For; Desire; Angel of Harlem; When Love Comes to Town; All I Want Is You; Sweetest Thing; All That You Can't Leave Behind; Vertigo*
Verve, The	Britain	Richard Ashcroft (vocals) Nick McCabe (guitar) Simon Tong (guitar) Simon Jones (bass) Peter Salisbury (drums)	1990s	*Bitter Sweet Symphony; Lucky Man; The Drugs Don't Work* Albums: *A Northern Soul; Urban Hymns*
Waits, Tom	USA		1970s–present	*Ol' 55; Downtown Train; Sea of Love;* Albums: *The Black Rider; Real Gone*
Warwick, Dionne	USA		1960s–80s	*Anyone Who Had a Heart; Walk On By; A Message to Martha; I Say a Little Prayer; Do You Know The Way To San José?; This Girl's In Love With You; You've Lost That Lovin' Feeling; I'll Never Fall In Love Again; Then Came You; I'll Never Love This Way Again; Heartbreaker; All The Love In The World; That's What Friends Are For*
Westlife	Britain	Shane Filton (vocals) Mark Freehily (vocals) Nicky Byrne (vocals) Kian Egan (vocals) Brian McFadden (vocals, left 2005)	1990s–present	Albums: *Coast to Coast; World of Our Own; Turnaround; Allow us To Be Frank; Face to Face*
White, Barry	USA		1970s–2003	*I'm Gonna Love You Just A Little More; Baby; Never Gonna Give You Up; I'm Under the Influence of Love; Can't Get Enough of Your Love Babe; You're The First The Last My What Am I Gonna Do With You?; Let The Music Play; You See The Trouble With Me; It's Ecstasy When You Lay Down Next To Me*
Who, The	Britain	Pete Townshend (guitar) Roger Daltrey (vocals) John Entwhistle (bass) Keith Moon (drums)	1960s–80s	*Can't Explain; Anyway Anyhow Anywhere; My Generation; Substitute; I'm A Boy; Happy Jack; Pictures of Lily; I Can See For Miles; Pinball Wizard; Won't Get Fooled Again; Squeeze Box; Who Are You? You Better You Bet*
Williams, Robbie	Britain		1990s–present	*Freedom; Angels; Let Me Entertain You; Millennium; No Regrets; Strong; Something Stupid* (with Nicole Kidman); *Radio; Tripping; Rudebox*

ARTS AND CULTURE

Name	Country of origin	Group members*	Period	Major hits
Wonder, Stevie	USA		1960s–present	*Fingertips – Pt 2; Uptight; A Place in the Sun; I Was Made to Love Her; For Once in My Life; My Cherie Amour; Yester-Me, Yester-You, Yesterday; Never Had A Dream Come True; Signed Sealed Delivered I'm Yours; You Are the Sunshine of My Life; Superstition; Living for the City; He's Misstra Know It All; I Wish; Sir Duke; Master Blaster; I Ain't Gonna Stand For It; Lately; Happy Birthday; Jammin'; Ebony and Ivory; I Just Called to Say I Love You; Part-Time Lover*
Young, Neil	Canada		1960s–present	Albums: *After The Goldrush; Harvest; Time Fades Away; Rust Never Sleeps; American Stars'n'Bars; Comes A Time; Live Rust; Trans; Neil Young; Unplugged; Decade; Prairie Wind*
Zappa, Frank	USA		1960s–1994	*Memories of El Monte* Albums: *Absolutely Free; Hot Rats; Burnt Weeny Sandwich; Weasels Ripped My Flesh; Over-Nite Sensation; Apostrophe; Sheik Yerbouti*

International music festivals

Festival	Date founded	Location	Time of year
Aldeburgh Festival	1948	Aldeburgh, Suffolk	Summer
Aspen Music Festival	1949	Aspen, Colorado	Summer
Bayreuth Festival (Richard Wagner Festival)	1876	Bayreuth, Bavaria	Summer
Berkshire Festival	1937	Stockbridge, Massachusetts	Summer
Glyndebourne Festival	1934	nr Lewes, East Sussex	Summer
Llangollen International Music Eisteddfod	1947	Llangollen, Clwyd, N Wales	Summer
Marlboro Music Festival	1951	Malboro, Vermont	Summer
Montreux International Jazz Festival	1967	Montreux, Switzerland	Summer
Newport Jazz Festival	1954	Newport, Rhode Island (until 1971, then in NYC)	Summer
Salzburg Festival	1920	Salzburg	Summer
Santa Fe Opera	1957	Santa Fe, New Mexico	Summer
Spoleto Festival (Festival of the Two Worlds)	1958	Spoleto, Italy	Summer

ARTS AND CULTURE

Pulitzer Prize in music

1943	*Secular Cantata No 2, A Free Song* William Schuman	1978	*Déjà Vu for Percussion Quartet and Orchestra* Michael Colgrass
1944	*Symphony No 4 (Op. 34)* Howard Hanson	1979	*Aftertones of Infinity* Joseph Schwantner
1945	*Appalachian Spring* Aaron Copland	1980	*In Memory of a Summer Day* David Del Tredici
1946	*The Canticle of the Sun* Leo Sowerby	1981	No award
1947	*Symphony No 3* Charles Ives	1982	*Concerto for Orchestra* Roger Sessions
1948	*Symphony No 3* Walter Piston	1983	*Three Movements for Orchestra* Ellen T Zwilich
1949	*Louisiana Story* music Virgil Thomson	1984	*Canti del Sole* Bernard Rands
1950	*The Consul* Gian Carlo Menotti	1985	*Symphony River Run* Stephen Albert
1951	Music for opera *Giants in the Earth* Douglas Stuart Moore	1986	*Wind Quintet IV* George Perle
		1987	*The Flight into Egypt* John Harbison
1952	*Symphony Concertante* Gail Kubik	1988	*12 New Etudes for Piano* William Bolcom
1954	*Concerto for Two Pianos and Orchestra* Quincy Porter	1989	*Whispers Out of Time* Roger Reynolds
		1990	*Duplicates: A Concerto for Two Pianos and Orchestra* Mel Powell
1955	*The Saint of Bleecker Street* Gian Carlo Menotti	1991	*Symphony* Shulamit Ran
1956	*Symphony No 3* Ernest Toch	1992	*The Face of the Night, The Heart of the Dark* Wayne Peterson
1957	*Meditations on Ecclesiastes* Norman Dello Joio		
1958	*Vanessa* Samuel Barber	1993	*Trombone Concerto* Christopher Rouse
1959	*Concerto for Piano and Orchestra* John La Montaine	1994	*Of Remembrances and Reflections* Gunther Schuller
1960	*Second String Quartet* Elliott Carter	1995	*Stringmusic* Morton Gould
1961	*Symphony No 7* Walter Piston	1996	*Lilacs* George Walker
1962	*The Crucible* Robert Ward	1997	*Blood on the Fields* Wynton Marsalis
1963	*Piano Concerto No 1* Samuel Barber	1998	*String Quartet No 2, Musica Instrumentalis* Aaron J Kernis
1966	*Variations for Orchestra* Leslie Bassett		
1967	*Quartet No 3* Leon Kirchner	1999	*Concerto for Flute, Strings and Percussion* Melinda Wagner
1968	*Echoes of Time and the River* George Crumb		
1969	*String Quartet No 3* Karel Husa	2000	*Life Is a Dream, Opera in Three Acts: Act II, Concert Version* Lewis Spratlan
1970	*Time's Encomium* Charles Wuorinen		
1971	*Synchronisms No 6 for Piano and Electronic Sound* Mario Davidovsky	2001	*Symphony No 2 for string orchestra* John Corigliano
1972	*Windows* Jacob Druckman	2002	*Ice Field* Henry Brant
1973	*String Quartet No 3* Elliott Carter	2003	*On The Transmigration of Souls* John Adams
1974	*Notturno* Donald Martino	2004	*Tempest Fantasy* Paul Moravec
1975	*From the Diary of Virginia Woolf* Dominick Argento	2005	*Second Concerto for Orchestra* Steven Stucky
1976	*Air Music* Ned Rorem	2006	*Piano Concerto: Chiavi in Mano* Yehudi Wyner
1977	*Visions of Terror and Wonder* Richard Wernick		

National anthems/songs from around the world

Country	Title (composer in brackets)
Australia[a]	*Advance Australia Fair*[a] (Peter Dodds McCormick)
Austria	*Bundeshymne der Republik Österreich* (Johan Holzer)
Canada	*O Canada* (Calixa Lavallée)
China	*March of the Volunteers*
England	*Land of Hope and Glory* (A C Benson)
France	*La Marseillaise* (Claude-Joseph Rouget de Lisle)
Germany	*Deutschland-Lied* (Haydn)
India	*Jana Gana Rana* (Rabindranath Tagore)
Ireland	*Amhrán Na bhFiann* (Peadar Kearney)
Italy	*Fratelli d'Italia* (Michele Novaro)
Japan	*Kimigayo* (Hayashi Hiromori)
New Zealand[a]	*God Defend New Zealand* (John Joseph Woods)
Russian Federation	*State Hymn of the Russian Federation* (Mikhail Glinka)
Scotland	*Flower of Scotland* (Roy Williamson)
UK	*God Save the Queen/King*
USA	*The Star Spangled Banner* (John Stafford Smith)
Wales	*Hen Wlad fy Nhadau* (Evan and James James)

[a]The royal anthem, *God Save the Queen/King*, is played when the Queen or a member of the royal family is present.

DANCE

Dance personalities

Name	Dates	Place of birth	Occupation
Acosta, Carlos	1973–	Havana	Dancer (ballet)
Ailey, Alvin	1931–89	Texas	Dancer, choreographer (ballet); formed the Alvin Ailey American Dance Theatre in 1958
Ailian, Dai	1916–2006	Trinidad	Dancer, choreographer (ballet); 1959 cofounder of Central Ballet of China
Alonso, Alicia	1921–	Havana	Dancer, choreographer; founder of Ballet de Cuba; formed the Alicia Alonso Company, 1948
Alston, Richard	1948–	Sussex	Choreographer (modern dance)
Amagatsu, Ushio	1949–	Yokosuka, Japan	Choreographer (modern dance)
Argentina, La	1890–1936	Buenos Aires	Dancer (Spanish dance)
Armitage, Karole	1954–	Madison, Wisconsin	Dancer, choreographer (ballet)
Ashton, Frederick	1904–88	Guayaquil, Ecuador	Dancer, choreographer (ballet)
Babilée, Jean	1923–	Paris	Dancer, choreographer (ballet)
Balanchine, George	1904–83	St Petersburg	Dancer, choreographer
Baryshnikov, Mikhail Nikolayevich	1948–	Riga	Dancer (ballet)
Bausch, Pina	1940–	Solingen, Germany	Dancer, choreographer, director (ballet)
Beauchamp, Pierre	1637–1705	Versailles	Dancer, choreographer, ballet master
Béjart, Maurice	1927–	Marseilles	Founder of Ballet Béjart, 1954 (modern ballet)
Benesh, Rudolph	1916–75	London	Dance notator
Bennett, Michael	1943–87	Buffalo, New York	Dancer, choreographer (musical)
Berkeley, Busby	1895–1976	Los Angeles	Choreographer (film)
Bessmertnova, Natalia	1941–	Moscow	Ballerina
Bintley, David	1957–	Huddersfield, West Yorkshire	Choreographer; resident choreographer with the Royal Ballet from 1986
Bolm, Adolph	1884–1951	St Petersburg	Dancer, choreographer, teacher (ballet)
Borovansky, Edouard	1902–59	Prerov	Dancer, choreographer, ballet director
Bournonville, August	1805–79	Copenhagen	Choreographer
Brown, Trisha	1936–	Aberdeen, Washington	Choreographer; cofounder of Judson Dance Company, 1962 (experimental dance)
Bruce, Christopher	1945–	Leicester	Choreographer (ballet/modern dance)
Bruhn, Erik	1928–86	Copenhagen	Dancer, ballet director
Bujones, Fernando	1955–	Florida	Dancer (ballet)
Bull, Deborah	1963–	Derby	Dancer (ballet)
Bussell, Darcey	1969–	London	Dancer (ballet)
Butcher, Rosemary	1947–	Bristol	Choreographer (experimental dance)
Camargo, Maria Anna de	1710–70	Brussels	Ballerina
Carlson, Carolyn	1943–	Oakland, California	Dancer, choreographer
Childs, Lucinda	1940–	New York	Choreographer
Clark, Michael	1962–	Aberdeen	Dancer, choreographer (ballet/modern dance)
Cohan, Robert	1925–	Brooklyn, New York	Choreographer, dancer, director (modern dance)
Cranko, John	1927–73	Rustenburg, S Africa	Dancer, choreographer director (ballet)
Cullberg, Birgit Ragnhild	1908–99	Nyköping, Sweden	Dancer, choreographer director (ballet)
Cunningham, Merce	1919–	Centralia, Washington	Dancer, choreographer, director, teacher (modern dance)
Danilova, Alexandra	1904–97	Peterhof	Dancer (ballet)
Dantzig, Rudi von	1933–	Amsterdam	Dancer, choreographer, ballet director
Davies, Siobhan	1950–	London	Choreographer, dancer; formed Siobhan Davies Company, 1988 (contemporary dance)
Dean, Laura	1945–	New York	Dancer, choreographer, teacher (ballet/modern dance)
Deane, Derek	1953–	Cornwall	Dancer, choreographer, ballet director
De Basil, Colonel Wassili	1881–1951	Kaunas	Ballet impresario
DeMille, Agnes	1909–93	New York City	Choreographer (ballet)

Dance personalities (continued)

Name	Dates	Place of birth	Occupation
Diaghilev, Sergei (Pavlovich)	1872–1929	Novgorod	Ballet impresario and founder of Ballets Russes
Dolin, Anton	1904–83	Slinfold, Sussex	Dancer, choreographer; cofounder of the Markova–Dolin Ballet
Dowell, Anthony	1943–	London	Dancer (ballet); director of the Royal Ballet
Duncan, Isadora	1877–1927	San Francisco	Dancer, choreographer (ballet)
Dunham, Katherine	1910–2006	Chicago	Dancer (ballet)
Dunn, Douglas	1942–	Palo Alto, California	Dancer, choreographer (experimental dance)
Dupond, Patrick	1959–	Paris	Dancer (ballet)
Fagan, Garth	1940–	Kingston, Jamaica	Dancer, choreographer
Falco, Louis	1942–93	New York City	Dancer, choreographer (contemporary dance)
Farrell, Suzanne	1945–	Cincinatti, Ohio	Dancer (ballet)
Feld, Eliot	1942–	Brooklyn, New York	Dancer, choregrapher (ballet/modern dance)
Flatley, Michael	1958–	Chicago	Dancer (tap), choreographer
Fokine, Michel	1880–1942	St Petersburg	Dancer, choreographer (creator of modern ballet)
Fonteyn, Margot	1919–91	Reigate	Ballerina
Forsythe, William	1949–	New York City	Dancer, choreographer (contemporary dance)
Fosse, Bob	1927–87	Chicago	Choreographer (film and theatre)
Franca, Celia	1921–	London	Dancer (ballet); National Ballet of Canada founded under her directorship, 1951
Franklin, Frederic	1914–	Liverpool	Dancer, teacher, ballet director
Fuller, Loie	1862–1928	Illinois	Dancer, choreographer (performance art)
Gable, Christopher	1940–98	London	Dancer (ballet)
Gielgud, Maina	1945–	London	Dancer, artistic director, teacher (modern dance)
Gilpin, John	1930–83	Southsea	Dancer (ballet)
Gordon, David	1936–	Brooklyn, New York	Choreographer (experimental dance)
Graham, Martha	1849–91	Pittsburgh, Pennsylvania	Dancer, teacher, choreographer (modern dance)
Grahn, Lucile	1819–1907	Copenhagen	Ballerina
Grant, Alexander	1925–	Wellington, New Zealand	Dancer (ballet)
Grey, Beryl	1927–	London	Ballerina
Grigorovich, Yuri	1927–	St Petersburg	Dancer, teacher, choreographer (ballet)
Guillem, Sylvie	1965–	Le Blanc Mestril, France	Ballerina
Hawkins, Erick	1909–94	Colorado	Dancer, choreographer, teacher (ballet/modern dance)
Haydée, Marcia	1939–	Niteroi, Brazil	Ballerina
Helpmann, Robert	1909–86	Mount Gambier, Australia	Dancer, choreographer (ballet)
Hightower, Rosella	1920–	Ardmore, Oklahoma	Dancer, teacher (ballet)
Holm, Hanya	1893–1992	Worms	Dancer, choreographer, teacher (modern dance)
Humphrey, Doris	1895–1958	Oak Park, Illinois	Dancer, choreographer, teacher (modern dance)
Ivanov, Lev	1834–1901	Moscow	Choreographer (ballet)
Jamison, Judith	1943–	Philadelphia	Dancer
Joffrey, Robert	1930–88	Seattle	Dancer, choreographer, teacher, ballet director
Jooss, Kurt	1901–79	Waaseralfingen	Choreographer (ballet)
Kain, Karen	1951–	Hamilton, Ontario	Ballerina
Karsavina, Tamara	1885–1978	St Petersburg	Ballerina
Kaye, Nora	1920–87	New York	Ballerina
Kemp, Lindsay	c.1939–	Isle of Lewis	Choreographer
Kidd, Michael	1919–	Brooklyn, New York	Dancer, choreographer, director (modern ballet/musical)
Kirkland, Gelsey	1952–	Bethlehem, Pennsylvania	Dancer (ballet)
Kirstein, Lincoln	1907–96	Rochester, New York	Impresario and ballet director

Name	Dates	Place of birth	Occupation
Kylian, Jiri	1947–	Prague	Dancer, choreographer (ballet)
Laban, Rudolf von	1879–1958	Pozsony, Hungary (now Bratislava, Slovakia)	Dancer, choreographer, dance theoretician (modern dance)
Lander, Harald	1905–71	Copenhagen	Dancer, choreographer, teacher (modern ballet)
Larrieu, Daniel	1957–	Marseilles	Dancer, choreographer (modern ballet)
Legat, Nicolai	1869–1937	St Petersburg	Dancer, choreographer, teacher, ballet master
Lifar, Serge	1905–86	Kiev	Dancer, choreographer (ballet)
Limon, Jose	1908–72	Culiacan, Mexico	Dancer, choreographer, teacher (modern dance)
Lophukov, Fyodor	1886–1973	St Petersburg	Dancer, choreographer, teacher (modern ballet/modern dance)
MacDonald, Elaine	1943–	Tadcaster	Ballerina
MacMillan, Kenneth	1929–92	Dunfermline	Dancer, choreographer, ballet company director; artistic director of Royal Ballet from 1970 and principal choreographer from 1977
Makarova, Nataliya	1940–	St Petersburg	Ballerina
Manen, Hans van	1932–	Amstel, Netherlands	Dancer, choreographer, director (ballet)
Marin, Maguy	1951–	Toulouse	Dancer, choreographer (modern ballet)
Markova, Alicia	1910–2004	London	Prima ballerina
Martins, Peter	1946–	Copenhagen	Dancer (ballet)
Massine, Leonide	1896–1979	Moscow	Dancer, choreographer (ballet)
Messerer, Asaf	1903–92	Vilnius	Dancer, teacher, choreographer (ballet)
Mitchell, Arthur	1934–	New York	Dancer, choreographer, director; founder of Dance Theater of Harlem, 1971 (ballet/modern dance)
Moiseyev, Igor Alexandrovich	1906–	Kiev	Dancer, choreographer, ballet director; founded the State Ensemble of Classical Ballet, 1967
Mordkin, Mikhail	1880–1944	Moscow	Dancer, teacher (ballet)
Morris, Mark	1956–	Seattle	Dancer, choreographer; founded Mark Morris Dance Group, 1980 (modern dance)
Murphy, Graeme	1951–	Melbourne	Dancer, choreographer, ballet director (ballet/contemporary dance)
Neumeier, John	1942–	Milwaukee	Choreographer; director of Hamburg Ballet from 1973
Nijinska, Bronislava	1891–1972	Minsk	Dancer, choreographer (ballet)
Nijinsky, Vaslav	1890–1950	Kiev	Dancer, choreographer (ballet/modern ballet)
Nikolais, Alwin	1912–93	Southington, Connecticut	Choreographer
North, Robert	1945–	Charleston, S Carolina	Dancer, choreographer (contemporary dance)
Noverre, Jean-Georges	1727–1810	Paris	Dancer, choreographer, ballet master
Nureyev, Rudolf	1938–93	Irkutsk, Siberia	Dancer (ballet); director at Paris Opéra from 1983
Page, Ashley	1956–	Rochester, Kent	Dancer, choreographer
Panov, Valeri	1938–	Vitebsk	Dancer (ballet)
Pavlova, Anna	1881–1931	St Petersburg	Ballerina
Paxton, Steve	1939–	Tucson, Arizona	Dancer, choreographer (experimental dance)
Petipa, Marius	1818–1910	Marseilles	Dancer, choreographer, ballet master; created *The Sleeping Beauty* and *Swan Lake*
Petit, Roland	1924–	Paris	Choreographer and dancer; founded Ballets de Paris de Roland Petit, 1948, and Ballet de Marseille, 1972
Petronio, Stephen	1956–	New Jersey	Dancer, choreographer (experimental dance)
Plisetskaya, Maya	1925–	Moscow	Ballerina
Praagh, Peggy van	1910–90	London	Dancer, teacher, ballet director
Rainer, Yvonne	1934–	San Francisco	Dancer, choreographer (experimental dance)

Dance personalities (continued)

Name	Dates	Place of birth	Occupation
Rambert, Marie	1888–1982	Warsaw	Dancer, teacher; founded Ballet Rambert, 1935 (ballet/modern dance)
Reitz, Dana	1948–	New York	Dancer, choreographer (ballet)
Robbins, Jerome	1918–98	New York City	Dancer, choreographer, director (musical)
Saint-Leon, Arthur	1821–70	Paris	Choreographer (ballet)
Sallé, Marie	1707–56	Paris	Ballerina
Schaufuss, Peter	1949–	Copenhagen	Dancer (ballet)
Seymour, Lynn	1939–	Wainright, Canada	Ballerina
Shearer, Moira	1926–2006	Dunfermline	Ballerina
Sibley, Antoinette	1939–	Bromley	Ballerina
Sleep, Wayne	1948–	Plymouth, Devon	Dancer
Sokolow, Anna	1912–2000	Hartford, Connecticut	Dancer, choreographer, teacher (modern dance)
Spoerli, Heinz	1941–	Basel	Dancer, choreographer, ballet director
Takei, Kei	1939–	Tokyo	Post-modern dancer and choreographer
Taylor, Paul	1930–	Pittsburgh	Choreographer (modern dance)
Tetley, Glen	1926–	Cleveland, Ohio	Dancer, choreographer (contemporary ballet)
Tharp, Twyla	1942–	Portland, Indiana	Dancer, choreographer (modern dance)
Tudor, Antony	1908–87	London	Choreographer (ballet)
Ulanova, Galina	1910–98	St Petersburgh	Ballerina
Valois, Ninette de	1898–2001	Co. Wicklow, Ireland	Ballerina; founder of Sadler's Wells Ballet, 1931
Villella, Edward	1936–	New York	Dancer (ballet)
Wagoner, Dan	1932–	Springfield, W Virginia	Dancer, choreographer (modern dance)
Wigman, Mary	1886–1973	Hanover	Dancer, choreographer, teacher (modern dance)
Zakharov, Rostislav	1907–84	Astrakhan	Dancer, choreographer, teacher, ballet director

Ballets

Ballet	Composer	Choreographer	First performed
Anastasia	Tchaikovsky	MacMillan	1971
Apollon Musagète	Stravinsky	Bolm	1928
Appalachian Spring	Copland	Graham	1944
L' Après-midi d'un Faune	Debussy	Nijinsky	1912
Bayadère, La	Minkus	Petipa	1877
Biches, Les	Poulenc	Nijinska	1924
Billy the Kid	Copland	Loring	1938
Bolero	Ravel	Nijinska	1928
Boutique Fantastique, La	Rossini	Massine	1919
Burrow, The	Martin	MacMillan	1958
Cain and Abel	Panufnik	MacMillan	1968
Carmen	Bizet	Petit	1949
Chant du Rossignol, Le	Stravinsky	Massine	1920
Cinderella	Prokofiev	Zakharov	1945
Concerto Barocco	Bach	Balanchine	1941
Coppélia	Delibes	Saint-Leon	1870
Don Quixote	Minkus	Petipa	1869
Ebony Concerto	Stravinsky	Page	1995
Elite Syncopations	Joplin	MacMillan	1974
Enigma Variations	Elgar	Ashton	1968
Fille Mal Gardée, La	Various (traditional French songs)	Dauberval	1789
Firebird, The	Stravinsky	Fokine	1910
Four Seasons, The	Vivaldi	MacMillan	1975
Giselle	Adam	Coralli/ Perrot	1841
Gods Go A-Begging, The	Handel	Balanchine	1928
Hamlet	Tchaikovsky	Helpmann	1942
Harlequinade	Drigo	Balanchine	1965
Hermanas, Las	Martin	MacMillan	1963
Illuminations	Britten	Ashton	1950
Invitation, The	Seiber	MacMillan	1960
Isadora	Rodney Bennett	MacMillan	1981
Ivan The Terrible	Prokofiev	Grigorovich	1975
Jeune Homme et La Mort, Le	Bach	Petit	1946
Judas Tree, The	Elias	MacMillan	1992
Knight Errant	Strauss (Richard)	Tudor	1968
Labyrinth	Schubert	Massine	1941
Lady and the Fool, The	Verdi	Cranko	1954
Lady of the Camellias	Chopin	Neumeier	1978
Lament of the Waves	Masson	Ashton	1970
Legend of Joseph	Strauss (Richard)	Fokine	1914
Luna, La	Bach	Béjart	1991
Malade Imaginaire, Le	Rota	Béjart	1976
Manon	Massenet	MacMillan	1974
Masques, Les	Poulenc	Ashton	1933
Mathilde	Wagner	Béjart	1965
Mayerling	Liszt	MacMillan	1978
Midsummer Night's Dream	Mendelssohn	Balanchine	1962
Month in the Country, A	Chopin	Ashton	1976
Night Journey	Schumann	Graham	1947
Night Shadow	Rieti	Balanchine	1946
Nocturne	Delius	Ashton	1936
Nutcracker, The	Tchaikovsky	Ivanov	1892
Ondine	Henze	Ashton	1958
Onegin	Tchaikovsky	Cranko	1965
Orpheus	Stravinsky	Balanchine	1948
Papillons, Les	Schumann	Fokine	1913
Parade	Satie	Massine	1917
Patineurs, Les	Meyerbeer	Ashton	1937
Petrushka	Stravinsky	Fokine	1911
Pineapple Poll	Sullivan	Cranko	1951
Present Histories	Schubert	Tuckett	1991
Prince Igor	Borodin	Ivanov	1890
Prince of the Pagodas, The	Britten	Cranko	1957
Prodigal Son, The	Prokofiev	Balanchine	1929
Rake's Progress, The	Gordon	De Valois	1935
Renard	Stravinsky	Page	1994
Rendez-Vous, Les	Auber	Ashton	1933
Rhapsody	Rachman-inov	Ashton	1980
Rite of Spring, The	Stravinsky	Nijinsky	1913
Rituals	Bartok	MacMillan	1975
Romeo and Juliet	Prokofiev	Psota	1938
Rooms	Hopkins	Sokolow	1955
Russian Soldier, The	Prokofiev	Fokine	1942
Saisons, Les	Glazunov	Petipa	1900
Scènes de Ballet	Stravinsky	Dolin	1944
Scheherezade	Rimsky-Korsakov	Fokine	1910
Scotch Symphony	Mendelssohn	Balanchine	1952
Serenade	Tchaikovsky	Balanchine	1934
Seven Deadly Sins	Weill	Balanchine	1933
Sleeping Beauty, The	Tchaikovsky	Petipa	1890
Song of the Earth	Mahler	MacMillan	1965
Spectre de la Rose, Le	Weber	Fokine	1911
Stoics Quartet	Mendelssohn	Burrows	1991
Summerspace	Feldman	Cunningham	1958
Swan Lake	Tchaikovsky	Reisinger	1877
Sylphides, Les	Chopin	Fokine	1907
Symphonic Variations	Franck	Ashton	1946
Symphonie Fantastique	Berlioz	Massine	1936
Symphony in C	Bizet	Balanchine	1991
Tales of Hoffmann	Offenbach	Darrell	1972
Taming of the Shrew	Scarlatti-Stolze	Cranko	1969
Three-Cornered Hat, The	De Falla	Massine	1919
Vainqueurs, Les	Wagner	Béjart	1969
Valse, La	Ravel	Nijinska	1929
Variations	Stravinsky	Balanchine	1966
Voluntaries	Poulenc	Tetley	1973
Walk to the Paradise Garden, The	Delius	Ashton	1972

Dance companies

Name	Date founded	Location
Alvin Ailey American Dance Theater	1958	New York
American Ballet Theatre	1940	New York
Australian Ballet Company	1962	Melbourne
Australian Dance Theatre	1965	Adelaide
Ballet Gulbenkian	1965	Lisbon
Ballet Jooss	1933	Cambridge, UK
Ballets de Paris	1948	France
Rambert Dance Company (formerly Ballet Rambert)	1926	London
Ballet Russe de Monte Carlo	1938	Monte Carlo
Ballets des Champs-Elysées	1944	Paris
Ballets Russes de Sergei Diaghilev (became the Kirov Ballet)	1909–29	St Petersburg
Ballets Suedois	1920	France
Ballet Théâtre Contemporain	1968	Amiens
Ballet Trockadero de Monte Carlo, Les	1974	New York
Ballet West	1968	Salt Lake City, Utah
Bejárt Ballet Lausanne (formerly Ballet Béjart and Ballet du Xième Siecle)	1987	Lausanne
Birmingham Royal Ballet (formerly the Sadler's Wells (1940) and the Royal Ballet (1956))	1946	Birmingham
Bolshoi Ballet	1776	Moscow
Borovansky Ballet	1942	Melbourne
Boston Ballet	1964	Boston
Central Ballet of China	1959	Beijing
Cholmondeleys, The	1984	London
Dance Bites	1994	London
Dance Theater of Harlem	1971	New York
Dutch National Ballet	1961	Amsterdam
DV8 Physical Theatre	1986	London
English National Ballet (originally London Festival Ballet)	1950	London
Extemporary Dance Theatre	1975	London
Feld Ballet NY	1974	New York
Grands Ballets Canadiens, Les	1956	Montreal
Houston Ballet	1968	Houston
Joffrey Ballet of Chicago (formerly Joffrey Ballet)	1954	New York
Jose Limon Dance Company	1946	New York
Kirov-Marinsky Ballet (formerly Kirov Ballet)	1935	St Petersburg
Lar Lubovitch Dance Company	1968	New York
London City Ballet	1978	London
London Contemporary Dance Theatre	1967–95	London
London Festival Ballet (now English National Ballet)	1950–88	London
Maly Ballet	1915	St Petersburg
Martha Graham Dance Company	1927	New York
Miami City Ballet	1986	Miami
National Ballet	1962	Washington
National Ballet of Canada	1951	Toronto
National Ballet of Cuba	1948	Havana
National Ballet of Mexico	1949	Mexico City
Netherlands Dance Theatre	1959	The Hague
New York City Ballet	1948	USA
Nikolais Dance Theatre	1951	New York
Northern Ballet	1969	Manchester
Paris Opéra Ballet	1661	Paris
Pennsylvania Ballet	1963	Philadelphia
Pilobolus Dance Theatre	1971	Vermont
Pittsburgh Ballet Theater	1970	Pittsburgh
Richard Alston Dance Company	1994	London
Royal Ballet	1931	Covent Garden, London
Royal Danish Ballet	16th-c	Copenhagen
Royal New Zealand Ballet Company (as from 1984)	1961	Wellington
Royal Swedish Ballet	1609	Stockholm
Royal Winnipeg Ballet	1938	Canada
San Francisco Ballet	1933	USA
School of American Ballet (now the American Ballet)	1933	New York
Scottish Ballet	1956	Glasgow
Stanislavsky Ballet	1929	Moscow
Stuttgart Ballet	1609	Germany
Sydney Dance Company	1971	Sydney
Washington Ballet	1962	Washington
Western Theatre Ballet	1957	Bristol

DESIGN

Design personalities

Name	Dates	Nationality	Field of work
Aalto, Alvar	1898–1976	Finnish	Furniture, particularly bentwood designs
Ashbee, Charles Robert	1863–1942	British	Arts and crafts designer, particularly jewellery, also wallpaper, pottery, and carpets; founded the Guild of Handicraft, 1888
Baillie Scott, Mackay Hugh	1865–1945	British	Stained glass, ironwork, mosaics, furniture, wallpaper
Banks, Jeff	1943–	British	Interior design, textiles, tableware
Barker, Linda	1961–	British	Interiors, soft furnishings, homewares, jewellery
Barnsley, Sidney	1865–1926	British	Furniture
Behrens, Peter	1868–1940	Austrian	Furniture, glass, cutlery, fabrics
Bell, Vanessa	1879–1961	British	Murals and interiors
Berlage, Hendrik Petrus	1856–1934	Dutch	Interior design, furniture, ironwork
Bindesboll, Thorvald	1846–1908	Danish	Ceramics
Brandt, Edgar	1880–1960	French	Metalwork
Brandt, Marianne	1893–1983	German	Metalwork and lighting; designed the Kandem bedside table light
Brangwyn, Frank	1867–1956	British	Graphics
Breuer, Marcel	1902–81	Hungarian	Furniture
Bugatti, Carlo	1855–1940	Italian	Furniture
Burges, William	1827–81	British	Furniture (Yatman cabinet, Great Bookcase) and interior design
Burne-Jones, Edward	1833–98	British	Stained glass and tapestries
Charpentier, Alexandre	1856–1909	French	Posters, furniture, metalwork, ceramics, interiors
Chermayeff, Serge	1900–96	Russian	Furniture, carpets, decorative work
Cliff, Clarice	1899–1972	British	Ceramics
Conran, Terence	1931–	British	Furniture, soft furnishings
Cooper, John Paul	1869–1933	British	Silversmith and jeweller
Crane, Walter	1845–1915	British	Illustrator and book designer
Czeschka, Carl Otto	1878–1960	Austrian	Jewellery, embroidery, stained glass
Daum, Auguste and Antonin	1853–1909 1864–1930	French	Glasswork
Day, Lewis F	1845–1910	British	Stained glass, wallpaper, textiles, jewellery, furniture
Deck, Theodore	1823–91	French	Pottery
Decoeur, Emile	1876–1953	French	Ceramics
Delaherche, Auguste	1857–1940	French	Ceramics
Doat, Taxile	1851–1938	French	Ceramics
Dorn, Marion	1900–64	American	Textiles
Dresser, Christopher	1834–1904	British	Silver plate, ceramics, glass, furniture, textiles
Dufrene, Maurice	1876–1955	French	Interior design
Dufy, Raoul	1877–1953	French	Textiles
Dunand, Jean	1877–1942	Swiss	Furniture, metalwork, lacquerwork
Eames, Charles	1907–78	American	Furniture
Eastlake, Charles	1836–1906	British	Furniture
Elmslie, George Grant	1871–1952	Scottish	Furniture, metalwork, stained glass, embroidery
Erp, Dirk van	1860–1933	American	Metalworker
Erté (Romain de Tirtoff)	1892–1990	Russian	Graphics
Fabergé, Carl	1846–1920	Russian	Jewellery
Farge, John La	1835–1910	American	Stained glass
Feure, Georges De	1869–1928	French	Interiors, furniture, porcelain, glass
Finch, Alfred William	1854–1930	Belgian	Ceramics
Fisher, Alexander	1864–1936	British	Enamelling
Follot, Paul	1877–1941	French	Jewellery, textiles, interiors, furniture, ceramics; designed the 'Pomone' dinner service for Wedgwood
Frankl, Paul	1886–1958	Austrian	Furniture
Fry, Roger	1866–1934	British	Founder of the Omega workshop, producing furniture, textiles, stained glass, pottery
Gaillard, Eugene	1862–1933	French	Textiles, furniture, interiors
Gallé, Emile	1846–1904	French	Glass and furniture
Gate, Simon	1883–1943	Swedish	Glass
Gaudi, Antonio	1852–1926	Spanish	Metalwork and furniture
Gill, Eric	1882–1940	British	Sculpture and typography

Design personalities (continued)

Name	Dates	Nationality	Field of work
Gimson, Ernest	1864–1919	British	Furniture
Gomperz, Lucie Marie	1902–95	Austrian	Pottery
Grant, Duncan	1885–1978	British	Murals
Grasset, Eugène	1841–1917	Swiss	Textiles, wallpapers, stained glass, ceramics, jewellery
Gray, Eileen	1879–1976	British	Lacquerwork
Greene, Charles Sumner	1868–1957	American	Furniture
Gropius, Walter	1883–1969	German	Furniture; director of Bauhaus
Grueby, William H	1867–1925	American	Pottery
Guimard, Hector	1867–1942	French	Ironwork, decorative work; designed the Paris metro entrance signs
Gullberg, Elsa	1886–1984	Swedish	Textiles
Hald, Edward	1883–1980	Swedish	Glass
Hansen, Frieda	1855–1931	Norwegian	Textiles
Heal, Ambrose	1872–1959	British	Furniture
Hoffmann, Josef	1870–1956	Austrian	Furniture (Kubus chair), metalwork, textiles, jewellery; founder of the Wiener Werkstatte, 1903
Holiday, Henry	1839–1927	British	Stained glass
Horta, Victor	1861–1947	Belgian	Interiors
Jensen, Georg	1866–1935	Danish	Silver and jewellery
Joel, Betty	1896–1985	British	Furniture and textiles
Knox, Archibald	1864–1933	British	Silver
Koehler, Florence	1861–1944	American	Jewellery
Krog, Arnold	1856–1931	Danish	Ceramics
Lalique, Réné	1860–1945	French	Goldsmith; jewellery and glass
Leach, Bernard	1887–1979	British	Ceramics
Lethaby, William	1857–1931	British	Furniture
Livemont, Privat	1861–1936	Belgian	Graphics
Llewelyn-Bowen, Laurence	1965–	British	Interiors, wallpapers, soft furnishings
Lurcat, Jean	1892–1966	French	Ceramics and tapestry
Mackintosh, Charles Rennie	1868–1928	British	Interiors, furniture, cutlery, stained glass, jewellery
Mackmurdo, Arthur	1851–1942	British	Metalwork, furniture, wallpaper, embroidery; founder of the Century Guild, 1884
Mathews, Arthur and Lucia	1860–1945 1870–1955	American	Murals; founded the Furniture Shop and Philopolis magazine
Morgan, William de	1839–1917	British	Ceramics
Morris, William	1834–96	British	Wallpaper, textiles, carpets, tapestry, typography; leader of the Arts and Crafts Movement
Moser, Koloman	1868–1918	Austrian	Graphics
Mucha, Alphonse	1860–1939	Czech	Art and poster design
Munthe, Gerhard	1849–1929	Norwegian	Furniture
Muthesius, Hermann	1861–1927	German	Interiors and furniture; founder of the Deutscher Werkbund, 1907
Nash, Paul	1889–1946	British	Textiles, upholstery, posters
Nilsson, Wiven	1870–1942	Swedish	Silver
Nordstrom, Patrick	1870–1929	Swedish	Pottery
Obseiger, Robert	1884–1940	Austrian	Pottery
Olbrich, Josef Maria	1867–1908	Austrian	Cofounder of the Vienna Secession
Pabst, Daniel	1826–1910	American	Furniture and cabinet making
Parrish, Maxfield	1870–1966	American	Graphics and poster design
Peche, Dagobert	1887–1923	Austrian	Art, metalwork
Pick, Frank	1878–1941	British	Poster design and typography; responsible for design for the London Underground
Poiret, Paul	1879–1944	French	Interior design, costume design
Ponti, Gio	1891–1979	Italian	Furniture
Prutscher, Otto	1880–1949	Austrian	Furniture and jewellery
Puiforcat, Jean	1897–1945	French	Silversmith
Quarti, Eugenio	1867–1931	Italian	Furniture
Redon, Odilon	1840–1916	French	Lithography, etching
Riegel, Ernst	1871–1946	German	Goldsmith and silversmith
Riemerschmied, Richard	1868–1957	German	Interiors, furniture, porcelain, glass, cutlery; founder member of Deutscher Werkbund
Rietveld, Gerritt Thomas	1888–1964	Dutch	Furniture
Robineau, Adelaide	1865–1929	American	Ceramics; edited the *Keramic Studio*
Rohe, Ludwig Mies van der	1886–1969	German	Furniture; last head of Bauhaus

Name	Dates	Nationality	Field of work
Rohlfs, Charles	1853–1936	American	Furniture
Rousseau, Clement	1872–1921	French	Furniture
Ruskin, John	1819–1900	British	Social critic and inspiration for the Arts and Crafts Movement
Russell, Gordon	1892–1980	British	Furniture
Ryggen, Hannah	1894–1970	Norwegian	Textiles
Serrurier-Bovy, Gustave	1858–1910	Belgian	Ironwork, furniture, wallpaper, stained glass
Staite-Murray, William	1861–1910	British	Ceramics
Stam, Mart	1899–1986	Dutch	Designed the first cantilever chair
Stickley, Gustav	1858–1942	American	Furniture; founded *The Craftsman* magazine, 1901
Taylor, William Howson	1876–1935	British	Ceramics; founded the Ruskin Pottery, 1898
Tiffany, Louis Comfort	1848–1933	American	Jewellery, stained glass, art glass, interiors
Voysey, Charles Annesley	1857–1941	British	Wallpaper and textile pattern design, furniture, tableware, lighting
Wagenfeld, Wilhelm	1900–90	German	Goldsmith; metalwork, glass, porcelain
Webb, Philip	1831–1915	British	Furniture
Wilson, Henry	1864–1934	British	Silversmith
Wimmer, Joseph Eduard	1882–1961	Austrian	Metalwork; co-director of the Wiener Werkstatte
Wolfe, Elsie de	1865–1950	American	Interior design
Wolfers, Philippe	1858–1929	Belgian	Jewellery
Zen, Carlo	1851–1918	Italian	Cabinet maker
Zen, Pietro	1879–1950	Italian	Furniture

na = not available

FASHION

Fashion designers

Name	Dates	Place of birth
Alaia, Azzedine	1940–	Busto Arsizio
Amies, Hardy	1909–2003	London
Armani, Giorgio	1934–	Piacenza
Ashley, Laura	1925–85	Merthyr Tydfil
Azagury, Jacques	1958–	Casablanca
Balenciaga, Cristobal	1895–1972	Guetaria, Spain
Balmain, Pierre	1914–82	St Jean de Maurienne
Banks, Jeff	1943–	Ebbw Vale, Wales
Beene, Geoffrey	1927–2004	Haynesville, Louisiana
Beretta, Anne-Marie	1937–	Beziers, France
Blass, Bill	1922–2002	Fort Wayne, Indiana
Bohan, Marc	1926–	Paris
Boss, Hugo	d.1948	Germany
Cacharel, Jean	1932–	Nîmes
Capucci, Roberto	1929–	Rome
Cardin, Pierre	1922–	Venice
Cassini, Oleg	1913–	Paris
Cerruti, Nino (Antonio)	1930–	Biella, Italy
Chanel, Gabrielle (Coco)	1883–1971	Saumur
Clements, Suzanne (of Clements Ribeiro)	1969–	Britain
Conran, Jasper	1959–	London
Courrèges, André	1923–	Pau, France
Daché, Lilly	1892–1989	Béigles, France
De la Renta, Oscar	1932–	Santo Domingo
Desses, Jean	1904–70	Alexandria
Dior, Christian	1905–57	Granville, Normandy
Dolce, Domenico (of Dolce & Gabbana)	1958–	Sicily
Erté (Romain de Tirtoff)	1892–1990	St Petersburg
Farhi, Nicole	1947–	Nice
Fassett, Kaffe	1937–	San Francisco, CA
Fiorucci, Elio	1935–	Milan
Fortuny, Mariano	1871–1949	Granada
Gabbana, Stefano (of Dolce & Gabbana)	1962–	Venice
Galliano, Sir John (Charles)	1960–	Gibraltar
Gaultier, Jean-Paul	1952–	Paris
Givenchy, Hubert James Marcel Taffin de	1927–	Beauvais
Gucci, Guccio	1881–1953	Florence, Italy
Halston (Roy Halston Frowick)	1932–90	Des Moines, Iowa
Hamnett, Katharine	1948–	Gravesend, Kent
Hartnell, Norman	1901–78	Honiton, Devon
Hechter, Daniel	1938–	Paris
Herrera, Caroline	1939–	Venezuela
Hilfiger, Tommy	1952–	Elmira, New York
Jackson, Betty	1949–	Backup, Lancashire
Karan, Donna	1948–	Forest Hills, New York
Kawakubo, Rei	1943–	Tokyo
Kenzo, Takada	1940–	Kyoto

Fashion designers (continued)

Name	Dates	Place of birth	Name	Dates	Place of birth
Klein, Anne Hannah	1921–74	New York	Rhodes, Zandra	1940–	Chatham, Kent
Klein, Calvin	1942–	New York	Ribeiro, Inacio	1963–	Brazil
Klein, Roland	1938–	Rouen	(of Clements Ribeiro)		
Lacroix, Christian	1951–	Arles	Ricci, Nina	1883–1970	Turin
Lagerfeld, Karl	1939–	Hamburg	Rocha, John	1953–	Hong Kong
Lanvin, Jeanne	1867–1946	Brittany	Rochas, Marcel	1902–55	Paris
Lapidus, Ted	1929–	Paris	Saint-Laurent, Yves	1936–	Oran, Algeria
Laroche, Guy	1923–89	La Rochelle, nr Bordeaux	Scherrer, Jean-Louis	1936–	Paris
			Schiaparelli, Elsa	1896–1973	Rome
Lauren, Ralph	1939–	New York City	Simonetta (Duchesa	1922–	Rome
Lelong, Lucien	1889–1958	Paris	Simonetta Colonna		
Macdonald, Julien	1972–	Merthyr Tydfil, S Wales	di Cesaro)		
			Smith, Paul	1946–	Nottingham
Mainbocher (Main Rousseau Bocher)	1891–1976	Chicago	Stavropoulos, George	1920–	Tripolis, Greece
			Stiebel, Victor	1907–76	Durban
Maxwell, Vera (Vera Huppe)	1901–95	New York	Strauss, Levi	1829–1902	Bavaria
			Tarlazzi, Angelo	1945–	Ascoli Piceno, Italy
McCartney, Stella	1971–	Britain			
McQueen, Alexander	1969–	London	Ungaro, Emmanuel	1933–	Aix-en-Provence
Michiko, Koshino	1950–	Osaka	Valentino	1933–	Voghera, Italy
Missoni, Tai Otavio	1921–	Yugoslavia	Versace, Donatella	1955–	Reggio Calabria, Italy
Miyake, Issey	1938–	Hiroshima			
Molyneux, Edward Henry	1891–1974	London	Versace, Gianni	1946–97	Calabria, Italy
			Von Furstenburg, Diane	1946–	Brussels
Montana, Claude	1949–	Paris	Westwood, Vivienne	1941–	Tintwistle, Derby
Mortensen, Erik	1926–	Denmark	Worth, Charles Frederick	1825–95	Bourn, Lincolnshire
Moschino, Franco	1950–95	Italy			
Mugler, Thierry	1948–	Strasbourg	Yamamoto, Yohji	1943–	Tokyo
Muir, Jean	1933–95	London			
Oldfield, Bruce	1950–	London			
Ozbek, Rifat	1955–	Istanbul			
Patou, Jean	1880–1936	Normandy			
Poiret, Paul	1879–1944	Paris			
Pucci, Emilio, Marchese di Barsento	1914–93	Naples			
Quant, Mary	1934–	London			
Rabanne, Paco	1934–	San Sebastian			
Réard, Louis	1897–1984	France			
Reger, Janet	1935–	London			

na = not available.

Clothes care

⊠ Do not iron

⊿ Can be ironed with *cool* iron (up to 110°C)

⊿ Can be ironed with *warm* iron (up to 150°C)

⊿ Can be ironed with *hot* iron (up to 200°C)

⊌ Hand wash only

⊟ Can be washed in a washing machine; the number shows the most effective washing temperature (in °C)

⊟ Reduced (medium) washing conditions

⊟ Much reduced (minimum) washing conditions (for wool products)

⊠ Do not wash

◉ Can be tumble-dried (one dot within the circle means a low temperature setting; two dots for higher temperatures)

⊠ Do not tumble-dry

⊗ Do not dry-clean

Ⓐ Dry-cleanable (letter indicates which solvents can be used) A: all solvents

Ⓕ Dry-cleanable F: white spirit and solvent 11 can be used

Ⓟ Dry-cleanable P: perchloroethylene (tetrachloroethylene), white spirt, solvent 113 and solvent 11 can be used

Ⓟ Dry-cleanable, if special care taken

▲ Chlorine bleach may be used with care

⊠ Do not use chlorine bleach

International clothing sizes

Size equivalents are approximate, and may display some variation between manufacturers.

Women's suits/dresses

UK	US	UK/Continent
8	6	36
10	8	38
12	10	40
14	12	42
16	14	44
18	16	46
20	18	48
22	20	50
24	22	52

Women's hosiery

UK/US	UK/Continent
8	0
$8^1/2$	1
9	2
$9^1/2$	3
10	4
$10^1/2$	5

Adults' shoes

UK	US	UK/Continent
Ladies		
$4^1/2$	6	$37^1/2$
5	$6^1/2$	38
$5^1/2$	7	39
6	$7^1/2$	$39^1/2$
$6^1/2$	8	40
7	$8^1/2$	$40^1/2$
Men		
7	$7^1/2$	$40^1/2$
$7^1/2$	8	41
8	$8^1/2$	42
9	$9^1/2$	43
10	$10^1/2$	$44^1/2$
11	$11^1/2$	46

Children's shoes

UK/US	UK/Continent
0	15
1	17
2	18
3	19
4	20
5	22
6	23
7	24
8	25
$8^1/2$	26
9	27
10	28
11	29
12	30
13	32

Men's suits and overcoats

UK/US	Continental
36	46
38	48
40	50
42	52
44	54
46	56

Men's shirts

UK/US	UK/Continent
12	30–1
$12^1/2$	32
13	33
$13^1/2$	34–5
14	36
$14^1/2$	37
15	38
$15^1/2$	39–40
16	41
$16^1/2$	42
17	43
$17^1/2$	44–5

Men's socks

UK/US	UK/Continent
$9^1/2$	38–9
10	39–40
$10^1/2$	40–1
11	41–2
$11^1/2$	42–3

International pattern sizes

Young junior/teenage

Size	Bust cm	in	Waist cm	in	Hip cm	in	Back waist length cm	in
5/6	71	28	56	22	79	31	34.5	$13^1/2$
7/8	74	29	58	23	81	32	35.5	14
9/10	78	$30^1/2$	61	24	85	$33^1/2$	37	$14^1/2$
11/12	81	32	64	25	89	35	38	15
13/14	85	$33^1/2$	66	26	93	$36^1/2$	39	$15^3/8$
15/16	89	35	69	27	97	38	40	$15^3/4$

Half-size

Size	Bust cm	in	Waist cm	in	Hip cm	in	Back waist length cm	in
$10^1/2$	84	33	69	27	89	35	38	15
$12^1/2$	89	35	74	29	94	37	39	$15^1/2$
$14^1/2$	94	37	79	31	99	39	39.5	$15^1/2$
$16^1/2$	99	39	84	33	104	41	40	$15^3/4$
$18^1/2$	104	41	89	35	109	43	40.5	$15^7/8$
$20^1/2$	109	43	96	$37^1/2$	116	$45^1/2$	40.5	16
$22^1/2$	114	45	102	40	122	48	41	$16^1/8$
$24^1/2$	119	47	108	$42^1/2$	128	$50^1/2$	41.5	$16^1/4$

Misses

Size	Bust cm	in	Waist cm	in	Hip cm	in	Back waist length cm	in
6	78	$30^1/2$	58	23	83	$32^1/2$	39.5	$15^1/2$
8	80	$31^1/2$	61	24	85	$33^1/2$	40	$15^3/4$
10	83	$32^1/2$	64	25	88	$34^1/2$	40.5	16
12	87	34	67	$26^1/2$	92	36	41.5	$16^1/4$
14	92	36	71	28	97	38	42	$16^1/2$
16	97	38	76	30	102	40	42.5	$16^3/4$
18	102	40	81	32	107	42	43	17
20	107	42	87	34	112	44	44	$17^1/4$

Women's

Size	Bust cm	in	Waist cm	in	Hip cm	in	Back waist length cm	in
38	107	42	89	35	112	44	44	$17^1/4$
38	107	42	89	35	112	44	44	$17^1/4$
42	117	46	99	39	122	48	44.5	$17^1/2$
44	122	48	105	$41^1/2$	127	50	45	$17^5/8$
46	127	50	112	44	132	52	45	$17^3/4$
48	132	52	118	$46^1/2$	137	54	45.5	$17^7/8$
50	137	54	124	49	142	56	46	18

ARCHITECTURE

Architects

Name	Dates	Place of birth	Selected works
Aalto, Alvar	1898–1976	Kuortane, Finland	Designed public and industrial buildings, and some furniture.
Abercrombie, Patrick	1879–1957	Ashton-upon-Mersey	Pioneer of town planning. His major work was the replanning of London – County of London Plan (1943) and Greater London Plan (1944).
Adam, Robert	1728–92	Kirkcaldy, Fife	Architect of the King's works in 1761–9. Examples of his work are Home House in London's Portland Square, Landsdown House, Derby House, and Register House in Edinburgh.
Alberti, Leon Battista	1404–72	Genoa	One of the most brilliant figures of the Renaissance, who worked in Florence from 1428.
Alessi, Galeazzo	1512–72	Perugia	Gained recognition in Europe for his designs for churches and palaces in Genoa.
Ammanti, Bartolommeo	1511–92	Settignano	Designed the Ducal Palace at Lucca and part of the Pitti palace and the Ponte Sta Trinita in Florence.
Archer, Thomas	1668–1743	Tanworth	Baroque architect responsible for the churches of St John's, Westminster (1714) and St Paul's, Deptford (1712). He also designed part of Chatsworth House.
Arnolfo di Cambio	1245–1302	Colle di Valdelsa, Tuscany	Major work is the design of Florence Cathedral.
Asplund, Erik Gunnar	1885–1940	Stockholm	Major works are concentrated in Stockholm: the Stockholm City Library (1924–7), the Woodland Chapel, Skandia Cinema. He was responsible for most of the exhibits in the Stockholm Exhibition of 1930.
Baker, Herbert	1862–1946	Kent	Designed Groote Schur, near Cape Town, the Union Government buildings in Pretoria, and worked with Edward Lutyens on the design of New Delhi, India. In Britain he designed the new Bank of England and South Africa House, and Rhodes House in Oxford.
Barry, Charles	1795–1860	London	Palace of Westminster (1840).
Basevi, George	1794–1845	London	In classic revivalist style he designed the Fitzwilliam Museum, Cambridge; laid out part of Belgravia; and designed a number of country houses and Gothic churches.
Behrens, Peter	1868–1940	Hamburg	Designed the AEG turbine assembly works in glass and steel. Also designed workers houses in Stuttgart and Vienna, and the German embassy in St Petersburg.
Berlage, Hendrick Petrus	1856–1934	Amsterdam	Designed the Amsterdam Bourse (1903); Holland House, London (1914); and the Gemeente Museum in the Hague (1934).
Blacket, Edmund Thomas	1817–83	Southwark	Government architect for New South Wales in 1849, but returned to private practice in 1854 and designed the New South Wales University. He adopted Victorian Gothic style for his work on ecclesiastical buildings, including Sydney and Perth cathedrals, but classical forms for his commercial projects, such as banks and hotels.
Borromini, Francesco	1599–1667	Bissone, Lake Lugano	San Carlo alle Quattro Fontane (1637–41), Rome.
Boullée, Etienne-Louis	1728–99	Paris	He became architect to the King of Prussia in 1762. His pre-Revolution Neo-Classical work includes the Hotel de Brunoy, Paris (1772).
Boyd, Robin Penleigh	1919–71	Melbourne	Influential critical works which shaped the future direction of Australian architecture.
Bramante, Donato	c.1444–1514	nr Urbino	Renovation of the Vatican and St Peter's (1505–6).

Name	Dates	Place of birth	Selected works
Breuer, Marcel	1902–81	Pécs	Student of the Bauhaus from 1921 and took charge of the furniture workshop in 1924. His architectural works were designed with Bernard Zehrfuss and Pier Luigi Nervi, and include the UNESCO building in Paris.
Brosse, Salomon de	1565–1626	Verneuil-sur-Oise	Designed the Luxembourg Palace, Paris (1615–20), and Louis XIII's hunting lodge at Versaille (1624–26).
Brunelleschi, Filippo	1377–1446	Florence	Dome of Florence Cathedral (1417–34).
Burges, William	1827–81	London	Architecture employed strong mediaeval style. Designed Castell Coch (1876–81) as a hunting lodge for the third marquess of Bute; Cardiff Castle (1876–81); Cork Cathedral (1862–76); and a house in Park Place (1870s).
Burton, Decimus	1800–81	London	Planned the Regent's Park colosseum and in 1825 designed the new layout of Hyde Park and the Triumphal Arch at Hyde Park Corner. Also designed the Palm House at Kew Gardens (1844–8).
Butterfield, William	1814–1900	London	Leading exponent of the Gothic revival and the architect of Keble College, Oxford; St Augustine's College, Canterbury; the chapel and quad at Rugby and St Albans, Holborn.
Campen, Jacob van	1595–1657	Haarlem	Built the first classical building in Holland. Most celebrated work was the Mauritshuis in The Hague (1633). Other works include the Amsterdam Theatre (1637) and Amsterdam Town Hall (1647–55).
Candela, Felix	1910–97	Spain	One of the world's foremost designers of reinforced concrete hyperbolic paraboloid shell roofs. His works include the Sports Palace for the Olympic Games in Mexico City (1968).
Casson, Hugh	1910–99	London	Directed the architecture of the Festival of Britain (1948–51).
Chambers, William	1726–96	Stockholm	Designed Somerset House (1776) and the pagoda in Kew Gardens.
Chermayeff, Serge	1900–96	Caucasus	Designed De La Warr Pavilion at Bexhill-on-Sea (1933–5).
Churriguera, Done Jose	1650–1725	Salamanca	Royal architect to Charles II and developed the Churrigueresque style. Designed Salamanca Cathedral.
Coates, Wells Wintemute	1895–1958	Tokyo	Leading figure in the modern movement of architecture. Responsible for the design of the BBC studios and the EKCO laboratories as well as many other buildings in Britain and Canada.
Cockerell, Charles Robert	1788–1863	London	Designed the Taylorian Institute and Ashmolean Museum at Oxford.
Costa, Lucio	1902–98	Toulouse	Designed the award-winning Eduardo Gunile apartments. Drew up plans for city of Brasilia.
Dance, George	1695–1768	London	Newgate Prison (1770–83).
Doshi, Balkrishna Vithaldas	1927–	Poona, India	Worked as a senior designer with Le Corbusier. Works include the City Hall, Toronto (1958); the Indian Institute of Management (1962–74) in Ahmedabad; and Vidyadhar Nagar New Town, Jaipur.
Dudok, Willem Marinus	1884–1974	Amsterdam	Became city architect of Hilversum in 1915. His most famous works are the Hilversum Town Hall (1928–30) and the Bijenkorf department store in Rotterdam.
Erickson, Arthur Charles	1924–	Vancouver	His work on the Simon Fraser University buildings (1963) in British Columbia brought him international recognition. He also designed the Lethbridge University (1971) in Alberta; the Museum of Anthropology, British Columbia (1971–7); and the Roy Thomson Hall, Toronto (1976–80).
Farrell, Terry	1938–	Newcastle-upon Tyne	Embankment Place, Charing Cross (1991)

Architects (continued)

Name	Dates	Place of birth	Selected works
Fischer von Erlach, Johann Bernard	1656–1723	Graz, Austria	Designer of churches and palaces, notably Karlskirche in Vienna and the University Church at Salzburg.
Fontana, Carlo	1638–1714	Rancate, nr Como	Papal architect in Rome where he designed many major works such as the fountain in the Piazza di San Petro. Also designed Loyola College in Spain and the Palazzo Durazzo at Genoa.
Fontana, Domenico	1543–1607	Melide, nr Lugano	Papal architect in Rome, employed on the Lateran Palace, the Vatican Library, and St Peter's Dome.
Foster, Norman	1935–	Manchester	Sainsbury Centre, University of East Anglia (1977); Hong Kong and Shanghai Bank, Hong Kong (1979–85); Terminal Tower, Stansted Airport (1991); Century Tower, Tokyo (1991); Millennium Bridge, London (2000); Swiss-Re Tower, London (2002); New Wembley National Stadium (begun 2003); Viaduc de Millau motorway bridge, France (2005); Hearst Tower office complex, NY (2006)
Fowke, Albert	1823–65	Belfast	Planned the Albert Hall, London, and produced the original designs for the Victoria and Albert Museum. Also planned the Royal Scottish Museum in Edinburgh.
Francesco di Giorgio	1439–1502	Siena	Chief architect of Siena Cathedral.
Freed, James Ingo	1930–	US	Holocaust Memorial Museum, Washington, DC (1993); Ronald Reagan International Trade Center, Washington, DC (1997); 1700K Street Office Complex, Washington DC (2005)
Gabriel, Jacques Ange	1698–1782	Paris	Court architect to Louis XV, he designed the Petit Trianon (1768) and also laid out the Place de la Concorde (1753).
Garnier, Tony	1869–1948	Lyon	His theoretical work, *Une Cité Industrielle*, made a major contribution to the development of 20th-c urban architecture. Works include the Grange Blanche hospital (1911–27); Stadium (1913–18), Lyon; Hôtel de Ville, Boulogne-Bilancourt (1931–3).
Gaudi, (I Cornet) Antonio	1852–1926	Riudoms, Catalonia	Exponent of Catalan 'modernism'; also famous for the Church of the Holy Family in Barcelona.
Gehry, Frank O	1929–	Toronto	Communication and Technology Centre, Bad Oeynhausen, Germany (1997); Guggenheim Museum, Bilbao (1997); Maggie's Centre, Dundee (2003)
Gilbert, Cass	1859–1934	Zanesville, Ohio	Architect of the first skyscraper, the 60-storey Woolworth Building in New York (1912). Public buildings include the US Customs House, New York City (1907); Supreme Court building, Washington DC (1935); university campuses at Minnesota (Minneapolis) and Texas (Austin).
Griffin, Walter Burley	1876–1937	Maywood, Illinois	Director of design and construction of the city of Canberra; designs adopted in 1925. Designed notable buildings and Castlecrag Estate in N Sydney
Grimshaw, Nicholas	1939–	Hove, Sussex	Financial Times printing plant, London (1988); British Pavilion, Expo'92, Seville (1992); Eden Project, Cornwall (2001)
Gropius, Walter	1883–1969	Berlin	Founder of Bauhaus movement.
Guarini, Guarino	1624–83	Modena	Designed several churches in Turin: San Lorenzo (1668–80) and Capella della SS Sindone (1668); also the Palazzo Carignano (1679), as well as palaces for Bavaria and Baden.
Guimard, Hector Germain	1867–1942	Lyon	The most important Art Nouveau architect in Paris before World War 1. Designed the Castel Béranger apartment block (1894–8) and is famous for the Paris Metro signs of the 1900s.
Hamilton, Thomas	1784–1858	Glasgow	Designs include the Burns Monument, Galloway (1820); Royal High School, Edinburgh (1823–29); Royal College of Physicians Hall (1844–45), Edinburgh.

Name	Dates	Place of birth	Selected works
Hardwick, Philip	1792–1870	London	Designer of Euston station, Lincoln's Inn Hall and Library, Goldsmith's Hall, and Limerick Cathedral.
Haussmann, Georges Eugene	1809–91	Paris	Restructured Paris by widening streets, laying out boulevards and parks, and building bridges.
Hawksmoor, Nicholas	1661–1736	East Drayton, Nottinghamshire	Work includes the London churches St Mary Woolnoth, St George's (Bloomsbury), and Christ Church (Spitalfields).
Hoffmann, Josef	1870–1956	Pirnitz, Austria	Leader of the Vienna Secession and founded the Wiener Werkstatte in 1903. His architectural achievements include the Purkersdorf Sanatorium (1903–5) and Stoclet House in Brussels (1905–11). He was city architect for Vienna from 1920.
Holland, Henry	1746–1806	Ledbury	Designed old Carlton House in London, the original Brighton Pavilion and Brook's Club.
Hood, Raymond Mathewson	1881–1934	Rhode Island	The leading designer of skyscrapers in the 1930s. Designed the American Radiator building, New York (1924), the Daily News building (1929–30), the Rockefeller Center (1930–40), and the McGraw-Hill building (1931).
Horta, Victor	1861–1947	Ghent	Regarded as the originator of Art Nouveau. In Brussels his works include the Maison Tassel (1892–3), the Maison Solray (1894–1900) and the Maison du Peuple (1895–99). He also designed the first department store there, L'Innovation (1901)
Howard, Ebenezer	1850–1928	London	Founder of the Garden City movement.
Jacobsen, Arne	1902–71	Copenhagen	Main public building in Copenhagen was the SAS skyscraper (1955). He also designed St Catherine's College, Oxford.
Johnson, Philip	1906–2005	Cleveland, Ohio	Designed the Seagram building, New York City (1945); New York State Theater, Lincoln Center (1964); Amon Carter Museum of Western Art, Texas (1961); and the American Telephone and Telegraph Company (1978–84); Cathedral of Hope, Dallas, Texas (1998).
Jones, Inigo	1573–1652	London	Introduced the Palladian style to England. His designs include the Queen's House at Greenwich (1616) and the Banqueting House in Westminster (1619–22).
Kahn, Louis Isadore	1901–74	Saaremaa, Estonia	Pioneer of functionalist architecture. Designed the Richards Medical Research Building in Pennsylvania (1957–61); the City Tower Municipal Building in Philadelphia; Yale University Art Gallery (1953); Salk Institute, La Jolla, California (1959–65); the Indian Institute of Management, Ahmedabad (with Doshi); and the Paul Mellon Center, Yale (1969–72).
Kent, William	1685–1748	Bridlington	Designed many public buildings in London, including the Royal Mews, Trafalgar Square, the Treasury buildings, and the Horse Guards block in Whitehall.
Larsen, Henning	1925–		Buildings include Trondheim University, institute of the Freie Universität, Danish Embassy in Riadh, Compton Verney opera house, Stratford-upon-Avon, Copenhagen Opera House (2005).
Lasdun, Denys	1914–2001	London	His best-known buildings include the Royal College of Musicians (1958–64); the University of East Anglia (1962–8); the National Theatre, London (1965–76); European Investment Bank, Luxembourg (1975); and the Institute of Education (1970–8).
Le Corbusier (Charles Edouard Jeanneret)	1887–1965	La-Chaux-de-Fonds	First building was the Unité d'Habitation, Marseilles (1945–50). Designed the plans for the city of Chandigarh, the capital of the Punjab. First use of piloti (stilts) in his designs was the Swiss Pavilion on the campus of the Cité Universitaire, Paris.
Ledoux, Claude Nicolas	1736–1806	Dormans, Champagne	Architect to Louis XVI, his major works include the Chateau at Louveciennes; the Saltworks at Arc-et-Senans (1775–80); theatre at Besançon (1771–3).

Architects (continued)

Name	Dates	Place of birth	Selected works
Lescot, Pierre	c.1515–78	Paris	Major work is the Louvre, Paris.
Loos, Adolf	1870–1933	Brno	One of the major architects of the 'Modern Movement'. He settled in Vienna in 1896.
Lutyens, Edwin	1869–1944	London	His best-known projects are Castle Drogo (1910–30); the Cenotaph in Whitehall; and laying out New Delhi, India (1912–30).
Mackintosh, Charles Rennie	1868–1928	Glasgow	A leader of 'Glasgow style', a movement related to Art Nouveau. Designs include interiors, furniture, and the Glasgow School of Art (1896–9 and 1906–9).
Maderno, Carlo	1556–1629	Capalgo, Italy	Appointed architect to St Peter's, 1603, added a large façade (1606–12). Other works are Sta Susanna (1597–1603) and the Palazzo Barberini (1628–38).
Mansard or Mansart, François	1598–1666	Paris	He brought a simplified adaptation of the Baroque style into France and made fashionable the high-pitched type of roof which bears his name.
Meier, Richard	1934–	Newark, New Jersey	Museum für Kunsthandwerk, Frankfurt (1984); City Hall and Central Library, The Hague (1996); J Paul Getty Center, Los Angeles (1997); Burda Collection Museum, Baden-Baden (2004).
Mendelsohn, Erich	1887–1953	Allenstein, Germany	Designed the Einstein Tower in Potsdam, and various hospitals and stores, also the Hebrew University in Jerusalem. From 1941 he worked in the United States, designing synagogues and hospitals.
Mies van der Rohe, Ludwig	1886–1969	Aachen	Designs include the German pavilion for the Barcelona Exhibition (1928), and the Seagram Building, New York (1956–9).
Moneo, José Rafael	1937–	Tudela, Spain	Attocha Railroad Station, Madrid (1982–94); Davis Museum and Cultural Centre, Wellesley College, MA (1993); Museum in Stockholm (1998); Cathedral of Our Lady of the Angels, Los Angeles (2002).
Nash, John	1752–1835	London	Designed Regent's Park and Marble Arch, recreated Buckingham Palace, and laid out Trafalgar Square and St James Park.
Nervi, Pier Luigi	1891–1979	Sondrio, Italy	Designed the Stadium for the Olympic games in Rome (1960) and San Francisco Cathedral (1970).
Neumann, Balthasar	1687–1753	Eger, Germany	Designed many outstanding examples of the Baroque style, notably Würzburg Palace and Schloss Bruchsal.
Niemeyer, Oscar	1907–	Rio de Janeiro	Church of São Francisco, Pampulha (1942–44); Exhibition Hall, São Paulo (1953); President's Palace, Cathedrals, and Law Courts, Brasilia; Oscar Niemeyer Museum of Art, Paraná, Brazil (2004).
Oud, Jacobus Johannes Pieter	1890–1963	Purmerend, Netherlands	Launched the review de Stijl and became a pioneer of modern architecture based on simplified forms. He became city architect to Rotterdam in 1918.
Palladio, Andrea	1508–80	Vicenza	Developed the style now known as 'Palladian', based on classical Roman principles. He remodelled the basilica at Vicenza and designed many villas, palaces, and churches, particularly in Venice.
Pei, Ieoh Meng	1917–	Canton	Mile High Center, Denver; John Hancock Tower, Boston; glass pyramid at the Louvre; Miho Museum, Kyoto (1998); Arts Center, Christopher Newport University, VA (2005); Suzhou Museum, China (2006).
Pelli, Cesar	1926–	Tucuman, Argentina	Canary Wharf Tower, London (1986); Ohio Center for Performing Arts (1991); Washington National Airport passenger terminal (1997); Petronas Towers, Kuala Lumpur (1998); New Segerstrom Concert Hall, Costa Mesa, CA (2006)
Peruzzi, Baldassare Tommaso	1481–1536	Ancajano	Villa Farnesina, Ossoli Palace, and Palazzo Massimo, Rome.
Piano, Renzo	1937–	Genoa, Italy	Pompidou Centre, Paris (1976); Kansai International Airport, Japan (1994–8); Lingotto Conference Centre, Turin (1998); Beyeler Museum, Basel (1998); Zentrum Paul Klee (2005); Morgan Library and Museum extension, NY City (2006).

Name	Dates	Place of birth	Selected works
Piranesi, Giovanni Battista	1720–78	Venice	Major influence on Neo-Classicism.
Playfair, William Henry	1789–1857	London	Designed most of Edinburgh's most important buildings, including the National Gallery of Scotland, the Royal Scottish Academy, and Donaldson's Hospital.
Poelzig, Hans	1869–1936	Berlin	Expressionist architect who served as the city architect for Dresden between 1916 and 1920. Early projects included the Luban Chemical Works, Posen, and the Water Tower and Exhibition Hall, Posen (1911–12). Later works were the remodelling of the Grosses Schauspielhaus, Berlin (1919); Salzburg Festival Theatre (1920–2); and the I G Farben Headquarters, Frankfurt (1928–31).
Pugin, Augustus	1812–52	London	Designed a large part of the decorations and sculpture for the new Houses of Parliament (1836–7) and did much to revive Gothic architecture in Britain.
Rietveld, Gerrit Thomas	1888–1964	Utrecht	Works include the Schroder House, Utrecht (1924), and the Van Gogh Museum, Amsterdam (completed posthumously 1973).
Rogers, Richard, Lord	1933–	Florence	Centre Pompidou, Paris (1971–9); Lloyds of London (1979–85); Channel 4 Television HQ, London (1995); Millennium Dome, London (2000); Terminal 5 Heathrow Airport (completion 2008).
Saarinnen, Eero	1910–61	Kirkonnumi, Finland	His designs for Expressionist buildings include the Trans-World Airline Kennedy Terminal, New York.
Sangallo, Antonio Giamberti da	1485–1546	Florence	Leading architect of the High Renaissance in Rome, designing the Palazzo Palma-Baldassini, Rome (c.1520), and the Palazzo Farnese, Rome (1534–46).
Scott, George Gilbert	1811–78	Gawcott, Buckinghamshire	The leading practical architect of the British Gothic Revival, as seen in the Albert Memorial (1862–3), St Pancras Station and Hotel (1865); and Glasgow University (1865).
Scott, Giles Gilbert	1880–1960	London	Designed the Anglican cathedral in Liverpool (1924); the new buildings at Clare College, Cambridge, and Cambridge University Library (1931–4); the new Bodleian Library, Oxford (1936–46). He designed the new Waterloo Bridge (1939–45); and was responsible for the rebuilding of the House of Commons after World War 2.
Shaw, Norman	1831–1912	Edinburgh	Major works include the Old Swan House, Chelsea (1876); New Scotland Yard (1888); the Gaiety Theatre, Aldwych (1902); and the Piccadilly Hotel (1905).
Smirke, Robert	1781–1867		Significant buildings include Covent Garden Theatre (1809) and the British Museum (1823–47). He also designed the General Post Office (1824–9) and the College of Physicians (1825).
Soane, John	1753–1837	Goring, Oxfordshire	His designs include The Bank of England (1792-1833) and Dulwich College Art Gallery (1811–14).
Soufflot, Jacques	1713–80	Irancy	Leading exponent of Neo-Classicism, designing the Panthéon and École de Droit, Paris; the Hotel Dieu, Lyon; and Rennes Cathedral.
Spence, Basil	1907–76	Bombay	The leading post-war architect; examples of his work include the pavilion for the Festival of Britain (1951) and the new Coventry Cathedral (1951).
Stirling, James	1926–92	Glasgow	Clore Gallery, Tate Gallery, London
Sullivan, Louis	1856–1924	Boston	His experimental, functional skeleton constructions of skyscrapers and office blocks, particularly the Gage Building and stock exchange, earned him the title of the 'Father of Modernism'.
Tait, Thomas Smith	1882–1954		Prominent architect of the inter-war period. Designed Adelaide House (1921–4) and the Daily Telegraph offices (1927) in London, and St Andrew's House, Edinburgh (1934).

ARTS AND CULTURE

Architects (continued)

Name	Dates	Place of birth	Selected works
Tange, Kenzo	1913–2005	Tokyo	Works include the Hiroshima Peace Centre (1949–55), the Shizoka Press and Broadcasting Centre (1966–7), and the National Gymnasium for the 1964 Olympic Games; also produced designs for new Nigerian Capital, Abuja.
Terry, Quinlan	1937–	London	Merks Hall, Great Dunmow, Essex (1982); Richmond Riverside project, London (1984); Downing College Library, Cambridge (1990–2)
Utzon, Jørn	1918–	Copenhagen	Designer of the Sydney Opera House; the Kuwait House of Parliament; Copenhagen's Bagsuaerd Church (1976); Paustian's House of Furniture (1987); Can Feliz, Mallorca (1995).
Venturi, Robert	1925–	Philadelphia	Seattle Art Museum, WA; Vanna Venturi House, PA; Provincial Capitol Building, Toulouse; Sainsbury Wing, National Gallery, London (1991); Life Sciences Institute, Michigan University (2004).
Vignola, Giacomo da	1507–73	Vignola	In Rome he designed the Villa di Papa Giulio and the Church of the Gesù.
Viñoly, Rafael	1944–	Montevideo, Uruguay	Performing Arts Centre, Philadelphia (1996); Tokyo International Forum (1996); Mahler 4 Office Tower, Amsterdam (2005)
Viollet-le-Duc, Eugene	1814–79	Paris	Restored the cathedrals of Notre Dame, Amiens, and Laon; and the Chateau de Pierrefonds.
Vitruvius (Marco Vitruvius Pollio)	1st-c AD	Rome	Architect and engineer. He wrote the *De Architectura*, the only extant Roman treatise on this subject.
Wagner, Otto	1841–1918	Vienna	Considered the founder of the 'modern movement'. His most influential works include Karlsplatz station (1898–9) and Am Steinhof Church (1905–7). His main hall of the K K Sportsparkasse (1904–6) was regarded as the first example of modern architecture in the 20th-c.
Waterhouse, Alfred	1830–1905	Liverpool	Built the romanesque Natural History Museum in London (1873–81); from his great use of red brick came the name 'red-brick university'.
Webb, Aston	1849–1930	London	Designed the Admiralty Arch, Imperial College of Science, and many other buildings in London.
Wilson, Colin St John	1922–	Cheltenham	British Library, London (1982–98)
Wood, John (the Elder)	1705–54	Yorkshire	Responsible for many of the well-known streets and buildings of Bath – North and South Parades, Queen Square, the Circus, and Prior Park.
Wren, Christopher	1632–1723	East Knoyle, Wiltshire	After the Great Fire of London he drew up plans for rebuilding the whole city, but the plans were never implemented. He designed the new St Paul's Cathedral in 1669 and then many other public buildings, such as the Greenwich Observatory; the Ashmolean Library, Oxford; part of Hampton Court; The Sheldonian Theatre, Oxford; the Royal Exchange, the Temple Bar, and Greenwich Hospital.
Wright, Frank Lloyd	1869–1959	Richland Center, Wisconsin	One of the leading designers of private dwellings, planned in conformity with the natural features of the land. Among his larger works is the Guggenheim Museum of Art in New York.
Wyatt, James	1746–1813	Burton Constable, Staffordshire	Designed the London Pantheon (1772), but his best known work is the Gothic-Revival Fonthill Abbey (1796–1807).

PAINTING

Artists

Name	Dates	Place of birth	Selected works
Albani, Francesco	1578–1660	Bologna	Altarpieces in the Chapel of the Annunciation, Quirinal Palace, and the choir of St Maria della Pace; frescoes in the chapel of St Diego, church of St Giacomo degli Spagnuoli; *Dance of the Amorini*
Angelico, Fra	c.1400–1455	Vicchio, Tuscany	San Marco frescoes, Florence; *Last Judgement; Orvieto; Coronation of the Virgin; Glory; Pietas*
Antonello da Messina	1430–79	Sicily	San Cassiano altarpiece; *Annunciation*
Bacon, Francis	1909–92	Dublin	*Studio of Velazquez*
Baselitz, Georg	1938–	Deutschbaselitz, Germany	*The Great Friend; The Brocken Choir; Rote Schwestern-Smyrna*
Bassano, Jacopo da	c.1510–92	Bassano	*Adoration of the Magi; Crucifixion*
Beardsley, Aubrey	1872–98	Brighton	*Isolde; Salome; Morte d'Arthur*
Bellini, Giovanni	c.1430–1516	Venice	San Giobbe altarpiece; *Madonna with Baptist and another Saint; Bacchanale; Pieta; The Doge Loredano*
Blake, William	1757–1827	London	Illustrations to the Book of Job
Bonnard, Pierre	1867–1947	Paris	*Nude in the Bath; Skating Rink; Red Bodice; La Toilette; Woman in Black Stockings*
Bosch, Hieronymus	1450–1516	Hertogenbosch	*The Garden of Earthly Delights; The Last Judgement*
Botticelli, Sandro	1445–1510	Florence	*Birth of Venus; Primavera; Nativity; Mars and Venus*
Boucher, François	1703–70	Paris	*Birth of Venus*
Boudin, Eugene	1824–98	Honfleur	*Deauville; Harbour at Trouville; Corvette Russe*
Braque, Georges	1882–1963	Argenteuil	*Piano and Lute; House at L'Estaque; Still Life*
Breughel, Pieter (the Elder)	1520–69	Breda	*Massacre of the Innocents; Peasant Wedding; Hunters in the Snow; The Triumph of Death*
Bronzino, Agnolo Filippo	1503–72	Monticelli	*Venus; Cupid; Folly and Time; Portrait of Lucrezia Panciatichi*
Canaletto	1697–1768	Venice	*The Stonemason's Yard; Venice: Piazza San Marco and the Colonnade of the Procurate Nuove; Scene in Venice; The Piazzetta Entrance to the Grand Canal*
Caravaggio	1573–1610	Caravaggio	*Madonna of the Rosary; Death of the Virgin; Christ at Emmaus; Deposition of Christ; The Conversion of St Paul; The Entombment; The Calling of St Matthew*
Carpacció, Vittore	c.1460–c.1525	Venice	*Young Knight in a Landscape; Stories of St Ursula; The Presentation in the Temple*
Cézanne, Paul	1839–1906	Aix-en-Provence	*The Bathers; La Maison du Pendu; Les Grandes Baigneuses; The Blue Vase; Man Standing with Hands on Hips*
Chagall, Marc	1887–1985	Vitebsk	*Self-Portrait with Seven Fingers; The Newspaper Seller; Paris Through the Window*
Christo (Christo Javacheff)	1935–	Gabrovo, Bulgaria	*Wrapped Coast, Little Bay, Sydney, Australia; Valley Curtain, Grand Hogback, Rifle, Colorado; Running Fence, California; The Pont Neuf Wrapped, Paris; Surrounded Islands; The Gates*
Clemente, Francesco	1952–	Naples	*Francesco Clemente Pinxit; Two Painters*
Constable, John	1776–1837	East Bergholt, Suffolk	*The Haywain; Weymouth Bay; Borrowdale; White Horse; Valley Farm; Cornfield*
Corbet, Christian Cardell	1966–	Ontario	*Elizabeth Holding Her Ribbon*
Corot, Jean-Baptiste-Camille	1796–1875	Paris	*The Bridge at Nantes; The Studio; Chartres Cathedral; Danse des Nymphes; Le Bûcheron; Orphée; Homère et les Bergers; Joueur de Flûte*
Correggio, Antonio	1494–1534	Correggio	*Adoration of the Shepherds; Madonna of St Francis; Madonna of St Sebastian; Jupiter and Io; Nativity; Jupiter and Antiope; Education of Cupid; Danae; Ecce Homo*
Courbet, Gustave	1819–77	Ornans	*The Painter's Studio; Funeral at Ornans; Girls on the Banks of the Seine; Peasants of Flazey*
Dali, Salvador	1904–89	Figueras	*Persistence of Memory; Christ of St John of the Cross*
Daumier, Honoré	1808–79	Marseilles	*La Rue Transnonain; The Washerwoman; Ecce Homo; Third-Class Carriage*
David, Jacques Louis	1748–1825	Paris	*Oath of the Horatii; The Death of Socrates; Portrait of Madame Recamier*

Artists (continued)

Name	Dates	Place of birth	Selected works
Degas, Edgar	1834–1917	Paris	Absinthe Drinker; Bellelli Family; Miss Lola at the Cirque Fernando; Dancer at the Bar; Cotton-brokers Office
de Kooning, Willem	1904–97	Rotterdam	Woman I–IV
Delacroix, Eugène	1798–1863	Charenton-Saint-Maurice	Women of Algiers; Liberty Guiding the People; The Massacre at Chios
Delaunay, Robert	1885–1941	Paris	Eiffel Tower; Fenêtres
Dix, Otto	1891–1969	Gera	The Hall of Mirrors; The Artist's Parents; Pimp and Girls; Two Sacrifices of Capitalism; Saul and David; Crucifixion
Dufy, Raoul	1877–1953	Le Havre	Nice; Bois de Boulogne; Deauville
Dürer, Albrecht	1471–1528	Nuremburg	Self-Portrait; Lamentation on the Dead Christ; Melancolia
Ernst, Max	1891–1976	Bruhl	The Elephant Celebes; The Hat Makes the Man; Two Children are Threatened By a Nightingale; Oedipus; Une Semaine de Bonté
Fantin-Latour, Henri	1836–1904	Grenoble	Hommage à Delacroix; Still Life; L' Anniversaire
Fragonard, Jean-Honoré	1732–1806	Grasse	La Belle Serveuse; The Swing; Bacchante Endormie; La Chemise Enlevée
Francesca, Piero della	1420–92	Borgo San Sepolcro	Annunciation; Flagellation; Brera Madonna
Freud, Lucian	1922–	Berlin	Woman with a Daffodil, Dead Monkey; Large Interior; David Dawson; The Painter Surprised by a Naked Admirer
Frost, Terry	1915–2003	Leamington Spa	Movement, Green and Black; Red, Black and White; Newlyn Blue Q; Zeus Flight
Gainsborough, Thomas	1727–88	Sudbury, Suffolk	The Morning Walk; Lady Brisco; Lord and Lady Howe; Mrs Portman; Blue Boy
Gauguin, Paul	1848–1903	Paris	The Moon and the Earth; La Belle Angele; Whence do we come? What are we? Where do we go?; The Yellow Christ; Vision after the Sermon; Nevermore
Gentile da Fabriano	c.1370–c.1427	Fabriano	Adoration of the Magi
Giotto	1267–1337	Vespignano	Stefaneschi Triptych; The Lamentation; Death of the Knight of Celano; The Betrayal; The Lives of Christ and the Virgin
Goya, Francisco	1746–1828	Saragossa	The Execution of the Rebels; Stilt Walkers; Blind Guitarist;
Greco, El	1541–1614	Crete	Baptism; Pentecost; Resurrection; Assumption of the Virgin
Grünewald, Mathias	1480–1528	Würzburg	Crucifixion; Isenheim altarpiece
Hals, Frans	c.1580–1666	Antwerp	Portrait of a Married Couple; Merry Drinkers; Banquet of the Officers of St George; The Laughing Cavalier; Gypsy Girl
Hiroshige, Ando	1797–1858	Edo, Japan	Ukiyo-e (Pictures of the Floating World); Fifty-three Stages on the Tōkaidō Progress; Portrait of an Artist
Hockney, David	1937–	Bradford, West Yorkshire	A Bigger Splash; Mr and Mrs Clark and Percy; Apples, Grapes, Lemons on a Table; Tjufjord, Nordkapp; Path Through Wheat Field
Hodler, Ferdinand	1853–1918	Berne	Night; The Elect; Eurhythmy; Day; The Battle of Nafels
Hogarth, William	1697–1764	London	Marriage à la Mode; Harlot's Progress; Rake's Progress
Hokusai, Katsushika	1760–1849		The Great Wave of Kanagawa; Hundred Views of Mount Fuji
Holbein, Hans (the Younger)	1497–1543	Augsburg	Portrait of Erasmus of Rotterdam; The Ambassadors
Hopper, Edward	1882–1967	New York	Window at Night; Early Sunday Morning; House by the Railroad; Room in Brooklyn; Nighthawks; Second Story Sunlight
Hunt, William Henry	1790–1864	London	Peaches and Grapes; Old Pollard; Wild Flowers
Ingres, Jean Auguste Dominique	1780–1867	Montauban	Napoleon on the Imperial Throne; Oedipus and the Sphinx; The Dream of Ossian; La Grande Odalisque; Apotheosis of Homer
John, Augustus	1878–1961	Tenby	Smiling Woman; portraits of James Joyce, G B Shaw, Mme Suggia, and Dylan Thomas
Kandinsky, Wasily	1866–1944	Moscow	Landscape with Red Spot; Painting with a Black Arch; Improvisation V; The Abstract Watercolour; White Line; Blue Segment; Dominant Curve; Affirmed Pink
Kaprow, Allan	1927–2006	Atlantic City, New Jersey	Eighteen Happenings in Six Parts
Kiefer, Anselm	1945–	Donaveschingen, Germany	Die Meistersinger; Departure from Egypt; The Red Sea; Jerusalem; Bohemia Lies By the Sea

Name	Dates	Place of birth	Selected works
Kirchner, Ernst	1880–1938	Aschaffenburg	*Five Women in the Street; Self-Portrait with Model; Woman at the Mirror*
Klee, Paul	1879–1940	Munchenbuchsee	*Red-Green Gardens; Around the Fish; Goldfish Wife; Twittering Machine*
Klein, Yves	1928–62	Nice	*Anthropometries*
Klimt, Gustav	1862–1918	Baumgarten, Austria	*The Kiss; Frau Fritza Riedler; Frau Adele Bloch-Bauer; Beethoven Frieze; Jurisprudence*
Klinger, Max	1857–1920	Leipzig	*The Judgement of Paris; Pietà; Christ in Olympus; Fantasy on Brahms; Eve of the Future; A Life; Of Death*
Kokoschka, Oskar	1886–1980	Pochlarn, Austria	*The Tempest; Knight Errant; Portrait of Dr Tietze and his Wife; Ambassador Maysky*
Laurencin, Marie	1883–1956	Paris	*The Assembly*
Leonardo da Vinci	1452–1519	Vinci, Florence	*Madonna Benois; Madonna Litta; Mona Lisa; The Virgin of the Rocks; Last Supper*
Le Parc, Julio	1928–	Mendoza, Argentina	*Continuel Lumière Formes en Contorsion*
Lichtenstein, Roy	1923–97	New York	*M-Maybe; Hopeless; New York City*
Lippi, Fra Filippo	c.1406–69	Florence	*Annunciation; Tarquinia Madonna; The Virgin and the Saints; The Vision of St Bernard; The Adoration of the Magi*
Long, Richard	1945–	Bristol	*A Line in Scotland; Parnassus Line, Karoo Crossing*
Lorenzetti, Pietro	c.1280/90 –c.1348	Siena	*Deposition; Birth of the Virgin*
Lowry, Lawrence Stephen	1887–1976	Manchester	*Coming from the Mill*
Macke, August	1887–1914	Meschede	*The Storm; Woman with a Green Jacket; The Zoo*
Magritte, René	1898–1967	Lessines	*Ceci n'est pas une Pipe; Duration Knifed; Le Plaisir; The Wind and the Song; The Human Condition*
Manet, Edouard	1832–83	Paris	*Déjeuner sur L'Herbe; Olympia; Portrait of Emile Zola; A Bar at the Folies-Bergères*
Mantegna, Andrea	1431–1506	Vicenza	*Agony in the Garden; Dead Christ; Martyrdom of St Sebastian; San Zeno altarpiece*
Masson, André	1896–1987	Balagny	*Fish in Sand; Dead Horses*
Matisse, Henri	1869–1954	Cateau-Cambresis	*The Yellow Curtain; Girl Swimming in the Aquarium; The Red Room; Portrait of Madame Matisse with a Green Streak; The Snail; Woman with the Hat*
Michelangelo (Buonarotti)	1475–1564	Caprese	*Tondo Doni; Birth of Eve; Universal Judgement; Holy Family of the Tribune; The Last Judgement*
Millais, John Everett	1829–96	Southampton	*Ophelia; Gambler's Wife; The Boyhood of Raleigh; Bubbles*
Millet, Jean-Francois	1814–75	Gruchy	*The Winnower; The Sower; Angelus*
Miró, Joán	1893–1983	Barcelona	*Dutch Interior; The Ploughed Field; Person Throwing a Stone at a Bird*
Modigliani, Amedeo	1884–1920	Livorno	*Red Nude; Portrait of Madame Anna Zborowska; Reclining Nude*
Mondrian, Piet	1872–1944	Amersfoort	*Composition with Red; Yellow and Blue; Tree*
Monet, Claude	1840–1926	Giverny	*Rouen Cathedral; Waterlilies; Women in the Garden; Impression: Sunrise*
Morisot, Berthe	1841–95	Bourges	*The Artist's Sister; Madame Pontillon; Seated on the Grass; The Artist's Sister Edma and their Mother*
Moroni, Giovanni Battista	1525–78	Bondo	*The Tailor*
Munch, Edvard	1863–1944	Loten	*The Scream; Angst; Girls on the Bridge; The Dance of Life; White Night; Marat's Death; Inttell–Self-Portrait*
Nicholson, Ben	1894–1982	Denham	*White Relief*
Nolan, Sidney	1917–92	Melbourne	*Boy and the Moon; Kelly; Leda and the Swan*
Noland, Kenneth	1924–	Asheville, Carolina	*Gift; The Other Side of Midnight*
Nolde, Emil	1867–1956	Nolde, Germany	*Dance Round the Golden Calf; Red and Yellow Roses; The Life of Christ; Marsh Landscape*
Ofili, Chris	1968–	Manchester	*Rara and Mala; Ongley; Double Captain Shit and the Legend of the Black Stars; The Upper Room*
O'Keefe, Georgia	1887–1986	Sun Prairie, Wisconsin	*Blue and Green Music; Black Iris; 'Near Abiquiu; New Mexico'*
Pechstein, Max	1881–1955	Zwickau	*Still Life with African Mask; Indian and Woman*
Picasso, Pablo	1881–1973	Malaga	*The Accordian Player; Les Demoiselles d'Avignon; Bottle of Vieux Marc; Guernica; Girl with a Mandolin; Two Women Running on the Beach*

ARTS AND CULTURE

Artists (continued)

Name	Dates	Place of birth	Selected works
Pisanello, Antonio	1395–1455	San Visilio	Vision of St Eustache; The Madonna with Saints Anthony and George; Margherita Gonzaga; Lionello d'Este
Pissarro, Camille	1830–1903	St Thomas, W Indies	Entrance to the Village of Voisins; Boulevard Montmartre; Place du Théâtre Français; Bridge at Bruges; 'Orchard with Flowering Fruit Trees, Springtime, Pontoise'; Peasant Girl with a Stick
Pollock, Jackson	1912–56	Cody, Wyoming	Number 1; Convergence; Number 12; Lucifer
Poussin, Nicolas	1594–1665	Les Andelys	Triumph of Neptune; Autumn; The Adoration of the Golden Calf
Raphael	1483–1520	Urbino	Conestabile Madonna; Holy Family; Sistine Madonna; Madonna of the Meadow; The Three Graces; Madonna and Child Enthroned with Saints; La Belle Jardinière; Coronation of the Virgin; Transfiguration; Madonna of Foligno; School of Athens
Rembrandt	1606–69	Leyden	Self-Portrait with Saskia; Self-Portrait; Flora; The Night Watch; The Jewish Bride; Syndics of the Cloth Drapers' Guild; Dr Tulp's Anatomy Lesson
Renoir, Pierre Auguste	1841–1919	Limoges	Le Moulin de la Galette; La Grenouillère; The Two Sisters; Luncheon of the Boating Party
Riley, Bridget	1931–	London	Fall; Nineteen Greys; Nataraja; Composition with Circles
Roberti, Ercole de	1450–96	Ferrara	Santa Maria in Porto altarpiece; Madonna; Pietà
Rossetti, Dante Gabriel	1828–82	London	Beata Beatrix; The Annunciation; The Girlhood of Mary Virgin; Ecce Ancilla Domini
Rothko, Mark	1903–70	Dvinsk, Russia	Number 10; Light Red Over Black
Rousseau, Henri (le Douanier)	1844–1910	Laval	The Sleeping Gypsy; Carnival Evening; Myself : Portrait Landscape; Yadivigha's Dream; The Hungry Lion
Rousseau, Théodore	1812–67	Paris	Path through the Forest of L'Isle Adam; Effet d'Orage; Forest of Compiègne
Rubens, Peter Paul	1577–1640	Siegen	Deposition; Henry IV Receiving the Portrait of Maria de' Medici; Allegory of War; Descent from the Cross; The Crucifixion of St Peter
Sargent, John Singer	1856–1925	Florence	Madame Gautreau; Madam X; The Wyndham Sisters; 'Carnation, Lily, Lily, Rose'; Mountain Fire
Schiele, Egon	1890–1918	Tulln	Self-Portrait; The Self-Seer; The Cardinal and the Nun; Embrace
Schnabel, Julian	1951–	Brooklyn, New York	The Sea; King of the Wood; Homo Painting; Humanity Asleep; The Conversion of St Paolo Malfi
Schwitters, Kurt	1887–1948	Hanover	The Constellation; Picture with Light Centers; Merzbilden
Seurat, Georges	1859–91	Paris	Bathers at Asnières; Sunday Afternoon on the Island of La Grande Jatte; La Baignade; Les Poseuses; Le Cirque
Signac, Paul	1863–1935	Paris	The Seine at Asnières; View of the Port of Marseilles
Signorelli, Luca	c.1441–1523	Cortona	The Preaching of the Anti-Christ; Last Judgement
Sisley, Alfred	1839–99	Paris	Flood at Port Marley; The Boat During the Flood
Spencer, Stanley	1891–1959	Cookham, Berkshire	Resurrection: Port Glasgow; Shipbuilding on the Clyde; The Resurrection
Steer, Philip Wilson	1860–1942	Birkenhead	Self-Portrait; The Music Room; Portrait of Mrs Hammersley
Tanguy, Yves	1900–55	Paris	Fear; Mama Papa is Wounded
Tiepolo, Giovanni Battista	1696–1770	Venice	Thetis Comforting Achilles; The Sacrifice of Isaac; Madonna of Carmelo and the Souls of Purgatory; The Banquet of Cleopatra; The Martyrdom of St Sebastian; Time Revealing Truth
Tintoretto	1518–94	Venice	Miracles of St Mark; Discovery of the Body of St Mark; The Last Supper; The Miracle of the Loaves and Fishes; The Golden Calf; Entombment
Titian	1490–1576	Pieve di Cadore	Pietà; Presentation of the Virgin in the Temple; Isabella d'Este; The Gypsy Madonna; Madonna of Frari; Assumption of the Virgin
Toulouse-Lautrec, Henri	1864–1901	Albi	Au Moulin Rouge; Les Deux Amis; The Bar; At the Races
Turner, Joseph Mallord William	1775–1851	London	Calais Pier; Fall of an Avalanche in the Grisons; Norham Castle; Hannibal Crossing the Alps; Burning of the Houses of Parliament
Utrillo, Maurice	1883–1955	Paris	Church at Chatillon; Sacré-Coeur de Montmartre
Van Dyck, Anthony	1599–1641	Antwerp	Iconographica; The Deposition; Le Roi à la Chasse
Van Eyck, Jan	1390–1441	Maastricht	Arnolfini Wedding Portrait; Adoration of the Lamb

Name	Dates	Place of birth	Selected works
Van Gogh, Vincent	1853–90	Groot Zundert	*The Night Café; Starry Night; The Potato Eaters; Sunflowers; The Bridge; The Chair and the Pipe*
Vasarely, Viktor	1908–97	Pecs, Hungary	*Sorata-T; Inflexion*
Velazquez, Diego	1599–1660	Seville	*The Drinkers; Christ in the House of Martha; The Coronation of the Virgin; The Toilet of Venus*
Vermeer, Jan	1632–75	Delft	*A Girl Asleep; Young Woman Reading a Letter; The Letter; The Kitchen Maid; View of Delft; The Love Letter; The Lacemaker*
Veronese, Paolo	c.1528–88	Verona	*Feast in the House of Levi; Mars and Venus United by Love; Venice Crowned Queen of the Sea; The Marriage Feast at Cana; The Adoration of the Magi*
Vuillard, Edouard	1868–1940	Cuiseaux	*Under the Trees; Jardin de Paris; Woman Sweeping*
Warhol, Andy	1927–87	Pittsburgh, Pennsylvania	*Campbell's Soup; Marilyn Monroe; Dick Tracy; 100 Soup Cans*
Watteau, Antoine	1684–1721	Valenciennes	*L'Indifférente; Enseigne de Gersaint; Fêtes Galantes; Embarquement pour Cythère*
Wearing, Gillian	1963–	Birmingham	*Homage to the Woman the Bandaged Face who I Saw Yesterday Down Walworth Road; Confess All on Video* (video); *Sixty Minute Silence* (video)
Whistler, James Abbott McNeill	1834–1903	Lowell, Massachusetts	*Portrait of the Artist's Mother; Old Battersea Bridge; The White Girl; Cremorne Gardens; No.2; Three Figures: Pink and Grey*
Witz, Konrad	1400–46	Rottweil	*Annunciation; Christ Walking on the Water; Miraculous Draft of Fishes*

The Turner Prize

1985	Howard Hodgkin	1993	Rachel Whiteread	2001	Martin Creed
1986	Gilbert and George	1994	Anthony Gormley	2002	Keith Tyson
1987	Richard Deacon	1995	Damien Hirst	2003	Grayson Perry
1988	Tony Cragg	1996	Douglas Gordon	2004	Jeremy Deller
1989	Richard Long	1997	Gillian Wearing	2005	Simon Starling
1990	*Prize suspended*	1998	Chris Ofili	2006	Tomma Abts
1991	Anish Kapoor	1999	Steve McQueen		
1992	Grenville Davey	2000	Wolfgang Tillmans		

SCULPTURE

Sculptors

Name	Dates	Place of birth	Selected works
Agostino di Duccio	1418–81	Florence	Tempio Malatestiano decorations, oratory of St Bernadino, Perugia
Andre, Carl	1935–	Massachusetts	*Equivalents; Cedar Piece; Isoclast*
Arp, Hans	1887–1966	Strasbourg	*Shell and Head*
Barlach, Ernst	1870–1938	Wedel	*The Avenger; Death*
Bernini, Gian Lorenzo	1598–1680	Naples	*Fontana dei Quattro Fiumi*; Rome, dome of San Carlo alle Quattro Fontane; *Apollo and Daphne*; Conaro Chapel
Brancusi, Constantin	1876–1957	Hobitza	*Bird in Space; The Kiss; Torso of a Young Man*
Brunelleschi, Filippo	1377–1446	Florence	Dome of Florence cathedral; *Sacrifice of Isaac*
Calder, Alexander	1898–1976	Philadelphia	*Josephine Baker; Romulus and Remus; The Horse; Spring; A Universe; Hanging Mobile; Lobster Trap and Fish Tail; Constellation with Red Object*
Canova, Antonio	1757–1822	Possagno	*Cupid and Psyche; Winged Cupid; Venus and Adonis; Psyche Holding a Butterfly; Penitent Magdalen; Perseus with the Head of the Medusa*

Sculptors (continued)

Name	Dates	Place of birth	Selected works
Caro, Anthony	1924–	London	Sailing Tonight; Ledge Piece; Goodwood Steps; Chair IV; Waltz Time
Cellini, Benvenuto	1500–71	Florence	Perseus with the Head of the Medusa; Nymph; Neptune and Ceres
Donatello di Niccolo	c.1386–1466	Florence	David; Judith and Holofernes; Cantoria; Magdalen; Gattamelata
Duchamp, Marcel	1887–1968	Blainville	The Bride Stripped Bare by her Bachelors, Even; Fountain; Bicycle Wheel
Duchamp-Villon, Ramond	1876–1918	Damville	Horse; Baudelaire; Maggy; The Seated Woman
Emin, Tracey	1963–	London	My Bed; Everyone I have ever slept with (1963–95); The Roman Standard
Epstein, Jacob	1880–1959	New York	Rima; Genesis; Ecce Homo; Christ in Majesty; St Michael and the Devil
Gabo, Naum	1890–1977	Bryansk, Russia	Head of a Woman; Kinetic Composition; Spiral Theme
Ghiberti, Lorenzo	c.1378–1455	Florence	Sacrifice of Isaac; John the Baptist; St Matthew; The Gates of Paradise
Giacommetti, Alberto	1901–66	Stampo	Suspended Square; Observing Head; Torso; Cubist Composition; Three Figures Outdoors; Tall Figures; City Square; Chariot
Giambologna, Jean de Boulogne	1529–1608	Douai	Rape of the Sabine Women; Mercury; Fountain of Neptune; Samson and a Philistine; Altar of Liberty
Gill, Eric	1882–1940	Brighton	Stations of the Cross; Mankind; Mother and Child; Prospero and Ariel; The Creation of Adam
Gormley, Antony	1950–	London	Three Ways: Mould, Hole and Passage; The Angel of the North; Quantum Leap; Domain Field; Another Place
Hanson, Duane	1925–96	Alexandria, Minnesota	Abortion; Woman with Shopping Trolley; Tourists
Hepworth, Barbara	1903–75	Wakefield	Figure of a Woman; Large and Small Forms; Reclining Figure; Wave; Four Squares; Orpheus
Hirst, Damien	1965–	Bristol	Mother and Child Divided; A Thousand Years; Away from the Flock; Some Comfort Gained from the Acceptance of the Inherent Lies in Everything; Amazing Revelations
Judd, Donald	1928–94	Excelsior Springs	Eight Modular Unit V-Channel Piece
Kapoor, Anish	1954–	Bombay	A Flower, A Drama Like Death; A Wing at the Heart of Things; Parabolic Waters; Marsyas; Cloud Gate
Laurens, Henri	1885–1954	Paris	The Farewell; Head of a Young Girl; Still Life
Leonardo da Vinci	1452–1519	Vinci	St John the Baptist
Leoncillo	1915–1968	Spoleto	St Sebastian
Lipchitz, Jacques	1891–1973	Druskininkai	Sailor with a Guitar; Harpist; The Couple; Prayer; Prometheus Strangling the Vulture II
Maitani, Lorenzo	c.1275–1330	Orvieto	Creation of the Animals; Eagle of St John; Angel of St Matthew
Manzù, Giacomo	1908–91	Bergamo, Italy	Bronze doors, St Peter's, Rome
Marini, Marino	1901–80	Pistoia	The Dancer; Horse and Rider; Portrait of Igor Stravinsky
Martini, Arturo	1889–1947	Treviso	Water Drinker; Moonlight; Thirst; Girl Swimming Under Water; Corporate Justice
Michelangelo (Buonarroti)	1475–1564	Caprese	Pietà; Madonna of the Steps; Victory
Moore, Henry	1898–1986	Castleford	Recumbent Figure; Fallen Warrior; Mother and Child; Family Group; Reclining Figure; King and Queen; Seated Figure Against Curved Wall
Morris, Robert	1931–	Kansas City	Untitled; In the Realm of the Carceral
Nash, David	1945–	Esher, Surrey	Rostrum with Bonks; Birch Crack and Warp; Sculpture from California
Noguchi, Isamu	1904–88	Los Angeles	Detroit Civic Center Plaza Fountain
Oldenburg, Claes	1929–	Stockholm	Giant Soft Fan; Lipstick (Ascending) on Caterpillar Tracks; Colossal Ashtray with Fagends; Mistos, or Match Cover; Museum à la Mode; Balzac Petanque
Parmiggiani, Claudio	1943–	Luzzara	Sineddoche; Polvere; Untitled
Pisano, Andrea	1270–1349	Pontedera	The Baptism of Christ; Bell Tower of Florence Cathedral
Pisano, Giovanni	1245–1317	Pisa	Annunciation; Nativity; Annunciation to the Shepherds; tomb sculpture for Margaret of Luxembourg
Rauschenberg, Robert	1925–	Port Arthur, Texas	Monogram; Bicycle; Wonder
Rodin, Auguste	1840–1917	Paris	L'Homme au Nez Cassé; Le Baiser; Le Penseur; Les Bourgeois de Calais; The Vanquished; The Age of Bronze

Name	Dates	Place of birth	Selected works
Rossellino, Antonio	1427–79	Florence	Bust of Florentine Matteo Palmieri; bust of Giovanni Chellini; *Madonna and Child; Shrine of the Marcolino de Forli*
Schlemmer, Oskar	1888–1943	Stuttgart	*Triadic Ballet; Abstrakte Rindplastik*
Segal, George	1925–2000	New York	*Rock'n Roll Combo; The Truck; The Laundromat; Hot Dog Stand; Bus Shelter*
Sluter, Claus	1350–1405	Haarlem	Bust of Christ; *Well of Moses*; chapel of Chartreuse de Champnol, Dijon, tomb of Philip the Bold, Duke of Burgundy
Tinguely, Jean	1925–91	Fribourg	*Machines à Peindre; Study for an End of the World; Metamécanique No.; Homage to New York*

PHOTOGRAPHY

Photographers

Name	Dates	Place of birth
Adams, Ansel	1902–84	San Francisco
Arbus, Diane	1923–71	New York City
Avedon, Richard	1923–2004	New York City
Bailey, David	1938–	London
Beaton, Cecil	1904–80	London
Bourke-White, Margaret	1906–71	New York City
Brady, Mathew	1823–96	Lake George, New York
Brandt, Bill	1904–83	London
Brassaï (Gyula Halasz)	1899–1984	Brasso, Transylvania
Cameron, Julia Margaret	1815–79	Calcutta
Capa, Robert (André Friedmann)	1913–54	Budapest
Cartier-Bresson, Henri	1908–2004	Paris
Cunningham, Imogen	1883–1976	Portland, Oregon
Curtis, Edward Sheriff	1868–1952	Madison, Wisconsin
Daguerre, Louis Jacques Mandé	1789–1851	Cormeilles
Eisenstaedt, Alfred	1898–95	Tczew, Poland (formerly Dirschau)
Evans, Frederick	1853–1943	Whitechapel, London
Evans, Walker	1903–75	St Louis, Missouri
Fenton, Roger	1819–69	Lancashire
Firth, Francis	1822–98	Chesterfield
Godwin, Fay Simmonds	1931–2005	Berlin
Hardy, Bert	1913–95	London
Hill, David Octavius	1802–70	Perth, Scotland
Hine, Lewis	1874–1940	Oshkosh, Wisconsin
Karsh, Yousuf	1908–2002	Mardin (Turkey)
Kertész, André	1894–1985	Budapest
Koudelka, Josef	1938–	Boskovice, Czech Republic
Lange, Dorothea	1895–1965	Hoboken, New Jersey
Lartigue, Jacques-Henri	1894–1986	Curbevoie, France
Leibovitz, Annie	1950–	Connecticut
Lichfield, Patrick	1939–2005	Britain
Martin, Paul	1864–1942	Herbenville, France
McBean, Angus Rowland	1904–90	Newbridge, Monmouth
McCullin, Don	1935–	London
Mapplethorpe, Robert	1946–89	New York
Moholy-Nagy, László	1895–1946	Bacsbarsod, Hungary
Muybridge, Eadweard (Edward James Muggeridge)	1830–1904	Kingston-on-Thames
Mydans, Carl	1907–2004	Boston, Massachusetts
Nadar (Gaspard-Felix Tournachon)	1820–1910	Paris
Newman, Arnold	1918–2006	New York City
Nilsson, Lennart	1922–	Strängnäs, Sweden
Parer, Damien	1912–44	Malvern, Victoria
Parkinson, Norman (Ronald William Parkinson Smith)	1913–90	London
Ray, Man (Emanuel Rabinovitch)	1870–1976	Philadelphia
Robinson, Henry Peach	1830–1901	Ludlow
Saint Joseph, John Kenneth Sinclair	1912–94	Worcestershire
Sander, August	1876–1964	Herdorf, Germany
Sheeler, Charles	1883–1965	Philadelphia
Snowdon, Earl of (Antony Armstrong Jones)	1930–	London
Steichen, Edward Jean	1879–1973	Luxembourg
Stieglitz, Alfred	1864–1946	Hoboken, New Jersey
Strand, Paul	1890–1976	New York City
Sutcliffe, Frank Meadow	1853–1941	Whitby, Yorkshire
Talbot, William Henry Fox	1800–77	Melbury Abbas, Deveon
Weston, Edward	1886–1958	Highland Park, Illinois
White, Minor	1908–76	Minneapolis

ARTS AND CULTURE

ACADEMIC STUDY

Museums and art galleries

Country	Location	Museum	Date established
Afghanistan	Kabul	Kabul Museum	1922
Albania	Tiranë	Albanian National Culture Museum	na
Algeria	Algiers	National Museum of Algiers	1930
Argentina	Buenos Aires	National History Museum	1889
Armenia	Yerevan	Armenian State Historical Museum	
		Armenian State Picture Gallery	1921
Australia	Sydney	Australian Museum	1827
		Art Gallery of New South Wales	1874
		Australian National Maritime Museum	1985
		Powerhouse Museum, Museum of Applied Arts and Sciences	1880
	Canberra	National Gallery of Australia	1975
		National Museum of Australia	1980
	Melbourne	Museum of Victoria	1854
		National Gallery of Victoria	1859
	Brisbane	Queensland Art Gallery	1895
		Queensland Museum	1871
	Adelaide	Art Gallery of South Australia	1881
		South Australian Museum	1856
	Perth	Art Gallery of Western Australia	1895
		Western Australian Museum	1891
	Launceston	Queen Victoria Museum and Art Gallery	1891
	Hobart	Tasmanian Museum and Art Gallery	1852
Austria	Salzburg	Residence Gallery	1789
	Vienna	Kunsthistorisches Museum	1891
		Belvedere Gallery	18th-c
		Schönbrunn Palace	1569, museum in 1922
Bahamas	Nassau	Bahamia Museum	na
Bahrain	Manama	Bahrain Museum	1970
Bangladesh	Dhaka	Bangladesh National Museum	1913
Barbados	St Ann's Garrison	Barbados Museum and Historical Society	1933
Belarus	Minsk	Belarussian State Art Museum	1939
Belgium	Antwerp	Ruben's House	17th-c
		Royal Museum of Fine Art	1890
	Brussels	Erasmus House	1515
Bhutan	Paro	National Museum	1968
Bolivia	La Paz	National Museum	1846
Brazil	Rio de Janerio	National Museum	1818
Brunei	Kota Batu	Brunei Museum	1965
Bulgaria	Sofia	National Art Gallery	1948
Canada	Ottawa	Canadian Museum of Nature	1905
		Museum of Civilization	1905
		National Gallery of Canada	na
		National Museum of Science and Technology	1967
	Toronto	Art Gallery of Ontario	1900
		Royal Ontario Museum	na
	Quebec	Musé du Québec	1933
		McCord Museum of Canadian History	1919
	Montreal	Montreal Museum of Fine Arts	1860
	Vancouver	Vancouver Art Gallery	1931
	Victoria	British Columbia Provincial Museum	1886
	Edmonton	Provincial Museum of Alberta	1964
	Winnipeg	Winnipeg Art Gallery	1912
		Manitoba Museum of Man and Nature	1970
	Regina	Saskatchewan Museum of Natural History	1955
	St John's	Newfoundland Museum	na
	Saint John	New Brunswick Museum	1842
	Halifax	Nova Scotia Museum	1868
Chile	Santiago	National Historical Museum	1911
China	Beijing	Museum of Chinese History	1920
	Tsimshatsui	Hong Kong Museum of History	1975

Museums and art galleries (continued)

Country	Location	Museum	Date established
Colombia	Carrera	National Museum	1823
Costa Rica	San Jose	National Museum of Costa Rica	1887
Croatia	Zagreb	Croatian Historical Museum	1844
Cuba	Havana	National Museum	1913
Cyprus	Nicosia	The Cyprus Museum	1883
Czech Republic	Prague	National Museum	1818
		National Gallery	1796
Denmark	Copenhagen	National Museum	1807
Dominican Republic	Santo Domingo	National Fine Arts Gallery	1943
Ecuador	Quito	Civic Museum of Arts and History	1930
Egypt	Cairo	Egyptian Museum	1857
El Salvador	San Salvador	National Museum	1976
Estonia	Tallinn	Art Museum of Estonia	1919
		Estonian History Museum	1864
Ethiopia	Addis Ababa	Museum of the Institute of Ethiopian Studies	1963
Finland	Helsinki	Museum of Applied Arts	1873
France	Beauvais	National Tapestry Gallery	1964
	Fontainebleau	The Royal Palace of Fontainebleau	12th-c
	Paris	Auguste Rodin Museum	1915
		The Louvre	1791
		Musée d'Orsay	1986
		Museum of Modern Art at the Pompidou Centre	1976
		Museum of Technology	1794
		Picasso Museum	1985
	Saint-Germain-en-Laye	Museum of National Antiquities	16th-c
	Versailles	Château de Versailles	1837
Georgia	Tbilisi	Georgian State Museum	1852
Germany	Berlin	Bauhaus Archives and Museum of Design	1969
		Berlin Museum	1962
		Deutsches Historisches Museum	1987
		Haus der Wannsee-Konferenz	1992
	Frankfurt-am-Main	Goethe Museum	1859
	Hamburg	Altona Museum	1863
		Hamburg Art Gallery	1869
	Mainz	Roman-Germanic Central Museum	1852
	Munich	Deutsches Museum	1925
		Bavarian National Museum	1859
Greece	Athens	National Archaeological Museum	1866
		Museum of Cycladic Art	1986
		Acropolis Museum	1865
	Heraklion (Crete)	Archaeological Museum	1904
	Olympia	Museum of Ancient Olympia	1888
Grenada	St George's	Grenada National Museum	1976
Guatemala	Guatemala City	National Museum of History	1975
Guyana	Georgetown	Guyana Museum	1853
Haiti	Port-au-Prince	National Museum	1983
Hungary	Budapest	Hungarian National Museum	1802
Iceland	Reykjavík	National Museum	1863
India	New Delhi	National Museum of India	1949
Indonesia	Jakarta	National Museum	1778
Iran	Tehran	Iran Bastan Museum	1946
Iraq	Baghdad	Archaeological Museum of Iraq	na
Ireland	Dublin	National Museum of Ireland	1731
		National Gallery of Ireland	1864
Israel	Tel Aviv	Eretz-Israel Museum	1948
	Jerusalem	Israel Museum	1965
Italy	Bologna	Archaeological Museum	1881
		Museum of the Middle Ages and Renaissance	1985
		National Art Gallery	1882
	Florence	Accademia Gallery	1784
		Museum of the History of Science	1929
		Bardini Museum	1924
		Bargello Museum	1857
		Uffizi Gallery	1581

Country	Location	Museum	Date established
	Milan	Brera Art Gallery	1776
		Leonardo da Vinci Museum of Science and Technology	1953
	Naples	National Archaeological Museum	18th-c
	Rome	Borghese Gallery	1902
		Vatican Museums	na
		National Museum of Popular Art	1923
	Siena	Siena Museum	na
	Turin	Sabauda Gallery	1832
	Venice	Accademia Gallery	1807
		Peggy Guggenheim Collection	1980
		Treasury of St Mark's	na
Japan	Tokyo	National Museum	1871
Jordan	Amman	Folklore Museum	1972
		Popular Life Museum	1973
Kazakhstan	Alma Ata	Central State Museum of Kazakhstan	na
Korea, North	Pyongyang	Korean Central Historical Museum	na
Korea, South	Seoul	National Museum of Korea	1908
Kuwait	Kuwait City	Kuwait National Museum	1957
Kyrgyzstan	Bishkek	State Historical Museum of Kyrgyzstan	na
Laos	Vientiane	National Museum	1965
Latvia	Riga	Latvian Historical Museum	1869
		State Museum of Latvian and Russian Art	
Lebanon	Beirut	National Museum of Lebanon	1920
Liechtenstein	Vaduz	Liechtenstein Museum	1954
Lithuania	Vilnius	Museum of History and Ethnography of Lithuania	1855
		Art Museum of Lithuania	1941
Luxembourg	Luxembourg-Ville	Luxembourg Museum	1845
Malaysia	Kuala Lumpur	National Museum of Malaysia	1963
Maldives	Dhivehi	National Museum	1952
Mexico	Mexico City	National Museum of Anthropology	1964
Monaco	Monaco-Ville	Oceanographic Museum	1910
Morocco	Rabat	Museum of Antiquities	1917
Nepal	Kathmandu	National Museum of Nepal	1928
Netherlands	Amsterdam	Rijksmuseum	1817
		Rijksmuseum Vincent Van Gogh	1973
		Stedelijk Museum	1893
	Utrecht	Catherine Convent State Museum	1921
New Zealand	Auckland	Auckland City Art Gallery	1888
		Auckland Institute and Museum	1852
	Wellington	Museum of New Zealand Te Papa Tongarewa	1992
Nicaragua	Managua	National Museum of Nicaragua	1896
Norway	Bergen	Bergen Art Gallery	1925
	Oslo	Edvard Munch Museum	1963
		National Gallery	1836
		National Museum of Contemporary Art	1902
Oman	Muscat	Oman Natural History Museum	1983
Pakistan	Islamabad	National Museum of Pakistan	1950
Panama	Apdo	Museum of the History of Panama	1977
Paraguay	Asunción	National Museum of Fine Arts	1887
Peru	Lima	National Museum of History	1836
Philippines	Manila	National Museum of the Philippines	1901
Poland	Warsaw	National Museum	1862
Portugal	Lisbon	National Museum of Natural History	1859
		Museum of Popular Art	1948
Qatar	Doha	Qatar National Museum	1975
Romania	Bucharest	National History Museum of Romania	1968
		National Museum of Art	1950
Russia	Moscow	Pushkin Museum of Fine Arts	1912
	St Petersburg	Hermitage Museum	1764
		State Russian Museum	1898
Saudi Arabia	Riyadh	Museum of Archaeology and Ethnography	1978
Singapore	Singapore City	National Museum	1849
Spain	Barcelona	Catalan Museum of Art	1929
		Ethnological Museum	1948
		Picasso Museum	1963

KNOWLEDGE

Museums and art galleries (continued)

Country	Location	Museum	Date established
	Bilbao	Museum of Fine Art	1914
	Madrid	Prado Museum	1819
		National Museum of Ethnology	1940
	Seville	Museum of the Alcazar of Seville	na
		Museum of Fine Art	1835
	Valencia	Museum of Fine Art	1839
Sri Lanka	Colombo	Colombo National Museum	1877
Suriname	Paramaribo	Stichting Suranaams Museum	1947
Sweden	Stockholm	National Museum of Antiquities	1647
		Nordic Museum	1873
Switzerland	Basel	Basel Historical Museum	1894
	Geneva	Museum of Art and History	1910
	Zürich	Swiss National Museum	1898
		House of Art	1910
Syria	Damascus	National Museum	1919
Tajikistan	Dushanbe	Tajik Historical State Museum	na
Thailand	Bangkok	National Museum	1926
Trinidad and Tobago	Port of Spain	National Museum and Art Gallery	1898
Tunisia	Tunis	National Museum of Bardo	1888
Turkey	Istanbul	Topkapi Palace Museum	na
		Hagia Sophia Museum	1934
		Museum of the Ancient Orient	na
		Archaeological Museum	1891
Turkmenistan	Ashkhabad	Turkmen State United Museum of History and Ethnography	1899
Ukraine	Kiev	Kiev State Historical Museum	1934
United Arab Emirates	Abu Dhabi	Al-Ain Museum	1971
United Kingdom	Bradford	National Museum of Photography, Film and Television	1983
	Cambridge	Fitzwilliam Museum	1848
	Cardiff	National Museum of Wales	1907
	Edinburgh	National Gallery of Scotland	1859
		Royal Museum of Scotland	1854
		Scottish National Portrait Gallery	1882
	Glasgow	Kelvingrove Art Gallery and Museum	1902
		Burrell Collection	1944
	London	British Museum	1824
		Imperial War Museum	1815
		National Gallery	1838
		National Maritime Museum	1934
		National Portrait Gallery	1896
		Natural History Museum	1963
		Science Museum	1857
		Tate Gallery	1897
		Victoria & Albert Museum	1850
	Oxford	Ashmolean Museum	1683
Uruguay	Montevideo	National Historical Museum	1900
USA	Boston	Museum of Fine Arts	1924
	Chicago	Field Museum of Natural History	1893
	Dallas	Dallas Museum of Fine Arts	1903
	Detroit	Henry Ford Museum	1929
	Los Angeles (Malibu)	John Paul Getty Museum	1953
	New York	Solomon R Guggenheim Museum	1937
		Metropolitan Museum of Art	1870
		Museum of Modern Art	1929
	Philadelphia	Philadelphia Museum of Art	1876
	San Francisco	MH de Young Memorial Museum	1895
	Washington Smithsonian Institution	National Air and Space Museum	1946
		National Museum of American Art	1846
		National Museum of American History	na
Uzbekistan	Tashkent	Tashkent Historical Museum of the People of Uzbekistan	1876
Venezuela	Los Caobos	Museum of Fine Arts	1938
Vietnam	Hanoi	Vietnam History Museum	1958

na = not available

Presidents of the Royal Academy

1768–92	Joshua Reynolds
1792–1805	Benjamin West
1805–6	James Wyatt
1806–20	Benjamin West
1820–30	Thomas Lawrence
1830–50	Martin Archer Shee
1850–66	Charles Eastlake
1866–78	Francis Grant
1878–96	Frederick, 1st Baron Leighton
1896	John Everett Millais
1896–1919	Edward Poynter
1919–24	Aston Webb
1924–8	Frank Dicksee
1928–33	William Llewellyn
1938–44	Edwin Lutyens
1944–9	Alfred Munnings
1949–54	Gerald Festus Kelly
1954–6	Albert Edward Richardson
1956–66	Charles Wheeler
1966–76	Thomas Monnington
1976–84	Hugh Casson
1984–93	Roger de Grey
1993–9	Philip Dowson
1999–2004	Philip King
2004–	Nicholas Grimshaw

Presidents of the Royal Society

1662–77	William, 2nd Viscount Brouncker
1677–80	Joseph Williamson
1680–2	Christopher Wren
1682–3	John Hoskins
1683–4	Cyril Wyche
1684–6	Samuel Pepys
1686–9	John, Earl of Carbery
1689–90	Thomas Herbert, Earl of Pembroke
1690–5	Robert Southwell
1695–8	Charles Montagu, 1st Earl of Halifax
1698–1703	John, 1st Baron Somers
1703–27	Isaac Newton
1727–41	Hans Sloane
1741–52	Martin Folkes
1752–64	George, Earl of Macclesfield
1764–8	Lord Morton
1768–72	James West
1772–8	John Pringle
1778–1820	Joseph Banks
1820–7	Humphrey Davy
1827–30	Davies Gilbert
1830–8	Augustus Frederick, Duke of Sussex
1838–47	Marquis of Northampton
1847–54	William Parsons, 3rd Earl of Rosse
1854–8	Lord Wrothesley
1858–61	Benjamin Brodie
1861–71	Edward Sabine
1871–3	George Airy
1873–8	Joseph Hooker
1878–83	William Spottiswoode
1883–5	Thomas H Huxley
1885–90	George Stokes
1890–5	William Thomson, 1st Baron Kelvin
1895–1900	Joseph, Lord Lister
1900–5	William Huggins
1905–8	John William Strutt, 3rd Baron Rayleigh
1908–13	Archibald Geikie
1913–15	William Crookes
1915–20	Joseph Thomson
1920–5	Charles Sherrington
1925–30	Ernest, 1st Baron Rutherford
1930–5	Frederick Hopkins
1935–40	William Bragg
1940–5	Henry Dale
1945–50	Robert Robinson
1950–5	Edgar, 1st Baron Adrian
1955–60	Cyril Hinshelwood
1960–5	Howard, Baron Florey
1965–70	Patrick Stuart, Baron Blackett
1970–5	Alan Hodgkin
1975–80	Alexander, Baron Todd
1980–5	Andrew Huxley
1985–90	George, Lord Porter
1990–95	Michael Atiyah
1995–2000	Aaron Klug
2000–5	Robert May
2005–	Martin Rees

Nobel Prizewinners

Physics

1901	Wilhelm Konrad von Röntgen	
1902	Hendrik Antoon Lorentz	
	Pieter Zeeman	
1903	Antoine Henri Becquerel	
	Pierre Curie	
	Marie Curie	
1904	John William Strutt, 3rd Baron Rayleigh	
1905	Philipp Eduard Anton Lenard	
1906	Joseph John Thomson	
1907	Albert Abraham Michelson	
1908	Gabriel Lippmann	
1909	Guglielmo, Marchese Marconi	
	Karl Braun	
1910	Johannes Diderik van der Waals	
1911	Wilhelm Wien	
1912	Nils Gustav Dalén	
1913	Heike Kamerlingh Onnes	
1914	Max von Laue	
1915	William Henry Bragg	
	(William) Lawrence Bragg	
1916	*No award*	
1917	Charles Glover Barkla	
1918	Max Karl Ernst Planck	
1919	Johannes Stark	
1920	Charles Édouard Guillaume	
1921	Albert Einstein	
1922	Niels (Henrik David) Bohr	
1923	Robert Andrews Millikan	
1924	Karl Manne Georg Siegbahn	
1925	James Franck	
	Gustav Ludwig Hertz	
1926	Jean Baptiste Perrin	
1927	Arthur Holly Compton	
	Charles Thomson Rees Wilson	
1928	Owen Willans Richardson	
1929	Louis Victor, 7th Duc de Broglie	
1930	Chandrasekhara Venkata Raman	
1931	*No award*	
1932	Werner Karl Heisenberg	
1933	Paul Adrien Maurice Dirac	
	Erwin Schrödinger	
1934	*No award*	
1935	James Chadwick	
1936	Victor Francis Hess	
	Carl David Anderson	
1937	Clinton Joseph Davisson	
	George Paget Thomson	
1938	Enrico Fermi	
1939	Ernest Orlando Lawrence	
1943	Otto Stern	
1944	Isidor Isaac Rabi	
1945	Wolfgang Pauli	
1946	Percy Williams Bridgman	
1947	Edward Victor Appleton	

1948	Patrick Maynard Stuart, Baron Blackett	
1949	Hideki Yukawa	
1950	Cecil Frank Powell	
1951	John Douglas Cockcroft	
	Ernest Thomas Sinton Walton	
1952	Felix Bloch	
	Edward Mills Purcell	
1953	Frits Zernike	
1954	Max Born	
	Walther Bothe	
1955	Willis Eugene Lamb, Jr	
	Polykarp Kusch	
1956	William Bradford Shockley	
	John Bardeen	
	Walter Hauser Brattain	
1957	Tsung-Dao Lee	
	Chen Ning Yang	
1958	Pavel Alekseevich Cherenkov	
	Ilya Mikhailovich Frank	
	Igor Yevgenyevich Tamm	
1959	Emilio Segrè	
	Owen Chamberlain	
1960	Donald Arthur Glaser	
1961	Robert Hofstadter	
	Rudolf Mössbauer	
1962	Lev Davidovich Landau	
1963	(Johannes) Hans (Daniel) Jensen	
	Maria Goeppert-Mayer	
	Eugene Paul Wigner	
1964	Charles Hard Townes	
	Nikolai Gennadiyevich Basov	
	Alexander Mikhailovich Prokhorov	
1965	Julian S Schwinger	
	Richard P Feynman	
	Shinichiro Tomonaga	
1966	Alfred Kastler	
1967	Hans Albrecht Bethe	
1968	Luis Walter Alvarez	
1969	Murray Gell-Mann	
1970	Louis Eugène Félix Néel	
	Hannes Olof Alvén	
1971	Dennis Gabor	
1972	John Bardeen	
	Leon Neil Cooper	
	John Robert Schrieffer	
1973	Leo Esaki	
	Ivar Giaever	
	Brian David Josephson	
1974	Martin Ryle	
	Antony Hewish	
1975	Aage Niels Bohr	
	Benjamin Roy Mottelson	
	(Leo) James Rainwater	
1976	Burton Richter	
	Samuel Chao Chung Ting	
1977	Philip Warren Anderson	
	Nevill Francis Mott	
	John Hasbrouck van Vleck	

1978	Pjotr Leonidovich (Peter) Kapitza	
	Arno Allan Penzias	
	Robert Woodrow Wilson	
1979	Steven Weinberg	
	Sheldon Lee Glashow	
	Abdus Salam	
1980	James Watson Cronin	
	Val Logsdon Fitch	
1981	Nicolas Bloembergen	
	Arthur Leonard Schawlow	
	Kai M Siegbahn	
1982	Kenneth Geddes Wilson	
1983	Subrahmanyan Chandrasekhar	
	William Alfred Fowler	
1984	Carlo Rubbia	
	Simon van der Meer	
1985	Klaus von Klitzing	
1986	Gerd Binnig	
	Heinrich Rohrer	
	Ernst Ruska	
1987	George Bednorz	
	Alex Müller	
1988	Leon Lederman	
	Melvin Schwartz	
	Jack Steinberger	
1989	Hans Dehmelt	
	Wolfgang Paul	
	Norman Ramsay	
1990	Jerome Friedman	
	Henry Kendall	
	Richard Taylor	
1991	Pierre-Gilles de Gennes	
1992	Georges Charpak	
1993	Joseph Taylor	
	Russell Hulse	
1994	Bertram N Brockhouse	
	Clifford G Shull	
1995	Martin Perl	
	Frederick Reines	
1996	Douglas Osheroff	
	David Lee	
	Robert Richardson	
1997	Steven Chu	
	William D Phillips	
	Claude Cohen-Tannoudji	
1998	Robert B Laughlin	
	Horst L Stormer	
1999	Gerardhus'T Hooft	
	Martinus JG Veltman	
2000	Zhores L Alferov	
	Herbert Kroemer	
	Jack S Kilby	
2001	Eric A Cornell	
	Wolfgang Ketterle	
	Carl E Wieman	
2002	Raymond Davis	
	Masatoshi Koshiba	
	Riccardo Giacconi	
2003	Alexei Abrikosov	
	Vitaly Ginzburg	
	Anthony Leggett	

2004	David Gross	2005	Roy R Glauber	2006	John C Mather
	David Politzer		John L Hall		George F Smoot
	Frank Wilczek		Theodor W Hänsch		

Chemistry

1901	Jacobus Henricus van t'Hoff	1948	Arne Wilhelm Kaurin Tiselius	1983	Henry Taube
1902	Emil Hermann Fischer			1984	(Robert) Bruce Merrifield
1903	Svante Arrhenius	1949	William Francis Giauque	1985	Herbert Aaron Hauptman
1904	William Ramsay	1950	Otto Diels		Jerome Karle
1905	Johann Friedrich Wilhelm Adolf von Baeyer		Kurt Alder	1986	Dudley R Herschbach
1906	Henri Moissan	1951	Edwin Mattison McMillan		Yuan Tseh Lee
1907	Eduard Buchner		Glenn Theodore Seaborg		John C Polanyi
1908	Ernest, 1st Baron Rutherford	1952	Archer (John Porter) Martin	1987	Charles Pedersen
1909	Friedrich Wilhelm Ostwald		Richard Laurence Millington Synge		Donald Cram
1910	Otto Wallach				Jean-Marie Lehn
1911	Marie Curie	1953	Hermann Staudinger	1988	Johann Deisenhofer
1912	(François Auguste) Victor Grignard	1954	Linus Carl Pauling		Robert Huber
		1955	Vincent du Vigneaud		Hartmut Michel
	Paul Sabatier	1956	Nikolai Nikilaevich Semenov	1989	Sydney Altman
1913	Alfred Werner		Cyril Norman Hinshelwood		Thomas Cech
1914	Theodore William Richards	1957	Alexander Robertus Todd, Baron Todd	1990	Elias James Corey
1915	Richard Willstätter			1991	Richard Ernst
1916	*No award*	1958	Frederick Sanger	1992	Rudolph Marcus
1917	*No award*	1959	Jaroslav Heyrovsky	1993	Kary Mulis
1918	Fritz Haber	1960	Willard Frank Libby		Michael Smith
1919	*No award*	1961	Melvin Calvin	1994	George A Olah
1920	Walther Hermann Nernst	1962	John Cowdery Kendrew	1995	Paul Crutzen
1921	Frederick Soddy		Max Ferdinand Perutz		Mario Molina
1922	Francis William Aston	1963	Giulio Natta		Sherwood Rowland
1923	Fritz Pregl		Karl Ziegler	1996	Harold Kroto
1924	*No award*	1964	Dorothy Mary Hodgkin		Robert Curl
1925	Richard Adolf Zsigmondy	1965	Robert Burns Woodward		Richard Smalley
1926	Theodor Svedberg	1966	Robert Sanderson Mulliken	1997	Jens Skou
1927	Heinrich Otto Wieland	1967	Manfred Eigen		John Walker
1928	Adolf Otto Reinhold Windaus		Ronald George Wreyford Norrish		Paul Boyer
1929	Arthur Harden			1998	Walter Kohn
	Hans Karl August Simon von Euler-Chelpin		George, Baron Porter		John A Pople
		1968	Lars Onsager	1999	Ahmed Zewail
1930	Hans Fischer	1969	Derek H R Barton	2000	Alan J Heeger
1931	Carl Bosch		Odd Hassel		Alan G MacDiarmid
	Friedrich Bergius	1970	Luis Federico Leloir		Hideki Shirakawa
1932	Irving Langmuir	1971	Gerhard Herzberg	2001	William S Knowles
1933	*No award*	1972	Stanford Moore		Ryoji Noyori
1934	Harold Clayton Urey		William Howard Stein		K Barry Sharpless
1935	Jean Frédéric Joliot-Curie		Christian Boehmer Anfinsen	2002	John B Fenn
	Irène Joliot-Curie	1973	Ernst Otto Fischer		Koichi Tanaka
1936	Peter Joseph Wilhelm Debye		Geoffrey Wilkinson		Kurt Wüthrich
1937	Walter Norman Haworth	1974	Paul John Flory	2003	Peter Agre
	Paul Karrer	1975	John Warcup Cornforth		Roderick MacKinnon
1938	Richard Kuhn, *declined*		Vladimir Prelog	2004	Aaron Ciechanover
1939	Adolf Friedrich Johann Butenandt, *declined*	1976	William Nunn Lipscomb		Avram Hershko
		1977	Ilya Prigogine		Irwin Rose
	Leopold Ruzicka	1978	Peter Dennis Mitchell	2005	Yves Chauvin
1940	George de Hevesy	1979	Herbert Charles Brown		Robert H Grubbs
1944	Otto Hahn		Georg Wittig		Richard R Shrock
1945	Artturi Ilmari Virtanen	1980	Paul Berg	2006	Roger D Kornberg
1946	James Batcheller Sumner		Walter Gilbert		
	John Knudsen Northrop		Frederick Sanger		
	Wendell Meredith Stanley	1981	Kenichi Fukui		
1947	Robert Robinson		Roald Hoffmann		
		1982	Aaron Klug		

Nobel Prizewinners (continued)

Literature

1901	René François Armand Sully-Prudhomme
1902	Theodor Mommsen
1903	Bjørnstjerne Martinius Bjørnson
1904	Frédéric Mistral
	José Echegaray y Eizaguirre
1905	Henryk Sienkiewicz
1906	Giosuè Carducci
1907	Rudyard Kipling
1908	Rudolf Christoph Eucken
1909	Selma Ottiliana Lovisa Lagerlöf
1910	Paul Johann von Heyse
1911	Count Maurice Maeterlinck
1912	Gerhart Hauptmann
1913	Rabindranath Tagore
1914	*No award*
1915	Romain Rolland
1916	(Karl Gustav) Verner von Heidenstam
1917	Karl Gjellerup
	Henrik Pontoppidan
1918	*No award*
1919	Carl Friedrich Georg Spitteler
1920	Knut Hamsun
1921	Anatole France
1922	Jacinto Benavente y Martínez
1923	William Butler Yeats
1924	Wladyslaw Stanislaw Reymont
1925	George Bernard Shaw
1926	Grazia Deledda
1927	Henri Bergson
1928	Sigrid Undset
1929	Thomas Mann
1930	(Harry) Sinclair Lewis
1931	Erik Axel Karlfeldt
1932	John Galsworthy
1933	Ivan Alexeievich Bunin
1934	Luigi Pirandello
1935	*No award*
1936	Eugene Gladstone O'Neill
1937	Roger Martin du Gard
1938	Pearl S Buck
1939	Frans Eemil Sillanpää
1943	*No award*
1944	Johannes Vilhelm (J V) Jensen
1945	Gabriela Mistral
1946	Hermann Hesse
1947	André (Paul Guillaume) Gide
1948	T S (Thomas Stearns) Eliot
1949	William Faulkner
1950	Bertrand (Arthur William, 3rd Earl) Russell
1951	Pär (Fabian) Lagerkvist
1952	François Mauriac
1953	Winston (Leonard Spencer) Churchill

1954	Ernest (Millar) Hemingway
1955	Halldór Kiljan Laxness
1956	Juan Ramón Jiménez
1957	Albert Camus
1958	Boris Leonidovich Pasternak
1959	Salvatore Quasimodo
1960	Saint-John Perse
1961	Ivo Andrić
1962	John (Ernest) Steinbeck
1963	George Seferis
1964	Jean-Paul Sartre, *declined*
1965	Mikhail (Alexandrovich) Sholokhov
1966	Shmuel Yosef Agnon
	Nelly (Leonie) Sachs
1967	Miguel Angel Asturias
1968	Kawabata Yasunari
1969	Samuel Beckett
1970	Alexandr Isayevich Solzhenitsyn
1971	Pablo (Neftali Reyes) Neruda
1972	Heinrich Böll
1973	Patrick White
1974	Eyvind Johnson
	Harry (Edmund) Martinson
1975	Eugenio Montale
1976	Saul Bellow
1977	Vicente Aleixandre
1978	Isaac Bashevis Singer
1979	Odysseus Elytis
1980	Czeslaw Milosz
1981	Elias Canetti
1982	Gabriel García Márquez
1983	William (Gerald) Golding
1984	Jaroslav Seifert
1985	Claude (Eugène Henri) Simon
1986	Wole Soyinka
1987	Joseph Brodsky
1988	Naguib Mahfouz
1989	Camilo José Cela
1990	Octavio Paz
1991	Nadine Gordimer
1992	Derek Walcott
1993	Toni Morrison
1994	Kenzaburo Oe
1995	Seamus Heaney
1996	Wislawa Szymborska
1997	Dario Fo
1998	Jose Saramago
1999	Gunther Grass
2000	Gao Xingjian
2001	V S Naipaul
2002	Imre Kertész
2003	J M Coetzee
2004	Elfriede Jelinek
2005	Harold Pinter
2006	Orhan Pamuk

Economics

1969	Ragnar Anton Kittil Frisch
	Jan Tinbergen
1970	Paul Anthony Samuelson
1971	Simon Smith Kuznets
1972	John Richard Hicks
	Kenneth Joseph Arrow
1973	Wassily Leontief
1974	(Karl) Gunnar Myrdal
	Friedrich August von Hayek
1975	Leonid Vitaliyevich Kantorovich
	Tjalling Charles Koopmans
1976	Milton Friedman
1977	James Edward Meade
	Bertil Gotthard Ohlin
1978	Herbert Alexander Simon
1979	(William) Arthur Lewis
	Theodore William Schultz
1980	Lawrence Robert Klein
1981	James Tobin
1982	George Joseph Stigler
1983	Gerard Debreu
1984	(John) Richard Nicholas Stone
1985	Franco Modigliani
1986	James McGill Buchanan
1987	Robert Merton Solow
1988	Maurice Allais
1989	Trygve Haavelmo
1990	Harry M Markovitz
	Merton Miller
	William Sharpe
1991	Ronald Coase
1992	Gary S Becker
1993	Douglas C North
	Robert W Fogel
1994	John Nash
	Reinhard Selten
	John Harsanyi
1995	Robert E Lucas Jr
1996	James Mirrlees
	William Vickrey
1997	Myron Scholes
	Robert Merton
1998	Amartya Sen
1999	Robert A Mundell
2000	James J Heckman
	Daniel L McFadden
2001	George A Akerlof
	A Michael Spence
	Joseph E Stiglitz
2002	Daniel Kahneman
	Vernon L Smith
2003	Robert Engle
	Clive Granger
2004	Finn Kydland
	Edward Prescott
2005	Robert J Aumann
	Thomas C Schelling
2006	Edmund S Phelps

Physiology or Medicine

1901	Emil von Behring
1902	Ronald Ross
1903	Niels Ryberg Finsen
1904	Ivan Petrovich Pavlov
1905	Robert Koch
1906	Camillo Golgi
	Santiago Ramón y Cajal
1907	Charles Louis Alphonse Laveran
1908	Paul Ehrlich
	Ilya Ilich Mechnikov
1909	Emil Theodor Kocher
1910	Albrecht Kossel
1911	Allvar Gullstrand
1912	Alexis Carrel
1913	Charles Robert Richet
1914	Robert Bárány
1915	*No award*
1916	*No award*
1917	*No award*
1918	*No award*
1919	Jules Jean Baptiste Vincent Bordet
1920	Schack August Steenberg Krogh
1921	*No award*
1922	Archibald Vivian Hill
	Otto Fritz Meyerhof
1923	Frederick Grant Banting
	John James Rickard Macleod
1924	Willem Einthoven
1925	*No award*
1926	Johannes Andreas Grib Fibiger
1927	Julius Wagner-Jauregg
1928	Charles Jules Henri Nicolle
1929	Christiaan Eijkman
	Frederick Gowland Hopkins
1930	Karl Landsteiner
1931	Otto Heinrich Warburg
1932	Edgar Douglas Adrian, 1st Baron Edgar
	Charles Scott Sherrington
1933	Thomas Hunt Morgan
1934	George Hoyt Whipple
	George Minot
	William Murphy
1935	Hans Spemann
1936	Henry Hallett Dale
	Otto Loewi
1937	Albert von Nagyrapolt Szent-Györgyi
1938	Corneille Jean François Heymans
1939	Gerhard (Johannes Paul) Domagk, *declined*
1940	Carl Peter Henrik Dam
	Edward Adelbert Doisy
1944	Joseph Erlanger
	Herbert Spencer Gasser
1945	Alexander Fleming
	Ernst Boris Chain
	Howard Walter, Baron Florey
1946	Hermann Joseph Müller

1947	Carl Ferdinand Cori
	Gerty Theresa Cori
	Bernardo Alberto Houssay
1948	Paul Hermann Müller
1949	Walter Rudolf Hess
	António Caetano de Abreu Freire
	Egas Moniz
1950	Philip Showalter Hench
	Edward Calvin Kendall
	Tadeusz Reichstein
1951	Max Theiler
1952	Selman Abraham Waksman
1953	Fritz Albert Lipmann
	Hans Krebs
1954	John Franklin Enders
	Thomas Huckle Weller
	Frederick Chapman Robbins
1955	(Axel) Hugo Theodor Theorell
1956	Werner Forssmann
	Dickinson Woodruff Richards
	André Frédéric Cournand
1957	Daniel Bovet
1958	George Wells Beadle
	Edward Lawrie Tatum
	Joshua Lederberg
1959	Severo Ochoa
	Arthur Kornberg
1960	Frank Macfarlane Burnet
	Peter Brian Medawar
1961	Georg von Békésy
1962	Francis Crick
	James Dewey Watson
	Maurice Hugh Frederick Wilkins
1963	John Carew Eccles
	Alan Lloyd Hodgkin
	Andrew Fielding Huxley
1964	Konrad Emil Bloch
	Feodor Felix Konrad Lynen
1965	François Jacob
	Jacques Monod
	André Lwoff
1966	Charles Brenton Huggins
	Francis Peyton Rous
1967	Haldan Keffer Hartline
	George Wald
	Ragnar Arthur Granit
1968	Robert William Holley
	Har Gobind Khorana
	Marshall Warren Nirenberg
1969	Max Delbrück
	Alfred Day Hershey
	Salvador Edward Luria
1970	Julius Axelrod
	Bernard Katz
	Ulf von Euler
1971	Earl W Sutherland
1972	Gerald Maurice Edelman
	Rodney Robert Porter
1973	Konrad Zacharias Lorenz
	Nikolaas Tinbergen

	Karl von Frisch
1974	Albert Claude
	George Emil Palade
	Christian René de Duve
1975	David Baltimore
	Renato Dulbecco
	Howard Martin Temin
1976	Baruch Samuel Blumberg
	Daniel Carleton Gajdusek
1977	Rosalyn Sussman Yalow
	Roger (Charles Louis) Guillemin
	Andrew Victor Schally
1978	Werner Arber
	Daniel Nathans
	Hamilton Othanel Smith
1979	Allan MacLeod Cormack
	Godfrey Newbold Hounsfield
1980	Baruj Benacerraf
	George Davis Snell
	Jean Dausset
1981	Roger Wolcott Sperry
	David Hunter Hubel
	Torsten Nils Wiesel
1982	Sune Karl Bergström
	Bengt I Samuelsson
	John Robert Vane
1983	Barbara McClintock
1984	Niels Kai Jerne
	Georges J F Köhler
	César Milstein
1985	Joseph Leonard Goldstein
	Michael Stuart Brown
1986	Stanley Cohen
	Rita Levi-Montalcini
1987	Susumu Tonegawa
1988	James Black
	Gertrude Elion
	George Hitchings
1989	(John) Michael Bishop
	Harold Elliot Varmus
1990	Joseph Edward Murray
	(Edward) Donnall Thomas
1991	Erwin Neher
	Bert Sakmann
1992	Edmund H Fisher
	Edwin G Krebs
1993	Richard J Roberts
	Phillip A Sharp
1994	Alfred G Gilman
	Martin Rodbell
1995	Edward B Lewis
	Christiane Nüesslein-Volhard
	Eric F Wieschaus
1996	Peter Doherty
	Rolf Zinkernagel
1997	Stanley Prusiner
1998	Robert Furchgott
	Louis J Ignarro
	Ferid Murad
1999	Gunter Blobel
2000	Arvid Carlsson
	Paul Greengard
	Eric Kandel

Nobel Prizewinners (continued)

Physiology or Medicine (continued)

2001	Leland H Hartwell	2003	Sir Peter Mansfield	2006	Andrew Z Fire
	R Timothy Hunt		Paul Lauterbur		Craig C Mello
	Paul M Nurse	2004	Richard Axel		
2002	John E Sulston		Linda B Buck		
	Sydney Brenner	2005	Barry J Marshall		
	H Robert Horvitz		J Robin Warren		

Peace

1901	Jean Henri Dunant	1937	Robert Cecil,	1974	Sato Eisaku
	Frédéric Passy		1st Viscount Cecil of	1975	Andrei Dimitrievich
1902	Élie Ducommun		Chelwood		Sakharov
	Charles Albert Gobat	1938	Nansen International Office	1976	Mairead Corrigan
1903	William Randall Cremer		for Refugees		Betty Williams
1904	Institute of International	1939	*No award*	1977	Amnesty International
	Law	1943	*No award*	1978	Menachem Begin
1905	Bertha Félice Bertha von	1944	International Red Cross		Mohammed Anwar el-Sadat
	Suttner		Committee	1979	Mother Theresa of Calcutta
1906	Theodore Roosevelt	1945	Cordell Hull	1980	Adolfo Pérez Esquivel
1907	Ernesto Teodoro Moneta	1946	Emily Greene Balch	1981	Office of the UN High
	Louis Renault		John Raleigh Mott		Commissioner for Refugees
1908	Klas Pontus Arnoldson	1947	American Friends Service	1982	Alfonso García Robles
	Fredrik Bajer		Committee		Alva Myrdal
1909	Baron d'Estournelles de		Friends Service Council	1983	Lech Walesa
	Constant	1948	*No award*	1984	Desmond Mpilo Tutu
	Auguste Beernaert	1949	John Boyd Orr, 1st Baron	1985	International Physicians for
1910	International Peace Bureau		Boyd Orr		the Prevention of Nuclear
1911	Tobias Michael Carel Asser	1950	Ralphe Johnson Bunche		War
	Alfred Fried	1951	Léon Jouhaux	1986	Elie Wiesel
1912	Elihu Root	1952	Albert Schweitzer	1987	Oscar Arias Sánchez
1913	Henri Lafontaine	1953	George Catlett Marshall	1988	UN Peacekeeping Forces
1914	*No award*	1954	Office of the United Nations	1989	Tenzin Gyatso (Dalai Lama)
1915	*No award*		High Commissioner for	1990	Mikhail Sergeevich
1916	*No award*		Refugees		Gorbachev
1917	International Red Cross	1955	*No award*	1991	Aung San Suu Kyi
	Committee	1956	*No award*	1992	Rigoberta Menchú
1918	*No award*	1957	Lester Bowles Pearson	1993	Nelson Mandela
1919	Thomas Woodrow Wilson	1958	(Dominique) Georges Pire		Frederik Willem de Klerk
1920	Léon Victor Auguste	1959	Philip Noel-Baker, Baron	1994	Yitzhak Rabin
	Bourgeois		Noel-Baker		Yasser Arafat
1921	Karl Hjalmar Branting	1960	Albert John Luthuli		Shimon Peres
	Christian Louis Lange	1961	Dag Hjalmar Agne Carl	1995	Joseph Rotblat
1922	Fridtjof Nansen		Hammarskjöld		Pugwash Conferences
1923	*No award*	1962	Linus Carl Pauling	1996	Calos Filipe Ximenes Belo
1924	*No award*	1963	International Red Cross		José Ramos-Horta
1925	(Joseph) Austen Chamberlain		Committee	1997	Jody Williams and the
	Charles Gates Dawes		League of Red Cross Societies		International Campaign to
1926	Aristide Briand	1964	Martin Luther King, Jr		Ban Landmines
	Gustav Stresemann	1965	United Nations Children's	1998	John Hume
1927	Ferdinand Buisson		Fund (UNICEF)		David Trimble
	Ludwig Quidde	1966	*No award*	1999	Médecins Sans Frontières
1928	*No award*	1967	*No award*	2000	Kim Dae-jung
1929	Frank Billings Kellogg	1968	René Cassin	2001	United Nations and Kofi
1930	Nathan Söderblom	1969	International Labour		Annan
1931	Jane Addams		Organisation	2002	Jimmy Carter
	Nicholas Murray Butler	1970	Norman E Borlaug	2003	Shirin Ebadi
1932	*No award*	1971	Willy Brandt	2004	Wangari Maathai
1933	Norman Angell	1972	*No award*	2005	Mohamed ElBaradei
1934	Arthur Henderson	1973	Henry Alfred Kissinger	2006	Muhammad Yunus and
1935	Carl von Ossietzky		Le Duc Tho (*declined*)		Grameen Bank
1936	Carlos Saavedra Lamas	1974	Sean MacBride		

Universities

Albania

Korçe	Fan S Noli University (1971)
Shkoder	Luigj Gurakuqi University of Shkoder (1991)
Tirana	Universiteti Bujqësor i Trianës (1971)
	Universiteti i Trianës (1957)

Armenia

Yerevan	Yerevan State University (1919)

Australia

Australian Capital Territory	University of Canberra (1990), Belconnen
	Australian National University (1946), Acton
New South Wales	Australian Catholic University (1991), Sydney
	Charles Sturt University (1989), Bathurst
	Macquarie University (1964), Sydney
	Southern Cross University (1993), Lismore
	University of Newcastle (1965), Newcastle
	University of New England (1954), Armidale
	University of New South Wales (1948), Sydney
	University of Sydney (1850), Sydney
	University of Technology, Sydney (1965), Sydney
	University of Western Sydney (1989), Richmond, Campbelltown, Kingswood
	University of Wollongong (1961), Wollongong
Northern Territory	Northern Territory University (1989), Casuarina
Queensland	Bond University (1987), Gold Coast
	Central Queensland University (1967), Rockhampton
	Griffith University (1971), Nathan, Brisbane, Mount Gravatt, Morningside, Gold Coast
	James Cook University of North Queensland (1970), Townsville
	Queensland University of Technology (1965), Brisbane
	University of Queensland (1910), Brisbane
	University of Southern Queensland (1992), Toowoomba
South Australia	Flinders University of South Australia (1966), Adelaide
	University of Adelaide (1874), Adelaide
	University of South Australia (1991), Adelaide
Tasmania	University of Tasmania (1991), Hobart
Victoria	Deakin University (1974), Geelong
	La Trobe University (1964), Melbourne
	Monash University (1958), Melbourne
	Royal Melbourne Institute of Technology (1887), Melbourne
	Swinburne University of Technology (1908), Melbourne
	University of Melbourne (1853), Melbourne
	Victoria University of Technology (1990), Melbourne
Western Australia	Curtin University of Technology (1967), Perth
	Edith Cowan University (1991), Perth
	Murdoch University (1973), Perth
	University of Western Australia (1911), Perth

Austria

Graz	Karl-Franzens-Universität (1585)
	Technische Universität Graz (1811)
	Hochschule für Musik und Darstellende (1963)
	Kunst in Graz (University of Music and Dramatic Art in Graz)
Innsbruck	Leopold-Franzens Universität Innsbruck (1669)
Klagenfurt	Universität Klagenfurt (1970)
Linz	Johannes Kepler Universität Linz (1966)
	Hochschule für Künstlerische und Industrielle Gestaltung (University of Art and Industrial Design) (1947)
Leoben	Montanuniversität Leoben (Leoben University of Mining and Metallurgy) (1840)
Salzburg	Universität Salzburg (1622; closed 1810, reconstituted 1962)
	Hochschule für Musik und Darstellende Kunst 'Mozarteum' in Salzburg ('Mozarteum' University of Music and Dramatic Art in Salzburg) (1841)
Vienna	Universität Wien (1365)
	Technische Universität Wien (1815)
	Universität für Bodenkultur Wien (Vienna Agricultural University) (1872)
	Wirtschaftsuniversität Wien (Vienna University of Economics and Business Administration) (1898)

Universities (continued)

Veterinärmedizinische Universität Wien (1767)
Akademie der Bildende Künste (Academy of Fine Arts) (1692)
Hochschule für Angewandte Kunst in Wien (University of Applied Arts in Vienna) (1868)
Hochschule für Musik und Darstellende Kunst (University of Music and Dramatic Art)
 (1909)

Azerbaijan
Baku   Azerbaijan Technical University (1950)
            Baku State University (1919)

Belarus
Homel   Homel F Skaryna State University (1969)
Hrodna   Hrodna State University (1978)
Minsk   Belarusan State University (1921)

Belgium
Brussels   Catholic University of Brussels (1991)
                Free University of Brussels (Flemish) (1834, present status 1970)
                Free University of Brussels (French) (1834, present status 1970)
Ghent   University of Ghent (1817)
Liège   University of Liège (1817)
Louvain   Catholic University of Louvain (Flemish) (1970)
Louvain-le-Neuve Catholic University of Louvain (French) (1425, present status 1970)
Mons   University of Mons (1965)

Bosnia and Herzegovina
Banja Luka   Univerzitet u Banjoj Luci (1975)
Mostar   Sveuciliste u Mostaru (1977)
Sarajevo   Univerzitet u Sarejeva (1949)
Tuzla   Univerzitet u Tuzli (1976)

Bulgaria
Blagoevgrad American University in Bulgaria (1991)
Burgas   Burgas University of Technology (1963)
Gabrovo   Technical University, Gabrovo (1964)
Plovdiv   Agricultural University of Plovdiv (1945)
             Higher Institute of Food and Flavour Industries (1953)
             Plovdivski Universitet 'Paisij Hilendarski' (1961)
Ruse   Ruse Technical University (1954)
Sofia   Sofia University of Technology – Higher Institute of Chemical Technology (1953)
             Sofiiski Universitet 'Sveti Kliment Ohridsky' (1961)
             University of Architecture, Civil Engineering, and Geodesy (1942)
             University of Mining and Geology (1953)
             University of National and World Economics (1970)
Svishtov   D Tsenov Economic University (1936)
Varna   Technical University (1962)
             Varna University of Economics (1920)
Veliko Tarnovo V Tarnovski University 'Kiril i Metodii' (1971)

Canada
Alberta   Alberta University (1906), Edmonton
                 Athabasca University (1910), Athabasca
                 University of Calgary (1945), Calgary
                 University of Lethbridge (1967), Lethbridge
British Columbia Simon Fraser University(1963), Burnaby
                 Trinity Western University (1962), Langley
                 University of British Columbia (1908), Vancouver
                 University of Northern British Columbia (1990), Prince George
                 University of Victoria (1963), Victoria
Manitoba   Brandon University(1899), Brandon
                 University of Manitoba (1877), Winnipeg
                 University of Winnipeg (1871), Winnipeg
New Brunswick   Mount Allison University (1840), Sackville
                 Université de Moncton (1864), Moncton
                 University of New Brunswick (1785), Fredericton
Newfoundland   Memorial University of Newfoundland (1925), St John's
Nova Scotia   Acadia University (1838), Wolfville
                 Atlantic School of Theology (1971), Halifax
                 Dalhousie University (from 1997 includes Technical University,

founded 1907) (1818), Halifax
Mount Saint Vincent University (1925), Halifax
Nova Scotia Agricultural College (1905), Truro
Nova Scotia College of Art and Design (1887), Halifax
St Francis Xavier University (1853), Antigonish
St Mary's University (1802), Halifax
Université Sainte-Anne (1890), Pointe-de-l'Église
University College of Cape Breton (1951), Sydney
University of King's College (1789), Halifax

Ontario	Brock University (1964), St Catharines
	Carleton University (1942), Ottawa
	Collège Dominicain de Philosophie et de Théologie (1909), Ottawa
	Lakehead University (1965), Thunder Bay
	Laurentian University of Sudbury (1960), Sudbury
	McMaster University (1887), Hamilton
	Queen's College at Kingston (1841), Kingston
	Redeemer College (1976), Ancaster
	Royal Military College of Canada (1876), Kingston
	Ryerson Polytechnic University (1963), Toronto
	Trent University (1963), Peterborough
	University of Guelph (1964), Guelph
	University of Ottawa (1848), Ottawa
	University of Toronto (1827), Toronto
	University of Waterloo (1957), Waterloo
	University of Western Ontario (1878), London
	University of Windsor (1857), Windsor
	Wilfrid Laurier University (1911), Waterloo
	York University (1959), North York
Prince Edward Island	University of Prince Edward Island (1969), Charlottetown
Quebec	Bishop's University (1843), Lennoxville
	Concordia University (1974), Montreal
	McGill University (1821), Montreal
	Université de Montréal (1878), Montreal
	Université de Québec (1968), Sainte-Foy
	Université de Sherbrooke (1954), Sherbrooke
	Université Laval (1852), Quebec
Saskatchewan	University of Regina (1974), Regina
	University of Saskatchewan (1907), Saskatoon

Croatia

Osijek	Sveuciliste Josipa Juraja Strossmayera u Osijeku (1975)
Rijeka	Sveuciliste u Rijeci (1973)
Split	Sveuciliste u Splitu (1974)
Zagreb	Sveuciliste u Zagrebu (1669)

Czech Republic

Brno	Univerzita Masarykova (Masaryk University) (1919)
	Vysoká Škola Veterinární A Farmaceutická v Brně (University of Veterinary Science and Pharmacy in Brno) (1918)
	Vysoké Učení Technické v Brně (Technical University of Brno) (1899)
	Mendelova Zemědělska a Lesnická (University of Agriculture and Forestry) (1919)
Liberec	Vysoká Škola Strojní a Textilní Liberci (Technical University of Mechanical and Textile Engineering in Liberec) (1953)
Olomouc	Univerzita Palackého v Olomouci (Palacky University) (1566, reopened 1946)
Ostrava	Vysoká Škola Báňská v Ostravě (Technical University of Mining and Metallurgy of Ostrava) (1716)
Pardubice	Vysoká Škola Chemicko-Technologická v Pardubicích (Institute of Chemical Technology in Pardubice) (1950)
Plzen	Západočeská Univerzita (University of West Bohemia) (1949, present name 1991)
Prague	České Vysoké Učení Technické v Praze (Czech Technical University) (1707, reorganized 1960)
	Univerzita Karlova (Charles University) (1348)
	Vysoká Škola Chemicko-Technologická v Praze (University of Chemistry and Technology, Prague) (1807)
	Vysoká Škola Ekonomická (Prague University of Economics) (1953)
	Česká Zemědělska Univerzita v Praze (Czech University of Agriculture in Prague) (1906)
Ústí nad Laben	Jan Evangelista Purkyne University (1991)

KNOWLEDGE

Universities (continued)
Denmark
Aalborg	Aalborg Universitets Center (1974)
Aarhus	University of Aarhus (1928)
	Jutland Open University (1982)
Copenhagen	University of Copenhagen (1479)
	Technical University of Denmark (1829)
Fredericksburg	Royal Veterinary and Agricultural University (1856)
Odense	University of Odense (1964)

Estonia
Tallinn	Tallinn Technical University (1918)
Tartu	University of Tartu (1632)

Finland
Åbo	Åbo Akademi (Finland-Swedish University of Åbo) (1918)
Helsinki	Helsingin Yliopisto/Helsingfors Universitet (1911)
	Teknillinen Korkeakoulu (Helsinki University of Technology) (1908)
Joensuu	Jeonsuun Yliopisto (Jeonsuu University) (1969)
Jyväskylä	Jyväskylän Yliopisto (1966)
Kuopio	Kuopion Yliopisto (University of Kuopio) (1966)
Rovaniemi	Lapin Yliopisto (University of Lapland) (1979)
Lappeenranta	Lappeenrannan Teknillinen Korkeakoulu (Lappeenranta University of Technology) (1969)
Oulu	Oulun Yliopisto (1958)
Tampere	Tampereen Tenknillinen Korkeakoulu (Tampere University of Technology) (1965)
	Tampereen Yliopisto (University of Tampere) (1925)
Turku	Turun Yliopisto (Turka University) (1920)
Vaasa	Vaasan Yliopisto (University of Vaasa) (1968)

France
Aix-en-Provence	Université d'Aix-Marseille III (Université de Droit, d'Economie et des Sciences) (1973)
Angers	Université d'Angers (1971)
Amiens	Université de Picardie (1965)
Avignon	Université d'Avignon (1973)
Besançon	Université de Franche-Comté (1423 at Dôle, 1691 at Besançon)
Bordeaux	Université de Bordeaux II (na)
Brest	Université de Bretagne Occidentale (na)
Caen	Université de Caen (1432, reorganized) (1985)
Chambéry	Université de Savoie (Chambéry) (1970)
Clermont-Ferrand	Université de Clermont-Ferrand I (1976, present status 1985)
	Université de Clermont-Ferrand II (Université Blaise Pascal) (1810, present status 1984)
Corti	Université de Corse 1 (1976, opened)
	Università di Corsica (1981)
Créteil	Université de Paris XII (Paris-Val-de-Marne) (1970)
Dijon	Université de Bourgogne
Grenoble	Université de Grenoble I (Université Joseph Fourier)
	Université de Grenoble II (Université Pierre Mendès- France) (1970)
	Université de Grenoble III (Université Stendhal) (1810)
Le Havre	Université du Havre (1984)
Le Mans	Université du Maine (1969)
Lille	Université de Lille II (Droit et Santé) (1969)
Limoges	Université de Limoges (1808, reopened 1965)
Lyon	Université Lyon II
	Université Lyon III (Université Jean Moulin) (1973)
Marseille	Université d'Aix-Marseille I (Université de Provence) (1970)
	Université d'Aix-Marseille II (1973)
Metz	Université de Metz (1971)
Montpellier	Université de Montpellier I (1970)
	Université de Montpellier II (Université des Sciences et Techniques de Languedoc) (na)
	Université de Montpellier III (Université Paul Valéry) (1970)
Mont-Saint-Aignan	Université de Rouen (1966)
Mulhouse	Université de Haute-Alsace (1975)
Nancy	Université de Nancy I (1970)
	Université de Nancy II (1970)
Nanterre	Université de Paris X (Paris-Nanterre) (na)
Nantes	Université de Nantes (1962)
Nice	Université de Nice (1971)

Orléans	Université d'Orléans (1961)
Orsay	Université de Paris XI (Paris-Sud) (1970)
Paris	Université de Paris I (Panthéon-Sorbonne) (1971)
	Université de Paris II (Université Panthéon-Assas) (1970)
	Université de Paris III (Sorbonne-Nouvelle) (1970)
	Université de Paris IV (Paris-Sorbonne) (1970)
	Université de Paris V (René Descartes) (1970)
	Université de Paris VI (Pierre et Marie Curie) (na)
	Université de Paris VII (1970)
	Université de Paris IX (Paris-Dauphine) (1968)
Pau	Université de Pau et des Pays de l'Adour (1970
Perpignan	Université de Perpignan (1971)
Poitiers	Université de Poitiers (1432)
Reims	Université de Reims Champagne-Ardenne (1548)
Rennes	Université de Rennes I (na)
	Université de Rennes II (Université de Haute Bretagne) (na)
St Denis	Université de Paris VIII (Vincennes à St-Denis) (1969)
St-Étienne	Université Jean Monnet (Université de St-Étienne) (1969, present name 1991)
Strasbourg	Université de Strasbourg I (Université Louis Pasteur) (1971)
	Université de Strasbourg II (Sciences Humaines) (1538)
	Université de Strasbourg III (Université Robert Schumann)
Talence	Université de Bordeaux I (na)
	Université de Bordeaux III (na)
Toulon/La Garde	Université de Toulon et du Var (1970)
Toulouse	Université de Toulouse I (Sciences Sociales) (1229)
	Université de Toulouse II (Le Mirail) (na)
	Université de Toulouse III (Université Paul Sabatier) (1969)
Tours	Université de Tours (Université François Rabelais) (1970)
Valenciennes	Université de Valenciennes et du Hainaut- Cambresis (1964)
Versailles	Université Versailles/Saint Quentin-en-Yvelines (1991)
Villeneuve d'Ascq	Université de Lille I (Université des Sciences et Techniques de Lille Flandres Artois) (1855 as Faculty of Sciences, present status 1971)
	Université de Lille III (Sciences Humaines, Lettres et Arts) (1560, present status 1985)
Villetaneuse	Université de Paris XIII (Paris-Nord) (1970)
Villeurbanne	Université Lyon I (Université Claude-Bernard) (1970)

Georgia

Sukhumi	Abkhazian A M Gorkii State University (1985)
Tbilisi	Georgian Technical University (1990)
	Ivan Dzhavakhiladze University of Tbilisi (1918)

Germany

Aachen	Rheinisch-Westfälische Technische Hochschule Aachen (1870, University status 1880)
Augsburg	Universität Augsburg (1970)
Bamberg	Otto Friedrich Universität Bamberg (1647)
Bayreuth	Universität Bayreuth (1972)
Berlin	Humboldt-Universität zu Berlin (1809)
	Freie Universität Berlin (1948)
	Technische Universität Berlin Bauakademie(f.1799) and Gewerbeakademie (f.1821), amalgamated (1879 as Technische Hochschule; opened under present title 1946)
Bielefeld	Universität Bielefeld (1969)
Bochum	Ruhr-Universität Bochum (1961)
Bonn	Rheinische Friedrich-Wilhelms-Universität Bonn (founded 1786; refounded 1818)
Braunschweig	Technische Universität Carolo Wilhelmina zu Braunschweig (1745, present title 1968)
Bremen	Universität Bremen (1971)
Chemnitz	Technische Universität (Karl-Marx-Stadt) Chemnitz (1836)
Clausthal-Zellerfeld	Technische Universität Clausthal (1775, university status 1968)
Darmstadt	Technische Hochschule Darmstadt (1836, University status 1895)
Dortmund-Eichlinghafen	Universität Dortmund (1966)
Dresden	Technische Universität Dresden (1828, University status 1961)
Duisburg	Universität Duisburg Gesamthochschule (1972)
Düsseldorf	Heinrich-Heine-Universität Düsseldorf (1965 formerly Medizinische Akademie f.1907)
Eichstätt	Katholische Universität Eichstätt (1972) (founded originally 1574)
Erlangen	Friedrich-Alexander-Universität Erlangen- Nürnberg (1743)
Essen	Universität Essen-Gesamthochschule (1972)
Frankfurt-am-Main	Johann Wolfgang Goethe-Universität Frankfurt (1914)

Universities (continued)

Freiburg	Universität Freiburg (1457)
Giessen	Justus-Liebig-Universität Giessen (1607)
Göttingen	George-August-Universität Göttingen (1737)
Greifswald	Ernst Moritz Arndt Universität (1456)
Hagen	Open University (1974)
Halle	Martin Luther-Universität Halle-Wittenberg (1502 Wittenberg; 1694 Halle; 1817 Halle-Wittenberg)
Hamburg	Universität Hamburg (1919)
Hannover	Universität Hannover (1831)
Heidelberg	Ruprecht-Karls-Universität Heidelberg (1386)
Hohenheim (Stuttgart)	Universität Hohenheim (1818)
Jena	Friedrich-Schiller Universität (1558)
Kaiserslautern	Universität Kaiserslautern (1975)
Karlsruhe	Universität Fridericiana Karlsruhe (1825)
Kassel	Gesamthochschule Kassel (1970)
Kiel	Christian-Albrechts Universität zu Kiel (1665)
Köln	Universität zu Köln (1388)
Konstanz	Universität Konstanz (1966)
Leipzig	Universität Leipzig (1409)
Lüneburg	Universität Lüneburg (1946)
Magdeburg	Otto von Guericke Universität (1993)
Mainz	Johannes Gutenburg-Universität Mainz (1477; closed 1816–1946)
Mannheim	Universität Mannheim (1907, university status 1967)
Marburg	Philipps-Universität Marburg (1527)
Munich	Ludwig-Maximilians-Universität München (1472)
	Technische Universität München (1868)
Münster	Westfälische Wilhelms-Universität Münster (1780)
Oldenburg	Universität Carl von Ossietzky Oldenburg (1974)
Osnabruck	Universität Osnabrück (1973)
Paderborn	Universität-Gesamthochschule Paderborn (1972)
Passau	Universität Passau (1972)
Regensburg	Universität Regensburg (1962)
Rostock	Universität Rostock (1419)
Saarbrücken	Universität des Saarlandes (1948)
Siegen	Universität-Gesamthochschule Siegen (1972)
Stuttgart	Universität Stuttgart (1829, university status 1967)
Trier	Universität Trier (1473)
Tübingen	Eberhard-Karls-Universität Tübingen (1477)
Ulm	Universität Ulm (1967)
Wuppertal	Bergische Universität-Gesamthochschule Wuppertal (1972)
Würzburg	Bayerische-Julius-Maximilians-Universität Würzburg (1582)

Greece

Athens	National and Capodistrian University of Athens (1837)
	National Technical University of Athens (1836)
	University of the Aegean (1984)
Crete	University of Crete (1973)
	Technical University of Crete (1977)
Ioannina	University of Ioannina (1964, independent status 1970)
Komotini	'Demokritos' University of Thrace (1973)
Patras	University of Patras (1964)
Thessaloniki	University of Macedonia (1957)
	Aristotelian University of Thessaloniki (1925)

Hungary

Budapest	Eötvös Loránd Tudományegyetem (Loránd Eötvös University) (1635)
	Semmelweis Orvostudományi Egyetem (1769, independent 1951)
	Budapesti Közgazdaságtudományi Egyetem (Budapest University of Economic Sciences) (1948)
	Haynal Imre Egészségtudományi Egyetem (Imre Haynal University of Health Sciences) (1987)
	Állatorvostudományi Egyetem (University of Veterinary Sciences) (1787)
	Budapesti Műszaki Egyetem (Technical University of Budapest) (1871)
	Kertészeti És Élelmiszeripari Egyetem (University of Horticulture and Food Technology) (1853)

Debrecen	Kossuth Lajos Tudományegyetem (1912)
	Debreceni Orvostudományi Egyetem (University Medical School of Debrecen) (1951)
	Debreceni Agrártudományi Egyetem (Debrecen University of Agrarian Sciences) (1868)
Gödöllö	Agrártudományi Egyetem (University of Agricultural Sciences) (1945)
Keszthely	Pannon Agrártudományi Egyetem (Pannon University of Agricultural Sciences) (1797)
Miskolc	Miskolci Egyetem (Miskolc University) (1949)
Pécs	Pécsi Jannus Pannonius Tudományegyetem (Janus Pannonius University of Pécs) (1367)
	Pécsi Orvostudományi Egyetem (Medical University of Pecs) (1951)
Szeged	Szent-Györgi Albert Orvostudományi Egyetem (Albert Szent-Györgi Medical University) (1951)
	József Attila Tudományegyetem (Attila József University) (1872)
Sopron	Erdészeti És Faipari Egyetem (University of Forestry and Wood Science) (1808)
Veszprém	Veszprémi Egyetem (Veszprem University) (1949)

Ireland

Cork	University College Cork[a] (1845 as Queen's College; 1908)
Dublin	University of Dublin Trinity College (1592)
	National University of Ireland (1908)
	University College Dublin[a] (1909)
	Dublin City University (1975, university status 1989)
Galway	University College Galway[a] (1845 as Queen's College; 1908)
Limerick	University of Limerick (1970, university status 1989)

[a]The National University of Ireland has three constituent Colleges.

Italy

Ancona	Università degli Studi di Ancona (1969)
L'Aquila	Università degli Studi dell' Aquila (1952)
Bari	Università degli Studi di Bari (1924)
Bologna	Università degli Studi di Bologna (1088)
Brescia	Università degli Studi di Brescia (1982)
Cagliari, Sardinia	Università di Cagliari (1606)
Camerino	Università di Camerino (1336, university status 1727)
Campobasso	Università degli Studi del Molise (1982)
Cassino	Università degli Studi di Cassino (1982)
Catania	Università di Catania (1434)
Commenda di Rende	Università di Calabria (1972)
Ferrara	Università degli Studi di Ferrara (1391)
Florence	Università degli Studi di Firenze (1321)
Fisciano (Salerno)	Università degli Studi di Salerno (1970)
Genoa	Università degli Studi di Genova (1471)
Lecce	Università degli Studi di Lecce (1956)
Macerata	Università degli Studi di Macerata (1290)
Messina	Università degli Studi di Messina (1548)
Milan	Università degli Studi di Milano (1924)
	Catholic University of the Sacred Heart (1920, present status 1924)
	Università Commerciale Luigi Bocconi (1902)
Modena	Università degli Studi di Modena (1175)
Naples	Università degli Studi di Napoli (1224)
Padua	Università degli Studi di Padova (1222)
Palermo	Università degli Studi di Palermo (1777)
Parma	Università degli Studi (12th-c)
Pavia	Università degli Studi di Pavia (1361)
Perugia	Università degli Studi di Perugia (1200)
	Università Italiana per Stranieri (1921)
Pisa	Università degli Studi di Pisa (1343)
Reggio Calabria	Università di Reggio Calabria (1982)
Rome	Università degli Studi di Roma 'La Sapienza' (1303)
	Università degli Studi di Roma 'Tor Vergata' (1970)
Sassari	Università degli Studi di Sassari (1562)
Siena	Università degli Studi di Siena (1240)
Trento	Università degli Studi di Trento (1962)
Trieste	Università degli Studi di Trieste (1938)
Turin	Università degli Studi di Torino (1404)
	Politecnico di Torino (1859)
Udine	Università degli Studi di Udine (1977)

KNOWLEDGE

Universities (continued)

Urbino	Università degli Studi di Urbino (1506)
Venice	Università degli Studi di Venezia (1868)
Verona	Università degli Studi di Verona (1982)
Viterbo	Università degli Studi della Tuscia (1981)

Kazakhstan

Almaty	Kazakh Al-Farabi State National University (1934)
Karaganda	Karaganda State University (1972)

Kyrgyzstan

Bishkek	Kyrgyz State University (1951)

Latvia

Riga	Riga Technical University (1990)
	University of Latvia (1919)

Lithuania

Kaunas	Kaunas University of Technology (1922)
	Vytautas Magnus University (1922)
Vilnius	Vilnaius Technikos Universitetas (1961)
	Vilnius University (1579)

Luxembourg

Luxembourg	Centre Universitaire de Luxembourg (1969)

Macedonia, Former Yugoslav Republic of

Bitola	St Clement of Ohrid University (1979)
Skopje	Ss Cyril and Methodius University (1949)

Moldova

Chisinau	Moldovan State University (1946)

Montenegro

Podgorica	Univerzitet Crne Gore, Podgorica (1974)

Mongolia

Ulan Bator	Mongolian Technical University (1969)
	National University of Mongolia (1942)

Netherlands

Amsterdam	University of Amsterdam (1632)
	Free University, Amsterdam (1880)
Delft	Delft University of Technology (1842)
Eindhoven	Eindhoven University of Technology (1956)
Enschede	Twente University of Technology (1961)
Groningen	University of Groningen (1614)
Heerlen	Open University (1984)
Leiden	Leiden University (1575)
Maastricht	University of Limburg (1976)
Nijmegen	University of Nijmegen (1923)
Rotterdam	Erasmus University, Rotterdam (1973)
Tilburg	Tilburg University (1927)
Utrecht	Utrecht University (1636)
Wageningen	Agricultural University (1918)

New Zealand

Auckland	University of Auckland (1883)
Canterbury	Lincoln University (1878)
Christchurch	University of Canterbury (1873)
Dunedin	University of Otago (1869)
Hamilton	University of Waikato (1964)
Palmerston North	Massey University (1926)
Wellington	Victoria University of Wellington (1899)

Norway

Ås	Universitetet for miljø- og biovitenskap (2005)
Bergen	Universitetet i Bergen (1948)
Oslo	Universitetet i Oslo (1811)
Stavanger	Universitetet i Stavanger (2005)
Tromsø	Universitetet i Tromsø (1968)
Trondheim	Norges teknisk-naturvitenskapelige universitet (1968)

Poland

Białystok	Politechnika Białostocka (Białystok Technical University) (1949)
Częstochowa	Politechnika Częstochowska (Częstochowa Technical University) (1949)
Gdańsk	Uniwersytet Gdański (University of Gdańsk) (1970)
	Politechnika Gdańska (Technical University of Gdańsk) (1945)
Gliwice	Politechnika Slaska Im. W. Pstrowskiego (Silesian Technical University) (1945)
Katowice	Uniwerystet Sląski (Silesian University) (1968)
Kielce	Politechnika Świętokrzyska (Kielce University of Technology) (1965)
Kraków	Uniwersytet Jagielloński (Jagiellonian University) (1364)
	Akademia Gorniczo-Hutnicza Im. Stanisława Staszica W Krakowie (Stanisław Staszic Academy of Mining and Metallurgy) (1919)
	Politechnika Krakowska Im. Tadeusza Kościuszki (Kraków Technical University) (1945)
Łódz	Uniwersytet Łódzki (University of Łódz) (1945)
	Politechnika Łódzka (Łódz Technical University) (1945)
Lublin	Katolicki Uniwersytet Lubelski (Catholic University of Lublin) (1918)
	Uniwersytet Marii Curie-Skłodowskiej (Marie-Curie Skłodowska University) (1944)
	Politechnika Lubelska (Technical University of Lublin) (1953)
Poznań	Uniwersytet Im Adama Mickiewicza w Poznaniu (Adam Mickiewicz University in Poznań) (1919)
	Politechnika Poznańska (Poznań Technical University) (1919)
Rzeszów	Politechnika Rzeszowska (Rzeszów Technical University) (1974)
Szczecin	Uniwersytet Szczeciński (Szczecin University) (1985
	Politechnika Szczecinska (Szczecin Technical University) (1946
Toruń	Uniwersytet Mikołaja Kopernika w Toruniu (Nicholas Copernicus University in Toruń) (1945)
Warsaw	Uniwersytet Warszawski (University of Warsaw) (1818
	Politechnika Warszawska (Warsaw University of Technology) (1826)
Wrocław	Uniwersytet Wrocławski (1702, rebuilt 1945)
	Politechnika Wrocławska (Wroclaw Technical University) (1945)

Portugal

Braga	Universidade de Minho (1973)
Coímbra	Universidade de Coímbra (1290)
Corvilla	Universidade de Beira Interior (1986)
Évora	Universidade de Évora (1973, university status 1979)
Lisbon	Universidade Autónoma de Lisboa 'Luis de Camões' (1977)
	Universidade Católica Portuguesa (1967)
	New University of Lisbon (1973)
	Universidade Técnica de Lisboa (1930)
	Universidade Lusíada (1986)
Porto	Universidade de Porto (1911)

Romania

Brasov	Universitatea 'Transilvania' din Bucaresti (1971)
Bucharest	'Politehnica' din Bucuresti (1818)
	Universitatea Bucaresti (1694)
Cluj-Napoca	Universitatea 'Babes-Bolyai' Cluj-Napoca (1919)
	Universitatea de Medicina si Farmacie 'Iuliu Hatieganu' Cluj-Napoca (1919)
	Cluj-Napoca Technica din Cluj-Napoca (1948)
Craiova	Universitatea din Craiova (1966)
Galati	Universitatea 'Dunarea de Jos' din Galati (1948)
Iasi	Universitatea 'Al I Cuza' Iasi (1860)
	Universitatea de Medicina si Farmacie 'Gr T Popa' Iasi (1879)
	Universitatea Technica 'Gheorghe Asachi' (1912)
Ploiesti	Universitatea Petrol-Gaze Ploiesti (1948)
Timişoara	Universitatea de Stiinte Agricole a Banatului Timisoara (1945)
	Universitatea din Timisoara (1962)
	Universitatea Technica Timisoara (1920)
Tîrgu-Mures	Universitatea de Medicina si Farmacie (1948)

Russia

Barnaul	Altai State University (1973)
Cheboksary	Chuvash I N Ulyanov State University (1967)
Chelyabinsk	Chelyabinsk State Technical University (1943)
	Chelyabinsk State University (1976)
Yekaterinburg	Urals A M Gorkii State University (1920)
Elista	Kalmyk State University (1970)
Groznyi	Checheno-Ingush State University (1972)
Ioshkar-Ola	Mari University (1972)

Universities (continued)

Irkutsk	Irkutsk State University (1918)
Ivanovo	Ivanovo State University (1974)
Izhevsk	Udmurt State University (1972)
Kaliningrad	Kaliningrad State University (1967)
Kazan	Kazan State University (1804)
Kemerovo	Kemerovo State University (1974)
Krasnodar	Kuban State University (1970)
Krasnoyarsk	Krasnoyarsk State University (1969)
Makhachkala	Dagestan State University (1931)
Moscow	Moscow M V Lomonosov State University (1755)
	Russian Peoples' Friendship University (1960)
Nalchik	Kabardino-Balkar State University (1957)
Nizhni Novgorod	N I Lobachevskii State University (1918)
Novosibirsk	Novosibirsk State University (1959)
Omsk	Omsk State University (1974)
Perm	Perm A M Gorkii State University (1916)
Petrozavodsk	Petrozavodsk State University (1940)
Rostov-on-Don	Rostov State University (1915)
St Petersburg	St Petersburg State University (1724)
	St Petersburg Technical University (1899)
Samara	Samara State University (1969)
Saransk	Mordovian N P Ogarev State University (1957)
Saratov	Saratov N G Chernyshevskii State University (1909)
Syktyvkar	Syktyvkar State University (1972)
Tomsk	Tomsk State University (1880)
Tver	Tver State University (1971)
Tyumen	Tyumen State University (na)
Vladikavkaz	North-Ossetian K L Khetagurov State University (1969)
Vladivostock	Far Eastern State University (1899)
Volgograd	Volgograd State University (1978)
Voronezh	Voronezh State University (1918)
Yakutsk	Yakutsk State University (1956)
Yaroslavl	Yaroslavl State University (1970)

San Marino

San Marino	Università degli Studi (1987)

Serbia

Belgrade	Univerzitet u Beogradu (1863)
	Univerzitet Umetnosti u Beogradu (1957)
Kragujevac	Univerzitet u Kragujevcu (1976)
Nis	Univerzitet u Nisu (1965)
Novi Sad	Univerzitet u Novom Sadu (1960)
Pristina	Univerzitet u Pristini (1970)

Slovak Republic

Bratislava	Univerzita Komenského Bratislava (Comenius University of Bratislava) (1919)
	Slovenská Technická Univerzita v Bratislave (Slovak Technical University) (1938)
	Vysoká Ekonomicka v Bratislave (School of Economics in Bratislava) (1940)
Košice	Univerzita Pavla Jozefa Šafárika (Safarik University) (1959)
	Vysoká Škola Veterinárská Košiciach (University of Veterinary Medicine in Košice) (1949)
	Technická Univerzita v Košiciach (Košice Technical University) (1952)
Nitra	Vysoka Škola Pol'Nohospodarska (College of Agriculture) (1946)
Žilina	Žilinská univerzita (University of Žilina in Žilina) (1953)
Zvolen	Technická univerzita (Technical University) (1807, reorganized 1952)

Slovenia

Ljubljana	Univerza v Ljubljani (from 1994 included Faculty of Theology, founded 1919) (1595)
Maribor	Univerza v Mariboru (1975)

South Africa

Alice	University of Fort Hare (1916)
Auckland Park	Rand Afrikaans University (1966)
Bellville	University of the Western Cape (1960)
Bloemfontein	University of the Orange Free State (1855)
Cape Town	University of Cape Town (1829)
Durban	University of Durban-Westville (1961)

	University of Natal (1910)
Garankuwa	Medical University of South Africa (1976)
Grahamstown	Rhodes University (1904)
Johannesburg	University of the Witwatersrand, Johannesburg (1922)
Kwa-Dlangezwa	University of Zululand (1960)
Mabatho	University of North West (1978)
Port Elizabeth	University of Port Elizabeth (1964)
Potchefstroom	Potchefstroom University for Christian Higher Education (1869)
Pretoria	University of Pretoria (1908)
	University of South Africa (1873)
	Vista University (1982)
Sovenga	University of the North (1959)
Stellenbosch	University of Stellenbosch (1918)
Thohoynando	University of North West (1981)
Umtata	University of Transkei (1976)

Spain

Alcalá de Henares (Madrid)	Universidad de Alcalá de Henares (1977)
Alicante	Universidad de Alicante (1979)
Barcelona	Universitat de Barcelona (1450)
Bellaterra	Universitat Autónoma de Barcelona (1968)
Bilbao	Universidad de Deusto (1886)
	University of the Basque Country (1968, reorganized 1980)
Cáceres	Universidad de Extremadura (1973)
Cádiz	Universidad de Cádiz (1979)
Ciudad Real	Universidad de Castilla-la-Mancha (1982)
Córdoba	Universidad de Córdoba (1972)
Granada	Universidad de Granada (1526)
La Laguna, Canary Is	Universidad de La Laguna (1792)
Las Palmas, Canary Is	Universidad de Las Palmas de Gran Canaria (1980)
León	Universidad de León (1979)
Madrid	Universidad Complutense de Madrid (1508)
	Universidad Pontificia 'Comillas' (1890 in Santander; moved to Madrid 1960)
	Universidad Autónoma de Madrid (1968)
	Open University (1972)
	Universidad Carlos III de Madrid (1989)
Málaga	Universidad de Málaga (1972)
Murcia	Universidad de Murcia (1915)
Oviedo	Universidad de Oviedo (1608)
Palma de Mallorca	Universitat de Les Illes Balears (1978)
Pamplona	Universidad de Navarra (1952)
Salamanca	Universidad Pontificia de Salamanca (1134 as Ecclesiastical School, university status 1219; defunct by end 18th-c, restored 1940)
	Universidad de Salamanca (1218, reorganized 1254)
Santander	Universidad de Cantabria (1972, as Universidad de Santander)
Seville	Universidad de Sevilla (1502)
Valencia	Universitat de València (1510)
Valladolid	Universidad de Valladolid (13th-c)
Zaragoza	Universidad de Zaragoza (1583)

Sweden

Gothenburg	Chalmers Tekniska Högskola (Chalmers University of Technology) (1829)
	Göteborgs Universitet (1891)
Karlstad	Högskolan Karlstad (Karlstad University) (1977)
Linköping	Universitet Linköping (1970)
Luleå	Luleå Tekniska Universitat/Luleå University of Technology) (1971)
Lund	Lunds Universitet (1666)
Örebro	Högskolan I Örebro (1967)
Stockholm	Kungliga Tekniska Högskolan (Royal Institute of Technology) (1827)
	Stockholms Universitet (1877, state university 1960)
Uppsala	Sveriges Lantbruksuniversitet (Swedish University of Agricultural Sciences) (1977)
	Uppsala Universitet (1477)
Umeå	Umeå Universitet (1963)
Växjö	Högskolan Växjö (Växjö University) (1967)

KNOWLEDGE

Universities (continued)

Switzerland

Basel	Universität Basel (1460)
Bern	Universität Bern (1834)
Fribourg	Université de Fribourg (1889)
Geneva	Université de Genève (1559)
Lausanne	Université de Lausanne (1537)
	École Polytechnique Fédérale de Lausanne (1853)
Neuchâtel	Université de Neuchâtel (1909)
Zürich	Universität Zürich (1833)
	Eidgenössische Technische Hochschule (1855)
	Zürich (Swiss Federal Institute of Technology)

Tajikistan

Dushanbe	Tajik State University (1948)

Turkey

Adana	Çukurova Üniversitesi (1973)
Ankara	Ankara Üniversitesi (1946)
	Bilkent Üniversitesi (1984)
	Gazi Üniversitesi (1982)
	Hacettepe Üniversitesi (1206)
	Orta Dogu Teknik Üniversitesi (1956)
Antalya	Akdeniz Üniversitesi (1982)
Bursa	Uludag Üniversitesi (1975)
Campus-Sivas	Cumhuriyet Üniversitesi (1974)
Diyarbakir	Dicle Üniversitesi (1966)
Edirne	Trakya Üniversitesi (1982)
Elazig	Firat Üniversitesi (1975)
Erzurum	Atatürk Üniversitesi (1957)
Eskisehir	Anadolu Üniversitesi (1958)
Gaziantep	Gaziantep Üniversitesi (na)
Istanbul	Bogaziçi Üniversitesi (1863)
	Istanbul Teknik Üniversitesi (1773)
	Istanbul Üniversitesi (15th century)
	Marmara Üniversitesi (1883)
	Mimar Sinan Üniversitesi (1883)
	Yildiz Teknik Üniversitesi (1911)
Izmir	Dokuz Eylül Üniversitesi (1982)
	Ege Üniversitesi (1955)
Kayseri	Erciyes Üniversitesi (1978)
Konya	Selçuk Üniversitesi (1975)
Samsun	Ondokuz Üniversitesi (1975)
Trabzon	Karadeniz Teknik Üniversitesi (1963)
Van	Yüzüncü Yil Üniversitesi (1982)

Turkmenistan

Ashkhabad	Turkmen A M Gorkii State University (1950)

Ukraine

Chernivsti	Chernivsti State University (1875)
Dnepropetrovsk	Dnepropetrovsk State University (1918)
Donetsk	Donetsk State University (1965)
Kharkov	Kharkov State University (1805)
Kiev	Kiev-Mohyla Academy (1992)
	Kiev T G Shevchenko State University (1834)
Lvov	Lvov State University (1661)
Odessa	Odessa I I Mechnikov State University (1865)
Simferopol	Simferopol State University (1918)
Uzhgorod	Uzhgorod State University (1945)

United Kingdom

Aberdeen	University of Aberdeen (1495)
	Robert Gordon (1885[a])
Aberystwyth	University of Wales, Aberystwyth (1872)
Bangor	University of Wales, Bangor (1884)
Bath	University of Bath (1966)
Bedford	Cranfield University (formerly Institute of Technology) (1969)

Belfast	The Queen's University of Belfast (1908)
Birmingham	Aston University (1966)
	The University of Birmingham (1900)
	University of Central England in Birmingham (1971[a])
Bradford	University of Bradford (1966[a])
Brighton	University of Brighton (1970[a])
	The University of Sussex (1961)
Bristol	The University of Bristol (1909)
	University of the West of England (1969[a])
Buckingham	University of Buckingham (1983[a])
Chelmsford and Cambridge	Anglia Polytechnic University (1905[a] as Chelmsford School of Science and Art)
Cambridge	The University of Cambridge
	Christ's College (1505)
	Churchill College (1960)
	Clare College (1326)
	Clare Hall (1966)
	Corpus Christi College (1352)
	Darwin College (1964)
	Downing College (1800)
	Emmanuel College (1584)
	Fitzwilliam College (1966)
	Girton College (1869)
	Gonville & Caius College (1348)
	Homerton College (1824)
	Hughes Hall (1885)
	Jesus College (1496)
	King's College (1441)
	Lucy Cavendish College (1965)
	Magdalene College (1542)
	New Hall (1954)
	Newnham College (1871)
	Pembroke College (1347)
	Peterhouse (1284)
	Queens' College (1448)
	Robinson College (1977)
	St Catharine's College (1473)
	St Edmund's College (1896)
	St John's College (1511)
	Selwyn College (1882)
	Sidney Sussex College (1596)
	Trinity College (1546)
	Trinity Hall (1350)
	Wolfson College (1965)
Canterbury	University of Kent at Canterbury (1965)
Cardiff	The University of Wales (federal body) (1893)
	University of Wales, Cardiff (1988)
	University of Wales Institute, Cardiff (1976)
	College of Medicine (1984)
Colchester	The University of Essex (1964)
Coleraine	University of Ulster (1985)
Coventry	Coventry University (1970[a])
	The University of Warwick (1965)
Derby	University of Derby (1851[a])
Dundee	University of Dundee (incorporating Duncan Jordanstone College of Art) (1967)
	University of Abertay Dundee (formerly Dundee Institute of Technology) (1888)
Durham	The University of Durham (1832)
Edinburgh	University of Edinburgh (1583)
	Heriot-Watt University (1966)
	Napier University (1964[a])
Exeter	The University of Exeter (1955)
Glasgow	University of Glasgow (1451)
	Glasgow Caledonian University (Queen's College 1875: Glasgow Polytechnic 1971[a]; merged 1992)
	University of Strathclyde (1964)
Guildford	University of Surrey (1966)
Hatfield	University of Hertfordshire (1952[a])

Universities (continued)

Huddersfield	University of Huddersfield (1841[a])
Hull	The University of Hull (1954)
	University of Lincolnshire and Humberside (1978[a])
Kingston-upon-Thames	Kingston University (1970[a])
Lampeter	St David's College, Lampeter (1822, present status 1971)
Lancaster	The University of Lancaster (1964)
Leeds	The University of Leeds (1904)
	Leeds Metropolitan University (1970[a])
Leicester	The University of Leicester (1957)
	De Montfort University (1969[a])
Liverpool	The University of Liverpool (1903)
	Liverpool John Moores University (1970[a])
London	The University of London (1836)
	Birkbeck College (1823)
	Goldsmiths' College (1904)
	Imperial College of Science, Technology, and Medicine (1907)
	Institute of Education (1902; controlled by London University since 1932; School of London University since 1987)
	King's College London (1829)
	London School of Economics and Political Science (1895)
	Queen Mary and Westfield College (Queen Mary 1887; Westfield 1882; merged 1989)
	Royal Holloway and Bedford New College (Egham) (Royal Holloway 1886; Bedford 1849; merged 1985)
	Royal Veterinary College (1791)
	School of Oriental and African Studies (1916)
	School of Pharmacy (1842)
	University College London (1826)
	Wye College (Ashford) (1447)
	City University (1966)
	City of London University (1970[a])
	University of East London (1970[a])
	Middlesex University (1973[a])
	University of North London (1971[a])
	South Bank University (1970[a])
	University of Westminster (1970[a])
	London Guildhall University (1970[a])
	University of Greenwich (1890[a])
Loughborough	Loughborough University of Technology (1966)
Luton	University of Luton (1993)
Manchester	University of Manchester (1851)
	University of Manchester Institute of Science and Technology (UMIST) (1824)
	Manchester Metropolitan University (1970[a])
Middlesbrough	University of Teesside (1929[a])
Milton Keynes	The Open University (1969)
Newcastle under Lyme	Keele University (1962)
Newcastle upon Tyne	The University of Newcastle upon Tyne (1851)
	University of Northumbria at Newcastle (1969[a])
Newport	University of Wales College, Newport (formerly, Gwent College of Higher Education; Newport Mechanics Institute, 1841) (1975)
Norwich	The University of East Anglia (1964)
Nottingham	City University Nottingham (1970[a])
	The University of Nottingham (1948)
	Nottingham Trent University (1970[a])
Oxford	The University of Oxford
	All Souls College (1438)
	Balliol College (1263)
	Brasenose College (1509)
	Christ Church (1546)
	Corpus Christi College (1517)
	Exeter College (1314)
	Green College (1979)
	Hertford College (1874)
	Jesus College (1571)
	Keble College (1868)
	Lady Margaret Hall (1878)

Linacre College (1962)
Lincoln College (1427)
Magdalen College (1458)
Mansfield College (1996)
Merton College (1263)
New College (1379)
Nuffield College (1937)
Oriel College (1326)
Pembroke College (1624)
Queen's College (1340)
Rewley House (Kellogg College) (1990)
St Anne's College (1952)
St Antony's College (1950)
St Catherine's College (1962)
St Cross College (1965)
St Edmund Hall (c.1278)
St Hilda's College (1893)
St Hugh's College (1886)
St John's College (1555)
St Peter's College (1929)
Somerville College (1879)
Trinity College (1554)
University College (1249)
Wadham College (1612)
Wolfson College (1966)
Worcester College (1714)
Oxford Brookes University (1970[a])

Paisley	University of Paisley (1897)
Plymouth	University of Plymouth (1970[a])
Pontypridd	University of Glamorgan (1913[a] as mining college)
Poole	Bournemouth University (1961 as Dorset Institute of Higher Education[a])
Portsmouth	University of Portsmouth (1870[a])
Preston	University of Central Lancashire (1956[a])
Reading	The University of Reading (1926)
Salford	University of Salford (1967)
Sheffield	The University of Sheffield (1905)
	Sheffield Hallam University (1969[a])
Southampton	The University of Southampton (1952)
St Andrews	University of St Andrews (1411)
Stirling	University of Stirling (1967)
Stoke-on-Trent	Staffordshire University (1970[a])
Sunderland	University of Sunderland (1969[a])
Swansea	University of Wales, Swansea (1920)
Uxbridge	Brunel University (1966)
West London	Thames Valley University (1991[b])
Wolverhampton	University of Wolverhampton (1969[a])
Woolwich	University of Greenwich (1890[a])
York	The University of York (1963)

[a]Founded as a polytechnic or other college; university status applied for in 1992
[b]Formerly Ealing College of Higher Education

United States

Alabama	Auburn University (1856), Auburn
	Tuskegee University (1881), Tuskegee
	University of Alabama (1831), Tuscaloosa
	University of Alabama at Birmingham (1969), Birmingham
	University of Alabama in Huntsville (1950), Huntsville
	University of South Alabama (1963), Mobile
Alaska	University of Alaska Anchorage (1954), Anchorage
	University of Alaska Fairbanks (1917), Fairbanks
Arizona	Arizona State University (1885), Tempe
	Northern Arizona University (1899), Flagstaff
	University of Arizona (1885),Tucson
Arkansas	University of Arkansas (1871), Fayetteville
	University of Arkansas at Little Rock (1927), Little Rock
	University of Arkansas at Pine Bluff (1873), Pine Bluff
California	California Institute of Technology (1891), Pasadena
	California Polytechnic State University(1901),San Luis Obispo

Universities (continued)

	California Polytechnic State University (1938), Pomona
	California State University (1970), Bakersfield
	California State University (1887), Chico
	California State University, Dominguez Hills (1960), Carson
	California State University (1911), Fresno
	California State University (1957), Fullerton
	California State University (1957), Hayward
	California State University (1949), Long Beach
	California State University (1847), Los Angeles
	California State University (1958), Northridge
	California State University (1947), Sacramento
	California State University (1965), San Bernardino
	Loyola Marymount University (1911), Los Angeles
	National University (1971), San Diego
	Pomona College (1887), Claremont
	San Diego State University (1897), San Diego
	San Francisco State University (1899), San Francisco
	San Jose State University (1857), San Jose
	Santa Clara University (1851), Santa Clara
	Stanford University (1891), Stanford
	University of California at Berkeley (1868), Berkeley
	University of California, Davis (1906), Davis
	University of California, Irvine (1965), Irvine
	University of California, Los Angeles (1919), Los Angeles
	University of California, Riverside (1954), Riverside
	University of California, San Diego (1959), La Jolla
	University of California, Santa Barbara (1891), Santa Barbara
	University of California, Santa Cruz (1965), Santa Cruz
	University of Southern California (1880),Los Angeles
Colorado	Colorado School of Mines (1874), Golden
	Colorado State University (1862), Fort Collins
	Metropolitan State College (1965), Denver
	University of Colorado at Boulder (1876), Boulder
	University of Northern Colorado (1890), Greeley
Connecticut	Central Connecticut State University (1849), New Britain
	Fairfield University (1942), Fairfield
	Southern Connecticut State University (1893), New Haven
	University of Connecticut (1881), Storrs
	Wesleyan University (1831), Middletown
	Yale University (1701), New Haven
Delaware	University of Delaware (1743), Newark
District of Columbia	American University (1893), Washington
	Catholic University of America (1887), Washington
	Gallaudet University (1856), Washington
	Georgetown University (1789), Washington
	George Washington University (1821), Washington
	Howard University (1867), Washington
	University of the District of Columbia (1976), Washington
Florida	Florida Atlantic University (1961), Boca Raton
	Florida International University (1965), Miami
	Florida State University (1857), Tallahassee
	Nova University (1964), Fort Lauderdale
	University of Central Florida (1963), Orlando
	University of Florida (1853), Gainsville
	University of Miami (1925), Coral Gables
	University of South Florida (1956), Tampa
Georgia	Emory University (1836), Atlanta
	Georgia Institute of Technology (1885), Atlanta
	Georgia Southern University (1906), Statesboro
	Georgia State University (1913), Atlanta
	University of Georgia (1785), Athens
Hawaii	University of Hawaii at Hilo (1970), Hilo
	University of Hawaii at Manoa (1907), Honolulu
Idaho	Boise State University (1932), Boise
	University of Idaho (1889), Moscow
Illinois	DePaul University (1898), Chicago

	Eastern Illinois University (1895), Charleston
	Illinois State University (1857), Normal
	Loyola University Chicago (1870), Chicago
	Northern Illinois University (1895), De Kalb
	Northeastern Illinois University (1961), Chicago
	Northwestern University (1851), Evanston
	Southern Illinois University of Carbondale (1869), Carbondale
	Southern Illinois University at Edwardsville (1957), Edwardsville
	University of Chicago (1891), Chicago
	University of Illinois at Chicago (1965),Chicago
	University of Illinois at Urbana – Champaign (1867), Urbana
	Western Illinois University (1899), Macomb
Indiana	Ball State University (1918), Muncie
	Indiana State Univesity (1865), Terre Haute
	Indiana State University Kokomo (1945), Kokomo
	Indiana University at Bloomington (1820), Bloomington
	Indiana University at South Bend (1922), South Bend
	Indiana University Northwest (1959), Gary
	Indiana University of Pennsylvania (1875), Indiana
	Indiana University – Purdue University at Fort Wayne (1917), Fort Wayne
	Indiana University – Purdue University at Indianapolis (1969), Indianapolis
	Indiana University Southeast (1941), New Albany
	Purdue University (1869), West Lafayette
	Purdue University Calumet (1951), Hammond
	Purdue University North Central (1967), Westville
	University of Notre Dame (1842), Notre Dame
	Valparaiso University (1859),Valparaiso
Iowa	Drake University (1881),Des Moines
	Grinnell College (1846), Grinnell
	Iowa State University of Science and Technology (1858), Ames
	University of Iowa (1947), Iowa City
	University of Northern Iowa (1876), Cedar Falls
Kansas	Kansas State University (1863), Manhattan
	University of of Kansas (1866), Lawrence
	Wichita State University (1895), Wichita
Kentucky	Bellarmine College (1950), Louisville
	University of Kentucky (1865), Lexington
	University of Louisville (1798),Louisville
	Western Kentucky University (1906), Bowling Green
Louisiana	Louisiana State University and A&M College (1860), Baton Rouge
	Louisiana Technical University (1894), Ruston
	Loyola University New Orleans (1912), New Orleans
	Northeast Louisiana University (1931), Monroe
	Southern University and A&M College (1880), Baton Rouge
	Tulane University (1834), New Orleans
	University of New Orleans (1958), New Orleans
	University of Southwestern Louisiana (1898), Lafayette
Maine	Bowdoin College (1794), Brunswick
	University of Maine (1865), Orono
	University of Southern Maine (1878), Portland
Maryland	Johns Hopkins University (1876), Baltimore
	Towson State University (1866), Towson
	University of Maryland Baltimore County (1966), Baltimore
	University of Maryland College Park (1856), College Park
	University of Maryland University College (1947), College Park
	Washington College (1782), Chestertown
Massachusetts	Amherst College (1821), Amherst
	Boston College (1863), Chestnut Hill
	Boston University (1839), Boston
	Brandeis University (1948), Waltham
	College of the Holy Cross (1843), Worcester
	Harvard University (1636), Cambridge
	Massachusetts Institute of Technology (1861), Cambridge
	Mt Holyoke College (1837), South Hadley
	Northeastern University (1898), Boston
	Smith College (1871), Northampton
	Tufts University (1852), Medford
	University of Lowell (1894), Lowell

KNOWLEDGE

Universities (continued)

	University of Massachusetts at Amherst (1863), Amherst
	University of Massachusetts at Boston (1964), Boston
	Wellesley College (1870), Wellesley
	Wheaton College (1834), Norton
	Williams College (1793), Williamstown
Michigan	Central Michigan University (1892), Mount Pleasant
	Eastern Michigan University (1849), Ypsilanti
	Ferris State University (1884), Big Rapids
	Grand Valley State University (1960), Allendale
	Michigan State University (1855), East Lansing
	Oakland University (1957), Rochester
	University of Michigan (1817), Ann Arbor
	University of Michigan – Dearborn (1959), Dearborn
	University of Michigan – Flint (1956), Flint
	Wayne State University (1868), Detroit
	Western Michigan University (1903), Kalamazoo
Minnesota	Mankato State University (1867), Mankato
	St Cloud State University (1869), St Cloud
	University of Minnesota, Twin Cities Campus (1851), Minneapolis
Mississippi	Mississippi State University (1878), Mississippi State
	University of Mississippi (1844), Oxford
	University of Southern Mississippi (1910), Hattiesburg
Missouri	Central Missouri State University (1871), Warrensburg
	Saint Louis University (1818), St Louis
	Southwest Missouri State University (1905), Springfield
	Stephens College (1833), Columbia
	University of Missouri – Columbia (1839), Columbia
	University of Missouri – Kansas City (1933), Kansas City
	University of Missouri – Rolla (1870), Rolla
	University of Missouri – St Louis (1963), St Louis
	Washington University (1853), St Louis
Montana	Montana State University (1893), Bozeman
	University of Montana (1893), Missoula
Nebraska	Creighton University (1878), Omaha
	University of Nebraska at Kearney (1903), Kearney
	University of Nebraska at Omaha (1908), Omaha
	University of Nebraska – Lincoln (1869), Lincoln
Nevada	University of Nevada, Las Vegas (1957), Las Vegas
	University of Nevada, Reno (1874), Reno
New Hampshire	Dartmouth College (1769), Hanover
	University of New Hampshire (1866), Durham
	Drew University (1866), Madison
New Jersey	Fairleigh-Dickinson University, Teaneck-Hackensack Campus (1954), Teaneck
	Kean College of New Jersey (1855), Union
	Montclair State College (1908), Upper Montclair
	Princeton University (1746), Princeton
	Rutgers, State University of New Jersey
	Douglas College (1918), New Brunswick
	Livingston College (1969), New Brunswick
	Newark College of Arts and Science (1946), Newark
	Rutgers College (1766), New Brunswick
	University College – New Brunswick (1934), New Brunswick
	Seton Hall University (1856), South Orange
	William Paterson College of New Jersey (1855), Wayne
New Mexico	New Mexico State University (1888), Las Cruces
	University of New Mexico (1889), Albuquerque
New York	Adelphi University (1896), Garden City
	Barnard College (1889), New York
	Baruch College of the City University of New York (1968), New York
	Brooklyn College of the City University of New York (1930), New York
	City College of the City University of New York (1847), New York
	Clarkson University (1896), Potsdam
	Colgate University (1819), Hamilton
	College of Staten Island of the City University of New York (1955), New York
	Columbia College (1754), New York

Columbia University School of Engineering and Applied Science (1864), New York
Columbia University School of General Studies (1754), New York
Cooper Union for the Advancement of Science and Art (1859), New York
Cornell University (1865), Ithaca
Fashion Institute of Technology (1944), New York
Fordham University (1841), New York
Hamilton College (1812), Clinton
Hartwick College (1797), Oneonta
Hofstra University (1935), Hempstead
Hunter College of the City University of New York (1870), New York
Ithaca College (1892), Ithaca
Juilliard School (1905), New York
Long Island University, Brooklyn Campus (1926), Brooklyn
Long Island University, CW Post Campus (1954), Brookville
New York Institute of Technology (1955), Old Westbury
New York University (1831), New York
Pace University (1906), New York
Parsons School of Design, New School for Social Research (1896), New York
Pratt Institute (1887), Brooklyn
Queens College of the City University of New York (1937), Flushing
Rensselaer Polytechnic Institute (1824), Troy
Rochester University (1850), Rochester
Rochester Institute of Technology (1829), Rochester
Sarah Lawrence College (1926), Bronxville
Skidmore College (1903), Saratoga Springs
St John's University (1870), Jamaica
State University of New York at Albany (1844), Albany
State University of New York at Binghamton (1946), Binghamton
State University of New York at Buffalo (1946), Buffalo
State University of New York at Stony Brook (1957), Brook
State University of New York, College at Brockport (1867), Brockport
State University of New York, College at Buffalo (1867), Buffalo
State University of New York, College at Cortland (1868), Cortland
State University of New York, College at Fredonia (1826), Fredonia
State University of New York, College at Geneseo (1867), Geneseo
State University of New York, College at New Paltz (1828), New Paltz
State University of New York, College at Old Westbury (1965), Old Westbury
State University of New York, College at Oneonta (1889), Oneonta
State University of New York, College at Oswego (1861), Oswego
State University of New York, College at Plattsburgh (1889), Plattsburgh
State University of New York, College at Potsdam (1816), Potsdam
State University of New York, Empire State College (1971), Saratoga Springs
Syracuse University (1870), Syracuse
Union College (1795), Schenectady
State University of New York, Regents College (1971), Albany
Vassar College (1861), Poughkeepsie
Yeshiva University (1886), New York

North Carolina	Appalachian State University (1899), Boone
	Duke University (1838), Durham
	East Carolina University (1907), Greenville
	North Carolina State University (1887), Raleigh
	University of North Carolina at Asheville (1927), Asheville
	University of North Carolina at Chapel Hill (1795), Chapel Hill
	University of North Carolina at Charlotte (1946), Charlotte
	University of North Carolina at Greensboro (1891), Greensboro
	University of North Carolina at Wilmington (1947), Wilmington
	Wake Forest University (1834), Winston-Salem
North Dakota	University of North Dakota (1883), Grand Forks
Ohio	Bowling Green State University (1910), Bowling Green
	Case Western Reserve University (1826), Cleveland
	Cleveland State University (1964), Cleveland
	John Carroll University (1886), University Heights
	Kent State University (1910), Kent
	Miami University (1809), Oxford
	Oberlin College (1833), Oberlin
	Ohio State University (1870), Columbus
	Ohio University (1804), Athens

Universities (continued)

	University of Akron (1870), Akron
	University of Cincinnati (1819), Cincinnati
	University of Dayton (1850), Dayton
	University of Toledo (1872), Toledo
	Wright State University (1964), Dayton
	Xavier University (1831), Cincinnati
	Youngstown State University (1908), Youngstown
Oklahoma	Central State University (1890), Edmond
	Oklahoma State University (1890), Stillwater
	Oral Roberts University (1963), Tulsa
	University of Oklahoma (1890), Norman
Oregon	Oregon State University (1868), Corvallis
	Portland State University (1946), Portland
	University of Oregon (1872), Eugene
Pennsylvania	Bryn Mawr College (1885), Bryn Mawr
	Bucknell University (1846), Lewisburg
	Carnegie Mellon University (1900), Pittsburgh
	Dickinson College (1773), Carlisle
	Drexel University (1891), Philadelphia
	Duquesne University (1878), Pittsburgh
	Haverford College (1833), Haverford
	La Salle University (1863), Philadelphia
	Lehigh University (1865), Bethlehem
	Moravian College (1742), Bethlehem
	Pennsylvania State University, University Park Campus (1855), University Park
	Swarthmore College (1864), Swarthmore
	Temple University (1884), Philadelphia
	Temple University, Ambler Campus (1910), Ambler
	University of Pennyslvania (1740), Philadelphia
	University of Pittsburgh (1787), Pittsburgh
	University of Pittsburgh at Johnstown (1927), Johnstown
	Villanova University (1842), Villanova
	Washington and Jefferson College (1781), Washington
	West Chester University of Pennsylvania (1871), West Chester
Rhode Island	Brown University (1764), Providence
	Rhode Island School of Design (1877), Providence
	University of Rhode Island (1892), Kingston
South Carolina	The Citadel, The Military College of South Carolina (1842), Charleston
	Clemson University (1889), Clemson
	Converse College (1889), Spartanburg
	University of South Carolina (1801), Columbia
	University of South Carolina at Spartanburg (1967), Spartanburg
	University of South Carolina – Coastal Carolina College (1954), Conway
Tennessee	East Tennessee State University (1911), Johnson City
	Memphis State University (1912), Memphis
	Middle Tennessee State University (1911), Murfreesboro
	University of Tennessee at Chattanooga (1886), Chattanooga
	University of Tennessee at Martin (1927), Martin
	University of Tennessee, Knoxville (1794), Knoxville
	Vanderbilt University (1873), Nashville
Texas	Abilene Christian University (1906), Abilene
	Baylor University (1845), Waco
	Lamar University (1923), Beaumont
	Rice University (1912), Houston
	Sam Houston State University (1879), Huntsville
	Southern Methodist University (1911), Dallas
	Southwest Texas State University (1899), San Marcos
	Stephen F Austin State University (1923), Nacogdoches
	Texas A&M University (1876), College Station
	Texas Christian University (1873), Fort Worth
	Texas Technical University (1923), Lubbock
	Trinity University (1869), San Antonio
	University of Houston (1927), Houston
	University of Houston – Clear Lake (1971), Houston
	University of Houston – Downtown (1974), Houston

KNOWLEDGE

	University of North Texas (1890), Denton
	University of Texas at Arlington (1895), Arlington
	University of Texas at Austin (1883), Austin
	University of Texas at Dallas (1969), Richardson
	University of Texas at El Paso (1913), El Paso
	University of Texas at San Antonio (1969), San Antonio
	University of Texas at Tyler (1972), Tyler
	University of Texas – Pan American (1927), Edinburg
Utah	Brigham Young University (1875), Provo
	University of Utah (1850), Salt Lake City
	Utah State University (1888), Logan
	Weber State College (1889), Ogden
Vermont	University of Vermont (1791), Burlington
Virginia	College of William and Mary (1693), Williamsburg
	George Mason University (1957), Fairfax
	Hampden-Sydney College (1776), Hampden-Sydney
	James Madison University (1908), Harrisonburg
	Liberty University (1971), Lynchburg
	Old Dominion University (1930), Norfolk
	University of Virginia (1810), Charlottesville
	Virginia Commonwealth University (1838), Richmond
	Virginia Polytechnic Institute and State University (1872), Blacksburg
	Washington and Lee University (1749), Lexington
Washington	Gonzaga University (1887), Spokane
	University of Washington (1861), Seattle
	Washington State University (1892), Pullman
West Virginia	Marshall University (1837), Huntington
	West Virginia University (1867), Morgantown
Wisconsin	Marquette University (1881), Milwaukee
	University of Wisconsin – Eau Claire (1916), Eau Claire
	University of Wisconsin – Green Bay (1968), Green Bay
	University of Wisconsin – La Crosse (1909), La Crosse
	University of Wisconsin – Madison (1848), Madison
	University of Wisconsin – Milwaukee (1956), Milwaukee
	University of Wisconsin – Oshkosh (1871), Oshkosh
	University of Wisconsin – Parkside (1968), Kenosha
	University of Wisconsin – Platteville (1866), Platteville
	University of Wisconsin – River Falls (1874), River Falls
	University of Wisconsin – Stevens Point (1894), Stevens Point
	University of Wisconsin – Stout (1891), Menomonie
	University of Wisconsin – Whitewater (1868), Whitewater
Wyoming	University of Wyoming (1886), Laramie

Uzbekistan

Nukus	Nukus State University (1979)
Samarkand	Samarkand State University (1933)
Tashkent	Tashkent State University (1920)

Vatican

City State	Rome Pontificia Universitas Gregoriana (1553)
	Pontificia Universitas Lateranensis (1773)
	Pontificia Università Salesiana (1940)
	Pontificia Università S Tommaso D'Aquino (1580)
	Pontificia Universitas Urbiana (1627)

KNOWLEDGE

PART FOURTEEN

Sports and Games

OLYMPIC GAMES

The first modern Olympic Games took place in 1896, founded by the Frenchman Baron de Coubertin. They are held every four years. Women first competed in 1900. The first separate Winter Games celebration was in 1924; beginning in 1994, the Winter Games takes place between Summer Games celebrations.

Venues

	Summer Games	Winter Games
1896	Athens, Greece	–
1900	Paris, France	–
1904	St Louis, USA	–
1908	London, UK	–
1912	Stockholm, Sweden	–
1920	Antwerp, Belgium	–
1924	Paris, France	Chamonix, France
1928	Amsterdam, Netherlands	St Moritz, Switzerland
1932	Los Angeles, USA	Lake Placid, NY, USA
1936	Berlin, Germany	Garmisch-Partenkirchen, Germany
1948	London, UK	St Moritz, Switzerland
1952	Helsinki, Finland	Oslo, Norway
1956	Melbourne, Australia	Cortina, Italy
1960	Rome, Italy	Squaw Valley, CA, USA
1964	Tokyo, Japan	Innsbruck, Austria
1968	Mexico City, Mexico	Grenoble, France
1972	Munich, Germany	Sapporo, Japan
1976	Montreal, Canada	Innsbruck, Austria
1980	Moscow, Russia	Lake Placid, NY, USA
1984	Los Angeles, USA	Sarajevo, Yugoslavia
1988	Seoul, South Korea	Calgary, Canada
1992	Barcelona, Spain	Albertville, France
1994	–	Lillehammer, Norway
1996	Atlanta, USA	–
1998	–	Nagano, Japan
2000	Sydney, Australia	–
2002	–	Salt Lake City, USA
2004	Athens, Greece	–
2006	–	Turin, Italy
2008	Beijing, China	–
2010	–	Vancouver, Canada
2012	London, UK	

Olympic Games were also held in 1906 in Athens, Greece, to commemorate the 10th anniversary of the birth of the modern Games.

Leading medal winners: 2004 Summer Olympics

		Gold	Silver	Bronze	Total
1	USA	35	39	29	103
2	China	32	17	14	63
3	Russia	27	27	38	92
4	Australia	17	16	16	49
5	Japan	16	9	12	37
6	Germany	14	16	18	48
7	France	11	9	13	33
8	Italy	10	11	11	32
9	South Korea	9	12	9	30
10	Great Britain	9	9	12	30
11	Cuba	9	7	11	27
12	Ukraine	9	5	9	23
13	Hungary	8	6	3	17
14	Romania	8	5	6	19
15	Greece	6	6	4	16
16	Norway	5	0	1	6
17	Netherlands	4	9	9	22
18	Brazil	4	3	3	10
19	Sweden	4	1	2	7
20	Spain	3	11	5	19
21	Canada	3	6	3	12
22	Turkey	3	3	4	10
23	Poland	3	2	5	10
24	New Zealand	3	2	0	5
25	Thailand	3	1	4	8
26	Belarus	2	6	7	15
27	Austria	2	4	1	7
28	Ethiopia	2	3	2	7
29	Iran	2	2	2	6
30	Slovakia	2	2	2	6
31	Taiwan	2	2	1	5
32	Georgia	2	2	0	4
33	Bulgaria	2	1	9	12
34	Jamaica	2	1	2	5

Medal winners: 2006 Winter Games

		Gold	Silver	Bronze	Total
1	Germany	11	12	6	29
2	USA	9	9	7	25
3	Austria	9	7	7	23
4	Russia	8	6	8	22
5	Canada	7	10	7	24
6	Sweden	7	2	5	14
7	South Korea	6	3	2	11
8	Switzerland	5	4	5	14
9	Italy	5	0	6	11
10	France	3	2	4	9
10	Netherlands	3	2	4	9
12	Estonia	3	0	0	3
13	Norway	2	8	9	19
14	China	2	4	5	11
15	Czech Republic	1	2	1	4
16	Croatia	1	2	0	3
17	Australia	1	0	1	2
18	Japan	1	0	1	2
19	Finland	0	6	3	9
20	Poland	0	1	1	2
21	Belarus	0	1	0	1
21	Bulgaria	0	1	0	1
21	Great Britain	0	1	0	1
21	Slovakia	0	1	0	1
25	Ukraine	0	0	2	2
26	Latvia	0	0	1	1

COMMONWEALTH GAMES

First held as the British Empire Games in 1930. They take place every four years and between Olympic celebrations. They became the British Empire and Commonwealth Games in 1954; the current title was adopted in 1970.

Venues

1930 Hamilton, Canada
1934 London, England
1938 Sydney, Australia
1950 Auckland, New Zealand
1954 Vancouver, Canada
1958 Cardiff, Wales
1962 Perth, Australia
1966 Kingston, Jamaica
1970 Edinburgh, Scotland
1974 Christchurch, New Zealand
1978 Edmonton, Canada
1982 Brisbane, Australia
1986 Edinburgh, Scotland
1990 Auckland, New Zealand
1994 Victoria, Canada
1998 Kuala Lumpur, Malaysia
2002 Manchester, England
2006 Melbourne, Australia
2010 Delhi, India

Leading medal winners (including 2002)

Nation	Gold	Silver	Bronze	Total
1 Australia	646	548	494	1688
2 England	521	510	531	1582
3 Canada	388	415	508	1311
4 New Zealand	118	157	221	496
5 India	82	78	75	225
6 South Africa	80	79	84	243
7 Scotland	71	87	143	301
8 Kenya	53	42	49	143
9 Wales	46	66	85	198
10 Nigeria	35	42	50	127

Medal winners: Manchester 2002 Games

Nation	Gold	Silver	Bronze	Total
1 Australia	82	62	62	206
2 England	54	51	60	165
3 India	32	21	19	72
4 Canada	31	41	42	114
5 New Zealand	11	13	21	45
6 South Africa	9	20	17	46
7 Cameroon	9	1	2	12
8 Malaysia	7	9	18	34
9 Scotland	6	8	16	30
10 Nigeria	5	4	11	20
11 Wales	4	15	12	31
12 Kenya	4	8	4	16
13 Jamaica	4	6	7	17
14 Singapore	4	2	7	13
15 Bahamas	4	0	4	8
16 Nauru	2	3	10	15
17 Northern Ireland	2	2	1	5
18 Cyprus	2	1	1	4
19 Pakistan	1	3	3	7
20 Fiji	1	1	1	3
21 Zambia	1	1	1	3
22 Zimbabwe	1	1	0	2
23 Namibia	1	0	4	5
24 United Republic of Tanzania	1	0	1	2
25 Bangladesh	1	0	0	1
25 Guyana	1	0	0	1
25 Mozambique	1	0	0	1
25 St Kitts and Nevis	1	0	0	1
29 Botswana	0	2	1	3
30 Uganda	0	2	0	2
31 Samoa	0	1	2	3
32 Trinidad and Tobago	0	1	0	1
33 Barbados	0	0	1	1
33 Cayman Islands	0	0	1	1
33 Ghana	0	0	1	1
33 Lesotho	0	0	1	1
33 Malta	0	0	1	1
33 Mauritius	0	0	1	1
33 St Lucia	0	0	1	1

ANGLING

World freshwater championship

First held in 1957; takes place annually.

Recent winners: individual
1991 Bob Nudd (England)
1992 David Wesson (Australia)
1993 Mario Barras (Portugal)
1994 Bob Nudd (England)
1995 Pierre Jean (France)
1996 Alan Scotthorne (England)
1997 Alan Scotthorne (England)
1998 Alan Scotthorne (England)
1999 Bob Nudd (England)
2000 Jacopo Falsini (Italy)
2001 Umberto Ballabeni (Italy)
2002 Juan Blasco (Spain)
2003 Alan Scotthorne (England)
2004 Tamas Walter (Hungary)
2005 Guido Nullens (Belgium)
2006 Tamas Walter (Hungary)

Recent winners: team
1991 England
1992 Italy
1993 Italy
1994 Italy
1995 France
1996 Italy
1997 Italy
1998 England
1999 Spain
2000 Italy
2001 England
2002 Spain
2003 Hungary
2004 France
2005 England
2006 England

Most wins: Individual (4), Bob Nudd (England) 1990 and as above. Team (14), France: 1959, 1963–4, 1966, 1968, 1972, 1974–5, 1978–9, 1981, 1990, 1995, 2004.

World fly-fishing championship

First held in 1981; takes place annually.

Winners: individual
1991 Brian Leadbetter (England)
1992 Pierluigi Cocito (Italy)
1993 Russell Owen (Wales)
1994 Pascal Cognard (France)
1995 Jeremy Herrmann
1996 Pierluigi Cocito (Italy)
1997 Pascal Cognard (France)
1998 Tomas Starychsojtu (Czech Republic)
1999 Ross Stewart (Australia)

2000 Pascal Cognard (France)
2001 Vladimir Sedivy (Czech Republic)
2002 Jerome Brossutti (France)
2003 Stefano Cotugno (Italy)
2004 Miroslav Antal (Slovakia)
2005 Bertrand Jacquemin (France)
2006 Antonin Pesek (Czech Republic)

Winners: team
1991 New Zealand
1992 Italy
1993 England
1994 Czech Republic
1995 England
1996 Czech Republic
1997 France
1998 Czech Republic
1999 Australia
2000 France
2001 France
2002 France
2003 France
2004 Slovakia
2005 France
2006 Czech Republic

Most wins: Individual (3), Pascal Cognard (France) as above. Team (6), France, as above.

ARCHERY

World championships

First held in 1931; took place annually until 1959; since then, every two years.

Recent winners: individual – men
1977 Richard McKinney (USA)
1979 Darrell Pace (USA)
1981 Kysti Laasonen (Finland)
1983 Richard McKinney (USA)
1985 Richard McKinney (USA)
1987 Vladimir Yesheyev (USSR)
1989 Stanislav Zabrodsky (USSR)
1991 Simon Fairweather (Australia)
1993 Kyung-mo Park (South Korea)
1995 Gary Broadhead (USA)
1997 Kyung-ho Kim (South Korea)
1999 Sung-chil Hong (South Korea)
2001 Jung-ki Yeon (South Korea)
2003 Keijo Kallunki (Finland)
2005 Morgan Lundin (Sweden)

Recent winners: team – men
1977 USA
1979 USA
1981 USA
1983 USA
1985 South Korea
1987 South Korea
1989 USSR

1991 South Korea
1993 France
1995 USA
1997 South Korea
1999 Italy
2000 South Korea
2003 USA
2005 USA

Most wins: Individual (4), Hans Deutgen (Sweden): 1947–50. Team (17), USA: 1957–83, 1995, 2003, 2005.

Recent winners: individual – women
1977 Luann Ryon (USA)
1979 Jin-ho Kim (South Korea)
1981 Natalia Butuzova (USSR)
1983 Jin-ho Kim (South Korea)
1985 Irina Soldatova (USSR)
1987 Ma Xiaojun (China)
1989 Soo-nyung Kim (South Korea)
1991 Soo-nyung Kim (South Korea)
1993 Hyo-jung Kim (South Korea)
1995 Angela Moscarelly (USA)
1997 Du-ri Kim (South Korea)
1999 Eun-kyung Lee (South Korea)
2001 Sung-hyun Park (South Korea)
2003 Bruna Coladarci (Italy)
2005 Sofya Goncharova (Russia)

Recent winners: team – women
1977 USA
1979 South Korea
1981 USSR
1983 South Korea
1985 USSR
1987 USSR
1989 South Korea
1991 South Korea
1993 South Korea
1995 USA
1997 South Korea
1999 Italy
2001 China
2003 South Korea
2005 France

Most wins: Individual (7), Janina Kurkowska (Poland): 1931–4, 1936, 1939, 1947. Team (9), USA: 1952, 1957–9, 1961, 1963, 1965, 1977, 1995.

Olympic Games

Gold medal winners: 2004
Individual (men)
Marco Galiazzo (Italy)

Team (men)
South Korea

Individual (women)
Sung-Hyun Park (Korea)

Team (women)
South Korea

ATHLETICS

Performance times are given in seconds, or minutes:seconds, or hours:minutes:seconds. Distances are given in metres. Performances in the decathlon, pentathlon, and heptathlon are given in points.

World championships

First held in Helsinki in 1983; then in Rome in 1987; Tokyo in 1991; Stuttgart in 1993; Gothenburg in 1995; Athens in 1997; Seville in 1999; Edmonton in 2001; Paris in 2003; Helsinki in 2005; takes place every two years.

Event winners: men

100 m
2001 Maurice Greene (USA) 9.85
2003 Kim Collins (St Kitts & Nevis) 10.07
2005 Justin Gatlin (USA) 9.88

200 m
2001 Konstadínos Kedéris (Greece) 20.04
2003 John Capel (USA) 20.30
2005 Justin Gatlin (USA) 20.04

400 m
2001 Avard Moncour (Bahamas) 44.64
2003 Jerome Young (USA) 44.50
2005 Jeremy Wariner (USA) 43.93

800 m
2001 André Bucher (Switzerland) 1:43.70
2003 Djabir Sad-Guerni (Algeria) 1:44.81
2005 Rashid Ramzi (Bahrain) 1:44.24

1500 m
2001 Hicham El Guerrouj (Morocco) 3:30.68
2003 Hicham El Guerrouj (Morocco) 3:31.77
2005 Rashid Ramzi (Bahrain) 3:37.88

5000 m
2001 Richard Limo (Kenya) 13:00.77
2003 Eliud Kipchoge (Kenya) 12:52.79
2005 Benjamin Limo (Kenya) 13:32.55

10000 m
2001 Charles Kamathi (Kenya) 27:53.25
2003 Kenenisa Bekele (Ethiopia) 26:49.57
2005 Kenenisa Bekele (Ethiopia) 27:08.33

Marathon
2001 Gezahegne Abera (Ethiopia) 2:12.42
2003 Jaouad Gharib (Morocco) 2:08.31
2005 Jaouad Gharib (Morocco) 2:10.10

3000 m steeplechase
2001 Reuben Kosgei (Kenya) 8:15.16
2003 Saif Saaeed Shaheen (Qatar) 8:04.39
2005 Saif Saaeed Shaheen (Qatar) 8:13.31

110 m hurdles
2001 Allen Johnson (USA) 13.04
2003 Allen Johnson (USA) 13.12
2005 Ladji Doucoure (France) 13.07

400 m hurdles
2001 Felix Sanchez (Dominican Republic) 47.49
2003 Felix Sanchez (Dominican Republic) 47.25
2005 Bershawn Jackson (USA) 47.30

High jump
2001 Martin Buss (Germany) 2.36
2003 Jacques Freitag (South Africa) 2.35
2005 Yuriy Krymarenko (Ukraine) 2.32

Pole vault
2001 Dmitri Markov (Australia) 6.05
2003 Giuseppe Gibilisco (Italy) 5.90
2005 Rens Blom (Netherlands) 5.80

Long jump
2001 Ivan Pedroso (Cuba) 8.40
2003 Dwight Phillips (USA) 8.32
2005 Dwight Phillips (USA) 8.60

Triple jump
2001 Jonathan Edwards (Great Britain) 17.92
2003 Christian Olsson (Sweden) 17.72
2005 Walter Davis (USA) 17.57

Shot
2001 John Godina (USA) 21.87
2003 Andrei Mikhnevich (Belarus) 21.69
2005 Adam Nelson (USA) 21.73

Discus
2001 Lars Riedel (Germany) 69.72
2003 Virgilijus Alekna (Lithuania) 69.69
2005 Virgilijus Alekna (Lithuania) 70.17

Hammer
2001 Szymon Ziolkowski (Poland) 83.38
2003 Ivan Tikhon (Belarus) 83.05
2005 Ivan Tikhon (Belarus) 83.89

Javelin
2001 Jan Zelezny (Czech Republic) 92.80
2003 Sergey Makarov (Russia) 85.44
2005 Andrus Värnik (Estonia) 87.17

Decathlon
2001 Tomas Dvorak (Czech Republic) 8902
2003 Tom Pappas (USA) 8750
2005 Bryan Clay (USA) 8732

4 × 100 m relay
2001 USA 37.96
2003 USA 38.06
2005 France 38.08

4 × 400 m relay
2001 USA 2:57.54
2003 USA 2:58.88
2005 USA 2:56.91

20 km walk
2001 Roman Rasskazov (Russia) 1:20.31
2003 Jefferson Pérez (Ecuador) 1:17.21
2005 Jefferson Pérez (Ecuador) 1:18.35

50 km walk
2001 Robert Korzeniowski (Poland) 3:42.08
2003 Robert Korzeniowski (Poland) 3:36.03
2005 Sergey Kirdyapkin (Russia) 3:38.08

Event winners: women

100 m
2001 Zhanna Pintusevich-Block (Ukraine) 10.82
2003 Kelli White (USA) 10.85
2005 Lauryn Williams (USA) 10.93

200 m
2001 Marion Jones (USA) 22.39
2003 Kelli White (USA) 22.05
2005 Allyson Felix (USA) 22.16

400 m
2001 Amy Mbacke Thiam (Senegal) 49.86
2003 Ana Guevara (Mexico) 48.89
2005 Tonique Williams-Darling (Bahamas) 49.55

800 m
2001 Maria Mutola (Mozambique) 1:57.17
2003 Maria Mutola (Mozambique) 1:59.89
2005 Zulia Calatayud (Cuba) 1:58.82

1500 m
2001 Gabriela Szabo (Romania) 4:00.57
2003 Tatyana Tomashova (Russia) 3:58.52
2005 Tatyana Tomashova (Russia) 4:00.35

5000 m
2001 Olga Yegorova (Russia) 15:03.39
2003 Tirunesh Dibaba (Ethiopia) 14:51.72
2005 Tirunesh Dibaba (Ethiopia) 14:38.59

10000 m
2001 Derartu Tulu (Ethiopia) 31:48.81
2003 Berhane Adere (Ethiopia) 30:04.18
2005 Tirunesh Dibaba (Ethiopia) 30:24.02

Marathon
2001 Lidia Simon (Romania) 2:26.01
2003 Catherine Ndereba (Kenya) 2:23.55
2005 Paula Radcliffe (Great Britain) 2:20.07

100 m hurdles
2001 Anjanette Kirkland (USA) 12.42
2003 Perdita Felicien (Canada) 12.53
2005 Michelle Perry (USA) 12.66

400 m hurdles
2001 Nezha Bidouane (Morocco) 53.34
2003 Jana Pittman (Australia) 53.22
2005 Yuliya Pechonkina (Russia) 52.90

High jump
2001 Hestrie Cloete (South Africa) 2.00
2003 Hestrie Cloete (South Africa) 2.06
2005 Kajsa Bergqvist (Sweden) 2.02

Long jump
2001 Fiona May (Italy) 7.02
2003 Eunice Barber (France) 6.99
2005 Tianna Madison (USA) 6.89

Triple jump
2001 Tatyana Lebedeva (Russia) 15.25
2003 Tatyana Lebedeva (Russia) 15.18
2005 Nadezhda Ostapchuk (Belarus) 20.51

Shot
2001 Yanina Korolchik (Belarus) 20.61
2003 Svetlana Krivelyova (Russia) 20.63
2005 Nadezhda Ostapchuk (Belarus) 20.51

Discus
2001 Natalya Sadova (Russia) 68.57
2003 Irina Yatchenko (Belarus) 67.32
2005 Franka Dietzsch (Germany) 66.56

Javelin
2001 Osleidys Menéndez (Cuba) 69.53
2003 Mirela Manjani (Greece) 66.52
2005 Osleidys Menéndez (Cuba) 71.70

Pole Vault
2003 Svetlana Feofanova (Russia) 4.75
2005 Yelena Isinbayeva (Russia) 5.01

Hammer
2003 Yipsi Morena (Cuba) 73.33
2005 Olga Kuzenkova (Russia) 75.10

Heptathlon
2001 Yelena Prokhorova (Russia) 6694
2003 Carolina Kluft (Sweden) 7001
2005 Carolina Kluft (Sweden) 6887

10 km walk
From 1999, 20 km walk

20 km walk
2001 Olimpiada Ivanova (Russia) 1:27.48
2003 Yelena Nikolayeva (Russia) 1:26.52
2005 Olimpiada Ivanova (Russia) 1:25.41

4 × 100 m relay		4 × 400 m relay	
1999	Bahamas 41.93	1999	Russia 3:21.98
2001	USA 41.71	2001	Jamaica 3:20.65
2003	France 41.78	2003	USA 3:22.63
2005	USA 41.78	2005	Russia 3:20.95

Olympic Games

Event winners: men

100 m
1904 Archie Hahn (USA) 11.0
1906 Archie Hahn (USA) 11.2
1908 Reginald Walker (S Africa) 10.8
1912 Ralph Craig (USA) 10.8
1920 Charles Paddock (USA) 10.8
1924 Harold Abrahams (Great Britain) 10.6
1928 Percy Williams (Canada) 10.8
1932 Eddie Tolan (USA) 10.3
1936 Jesse Owens (USA) 10.3
1948 Harrison Dillard (USA) 10.3
1952 Lindy Remigino (USA) 10.4
1956 Bobby Morrow (USA) 10.5
1960 Armin Hary (W Germany) 10.2
1964 Bob Hayes (USA) 10.06
1968 James Hines (USA) 9.95
1972 Valeriy Borzov (USSR) 10.14
1976 Hasely Crawford (Trinidad) 10.06
1980 Allan Wells (Great Britain) 10.25
1984 Carl Lewis (USA) 9.99
1988 Carl Lewis (USA) 9.92
1992 Linford Christie (Great Britain) 9.96
1996 Donovan Bailey (Canada) 9.84
2000 Maurice Greene (USA) 9.87
2004 Justin Gatlin (USA) 9.85

Athletics, Olympic games (continued)

200 m
1908	Robert Kerr (Canada)	22.6
1912	Ralph Craig (USA)	21.7
1920	Allen Woodring (USA)	22.0
1924	Jackson Scholz (USA)	21.6
1928	Percy Williams (Canada)	21.8
1932	Eddie Tolan (USA)	21.2
1936	Jesse Owens (USA)	20.7
1948	Melvin Patton (USA)	21.1
1952	Andrew Stanfield (USA)	20.7
1956	Bobby Morrow (USA)	20.5
1960	Livio Berruti (Italy)	20.6
1964	Henry Carr (USA)	20.36
1968	Tommie Smith (USA)	19.83
1972	Valeriy Borzov (USSR)	20.00
1976	Donald Quarrie (Jamaica)	20.3
1980	Pietro Mennea (Italy)	20.19
1984	Carl Lewis (USA)	19.80
1988	Joe DeLoach (USA)	19.75
1992	Michael Marsh (USA)	20.01
1996	Michael Johnson (USA)	19.32
2000	Konstantínos Kedéris (Greece)	20.09
2004	Shawn Crawford (USA)	19.79

400 m
1904	Harry Hilllman (USA)	49.2
1906	Paul Pilgrim (USA)	53.2
1908	Wyndham Halswelle (Great Britain)	50.0
1912	Charles Reidpath (USA)	48.2
1920	Bevil Rudd (S Africa)	49.6
1924	Eric Liddell (Great Britain)	47.6
1928	Ray Barbuti (USA)	47.8
1932	Bill Carr (USA)	46.28
1936	Archie Williams (USA)	46.66
1948	Arthur Wint (Jamaica)	46.2
1952	George Rhoden (Jamaica)	46.09
1956	Charles Jenkins (USA)	46.86
1960	Otis Davis (USA)	45.07
1964	Michael Larrabee (USA)	45.15
1968	Lee Evans (USA)	43.86
1972	Vincent Matthews (USA)	44.66
1976	Alberto Juantoreno (Cuba)	44.26
1980	Viktor Markin (USSR)	44.60
1984	Alonzo Babers (USA)	44.27
1988	Steve Lewis (USA)	43.87
1992	Quincy Watts (USA)	43.50
1996	Michael Johnson (USA)	43.49
2000	Michael Johnson (USA)	43.84
2004	Jeremy Wariner (USA)	44.0

800 m
1904	James Lightbody (USA)	1:56.0
1906	Paul Pilgrim (USA)	2:01.5
1908	Mel Sheppard (USA)	1:52.8
1912	James Meredith (USA)	1:51.9
1920	Albert Hill (Great Britain)	1:53.4
1924	Douglas Lowe (Great Britain)	1:52.4
1928	Douglas Lowe (Great Britain)	1:51.8
1932	Tom Hampson (Great Britain)	1:49.70
1936	John Woodruff (USA)	1:52.9
1948	Malvin Whitfield (USA)	1:49.2
1952	Malvin Whitfield (USA)	1:49.34
1956	Thomas Courtney (USA)	1:47.75
1960	Peter Snell (New Zealand)	1:46.48
1964	Peter Snell (New Zealand)	1:45.1
1968	Ralph Doubell (Australia)	1:44.40
1972	David Wottle (USA)	1:45.86

1976	Alberto Juantorena (Cuba)	1:43.50
1980	Steven Ovett (Great Britain)	1:45.40
1984	Joaquim Cruz (Brazil)	1:43.00
1988	Paul Ereng (Kenya)	1:43.45
1992	William Tanui (Kenya)	1:43.66
1996	Vebjoern Rodal (Norway)	1:42.58
2000	Nils Schumann (Germany)	1:45.08
2004	Yuriy Borzakovskiy (Russia)	1:44.45

1500 m
1904	James Lightbody (USA)	4:05.4
1906	James Lightbody (USA)	4:12.0
1908	Mel Sheppard (USA)	4:03.4
1912	Arnold Jackson (Great Britain)	3:56.8
1920	Albert Hill (Great Britain)	4:01.8
1924	Paavo Nurmi (Finland)	3:53.6
1928	Harri Larva (Finland)	3:53.2
1932	Luigi Beccali (Italy)	3:51.20
1936	Jack Lovelock (New Zealand)	3:47.8
1948	Henry Eriksson (Sweden)	3:49.8
1952	Josef Barthel (Luxembourg)	3:45.28
1956	Ron Delany (Ireland)	3:41.49
1960	Herbert Elliott (Australia)	3:35.6
1964	Peter Snell (New Zealand)	3:38.1
1968	Kipchoge Keino (Kenya)	3:34.91
1972	Pekkha Vasala (Finland)	3:36.33
1976	John Walker (New Zealand)	3:39.17
1980	Sebastian Coe (Great Britain)	3:38.40
1984	Sebastian Coe (Great Britain)	3:32.53
1988	Peter Rono (Kenya)	3:35.96
1992	Fermin Cacho (Spain)	3:40.12
1996	Noureddine Morceli (Algeria),	3:35.79
2000	Noah Ngeny (Kenya)	3:32.07
2004	Hicham El Guerrouj (Morocco)	3:34.18

5000 m
1924	Paavo Nurmi (Finalnd)	14:31.2
1928	Ville Ritola (Finland)	14:38.0
1932	Lauri Lehtinen (Finland)	14:29.91
1936	Gunnar Höckert (Finland)	14:22.2
1948	Gaston Reiff (Belgium)	14:17.6
1952	Emil Zátopek (Czechoslovakia)	14:06.72
1956	Vladimir Kuts (USSR)	13:39.86
1960	Murray Halberg (New Zealand)	13:43.4
1964	Robert Schul (USA)	13:48.8
1968	Mohamed Gammoudi (Tunisia)	14:05.0
1972	Lasse Viren (Finland)	13:26.42
1976	Lasse Viren (Finland)	13:24.76
1980	Miruts Yifter (Ethiopia)	13:20.91
1984	Saïd Aouita (Morocco)	13:05.59
1988	John Ngugi (Kenya)	13:11.70
1992	Dieter Baumann (Germany)	13:12.52
1996	Venuste Niyongabo (Burundi)	13:07.97
2000	Millon Wolde (Ethiopia)	13:35.49
2004	Hicham El Guerrouj (Morocco)	13:14.39

10 000 m
1924	Ville Ritola (Finland)	30:23.1
1928	Paavo Nurmi (Finland)	30:18.8
1932	Janusz Kusocinski (Poland)	30:11.4
1936	Ilmari Salminen (Finland)	30:15.4
1948	Emil Zátopek (Czechoslovakia)	29:59.6
1952	Emil Zátopek (Czechoslovakia)	29:17.0
1956	Vladimir Kuts (USSR)	28:45.60
1960	Pyotr Bolotnikov (USSR)	28:32.18
1964	William Mills (USA)	28:24.4
1968	Naftali Temu (Kenya)	29:27.45
1972	Lasse Viren (Finland)	27:38.35
1976	Lasse Viren (Finland)	27:40.38

1980	Miruts Yifter (Ethiopia) 27:42.69
1984	Alberto Cova (Italy) 27:47.54
1988	Brahim Boutayeb (Morocco) 27:21.46
1992	Khalid Skah (Morocco) 27:46.70
1996	Haile Gebrselassie (Ethiopia) 27:07.34
2000	Haile Gebrselassie (Ethiopia) 27:18.20
2004	Kenenisa Bekele (Ethiopia) 27:05.10

Marathon*

1904	Thomas Hicks (USA) 3:28:35.0 *(40 km)*
1906	William Sherring (Canada) 2:51:23.6 *(41.86 km)*
1908	John Hayes (USA) 2:55:18.4
1912	Kenneth McArthur (S Africa) 2:36:54.8 *(40.2 km)*
1920	Hannes Kolehmainen (Finland) 2:32:35.8 *(42.75 km)*
1924	Albin Stenroos (Finland) 2:41:22.6
1928	Mohamed Boughéra El Ouafi (France) 2:32:57.0
1932	Juan Carlos Zabala (Argentina) 2:31:36.0
1936	Kitei Son (Japan) 2:29:19.2
1948	Delfo Cabrera (Argentina) 2:34:51.6
1952	Emil Zátopek (Czechoslovakia) 2:23:03.2
1956	Alain Mimoun (France) 2:25:00.0
1960	Abebe Bikila (Ethiopia) 2:15:16.2
1964	Abebe Bikila (Ethiopia) 2:12:11.2
1968	Mamo Wolde (Ethiopia) 2:20:26.4
1972	Frank Shorter (USA) 2:12:19.8
1976	Waldemar Cierpinski (E Germany) 2:09:55
1980	Waldemar Cierpinski (E Germany) 2:11:03
1984	Carlos Lopes (Portugal) 2:09:21
1988	Gelindo Bordin (Italy) 2:10:32
1992	Hwang Young-jo (S Korea) 2:13:23
1996	Josia Thugwane (S Africa) 2:12.36
2000	Gezahgne Abera (Ethiopia) 2:10.11
2004	Stefano Baldini (Italy) 2:10.55

*Unless shown as otherwise above, the Marathon is run over a distance of 42 km 195 m/26 mi 385 yd.

110 m hurdles

1904	Fred Schule (USA) 16.0
1906	Robert Leavitt (USA) 16.2
1908	Forrest Smithson (USA) 15.0
1912	Fred Kelly (USA) 15.1
1920	Earl Thomson (Canada) 14.8
1924	Daniel Kinsey (USA) 15.0
1928	Sydney Atkinson (S Africa) 14.8
1932	George Saling (USA) 14.57
1936	Forrest Towns (USA) 14.2
1948	William Porter (USA) 13.9
1952	Harrison Dillard (USA) 13.91
1956	Lee Calhoun (USA) 13.70
1960	Lee Calhoun (USA) 13.98
1964	Hayes Jones (USA) 13.67
1968	Willie Davenport (USA) 13.33
1972	Rodney Milburn (USA) 13.24
1976	Guy Drut (France) 13.30
1980	Thomas Munkelt (E Germany) 13.39
1984	Roger Kingdom (USA) 13.20
1988	Roger Kingdom (USA) 12.98
1992	Mark McKoy (Canada) 13.12
1996	Allen Johnson (USA) 12.95
2000	Anier Garcia (Cuba) 13.00
2004	Liu Xiang (China) 12.91

400 m hurdles

1908	Charles Bacon (USA) 55.0
1920	Frank Loomis (USA) 54.0
1924	Morgan Taylor (USA) 52.6
1928	Lord Burghley (Great Britain) 53.4
1932	Robert Tisdall (Ireland) 51.67

1936	Glenn Hardin (USA) 52.4
1948	Roy Cochran (USA) 51.1
1952	Charles Moore (USA) 51.06
1956	Glenn Davis (USA) 50.29
1960	Glenn Davis (USA) 49.51
1964	Rex Cawley (USA) 49.69
1968	David Hemery (Great Britain) 48.12
1972	John Akii-Bua (Uganda) 47.82
1976	Edwin Moses (USA) 47.63
1980	Volker Beck (E Germany) 48.70
1984	Edwin Moses (USA) 47.75
1988	Andre Phillips (USA) 47.19
1992	Kevin Young (USA) 46.78
1996	Derrick Adkins (USA) 47.54
2000	Angelo Taylor (USA) 47.50
2004	Felix Sánchez (Dominican Republic) 47.63

Steeplechase*

1904	James Lightbody (USA) 7:39.6 *(2590 m)*
1908	Arthur Russell (Great Britain) 10:47.8 *(3200 m)*
1920	Percy Hodge (Great Britain) 10:00.4
1924	Ville Ritola (Finland) 9:33.6
1928	Toivo Loukola (Finland) 9:21.8
1932	Volmari Iso-Hollo (Finland) 10:33.4**
1936	Volmari Iso-Hollo (Finland) 9:03.8
1948	Tore Sjöstrand (Sweden) 9:04.6
1952	Horace Ashenfelter (USA) 8:45.68
1956	Christopher Brasher (Great Britain) 8:41.35
1960	Zdzislaw Kryszkowiak (Poland) 8:34.31
1964	Gaston Roelants (Belgium) 8:30.8
1968	Amos Biwott (Kenya) 8:51.0
1972	Kipchoge Keino (Kenya) 8:23.64
1976	Anders Gärderud (Sweden) 8:08.02
1980	Bronislaw Malinowski (Poland) 8:09.70
1984	Julius Korir (Kenya) 8:11.80
1988	Julius Kariuki (Kenya) 8:05.51
1992	Matthew Birir (Kenya) 8:08.94
1996	Joseph Keter (Kenya) 8:07.12
2000	Reuben Kosgei (Kenya) 8:21.43
2004	Ezekiel Kemboi (Kenya) 8:05.81

*Unless shown otherwise above, distance is 3000 m.
**Athletes ran an extra lap in error – distance 3460 m.

High jump

1904	Samuel Jones (USA) 1.80
1906	Con Leahy (Ireland)[b] 1.77
1908	Harry Porter (USA) 1.90
1912	Alma Richards (USA) 1.93
1920	Richard Landon (USA) 1.94
1924	Harold Osborn (USA) 1.98
1928	Robert King (USA) 1.94
1932	Duncan McNaughton (Canada) 1.97
1936	Cornelius Johnson (USA) 2.03
1948	John Winter (Austrialia) 1.98
1952	Walter Davis (USA) 2.04
1956	Charles Dumas (USA) 2.12
1960	Robert Shavlakadze (USSR) 2.16
1964	Valeriy Brumel (USSR) 2.18
1968	Dick Fosbury (USA) 2.24
1972	Jüri Tamak (USSR) 2.23
1976	Jacek Wszola (Poland) 2.25
1980	Gerd Wessig (E Germany) 2.36
1984	Dietmar Mögenburg (W Germany) 2.35
1988	Gennadiy Avdeyenko (USSR) 2.38
1992	Javier Sotomayor (Cuba) 2.34
1996	Charles Austin (USA) 2.39
2000	Sergey Kliugin (Russia) 2.35
2004	Stefan Holm (Sweden) 2.36

Athletics, Olympic games (continued)

Pole vault
1904 Charles Dvorak (USA) 3.50
1906 Fernand Gonder (France) 3.40
1908 Edward Cooke & Alfred Gilbert (USA) 3.71
1912 Harry Babock (USA) 3.95
1920 Frank Foss (USA) 4.09
1924 Lee Barnes (USA) 3.95
1928 Sabin Carr (USA) 4.20
1932 Bill Miller (USA) 4.31
1936 Earle Meadows (USA) 4.35
1948 Guinn Smith (USA) 4.30
1952 Robert Richards (USA) 4.55
1956 Robert Richards (USA) 4.56
1960 Donald Bragg (USA) 4.70
1964 Frederick Hansen (USA) 5.10
1968 Bob Seagren (USA) 5.40
1972 Wolfgang Nordwig (E Germany) 5.50
1976 Tadeusz Slusarski (Poland) 5.50
1980 Wladyslaw Kozakiewicz (Poland) 5.78
1984 Pierre Quinon (France) 5.75
1988 Sergey Bubka (USSR) 5.90
1992 Maksim Tarasov (Unified Team) 5.80
1996 Jean Galfione (France) 5.92
2000 Nick Hysong (USA) 5.90
2004 Timothy Mack (USA) 5.95

Long jump
1904 Myer Prinstein (USA) 7.34
1906 Myer Prinstein (USA) 7.20
1908 Francis Irons (USA) 7.48
1912 Albert Gutterson (USA) 7.60
1920 William Pettersson (Sweden) 7.15
1924 William De Hart Hubbard (USA) 7.44
1928 Edward Hamm (USA) 7.73
1932 Edward Gordon (USA) 7.64
1936 Jesse Owens (USA) 8.06
1948 William Steele (USA) 7.82
1952 Jerome Biffle (USA) 7.57
1956 Gregory Bell (USA) 7.83
1960 Ralph Boston (USA) 8.12
1964 Lynn Davies (Great Britain) 8.07
1968 Bob Beamon (USA) 8.90
1972 Randy Williams (USA) 8.24
1976 Arnie Robinson (USA) 8.35
1980 Lutz Dombrowski (E Germany) 8.54
1984 Carl Lewis (USA) 8.54
1988 Carl Lewis (USA) 8.72
1992 Carl Lewis (USA) 8.67
1996 Carl Lewis (USA) 8.50
2000 Ivan Pedroso (Cuba) 8.55
2004 Dwight Phillips (USA) 8.59

Triple jump
1904 Myer Prinstein (USA) 14.35
1906 Peter O'Connor (Ireland) 14.07
1908 Tim Ahearne (Ireland) 14.91
1912 Gustaf Lindblom (Sweden) 14.76
1920 Viho Tuulos (Finland) 14.50
1924 Anthony Winter (Australia) 15.52
1928 Mikio Oda (Japan) 15.21
1932 Chuhei Nambu (Japan) 15.72
1936 Naoto Tajima (Japan) 16.00
1948 Arne Åhman (Sweden) 15.40
1952 Adhemar Ferreira da Silva (Brazil) 16.22
1956 Adhemar Ferreira da Silva (Brazil) 16.35
1960 Jozef Schmidt (Poland) 16.81
1964 Jozef Schmidt (Poland) 16.85

1968 Viktor Saneyev (USSR) 17.39
1972 Viktor Saneyev (USSR) 17.35
1976 Viktor Saneyev (USSR) 17.29
1980 Jaak Uudmäe (USSR) 17.35
1984 Al Joyner (USA) 17.26
1988 Khristo Markov (Bulgaria) 17.61
1992 Mike Conley (USA) 18.17
1996 Kenny Harrison (USA) 18.09
2000 Jonathan Edwards (Great Britain) 17.71
2004 Christian Olsson (Sweden) 17.79

Shot
1904 Ralph Rose (USA) 14.80
1906 Martin Sheridan (USA) 12.32
1908 Ralph Rose (USA) 14.21
1912 Patrick McDonald (USA) 15.34
1920 Ville Pörhölä (Finland) 14.81
1924 Clarence Houser (USA) 14.99
1928 John Kuck (USA) 15.87
1932 Leo Sexton (USA) 16.00
1936 Hans Woellke (Germany) 16.20
1948 Wilbur Thompson (USA) 17.12
1952 Parry O'Brien (USA) 17.41
1956 Parry O'Brien (USA) 18.57
1960 William Nieder (USA) 19.68
1964 Dallas Long (USA) 20.33
1968 Randy Matson (USA) 20.54
1972 Wladyslaw Komar (Poland) 21.18
1976 Udo Beyer (E Germany) 21.05
1980 Vladimir Kiselyov (USSR) 21.35
1984 Alessandro Andrei (Italy) 21.26
1988 Ulf Timmermann (E Germany) 22.47
1992 Mike Stulce (USA) 21.70
1996 Randy Barnes (USA) 21.62
2000 Arsi Harju (Finland) 21.29
2004 Yuriy Bilonog (Ukraine) 21.16

Discus
1904 Martin Sheridan (USA) 39.28
1906 Martin Sheridan (USA) 41.46
1904 Martin Sheridan (USA) 40.89
1912 Armas Taipale (Finland) 45.21
1920 Elmer Niklander (Finland) 44.68
1924 Clarence Houser (USA) 46.15
1928 Clarence Houser (USA) 47.32
1932 John Anderson (USA) 49.49
1936 Ken Carpenter (USA) 50.48
1948 Adolfo Consolini (Italy) 52.78
1952 Sim Iness (USA) 55.03
1956 Al Oerter (USA) 56.36
1960 Al Oerter (USA) 59.18
1964 Al Oerter (USA) 61.00
1968 Al Oerter (USA) 64.78
1972 Ludvik Danek (Czechloslovakia) 64.40
1976 Mac Wilkins (USA) 67.50
1980 Viktor Rashchupkin (USSR) 66.64
1984 Rolf Danneberg (W Germany) 66.60
1988 Jürgen Schult (E Germany) 68.82
1992 Romas Ubartas (Lithuania) 65.12
1996 Lars Riedel (Germany) 69.40
2000 Virgilijus Alekna (Lithuania) 69.30
2004 Robert Fazekas (Hungary) 70.93

Hammer
1908 John Flanagan (USA) 51.92
1912 Matt McGrath (USA) 54.74
1920 Patrick Ryan (USA) 52.87
1924 Fred Tootell (USA) 53.29
1928 Patrick O'Callaghan (Ireland) 51.39
1932 Patrick O'Callaghan (Ireland) 53.92

1936 Karl Hein (Germany) 56.49
1948 Imre Németh (Hungary) 56.07
1952 József Csermak (Hungary) 60.34
1956 Harold Connolly (USA) 63.19
1960 Vasiliy Rudenkov (USSR) 67.10
1964 Romuald Klim (USSR) 69.74
1968 Gyula Zsivótzky (Hungary) 73.36
1972 Anatoliy Bondarchuk (USSR) 75.50
1976 Yuriy Sedykh (USSR) 77.52
1980 Yuriy Sedykh (USSR) 81.80
1984 Juha Tiainen (Finland) 78.08
1988 Sergey Litvinov (USSR) 84.80
1992 Andrei Abduyvaliyev (Unified Team) 82.54
1996 Balazs Kiss (Hungary) 81.24
2000 Szymon Ziolkowski (Russia) 80.02
2004 Adrian Annus (Hungary) 83.19

Javelin*
1912 Erik Lemming (Sweden) 60.64
1920 Jonni Myyrä (Finland) 65.78
1924 Jonni Myyrä (Finland) 62.96
1928 Erik Lundkvist (Sweden) 66.60
1932 Matti Järvinen (Finland) 72.71
1936 Gerhard Stöck (Germany) 71.84
1948 Tapio Rautavaara (Finland) 69.77
1952 Cyrus Young (USA) 73.78
1956 Egil Danielsen (Norway) 85.71
1960 Viktor Tsibulenko (USSR) 84.64
1964 Pauli Nevala (Finland) 82.66
1968 Janis Lusis (USSR) 90.10
1972 Klaus Wolfermann (W Germany) 90.48
1976 Miklós Németh (Hungary) 94.58
1980 Dainis Kula (USSR) 91.20
1984 Arto Harkönen (Finland) 86.76
1988 Tápio Korjus (Finland) 84.28
1992 Jan Zelezny (Czechoslovakia) 89.66
1996 Jan Zelezny (Czech Republic) 88.16
2000 Jan Zelezny (Czech Republic) 90.17
2004 Andreas Thorkildsen (Norway) 86.50

*New javelin specification introduced in 1984.

Decathlon*
1928 Paavo Yrjölä (Finland) 6587
1932 James Bausch (USA) 6735
1936 Glenn Morris (USA) 7254
1948 Robert Mathias (USA) 6628
1952 Robert Mathias (USA) 7592
1956 Milton Campbell (USA) 7614
1960 Rafer Johnson (USA) 7926
1964 Willi Holdorf (W Germany) 7794
1968 Bill Toomey (USA) 8144
1972 Nikolay Avilov (USSR) 8466
1976 Bruce Jenner (USA) 8634
1980 Daley Thompson (Great Britain) 8522
1984 Daley Thompson (Great Britain) 8847
1988 Christian Schenk (E Germany) 8488
1992 Robert Zmelik (Czechoslovakia) 8611
1996 Dan O'Brien (USA) 8824
2000 Erki Nool (Estonia) 8641
2004 Roman Sebrle (Czech Republic) 8893

*All points given here are rescored using 1984 tables.

Modern Pentathlon
2000 Dmitri Svatkovski (Russia) 5376
2004 Andrey Moiseev (Russia) 5480

20 km walk
1964 Kenneth Matthews (Great Britain) 1:29:34.0

1968 Vladimir Golubnichiy (USSR) 1:33:58.4
1972 Peter Frenkel (E Germany) 1:26:42.4
1976 Daniel Bautista (Mexico) 1:24:40.6
1980 Maurizio Damilano (Italy) 1:23:35.5
1984 Ernesto Canto (Mexico) 1:23:13
1988 Jozef Pribilinec (Czechoslovakia) 1:19:57
1992 Daniel Plaza (Spain) 1:21:45
1996 Jefferson Pérez (Ecuador) 1:20:06
2000 Robert Korzeniowski (Poland) 1:18:59
2004 Ivano Brugnetti (Italy) 1:19.40

50 km walk
1948 John Ljunggren (Sweden) 4:41:52.0
1952 Giuseppe Dordoni (Italy) 4:28:07.8
1956 Norman Read (New Zealand) 4:30:42.8
1960 Don Thompson (Great Britain) 4:25:30.0
1964 Abdon Pamich (Italy) 4:11:12.4
1968 Christophe Höhne (E Germany) 4:20:13.6
1972 Bernd Kannenberg (E Germany) 3:56:11.6
1980 Hartwig Gauder (E Germany) 3:49:24
1984 Raúl Gonzales (Mexico) 3:47:26
1988 Vyacheslav Ivanenko (USSR) 3:38:29
1992 Andrei Perlov (Unified Team) 3:50:13
1996 Robert Korzeniowski (Poland) 3:43:30
2000 Robert Korzeniowski (Poland) 3:42:22
2004 Robert Korzeniowski (Poland) 3:38.46

4 × 100 m relay
1924 USA 41.0
1928 USA 41.0
1932 USA 40.1
1936 USA 39.8
1948 USA 40.6
1952 USA 40.26
1956 USA 39.59
1960 W Germany 39.66
1964 USA 39.06
1968 USA 38.23
1972 USA 38.19
1976 USA 38.83
1980 USSR 38.26
1984 USA 37.83
1988 USSR 38.19
1992 USA 37.40
1996 Canada 37.69
2000 USA 37.61
2004 Great Britain 38.07

4 × 400 m relay
1928 USA 3:16.0
1928 USA 3:14.2
1932 USA 3:08.14
1936 Great Britain 3:09.0
1948 USA 3:10.4
1952 Jamaica 3:04.04
1956 USA 3:04.80
1960 USA 3:02.37
1964 USA 3:00.71
1968 USA 2:56.16
1972 Kenya 2:59.83
1976 USA 2:58.66
1980 USSR 3:01.08
1984 USA 3:57.91
1988 USA 2:56.16
1992 USA 2:55.74
1996 USA 2:55.99
2000 USA 3:22.62
2004 USA 2:55.91

Athletics, Olympic games (continued)

Event winners: women

100 m
1936 Helen Stephens (USA) 11.5
1948 Fanny Blankers-Koen (Netherlands) 11.9
1952 Marjorie Jackson (Australia) 11.65
1956 Betty Cuthbert (Australia) 11.82
1960 Wilma Rudolph (USA) 11.08
1964 Wyomia Tyus (USA) 11.49
1968 Wyomia Tyus (USA) 11.08
1972 Renate Stecher (E Germany) 11.07
1976 Annegret Richter (W Germany) 11.08
1980 Lyudmila Kondratyeva (USSR) 11.06
1984 Evelyn Ashford (USA) 10.97
1988 Florence Griffith-Joyner (USA) 10.54ᶜ
1992 Gail Devers (USA) 10.82
1996 Gail Devers (USA) 10.94
2000 Marion Jones (USA) 10.75
2004 Yuliya Nesterenko (Belarus) 10.93

200 m
1956 Betty Cuthbert (Australia) 23.55
1960 Wilma Rudolph (USA) 24.03
1964 Edith Maguire (USA) 23.05
1968 Irena Szewinska (Poland) 22.58
1972 Renate Stecher (E Germany) 22.40
1976 Bärbel Eckert (E Germany) 22.37
1980 Bärbel Wöckel (E Germany) 22.03
1984 Valerie Brisco-Hooks (USA) 21.81
1988 Florence Griffith-Joyner (USA) 21.34
1992 Gwen Torrence (USA) 21.81
1996 Marie-José Pérec (France) 22.12
2000 Marion Jones (USA) 21.84
2004 Veronica Campbell (Jamaica) 22.05

400 m
1972 Monika Zehrt (E Germany) 51.08
1976 Irena Szewinska (Poland) 49.29
1980 Marita Koch (E Germany) 48.88
1984 Valerie Brisco-Hooks (USA) 48.83
1988 Olga Bryzgina (USSR) 48.65
1992 Marie-José Pérec (France) 48.83
1996 Marie-José Pérec (France) 48.25
2000 Cathy Freeman (Australia) 49.11
2004 Tonique Williams-Darling (Bahamas) 49.41

800 m
1968 Madeline Manning (USA) 2:00.92
1972 Hilde Falck (W Germany) 1:58.55
1976 Tatyana Kazankina (USSR) 1:54.94
1980 Nadezhda Olizarenko (USSR) 1:53.43
1984 Doina Melinte (Romania) 1:57.60
1988 Sigrun Wodars (E Germany) 1:56.10
1992 Ellen van Langen (Netherlands) 1:55.54
1996 Svetlana Masterkova (Russia) 1:57.73
2000 Maria Mutola (Mozambique) 1:56.15
2004 Kelly Holmes (Great Britain) 1:56.38

1 500 m
1980 Tatyana Kazankina (USSR) 3:56.56
1984 Gabriella Doria (Italy) 4:03.25
1988 Paula Ivan (Romania) 3:53.96
1992 Hassiba Boulmerka (Algeria) 3:55:30
1996 Svetlana Masterkova (Russia) 4:00.83
2000 Nouria Merah-Benida (Algeria) 4:05.10
2004 Kelly Holmes (Great Britain) 3:57.90

5 000 m (3 000 m to 1996)
1988 Tatyana Samolenko (USSR) 8:26.53
1992 Yelena Romanova (Unified Team) 8:46.04

1996 Yunxia Wang (China) 14: 59.88
2000 Gabriela Szabo (Romania) 14:40.79
2004 Meseret Defar (Ethiopia) 14:45.65

10 000 m
1992 Derartu Tulu (Ethiopia) 31:06.02
1996 Fernanda Ribeiro (Portugal) 31:01.63
2000 Derartu Tulu (Ethiopia) 30:17.49
2004 Huina Xing (China) 30:24.36

Marathon
1988 Rosa Mota (Portugal) 2:25.40
1992 Valentina Yegorova (Unified Team) 2:32:41
1996 Fatuma Roba (Ethiopia) 2:26:5
2000 Naoko Takahashi (Japan) 2:23:14
2004 Mizuki Noguchi (Japan) 2:26.20

100 m hurdles
1976 Johanna Schaller (E Germany) 12.77
1980 Vera Komisova (USSR) 12.56
1984 Benita Fitzgerald-Brown (USA) 12.84
1988 Yordanka Donkova (Bulgaria) 12.38
1992 Paraskevi Patoulidou (Greece) 12.64
1996 Ludmila Enquist (Sweden) 12.58
2000 Olga Shishigina (Kazakhstan) 12.65
2004 Joanna Hayes (USA) 12.37

400 m hurdles
1988 Debbie Flintoff-King (Australia) 53.17
1992 Sally Gunnell (Great Britain) 53.23
1996 Deon Hemmings (Jamaica) 52.82
2000 Irina Privalova (Russia) 53.02
2004 Fani Halkia (Greece) 52.82

Triple Jump
2000 Tereza Marinova (Bulgaria) 15.20
2004 Françoise Mbango Etone (Cameroon) 15.30

High jump
1932 Jean Shiley (USA) 1.65
1936 Ibolya Csák (Hungary) 1.60
1948 Alice Coachman (USA) 1.68
1952 Esther Brand (S Africa) 1.67
1956 Mildred McDaniel (USA) 1.76
1960 Iolanda Balas (Romania) 1.85
1964 Iolanda Balas (Romania) 1.90
1968 Miloslava Rezková (Czechoslovakia) 1.82
1972 Ulrike Meyfarth (W Germany) 1.92
1976 Rosemarie Ackermann (E Germany) 1.93
1980 Sara Simeoni (Italy) 1.97
1984 Ulrike Meyfarth (W Germany) 2.02
1988 Louise Ritter (USA) 2.03
1992 Heike Henkel (Germany) 2.02
1996 Stefka Kostadinova (Bulgaria) 2.05
2000 Yelena Yelesina (Russia) 2.01
2004 Yelena Slesarenko (Russia) 2.06

Long jump
1956 Elzbieta Krzesinska (Poland) 6.35
1960 Vyera Krepkina (USSR) 6.37
1964 Mary Rand (Great Britain) 6.76
1968 Viorica Viscopoleanu (Romania) 6.82
1972 Heide Rosendahl (W Germany) 6.78
1976 Angela Voigt (E Germany) 6.72
1980 Tatyana Kolpakova (USSR) 7.06
1984 Anisoara Stanciu (Romania) 6.96
1988 Jackie Joyner-Kersee (USA) 7.40
1992 Heike Drechsler (Germany) 7.14
1996 Chioma Ajunwa (Nigeria) 7.12
2000 Heike Drechsler (Germany) 6.99
2004 Tatyana Lebedeva (Russia) 7.07

Shot
1956   Tamara Tishkyevich (USSR) 16.59
1960   Tamara Press (USSR) 17.32
1964   Tamara Press (USSR) 18.14
1968   Margitta Gummel (E Germany) 19.61
1972   Nadezhda Chizhova (USSR) 21.03
1976   Ivanka Khristova (Bulgaria) 21.16
1980   Ilona Slupianek (E Germany) 22.41
1984   Claudia Losch (W Germany) 20.48
1988   Natalya Lisovskaya (USSR) 22.24
1992   Svetlana Krivelyova (Unified Team) 21.06
1996   Astrid Kumbernuss (Germany) 20.56
2000   Yanina Korolchik (Belarus) 20.56
2004   Yumileidi Cumba (Cuba) 19.59

Discus
1936   Gisela Mauermayer (Germany)
1948   Micheline Ostermeyer (France) 41.92
1952   Nina Ponomaryeva (USSR) 51.42
1956   Olga Fikotová (Czechoslovakia) 53.69
1960   Nina Ponomaryeva (USSR) 55.10
1964   Tamara Press (USSR) 57.27
1968   Lia Manoliu (Romania) 58.28
1972   Faina Melnik (USSR) 66.62
1976   Evelin Schlaak (E Germany) 69.00
1980   Evelin Jahl (E Germany) 69.96
1984   Ria Stalmach (Netherlands) 65.36
1988   Martina Hellmann (E Germany) 72.30
1992   Maritza Marten (Cuba) 70.06
1996   Like Wyludda (Germany) 69.66
2000   Ellina Zvereva (Belarus) 68.40
2004   Natalya Sadova (Russia) 67.02

Javelin
1936   Tilly Fleischer (Germany) 45.18
1948   Herma Bauma (Australia) 45.57
1952   Dana Zátopková (Czechoslovakia) 50.47
1956   Inese Jaunzeme (USSR) 53.86
1960   Elvira Ozolina (USSR) 55.98
1964   Mihaela Penes (Romania) 60.54
1968   Angéla Németh (Hungary) 60.36
1972   Ruth Fuchs (E Germany) 63.88
1976   Ruth Fuchs (E Germany) 65.94
1980   Maria C. Colón (Cuba) 68.40
1984   Tessa Sanderson (Great Britain) 69.56
1988   Petra Felke (E Germany) 74.68
1992   Silke Renk (Germany) 68.34
1996   Heller Rantanen (Finland) 67.94
2000   Trine Hattestad (Norway) 68.91
2004   Osleidys Menendez (Cuba) 71.53

Pole vault
2000   Stacy Draglia (USA) 4.60
2004   Yelena Isinbayeva (Russia) 4.91

Hammer
2000   Kamila Skolimowska (Poland) 71.16
2004   Olga Kuzenkova (Russia) 75.02

Pentathlon
1964   Irina Press (USSR) 4702
1968   Ingrid Becker (W Germany) 4559
1972   Mary Peters (Great Britain) 4801
1976   Sigrun Siegl (E Germany) 4745
1980   Nadezhda Tkachenko (USSR) 5083

Modern pentathlon
2000   Stephanie Cook (Great Britain) 5318
2004   Zsuzsanna Vores (Hungary) 5448

Heptathlon
1988   Jackie Joyner-Kersee (USA) 7291
1992   Jackie Joyner-Kersee (USA) 7044
1996   Ghada Shouaa (Syria) 6780
2000   Denise Lewis (Great Britain) 6584
2004   Carolina Kluft (Sweden) 6952

20 km walk
2000   Wang Liping (China) 1:29.05
2004   Athanasia Tsoumeleka (Greece) 1:29.12

4 × 100 m relay
1932   USA 46.86
1936   USA 46.9
1948   Netherlands 47.5
1952   USA 46.14
1956   Australia 44.65
1960   USA 44.72
1964   Poland 43.69
1968   USA 42.87
1972   W Germany 42.81
1976   E Germany 42.55
1980   E Germany 41.60
1984   USA 41.65
1988   USA 41.98
1992   USA 42.11
1996   USA 41.95
2000   Bahamas 41.95
2004   Jamaica 41.73

4 × 400 m relay
1976   E Germany 3:19.23
1980   USSR 3:20.12
1984   USA 3:18.29
1988   USSR 3:15.18
1992   Unified Team 3:20.20
1996   USA 3:20.91
2000   USA 3:22.62
2004   USA 3:19.01

Marathon

Run over 42 km 195 m/26 mi 385 yd; a distance which became standard from 1924. Women first competed officially in 1972.

Boston
The world's oldest annual race; first held in 1897.

Men
1992	Ibrahim Hussein (Kenya) 2:08.14
1993	Cosmas N'deti (Kenya) 2:09.33
1994	Cosmas N'deti (Kenya) 2:07.15
1995	Cosmas N'deti (Kenya) 2:09.16
1996	Moses Tanui (Kenya) 2:09.16
1997	Lameck Aguta (Kenya) 2:10.34
1998	Moses Tanui (Kenya) 2:07.52
1999	Joseph Chebet (Kenya) 2:09.16
2000	Elijah Lagat (Kenya) 2:09.47
2001	Bong-Ju Lee (South Korea) 2:09.43
2002	Rodgers Rop (Kenya) 2:09.02
2003	Robert Kipkoech Cheruiyot (Kenya) 2:10.11
2004	Timothy Cherigat (Kenya) 2:10.40
2005	Hailu Negussie (Ethiopia) 2:11.45
2006	Robert Kipkoech Cheruiyot (Kenya) 2:07:14

Most wins: (7) Clarence De Mar (USA): 1911, 1922–4, 1927–8, 1930.

Women
1992	Olga Markova (Russia) 2:23.43
1993	Olga Markova (Russia) 2:25.37
1994	Uta Pippig (Germany) 2:21.45
1995	Uta Pippig (Germany) 2:25.11
1996	Uta Pippig (Germany) 2:27.12
1997	Fatuma Roba (Ethiopia) 2:26.23
1998	Fatuma Roba (Ethiopia) 2:23.21
1999	Fatuma Roba (Ethiopia) 2:23.25
2000	Catherine Ndereba (Kenya) 2:26.11
2001	Catherine Ndereba (Kenya) 2:23.53
2002	Margaret Okayo (Kenya) 2:20.43
2003	Svetlana Zakharova (Russia) 2:25.20
2004	Catherine Ndereba (Kenya) 2:24.27
2005	Catherine Ndereba (Kenya) 2:25.13
2006	Rita Jeptoo (Kenya) 2:23:38

Most wins: (4) Catherine Ndebera (Kenya) as above.

London
First run in 1981.

Men
1991	Yakov Tolstikov (USSR) 2:09.17
1992	António Pinto (Portugal) 2:10.02
1993	Eamonn Martin (Great Britain) 2:10.50
1994	Dionicio Ceron (Mexico) 2:08.53
1995	Dionicio Ceron (Mexico) 2:08.30
1996	Dionicio Ceron (Mexico) 2:10.00
1997	António Pinto (Portugal) 2:07.55
1998	Abel Anton (Spain) 2:07.57
1999	Abdel Kader El Mouaziz (Morocco) 2:07.57
2000	António Pinto (Portugal) 2:06.35
2001	Abdel Kader El Mouaziz (Morocco) 2:07.11
2002	Khalid Khannouchi (Morocco/USA) 2:05.38
2003	Gezahegne Abera (Ethiopia) 2:07.56
2004	Evans Rutto (Kenya) 2:06.18
2005	Martin Lel (Kenya) 2:07.26
2006	Felix Limo (Kenya) 2:06:39

Most wins: (3) Dionicio Ceron (Mexico); António Pinto (Portugal) as above.

Women
1991	Rosa Mota (Portugal) 2:26.14
1992	Katrin Dörre (Germany) 2:29.39
1993	Katrin Dörre (Germany) 2:27.09
1994	Katrin Dörre (Germany) 2:32.34
1995	Malgorzata Sobanska (Poland) 2:27.43
1996	Liz McColgan (Great Britain) 2:27.54
1997	Joyce Chepchumba (Kenya) 2:26.51
1998	Catherina McKiernan (Ireland) 2:26.26
1999	Joyce Chepchumba (Kenya) 2:23.22
2000	Tegla Loroupe (Kenya) 2:24.33
2001	Derartu Tulu (Ethiopia) 2:23.57
2002	Paula Radcliffe (Great Britain) 2:18.56
2003	Paula Radcliffe (Great Britain) 2:15.25
2004	Margaret Okayo (Kenya) 2:22.35
2005	Paula Radcliffe (Great Britain) 2:17.42
2006	Deena Kastor (USA) 2:19:36

Most wins: (4) Ingrid Kristiansen (Norway): 1984–5, 1987–8.

New York
First run in 1970.

Men
1990	Douglas Wakihuri (Kenya) 2:12.39
1991	Salvador Garcia (Mexico) 2:09.28
1992	Willie Mtolo (South Africa) 2:09.29
1993	Andreas Espinosa (Mexico) 2:10.04
1994	German Silva (Mexico) 2:11.21
1995	German Silva (Mexico) 2:11.00
1996	Giacomo Leone (Italy) 2:09.54
1997	John Kagwe (Kenya) 2:08.12
1998	John Kagwe (Kenya) 2:08.45
1999	Joseph Chebet (Kenya) 2:09.13
2000	Abdel Kader El Mouaziz (Morocco) 2:10.09
2001	Tesfaye Jifar (Ethiopia) 2:07.43
2002	Rodgers Rop (Kenya) 2:08.07
2003	Martin Lel (Kenya) 2:10.30
2004	Hendrik Ramaala (South Africa) 2:9:28
2005	Paul Tergat (Kenya) 2:09:29
2006	Marilson dos Santos (Brazil) 2:09.58

Most wins: (4) Bill Rodgers (USA): 1976–9.

Women
1990	Wanda Panfil (Poland) 2:30.45
1991	Liz McColgan (Great Britain) 2:27.23
1992	Lisa Ondieki (Australia) 2:24.40
1993	Uta Pippig (Germany) 2:26.24
1994	Tecla Loroupe (Kenya) 2:27.37
1995	Tecla Loroupe (Kenya) 2:28.06
1996	Anuta Katuna (Romania) 2:28.18
1997	Franziska Rochat-Moser (Switzerland) 2:28.43
1998	Franca Fiacconi (Italy) 2:25.17
1999	Adriana Fernandez (Mexico) 2:25.06
2000	Ludmila Petrova (Russia) 2:25.45
2001	Margaret Okayo (Kenya) 2:24.21
2002	Joyce Chepchumba (Kenya) 2:25.56
2003	Margaret Okayo (Kenya) 2:22.31
2004	Paula Radcliffe (Great Britain) 2:23.10
2005	Jelena Prokopcuka (Latvia) 2:24:41
2006	Jelena Prokopcuka (Latvia) 2:25.05

Most wins: (9) Grete Waitz (Norway): 1978–80, 1982–6, 1988.

BADMINTON

World championships

First held in 1977; initially took place every three years, since 1983 usually every two years.

Singles winners: men
1995 Heryanto Arbi (Indonesia)
1997 Peter Rasmussen (Denmark)
1999 Sun Jun (China)
2001 H Hendrawan (Indonesia)
2003 Xia Xuanze (China)
2005 Taufik Hidayat (Indonesia)
2006 Lin Dan (China)

Singles winners: women
1995 Ye Zhaoying (China)
1997 Ye Zhaoying (China)
1999 Camilla Martin (Denmark)
2001 Gong Ruina (China)
2003 Zhang Ning (China)
2005 Xie Zingfang (China)
2006 Xie Xingfang (China)

Most titles: (4) Park JooBong (South Korea): men's doubles 1985, 1991; mixed doubles 1989, 1991.

Thomas cup

An international event for men's teams: inaugurated in 1949, now held every two years.

Recent winners
1982 China
1984 Indonesia
1986 China
1988 China
1990 China
1992 Malaysia
1994 Indonesia
1996 Indonesia
1998 Indonesia
2000 Indonesia
2002 Indonesia
2004 China
2006 China

Most wins: (13) Indonesia: 1958, 1961, 1964, 1970, 1973, 1976, 1979, and as above.

Uber cup

An international event for women's teams; first held in 1957, now held every two years.

Recent winners
1981 Japan
1984 China
1986 China
1988 China
1990 China
1992 China
1994 Indonesia
1996 Indonesia
1998 China
2000 China
2002 China
2004 China
2006 China

Most wins: (10) China: as above.

All-England championship

Badminton's premier event prior to the inauguration of the World Championships; first held in 1899.

Recent winners: singles – men
1987 Morten Frost (Denmark)
1988 Ib Frederikson (Denmark)
1989 Yang Yang (China)
1990 Zhao Jianhua (China)
1991 Ardi Wiranata (Indonesia)
1992 Liu Jun (China)
1993 Heryanto Arbi (Indonesia)
1994 Heryanto Arbi (Indonesia)
1995 Poul-Erik Hoyer Larsen (Denmark)
1996 Poul-Erik Hoyer Larsen (Denmark)
1997 Dong Jiong (China)
1998 Sun Jun (China)
1999 Peter Gade Christensen (Denmark)
2000 Xia Xuanze (China)
2001 Pullela Gopichand (India)
2002 Chen Hong (China)

2003 Muhammad Hafiz Hashim (Malaysia)
2004 Lin Dan (China)
2005 Chen Hong (China)
2006 Lin Dan (China)

Recent winners: singles – women
1987 Kirsten Larsen (Denmark)
1988 Gu Jiaming (China)
1989 Li Lingwei (China)
1990 Susi Susanti (Indonesia)
1991 Susi Susanti (Indonesia)
1992 Tang Jiuhong (China)
1993 Susi Susanti (Indonesia)
1994 Susi Susanti (Indonesia)
1995 Lin Xiao Qing (Sweden)
1996 Bang Soo-Hyun (South Korea)
1997 Ye Zhaoying (China)
1998 Ye Zhaoying (China)
1999 Ye Zhaoying (China)
2000 Gong Zhichao (China)
2001 Gong Zhichao (China)
2002 Camilla Martin (Denmark)
2003 Zhou Mi (China)
2004 Gong Ruina (China)
2005 Xie Xingfang (China)
2006 Xie Xingfang (China)

Most titles: (21; 4 singles, 9 men's doubles, 8 mixed doubles), George Thomas (England): 1903–28.

Olympic Games

Gold medal winner: 2004
Singles (men)
Taufik Hidayat (Indonesia)

Doubles (men)
Kim Moon-Dong/Ha Kwon-Tae (South Korea)

Singles (women)
Zhang Ning (China)

Doubles (women)
Zhang Jiewen/Yang Wei (China)

Mixed Doubles
Zhang Jun/Gao Ling (China)

BASEBALL

There are two leagues in the North American Major League – the National League (NL) and the American League (AL). Each league consists of an Eastern, Western, and (since 1994) Central division. Each division winner and a wild-card team (the second-place team with the best record) meet in a best-of-five playoff in the first round, then in a best-of-seven for the League Pennant, and then in the best-of-seven World Series.

World Series

First held in 1903; takes place each October; not held in 1904, 1994.

1903 Boston (AL) 5, Pittsburg (NL) 2
1905 New York (NL) 4, Philadelphia (AL) 1
1906 Chicago (AL) 4, Chicago (NL) 2
1907 Chicago (NL) 4, Detroit (AL) 0; 1 tie
1908 Chicago (NL) 4, Detroit (AL) 1
1909 Pittsburgh (NL) 4, Detroit (AL) 3

Baseball (continued)

1910 Philadelphia (AL) 4, Chicago (NL) 1
1911 Philadelphia (AL) 4, New York (NL) 2
1912 Boston (AL) 4, New York (NL) 3; 1 tie
1913 Philadelphia (AL) 4, New York (NL) 1
1914 Boston (NL) 4, Philadelphia (AL) 0
1915 Boston (AL) 4, Philadelphia (NL) 1
1916 Boston (AL) 4, Brooklyn (NL) 1
1917 Chicago (AL) 4, New York (NL) 2
1918 Boston (AL) 4, Chicago (NL) 2
1919 Cincinnati (NL) 5, Chicago (AL) 3
1920 Cleveland (AL) 5, Brooklyn (NL) 2
1921 New York (NL) 5, New York (AL) 3
1922 New York (NL) 4, New York (AL) 0; 1 tie
1923 New York (AL) 4, New York (NL) 2
1924 Washington (AL) 4, New York (NL) 3
1925 Pittsburgh (NL) 4, Washington (AL) 3
1926 St Louis (NL) 4, New York (AL) 3
1927 New York (AL) 4, Pittsburgh (NL) 0
1928 New York (AL) 4, St Louis (NL) 0
1929 Philadelphia (AL) 4, Chicago (NL) 1
1930 Philadelphia (AL) 4, St Louis (NL) 2
1931 St Louis (NL) 4, Philadelphia (AL) 3
1932 New York (AL) 4, Chicago (NL) 0
1933 New York (NL) 4, Washington (AL) 1
1934 St Louis (NL) 4, Detroit (AL) 3
1935 Detroit (AL) 4, Chicago (NL) 2
1936 New York (AL) 4, New York (NL) 2
1937 New York (AL) 4, New York (NL) 1
1938 New York (AL) 4, Chicago (NL) 0
1939 New York (AL) 4, Cincinnati (NL) 0
1940 Cincinnati (NL) 4, Detroit (AL) 3
1941 New York (AL) 4, Brooklyn (NL) 1
1942 St Louis (NL) 4, New York (AL) 1

1943 New York (AL) 4, St Louis (NL) 1
1944 St Louis (NL) 4, St Louis (AL) 2
1945 Detroit (AL) 4, Chicago (NL) 3
1946 St Louis (NL) 4, Boston (AL) 3
1947 New York (AL) 4, Brooklyn (NL) 3
1948 Cleveland (AL) 4, Boston (NL) 2
1949 New York (AL) 4, Brooklyn (NL) 1
1950 New York (AL) 4, Philadelphia (NL) 0
1951 New York (AL) 4, New York (NL) 2
1952 New York (AL) 4, Brooklyn (NL) 3
1953 New York (AL) 4, Brooklyn (NL) 2
1954 New York (NL) 4, Cleveland (AL) 0
1955 Brooklyn (NL) 4, New York (AL) 3
1956 New York (AL) 4, Brooklyn (NL) 3
1957 Milwaukee (NL) 4, New York (AL) 3
1958 New York (AL) 4, Milwaukee (NL) 3
1959 Los Angeles (NL) 4, Chicago (AL) 2
1960 Pittsburgh (NL) 4, New York (AL) 3
1961 New York (AL) 4, Cincinnati (NL) 1
1962 New York (AL) 4, San Francisco (NL) 3
1963 Los Angeles (NL) 4, New York (AL) 0
1964 St Louis (NL) 4, New York (AL) 3
1965 Los Angeles (NL) 4, Minnesota (AL) 3
1966 Baltimore (AL) 4, Los Angeles (NL) 0
1967 St Louis (NL) 4, Boston (AL) 3
1968 Detroit (AL) 4, St Louis (NL) 3
1969 New York (NL) 4, Baltimore (AL) 1
1970 Baltimore (AL) 4, Cincinnati (NL) 1
1971 Pittsburgh (NL) 4, Baltimore (AL) 3
1972 Oakland (AL) 4, Cincinnati (NL) 3
1973 Oakland (AL) 4, New York (NL) 3
1974 Oakland (AL) 4, Los Angeles (NL) 1
1975 Cincinnati (NL) 4, Boston (AL) 3
1976 Cincinnati (NL) 4, New York

(AL) 0
1977 New York (AL) 4, Los Angeles (NL) 2
1978 New York (AL) 4, Los Angeles (NL) 2
1979 Pittsburgh (NL) 4, Baltimore (AL) 3
1980 Philadelphia (NL) 4, Kansas City (AL) 2
1981 Los Angeles (NL) 4, New York (AL) 2
1982 St Louis (NL) 4, Milwaukee (AL) 3
1983 Baltimore (AL) 4, Philadelphia (NL) 1
1984 Detroit (AL) 4, San Diego (NL) 1
1985 Kansas City (AL) 4, St Louis (NL) 3
1986 New York (NL) 4, Boston (AL) 3
1987 Minnesota (AL) 4, St Louis (NL) 3
1988 Los Angeles (NL) 4, Oakland (AL) 1
1989 Oakland (AL) 4, San Francisco (NL) 0
1990 Cincinnati (NL) 4, Oakland (AL) 0
1991 Minnesota (AL) 4, Atlanta (NL) 3
1992 Toronto (AL) 4, Atlanta (NL) 2
1993 Toronto (AL) 4, Philadelphia (NL) 2
1995 Atlanta (NL) 4, Cleveland (AL) 2
1996 New York (AL) 4, Atlanta (NL) 2
1997 Florida (NL) 4, Cleveland (AL) 3
1998 New York Yankees (AL) 3 San Diego Padres (NL) 0
1999 New York Yankees (AL) 4 Atlanta Braves (NL) 0
2000 New York Yankees (AL) 4, New York Mets (NL) 1
2001 Arizona Diamondback (NL) 4, New York Yankees (AL) 3
2002 Anaheim Angels (AL) 4, San Francisco Giants (NL) 3
2003 Florida Marlins (NL) 4, New York Yankees (AL) 2
2004 Boston Red Sox (AL) 4, St Louis Cardinals (NL) 0
2005 Chicago White Sox (AL) 4, Houston Astros (NL) 0
2006 St Louis Cardinals (NL) 4, Detroit Tigers (AL) 2

Most wins: (26) New York Yankees (AL): 1923, 1927–8, 1932, 1936–9, 1941, 1943, 1947, 1949–53, 1956, 1958, 1961–2, 1977–8, 1996, 1998, 1999, 2000.

Most valuable player

Each year since 1931 the Baseball Writers' Association has voted to determine the year's most outstanding player. There are two awards – one for each of the two leagues which comprise the North American Major League – the National League (NL) and the American League (AL). There was no award in 1995.

National League

1931	Frank Frisch, St Louis Cardinals
1932	Charles Klein, Philadelphia Phillies
1933	Carl Hubbell, New York Mets
1934	Dizzy Dean, St Louis Cardinals
1935	Gabby Hartnett, Chicago Cubs
1936	Carl Hubbell, New York Mets
1937	Joe Medwick, St Louis Cardinals
1938	Ernie Lombardi, Cincinnati Reds
1939	Bucky Walters, Cincinnati Reds
1940	Frank McCormick, Cincinnati Reds
1941	Dolph Carnitti, Brooklyn Dodgers
1942	Mort Cooper, St Louis Cardinals
1943	Stan Musial, St Louis Cardinals
1944	Martin Marion, St Louis Cardinals
1945	Phil Cavarretta, Chicago Cubs
1946	Stan Musial, St Louis Cardinals
1947	Bob Elliottt, Boston Braves
1948	Stan Musial, St Louis Cardinals
1949	Jackie Robinson, Brooklyn Dodgers
1950	Jim Konstanty, Philadelphia Phillies
1951	Roy Campanella, Brooklyn Dodgers
1952	Hank Sauer, Chicago Cubs
1953	Roy Campanella, Brooklyn Dodgers
1954	Willie Mays, New York Mets
1955	Roy Campanella, Brooklyn Dodgers
1956	Don Newcombe, Brooklyn Dodgers
1957	Henry Aaron, Milwaukee Braves
1958	Ernie Banks, Chicago Cubs
1959	Ernie Banks, Chicago Cubs
1960	Dick Groat, Pittsburgh Pirates
1961	Frank Robinson, Cincinnati Reds
1962	Maury Wills, Los Angeles Dodgers
1963	Sandy Koufax, Los Angeles Dodgers
1964	Ken Boyers , St Louis Cardinals
1965	Willie Mays, San Francisco Giants
1966	Roberto Clemente, Pittsburgh Pirates
1967	Orlando Cepeda, St Louis Cardinals
1968	Bob Gibson, St Louis Cardinals
1969	Willie McCovey, San Francisco Giants
1970	Johnny Bench, Cincinnati Reds
1971	Joe Torre, St Louis Cardinals
1972	Johnny Bench, Cincinnati Reds
1973	Pete Rose, Cincinnati Reds
1974	Steve Garvey, Los Angeles Dodgers
1975	Joe Morgan, Cincinnati Reds
1976	Joe Morgan, Cincinnati Reds
1977	George Foster, Cincinnati Reds
1978	Dave Parker, Pittsburgh Pirates
1979	Willie Stargell, Pittsburgh Pirates; Keith Hernandez, St Louis Cardinals
1980	Mike Schmidt, Philadelphia Phillies
1981	Mike Schmidt, Philadelphia Phillies
1982	Dale Murphy, Atlanta Braves
1983	Dale Murphy, Atlanta Braves
1984	Ryne Sandberg, Chicago Cubs
1985	Willie McGee, St Louis Cardinals
1986	Mike Schmidt, Philadelphia Phillies
1987	Andre Dawson, Chicago Cubs
1988	Kirk Gibson, Los Angeles Dodgers
1989	Kevin Mitchell, San Francisco Giants
1990	Barry Bonds, Pittsburgh Pirates
1991	Terry Pendleton, Atlanta Braves
1992	Barry Bonds, Pittsburgh Pirates
1993	Barry Bonds, San Francisco Giants
1994	Jeff Bagwell, Houston Astros
1995	Barry Larkin, Cincinnati Reds
1996	Ken Caminiti, San Diego
1997	Larry Walker, Colorado Rockies
1998	Sammy Sosa, Chicago Cubs
1999	Chipper (Larry) Jones, Atlanta Braves
2000	Jeff Kent, San Francisco Giants
2001	Barry Bonds, San Francisco Giants
2002	Barry Bonds, San Francisco Giants
2003	Barry Bonds, San Francisco Giants
2004	Barry Bonds, San Francisco Giants
2005	Albert Pujols, St Louis Cardinals
2006	Ryan Howard, Philadelphia Phillies

American League

1931	Lefty Grove, Philadelphia Athletics
1932	Jimmie Foxx, Philadelphia Athletics
1933	Jimmie Foxx, Philadelphia Athletics
1934	Mickey Cochrane, Detroit Tigers
1935	Hank Greenberg, Detroit Tigers
1936	Lou Gehrig, New York Yankees
1937	Charley Gehringer, Detroit Tigers
1938	Jimmie Foxx, Boston Red Sox
1939	Joe DiMaggio, New York Yankees
1940	Hank Greenberg, Detroit Tigers
1941	Joe DiMaggio, New York Yankees
1942	Joe Gordon, New York Yankees
1943	Spurgeon Chandler, New York Yankees
1944	Hal Newhouser, Detroit Tigers
1945	Hal Newhouser, Detroit Tigers
1946	Ted Williams, Boston Red Sox
1947	Joe DiMaggio, New York Yankees
1948	Lou Boudreau, Cleveland Indians
1949	Ted Williams, Boston Red Sox
1950	Phil Rizzuto, New York Yankees
1951	Yogi Berra, New York Yankees
1952	Bobby Shantz, Philadelphia Athletics
1953	Al Rosen, Cleveland Indians
1954	Yogi Berra, New York Yankees
1955	Yogi Berra, New York Yankees
1956	Mickey Mantle, New York Yankees
1957	Mickey Mantle, New York Yankees
1958	Jackie Jensen, Boston Red Sex
1959	Nellie Fox, Chicago White Sox
1960	Roger Maris, New York Yankees
1961	Roger Maris, New York Yankees
1962	Mickey Mantle, New York Yankees
1963	Elston Howard, New York Yankees
1964	Brooks Robinson, Baltimore Orioles
1965	Zoilo Versalles, Minnesota Twins
1966	Frank Robinson, Baltimore Orioles
1967	Carl Yastrzemski, Boston Red Sox
1968	Denny McLain, Detroit Tigers
1969	Harmon Killebrew, Minnesota Twins
1970	John (Boog) Powell, Baltimore Orioles
1971	Vida Blue, Oakland A's
1972	Dick Allen, Chicago White Sox
1973	Reggie Jackson, Oakland A's

Baseball (continued)

1974	Jeff Burroughs, Texas Rangers
1975	Fred Lynn, Boston Red Sox
1976	Thurman Munson, New York Yankees
1977	Rod Carew, Minnesota Twins
1978	Jim Rice, Boston Red Sox
1979	Don Baylor, California Angels
1980	George Brett, Kansas City Royals
1981	Rollie Fingers, Milwaukee Brewers
1982	Robin Yount, Milwaukee Brewers
1983	Cal Ripken Jr, Baltimore Orioles
1984	Willie Hernandez, Detroit Tigers
1985	Don Mattingly, New York Yankees
1986	Roger Clemens, Boston Red Sox
1987	George Bell, Toronto Blue Jays
1988	Jose Canseco, Oakland A's
1989	Robin Yount, Milwaukee Brewers
1990	Rickey Henderson, Oakland A's
1991	Cal Ripken Jr, Baltimore Orioles
1992	Dennis Eckersley, Oakland A's
1993	Frank Thomas, Chicago White Sox
1994	Frank Thomas, Chicago White Sox
1995	Mo Vaughn, Boston Red Sox
1996	Juan Gonzalez, Texas Rangers
1997	Ken Griffey Jnr, Seattle Mariners
1998	Juan Gonzalez, Texas Rangers
1999	Ivan Rodriguez, Texas Rangers
2000	Jason Giambi, Oakland A's
2001	Ichiro Suzuki, Seattle Mariners
2002	Miguel Tejada, Oakland A's
2003	Alex Rodriguez, Texas Rangers
2004	Vladimir Guerrero, Anaheim Angels
2005	Alex Rodriguez, New York Yankees
2006	Justin Morneau, Minnesota Twins

Cy Young Award
An award for the most outstanding pitcher of the year in each of the two leagues. First given in 1956. Pre-1967 there was just one award covering both leagues.

1956	Don Newcombe, Brooklyn Dodgers (NL)
1957	Warren Spahn, Milwaukee Braves (NL)
1958	Bob Turley, New York Yankees (AL)
1959	Early Wynn, Chicago White Sox (AL)
1960	Vernon Law, Pittsburgh Pirates (NL)
1961	Whitey Ford, New York Yankees (AL)
1962	Don Drysdale, Los Angeles Dodgers (NL)
1963	Sandy Koufax, Los Angeles Dodgers (NL)
1964	Dean Chance, California Angels (AL)
1965	Sandy Koufax, Los Angeles Dodgers (NL)
1967	Sandy Koufax, Los Angeles Dodgers (NL)

National League
1967	Mike McCormick, San Francisco Giants
1968	Bob Gibson, St Louis Cardinals
1969	Tom Seaver, New York Mets
1970	Bob Gibson, St Louis Cardinals
1971	Ferguson Jenkins, Chicago Cubs
1972	Steve Carlton, Philadelphia Phillies
1973	Tom Seaver, New York Mets
1974	Mike Marshall, Los Angeles Dodgers
1975	Tom Seaver, New York Mets
1976	Randy Jones, San Diego Padres
1977	Steve Carlton, Philadelphia Phillies
1978	Gaylord Perry, San Diego Padres
1979	Bruce Sutter, Chicago Cubs
1980	Steve Carlton, Philadelphia Phillies
1981	Fernando Valenzuela, Los Angeles Dodgers

1982	Steve Carlton, Philadelphia Phillies
1983	John Denny, Philadelphia Phillies
1984	Rick Sutcliffe, Chicago Cubs
1985	Dwight Gooden, New York Mets
1986	Mike Scott, Houston Astros
1987	Steve Bedrosian, Philadelphia Phillies
1988	Orel Hershiser, Los Angeles Dodgers
1989	Mark Davis, San Diego Padres
1990	Doug Drabek, Pittsburgh Pirates
1991	Tom Glavine, Atlanta Braves
1992	Greg Maddux, Chicago Cubs
1993	Greg Maddux, Atlanta Braves
1994	Greg Maddux, Atlanta Braves
1995	Greg Maddux, Atlanta Braves
1996	John Smoltz, Atlanta Braves
1997	Pedro Martinez, Montreal Expos
1998	Tom Glavine, Atlanta Braves
1999	Randy Johnson, Arizona Diamondbacks
2000	Randy Johnson, Arizona Diamondbacks
2001	Randy Johnson, Arizona Diamondbacks
2002	Randy Johnson, Arizona Diamondbacks
2003	Eric Gagne, Los Angeles Dodgers
2004	Roger Clemens, Houston Astros
2005	Chris Carpenter, St Louis Cardinals

American League
1967	Jim Lonborg, Boston Red Sox
1968	Denny McLain, Detroit Tigers
1969	Denny McLain, Detroit Tigers; Mike Cuellar, Baltimore Orioles
1970	Jim Perry, Minnesota Twins
1971	Vida Blue, Oakland A's
1972	Gaylord Perry, Cleveland Indians
1973	Jim Palmer, Baltimore Orioles
1974	Jim 'Catfish' Hunter, Oakland A's
1975	Jim Palmer, Baltimore Orioles
1976	Jim Palmer, Baltimore Orioles
1977	Sparky Lyle, New York Yankees
1978	Ron Guidry, New York Yankees
1979	Mike Flanagan, Baltimore Orioles
1980	Steve Stone, Baltimore Orioles
1981	Rollie Fingers, Milwaukee Brewers
1982	Pete Vuckovich, Milwaukee Brewers
1983	La Marr Hoyt, Chicago White Sox
1984	Willie Hernandez, Detroit Tigers
1985	Bret Saberhagen, Kansas City Royals
1986	Roger Clemens, Boston Red Sox
1987	Roger Clemens, Boston Red Sox
1988	Frank Viola, Minnesota Twins
1989	Bret Saberhagen, Kansas City Royals
1990	Bob Welch, Oakland A's
1991	Roger Clemens, Boston Red Sox
1992	Dennis Eckersley, Oakland A's
1993	Jack McDowell, Chicago White Sox
1994	David Cone, Kansas City Royals
1995	Randy Johnson, Seattle Mariners
1996	Pat Hentgen, Toronto Blue Jays
1997	Roger Clemens, Toronto Blue Jays
1998	Roger Clemens, Toronto Blue Jays
1999	Pedro Martinez, Boston Red Sox
2000	Pedro Martinez, Boston Red Sox
2001	Roger Clemens, New York Yankees
2002	Barry Zito, Oakland A's
2003	Roy Halladay, Toronto Blue Jays
2004	Johan Santana, Minnesota Twins
2005	Bartolo Colon, Los Angeles Angels
2006	Johan Santana, Minnesota Twins

World Cup

Instituted in 1938; since 1974 usually held every two years.

Recent winners
1982	South Korea
1984	Cuba
1986	Cuba
1988	Cuba
1990	Cuba
1992	Cuba
1994	Cuba
1996	Cuba
1998	Cuba
2001	Cuba
2003	Cuba
2005	Cuba

Most wins: (27) Cuba: 1939–40, 1942–3, 1950, 1952–3, 1961, 1969–73, 1976, 1978, 1980, and as above.

Olympic Games

Became an Olympic event in 1992.

1992	Cuba
1996	Cuba
2000	USA
2004	Cuba

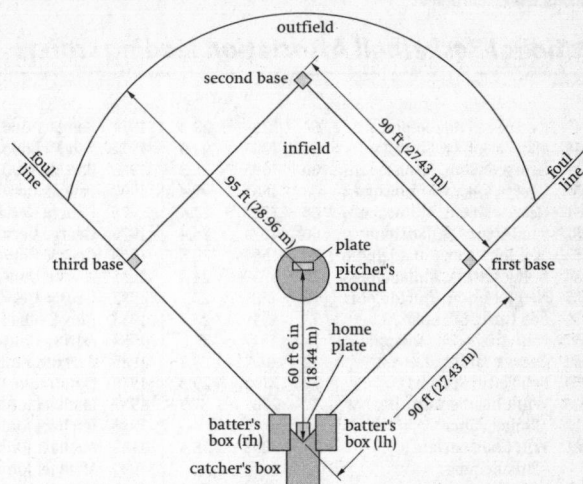

Minimum distance along each foul line is 250 ft (72.2 m)
Distance to the farthest point in centre field is at least 400 ft (122 m)

Baseball diamond

BASKETBALL

In the USA the game's governing body is the National Basketball Association (NBA), which comprises two 'conferences': Eastern (Atlantic Division and Central Division) and Western (Midwest Division and Pacific Division). At the end of the season each conference title is decided in a series of play-offs involving the divisional leaders and the next six best teams; the two conference title-holders compete in a best-of-seven series for the NBA Championship.

National Basketball Association championship

First held in 1947; the major competition in professional basketball in the USA.

1947	Philadelphia 4, Chicago 1
1948	Baltimore 4, Philadelphia 2
1949	Minneapolis 4, Washington 2
1950	Minneapolis 4, Syracuse 2
1951	Rochester 4, New York 3
1952	Minneapolis 4, New York 3
1953	Minneapolis 4, New York 1
1954	Minneapolis 4, Syracuse 3
1955	Syracuse 4, Ft Wayne 3
1956	Philadelphia 4, Ft Wayne 4
1957	Boston 4, St Louis 3
1958	St Louis 4, Boston 2
1959	Boston 4, Minneapolis 0
1960	Boston 4, St Louis 3
1961	Boston 4, St Louis 1
1962	Boston 4, LA Lakers 3
1963	Boston 4, LA Lakers 2
1964	Boston 4, San Francisco 1
1965	Boston 4, LA Lakers 1
1966	Boston 4, LA Lakers 3
1967	Philadelphia 4, San Francisco 2
1968	Boston 4, LA Lakers 2
1969	Boston 4, LA Lakers 3

1970	New York 4, LA Lakers 3
1971	Milwaukee 4, Baltimore 0
1972	LA Lakers 4, New York 1
1973	New York 4, LA Lakers 1
1974	Boston 4, Milwaukee 3
1975	Golden State 4, Washington 0
1976	Boston 4, Phoenix 2
1977	Portland 4, Philadelphia 2
1978	Washington 4, Seattle 3
1979	Seattle 4, Washington 1
1980	LA Lakers 4, Philadelphia 2
1981	Boston 4, Houston 2
1982	LA Lakers 4, Philadelphia 2
1983	Philadelphia 4, LA Lakers 0
1984	Boston 4, LA Lakers 3
1985	LA Lakers 4, Boston 2
1986	Boston 4, Houston 2
1987	LA Lakers 4, Boston 2
1988	LA Lakers 4, Detroit 3
1989	Detroit 4, LA Lakers 0
1990	Detroit 4, Portland 1
1991	Chicago 4, LA Lakers 1
1992	Chicago 4, Portland 1
1993	Chicago 4, Phoenix 2

1994	Houston 4, New York 3
1995	Houston 4, Orlando 0
1996	Chicago 4, Seattle 2
1997	Chicago 4, Utah 2
1998	Chicago 4, Utah 2
1999	San Antonio 4, New York 1
2000	LA Lakers 4, Indiana 2
2001	LA Lakers 4, Philadelphia 1
2002	LA Lakers 4, New Jersey 0
2003	San Antonio 4, New Jersey 2
2004	Detroit 4, LA Lakers 1
2005	San Antonio 4, Detroit 3
2006	Miami Heat 4, Dallas 2

Most wins: (16) Boston Celtics: 1957, 1959–66, 1968–9, 1974, 1976, 1981, 1984, 1986.

Basketball (continued)

National Basketball Association leading scorers

		games	points	average			games	points	average
1947	Joe Fulks, Philadelphia	60	1389	23.2	1974	Bob McAdoo, Buffalo	74	2261	30.6
1948	Max Zaslofsky, Chicago	48	1007	21.0	1975	Bob McAdoo, Buffalo	82	2831	34.5
1949	George Mikan, Minneapolis	60	1698	28.3	1976	Bob McAdoo, Buffalo	78	2427	31.1
1950	George Mikan, Minneapolis	68	1865	27.4	1977	Pete Maravich, New Orleans	73	2273	31.1
1951	George Mikan, Minneapolis	68	1932	28.4	1978	George Gervin, San Antonio	82	2232	27.2
1952	Paul Arizin, Philadelphia	66	1674	25.4	1979	George Gervin, San Antonio	80	2365	29.6
1953	Neil Johnston, Philadelphia	70	1564	22.3	1980	George Gervin, San Antonio	78	2585	33.1
1954	Neil Johnston, Philadelphia	72	1759	24.4	1981	Adrian Dantley, Utah	80	2452	30.7
1955	Neil Johnston, Philadelphia	72	1631	22.7	1982	George Gervin, San Antonio	79	2551	32.3
1956	Bob Pettit, St Louis	72	1849	25.7	1983	Alex English, Denver	82	2326	28.4
1957	Paul Arizin, Philadelphia	71	1817	25.6	1984	Adrian Dantley, Utah	79	2418	30.6
1958	George Yardley, Detroit	72	2001	27.8	1985	Bernard King, New York	55	1809	32.9
1959	Bob Pettit, St Louis	72	2105	29.2	1986	Dominique Wilkins, Atlanta	78	2366	30.3
1960	Wilt Chamberlain, Philadelphia	72	2707	37.9	1987	Michael Jordan, Chicago	82	3041	37.1
					1988	Michael Jordan, Chicago	82	2868	35.0
1961	Wilt Chamberlain, Philadelphia	79	3033	38.4	1989	Michael Jordan, Chicago	81	2633	32.5
					1990	Michael Jordan, Chicago	82	2753	33.6
1962	Wilt Chamberlain, Philadelphia	80	4029	50.4	1991	Michael Jordan, Chicago	82	2580	31.5
					1992	Michael Jordan, Chicago	80	2404	30.1
1963	Wilt Chamberlain, San Francisco	80	3586	44.8	1993	Michael Jordan, Chicago	78	2541	32.3
					1994	David Robinson, San Antonio	80	2383	29.8
1964	Wilt Chamberlain, San Francisco	80	2948	36.5	1995	Shaquille O'Neal, Orlando	79	2315	29.3
					1996	Michael Jordan, Chicago	82	2491	30.04
1965	Wilt Chamberlain, San Francisco/Philadelphia	80	2534	34.7	1997	Michael Jordan, Chicago	82	2431	29.6
					1998	Michael Jordan, Chicago	82	2357	28.7
1966	Wilt Chamberlain, Philadelphia	79	2649	33.5	1999	Allen Iverson, Philadelphia	42	1284	26.8
					2000	Shaquille O'Neal, LA Lakers	79	2344	29.7
1967	Rick Barry, San Francisco	79	2775	35.6	2001	Allen Iverson, Philadelphia	71	2207	31.1
1968	Dave Bing, Detroit	79	2142	27.1	2002	Allen Iverson, Philadelphia	60	1883	31.4
1969	Elvin Hayes, San Diego	82	2327	28.4	2003	Tracy McGrady, Orlando	75	2407	32.1
1970	Jerry West, Los Angeles	74	2309	31.2	2004	Allen Iverson, Philadelphia	60	1819	30.3
1971	Lew Alcindor, Milwaukee	82	2596	31.7	2005	Allen Iverson, Philadelphia	75	2302	30.7
1972	Kareem Abdul-Jabbar (Lew Alcindor), Milwaukee	81	2822	34.8	2006	Kobe Bryant, LA Lakers	80	2832	35.4
1973	Nate Archibald, Kansas City Omaha	80	2719	34.0					

Most times: (10), Michael Jordan, as above.

National Basketball Association most valuable player

Each year the NBA players vote to decide which player will receive the Maurice Podoloff Trophy as the year's Most Valuable Player.

Recent winners:

1964	Oscar Robertson, Cincinnati
1965	Bill Russell, Boston
1966	Wilt Chamberlain, Philadelphia
1967	Wilt Chamberlain, Philadelphia
1968	Wilt Chamberlain, Philadelphia
1969	Wes Unseld, Baltimore
1970	Willis Reed, New York
1971	Lew Alcindor, Milwaukee
1972	Kareem Abdul-Jabbar (Lew Alcindor), Milwaukee
1973	Dave Cowens, Boston
1974	Kareem Abdul-Jabbar, Milwaukee
1975	Bob McAdoo, Buffalo
1976	Kareem Abdul-Jabbar, LA Lakers
1977	Kareem Abdul-Jabbar, LA Lakers
1978	Bill Walton, Portland
1979	Moses Malone, Houston
1980	Kareem Abdul-Jabbar, LA Lakers
1981	Julius Erving, Philadelphia
1982	Moses Malone, Houston
1983	Moses Malone, Philadelphia
1984	Larry Bird, Boston
1985	Larry Bird, Boston
1986	Larry Bird, Boston
1987	Magic Johnson, LA Lakers
1988	Michael Jordan, Chicago
1989	Magic Johnson, LA Lakers
1990	Magic Johnson, LA Lakers
1991	Michael Jordan, Chicago
1992	Michael Jordan, Chicago
1993	Charles Barkley, Phoenix
1994	Hakeem Olajuwon, Houston
1995	David Robinson, San Antonio
1996	Michael Jordan, Chicago
1997	Karl Malone (Utah)
1998	Michael Jordan (Chicago)
1999	Karl Malone (Utah)
2000	Shaquille O'Neal, LA Lakers
2001	Allen Iverson, Philadelphia
2002	Tim Duncan, San Antonio
2003	Tim Duncan, San Antonio
2004	Kevin Garnett, Minnesota
2005	Steve Nash, Phoenix
2006	Steve Nash, Phoenix

Most time MVP: (6) Kareem Abdul-Jabbar, as above

World championship

First held 1950 for men, 1953 for women; usually now takes place every four years.

Winners (men)		Winners (women)	
1967	USSR	1967	USSR
1970	Yugoslavia	1971	USSR
1974	USSR	1975	USSR
1978	Yugoslavia	1979	USA
1982	USSR	1983	USSR
1986	USA	1987	USA
1990	Yugoslavia	1991	USA
1994	USA	1994	Brazil
1998	Yugoslavia	1998	USA
2002	Yugoslavia	2002	USA
2006	Spain	2006	Australia

Most wins: (5) Yugoslavia: as above.

Most wins: (6) USSR: 1959, 1964 and as above; USA: 1957 and as above.

Olympic Games

Became an Olympic event for men in 1936, for women in 1976.

Winners (men)		Winners (women)	
1956	USA	1976	USSR
1960	USA	1980	USSR
1964	USA	1984	USA
1968	USA	1988	USA
1972	USSR	1992	Unified Team
1976	USA	1996	USA
1980	Yugoslavia	2000	USA
1984	USA	2004	USA
1988	USSR		
1992	USA	*Most wins:* (5) USA: as above.	
1996	USA		
2000	USA		
2004	Argentina		

Most wins: (12) USA: 1936, 1948, 1952 and as above.

BIATHLON

World championships

First held in 1958; take place annually; the Olympic champion is the automatic world champion in Olympic years; women's championship first held in 1984.

Recent winners: individual – men

10 km
1992	Mark Kirchner (Germany)
1993	Mark Kirchner (Germany)
1994	Serguei Tchepikov (Russia)
1995	Patrice Bailly-Salins (France)
1996	Vladimir Dratshev (Russia)
1997	Erik Lundström (Sweden)
1998	Ole Einar Bjoerndalen (Norway)
1999	Frank Luck (Germany)
2000	Frode Andreson (Norway)
2001	Raphael Poiree (France)
2002	Ole Einar Bjoerndalen (Norway)
2003	Ole Einar Bjoerndalen (Norway)
2004	Lars Berger (Norway)
2005	Ole Einar Bjoerndalen (Norway)
2006	Sven Fischer (Germany)

20 km (now 12.5 km *pursuit*)
1992	Yevgeniy Redkine (Unified Team)
1993	Franz Zingerle (Austria)
1994	Sergei Tarasov (Russia)
1995	Tomaz Sikora (Poland)
1996	Sergei Tarasov (Russia)
1997	Ricco Gross (Germany)
1998	Halvard Hanevold (Norway)
1999	Ricco Gross (Germany)
2000	Wolfgang Rottmann (Austria)
2001	Paavo Puurunen (Finland)
2002	Ole Einar Bjoerndalen (Norway)
2003	Rico Gross (Germany)
2004	Raphael Poiree (France)
2005	Roman Dostal (Czech Republic)
2006	Michael Greis (Germany)

Most individual titles: (6): Frank Ullrich (E Germany) 1978–81, 10 km; 1982–3, 20 km.

Olympic Games - winter

4 x 7.5 km relay (first held 1965)
1998	Germany
2002	Norway
2006	Germany

Recent winners: individual – women

7.5 km (5 km before 1988) – sprint
1996	Olga Romasko (Russia)
1997	Olga Romasko (Russia)
1998	Galina Koukleva (Russia)
1999	Martina Zellner (Germany)
2000	Liv Grete Skjelbreid (Norway)
2001	Kati Wilhelm (Germany)
2002	Kati Wilhelm (Germany)
2003	Sylvie Becaert (France)
2004	Olga Pyleva (Russia)
2005	Uschi Disl (Germany)
2006	Florence Baverel-Robert (France)

15 km (10 km before 1988) – pursuit
1994	Myriam Bedard (Canada)
1995	Corrine Miogret (France)
1996	Emmanuelle Claret (France)
1997	Magdalena Forsberg (Sweden)
1998	Ekaterina Dafovska (Bulgaria)
1999	Olena Zubrilova (Ukraine)
2000	Corrine Niogret (France)
2001	Magdalena Forsberg (Sweden)
2002	Andrea Henkel (Germany)
2003	Sandrine Bailly (France)
2004	Olga Pyleva (Russia)
2005	Andrea Henkel (Germany)
2006	Svetlana Ishmouratova (Russia)

Most individual titles: (4) Petra Schaaf (Germany) 1988, 7.5 km, 1989, 1991, 1993, 15 km.

Olympic Games - winter

4 x 7.5 km relay (3 x 5 km before 1989)
1998	Germany
2002	Germany
2006	Russia

SPORTS AND GAMES

BILLIARDS

World professional championship

First held in 1870, organized on a challenge basis. Became a knockout event in 1909; discontinued in 1934; revived in 1951 as a challenge system; reverted to a knockout event in 1980.

Recent winners

1993	Geet Sethi (India)	2002	Mike Russell (England)
1994	Peter Gilchrist (England)	2003	Lee Lagan (England)
1995	Geet Sethi (India)	2004	Mike Russell (England)
1996	Mike Russell (England)	2005	Chris Shutt (England)
1997	Mike Russell (England)	2006	Geet Sethi (India)
1998	Geet Sethi (India)		
1999	Mike Russell (England)		
2001	Peter Gilchrist (England)		

Most wins: Knockout (6) Tom Newman (England): 1921–2, 1924–7. Challenge (8) John Roberts, Jnr (England): 1870–85.

BOBSLEIGHING AND TOBOGGANING/LUGE

World championships

First held in 1930 (four-man) and in 1931 (two-man). Olympic champions automatically become world champions. Women's event introduced at 2002 Olympics.

Recent winners: two-man
1999 Günter Huber/Ubaldo Ranzi (Italy)
2000 Cristoph Langen/Markus Zimmerman (Germany)
2001 Cristoph Langen/Marco Jakobs (Germany)
2002 Cristoph Langen/Markus Zimmerman (Germany)
2003 Andre Lange/Kevin Kuske (Germany)
2004 Pierre Lueders/Giulio Zardo (Canada)
2005 Pierre Lueders/Lascelles Brown (Canada)
2006 Andre Lange/Kevin Kuske (Germany)

Recent winners: women
2002 Jill Bakken/Vonetta Flowers (USA)
2003 Susi Erdmann/Annegret Richter (Germany)
2004 Susi Erdmann/Kristina Bader (Germany)
2005 Sandra Kiriasis/Anja Schneiderheinze (Germany)
2006 Sandra Kiriasis/Anja Schneiderheinze (Germany)

Recent winners: four-man

1992	Austria	1999	France
1993	Switzerland	2000	Germany
1994	Switzerland	2001	Germany
1995	Germany	2002	Germany
1996	Germany	2003	Germany
1997	Germany	2004	Germany
1998	Germany	2005	Germany

Most wins: Two-man (8) Eugenio Monti (Italy): 1957–61, 1963, 1966, 1968. Four-man (17), Switzerland: 1939, 1947, 1954–5, 1957, 1971, 1973, 1975, 1982–3, 1986–90, 1993–4.

Luge world championships

First held in 1955; annually until 1981, then usually every two years. The Olympic champion automatically becomes the world champion.

Recent winners: men's single-seater
1993 Werdel Suckow (USA)
1995 Armin Zoeggeler (Italy)
1996 Marcus Prock (Austria)
1997 Georg Hackl (Germany)
1999 Armin Zoeggeler (Italy)
2000 Jens Müller (Germany)
2001 Armin Zoeggeler (Italy)
2002 Armin Zoeggeler (Italy)
2003 Armin Zoeggeler (Italy)
2004 David Moeller (Germany)
2005 Armin Zoeggeler (Italy)
2006 Armin Zoeggeler (Italy)

Most wins: (7) Armin Zoeggeler (Italy), as above.

Recent winners: women's single-seater
1993 Gerda Weissensteiner (Italy)
1994 Gerda Weissensteiner (Italy)
1995 Gabriele Kohlisch (Germany)
1997 Susi Erdmann (Germany)
1999 Sonja Wiedmann (Germany)
2000 Sylke Otto (Germany)
2001 Sylke Otto (Germany)
2002 Sylke Otto (Germany)
2003 Sylke Otto (Germany)
2004 Silke Kraushaar (Germany)
2005 Sylke Otto (Germany)
2006 Sylke Otto (Germany)

Most wins: (6) Sylke Otto (Germany), as above.

Olympic Games, luge

Winners: men's single-seater
1992 Georg Hackl (Germany)
1994 Georg Hackl (Germany)
1998 Georg Hackl (Germany)
2002 Armin Zoeggeler (Italy)
2006 Armin Zoeggeler (Italy)

Winners: pairs (men)

1992	Germany	1998	Germany	2006	Austria
1994	Italy	2002	Germany		

Most wins: Singles (3) Georg Hackl (Germany), as above. Pairs (5) E Germany: 1968, 1972, 1976, 1980, 1988.

Winners: women's single-seater
1992 Doris Neuner (Austria)
1994 Gerda Weissensteiner (Italy)
1998 Silke Kraushaar (Germany)
2002 Sylke Otto (Germany)
2006 Sylke Otto (Germany)

Most wins: (2) Steffi Martin Walter (E Germany): 1984, 1988; Sylke Otto (Germany(, as above.

BOWLS

World championships

Instituted for men in 1966 and for women in 1969; held every four years.

Men's singles
1980	David Bryant (England)
1984	Peter Bellis (New Zealand)
1988	David Bryant (England)
1992	Tony Allcock (England)
1996	Tony Allcock (England)
2000	Jeremy Henry (Ireland)
2004	Steve Glasson (Australia)

Men's pairs
1980	Australia
1984	USA
1988	New Zealand
1992	Scotland
1996	Ireland
2000	Scotland
2004	Canada

Men's triples
1980	England
1984	Ireland
1988	New Zealand
1992	Israel
1996	Scotland
2000	New Zealand
2004	Scotland

Men's fours
1980	Hong Kong
1984	England
1988	Ireland
1992	Scotland
1996	England
2000	Wales
2004	N Ireland

Most wins: (5) David Bryant (singles: as above and 1966; triples: 1988; team: 1980).

Women's singles
1985	Merle Richardson (Australia)
1988*	Janet Ackland (Wales)
1992	Margaret Johnston (N Ireland)
1996	Carmen Anderson (Norfolk Island)
2000	Margaret Johnston (N Ireland)
2004	Margaret Johnston (N Ireland)

Women's pairs
1981	Ireland
1985	Australia
1988*	Ireland
1992	Ireland
1996	Ireland
2000	Scotland
2004	New Zealand

Women's triples
1981	Hong Kong
1985	Australia
1988*	Australia
1992	Scotland
1996	South Africa
2000	New Zealand
2004	South Africa

Women's fours
1981	England
1985	Scotland
1988*	Australia
1992	Scotland
1996	Australia
2000	New Zealand
2004	England

Women's team
1981	England
1985	Australia
1988*	England
1992	Scotland
1996	South Africa
2000	England
2004	England

Most wins: (3) Merle Richardson (fours: 1977; singles and pairs: 1985); Margaret Johnston (singles as above).

*The women's event was advanced to December 1988 (Australia).

World indoor championships

First held in 1979, became fully professional in 1995, and gender-free in 1997. Women's amateur first held in 1998; both held annually.

Winners: men
1997	Hugh Duff (Scotland)
1998	Paul Foster (Scotland)
1999	Alex Marshall (Scotland)
2000	Robert Wheale (Wales)
2001	Paul Foster (Scotland)
2002	Tony Allcock (England)
2003	Alex Marshall (Scotland)
2004	Alex Marshall (Scotland)
2005	Paul Foster (Scotland)
2006	Mervyn King (England)

Most wins: (3) David Bryant: 1979–81; Tony Allcock: 1986–7, 2002; Richard Corsie: 1989, 1991, 1993; Paul Foster, Alex Marshall, as above.

Winners: women
1997	Norma Shaw (England)
1998	Caroline McAllister (Scotland)
1999	Caroline McAllister (Scotland)
2000	Marlene Castle (New Zealand)
2001	Betty Brown (Scotland)
2002	Carol Ashby (England)
2003	Carol Ashby (England)
2004	Carol Ashby (England)
2005	Ellen Falkner (England)
2006	Ellen Falkner (Scotland)

Most wins: (3) Carol Ashby, as above.

Waterloo Handicap

First held in 1907 and annually at Blackpool's Waterloo Hotel; the premier event of Crown Green Bowling.

Recent winners: men
2000	Carl Armitage
2001	Glynn Cookson
2002	Stan Frith
2003	Gary Ellis
2004	Noel Burrows
2005	John Bailey
2006	Andrew Moss

Recent winners: women
2000	Lynn Pritchett
2001	Lesley Smith
2002	Karen Johnstone
2003	Joan Jolly
2004	Ann Roberts
2005	Barbara Rawcliffe

BOXING

World heavyweight champions

Undisputed
1882	John L Sullivan (USA)
1892	James J Corbett (USA)*
1897	Bob Fitzsimmons (Great Britain)
1899	James J Jefferies (USA)
1905	Marvin Hart (USA)
1906	Tommy Burns (Can)
1908	Jack Johnson (USA)
1915	Jess Willard (USA)
1919	Jack Dempsey (USA)
1926	Gene Tunney (USA)
1930	Max Schmeling (Germany)
1932	Jack Sharkey (USA)
1933	Primo Carnera (Italy)
1934	Max Baer (USA)
1935	James J Braddock (USA)
1937	Joe Louis (USA)
1949	Ezzard Charles (USA)
1951	Jersey Joe Walcott (USA)
1952	Rocky Marciano (USA)
1956	Floyd Patterson (USA)
1959	Ingemar Johansson (Sweden)
1960	Sonny Liston (USA)
1964	Cassius Clay (USA)[a]
1970	Joe Frazier (USA)
1973	George Foreman (USA)
1974	Muhammad Ali (USA)[a]
1978	Leon Spinks (USA)
1987	Mike Tyson (USA)
1999	Lennox Lewis (UK)

*The first world heavyweight champion under Queensberry rules with gloves.

Boxing (continued)

In recent years, 'world champions' have been recognized by up to four different governing bodies.

Champions since 1986	Recognizing body
1986 Tim Witherspoon (USA)	WBA
1986 Trevor Berbick (Canada)	WBC
1986 Mike Tyson (USA)	WBC
1986 James Smith (USA)	WBA
1987 Tony Tucker (USA)	IBF
1987 Mike Tyson (USA)	WBA/WBC
1987 Mike Tyson (USA)	UND
1989 Francesco Damiani (Italy)	WBO
1990 James (Buster) Douglas (USA)	WBA/WBC/IBF
1990 Evander Holyfield (USA)	WBA/WBC/IBF
1991 Ray Mercer (USA)	WBO
1992 Riddick Bowe (USA)	WBA/WBC/IBF
1992 Michael Moorer (USA)	WBO
1992 Lennox Lewis (Great Britain)	WBC
1993 Tommy Morrison (USA)	WBO
1994 Oliver McCall (UK)	WBC
1994 Herbie Hide (USA)	WBO
1994 George Foreman (USA)	IBF
1995 Frank Bruno (UK)	WBC
1996 Mike Tyson (USA)	WBC
1996 Henry Akinwande (UK)	WBO
1996 Evander Holyfield (USA)	WBA
1996 Michael Moorer (USA)	IBF
1997 Lennox Lewis (UK)	WBC
1997 Herbie Hide (UK)	WBO
1997 Evander Holyfield (USA)	WBA/IBF
1998 Lennox Lewis (UK)	WBC
1999 Vitali Klitschko (Ukraine)	WBO
1999 Lennox Lewis (UK)	WBO/WBA[b]/WBC/IBF/UND
2000 John Ruiz (USA)	WBA
2000 Chris Byrd (USA)	WBO
2000 Vitali Klitschko (Ukraine)	WBO
2001 Hasim Rahman (USA)	WBC, IBF
2001 Lennox Lewis (UK)	WBC, IBF
2002 Lennox Lewis (UK)	WBC, IBF
2003 Roy Jones, Jr (USA)	WBA
2003 Lennox Lewis (UK)	WBC
2003 Corrie Sanders (South Africa)	WBO
2004 John Ruiz (USA)	WBA
2004 Vitali Klitschko (Ukraine)	WBC
2004 Lamon Brewster (USA)	WBO
2005 Vitali Klitschko (Ukraine	WBC
2005 John Ruiz (USA)	WBA
2005 Chris Byrd (USA)	IBF
2005 Lamon Brewster (USA)	WBO
2005 Nikolay Valuev (Russia)	WBA
2006 Oleg Maskaev (Kazakhstan)	WBC

[a]Cassius Clay changed his name to Muhammad Ali upon joining the Black Muslims.
[b]He was stripped of this award by a New York court in 2000.

IBF = International Boxing Federation   WBC = World Boxing Council
UND = Undisputed Champion   WBO = World Boxing Organization
WBA = World Boxing Association

CANOEING

Olympic Games

Single kayak: 1000 m – men
1936	Gregor Hradetzky (Austria)
1948	Gert Fredriksson (Sweden)
1952	Gert Fredriksson (Sweden)
1956	Gert Fredriksson (Sweden)
1960	Erik Hansen (Denmark)
1964	Rolf Peterson (Sweden)
1968	Mihaly Hesz (Hungary)
1972	Aleksandr Shaparenko (USSR)
1976	Rüdiger Helm (E Germany)
1980	Rüdiger Helm (E Germany)
1984	Alan Thompson (New Zealand)
1988	Greg Barton (USA)
1992	Clint Robinson (Australia)
1996	Oliver Fix (Germany)
2000	Thomas Schmidt (Germany)
2004	Eirik Veraas Larsen (Norway)

Single kayak: 500 m – women
1948	Keren Hoff (Denmark)
1952	Sylvi Saimo (Finland)
1956	Elisaveta Dementyeva (USSR)
1960	Antonina Seredina (USSR)
1964	Lyudmila Khvedosyuk (USSR)
1968	Lyudmila Pinayeva (USSR)
1972	Yulia Ryabchinskaya (USSR)
1976	Carola Zirzow (E Germany)
1980	Birgit Fischer (E Germany)
1984	Agneta Andersson (Sweden)
1988	Vania Gecheva (USSR)
1992	Brigit Schmidt (Germany)
1996	Stepanka Hilgertova (Czech Republic)
2000	Stepanka Hilgertova (Czech Republic)
2004	Natasa Janics (Hungary)

Most wins: Men (3) Gert Fredriksson: as above. Women (2) Stepanka Hilgertova: as above.

CHESS

World champions

World champions have been recognized since 1886; first women's champion recognized in 1927. A split between the World Chess Federation (FIDE) and the new Professional Chess Association (PCA) resulted in two championship matches in 1993. Following the collapse of the PCA and subsequent collapse of the World Chess Council set up to replace it, the 2000 world championship was contested under the aegis of Braingames Network, an Internet company.

Recent champions: men

1972–5	Bobby Fischer (USA)
1975–85	Anatoly Karpov (USSR)

1985–2000	Gary Kasparov (USSR/Azerbaijan) PCA
1993–9	Anatoly Karpov (Russia) FIDE
1999–2000	Alexander Khalifman (Russia) FIDE
2000–02	Vishwanathan Anand (India) FIDE
2000	Vladimir Kramnik (Russia) Braingames Network
2002–4	Ruslan Ponomariov (Ukraine) FIDE
2004–5	Rustam Kasimdzhanov (Uzbekistan) FIDE
2005–	Veselin Topalov (Bulgaria) FIDE

Longest reigning champion: 27 years, Emanuel Lasker (Germany): 1894–1921.

Champions: women

1950–3	Lyudmila Rudenko (USSR)
1953–6	Elizaveta Bykova (USSR)
1956–8	Olga Rubtsova (USSR)
1958–62	Elizaveta Bykova (USSR)
1962–78	Nona Gaprindashvili (USSR)
1978–92	Maya Chiburdanidze (USSR)
1992–5	Xie Jun (China)
1996–9	Zsusza Polgar (Hungary)
1999–2000	Xie Jun (China)
2001–5	Zhu Chen (China) FIDE
2004–6	Antoaneta Stefanova (Bulgaria) FIDE
2006–	Xu Yuhua (China) FIDE

Longest reigning champion: 17 years, Vera Menchik-Stevenson (UK): 1927–44.

Chess notation

The opening position[a]

Abbreviations

B	Bishop
K	King
KB	King's bishop
KN	King's knight
KR	King's rook
N	Knight
P	Pawn
Q	Queen
QB	Queen's bishop
QN	Queen's knight
QR	Queen's rook
R	Rook

Descriptive notation

Each file is named by the piece on the first rank; ranks are numbered 1–8 away from the player.

x	captures (Q x P = Queen takes Pawn)
–	moves to (Q–KB4)
ch	check (R–QB3 ch)
dis ch	discovered check
dbl ch	double check
e.p.	en passant
mate	checkmate
0–0	castles, King's side
0–0–0	castles, Queen's side
!	good move (P x R!)
!!	very good move
!!!	outstanding move
?	bad move
!?	good or bad move (depends on response of the other player)

Algebraic notation

Each square is named by a combination of file letter and rank number.

Chess pieces in other languages

French

B	fou (fool)
K	roi (king)
N	cavalier (horseman)
P	pion (pawn)
Q	dame, reine (lady), (queen)
R	tour (tower)

German

B	Läufer (runner)
K	König (king)
N	Springer (jumper)
P	Bauer (peasant)
Q	Königin (queen)
R	Turm (tower)

[a] The white queen is placed on a white square, and the black queen on a black square.

CONTRACT BRIDGE

World team championship

The game's biggest championship; men's contest (The Bermuda Bowl) first held in 1951, and now takes place every two years; women's contest (The Venice Cup) first held in 1974, and since 1985 is concurrent with the men's event.

Bermuda Bowl winners: men

1979	USA	1993	Netherlands
1981	USA	1995	USA
1983	USA	1997	France
1985	USA	2000	USA
1987	USA	2001	USA
1989	Brazil	2003	USA
1991	Iceland	2005	Italy

Most wins: (13) Italy: 1957–9, 1961–3, 1965–7, 1969, 1973–5.

Venice Cup winners: women

1978	USA	1993	USA
1981	UK	1995	Germany
1983	*Not held*	1997	USA
1985	UK	2000	Netherlands
1987	Italy	2001	Germany
1989	USA	2003	USA
1991	USA	2005	France

Most wins: (8) USA: 1974 and as above

World team olympiad

First held in 1960; takes place every four years.

Winners: men

1960	France	1984	Poland
1964	Italy	1988	USA
1968	Italy	1992	France
1972	Italy	1996	France
1976	Brazil	2000	Italy
1980	France	2004	Italy

Winners: women

1964	UK	1988	Denmark
1968	Sweden	1992	Austria
1972	Italy	1996	USA
1976	USA	2000	USA
1980	USA	2004	Russia
1984	USA		

Most wins: Men (5) Italy: as above. Women (5) USA: as above.

CRICKET

World cup

First played in England in 1975 (women's match from 1973); held every four years. The 1987 competition was the first to be played outside England, in India and Pakistan.

Winners

1975	West Indies	1992	Pakistan
1979	West Indies	1996	Sri Lanka
1983	India	1999	Australia
1987	Australia	2003	Australia

County championship

The oldest cricket competition in the world; first won by Sussex in 1827. Not officially recognized until 1890, when a proper points system was introduced.

Recent winners

1993	Middlesex
1994	Warwickshire
1995	Warwickshire
1996	Leicestershire
1997	Glamorgan
1998	Leicestershire
1999	Surrey
2000	Surrey
2001	Yorkshire
2002	Surrey
2003	Sussex
2004	Warwickshire
2005	Nottinghamshire
2006	Sussex

Most outright wins: (30) Yorkshire: 1893, 1896, 1898, 1900–2, 1905, 1908, 1912, 1919, 1922–5, 1931–3, 1935, 1937–9, 1946, 1959–60, 1962–3, 1966–8, 2001.

The Ashes

One of cricket's oldest international contests; originating in 1882, when England was defeated by Australia on home soil. The ashes of a stump from that match remain at Lords' cricket ground. Usually held every two years.

Recent winners

1989	Australia 4 – 0 England
1991	Australia 3 – 0 England
1993	Australia 4 – 1 England
1995	Australia 3 – 1 England
1997	Australia 3 – 2 England
1999	Australia 3 – 1 England
2001	Australia 4 – 1 England
2003	Australia 4 – 1 England
2005	England 2 – 1 Australia
2006	Australia 5 – 0 England

NPower Twenty20 Cup

First held in 2003. Replaced the Benson and Hedges Cup.

Recent winners

2003	Surrey
2004	Leicestershire
2005	Somerset
2006	Leicestershire

Cheltenham and Gloucester trophy

First held in 1963; known as the Gillette Cup until 1981 and the NatWest Bank trophy until 2000.

Recent winners

1996	Lancashire
1997	Essex
1998	Lancashire
1999	Gloucestershire
2000	Gloucestershire
2001	Somerset
2002	Yorkshire
2003	Gloucestershire
2004	Gloucestershire
2005	Hampshire
2006	Sussex

Most wins: (7) Lancashire: 1970–2, 1975, 1990, 1996, 1998.

NatWest Pro40 National League

First held in 1969; known as the John Player League 1969–86; the Refuge Assurance League to 1991; the AXA Equity and Law League to 1999; the CGU National Cricket League to 2000; the Norwich Union National League to 2003, and the Totesport National League to 2005.

Recent winners

1996	Surrey
1997	Warwickshire
1998	Lancashire
1999	Lancashire
2000	Gloucestershire
2001	Kent
2002	Glamorgan
2003	Surrey
2004	Glamorgan
2005	Essex
2006	Essex

Most wins: (5) Lancashire: 1969–70, 1989, 1998–9; Kent: 1972–3, 1976, 1995, 2001; Essex: 1981, 1984–5, and as above.

Pura Milk Cup

Australia's leading domestic competition; contested inter-state since 1891, known as the Sheffield Shield until 1999.

Recent winners
1995	Queensland
1996	South Australia
1997	Queensland
1998	Western Australia
1999	Queensland
2000	Queensland
2001	Queensland
2002	Queensland
2003	New South Wales
2004	Victoria
2005	New South Wales
2006	Queensland

Most wins: (44) New South Wales, 1896–7, 1900, 1902–7, 1909, 1911–12, 1914, 1920–1, 1923, 1926, 1929, 1932–3, 1938, 1940, 1949–50, 1952, 1954–62, 1965–6, 1983, 1985–6, 1993, 1994, and as above.

Cricket field positions[a]

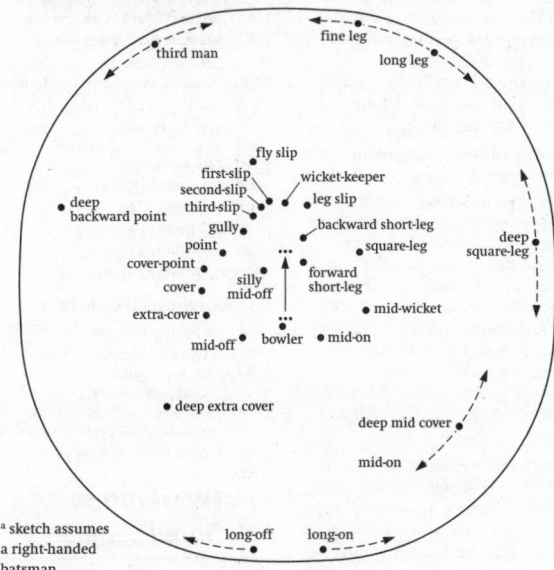

[a] sketch assumes a right-handed batsman

CROQUET

MacRobertson Shield

Croquet's leading tournament; held spasmodically since 1925; contested by teams from Great Britain, New Zealand, Australia, and USA.

Winners
1935	Australia
1937	Great Britain
1950	New Zealand
1956	Great Britain
1963	Great Britain
1969	Great Britain
1974	Great Britain
1979	New Zealand
1982	Great Britain
1986	New Zealand
1990	Great Britain
1993	Great Britain
1996	Great Britain
2000	Great Britain
2003	Great Britain
2006	Great Britain

Most wins: (13) Great Britain: 1925 and as above.

World singles championships

Inaugurated in 1989. Held every two to three years.

Winners
1992	Robert Fulford (Britain)
1994	Robert Fulford (Britain)
1995	Chris Clarke (Britain)
1997	Robert Fulford (Britain)
2001	Reg Bamford (South Africa)
2002	Robert Fulford (Britain)
2005	Reg Bamford (South Africa)

Most wins: (5) Robert Fulford (Britain): 1990 and as above.

CROSS-COUNTRY RUNNING

World championships

First international championship held in 1903, but only included runners from England, Ireland, Scotland, and Wales. Recognized as an official world championship from 1973; first women's race in 1967.

Recent winner: individual – men
1997	Paul Tergat (Kenya)
1998	Paul Tergat (Kenya)
1999	Paul Tergat (Kenya)
2000	Mohammad Mourhit (Belgium)
2001	Mohammad Mourhit (Belgium)
2002	Kenenisa Bekele (Ethiopia)
2003	Kenenisa Bekele (Ethiopia)
2004	Kenenisa Bekele (Ethiopia)
2005	Kenenisa Bekele (Ethiopia)
2006	Kenenisa Bekele (Ethiopia)

Recent winners: team – men
1997	Kenya	2002	Kenya
1998	Kenya	2003	Kenya
1999	Kenya	2004	Ethiopia
2000	Kenya	2005	Ethiopia
2001	Kenya	2006	Kenya

Most wins: Individual (5) John Ngugi (Kenya): 1986–9, 1991–2; Paul Tergat (Kenya) 1995, 1996, and as above; Kenenisa Bekele (Ethiopia), as above. Team (45), England: between 1903 and 1980.

Recent winners: individual – women
1997	Derartu Tulu (Ethiopia)
1998	Sonia O'Sullivan (Ireland)
1999	Gete Wami (Ethiopia)
2000	Derartu Tulu (Ethiopia)
2001	Paula Radcliffe (Great Britain)
2002	Paula Radcliffe (Great Britain)
2003	Werknesh Kidane (Ethiopia)
2004	Benita Johnson (Australia)
2005	Tirunesh Dibaba (Ethiopia)
2006	Tirunesh Dibaba (Ethiopia)

Recent winners: team – women
1994	Portugal	2000	Portugal
1995	Kenya	2001	Kenya
1996	Kenya	2002	Kenya
1997	Ethiopia	2003	Ethiopia
1998	Kenya	2004	Ethiopia
1999	France	2005	Ethiopia

Most wins: Individual (5) Doris Brown (USA): 1967–71; Grete Waitz (Norway): 1978–81, 1983. Team (8), USA: 1968–9, 1975, 1979, 1983–5, 1987, 1988–9; Kenya: 1991 (tied), 1992, 1993, and as above.

SPORTS AND GAMES

CURLING

World championships

First men's championship held in 1959; first women's championship in 1979. Takes place annually.

Recent winners: men

1991	Scotland	1999	Scotland
1992	Switzerland	2000	Canada
1993	Canada	2001	Sweden
1994	Canada	2002	Canada
1995	Canada	2003	Canada
1996	Canada	2004	Sweden
1997	Sweden	2005	Canada
1998	Canada	2006	Scotland

Recent winners: women

1991	Norway	1999	Sweden
1992	Sweden	2000	Canada
1993	Germany	2001	Canada
1994	Canada	2002	Scotland
1995	Canada	2003	USA
1996	Canada	2004	Canada
1997	Canada	2005	Sweden
1998	Sweden	2006	Sweden

Most wins: Men (29) Canada: 1959–64, 1966, 1968–72, 1980, 1982–3, 1985–7, 1989, and as above. Women (13) Canada: 1980, 1984–7, 1989, and as above.

CYCLING

Tour de France

World's premier cycling event; first held in 1903.

Recent winners

1987	Stephen Roche (Ireland)
1988	Pedro Delgado (Spain)
1989	Greg LeMond (USA)
1990	Greg LeMond (USA)
1991	Miguel Induráin (Spain)
1992	Miguel Induráin (Spain)
1993	Miguel Induráin (Spain)
1994	Miguel Induráin (Spain)
1995	Miguel Induráin (Spain)
1996	Bjarne Riis (Denmark)
1997	Jan Ullrich (Germany)
1998	Marco Pantani (Italy)
1999	Lance Armstrong (USA)
2000	Lance Armstrong (USA)
2001	Lance Armstrong (USA)
2002	Lance Armstrong (USA)
2003	Lance Armstrong (USA)
2004	Lance Armstrong (USA)
2005	Lance Armstrong (USA)
2006	Oscar Pereiro (Spain)

Most wins: (7) Lance Armstrong (USA), as above.

World road race championships

Men's race first held in 1927; takes place annually. First women's race in 1958; takes place annually.

Recent winners: professional men

1995	Abraham Olano (Spain)
1996	Johan Museeuw (Belgium)
1997	Laurent Brochard (France)
1998	Oscar Camenzind (Switzerland)
1999	Oscar Freire Gomez (Spain)
2000	Romans Vainsteins (Latvia)
2001	Oscar Freire Gomez (Spain)
2002	Mario Cipollini (Italy)
2003	Igor Astarloa (Spain)
2004	Oscar Freire Gomez (Spain)
2005	Tom Boonen (Belgium)
2006	Paolo Bettini (Italy)

Recent winners: women

1995	Jeannie Longo (France)
1996	Jeannie Longo (France)
1997	Alessandra Cappelloto (Italy)
1998	Diana Ziliute (Lithuania)
1999	Edita Pucinskaite (Lithuania)
2000	Zinaida Stahurskai (Bulgaria)
2001	Rasa Polikeviciute (Lithuania)
2002	Susanne Ljungskog (Sweden)
2003	Susanne Ljungskog (Sweden)
2004	Judith Arndt (Germany)
2005	Regina Schleicher (Germany)
2006	Marianne Vos (Netherlands)

Most wins: Men (3) Alfredo Binda (Italy): 1927, 1930, 1932; Rik Van Steenbergen (Belgium): 1949, 1956–7; Eddy Merckx (Belgium): 1967, 1971, 1974; Oscar Freire Gomez (Spain): as above. Women (7); Jeannie Longo (France): 1985, 1986, 1987, 1988, 1989, and as above.

Olympic Games

Gold medal winners: 2004 – men

Individual road race
Paulo Bettini (Italy)

1000 m sprint
Ryan Baley (USA)

4000 m individual pursuit
Bradley Wiggins (Great Britain)

Gold medal winners: 2004 – women

Individual road race
Sara Carrigan (Australia)

1000 m sprint
Lori-Ann Muenzer (Canada)

3000 m individual pursuit
Sarah Ulmer (New Zealand)

CYCLO-CROSS

World championships

First held in 1950 as an open event; separate professional and amateur events since 1967; both events combined from 1994 to form the Open; since 1995, called the Elite.

Recent winners: professional

1981	Johannes Stamsnijder (Netherlands)
1982	Roland Liboton (Belgium)
1983	Roland Liboton (Belgium)
1984	Roland Liboton (Belgium)
1985	Klaus-Peter Thaler (W Germany)
1986	Albert Zweifel (Switzerland)
1987	Klaus-Peter Thaler (W Germany)
1988	Pascal Richard (Switzerland)
1989	Danny De Bie (Belgium)
1990	Henk Baars (Netherlands)
1991	Radomir Simunek (Czechoslovakia)
1992	Mike Kluge (Germany)
1993	Dominique Arnaud (France)

Recent winners: amateur

1981	Milos Fisera (Czechoslovakia)
1982	Milos Fisera (Czechoslovakia)
1983	Radomir Simunek (Czechoslovakia)
1984	Radomir Simunek (Czechoslovakia)
1985	Mike Kluge (W Germany)
1986	Vito di Tano (Italy)
1987	Mike Kluge (W Germany)
1988	Karol Camrola (Czechoslovakia)
1989	Ondrej Glaja (Czechoslovakia)
1990	Andreas Buesser (Switzerland)
1991	Thomas Frischknecht (Switzerland)
1992	Daniele Pontoni (Italy)
1993	Henrik Djemis (Denmark)

Recent Winners: Elite

1997	Daniele Pontoni (Italy)
1998	Mario De Clercq (Belgium)
1999	Mario De Clercq (Belgium)
2000	Richard Groenendaal (Netherlands)
2001	Erwin Vervecken (Belgium)
2002	Mario De Clercq (Belgium)
2003	Bart Wellens (Belgium)
2004	Bart Wellens (Belgium)
2005	Sven Nys (Belgium)
2006	Erwin Vervecken (Belgium)

Most wins: Professional (7) Eric de Vlaeminck (Belgium): 1966, 1968–73. Amateur (5) Robert Vermiere (Belgium): 1970–1, 1974–5, 1977.

DARTS

World professional championship (BDO)

British Darts Organisation: first held at Nottingham, 1978; held at Frimley Green, Surrey, since 1986; women's tournament first held in 2001.

Winners: men
2001 John 'Boy' Walton (England)
2002 Tony David (Australia)
2003 Raymond Barneveld (Netherlands)
2004 Andy Fordham (England)
2005 Raymond Barneveld (Netherlands)
2006 Jelle Klaasen (Netherlands)
2007 Martin Adams (England)

Winners: women
2001 Trina Gulliver (England)
2002 Trina Gulliver (England)
2003 Trina Gulliver (England)
2004 Trina Gulliver (England)
2005 Trina Gulliver (England)
2006 Trina Gulliver (England)

Most wins: Men (5) Eric Bristow 1980–1, 1984–6. Women (6) Trina Gulliver, as above.

World cup

A team competition first held at Wembley in 1977; takes place every two years.

Winners: team
1989 England
1991 England
1993 Wales
1995 England
1997 Wales
1999 England
2001 England
2003 England
2005 Finland

Winners: individual
1987 Eric Bristow (England)
1989 Eric Bristow (England)
1991 John Lowe (England)
1993 Roland Schollen (Denmark)
1995 Martin Adams (England)
1997 Raymond Barneveld (Netherlands)
1999 Raymond Barneveld (Netherlands)
2001 Martin Adams (England)
2003 Raymond Barneveld (Netherlands)
2005 Dick van Dejk (Netherlands)

Most wins: Team (11) England: 1979, 1981, 1983, 1985, 1987, and as above. Individual (4) Eric Bristow (England) 1983, 1985, and as above.

DRAUGHTS

World championship

Held on a challenge basis.
1991–94 D Oldbury (Great Britain)
1994–2003 R King (Barbados)
2003–5 Alexander Georgiev (Russia)
2005– Alexey Chizhov (Russia)

British Open championship

The leading championship in Britain. First held in 1926; now takes place every two years.

Recent winners
1980 T Watson (Great Britain)
1982 T Watson (Great Britain)
1984 A Long (USA)
1986 H Devlin (Great Britain)
1988 D Oldbury (Great Britain)
1990 T Watson (Great Britain)
1992 H Devlin (Great Britain)
1994 W J Edwards (Great Britain)
1996 W J Edwards (Great Britain)
1998 Pat McCarthy (Ireland)
2000 W Doherty (Scotland)
2002 Ronald King (Barbados)
2004 Colin Young (Scotland)
2006 Mustafa Durdyev (Turkmenistan)

EQUESTRIAN EVENTS

World championships

Show-jumping championships first held in 1953 (for men) and 1965 (for women); since 1978 men and women have competed together and on equal terms. Team competition introduced in 1978; three-day event and dressage championships introduced in 1966. All three now held every four years.

Winners: show jumping – men
1953 Francisco Goyoago (Spain)
1954 Hans-Günter Winkler (W Germany)
1955 Hans-Günter Winkler (W Germany)
1956 Raimondo D'Inzeo (Italy)
1960 Raimondo D'Inzeo (Italy)
1966 Pierre d'Oriola (France)
1970 David Broome (Great Britain)
1974 Hartwig Steenken (W Germany)

Winners: show jumping – women
1965 Marion Coakes (Great Britain)
1970 Janou Lefèbvre (France)
1974 Janou Tissot (France)

Winners: individual
1994 Franke Sloothaak (Germany)
1998 Rodrigo Pessoa (Brazil)
2002 Dermot Lennon (Ireland)
2006 Jos Lansink (Belgium)

Winners: team
1994 Germany
1998 Germany
2002 France
2006 Netherlands

Winners: three-day event – individual
1990 Blyth Tait (New Zealand)
1994 Vaughn Jefferis (New Zealand)
1998 Blyth Tait (New Zealand)
2002 Jean Teulere (France)
2006 Zara Phillips (Great Britain)

Winners: three-day event – team
1986 Great Britain
1990 New Zealand
1994 Great Britain
1998 New Zealand
2002 USA
2006 Germany

Winners: dressage – individual
1990 Nicole Uphoft (W Germany)
1994 Isabell Werth (Germany)
1998 Isabell Werth (Germany)
2002 Nadine Capellmann (Germany)
2006 Isabell Werth (Germany)

Winners: dressage – team
1986	W Germany	1998	Germany
1990	W Germany	2002	Germany
1994	Germany	2006	Germany

Olympic Games

Gold medal winners: 2004 – individual
Three-day event
Leslie Law (Great Britain)

Dressage
Anky van Grunsven (Netherlands)

Jumping
Cian O'Connor (Ireland)

Gold medal winners: 2004 – team
Three-day event	France
Dressage	Germany
Jumping	Germany

FENCING

World championships

Held annually since 1921 (between 1921–35, known as European Championships). Not held in Olympic years.

Recent winners
Foil: individual – men

1986	Andrea Borella (Italy)
1987	Mathias Gey (W Germany)
1989	Alexander Koch (W Germany)
1990	Philippe Omnes (France)
1991	Ingo Weissenborn (Germany)
1993	Alexander Koch (Germany)
1994	Rolando Tucker (Cuba)
1995	Dimitriy Chevtchenko (Russia)
1997	Sergey Golubitsky (Ukraine)
1998	Sergey Golubitsky (Ukraine)
1999	Sergey Golubitsky (Ukraine)
2001	Salvatore Sanzo (Italy)
2002	Simone Vanni (Italy)
2003	Peter Joppich (Germany)
2005	Salvatore Sanzo (Italy)
2006	Peter Joppich (Germany)

Foil: team – men

1986	Italy	1997	France
1987	USSR	1998	Poland
1989	USSR	1999	France
1990	Italy	2001	France
1991	Cuba	2002	Germany
1993	Germany	2003	Italy
1994	Italy	2005	France
1995	Cuba	2006	France

Most wins: Individual (5) Alexander Romankov (USSR): 1974, 1977, 1979, 1982–3. Team (15) USSR: between 1959–89.

Foil: individual – women

1986	Anja Fichtel (W Germany)
1987	Elisabeta Tufan (Romania)
1989	Olga Velitschko (USSR)
1990	Anja Fichtel (W Germany)
1991	Giovanna Trillini (Italy)
1993	Francesca Bortolozzi (Italy)
1994	Reka Szabo-Lazar (Romania)
1995	Laura Badea (Romania)
1997	Giovanna Trillini (Italy)
1998	Sabine Bau (Germany)
1999	Valentina Vezzali (Italy)
2001	Valentina Vezzali (Italy)
2002	Svetlana Bojko (Russia)
2003	Valentina Vezzali (Italy)
2005	Valentina Vezzali (Italy)
2006	Margherita Granbassi (Italy)

Foil: team – women

1986	USSR	1997	Italy
1987	Hungary	1998	Italy
1989	W Germany	1999	Germany
1990	Italy	2001	Italy
1991	Cuba	2002	Russia
1993	Germany	2003	Italy
1994	Romania	2005	S Korea
1995	Italy	2006	Russia

Most wins: Individual (4) Valentina Vezzali (Italy), as above. Team (15) USSR: between 1956–86.

Epée: individual – men

1986	Philippe Riboud (France)
1987	Volker Fischer (W Germany)
1989	Manuel Pereira (Spain)
1990	Thomas Gerull (W Germany)
1991	Andrei Shuvalov (USSR)
1993	Pavel Kolobkov (Russia)
1994	Pavel Kolobkov (Russia)
1995	Eric Srecki (France)
1997	Eric Srecki (France)
1998	Hugues Obry (France)
1999	Arnd Schmitt (Germany)
2001	Paolo Milanoli (Italy)
2002	Pavel Kolobkov (Russia)
2003	Fabrice Jeannet (France)
2005	Pavel Kolobkov (Russia)
2006	Lei Wang (China)

Epée: team – men

1986	W Germany	1997	Cuba
1987	W Germany	1998	Hungary
1989	Italy	1999	France
1990	Italy	2001	Hungary
1991	USSR	2002	France
1993	Italy	2003	Russia
1994	Germany	2005	France
1995	Germany	2006	France

Most wins: Individual (4) Pavel Kolobkov (Russia), as above. Team (15) France: between 1934–83, 1999–2006.

Epée: individual – women

1989	Anja Straub (Switzerland)
1990	Taime Chappe (Cuba)
1991	Marianne Horvath (Hungary)
1993	Oksana Ermakova (Estonia)
1994	Laura Chiesa (Italy)
1995	Joanna Jakimiuk (Poland)
1997	Miraide Garcia-Soto (Cuba)
1998	Laura Flessel (France)
1999	Laura Flessel-Colovic (France)
2001	Claudia Bokel (Germany)
2002	Hyun Hee (Korea)
2003	Natalia Conrad (Ukraine)
2005	Danuta Dmowska (Poland)
2006	Timea Nagy (Hungary)

Epée: team – women

1989	Hungary	1998	France
1990	W Germany	1999	Hungary
1991	Hungary	2001	France
1993	Hungary	2002	Hungary
1994	Spain	2003	Russia
1995	Hungary	2005	France
1997	Hungary	2006	China

Most wins: Individual (2) Laura Flessel-Colovic (France), as above. Team (7); Hungary: as above.

Sabre: individual – men

1997	Stanislaw Pozdniakov (Russia)
1998	Luigo Tarantino (Italy)
1999	Damien Touya (France)
2001	Stanislaw Pozdniakov (Russia)
2002	Stanislaw Pozdniakov (Russia)
2003	Vladimir Lukashenko (Ukraine)
2005	Mihai Covaliu (Romania)
2006	Stanislaw Pozdniakov (Russia)

Sabre: team – men

1995	Italy	2002	Russia
1997	France	2003	Russia
1998	Hungary	2005	Russia
1999	France	2006	France
2001	Russia		

Sabre: individual – women

2001	Anne-Lise Touya (France)
2002	Tan Xue (China)
2003	Dorina Mihai (Romania)
2005	Anne-Lise Touya (France)
2006	Rebecca Ward (USA)

Sabre: team – women

1999	Italy	2005	USA
2001	Russia	2006	France
2002	Russia		
2003	Italy		

Most wins: Individual (4) Grigory Kirienko (Russia): 1989, 1991, 1993, 1995; Stanislaw Pozdniakov (Russia): as above. Team (20) Hungary: between 1930–98.

Olympic Games

Gold medal winners: 2004 – men

Individual foil
Brice Guyart (France)

Team foil
Italy

Individual epée
Marcel Fischer (Switzerland)

Team epée
France

Individual sabre
Aldo Montano (Italy)

Team sabre
France

Gold medal winners: 2004 – women

Individual foil
Valentina Vezzali (Italy)

Individual epée
Timea Nagy (Hungary)

Individual sabre
Mariel Zagunis (USA)

Team epée
Russia

FOOTBALL (AMERICAN)

National Football League (NFL)

In its existing form since 1970, the NFL consists of two 'conferences': the American Football Conference (AFC) and the National Football Conference (NFC). Each of these comprises three divisions (Eastern, Central, and Western), which are made up of either four or five teams. The season is played over sixteen games, with the championship of each conference being decided by two rounds of play-offs involving the three winners of the divisions, plus a number of 'wild cards', ie the best of the rest.

Super Bowl

First held in 1967; takes place each January; since 1971 an end of season meeting between the AFC and NFC champions.

1968 Green Bay Packers (NFL) 33, Oakland Raiders (AFL) 14
1969 New York Jets (AFL) 16, Baltimore Colts (NFL) 7
1970 Kansas City Chiefs (AFL) 23, Minnesota Vikings (NFL) 7
1971 Baltimore Colts (AFC) 16, Dallas Cowboys (NFC) 13
1972 Dallas Cowboys (NFC) 24, Miami Dolphins (AFC) 3
1973 Miami Dolphins (AFC) 14, Washington Redskins (NFC) 7
1974 Miami Dolphins (AFC) 24, Minnesota Vikings (NFL) 7
1975 Pittsburgh Steelers (AFC) 16, Minnesota Vikings (NFC) 6
1976 Pittsburgh Steelers (AFC) 21, Dallas Cowboys (NFC) 17
1977 Oakland Raiders (AFC) 32, Minnesota Vikings (NFC) 14
1978 Dallas Cowboys (NFC) 27, Denver Broncos (AFC) 10
1979 Pittsburgh Steelers (AFC) 35, Dallas Cowboys (NFC) 31
1980 Pittsburgh Steelers (AFC) 31, Los Angeles Rams (NFC) 19
1981 Oakland Raiders (AFC) 27, Philadelphia Eagles (NFC) 10
1982 San Francisco 49ers (NFC) 26, Cincinnati Bengals (AFC) 21
1983 Washington Redskins (NFC) 27, Miami Dolphins (AFC) 17
1984 Los Angeles Raiders (AFC) 38, Washington Redskins (NFC) 9
1985 San Francisco 49ers (NFC) 38, Miami Dolphins (AFC) 16
1986 Chicago Bears (NFC) 46, New England Patriots (AFC) 10
1987 New York Giants (NFC) 39, Denver Broncos (AFC) 20
1988 Washington Redskins (NFC) 42, Denver Broncos (AFC) 10
1989 San Francisco 49ers (NFC) 20, Cincinnati Bengals (AFC) 16
1990 San Francisco 49ers (NFC) 55, Denver Broncos (AFC) 10
1991 New York Giants (NFC) 20, Buffalo Bills (AFC) 19
1992 Washington Redskins (NFC) 37, Buffalo Bills (AFC) 24
1993 Dallas Cowboys (NFC) 52, Buffalo Bills (AFC) 17
1994 Dallas Cowboys (NFC) 30, Buffalo Bills (AFC) 13
1995 San Franscisco 49ers (NFC) 49, San Diego Chargers (NFC) 26
1996 Dallas Cowboys (NFC) 27, Pittsburgh Steelers (AFC) 17

American football field

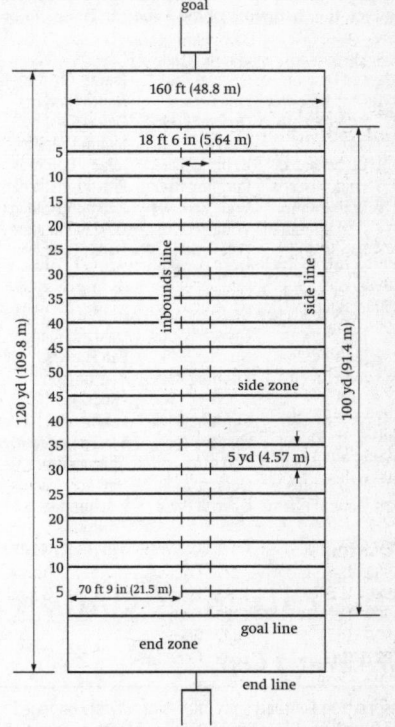

1997 Green Bay Packers (NFC) 35, New England Patriots (AFC) 21
1998 Denver Broncos (AFC) 31, Green Bay Packers (NFC) 24
1999 Denver Broncos (AFC) 34, Atlanta Falcons (NFC) 19
2000 St Louis Rams (NFC) 23, Tennessee Titans (AFC) 16
2001 Baltimore Ravens (AFC) 24, New York Giants (NFC) 7
2002 New England Patriots (AFC) 20, St Louis Rams (NFC) 17
2003 Tampa Bay Buccaneers (NFC) 48, Oakland Raiders (AFC) 21
2004 New England Patriots (AFC) 32, Carolina Panthers (NFC) 29
2005 New England Patriots (AFC) 24, Philadelphia Eagles (NFC) 21
2006 Pittsburgh Steelers (AFC) 21, Seattle Seahawks (NFC) 10

Most wins: (5) San Francisco 49ers: 1982, 1985, 1989–90, 1994; Dallas Cowboys: 1971, 1977, 1992–3, 1995; Pittsburgh Steelers: 1975–6, 1979–80, 2006.

Football (American) (continued)

Super Bowl most valuable player

The player judged to have made the most outstanding contribution in the Super Bowl – the end of season meeting between the champions of the American Football Conference (AFC) and the National Football Conference (NFC).

1969	Joe Namath	Quarter Back	New York Jets	1990 Joe Montana	Quarter Back	San Francisco 49ers
1970	Len Dawson	Quarter Back	Kansas City Chiefs	1991 Ottis Anderson	Running Back	New York Giants
1971	Chuck Howley	Line Backer	Dallas Cowboys	1992 Mark Rypien	Quarter Back	Washington Redskins
1972	Roger Staubach	Quarter Back	Dallas Cowboys			
1973	Jake Scott	Safety	Miami Dolphins	1993 Troy Aikman	Quarter Back	Dallas Cowboys
1974	Larry Csonka	Running Back	Miami Dolphins	1994 Emmit Smith	Running Back	Dallas Cowboys
1975	Franco Harris	Running Back	Pittsburgh Steelers	1995 Steve Young	Quarter Back	San Francisco 49ers
1976	Lynn Swann	Wide Receiver	Pittsburgh Steelers	1996 Larry Brown	Corner Back	Dallas Cowboys
1977	Fred Biletnikoff	Wide Receiver	Oakland Raiders	1997 Desmond Howard	Wide Receiver	Green Bay Packers
1978	Randy White	Defensive Tackle	Dallas Cowboys			
	Harvey Martin	Defensive End	Dallas Cowboys	1998 Terrell Davis	Running Back	Denver Broncos
1979	Terry Bradshaw	Quarter Back	Pittsburgh Steelers	1999 John Elway	Quarter Back	Denver Broncos
1980	Terry Bradshaw	Quarter Back	Pittsburgh Steelers	2000 Kurt Warner	Quarter Back	St Louis Rams
1981	Jim Plunkett	Quarterback	Oakland Raiders	2001 Ray Lewis	Line Back	Baltimore Ravens
1982	Joe Montana	Quarter Back	San Francisco 49ers	2002 Tom Brady	Quarter Back	New England Patriots
1983	John Riggins	Running Back	Washington Redskins	2003 Dexter Jackson	Defensive Back	Tampa Bay Buccaneers
1984	Marcus Allen	Running Back	Los Angeles Raiders	2004 Tom Brady	Quarter Back	New England Patriots
1985	Joe Montana	Quarter Back	San Francisco 49ers			
1986	Richard Dent	Defensive End	Chicago Bears	2005 Deion Branch	Wide Receiver	New England Patriots
1987	Phil Simms	Quarter Back	New York Giants			
1988	Doug Williams	Quarter Back	Washington Redskins	2006 Hines Ward	Wide Receiver	Pittsburgh Steelers
1989	Jerry Rice	Wide Receiver	San Francisco 49ers			

FOOTBALL (ASSOCIATION FOOTBALL/SOCCER)

FIFA World Cup

Association Football's premier event. First contested for the Jules Rimet Trophy in 1930; Brazil won outright after winning for the third time in 1970. Since then teams have competed for the FIFA (*Fédération Internationale de Football Association*) World Cup; held every four years.

	Winner	Score	Runner-up	Final held in
1930	Uruguay	4–2	Argentina	Montevideo
1934	Italy	2–1	Czechoslovakia	Rome
1938	Italy	4–2	Hungary	Paris
1950	Uruguay	2–1	Brazil	Rio de Janeiro
1954	W Germany	3–2	Hungary	Berne
1958	Brazil	5–2	Sweden	Stockholm
1962	Brazil	3–1	Czechoslovakia	Santiago
1966	England	4–2	W Germany	London
1970	Brazil	4–1	Italy	Mexico City
1974	W Germany	2–1	Holland	Munich
1978	Argentina	3–1	Holland	Buenos Aires
1982	Italy	3–1	W Germany	Madrid
1986	Argentina	3–2	W Germany	Mexico City
1990	W Germany	1–0	Argentina	Rome
1994	Brazil	0–0	Italy (3–2 pso*)	California
1998	France	3–0	Brazil	Paris
2002	Brazil	2–0	Germany	Yokohama
2006	Italy	0–0 (5–3 pso*)	France	Berlin

*penalty shoot-out

Most wins: (5) Brazil, as above.

Association football field

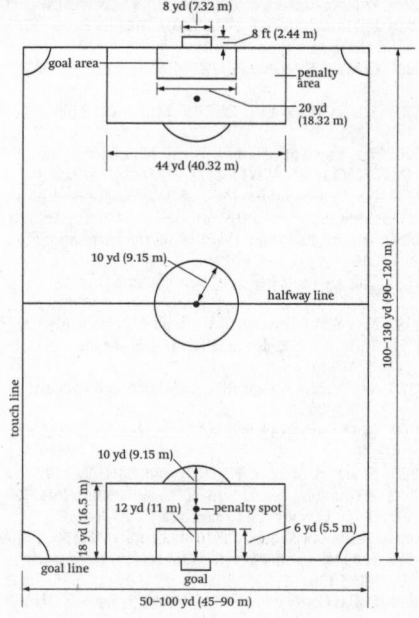

8 yd (7.32 m)
8 ft (2.44 m)
goal area
penalty area
20 yd (18.32 m)
44 yd (40.32 m)
10 yd (9.15 m)
halfway line
100–130 yd (90–120 m)
touch line
10 yd (9.15 m)
18 yd (16.5 m)
12 yd (11 m) — penalty spot
6 yd (5.5 m)
goal line
goal
50–100 yd (45–90 m)

European Champions Cup

The leading club competition in Europe. Open to the League champions of countries affiliated to UEFA (Union of European Football Associations); commonly known as the 'European Cup'. Inaugurated in the 1955–6 season; played annually.

Recent winners

1985	Juventus	1–0	Liverpool
1986[b]	Steaua Bucharest	0–0	Barcelona
1987	FC Porto	2–1	Bayern Munich
1988[c]	PSV Eindhoven	0–0	Benfica
1989	AC Milan	4–0	Steaua Bucharest
1990	AC Milan	1–0	Benfica
1991[d]	Red Star Belgrade	0–0	Olympique Marseilles
1992	Barcelona	1–0	Sampdoria
1993	Olympique Marseilles[f]	1–0	AC Milan
1994	AC Milan	4–0	Barcelona
1995	Ajax	1–0	AC Milan
1996[e]	Juventus	1–1	Ajax
1997	Borussia Dortmund	3–1	Juventus
1998	Real Madrid	1–0	Juventus
1999	Manchester United	2–1	Bayern Munich
2000	Real Madrid	3–0	Valencia
2001[g]	Bayern Munich	1–1	Valencia
2002	Real Madrid	2–1	Bayer Leverkusen
2003	AC Milan[h]	0–0	Juventus
2004	FC Porto	3–0	AC Monaco
2005[i]	Liverpool	3–3	AC Milan
2006	Barcelona	2–1	Arsenal

[a] Liverpool won 4–2 on penalties.
[b] Steaua won 2–0 on penalties.
[c] Eindhoven won 6–5 on penalties.
[d] Red Star won 5–3 on penalties.
[e] Juventus won 4–2 on penalties.
[f] Victory later cancelled following bribery allegations.
[g] Bayern Munich won 5–4 on penalties.
[h] AC Milan won 3–2 on penalties.
[i] Liverpool won 3–2 on penalties.

Most wins: (9) Real Madrid (Spain): 1956–60, 1966, 1998, 2000, 2002.

South American championship

First held in 1916, for South American national sides. Discontinued in 1967, but revived eight years later; now played every two years; known as the Copa America.

Recent winners

1983	Uruguay
1987	Uruguay
1989	Brazil
1991	Argentina
1993	Argentina
1995	Uruguay
1997	Brazil
1999	Brazil
2001	Colombia
2004	Brazil

Most wins: (14) Uruguay: 1916–17, 1920, 1923–4, 1926, 1935, 1942, 1956, 1959, 1967, and as above; Argentina: 1921, 1925, 1927, 1929, 1937, 1941, 1945–7, 1955, 1957, 1959, and as above.

European Cup-Winners' Cup

Annual club competition, open to the main cup winners from all the UEFA countries; inaugurated in 1961, when the final was played over two legs. Since 1962 there has been a single game final. The competition ceased in 1999.

Recent winners

1986	Dynamo Kiev	1993	Parma
1987	Ajax	1994	Arsenal
1988	Mechelen	1995	Real Zaragoza
1989	Barcelona	1996	Paris St Germain
1990	Sampdoria	1997	Barcelona
1991	Manchester United	1998	Chelsea
1992	Werder Bremen	1999	Lazio

Most wins: (4) Barcelona: 1979, 1982, 1989, 1997.

UEFA Cup

Originally the International Industries Fairs Inter-Cities Cup (more commonly the 'Fairs Cup'). It was first contested in 1955, and became the UEFA Cup in 1971. Each participating nation is allotted a certain number of team places. The final is played over two legs.

Recent winners

1986	Real Madrid	1997	Schalke
1987	IFK Gothenburg	1998	Inter Milan
1988	Bayer Leverkusen	1999	Parma
1989	Napoli	2000	Galatasaray
1990	Juventus	2001	Liverpool
1991	Inter Milan	2002	Feyenoord
1992	Ajax	2003	FC Porto
1993	Juventus	2004	Valencia
1994	Inter Milan	2005	CSKA Moscow
1995	Parma	2006	Sevilla
1996	Bayern Munich		

Most wins: (3) Barcelona: 1958, 1960, 1966; Inter Milan, as above.

European championship

Held every four years since 1960; qualifying group matches held over the two years preceding the final.

	Winner	Score	Runner-up	Final held in
1960	USSR	2–1	Yugoslavia	Paris
1964	Spain	2–1	USSR	Madrid
1968[a]	Italy	2–1	Yugoslavia	Rome
1972	W Germany	3–0	USSR	Brussels
1976[b]	Czechoslovakia	2–2	W Germany	Belgrade
1980	W Germany	2–1	Belgium	Rome
1984	France	2–0	Spain	Paris
1988	Holland	2–0	USSR	Munich
1992	Denmark	2–0	Germany	Gothenburg
1996	Germany	2–1	Czech Republic	London
2000	France	2–1	Italy	Rotterdam
2004	Greece	1–0	Portugal	Lisbon

[a] Replay after 1–1 draw.
[b] Czechoslovakia won 5–2 on penalties.

Most wins: (3) Germany: as above.

Football League

The oldest league in the world, founded in 1888; consists of four divisions; the current complement of 92 teams achieved in 1950. Before the start of the 1992–93 season, the 22 teams of the 1st division voted to form the FA Premier League, divisions 2, 3, and 4 becoming League divisions 1, 2, and 3 respectively; the system of promotion and relegation remained unchanged. From the start of the 2004–5 season, the 1st division was renamed the Championship, and divisions 2 and 3 became Leagues 1 and 2 respectively. Sponsors of the Premier League have been Carling (1993–2001), Barclaycard (2001–4), and Barclays (2004–8).

League champions

1888–89	Preston North End
1889–90	Preston North End
1890–91	Everton
1891–92	Sunderland
1892–93	Sunderland
1893–94	Aston Villa
1894–95	Sunderland
1895–96	Aston Villa
1896–97	Aston Villa
1897–98	Sheffield United
1898–99	Aston Villa
1899–1900	Aston Villa
1900–01	Liverpool
1901–02	Sunderland
1902–03	Sheffield Wednesday
1903–04	Sheffield Wednesday
1904–05	Newcastle United
1905–06	Liverpool
1906–07	Newcastle United
1907–08	Manchester United
1908–09	Newcastle United
1909–10	Aston Villa
1910–11	Manchester United
1911–12	Blackburn Rovers
1912–13	Sunderland
1913–14	Blackburn Rovers
1914–15	Everton
1919–20	West Bromwich Albion
1920–21	Burnley
1921–22	Liverpool
1922–23	Liverpool
1923–24	Huddersfield Town
1924–25	Huddersfield Town
1925–26	Huddersfield Town
1926–27	Newcastle United
1927–28	Everton
1928–29	Sheffield Wednesday
1929–30	Sheffield Wednesday
1930–31	Arsenal
1931–32	Everton
1932–33	Arsenal
1933–34	Arsenal
1934–35	Arsenal
1935–36	Sunderland
1936–37	Manchester City
1937–38	Arsenal
1938–39	Everton
1946–47	Liverpool
1947–48	Arsenal
1948–49	Portsmouth
1949–50	Portsmouth
1950–51	Tottenham Hotspur
1951–52	Manchester United
1952–53	Arsenal
1953–54	Wolverhampton Wanderers
1954–55	Chelsea
1955–56	Manchester United
1956–57	Manchester United
1957–58	Wolverhampton Wanderers
1958–59	Wolverhampton Wanderers
1959–60	Burnley
1960–61	Tottenham Hotspur
1961–62	Ipswich Town
1962–63	Everton
1963–64	Liverpool
1964–65	Manchester United
1965–66	Liverpool
1966–67	Manchester United
1967–68	Manchester City
1968–69	Leeds United
1969–70	Everton
1970–71	Arsenal
1971–72	Derby County
1972–73	Liverpool
1973–74	Leeds United
1974–75	Derby County
1975–76	Liverpool
1976–77	Liverpool
1977–78	Nottingham Forest
1978–79	Liverpool
1979–80	Liverpool
1980–81	Aston Villa
1981–82	Liverpool
1982–83	Liverpool
1983–84	Liverpool
1984–85	Everton
1985–86	Liverpool
1986–87	Everton
1987–88	Liverpool
1988–89	Arsenal
1989–90	Liverpool
1990–91	Arsenal
1991–92	Leeds United
1992–93	Manchester United
1993–94	Manchester United
1994–95	Blackburn Rovers
1995–96	Manchester United
1996–97	Manchester United
1997–98	Arsenal
1998–99	Manchester United
1999–2000	Manchester United
2000–1	Manchester United
2001–2	Arsenal
2002–3	Manchester United
2003–4	Arsenal
2004–5	Chelsea
2005–6	Chelsea

Most wins: (18) Liverpool: 1901, 1906, 1922–3, 1947, 1964, 1966, 1973, 1976–7, 1979–80, 1982–4, 1986, 1988, 1990.

Football League Cup

Inaugurated in 1961, it is competed for by the 92 clubs of the Football League. From 1982 to 1986 it was known as the Milk Cup; 1986–90 as the Littlewoods Cup; 1990–2 as the Rumbelows Cup; 1992–3 as the Coca-Cola Cup; 1998–9 as the Worthington Cup; and from 2003 as the Carling Cup.

Recent winners

1981	Liverpool
1982	Liverpool
1983	Liverpool
1984	Liverpool
1985	Norwich City
1986	Oxford United
1987	Arsenal
1988	Luton Town
1989	Nottingham Forest
1990	Nottingham Forest
1991	Sheffield Wednesday
1992	Manchester United
1993	Arsenal
1994	Aston Villa
1995	Liverpool
1996	Aston Villa
1997	Leicester City
1998	Chelsea
1999	Tottenham Hotspur
2000	Leicester City
2001	Liverpool
2002	Blackburn Rovers
2003	Liverpool
2004	Middlesbrough
2005	Chelsea
2006	Manchester United

Most wins: (7) Liverpool, as above.

Football Association Challenge Cup

The world's oldest club knockout competition (the 'FA cup'), held annually, it is open to both League and non-League teams; first contested in the 1871–2 season; first final at the Kennington Oval on 16 March 1872; first winners were the Wanderers. Played at Wembley since 1923.

1871–72	Wanderers	1–0	Royal Engineers
1872–73	Wanderers	2–0	Oxford University
1873–74	Oxford University	2–0	Royal Engineers
1874–75	Royal Engineers	1–1, 2–0	Old Etonians
1875–76	Wanderers	1–1, 3–0	Old Etonians
1876–77	Wanderers	2–1	Oxford University
1877–78	Wanderers	3–1	Royal Engineers
1878–79	Old Etonians	1–0	Clapham Rovers
1879–80	Clapham Rovers	1–0	Oxford University
1880–81	Old Carthusians	3–0	Old Etonians
1881–82	Old Etonians	1–0	Blackburn Rovers
1882–83	Blackburn Olympic	2–1	Old Etonians
1883–84	Blackburn Rovers	2–1	Queen's Park
1884–85	Blackburn Rovers	2–0	Queen's Park
1885–86	Blackburn Rovers	0–0, 2–0	West Bromwich Albion
1886–97	Aston Villa	2–0	West Bromwich Albion
1887–88	West Bromwich Albion	2–1	Preston North End
1888–89	Preston North End	3–0	Wolverhampton Wanderers
1889–90	Blackburn Rovers	6–1	Sheffield Wednesday
1890–91	Blackburn Rovers	3–1	Notts County
1891–92	West Bromwich Albion	3–0	Aston Villa
1892–93	Wolverhampton Wanderers	1–0	Everton
1893–94	Notts County	4–1	Bolton Wanderers
1894–95	Aston Villa	1–0	West Bromwich Albion
1895–96	Sheffield Wednesday	2–1	Wolverhampton Wanderers
1896–97	Aston Villa	3–2	Everton
1897–98	Nottingham Forest	3–1	Derby County
1898–99	Sheffield United	4–1	Derby County
1899–1900	Bury	4–0	Southampton
1900–01	Tottenham Hotspur	2–2, 3–1	Sheffield United
1901–02	Sheffield United	1–1, 2–1	Southampton
1902–03	Bury	6–0	Derby County
1903–04	Manchester City	1–0	Bolton Wanderers
1904–05	Aston Villa	2–0	Newcastle United
1905–06	Everton	1–0	Newcastle United
1906–07	Sheffield Wednesday	2–1	Everton
1907–08	Wolverhampton Wanderers	3–1	Newcastle United
1908–09	Manchester United	1–0	Bristol City
1909–10	Newcastle United	1–1, 2–0	Barnsley
1910–11	Bradford City	0–0, 1–0	Newcastle United
1911–12	Barnsley	0–0, 1–0	West Bromwich Albion
1912–13	Aston Villa	1–0	Sunderland
1913–14	Burnley	1–0	Liverpool
1914–15	Sheffield United	3–0	Chelsea
1919–20	Aston Villa	1–0	Huddersfield Town
1920–21	Tottenham Hotspur	1–0	Wolverhampton Wanderers
1921–22	Huddersfield Town	1–0	Preston North End
1922–23	Bolton Wanderers	2–0	West Ham United
1923–24	Newcastle United	2–0	Aston Villa
1924–25	Sheffield United	1–0	Cardiff City
1925–26	Bolton Wanderers	1–0	Manchester City
1926–27	Cardiff City	1–0	Arsenal
1927–28	Blackburn Rovers	3–1	Huddersfield Town
1928–29	Bolton Wanderers	2–0	Portsmouth
1929–30	Arsenal	2–0	Huddersfield Town
1930–31	West Bromwich Albion	2–1	Birmingham City
1931–32	Newcastle United	2–1	Arsenal
1932–33	Everton	3–0	Manchester City
1933–34	Manchester City	2–1	Portsmouth
1934–35	Sheffield Wednesday	4–2	West Bromwich Albion
1935–36	Arsenal	1–0	Sheffield United

Football Association Challenge Cup (continued)

	Winners	Score	Runner-up
1936–37	Sunderland	3–1	Preston North End
1937–38	Preston North End	1–0	Huddersfield Town
1938–39	Portsmouth	4–1	Wolverhampton Wanderers
1945–46	Derby County	4–1	Charlton Athletic
1946–47	Charlton Athletic	1–0	Burnley
1947–48	Manchester United	4–2	Blackpool
1948–49	Wolverhampton Wanderers	3–1	Leicester City
1949–50	Arsenal	2–0	Liverpool
1950–51	Newcastle United	2–0	Blackpool
1951–52	Newcastle United	1–0	Arsenal
1952–53	Blackpool	4–3	Bolton Wanderers
1953–54	West Bromwich Albion	3–2	Preston North End
1954–55	Newcastle United	3–1	Manchester City
1955–56	Manchester City	3–1	Birmingham City
1956–57	Aston Villa	2–1	Manchester United
1957–58	Bolton Wanderers	2–0	Manchester United
1958–59	Nottingham Forest	2–1	Luton Town
1959–60	Wolverhampton Wanderers	3–0	Blackburn Rovers
1960–61	Tottenham Hotspur	2–0	Leicester City
1961–62	Tottenham Hotspur	3–1	Burnley
1962–63	Manchester United	3–1	Leicester City
1963–64	West Ham United	3–2	Preston North End
1964–65	Liverpool	2–1	Leeds United
1965–66	Everton	3–2	Sheffield Wednesday
1966–67	Tottenham Hotspur	2–1	Chelsea
1967–68	West Bromwich Albion	1–0	Everton
1968–69	Manchester City	1–0	Leicester City
1969–70	Chelsea	2–2, 2–1	Leeds United
1970–71	Arsenal	2–1	Liverpool
1971–72	Leeds United	1–0	Arsenal
1972–73	Sunderland	1–0	Leeds United
1973–74	Liverpool	3–0	Newcastle United
1974–75	West Ham United	2–0	Fulham
1975–76	Southampton	1–0	Manchester United
1976–77	Manchester United	2–1	Liverpool
1977–78	Ipswich Town	1–0	Arsenal
1978–79	Arsenal	3–2	Manchester United
1979–80	West Ham United	1–0	Arsenal
1980–81	Tottenham Hotspur	1–1, 3–2	Manchester City
1981–82	Tottenham Hotspur	1–1, 1–0	Queen's Park Rangers
1982–83	Manchester United	2–2, 4–0	Brighton & Hove Albion
1983–84	Everton	2–0	Watford
1984–85	Manchester United	1–0	Everton
1985–86	Liverpool	3–1	Everton
1986–87	Coventry City	3–2	Tottenham Hotspur
1987–88	Wimbledon	1–0	Liverpool
1988–89	Liverpool	3–2	Everton
1989–90	Manchester United	3–3, 1–0	Crystal Palace
1990–91	Tottenham Hotspur	2–1	Nottingham Forest
1991–92	Liverpool	2–0	Sunderland
1992–93	Arsenal	1–1, 2–1	Sheffield Wednesday
1993–94	Manchester United	4–0	Chelsea
1994–95	Everton	1–0	Manchester United
1995–96	Manchester United	1–0	Liverpool
1996–97	Chelsea	2–0	Middlesbrough
1997–98	Arsenal	2–0	Newcastle United
1998–99	Manchester United	2–0	Newcastle United
1999–2000	Chelsea	1–0	Aston Villa
2000–1	Liverpool	2–1	Arsenal
2001–2	Arsenal	2–0	Chelsea
2002–3	Arsenal	1–0	Southampton
2003–4	Manchester United	3–0	Millwall
2004–5	Arsenal	0–0, 5–4	Manchester United
2005–6	Liverpool	3–3, 3–1	West Ham United

Most wins: (11) Manchester United, as above.

Scottish Premier League

Formed in 1890, with a second division added in 1893. The present format (Premier Division, Division 1, Division 2) was arrived at in 1975.

Recent winners

1985–86	Celtic
1986–87	Rangers
1987–88	Celtic
1988–89	Rangers
1989–90	Rangers
1990–91	Rangers
1991–92	Rangers
1992–93	Rangers
1993–94	Rangers
1994–95	Rangers
1995–96	Rangers
1996–97	Rangers
1997–98	Celtic
1998–9	Rangers
1999–2000	Rangers
2000–1	Celtic
2001–2	Celtic
2002–3	Rangers
2003–4	Celtic
2004–5	Rangers
2005–6	Celtic

Most wins: (52) Rangers.

Scottish FA Cup

First played in 1874; held at Hampden Park.

Recent winners

1990	Aberdeen
1991	Motherwell
1992	Rangers
1993	Rangers
1994	Dundee United
1995	Celtic
1996	Rangers
1997	Kilmarnock
1998	Heart of Midlothian
1999	Rangers
2000	Rangers
2001	Celtic
2002	Rangers
2003	Rangers
2004	Celtic
2005	Celtic
2006	Heart of Midlothian

Most wins: (33) Celtic.

Clubs of the English Football League

Team	Nickname	Ground	Team	Nickname	Ground
Accrington Stanley	Stanley	Fraser Eagle Stad.	Luton Town	Hatters	Kenilworth Road
			Macclesfield Town	Silkmen	Mose Rose
Arsenal	Gunners	Emirates Stad.	Manchester City	Blues/	City of
Aston Villa	Villans	Villa Park		Citizens	Manchester
Barnet	Bees	Underhill Stad.			Stad.
Barnsley	Tykes	Oakwell	Manchester United	Red Devils	Old Trafford
Birmingham City	Blues	St Andrews	Mansfield Town	Stags	Field Mill
Blackburn Rovers	Blue-and-Whites	Ewood Park	Middlesbrough	Boro	Cellnet Riverside Stad.
Blackpool	Seasiders	Bloomfield Road	Millwall	Lions	The New Den
Bolton Wanderers	Trotters	Reebok Stad.	Newcastle United	Magpies/	St James' Park
Boston United	Pilgrims	York Street Stad.		The Toon	
Bournemouth	Cherries	Dean Court	Northampton Town	Cobblers	Sixfields Stad.
Bradford City	Bantams	Bradford and Bingley Stad.	Norwich City	Canaries	Carrow Road
			Nottingham Forest	Reds	City Ground
Brentford	Bees	Griffin Park	Notts County	Magpies	Meadow Lane
Brighton and Hove Albion	Seagulls	Withdean	Oldham Athletic	Latics	Boundary Park
			Peterborough United	Posh	London Road
Bristol City	Robins	Ashton Gate	Plymouth Argyle	Pilgrims	Home Park
Bristol Rovers	Pirates	Memorial Ground	Portsmouth	Pompey	Fratton Park
			Port Vale	Valiants	Vale Park
Burnley	Clarets	Turf Moor	Preston North End	Lillywhites	Deepdale
Bury	Shakers	Gigg Lane	Queen's Park Rangers	Superhoops	Loftus Road
Cardiff City	Bluebirds	Ninian Park	Reading	Royals	Madejski Stad.
Carlisle United	Cumbrians	Brunton Park	Rochdale	Dale	Spotland
Charlton Athletic	Addicks	The Valley	Rotherham United	Millers	Millmoor
Chelsea	Blues	Stamford Bridge	Scunthorpe United	Irons	Glanford Park
Cheltenham Town	Robins	Whaddon Road	Sheffield United	Blades	Bramall Lane
Chester City	Blues	Saunders Honda Stad.	Sheffield Wednesday	Owls	Hillsborough
			Shrewsbury Town	Shrews	Gay Meadow
Chesterfield	Spireites	Saltergate	Southampton	Saints	Friends Provident St Mary's Stad.
Colchester United	'U's	Layer Road			
Coventry City	Sky Blues	Ricoh Arena	Southend United	Shrimpers	Roots Hall
Crewe Alexandra	Railwaymen	Gresty Road	Stockport County	Hatters	Edgeley Park
Crystal Palace	Eagles	Selhurst Park	Stoke City	Potters	Britannia Ground
Darlington	Quakers	Williamson Motors Stad.	Sunderland	Black Cats/ Rokerites	Stad. of Light
Derby County	Rams	Pride Park	Swansea City	Swans	Liberty Stad.
Doncaster Rovers	Rovers	Belle Vue	Swindon Town	Robins	County Ground
Everton	Toffeemen	Goodison Park	Torquay United	Gulls	Plainmoor
Fulham	Cottagers	Craven Cottage	Tottenham Hotspur	Spurs	White Hart Lane
Gillingham	Gills	Priestfield	Tranmere Rovers	Rovers	Prenton Park
Grimsby Town	Mariners	Blundell Park	Walsall	Saddlers	Bescot Stad.
Hartlepool United	Pool	Victoria Ground	Watford	Hornets	Vicarage Road
Hereford United	Bulls	Edgar Street Athletic Ground	West Bromwich Albion	Baggies	The Hawthorns
			West Ham United	Hammers	Boleyn Ground (Upton Park)
Huddersfield Town	Terriers	MacAlpine Stad.	Wigan Athletic	Latics	JJB Stad.
Hull City	Tigers	KC Stad.	Wolverhampton Wanderers	Wolves	Molineux
Ipswich Town	Blues/Tractor Boys	Portman Road	Wrexham	Robins	Racecourse Ground
Leeds United	The Whites	Elland Road			
Leicester City	Foxes	Walkers Stad.	Wycombe Wanderers	Chairboys	Causeway Stad.
Leyton Orient	'O's	Matchroom Stad.	Yeovil Town	Glovers	Huish Park
Lincoln City	Imps	Sincil Bank			
Liverpool	Reds	Anfield	*Stad. = Stadium*		

SPORTS AND GAMES

FOOTBALL (AUSTRALIAN)

Australian Football League

Known as the Victoria Football League until 1987, when teams from Western Australia and Queensland joined the league. The top prize is the annual VFL/AFL Premiership Trophy.

Premiership Trophy

First contested in 1897 and won by Essendon.

Recent winners

1991	Hawthorn	1999	North Melbourne
1992	West Coast Eagles	2000	Essendon
1993	Essendon	2001	Brisbane Lions
1994	West Coast Eagles	2002	Brisbane Lions
1995	Carlton	2003	Brisbane Lions
1996	North Melbourne	2004	Port Adelaide
1997	Adelaide Crows	2005	Sydney Swans
1998	Adelaide Crows	2006	West Coast Eagles

Most wins: (16) Carlton: 1906–8, 1914–15, 1938, 1945, 1947, 1968, 1970, 1972, 1979, 1981–2, 1987, 1995.

Australian football field

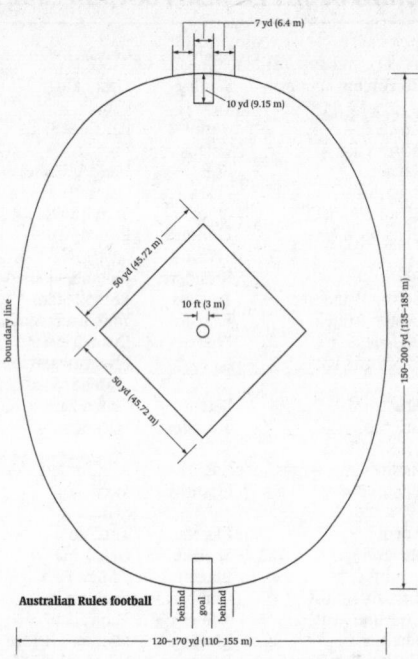

Australian Rules football

FOOTBALL (GAELIC)

All-Ireland championship

First held in 1887. Takes place in Dublin in September each year.

Recent winners

1989	Cork	1998	Galway
1990	Cork	1999	Meath
1991	Down	2000	Kerry
1992	Donegal	2001	Galway
1993	Derry	2002	Armagh
1994	Down	2003	Tyrone
1995	Dublin	2004	Kerry
1996	Meath	2005	Tyrone
1997	Kerry	2006	Kerry

Most wins: (34) Kerry: 1903–4, 1909, 1913–14, 1924, 1926, 1929–32, 1937, 1939–41, 1946, 1953, 1955, 1959, 1962, 1969–70, 1975, 1978–81, 1984–6, 1997, 2000, 2004, 2006.

GLIDING

World championships

First held in 1937. Current classes are Open, Standard, and 15 metres. The Open class is the principal event, held every two years until 1978 and again since 1981.

Recent winners: open category

1974	George Moffat (USA)
1976	George Lee (Great Britain)
1978	George Lee (Great Britain)
1981	George Lee (Great Britain)
1983	Ingo Renner (Australia)
1985	Ingo Renner (Australia)
1987	Ingo Renner (Australia)
1989	Claude Lopitaux (France)
1991	Janusz Centka (Poland)
1993	Andy Davis (Great Britain)
1995	Raymond Lynskey (New Zealand)
1997	Gerard Lherm (France)
1999	Holger Karow (Germany)
2001	Oscar Goudriaan (South Africa)
2003	Holger Karow (Germany)
2005	*Not held*
2006	Michael Sommer (Germany)

Most wins: (3) George Lee and Ingo Renner: as above.

GOLF

Open

First held at Prestwick, UK, in 1860, and won by Willie Park. Takes place annually; regarded as the world's leading golf tournament.

Recent winners

1987	Nick Faldo (Great Britain)
1988	Severiano Ballesteros (Spain)
1989	Mark Calcavecchia (USA)
1990	Nick Faldo (Great Britain)
1991	Ian Baker-Finch (Australia)
1992	Nick Faldo (Great Britain)
1993	Greg Norman (Australia)
1994	Nick Price (Zimbabwe)
1995	John Daly (USA)
1996	Tom Lehman (USA)
1997	Justin Leonard (USA)
1998	Mark O'Meara (USA)
1999	Paul Lawrie (Great Britain)
2000	Tiger Woods (USA)
2001	Tiger Woods (USA)
2002	Ernie Els (South Africa)
2003	Ben Curtis (USA)
2004	Todd Hamilton (USA)
2005	Tiger Woods (USA)
2006	Tiger Woods (USA)

Most wins: (6) Harry Vardon (Great Britain): 1896, 1898–9, 1903, 1911, 1914.

United States Open

First held at Newport, Rhode Island, in 1895, and won by Horace Rawlins. Takes place annually.

Recent winners
1993 Lee Janzen (USA)
1994 Ernie Els (South Africa)
1995 Corey Pavin (USA)
1996 Steve Jones (USA)
1997 Ernie Els (South Africa)
1998 Lee Janzen (USA)
1999 Payne Stewart (USA)
2000 Tiger Woods (USA)
2001 Retief Goosen (South Africa)
2002 Tiger Woods (USA)
2003 Jim Furyk (USA)
2004 Retief Goosen (South Africa)
2005 Michael Campbell (New Zealand)
2006 Geoff Ogilvy (Australia)

Most wins: (4) Willie Anderson (USA): 1901, 1903–5; Bobby Jones (USA): 1923, 1926, 1929–30; Ben Hogan (USA): 1948, 1950–1, 1953; Jack Nicklaus (USA): 1962, 1967, 1972, 1980.

US Masters

First held in 1934. Takes place at the Augusta National course in Georgia every April.

Recent winners
1993 Bernard Langer (Germany)
1994 José María Olázabal (Spain)
1995 Ben Crenshaw (USA)
1996 Nick Faldo (Great Britain)
1997 Tiger Woods (USA)
1998 Mark O'Meara (USA)
1999 José María Olázabal (Spain)
2000 Vijay Singh (Fiji)
2001 Tiger Woods (USA)
2002 Tiger Woods (USA)
2003 Mike Weir (Canada)
2004 Phil Mickelson (USA)
2005 Tiger Woods (USA)
2006 Phil Mickelson (USA)

Most wins: (6) Jack Nicklaus (USA): 1963, 1965–6, 1972, 1975, 1986.

United States PGA championship

The last of the season's four 'Majors'; first held in 1916, and a match-play event until 1958. Held annually.

Recent winners
1992 Nick Price (Zimbabwe)
1993 Paul Azinger (USA)
1994 Nick Price (Zimbabwe)
1995 Steve Elkington (Australia)
1996 Mark Brooks (USA)
1997 Davis Love III (USA)
1998 Vijay Singh (Fiji)

1999 Tiger Woods (USA)
2000 Tiger Woods (USA)
2001 David Toms (USA)
2002 Rich Beem (USA)
2003 Shaun Micheel (USA)
2004 Vijay Singh (Fiji)
2005 Phil Mickelson (USA)
2006 Tiger Woods (USA)

Most wins: (5) Walter Hagen (USA): 1921, 1924–7; Jack Nicklaus (USA): 1963, 1971, 1973, 1975, 1980.

Ryder Cup

The leading international team tournament, first held at Worcester, Massachusetts, in 1927. Takes place every two years between teams from the USA and Europe (Great Britain 1927–71; Great Britain and Ireland 1973–7).

Recent winners
1985	Europe	$16^1/_2$–$11^1/_2$
1987	Europe	15–13
1989	Drawn	14–14
1991	USA	$14^1/_2$–$13^1/_2$
1993	USA	15–13
1995	Europe	$14^1/_2$–$13^1/_2$
1997	Europe	$14^1/_2$–$13^1/_2$
1999	USA	$14^1/_2$–$13^1/_2$
2001	*not held*	
2002	Europe	$15^1/_2$–$12^1/_2$
2004	Europe	$18^1/_2$–$9^1/_2$
2006	Europe	$18^1/_2$–$9^1/_2$

Wins: (24) USA: during 1927–99. (3), Great Britain: 1929, 1933, 1957. (7), Europe: during 1985–2006, (2), Drawn: 1969, 1989.

GREYHOUND RACING

Greyhound Derby

The top race of the British season, first held in 1927. Run at the White City every year (except 1940) until its closure in 1985; since then all races run at Wimbledon.

Recent winners
1989 Lartigue Note
1990 Slippy Blue
1991 Ballinderry Ash
1992 Farloe Melody
1993 Arfur Daley
1994 Ringa Hustle
1995 Moaning Lad
1996 Shanless Slippy
1997 Some Picture
1998 Toms The Best
1999 Chart King
2000 Rapid Ranger
2001 Rapid Ranger

2002 Allen Gift
2003 Droopys Hewitt
2004 Droopys Scholes
2005 Westmead Hawk
2006 Westmead Hawk

Most wins: (2) Mick the Miller: 1929–30; Patricia's Hope: 1972–3; Rapid Ranger: 2000–1; Westmead Hawk: 2005–6.

GYMNASTICS

World championships

First held in 1903. Held every four years, 1922–78; since 1979, usually every two years.

Recent winners: individual combined exercises – men
1985 Yuriy Korolev (USSR)
1987 Dmitri Belozerchev (USSR)
1989 Igor Korobichensky (USSR)
1991 Grigoriy Misutin (USSR)
1993 Vitaly Shcherbo (Belarus)
1994 Ivan Ivankov (Belarus)
1995 Li Xiaoshuang (China)
1997 Ivan Ivankova (Belarus)
1999 Nikolay Krukov (Russia)
2001 Feng Jing (China)
2003 Paul Hamm (USA)
2005 Hiroyuki Tomita (Japan)
2006 Yang Wei (China)

Recent winners: team – men
1983	China	1995	China
1985	USSR	1997	China
1987	USSR	1999	China
1989	USSR	2001	Belarus
1991	USSR	2003	China
1994	China	2006	China

Most wins: Individual (2) Marco Torrès (France): 1909, 1913; Peter Sumi (Yugoslavia): 1922, 1926; Dmitri Belozerchev: 1983, 1987; Yuriy Korolev as above. Team (8) USSR: 1954, 1958, 1981 and as above.

Recent winners: individual combined exercises – women
1981 Olga Bitcherova (USSR)
1983 Natalia Yurchenko (USSR)
1985 Yelena Shoushounova (USSR) and Oksana Omeliantchuk (USSR)
1987 Aurelia Dobre (Romania)
1989 Svetlana Boginskaya (USSR)
1991 Kim Zmeskal (USA)
1993 Shannon Miller (USA)
1994 Shannon Miller (USA)
1995 Lilia Podkopayeva (Ukraine)
1997 Svetlana Khorkina (Russia)
1999 Maria Olaru (Romania)
2001 Svetlana Khorkina (Russia)
2003 Svetlana Khorkina (Russia)
2005 Chellsie Memmel (USA)
2006 Vanessa Ferrari (Italy)

Gymnastics (continued)

Recent winners team – women

1983	USSR	1995	Romania
1985	USSR	1997	Romania
1987	Romania	1999	Romania
1989	USSR	2001	Romania
1991	USSR	2003	USA
1994	Romania	2006	China

Most wins: Individual (3) Svetlana Khorkina (Russia): as above. Team (10) USSR: 1954, 1958, 1970, 1974, 1978, 1981 and as above.

Olympic Games

Gold medal winners: 2004

Combined exercises: men
Individual
Paul Hamm (USA)

Team
Japan

Gold medal winners: 2004

Combined exercises: women
Individual
Carly Patterson (USA)

Team
Romania

HANDBALL

World championships

First men's championships held in 1938, both indoors and outdoors (latter discontinued in 1966). First women's outdoor championships in 1949 (discontinued in 1960); first women's indoor championships in 1957.

Winners: indoors – men

1964	Romania
1967	Czechoslovakia
1970	Romania
1974	Romania
1978	W Germany
1982	USSR
1986	Yugoslavia
1990	Sweden
1993	Russia
1995	France
1997	Russia
1999	Sweden
2001	France
2003	Croatia
2005	Spain

Winners: outdoors – men

1938	Germany
1948	Sweden
1952	W Germany
1955	W Germany
1959	E/W Germany (combined)
1963	E Germany
1966	W Germany

Most wins: Indoors (4) Romania as above, Sweden: 1954, 1958 and as above. Outdoors (4) W Germany (including 1 as combined E/W German team): as above.

Winners: indoors – women

1962	Romania
1965	Hungary
1971	E Germany
1973	Yugoslavia
1975	E Germany
1979	E Germany
1982	USSR
1986	USSR
1990	USSR
1993	Germany
1995	Germany
1997	Denmark
1999	Norway
2001	Russia
2003	France
2005	Russia

Winners: outdoors – women

1949	Hungary
1956	Romania
1960	Romania

Most wins: Indoors (3) USSR/Russia: as above: as above. Outdoors (2) Romania: as above.

Olympic Games

Gold medal winners: 2004

Men	Croatia
Women	Denmark

HANG GLIDING

World championships

First held officially in 1976; since 1979, usually takes place every two years.

Winners: individual – class 1

1985	John Pendry (Great Britain)
1987	Rich Duncan (Australia)
1989	Robert Whittall (Great Britain)
1991	Tomás Suchanek (Czechoslovakia)
1993	Tomás Suchanek (Czech Republic)
1995	Tomás Suchanek (Czech Republic)
1998	Guido Gehrmann (Germany)
1999	Manfred Ruhmer (Austria)
2001	Manfred Ruhmer (Austria)
2003	Manfred Ruhmer (Austria)
2005	Oleg Bondarchuk (Ukraine)

Winners: team

1985	Great Britain
1987	Australia
1989	Great Britain
1991	Great Britain
1993	USA
1995	Austria
1998	Austria
1999	Brazil
2001	Austria
2003	Austria
2005	Australia

Most wins: Individual (3) Tomás Suchanek (Czech Republic) as above; Manfred Ruhmer (Austria) as above. Team (5) Austria: 1976 and as above.

HOCKEY

World Cup

Men's tournament first held in 1971, and every four years since 1978. Women's tournament first held in 1974, and now takes place every four years.

Recent winners: men	Recent winners: women
1982 Pakistan	
1986 Australia	1983 Netherlands
1990 Netherlands	1986 Netherlands
1994 Pakistan	1990 Netherlands
1998 Netherlands	1994 Australia
2002 Germany	1998 Australia
2006 Germany	2002 Argentina
	2006 Netherlands

Most wins: (4) Pakistan: 1971, 1978, and as above.

Most wins: (5) Netherlands: 1974, 1978, and as above.

Olympic Games

Regarded as hockey's leading competition. First held in 1908; included at every celebration since 1928; women's competition first held in 1980.

Recent winners: men	Recent winners: women
1956 India	
1960 Pakistan	1980 Zimbabwe
1964 India	1984 Netherlands
1968 Pakistan	1988 Australia
1972 W Germany	1992 Spain
1976 New Zealand	1996 Australia
1980 India	2000 Australia
1984 Pakistan	2004 Germany
1988 Great Britain	
1992 Germany	
1996 Netherlands	
2000 Netherlands	
2004 Australia	

Most wins: Men (8) India: 1928, 1932, 1936, 1948, 1952 and as above. Women (3) Australia: as above.

Hockey field

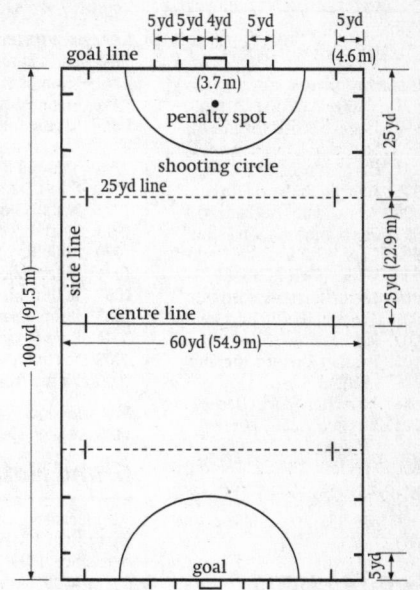

HORSE RACING

The English Classics are five races run from April to September each year for three-year-olds: The Derby; The Oaks; One Thousand Guineas; Two Thousand Guineas; and St Leger.

The Derby

The 'Blue Riband' of the Turf; run at Epsom over 1 1/2 miles. First run in 1780.

Recent winners
1989	Nashwan (Willie Carson)
1990	Quest for Fame (Pat Eddery)
1991	Generous (Alan Munro)
1992	Dr Devious (John Reid)
1993	Commander-In-Chief (Michael Kinane)
1994	Erhaab (Willie Carson)
1995	Lammtarra (Walter Swinburn)
1996	Shaamit (Michael Hills)
1997	Benny The Dip (Willie Ryan)
1998	High Rise (Olivier Peslier)
1999	Oath (Kieren Fallon)
2000	Sinndar (Johnny Murtagh)
2001	Galileo (Michael Kinane)
2002	High Chaparral (Johnny Murtagh)
2003	Kris Kin (Kieren Fallon)
2004	North Light (Kieren Fallon)
2005	Motivator (Johnny Murtagh)
2006	Sir Percy (Martin Dwyer)

Most wins: Jockey (9) Lester Piggott: 1954, 1957, 1960, 1968, 1970, 1972, 1976–7, 1983.

The Oaks

Raced at Epsom over 1 1/2 miles; for fillies only. First run in 1779.

Recent winners
1989	Snow Bride (Steve Cauthen)
1990	Salsabil (Willie Carson)
1991	Jet Ski Lady (Christy Roche)
1992	User Friendly (George Duffield)
1993	Intrepidity (Michael Roberts)
1994	Balanchine (Frankie Dettori)
1995	Moonshell (Frankie Dettori)
1996	Lady Carla (Pat Eddery)
1997	Reams of Verse (Kieren Fallon)
1998	Shahtoush (Michael Kinane)
1999	Ramruma (Kieren Fallon)
2000	Love Divine (Richard Quinn)
2001	Imagine (Michael Kinane)
2002	Kazzia (Frankie Dettori)
2003	Casual Look (Martin Dwyer)
2004	Ouija Board (Kieren Fallon)
2005	Eswarah (Richard Hills)
2006	Alexandrova (Kieron Fallon)

Most wins: Jockey (9) Frank Buckle: 1797–9, 1802–3, 1805, 1817–18, 1823.

Horse racing (continued)

One Thousand Guineas

Run over 1 mile at Newmarket; for fillies only. First run in 1814.

Recent winners
1991 Shadayid (Willie Carson)
1992 Hatoof (Walter Swinburn)
1993 Sayyedati (Walter Swinburn)
1994 Las Meninas (John Reid)
1995 Harayir (Richard Ellis)
1996 Bosra Sham (Pat Eddery)
1997 Sleepytime (Kieren Fallon)
1998 Cape Verdi (Frankie Dettori)
1999 Wince (Kieren Fallon)
2000 Lahan (Richard Hills)
2001 Ameerat (Philip Johnson)
2002 Kazzia (Frankie Dettori)
2003 Russian Rhythm (Kieren Fallon)
2004 Attraction (Kevin Darley)
2005 Virginia Waters (Kieren Fallon)
2006 Speciosa (Michael Fenton)

Most wins: Jockey (7) George Fordham: 1859, 1861, 1865, 1868–9, 1881, 1883.

Two Thousand Guineas

Run at Newmarket over 1 mile. First run in 1809.

Recent winners
1990 Tirol (Michael Kinane)
1991 Mystiko (Michael Roberts)
1992 Rodrigo de Triano (Lester Piggott)
1993 Zafonic (Pat Eddery)
1994 Mister Baileys (Jason Weaver)
1995 Pennekamp (Thierry Jarnet)
1996 Mark of Esteem (Frankie Dettori)
1997 Entrepreneur (Michael Kinane)
1998 King of Kings (Michael Kinane)
1999 Island Sands (Frankie Dettori)
2000 King's Best (Kieren Fallon)
2001 Golan (Kieren Fallon)
2002 Rock of Gibraltar (Johnny Murtagh)
2003 Refuse To Bend (Pat Smullen)
2004 Haafhd (Richard Hills)
2005 Footsteps in the Sand (Kieren Fallon)
2006 George Washington (Kieren Fallon)

Most wins: Jockey (9) Jem Robinson: 1825, 1828, 1831, 1833, 1847–8.

St Leger

The oldest of the five English classics, first run in 1776. Raced at Doncaster annually over 1 mile 6 furlongs 127 yards.

Recent winners
1993 Bob's Return (Philip Robinson)
1994 Moonax (Pat Eddery)
1995 Classic Cliche (Frankie Dettori)
1996 Shantou (Frankie Dettori)
1997 Silver Patriarch (Pat Eddery)
1998 Nedawi (John Reid)
1999 Mustafaweq (Richard Hills)
2000 Millenary (Richard Quinn)
2001 Milan (Michael Kinane)
2002 Bollin Eric (Kevin Darley)
2003 Brian Boru (Jamie Spencer)
2004 Rule of Law (Kerrin McEvoy)
2005 Scorpion (Frankie Dettori)
2006 Sixties Icon (Frankie Dettori)

Most wins: Jockey (9) Bill Scott: 1821, 1825, 1828–9, 1938–41, 1846.

Grand National

Steeplechasing's most famous race. First run at Maghull in 1836; at Aintree since 1839; war-time races at Gatwick, 1916–18.

Recent winners
1989 Little Polveir (Jimmy Frost)
1990 Mr Frisk (Marcus Armytage)
1991 Seagram (Nigel Howke)
1992 Party Politics (Carl Llewellyn)
1993* Void
1994 Minnehoma (Richard Dunwoody)
1995 Royal Athlete (Jason Titley)
1996 Rough Quest (Mick Fitzgerald)
1997 Lord Gyllene (Tony Dobbin)
1998 Earth Summit (Carl Llewellyn)
1999 Bobbyjo (Paul Carberry)
2000 Papillon (Ruby Walsh)
2001 Red Marauder (Richard Guest)
2002 Bindaree (Jim Culloty)
2003 Monty's Pass (Barry Geraghty)
2004 Amberleigh House (Graham Lee)
2005 Hedgehunter (Ruby Walsh)
2006 Numbersixvalverde (Niall Madden)

*After a 2nd false start, the field was not called back.

Most wins: Jockey (5) George Stevens: 1856, 1863–4, 1869–70. Horse (3) Red Rum: 1973–4, 1977.

Prix de l'Arc de Triomphe

The leading end-of-season race in Europe; raced over 2 400 metres at Longchamp, France. First run in 1920.

Recent winners
1996 Helissio (Olivier Peslier)
1997 Peintre Celebre (Olivier Peslier)
1998 Sagamix (Olivier Peslier)
1999 Montjeu (Michael Kinane)
2000 Sinndar (Johnny Murtagh)
2001 Sakhee (Frankie Dettori)
2002 Marienbard (Frankie Dettori)
2003 Dalakhani (Christophe Soumillon)
2004 Bago (Thierry Gillet)
2005 Hurricane Run (Kieren Fallon)
2006 Rail Link (Stephane Pasquier)

Most wins: Jockey (4) Jacko Doyasbère: 1942, 1944, 1950–1; Freddy Head: 1966, 1972, 1976, 1979; Yves Saint-Martin: 1970, 1974, 1982, 1984; Pat Eddery, 1980, 1985, 1986, 1987. Horse (2) Ksar: 1921–2; Motrico: 1930, 1932; Corrida: 1936–7; Tantième: 1950–1; Ribot: 1955–6; Alleged: 1977–8.

The American Triple Crown comprises three races for three-year olds; The Kentucky Derby, the Preakness Stakes, and the Belmont Stakes.

Kentucky Derby

Raced at Churchill Downs, Louisville, over 1 mile 2 furlongs. First run in 1875.

Recent winners
1993 Sea Hero (J Bailey)
1994 Go for Gin (Chris McCarron)
1995 Thunder Gulch (Gary Stevens)
1996 Grindstone (Jerry Bailey)
1997 Silver Charm (Gary Stevens)
1998 Real Quiet (Kent Desormeaux)
1999 Charismatic (Chris Antley)
2000 Fusaichi Pegasus (Kent Desormeaux)
2001 Monarchos (Jorge Chavez)
2002 War Emblem (Victor Espinoza)
2003 Funny Cide (Jose Santos)
2004 Smarty Jones (Stewart Elliott)
2005 Giacomo (Mike Smith)
2006 Barbaro (Edgar Prado)

Most wins: Jockey (5) Eddie Arcaro: 1938, 1941, 1945, 1948, 1952; Bill Hartack: 1957, 1960, 1962, 1964, 1969.

Preakness Stakes

Raced at Pimlico, Baltimore, Maryland, over 1 mile 1½ furlongs. First run in 1873.

Recent winners
1989	Sunday Silence (Pat Valenzuela)
1990	Summer Squall (Pat Day)
1991	Hansel (Jerry Bailey)
1992	Pine Bluff (Chris McCarron)
1993	Prairie Bayou (Mike Smith)
1994	Tabasco Cat (Pat Day)
1995	Timber Country (Pat Day)
1996	Louis Quatorze (Pat Day)
1997	Silver Charm (Gary Stevens)
1998	Real Quiet (Kent Desormeaux)
1999	Charismatic (Chris Antley)
2000	Red Bullet (Jerry Bailey)
2001	Point Given (Gary Stevens)
2002	War Emblem (Victor Espinoza)
2003	Funny Cide (Jose Santos)
2004	Smarty Jones (Stewart Elliott)
2005	Afleet Alex (Jeremy Rose)
2006	Bernardini (Javier Castellano)

Most wins: Jockey (6) Eddie Arcaro: 1941, 1948, 1950–1, 1955, 1957.

Belmont Stakes

Raced at Belmont Park, New York, over 1 mile 4 furlongs. First run in 1867, at Jerome Park.

Recent winners
1989	Easy Goer (Pat Day)
1990	Go And Go (Michael Kinane)
1991	Hansel (Jerry Bailey)
1992	A.P. Indy (Eddie Delahoussaye)
1993	Colonial Affair (Julie Krone)
1994	Tabasco Cat (Pat Day)
1995	Thunder Gulch (Gary Stevens)
1996	Editor's Note (R Douglas)
1997	Touch Gold (Chris McCarron)
1998	Victory Gallup (Gary Stevens)
1999	Lemon Drop Kid (Jose Santos)
2000	Commendable (Pat Day)
2001	Point Given (Gary Stevens)
2002	Sarava (Edgar Prado)
2003	Empire Maker (Jerry Bailey)
2004	Birdstone (Edgar Prado)
2005	Afleet Alex (Jeremy Rose)
2006	Afleet (Fernando Jara)

Most wins: Jockey (6) Jimmy McLaughlin: 1882–4, 1886–8; Eddie Arcaro: 1941–2, 1945, 1948, 1952, 1955.

HURLING

All-Ireland championship

First contested in 1887. Played on the first Sunday in September each year.

Recent winners
1990	Cork
1991	Tipperary
1992	Limerick
1993	Kilkenny
1994	Offaly
1995	Clare
1996	Wexford
1997	Clare
1998	Offaly
1999	Cork
2000	Kilkenny
2001	Tipperary
2002	Kilkenny
2003	Kilkenny
2004	Cork
2005	Cork
2006	Kilkenny

Most wins: (30) Cork: 1890, 1892–4, 1902–3, 1919, 1926, 1928–9, 1931, 1941–4, 1946, 1952–4, 1966, 1970, 1976–8, 1984, 1986, and as above.

ICE HOCKEY

World championship

First held in 1920; takes place annually (except 1980). Up to 1968, the Olympic champions were also regarded as world champions. Women's matches held since 1990.

Recent winners
1992	Sweden
1993	Russia
1994	Canada
1995	Finland
1996	Czech Republic
1997	Canada
1998	Sweden
1999	Czech Republic
2000	Czech Republic
2001	Czech Republic
2002	Slovakia
2003	Canada
2004	Canada
2005	Czech Republic
2006	Sweden

Most wins: (23) Canada.

Stanley Cup

The most sought-after trophy at club level; the end-of-season meeting between the winners of the two conferences in the National Hockey League in the USA and Canada.

Recent winners
1989	Calgary Flames	1998	Detroit Redwings
1990	Edmonton Oilers	1999	Dallas Stars
1991	Pittsburgh Penguins	2000	New Jersey Devils
1992	Pittsburgh Penguins	2001	Colorado Avalanche
1993	Montreal Canadiens	2002	Detroit Red Wings
1994	New York Rangers	2003	New Jersey Devils
1995	New Jersey Devils	2004	Tampa Bay Lightning
1996	Colorado Avalanche	2005	*Not awarded*
1997	Detroit Redwings	2006	Carolina Hurricanes

Most wins: (24) Montreal Canadiens: 1916, 1924, 1930–1, 1944, 1946, 1953, 1956–60, 1965–6, 1968–9, 1971, 1973, 1976–9, 1986, 1993.

Olympic Games

Gold medal winners
Men		Women	
1988	USSR	1998	USA
1992	Unified Team	2002	Canada
1994	Sweden	2006	Canada
1998	Czech Republic		
2002	Canada		
2006	Sweden		

ICE SKATING

World championships

First men's championships in 1896; first women's event in 1906; pairs first contested in 1908. Ice dance officially recognized in 1952.

Recent winners: men

1995	Elvis Stojko (Canada)
1996	Todd Eldredge (USA)
1997	Elvis Stojko (Canada)
1998	Alexie Yagudin (Russia)
1999	Alexie Yagudin (Russia)
2000	Alexie Yagudin (Russia)
2001	Evgeni Plushenko (Russia)
2002	Alexie Yagudin (Russia)
2003	Evgeni Plushenko (Russia)
2004	Evgeni Plushenko (Russia)
2005	Stephane Lambiel (Switzerland)
2006	Stephane Lambiel (Switzerland)

Most wins: (10) Ulrich Salchow (Sweden): 1901–5, 1907–11.

Recent winners: women

1995	Lu Chen (China)
1996	Michele Kwan (USA)
1997	Tara Lipinski (USA)
1998	Michelle Kwan (USA)
1999	Maria Butyrskaya (Russia)
2000	Michelle Kwan (USA)
2001	Michelle Kwan (USA)
2002	Irina Slutskaya (Russia)
2001	Michelle Kwan (USA)
2004	Shizuka Arakawa (Japan)
2005	Irina Slutskaya (Russia)
2006	Kimmie Meissner (USA)

Most wins: (10) Sonja Henie (Norway): 1927–36.

Recent winners (pairs)

1993	Isabelle Brasseur/Lloyd Eisler (Canada)
1994	Yekaterina Gordeyeva/Sergey Grinkov (Russia)
1995	Radka Kovarikova/Rene Novotny (Czech Republic)
1996	Marina Eltsova/Andrey Bushkov (Russia)
1997	Mandy Woetzel/Ingo Steuer (Germany)
1998	Elena Berzhnaya/Anton Sikharulidze (Russia)
1999	Elena Berzhnaya/Anton Sikharulidze (Russia)
2000	Maria Petrova/Alexei Tikhonov (Russia)
2001	Jamie Sala/David Pelletier (Canada)
2002	Xue Shen/Hongbo Zhao (China)
2003	Xue Shen/Hongbo Zhao (China)
2004	Tatiana Totmianina/Maxim Marinin (Russia)
2005	Tatiana Totmianina/Maxim Marinin (Russia)
2006	Pang Qing/Tong Jian (China)

Most wins: (10) Irina Rodnina (USSR): 1969–72 (with Aleksey Ulanov), 1973–8 (with Aleksander Zaitsev).

Recent winners: ice dance

1993	Maia Usova/Alexandr Zhulin (Unified Team)
1994	Oksana Grichtchuk/Yevgeny Platov (Russia)
1995	Oksana Grichtchuk/Yevgeny Platov (Russia)
1996	Oksana Grichtchuk/Yevgeny Platov (Russia)
1997	Oksana Grichtchuk/Yevgeny Platov (Russia)
1998	Anjelika Krylova/Oleg Ovsyannikov (Russia)
1999	Anjelika Krylova/Oleg Ovsyannikov (Russia)
2000	Marina Anissina/Gwendal Peizerat (France)
2001	Barbara Fusar-Poli/Maurizo Margaglia (Italy)
2002	Irina Lobacheva/Ilia Averbukh (Russia)
2003	Shae-Lynn Bourne/Victor Kraatz (Canada)
2004	Tatiana Navka/Roman Kostomarov (Russia)
2005	Tatiana Navka/Roman Kostomarov (Russia)
2006	Albena Denkova/Maxim Staviski (Bulgaria)

Most wins: (6) Aleksander Gorshkov and Lyudmila Pakhomova (USSR): 1970–4, 1976.

JUDO

World championships

First held in 1956, now contested every two years. Current weight categories established in 1999; women's championship instituted in 1980.

Recent winners: open – men

1993	Rafael Kubacki (Poland)
1995	David Douillet (France)
1997	Rafael Kubacki (Poland)
1999	Shinichi Shinohara (Japan)
2001	Alexandre Mikhaylin (Russia)
2003	Keiji Suzuki (Japan)
2005	Dennis van der Gheest (Netherlands)

Recent winners: +100 kg – men

1993	David Douillet (France)
1995	David Douillet (France)
1997	David Douillet (France)
1999	Shinichi Shinohara (Japan)
2001	Alexander Mikhaylin (Russia)
2003	Yasuyuki Muneta (Japan)
2005	Alexander Mikhaylin (Russia)

Recent winners: –100 kg – men

1993	Antal Kovacs (Hungary)
1995	Pawel Nastula (Poland)
1997	Pawel Nastula (Poland)
1999	Kosie Inoue (Japan)
2001	Kosie Inoue (Japan)
2003	Kosie Inoue (Japan)
2005	Keiji Suzuki (Japan)

Recent winners: –90 kg – men

1993	Yoshio Nakamura (Japan)
1995	Ki-young Chun (S Korea)
1997	Ki-young Chun (S Korea)
1999	Hidehiko Yoshida (Japan)
2001	Frédéric Demontfaucon (France)
2003	Hee-tae Hwang (S Korea)
2005	Hiroshi Izumi (Japan)

Recent winners: –81 kg – men

1993	Ki-young Chun (S Korea)
1995	Toshihiko Koga (Japan)
1997	Cho In-chul (S Korea)
1999	Graeme Randall (Great Britain)
2001	Cho In-chul (S Korea)
2003	Florian Wanner (Germany)
2005	Guillaume Elmont (Netherlands)

Recent winners: –73 kg – men

1993	Hoon Chung (S Korea)
1995	Daisuke Hideshima (Japan)
1997	Kenzo Nakamura (Japan)
1999	Jimmy Pedro (USA)
2001	Vitali Makarov (Russia)
2003	Won-hee Lee (S Korea)
2005	Akos Braun (Hungary)

Recent winners: –66 kg – men

1993	Yukimasa Nakamura (Japan)
1995	Udo Quellmalz (Germany)

1997 Hyuk Kim (S Korea)
1999 Lardi Benboudaoud (France)
2001 Arash Miresmaeili (Iran)
2003 Arash Miresmaeili (Iran)
2005 Arash Miresmaeili (Iran)

Recent winners: −60 kg – men

1993 Ryudi Sanoda (Japan)
1995 Nikolai Ojeguine (Russia)
1997 Tadahiro Nomura (Japan)
1999 Manuel Poulot (Cuba)
2001 Anis Lounif (Tunisia)
2003 Min-Ho Choi (South Korea)
2005 Craig Fallon (Great Britain)

Most titles: (4) Yashiro Yamashita (Japan): 1981 (Open), 1979, 1981, 1983 (over 95 kg); Shozo Fujii (Japan): 1971, 1973, 1975 (under 80 kg), 1979 (under 78 kg).

Recent winners: open – women

1993 Beata Maksymow (Poland)
1995 Monique Van Der Lee (Netherlands)
1997 Daina Beltran (Cuba)
1999 Daina Beltran (Cuba)
2001 Celine Lebrun (France)
2003 Wen Tong (China)
2005 Midori Shintani (Japan)

Recent winners: +78 kg – women

1993 Johanna Hagen (Germany)
1995 Angelique Seriese (Netherlands)
1997 Christine Cicot (France)
1999 Beata Maksymow (Poland)
2001 Yuan Hua (China)
2003 Fuming Sun (China)
2005 Wen Tong (China)

Recent winners: −78 kg – women

1993 Chun Huileng (China)
1995 Diadenis Luna (Cuba)
1997 Noriko Anno (Japan)
1999 Noriko Anno (Japan)
2001 Noriko Anno (Japan)
2003 Noriko Anno (Japan)
2005 Yurisel Laborde (Cuba)

Recent winners: −70 kg (women)

1993 Min-sun Cho (S Korea)
1995 Min-sun Cho (S Korea)
1997 Kate Howey (Great Britain)
1999 Sibelis Veranes (Cuba)
2001 Masae Ueno (Japan)
2003 Masae Ueno (Japan)
2005 Edith Bosch (Netherlands)

Recent winners: −63 kg (women)

1993 Caveye de Van (Belgium)
1995 Sung-sook Young (S Korea)
1997 Servenr Vendenhende (France)
1999 Keiko Maeda (Japan)

2001 Gella Vandecaveye (Belgium)
2003 Daniela Krukower (Argentina)
2005 Lucie Decosse (France)

Recent winners: −57 kg – women

1991 Miriam Blasco Soto (Spain)
1993 Nicola Fairbrother (Great Britain)
1995 Driulis Gonzalez (Cuba)
1997 Isabel Fernandez (Spain)
1999 Druilis Gonzalez (Cuba)
2001 Yurisleidis Lupetey (Cuba)
2003 Kye Sun-Hui (North Korea)
2005 Kye Sun-Hui (North Korea)

Recent winners: −52 kg – women

1993 Rodriguez Verdecia (Cuba)
1995 Marie-Claire Restoux (France)
1997 Marie-Claire Restoux (France)
1999 Noriko Narasaki (Japan)
2001 Kye Sun-Hui (North Korea)
2003 Amarlis Savon (Cuba)
2005 Li Ying (China)

Recent winners: −48 kg – women

1993 Ryoko Tamura (Japan)
1995 Ryoko Tamura (Japan)
1997 Ryoko Tamura (Japan)
1999 Ryoko Tamura (Japan)
2001 Ryoko Tamura (Japan)
2003 Ryoko Tamura (Japan)
2005 Yanet Bermoy (Cuba)

Most titles: (6) Ingrid Berghmans (Belgium): 1980, 1982, 1984, 1986 (open), 1984, 1989 (under 72 kg); Ryoko Tamura (Japan): as above (−48 kg).

KARATE

World championships

First held in Tokyo 1970; have taken place every two years since 1980, when women first competed; there is a team competition plus individual competitions – Kumite (seven weight categories for men and three for women) and Kata. Separate men and women's teams started in 1992.

Kumite team winners: men

1998	France	2006	Spain
2000	France		
2002	Spain		
2004	France		

Kumite team winners: women

1998	Turkey	2006	Japan
2000	France		
2002	Spain		
2004	Turkey		

LACROSSE

World championships

First held for men in 1967; and for women in 1969. Have taken place every four years since 1974; since 1982 the women's event has been called the World Cup.

Winners: men

1974	USA	1994	USA
1978	Canada	1998	USA
1982	USA	2002	USA
1986	USA	2006	Canada
1990	USA		

Most wins: (8) USA: 1967 and as above.

Winners: women

1974	USA	1994	USA
1978	Canada	1998	USA
1982	USA	2001	USA
1986	Australia	2005	Australia
1990	USA		

Most wins: (7) USA: 1967 and as above.

Iroquois Cup

The sport's best-known trophy; contested by English club sides annually since 1890.

Recent winners

1983 Sheffield University
1984 Cheadle
1985 Cheadle
1986 Heaton Mersey
1987 Stockport
1988 Mellor
1989 Stockport
1990 Cheadle
1991 Cheadle
1992 Cheadle
1993 Heaton Mersey
1994 Cheadle
1995 Cheadle
1996 Stockport
1997 Mellor
1998 *Not played*
1999 Cheadle
2000 Cheadle
2001 Cheadle
2002 Cheadle
2003 Cheadle
2004 Stockport
2005 *Not played*
2006 *Not played*

Most wins: (19) Stockport: 1897–1901, 1903, 1905, 1911–13, 1923–4, 1926, 1928, 1934, 1987, 1989, 1996, 2004.

SPORTS AND GAMES

MODERN PENTATHLON

World championships

Men's individual championship held annually since 1949 with the exception of Olympic years, when Olympic champions automatically become world champions; team championship held annually. Women's individual and team events held annually. From 2000 World Championships held annually for men and women. Inaugural women's Olympic competition in 2000.

Recent winners: individual men

2003	Eric Walther (Germany)
2004	Andrejus Zadneprovski (Lithuania)
2005	Qian Zhenhua (China)
2006	Edvinas Krungolcas (Lithuania)

Recent winners: individual women

2003	Zsuzsanna Voros (Hungary)
2004	Zsuzsanna Voros (Hungary)
2005	Claudia Corsini (Italy)
2006	Marta Dziadura (Poland)

Recent winners: team

	Men	Women
2003	Hungary	Great Britain
2004	Russia	Great Britain
2005	Russia	Russia
2006	Lithuania	Poland

Olympic Games
Gold medal winner 2004 – men
Andrey Moiseev (Russia)

Gold medal winner 2004 – women
Zsuzsanna Voros (Hungary)

MOTOR CYCLING

World championships

First organized in 1949; current titles for 500 cc, 250 cc, 125 cc, 80 cc and Sidecar. Formula One and Endurance world championships also held annually. The most prestigious title is the 500 cc category.

Recent winners: 500 cc

1993	Kevin Schwantz (USA)
1994	Michael Doohan (Australia)
1995	Michael Doohan (Australia)
1996	Michael Doohan (Australia)
1997	Michael Doohan (Australia)
1998	Michael Doohan (Australia)
1999	Alex Criville (Spain)
2000	Kenny Roberts Jr (USA)
2001	Valentino Rossi (Italy)
2002	Valentino Rossi (Italy)
2003	Valentino Rossi (Italy)
2004	Valentino Rossi (Italy)
2005	Valentino Rossi (Italy)
2006	Nicky Hayden (USA)

Most wins: (8) Giacomo Agostini (Italy): 1966–72, 1975.

Most world titles: (15) Giacomo Agostini (Italy): 350 cc 1968–74, 500 cc as above.

Isle of Man TT races

The most famous of all motor-cycle races; first held 1907; takes place each June. Principal race is the Senior TT.

Recent winners: senior TT

1993	Phil McCallen (Ireland)
1994	Steve Hislop (Great Britain)
1995	Joey Dunlop (Ireland)
1996	Phil McCallen (Ireland)
1997	Phil McCallen (Ireland)
1998	Ian Simpson (Scotland)
1999	David Jefferies (England)
2000	David Jefferies (England)
2001	*Not held*
2002	David Jefferies (England)
2003	Adrian Archibald (N Ireland)
2004	Adrian Archibald (N Ireland)
2005	John McGuinness (England)
2006	John McGuinness (England)

Most senior TT wins: (7) Mike Hailwood (Great Britain): 1961, 1963–7, 1979.

MOTOR RACING

World championship

A Formula One drivers' world championship instituted in 1950; constructor's championship instituted in 1958.

Recent winners

1996	Damon Hill (Great Britain); Williams-Renault
1997	Jacques Villeneuve (Canada); Williams-Renault
1998	Mika Hakkinen (Finland); McLaren-Mercedes
1999	Mika Hakkinen (Finland); McLaren-Mercedes
2000	Michael Schumacher (Germany); Ferrari
2001	Michael Schumacher (Germany); Ferrari
2002	Michael Schumacher (Germany); Ferrari
2003	Michael Schumacher (Germany); Ferrari
2004	Michael Schumacher (Germany); Ferrari
2005	Fernando Alonso (Spain); Renault
2006	Fernando Alonso (Spain); Renault

Most wins: Driver (7) Michael Schumacher (Germany): 1994, 1995, and as above. Constructor (11) Ferrari: 1958, 1961, 1964, 1975, 1977, 1979, 2000–4.

Le Mans 24-Hour Race

The greatest of all endurance races. First held in 1923.

Recent winners

1993	Geoff Brabham (Australia) Christophe Bouchut (France) Eric Helary (France)
1994	Yannick Dalmas (France) Mauro Baldi (Italy) Hurley Haywood (USA)
1995	Yannick Dalmas (France) J J Lehto (Finland) Masanori Sekiya (Japan)
1996	Manuel Reuter (Germany) Davey Jones (USA) Alexander Wurz (Austria)
1997	Michele Alboreto (Italy) Stefan Johansson (Sweden) Tom Kristensen (Denmark)
1998	Allan McNish (Great Britain) Laurent Aiello (France) Stephane Ortelli (France)
1999	Pierluigi Martini (Italy) Joachim Winkelhock (Germany) Yannick Dalmas (France)
2000	Emanuele Pirro (Italy) Frank Biela (Germany) Tom Kristensen (Denmark)
2001	Emanuele Pirro (Italy) Frank Biela (Germany) Tom Kristensen (Denmark)
2002	Emanuele Pirro (Italy) Frank Biela (Germany) Tom Kristensen (Denmark)
2003	Rinaldo Capello (Italy) Guy Smith (UK) Tom Kristensen (Denmark)
2004	Rinaldo Capello (Italy) Seiji Ara (Japan) Tom Kristensen (Denmark)
2005	Tom Kristensen (Denmark) J J Lehto (Finland) Marco Werner (Germany)
2006	Emanuele Pirro Italy) Frank Biela (Germany) Marco Werner (Germany)

Most wins: (7) Tom Kristensen (Denmark) as above.

Indianapolis 500

First held in 1911. Raced over the Indianapolis Raceway as part of the Memorial Day celebrations at the end of May each year.

Recent winners
1993 Emerson Fittipaldi (Brazil)
1994 Al Unser Jr (USA)
1995 Jacques Villeneuve (Canada)
1996 Buddy Lazier (USA)
1997 Arie Luyendyk (Netherlands)
1998 Eddie Cheever Jr (USA)
1999 Kenny Brack (Sweden)
2000 Juan Montoya (Colombia)
2001 Helio Castroneves (Brazil)
2002 Helio Castroneves (Brazil)
2003 Gil de Ferran (Brazil)
2004 Buddy Rice (USA)
2005 Dan Wheldon (Great Britain)
2006 Sam Hornish Jr (USA)

Most wins: (4) A J Foyt (USA): 1961, 1964, 1967, 977; Al Unser (USA): 1970–1, 1978, 1987; Rick Mears (USA): 1979, 1984, 1988, 1991.

Monte Carlo rally

The world's leading rally; first held in 1911.

Recent winners
1994 François Delecour/Daniel
       Grataloup (France)
1995 Carlos Sainz/Luis Moia
       (Spain)
1996 Patrick Bernardini/Bernard
       Occelli (France)
1997 Piero Liatti/Fabrizia Pons
       (Italy)
1998 Carlos Sainz/Luis Moya
       (Spain)
1999 Tommi Makinen/Risto
       Mannisenmaki (Finland)
2000 Tommi Makinen/Risto
       Mannisenmaki (Finland)
2001 Tommi Makinen (Finland)/
       Nicky Grist (Wales)
2002 Tommi Makinen/Kaj
       Lindstrom (France)
2003 Sebastien Loeb/Daniel Elena
       (France)
2004 Sebastien Loeb/Daniel Elena
       (France)
2005 Sebastien Loeb/Daniel Elena
       (France)
2006 Marcus Gronhölm/Timo
       Rautiainen (Finland)

Most wins: (4) Sandro Munari (Italy): 1972, 1975–7; Walter Röhrl (W Germany): 1980, 1982, 1983, 1984. Tommi Makinen (Finland): as above; Most successful co-driver: (4) Christian Geistdorfer all with Walter Röhrl; Bernard Occelli, 1992, 1993, 1996.

NETBALL

World championships

First held in 1963, then every four years.

Winners
1963 Australia
1967 New Zealand
1971 Australia
1975 Australia
1979 Australia, New Zealand,
       Trinidad & Tobago (*shared*)
1983 Australia
1987 New Zealand
1991 Australia
1995 Australia
1999 Australia
2003 New Zealand

Most wins: (8) Australia: as above.

ORIENTEERING

World championships

First held in 1966. Usually every two years, annually from 2003.

Winners: individual – men
Classic distance until 2002;
Long distance from 2003
1987 Kent Olsson (Sweden)
1989 Peter Thoresen (Norway)
1991 Jörgen Mårtensson (Sweden)
1993 Allan Mogensen (Denmark)
1995 Jörgen Mårtensson (Sweden)
1997 Peter Thoresen (Norway)
1999 Bjørnar Valstad (Norway)
2001 Jörgen Rostrup (Norway)
2003 Thomas Bührer
       (Switzerland)
2004 Bjørnar Valstad (Norway)
2005 Andrey Khramov (Russia)
2006 Jani Lakanen (Finland)

Winners: individual –
women.
Classic distance until 2002;
Long distance from 2003
1987 Arja Hannus (Sweden)
1989 Marita Skogum (Sweden)
1991 Katalin Olah (Hungary)
1993 Marita Skogurn (Sweden)
1995 Katalin Olah (Hungary)
1997 Hanne Staff (Norway)
1999 Kirsi Bostrom (Finland)
2001 Simone Luder (Switzerland)
2003 Simone Luder (Switzerland)
2004 Karolina Höjsgaard (Sweden)
2005 Simone Niggli-Luder
       (Switzerland)
2006 Simone Niggli-Luder-
       (Switzerland)

Most wins: Men (2), Age Hadler (Norway): 1966, 1972; Egil Johansen (Norway); Oyvin Thon (Norway): 1979, 1981; Peter Thoresen (Norway); Jörgen Mårtensson (Sweden); Bjørnar Valstad (Norway), as above. Women (4), Simone Niggli-Luder, as above.

Winners: relay – men
1979 Sweden	1995 Switzerland
1981 Norway	1997 Switzerland
1983 Norway	1999 Denmark
1985 Norway	2001 Norway
1987 Norway	2003 Sweden
1989 Norway	2004 Norway
1991 Switzerland	2005 Norway
1993 Switzerland	2006 Russia

Winners: relay – women
1976 Sweden	1993 Sweden
1978 Finland	1995 Finland
1979 Finland	1997 Sweden
1981 Sweden	1999 Norway
1983 Sweden	2001 Finland
1985 Sweden	2003 Switzerland
1987 Norway	2004 Sweden
1989 Sweden	2005 Switzerland
1991 Sweden	2006 Finland

Most wins: Men (10) Norway: 1968, 1978, and as above. Women (12) Sweden: 1966, 1970, 1974, and as above.

POLO

British Open Polo Championship

First held in 1956, replacing the Champion Cup. The British Open Championship for club sides: finalists compete for the Veuve Clicquot Gold Cup, once known as the Cowdray Park Gold Cup.

Recent winners
1990 Hildon
1991 Tramontana
1992 Black Bears
1993 Alcatel
1994 Ellerston Blacks
1995 Ellerston Whites
1996 C S Brooks
1997 Labegorce
1998 Ellerston White
1999 Pommery
2000 Dubai
2001 Dubai
2002 Black Bears
2003 Hildon
2004 Azzurra
2005 Dubai
2006 Black Bears

Most wins: (5) Stowell Park: 1973–4, 1976, 1978, 1980; Tramontana: 1986–9, and as above.

POWERBOAT RACING

World championships

Instituted in 1982; held in many categories, with Formula One and Formula Two being the principal competitions. Formula Two, known as Formula Grand Prix, was discontinued in 1989.

Winners: Formula One
1983 Renato Molinari (Italy)
1984 Renato Molinari (Italy)
1985 Bob Spalding (Great Britain)
1986 Gene Thibodaux (USA)
1987 Ben Robertson (USA)
1990 John Hill (Great Britain)
1991 Jonathan Jones (Great Britain)
1992 Fabrizio Bacca (Italy)
1993 Guido Capellini (Italy)
1994 Guido Capellini (Italy)
1995 Guido Capellini (Italy)
1996 Guido Capellini (Italy)
1997 Scott Gillman (USA)
1998 Scott Gillman (USA)
1999 Guido Capellini (Italy)
2000 Scott Gillman (USA)
2001 Guido Capellini (Italy)
2002 Guido Capellini (Italy)
2003 Guido Capellini (Italy)
2004 Scott Gillman (USA)
2005 Guido Capellini (Italy)
2006 Scott Gillman (USA)

Most wins: (9) Guido Capellini (Italy): as above.

Winners: Formula Two/Formula Grand Prix
1982 Michael Werner (W Germany)
1983 Michael Werner (W Germany)
1984 John Hill (Great Britain)
1985 John Hill (Great Britain)
1986 Jonathan Jones (Great Britain) and Buck Thornton (USA) (*shared*)
1987 Bill Seebold (USA)
1988 Chris Bush (USA)
1989 Jonathan Jones (Great Britain)

Most wins: (2) Michael Werner (W Germany): as above; John Hill (Great Britain): as above; Jonathan Jones (Great Britain): as above.

RACKETS

World championship

Organized on a challenge basis, the first champion in 1820 was Robert Mackay (Great Britain).

Recent winners
1929–37 Charles Williams (Great Britain)
1937–47 Donald Milford (Great Britain)
1947–54 James Dear (Great Britain)
1954–72 Geoffrey Atkins (Great Britain)
1972–3 William Surtees (USA)
1973–4 Howard Angus (Great Britain)
1975–1 William Surtees (USA)
1981–4 John Prenn (Great Britain)
1984–6 William Boone (Great Britain)
1986–8 John Prenn (Great Britain)
1988–99 James Male (Great Britain)
1999– Neil Smith (Great
2001 Britain)
2001–5 James Male (Great Britain)
2005– Harry Foster (Great Britain)

Longest-reigning champion: 18 years, Geoffrey Atkins: as above.

REAL TENNIS

World championship

The first world champion was M Clerge (France), c. 1740, regarded as the first world champion of any sport. Held on a challenge basis; first held for women in 1985, and then every two years.

Recent winners: men
1916–28 Fred Covey (Great Britain)
1928–55 Pierre Etchebaster (France)
1955–7 James Dear (Great Britain)
1957–9 Albert Johnson (Great Britain)
1959–69 Northrup Knox (USA)
1969–72 Pete Bostwick (USA)
1972–5 Jimmy Bostwick (USA)
1976–81 Howard Angus (Great Britain)
1981–7 Chris Ronaldson (Great Britain)
1987–94 Wayne Davis (Australia)
1994– Robert Fahey (Australia)

Longest-reigning champion: 33 years, Edmond Barre (France): 1829–62.

Winners – women
1985–9 Judy Clarke (Australia)
1989–93 Penny Fellows (Great Britain)
1993–5 Sally Jones (Great Britain)
1995– Penny Fellows Lumley
2001 (Great Britain)
2001–3 Charlotte Cornwallis (Great Britain)
2003–5 Penny Fellows Lumley (Great Britain)
2005– Charlotte Cornwallis (Great Britain)

Most wins: (6) Penny Fellows Lumley (Great Britain): as above.

ROLLER SKATING

World championships

Figure-skating world championships were first organized in 1947.

Recent winners: combined – men
1993   Samo Kokorovec (Italy)
1994   Steven Findlay (USA)
1995   Jason Sutcliffe (Australia)
1996   Francesco Ceresola (Italy)
1997   Mauro Mazzoni (Italy)
1998   Daniele Tofani (Italy)
1999   Adrian Stolzenberg (Germany)
2000   Adrian Stolzenberg (Germany)
2001   Leonardo Pancani (Italy)
2002   Frank Albiez (Germany)
2003   Luca D'Alisera (Italy)
2004   Luca D'Alisera (Italy)
2006   Roberto Riva (Italy)

Most wins: (5) Karl-Heinz Losch (W Germany): 1958–9, 1961–2, 1966.

Recent winners: combined – women
1993   Letitia Tinghi (Italy)
1994   April Dayney (USA)
1995   Letitia Tinghi (Italy)
1996   Giusy Loncani (Italy)
1997   Sabrini Tommasini (Italy)
1998   Christine Bartolozzi (Italy)
1999   Elisa Facciotti (Italy)
2000   Elisa Facciotti (Italy)
2001   Elisa Facciotti (Italy)
2002   Tanja Romano (Italy)
2003   Tanja Romano (Italy)
2004   Tanja Romano (Italy)
2006   Tanja Romano (Italy)

Most wins: (5) Rafaella Del Vinaccio (Italy): 1988–92.

Recent winners: pairs
1993   Patrick Venerucci/Maura Ferri (Italy)
1994   Patrick Venerucci/Beatrice Pallazzi Rossi (Italy)
1995   Patrick Venerucci/Beatrice Pallazzi Rossi (Italy)
1996   Patrick Venerucci/Beatrice Pallazzi Rossi (Italy)
1997   Patrick Venerucci/Beatrice Pallazzi Rossi (Italy)
1998   Patrick Venerucci/Beatrice Pallazzi Rossi (Italy)
1999   Patrick Venerucci/Beatrice Pallazzi Rossi (Italy)
2000   Patrick Venerucci/Beatrice Pallazzi Rossi (Italy)
2001   Patrick Venerucci/Beatrice Pallazzi Rossi (Italy)
2002   Patrick Venerucci/Beatrice Pallazzi Rossi (Italy)
2003   Marika Zanforlin/Federico Degli Esposti (Italy)
2004   Marika Zanforlin/Federico Degli Esposti (Italy)
2006   Marika Zanforlin/Federico Degli Esposti (Italy)

Most wins: (11) Patrick Venerucci (Italy): 1992 and as above.

Recent winners: dance
1992   Doug Wait/Deanna Monaham (USA)
1993   Doug Wait/Deanna Monaham (USA)
1994   Tim Patten/Lisa Friday (USA)
1995   Tim Patten/Lisa Friday (USA)
1996   Axel Haber/Swansi Gebauer (Germany)
1997   Axel Haber/Swansi Gebauer (Germany)
1998   Roland Bren/Candy Powderly (USA)
1999   Timothy Patten/Tara Graney (USA)
2000   Adam White/Melissa Quinn (USA)
2001   Adam White/Melissa Quinn (USA)
2002   Marco Bornati/Emanuela Bornati (Italy)
2003   Fabio Grossi/Michela Pizzi (Italy)
2004   Marco Bornati/Monica Coffele (Italy)
2006   Melissa Comin de Candido/Mirko Pontello (Italy)

Most wins: (3) Jane Puracchio (USA): 1973, 1975–6; Dan Littel and Florence Arsenault (USA): 1977–9; Greg Goody and Jodee Viola (USA): 1989, 1990, 1991.

ROWING

World championships

First held for men in 1962 and for women in 1974; Olympic champions assume the role of world champion in Olympic years. Principal events are the single sculls.

Recent winners: single sculls – men
1994   Andre Willms (Germany)
1995   Iztok Cop (Slovenia)
1996   Xeno Müller (Switzerland)
1997   James Koven (USA)
1998   Rob Waddell (New Zealand)
1999   Rob Waddell (New Zealand)
2000   Rob Waddell (New Zealand)
2001   Olaf Tufte (Norway)
2002   Marcel Hacker (Germany)
2003   Olaf Tufte (Norway)
2004   Olaf Tufte (Norway)
2005   Mahe Drysdale (New Zealand)
2006   Mahe Drysdale (New Zealand)

Most wins: (5) Thomas Lange (Germany): 1987–9, 1991–2.

Recent winners: sculls – women
1994   Trine Hansen (Denmark)
1995   Maria Brandin (Sewden)
1996   Yekaterina Karsten (Belarus)
1997   Yekaterina Karsten (Belarus)
1998   Irina Fedotova (Russia)
1999   Yekaterina Karsten-Khodotovich (Belarus)
2000   Yekaterina Karsten-Khodotovich (Belarus)
2001   Katrin Rutschow-Stomporowski (Germany)
2002   Rumyana Neykova (Bulgaria)
2003   Rumyana Neykova (Bulgaria)
2004   Rumyana Neykova (Bulgaria)
2005   Yekaterina Karsten-Khodotovich (Belarus)
2006   Yekaterina Karsten-Khodotovich (Belarus)

Most wins: (6) Yekaterina Karsten-Khodotovich (Belarus), as above

University Boat Race

An annual contest between the crews from the Oxford and Cambridge University rowing clubs, first contested in 1829. The current course is from Putney to Mortlake.

Recent winners
1989 Oxford	1995 Cambridge	2001 Cambridge
1990 Oxford	1996 Cambridge	2002 Oxford
1991 Oxford	1997 Cambridge	2003 Oxford
1992 Oxford	1998 Cambridge	2004 Cambridge
1993 Cambridge	1999 Cambridge	2005 Oxford
1994 Cambridge	2000 Oxford	2006 Oxford

Wins: 78 Cambridge; 73 Oxford; 1 dead-heat (1877).

Diamond Sculls

Highlight of Henley Royal Regatta held every July; first contested in 1844.

Recent winners

1989	Vaclav Chalupa (Czechoslovakia)
1990	Eric Verdonk (New Zealand)
1991	Wim van Belleghem (Belgium)
1992	Rorie Henderson (Great Britain)
1993	Thomas Lange (Germany)
1994	Xeno Müller (Switzerland)
1995	Yuri Jaanson (Estonia)
1996	Merlin Vervoorn (Netherlands)
1997	Greg Searle (Great Britain)
1998	James Coven (USA)
1999	Marcel Hacker (Germany)
2000	Aquil H Abdulla (USA)
2001	Duncan S Free (Australia)
2002	Peter Wells (Great Britain)
2003	Alan Campbell (Great Britain)
2004	Marcel Hacker (Germany)
2005	Wyatt Allen (USA)
2006	Mahe Drysdale (New Zealand)

Most wins: (6) Stuart Mackenzie (Australia): 1957–62.

RUGBY LEAGUE

World Cup/International championship

First contested in 1954 between Great Britain, France, New Zealand, and Australia. In 1975, England and Wales replaced Great Britain. The competition was discontinued after the 1977 World Cup, but was revived in 1988.

Winners

1960	Great Britain	1977	Australia
1968	Australia	1988	Australia
1970	Australia	1992	Australia
1972	Great Britain	1995	Australia
1975	Australia	2000	Australia

Most wins: (9) Australia: 1957 and as above.

Engage Super League

The original Northern Union was formed in 1895–6, and was won by Manningham. There have since been many changes to the rules and structure of the league, which from 1906–73 featured a Championship Play-off. The present structure, with Divisions One and Two, dates from the 1973–4 season. Known as the JJB Super League until 2000, and the Tetley's Bitter Super League until 2005.

Recent winners

1984–85	Hull Kingston Rovers	1995–96	Wigan
1985–86	Halifax	1996–97	Bradford
1986–87	Wigan	1997–98	Wigan
1987–88	Widnes	1998–99	Wigan
1988–89	Widnes	1999–2000	Wigan
1989–90	Wigan	2000–1	Bradford
1990–91	Wigan	2001–2	St Helens
1991–92	Wigan	2002–3	Bradford
1992–93	Wigan	2003–4	Leeds
1993–94	Wigan	2004–5	Bradford
1994–95	Wigan	2005–6	St Helens

Challenge Cup final

First contested in 1897 and won by Batley; first final at Wembley Stadium in 1929.

Recent winners

1993	Wigan	2000	Bradford Bulls
1994	Wigan	2001	St Helens
1995	Wigan	2002	Wigan Warriors
1996	St Helens	2003	Bradford Bulls
1997	St Helens	2004	St Helens
1998	Sheffield Eagles	2005	Hull
1999	Leeds Rhinos	2006	St Helens

Most wins: (17) Wigan: 1924, 1929, 1948, 1951, 1958–9, 1965, 1984, 1985, 1988–91, 1992 and as above.

Super League Grand Final

End-of-season knockout competition involving the top eight teams in the first division. First contested at the end of the 1974–5 season. Before 1998 known as the Premiership trophy.

Recent winners

1993	St Helens	2000	St Helens
1994	Wigan	2001	Bradford Bulls
1995	Wigan	2002	St Helens
1996	Wigan	2003	Bradford Bulls
1997	Wigan	2004	Leeds Rhinos
1998	Wigan	2005	Bradford Bulls
1999	St Helens	2006	St Helens

Most wins: (7) Wigan: 1987 and as above.

Regal trophy

A knockout competition, first held in 1971–2. Formerly known as the John Player Special Trophy, it adopted its current name/title in 1989–90, and ended in 1995–6.

Recent winners

1983	Wigan	1990	Wigan
1984	Leeds	1991	Warrington
1985	Hull Kingston Rovers	1992	Widnes
1986	Wigan	1993	Wigan
1987	Wigan	1994	Castleford
1988	St Helens	1995	Wigan
1989	Wigan	1996	Wigan

Most wins: (8) Wigan: as above.

Sydney Premiership

The principal competition in Australia, first held in 1908. The culmination of the competition is the Grand Final; the winning team receives the Winfield Cup.

Recent winners

1992	Brisbane Broncos
1993	Brisbane Broncos
1995	Sydney Bulldogs
1997	Newcastle Knights
1998	Brisbane Broncos
1999	Melbourne Storm
2000	Brisbane Broncos
2001	Newcastle Knights
2002	Sydney Roosters
2003	Penrith
2004	Canterbury Bulldogs
2005	Wests Tigers
2006	Brisbane Broncos

RUGBY UNION

World Cup

The first Rugby Union World Cup was held in 1987.

Recent winners

1987	New Zealand	2003	England
1991	Australia		
1995	South Africa		
1999	Australia		

Six Nations championship

A round-robin competition involving England, Ireland, Scotland, Wales and France; first contested in 1884. Italy joined in 2000.

Recent winners

1989	France	1998	France
1990	Scotland	1999	Scotland
1991	England	2000	England
1992	England	2001	England
1993	France	2002	France
1994	Wales	2003	England
1995	England	2004	France
1996	England	2005	Wales
1997	France	2006	Ireland

Most outright wins: (23) Wales: 1893, 1900, 1902, 1905, 1908–9, 1911, 1922, 1931, 1936, 1950, 1952, 1956, 1965–6, 1969, 1971, 1975–6, 1978–9, 1994, 2005.

County championship

First held in 1889.

Recent winners

1989	Durham	1998	Cheshire
1990	Lancashire	1999	Cornwall
1991	Cornwall	2000	Yorkshire
1992	Lancashire	2001	*not contested*
1993	Lancashire	2002	Gloucestershire
1994	Yorkshire	2003	Gloucestershire
1995	Warwickshire	2004	Devon
1996	Gloucestershire	2005	Devon
1997	Cumbria	2006	Lancashire

Most wins: (18) Gloucestershire: 1910, 1913, 1920–2, 1930–2, 1937, 1972, 1974–6, 1983–4, 1996, 2002–3.

Powergen Cup

An annual knockout competition for English club sides; first held in the 1971–2 season. Known as the John Player Special Cup until 1988, the Pilkington Cup until 1997, and the Tetley's Bitter Cup until 2001.

Recent winners

1991	Harlequins	1999	Wasps
1992	Bath	2000	Wasps
1993	Leicester	2001	Newcastle
1994	Bath	2002	London Irish
1995	Bath	2003	Gloucester
1996	Bath	2004	Newcastle
1997	Leicester	2005	Leeds
1998	Saracens	2006	Wasps

Most wins: (10) Bath: 1984–7, 1990, and as above.

Rugby Union football field

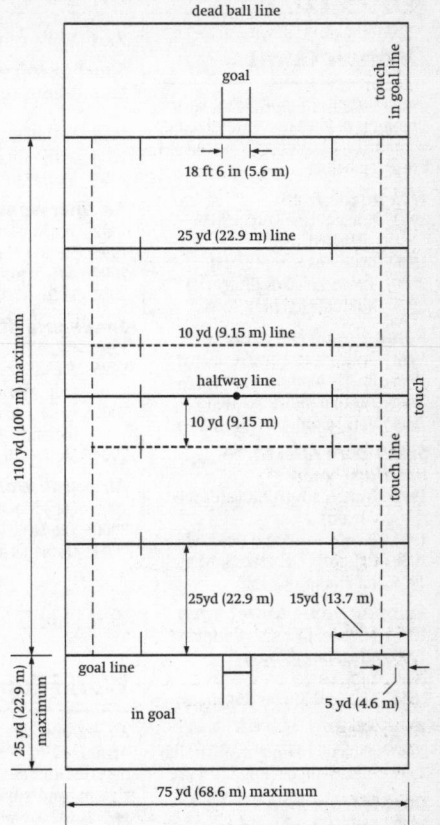

The Konica Minolta Cup

The knockout tournament for Welsh clubs; first held in 1971–2; formerly called the Schweppes Welsh Cup and (to 1999) the Swalec Cup, the Welsh Rugby Union Challenge Cup to 2000, and the Principality Cup to 2003.

Recent winners

1984	Cardiff	1996	Pontypridd
1985	Llanelli	1997	Cardiff
1986	Cardiff	1998	Llanelli
1987	Cardiff	1999	Swansea
1988	Llanelli	2000	Llanelli
1989	Neath	2001	Newport
1990	Neath	2002	Pontypridd
1991	Llanelli	2003	Llanelli
1992	Llanelli	2004	Neath
1993	Llanelli	2005	Llanelli
1994	Cardiff	2006	Pontypridd
1995	Swansea		

Most wins: (13) Llanelli: 1973–6, and as above.

SHOOTING

Olympic Games

The Olympic competition is the highlight of the shooting calendar; winners in all categories since 1984 are given below.

Free pistol: men
1992 Konstantine Loukachik (Unified Team)
1996 Boris Kokorev (Russia)
2000 Tanyu Kiriakov (Bulgaria)
2004 Mikhail Nestruev (Russia)

Rapid fire pistol: men
1992 Ralf Schumann (Germany)
1996 Ralf Schumann (Germany)
2000 Serguei Alifirenko (Russia)
2004 Ralf Schumann (Germany)

Small-bore rifle: three position – men
1992 Gratchia Petrikiane (Unified Team)
1996 Jean-Pierre Amat (France)
2000 Rajmond Debevec (Slovenia)
2004 Jia Zhanbo (China)

Running game target: men
1992 Michael Jakositz (Germany)
1996 Yang Ling (China)
2000 Yang Ling (China)
2004 Manfred Kurzer (Germany)

Trap: Men
2000 Michael Diamond (Australia)
2004 Alexei Alipov (Russia)

Double trap: men
2000 Richard Faulds (Great Britain)
2004 Ahmed al-Maktoum (UAE)

Double trap: women
2000 Pia Hansen (Sweden)
2004 Kimberly Rhode (USA)

Skeet: men
2000 Mykola Milchev (Ukraine)
2004 Andrea Benelli (Italy)

Small-bore rifle: prone – men
1992 Lee Eun Chul (S Korea)
1996 Christian Klees (Germany)
2000 Jonas Edman (Sweden)
2004 Matthew Emmons (USA)

Air rifle: men
1988 Goran Maksimovic (Yugoslavia)
1992 Iouri Fedkine (Unified Team)
1996 Artem Khadzhibekov (Russia)
2000 Cai Yalin (China)
2004 Qinan Zhu (China)

Air pistol: men
1996 Roberto Di Donna (Italy)
2000 Franck Dumoulin (France)
2004 Wang Yifu (China)

Sport pistol: women
1992 Marina Logvinenko (Unified Team)
1996 Li Duihong (China)
2000 Maria Grozdeva (Bulgaria)
2004 Maria Grozdeva (Bulgaria)

Air rifle: women
1992 Yeo Kab-Soon (S Korea)
1996 Renata Mauer (Poland)
2000 Nancy Johnson (USA)
2004 Li Du (China)

Small-bore rifle: women
1992 Lauri Melli (USA)
1996 Alexandra Ivosev (Yugoslavia)
2000 Renata Mauer-Rozanka (Poland)
2004 Lioubov Galkina (Russia)

Air pistol: women
1996 Olga Klochneva (Russia)
2000 Tao Luna (China)
2004 Olena Kostevych (Ukraine)

SKIING

World Cup

A season-long competition first organized in 1967. Champions are declared in downhill, slalom, giant slalom, and super-giant slalom, as well as the overall champion; points are obtained for performances in each category.

Recent overall winners: men
1992 Paul Accola (Switzerland)
1993 Marc Girardelli (Luxembourg)
1994 Kjetel Andre Aamodt (Norway)
1995 Alberto Tomba (Italy)
1996 Lasse Kjus (Norway)
1997 Luc Alphand (France)
1998 Hermann Maier (Austria)
1999 Lasse Kjus (Norway)
2000 Hermann Maier (Austria)
2001 Hermann Maier (Austria)
2002 Stephan Eberharter (Austria)
2003 Stephan Eberharter (Austria)
2004 Hermann Maier (Austria)
2005 Bode Miller (USA)
2006 Benjamin Raich (Austria)

Recent overall winners: women
1992 Petra Kronberger (Austria)
1993 Anita Wachter (Austria)
1994 Vreni Schneider (Switzerland)
1995 Vreni Schneider (Switzerland)
1996 Katja Seizinger (Germany)
1997 Pernilla Wiberg (Sweden)
1998 Katja Seizinger (Germany)
1999 Alexandra Meissnitzer (Austria)
2000 Renata Götschl (Austria)
2001 Janica Kostelic (Croatia)
2002 Michaela Dorfmeister (Austria)
2003 Janica Kostelic (Croatia)
2004 Anja Paerson (Sweden)
2005 Anja Paerson (Sweden)
2006 Janica Kostelic (Croatia)

Most wins: Men (5) Marc Girardelli (Luxembourg): 1985–6, 1989 and as above. Women (6) Annemarie Moser-Pröll (Austria): 1971–5, 1979.

Olympic Games

Gold medal winners
Men's Alpine combination
1998 Mario Reiter (Austria)
2002 Kjetil André Aamodt (Norway)
2006 Ted Ligety (USA)

Women's Alpine combination
1998 Katja Seizinger (Germany)
2002 Janica Kostelic (Croatia)
2006 Janica Kostelic (Croatia)

SNOOKER

World Professional championship

Instituted in the 1926–7 season. A knockout competition open to professional players who are members of the World Professional Billiards and Snooker Association; played at the Crucible Theatre, Sheffield.

Recent winners
1993 Stephen Hendry (Scotland)
1994 Stephen Hendry (Scotland)
1995 Stephen Hendry (Scotland)
1996 Stephen Hendry (Scotland)
1997 Ken Doherty (Ireland)
1998 John Higgins (Scotland)
1999 Stephen Hendry (Scotland)
2000 Mark Williams (Wales)
2001 Ronnie O'Sullivan (England)
2002 Peter Ebdon (England)
2003 Mark Williams (Wales)
2004 Ronnie O'Sullivan (England)
2005 Shaun Murphy (England)
2006 Graeme Dott (Scotland)

Most wins: (15) Joe Davis (England): 1927–40, 1946.

Grand Prix

Originally the Professional Players Tournament; Rothmans Grand Prix to 1993; New Skoda Grand Prix to 1996; Bournemouth Grand Prix in 1997; Preston Grand Prix to 2001; LG Cup to 2003; Totesport Grand Prix to 2005; Royal London Watches from 2006. A ranking tournament.[a]

Winners

1997	Dominic Dale (Wales)
1998	Stephen Lee (England)
1999	John Higgins (Scotland)
2000	Mark Williams (Wales)
2001	Stephen Lee (England)
2002	Chris Small (Scotland)
2003	Mark Williams (Wales)
2004	Ronnie O'Sullivan (England)
2005	John Higgins (Scotland)
2006	Neil Robertson (Australia)

Most wins: (4) Stephen Hendry (Scotland): 1987, 1990–1, 1995.

British Open

Became a ranking tournament[a] in 1985. 1999 tournaments were held in April and September.

Recent winners

1992	Jimmy White (England)
1993	Steve Davies (England)
1994	Ronnie O'Sullivan (England)
1995	John Higgins (Scotland)
1996	Nigel Bond (England)
1997	Mark J Williams (Wales)
1998	John Higgins (Scotland)
1999	Fergal O'Brien (Ireland)
1999	Stephen Hendry (Scotland)
2000	Peter Ebdon (England)
2001	John Higgins (Scotland)
2002	Paul Hunter (England)
2003	Stephen Hendry (Scotland)
2004	John Higgins (Scotland)
2005/6	Not held

Most wins: (5) Steve Davis (England): 1981, 1982, 1984, 1986 and as above.

The Masters

First contested in 1975 and won by John Spencer. Held at the Wembley Conference Centre, it is the most prestigious non-ranking tournament of the season. Known as the Benson & Hedges Masters until 2003.

Recent winners

1995	Ronnie O'Sullivan (England)
1996	Stephen Hendry (Scotland)
1997	Steve Davis (England)
1998	Mark Williams (Wales)
1999	John Higgins (Scotland)
2000	Matthew Stevens (Wales)
2001	Paul Hunter (England)
2002	Paul Hunter (England)

2003	Mark Williams (Wales)
2004	Paul Hunter (England)
2005	Ronnie O'Sullivan (England)
2006	John Higgins (Scotland)

Most wins: (6) Stephen Hendry (Scotland): 1989, 1990–2 and as above.

World amateur championship

First held in 1963, originally every two years, but annually since 1984.

Recent winners

1991	Noppodol Noppachorn (Thailand)
1992	Neil Moseley (England)
1993	Neil Moseley (England)
1994	Mohammed Yusuf (Pakistan)
1995	Sackai Sim-ngan (Thailand)
1996	Stuart Bingham (England)
1997	Marco Fu (Hong Kong)
1998	Luke Simmonds (England)
1999	Ian Preece (Wales)
2000	Stephen Maguire (Scotland)
2001	Not held
2002	Steve Mifsud (Australia)
2003	Pankaj Advani (India)
2004	Mark Allen (N Ireland)
2005	Mark Allen (N Ireland)
2006	Michael White (Wales)

Most wins: (2) Gary Owen (England): 1963, 1966; Ray Edmonds (England): 1972, 1974; Paul Mifsud (Malta): 1985–6; Neil Moseley (England) 1992–3; Mark Allen (N Ireland) 2004-5.

[a]At a ranking tournament players may gather world-ranking points.

SOFTBALL

World championships

First held for women in 1965 and for men the following year; now held every four years.

Winners: men

1976	Canada, New Zealand, USA shared
1980	USA
1984	New Zealand
1988	USA
1992	Canada
1996	New Zealand
2000	New Zealand
2004	New Zealand

Most wins: (5) USA: 1966, 1968, and as above.

Winners: women

1974	USA
1978	USA
1982	New Zealand

1986	USA
1990	USA
1994	USA
1998	USA
2002	USA

Most wins: (7) USA: as above.

SPEEDWAY

World championships

Individual championships inaugurated in 1936; team championship instituted in 1960; first official pairs world championship in 1970; world team cup in 1994; Speedway World Cup in 2001.

Recent winners: individual

1995	Hans Nielsen (Denmark)
1996	Billy Hamill (USA)
1997	Greg Hancock (USA)
1998	Tony Rickardsson (Sweden)
1999	Tony Rickardsson (Sweden)
2000	Mark Loram (England)
2001	Tony Rickardsson (Sweden)
2002	Tony Rickardsson (Sweden)
2003	Nicki Pedersen (Denmark)
2004	Jason Crump (Australia)
2005	Tony Rickardsson (Sweden)
2006	Jason Crump (Australia)

Most wins: (6) Ivan Mauger (New Zealand): 1968–70, 1972, 1977, 1979; Tony Rickardsson (Sweden): 1994 and as above.

Recent winners: world cup

1999	Jason Crump/Jason Lyons/ Leigh Adams (Australia)
2000	Tony Rickardsson/Henrik Gustafsson/Mikael Karlsson/ Peter Karlsson (Sweden)
2001	Jason Crump/Todd Wiltshire/ Craig Boyce/Ryan Sullivan/ Leigh Adams (Australia)
2002	Jason Crump/Todd Wiltshire/ Leigh Adams/Ryan Sullivan/ Jason Lyons (Australia)
2003	Mikael Max/Andreas Jonsson/ Peter Ljung/Peter Karlsson/ David Ruud (Sweden)
2004	Peter Karlsson/Tony Rickardsson/ Antonio Lindback/Mikael Max/ Andreas Jonsson (Sweden)
2005	Tomasz Gollob/Krzysztof Kasprzak/Piotr Protasiewicz/ Rune Holta/Jaroslaw Hampel (Poland)
2006	Nicki Pedersen/Hans Andersen/Bjarne Pedersen/ Charlie Gjedde/Niels-Kristian Iversen (Denmark)

Most wins: (9) Hans Nielsen (Denmark): 1979, 1986–91, 1995, 1997.

SPORTS AND GAMES

Speedway (continued)

Recent winners: team

1989	England
1990	USA
1991	Denmark
1992	USA
1993	USA
1994	Sweden

World Team Cup

1999	Australia
2000	Sweden
2001	Australia
2002	Australia
2003	Sweden
2004	Sweden
2005	Poland
2006	Denmark

Most wins: (11) Denmark: 1981, 1983–8, 1995 and as above.

SQUASH

World Open championship

First held in 1976: held annually for men, every two years for women, then annually from 1990.

Recent winners: men

1994	Jansher Khan (Pakistan)
1995	Jansher Khan (Pakistan)
1996	Jansher Khan (Pakistan)
1997	Rodney Eyles (Australia)
1998	Jonathon Power (Canada)
1999	Peter Nicol (UK)
2000	Not held
2001	Not held
2002	David Palmer (Australia)
2003	Amr Shabana (Egypt)
2004	Thierry Lincou (France)
2005	Amr Shabana (Egypt)
2006	Thierry Lincou (France)

Most wins: (8) Jansher Khan (Pakistan): 1987–9, 1990, 1992, 1993, and as above.

Recent winners: women

1994	Michelle Martin (Australia)
1995	Michelle Martin (Australia)
1996	Sarah Fitzgerald (Australia)
1997	Sarah Fitzgerald (Australia)
1998	Sarah Fitzgerald (Australia)
1999	Cassie Campion (England)
2000	Carol Owens (New Zealand)
2001	Sarah Fitzgerald (Australia)
2002	Sarah Fitzgerald (Australia)
2003	Carol Owens (New Zealand)
2004	Vanessa Atkinson (Netherlands)
2005	Nicol David (Malaysia)
2005	Nicol David (Malaysia)

Most wins: (5) Sarah Fitzgerald (Australia): as above.

SURFING

World professional championship

A season-long series of Grand Prix events. First held in 1970.

Recent winners: men		**Recent winners: women**	
1984	Tom Carroll (Australia)	1984	Kim Mearig (USA)
1985	Tommy Curren (USA)	1985	Frieda Zamba (USA)
1986	Tommy Curren (USA)	1986	Frieda Zamba (USA)
1987	Damien Hardman (Australia)	1987	Wendy Botha (S Africa)
1988	Barton Lynch (Australia)	1988	Frieda Zamba (USA)
1989	Martin Potter (Great Britain)	1989	Wendy Botha (S Africa)
1990	Tommy Curren (USA)	1990	Pam Burridge (Australia)
1991	Damien Hardman (Australia)	1991	Wendy Botha (Australia)
1992	Kelly Slater (USA)	1992	Wendy Botha (Australia)
1993	Derek Ho (Hawaii)	1993	Pauline Menczer (Australia)
1994	Kelly Slater (USA)	1994	Lisa Anderson (USA)
1995	Kelly Slater (USA)	1995	Lisa Anderson (USA)
1996	Kelly Slater (USA)	1996	Lisa Anderson (USA)
1997	Kelly Slater (USA)	1997	Lisa Anderson (USA)
1998	Kelly Slater (USA)	1998	Layne Beachley (Australia)
1999	Mark Occhilupa (Australia)	1999	Layne Beachley (Australia)
2000	Sunny Garcia (USA)	2000	Layne Beachley (Australia)
2001	C J Hopgood (USA)	2001	Layne Beachley (Australia)
2002	Andy Irons (Hawaii)	2002	Layne Beachley (Australia)
2003	Andy Irons (Hawaii)	2003	Layne Beachley (Australia
2004	Andy Irons (Hawaii)	2004	Sofia Mulanovich (Peru)
2005	Kelly Slater (USA)	2005	Chelsea Georgeson (Australia)
2006	Kelly Slater (USA)	2006	Layne Beachley (Australia)

Most wins: Men (8) Kelly Slater (USA) as above. Women (7) Layne Beachley (Australia) as above

SWIMMING AND DIVING

World championships

First held in 1973, the World Championships have since taken place in 1975, 1978, 1982, 1986, 1991, 1994, 1998, 2001, and 2003.

World champions: 2005 – men

50 m freestyle	Roland Schoeman (South Africa)
100 m freestyle	Filippo Magnini (Italy)
200 m freestyle	Michael Phelps (USA)
400 m freestyle	Grant Hackett (Australia)
800 m freestyle	Grant Hackett (Australia)
1500 m freestyle	Grant Hackett (Australia)
50 m backstroke	Aristeidis Grigoriadis (Greece)
100 m backstroke	Aaron Peirsol (USA)
200 m backstroke	Aaron Peirsol (USA)
50 m breaststroke	Mark Warnecke (Germany)
100 m breaststroke	Brendan Hansen (USA)
200 m breaststroke	Brendan Hansen (USA)
50 m butterfly	Roland Schoeman (South Africa)
100 m butterfly	Ian Crocker (USA)
200 m butterfly	Pawel Korzeniowski (Poland)
200 m individual medley	Michael Phelps (USA)
400 m individual medley	Laszlo Csech (Hungary)
4 x 100 m freestyle relay	USA
4 x 200 m freestyle relay	USA
4 x 100 m medley relay	USA
1 m springboard diving	Alexandre Despatie (Canada)
3 m springboard diving	Alexandre Despatie (Canada)
10 m platform diving	Hu Jia (China)

World champions: 2005 – women

50 m freestyle	Lisbeth Lenton (Australia)
100 m freestyle	Jodie Henry (Australia)
200 m freestyle	Solenne Figues (France)
400 m freestyle	Laure Manaudou (France)
800 m freestyle	Kate Ziegler (USA)
1500 m freestyle	Kate Ziegler (USA)
50 m backstroke	Giaan Rooney (Australia)
100 m backstroke	Kirsty Coventry (Zimbabwe)
200 m backstroke	Kirsty Coventry (Zimbabwe)
50 m breaststroke	Jade Edmistone (Australia)
100 m breaststroke	Leisel Jones (Australia)
200 m breaststroke	Leisel Jones (Australia)
50 m butterfly	Danni Miatke (Australia)
100 m butterfly	Jessica Schipper (Australia)
200 m butterfly	Otylia Jedrzejczak (Poland)
200 m individual medley	Katie Hoff (USA)
400 m individual medley	Katie Hoff (USA)
4 x 100 m freestyle relay	Australia
4 x 200 m freestyle relay	USA
4 x 100 m medley relay	Australia
1 m springboard diving	Blythe Hartley (Canada)
3 m springboard diving	Jingjing Guo (China)
10 m platform diving	Laura Ann Wilkinson (USA
Synchronized swimming	
Solo	Virginie Dedieu (France)
Duet	Russia
Team	Russia

Olympic Games

Gold medal winners: 2004 – men

50 m freestyle	Gary Hall Jr (USA)
100 m freestyle	Pieter van den Hoogenband (Netherlands)
200 m freestyle	Ian Thorpe (Australia)
400 m freestyle	Ian Thorpe (Australia)
1500 m freestyle	Grant Hackett (Australia)
100 m breaststroke	Kosuke Kitajima (Japan)
200 m breaststroke	Kosuke Kitajima (Japan)
100 m butterfly	Michael Phelps (USA)
200 m butterfly	Michael Phelps (USA)
100 m backstroke	Aaron Peirsol (USA)
200 m backstroke	Aaron Peirsol (USA)
200 m individual medley	Michael Phelps (USA)
400 m individual medley	Michael Phelps (USA)
400 m freestyle relay	South Africa
800 m freestyle relay	USA
400 m medley relay	USA

Gold medal winners: 2004 – women

50 m freestyle	Inge de Bruijn (Netherlands)
100 m freestyle	Jodie Henry (Australia)
200 m freestyle	Camelia Potec (Romania)
400 m freestyle	Laure Manaudou (France)
800 m freestyle	Ai Shibata (Japan)
100 m breaststroke	Xuejuan Luo (China)
200 m breaststroke	Amanda Beard (USA)
100 m backstroke	Natalie Coughlin (USA)
200 m backstroke	Kirsty Coventry (Zimbabwe)
100 m butterfly	Petria Thomas (Australia)
200 m butterfly	Otylia Jedrzejczak (Poland)
200 m individual medley	Yana Klochkova (Ukraine)
400 m individual medley	Yana Klochkova (Ukraine)
400 m freestyle relay	Australia
400 m medley relay	Australia
800 m freestyle relay	USA

TABLE TENNIS

World championships

First held in 1926 and usually every two years since 1957.

Recent winners: Swaythling Cup – men's team

1983	China	1995	China
1985	China	1997	China
1987	China	2000	Sweden
1989	Sweden	2001	China
1991	Sweden	2004	China
1993	Sweden	2006	China

Recent winners: Corbillon Cup – women's team

1983	China	1995	China
1985	China	1997	China
1987	China	1999	China
1989	China	2001	China
1991	S Korea	2004	China
1993	China	2006	China

Most wins: Swaythling Cup (15) China: 1961 1963, 1965, 1971, 1975, 1977, 1981, and as above. Corbillon Cup (16) China: 1965, 1975, 1977, 1979, 1981 and as above.

Recent winners: men

1971	Stellan Bengtsson (Sweden)
1973	Hsi En-Ting (China)
1975	Istvan Jonyer (Hungary)
1977	Mitsuru Kohno (Japan)
1979	Seiji Ono (Japan)
1981	Guo Yuehua (China)
1983	Guo Yuehua (China)
1985	Jiang Jialiang (China)
1987	Jiang Jialiang (China)
1989	Jan-Ove Waldner (Sweden)
1991	Jörgen Persson (Sweden)
1993	Jean-Philippe Gatien (France)
1995	Kong Linghui (China)
1997	Jan-Ove Waldner (Sweden)
1999	Liu Guoliang (China)
2001	Wang Liqin (China)
2003	Werner Schlager (Austria)
2005	Wang Liqin (China)

Most wins: (5) Viktor Barna (Hungary): 1930, 1932–5.

SPORTS AND GAMES

Table tennis, world championships
(continued)

Recent winners: women

1983 Cao Yanhua (China)
1985 Cao Yanhua (China)
1987 He Zhili (China)
1989 Qiao Hong (China)
1991 Deng Yaping (China)
1993 Hyun Jung-hwa (S Korea)
1995 Deng Yaping (China)
1997 Deng Yaping (China)
1999 Wang Nan (China)
2001 Wang Nan (China)
2003 Wang Nan (China)
2005 Zhang Yining (China)

Most wins: (6) Angelica Rozeanu (Romania): 1950–5.

Recent winners: doubles – men

1983 Dragutin Surbek/Zoran Kalinic (Yugoslavia)
1985 Mikael Applegren/Ulf Carlsson (Sweden)
1987 Chen Longcan/Wei Quinguang (China)
1989 Joerg Rosskopf/Stefen Fetzner (W Germany)
1991 Peter Karlson/Thomas von Scheele (Sweden)
1993 Wang Tao/Lu Lin (China)
1995 Wang Tao/Lu Lin (China)
1997 Kong Linghui/Liu Guoliang (China)
1999 Kong Linghui/Liu Guoliang (China)
2001 Wang Liqin/Yan Sen (China)
2003 Wang Liqin/Yan Sen (China)
2005 Kong Linghui/Wang Hao (China)

Most wins: (8) Viktor Barna (Hungary/England): 1929–33 (won two titles 1933), 1935, 1939.

Recent winners: doubles – women

1981 Zhang Deying/Cao Yanhua (China)
1983 Shen Jianping/Dai Lili (China)
1985 Dai Lili/Geng Lijuan (China)
1987 Yang Young-Ja/Hyun Jung-Hwa (Korea)
1989 Quio Hong/Deng Yaping (China)
1991 Chen Zhie/Gao Jun (China)

1993 Liu Wei/Qiao Yunping (China)
1995 Deng Yaping/Qiao Hong (China)
1997 Deng Yaping/Yang Ying (China)
1999 Wang Nan/Li Ju (China)
2001 Wang Nan/ Li Ju (China)
2003 Wang Nan/Zhang Yining (China)
2005 Wang Nan/Zhang Yining (China)

Most wins: (7) Maria Mednyanszky (Hungary): 1928, 1930–5.

Recent winners: mixed doubles

1981 Xie Saike/Huang Junqun (China)
1983 Guo Yuehua/Ni Xialian (China)
1985 Cai Zhenua/Coa Yanhua (China)
1987 Hui Jun/Geng Lijuan (China)
1989 Yoo Nam-Kyu/Hyun Jung-Hwa (S Korea)
1991 Wang Tao/Liu Wei (China)
1993 Wang Tao/Liu Wei (China)
1995 Wang Tao/Liu Wei (China)
1997 Liu Guoliang/Wu Na (China)
1999 Ma Lin/Zhang Yingying (China)
2001 Qin Zhijian/Yang Ying (China)
2003 Ma Lin/Wang Nan (China)
2005 Guo Yue/Wang Liqin (China)

Most wins: (6) Maria Mednyanszky (Hungary): 1927–8, 1930–1, 1933 (two titles).

Olympic Games

Gold medal winners: 2004

Men's singles
Ryu Min-Seung (South Korea)

Men's doubles
Chen Qi/Ma Lin (China)

Women's singles
Zhang Yining (China)

Women's doubles
Wang Nan/Li Ju (China)

TENNIS (LAWN)

Wimbledon Championships

The All-England Championships at Wimbledon are lawn tennis's most prestigious championships. First held in 1877.

Recent winners: men's singles

1992 Andre Agassi (USA)
1993 Pete Sampras (USA)
1994 Pete Sampras (USA)
1995 Pete Sampras (USA)
1996 Richard Krajicek (Netherlands)
1997 Pete Sampras (USA)
1998 Pete Sampras (USA)
1999 Pete Sampras (USA)
2000 Pete Sampras (USA)
2001 Goran Ivanisevic (Croatia)
2002 Lleyton Hewitt (Australia)
2003 Roger Federer (Switzerland)
2004 Roger Federer (Switzerland)
2005 Foger Federer (Switzerland)
2006 Roger Federer (Switzerland)

Most wins: (7) William Renshaw (Great Britain): 1881–6, 1889; Pete Sampras (USA): as above.

Recent winners: women's singles

1992 Steffi Graf (Germany)
1993 Steffi Graf (Germany)
1994 Conchita Martinez (Spain)
1995 Steffi Graf (Germany)
1996 Steffi Graf (Germany)
1997 Martina Hingis (Switzerland)
1998 Jana Novotná (Czech Republic)
1999 Lindsay Davenport (USA)
2000 Venus Williams (USA)
2001 Venus Williams (USA)
2002 Serena Williams (USA)
2003 Serena Williams (USA)
2004 Maria Sharapova (Russia)
2005 Venus Williams (USA)
2006 Amelie Mauresmo (France)

Most wins: (9) Martina Navratilova (Czechoslovakia/USA): 1978–9, 1982–7, 1990.

Recent winners: men's doubles

1993 Todd Woodbridge/Mark Woodforde (Australia)
1994 Todd Woodbridge/Mark Woodforde (Australia)
1995 Todd Woodbridge/Mark Woodforde (Australia)
1996 Todd Woodbridge/Mark Woodforde (Australia)
1997 Todd Woodbridge/Mark Woodforde (Australia)
1998 Jacco Eltingh/Paul Haarhuis (The Netherlands)
1999 Leander Paes/Mahesh Bhupathi (India)
2000 Todd Woodbridge/Mark Woodforde (Australia)
2001 Donald Johnson/Jared Palmer (USA)
2002 Todd Woodbridge (Australia)/Jonas Bjorkman (Sweden)
2003 Todd Woodbridge (Australia)/Jonas Bjorkman (Sweden)
2004 Todd Woodbridge (Australia)/Jonas Bjorkman (Sweden)
2005 Stephen Huss (Australia)/Wesley Moodie (South Africa)
2006 Bob Bryan/Mike Bryan (USA)

Most wins: (9) Todd Woodbridge (Australia): 6 with Mark Woodforde, 3 with Jonas Bjorkman, all as above.

Recent winners: women's doubles

1993 Gigi Fernandez (USA)/Natalya Zvereva (Belarus)
1994 Gigi Fernandez (USA)/Natalya Zvereva (Belarus)
1995 Jana Novotna (Czech Republic)/Arantxa Sanchez Vicario (Spain)
1996 Helena Sukova (Czech Republic)/Martina Hingis (Switzerland)
1997 Gigi Fernandez (USA)/Natalya Zvereva (Belarus)
1998 Jana Novotná (Czech Republic)/Martina Hingis (Switzerland)
1999 Lindsay Davenport/Corina Morariu (USA)
2000 Serena Williams/Venus Williams (USA)
2001 Lisa Raymond (USA)/Rennae Stubbs (Australia)
2002 Serena Williams/Venus Williams (USA)
2003 Kim Clijsters (Belgium)/Ai Sugiyama (Japan)
2004 Cara Black (Zimbabwe)/Rennae Stubbs (Australia)
2005 Cara Black (Zimbabwe)/Liezel Huber (South Africa)
2006 Zi Yan/Jie Zheng (China)

Most wins: (12) Elizabeth Ryan (USA): 1914, 1919–23, 1925–7, 1930, 1933–4.

Recent winners: mixed doubles

1993 Mark Woodforde (Australia)/Martina Navratilova (USA)
1994 Helena Sukova (Czech Republic)/Todd Woodbridge (Australia)
1995 Martina Navratilova/Jonathan Stark (USA)
1996 Helena Sukova/Cyril Suk (Czech Republic)
1997 Helena Sukova/Cyril Suk (Czech Republic)
1998 Serena Williams (USA)/Max Mirnyi (Belarus)
1999 Leander Paes (India)/Lisa Raymond (USA)
2000 Donald Johnson/Kimberly Po (USA)
2001 Daniela Hantuchova (Russia)/Leos Friedl (Czech Republic)
2002 Elena Likhovtseva (Russia)/Mahesh Bhupathi (India)
2003 Martina Navratilova (USA)/Leander Paes (India)
2004 Cara Black/Wayne Black (Zimbabwe)
2005 Mary Pierce (France)/Mahesh Bhupathi (India)
2006 Vera Zvonareva (Russia)/Andy Ram (Israel)

Most wins: (7) Elizabeth Ryan (USA): 1919, 1921, 1923, 1927–8, 1930, 1932.

Tennis court

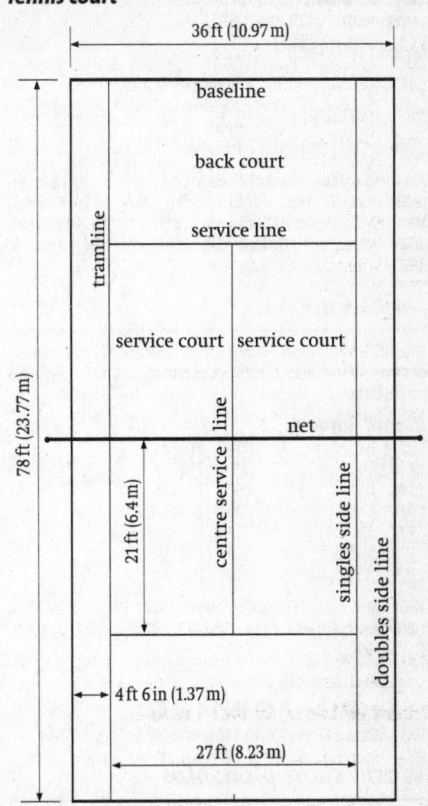

United States Open

First held in 1891 as the United States Championship; became the United States Open in 1968.

Recent winners: men's singles

1994 Andre Agassi (USA)
1995 Pete Sampras (USA)
1996 Pete Sampras (USA)
1997 Patrick Rafter (Australia)
1998 Patrick Rafter (Australia)
1999 Andre Agassi (USA)
2000 Marat Safin (Russia)
2001 Lleyton Hewitt (Australia)
2002 Pete Sampras (USA)
2003 Andy Roddick (USA)
2004 Roger Federer (Switzerland)
2005 Roger Federer (Switzerland)
2006 Roger Federer (Switzerland)

Recent winners: women's singles

1994 Arantxa Sánchez Vicario (Spain)
1995 Steffi Graf (Germany)
1996 Steffi Graf (Germany)
1997 Martina Hingis (Switzerland)
1998 Lindsay Davenport (USA)
1999 Serena Williams (USA)

Tennis (lawn) (continued)
2000 Venus Williams (USA)
2001 Venus Williams (USA)
2002 Serena Williams (USA)
2003 Justine Henin-Hardenne (Belgium)
2004 Svetlana Kuznetsova (Russia)
2005 Kim Clijsters (Belgium)
2006 Maria Sharapova (Russia)

Most wins: Men (7) Richard Sears (USA): 1881–7; Bill Larned (USA), 1901–2, 1907–11; Bill Tilden (USA): 1920–5, 1929. Women (7) Molla Mallory (née Bjurstedt) (USA): 1915–16, 1928, 1920–2, 1926; Helen Wills-Moody (USA): 1923–5, 1927–9, 1931.

Davis Cup

International team competition organized on a knock-out basis. First held in 1900; contested on a challenge basis until 1972.

Recent winners
1993	Germany	2000	Spain
1994	Sweden	2001	France
1995	USA	2002	Russia
1996	France	2003	Australia
1997	Sweden	2004	Spain
1998	Sweden	2005	Croatia
1999	Australia	2006	Russia

Most wins: (31) USA: 1900, 1902, 1913, 1920–6, 1937–8, 1946–9, 1954, 1958, 1963, 1968–72, 1978–9, 1981–2, 1990, 1992, 1995.

TENPIN BOWLING

World championships

First held in 1923 by the International Bowling Association; since 1954 organized by the Fédération Internationale des Quillieurs (FIQ). Since 1963, when women first competed, held every four years.

Recent winners: individual – men
1960 Tito Reynolds (Mexico)
1963 Les Zikes (USA)
1967 David Pond (Great Britain)
1971 Ed Luther (USA)
1975 Bud Staudt (USA)
1979 Ollie Ongtawco (Philippines)
1983 Armando Marino (Colombia)
1987 Rolland Patrick (France)
1991 Ma Ying-chei (Taiwan)
1995 Marc Doi (Canada)
1999 Ahmed Shaheen (Qatar)
2003 Michael Little (Australia)

Recent winners: individual – women
1975 Annedore Haefker (W Germany)
1979 Lita de la Roas (Philippines)
1983 Lena Sulkanen (Sweden)
1987 Edda Piccini (Italy)
1991 Martha Beckel (Germany)
1995 Debby Ship (Canada)
1999 Ann-Marie Putney (Australia)
2003 Diandra Hyman (USA)

Most wins: No one has won more than once.

TRAMPOLINING

World championships

First held in 1964 and annually until 1968; since then, usually every two years.

Recent winners: individual – men
1982 Carl Furrer (Great Britain)
1984 Lionel Pioline (France)
1986 Lionel Pioline (France)
1988 Vadim Krasnoshapka (USSR)
1990 Alexander Moskalenko (USSR)
1992 Alexander Moskalenko (Russia)
1994 Alexander Moskalenko (Russia)
1996 Dimitri Poliarauch (Belarus)
1998 German Khnivchev (Russia)
1999 Alexander Moskalenko (Russia)
2001 Alexander Moskalenko (Russia)
2003 Henrik Stehlik (Germany)
2005 Aleksander Rusakov (Russia)

Most wins: (5) Alexander Moskalenko (Russia): as above.

Recent winners: individual – women
1982 Ruth Keller (Switzerland)
1984 Sue Shotton (Great Britain)
1986 Tatyana Lushina (USSR)
1988 Rusadan Khoperia (USSR)
1990 Yelena Merkulova (USSR)
1992 Yelena Merkulova (Russia)
1994 Irina Karavaeva (Russia)
1996 Tatyana Kovaleva (Russia)
1998 Irina Karavaeva (Russia)
1999 Irina Karavaeva (Russia)
2001 Anna Dogonadze (Germany)
2003 Karen Cockburn (Canada)
2005 Irina Karavaeva (Russia)

Most wins: (5) Judy Wills (USA): 1964–8.

TUG OF WAR

World championships

Instituted in 1975. Held every two years; contested at 560 kg from 1982.

Winners
	720 kg	640 kg	560 kg	Catchweight (no specification)
1984	Ireland	Ireland	England	England
1985	Switzerland	Switzerland	Switzerland	–
1986	Ireland	Ireland	England	–
1988	Ireland	England	England	–
1990	Ireland	Ireland	Switzerland	–
1992	Switzerland	Switzerland	Spain	
1994	Switzerland	Switzerland	Spain	
1996	Netherlands	Switzerland	Spain	
1998	Netherlands	England	Spain	
2000	Switzerland	Switzerland	Switzerland	
2002	Netherlands	Switzerland	Switzerland	
2004	Netherlands	Switzerland	England	
2006	Switzerland	Germany	Switzerland	

Most titles: (17) England: 1975–82 and as above.

VOLLEYBALL

World championships

Inaugurated in 1949; first women's championships in 1952. Now held every four years, but Olympic champions are also world champions in Olympic years.

Recent winners: men

1982	USSR	1994	Italy
1984	USA	1996	Netherlands
1986	USA	1998	Italy
1988	USA	2002	Brazil
1990	Italy	2004	Brazil
1992	Brazil	2006	Brazil

Recent winners: women

1982	China	1994	Cuba
1984	China	1996	Cuba
1986	China	1998	Cuba
1988	USSR	2002	Italy
1990	USSR	2004	China
1992	Cuba	2006	Russia

Most wins: Men (9), USSR: 1949, 1952, 1960, 1962, 1964 1968, 1978, 1980, 1982. Women (9) USSR: 1952, 1956, 1960, 1968, 1970, 1972, 1980, 1988, 1990.

WALKING

World Race Walking Cup

Men's competition, formerly the Lugano Trophy (to 1999), held 1961–79. Separate men's team competition for 20 km and 50 km introduced in 1993. Women's competition, formerly the 5 km Eschborn Cup, first held in 1979; changed to 10 km (1983) and 20 km (1999). Competitions take place every two years.

Recent winners: men

20 km

1999	Russia
2002	Russia
2004	China
2006	Spain

50 km

1999	Russia
2002	Russia
2004	Russia
2006	Spain

Recent winners: women

20 km

1997	Russia
1999	China
2002	Russia
2004	China
2006	Russia

WATER POLO

World championship

First held in 1973, and usually every four years since 1978. It is usually included in the world swimming championships, but is occasionally held separately. First women's event held in 1986.

Recent winners: men

1982	USSR	1998	Spain
1986	Yugoslavia	2001	Spain
1991	Yugoslavia	2005	Serbia &
1994	Italy		Montenegro

Winners: women

1986	Australia	2001	Italy
1991	Netherlands	2003	USA
1994	Hungary	2005	Hungary
1998	Italy		

World Cup

Inaugurated in 1979 and usually held every two years. Women's event unofficial until 1989.

Recent winners: men

1985	W Germany	1997	USA
1987	Yugoslavia	1999	Hungary
1989	Yugoslavia	2002	Russia
1991	USA	2006	Serbia &
1993	Italy		Montenegro
1995	Hungary		

Most wins: (3) USSR/Russia: 1981, 1983, 2002.

Recent winners: women

1993	Netherlands
1995	Australia
1997	Netherlands
1999	Netherlands
2002	Hungary
2006	Australia

Most wins: (8) Netherlands: 1980–93, 1997, 1999

WATER SKIING

World championships

First held in 1949; take place every two years.

Recent winners: overall – men

1983	Sammy Duvall (USA)
1985	Sammy Duvall (USA)
1987	Sammy Duvall (USA)
1989	Patrice Martin (France)
1991	Patrice Martin (France)
1993	Patrice Martin (France)
1995	Patrice Martin (France)
1997	Patrice Martin (France)
1999	Patrice Martin (France)
2001	Jaret Llewellyn (Canada)
2003	Jimmy Siemers (USA)
2005	Jimmy Siemens (USA)

Most wins: (6) Patrice Martin (France): as above.

Recent winners: overall – women

1983	Ana-Maria Carrasco (Venezuela)
1985	Karen Neville (Australia)
1987	Deena Brush (USA)
1989	Deena Mapple (USA)
1991	Karen Neville (Australia)
1993	Natalia Rumiantseva (Russia)
1995	Judy Messer (Canada)
1997	Elena Milakova (Russia)
1999	Elena Milakova (Russia)
2001	Elena Milakova (Russia)
2003	Regina Jaquess (USA)
2005	Regina Jaquess (USA)

Most wins: (3) Willa McGuire (USA): 1949–50, 1955; Liz Allan-Shetter (USA): 1965, 1969, 1975; Elena Milakova (Russia) 1997–2001.

WEIGHTLIFTING

World championships

First held in 1898. 11 weight divisions; the most prestigious is the 105+ kg category (formerly known as Super Heavyweight). Olympic champions are automatically world champions in Olympic years.

Recent champions: over 105+ kg

1992	Alexander Kurlovich (USSR)
1992	Alexander Kurlovich (Unified Team)
1993	Ronnie Weller (Germany)
1994	Alexander Kurlovich (Belarus)
1995	Alexander Kurlovich (Belarus)
1996	Andrey Chermerkin (Russia)
1997	Andrey Chermerkin (Russia)
1998	Andrey Chermerkin (Russia)
1999	Andrey Chermerkin (Russia)
2000	Hossein Rezazadeh (Iran)
2001	Saeed Salem Jaber (Quatar)
2002	Hossein Rezazadeh (Iran)
2003	Hossein Rezazadeh (Iran)
2004	Hossein Rezazadeh (Iran)
2005	Hossein Rezazadeh (Iran)
2006	Hossein Rezazadeh (Iran)

Most titles (all categories): (8) John Davies (USA): 1938 (82.5 kg), 1946–50 (over 82.5 kg), 1951–2 (over 90 kg), Tommy Kono (USA): 1952 (67.5 kg), 1953, 1957–9 (75 kg), 1954–6 (82.5 kg) Vasiliy Alexseyev (USSR): 1970–7 (over 110 kg).

WRESTLING

World championships

Graeco-Roman world championships first held in 1921. First freestyle championships in 1951; each style contests 10 weight divisions, the heaviest being the 130 kg (formerly over 100 kg) category. Olympic champions become world champions in Olympic years.

Recent winners: freestyle – super-heavyweight/96–120 kg

1984	Bruce Baumgartner (USA)
1985	David Gobedzhishvili (USSR)
1986	Bruce Baumgartner (USA)
1987	Khadartsv Aslam (USSR)
1988	David Gobedzhishvili (USSR)
1989	Ali Reiza Soleimani (Iran)
1990	David Gobedzhishvili (USSR)
1991	Andreas Schroder (Germany)
1992	Bruce Baumgartner (USA)
1993	Mikael Ljunberg (Sweden)
1994	Mahmut Demir (Turkey)
1995	Bruce Baumgartner (USA)
1996	Mahmut Demir (Turkey)
1997	Zekeriya Güglü (Turkey)
1998	Alexis Rodriguez (Cuba)
1999	Stephen Neal (USA)
2000	David Moussoulbes (Russia)
2001	David Moussoulbes (Russia)
2002	David Moussoulbes (Russia)
2003	Artur Taymazov (Uzbekistan)
2004	Artur Taymazov (Uzbekistan)
2005	Aydin Polatci (Turkey)
2006	Artur Taymazov (Uzbekistan)

Recent winners: Graeco-Roman – super-heavyweight/96–120 kg

1983	Jevgeniy Artiochin (USSR)
1984	Jeffrey Blatnick (USA)
1985	Igor Rostozotskiy (USSR)
1986	Thomas Johansson (Sweden)
1987	Igor Rostozotskiy (USSR)
1988	Alexander Karelin (USSR)
1989	Alexander Karelin (USSR)
1990	Alexander Karelin (USSR)
1991	Alexander Karelin (USSR)
1992	Alexander Karelin (Unified Team)
1993	Alexander Karelin (Russia)
1994	Alexander Karelin (Russia)
1995	Alexander Karelin (Russia)
1996	Alexander Karelin (Russia)
1997	Alexander Karelin (Russia)
1998	Alexander Karelin (Russia)
1999	Alexander Karelin (Russia)
2000	Rulon Gardner (USA)
2001	Rulon Gardner (USA)
2002	Dremiel Byers (USA)
2003	Khassan Baroev (Russia)
2004	Khassan Baroev (Russia)
2005	Mijail Lopez (Cuba)
2006	Khassan Baroev (Russia)

Most titles (all weight divisions): Freestyle (10) Alexander Medved (USSR): 1962–4, 1966 (90 kg), 1967–8 (100 kg), 1969–72 (over 100 kg). Graeco-Roman (12) Alexander Karelin (Russia): as above (over 100 kg).

YACHTING

America's Cup

One of sport's famous trophies, first won by the schooner *Magic* in 1870. Now held approximately every four years, when challengers compete in a series of races to find which of them races against the holder. All 25 winners up to 1983 were from the United States.

Recent winners

1958	*Columbia* (USA) (Briggs Cunningham)
1962	*Weatherly* (USA) (Emil Mosbacher)
1964	*Constellation* (USA) (Bob Bavier)
1967	*Intrepid* (USA) (Emil Mosbacher)
1970	*Intrepid* (USA) (Bill Ficker)
1974	*Courageous* (USA) (Ted Hood)
1977	*Courageous* (USA) (Ted Turner)
1980	*Freedom* (USA) (Dennis Conner)
1983	*Australia II* (Australia) (John Bertrand)
1987	*Stars & Stripes* (USA) (Dennis Conner)
1988	*Stars & Stripes* (USA) (Dennis Conner)[a]
1992	*America 3* (USA) (Bill Koch)
1995	*Black Magic* (New Zealand) (Russell Coutts)
2000	*Black Magic* (New Zealand) (Russell Coutts)
2003	*Alinghi* (Switzerland) (Russell Coutts)

[a]*Stars & Stripes* won a special challenge match but on appeal the race was awarded to *New Zealand*, skippered by Davis Barnes. However, after much legal wrangling, the cup was retained by *Stars & Stripes*.

Most wins: (Skipper) (3) Charlie Barr (USA): 1899, 1901, 1903; Harold Vanderbilt (USA): 1930, 1934, 1937; Dennis Conner (USA): as above.

Admiral's Cup

A two-yearly series of races in the English Channel, around Fastnet rock and at Cowes; national teams of three boats per team. First held in 1957.

Recent winners

1975	Great Britain	1991	France
1977	Great Britain	1993	Germany
1979	Australia	1995	Italy
1981	Great Britain	1997	USA
1983	W Germany	1999	The Netherlands
1985	W Germany	2001	*Not held*
1987	New Zealand	2003	Australia
1989	Great Britain	2005	*Not held*

Most wins: (9) Great Britain: 1957, 1959, 1963, 1965, 1971, 1975, 1977, 1981, 1989.

International racing yacht classes

Class	Crew	Type of craft
Finn	1	Centre-board dinghy
Flying Dutchman	2	Centre-board dinghy
International 470	2	Centre-board dinghy
International Soling	3	Keel boat
International Star	2	Keel boat
International Tornado	2	Catamaran
Windglider	1	Single board

WORLD RECORDS

Athletics

World outdoor records

World outdoor records have been recognized by the International Amateur Federation (IAAF) since 1913; marathon events designated as "world best performances".

Men

100m	9.77	2005	Asafa Powell (Jamaica)
200m	19.32	1996	Michael Johnson (USA)
400m	43.18	1999	Michael Johnson (USA)
800m	1:41.11	1997	Wilson Kipketer (Denmark)
1000m	2:11.96	1999	Noah Ngeny (Kenya)
1500m	3:26.00	1998	Hicham El Guerrouj (Morocco)
Mile	3:43.13	1999	Hicham El Guerrouj (Morocco)
2000m	4:44.79	1999	Hicham El Guerrouj (Morocco)
3000m	7:20.67	1996	Daniel Komen (Kenya)
3000m steeplechase	7.53.17	2002	Brahim Boulami (Morocco)
5000m	12:37.35	2004	Kenenisa Bekele (Ethiopia)
10000m	26:17.53	2005	Kenenisa Bekele (Ethiopia)
20000m	56:55.6	1991	Arturo Barrios (Mexico)
Hour	21.101	1991	Arturo Barrios (Mexico)
25000m	1:13:55.8	1981	Toshihiko Seko (Japan)
30000m	1:29:18.8	1981	Toshihiko Seko (Japan)
Marathon	2:04.55	2003	Paul Tergat (Kenya)
110m hurdles	12.88	2006	Liu Xiang (China)
400m hurdles	46.78	1992	Kevin Young (USA)
20km track walk	1:17:21	2003	Jefferson Pérez (Ecuador)
30000m track walk	2:01:44.1	1992	Maurizio Damilano (Italy)
50km track walk	3:36:03	2003	Robert Korzeniowski (Poland)
4×100m relay	37.40	1993	Jon Drummond, Leroy Burrell, Dennis Mitchell, Andre Cason (USA)
4×200m relay	1:18.68	1994	Mike Marsh, Leroy Burrell, Floyd Heard, Carl Lewis (USA)
4×400m	2:54.20	1998	Jerome Young, Antonio Pettigrew, Michael Johnson, Tyree Washington (USA)
4×800m relay	7:03.89	1982	Peter Elliott, Garry Cook, Steve Cram, Sebastian Coe (Great Britain)
4×1500m	14:38.8	1977	Thomas Wessinghage, Harald Hudak, Michael Lederer, Karl Fleschen (West Germany)
High jump	2.45m	1993	Javier Sotomayor (Cuba)
Pole vault	6.14m	1994	Sergey Bubka (Ukraine)
Long jump	8.95m	1991	Mike Powell (USA)
Triple jump	18.29m	1995	Jonathan Edwards (Great Britain)
Shot	23.12m	1990	Randy Barnes (USA)
Discus	74.08m	1986	Jurgen Schult (East Germany)
Hammer	86.74m	1986	Yuri Syedikh (USSR)
Javelin	98.48m	1996	Jan Zelezny (Czech Republic)
Decathlon	9026 points	2001	Roman Šebrle (Czech Republic)

Women

100m	10.49	1988	Florence Griffith Joyner (USA)
200m	21.34	1988	Florence Griffith Joyner (USA)
400m	47.60	1985	Marita Koch (East Germany)
800m	1:53.28	1983	Jarmila Kratochvilova (Czechoslovakia)
1000m	2:28.98	1996	Svetlana Masterkova (Russia)
1500m	3:50.46	1993	Qu Yunxia (China)
Mile	4: 12.56	1996	Svetlana Masterkova (Russia)
2000m	5:25.36	1994	Sonia O'Sullivan (Ireland)
3000m	8:06.11	1993	Wang Yunxia (China)
5000m	14:24.53	2006	Meseret Defar (Ethiopia)
10000m	29:31.78	1993	Wang Yunxia (China)
20000m	1:05:26.6	2000	Tegla Loroupe (Kenya)
Hour	18.340	1998	Tegla Loroupe (Kenya)
25000m	1:27:05.84	2002	Tegla Loroupe (Kenya)

World records (continued)

30 000m	1:45:50.0	2003	Tegla Loroupe (Kenya)
Marathon	2:15:25	2003	Paula Radcliffe (Great Britain)
100m hurdles	12.21	1988	Yordanka Donkova (Bulgaria)
400m hurdles	52.34	2003	Yuliya Pechonkina (Russia)
10 000m track walk	41:56.23	1990	Nadezhea Ryashkina (USSR)
20km track walk	1:25:41.5	2001	Olimpiada Ivanova (Russia)
50km track walk	4:55:19.4	1998	Svetlana Bychenkova (Russia)
4×100m relay	41.37	1985	Silke Gladisch, Sabine Reiger, Ingrid Auerswald, Marlies Göhr (East Germany)
4×200m relay	1:27.46	2000	Latasha Jenkins, La Tasha Colander Richardson, Nanceen Perry, Marion Jones (USA)
4×400m	3:15.17	1988	Tatyana Ledovskaya, Olga Nazarove, Maria Pinigina, Olga Bryzgina (USSR)
4×800m relay	7:50.17	1984	Nadezhda Olizarenko, Lyubov Gurina, Lyudmila Borisova, Irina Podyalovskaya (USSR)
High jump	2.09 m	1987	Stefka Kostadinova (Bulgaria)
Pole vault	4.91 m	2006	Yelena Isinbayeva (Russia)
Long jump	7.52 m	1988	Galina Chistyakova (USSR)
Triple jump	15.50 m	1995	Inessa Kravets (Ukraine)
Shot	22.63 m	1987	Natalya Lisovskaya (USSR)
Discus	76.80 m	1988	Gabriele Reinsch (East Germany)
Hammer	77.80 m*	2006	Tatyana Lysenko (Russia) *awaiting IAAF ratification
Javelin	71.70 m	2005	Osleidys Menendez (Cuba)
Heptathlon	7291 points	1988	Jackie Joyner-Kersee (USA)

World indoor records

World indoor records have been recognized by the International Amateur Federation (IAAF) since 1 Jan 1987.

Men

50m	5.56	1996	Donovan Bailey (Canada)
60m	6.39	1998	Maurice Greene (USA)
200m	19.92	1996	Frankie Fredericks (Namibia)
400m	44.57	2005	Kerron Clement (USA)
800m	1:42.67	1997	Wilson Kipketer (Denmark)
1000m	2: 14.96	2000	Wilson Kipketer (Denmark)
1500m	3:31.18	1997	Hicham El Guerrouj (Morocco)
Mile	3:48.45	1997	Hicham El Guerrouj (Morocco)
2000m	4:52.86	1998	Haile Gebrselassie (Ethiopia)
3000m	7:24.90	1998	Daniel Komen (Kenya)
5 000m	12:49.60	2004	Kenenisa Bekele (Ethiopia)
50m hurdles	6.25	1986	Mark McKoy (Canada)
60m hurdles	7.30	1994	Colin Jackson (Great Britain)
5 000m walk	18:07.08	1995	Mikhail Schennikov (Russia)
4×200m relay	1:22.11	1991	Linford Christie, Darren Braithwaite, Ade Mafe, John Regis (Great Britain)
4×400m relay	3:02.83	1999	Andre Morris, Dameon Johnson, Deon Minor, Milton Campbell (USA)
High jump	2.43	1989	Javier Sotomayor (Cuba)
Pole vault	6. 15	1993	Sergey Bubka (Unified Team)
Long jump	8.79	1984	Carl Lewis (USA)
Triple jump	17.83	1997	Aliacer Urrutia (Cuba)
Shot	22.66	1989	Randy Barnes (USA)
Pentathlon	4440 points	1990	Christian Plaziat (France)
Heptathlon	6476 points	1993	Dan O'Brien (USA)

Women

50m	5.96	1995	Irina Privalova (Russia)
60m	6.92	1995	Irina Privalova (Russia)
200m	21.87	1993	Merlene Ottey (Jamaica)
400m	49.59	1982	Jarmila Kratochvilova (Czechoslovakia)
800m	1:55.82	2002	Jolanda Ceplak (Slovenia)
1000m	2:30.94	1999	Maria Mutola (Mozambique)
1500m	3:58.28	2006	Yelena Soboleva (Russia)
Mile	4:17.14	1990	Doina Melinte (Romania)
3 000m	8:27.86	2006	Liliya Shobukhova (Russia)
5 000m	14:32.93	2005	Tirunesh Dibaba (Ethiopia)
50m hurdles	6.58	1988	Cornelia Oschkenat (East Germany)

60m hurdles	7.69	1990	Lyudmila Narozhilenko (USSR)
3000m walk	11:35.34	2003	Gillian O'Sullivan (Ireland)
4×200m relay	1:32.41	2005	Yekaterina Kondratyeva, Irina Khabarova, Yuliya Pechonkina, Yuliya Gushchina (Russia)
4×400m relay	3:23.37	2006	Yuliya Gushchina, Olga Kotlyarova, Olga Zaytseva, Olesya Krasnomovets (Russia)
High jump	2.08 m	2006	Kajsa Bergqvist (Sweden)
Pole vault	4.91 m	2006	Yelena Isinbayeva (Russia)
Long jump	7.37 m	1992	Heike Drechsler (East Germany)
Triple jump	15.36 m	2004	Tatyana Lebedeva (Russia)
Shot	22.50 m	1977	Helena Fibingerova (Czechoslovakia)
Pentathlon	4991 points	1992	Irina Byelova (Unified Team)

Swimming

World records
Men
Freestyle

50m	0:21.64	2000	Alexander Popov (Russia)
100m	0:47.84	2000	Pieter van den Hoogenband (Netherlands)
200m	1:44.06	2001	Ian Thorpe (Australia)
400m	3:40.08	2002	Ian Thorpe (Australia)
800m	7:38.65	2005	Grant Hackett (Australia)
1500m	14:34.56	2001	Grant Hackett (Australia)

Breaststroke

100m	0:59.13	2006	Brendan Hansen (USA)
200m	2:08.74	2006	Brendan Hansen (USA)

Butterfly

100m	0:50.40	2005	Ian Crocker (USA)
200m	1:53.80	2006	Michael Phelps (USA)

Backstroke

100m	0:53.17	2005	Aaron Peirsol (USA)
200m	1:54.44	2006	Aaron Peirsol (USA)

Individual medley

200m	1:55.84	2006	Michael Phelps (USA)
400m	4:08.26	2004	Michael Phelps (USA)

Freestyle relays

4×100m	3:12.46	2006	Michael Phelps, Cullen Jones, Neil Walker, Jason Lezak (USA)
4×200m	7:04.66	2001	Grant Hackett, Michael Klim, William Kirby, Ian Thorpe (Australia)

Medley relays

4×100m	3:30.68	2004	Aaron Peirsol, Ian Crocker, Brendan Hansen, Jason Lezak (USA)

Women
Freestyle

50m	0:24.13	2000	Inge de Bruijn (Netherlands)
100m	0:53.30	2006	Britta Steffen (Germany)
200m	1:56.64	2002	Franziska van Almsick (Germany)
400m	4:02.13	2006	Laure Manadou (France)
800m	8:16.22	1989	Janet Evans (USA)
1500m	15:52.10	1988	Janet Evans (USA)

Breaststroke

100m	1:05.09	2006	Leisel Jones (Australia)
200m	2:20.54	2006	Leisel Jones (Australia)

Butterfly

100m	0:56.61	2000	Inge de Bruijn (Netherlands)
200m	2:05.40	2006	Jessicah Schipper (Australia)

Backstroke

100m	59.58	2002	Natalie Coughlin (USA)
200m	2:06.62	1991	Kristina Egerszegi (Hungary)

World records (continued)

Individual medley

200m	2:09.72	1997	Wu Yanyan (China)
400m	4:33.59	2000	Yana Klochkova (Ukraine)

Freestyle relays

4×100m	3:35.22	2006	Petra Dallmann, Daniela Götz, Britta Steffen, Annika Liebs (Germany)
4×200m	7:50.82	2006	Petra Dallmann, Daniela Samulski, Britta Steffen, Annika Liebs (Germany)

Medley relays

4×100m	3:56.30	2006	Jessicah Schipper, Leisel Jones, Lisbeth Lenton, Sophie Edington (Australia)

SPORTS PERSONALITIES

Name	Dates	Nationality	Sport	Achievements
Aaron, Hank	1934–	American	Baseball	Batting outfielder with Milwaukee Braves, Atlanta Braves, Milwaukee Brewers; hit 755 home runs
Abdul-Jabbar, Kareem	1947–	American	Basketball	Played for Milwaukee Bucks, LA Lakers; set individual points record of 38 387
Agassi, Andre	1970–	American	Tennis	Titles: Wimbledon singles 1992; US Open singles 1994, 1999; Australian Open singles 1995, 2000–1, 2003; Olympic singles gold medal 1996; French Open 1999
Agostini, Giacomo	1944–	Italian	Motor cycling	Record 15 world titles, 1966–75, including 500 cc title record eight times, 1966–72, 1975
Alekhine, Alexander	1892–1946	French	Chess	World champion, 1927–35, 1937–46
Alexeev, Vasiliy	1942–	Russian	Weightlifting	Olympic super-heavyweight champion, 1972, 1976, world champion, 1970–1,1973–5, 1977; European champion, 1970–8; broke 80 world records
Ali, Muhammad (Cassius Marcellus Clay)	1942–	American	Boxing	World heavyweight champion, 1964–7, 1974–8, 1978–81
Aouita, Said	1960–	Moroccan	Athletics	World records in 1500m, 5000m, 2 mile, 2000m; Olympic 500m gold medallist, 1984, 1987
Armstrong, Lance	1971–	American	Cycling	Won Tour de France a record 7 times, 1999–2005
Ashe, Arthur	1943–93	American	Tennis	US national singles and Open champion, 1968; Wimbledon singles champion, 1975
Ballesteros, Severiano	1957–	Spanish	Golf	British Open champion, 1979, 1984, 1988; US Masters, 1980, 1983
Bannister, Sir Roger	1929–	British	Athletics	First man to run mile in under 4 minutes (3 min 59.4 s), 1954
Barneveld, Raymond	1968–	Dutch	Darts	Wins include World Cup (individual) 1997, 1999, 2003, British Open 1998, World Championship 1998–9, 2003, 2005
Barrington, Jonah	1941–	British	Squash	British Open champion, 1967–73
Beamon, Bob	1946–	American	Athletics	At 1968 Olympics set long-standing 8.9m long jump record
Beckenbauer, Franz	1945–	German	Football	Captained West Germany to victory in 1974 World Cup; European Footballer of the Year, 1972; manager of Germany 1986
Becker, Boris	1967–	German	Tennis	Youngest ever Wimbledon men's singles winner, 1985; Wimbledon champion, 1986, 1989, US Open champion, 1989, Australian Open champion, 1991, 1996, ATP world title-holder, 1992
Beckham, David	1975–	British	Football	Manchester United 1993–2003, England 1996; Real Madrid 2003; FA Cup, League Championship, European Cup medals 1998–9 with United; England captain 2002–6

Name	Dates	Nationality	Sport	Achievements
Berra, Yogi	1925–	American	Baseball	Record 14 World Series with New York Yankees, 1946–63; record 313 home runs by a catcher; managed Yankees, New York Mets, Houston Astros
Best, George	1946–2005	Northern Ireland	Football	Leading scorer with Manchester United, 1967–8; European Cup-winner's medal and European Footballer of the Year, 1968
Biondi, Matt	1965–	American	Swimming	Triple gold medallist, 1986 world championships; five Olympic golds, 1988
Blanco, Serge	1958–	French	Rugby union	Fullback, played in record 93 internationals; in Grand Slam-winning sides 1981, 1987
Bonington, Chris	1934–	British	Mountaineering	Climbed Everest, 1985, led expeditions on Annapurna II, Nuptse, Eiger, Mt Vinson, and other peaks
Border, Allan	1955–	Australian	Cricket	Batsman, first captained Australia 1984–5; set record 10123 runs in Test cricket, 1993
Borg, Björn	1956–	Swedish	Tennis	Wimbledon singles champion, 1976–80; won two Italian championships, six French Open titles 1974–81
Borotra, Jean	1898–1994	French	Tennis	Wimbledon singles champion, 1924; also won French and Australian championships
Botham, Ian	1955–	British	Cricket	Batsman/bowler for Somerset, Worcestershire, Durham, England; scored 14 centuries, 5200 runs in Test cricket, took record 383 Test wickets
Botvinnik, Mikhail Moiseyevich	1911–95	Russian	Chess	World champion, 1948–57, 1958–60, 1961–3
Boycott, Geoffrey	1940–	British	Cricket	Batsman with Yorkshire and England; won 108 caps, scored 48 426 runs, including record 8114 in Test matches
Brabham, Sir Jack	1926–	Australian	Motor racing	Formula One world champion, 1959, 1960, 1966
Bradman, Sir Donald	1908–2001	Australian	Cricket	Captain of Australia; averaged 99.94 runs per Test innings, scored record Australian Test 334 runs against England, 1930
Bristow, Eric	1957–	British	Darts	World professional champion record five times, 1980–1, 1984–6
Broome, David	1940–	British	Show jumping	World champion show jumper, 1970; European champion, 1961,1967, 1969; Olympic bronze medallist, 1960, 1968
Brough, Louise	1923–	American	Tennis	Wimbledon singles champion, 1948–50, 1955; US national singles title, 1947, Australian singles title, 1950, many doubles titles
Bruno, Frank	1961–	British	Boxing	World heavyweight champion, 1995
Bryant, David	1931–	British	Bowling	World outdoor champion, 1966, 1980, 1988; world indoor champion, 1979–81
Budge, Don	1916–2000	American	Tennis	First player to win all four Grand Slam events in one year, 1938; Wimbledon singles, men's doubles, mixed doubles champion, 1937, 1938
Bueno, Maria	1939–	Brazilian	Tennis	Wimbledon singles champion, 1959, 1960, 1964; four US singles, five Wimbledon doubles, four US doubles titles
Busby, Sir Matt	1909–94	British	Football	Manager of Manchester United, 1945–69, won FA Cup, 1948, 1963, League championship, 1952, 1956, 1957, 1965, 1967, European Cup, 1968
Campbell, Donald	1921–67	British	Speed records	Reached record 403.1 mph on land, 276.33 mph on water, both 1964; killed in water speed record attempt on L Coniston
Campbell, Sir Malcolm	1885–1949	British	Speed records	Reached record 301.13 mph on land, 1935, 141.74 mph on water, 1939
Campese, David	1962–	Australian	Rugby union	Record 52 international tries, by 1993; holds record for Australian caps

Sports personalities (continued)

Name	Dates	Nationality	Sport	Achievements
Cantona, Eric	1966 –	French	Football	Striker with Marseille, Leeds United, Manchester United; 1994 FA Cup, League championship medals; first foreign player to win British PFA Player of the Year, 1994
Capablanca, José Raúl	1888–1942	Cuban	Chess	World champion, 1921–7
Carson, Willie	1942–	British	Horse racing	Champion jockey, 1972–3, 1978, 1980, 1983; won three Derby races, 1979, 1980, 1989
Caslavska, Vera	1943–	Czech	Gymnastics	Record 21 world, Olympic, and European gold medals, 1959–68
Cawley, Evonne (Yvonne Goolagong)	1951–	Australian	Tennis	Wimbledon singles champion, 1971, 1981; won Australian Open four times
Charlton, Bobby	1937–	British	Football	Five League Championship medals, one FA Cup-winner's medal, one European Cup-winner's medal with Manchester United; 106 caps for England; in 1996 World Cup-winning side
Charlton, Jack	1935–	British	Football	Played for Leeds United, and England in 1966 World Cup-winning squad; manager of the Republic of Ireland 1986–96
Chamberlain, Wilt	1936–99	American	Basketball	Scored record 100 points in one game, 4029 points in one season, with Philadelphia 76ers, 1962; leading scorer in National Basketball Association, 1960–6
Christie, Linford	1960–	British	Athletics	Olympic 100m gold medallist, 1992; 100m gold medallist Commonwealth Games, 1990, European championships, 1986, 1990, world championships, 1989, 1992, world athletic championships, 1993
Clark, Jim	1937–68	British	Motor racing	Formula One world champion, 1963, 1965; won 25 Grands Prix
Cobb, Ty	1886–1961	American	Baseball	Base runner and batter for Detroit and Philadelphia; set record of over 4000 base hits and record .367 career batting average
Coe, Sebastian (Lord Coe)	1956–	British	Athletics	Olympic 1500m gold medallist, 1980, 1984, Olympic 800m silver medallist, 1980, 1984; broke eight world records
Comaneci, Nadia	1961–	Romanian	Gymnastics	Olympic gold medals in beam, vault, floor disciplines, 1976; beam, parallel bars, 1980
Compton, Denis	1918–97	British	Cricket, football	Batsman/bowler for Middlesex and England, scored 38 942 runs, took 622 wickets; football for Arsenal and England
Connolly, Maureen	1934–69	American	Tennis	Wimbledon singles champion, 1952–4; first woman to win all four Grand Slam events, 1953
Connors, Jimmy	1952–	American	Tennis	Wimbledon singles champion, 1974, 1982; US Open champion, 1974, 1976, 1978, 1982–3
Constantine, Learie Nicholas, Baron	1902–71	West Indian	Cricket	First West Indian cricketer to score 1000 runs and take 100 wickets in one season, 1928
Cordobés, El (Manuel Benitez Pérez)	c. 1936–	Spanish	Bullfighting	Highest paid matador in history
Court, Margaret	1942–	Australian	Tennis	Record 66 Grand Slam events; Wimbledon singles champion, 1963, 1965, 1970
Cowdrey, Colin	1932–2000	British	Cricket	Batsman and captain of Kent and England; scored 107 centuries, 7264 Test runs
Cram, Steve	1960–	British	Athletics	World 1500m champion, 1983; Commonwealth 1500m gold medallist, 1982, 1986; 800m champion, 1986
Cruyff, Johan(nes)	1947–	Dutch	Football	11 League and Cup titles, three European Cups, 1971–3, with Ajax; captained Holland, 1974 World Cup Final; played for Barcelona and Feyenoord

Name	Dates	Nationality	Sport	Achievements
Curry, John Anthony	1949–94	British	Ice-skating	British figure-skating champion, 1970; Olympic figure-skating gold medallist, 1976
Dalglish, Kenny	1951–	British	Football	Record 102 caps for Scotland; as player and manager of Liverpool won nine League championships, four European Cups, two FA Cups, 1977–90; played for Celtic and managed Blackburn Rovers; manager Newcastle United, 1997–8
Davis, Joe	1901–78	British	Snooker, billiards	World champion snooker player, 1927–46; first to score official maximum break of 147, 1955
Davis, Steve	1957–	British	Snooker	World champion, 1981,1983–4, 1987–9; Benson & Hedges Masters title 1997
Dean, Dixie	1907–80	British	Football	Forward with Everton, scored 349 goals in 399 games and record 60 goals in one season
Dempsey, Jack	1895–1983	American	Boxing	World heavyweight champion, 1919–26
Dettori, Frankie	1970–	Italian	Horse racing	Champion jockey 1994–5, 2004; won Prix de l'Arc de Triomphe 1995, 2001, The Oaks 1994–5, 2002, St Leger 1995–6, 2005–6, One Thousand Guineas 1998, 2002, Two Thousand Guineas 1996, 1999
Devers, Gail	1966–	American	Athletics	Sprinter-hurdler, Olympic 100m sprint gold medallist 1992, 1996; World Championship 100m title in 1993; 100m hurdles winner also 1993, 1995, 1999
DiMaggio, Joe	1914–99	American	Baseball	Played with New York Yankees, 1936–51; hit safely in record 56 games, 1941
Di Stefano, Alfredo	1926–	Argentinian	Football	Won five European Cup-winner's medals with Real Madrid, 1956–60; European Footballer of the Year, 1957, 1959; also played for Spain, Millionarios, Español
D'Oliviera, Basil	1931–	South African	Cricket	Batsman for Lancashire, Worcestershire, England; won 44 caps, scored five Test centuries
Doohan, Mick	1965–	Australia	Motor-cycling	46 Grand Prix wins 1990–mid-1998; in 1998 became only third rider to win five successive 500cc world championships; set new record of 12 wins in a season in 1997
Edberg, Stefan	1966–	Swedish	Tennis	Wimbledon singles champion, 1988, 1990; won Australian Open, 1985, 1987, US Open, 1991, 1992, Grand Prix Masters, 1989
Eddery, Pat	1952–	Irish	Horse racing	Champion jockey, 1974–7, 1986, 1988–91, 1993, 1996; won Derby, 1975, 1982, 1990, Prix de l'Arc de Triomphe, 1980, 1985–7, Oaks 1996, St Leger 1997
Edwards, Gareth	1949–	British	Rugby union	Won 63 caps as halfback and captain of Wales, scoring record 20 tries
Edwards, Jonathan	1966–	British	Athletics	Triple jump world champion in 1995, 2001; Olympic silver medallist 1996, gold 2000
Eusebio (Ferreira da Silva)	1942–	Mozambican	Football	Won 15 domestic titles with Benfica and 77 caps with Portugal
Evert (Lloyd), Christine	1954–	American	Tennis	Wimbledon singles champion, 1974,1976, 1981; US singles champion, 1975-80, 1982, French Open champion, 1974–5, 1979–80, 1984, Australian Open champion, 1982, 1984
Faldo, Nick	1957–	British	Golf	Won PGA championships, 1978, 1980–1, 1989, Open, 1987, 1989, 1992, US Masters, 1989, 1990, 1996 European Open and World Match Play championship, 1992
Fangio, Juan Manuel	1911–95	Argentinian	Motor racing	World champion five times, 1951, 1954–7; won 24 Grands Prix

Sports personalities (continued)

Name	Dates	Nationality	Sport	Achievements
Favre, Brett	1969–	American	American Football	Played NFL football for Atlanta Falcons, joined Green Bay Packers as quarterback; only the second player to win NFL's Most Valuable Player in consecutive years 1995–6, shared the award in 1997
Federer, Roger	1981–	Swiss	Tennis	Wimbledon singles title 2003–6, US Open 2004–6, Australian Open 2004, 2006
Ferguson, Sir Alex(ander)	1941–	British	Football	Manager of Manchester United 1986–, won FA Cup 1990, 1994, 1996, 1999, 2004, European Cup Winners' Cup 1991, Premier Division Championship 1993–4, 1996–7, 1999–2001, 2003, League and Cup double 1994, 1996, 1999, European Cup 1999
Flintoff, Andrew	1977–	British	Cricket	Bowler/batsman for Lancashire and England; in England's winning 2005 Ashes Test, took 24 wickets, made 402 runs, won Man of the Series Award
Finney, Tom	1929–	British	Football	Winger for Preston North End and England; won 76 caps, first to be Footballer of the Year twice, 1954, 1957
Fischer, Bobby	1943–	American	Chess	World champion, 1972–5; ranked highest of all Grand Masters
Fitzsimmons, Bob	1862–1917	New Zealand	Boxing	World middleweight champion, from 1891, world heavyweight champion, from 1897, light heavyweight champion, from 1903
Foreman, George	1948–	American	Boxing	Olympic heavyweight gold medallist, 1968; world heavyweight champion, 1973–4, 1994
Foyt, A J	1935–	American	Motor racing	Won Indianapolis 500 four times, 1961, 1964, 1967, 1977
Francome, John	1952–	British	Horse racing	Rode record 1138 winners over fences, 1970–85; seven times National Hunt champion jockey, 1976,1979,1981–5
Frazier, Joe	1944–	American	Boxing	Olympic heavyweight gold medallist, 1964, and world heavyweight champion, 1970–3
Fry, C B	1872–1956	British	Athletics, cricket, football	Represented England in all three sports; as cricketer, played in 26 Tests and scored record six consecutive centuries
Gascoigne, Paul	1967–	British	Football	Striker with Tottenham Hotspur, Lazio, Rangers, Middlesbrough and England
Gavaskar, Sunil	1949–	Indian	Cricket	Scored 25 834 runs, including record 10 122 runs in Test cricket; hit Indian Test record of 236 not out against West Indies, 1983–4
Gebrselassie, Haile	1973–	Ethiopian	Athletics	World Championship 10 000 m gold medallist 1993, 1995, 1997, 1999; Olympic gold 10 000 m 1996, 2000
Gehrig, Lou	1903–41	American	Baseball	First baseman with New York Yankees, 1925–39, hit 493 home runs, batting average 340
Giggs, Ryan	1973–	British	Football	Joined Manchester United 1991, becoming youngest-ever Welsh cap; PFA Young Player of the Year 1991, 1992; honours include FA Cup, League Championship and European Cup medals 1998–9 season
Gooch, Graham	1953–	British	Cricket	Played for Essex and England; reached 100 centuries, 1993; scored record 456 runs in Test match against India, 1990
Gower, David	1957–	British	Cricket	Played for Leicestershire, Hampshire, and England; England's highest-scoring batsman in test cricket, 1992
Grace, William Gilbert	1848–1915	British	Cricket	Captain, batsman, and bowler for Gloucestershire and England, 1865–1908; scored 126 centuries and 54 896 runs took 2876 wickets

Name	Dates	Nationality	Sport	Achievements
Graf, Steffi	1969–	German	Tennis	Wimbledon singles champion, 1988–9, 1991–3, 1995–6; US Open, 1988–9, 1995, French Open, 1987–8, 1993, 1995, 1999; Australian Open, 1988–90, 1994, Olympic title, 1988
Green, Lucinda (Prior-Palmer)	1953–	British	Horse riding	Record six Badminton horse trials, 1973, 1976–7, 1979, 1983–4; European champion, 1975; world individual champion, 1982
Greene, Maurice	1974–	American	Athletics	100m gold at World Championships 1997, 1999 (world record), 2001, and for 200m at 1999 Championships
Greig, Tony	1946–	South African	Cricket	Captain, batsman, and bowler for England; scored eight centuries and 3599 runs, took 141 Test wickets
Gretzky, Wayne	1961–	Canadian	Ice hockey	Played with Edmonton Oilers, Los Angeles Kings and New York Rangers; broke record of 1850 goals; National Hockey League's Most Valuable Player record nine times
Grey-Thompson, Dame Tanni	1969–	British	Athletics	Wheelchair-racing paralympian; won total of 11 gold medals at 1998–2004 Olympic Games
Griffith-Joyner, Delorez Florence	1959–98	American	Athletics	Triple gold medallist, in 100m, 200m, sprint relay, 1988 Olympics
Gullit, Ruud	1962–	Dutch	Football	Debut for Holland, 1981, captained team to win 1998 European Championship; 1987 European Footballer of the Year; European Cup with AC Milan 1989, 1990; player-manager with Chelsea, 1995–7, FA Cup 1996–7; Newcastle United Manager 1998–9, coach at Feyenoord 2004–5
Hadlee, Sir Richard	1951–	New Zealand	Cricket	Played for Canterbury, Nottinghamshire, and New Zealand; took record 431 Test wickets
Hagen, Walter Charles	1892–1969	American	Golf	Won 11 championship titles
Hailwood, Mike	1940–81	British	Motor cycling	Won nine world titles and record 14 Isle of Man TT races, 1961–79
Hakkinen, Mika	1968–	Finnish	Moor Racing	Formula One World Champion 1998, 1999
Hamed, "Prince" Naseem	1975–	British	Boxing	WBO world featherweight champion 1995–99
Hammond, Wally	1903–65	British	Cricket	Scored over 50 000 runs for Gloucestershire and England; took record 10 catches against Surrey, 1928
Hanley, Ellery	1965–	British	Rugby league	Played for Bradford Northern, Wigan, and Leeds; won all top honours in British game
Hendry, Stephen	1970–	British	Snooker	World professional champion, 1990, 1992–6, 1999; British Open title, 2003
Henman, Tim(othy)	1974–	British	Tennis	British National Championships singles title 1995, 1996; Olympic silver men's doubles 1996; ATP tour title 1997; Davis Cup team member; Paris Masters title 2003
Hick, Graeme	1966–	Zimbabwean	Cricket	Batsman for Worcestershire and England; hit record 405 not out against Somerset, 1988
Higgins, Alex 'Hurricane'	1949–	British	Snooker	World champion, 1972, 1982
Higgins, John	1975–	British	Snooker	German Open 1995, 1997, British Open 1995, 1998, 2004, European Open 1997, World Championship 1998, 1999, UK Championship 2000, Masters 1999, 2006
Hill, Damon	1952–	British	Motor racing	Runner-up in Formula One world championship, 1994 and 1995; won 1996

Sports personalities (continued)

Name	Dates	Nationality	Sport	Achievements
Hill, Graham	1929–75	British	Motor racing	Formula One world champion, 1962, 1968; won 14 Grand Prix races
Hingis, Martina	1981–	Slovakian /Swiss	Tennis	Youngest singles Grand Slam winner of 20th-c, 1997; 1997 Wimbledon singles and 1998 doubles title; Australian Open singles and doubles titles 1997, 1998, 1999, mixed doubles 2006; French doubles 1998, 2000
Hoad, Lewis Alan	1934–94	Australian	Tennis	Wimbledon singles champion, 1956–7
Hobbs, Sir Jack	1882–1963	British	Cricket	Batsman for Cambridgeshire, Surrey, and England; scored 197 centuries, 61 167 runs
Hogan, Ben	1912–97	American	Golf	First player for 26 years to win all three US major titles, 1948, 1953; four US Open championships
Holmes, Dame Kelly	1970–	British	Athletics	1500m gold medal at 2002 Commonwealth Games; Olympic gold in 800 m and 1500m at Athens, 2004
Howe, Gordie	1926–	Canadian	Ice hockey	Played for Detroit Red Wings and New England Whalers; scored record 801 goals, 1049 assists, 1850 points
Hunt, James	1947–93	British	Motor racing	Formula One world champion, 1976
Hutton. Sir Len	1916–90	British	Cricket	Batsman with Yorkshire and England; scored 129 centuries, 40 140 runs, including record 364 runs in Test against Australia, 1938
Indurain, Miguel	1964–	Spanish	Cycling	Record five successive Tours de France 1991–5; Olympic gold in 1996 time trial
Jacklin, Tony	1944–	British	Golf	British Open champion, 1969; US Open champion, 1970; captain of British Ryder Cup team, 1983–9
Jackson, Colin	1967–	British	Athletics	Hurdler at 110m; World Championship gold medals 1993, 1999, silver, 1997; European Championship gold medal, 1994, 2002
Jenkins, Neil	1972–	British	Rugby Union	Fly-half for Pontypridd; world record career points in International Rugby Union 1999; equal most capped player for Wales
John, Barry	1945–	British	Rugby union	Scored record 90 points as outside-half for Wales; also played for Llanelli and Cardiff
Johnson, Ben	1961–	Canadian	Athletics	Set record for 100m at 1988 Olympics, but stripped of gold medal for drug taking
Johnson, Earvin 'Magic'	1959–	American	Basketball	National Basketball Association's Most Valuable Player, 1979; NBA championship-winning teams, 1980, 1982, 1985, 1987–8
Johnson, Jack	1878–1946	American	Boxing	World heavyweight champion, 1908–15
Johnson, Michael	1967–	American	Athletics	Olympic gold medals 200m, 400m 1996; World Championship gold medals 200m 1991, 1995; 400m 1993, 1995, 1997, 1999
Jones, Bobby	1902–71	American	Golf	British Open champion, 1926–7, 1930; US Open champion, 1923, 1926, 1929–30; won Grand Slam of both US and British amateur and Open titles, 1930
Jordan, Michael	1963–	American	Basketball	Played for Chicago Bulls; National Basketball Association's Most Valuable Player, 1988, 1991–2, 1996–7; took NBA scoring title nine times
Joyner-Kersee, Jackie	1962–	American	Athletics	Gold medallist in heptathlon and long jump, 1988 Olympics; Olympic heptathlon silver medallist, 1984; gold medallist 1992; world champion in long jump 1987, 1991; heptathlon 1987, 1993
Karpov, Anatoly	1951–	Russian	Chess	World champion, 1975–85; 1993

Name	Dates	Nationality	Sport	Achievements
Keegan, Kevin	1951–	British	Football	Inside forward for Scunthorpe, Liverpool, Hamburg, Southampton, Newcastle, and England; European Footballer of the Year, 1978, 1979; managed Newcastle 1992–7, Fulham 1997–9, England 1999–2000, Manchester City 2001–
Khan, Imran	1952–	Pakistani	Cricket	Fast bowler for Sussex, Worcestershire, and Pakistan; scored 3000 runs, took 300 wickets in Tests; as captain led Pakistan to victory in 1992 World Cup
Khan, Jahangir	1963–	Pakistani	Squash	World Open champion, 1981–5, 1988; British Open champion, 1982–91
Killy, Jean-Claude	1943–	French	Skiing	World champion in downhill and combined events, 1966; Olympic gold medallist slalom, giant slalom, downhill events, 1968
King, Billie Jean	1943–	American	Tennis	Won record 20 Wimbledon titles, including singles in 1966–8, 1972–3, 1975; also 13 US titles, four French, two Australian
Klammer, Franz	1953–	Austrian	Skiing	Olympic gold medallist in downhill event, 1976; world downhill champion, 1975–8, 1983
Korbut, Olga	1956–	Russian	Gymnastics	Won three gold medals and one silver medal at 1972 Olympics
Koufax, Sandy	1935–	American	Baseball	Played for Los Angeles Dodgers; won two World Series, 1963, 1965; Most Valuable Player, 1963
Kristiansen, Ingrid	1956–	Norwegian	Athletics	Broke world records in 5000m, 10 000m, marathon, 1985–6; won all major marathons
Lara, Brian	1969–	Trinidadian	Cricket	First batsmen to score over 500 runs in one innings in first-class cricket 1994; broke own world Test record with 400 runs in a single innings 2004; highest run-scorer in Test history when surpassed Allan Border's record of 11,174 runs, 2005
Larwood, Harold	1904–95	British	Cricket	Fast bowler, centre of controversy during 1932/3 'bodyline' tour of Australia
Lasker, Emanuel	1868–1941	German	Chess	World champion, 1894–1921
Latynina, Larissa	1934–	Ukrainian	Gymnastics	First woman athlete to win nine Olympic gold medals
Lauda, Niki	1949–	Austrian	Motor racing	Formula One world champion, 1975, 1977, 1984
Laver, Rod	1938–	Australian	Tennis	Wimbledon singles champion, 1961, 1962, 1968, 1969; world singles champion five times 1964–70
Lenglen, Suzanne	1899–1938	French	Tennis	French champion, 1920–3, 1925–6; Wimbledon singles and doubles champion, 1919–23, 1925; mixed doubles, 1920, 1922, 1925; Olympic gold medallist, 1920
Leonard, Sugar Ray	1956–	American	Boxing	Won world titles at five weights, 1976–88
Lewis, Carl	1961–	American	Athletics	Nine gold medals, one silver, in four successive Olympic Games: 100m, 200m, 400m relay, long jump, 1984; 100m, long jump (silver in 200m), 1988, 400m relay, long jump, 1992; long jump, 1996
Lewis, Lennox	1965–	British	Boxing	1988 Olympic Super-heavyweight gold medal; WBC heavyweight champion 1992–4, 1997–9, 2001–3
Lillee, Dennis	1949–	Australian	Cricket	Fast bowler; took 330 wickets in 70 Tests
Lindwall, Ray	1921–96	Australian	Cricket	Took 228 wickets in 61 Tests for Australia, scored more than 1500 runs, including two Test centuries

Sports personalities (continued)

Name	Dates	Nationality	Sport	Achievements
Lineker, Gary	1960–	British	Football	Played for Leicester, Everton, Barcelona, Tottenham Hotspur, Grampus Eight, and England; Footballer of the Year, 1986, 1992; scored 48 goals for England
Liston, Sonny	1919–70	American	Boxing	World heavyweight champion, 1962–4
Lloyd, Clive	1944–	West Indian	Cricket	Batsman for Lancashire and West Indies; scored 7515 runs, 19 centuries; captained West Indies to victory in World Cup, 1975, 1979
Locke, Bobby	1917–87	South African	Golf	British Open champion, 1949, 1950, 1952, and 1957; won 11 events on US circuit, 1947–50
Lombardi, Vince	1913–70	American	American football	Won five league titles, two Super Bowls, as coach of Green Bay Packers, 1959–69; coached New York Giants, 1954–9
Longo, Jeannie	1958–	French	Cycling	World Road Race champion 1985–9, 1995–6; Olympic gold medallist, 1996 Individual Road Race
Lopez, Nancy	1957–	American	Golf	Ladies' Professional Golf Association champion, 1978,1985, 1989
Louis, Joe	1914–81	American	Boxing	World heavyweight champion, 1937–49; record 25 defences of world title; won 67 of 70 professional fights
MacArthur, Dame Ellen	1976–	British	Sailing	Fastest woman to sail solo round the world, 2002; sailed solo round the world in record 13 days, 13 hrs, 31 min, 47 s aboard *Kingfisher*, 2005
McBride, Willie John	1939–	British	Rugby union	Played with Ballymena, Ireland, and British Lions; won 63 caps with Ireland, record 17 with Lions
McEnroe, John	1959–	American	Tennis	Won four US Open singles titles, 1979–81, 1984, three Wimbledon singles titles, 1981, 1983–4; World Championship Tennis champion, 1979,1981, 1983–4
Malone, Karl	1963–	American	Basketball	Player with Utah Jazz, holds various NBA records; named NBA Most Valuble Player 1996–7, 1998–9
Mansell, Nigel	1954–	British	Motor racing	Formula One world champion 1992; US Indy-car champion, 1993
Mantle, Mickey	1931–95	American	Baseball	Played for New York Yankees; hit record 177m home run, won Triple Crown in batting, home runs, runs batted, 1956
Maradona, Diego	1960–	Argentinian	Football	Played for Boca Juniors, Barcelona, Napoli, and Seville; as captain of Argentina, won World Cup, 1986
Marciano, Rocky	1923–69	American	Boxing	World heavyweight champion, 1952–6
Matthews, Sir Stanley	1915–2000	British	Football	Played for Stoke City, Blackpool, England; won FA Cup-winner's medal, 1953; twice Footballer of the Year; inaugural winner of European Footballer of the Year Award, 1956
Mays, Willie	1931–	American	Baseball	Played for New York, San Francisco Giants, and New York Mets; scored over 3000 hits, 600 home runs; Baseball Player of the Decade, 1960–9
Meade, Richard	1938–	British	Show jumping	Won three Olympic gold medals, in three-day event 1968, 1972, individual title, 1972; also won world championship team gold medals, 1970, 1982, and European team gold medals, 1967, 1971, 1981
Meads, Colin Earl	1935–	New Zealand	Rugby union	Lock forward; played for All Blacks in 133 matches, including record 55 Test matches

Name	Dates	Nationality	Sport	Achievements
Merckx, Eddy	1945–	Belgian	Cycling	Won record-equalling five Tours de France, 1969–72, 1974; world amateur champion, 1964, world professional champion, 1967, 1971, 1974
Mikan, George	1924–	American	Basketball	Won five championships with Minneapolis, 1948–56; top scorer three times
Milo of Croton	late 6c. BC	Greek	Wrestling	Won five successive Olympic wrestling titles
Montana, Joe	1956–	American	American football	Quarterback with Notre Dame; led San Francisco 49ers to four Super Bowl victories, 1980s; Most Valuable Player, 1989
Moore, Bobby	1941–93	British	Football	Defender with West Ham United and Fulham; captained England to victory in World Cup, 1966; record 108 caps
Morphy, Paul Charles	1837–84	American	Chess	Unofficial world champion, beat all challengers until no more came forward
Moses, Ed	1955–	American	Athletics	World Cup 40m hurdles gold medallist, 1977, 1979, 1981; world champion, 1983; Olympic champion, 1976, 1984; Olympic bronze medallist, 1988; broke world record four times
Moss, Sir Stirling	1929–	British	Motor racing	Runner-up in Formula One championship, 1955–8; won 16 of 66 races, 1951–61
Musial, Stan	1920–	American	Baseball	Played for St Louis Cardinals; topped National League's batting list seven times, 1943–57; hit record 3630 hits; three times Most Valuable Player
Namath, Joe	1943–	American	American football	Quarterback with New York Jets in 1960s
Navratilova, Martina	1956–	Czech/ American	Tennis	Won record nine Wimbledon singles titles, 1978–9, 1982 7, 1990; won 54 Grand Slam events, including 36 doubles titles; won mixed doubles, 2003, a record-equalling 20th Wimbledon title
Newcombe, John	1944–	Australian	Tennis	Wimbledon singles champion, 1967, 1970, 1971; won Wimbledon doubles title, 1965, 1968–70; Australian singles, 1973, 1975
Nicklaus, Jack	1940–	American	Golf	Won record 18 major tournaments, including British Open three times, US Open four times, US Professional Golfers Association tournament five times, US Masters a record six times
Norman, Greg	1955–	Australian	Golf	Australian Open champion, 1980, 1985, 1987; won British Open, 1986, 1993, World Match Play Championship, 1986
Nurmi, Paavo Johannes	1897–1973	Finnish	Athletics	Won nine Olympic gold medals, 1920–8; set 22 world records at distances ranging from 1500m to 10 000m
Oerter, Al	1936–	American	Athletics	Won four consecutive Olympic gold discus medals, 1956, 1960, 1964, 1968
O'Meara, Mark	1957–	American	Golf	US Masters title 1998; Open 1998
O'Sullivan, Ronnie	1975–	British	Snooker	World championship 2001,2004; European Open, 2003; Masters, 1995, 2005
Ovett, Steve	1955–	British	Athletics	800m gold medallist, 1500m bronze medallist in 1980 Olympics; set world records in 1500m, one mile, two mile events
Owen, Michael	1979–	British	Football	Centre forward with Liverpool 1996–2004; Real Madrid, 2004; Newcastle United, 2005; FA Young Player of the Year 1997–8; England team's youngest member and scorer, World Cup team, 1998, 2002, 2006
Owens, Jesse	1913–80	American	Athletics	Set five world records (100 yd, long jump, 220yd, 220yd hurdles, 200m hurdles), 1935; won record four gold medals in 1936 Olympics

Sports personalities (continued)

Name	Dates	Nationality	Sport	Achievements
Paige, Satchel	c.1906–82	American	Baseball	Pitcher with Cleveland Indians; helped team to win 1948 World Series
Palmer, Arnold	1929–	American	Golf	Won Canadian Open, 1960, British Open, 1961–2, US Open, 1960, US Masters, 1958, 1960, 1962, 1964
Pelé (Edison Arantes do Nascimento)	1940–	Brazilian	Football	World Cup-winner's medal with Brazil, 1958, 1962, 1970; played for Santos and New York Cosmos; scored 1281 goals in 1363 games
Perkins, Kieren	1973–	Australian	Swimming	Freestyle swimmer, won 1500m silver medal at 1990 Commonwealth Games; 400m and 1500m gold medallist, 1994 World Championships; Olympic gold medallist in 1500m, 1992, 1996
Perry, Fred	1909–95	British	Tennis, table-tennis	Wimbledon singles champion, 1934–6; won French, Australian, and US singles titles, was first man to win all four major titles
Petrosian, Tigran	1929–84	Soviet	Chess	World champion, 1963–9
Pettit, Bob	1932–	American	Basketball	Played for Milwaukee (later St Louis) Hawks; twice voted National Basketball Association's Most Valuable Player
Piggott, Lester	1935–	British	Horse racing	Flat racing jockey; rode over 4000 winners, 1948–93, including 30 classics and record nine Epsom Derby wins; champion jockey 11 times
Piquet, Nelson	1952–	Brazilian	Motor racing	Formula One world champion, 1981, 1983, 1987
Platini, Michel	1955–	French	Football	Scored record 41 goals in 72 games for France; first European Footballer of the Year three years in a row, 1983–5
Player, Gary	1935–	South African	Golf	British Open champion, 1959, 1968, 1974; US Open, 1965, US PGA, 1962, 1972, US Masters, 1961, 1974, 1978, South African Open 12 times, World Match Play title a record five times
Popov, Alexander	1971–	Russian	Swimming	Freestyle swimmer, 50m and 100m Olympic champion, 1992, 1996; world champion in same events, 1994; 100m, 1998; 50m, 2000
Prost, Alain	1955–	French	Motor racing	Formula One world champion, 1985–6, 1989, 1993; set world record of 699.5 championship points and 44 Grand Prix victories
Radcliffe, Paula	1973–	British	Athletics	5000m gold, Commonwealth Games, 2002; 10 000m gold, European Championships; 3 times London Marathon winner, 2002–3, 2005; World Championship gold in women's marathon, 2005
Ramsey, Sir Alf	1922–99	British	Football	Played for Southampton and Tottenham Hotspur; as manager, 1963–74, led England to victory in 1966 World Cup
Ranjitsinhji, Prince	1872–1933	Indian	Cricket	Batsman with Sussex and England; formed celebrated partnership with C B Fry
Reardon, Ray	1932–	British	Snooker	World professional champion, 1970, 1973–6, 1978
Redgrave, Sir Steven	1962–	British	Rowing	Winner of five consecutive Olympic gold medals in coxless pairs and fours, 1984–2000, three with Matthew Pinsent; record seven world championships in the coxless pairs 1991–9
Rhodes, Wilfred	1877–1973	British	Cricket	Batsman and bowler for Yorkshire and England; scored 39 722 runs, took record 4187 wickets; scored 1000 runs and took 100 wickets in a season 16 times

Name	Dates	Nationality	Sport	Achievements
Richards, Sir Gordon	1904–86	British	Horse racing	Rode record 4870 winners in Britain, champion jockey record 26 times, winning 14 English classics
Richards, Viv	1952–	West Indian	Cricket	Batsman and captain of West Indies; scored 8540 runs in 121 Test matches, including 24 centuries; scored record 1710 runs in a calendar year, 1976
Rivaldo (Vito Barba Ferreira)	1972–	Brazilian	Football	Striker with Brazilian team Palmeiras, then Spanish side Deportivo La Coruna; joined Barcelona 1997–2002, AC Milan 2002–3, Cruzeiro 2004, Olympiakos 2004
Robinson, Sugar Ray	1920–89	American	Boxing	World welterweight champion, 1946–51; world middleweight champion, 1950–1
Robson, Bobby	1933–	British	Football	Played for Fulham, West Bromwich Albion, England; manager of Ipswich Town, and England 1982–90, then PSV Eindhoven, Sporting Lisbon, Barcelona, and Newcastle United 1999–2004
Rockne, Knute	1888–1931	American	American football	Influential coach of Notre Dame from 1914
Rodnina, Irina	1949–	Soviet	Ice skating	Won 23 world, Olympic, and European gold medals in pairs competitions
Ronaldo (Luis Nazario de Lima)	1976–	Brazilian	Football	Forward for Cruzeiro, Brazil, PSV Eindhoven, Barcelona, Inter Milan, Real Madrid; won European Cup Winner's Cup, Spanish Cup Final medals with Barcelona; twice International Footballer of the Year 1996, 1997; European Player of the Year 1997
Rooney, Wayne	1985–	British	Football	Played for Everton 2002–4; Manchester United, 2004–; England Young Player of the Year, FIFPro World Player of the Year, 2005; PFA Young Player of the Year 2005, 2006
Rosewall, Ken	1934–	Australian	Tennis	Barring Wimbledon singles, won all major titles; professional world champion, 1971–2
Rusedski, Greg	1973–	Canadian/ British	Tennis	In Canada won six junior titles 1985–90; British citizen in 1995, Britain's No 1, 1997
Russell, Bill	1934–	American	Basketball	Won 11 championships with Boston Celtics, 1956–69; five times National Basketball Association's Most Valuable Player
Ruth, Babe	1895–1948	American	Baseball	Pitcher with Boston Red Sox and New York Yankees; first to hit three home runs in one game, 1926; hit record 60 home runs in a season, 1927; in all, hit record 714 home runs
Sampras, Pete	1971–	American	Tennis	Wimbledon singles champion record 7 times, 1993–5, 1997–2000; US Open 1990, 1993, 1995–6, 2002, Australian Open 1997
Sawchuk, Terry	1929–70	Canadian	Ice hockey	Goaltender for Detroit Red Wings, Boston Bruins, Toronto Maple Leafs, Los Angeles Kings, New York Rangers; set National Hockey League record of 103 shutouts, played in record 971 games
Schumacher, Michael	1969–	German	Motor racing	Formula One world champion a record 7 times, 1994–5, 2000–4
Scudamore, Peter	1958–	British	Horse racing	Champion jockey, 1982, 1986–92; rode world record 1677 winners
Seaman, David	1963–	British	Footballer	Goal keeper with Leeds Utd, Peterborough, Birmingham City, Queens Park Rangers, Arsenal 1990–2003, Manchester United 2003–4; England goalkeeper 1988–2003
Seles, Monica	1973–	Yugoslavian	Tennis	Youngest winner of a Grand Slam event, 1990; won US Open, 1991–2, French Open, 1990–3, Australian Open, 1991–3, 1996

SPORTS AND GAMES

Sports personalities (continued)

Name	Dates	Nationality	Sport	Achievements
Senna, Ayrton	1960–94	Brazilian	Motor racing	Formula One world champion, 1988, 1990–1
Shearer, Alan	1970–	British	Football	Striker for Southampton, Blackburn Rovers, Newcastle United; joined England 1992, captain 1996–2000; Footballer of the Year, 1994; Professional Footballers' Association Player of the Year, 1995; Domestic Player of the Decade, 2003; equalled Jackie Milburn's record of 200 goals for Newcastle, 2006
Shilton, Peter	1949–	British	Football	Goalkeeper for Leicester City, Stoke City, Nottingham Forest, Southampton, Derby County, England; won record 125 England caps
Shoemaker, Willie	1931–	American	Horse racing	Won record 8833 winners, 1949–89
Simpson, O J	1947–	American	American football	Played for Buffalo Bills; top League rusher four times, 1972–6; set record of 23 touchdowns in one season, 1975
Smith, Harvey	1938–	British	Show jumping	Won British championships several times; competed in Olympics, 1968, 1972
Smythe, Pat	1928–96	British	Show jumping	European champion, 1957, 1961–3; Olympic bronze medallist, 1956
Snead, Sam	1912–2002	American	Golf	British Open champion, 1946, US Professional Golfers Association championship, 1942, 1949, 1951, US Masters, 1949, 1952, 1954; won record six Senior Championships
Sobers, Sir Gary	1936–	West Indian	Cricket	Batsman and bowler for Nottinghamshire and West Indies; scored 28 315 runs, took 1043 wickets; set records of 8000 runs and 200 wickets in Tests, 365 not out in 1958 Test against Pakistan
Sosa, Sammy	1968–	Dominican Republic/ American	Baseball	Player with Texas Rangers, Chicago White Sox, Chicago Cubs from 1992; holds National League (NL) record for most home runs in consecutive seasons 102 (1997–8), NL Most Valuable Player 1998
Spassky, Boris	1937–	Russian	Chess	World champion, 1969–72
Spitz, Mark	1950–	American	Swimming	Gold medallist in team events at 1968 Olympic Games; won seven gold medals at 1972 Olympics
Stengel, Casey	1889–1975	American	Baseball	Outfielder for Brooklyn Dodgers and other teams; as manager led New York Yankees to seven World Series victories 1949–60; managed New York Mets, 1962–5
Stewart, Sir Jackie	1939–	British	Motor racing	Formula One world champion, 1969, 1971, 1973; won record 27 Grands Prix
Sullivan, John Lawrence	1858–1918	American	Boxing	World heavyweight champion, 1882–92
Surtees, John	1934–	British	Motor racing, motorcycling	Won 350 cc motor cycling world title, 1958–60, 500 cc title, 1956, 1958–60; Formula One championship, 1964
Szewinska, Irena	1946–	Polish	Athletics	Silver medallist in long jump and gold medallist in relay, 1964 Olympics; three gold medals, 1966 European Championships; 200m gold, 1968 Olympics; 400m gold, 1976 Olympics
Thompson, Daley	1958–	British	Athletics	Gold medal in decathlon at Commonwealth Games, 1978, 1982, 1986, world champion, 1983, European champion, 1982, 1986; Olympic champion, 1980, 1984; broke world record four times 1980–4
Thorpe, Jim	1888–1953	American	American football, athletics, baseball	Won pentathlon and decathlon at 1912 Olympics; played baseball, 1913–19, for New York Giants, Cincinnati Reds, Boston Braves

Name	Dates	Nationality	Sport	Achievements
Torvill, Jayne and Dean, Christopher	1957–	British	Ice skating	World ice dance champions, 1981–4; Olympic champions, 1984; European champions, Olympic bronze medallists, 1994
Trevino, Lee	1939–	American	Golf	Won three Open championships (US, Canadian, British) in a single year, 1971; retained British title in 1972
Trueman, Fred	1931–2006	British	Cricket	Fast bowler for Yorkshire and England; took 2304 wickets, including record 307 Test wickets
Tunney, Gene	1897–1978	American	Boxing	World heavyweight champion, 1926–8
Tyson, Mike	1966–	American	Boxing	Undisputed world heavyweight champion, 1987–92; regained WBC heavyweight title briefly in 1996
Unser, Al	1939–	American	Motor racing	Won Indianapolis 500, 1970–1, 1978, 1987
Venables, Terry	1943–	British	Football	Player with Chelsea, Tottenham Hotspur, Queens Park Rangers; manager of Crystal Palace, Queens Park Rangers, Barcelona (won Spanish Championship 1984), Tottenham Hotspur; England team coach 1994–6, then Australian national side; manager of Middlesbrough 2000, Leeds 2002–3; England assistant coach 2006–
Villeneuve, Jacques	1971–	Canadian	Motor racing	Won PPG Indy Car World Series, 1995; Formula One world champion, 1997
Wade. Virginia	1945–	British	Tennis	US Open singles champion, 1968; Italian singles champion, 1971; French singles champion, 1972; Wimbledon singles champion, 1977
Warne, Shane	1969–	Australian	Cricket	Leg-spin bowler for Hampshire and Australia; reached record 700 Test wickets during 2006–7 Ashes series, making him the most successful bowler in Test history
Weissmuller, Johnny	1904–84	American	Swimming	First to swim 100m in under one minute, 1922; Olympic gold medallist in 100m freestyle, 1924, 1928; Olympic 400m, 1928
Whymper, Edward	1840–1911	British	Mountaineering	First to climb the Matterhorn, 1865
Wilkinson, Jonny	1979–	British	Rugby union	Fly-half with Newcastle; England debut 1998; outstanding performances in 1999 World Cup, 2000 Six Nations; scored winning drop-goal in 2003 World Cup final
Williams, J P R	1949–	British	Rugby union	Fullback with London Welsh, Bridgend, Wales, British Lions; won record 55 Welsh caps
Wills Moody, Helen	1905–98	American	Tennis	Wimbledon champion, 1927–30, 1932–3, 1935, 1938; winner of 32 Grand Slam events
Winkler, Hans-Gunter	1926–	German	Show jumping	Only man to win five Olympic show jumping gold medals (two in 1956 and one in 1960, 1964, 1972)
Witt, Katerina	1965–	German	Ice-skating	European champion, 1983–9; world champion, 1984–5, 1987–8; Olympic champion, 1984, 1988
Woods, Tiger	1976–	American	Golf	Titles include US Masters 1997, 2000, 2002, 2005; US PGA 1999, 2000, 2006; US Open 2000, 2002, the Open 2000, 2005, 2006; US PGA Tour Player of the Year (seven times)
Zatopek, Emil	1922–2000	Czech	Athletics	Gold medallist in 10 000m at 1948 Olympics; triple gold medallist (10 000m, 5000m, marathon) in 1952 Olympics; broke 13 long-distance running world records

GOVERNING BODIES IN SPORT

AAU	Amateur Athletic Union (USA)
ACU	Auto Cycle Union
AIBA	International Amateur Boxing Federation
ASA	Amateur Swimming Association
BBBC	British Boxing Board of Control
BDO	British Darts Organization
ECB	England and Wales Cricket Board
FA	Football Association
FAI	International Aeronautics Federation
FEI	International Equestrian Federation
FIA	International Automobile Association
FIBA	International Basketball Federation
FIBT	International Bobsleigh and Tobogganing Federation
FIC	International Canoeing Federation
FIDE	International Chess Federation
FIE	International Fencing Federation
FIFA	International Football Association Federation
FIG	International Gymnastic Federation
FIH	International Hockey Federation
FILA	International Amateur Wrestling Federation
FIM	International Motorcycling Federation
FINA	International Amateur Swimming Federation
FIP	International Polo Federation
FIQ	International Bowling Federation
FIRA	International Amateur Rugby Federation
FIRS	International Roller Skating Federation
FIS	International Ski Federation
FISA	International Rowing Federation
FIT	International Trampoline Federation
FITA	International Archery Federation
FIVB	International Volleyball Federation
FMK	World Karate Federation
GAA	Gaelic Athletic Association
IAAF	International Amateur Athletic Federation
IBA	International Baseball Association
IBF	International Badminton Federation
IBF	International Boxing Federation
IBSF	International Billiards and Snooker Federation Association
IBU	International Biathlon Union
IFNA	International Federation of Netball Associations
IHF	International Handball Federation
IIHF	International Ice Hockey Federation
IJF	International Judo Federation
ILF	International Lacrosse Federation
IOC	International Olympic Committee
IOF	International Orienteering Federation
IRFB	International Rugby Football Board
ISA	International Surfing Association
ISF	International Softball Association
ISRF	International Squash Rackets Federation
ISU	International Skating Union
ITF	International Tennis Federation
ITF	International Trampoline Federation
ITTF	International Table Tennis Federation
IWF	International Weightlifting Federation
IWSF	International Water Ski Federation
IYRU	International Yacht Racing Union
LPGA	Ladies' Professional Golfers' Association
LTA	Lawn Tennis Association
MCC	Marylebone Cricket Club
NBA	National Basketball Association (USA)
NCAA	National Collegiate Athletic Association (USA)
NFA	National Federation of Anglers
NFL	National Football League (USA)
NHL	National Hockey League (USA)
PCA	Professional Chess Association
PGA	Professional Golfers' Association
RFU	Rugby Football Union
RL	Rugby League
TCCB	Test and County Cricket Board
TWIF	Tug of War International Federation
UCI	International Cycling Union
UEFA	Union of European Football Associations
UIM	Union Internationale Motonautique
UIPMB	International Union of Modern Pentathlon and Biathlon
UIT	International Shooting Union
UK Athletics (replaced the British Athletic Federation)	
USGA	United States Golf Association
USPGA	United States Professional Golfers' Association
WBA	World Boxing Association
WBB	World Bowls Board
WBC	World Boxing Council
WBO	World Boxing Organisation
WCF	World Curling Federation
WPBSA	World Professional Billiards and Snooker Association
WWSU	World Water Skiing Union

INDEX

Guide to the Index

The alphabetical arrangement of this index is letter-by-letter. The order follows the English alphabet, ignoring capital letters, accents, diacritics, and apostrophes.

In cases where a series of headwords have the same spelling, places are ordered before people, and people precede general topics.

Rulers are listed chronologically, ordering them by country if their names are the same (eg Charles I of England would precede Charles I of Spain, and these would be followed by Charles II).

When a number of people have the same name, monarchs are given before saints and popes, and these are followed by lay people. Compound names (eg John of Gaunt) appear later than single-element surnames (eg John, Elton), and are taken in strict letter-by-letter order, including grammatical words (eg John of Gaunt precedes John the Baptist).

Entries involving numbers are located on the basis of their spoken form (eg 10 will be found under 'ten').

Names beginning with St are ordered under Saint, and all Mc prefixes are ordered as if they were Mac.

Cross-references between index entries are shown with the symbol >>.

Conventional abbreviations are used for American states; these are explained on pp. 362-3.

Most of the entries consist of a single reference to a page in the first part of this book. In a few cases, sets of references have been compiled on points of special interest.

INDEX

ACKNOWLEDGEMENTS

We would like to thank the following for their help in the preparation of this book:

Audit Bureau of Circulations; Geoffrey Briggs, NASA; British Rail; British Standards Institution; British Telecom; Dr Michael Brooke, Cambridge; Professor A. Brown and Mrs P. Brown, Oxford; Calmann and King; Carol-June Cassidy; Central Statistical Office; Civil Aviation Authority; Department of Health; Food and Agriculture Organization; Dr J.T. Houghton, Hadley Climate Centre (Met Office); International Civil Aviation Organization; International Energy Agency; International Institute For Strategic Studies; International Monetary Fund; International Phonetic Association; Organization for Economic Co-operation and Development; David Pickering; Maureen Storey; United Nations Populations Division; Wine Institute; World Conservation Monitoring Centre; World Health Organization; World Resources Institute; UNESCO.